Financial Accounting

AUDITING: AN INTEGRATED APPROACH, 7/E
Arens/Loebbecke

KOHLER'S DICTIONARY FOR ACCOUNTANTS, 6/E
Cooper/Ijiri

FINANCIAL STATEMENT ANALYSIS, 2/E
Foster

GOVERNMENTAL AND NONPROFIT ACCOUNTING: THEORY AND PRACTICE, 5/E
Freeman/Shoulders

FINANCIAL ACCOUNTING, 3/E
Harrison/Horngren

COST ACCOUNTING: A MANAGERIAL EMPHASIS, 9/E
Horngren/Foster/Datar

ACCOUNTING, 3/E
Horngren/Harrison/Robinson

CASES IN FINANCIAL REPORTING, 2/E
Hirst/McAnally

PRINCIPLES OF FINANCIAL AND MANAGEMENT ACCOUNTING:
A SOLE PROPRIETORSHIP APPROACH
Horngren/Harrison/Robinson

PRINCIPLES OF FINANCIAL AND MANAGEMENT ACCOUNTING:
A CORPORATE APPROACH
Horngren/Harrison/Robinson

INTRODUCTION TO FINANCIAL ACCOUNTING, 6/E
Horngren/Sundem/Elliott

INTRODUCTION TO MANAGEMENT ACCOUNTING, 10/E
Horngren/Sundem/Stratton

BUDGETING, 5/E
Welsch/Hilton/Gordon

Financial Accounting

Third Edition

Walter T. Harrison, Jr.
Baylor University

Charles T. Horngren
Stanford University

PRENTICE-HALL Upper Saddle River, New Jersey 07458

Acquisitions Editor:	Annie Todd
Executive Editor:	P.J. Boardman
Marketing Manager:	Deborah Hoffman Emry
Development Editor:	Steven A. Rigolosi
Assistant Editor:	Natacha St. Hill
Editorial Assistant:	Elaine Oyzon-Mast
Director of Development:	Steve Deitmer
Production by:	Progressive Publishing Alternatives
Production Coordinator:	Cindy Spreder
Managing Editor:	Katherine Evancie
Senior Manufacturing Supervisor:	Paul Smolenski
Manufacturing Manager:	Vincent Scelta
Senior Designer:	Suzanne Behnke
Interior Design:	Kenny Beck
Cover Design:	Maureen Eide
Composition by:	TSI Graphics
Cover Art:	Valerie Sinclair

Photo Credits: **1** Lands' End, Inc.; **3** Lands' End, Inc.; **8** Boeing Commercial Airplane Group; **16** Newman Brown/Monkmeyer Press; **17** Dale Spartas/Gamma-Liaison, Inc.; **49** Teri Stratford; **51** Teri Stratford; **61** Coca Cola; **69** Mark Burnett/Stock Boston; **77** R. Lord/The Image Works; **105** Andrea McGinty; **107** Andrea McGinty; **108** Richard Pasley/Gamma-Liaison, Inc.; **133** Sographs/Gamma-Liaison, Inc.; **141** SuperStock, Inc.; **171** Michael Rosenfeld/Tony Stone Images; **173** Michael Rosenfeld/Tony Stone Images; **178a** Mark Antman/The Image Works; **178b** SuperStock, Inc.; **199** Nancy Richmond/The Image Works; **221** Lincoln Potter/Gamma-Liaison, Inc.; **223** Lincoln Potter/Gamma-Liaison, Inc.; **233** J. Albertson/Stock Boston; **242** Ford Motor Credit Company; **261** Steven Peters/Tony Stone Images; **263** Steven Peters/Tony Stone Images; **265** Frito-Lay, Inc.; **275** Owens Corning; **283** Simon Wolfe/The Stock Market; **319** Zigy Kaluzny/Gamma-Liaison, Inc.; **321** Zigy Kaluzny/Tony Stone Images; **324** Zigy Kaluzny/Tony Stone Images; **337** Tony Stone Images; **344** John McDermott/Tony Stone Images; **365** America West Airlines; **367** America West Airlines; **371** M. Farrell/The Image Works; **373** Joe Towers/The Stock Market; **378** IBM; **396** Don Smetzer/Tony Stone Images; **417** Dennis M. Gottlieb/The Stock Market; **419** Dennis M. Gottlieb/The Stock Market; **425** Kimberly Clark; **436** Michael Newman/Photoedit; **443** Honeywell; **467** Saturn Corporation; **469** Saturn Corporation; **470** Prudential Securities, Inc.; **477** Reinhold Spiegler/Reinhold Spiegler Photography; **489** Teri Stratford; **495** Teri Stratford; **515** Michael Quackenbush/The Image Bank; **517** Michael Quackenbush/The Image Bank; **522** Kentucky Fried Chicken; **530** Teri Stratford; **536** Lee Snider/The Image Works; **591** James Blank/FPG International; **592** Northrup Grumman Corporation; **609** Gamma-Liaison, Inc.; **643** Tony Stone Images; **645** Tony Stone Images; **646** Teri Stratford; **656** Rubbermaid, Inc.; **659** General Mills.

The annual report material in Appendix A, pages 693–719, is provided courtesy of Lands' End, Inc.

Library of Congress Cataloging-in Publication Data

Harrison, Walter T.
Financial accounting / Walter T. Harrison, Jr., Charles T. Horngren. — 3rd ed.
p. cm.
Includes index.
ISBN 0-13-915919-3
1. Accounting. I. Horngren, Charles T. II. Title
HF5635.H333 1997
657—dc21 97-3147 CIP

Prentice-Hall International (UK) Limited, London
Prentice-Hall of Australia Pty. Limited, Sydney
Prentice-Hall Canada, Inc., Toronto
Prentice-Hall Hispanoamericana, S.A., Mexico
Prentice-Hall of India Private Limited, New Delhi
Prentice-Hall of Japan, Inc., Tokyo
Simon & Schuster Asia Pte. Ltd., Singapore
Editora Prentice-Hall do Brasil, Ltda., Rio de Janeiro

Printed in the United States of America

10 9 8 7 6 5 4 3 2

For our wives,

Nancy and Joan

Third Edition Report

FINANCIAL ACCOUNTING

HARRISON HORNGREN

PRENTICE HALL BUSINESS PUBLISHING

LETTER TO OUR STAKEHOLDERS

DEAR STAKEHOLDERS:

We are pleased to introduce the third edition of *Financial Accounting*. To reflect the changing nature of the course, we have significantly reengineered our book.

OUR MISSION

It's not information until you use it to make a decision. This is the theme of our text. The financial statements contain a wealth of information that managers, investors, and creditors need to evaluate a company's operations. But to fully understand those statements, managers must know how they've been prepared. Thus we take a two-pronged approach throughout this book—simultaneously showing how the statements are prepared *and* how decision makers use those statements.

A LEANER ORGANIZATION

We are all aware of the constraints on our time, as well as the demands of our stakeholders (both instructors and students). Thus this new edition focuses on presenting the *core* of financial accounting along with applications. We have cut more than 100 pages and reduced the book from 19 chapters to 13 chapters.

WE'D LIKE TO HEAR FROM YOU

The bases of our success are simple: (1) quality, and (2) customer service. We are dedicated to continuous improvement, to achieving 100% satisfaction in our relationships with our customers. If you have any suggestions, we'd like to hear from you. Please write to us at the addresses below, and we will respond promptly.

Tom Harrison

Walter T. Harrison, Jr.
Baylor University
tom_harrison@ baylor.edu

Charles T. Horngren

Charles T. Horngren
Stanford University
horngren_charles@gsb.stanford.edu

At a glance

A Summary of Product Enhancements

Quality Assurance

New to the Third Edition

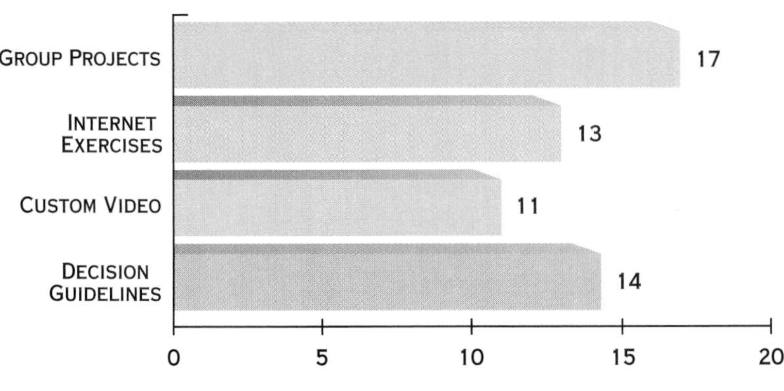

Number of Chapters

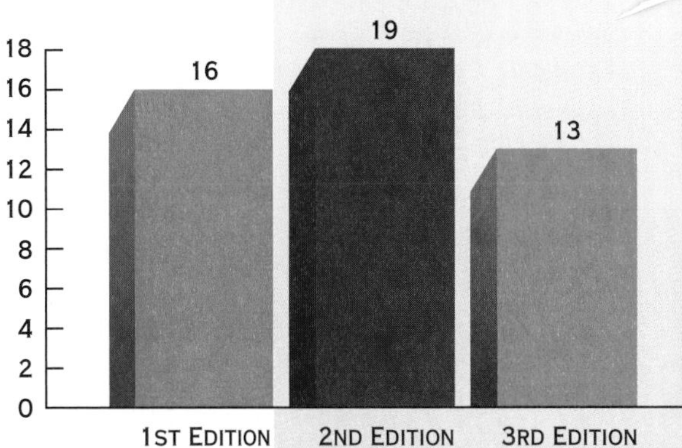

Number of Pages

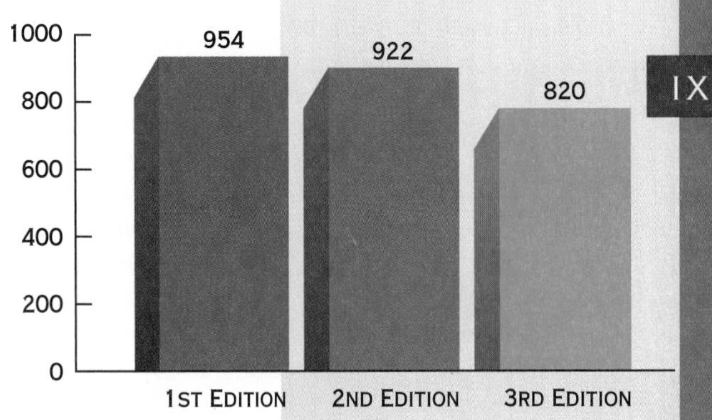

Sources and Uses of Cash

Coverage of the Statement of Cash Flows

Chapter	New Material
1	Introduction to the Statement of Cash Flows (SCF)
3	Analyzing the Financial Statements of a Real Company (Hawaiian Airlines, Inc.), Including the SCF
5	Relating Short-Term Investments and Receivables to the SCF
6	Reporting Inventory Transactions on the SCF
7	Reporting Plant Asset Transactions on the SCF
8	Reporting Financing Activities on the SCF
9	Reporting Stockholders' Equity Transactions on the SCF
10	Using the SCF to Interpret a Company's Investment Activities
12	Preparing the SCF; Investors' and Creditors' use of Cash-Flow and Related Information
13	Using the SCF in Decision Making

product profile

"Excellent. I especially like the Lands' End financial statements. This chapter is very effective in illustrating basic concepts from a user's perspective."
Pat Evans
Auburn University

"The section on 'How Managers and Owners Use the Bank Reconciliation' is a very good addition. But perhaps the part that I like most is the new section on 'Using a Budget to Manage Cash.' It is a feature like this that really distinguishes a textbook."
Patrick M. Premo
St. Bonaventure University

"Finally somebody has eliminated the redundancy of the separate chapters on merchandising and inventories. Harrison/Horngren have accomplished this splendidly."
Gregory S. Kordecki
Clayton State University

PRODUCT ENHANCEMENTS	FEATURED COMPANY AND VIDEO
Chapter 1: Summarizing Business Activity and Using the Financial Statements •Introduction to all the major financial statements, including the statement of cash flows •Transaction analysis eliminated; decision making emphasized	Lands' End, Part 1
Chapter 2: Processing Accounting Information •Accounting cycle now covered in 2 chapters rather than 3 •Transactions analyzed first in terms of their effects on the accounting equation and second in terms of debits and credits	Lands' End, Part 2
Chapter 3: Accrual Accounting and the Financial Statements •Worksheet moved to end-of-chapter appendix •New applied material: Using the Current Ratio and Using the Debt Ratio	It's Just Lunch
Chapter 4: Internal Control and Managing Cash •New section: Managing Cash and Budgeting	Grant LeForge & Co./ José Gomez
Chapter 5: Accounting for Short-Term Investments and Receivables •New applied material: Using the Quick Ratio and Day's Sales in Receivables; Using Receivables to Finance Operations	Intel
Chapter 6: Accounting for Merchandise Inventory, Cost of Goods Sold, and the Gross Margin •Inventory methods and COGS now treated in one chapter •New material: Managers', Investors', and Creditors' Use of the COGS Model for Decision Making	Huntington Galleries
Chapter 7: Accounting for Plant Assets, Intangible Assets, and Related Expenses •New applied material: Making Decisions on Plant Assets and Related Expenses	Home Depot
Chapter 8: Accounting for Current and Long-Term Liabilities •Combines short-term and long-term liabilities into one chapter; payroll accounting discussed only briefly •Time value of money discussed in optional end-of-book appendix •New applied material: Financing with Debt versus Stock	America West Airlines

PRODUCT PROFILE

PRODUCT ENHANCEMENTS	FEATURED COMPANY AND VIDEO
Chapter 9: Measuring and Reporting Stockholders' Equity •New decision-oriented material: Investing in Stock	IHOP
Chapter 10: Accounting for Long-Term Investments and International Operations •Improved material on managing cash in international transactions	General Motors/GMAC
Chapter 11: Using the Income Statement and Financial Statement Notes: Additional Corporate Reporting Issues •New section on quality of earnings and the investment capitalization rate •Includes extended discussion of the notes to the financial statements, MD&A, and auditors' report	May Department Stores
Chapter 12: Preparing and Using the Statement of Cash Flows •New section on free cash flow •New decision-oriented material: Investors' and Creditors' Use of Cash-Flow and Related Information	W.T. Grant & Company
Chapter 13: Financial Statement Analysis for Decision Making •New material on benchmarking versus the industry and key competitors •New discussion of economic value added (EVA)	Bristol-Myers Squibb, Procter & Gamble

APPENDIXES

A: The Annual Report of Lands' End, Inc.
- Featured in the Financial Statement Cases at the end of each chapter

B: Time Value of Money: Future Value and Present Value*

C: Summary of Generally Accepted Accounting Principles
- Replaces a complete chapter on GAAP; GAAP is fully integrated throughout the text

D: Accounting for Partnerships*

E: Modern Accounting Information Systems
- An introduction to electronic spreadsheets and databases

F: Special Accounting Journals*

G: Check Figures

*Includes exercises and problems.

"A significant improvement with combining [two chapters] from the previous edition. This adds continuity, clarity, and conciseness. In Chapter 9, the authors have done an excellent job of covering the fundamental issues related to equity."
Timothy B. Griffin
University of Missouri, Kansas City

"The 'Decision Guidelines' and 'Using Cash Flow Information' sections are valuable additions to Chapter 12."
Sue Gunckel
Albuquerque TVI

"The authors have done an excellent job integrating AIS and GAAP throughout."
Carolyn Streuly
Marquette University

Financial Highlights

Decision Guidelines

Decision Guidelines provide tips on how managers, creditors, and investors use financial statements and other forms of accounting information.

Decision Guidelines

Financing With Debt or With Stock

Decision	Guidelines
How will you finance your business's operations?	Your financing plan depends on several factors, including the ability of the business's operations to generate cash flow, your willingness to give up some control of the business, the amount of financing risk you are willing to take, and the business's credit rating.
Do the business's operations generate enough cash flow to meet all its financing needs?	If yes, the business needs little outside financing. There is no need for debt. If no, the business will need to issue additional stock or borrow the money it needs.
Are you willing to give up some of your control of the business?	If yes, then issue stock to other stockholders, who can vote their shares to elect the company's directors. If no, then borrow from bondholders, who have no vote in the management of the company.
How much financing risk are you willing to take?	If much, then borrow as much as you can. This will increase the business's debt ratio and the risk that it will be unable to pay its debts. If little, then borrow sparingly. This will hold the debt ratio down and reduce the risk of default on borrowing agreements.
How good i...	The better t... the

Real Financial Statements with Custom On Location Videos

Each chapter begins with the financial statement of a well-known organization and a story that draws students into accounting concepts. Each example is accompanied by a **high-interest video clip**, produced especially for this book. Among the companies featured:

- Lands' End
- Intel
- General Motors Acceptance Corp.
- America West Airlines
- May Department Stores
- IHOP

Internet Exercises

A huge assortment of financial information is available on the World Wide Web. Each chapter features an Internet Exercise tied to the chapter's opening story and video. Check out the Harrison/Horngren *Financial Accounting* site at **http://www.prenhall.com/phbusiness**, which remains up-to-date even as company addresses and URLs change. The Harrison/Horngren Web site also contains links to many of the companies featured as examples in the text.

LEARNING BY DOING

STOP & THINK

To learn accounting, students must use accounting. Stop & Think features ask students to pause and think about what they've read—to put the concepts they've learned into practice.

STOP & THINK Test your ability to use the cash-flow statement. During the fiscal year ended January 28, 1996, The Home Depot paid $1,278.1 million for plant assets. The cash-flow statement reports this cash payment as Capital Expenditures, a common description. During the year the company sold property and equipment, receiving cash of $29.4 million. The Home Depot labels the cash received as Proceeds from Sales of Property and Equipment, also a common reporting practice. The $29.4 million is the amount of cash received from the sale of plant assets. It is neither the cost nor the book value of the assets sold. If the cash received from the sale differs from the asset's book value, the company reports a gain or a loss on the sale in the income statement.

1. Make an entry in the journal to record The Home Depot's capital expenditures during the year.

2. Suppose the book value of the property and equipment that The Home Depot sold was $31.5 million. The assets' cost was $52.7 million and their accumulated depreciation was $21.2 million. Record the company's transaction to sell the property and equipment. Also write a sentence to explain why the sale transaction resulted in a loss for The Home Depot.

Answer:

		Millions	
1.	Property and Equipment............................	1,2781.1	
	Cash...		1,278.1
	Made capital expenditures.		
2.	Cash..	29.4	
	Accumulated Depreciation.........................	21.2	
	Loss on Sale of Property and Equipment...	2.1	
	Property and Equipment		52.7
	Sold property and equipment.		

The company sold for $29.4 million assets that had book value of $31.5 million. The result of the sale was a loss of $2.1 million.

MID-CHAPTER AND END-OF-CHAPTER SUMMARY PROBLEMS

Accounting knowledge is cumulative. Students cannot simply discard what they've learned after they've taken the first exam if they hope to do well on the next one. Each chapter features two summary problems that ask students to work with the material encountered in the chapter thus far. Complete solutions are provided.

Mid-Chapter

SUMMARY PROBLEM FOR YOUR REVIEW

Humana, Inc. is one of the largest U.S. managed health-care companies. It provides a full array of health plans, including health maintenance organizations (HMOs) and administrative-services-only plans. The largest current asset on Humana's balance sheet is Marketable Securities (short-term investments). Note 4 to Humana's financial statements indicates that U.S. government securities, tax-exempt bonds, and corporate bonds make up the bulk of the company's marketable securities.

Assume Humana paid $1,136 million when it purchased the marketable securities in November 19X5. At December 31, 19X5, their amortized cost is $1,144 million, and their market value is $1,156 million.

Required

Test your understanding of accounting for short-term investments by answering these questions about Humana's marketable securities.

1. If Humana plans to hold the marketable securities until their maturity, will these securities be classified as held-to-maturity, trading, or available-for-sale? At what amount will Humana report the investment on the balance sheet at December 31, 19X5? What will Humana report on its income statement for 19X5?

Answer

1. Held-to-maturity securities, reported as follows on the balance sheet:

Current assets:	Millions
Cash..	$ XX
Marketable securities (or short-term investments), at amortized cost.......	1,144

Humana's income statement will report:

Other revenue and expense:	Millions
Interest revenue ($1,144 million - $1,136 million).......................................	$ 8

THE BEST IN BRIEF

OTHER FEATURES THAT CONTRIBUTE TO OUR SUCCESS:

- *Integrated coverage of the* ***statement of cash flows***
- *Analysis of transactions through the* ***accounting equation***
- *Hundreds of examples from real-world companies like Coca-Cola and Toys"Я"Us*
- *New* ***group projects*** *in every chapter*
- ***Concept highlights*** *that summarize key material*
- *The finest exercises and problems of any textbook, many featuring* ***decision settings*** *at real companies like Sprint and Wal-Mart*
- ***Concept links*** *that help students review earlier discussions of technical material*
- ***Writing exercises*** *in every chapter*

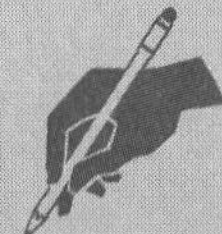

Underlying our operations is a series of beliefs that provides a foundation for our main product— the Financial Accounting, 3/E text.

CORPORATE PROFILE

THEME	MISSION STATEMENT	FIND IT HERE
Cash Management	*Businesses must carefully monitor their inflows and outflows of cash.*	•*Chapter 4* presents new material on budgeting, managing cash, and speeding the collection of cash from sales. •The statement of cash flows (SCF) is introduced as an instrument of analysis in Chapter 1, and revisited throughout the text. See, for example, the following optional sections: •*Chapter 5*: Relating short-term investments and receivables to the SCF •*Chapter 7*: Reporting plant asset transactions on the SCF •*Chapter 8*: Reporting financing activities on the SCF •*Chapter 10*: Using the SCF to interpret a company's investing activities •*Chapter 12* explains the preparation of the statement of cash flows, step by step.
Internal Control	*Managers must use an effective internal control system to safeguard the organization's assets.*	•Internal control issues are introduced and discussed in detail in Chapter 4. •Internal control is addressed in relevant chapter sections—for example: •*Chapter 5*: Establishing internal control over the collection of receivables •*Chapter 6*: Internal control over inventory •*Chapter 7*: Internal control over plant assets
Accounting Information Systems	*Computers and management information systems have revolutionized accounting, freeing accountants to spend more time on management and consulting activities.*	•The role of computers in accounting is introduced in Chapter 1. Each chapter discusses the uses of computers in the various accounting processes. For example: •*Chapter 3*: Automatic monthly depreciation calculated and posted by computer •*Chapter 5*: Calculating interest payments with computers •*Chapter 10*: Using computers for consolidation accounting •*Chapter 12*: Using computers to prepare the statement of cash flows •*Chapter 13*: Using computers to calculate financial ratios and to compare companies' performance •*Appendix E* provides an introduction to spreadsheets and databases.
Ethics	*Accountants must subscribe to the highest ethical standards.*	•Ethical Issues are featured in every chapter's problem material. •In-chapter discussions throughout the text—for example: •*Chapter 3*: Ethical issues in accrual accounting •*Chapter 6*: Ethical issues in inventory accounting •*Chapter 7*: Ethical issues in accounting for plant assets and intangibles •*Chapter 8*: Ethics of reporting contingent liabilities

Management Discussion & Analysis

We had a successful and fulfilling year of product revision, and we feel very confident in our book's ability to meet our customers' needs.

Because *Financial Accounting, 3/E* focuses on the most widely used accounting theory and practice, it falls clearly into the mainstream of modern accounting. At the same time, the book incorporates many of the pedagogical improvements suggested by the Accounting Education Change Commission (AECC)—a user perspective, an emphasis on critical thinking skills and decision making, group learning activities, a business context for accounting, and the integration of ethical and international issues.

The text follows the authors' teaching method, which is to lead students into accounting through a series of dynamic examples from the real world of business. Each chapter begins with an application that eases students into the accounting concepts being discussed. How different from the days when educators assumed that students were naturally interested in accounting! They are not. It is the text's job, and the educator's job, to spark students' interest in the material, to show the application of accounting to their lives. Once they see the relevance of accounting, students will learn it.

Report of Independent Auditors

To the stakeholders of Harrison and Horngren's *Financial Accounting, 3/E*:

We understand that textbooks and their ancillary materials need to be 100% error-free. Ensuring this type of accuracy is a major undertaking, given that accounting books are generally typeset by nonaccountants. Thus, to ensure complete accuracy in the text, we, the undersigned accountants, have checked every stage of proof, from original manuscript through final typeset pages. Through careful examination of every stage of the publishing process, we have also made every effort to ensure that the book's accompanying Solutions Manual is also error-free.

Betsy Willis
Baylor University

Becky Jones
Baylor University

Robert H. Bauman
Allan Hancock College

Thomas Hoar
Houston Community College

Fred R. Jex
Macomb Community College

Brian F. Ready, MBA

Carolyn Streuly
Marquette University

Timothy B. Griffin
University of Missouri, Kansas City

Harrison & Horngren's Financial Accounting, 3/E comes with a number of innovative supplements.

SUBSIDIARIES

ON LOCATION VIDEO PACKAGE

This video series, created exclusively for Prentice Hall, uses TV's fast-paced and engaging qualities to focus on the financial accounting activities of real-world companies. These high-impact videos take students on location at such companies as Lands' End, Intel, Home Depot, General Motors Acceptance Corp., and many more. The *Video Guide*, in the Instructor's Manual, provides suggestions for integrating the videos into classroom lectures.

TEACHING TRANSPARENCIES

These teaching acetates provide overviews and outlines of chapter topics. Many of these acetates feature *additional* exhibits, examples, and step-by-step explanations not provided in the text. The *Instructor's Manual* provides Lecture Notes for each teaching transparency.

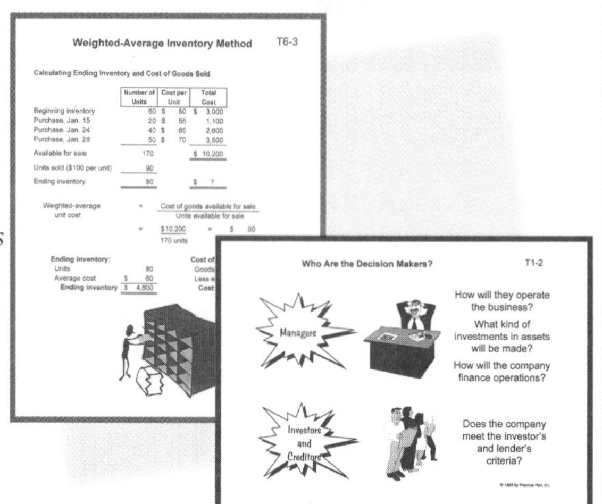

PH PROFESSOR: CLASSROOM PRESENTATIONS ON POWERPOINT

A PowerPoint presentation is available for each chapter of the text. Each module presents chapter material using colorful graphics and charts, innovative ways of explaining text concepts, and interactive activities for students. PowerPoint also provides instructors with the flexibility to add, delete, or modify existing slides.

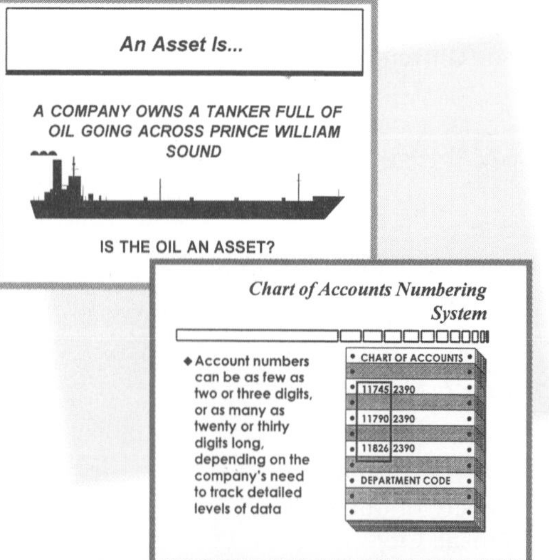

OUR CORE SUBSIDIARIES:

Solutions Manual • Instructor's Manual and Video Guide • Test Item File • Prentice Hall Custom Test software

FOR OUR MOST IMPORTANT CUSTOMERS, THE STUDENTS:

Working Papers • Study Guide • Power Notes on the Web • Activities in Financial Accounting, by Martha S. Doran • Interpreting and Analyzing Financial Statements, by Karen Schoenebeck • Spreadsheet Templates (Excel and Lotus) to accompany text exercises and problems

We offer a number of options for instructors who wish to use technology and multimedia in the classroom.

Technological Ventures

Career Paths in Accounting CD-ROM

Winner of the New Media INVISION Gold Award in Education

This CD-ROM provides students with a dynamic, interactive job-search tool. The CD includes workshops in career planning, résumé writing, and interviewing skills. Students can learn about the latest market trends, facts about the profession, and the skills they need to land the right job. The CD also provides salary information, video clips describing specific jobs, and profiles of accounting professionals.

PH Re-Enforcer Tutorial Software 3.0 for Windows

This enhanced interactive tutorial allows students to work through accounting problems to reinforce concepts and skills covered in the text. Users can work through multiple-choice questions, short exercises, vocabulary games, and case problems using multimedia graphics and a computer tutorial environment. This release has new printing capabilities, and students can now retrieve questions based on learning objective and/or difficulty level. A *Teacher's Edition* allows instructors to edit, change, and add existing or additional material.

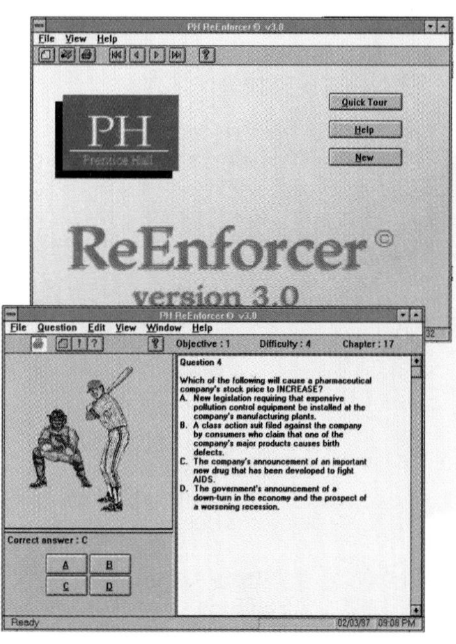

New

Prentice Hall Accounting Web Site

For the best in accounting on the Internet, visit our home page at **http://www.prenhall.com/phbusiness**. Both faculty and student supplements are available on this Web site, including PowerPoint presentations, Power Notes, Teaching Transparencies, and Spreadsheet Templates.

New

Quick Tours

Interested in learning about Re-Enforcer or the Prentice Hall Accounting Software (PHAS) quickly and easily? Both packages now include Quick Tours that provide students with step-by-step instructions on how to use the program. Quick Tours also allow students to run practice drills on all the types of problems within each software package.

Our Core Technology Products:

- *Prentice Hall Accounting Software (PHAS)—* *A general ledger package to accompany textbook exercises and problems.*
- *Training Video, by Jean Insinga—to teach instructors how to use Prentice Hall's technology products.*

We rely on the help of trained professionals to help us maintain our commitment to quality.

Third Edition Consultants

Text Reviewers

Kim L. Anderson
Indiana University of Pennsylvania

James M. Emig
Villanova University

Pat Evans
Auburn University

Kevin Feeney
Southern Connecticut State University

Timothy B. Griffin
University of Missouri - Kansas City & Johnson County Community College

Sue Gunckel
Albuquerque TVI Community College

Jim Haischer
Polk Community College

Gregory S. Kordecki
Clayton State College

Keith R. Leeseburg
Manatee Community College

Alfonso Oddo
Niagara University

Patrick M. Premo
St. Bonaventure University

Victoria Rymer
University of Maryland at College Park

Margaret Shelton
University of Houston - Downtown

Carolyn Streuly
Marquette University

Diane L. Tanner
University of North Florida

Focus Group Participants

John Aheto
Pace University

Ashton Bishop
James Madison University

Bill Geary
College of William & Mary

Ken Hiltebeitel
Villanova University

Rita Kingery
University of Delaware - Newark

Frank Lordi
Widener University

John Rude
St. John's University

John Sigler
University of Baltimore

Supplements Authors

Instructor's Manual
Becky Jones
Betsy Willis
Baylor University

PowerPoint Presentations/ Power Notes
Grace F. Johnson-Page
Marietta College

Software Consultant
Jean Insinga
Middlesex Community College

Spreadsheet Templates
Albert Fisher
Community College of Southern Nevada

Study Guide
Stephen C. Schaefer
Contra Costa College

Teaching Transparencies
Diane L. Tanner
University of North Florida

Test Item File
Alice B. Sineath, CPA
Forsyth Technical Community College

Video Producer
Beverly Amer
Northern Arizona University

Working Papers
Ellen Sweatt
DeKalb College - North

Text Reviewers, First & Second Editions

Salvador D. Aceves
Napa Valley College

Nina Brown
Tarrant County Junior College - Northwest

Kurt H. Buerger
Angelo State University

Glenn Bushnell
DeAnza College

Eric Carlson
Kean College of New Jersey

Wallace P. Carroll
J. Sargeant Reynolds Community College

Donna Chadwick
Sinclair Community College

Darrel W. Davis
University of Northern Iowa

S.T. Desai
Cedar Valley College

Carl J. Fisher
Foothill College

Jessica Frazier
Eastern Kentucky University

Marilyn Fuller
Paris Junior College

Roger Gee
San Diego Mesa College

Lucille Genduso
Nova University

James Genseal
Joliet Junior College

Barbara Gerrity
Berkeley School of Westchester

Gloria Grayless
Sam Houston State University

Ann Gregory
South Plains College

Debby Halik
Ivy Technical College

Jim Hansen
North Dakota State University

Saad Hassanein
Marymount University

Jimmie Henslee
El Centro College

Cynthia Holloway
Tarrant County Junior College - Northeast

Andrew Hrechek
Seton Hall University

Jean Insinga
Middlesex Community College

Tyronne James
Southern University of New Orleans

Fred R. Jex
Macomb Community College

Mary Thomas Keim
Indiana University of Pennsylvania

Nancy L. Kelly
Middlesex Community College

Randy Kidd
Penn Valley Community College

Raymond L. Larson
Appalachian State University

Cathy Larson
Middlesex Community College

Linda Lessing
SUNY College of Technology - Farmingdale

Lola Locke
Tarrant County Junior College

Cathy Lumbattis
Southern Illinois University

Paul Mihalek
University of Hartford

Graham Morris

Bruce Neumann
University of Colorado - Denver

Alfonso R. Oddo
Niagara University

Linda Overstreet
Hillsborough Community College

Robert Palmer
Troy State University

Karen Russom
North Harris College

Sherry Shively
Johnson County Community College

Kathleen Simione
Quinnipiac College

Dorothy Steinsapir
Middlesex Community College

Gracelyn Stuart
Palm Beach Community College

Diane L. Tanner
University of North Florida

Kathy Terrell
University of Central Oklahoma

Cynthia Thomas
Central Missouri State University

John Vaccaro
Bunker Hill Community College

Paul Waite
Niagara Community College

Martin Ward
DeVry Institute of Technology

Jim Weglin
North Seattle Community College

Bill Wempe
Wichita State University

Dale Westfall
Midland College

Joe Zernick
Ivy Technical College

English as a Second Language Reviewer

Zhu Zhu
Phoenix College

Focus Group Participants

Richard Ahrens
Los Angeles Pierce College

Charles Alvis
Winthrop University

Juanita Ardavant
Los Angeles Valley College

Patricia Ayres
Arapahoe Community College

Carl Ballard
Central Piedmont Community College

Maria Barillas
Phoenix College

Dorcus Berg
Wingate College

Angela Blackwood
Belmont Abbey College

Gary R. Bower
Community College of Rhode Island

Jack Brown
Los Angeles Valley College

Virginia Brunell
Diablo Valley College

James Carriger
Ventura College

Stan Carroll
New York City Technical College

Janet Cassagio
Nassau Community College

Les Chadwick
University of Delaware

Stanley Chu
Borough of Manhattan Community College

Kerry Colton
Aims Community College

Shaun Crayton
New York City Technical College

Susan Crosson
Santa Fe Community College

Don Daggett
Mankato State University

Joneal W. Daw
Los Angeles Valley College

Lyle E. Dehning
Metropolitan State College

Wanda Deleo
Winthrop University

Jim Donnelly
Bergen Community College

Bruce England
Massasoit Community College

Dave Fellows
Red Rocks Community College

Roger Gee
San Diego Mesa College

Marty Ginsberg
Rockland Community College

Earl Godfrey
Gardner Webb University

Jean Gutmann
University of Southern Maine

Ralph W. Hernandez
New York City Technical College

Carl High
New York City Technical College

Mary Hill
University of North Carolina - Charlotte

Jean Insinga
Middlesex Community College

Bernard Johnson
Santa Monica College

Diane G. Kanis
Bergen Community College

John Keelan
Massachusetts Bay Community College

Mary Thomas Keim
Indiana University of Pennsylvania

Cynthia Kreisner
Austin Community College

Cathy Larson
Middlesex Community College

Raymond L. Larson
Appalachian State University

Linda Lessing
SUNY College of Technology - Farmingdale

Angela LeTourneau
Winthrop University

Frank Lordi
Widener University

Audra Lowray
New York City Technical College

Grace Lyons
Bergen Community College

Ed Malmgren
University of North Carolina - Charlotte

Paola Marocchi
New York City Technical College

Larry McCarthy
Slippery Rock University

Linda Spotts Michael
Maple Woods Community College

Greg Mostyn
Mission College

Kitty Nessmith
Georgia Southern University

Lee Nicholas
University of Northern Iowa

Terry Nunnelly
University of North Carolina - Charlotte

Al Partington
Los Angeles Pierce College

Juan Perez
New York City Technical College

Ron Pierno
University of Missouri

Geraldine Powers
Northern Essex Community College

Harry Purcell
Ulster County Community College

John Ribezzo
Community College of Rhode Island

Rosemarie Ruiz
York University

Stephen C. Schaefer
Contra Costa College

Parmar Sejal
Bergen Community College

Lynn Shoaf
Belmont Abbey College

Walter J. Silva
Roxbury Community College

Leon Jo Singleton
Santa Monica College

David Skougstad
Metropolitan State College

Paul Sunko
Olive-Harvey College

Chandra Taylor
New York City Technical College

Phillip Thornton
Metropolitan State College

John L. Vaccaro
Bunker Hill Community College

The excellence of our products owes much to the people who help us develop, produce, and market them:

DIRECTORS AND OFFICERS

Annie Todd
Senior Acquisitions Editor

Steven Rigolosi
Managing Editor, Book Development

Deborah Hoffman Emry
Executive Marketing Manager

Katherine Evancie
Managing Editor, Production

Suzanne Behnke
Senior Designer

P.J. Boardman
Editor-in-Chief

Patti Dant
Customer Service and Events Manager

Chris Smerillo
Customer Service Representative

Vincent Scelta
Manufacturing Manager

Paul Smolenski
Senior Manufacturing Supervisor

Alana Zdinak
Manufacturing Buyer

Natacha St. Hill
Assistant Editor

Elaine Oyzon-Mast
Editorial Assistant

Robert Prokop
Marketing Assistant

Cindy Spreder
Production Coordinator

In addition, we thank Betsy Willis and Becky Jones for coordinating the team of solutions checkers, and for providing many of the Learning Tips and Concept Links. We also thank J. R. Dietrich, Barbara Gerrity, Carl High, Jean Marie Hudson, Alfonso R. Oddo, and Beverly Terry for providing a variety of helpful suggestions. Our gratitude also to Eve Adams for designing our annual report, to Phil Drake for preparing the Internet exercises, and to Beverly Amer for producing the video series.

INVESTOR INFORMATION

Ask your Prentice Hall sales representative for more information about any of our products or subsidiaries. Or call the ***Prentice Hall Accounting and Taxation Hotline*** *at* ***1-800-227-1816*** *for all your information, textbook, and supplement needs.*

Harrison and Horngren,
Financial Accounting 3/E
ISBN 013-741984-8

CP083AC

Contents

CHAPTER 4

Internal Control and Managing Cash 169

CHAPTER 5

Accounting for Short-Term Investments and Receivables 219

CHAPTER 6

Accounting for Merchandise Inventory, Cost of Goods Sold, and the Gross Margin 261

CHAPTER 7

Accounting for Plant Assets, Intangible Assets, and Related Expenses 319

CHAPTER 8

Accounting for Current and Long-Term Liabilities 365

CHAPTER 9
Measuring and Reporting Stockholders' Equity 417

CHAPTER 10
Accounting for Long-Term Investments and International Operations 467

CHAPTER 13
Financial Statement Analysis for Decision Making 643

APPENDIX A
The Annual Report of Lands' End, Inc. 693

APPENDIX B
Time Value of Money: Future Value and Present Value 720

APPENDIX C
Summary of Generally Accepted Accounting Principles (GAAP) 729

APPENDIX D
Accounting for Partnerships 731

APPENDIX E
Modern Accounting Information Systems 748

APPENDIX F
Special Accounting Journals 755

APPENDIX G
Check Figures 768

GLOSSARY G1

COMPANY AND PRODUCT INDEX I1

SUBJECT INDEX I3

Decision Guidelines

Thematic Examples

Computerized Accounting Systems

Chapter	Example	Page
1	General introduction to the role of computers in accounting	10
	The virtual office	47
2	Debits and credits in a computerized accounting system	64
	Using computers to record and journalize transactions immediately; computerized ledgers	69
	Computer preparation of trial balances	75
3	Use of computers to prepare monthly trial balances	113
	Adjusting prepaid expenses automatically each month with computer software	115
	Automatic monthly depreciation calculated and posted by computer	116
	Computerized payroll modules for end-of-month adjustments	120
	Closing entries done automatically by computer	136
	Correcting errors in computerized accounting systems	136–137
4	Separation of duties in computerized systems	174
	Automatic creation of permanent sales records in a computerized system and other computerized controls	175
	Electronic fund transfer	178–179
	Prevention of errors in account balances with computers	181
	Using computers to keep track of accounts receivable	189
	Computers used to control cash receipts and disbursements	191, 193
5	Using computers in the aging of accounts receivable	233
	Computer databases of bad credit risks	235
	Calculating interest payments with computers	238
6	Use of computers in a perpetual inventory system	265
	Maintaining weighted-average cost records by computer	278
	Using computers to report inventory at LCM	280
	Using optical scanners to update the cost of goods sold account	314
7	Accounting for the cost of buildings during construction with computers	323
	Using computerized systems to account for fixed assets and changes in accounting estimates	336
8	Accounting for current liabilities arising from many similar transactions; using computers to link the accounts payable	368
	Computerizing the payment of interest on notes payable	369
	Use of computers to answer "what if" questions regarding financing options	394
10	Using computers for consolidation accounting	483
12	Using computers to prepare the statement of cash flows	592
	Computers and the indirect method of generating the statement of cash flows	610
	Using a computerized work sheet to prepare the statement of cash flows	637
13	Using computers to calculate financial ratios and to compare companies' performance	659

Generally Accepted Accounting Principles (GAAP)

Chapter	Example	Page
1	Introduction to generally accepted accounting principles: entity concept, reliability principle, cost principle, going-concern principle, stable-monetary unit concept	10–13
3	GAAP requirement that the accrual basis of accounting be used rather than the cash basis	108
	The time-period concept, revenue principle, and matching principle	109–112
4	GAAP rules regarding preparation of the statement of cash flows	196–197
5	Reasons not to use the direct write-off method of accounting for bad debts	236
6	Four inventory costing methods allowed by GAAP: specific unit cost, weighted-average cost, FIFO, and LIFO	271–273
	GAAP and practical considerations: a comparison of inventory methods	274–276
	GAAP's lower-of-cost-or-market rule	280–281
7	Accounting for plant assets and intangibles according to GAAP	322
	Matching an asset's expense against the revenue produced by that asset	332
	GAAP requirements for a change in accounting estimate	337
	Rules regarding amortization, including goodwill	343, 345
	GAAP rules regarding the expensing of R&D costs	346
8	Accounting for contingent liabilities	377–378
	GAAP rules regarding use of the straight-line amortization	391
	Procedures for recording extraordinary gains and losses on the early retirement of debt	392
9	Reporting of donated capital	431
	Recording small (0-20%) versus large (25%+) stock dividends	441–443
10	Bringing foreign subsidiaries' statements into conformity with American GAAP	492
	Comparison of GAAP in the United States with accounting principles in other countries	494
11	GAAP requirement that companies report the cumulative effect of a change in accounting principle	523
	GAAP requirement that earnings per share data be reported on the income statement	524
	GAAP requirement that companies disclose upcoming debt payments for the next five years	539
	Conformity to GAAP as explained in the statement of management responsibility	543
12	Accrual-basis accounting vs. cash-basis accounting	588
	Ensuring that the statement of cash flows, as prepared by computer, corresponds to GAAP	610
13	GAAP requirement that companies disclose EPS on the income statement	672
Appendix C	Summary of GAAP	729

Internal Control

Chapter	Example	Page
4	Full chapter on "Internal Control and Managing Cash"	169–218
5	Establishing internal control over the collection of receivables	229–230
6	Internal control over inventory	286–288
7	Internal control of plant assets	341–342

Ethics

(Ethical Issue exercises appear at the end of every chapter)

Chapter	Example	Page
1	Introduction to ethical considerations in accounting and business	8
3	Ethical issues in accrual accounting	131–132
4	Ethics and internal/external controls	198–201
6	Ethical issues in inventory accounting	282–283
7	Ethical issues in accounting for plant assets and intangibles	347–348
8	Ethics of reporting contingent liabilities	377–378
9	Ethical considerations in accounting for the issuance of stock	431
	Ethical implications of treasury stock transactions	434

Financial Accounting

1

Summarizing Business Activity and Using the Financial Statements

Learning Objectives

After studying this chapter, you should be able to

1. Understand accounting vocabulary and use it in decision making
2. Analyze business activity with accounting concepts and principles
3. Use the accounting equation to describe an organization's financial position
4. Use a company's financial statements to evaluate its operating performance and financial position
5. Understand the relationships among the financial statements

Lands' End, Inc. & Subsidiaries
Consolidated Statement of Operations (adapted)

	(In thousands)	*For the fiscal years ended* February 2, 1996	*For the fiscal years ended* January 27, 1995
1	**Net sales**	**$1,031,548**	$992,106
2	Cost of sales	**588,017**	571,265
3	**Gross profit**	**443,531**	420,841
4	Selling, general, and administrative expenses	**392,484**	357,516
5	Charges from sale of subsidiary	**1,882**	3,500
6	**Income from operations**	**49,165**	59,825
7	Other income (expense):		
8	Interest expense	**(2,771)**	(1,769)
9	Interest income	**253**	307
10	Other	**4,278**	1,300
11	Total other income (expense), net	**1,760**	(162)
12	**Income before income taxes**	**50,925**	59,663
13	Income tax provision	**20,370**	23,567
14	**Net income**	**$ 30,555**	$ 36,096

> "*All the activities and events at Lands' End relate to the financial statements. We report all the activities in the financial statements, whether it's payroll on a weekly basis, catalog costs, or investing in buildings or equipment. . . . Everything that happens at Lands' End in some way will end up coming through the financial statements.*"
>
> —DON HUGHES, VICE PRESIDENT–FINANCE, LANDS' END, INC.

A major catalog merchant located in Dodgeville, Wisconsin is **Lands' End, Inc.** The company, best known for its shirts, slacks, and luggage, began in 1963 as a retailer of boat hardware and other sailing equipment. In 1978, founder Gary Comer listed some clothing in a Lands' End catalog, and the business took off. Today Lands' End sells over $1 billion of merchandise a year and earns an annual profit exceeding $30 million.

Suppose Lands' End is considering expanding its Dodgeville facility. What factors must its top managers consider as they decide whether the expansion will be worth the investment? First and foremost, Lands' End must expect to earn a profit on its new venture. Otherwise the company would decide not to undertake the expansion. If the company expected a loss on the new venture, it would look for investment opportunities elsewhere.

Operating, Investing, and Financing Activities

A firm's **operating activities** relate directly to its *net income*. The table on page 2 is Lands' End's *statement of operations,* taken from its annual report for 1996; the last line reports the company's net income (profits) for the year. The statement of operations is also called the *income statement* because it focuses on net income, the "bottom line" of the statement.

Before Lands' End began operating in 1963, it had to invest in assets that the company needed to conduct its business. *Assets* are the resources that a business uses to produce a product or deliver a service. **Investing activities** relate to the purchase and sale of assets such as land, buildings, and equipment. Lands' End owns land in Wisconsin, warehouses its goods in buildings, and uses equipment to move merchandise through the warehouse en route to United Parcel Service and other shippers.

To purchase these assets, Lands' End had to undertake financing activities. **Financing activities** relate to the ways a company obtains money for investing and operating activities. There are two basic ways to finance a business: (1) borrow money from banks and other lenders, and/or (2) obtain funds from the business's owners. Most companies finance their operations with a combination of the two.

In new businesses, financing generally comes first, because a company must have money before it can invest and operate. Investing typically occurs next as the business invests in the assets it needs for operations. Operating activities follow as the company conducts its core business. At Lands' End, operations consist of buying and selling merchandise. The operations of IBM and Xerox consist of manufacturing and selling business machines. Lawyers and accounting firms perform professional services as their core business operations. Exhibit 1-1 diagrams the flow of business activity for all types of businesses.

Once a business is up and running, which type of activity is most important? Operating activities are, because successful companies generate most of their money—year in and year out—from their main line of business. If a company operates successfully (that is, earns high levels of profit and generates a lot of cash) from its core operations, then investors will line up to buy its stock, and banks will be happy to lend the company money.

Investing activities are typically next most important because how much money comes in also depends on how wisely a business invests. Good investments generate a lot of cash, while bad investments lose money. For Lands' End, a good investment may be robotic equipment that speeds the process of order filling and reduces labor costs. A bad investment for Lands' End may be an expansion into electronic products, which Lands' End managers may not understand well and which may cause the company to lose money.

For most ongoing businesses, financing activities are less important than operating and investing activities. It is more important that the business buy and

EXHIBIT 1-1
Financing, Investing, and Operating Activities

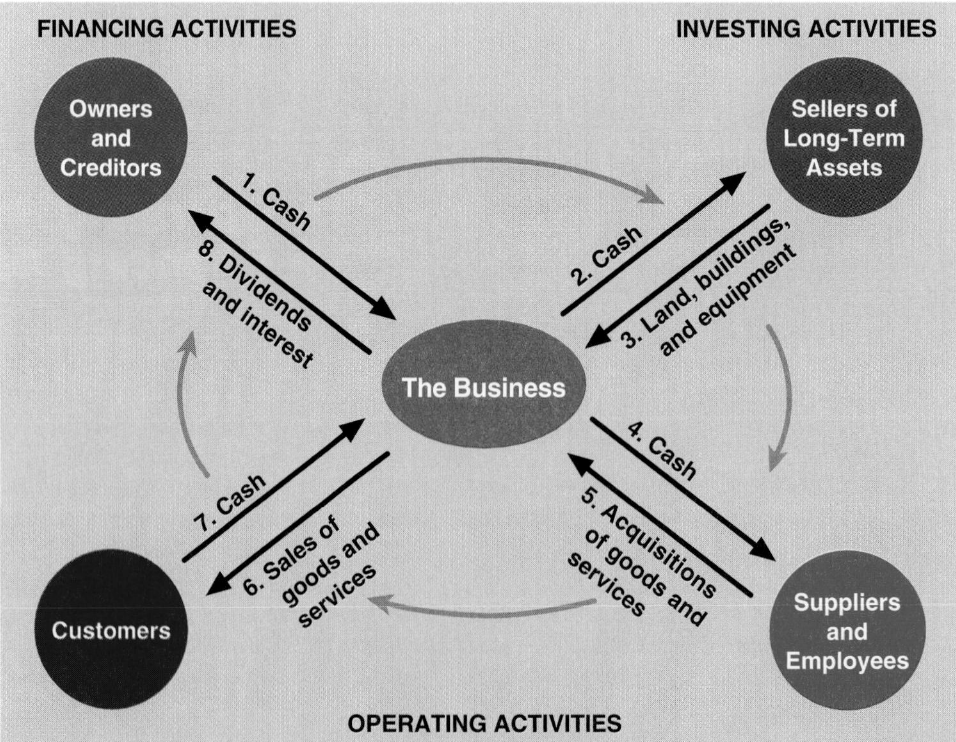

sell the right merchandise—that is, operate—and invest wisely because these activities are at the core of the company. A company that operates successfully and makes intelligent investments will have no trouble financing its operations.

Managerial Decisions

In deciding how they will operate the business, Lands' End managers must determine what merchandise they will sell and how they will market these goods. To make these decisions, these managers need to estimate the revenue that Lands' End can expect to earn from selling the goods and how much the goods will cost Lands' End. Clearly, the company wants its revenues to exceed its expenses so that the company will earn a profit. Accounting helps managers measure the revenue, the expenses, and the profit of the business.

The income statement on page 2 reports that Lands' End earned net sales revenue of over a billion dollars during 1996 (line 1). Cost of sales, an expense (line 2), consumed almost $600 million, leaving gross profit of $443 million (line 3). The other major expense category was selling, general, and administrative expenses (line 4, $392 million), and net income, after all expenses, was $30.6 million (line 14).

Lands' End managers must also determine what kinds of investments to make. In what types of assets should they invest? For example, should they automate the warehouse and use robotic equipment to handle their merchandise? If so, they will want to purchase the merchandise-handling equipment that moves goods rapidly and at the lowest cost. Accounting measures the cost of the equipment.

Finally, Lands' End's managers must decide how the company will finance its operations. Which way of financing the business is better—selling stock (ownership shares) to the owners or borrowing from outsiders? There is no standard answer. Sometimes there is an advantage to borrowing. In other cases, it is better to issue stock. However the company finances operations, accounting measures the cost of obtaining the funds.

Investor Decisions

Suppose you have $50,000 to invest. You can deposit the money in a bank and earn interest. Your investment would be safe because deposits in U.S. banks are insured, but it will not grow very fast in a bank account. Another possibility is for you to invest in land on the outskirts of town. There has been some talk that Wal-Mart may open a store in the vicinity, and the land may increase in value. If so, your investment may double or triple in value, but it is also quite risky because Wal-Mart may not locate near your land. Besides, others also know of Wal-Mart's plan, and you will have to pay a high price for the land.

A third possible investment is for you to buy stock in Lands' End. This investment is more risky than depositing money in a bank account but less risky than buying land in hopes of selling to Wal-Mart at a higher price. What information would you need before deciding to invest in Lands' End stock? You would prefer that Lands' End have a track record of profitable operations—earning a profit (net income) year after year. The company would need a steady stream of cash coming in and a manageable level of debt. How would you determine whether the company meets these criteria? The company's *financial statements* can provide you with the information you need.

Accounting—The Basis of Decision Making

Objective 1

Understand accounting vocabulary and use it in decision making

Accounting is the information system that measures business activities, processes that information into reports, and communicates the results to decision makers. For this reason, it is called "the language of business." The better you understand this language, the better you can manage the financial aspects of living, and the better your financial decisions will be. Personal financial planning, education expenses, loans, car payments, income taxes, and investments are all based on the information system we call accounting.

A key product of an accounting information system is a series of financial statements that allow people to make informed business decisions. **Financial statements** are the documents that report financial information about a business entity to decision makers. They tell us how well a business is performing and where it stands. In this chapter we focus on the financial statements of Lands' End, Inc. By the time you complete this first chapter, you will be familiar with the financial statements that this well-known company uses to represent itself to the public. This is the first step in this book's major goal: to acquaint you with financial statements and to give you the expertise you need to use them for financial decision making.

Please don't mistake bookkeeping for accounting. *Bookkeeping* is a procedural element of accounting, just as arithmetic is a procedural element of mathematics. Exhibit 1-2 illustrates the role of accounting in business. The process starts and ends with people making decisions.

The Users of Accounting Information: Decision Makers

Decision makers need information. The more important the decision, the greater the need for accurate information. Virtually all businesses and most individuals keep accounting records to aid in making decisions. The chapter opening story discussed some of the decisions that Lands' End managers and investors might be called on to make about an expansion of the company. One piece of financial information these decision makers might consult is the company's income statement (page 2), which we also saw earlier. We will examine this and other financial statements in detail as we proceed through this chapter.

Most of the material in this text describes business situations, but the principles of accounting apply to the financial affairs of other organizations and individuals as well. The following people and groups use accounting information regularly.

INDIVIDUALS People use accounting information in their day-to-day affairs to manage bank accounts, to evaluate job prospects, to make investments, and to decide whether to rent an apartment or buy a house.

EXHIBIT 1-2
The Accounting System: The Flow of Information

BUSINESSES Managers of businesses use accounting information to set goals for their organizations, to evaluate progress toward those goals, and to take corrective action if necessary. Decisions based on accounting information may include which building to purchase, how much merchandise inventory to keep on hand, and how much cash to borrow. In our chapter opening story, the managers of Lands' End needed to know how much the company could spend on an expansion of the business.

INVESTORS AND CREDITORS Investors and creditors provide the money a business needs to begin operations. To decide whether to help start a new venture, potential investors evaluate what income they can expect on their investment. This means analyzing the financial statements of the business. Before deciding to invest in Lands' End, for example, you or your investment adviser may examine Lands' End's financial statements. You would also keep up with developments in the company as reported in the business press—for example, *The Wall Street Journal, Business Week, Forbes,* and *Fortune.* Before making a loan, banks determine the borrower's ability to meet scheduled payments. This evaluation includes a projection of future operations and revenue, which is based on accounting information.

GOVERNMENT REGULATORY AGENCIES Most organizations face government regulation. For example, the *Securities and Exchange Commission (SEC),* a federal agency, requires businesses to disclose certain financial information to the investing public. Like many government agencies, the SEC bases its regulations in part on the accounting information it receives from firms.

TAXING AUTHORITIES Local, state, and federal governments levy taxes on individuals and businesses. The amount of the tax is figured using accounting information. Businesses determine the amount of sales tax they owe from accounting records that show how much they have sold. Individuals and businesses compute the income tax they owe from their recorded earnings.

NONPROFIT ORGANIZATIONS Nonprofit organizations—such as churches, hospitals, government agencies, and colleges, which operate for purposes other than profit—use accounting information in much the same way that profit-oriented businesses do. Both for-profit organizations and nonprofit organizations deal with budgets, payrolls, rent payments, and the like—all information that comes from the accounting system.

OTHER USERS Employees and labor unions make wage demands based on their employer's reported income. Consumer groups and the general public are also interested in the amount of income businesses earn. For example, during fuel shortages consumer groups have charged that oil companies have earned "obscene profits." And newspapers report "improved profit pictures" of companies as the nation emerges from economic recession. Such news, based on accounting information, is related to our standard of living.

Financial Accounting and Management Accounting

The users of accounting information are a diverse population, but they may be categorized as external users or internal users. This distinction allows us to classify accounting into two fields—financial accounting and management accounting.

Financial accounting provides information to managers and to people outside the firm, such as investors on Wall Street. Creditors and stockholders are not part of the day-to-day management of the company. Likewise, government agencies, such as the SEC, and the general public are external users of a firm's accounting information. Financial accounting information must meet certain standards of relevance and reliability. This book deals primarily with financial accounting.

Management accounting generates confidential information for internal decision makers, such as top executives, department heads, college deans, and hospital administrators. Management accounting information is tailored to the needs of the managers and thus does not have to meet external standards of reliability.

Ethical Considerations in Accounting and Business

Ethical considerations pervade all areas of accounting and business. Consider the following situation:

> **Texaco, Inc.,** was the defendant in a major lawsuit that threatened to put the company out of business. Texaco's managers wanted to downplay this lawsuit because they feared that customers would stop buying the company's products, which include gasoline, motor oil, and antifreeze; that Texaco's stock price would fall; and that banks would stop loaning money to the company. Should Texaco have disclosed this sensitive information? Yes, and Texaco did report the lawsuit, along with the potential effects on the company. Accounting guidelines required Texaco to describe this situation in its financial statements. And the company's auditor was required to state whether the Texaco disclosure was adequate.

By what criteria do accountants address questions that challenge their ethical conduct? The *American Institute of Certified Public Accountants (AICPA)*, other professional accounting organizations, and most large companies have codes of ethics that require their members and employees to have high levels of ethical conduct. The AICPA is the country's largest organization of professional accountants, similar to the American Medical Association for physicians and the American Bar Association for attorneys.

STANDARDS OF PROFESSIONAL CONDUCT FOR ACCOUNTANTS The Code of Professional Conduct was adopted by the members of the AICPA to provide guidance in performing their professional duties. Ethical standards in accounting are designed to produce accurate information for decision making. The preamble to the Code states: "[A] certified public accountant assumes an obligation of self-discipline above and beyond the requirements of laws and regulations . . . [and] an unswerving commitment to honorable behavior, even at the sacrifice of personal advantage." Key terms in the Code include *self-discipline, honorable behavior, moral judgments, the public interest, professionalism, integrity,* and *technical and ethical standards.*

The Boeing Company, a leading manufacturer of aircraft, has a highly developed set of business conduct guidelines.

THE BOEING COMPANY'S BUSINESS CONDUCT GUIDELINES Most organizations set standards of ethical conduct for their employees. For example, **The Boeing Company,** a leading manufacturer of aircraft, has a highly developed set of business conduct guidelines. In the introduction to those guidelines, the chairperson of the board and chief executive officer state: "We owe our success as much to our reputation for integrity as we do to the quality and dependability of our products and services. This reputation is fragile and can easily be lost."

Types of Business Organizations

A business takes one of three forms of organization, and in some cases, accounting procedures depend on which form the organization takes. Therefore, you should understand the differences among the three types of business organizations: proprietorships, partnerships, and corporations. Exhibit 1-3 compares the three types.

PROPRIETORSHIPS A **proprietorship** has a single owner, called the proprietor, who is generally also the manager. Lands' End started out as a proprietorship, with Gary Comer as the owner. Proprietorships tend to be small retail establish-

	Proprietorship	Partnership	Corporation
Owner(s)	Proprietor—one owner	Partners—two or more owners	Stockholders—generally many owners
Life of entity	Limited by owner's choice or death	Limited by owners' choices or death	Indefinite
Personal liability of owner(s) for business debts	Proprietor is personally liable	Partners are personally liable	Stockholders are not personally liable
Accounting status	Accounting entity is separate from proprietor	Accounting entity is separate from partners	Accounting entity is separate from stockholders

EXHIBIT 1-3
Comparison of the Three Forms of Business Organization

ments or individual professional businesses, such as those of physicians, attorneys, and accountants. From the accounting viewpoint, each proprietorship is distinct from its proprietor. Thus, the accounting records of the proprietorship do *not* include the proprietor's personal financial records. From a legal perspective, however, the business is the proprietor, which means that the proprietor is personally liable for the debts of the business.

PARTNERSHIPS A **partnership** joins two or more individuals together as co-owners. Each owner is a partner. Many retail establishments, as well as some professional organizations of physicians, attorneys, and accountants, are partnerships. Most partnerships are small or medium-sized, but some are gigantic, exceeding 2,000 partners. Accounting treats the partnership as a separate organization, distinct from the personal affairs of each partner. But, similar to a proprietorship, the law views a partnership as the partners. Therefore, each partner is personally liable for all the debts of the partnership. For this reason, partnerships are viewed as quite risky.

CORPORATIONS A **corporation** is a business owned by **stockholders,** or **shareholders,** people who own **stock,** or shares of ownership, in the business. The corporation is the dominant form of business organization in the United States. Although proprietorships and partnerships are more numerous, corporations transact more business and are larger in terms of total assets, income, and number of employees. Most well-known companies, such as Lands' End, General Motors, and American Airlines, are corporations. Their full names include *Corporation* or *Incorporated* (abbreviated *Corp.* and *Inc.*) to indicate that they are corporations—for example, Lands' End, Inc., and General Motors Corporation. Some corporations bear the name "Company," such as Ford Motor Company. This title does not clearly identify the organization as a corporation because a proprietorship and a partnership can also bear the name "Company."

A corporation is a business entity formed under state law. From a legal perspective, a corporation is a distinct entity. The corporation operates as an artificial person that exists apart from its owners. The corporation has many of the rights that a person has. For example, a corporation may buy, own, and sell property. Assets and debts in the business belong to the corporation. The corporation may enter into contracts, sue, and be sued. Unlike proprietors and partners, a stockholder has no personal obligation for corporation debts. The most that a stockholder can lose on an investment in a corporation's stock is the cost of the investment. But proprietors and partners are personally liable for the debts of their businesses.

The ownership interest of a corporation is divided into shares of stock. A person becomes a stockholder by purchasing the corporation's stock. Lands' End, for example, has over 40 million shares of stock owned by some several thousand shareholders. An investor with no personal relationship either to

Lands' End or to any other stockholder can become a co-owner by buying 1, 30, 100, 5,000, or any number of shares of its stock through the New York Stock Exchange.

The ultimate control of the corporation rests with the stockholders, who receive one vote for each share of stock they own. The stockholders elect the members of the **board of directors,** which sets policy for the corporation and appoints the officers. The board elects a *chairperson,* who usually is the most powerful person in the corporation and often carries the title chief executive officer (CEO). The board also designates the president, who is the chief operating officer (COO) in charge of managing day-to-day operations. Most corporations also have vice presidents in charge of sales, manufacturing, accounting and finance, and other key areas.

Accounting and Computers

Computers have revolutionized accounting in the late twentieth century. Tasks that are time-consuming when done by hand can be performed by computer in a fraction of the time. In addition to helping with accounting itself, microcomputers—personal computers, such as Apples, IBMs, and Compaqs—assist with many financial applications of accounting information and in business correspondence. Also, thanks to telecommunications, microcomputers can tap into the Internet. As we progress through the study of accounting, we will consider computer applications that fit the topics under discussion. We also provide an overview of computerized accounting systems in Appendix E at the end of the book.

STOP & THINK In an important trend in the health-care industry, many people are joining managed health-care groups. Suppose you want to invest in a company in this growth industry, such as U.S. Healthcare, Inc. (located in Blue Bell, Pennsylvania) or Humana, Inc. (headquartered in Louisville, Kentucky). Or perhaps you are more interested in the airline industry and have your eye on American Airlines (located in Dallas) or Delta Airlines (in Atlanta). How do you go about finding the information necessary to help make these decisions?

Answer: You can obtain the annual reports of most large corporations simply by requesting them from the company. EDGAR, a Securities and Exchange Commission database, gives addresses and other company data via the Internet, or you can obtain company addresses from *Moody's Industrial Manual* and other corporate directories available in most libraries.

Accounting Principles and Concepts

Objective 2

Analyze business activity with accounting concepts and principles

Accounting practices follow certain guidelines. The rules that govern how accountants measure, process, and communicate financial information fall under the heading **GAAP,** which stands for **generally accepted accounting principles.**

In the United States, the *Financial Accounting Standards Board (FASB)* determines how accounting is practiced. The FASB works with the SEC and AICPA. Exhibit 1-4 diagrams the relationships among these organizations and the rules that govern them. (In the diagram, start at the top, and move to your right.)

GAAP rests on a conceptual framework written by the FASB. *The primary objective of financial reporting is to provide information useful for making investment and lending decisions.* To be useful, information must be relevant, reliable, and comparable. Accountants strive to meet those goals in the information they produce. This course will expose you to the generally accepted methods of accounting; we will discuss these as they become relevant in each chapter. We also summarize them in Appendix C at the end of the book. Before we do so, however, you need to understand several basic concepts that underlie accounting practice.

EXHIBIT 1-4
Key Accounting Organizations

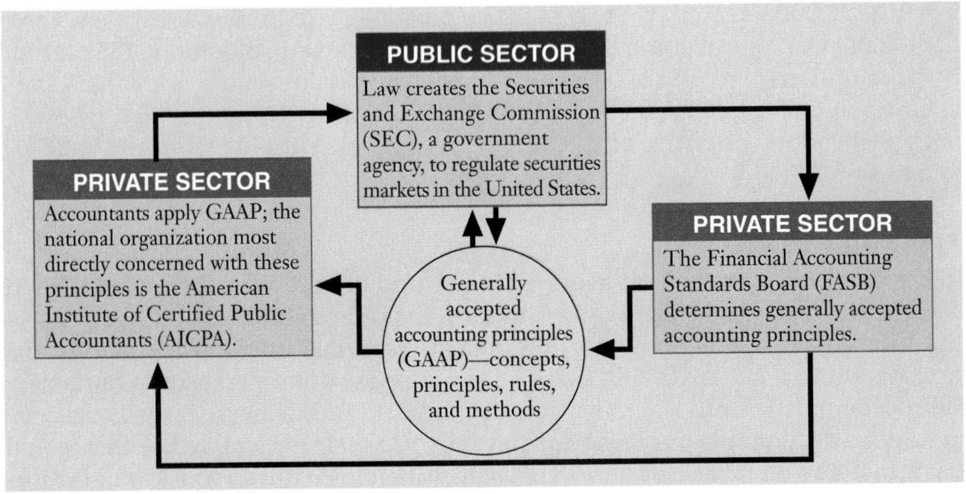

PUBLIC SECTOR
Law creates the Securities and Exchange Commission (SEC), a government agency, to regulate securities markets in the United States.

PRIVATE SECTOR
Accountants apply GAAP; the national organization most directly concerned with these principles is the American Institute of Certified Public Accountants (AICPA).

Generally accepted accounting principles (GAAP)—concepts, principles, rules, and methods

PRIVATE SECTOR
The Financial Accounting Standards Board (FASB) determines generally accepted accounting principles.

The Entity Concept

The most basic concept in accounting is that of the **entity.** An accounting entity is an organization or a section of an organization that stands apart from other organizations and individuals as a separate economic unit. From an accounting perspective, sharp boundaries are drawn around each entity so as not to confuse its affairs with those of other entities.

Consider Julie DeFilippo, the owner of the catering firm An Extra Hand. Suppose that her bank account shows a $2,000 balance at the end of the year. Only $1,200 of that amount came from the business's operations. The other $800 was a gift from her grandparents. If DeFilippo follows the entity concept, she will account for the $1,200 generated by the business—one economic unit—separately from the $800 she received from her family, a second economic unit. This separation makes it possible to view An Extra Hand's financial position clearly.

Suppose DeFilippo disregards the entity concept and treats the full $2,000 as the product of An Extra Hand's operations. She will be misled into believing that the business has produced more cash than it has and therefore may not take the actions necessary to make the business more successful.

Now consider **Toyota,** a huge organization made up of several divisions. Toyota management evaluates each division as a separate accounting entity. If sales in the Lexus division are dropping drastically, Toyota would do well to identify the reason. But if sales figures from all divisions of the company are analyzed as a single amount, then management will not know that the company is not selling enough Lexus automobiles. Thus, the entity concept also applies to the parts of a large organization—in fact, to any entity that needs to be evaluated separately.

In summary: The transactions of different entities should not be accounted for together. Each entity should be evaluated separately.

The Reliability (or Objectivity) Principle

Accounting records and statements are based on the most reliable data available so that they will be as accurate and as useful as possible. This guideline is the *reliability principle,* also called the *objectivity principle.* Reliable data are verifiable. They may be confirmed by an independent observer. Ideally, accounting records are based on information that flows from activities documented by objective evidence. For example, an $18 purchase of a shirt by Lands' End is supported by a paid invoice. This invoice is objective evidence of the company's cost of the shirt. Without the reliability principle, accounting records would be based on whims and opinions and subject to dispute.

Suppose you want to open a stereo shop. To have a place for retail operations, you transfer a small building to the business. You believe the building is worth $155,000. To confirm its cost to the business, you hire two real estate professionals who appraise the building at $147,000. Is your opinion ($155,000) or is the appraisers' opinion ($147,000) the more reliable estimate of the building's value? The real estate appraisal of $147,000 is, because it is supported by external, independent, objective observation. The business should record the building at cost of $147,000.

The Cost Principle

The *cost principle* states that acquired assets and services should be recorded at their actual cost (also called *historical cost*). Even though the purchaser may believe the price paid is a bargain, the item is recorded at the price paid in the transaction and not at the "expected" cost. Suppose your stereo shop purchases stereo equipment from a supplier who is going out of business. Assume that you get a good deal on this purchase and pay only $2,000 for merchandise that would have cost you $3,000 elsewhere. The cost principle requires you to record this merchandise at its actual cost of $2,000, not the $3,000 that you believe the equipment is worth.

The cost principle also holds that accounting records should maintain the historical cost of an asset for as long as the business holds the asset. Why? Because cost is a reliable measure. Suppose your store holds the stereo equipment for six months. During that time, stereo prices increase and the equipment can be sold for $3,500. Should its accounting value—the figure "on the books"—be the actual cost of $2,000 or the current market value of $3,500? According to the cost principle, the accounting value of the equipment remains at actual cost, $2,000.

The Going-Concern Concept

Another reason for measuring assets at historical cost is the *going-concern concept,* which holds that the entity will remain in operation for the foreseeable future. Most assets—that is, the firm's resources, such as supplies, land, buildings, and equipment—are acquired to use rather than to sell. Under the going-concern concept, accountants assume that the business will remain in operation long enough to use existing assets for their intended purpose. The market value of an asset—the price for which the asset can be sold—may change during the asset's life. Moreover, historical cost is a more reliable accounting measure for assets than market value is because cost is a historical fact. By contrast, there may be wide disagreement about the current market value of an asset.

To understand the going-concern concept better, consider the alternative, which is to go out of business. A store that is holding a going-out-of-business sale is trying to sell all its assets. In that case, the relevant measure of the assets is their current market value. However, going out of business is the exception rather than the rule, and for this reason the accounting records of a going concern list the assets at their historical cost.

The Stable-Monetary-Unit Concept

We think of a loaf of bread and a month's rent in terms of their dollar value. In the United States, accountants record transactions in dollars because the dollar is the medium of exchange. British accountants record transactions in pounds sterling, and Japanese accountants record transactions in yen.

Unlike the value of a liter, a mile, or an acre, the value of a dollar or of a Mexican peso changes over time. A rise in the general price level is called *inflation.* During inflation a dollar will purchase less milk, less toothpaste, and less of other goods. When prices are stable—when there is little inflation—a dollar's purchasing power is also stable.

Accountants assume that the dollar's purchasing power is relatively stable. The *stable-monetary-unit concept* is the basis for ignoring the effect of inflation in the accounting records. It allows accountants to add and subtract dollar amounts as though each dollar has the same purchasing power as any other dollar at any other time. In South America, where inflation rates are often high, accountants make adjustments to report monetary amounts in units of current buying power—a very different concept.

STOP & THINK You are considering the purchase of land for future expansion. The seller is asking $50,000 for land that cost him $35,000. An appraisal shows a value of $47,000. You first offer $44,000, the seller makes a counter offer of $48,000, and you agree on $46,000. What dollar value is reported for the land on your financial statements?

Answer: The land's historical cost, $46,000.

The Accounting Equation

Objective 3

Use the accounting equation to describe an organization's financial position

As we saw earlier, financial statements tell us how a business is performing and where it stands. They are the final product of the accounting process. But how do we arrive at the items and amounts that make up the financial statements?

Assets and Liabilities

The financial statements are based on the most basic tool of accounting, the **accounting equation.** This equation presents the resources of the business and the claims to those resources. **Assets** are the economic resources of a business that are expected to be of benefit in the future. Cash, office supplies, merchandise, furniture, land, and buildings are examples of assets.

Claims to assets come from two sources. **Liabilities** are "outsider claims." They are economic obligations—debts—payable to outsiders, called *creditors*. For example, a creditor who has loaned money to a business has a claim—a legal right—to a part of the company's assets until the business repays the debt. "Insider claims" are called **owners' equity,** or **capital.** These are the claims held by the owners of the business. An owner has a claim to the entity's assets because he or she has invested in the business. The amount that Gary Comer invested to start Lands' End is an example. Owners' equity is measured by subtracting liabilities from assets.

The accounting equation shows the relationship among assets, liabilities, and owners' equity. Assets appear on the left-hand side of the equation. The legal and economic claims against the assets—the liabilities and owners' equity—appear on the right-hand side of the equation. As Exhibit 1-5 shows, the two sides must be equal:

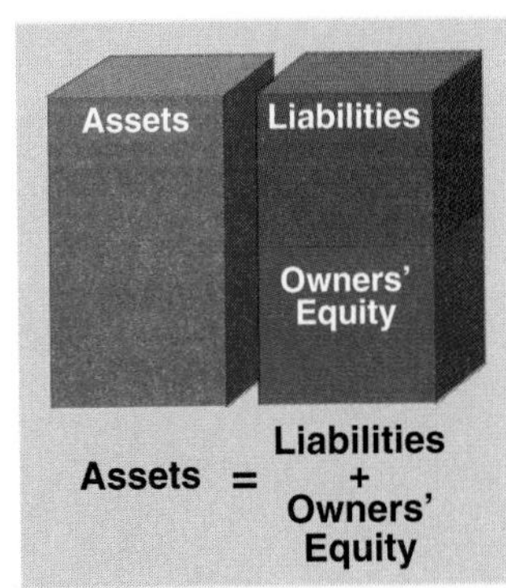

EXHIBIT 1-5
The Accounting Equation

Economic Resources	=	**Claims to Economic Resources**
Assets	=	**Liabilities + Owners' Equity**

Let's take a closer look at the elements that make up the accounting equation. Suppose you run a business that supplies meat to McDonald's and other restaurants. Some customers pay you in cash when you deliver the meat. Cash is an asset. Other customers buy on credit and promise to pay you within a certain time after delivery. This promise is also an asset because it is an economic resource that will benefit you in the future when you receive cash from the customer. To you (the meat supplier), this promise is an **account receivable.** If the promise that entitles you to receive cash in the future is formally written out, it is called a **note receivable.** All receivables are assets.

McDonald's promise to pay for its credit purchases creates a debt for the restaurant. This liability is an **account payable** of McDonald's—the debt is not written out. It is backed up by McDonald's reputation and credit standing. A written promise of future payment is a **note payable.** All payables are liabilities.

Owners' equity is the amount of assets that remain after the liabilities are subtracted. For this reason, owners' equity is often referred to as *net assets.* We often write the accounting equation to show that the owners' claim to business assets is a *residual,* something that is left over after a subtraction process:

Assets − Liabilities = Owners' Equity

Owners' Equity

The owners' equity of a corporation—called **stockholders' equity**—is divided into two main categories, paid-in capital and retained earnings. For a corporation the accounting equation can be written as

Assets = Liabilities + Stockholders' Equity

Assets = Liabilities + Paid-in Capital + Retained Earnings

Paid-in, or **contributed, capital** is the amount invested in the corporation by its owners. The basic component of paid-in capital is **common stock,** which the corporation issues to its stockholders as evidence of their ownership.

Retained earnings is the amount earned by income-producing activities and kept for use in the business. Two types of transactions that affect retained earnings are revenues and expenses. **Revenues** are increases in retained earnings from delivering goods or services to customers or clients. For example, a laundry's receipt of cash from a customer for cleaning a coat brings in revenue and increases the laundry's retained earnings. **Expenses** are decreases in retained earnings that result from operations. For example, the wages that the laundry pays its employees is an expense and decreases retained earnings. Expenses are the cost of doing business and are the opposite of revenues. Expenses include office rent, salaries, advertisements, and utility payments for light, electricity, gas, and so forth.

Businesses strive for profitability. When total revenues exceed total expenses, the result of operations is called **net income, net earnings,** or **net profit.** When expenses exceed revenues, the result is a **net loss.**

If the business is successful in earning a net income, it may pay dividends, the third type of transaction that affects retained earnings. **Dividends** are distributions to stockholders of assets (usually cash) generated by net income. Dividends are not expenses because the decision of whether to distribute dividends is made after expenses and revenues are recorded. First, the business measures its net income or net loss. Then it may (or may not) pay dividends. Exhibit 1-6 shows the relationships among retained earnings, revenues, expenses, net income or net loss, and dividends.

The owners' equity of proprietorships and of partnerships is different. These types of businesses make no distinction between paid-in capital and retained earnings. Instead, the equity of each owner is accounted for under the

EXHIBIT 1-6
Components of Retained Earnings

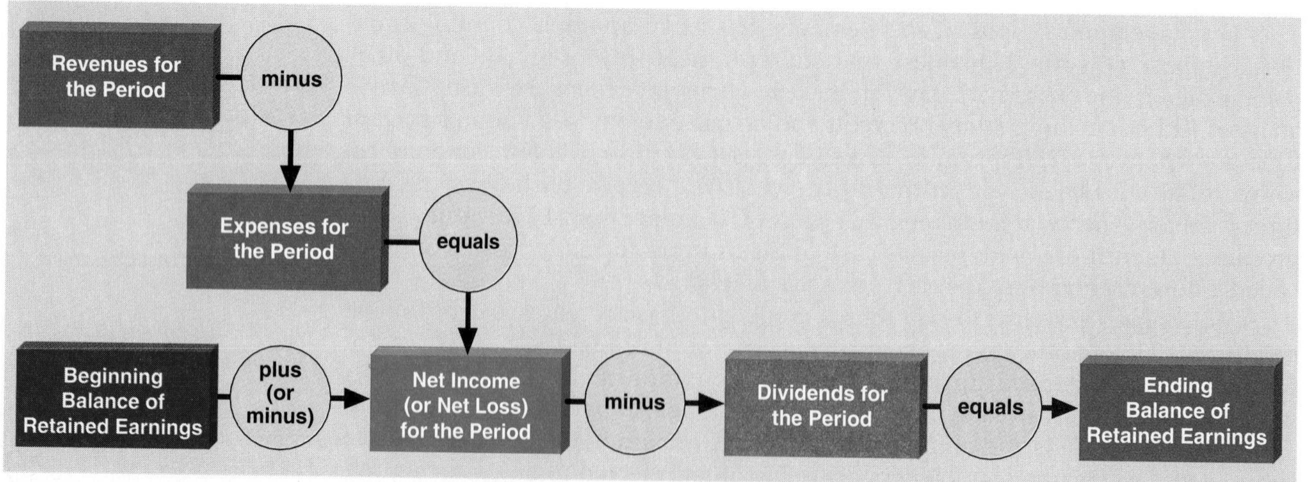

single heading of Capital—for example, Gary Comer, Capital for Lands' End if the company were a proprietorship. The partnership of Pratt and Muesli has a separate record for the capital of each partner: Pratt, Capital and Muesli, Capital.

STOP & THINK

1. If the assets of a business are $174,300 and the liabilities are $82,000, how much is the owners' equity?
2. If the owners' equity in a business is $22,000 and the liabilities are $36,000, how much are the assets?
3. A company reported monthly revenues of $77,600 and expenses of $81,300. What is the result of operations for the month?

Answers

1. $92,300
2. $58,000
3. Net loss of $3,700 ($77,600 – $81,300); expenses minus revenues.

The Financial Statements

Objective 4

Use a company's financial statements to evaluate its operating performance and financial position

The end product of the accounting process is a set of financial statements that portrays the company in financial terms. Each financial statement relates to a specific date or covers a specific period of business activity, such as a year. What would managers and investors want to know about a company at the end of a period? Exhibit 1-7 summarizes the four basic questions that decision makers are likely to ask. The answer to each question is given by one of the financial statements: the income statement, the statement of retained earnings, the balance sheet, and the statement of cash flows.

To examine what the financial statements include and how to read them, let's look at the Lands' End financial statements for fiscal year 1996. At this point, we will be looking at the big picture—our goal is an overall understanding of the four basic financial statements and the information they provide for decision makers. At this early stage it will be necessary to ignore some details on each

EXHIBIT 1-7
Information Reported on the Financial Statements

Question	Answer	Financial Statement
How well did the company perform (or operate) during the period?	Revenues – Expenses Net income (or Net loss)	Income statement (also called the Statement of operations)
Why did the company's retained earnings change during the period?	Beginning retained earnings + Net income (or – Net loss) – Dividends Ending retained earnings	Statement of retained earnings (or Statement of stockholders' equity)
What is the company's financial position at the end of the period?	Assets = Liabilities + Owners' Equity	Balance sheet (also called the Statement of financial position)
How much cash did the company generate and spend during the period?	Operating cash flows ± Investing cash flows ± Financing cash flows Increase (or Decrease) in cash during the period	Statement of cash flows

statement. As we progress through the text, we will examine these details carefully so that you can perform your analyses in more depth.

Let's begin with the income statement (statement of operations) in Exhibit 1-8. Its final amount, net income, feeds into the statement of retained earnings (Exhibit 1-9), which also appears on the balance sheet (Exhibit 1-10). As you can see, there is a natural progression from the income statement, to the statement of retained earnings, to the balance sheet, and finally to the statement of cash flows (Exhibit 1-11). We will see these exhibits in the pages that follow.

Income Statement (Statement of Operations)

The **income statement,** or **statement of operations,** reports the company's revenues, expenses, and net income or net loss for the period. At the top of Exhibit 1-8 (which is the same as the income statement we saw in the chapter opening story) is the company's name, Lands' End, Inc. & Subsidiaries. Lands' End, the parent company, owns other companies that are its subsidiaries. The amounts reported on the statements include figures for both Lands' End and its subsidiaries to give a full picture of all the resources that Lands' End controls. Most companies' financial statements show the consolidation of the parent company and one or more subsidiaries.

JC Penney, Wal-Mart Stores, and most other retailers also use a fiscal year that ends on January 31.

The date of the income statement is "For the fiscal years ended February 2, 1996 and January 27, 1995." A *fiscal year* is the year used for accounting purposes. The Lands' End fiscal year ends on the Friday closest to January 31 of each year. If Lands' End followed the calendar year, its accounting year would end on December 31, and its income statement would be dated "For the year ended December 31, 1995." Lands' End uses a fiscal year that ends around January 31 because the company's big selling period winds down about a month after Christmas. **JC Penney, Wal-Mart Stores,** and most other retailers also use a fiscal year that ends on January 31. This is a general principle: Most companies adopt an accounting year that ends with the low

EXHIBIT 1-8
Consolidated Income Statement (Statement of Operations) (adapted)

LANDS' END, INC. & SUBSIDIARIES
Consolidated Statement of Operations

		For the fiscal years ended	
	(In thousands)	February 2, 1996	January 27, 1995
1	**Net sales**	**$1,031,548**	$992,106
2	Cost of sales	**588,017**	571,265
3	Gross profit	**443,531**	420,841
4	Selling, general, and administrative expenses	**392,484**	357,516
5	Charges from sale of subsidiary	**1,882**	3,500
6	**Income from operations**	**49,165**	59,825
7	Other income (expense):		
8	Interest expense	**(2,771)**	(1,769)
9	Interest income	**253**	307
10	Other	**4,278**	1,300
11	Total other income (expense), net	**1,760**	(162)
12	**Income before income taxes**	**50,925**	59,663
13	Income tax provision	**20,370**	23,567
14	**Net income**	**$ 30,555**	$ 36,096

point in their annual operations. For over 60% of large companies, the low point is December 31.

The Lands' End income statement reports operating results for two fiscal years, 1996 and 1995. The income statement includes more than one year's data to let owners and creditors examine the company's sales and net income trends. To avoid cluttering the statement with zeros, Lands' End reports its figures in thousands of dollars. Some companies report their financial statement amounts in millions. During 1996, Lands' End increased net sales from $992 million to over $1 billion (see line 1), but net income dropped from $36 million to under $31 million (line 14). Continuation of this downward trend in net income would concern the company's managers and investors.

The income statement reports two main categories:

- Revenues (also called income, such as interest income) and gains
- Expenses and losses

Net Income[1] = Total Revenues and Gains − Total Expenses and Losses

REVENUES Revenues and expenses do not always carry the terms *revenue* and *expense* in their titles. For example, *net sales* is really net sales revenue, but the term "revenue" is often omitted. During fiscal year 1996, Lands' End had net sales of $1,031,548,000 (line 1). The term "net" sales means that the company has subtracted from its total sales the sales value of the goods that Lands' End customers returned to the company.

EXPENSES *Cost of sales* (or cost of goods sold, line 2) represents the cost to Lands' End of the goods it sold to customers during the year. For example, suppose Lands' End buys a shirt for $16 and sells the shirt for $30. Sales revenue is $30, and cost of goods sold is $16.

On the Lands' End income statement, Net sales − Cost of sales = Gross profit (line 3). *Gross profit* is profit before operating expenses have been deducted. To earn its revenue, Lands' End incurs expenses in addition to Cost of sales. For catalog merchants such as Lands' End and **L. L. Bean,** the second highest major expense (behind Cost of sales) is *selling expense,* which includes the cost of producing and mailing catalogs to prospective customers nationwide. All companies—Lands' End included—also have general expenses such as utilities, maintenance, and property taxes, as well as administrative expenses for the home office and for executive and other employee salaries. Most companies combine all three expense categories and report a single amount for Selling, general, and administrative expenses (line 4, often abbreviated as *SG&A expense*). During fiscal year 1996, Lands' End incurred SG&A expenses of just over $392 million (line 4).

Income before income taxes totaled $50.9 million (line 12), and income tax expense (here labeled as "Income tax provision") absorbed $20.4 million of the company's pretax income (line 13). For fiscal year 1996, Lands' End earned net income of $30.6 million after covering all expenses including income tax. Let's now move on to the Statement of Retained Earnings in Exhibit 1-9 on page 18.

Statement of Retained Earnings

Lands' End's *retained earnings* represent exactly what the words imply: that portion of net income the company has retained, or kept for use in the business. As we saw in the income statement, during 1996, the company earned net income of $30.6 million. This number from the income statement also appears on the

[1]For fiscal years after December 15, 1997, FASB Statement No. 130 requires companies to report both net income and a new measure called comprehensive income. *Comprehensive income* includes net income plus several other components that we discuss in chapters 10 and 11.

EXHIBIT 1-9
Consolidated Statement of Retained Earnings

LANDS' END, INC. & SUBSIDIARIES
Consolidated Statement of Retained Earnings

(In thousands)	For the fiscal years ended February 2, 1996	January 27, 1995
Retained Earnings		
1 Beginning balance	**$229,554**	$193,460
2 Net income	**30,555**	36,096
3 Cash dividends paid	—	—
4 Issuance of treasury stock	—	(2)
5 Ending balance	**$260,109**	$229,554

statement of retained earnings (line 2 in Exhibit 1-9). Thus, net income is the link between these two financial statements. After Lands' End earns net income, the board of directors must decide whether to retain the income for use in the business or to pay a dividend to the stockholders. In both 1996 and 1995, Lands' End decided not to pay dividends (line 3). Rather, it kept all its net income as retained earnings.

Note the $2,000 decrease in retained earnings due to the Issuance of treasury stock in fiscal year 1995 (line 4). This item illustrates a general rule in financial reporting:

- **Positive amounts in tabular displays usually appear with no sign—neither a plus (+) nor a minus (−).**
- **Negative amounts often appear in parentheses.**

On the statement of retained earnings, net income (line 2) has no sign, which means that it is positive and thus added to the beginning balance of retained earnings (line 1). The issuance of treasury stock during fiscal year 1995 decreased retained earnings, so the ending balance for 1995 is computed as follows:

$$\$193{,}460 + \$36{,}096 - \$2 = \$229{,}554$$

During fiscal years 1996 and 1995, Lands' End paid no dividends, so the statement of retained earnings shows no subtraction for dividends. During 1996, Lands' End's retained earnings grew from $229.6 million to $260.1 million because net income increased retained earnings by $30.6 million in 1996. This means that the company had $30 million more to work with in 1996 than it had in 1995.

Balance Sheet

The Lands' End balance sheet appears in Exhibit 1-10. Notice that the balance sheet is dated February 2, 1996, the end of the company's fiscal year. The balance sheet gives a still picture (a snapshot) of the company's financial position at a moment in time—specifically the stroke of midnight on that day. This is in contrast to the dates of the other three statements: *For the fiscal year ended* February 2, 1996. The income statement, the statement of retained earnings, and the statement of cash flows (which we discuss in the next section) report on events that occurred throughout the year, from beginning to end.

A company's **balance sheet,** sometimes called its **statement of financial position,** reports three main categories of items: Assets, Liabilities, and Owners' equity (which Lands' End calls "Shareholders' investment").

ASSETS Assets are subdivided into two categories: current assets and long-term assets. **Current assets** are those assets that the company expects to convert to cash, sell, or consume during the next 12 months or within the business's normal operating cycle if longer than a year. The *operating cycle* is the time span during which (1) cash is used to acquire goods and services, and (2) these goods and services are sold to customers, from whom the business collects cash.

EXHIBIT 1-10
Consolidated Balance Sheet (adapted)

LANDS' END, INC. & SUBSIDIARIES
Consolidated Balance Sheet

	(In thousands)	February 2, 1996	January 27, 1995
	ASSETS		
	Current assets:		
1	Cash	**$ 17,176**	$ 5,426
2	Receivables	**8,064**	4,459
3	Inventory	**164,816**	168,652
4	Prepaid advertising and other expenses	**32,033**	19,631
5	Total current assets	**222,089**	198,168
	Property, plant, and equipment, at cost:		
6	Land and buildings	**72,248**	69,798
7	Fixtures and equipment	**83,880**	74,745
8	Leasehold improvements	**2,912**	1,862
9	Total property, plant, and equipment	**159,040**	146,405
10	Less accumulated depreciation and amortization	**60,055**	49,414
11	Property, plant, and equipment, net	**98,985**	96,991
12	Intangibles, net	**2,423**	2,453
13	Total assets	**$323,497**	$297,612
	LIABILITIES AND SHAREHOLDERS' INVESTMENT		
	Current liabilities:		
14	Lines of credit	**$ 9,319**	$ 7,539
15	Accounts payable	**62,380**	52,762
16	Reserve for returns	**4,555**	5,011
17	Accrued liabilities	**23,751**	25,959
18	Accrued profit sharing	**1,483**	1,679
19	Income taxes payable	**13,256**	9,727
20	Current maturities of long-term debt	**—**	40
21	Total current liabilities	**114,744**	102,717
22	**Deferred income taxes**	**7,212**	5,379
23	**Long-term liabilities**	**349**	388
	Shareholders' investment:		
24	Common stock, 40,221 shares issued	**26,567**	26,219
25	Retained earnings	**260,109**	229,554
26	Other	**(85,484)**	(66,645)
27	Total shareholders' investment	**201,192**	189,128
28	Total liabilities and shareholders' investment	**$323,497**	$297,612

Current assets for Lands' End consist of Cash, Receivables, Inventory, and Prepaid advertising and other expenses (lines 1–4). Total current assets (line 5) were $222 million at the close of business on February 2, 1996. Lands' End had over $17 million of cash in the bank. The company sells to customers on credit, which explains the $8 million in Receivables that Lands' End expects to collect within a short time. Inventory is the company's largest asset, totaling almost $165 million. *Inventory* is an abbreviation for *merchandise inventory*—the shirts, slacks, and other goods the company sells as its core operations. Because the company markets its products through catalogs, advertising is important.

Prepaid advertising represents prepayments for advertisements that have not yet run. Prepaid expenses are assets because the company expects to benefit from these expenditures in the future.

The main category of *long-term assets* is Property, plant, and equipment (lines 6–8). These assets cost a total of $159 million (line 9). The property, plant, and equipment are partially used up, as indicated by the accumulated depreciation of $60 million (line 10). (*Depreciation* is the accounting process of allocating an asset's cost to expense; we discuss this concept in detail in later chapters.) The net amount of property, plant, and equipment is $99 million (cost of $159 million – accumulated depreciation of $60 million = net of $99 million, line 11). At the end of fiscal year 1996, Lands' End had total assets of more than $323 million (line 13).

LIABILITIES Liabilities are also divided into current and long-term categories. **Current liabilities** (lines 14–20) are debts that are due to be paid within one year or within the entity's normal operating cycle if longer than a year. Chief among the current liabilities for Lands' End are Accounts payable, Accrued liabilities, Income taxes payable, and Lines of credit. *Long-term liabilities* are payable after one year.

Accounts payable (line 15) represents amounts owed for goods and services that Lands' End has purchased but not yet paid for. (The word *payable* always indicates a liability.) Accounts payable exceeded $62 million on February 2, 1996. The company's second largest current liability is Accrued liabilities (line 17)—almost $24 million. Included among the accrued liabilities are salaries payable to Lands' End employees, payroll taxes the company owes to the government, and interest owed on borrowed money. Income taxes payable (line 19) are amounts the company owes the federal government for income taxes. The Lines of credit (line 14) are short-term notes payable to banks.

On February 2, 1996, Lands' End owed current liabilities of almost $115 million that will be paid within a few months (line 21). How will the company pay this huge amount? They will pay it with cash generated from selling inventory and collecting cash from customers. Recall that current assets totaled $222 million. Would you feel safe if you had $222 million of current assets to pay $115 million of current liabilities within a year? Most managers of large businesses would feel safe because of the high proportion of current assets to current liabilities.

Lands' End is in the enviable position of having almost no long-term liabilities. This is unusual because most companies finance their operations with larger amounts of long-term debt. The company's long-term liabilities of $7.5 million consist of Deferred income taxes (line 22, $7.2 million)—tax debts whose payment can be deferred beyond a year—and other long-term liabilities (line 23, $0.3 million). In sum, Lands' End has total liabilities of around $122 million (current liabilities of $115 million + long-term liabilities of $7 million), which is quite low relative to total assets of $323 million.

The accounting equation states that

Assets – Liabilities = Owners' Equity

The assets (resources) and the liabilities (debts) of Lands' End are fairly easy to understand. Owners' equity is harder to pin down.

OWNERS' EQUITY At a purely mathematical level, owners' equity is simple to calculate:

Assets – Liabilities = Owners' Equity

But what does owners' equity really *mean?* Lands' End labels its owners' equity as Total shareholders' investment (line 27), and this title is descriptive. Remember that a company's owners' equity represents the shareholders' investment in the assets of the business. Owners' equity for Lands' End consists of common stock, represented by 40.2 million shares that the company has sold to stockholders for approximately $26.6 million (line 24). The largest part of the owners' equity is retained earnings of $260 million (line 25). This large amount may explain why long-term liabilities are so low: Profitable operations, not long-term debt, have financed the company's operations. You should trace the $260 million ending balance of retained earnings from the statement of retained earnings in Exhibit 1-9 to the balance sheet. This is the link between these two financial statements.

On February 2, 1996, total shareholders' investment (owners' equity) for Lands' End was $201 million (line 27). For now you may ignore the Other equity in line 26 (negative amount of $85 million). We will explain the components of this item as we move through the text.

The bottom line of the balance sheet shows Total liabilities and shareholders' investment of $323 million, which (as the accounting equation tells us) must equal the company's total assets ($323 million). The balance sheet thus reports that Lands' End, Inc., has $323 million of assets with which to work. Of this amount, the company owes $122 million, and the company's stockholders own $201 million of the company's assets free and clear of any debt.

Statement of Cash Flows

To examine the statement of cash flows, we return to the discussion with which we began the chapter. Managers engage in three basic activities: They *finance* the organization to obtain the funds needed to *invest* in assets and *operate* the company. The **statement of cash flows** is organized around these three activities.

The Lands' End statement of cash flows appears in Exhibit 1-11. Each of the three main categories of cash flows includes cash receipts and cash

EXHIBIT 1-11
Consolidated Statement of Cash Flows (adapted)

LANDS' END, INC. & SUBSIDIARIES
Consolidated Statement of Cash Flows

	(In thousands)	For the fiscal years ended February 2, 1996	January 27, 1995
	Cash flows from operating activities:		
1	Cash received from customers	**$1,027,943**	$991,291
2	Cash received from interest	**253**	307
3	Cash paid to suppliers and employees	**(967,075)**	(926,714)
4	Cash paid for interest	**(2,833)**	(2,828)
5	Cash paid for income taxes	**(16,896)**	(27,595)
6	Net cash flows from operating activities	**41,392**	34,461
	Cash flows from investing activities:		
7	Cash paid for capital additions and businesses acquired	**(13,904)**	(32,102)
8	Proceeds from divestiture	**1,665**	—
9	Net cash flows used for investing activities	**(12,239)**	(32,102)
	Cash flows from financing activities:		
10	Proceeds from short-term and long-term debt	**1,780**	7,539
11	Payment of long-term debt	**(40)**	(40)
12	Purchases of treasury stock	**(20,001)**	(27,979)
13	Issuance of treasury stock	**858**	1,978
14	Cash dividends paid	**—**	—
15	Net cash flows used for financing activities	**(17,403)**	(18,502)
16	**Net increase (decrease) in cash**	**11,750**	(16,143)
17	**Beginning cash**	**5,426**	21,569
18	**Ending cash**	**$ 17,176**	$ 5,426

payments. Cash receipts are positive amounts with no signs. Cash payments are negative amounts indicated by parentheses.

Operating activities generate the lion's share of the company's cash (over $41 million in fiscal year 1996; see line 6). Investing activities include more cash payments than cash receipts, for a net cash outflow of $12 million (line 9). Financing activities resulted in a net cash outflow of $17 million (line 15). Overall, the company increased its cash balance by $11.75 million during 1996 (line 16) to end the year with cash of $17.2 million (line 18). Note that you can trace the ending cash balance to the balance sheet. The cash balance is the link between the statement of cash flows and the balance sheet.

Let's now examine the three major sections of the statement of cash flows more closely.

CASH FLOWS FROM OPERATING ACTIVITIES The bulk of the operating cash flows at Lands' End took the form of cash received from customers (line 1). This is a strong positive indicator because core operations are a company's largest source of cash for paying the bills and expanding the business. Consider an alternative: Suppose the company's main source of cash is borrowing. This would suggest that operations are not very successful and that borrowing is necessary to keep the company afloat. This is clearly not the case at Lands' End. The largest cash payments went to Lands' End suppliers and to the company's 7,900 employees (line 3). Because Lands' End buys worldwide, the suppliers are scattered around the globe. Most company employees live in Wisconsin, Illinois, or Iowa.

What does management expect regarding the adequacy of cash flows from operations in the future? The company's annual report includes a section titled "Management Discussion and Analysis," which states on page 11 that "The company believes that its cash flow from operations and borrowings under its current credit facilities will provide adequate resources to meet its [investment] requirements and operational needs for the foreseeable future."

CASH FLOWS FROM INVESTING ACTIVITIES During 1996, Lands' End spent $13.9 million to purchase new computer hardware and merchandise-handling equipment (capital additions) and to acquire new businesses (line 7). The company also sold property, plant, and equipment (divestitures) for $1.665 million (line 8)—a relatively small amount. The net cash *outflows* from investing activities thus totaled $12.2 million over the course of fiscal year 1996 (line 9). A net cash outflow from investing activities is generally healthy because it indicates that the business is buying new assets. Again, consider the alternative: What would you think of a company that year after year had a net cash *inflow* from investing activities? This would reveal that the company is shrinking as it sells off its long-term assets. The outlook would be cloudy.

What investing activities was Lands' End planning for 1997 and beyond? The 1996 Management Discussion and Analysis states (page 11) that "In the coming year, the company plans to invest about $16 million in capital improvements [same as long-term assets]." Also, "The company continues to explore investment opportunities arising from the expansion of its international businesses and the development of new businesses."

CASH FLOWS FROM FINANCING ACTIVITIES Borrowing is labeled *Proceeds from short-term and long-term debt* on the Lands' End statement of cash flows. During the year the company borrowed a modest amount of cash, only $1.78 million (line 10).

The largest financing cash flow was a $20 million payment for the purchase of treasury stock (line 12). This means that Lands' End bought back some of its own stock that it had issued earlier to its stockholders. (We explain treasury stock in more detail in Chapter 9.) Consistent with the information provided by the statement of retained earnings, the cash flow statement reports no dividend payments during fiscal year 1996 (line 14). The overall effect of financing activities on the Lands' End cash position during fiscal 1996 was a net cash outflow of $17.4 million (line 15).

STOP & THINK

1. Suppose you are considering investing in the stock of Lands' End, Inc. Which financial statement would you examine to see whether the company is profitable? What would you look for?
2. Suppose you are a bank considering lending $1 million to Lands' End. Which financial statement would you look at to see how much the company already owes other creditors? What would you look for?

Answers

1. Look for net income on the income statement.
2. Look for liabilities on the balance sheet.

Relationships Among the Financial Statements

Objective 5

Understand the relationships among the financial statements

Exhibit 1-12 summarizes the relationships among the financial statements. Study the exhibit carefully because you will use these relationships throughout your business career. Specifically, note the following:

EXHIBIT 1-12
Relationships Among the Lands' End Financial Statements (Amounts in thousands)

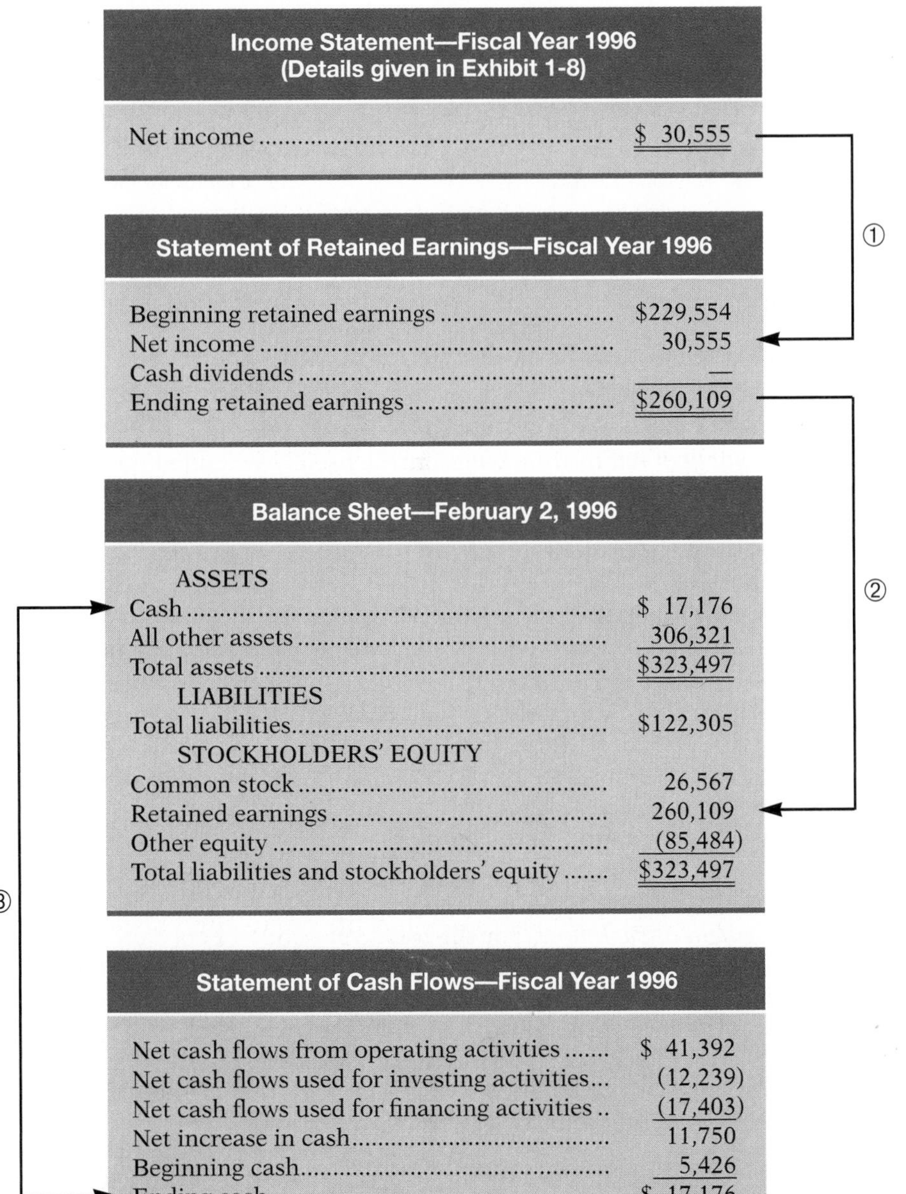

Income Statement—Fiscal Year 1996 (Details given in Exhibit 1-8)

Net income	$ 30,555

①

Statement of Retained Earnings—Fiscal Year 1996

Beginning retained earnings	$229,554
Net income	30,555
Cash dividends	—
Ending retained earnings	$260,109

②

Balance Sheet—February 2, 1996

ASSETS	
Cash	$ 17,176
All other assets	306,321
Total assets	$323,497
LIABILITIES	
Total liabilities	$122,305
STOCKHOLDERS' EQUITY	
Common stock	26,567
Retained earnings	260,109
Other equity	(85,484)
Total liabilities and stockholders' equity	$323,497

③

Statement of Cash Flows—Fiscal Year 1996

Net cash flows from operating activities	$ 41,392
Net cash flows used for investing activities	(12,239)
Net cash flows used for financing activities	(17,403)
Net increase in cash	11,750
Beginning cash	5,426
Ending cash	$ 17,176

Decision Guidelines

How Stockholders and Creditors Use the Financial Statements

Group	Mainly Interested In	Reason	What They Look For
Stockholders	Net income	*Net income* means the company is profitable. Stockholders enhance their personal wealth through (a) an increase in the market price of the company's stock, and (b) dividends received. Net income affects both stock prices and dividends.	Steadily rising level of net income over time means the company's profits look solid.
	Cash flows	*Cash flows* report how the company generates and uses its cash. Wise use of cash produces net income and more cash.	Operating activities should be the main source of cash.
Bankers and other creditors	Assets and liabilities	*Liabilities* indicate how much the company owes other creditors. *Assets* show what the company can pledge as collateral that a creditor can take if the company fails to pay its debts.	Assets far in excess of liabilities, or assets increasing faster than liabilities over time.
	Net income	Profitable companies can usually pay their debts.	Same as for stockholders.
	Cash flows	Same as for stockholders.	Same as for stockholders.

1. The *income statement* for the fiscal year ended February 2, 1996
   a. Reports all *revenues* and all *expenses* during the period. Revenues and expenses are reported only on the income statement.
   b. Reports *net income* of the period if total revenues exceed total expenses, as in the case of Lands' End, Inc.'s operations for fiscal year 1996. If total expenses exceed total revenues, a *net loss* is reported instead.
2. The *statement of retained earnings* for the fiscal year ended February 2, 1996
   a. Opens with the retained earnings balance at the beginning of the period.
   b. Adds *net income* (or subtracts *net loss,* as the case may be). Net income (or net loss) comes directly from the income statement (see arrow ① in Exhibit 1-12).
   c. Subtracts *dividends,* if appropriate. (There are no dividends in this example.)
   d. Ends with the retained earnings balance at the end of the period.
3. The *balance sheet* at February 2, 1996, the end of the fiscal year
   a. Reports all *assets,* all *liabilities,* and *stockholders' equity* of the business at the end of the period. No other financial statement reports assets and liabilities.
   b. Reports that total assets equal the sum of total liabilities plus total stockholders' equity. This balancing feature gives the balance sheet its name; it is based on the accounting equation.
   c. Reports the ending retained earnings, taken directly from the statement of retained earnings (see arrow ②).
4. The *statement of cash flows* for the fiscal year ended February 2, 1996
   a. Reports cash flows from three types of business activities (*operating, investing,* and *financing* activities) during the year. Each category results in a net cash inflow or a net cash outflow for the period.
   b. Reports a net increase (or a net decrease) in cash during the year and ends with the cash balance on February 2, 1996. This is the amount of cash reported on the balance sheet (see arrow ③).

The Decision Guidelines feature summarizes how stockholders and creditors use the financial statements. Decision Guidelines features appear throughout this book; they summarize how to make key decisions.

SUMMARY PROBLEM FOR YOUR REVIEW

A travel agency, Air & Sea Travel, Inc., began operations on April 1, 19X1, when the business received $50,000 and issued common stock to Gary and Monica Lyon, the stockholders. During April, the business provided travel services for clients. It is now April 30, and the Lyons wonder how well Air & Sea Travel performed during its first month. They also want to know the business's financial position at the end of April and its cash flows during the month.

They have assembled the following data, listed in alphabetical order. They have requested your help in preparing the Air & Sea Travel financial statements at the end of April 19X1.

Accounts payable	$ 100	Office supplies	$ 500
Accounts receivable	2,000	Payments of cash:	
Cash balance at beginning of April	-0-	Acquisition of land	40,000
Cash balance at end of April	33,300	Dividends	2,100
Cash receipts:		To suppliers and employees	3,100
Collections from customers	6,500	Rent expense	1,100
Issuance (sale) of stock to owners	50,000	Retained earnings at beginning of April	-0-
Sale of land	22,000	Retained earnings at end of April	?
Common stock	50,000	Salary expense	1,200
Dividends	2,100	Service revenue	8,500
Land	18,000	Utilities expense	400

Required

1. Prepare the income statement, the statement of retained earnings, and the statement of cash flows for the month ended April 30, 19X1, and the balance sheet at April 30, 19X1. Draw arrows linking the pertinent items in the statements.
2. Answer the owners' underlying questions.
   a. How well did Air & Sea Travel perform during its first month of operations?
   b. Where does Air & Sea Travel stand financially at the end of the first month?
3. If you were a banker, would you be willing to lend money to Air & Sea Travel, Inc.?

ANSWERS

Requirement 1

Financial statements of Air & Sea Travel, Inc.

AIR & SEA TRAVEL, INC.
Income Statement
Month Ended April 30, 19X1

Revenue:		
Service revenue		$8,500
Expenses:		
Salary expense	$1,200	
Rent expense	1,100	
Utilities expense	400	
Total expenses		2,700
Net income		$5,800

(Continued)

①

①

AIR & SEA TRAVEL, INC.
Statement of Retained Earnings
Month Ended April 30, 19X1

Retained earnings, April 1, 19X1	$ 0
Add: Net income for the month	5,800
	5,800
Less: Dividends	2,100
Retained earnings, April 30, 19X1	$3,700

②

AIR & SEA TRAVEL, INC.
Balance Sheet
April 30, 19X1

Assets		Liabilities	
Cash	$33,300	Accounts payable	$ 100
Accounts receivable	2,000		
Office supplies	500	**Stockholders' Equity**	
Land	18,000	Common stock	50,000
		Retained earnings	3,700
		Total stockholders' equity	53,700
		Total liabilities and	
Total assets	$53,800	stockholders' equity	$53,800

③

AIR & SEA TRAVEL, INC.
Statement of Cash Flows
Month Ended April 30, 19X1

Cash flows from operating activities:		
Receipts:		
Collections from customers		$ 6,500
Payments:		
To suppliers and employees		(3,100)
Net cash inflow from operating activities		3,400
Cash flows from investing activities:		
Acquisition of land	$(40,000)	
Sale of land	22,000	
Net cash outflow from investing activities		(18,000)
Cash flows from financing activities:		
Issuance (sale) of stock to owners	$ 50,000	
Dividends	(2,100)	
Net cash inflow from financing activities		47,900
Net increase in cash		$33,300
Cash balance, April 1, 19X1		0
Cash balance, April 30, 19X1		$33,300

Requirements 2 and 3

The company performed rather well in April. Business net income was $5,800—very good in relation to service revenue of $8,500. Gary and Monica Lyon were able to receive cash dividends of $2,100 for personal use. The business ended April with cash of $33,300. The total assets of $53,800 far exceed the total liabilities of $100. The stockholders' equity of $53,700 provides a good cushion against which the business can borrow. The business's financial position at April 30, 19X1, is strong. What identifies a strong financial position? Plenty of cash and assets far in excess of liabilities—hence a large amount of stockholders' equity. Lenders like to see these features before making a loan: "Those most able to borrow money need it the least." Thus, most bankers would be willing to lend to Air & Sea Travel at this time.

SUMMARY OF LEARNING OBJECTIVES

1. *Understand accounting vocabulary and use it in decision making.* *Accounting* is an information system for measuring, processing, and communicating financial information. As the "language of business," accounting helps a wide range of decision makers. Accountants are expected to perform their jobs in an ethical manner consistent with generally accepted accounting principles (GAAP).

The three forms of business organization are the proprietorship, the partnership, and the corporation. In some cases, accounting procedures depend on which form of organization the business adopts.

2. *Analyze business activity with accounting concepts and principles.* Accountants use the *entity concept* to keep the business's records separate from the personal records of the people who run it, and to separate corporate divisions from one another. Other important concepts that guide accountants are the *reliability principle,* the *cost principle,* the *going-concern concept,* and the *stable-monetary-unit concept.*

3. *Use the accounting equation to describe an organization's financial position.* In its most common form, the accounting equation is

Assets = Liabilities + Owners' Equity

Assets are the economic resources of a business that are expected to be of benefit in the future. *Liabilities* are economic debts payable to people or organizations outside the firm. *Owners' equity* refers to the claims held by the owners of a proprietorship or partnership. In a corporation, owners' equity is usually called *stockholders' equity* and is subdivided into two categories: *paid-in capital* and *retained earnings.*

4. *Use a company's financial statements to evaluate its operating performance and financial position.* The *financial statements* communicate financial information about a business entity to decision makers. The *income statement* reports the company's revenues, expenses, and net income or net loss for a period. The *statement of retained earnings* summarizes the changes in a corporation's retained earnings during the period. The *balance sheet* is a snapshot of a business on a particular day; it reports on three main categories of items—assets, liabilities, and owners' equity. The *statement of cash flows* reports cash receipts and disbursements over a period, classified according to the entity's major activities: operating, investing, and financing.

5. *Understand the relationships among the financial statements.* The bottom line of the income statement, net income, feeds into the statement of retained earnings. The final value of retained earnings then appears on the balance sheet. The final cash balance on the statement of cash flows also appears on the balance sheet.

ACCOUNTING VOCABULARY

Accounting, like many other subjects, has a special vocabulary. It is important that you understand the following terms. They are explained in the chapter and also in the Glossary at the end of the book.

account payable *(p. 13).*
account receivable *(p. 13).*
accounting *(p. 5).*
accounting equation *(p. 13).*
asset *(p. 13).*
balance sheet *(p. 18).*
board of directors *(p. 10).*
capital *(p. 13).*
common stock *(p. 14).*
contributed capital *(p. 14).*
corporation *(p. 9).*
current assets *(p. 18).*
current liabilities *(p. 20).*
dividend *(p. 14).*
entity *(p. 11).*
expense *(p. 14).*
financial accounting *(p. 7).*
financial statements *(p. 6).*
financing activities *(p. 4).*
generally accepted accounting principles (GAAP) *(p. 10).*
income statement *(p. 16).*
investing activities *(p. 4).*
liability *(p. 13).*
management accounting *(p. 8).*
net earnings *(p. 14).*
net income *(p. 14).*

net loss *(p. 14).*
net profit *(p. 14).*
note payable *(p. 13).*
note receivable *(p. 13).*
operating activities *(p. 3).*
owners' equity *(p. 13).*
paid-in capital *(p. 14).*
partnership *(p. 9).*
proprietorship *(p. 8).*
retained earnings *(p. 14).*
revenue *(p. 14).*
shareholder *(p. 9).*
statement of cash flows *(p. 21).*
statement of financial position *(p. 18).*
statement of operations *(p. 16).*
statement of retained earnings *(p. 18).*
stock *(p. 9).*
stockholder *(p. 9).*
stockholders' equity *(p. 14).*

QUESTIONS

1. Distinguish between accounting and bookkeeping.
2. Identify five users of accounting information, and explain how they use it.
3. What organization formulates generally accepted accounting principles? Is this organization a government agency?
4. What are the owner(s) of a proprietorship, a partnership, and a corporation called?
5. Why do ethical standards exist in accounting?
6. Why is the entity concept so important to accounting?
7. Give four examples of accounting entities.
8. Briefly describe the reliability principle.
9. What role does the cost principle play in accounting?
10. If *assets = liabilities + owners' equity,* then how can liabilities be expressed?
11. Explain the difference between an account receivable and an account payable.
12. In what two ways can a business use its net income?
13. Give a more descriptive title for the balance sheet.
14. What feature of the balance sheet gives this financial statement its name?
15. Give another title for the income statement.
16. Which financial statement is like a snapshot of the entity at a specific time?
17. What information does the statement of retained earnings report?
18. What piece of information flows from the income statement to the statement of retained earnings? What information flows from the statement of retained earnings to the balance sheet?
19. List the cash flow activities in the order they are likely to occur for a new business. Rank the activities in the order of their importance to investors.

EXERCISES

Explaining the income statement and the balance sheet
(Obj. 1)

E1-1 Sal and Sophia Molnari want to open an Italian restaurant in Los Angeles. In need of cash, they ask City Bank & Trust for a loan. The bank's procedures require borrowers to submit financial statements to show likely results of their operations for the first year and their likely financial position at the end of the first year. With little knowledge of accounting, Sal and Sophia don't know how to proceed. Explain to them the information provided by the statement of operations (the income statement) and the statement of financial position (the balance sheet). Indicate why a lender would require this information.

Organizing a business
(Obj. 1)

E1-2 Lang Enterprises is being formed to develop World Wide Web sites on the Internet for other companies. Lang needs funds, and Alden Lang, the president, has asked you to consider investing in the business. Answer the following questions about the different ways that Lang might organize the business. Explain each of your answers.

a. What form of business organization will give Lang the most freedom to manage the business as he wishes?
b. What form of organization will give creditors the maximum protection in the event that Lang Enterprises fails and cannot pay its liabilities?
c. What form of organization will enable the owners of Lang Enterprises to limit their risk of loss to the amount they have invested in the business?
d. Under what form of organization will Lang Enterprises be likely to have the longest life?
e. What form of organization will probably enable Lang Enterprises to raise the most money from owners' equity over the life of the business?

If you were Lang and could organize the business as you wish, what form of organization would you choose for Lang Enterprises? Explain your reasoning.

Applying accounting concepts and principles
(Obj. 2)

E1-3 Paul Harvey is a famous broadcaster reputed to earn $13 million a year. Harvey owns several organizations that take care of various aspects of his broadcasting and related endeavors. Consider Paul Harvey News and Paul Harvey Products, two of those organizations.

Required

Identify the accounting concept or principle that would guide the accounting for each of the following business transactions or events.

a. Paul Harvey suspects that Paul Harvey News is profitable and that Paul Harvey Products is losing money. He knows that overall his business endeavors are profitable, but he wishes to know the profit or loss of each separate organization.

b. It turns out that Paul Harvey Products is losing money and Harvey wishes to shut down the business, sell its assets, and pay off the liabilities. He hopes to have a little cash left over.

c. Paul Harvey News purchases an office building for its headquarters. The real estate appraisal on the building is $500,000, but Paul Harvey News is able to buy the building for $450,000. What amount should Paul Harvey News record for the building?

d. Paul Harvey the man wishes to keep his personal affairs separate from the finances of his businesses.

e. Paul Harvey News reports a balance sheet to show the business's financial position each year. The assets and liabilities have current values that differ significantly from the reported amounts. As a result, the owners' equity of the business is undervalued on the balance sheet. What accounting principle keeps Paul Harvey News from changing the reported amount of its owners' equity?

E1-4 Compute the missing amount in the accounting equation for each entity:

Accounting equation (Obj. 3)

	Assets	Liabilities	Owners' Equity
Entity A	$?	$81,800	$84,400
Entity B	85,900	?	34,000
Entity C	81,700	49,800	?

E1-5 **PepsiCo, Inc.,** has current assets of $5,072 million; property, plant, and equipment of $9,883 million; and other assets totaling $9,837 million. Current liabilities are $5,270 million, long-term debt is $8,841 million, and other long-term liabilities add up to $3,825 million.

Accounting equation (Obj. 3, 4)

Required

1. Use these data to write PepsiCo's accounting equation.
2. How much in resources does PepsiCo have to work with?
3. How much does PepsiCo owe?
4. How much of the company's assets do the PepsiCo stockholders actually own?

E1-6 Renaissance Travel Agency balance sheet data at May 31, 19X2, and June 30, 19X2, follow:

Accounting equation (Obj. 3)

	May 31, 19X2	June 30, 19X2
Total assets	$150,000	$195,000
Total liabilities	109,000	131,000

Required

Three situations about investments and dividends of the business during June are given. For each situation, compute the amount of the business's net income or net loss during June 19X2.

1. The owners invested $8,000 in the business and received no dividends.
2. The owners made no additional investments in the business but received dividends of $30,000.
3. The owners invested $39,000 in the business and received dividends of $6,000.

E1-7 Answer these questions about two actual companies.

Accounting equation (Obj. 3, 4)

1. **Johnson & Johnson,** famous for Band-Aids and other health-care products, began the year with total assets of $12.2 billion and total liabilities of $6.7 billion. Net income for the year was $2.0 billion, and dividends and other decreases in stockholders' equity totaled $0.4 billion. How much is stockholders' equity at the end of the year?
2. **The Gap** clothing company began the year with total liabilities of $0.63 billion and total stockholders' equity of $1.37 billion. During the year, total assets increased by 17 percent. How much are total assets at the end of the year?

E1-8 Managers at The Coca-Cola Company are planning an expansion of their bottling operations in Canada. They must decide where to locate the bottling plant, how much to spend on the building, and how to finance its construction. Of central importance is the level of net income they can expect to earn from operating the new plant. Identify the financial statement where these decision makers can find the following information about The Coca-Cola Company. (In some cases, more than one statement will report the needed data.)

Identifying financial statement information (Obj. 4)

a. Liabilities that must be paid next year
b. Net income
c. Total assets
d. Cash spent to acquire the building
e. Selling, general, and administrative expenses
f. Cash collections from customers
g. Ending cash balance
h. Long-term debt
i. Revenue
j. Common stock
k. Cash spent for income tax
l. Dividends
m. Income tax expense
n. Ending balance of retained earnings
o. Cost of goods sold

Business organization, balance sheet
(Obj. 2, 5)

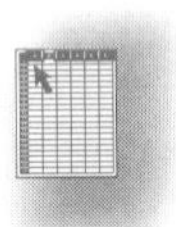

E1-9 Balances of the assets and liabilities of King's Copy Service as of September 30, 19X2 are given. Also included are the revenue and expense figures of the business for September.

Copy service revenue	$8,100	Copy equipment	$15,500
Accounts receivable	1,900	Supplies	600
Accounts payable	1,750	Note payable	6,000
Common stock	7,000	Rent expense	500
Salary expense	2,000	Cash	750
Supplies expense	1,600	Retained earnings	?

Required

1. What type of business organization is King's Copy Service? How can you tell?
2. Prepare the balance sheet of King's Copy Service as of September 30, 19X2.

Income statement
(Obj. 2, 5)

E1-10 Balances of the assets, liabilities, owners' equity, revenues, and expenses are given for Eagle Tax Service, Inc., at December 31, 19X3, the end of its first year of business. During the year, the owners invested $10,000 in the business.

Note payable	$ 30,000	Office furniture	$45,000
Utilities expense	6,800	Rent expense	24,000
Accounts payable	3,300	Cash	3,600
Retained earnings	17,100	Office supplies	4,800
Service revenue	171,200	Salary expense	49,000
Accounts receivable	9,000	Salaries payable	2,000
Supplies expense	4,000	Property tax expense	1,200
Common stock	10,000	Dividends	?

Required

1. Prepare the income statement of Eagle Tax Service, Inc., for the year ended December 31, 19X3.
2. What was the amount of the dividends during the year?

Statement of cash flows
(Obj. 2, 4, 5)

E1-11 **Sprint Corporation,** the telecommunications company, began the year 19X5 with $113.7 million in cash. During 19X5, Sprint earned a net income of $395.3 million. Assume the company collected $12,629.3 million in cash from customers and paid $9,900.4 million to suppliers and employees during the year. Investing activities used cash of $3,141.0 million, and financing activities provided a net cash inflow of $422.6 million. Sprint ended 19X5 with total assets of $15,195.9 million and total liabilities of $10,553.3 million.

Required

Prepare Sprint Corporation's statement of cash flows for the year ended December 31, 19X5. Identify the data items given that do not appear on the statement of cash flows, and note which financial statement reports these items.

Preparing an income statement and a statement of retained earnings
(Obj. 5)

E1-12 Campus Apartment Locators, Inc., completed the month of July 19X1, with these data:

Accounts payable	$ 250	Payments of cash:	
Cash balance at beginning of July	-0-	Acquisition of land	$30,000
Cash balance at end of July	5,250	Dividends	1,200
Cash receipts:		To suppliers	450
Collections from customers	1,900	Rent expense	400
Issuance (sale) of stock to owners	35,000	Retained earnings at beginning of July	-0-
Common stock	35,000	Retained earnings at end of July	?
Dividends	1,200	Service revenue	1,900
Land	30,000	Utilities expense	100
Office supplies	200		

Required

Prepare the income statement and the statement of retained earnings of Campus Apartment Locators, Inc., for the month ended July 31, 19X1.

Preparing a balance sheet
(Obj. 5)

E1-13 Refer to the data in the preceding exercise. Prepare the balance sheet of Campus Apartment Locators, Inc., at July 31, 19X1.

Preparing a statement of cash flows
(Obj. 5)

E1-14 Refer to the data in Exercise 1-12. Prepare the statement of cash flows of Campus Apartment Locators, Inc., for the month ended July 31, 19X1. Draw arrows linking the pertinent items in the statements you prepared for Exercises 1-12 through 1-14.

E1-15 This exercise should be used in conjunction with Exercises 1-12 through 1-14.

The owners of Apartment Locators, Inc., now seek your advice as to whether they should cease operations or continue the business. Write a report giving them your opinion of the operating results, dividends, financial position, and cash flows during their first month of operations. Cite specifics from the financial statements to support your opinion, and end your report with advice on whether to stay in business or cease operations.

Advising a business **(Obj. 4, 5)**

E1-16 Apply your understanding of the relationships among the financial statements to answer these questions.

Applying accounting concepts to explain business activity **(Obj. 2, 5)**

a. Give two reasons why a business can have a steady stream of net income over a five-year period and still experience a shortage of cash.

b. How can a business lose money several years in a row and still have plenty of cash?

c. How can a business earn large profits but have a small balance of retained earnings?

d. Suppose your business has $100,000 of current liabilities that must be paid within the next three months. Your current assets total only $70,000, and your sales and collections from customers are slow. Identify two ways to finance the extra $30,000 you will need to pay your current liabilities when they come due.

e. If you could pick a single source of cash for your business, what would it be? Why?

PROBLEMS

(GROUP A)

P1-1A As an analyst for Quaker State Bank, it is your job to write recommendations to the bank's loan committee. Acura Enterprises has submitted these summary data to support the company's request for a $400,000 loan.

Analyzing a loan request **(Obj. 1, 5)**

INCOME STATEMENT DATA	19X5	19X4	19X3
Total revenues	$890,000	$830,000	$820,000
Total expenses	640,000	570,000	540,000
Net income	$250,000	$260,000	$280,000
SELECTED STATEMENT OF RETAINED EARNINGS DATA			
Dividends	$290,000	$280,000	$270,000
BALANCE SHEET DATA			
Total assets	$730,000	$700,000	$660,000
Total liabilities	$390,000	$320,000	$260,000
Total stockholders' equity	340,000	380,000	400,000
Total liabilities and stockholders' equity	$730,000	$700,000	$660,000
STATEMENT OF CASH FLOW DATA			
Net cash flow from operations	$ 70,000	$ 90,000	$110,000
Net cash flow from investing	(40,000)	(100,000)	60,000
Net cash flow from financing	(80,000)	(40,000)	(190,000)
Increase (decrease) in cash	$ (50,000)	$ (50,000)	$ (20,000)

Required

Analyze these financial statement data to determine whether the bank should lend $400,000 to Acura Enterprises. Write a one-paragraph recommendation to the loan committee.

P1-2A Assume that Chrysler Corporation, the automaker, experienced the following transactions during the year ended December 31, 19X4:

Applying accounting concepts and principles to the income statement **(Obj. 2, 4, 5)**

a. Chrysler sold automobiles and other manufactured products for $49.4 billion. Company management believes that the value of these products is approximately $53 billion. Other revenues totaled $2.8 billion.

b. It cost Chrysler $38.0 billion to manufacture the products it sold. If Chrysler had purchased the products instead of manufacturing them, the cost would have been $41.6 billion.

c. Selling and administrative expenses were $3.9 billion. All other expenses, excluding income taxes, totaled $4.5 billion for the year. Income tax expense was 36% of income before tax.

d. If Chrysler were to go out of business, the sale of its assets would bring in over $50 billion in cash.

e. Chrysler has several operating divisions: Plymouth, Dodge, Chrysler, Jeep, and Eagle. Each division is accounted for separately so that top management can see how well each division is performing. However, the company's financial statements combine the statements of all the divisions in order to show the operating results of the company as a whole.

f. Inflation affects the amounts that Chrysler must pay for steel and other components of the company's manufactured goods. If Chrysler's financial statements were to show the effects of inflation, the company's reported net income would drop by $0.4 billion.

Required

1. Prepare Chrysler Corporation's income statement for the year ended December 31, 19X4.
2. For *a* through *f*, identify the accounting concept or principle that provides guidance in accounting for the item described. State how you have applied the concept or principle in preparing Chrysler's income statement.

Using the accounting equation
(Obj. 3)

P1-3A Compute the missing amounts (?) for each company.

	Alpha Co.	Beta Co.	Omega Co.
BEGINNING:			
Assets	$ 60,000	$ 80,000	$120,000
Liabilities	30,000	60,000	50,000
ENDING:			
Assets	$ 90,000	$?	$160,000
Liabilities	55,000	80,000	70,000
OWNERS' EQUITY:			
Investments by owners	$ 0	$ 10,000	$?
Dividends	40,000	30,000	70,000
INCOME STATEMENT:			
Revenues	$240,000	$400,000	$400,000
Expenses	?	300,000	320,000

Balance sheet
(Obj. 2, 5)

P1-4A The manager of Allstate Travel Agency, Inc., prepared the company's balance sheet while the accountant was ill. The balance sheet contains numerous errors. In particular, the manager knew that the balance sheet should balance, so he plugged in the stockholders' equity amount needed to achieve this balance. The stockholders' equity amount, however, is not correct. All other amounts are accurate.

ALLSTATE TRAVEL AGENCY, INC.
Balance Sheet
Month Ended October 31, 19X7

Assets		Liabilities	
Cash	$ 3,400	Notes receivable	$14,000
Advertising expense	300	Interest expense	2,000
Land	80,500	Office supplies	800
Salary expense	3,300	Accounts receivable	2,600
Office furniture	6,700	Note payable	50,000
Accounts payable	3,000		
Utilities expense	2,100	**Stockholders' Equity**	
		Stockholders' equity	29,900
Total assets	$99,300	Total liabilities	$99,300

Required

1. Prepare the correct balance sheet and date it correctly. Compute total assets, total liabilities, and stockholders' equity.

2. Identify the accounts listed on the incorrect balance sheet that should *not* be presented on the balance sheet. State why you excluded them from the correct balance sheet you prepared for Requirement 1. On which financial statement should these accounts appear?

Balance sheet, entity concept ***(Obj. 2, 5)***

P1-5A Dean Childres is a realtor. He buys and sells properties on his own, and he also earns commission as a real estate agent for buyers and sellers. He organized his business as a corporation on March 10, 19X2, by investing $60,000 to acquire the business's common stock. Consider the following facts as of March 31, 19X2:

a. Childres had $25,000 in his personal bank account and $6,000 in his business bank account.

b. Office supplies on hand at the real estate office totaled $1,000.

c. Childres's business had spent $15,000 for an Electronic Realty Associates (ERA) franchise, which entitles him to represent himself as an ERA agent. The ERA is a national affiliation of independent real estate agents. This franchise is a business asset.

d. Childres owed $33,000 on a note payable for some undeveloped land that his business acquired for a total price of $70,000.

e. Childres owed $65,000 on a personal mortgage on his personal residence, which he acquired in 19X1 for a total price of $90,000.

f. Childres owed $950 on a personal charge account with Sears.

g. Childres had acquired business furniture for $12,000 on March 26. Of this amount, Childres's business owed $6,000 on open account at March 31.

Required

1. Prepare the balance sheet of the real estate business of Dean Childres, Realtor, Inc., at March 31, 19X2.
2. Identify the personal items given in the preceding facts that would not be reported on the balance sheet of the business.

Income statement, statement of retained earnings, balance sheet ***(Obj. 5)***

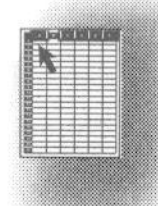

P1-6A Given are the amounts of (a) the assets and liabilities of Boston Express Service, Inc., as of December 31, and (b) the revenues and expenses of the company for the year ended on that date. The items are listed in alphabetical order.

Accounts payable	$12,000	Land	$ 8,000
Accounts receivable	6,000	Note payable	31,000
Building	26,000	Property tax expense	2,000
Cash	4,000	Rent expense	14,000
Common stock	10,000	Salary expense	38,000
Equipment	31,000	Service revenue	130,000
Interest expense	4,000	Supplies	17,000
Interest payable	1,000	Utilities expense	3,000

The beginning amount of retained earnings was $11,000, and during the year dividends were $42,000.

Required

1. Prepare the income statement of Boston Express Service, Inc., for the year ended December 31 of the current year.
2. Prepare the company's statement of retained earnings for the year ended December 31.
3. Prepare the company's balance sheet at December 31.

Analyzing a company's financial statements ***(Obj. 4, 5)***

P1-7A McDonnell Douglas Corporation manufactures the DC-9 and other commercial aircraft in the DC line. Condensed versions of the company's financial statements, with certain items omitted, are given for two recent years.

	19X4	19X3
STATEMENT OF OPERATIONS	**(In millions)**	
Revenues	$ k	$14,487
Cost of products, services, and rentals	11,026	a
Other expenses	1,230	1,169
Earnings before income taxes	920	496
Income taxes (35% in 19X4)	l	100
Net earnings	$ m	$ b

(Continued)

(Continued)

	19X4	19X3
STATEMENT OF RETAINED EARNINGS		
Beginning balance	$ n	$ 2,702
Net earnings	o	c
Dividends	(65)	(55)
Ending balance	$ p	$ d
BALANCE SHEET		
Assets		
Cash	$ q	$ e
Property, plant, and equipment	1,597	1,750
Other assets	r	10,190
Total assets	$ s	$12,026
Liabilities		
Current liabilities	$ t	$ 5,403
Notes payable and long-term debt	2,569	3,138
Other liabilities	69	72
Total liabilities	$ 8,344	$ f
Shareholders' Equity		
Common stock	$ 117	$ 118
Retained earnings	u	g
Other shareholders' equity	179	252
Total shareholders' equity	v	3,413
Total liabilities and shareholders' equity	$ w	$ h
STATEMENT OF CASH FLOWS		
Net cash provided by operating activities	$ x	$ 475
Net cash provided by investing activities	58	574
Net cash used by financing activities	(709)	(1,045)
Increase (decrease) in cash	335	i
Cash at beginning of year	y	82
Cash at end of year	$ z	$ j

Required

1. Determine the missing amounts denoted by the letters.
2. Use McDonnell Douglas's financial statements to answer these questions about the company. Explain each of your answers.
   a. Did operations improve or deteriorate during 19X4?
   b. What is the company doing with most of its income—retaining it for use in the business or using it for dividends?
   c. How much in total resources does the company have to work with as it moves into the year 19X5?
   d. At the end of 19X3, how much did the company owe outsiders? At the end of 19X4, how much did the company owe? Is this trend good or bad in comparison to the trend in assets?
   e. What is the company's major source of cash? Is cash increasing or decreasing? What is your opinion of the company's ability to generate cash?

(GROUP B)

P1-1B As an analyst for Providence Bank, it is your job to write recommendations to the bank's loan committee. Eisner Company has submitted these summary data to support Eisner's request for a $250,000 loan.

Analyzing a loan request
(Obj. 1, 5)

INCOME STATEMENT DATA			
	19X5	**19X4**	**19X3**
Total revenues	$850,000	$770,000	$720,000
Total expenses	640,000	570,000	540,000
Net income	$210,000	$200,000	$180,000
SELECTED STATEMENT OF RETAINED EARNINGS DATA			
Dividends	$160,000	$140,000	$120,000
BALANCE SHEET DATA			
Total assets	$740,000	$670,000	$590,000
Total liabilities	$240,000	$220,000	$200,000
Total stockholders' equity	500,000	450,000	390,000
Total liabilities and stockholders' equity	$740,000	$670,000	$590,000
STATEMENT OF CASH FLOW DATA			
Net cash flow from operations	$190,000	$170,000	$170,000
Net cash flow from investing	(180,000)	(180,000)	(50,000)
Net cash flow from financing	30,000	(10,000)	(110,000)
Increase (decrease) in cash	$ 40,000	$ (20,000)	$ 10,000

Required

Analyze these financial statement data to decide whether the bank should lend $250,000 to Eisner Company. Write a one-paragraph recommendation to the loan committee.

P1-2B Assume Ford Motor Company, the automaker, experienced the following transactions during the year ended December 31, 19X4:

Applying accounting concepts and principles to the income statement
(Obj. 2, 4, 5)

a. Ford sold automobiles and other manufactured products for $110.5 billion. Company management believes that the value of these products is approximately $116 billion. Other revenues totaled $26.6 billion.

b. It cost Ford $101.2 billion to manufacture the products it sold. If Ford had purchased the products instead of manufacturing them, Ford's cost would have been $122.6 billion.

c. Selling and administrative expenses were $6.0 billion. All other expenses, excluding income taxes, totaled $23.4 billion for the year. Income tax expense was 36% of income before tax.

d. If Ford were to go out of business, the sale of its assets would bring in over $250 billion in cash.

e. Ford has several operating divisions: Ford, Mercury, Lincoln, and Financial Services. Each division is accounted for separately so that top management can see how well each division is performing. However, the company's financial statements combine the statements of all the divisions in order to show the operating results of the company as a whole.

f. Inflation affects the amounts that Ford must pay for steel and other components of the company's manufactured goods. If Ford's financial statements were to show the effects of inflation, assume the company's reported net income would drop by $0.7 billion.

Required

1. Prepare Ford Motor Company's income statement for the year ended December 31, 19X4.

2. For *a* through *f*, identify the accounting concept or principle that provides guidance in accounting for the item described. State how you have applied the concept or principle in preparing Ford's income statement.

Using the accounting equation
(Obj. 3)

P1-3B Compute the missing amounts for each company.

	Red Co.	White Co.	Blue Co.
BEGINNING:			
Assets	$ 40,000	$100,000	$110,000
Liabilities	20,000	60,000	50,000
ENDING:			
Assets	$ 70,000	$?	$160,000
Liabilities	35,000	80,000	70,000
OWNERS' EQUITY:			
Investments by owners	$ 0	$ 10,000	$?
Dividends	40,000	70,000	100,000
INCOME STATEMENT:			
Revenues	$210,000	$400,000	$430,000
Expenses	?	300,000	320,000

Balance sheet
(Obj. 2, 5)

P1-4B The manager of H&R Auction Co. prepared the balance sheet of the company while the accountant was ill. The balance sheet contains numerous errors. In particular, the manager knew that the balance sheet should balance, so he plugged in the stockholders' equity amount needed to achieve this balance. The stockholders' equity amount, however, is not correct. All other amounts are accurate.

H&R AUCTION CO.
Balance Sheet
Month Ended July 31, 19X3

Assets		Liabilities	
Cash	$ 3,000	Accounts receivable	$12,000
Office supplies	1,000	Service revenue	50,000
Land	44,000	Property tax expense	800
Advertising expense	2,500	Accounts payable	9,000
Office furniture	10,000		
Note payable	16,000	**Stockholders' Equity**	
Rent expense	4,000	Stockholders' equity	8,700
Total assets	$80,500	Total liabilities	$80,500

Required

1. Prepare the correct balance sheet and date it correctly. Compute total assets, total liabilities, and stockholders' equity.
2. Identify the accounts listed above that should *not* be presented on the balance sheet. State why you excluded them from the correct balance sheet you prepared for Requirement 1. Which financial statement should these accounts appear on?

Balance sheet, entity concept
(Obj. 2, 5)

P1-5B Monica Peres is a realtor. She buys and sells properties on her own, and she also earns commission as a real estate agent for buyers and sellers. She organized her business as a corporation on November 24, 19X4, by investing $50,000 to acquire the business's common stock. Consider these facts, which were accurate as of November 30, 19X4:

a. Peres owed $55,000 on a note payable for some undeveloped land that her business had acquired for a total price of $110,000.
b. Peres's business had spent $20,000 for a Century 21 real estate franchise, which entitles her to represent herself as a Century 21 agent. Century 21 is a national affiliation of independent real estate agents. This franchise is a business asset.
c. Peres owed $120,000 on a personal mortgage on her personal residence, which she acquired in 19X1 for a total price of $170,000.
d. Peres had $10,000 in her personal bank account and $12,000 in her business bank account.
e. Peres owed $1,800 on a personal charge account with the Nordstrom department store.
f. Peres acquired business furniture for $17,000 on November 25. Of this amount, her business owed $6,000 on open account at November 30.
g. Office supplies on hand at the real estate office totaled $1,000.

Required

1. Prepare the balance sheet of the real estate business of Monica Peres, Realtor, Inc., at November 30, 19X4.
2. Identify the personal items given in the preceding facts that would not be reported on the balance sheet of the business.

Income statement, statement of retained earnings, balance sheet ***(Obj. 5)***

P1-6B Given are the amounts of (a) the assets and liabilities of Eastman Corporation as of December 31, and (b) the revenues and expenses of the company for the year ended on that date. The items are listed in alphabetical order.

Accounts payable	$ 19,000	Land	$ 98,000
Accounts receivable	12,000	Note payable	85,000
Advertising expense	13,000	Property tax expense	4,000
Building	170,000	Rent expense	23,000
Cash	10,000	Salary expense	63,000
Common stock	100,000	Salary payable	1,000
Furniture	20,000	Service revenue	240,000
Interest expense	9,000	Supplies	3,000

The beginning amount of retained earnings was $50,000, and during the year dividends were $70,000.

Required

1. Prepare the income statement of Eastman Corporation for the year ended December 31 of the current year.
2. Prepare Eastman's statement of retained earnings for the year ended December 31.
3. Prepare Eastman's balance sheet at December 31.

Analyzing a company's financial statements ***(Obj. 4, 5)***

P1-7B Wal-Mart Stores, Inc., is the world's largest retailer, with almost 3,000 stores and over 675,000 employees. Condensed versions of the company's financial statements, with certain items omitted, follow for two recent years.

	19X6	19X5
STATEMENT OF INCOME	**(In millions)**	
Revenues	$ k	$83,412
Cost of sales	74,564	a
Other expenses	15,839	13,564
Income before income taxes	4,346	4,262
Income taxes (36.95% in 19X6)	1	1,581
Net income	$ m	$ b
STATEMENT OF RETAINED EARNINGS		
Beginning balance	$ n	$ 9,987
Net income	o	c
Dividends and other	(559)	(455)
Ending balance	$ p	$ d
BALANCE SHEET		
Assets:		
Cash	$ q	$ e
Property, plant, and equipment	18,894	15,874
Other assets	r	16,900
Total assets	$ s	$32,819
Liabilities:		
Current liabilities	$ t	$ 9,973
Long-term debt and other liabilities	11,331	10,120
Total liabilities	22,785	f

(Continued)

(Continued)

	19X6	19X5
Shareholders' Equity:		
Common stock	$ 229	$ 230
Retained earnings	u	g
Other shareholders' equity	133	283
Total shareholders' equity	v	12,726
Total liabilities and shareholders' equity	$ w	$ h
STATEMENT OF CASH FLOWS		
Net cash provided by operating activities	$ x	$ 2,906
Net cash used in investing activities	(3,332)	(3,792)
Net cash provided by financing activities	987	911
Increase (decrease) in cash	38	i
Cash at beginning of year	y	20
Cash at end of year	$ z	$ j

Required

1. Determine the missing amounts denoted by the letters.
2. Use Wal-Mart's financial statements to answer these questions about the company. Explain each of your answers.
   - **a.** Did operations improve or deteriorate during 19X6?
   - **b.** What is the company doing with most of its income—retaining it for use in the business or using it for dividends?
   - **c.** How much in total resources does the company have to work with as it moves into the year 19X7? How much in total resources did the company have at the end of 19X5?
   - **d.** At the end of 19X5, how much did the company owe outsiders? At the end of 19X6, how much did the company owe?
   - **e.** What is the company's major source of cash? What is your opinion of the company's ability to generate cash? How is the company using most of its cash? Is the company growing or shrinking?

EXTENDING YOUR KNOWLEDGE

DECISION CASES

Using financial statements to evaluate a request for a loan ***(Obj. 1, 2)***

Case 1. Two businesses, Alcoa Drug Company and Whitman Home Decorators, Inc., have sought business loans from you. To decide whether to make the loans, you have requested their balance sheets.

ALCOA DRUG COMPANY
Balance Sheet
August 31, 19X4

Assets		Liabilities	
Cash	$ 9,000	Accounts payable	$ 12,000
Accounts receivable	14,000	Note payable	18,000
Merchandise inventory	85,000	Total liabilities	30,000
Store supplies	500		
Furniture and fixtures	9,000	**Stockholders' Equity**	
Building	82,000	Stockholders' equity	183,500
Land	14,000	Total liabilities and	
Total assets	$213,500	stockholders' equity	$213,500

WHITMAN HOME DECORATORS, INC.
Balance Sheet
August 31, 19X4

Assets		Liabilities	
Cash	$ 11,000	Accounts payable	$ 3,000
Accounts receivable	4,000	Note payable	88,000
Office supplies	1,000	Total liabilities	91,000
Office furniture	36,000		
Land	79,000	**Owners' Equity**	
		Owners' equity	40,000
Total assets	$131,000	Total liabilities and owners' equity	$131,000

Required

1. Solely on the basis of these balance sheets, to which entity would you be more comfortable lending money? Explain fully, citing specific items and amounts from the balance sheets.
2. In addition to the balance sheet data, what other information would you require? Be specific.

Using accounting information ***(Obj. 1, 2, 3, 4, 5)***

Case 2. A friend learns that you are taking an accounting course. Knowing that you do not plan a career in accounting, the friend asks you why you are "wasting your time." Explain to the friend:

1. Why you are taking the course.
2. How accounting information is used and will be used.
   - **a.** in your personal life.
   - **b.** in the business life of your friend, who plans to be a farmer.
   - **c.** in the business life of another friend, who plans a career in sales.

ETHICAL ISSUE

The board of directors of Ultramar Corporation is meeting to discuss the past year's results before releasing financial statements to the public. The discussion includes this exchange:

Lisa Todd, company president: "Well, this has not been a good year! Revenue is down and expenses are up—way up. If we don't do some fancy stepping, we'll report a loss for the third year in a row. I can temporarily transfer some land that I own into the company's name, and that will beef up our balance sheet. Ralph, can you shave $500,000 from expenses? Then we can probably get the bank loan that we need."

Ralph Nettle, company chief accountant: "Lisa, you are asking too much. Generally accepted accounting principles are designed to keep this sort of thing from happening."

Required

1. What is the fundamental ethical issue in this situation?
2. Discuss how Todd's proposals violate generally accepted accounting principles. Identify the specific concept or principle involved, and also refer to specifics from the AICPA Code of Professional Conduct.

FINANCIAL STATEMENT CASES

Identifying items from a company's financial statements ***(Obj. 4)***

Case 1. This and similar problems in succeeding chapters focus on the financial statements of Lands' End, Inc., the catalog merchandising company. As you study each problem, you will gradually build the confidence that you can understand and use actual financial statements.

Required

Refer to the Lands' End financial statements in Appendix A at the end of the book.

1. Use the Lands' End *income statement* for the current year to answer these questions: Suppose you own stock in Lands' End, Inc. If you could pick one item on the company's income statement to increase year after year, what would it be? Why is this item so important? Did this item increase or decrease during fiscal year 1996? Is this good news or

bad news for the company? What other item is chiefly responsible for making the first item increase or decrease? Did the second item increase or decrease in fiscal year 1996? What caused one item to increase and the other to decrease?

2. Use the Lands' End *statement of retained earnings* to answer these questions: What is Lands' End doing with its net income? How can you tell?
3. Use the most recent *balance sheet* of Lands' End to answer these questions: At the end of fiscal year 1996, how much in total resources did Lands' End have to work with? How much did the company owe? How much of its assets did the company's stockholders actually own? Use these amounts to write the company's accounting equation at February 2, 1996.
4. Use the Lands' End *statement of cash flows* on page 21 (not the cash-flow statement in Appendix A at the back of the book) to answer these questions: It takes a lot of money to operate a company the size of Lands' End. Where does Lands' End get its cash? How does the company spend its cash? How much cash did it have at the beginning of the most recent year? How much cash did it have at the end of the year?

Identifying items from a company's financial statements ***(Obj. 4)***

Case 2. Obtain the annual report of a company of your choosing. Annual reports are available in various forms, including the original document in hard copy and computerized databases such as that provided by Disclosure, Inc., and the SEC's EDGAR database.

Required

Answer the following questions about the company. Concentrate on the current year in the annual report you select, except as directed for particular questions.

1. How much in cash (which may include cash equivalents) did the company have at the end of the current year? At the end of the preceding year? Did cash increase or decrease during the current year? By how much?
2. What were total assets at the end of the current year? At the end of the preceding year?
3. Write the company's accounting equation at the end of the current year by filling in the dollar amounts:

Assets = Liabilities + Owners' or Stockholders' Equity

4. Identify net sales revenue for the current year. The company may label this as *Net sales, Sales, Net revenue,* or as some other title. How much was the corresponding revenue amount for the preceding year?
5. How much net income or net loss did the company experience for the current year? For the preceding year? Evaluate the current year's operations in comparison with the preceding year.

GROUP PROJECTS

Project 1. As instructed by your professor, obtain the annual report of a well-known company.

Required

1. Take the role of a loan committee of Nation's Bank, a large banking company headquartered in Charlotte, North Carolina. Assume the company has requested a loan from Nation's Bank. Analyze the company's financial statements and any other information you need to reach a decision regarding the largest amount of money you would be willing to lend. Go as deeply into the analysis and the related decision as you can. Specify the following:
   - **a.** The length of the loan period—that is, over what period will you allow the company to pay you back?
   - **b.** The interest rate you will charge on the loan. Will you charge the prevailing interest rate, a lower rate, or a higher rate? Why?
   - **c.** Any restrictions you will impose on the borrower as a condition for making the loan.

   Note: The long-term debt note to the financial statements gives details of the company's existing liabilities.
2. Write your group decision in a report addressed to the bank's board of directors. Limit your report to two double-spaced word-processed pages.
3. If your professor directs, present your decision and your analysis to the class. Limit your presentation to 10–15 minutes.

Project 2. You are the owner of a company that is about to "go public"—that is, issue its stock to outside investors. You wish to make your company look as attractive as possible in order to raise $1 million of cash to expand the business. At the same time, you want to give potential investors a realistic picture of your company.

Required

1. Design a booklet to portray your company in a way that will enable outsiders to reach an informed decision as to whether to buy some of your stock. The booklet should include the following:

a. Name and location of your company.
b. Nature of the company's business (be as detailed as possible).
c. How you plan to spend the money you raise.
d. The company's comparative income statement, statement of retained earnings, balance sheet, and statement of cash flows for two years: the current year and the preceding year. Make the data as realistic as possible with the intent of receiving $1 million.

2. Word-process your booklet, not to exceed five pages.
3. If directed by your professor, make a copy for each member of your class. Distribute copies to the class, and present your case with the intent of interesting your classmates in investing in the company. Limit your presentation to 10–15 minutes.

INTERNET EXERCISE

LANDS' END, INC.

The Internet and its multimedia component, the World Wide Web, contain a wealth of information at the click of a mouse. The Internet exercises (which you will find at the end of each chapter) are designed to help you explore the opportunities and information available on the Net. This first exercise builds on the book's annual-report example (Lands' End) and is designed to get you acquainted with the Net.

From Lands' End home page, the Web site's starting point, you can view the company's Internet catalog, get gift ideas, place orders, or e-mail the company. Lands' End also uses its Web site to give visitors a sense of the company's history, vision, and values. Finally, much of the information in the Lands' End annual report is available.

Required

1. Go to **http://www.landsend.com/.** There you will find the Lands' End welcome page.*
2. At the bottom of the page (you may have to scroll down), click on the **Home** button. Doing so takes you to a list of Lands' End sites on the Internet (Internet Store, Catalogs, Services, and so forth).
3. To learn about Lands' End, answer the following questions by exploring the section labeled **The Company Inside and Out,** where the firm's history and corporate information are presented with its annual report.
   a. What are Lands' End's Principles of Doing Business?
   b. Describe the typical Lands' End customer.
   c. Why do the people at Lands' End consider themselves direct merchants instead of direct marketers?
   d. Why is the apostrophe in Lands' End in the wrong place?
   e. What is the Lands' End Guarantee?
   f. How does the president and CEO of Lands' End describe last year's performance?
   g. How much cash was generated (or used) by Lands' End operations?

APPENDIX TO CHAPTER 1
Accounting's Role in Business

Accounting's Relationship to the Other Areas of Business

As we approach the new millennium, accounting professionals will be more in demand than ever. The U.S. Labor Department predicts that the demand for accountants will increase 40% between 1996 and the year 2000. Why do you

*Note: Internet addresses and content change frequently. If you are having trouble connecting to a site, the address may have changed. In that case, visit the Prentice Hall Web Site for this text at **http://www.prenhall.com/phbusiness.** The textbook site is updated weekly and will have the company's most current address.

suppose this is occurring? Let's step back for a moment and examine how organizations operate. Every organization has a primary mission. Hospitals provide health care. Law firms advise clients on legal matters. Automobile manufacturers produce cars. Auto dealers sell the cars. All these organizations use *accounting* because it is impossible to physically observe all the aspects of a business. Accounting helps an organization understand its operations the same way a model helps an architect construct a building; that is, accounting helps the manager get a handle on the organization as a whole without drowning in all its details. Specifically, let's discuss how businesspeople use accounting to understand their business and make decisions.

How Owners and Managers Use Accounting

Suppose you own your own business, a consulting firm. How will you decide how much to spend on office rent, employee salaries, and computer hardware and software? You will be limited by the amount of cash you have in the bank, and you will know your cash balance because you've kept accounting records. After the business becomes a smashing success, how will you decide how much to spend on a business expansion? Observation, good contacts, and raw intelligence will give you ideas that are very important but inadequate for sound decision making. You will need to "run the numbers" to measure precisely how much you expect to earn from expanding the business. And others whom you invite to invest in the business will be more impressed with a carefully thought-out business plan than with a few vague ideas. Accounting will help you develop a business plan.

In fact, familiarity with accounting terms and practices is crucial for gaining entry to management positions. Accounting and finance are the main tools for setting goals, measuring results, and making decisions. Indeed, some companies are even adopting a policy called "open book management." Managers train all employees to understand the company's financial data and share those once-secret numbers with the work force. Clearly, as businesses "open their books," those who know how to use financial statements and other accounting information will advance rapidly.

Good managers plan their activities in advance. They write their business plans in terms of a *budget,* which is a formal plan often expressed in monetary terms. For example, a sales manager for Xerox Corporation will have an annual sales budget for which she is responsible. If she makes more sales than specified in the budget, she will receive a bonus. If you were this sales manager, would you become acquainted with the budgeting process that gives you your marching orders each year? You certainly would. Budgeting is an important part of accounting.

How Lenders and Investors Use Accounting

Accounting helps banks decide to whom they will lend money. Bankers cannot spend all their time observing borrowers' operations. But the bankers can study loan applicants' financial reports to get an idea of their ability to repay the loan. After making loans, bankers can monitor borrowers' progress by examining their financial reports. All financial reports are the result of accounting practices and procedures.

Accounting also provides important information that investors use to decide which stocks to buy and sell. An investor in Kansas may not have the time or the expertise to check on every detail of a company in Florida before buying its stock. But the investor can examine the company's financial reports to decide whether the company appears to be profitable and well managed. It may seem amazing to you that investors buy the stock of a company that they have barely heard of. Why are investors willing to spend their money this way? Because accounting statements and other reports give a picture of the business that people trust. The accounting reports tell whether the company is profitable or is losing money. They report the business's assets, how much it owes, and how much profit it is earning. In this course, you will learn how to use accounting to make some basic decisions, such as whether or not to invest in or lend money to a company.

Accounting is usually divided into two areas: private accounting and public accounting.

Private Accounting

Private accountants work for a single business, such as a local department store, the McDonald's restaurant chain, or the Eastman Kodak Company. Charitable organizations, educational institutions, and government agencies also employ private accountants. You'll find private accountants in a Wall Street brokerage firm, an agency for the homeless, and a rock-and-roll band organization. Accountants' goals vary according to the business or industry in which they operate. For instance, private accountants working for banks and insurance companies must help their companies adapt to the restructuring of financial markets and enterprises. Accountants in health-care organizations are playing a vital role in restructuring the nation's health-care delivery system by guiding their companies through a maze of government regulations. In the fast-paced world of entertainment and media, a private accountant might advise management on how to adapt to rapid technological changes. Private accountants for state or government agencies may help to "reinvent government" to provide more value for less cost.

While the specific missions of accountants vary, private accountants generally provide these services for their companies:

- *Budgeting* sets sales and profit goals and develops detailed plans for achieving those goals. Some of the most successful companies in the United States have been pioneers in the field of budgeting—**Procter & Gamble** and **General Electric,** for example.
- *Information systems design* identifies the organization's information needs, both internal and external. Systems designers develop and implement an information system to meet those needs.
- *Cost accounting* analyzes a business's costs to help managers control expenses. Cost accounting records guide managers in pricing their products and services to achieve greater profits. Also, cost accounting information shows management when a product is not profitable and should be dropped.
- *Internal auditing* is performed by a business's own accountants. Large organizations—**Motorola, Bank of America,** and **3M** among them—maintain a staff of internal auditors. These accountants evaluate the firm's own accounting and management systems to improve operating efficiency and ensure that employees follow company policies.

A company's chief accounting officer usually has the title of controller, treasurer, or chief financial officer (CFO). Whatever the title, this person usually carries the status of a vice president. Accountants who have met certain professional requirements in the area of management accounting are designated as *certified management accountants (CMAs).*

The CFO and other accounting professionals have become increasingly important as businesses compete in global markets. Accountants provide data that present a picture of the company as it is today and information that helps managers steer the company into tomorrow. For instance, accountants often measure the company against its toughest competitors. This practice is called "benchmarking," and it requires accountants to visit other companies to gather information. At **Federal Express,** some financial managers visited Intel to learn how to improve mailroom efficiency. At **Frito-Lay,** financial people use benchmarking to set goals and stimulate the company's creativity. For instance, they might ask, "How can our competitor produce a quality product at a lower price? How can we do the same?" These are the kinds of vital business questions that accountants help to answer.

Clearly, this is a far cry from the old stereotype of the accountant sitting in a back room with record books and calculator in hand. Stephen Bollenbach, CFO of **Walt Disney Company** recalls, "During the sixties the CFO, as scorekeeper, was mainly concerned with accounting and budgets. Now the CFO's role encompasses critical functions like strategic planning—charting the company's long-term direction."

In many companies, accountants have become coaches and team players as they have shifted the most routine tasks to computers. This is exactly what happened at **Solectron,** a maker of electronic components. Accountants taught Solectron's salespeople how to evaluate a customer's creditworthiness and even how to determine how much credit to give them. This new procedure not only speeds up the process of getting new customers, but also frees up the accountants' time for more interesting and important jobs. They might, for example, help determine what kind of customers are most profitable or how to reduce the cost of gaining customers.

The changing nature of accountants' jobs means that people who choose accounting as a career need to have more than a sound financial and accounting background. They must be good communicators, analysts, and problem solvers, and they must be able to work in cross-functional teams composed of members from the company's different departments: operations, production, distribution, sales, and marketing.

Public Accounting

Public accountants serve the general public and collect professional fees for their work, much as doctors and lawyers do. Public accountants are a small fraction (about 10%) of all accountants. Accountants who have met certain professional requirements in law, auditing, and accounting are designated as *certified public accountants (CPAs).*

Like private accountants, public accountants provide many valuable services:

- **Auditing** is one of the accounting profession's most important services. In conducting an audit, CPAs from outside a business examine the business's financial statements. The CPAs report a professional opinion stating whether the firm's financial statements agree with generally accepted accounting principles. Why is the audit so important? Creditors want assurance that the facts and figures submitted by borrowers are reliable. Stockholders, who have invested in the company, need to know that the financial picture management shows them is complete. Government agencies also need accurate information from businesses.
- *Tax accounting* has two aims: complying with the tax laws and minimizing the company's tax bill. Because federal income tax rates run as high as 39.6% for individuals and 35% for corporations, reducing the company's tax bill is an important management consideration. Accountants prepare tax returns and plan business transactions to minimize taxes. CPAs advise individuals on what type of investments to make and on how to structure their transactions.
- *Management consulting* is a catchall term that describes the wide scope of advice CPAs provide to help managers run a business. As CPAs conduct audits, they look deep into a business's operations. With the insights they gain, they often make suggestions for improvements in the business's management structure and accounting systems.

Some public accountants pool their talents and work together within a single firm. Most professional employees of the public accounting firms are CPAs. The accounting firms vary greatly in size. Some are small businesses, and others are large partnerships. Exhibit 1A-1 gives data on the ten largest U.S. accounting firms.

These firms are very large. **Andersen Worldwide** (the combination of **Arthur Andersen** and **Andersen Consulting**) generates annual revenues of almost $4 billion. The firm has over 1,500 partners, more than 35,000 employees, and operates 91 offices around the world. The average Andersen partner brings in annual revenues exceeding $2.5 million and is paid $300,000–$400,000 per year. Partners in the other large accounting firms receive similar compensation.

The rightmost column of Exhibit 1A-1 shows how the accounting firms earn their revenue. Andersen's fee split of 32/16/52 indicates that the firm earns 32% of its revenue from accounting and auditing services, 16% from tax services, and 52% from consulting, or management advisory, services. Thus, Andersen Worldwide earns the majority of its revenue as a management consulting firm. The other five leading firms earn approximately 36% of their revenue from consulting, and this percentage is growing.

Indeed, the accounting firms in Exhibit 1A-1 are the largest consulting firms in the world.

Accountants working as management consultants can have a major impact on their clients. The following actual examples describe how public accountants have affected their clients:

- A consultant specializing in health care simplified the way medical personnel interact with computers so that they can give more personal attention to patients. Meanwhile, the computer keeps track of important medical information, such as whether or not the patient got well and how long the recovery took.

EXHIBIT 1A-1
The Largest U.S. Accounting Firms

Rank (1996)	Firm Location	Net revenue (in millions)	Partners	Employees	Number of Offices	Revenue per partner (in millions)	Fee split* (% of total revenue) A&A/Taxes/MAS
1	Andersen Worldwide New York	$3,860.2	1,529	35,015	91	$2.525	32/16/52
2	Ernst & Young New York	$2,974.0	1,864	21,690	91	$1.595	43/22/35
3	Deloitte & Touche Wilton, Connecticut	$2,570.0	1,477	16,483	110	$1.745	44/20/36
4	KPMG Peat Marwick New York	$2,289.0	1,425	16,025	124	$1.606	45/19/36
5	Coopers & Lybrand New York	$1,905.0	1,229	16,335	117	$1.550	45/20/35
6	Price Waterhouse New York	$1,770.0	957	15,221	106	$1.850	40/24/36
7	H&R Block Tax Services** Kansas City, Missouri	$ 657.0	8,200	83,000	8,268	$0.082	0/100/0
8	Grant Thornton Chicago	$ 240.0	282	2,605	48	$0.851	46/32/22
9	McGladrey & Pullen Davenport, Iowa	$ 229.8	387	2,725	73	$0.594	49/33/18
10	BDO Seidman New York	$ 202.5	230	1,650	40	$0.880	54/29/17

*A&A = Accounting and auditing
Taxes = Income and other taxes
MAS = Management advisory services
**H&R Block, unlike the other accounting firms, is not a partnership.
Source: Adapted from *Accounting Today* (March 18–April 7, 1996), p. 17.

- At a large regulated utility in the United Kingdom, consulting accountants brought 85 managers, regulators, and shippers together for a three-day conference. The purpose was to revamp one of the utility's core business processes. The group agreed to significant and far-reaching changes, and within three weeks, the utility company had cut the time it takes to complete the process from 28 days to five.
- A CPA devised an ownership-succession plan for a small family-owned business. She had to bring together quarreling family members, the ailing company founder, and anxious employees. By the end of her engagement, the company had hammered out an agreement for a smooth transition of ownership that was acceptable to both family members and the other employees.

Public accountants spend most of their time at their clients' locations: across town, around the country, or even around the world. Public accountants may even find themselves in some unlikely places. Consider the following examples:

- Josh Young's first consulting engagement for Arthur Andersen found him on the site of the Northridge earthquake outside of Los Angeles. One of his clients was a large supermarket chain with 150 damaged stores. Young helped prepare insurance claims for his client and needed to visit the actual site at 4:00 A.M.—as the tremors continued—to determine how much damage had occurred.
- Mike Nugent, a supervising senior at **KPMG Peat Marwick,** took on a consulting job, unaware that his business attire might include boots, overalls, and a hairnet. To conduct an audit for a chicken producer recently acquired by a Japanese holding company, Nugent drove to Heartland, Indiana. "Of course there was an inventory involved in this assignment," says Nugent, who soon found himself surrounded by 2,000 screaming chickens!
- Jennifer Tufer is a **Deloitte & Touche** senior manager on assignment in Moscow. At the end of the day, she sifts through stacks of faxes that have arrived from various Deloitte & Touche offices around the world. A typical request comes from a U.S. manufacturer interested in setting up operations in Russia. "The company wanted to know how they would be taxed," Ms. Tufer says.

Because they work with a cross section of businesses and industries, public accountants bring a valuable outsider's perspective to client problems. The ability to work with a wide array of companies is an important skill for people who choose a public accounting career. Caroline King, a manager at Deloitte & Touche in New York, says that when she began her career, "Diversity was very important to me. I wanted the opportunity to explore different industries and a variety of functions within those industries." The work has exceeded her expectations: "I've worked with a variety of clients—insurance companies, manufacturers, and retailers—on projects ranging from cash management and strategy development to creating business plans and helping companies reorganize. All of my assignments have been interesting and challenging." Public accountants working for a client often work with people at a higher level than they would if they were full-time employees of the client. Consulting with clients often gives public accountants access to some of the company's top executives.

Accounting Today

Today's accountants are as diverse as their job assignments. Accountants may be male or female, outgoing or conservative, but they are all analytical. They may have backgrounds in art history or computer programming. Their hobbies include rock climbing, scuba diving, and gourmet cooking. And they come from every ethnic and cultural background.

Accounting was once dominated by men, particularly in the "Big Six" firms—the six largest public accounting firms. Today, the Big Six, smaller CPA firms, and companies in general are hiring more women as professionals than ever before. Women are rising to top positions, such as CFO or partner. In 1995, Deloitte & Touche, a Big Six firm that has made a major initiative for the advancement of women, admitted 22 women to the partnership. That was 21% of new partners, compared to only 8% in 1991.

Both men and women accountants are benefiting from today's flexible work arrangements. "I'm probably one of the first people who stayed in public accounting because of quality-of-life advantages," says Eileen Garvey, an audit partner at **Ernst & Young** in New York. Garvey was an early participant in flexible scheduling and spent six years working a three-day-a-week schedule. The mother of two young girls, Garvey was admitted to the partnership as a part-timer. Flexibility works for men, too. Carl Moellenkamp, a manager with Arthur Andersen in Chicago, took a summer's leave to pursue his other career as a chef.

Since the tools of the accounting trade are computers, phones, and fax machines, some accountants are now balancing career and family by working from home. They can set up shop at home to save on office rent. Janet Caswell, a Michigan accountant with her own business, has a staff but no office. Her files, computer file server, and other equipment are located in a rented storage space. Her telephone is a personal 800 number that can be programmed to follow her staff wherever they go. Her employees communicate and "meet" electronically. Caswell is one of a growing number of public accountants with this type of "virtual office."

What are the prospects for people entering the accounting field? Exhibit 1A-2 shows the accounting positions within public accounting firms and other organizations. Note the upward movement of accounting personnel, as indicated by the arrows. In particular, note how accountants may move from positions in public accounting firms to similar or higher positions in industry and government. This is a frequently traveled career path. An accounting background can open doors in most lines of business. In addition to providing the foundation for becoming a partner in an accounting firm, accounting can lead to a career in finance or corporate management, or to a leadership position in a government agency or a charitable organization. Knowing how to design a business plan, prepare a budget, and analyze costs, profits, and losses also equips a person to become an entrepreneur. In short, because accounting deals with all facets of an organization—such as purchasing, manufacturing, marketing, and distribution—it provides an excellent basis for gaining broad business experience.

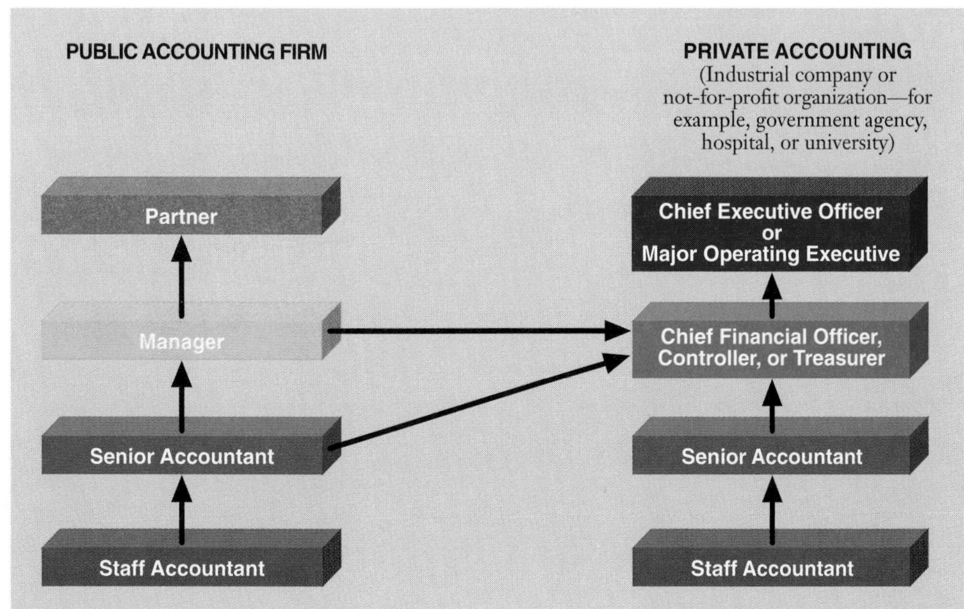

EXHIBIT 1A-2
Accounting Positions within Organizations

2

Processing Accounting Information

Learning Objectives

After studying this chapter, you should be able to

1. Define and use key accounting terms: account, asset, liability, stockholders' equity, revenue, and expense
2. Use the accounting equation to analyze business transactions
3. Understand how double-entry accounting works
4. Record transactions in the journal, and post from the journal to the ledger
5. Prepare and use a trial balance
6. Set up a chart of accounts for a business
7. Analyze transactions without a journal

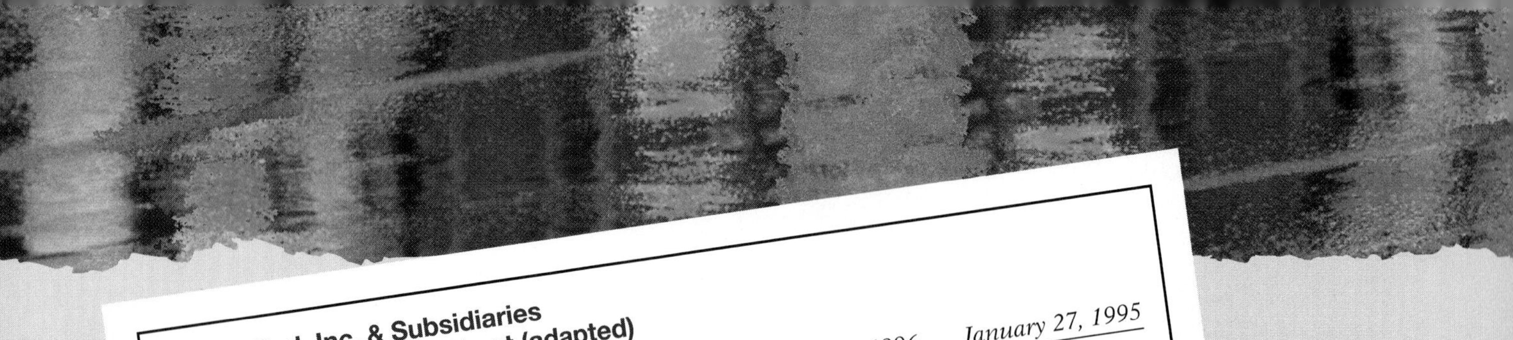

Lands' End, Inc. & Subsidiaries
Consolidated Balance Sheet (adapted)

	(In thousands)	*February 2, 1996*	*January 27, 1995*
	ASSETS		
	Current assets:		
1	Cash	**$ 17,176**	$ 5,426
2	Receivables	**8,064**	4,459
3	Inventory	**164,816**	168,652
4	Prepaid advertising and other expenses	**32,033**	19,631
5	Total current assets	**222,089**	198,168
	Property, plant, and equipment, at cost:		
6	Land and buildings	**72,248**	69,798
7	Fixtures and equipment	**83,880**	74,745
8	Leasehold improvements	**2,912**	1,862
9	Total property, plant, and equipment	**159,040**	146,405
10	Less: Accumulated depreciation and amortization	**60,055**	49,414
11	Property, plant, and equipment, net	**98,985**	96,991
12	Intangibles, net	**2,423**	2,453
13	Total assets	**$323,497**	$297,612
	LIABILITIES AND SHAREHOLDERS' INVESTMENT		
	Current liabilities:		
14	Lines of credit	**$ 9,319**	$ 7,539
15	Accounts payable	**62,380**	52,762
16	Reserve for returns	**4,555**	5,011
17	Accrued liabilities	**23,751**	25,959
18	Accrued profit sharing	**1,483**	1,679
19	Income taxes payable	**13,256**	9,727
20	Current maturities of long-term debt	**—**	40
21	Total current liabilities	**114,744**	102,717
22	**Deferred income taxes**	**7,212**	**5,379**
23	**Long-term liabilities**	**349**	**388**
	Shareholders' investment:		
24	Common stock, 40,221 shares issued	**26,567**	26,219
25	Retained earnings	**260,109**	229,554
26	Other	**(85,484)**	(66,645)
27	Total shareholders' investment	**201,192**	189,128
28	Total liabilities and shareholders' investment	**$323,497**	$297,612

"I want everything that appears in the Lands' End annual report to help the potential shareholder or the active shareholder to understand the business."

—CHARLOTTE LA COMB, MANAGER, INVESTOR RELATIONS, LANDS' END, INC.

Like all other companies, **Lands' End** represents itself to outsiders through its financial statements. But the financial statements are also used internally. Lands' End managers at all levels use financial statement data for decision making. For example, Lands' End purchases some of its merchandise from manufacturers in Hong Kong. How does the purchasing manager know how much merchandise to order? The inventory balance (line 3 of the balance sheet) will affect the amounts and timing of various orders. When you phone Lands' End with an order, the customer service representative can tell you whether the merchandise is available because the accounting records keep a running tally of the inventory on hand. How does the company know when its liabilities (lines 14–23) are due and how much to pay for them? Again, the balance sheet and the related accounting records provide the information.

Chapter 1 gave you a good grounding in the financial statements, which are the focus of this course. But that chapter did not show how the financial statements are prepared. Chapters 2 and 3 cover the accounting process that results in the financial statements.

Chapter 2 discusses the processing of accounting information. It begins with an intuitive approach that is based on the accounting equation we studied in Chapter 1. The second half of the chapter extends the discussion to illustrate the way accounting systems work. Chapter 3 goes more deeply into how income is measured. It covers the end-of-period accounting process that results in the financial statements.

Throughout this chapter and the next we illustrate service businesses such as a travel agency, a law practice, or a sports franchise like the Chicago Bulls. In later chapters we move into merchandising businesses such as Macy's and Wal-Mart.

By learning how accounting information is processed, you will understand where the facts and figures reported in the financial statements come from. This knowledge will increase your confidence as you make decisions. It will also speed your progress in your business career.

The Account

Objective 1

Define and use key accounting terms: account, asset, liability, stockholders' equity, revenue, and expense

Recall that in Chapter 1, page 13, we learned that the accounting equation is the most basic tool in accounting. It measures the assets of the business and the claims to those assets.

The basic summary device of accounting is the **account,** the detailed record of the changes that have occurred in a particular asset, liability, or stockholders' (or owners') equity during a period of time. Accounts are grouped in three broad categories, according to the accounting equation:

Assets = Liabilities + Stockholders' (or Owners') Equity

Assets

Assets are the economic resources that benefit the business and will continue to do so in the future. Most firms use the following asset accounts.

CASH The Cash account shows the cash effects of a business's transactions. *Cash* means money and any medium of exchange that a bank accepts at face value, such as bank account balances, paper currency, coins, certificates of deposit, and checks. Most business failures result from a shortage of cash.

ACCOUNTS RECEIVABLE A business may sell its goods or services in exchange for an oral or implied promise for future cash receipt. Such sales are made on credit ("on account"). The Accounts Receivable account contains these amounts. Most sales in the United States and in other developed countries are made on accounts receivable. Look at the Receivables balance in the Lands' End balance sheet on page 50. This balance is low because most of the company's sales are by credit card, and credit-card collections are rapid.

INVENTORY Lands' End's most important asset is its inventory—the shirts, slacks, luggage, and other goods that the company sells to customers. Other titles used for this account include Merchandise and Merchandise Inventories.

NOTES RECEIVABLE A business may sell its goods or services in exchange for a *promissory note,* which is a written pledge that the customer will pay a fixed amount of money by a certain date. The Notes Receivable account is a record of the promissory notes the business expects to collect in cash. A note receivable offers more security for collection than a mere account receivable does.

PREPAID EXPENSES A business often pays certain expenses in advance. A prepaid expense is an asset because the business avoids having to pay cash in the future for the specified expense. Each prepaid expense has a separate asset account. Prepaid Rent, Prepaid Insurance, and Office Supplies are accounted for as prepaid expenses. The largest prepaid expense for Lands' End is Prepaid Advertising.

LAND The Land account is a record of the cost of land a business owns and uses in its operations. Land held for sale is accounted for separately in an investment account.

BUILDINGS The cost of a business's buildings—office, warehouse, garage, and the like—appear in the Buildings account. Buildings held for sale are separate assets accounted for as investments.

EQUIPMENT, FURNITURE, AND FIXTURES A business has a separate asset account for each type of equipment—Office Equipment and Store Equipment, for example. The Furniture and Fixtures account shows the cost of these assets, which are similar to equipment.

We will discuss the other asset categories and accounts as needed. For example, many businesses have an Investments account for their investments in the stocks and bonds of other companies.

Liabilities

Recall that a *liability* is a debt. Here are some of the most common types of liability accounts:

NOTES PAYABLE The Notes Payable account is the opposite of the Notes Receivable account. Notes Payable includes the amounts that the business must pay because it signed a promissory note to borrow money or to purchase goods or services. The Lines of Credit account of Lands' End (line 14 of the balance sheet on page 50) is like a note payable.

ACCOUNTS PAYABLE The Accounts Payable account is the opposite of the Accounts Receivable account. The oral or implied promise to pay off debts arising from credit purchases of inventory and other goods appears in the Accounts Payable account. Such a purchase is said to be made "on account." Lands' End will pay most of its accounts payable within 30 days.

ACCRUED LIABILITIES An *accrued liability* is a liability for an expense that has not been paid. Accrued liability accounts are added as needed. Interest Payable and Salary Payable are accrued liability accounts of most companies. Income Taxes Payable is also an accrued liability. Like many other companies, Lands' End reports Income Taxes Payable separately from the other accrued liabilities.

> LEARNING TIP A receivable is always an asset. A payable is always a liability.

Stockholders' (Owners') Equity

The owners' claims to the assets of a corporation are called *stockholders' equity, shareholders' equity,* or simply *owners' equity.* In a proprietorship or a partnership, owner equity is often split into separate accounts for each owner's capital balance and each owner's withdrawals. A corporation has a similar setup but uses Common Stock, Retained Earnings, and Dividends accounts.

COMMON STOCK The Common Stock account represents the owners' investment in the corporation. A person invests in a corporation by purchasing common stock. The corporation issues a stock certificate imprinted with the stockholder's name as proof of ownership.

RETAINED EARNINGS A for-profit business must earn a profit to remain in operation. The Retained Earnings account shows the cumulative net income earned by the corporation over its lifetime, minus cumulative net losses and dividends. We will study this account more in the chapters that follow and include it here merely for completeness.

DIVIDENDS The owners of a corporation demand cash from their business. After profitable operations, the board of directors may (or may not) declare a cash dividend to be paid at a later date. Dividends are not required but are optional and depend on the decision of the board of directors. The corporation may keep a separate account titled *Dividends,* which indicates a decrease in Retained Earnings.

REVENUES The increase in stockholders' equity created by delivering goods or services to customers or clients is called *revenue.* The company uses as many revenue accounts as needed. Lands' End uses a Sales Revenue account for amounts earned by selling merchandise to customers. A lawyer provides legal services for clients and thus uses a Service Revenue account. If a business loans money to an outsider, it will need an Interest Revenue account for the interest earned on the loan. If the business rents a building to a tenant, it will need a Rent Revenue account.

EXPENSES The cost of operating a business is called *expense.* Expenses have the opposite effect of revenues; they *decrease* stockholders' equity. A business needs a separate account for each type of expense, such as Salary Expense, Rent Expense, Advertising Expense, and Utilities Expense. Businesses strive to minimize their expenses and thereby maximize net income.

STOP & THINK Name two things that (1) increase stockholders' equity; (2) decrease stockholders' equity.

Answer: (1) Sale of stock and net income (revenue greater than expenses). (2) Declaration and payment of dividends and net loss (expenses greater than revenue).

Accounting for Business Transactions

Objective 2

Use the accounting equation to analyze business transactions

In accounting terms, a **transaction** is any event that *both* affects the financial position of the business entity *and* can be reliably recorded. Many events may affect a company, including (1) elections, (2) economic booms and recessions, (3) purchases and sales of merchandise inventory, (4) payment of rent, (5) collection of cash from customers, and so on. But accountants record only events with effects that can be measured reliably as transactions.

Which of the above five events would an accountant record? The answer is events (3), (4), and (5) because their dollar amounts can be measured reliably. The dollar effects of elections and economic trends cannot be measured reliably. Therefore, an accountant would not record a key election or a trend even though it might affect the business more than events (3), (4), and (5).

To illustrate accounting for business transactions, let's return to Gary and Monica Lyon. We met Gary and Monica in Chapter 1, when they opened a travel agency in April, 19X1 and incorporated it as Air & Sea Travel, Inc. We will consider 11 events and analyze each in terms of its effect on the accounting equation of Air & Sea Travel. Transaction analysis is the essence of accounting.

TRANSACTION 1 The Lyons invest $50,000 of their money to begin the business. Specifically, they deposit $50,000 in a bank account entitled Air & Sea Travel, Inc. As evidence of the corporation, Air & Sea Travel issues common stock to Gary and Monica Lyon. The stock is printed on certificates and issued by the corporation. It provides tangible evidence that the Lyons have an ownership interest in the corporation. The effect of this transaction on the accounting equation of the business entity Air & Sea Travel, Inc., is

	Assets	=	Liabilities	+	Stockholders' Equity	Type of Stockholders' Equity Transaction
	Cash				Common Stock	
(1)	+50,000				+50,000	Issued stock to owners

For every transaction, the amount on the left side of the equation must equal the amount on the right side. The first transaction increases both the assets (in this case, Cash) and the owners' equity of the business (Common Stock). The transaction involves no liabilities because it creates no obligation for Air & Sea Travel to pay an outside party. To the right of the transaction we write "Issued stock to owners" to keep track of the reason for the effect on stockholders' equity. Most businesses start with an issuance of stock to the owners, *not* with borrowed money. Why? Because lenders usually require the owners to have some of their own money in the business.

TRANSACTION 2 Air & Sea Travel purchases land for a future office location, paying cash of $40,000. The effect of this transaction on the accounting equation is

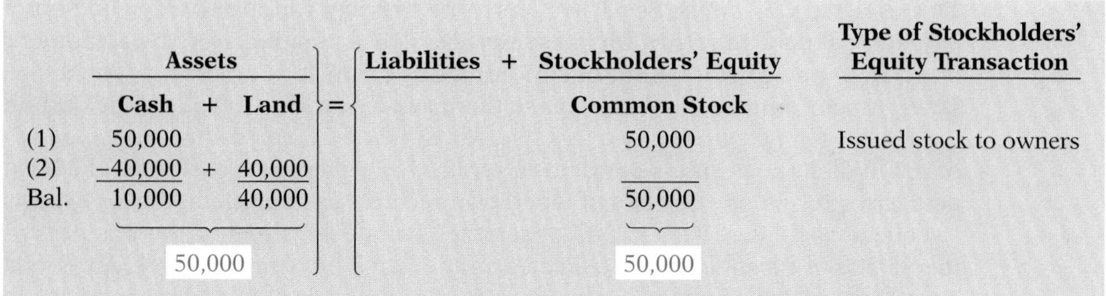

	Assets			Liabilities + Stockholders' Equity	Type of Stockholders' Equity Transaction
	Cash	+	Land	Common Stock	
(1)	50,000			50,000	Issued stock to owners
(2)	−40,000	+	40,000		
Bal.	10,000		40,000	50,000	
	50,000			50,000	

The cash purchase of land increases one asset (Land) and decreases another asset (Cash) by the same amount. After the transaction is completed, Air & Sea Travel has cash of $10,000, land of $40,000, no liabilities, and stockholders' equity of $50,000. Note that the sums of the balances (which we abbreviate Bal.) on both sides of the equation are equal. This equality must always exist.

TRANSACTION 3 The business buys stationery and other office supplies, agreeing to pay $500 to the office-supply store within 30 days. This transaction increases both the assets and the liabilities of the business. Its effect on the accounting equation is

	Assets					Liabilities	+	Stockholders' Equity
	Cash	+	Office Supplies	+	Land	Accounts Payable	+	Common Stock
Bal.	10,000				40,000			50,000
(3)			+500			+500		
Bal.	10,000		500		40,000	500		50,000
			50,500				50,500	

The asset affected is Office Supplies, and the liability is an Account Payable. Because Air & Sea Travel is obligated to pay $500 in the future but signs no formal promissory note, we record the liability as an account payable, not as a note payable. We say that purchases supported by the buyer's general credit standing are made on *open account.*

TRANSACTION 4 Air & Sea Travel earns service revenue by providing travel arrangement services for customers. Assume the business earns $5,500 and collects this amount in cash. The effect on the accounting equation is an increase in the asset Cash and an increase in Retained Earnings, as follows:

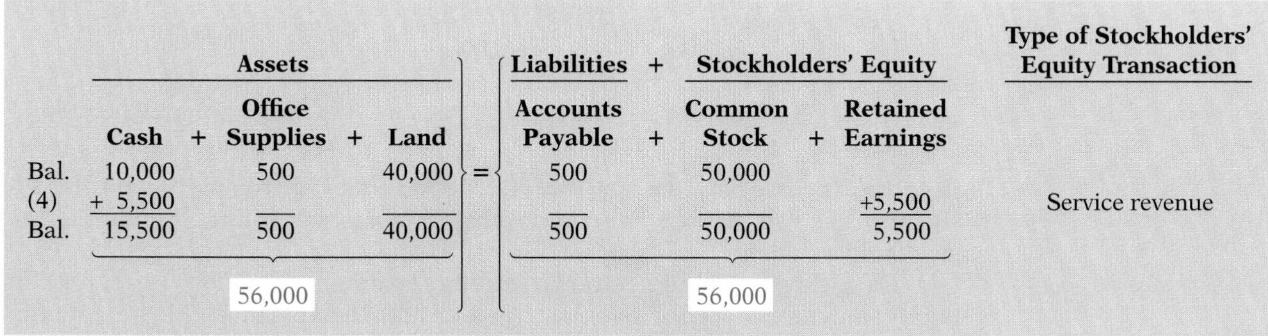

	Assets					Liabilities	+	Stockholders' Equity			Type of Stockholders' Equity Transaction
	Cash	+	Office Supplies	+	Land	Accounts Payable	+	Common Stock	+	Retained Earnings	
Bal.	10,000		500		40,000	500		50,000			
(4)	+ 5,500									+5,500	Service revenue
Bal.	15,500		500		40,000	500		50,000		5,500	
			56,000					56,000			

This revenue transaction caused the business to grow, as shown by the increase in total assets and in total liabilities plus stockholders' equity. Air & Sea Travel performs services for clients, so its revenue is called *service revenue.*

TRANSACTION 5 Air & Sea Travel performs services for customers who do not pay immediately. In return for these services, Air & Sea receives the customers' promise to pay $3,000 within one month. This promise is an asset to Air & Sea Travel, an account receivable because the business expects to collect the cash in the future. (In accounting, we say that Air & Sea performed this service *on account*.) When the business performs a service for a client or a customer, the business earns revenue regardless of whether it receives cash immediately or expects to collect cash later. This $3,000 of service revenue is as real to the business as the $5,500 of revenue that it collected immediately in Transaction 4. Air & Sea Travel records an increase in the asset Accounts Receivable and an increase in Retained Earnings as follows:

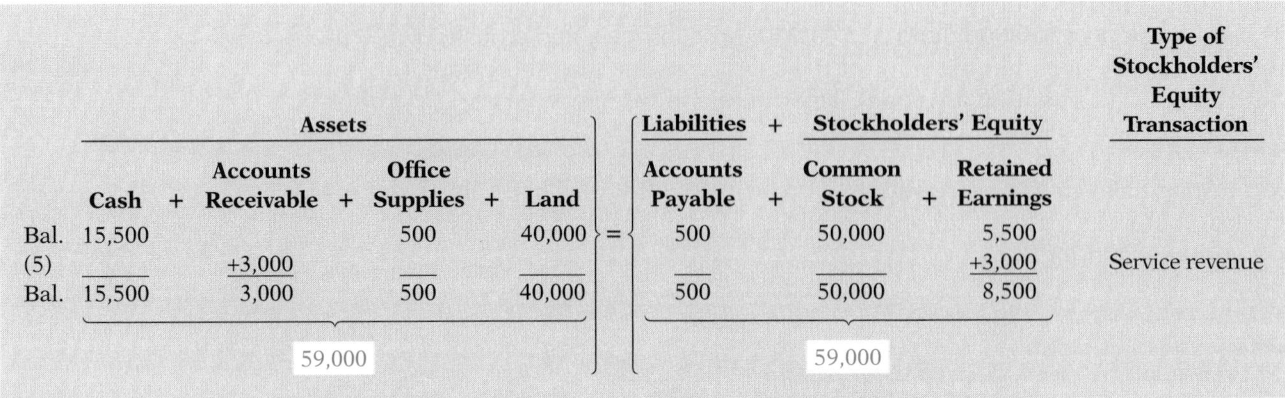

	Assets				=	Liabilities +	Stockholders' Equity		Type of Stockholders' Equity Transaction
	Cash +	Accounts Receivable +	Office Supplies +	Land		Accounts Payable +	Common Stock +	Retained Earnings	
Bal.	15,500		500	40,000	=	500	50,000	5,500	
(5)		+3,000						+3,000	Service revenue
Bal.	15,500	3,000	500	40,000		500	50,000	8,500	
	59,000					59,000			

Like Transaction 4, this revenue transaction caused the business to grow.

TRANSACTION 6 During the month, Air & Sea Travel pays $2,700 in cash expenses: office rent, $1,100; employee salary, $1,200 (for a part-time assistant); and total utilities, $400. The effect on the accounting equation is

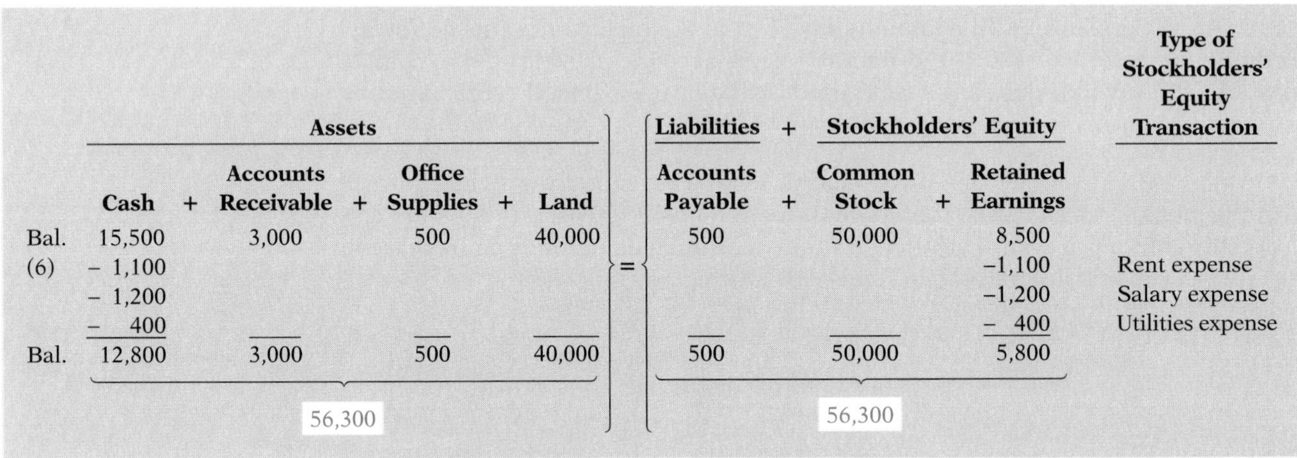

	Assets				=	Liabilities +	Stockholders' Equity		Type of Stockholders' Equity Transaction
	Cash +	Accounts Receivable +	Office Supplies +	Land		Accounts Payable +	Common Stock +	Retained Earnings	
Bal.	15,500	3,000	500	40,000		500	50,000	8,500	
(6)	− 1,100				=			−1,100	Rent expense
	− 1,200							−1,200	Salary expense
	− 400							− 400	Utilities expense
Bal.	12,800	3,000	500	40,000		500	50,000	5,800	
	56,300					56,300			

Because expenses have the opposite effect of revenues, they cause the business to shrink, as shown by the smaller amounts of total assets and total liabilities and stockholders' equity.

Each expense should be recorded in a separate transaction. Here, for simplicity, they are recorded together. As a result, the "balance" of the equation holds, as we know it must.

TRANSACTION 7 Air & Sea Travel pays $400 to the store from which it purchased $500 worth of office supplies in Transaction 3. (In accounting, we say that Air & Sea Travel pays $400 *on account*.) The effect on the accounting equation is a decrease in the asset Cash and a decrease in the liability Accounts Payable as follows:

	Assets					Liabilities +	Stockholders' Equity	
	Cash	+ Accounts Receivable	+ Office Supplies	+ Land		Accounts Payable	+ Common Stock	+ Retained Earnings
Bal.	12,800	3,000	500	40,000	=	500	50,000	5,800
(7)	− 400					−400		
Bal.	12,400	3,000	500	40,000		100	50,000	5,800
	55,900					55,900		

The payment of cash on account has no effect on the asset Office Supplies because the payment does not increase or decrease the supplies available to the business. The payment is not an expense; instead the business is paying off a liability.

Transaction 8 The Lyons remodel their home at a cost of $30,000, paying cash from personal funds. This event is *not* a transaction of Air & Sea Travel, Inc. It has no effect on Air & Sea's business affairs and therefore is not recorded by the business. It is a transaction of the *personal* entity the Lyon family, not the *business* entity Air & Sea Travel. We are focusing now solely on the business entity, and this event does not affect it. This transaction illustrates the application of the *entity concept* (see Chapter 1).

Transaction 9 In Transaction 5, Air & Sea Travel performed service for customers on account. The business now collects $1,000 from a customer. (We say that it collects the cash *on account*.) Air & Sea will record an increase in the asset Cash. Should it also record an increase in service revenue? No, because Air & Sea already recorded the revenue when it performed the service in Transaction 5. The phrase "collect cash on account" means to record an increase in Cash and a decrease in the asset Accounts Receivable. The effect on the accounting equation is

	Assets					Liabilities +	Stockholders' Equity	
	Cash	+ Accounts Receivable	+ Office Supplies	+ Land		Accounts Payable	+ Common Stock	+ Retained Earnings
Bal.	12,400	3,000	500	40,000	=	100	50,000	5,800
(9)	+ 1,000	−1,000						
Bal.	13,400	2,000	500	40,000		100	50,000	5,800
	55,900					55,900		

Total assets are unchanged from the preceding transaction's total. Why? Because Air & Sea Travel merely exchanged one asset for another. Also, liabilities and stockholders' equity are unchanged.

Transaction 10 An individual approaches the Lyons about selling a piece of the land owned by Air & Sea Travel. They and the other person agree to a sale price of $22,000, which is equal to the business's cost of the land. Air & Sea sells the land and receives $22,000 cash, and the effect on the accounting equation is

	Assets					Liabilities +	Stockholders' Equity	
	Cash	+ Accounts Receivable	+ Office Supplies	+ Land		Accounts Payable	+ Common Stock	+ Retained Earnings
Bal.	13,400	2,000	500	40,000	=	100	50,000	5,800
(10)	+22,000			−22,000				
Bal.	35,400	2,000	500	18,000		100	50,000	5,800
	55,900					55,900		

Note that the company did not sell all its land; it still owns $18,000 worth of land.

TRANSACTION 11 The corporation declares a dividend and pays Gary and Monica Lyon $2,100 cash for their personal use. The effect on the accounting equation is

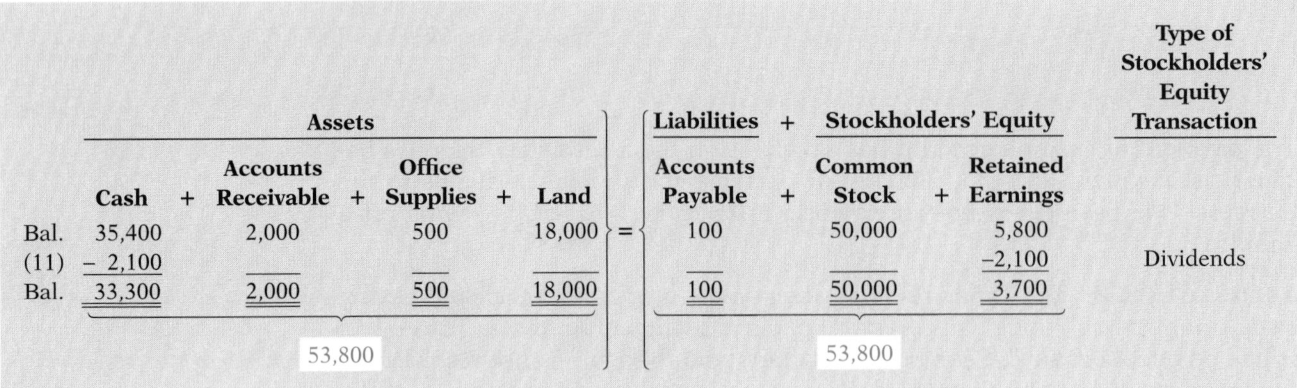

	Assets					Liabilities +	Stockholders' Equity		Type of Stockholders' Equity Transaction
	Cash +	Accounts Receivable +	Office Supplies +	Land		Accounts Payable +	Common Stock +	Retained Earnings	
Bal.	35,400	2,000	500	18,000	=	100	50,000	5,800	
(11)	− 2,100							−2,100	Dividends
Bal.	33,300	2,000	500	18,000		100	50,000	3,700	
	53,800					53,800			

The dividend decreases the asset Cash and also the retained earnings of the business.

Does the dividend decrease the business entity's holdings? The answer is yes, because the cash paid to the stockholders is no longer available for Air & Sea's business use. The dividend does *not* represent a business expense, however, because the cash is paid to the owners for their personal use. Therefore, we record this decrease in stockholders' equity as Dividends, *not* as an expense.

Business Transactions and the Financial Statements

Exhibit 2-1 summarizes the 11 preceding transactions. Panel A summarizes the details of the transactions, and Panel B presents the financial analysis. As you study the exhibit, note that every transaction maintains the equality

Assets = Liabilities + Stockholders' Equity

Exhibit 2-1 provides the data that Air & Sea Travel will use to create its financial statements. Data for the *statement of cash flows* are aligned under the Cash account. Cash receipts show up as increases in cash, and cash payments appear as decreases. *Income statement* data appear as revenues and expenses under Retained Earnings. The revenues increase retained earnings; the expenses decrease retained earnings. The *balance sheet* data are composed of the ending balances of the assets, liabilities, and stockholders' equities shown at the bottom of the exhibit. The accounting equation shows that total assets ($53,800) equal total liabilities plus stockholders' equity ($53,800). The *statement of retained earnings,* which shows net income (or net loss) and dividends, can be prepared from the income statement data.

Exhibit 2-2 on page 60 shows Air & Sea Travel's financial statements at the end of April, the business's first month of operations. You will recognize the Air & Sea Travel statements from the solution to the summary problem at the end of Chapter 1. We repeat the financial statements here to reinforce your learning. Follow the flow of data to observe that

1. The income statement reports revenues, expenses, and either a net income or a net loss for the period. During April, Air & Sea earned net income of $5,800.

2. The statement of retained earnings starts with the beginning balance of retained earnings, which for a new business is zero. Add net income for the period (arrow ①), subtract dividends, and obtain the ending balance of retained earnings ($3,700).

EXHIBIT 2-1
Analysis of Air & Sea Travel, Inc., Transactions

PANEL A—Details of transactions

(1) Issued stock to the owners who invested $50,000 cash in the business.
(2) Paid $40,000 cash for land.
(3) Bought $500 of office supplies on account.
(4) Received $5,500 cash from customers for service revenue earned.
(5) Performed services for customers on account, $3,000.
(6) Paid cash expenses: rent, $1,100; employee salary, $1,200; utilities, $400.
(7) Paid $400 on the account payable created in Transaction 3.
(8) Owners paid personal funds to remodel home. This is *not* a transaction of the business.
(9) Received $1,000 on the account receivable created in Transaction 5.
(10) Sold land for cash at its cost of $22,000.
(11) Declared and paid a dividend of $2,100 to the stockholders.

PANEL B—Analysis of transactions

	Assets				=	Liabilities +	Stockholders' Equity		Type of Stockholders' Equity Transaction
	Cash	+ Accounts Receivable	+ Office Supplies	+ Land		Accounts Payable	+ Common Stock	+ Retained Earnings	
(1)	+50,000						+50,000		Issued stock to owners
(2)	−40,000			+40,000					
(3)			+500			+500			
(4)	+ 5,500							+5,500	Service revenue
(5)		+3,000						+3,000	Service revenue
(6)	− 1,100							−1,100	Rent expense
	− 1,200							−1,200	Salary expense
	− 400							− 400	Utilities expense
(7)	− 400					−400			
(8)	Not a transaction of the business								
(9)	+ 1,000	−1,000							
(10)	+22,000			−22,000					
(11)	− 2,100							−2,100	Dividends
Bal.	33,300	2,000	500	18,000		100	50,000	3,700	
	53,800					53,800			

Statement of Cash Flows Data (transactions (1)–(11), Cash column)

Income Statement Data (transactions (4)–(6))

Balance Sheet Data

EXHIBIT 2-2
Financial Statements of Air & Sea Travel, Inc.

AIR & SEA TRAVEL, INC.
Income Statement
Month Ended April 30, 19X1

Revenue:		
Service revenue ($5,500 + $3,000)		$8,500
Expenses:		
Salary expense	$1,200	
Rent expense	1,100	
Utilities expense	400	
Total expenses		2,700
Net income		$5,800

①

AIR & SEA TRAVEL, INC.
Statement of Retained Earnings
Month Ended April 30, 19X1

Retained earnings, April 1, 19X1	$ 0
Add: Net income for the month	5,800
	5,800
Less: Dividends	2,100
Retained earnings, April 30, 19X1	$3,700

②

AIR & SEA TRAVEL, INC.
Balance Sheet
April 30, 19X1

Assets		**Liabilities**	
Cash	$33,300	Accounts payable	$ 100
Accounts receivable	2,000	**Stockholders' Equity**	
Office supplies	500		
Land	18,000	Common stock	50,000
		Retained earnings	3,700
		Total stockholders' equity	53,700
		Total liabilities and	
Total assets	$53,800	stockholders' equity	$53,800

AIR & SEA TRAVEL, INC.
Statement of Cash Flows
Month Ended April 30, 19X1

③

Cash flows from operating activities:		
Receipts:		
Collections from customers ($5,500 + $1,000)		$ 6,500
Payments:		
To suppliers and employees ($2,700 + $400)		(3,100)
Net cash inflow from operating activities		3,400
Cash flows from investing activities:		
Acquisition of land	$(40,000)	
Sale of land	22,000	
Net cash outflow from investing activities		(18,000)
Cash flows from financing activities:		
Issuance (sale) of stock to owners	$ 50,000	
Dividends	(2,100)	
Net cash inflow from financing activities		47,900
Net increase in cash		$33,300
Cash balance, April 1, 19X1		0
Cash balance, April 30, 19X1		$33,300

3. The balance sheet lists the assets, liabilities, and stockholders' equity of the business at the end of the period. Included in stockholders' equity is retained earnings, which comes from the statement of retained earnings (arrow ②).

4. The statement of cash flows summarizes cash receipts and cash payments under three categories of activities: operating, investing, and financing. The result is an increase or a decrease in cash during the period. Add the beginning cash balance to the change in cash and obtain the ending cash balance, which is reported on the balance sheet (arrow ③).

The transaction analysis we've just examined can be used to prepare the financial statements. However, the analysis in Exhibit 2-1 can become cumbersome for even the smallest of organizations. Consider the **Coca-Cola Company** with its hundreds of accounts and thousands of transactions. The spreadsheet to account for Coca-Cola's transactions would be too large to use. For this reason, accountants use a different accounting system called *double-entry accounting* to create the financial statements. In the second half of this chapter we discuss double-entry accounting as it is used by most businesses. But first, let's put into practice what you have learned thus far.

Consider the Coca-Cola Company with its hundreds of accounts and thousands of transactions. The spreadsheet to account for Coca-Cola's transactions would be too large to use. For this reason, accountants use a different accounting system called **double-entry accounting** *to create the financial statements.*

Mid-Chapter
SUMMARY PROBLEM FOR YOUR REVIEW

Mike Cassell opens a research service near a college campus. He names the corporation Cassell Researchers, Inc. During the first month of operations, July 19X1, the business engages in the following transactions:

a. Mike Cassell invests $25,000 of personal funds, and the corporation issues its common stock to Cassell.

b. The company purchases on account office supplies costing $350.

c. Cassell Researchers pays cash of $20,000 to acquire a lot next to the campus. The company intends to use the land as a future building site for a business office.

d. Cassell Researchers performs research for clients and receives cash of $1,900.

e. Cassell Researchers pays $100 on the account payable it created in Transaction b.

f. Mike Cassell pays $2,000 of personal funds for a vacation.

g. Cassell Researchers pays cash expenses for office rent ($400) and utilities ($100).

h. The business sells a small parcel of the land for its cost of $5,000.

i. The business declares and pays a cash dividend of $1,200.

Required

1. Analyze the preceding transactions in terms of their effects on the accounting equation of Cassell Researchers, Inc. Use Exhibit 2-1 as a guide.
2. Prepare the income statement, statement of retained earnings, balance sheet, and statement of cash flows of the business after recording the transactions. Draw arrows linking the statements.

ANSWERS

Requirements 1 and 2

PANEL A—Details of Transactions

(a) Cassell invested $25,000 cash to acquire the common stock of the corporation.

(b) Purchased $350 of office supplies on account.

(c) Paid $20,000 to acquire land as a future building site.

(d) Earned service revenue and received cash of $1,900.

(e) Paid $100 on account.

(f) Paid for a personal vacation, which is not a transaction of the business.

(g) Paid cash expenses for rent ($400) and utilities ($100).

(h) Sold land for $5,000, its cost.

(i) Declared and paid dividends of $1,200.

PANEL B—Analysis of Transactions

	Assets				=	Liabilities +		Stockholders' Equity			Type of Stockholders' Equity Transaction
	Cash	**+ Office Supplies**	**+**	**Land**		**Accounts Payable**	**+**	**Common Stock**	**+**	**Retained Earnings**	
(a)	+25,000							+25,000			Issued stock to owner
(b)		+350				+350					
(c)	−20,000			+20,000							
(d)	+ 1,900									+1,900	Service revenue
(e)	− 100					−100					
(f)	Not a transaction of the business										
(g)	− 400									− 400	Rent expense
	− 100									− 100	Utilities expense
(h)	+ 5,000			− 5,000							
(i)	− 1,200									−1,200	Dividends
Bal.	10,100	350		15,000		250		25,000		200	
	25,450					25,450					

CASSELL RESEARCHERS, INC.
Income Statement
Month Ended July 31, 19X1

Revenue:		
Service revenue		$1,900
Expenses:		
Rent expense	$400	
Utilities expense	100	
Total expenses		500
Net income		$1,400

CASSELL RESEARCHERS, INC.
Statement of Retained Earnings
Month Ended July 31, 19X1

Retained earnings, July 1, 19X1	$ 0
Add: Net income for the month	1,400
	1,400
Less: Dividends	1,200
Retained earnings, July 31, 19X1	$ 200

(Continued)

(Continued)

CASSELL RESEARCHERS, INC.
Balance Sheet
July 31, 19X1

Assets		Liabilities	
Cash	$10,100	Accounts payable	$ 250
Office supplies	350		
Land	15,000	**Stockholders' Equity**	
		Common stock	25,000
		Retained earnings	200
		Total stockholders' equity	25,200
		Total liabilities and	
Total assets	$25,450	stockholders' equity	$25,450

CASSELL RESEARCHERS, INC.
Statement of Cash Flows
Month Ended July 31, 19X1

Cash flows from operating activities:		
Receipts:		
Collections from customers		$ 1,900
Payments:		
To suppliers ($100 + $400 + $100)		(600)
Net cash inflow from operating activities		1,300
Cash flows from investing activities:		
Acquisition of land	$(20,000)	
Sale of land	5,000	
Net cash outflow from investing activities		(15,000)
Cash flows from financing activities:		
Issuance (sale) of stock to owner	$ 25,000	
Dividends	(1,200)	
Net cash inflow from financing activities		23,800
Net increase in cash		$10,100
Cash balance, July 1, 19X1		0
Cash balance, July 31, 19X1		$10,100

Double-Entry Accounting

Objective 3

Understand how double-entry accounting works

Accounting is based on a **double-entry system,** which means that we record the *dual effects* of a business transaction. *Each transaction affects at least two accounts.* For example, Gary and Monica Lyon's $50,000 cash investment in their travel agency increased both the Cash and the Common Stock accounts of the business. It would be incomplete to record only the increase in the entity's cash without recording the increase in its stockholders' equity.

Consider a *cash purchase of supplies.* What are the dual effects of this transaction? The purchase (1) decreases cash and (2) increases supplies. A *purchase of supplies on credit* (1) increases supplies and (2) increases accounts payable. A *cash payment on account* (1) decreases cash and (2) decreases accounts payable. All transactions have at least two effects on the entity.

The T-Account

To record transactions, accountants often use *T-accounts.* The term gets its name from the capital letter "T." The vertical line in the letter divides the account into its left and right sides. The account title rests on the horizontal line. For example, the Cash account of a business appears in the following T-account format:

Cash	
(Left side) *Debit*	(Right side) *Credit*

The left side of the account is called the **debit** side, and the right side is called the **credit** side. Often, beginners in the study of accounting are confused by the words *debit* and *credit*. To become comfortable using them, remember that

Debit = Left side

Credit = Right side

Even though *left side* and *right side* are more descriptive, the terms *debit* and *credit* are deeply entrenched in business.[1] Every business transaction involves both a debit and a credit.

Increases and Decreases in the Accounts

The type of account determines how increases and decreases in it are recorded. For any given account, all increases are recorded on one side, and all decreases are recorded on the other side. Increases in *assets* are recorded in the left (debit) side of the account. Decreases in assets are recorded in the right (credit) side. Conversely, increases in *liabilities* and *stockholders' equity* are recorded by *credits*. Decreases in liabilities and stockholders' equity are recorded by *debits*. These are the *rules of debit and credit*.

In everyday conversation, we may praise someone by saying, "She deserves credit for her good work." In your study of accounting, forget this general usage. Remember only that *debit means left side* and *credit means right side*. Whether an account is increased or decreased by a debit or credit depends on the type of account (Exhibit 2-3).

In a computerized accounting system, the computer interprets debits and credits as increases or decreases by account type. For example, a computer reads a debit to Cash as an increase to that account. But *debit* and *credit* are so deeply ingrained in accounting vocabulary that we use them even for computerized systems.

This pattern of recording debits and credits is based on the accounting equation:

Assets = Liabilities + Stockholders' Equity

Assets are on the opposite side of the equation from liabilities and stockholders' equity. Therefore, increases and decreases in assets are recorded in the *opposite* manner from those in liabilities and stockholders' equity. And liabilities and stockholders' equity, which are on the same side of the equal sign, are treated in the same way. Exhibit 2-3 shows the relationship between the accounting equation and the rules of debit and credit.

To illustrate the ideas diagrammed in Exhibit 2-3, reconsider the first transaction from page 54. Air & Sea Travel received $50,000 cash and issued common stock to Gary and Monica Lyon. Which accounts of Air & Sea Travel are affected?

EXHIBIT 2-3
Accounting Equation and the Rules of Debit and Credit (The Effects of Debits and Credits on Assets, Liabilities, and Stockholders' Equity)

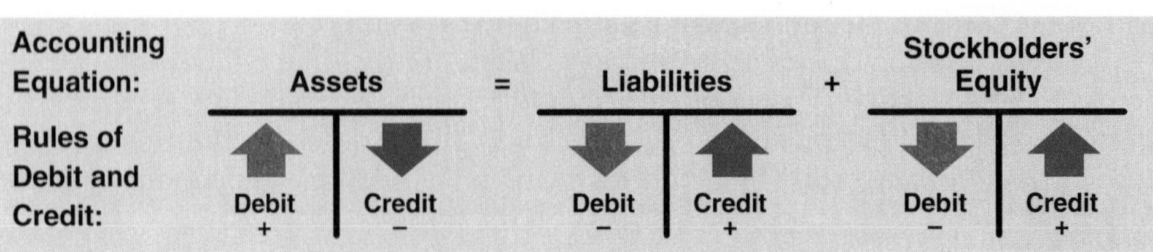

[1]The words *debit* and *credit* have a Latin origin (*debitum* and *creditum*). Pacioli, the Italian monk who wrote about accounting in the fifteenth century, used these terms.

By what amounts? On what side (debit or credit)? The answer is that Assets and Common Stock would increase by $50,000, as the following T-accounts show:

Assets = Liabilities + Stockholders' Equity

Cash	
Debit for Increase, 50,000	

Common Stock	
	Credit for Increase, 50,000

Notice that Assets = Liabilities + Stockholders' Equity *and* that total debit amounts = total credit amounts.

The amount remaining in an account is called its *balance.* This first transaction gives Cash a $50,000 debit balance and Common Stock a $50,000 credit balance.

STOP & THINK Can you prepare a balance sheet and an income statement for Air & Sea Travel at this point? What would the business's financial statements report?

Answer: You could prepare a balance sheet that would report Cash, an asset, of $50,000 and Common Stock, a stockholders' equity, of $50,000. You would not yet prepare an income statement because the business has experienced no revenues or expenses.

The second transaction is a $40,000 cash purchase of land. This transaction affects two assets: Cash and Land. It decreases (credits) Cash and increases (debits) Land, as shown in the T-accounts:

Assets = Liabilities + Stockholders' Equity

Cash	
Bal. 50,000	Credit for Decrease, 40,000

Land	
Debit for Increase, 40,000	

Common Stock	
	Bal. 50,000

After this transaction, Cash has a $10,000 debit balance ($50,000 debit balance minus the $40,000 credit amount), Land has a debit balance of $40,000, and Common Stock has a $50,000 credit balance, as shown in Exhibit 2-4.

Transaction 3 is a $500 purchase of office supplies on account. This transaction increases the asset Office Supplies and the liability Accounts Payable, as shown in the following T-accounts and in Exhibit 2-4 on page 66:

Assets = Liabilities + Stockholders' Equity

Cash	
Bal. 10,000	

Office Supplies	
Debit for Increase, 500	

Land	
Bal. 40,000	

Accounts Payable	
	Credit for Increase, 500

Common Stock	
	Bal. 50,000

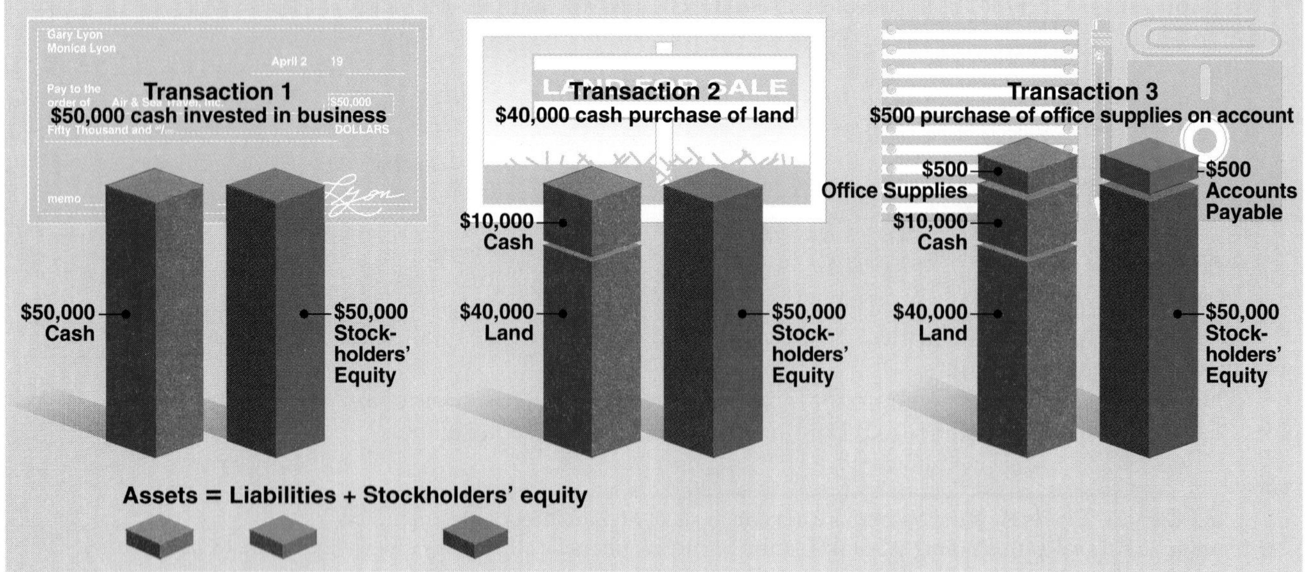

EXHIBIT 2-4
The Accounting Equation and the First Three Transactions of Air & Sea Travel, Inc.

We can create new accounts as needed. The process of creating a new T-account in preparation for recording a transaction is called *opening the account.* For Transaction 1, we opened the Cash account and the Common Stock account. For Transaction 2, we opened the Land account. For Transaction 3, we opened Office Supplies and Accounts Payable.

LEARNING TIP The accounting equation must balance after every transaction. But verifying that total assets = total liabilities + stockholders' equity is no longer necessary after every transaction. The equation will balance as long as the debits in each transaction equal the credits in the transaction. Remember that every transaction involves both a debit and a credit, and that the total amount debited in a transaction must always equal the total amount credited.

Additional Stockholders' Equity Accounts: Revenues and Expenses

The stockholders' equity category includes the two income statement accounts Revenues and Expenses. As we have discussed, *revenues* are increases in stockholders' equity that result from delivering goods or services to customers. *Expenses* are decreases in stockholders' equity due to the cost of operating the business. Therefore, the accounting equation may be expanded as shown in Exhibit 2-5. Revenues and expenses appear in parentheses because their net effect—revenues minus expenses—equals net income, which increases stockholders' equity. If expenses are greater, the net effect is a net loss, which decreases stockholders' equity.

We can now express the rules of debit and credit in final form, as shown in Exhibit 2-6. **You should not proceed until you have learned the rules of debit and credit.**

Objective 4

Record transactions in the journal, and post from the journal to the ledger

Recording Transactions in the Journal

We could record all transactions directly in the T-accounts. However, this method of accounting is not practical because it does not leave a clear record of each transaction. For this reason, accountants record transactions first in a **journal,** which is a chronological record of the entity's transactions. The journalizing process follows these five steps:

EXHIBIT 2-5
Expansion of the Accounting Equation

1. Identify the transaction from source documents, such as bank deposit slips, sale receipts, and check stubs.
2. Specify each account affected by the transaction and classify it by type (asset, liability, stockholders' equity, revenue, or expense).
3. Determine whether each account is increased or decreased by the transaction.
4. Using the rules of debit and credit, determine whether to debit or credit the account to record its increase or decrease.
5. Enter the transaction in the journal, including a brief explanation for the journal entry. The debit side of the entry is entered first and the credit side next.

EXHIBIT 2-6
Expanded Rules of Debit and Credit

Account	Debit	Credit
Assets	Debit for Increase +	Credit for Decrease –
= Liabilities	Debit for Decrease –	Credit for Increase +
+ Common Stock	Debit for Decrease –	Credit for Increase +
Retained Earnings	Debit for Decrease –	Credit for Increase +
Dividends	Debit for Increase +	Credit for Decrease –
Revenues	Debit for Decrease –	Credit for Increase +
Expenses	Debit for Increase +	Credit for Decrease –

Step 5, "Enter the transaction in the journal," means to record the transaction in the journal. This step is also called "making the journal entry" or "journalizing the transaction." Let's apply the five steps to journalize the first transaction of Air & Sea Travel, Inc.—receiving cash of $50,000 and issuing common stock.

Step 1: The source documents are Air & Sea Travel's bank deposit slip and the stock certificate the business issued to Gary and Monica Lyon.

Step 2: *Cash* and *Common Stock* are the accounts affected by the transaction. Cash is an asset account, and Common Stock is a stockholders' equity account.

Step 3: Both accounts increase by $50,000. Cash is an asset account that is increased, and Common Stock is a stockholders' equity account that is increased.

Step 4: Debit Cash to record an increase in this asset account. Credit Common Stock to record an increase in this stockholders' equity account.

Step 5: The journal entry is

Date	Accounts and Explanation	Debit	Credit
Apr. 2[(a)]	Cash[(b)]	50,000[(d)]	
	Common Stock[(c)]		50,000[(e)]
	Issued common stock to owners.[(f)]		

The journal entry includes (a) the date of the transaction, (b) the title of the account debited (placed flush left), (c) the title of the account credited (indented slightly), the dollar amounts of the (d) debit (left) and (e) credit (right)—dollar signs are omitted in the money columns—and (f) a short explanation of the transaction (not indented). Journal entries should always be recorded in this format.

LEARNING TIP To get off to the best start when analyzing a transaction, first pinpoint its effects (if any) on cash. Did cash increase or decrease? Then find its effect on other accounts. Typically, it is easier to identify a transaction's cash effect than to identify its effects on other accounts.

The journal offers information that T-accounts do not provide. Each journal entry shows the complete effect of a business transaction. Let's examine Air & Sea Travel's initial receipt of cash and issuance of stock again. The Cash T-account shows a single figure, the $50,000 debit. We know that every transaction has a credit, so in which account will we find the corresponding $50,000 credit? In this simple illustration, we know that the Common Stock account holds this figure. But imagine the difficulties you would face trying to link debits and credits for hundreds of daily transactions—without a separate record of each transaction. The journal solves this problem and presents the full story for each transaction. Exhibit 2-7 shows how a journal page might look after the first transaction is recorded.

EXHIBIT 2-7
The Journal

Journal — Page 1

Date	Accounts and Explanation	Debit	Credit
Apr. 2	Cash	50,000	
	Common Stock		50,000
	Issued common stock to owners.		

In the introductory discussions that follow, we temporarily ignore the date of each transaction to focus on the accounts and their dollar amounts.

Regardless of the accounting system in use, an accountant must analyze every business transaction in the manner we have presented. Once the transaction has been analyzed, a computerized accounting package can perform the same actions as accountants do in a manual system. For example, when a sales clerk runs your VISA card through the credit-card reader, the underlying accounting system automatically records the store's sales revenue and receivable from VISA. The computer automatically records the transaction as a journal entry, but an accountant had to program the computer to do so. A computer's ability to perform routine tasks and mathematical operations fast and without error frees accountants for decision making and management consulting.

When a sales clerk runs your VISA card through the credit-card reader, the underlying accounting system automatically records the store's sales revenue and receivable from VISA.

Copying Information (Posting) from the Journal to the Ledger

The journal is a record of all company transactions. But the journal does not indicate how much cash the business has to use. Another part of the accounting system, called the ledger, gives the balance in each account. The **ledger** is a grouping of all the accounts with their balances. For example, the balance of the Cash account shows how much cash the business has. The balance of Accounts Receivable indicates the amount due from customers. The balance of Accounts Payable tells how much the business owes suppliers on open account, and so on.

In the phrase "keeping the books," *books* refers to the ledger. In most accounting systems, the ledger is computerized. Exhibit 2-8 shows how the asset, liability, and stockholders' equity accounts are grouped in the ledger.

Entering transaction data in the journal does not place the data into the ledger. Data must be copied, or **posted,** to the appropriate accounts in the ledger. Debits in the journal are posted as debits in the ledger, and credits in the journal as credits in the ledger. Exhibit 2-9 on page 70 shows how the initial investment transaction of Air & Sea Travel is posted to the ledger. Computers perform this task quickly and without error.

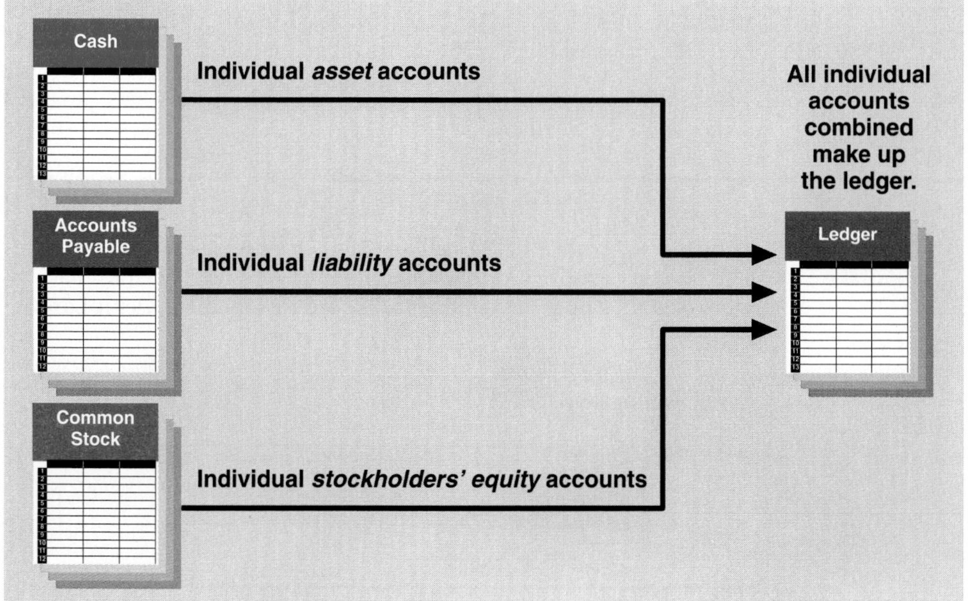

EXHIBIT 2-8
The Ledger (Asset, Liability, and Stockholders' Equity Accounts)

EXHIBIT 2-9
Journal Entry and Posting to the Ledger

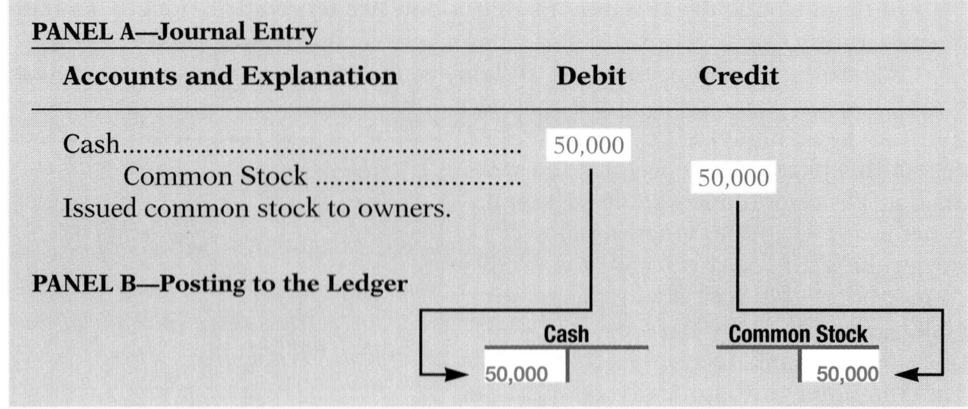

The Flow of Accounting Data: Putting Theory into Practice

Exhibit 2-10 summarizes the flow of accounting data from the business transaction to the ledger. Let's continue the example of Air & Sea Travel, Inc., and account for the same 11 transactions we illustrated earlier in terms of their effects on the accounting equation, the journal, and the ledger.

1. *Transaction analysis:* Air & Sea Travel, Inc., received $50,000 cash from the Lyons as their investment in the business and in turn issued common stock to them. Air & Sea Travel increased its asset cash; to record this increase, debit Cash. The corporation's issuance of stock to the owners increased the stockholders' equity of the corporation; to record this increase, credit Common Stock.

Journal entry:

	Debit	Credit
Cash	50,000	
Common Stock		50,000
Issued common stock to owners.		

After making the journal entry, we normally post directly to the accounts. To give you a sense of the entry's effects on the big picture, we also show how the entry affects the accounting equation.

Accounting equation:	Assets	=	Liabilities	+	Stockholders' Equity
	50,000	=	0	+	50,000

Ledger accounts:

STOP & THINK Suppose you are a lender and Gary and Monica Lyon ask you to make a $10,000 business loan to Air & Sea Travel, Inc. After the initial investment of $50,000, how would you evaluate Air & Sea Travel as a credit risk?

Answer: You would probably view the loan request favorably. The Lyons have invested $50,000 of their own money in the business. The travel agency has no debts, so it should be able to repay you.

2. *Transaction analysis:* The business paid $40,000 cash for land as a future office location. The purchase decreased cash; therefore, credit Cash. The purchase increased the entity's asset land; to record this increase, debit Land.

Journal entry:

	Debit	Credit
Land	40,000	
Cash		40,000
Paid cash for land.		

Accounting equation:	Assets	=	Liabilities	+	Stockholders' Equity
	+40,000 −40,000	=	0	+	0

Ledger accounts:

Cash (Dr)		Cash (Cr)		Land (Dr)	
(1)	50,000	(2)	40,000	(2)	40,000

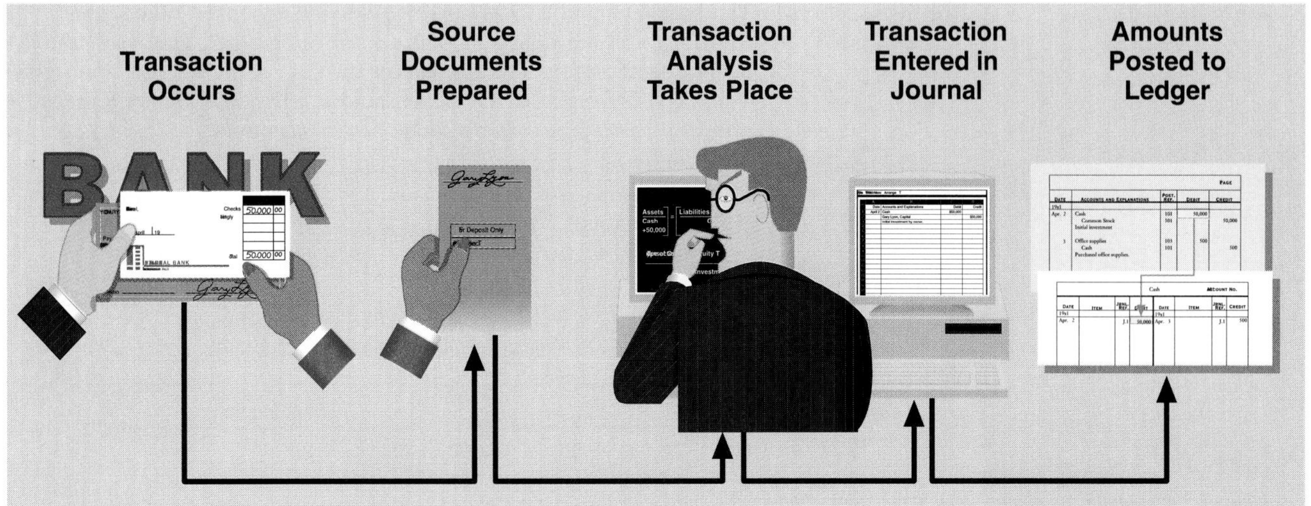

Concept Highlight

EXHIBIT 2-10
Flow of Accounting Data

3. *Transaction analysis:* The business purchased $500 office supplies on account payable. The credit purchase of office supplies increased this asset; to record this increase, debit Office Supplies. The purchase also increased the liability accounts payable; to record this, credit Accounts Payable.

Journal entry:

	Debit	Credit
Office Supplies	500	
Accounts Payable		500
Purchased office supplies on account.		

Accounting equation:	Assets	=	Liabilities	+	Stockholders' Equity
	+500	=	+500	+	0

Ledger accounts:

Office Supplies			
(3)	500		

Accounts Payable			
		(3)	500

4. *Transaction analysis:* The business performed travel service for clients and received cash of $5,500. The transaction increased the business's cash, so debit Cash. Service revenue was increased. To record an increase in revenue, credit Service Revenue.

Journal entry:

	Debit	Credit
Cash	5,500	
Service Revenue		5,500
Performed services for cash.		

Accounting equation:	Assets	=	Liabilities	+	Stockholders' Equity	+	Revenues
	+5,500	=	0	+		+	5,500

Ledger accounts:

Cash			
(1)	50,000	(2)	40,000
(4)	5,500		

Service Revenue			
		(4)	5,500

5. *Transaction analysis:* The business performed services for clients who did not pay immediately. Air & Sea Travel billed the clients for $3,000 on account. The transaction increased the asset accounts receivable; therefore, debit Accounts Receivable. Service revenue was also increased, so credit Service Revenue.

Journal entry:

	Debit	Credit
Accounts Receivable	3,000	
Service Revenue		3,000
Performed services on account.		

Accounting equation:	Assets	=	Liabilities	+	Stockholders' Equity	+	Revenues
	+3,000	=	0	+		+	3,000

Ledger accounts:

Accounts Receivable			
(5)	3,000		

Service Revenue			
		(4)	5,500
		(5)	3,000

6. *Transaction analysis:* The business paid $2,700 for the following expenses: office rent, $1,100; employee salary, $1,200; and utilities, $400. The asset cash is decreased; therefore, credit Cash for the sum of the expense amounts. The following expenses are increased: Rent Expense, Salary Expense, and Utilities Expense. Debit each of these accounts.

Journal entry:

	Debit	Credit
Rent Expense	1,100	
Salary Expense	1,200	
Utilities Expense	400	
Cash		2,700

Paid expenses.

Accounting equation:	Assets	=	Liabilities	+	Stockholders' Equity	−	Expenses
	−2,700	=	0	+		−	2,700

Ledger accounts:

Cash

(1) 50,000		(2) 40,000	
(4) 5,500		(6) 2,700	

Rent Expense

(6) 1,100	

Salary Expense

(6) 1,200	

Utilities Expense

(6) 400	

7. *Transaction analysis:* The business paid $400 on the account payable created in Transaction 3. The payment decreased the asset cash; therefore, credit Cash. The payment also decreased the liability accounts payable; to record this decrease, debit Accounts Payable.

Journal entry:

	Debit	Credit
Accounts Payable	400	
Cash		400

Paid cash on account.

Accounting equation:	Assets	=	Liabilities	+	Stockholders' Equity
	−400	=	−400	+	0

Ledger accounts:

Cash

(1) 50,000	(2) 40,000
(4) 5,500	(6) 2,700
	(7) 400

Accounts Payable

(7) 400	(3) 500

8. *Transaction:* The Lyons remodeled their personal residence. This is not a transaction of the travel agency, so no journal entry is made.

9. *Transaction analysis:* The business collected $1,000 cash on account from the clients in Transaction 5. The receipt of cash increased this asset, so debit Cash. The asset accounts receivable decreased; therefore, credit Accounts Receivable.

Journal entry:

	Debit	Credit
Cash	1,000	
Accounts Receivable		1,000

Collected cash on account.

Accounting equation:	Assets	=	Liabilities	+	Stockholders' Equity
	+1,000	=	0	+	0
	−1,000				

Ledger accounts:

Cash

(1) 50,000	(2) 40,000
(4) 5,500	(6) 2,700
(9) 1,000	(7) 400

Accounts Receivable

(5) 3,000	(9) 1,000

10. *Transaction: analysis:* The business sold land for its cost of $22,000, receiving cash. The asset cash increased; debit Cash. The asset land decreased, so credit Land.

Journal entry:

	Debit	Credit
Cash	22,000	
Land		22,000

Sold land.

Accounting equation:	Assets	=	Liabilities	+	Stockholders' Equity
	+22,000	=	0	+	0
	−22,000				

Ledger accounts:

Cash

	Debit		Credit
(1)	50,000	(2)	40,000
(4)	5,500	(6)	2,700
(9)	1,000	(7)	400
(10)	22,000		

Land

	Debit		Credit
(2)	40,000	(10)	22,000

11. *Transaction analysis:* Air & Sea Travel, Inc., paid the Lyons cash dividends of $2,100. The dividends decreased the entity's cash; therefore, credit Cash. The transaction also decreased the stockholders' equity of the entity and must be recorded by a debit to a stockholders' equity account. Decreases in a corporation's stockholders' equity that result from distributions to owners are debited to a separate stockholders' equity account entitled Dividends. Therefore, debit Dividends.

Journal entry:

Dividends	2,100	
Cash		2,100
Declared and paid dividends.		

	Assets	=	Liabilities	+	Stockholders' Equity	−	Dividends
Accounting equation:	−2,100	=	0	+		−	2,100

Ledger accounts:

Cash

	Debit		Credit
(1)	50,000	(2)	40,000
(4)	5,500	(6)	2,700
(9)	1,000	(7)	400
(10)	22,000	(11)	2,100

Dividends

	Debit		Credit
(11)	2,100		

Each journal entry posted to the ledger is keyed by date or by transaction number. In this way, any transaction can be traced from the journal to the ledger and, if need be, back to the journal. This linking allows you to locate efficiently any information needed.

Accounts after Posting

Exhibit 2-11 shows how the ledger accounts look when the amounts of the preceding transactions have been posted. The exhibit groups the accounts under the accounting equation's headings.

Each account has a balance, denoted as Bal. This amount is the difference between the account's total debits and its total credits. For example, the balance in the Cash account is the difference between the debits, $78,500 ($50,000 + $5,500 + $1,000 + $22,000) and the credits, $45,200 ($40,000 + $2,700 + $400 +

EXHIBIT 2-11
Air & Sea Travel's Ledger Accounts After Posting

ASSETS = LIABILITIES + STOCKHOLDERS' EQUITY

ASSETS

Cash

	Debit		Credit
(1)	50,000	(2)	40,000
(4)	5,500	(6)	2,700
(9)	1,000	(7)	400
(10)	22,000	(11)	2,100
Bal.	33,300		

Accounts Receivable

	Debit		Credit
(5)	3,000	(9)	1,000
Bal.	2,000		

Office Supplies

	Debit		Credit
(3)	500		
Bal.	500		

Land

	Debit		Credit
(2)	40,000	(10)	22,000
Bal.	18,000		

LIABILITIES

Accounts Payable

	Debit		Credit
(7)	400	(3)	500
		Bal.	100

STOCKHOLDERS' EQUITY

Common Stock

	Debit		Credit
		(1)	50,000
		Bal.	50,000

Dividends

	Debit		Credit
(11)	2,100		
Bal.	2,100		

REVENUE

Service Revenue

	Debit		Credit
		(4)	5,500
		(5)	3,000
		Bal.	8,500

EXPENSES

Rent Expense

	Debit		Credit
(6)	1,100		
Bal.	1,100		

Salary Expense

	Debit		Credit
(6)	1,200		
Bal.	1,200		

Utilities Expense

	Debit		Credit
(6)	400		
Bal.	400		

EXHIBIT 2-12
Trial Balance

AIR & SEA TRAVEL, INC. Trial Balance April 30, 19X1		
	Balance	
Account Title	Debit	Credit
Cash	$33,300	
Accounts receivable	2,000	
Office supplies	500	
Land	18,000	
Accounts payable		$ 100
Common stock		50,000
Dividends	2,100	
Service revenue		8,500
Rent expense	1,100	
Salary expense	1,200	
Utilities expense	400	
Total	$58,600	$58,600

$2,100). Thus, the cash balance is $33,300. The balance amounts are not journal entries posted to the accounts, so we set an account balance apart from the individual amounts by horizontal lines.

If the sum of an account's debits is greater than the sum of its credits, that account has a debit balance, as the Cash account does here. If the sum of its credits is greater, that account has a credit balance, as Accounts Payable does.

The Trial Balance

Objective 5

Prepare and use a trial balance

A **trial balance** is a list of all accounts with their balances—assets first, followed by liabilities and then stockholders' equity. It provides a check on accuracy by showing whether the total debits equal the total credits. A trial balance may be taken at any time the postings are up to date, but the most common time is at the end of the period. Exhibit 2-12 is the trial balance of the ledger of Air & Sea Travel, Inc., after its first 11 transactions have been journalized and posted.

Do not confuse the trial balance with the balance sheet. Accountants prepare a trial balance for their internal records. The company reports its financial position on the balance sheet, which is a formal financial statement. And remember that the financial statements are the focal point of the accounting process; the trial balance is merely a step in the preparation of the financial statements.

STOP & THINK Refer to the Air & Sea Travel trial balance in Exhibit 2-12. Suppose you are Monica Lyon, one of the owners. Your accountant is out of town, and the only accounting record available to you is the trial balance. You need a business loan, and your banker requests some information. Answer the following questions by developing the information from the trial balance:

1. How much are Air & Sea Travel's total assets?
2. Does the business already have any loans payable to other banks?
3. How much does the business owe in total?
4. How much equity do the owners have in the business? Compute owners' equity by the accounting equation.
5. What was the business's net income or net loss during April?

Answers

1. $53,800 ($33,300 + $2,000 + $500 + $18,000)
2. No loans payable to other banks.

3. $100 for accounts payable.
4. $53,700 (Assets of $53,800 – Liabilities of $100)
5. Net income was $5,800 [Revenues of $8,500 – Expenses of $2,700 ($1,100 + $1,200 + $400)].

Correcting Accounting Errors

The term *trial balance* is appropriate. The list is prepared to *test* the accounts' balances by showing whether total debits equal total credits. If they are not equal, then accounting errors exist. Most computerized accounting systems prohibit the recording of unbalanced journal entries. Because the journal amounts are posted exactly as they have been journalized, trial balances will always balance. Hence, computers minimize accounting errors. But they cannot *eliminate* errors, because human operators might input the amounts incorrectly.

You can detect the reason(s) behind many out-of-balance conditions by computing the difference between total debits and total credits on the trial balance. Then perform one or more of the following actions:

1. Search the trial balance for a missing account. Trace each account and its balance from the ledger to the trial balance.

2. Search the journal for the amount of the difference. For example, suppose the total credits on Air & Sea Travel's trial balance equal $58,600 and total debits are $58,400. A $200 transaction may have been recorded incorrectly in the journal or posted incorrectly to the ledger. Search the journal for a $200 transaction.

3. Divide the difference between total debits and total credits by 2. A debit treated as a credit, or vice versa, doubles the amount of error. Suppose Air & Sea Travel debited $300 to Cash instead of crediting the Cash account, or assume the accountant posted a $300 credit as a debit. Total debits contain the $300, and total credits omit the $300. The out-of-balance amount is $600, and dividing by 2 identifies the $300 of the transaction. Then search the journal for the $300 transaction and trace to the account affected.

4. Divide the out-of-balance amount by 9. If the result is evenly divisible by 9, the error may be a *slide* (example: writing $61 as $610) or a *transposition* (example: treating $61 as $16). Suppose Air & Sea Travel listed the $2,100 Dividends balance as $21,000 on the trial balance—a slide-type error. Total debits would differ from total credits by $18,900 ($21,000 – $2,100 = $18,900). Dividing $18,900 by 9 yields $2,100, the correct amount of the dividends. Trace this amount through the journal and then to the account affected.

Using Journals, Ledgers, and Posting to Trace Information

To focus on the main points of journalizing and posting, we purposely omitted certain essential data. In practice, the journal and the ledger provide additional details that create a "trail" through the accounting records for future reference. For example, a supplier may bill us twice for the same item we purchased on account. To prove we paid the bill, we would search the accounts payable records and work backward to the journal entry that recorded our payment. To see how this process works, let's take a closer look at the journal and the ledger.

JOURNAL Exhibit 2-13, Panel A (page 76), presents a widely used journal format. The journal page number appears in the upper-right corner. As the column headings indicate, the *journal* displays the following information:

- The *date,* which indicates when the transaction occurred. The year 19X1 appears only when the journal is started or when the year has changed. For our purposes, the year appears with an X in the third, or decade's, position. Thus, 19X1 is followed by 19X2, and so on. The date of the transaction is recorded for every transaction.
- The *account title* and explanation of the transaction.

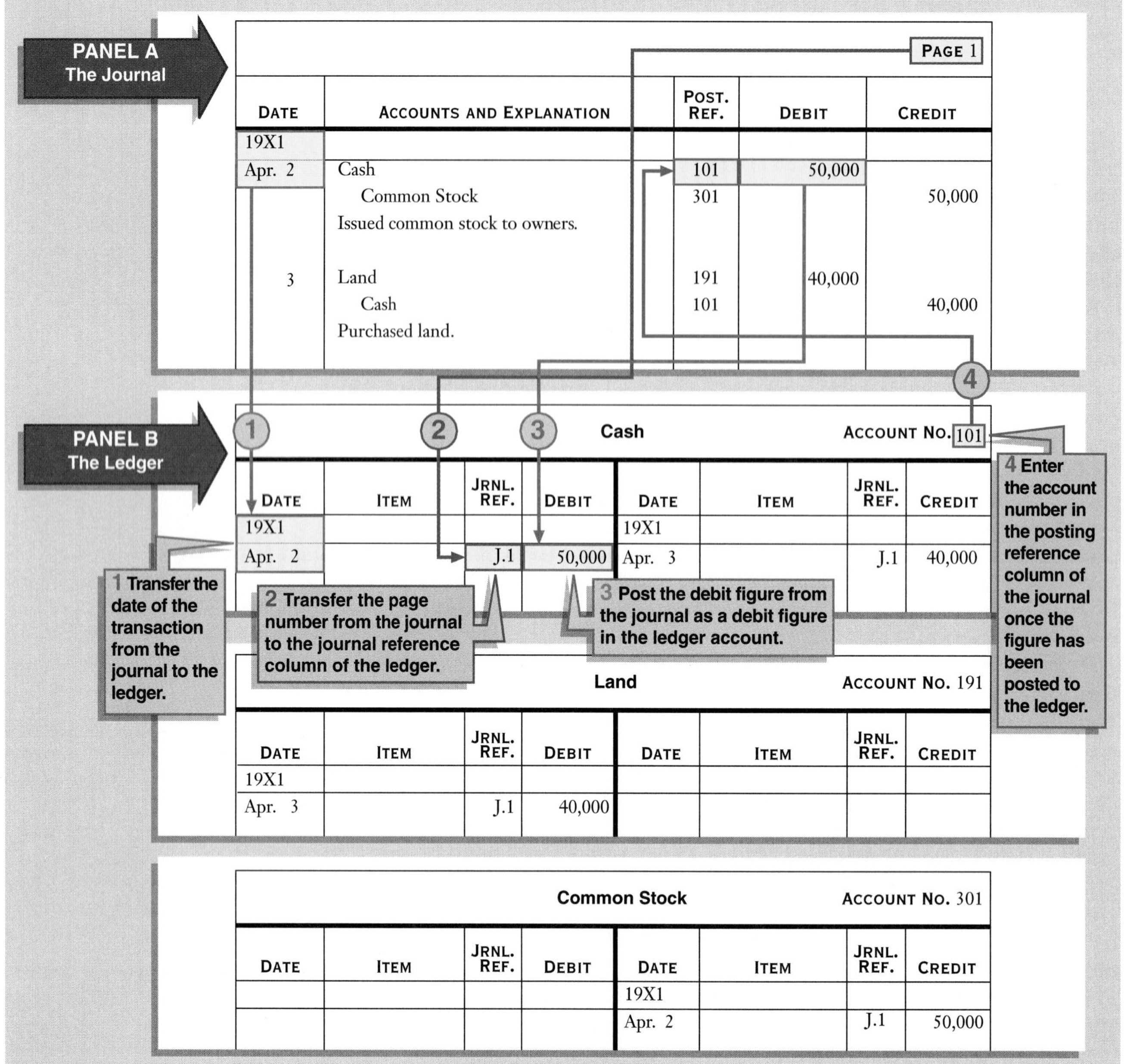

EXHIBIT 2-13
Details of Journalizing and Posting

- The *posting reference,* abbreviated Post. Ref., used to indicate whether the amount has been posted.
- The *debit* column, which shows the amount debited.
- The *credit* column, which shows the amount credited.

LEDGER Exhibit 2-13, Panel B, presents the *ledger* in T-account format. Each account has its own record in the ledger. Our example shows Air & Sea Travel's Cash, Land, and Common Stock accounts. These accounts maintain the basic format of the T-account but offer more information—for example, the account number at the upper-right corner. Each account has its own identification number.

The column headings identify the ledger account's features:

- The date.
- The item column. This space is used for any special notation.

- The journal reference column, abbreviated Jrnl. Ref., which refers to the journal page from which the amount was posted.
- The debit column, with the amount debited.
- The credit column, with the amount credited.

POSTING We know that posting means transferring information from the journal to the ledger accounts. But how do we handle the additional details that appear in the journal and the ledger formats that we have just seen? Exhibit 2-13 illustrates the steps in full detail.

Because the flow of accounting data moves from the journal to the ledger, you would first record the journal entry, as shown in Panel A. The date of the entry is printed in the ledger account (arrow ①). The journal page number is transferred to the ledger account to show where the data originated (arrow ②). The individual debit and credit amounts are posted to the account (arrow ③). Once a dollar amount is posted to the ledger account, that account's number is entered in the journal's posting reference column (arrow ④). This step indicates that the information for that account has been transferred from the journal to the ledger.

Chart of Accounts

Objective 6

Set up a chart of accounts for a business

As you know, the ledger contains the business's accounts grouped under these headings:

1. Balance sheet accounts: Assets, Liabilities, and Stockholders' Equity
2. Income statement accounts: Revenues and Expenses

To keep track of their accounts, organizations have a **chart of accounts,** which lists all the accounts and their account numbers. These account numbers are used as posting references, as illustrated by arrow ④ in Exhibit 2-13. It is easier to input the account number, 101, in the posting reference column of the journal than to input the account title, Cash. Also, this numbering system makes it easy to locate individual accounts in the ledger.

We learned in Chapter 1, page 18, that balance sheet amounts report the assets, liabilities, and stockholders' equity of an entity as of a specific date; the income statement amounts report the revenues and expenses of the entity for a specific period of time.

Account numbers usually have two or more digits. Assets are often numbered beginning with 1, liabilities with 2, stockholders' equity with 3, revenues with 4, and expenses with 5. The second, third, and higher digits in an account number indicate the position of the individual account within the category. For example, Cash may be account number 101, which is the first asset account. Accounts Payable may be number 201, the first liability account. All accounts are numbered by this system.

Yankelovich-Clancy-Shulman, a leading marketing research firm, uses five-digit account numbers.

Organizations with many accounts use lengthy account numbers. For example, the chart of accounts of **Yankelovich-Clancy-Shulman**, a leading marketing research firm, uses five-digit account numbers. Exhibit 2-14 on page 78 lists some of Yankelovich's asset accounts.

The chart of accounts for Air & Sea Travel, Inc., appears in Exhibit 2-15 on page 78. Notice the gap between the account numbers 111 and 141. The Lyons realize that at some later date the business may need to add another category of receivables—for example, Notes Receivable, which may be numbered 121.

The chapter appendix gives two expanded charts of accounts that you will find helpful as you work through this course. The first chart lists the typical accounts of a large service corporation, such as Air & Sea Travel would be after a period of growth. The second chart is for a merchandising corporation, one that sells a product rather than a service. Study the service corporation chart of accounts now, and refer to the second chart of accounts as needed later.

EXHIBIT 2-14
Partial Chart of Accounts of Yankelovich-Clancy-Shulman

Account Number	Account Title
10100	Cash Chase [cash in Chase Manhattan Bank]
10130	Cash—Petty Cash [cash on hand]
10200	Accounts Receivable—Trade
10300	Accounts Receivable—Rent
10520	Prepaid Insurance
10530	Prepaid Rent
11110	Furniture & Fixtures
11140	Machinery & Equipment

EXHIBIT 2-15
Chart of Accounts—Air & Sea Travel, Inc.

BALANCE SHEET ACCOUNTS:

Assets	Liabilities	Stockholders' Equity
101 Cash	201 Accounts Payable	301 Common Stock
111 Accounts Receivable	231 Notes Payable	311 Dividends
141 Office Supplies		312 Retained Earnings
151 Office Furniture		
191 Land		

INCOME STATEMENT ACCOUNTS (PART OF STOCKHOLDERS' EQUITY):

Revenues	Expenses
401 Service Revenue	501 Rent Expense
	502 Salary Expense
	503 Utilities Expense

The Normal Balance of an Account

An account's *normal balance* is on the side of the account—debit or credit—where *increases* are recorded. That is, the normal balance is on the side that is positive. For example, Cash and other assets usually have a debit balance (the debit side is positive and the credit side negative), so the normal balance of assets is on the debit side, and assets are called *debit-balance accounts.* Conversely, liabilities and stockholders' equity usually have a credit balance, so their normal balances are on the credit side, and they are called *credit-balance accounts.* Exhibit 2-16 illustrates the normal balances of all the assets, liabilities, and stockholders' equities, including revenues and expenses.

An account that normally has a debit balance may occasionally have a credit balance, which indicates a negative amount of the item. For example, Cash will have a temporary credit balance if the entity overdraws its bank account. Similarly, the liability Accounts Payable—normally a credit-balance account—will have a debit balance if the entity overpays its account. In other instances, the shift of a balance amount away from its normal column indicates an accounting error. For example, a credit balance in Office Supplies, Office Furniture, or Buildings indicates an error because negative amounts of these assets cannot exist.

As explained earlier, stockholders' equity usually contains several accounts. In total, these accounts show a normal credit balance for the stockholders' equity of the business. Each stockholders' equity account has a normal credit balance if

EXHIBIT 2-16
Normal Balances of the Accounts

Account	Debit	Credit
Assets	Debit	
Liabilities		Credit
Stockholders' Equity—overall		Credit
Common stock		Credit
Retained earnings		Credit
Dividends	Debit	
Revenues		Credit
Expenses	Debit	

Account: **Cash** Account No. 101

Date	Item	Jrnl. Ref.	Debit	Credit	Balance Debit	Balance Credit
19X1						
Apr. 2		J.1	50,000		50,000	
3		J.1		40,000	10,000	

EXHIBIT 2-17
Account in Four-Column Format

it represents an *increase* in stockholders' equity (for example, the Common Stock account in Exhibit 2-16). However, if the individual stockholders' equity account represents a *decrease* in stockholders' equity, the account will have a normal debit balance (for example, the Dividends account in Exhibit 2-16).

Four-Column Account Format

The ledger accounts illustrated thus far have been in a two-column T-account format, with the debit column on the left and the credit column on the right. The T-account clearly distinguishes debits from credits and is often used for illustrative purposes that do not require much detail.

Another standard format has four amount columns, as illustrated for the Cash account in Exhibit 2-17. The first pair of amount columns are for the debit and credit amounts posted from individual entries. The second pair of amount columns are for the account's balance. This four-column format keeps a running balance in the account. For this reason, it is used more often than the two-column format. In Exhibit 2-17, Cash has a debit balance of $50,000 after Air & Sea's first transaction is posted and a debit balance of $10,000 after its second transaction.

This chapter has covered a lot of material on the processing of accounting information. The Decision Guidelines feature on page 80, "Analyzing and Recording Transactions," should help you focus on the essential elements covered in the chapter. The guidelines start with the most fundamental consideration in accounting: Has a transaction occurred? As you work through the guidelines, don't lose sight of your goal. The final guideline zeroes in on the financial statements, which are the end product of the accounting process.

The statements are where the fun begins—the place people go for information to make decisions. As we proceed through this book, we will emphasize the use of the information for decision making. The more accounting you learn, the better equipped you will be to make decisions in your organization.

Using Accounting Information for Quick Decision Making

Objective 7

Analyze transactions without a journal

What dominates the accountant's analysis of transactions: the accounting equation, the journal, or the ledger? The accounting equation is most fundamental. And the ledger is more useful than the journal in providing an overall model of the organization. The ledger includes all the accounts, which represent all the entity's assets, liabilities, stockholders' equity, revenues, and expenses. The journal is merely a record of transactions.

Businesspeople must often make quick decisions without the benefit of a complete accounting system. For example, Norman Erickson, a barber in New

Decision Guidelines

Analyzing and Recording Transactions

Decision	Guidelines
Has a transaction occurred?	If the event affects the entity's financial position and can be reliably recorded—*Yes* If either condition is absent—*No*
Where to record the transaction?	In the journal, the chronological record of transactions
What to record for each transaction?	Increases and/or decreases in all the accounts affected by the transaction
How to record an increase/decrease in the following accounts?	Rules of debit and credit:

Account	Increase	Decrease
Asset	Debit	Credit
Liability	Credit	Debit
Stockholders' equity	Credit	Debit
Revenue	Credit	Debit
Expense	Debit	Credit

Decision	Guidelines
Where to store all the information for each account?	In the ledger, the book of accounts and their balances
Where to list all the accounts and their balances?	In the trial balance
Where to report the Results of operations?	In the income statement (revenues – expenses = net income or net loss)
Financial position?	In the balance sheet (assets = liabilities + stockholders' equity)

Preston, Connecticut, may be renegotiating the lease on his shop. He may not have the time for a thorough recording of the effects of all the barber shop's transactions. One who knows accounting can skip the journal and go directly to the ledger, thus compressing transaction analysis, journalizing, and posting into one step. This type of analysis saves time that may make the difference between a good business decision and a lost opportunity.

Erickson needs to compare the expense of renting the shop for $800 per month with the $75,000 cost of buying his own building. In the heat of negotiation, he doesn't have time to journalize and post all the likely transactions and prepare a trial balance. But if he knows some accounting, he can make this quick comparison:

RENT THE SHOP				BUY THE BUILDING			
Cash		Rent Expense		Cash		Building	
	800	800			75,000	75,000	

Erickson can immediately see that buying the building will require more cash, but he can also see that he will obtain the building as an asset. This may motivate him to borrow cash and buy the building.

Companies do not actually keep their records in this short-cut fashion. But a decision maker who needs information immediately need not perform all the accounting steps to analyze the effect of a set of transactions on the company's financial statements.

SUMMARY PROBLEM FOR YOUR REVIEW

The trial balance of Calderon Computer Service Center, Inc., on March 1, 19X2, lists the entity's assets, liabilities, and stockholders' equity on that date.

Account Title	Balance Debit	Balance Credit
Cash	$26,000	
Accounts receivable	4,500	
Accounts payable		$ 2,000
Common stock		10,000
Retained earnings		18,500
Total	$30,500	$30,500

During March, the business engaged in the following transactions:

a. Borrowed $45,000 from the bank. Calderon signed a note payable in the name of the business.
b. Paid cash of $40,000 to a real estate company to acquire land.
c. Performed service for a customer and received cash of $5,000.
d. Purchased supplies on credit, $300.
e. Performed customer service and earned revenue on account, $2,600.
f. Paid $1,200 on account.
g. Paid the following cash expenses: salaries, $3,000; rent, $1,500; and interest, $400.
h. Received $3,100 on account.
i. Received a $200 utility bill that will be paid next week.
j. Paid dividend of $1,800.

Required

1. Open the following accounts, with the balances indicated, in the ledger of Calderon Computer Service Center, Inc. Use the T-account format.
   - Assets—Cash, $26,000; Accounts Receivable, $4,500; Supplies, no balance; Land, no balance
   - Liabilities—Accounts Payable, $2,000; Note Payable, no balance
   - Stockholders' Equity—Common Stock, $10,000; Retained Earnings, $18,500; Dividends, no balance
   - Revenues—Service Revenue, no balance
   - Expenses—(none have balances) Salary Expense, Rent Expense, Interest Expense, Utilities Expense
2. Journalize the preceding transactions. Key journal entries by transaction letter.
3. Post to the ledger and show the balance in each account after all the transactions have been posted.
4. Prepare the trial balance of Calderon Computer Service Center, Inc., at March 31, 19X2.
5. To determine the net income or net loss of the entity during the month of March, prepare the income statement for the month ended March 31, 19X2. List expenses in order from the largest to the smallest.
6. Suppose the organizers of Calderon Computer Service Center ask you to invest $5,000 in the company's stock. Cite specifics from the income statement and the trial balance to support your decision.

ANSWERS

Requirement 1

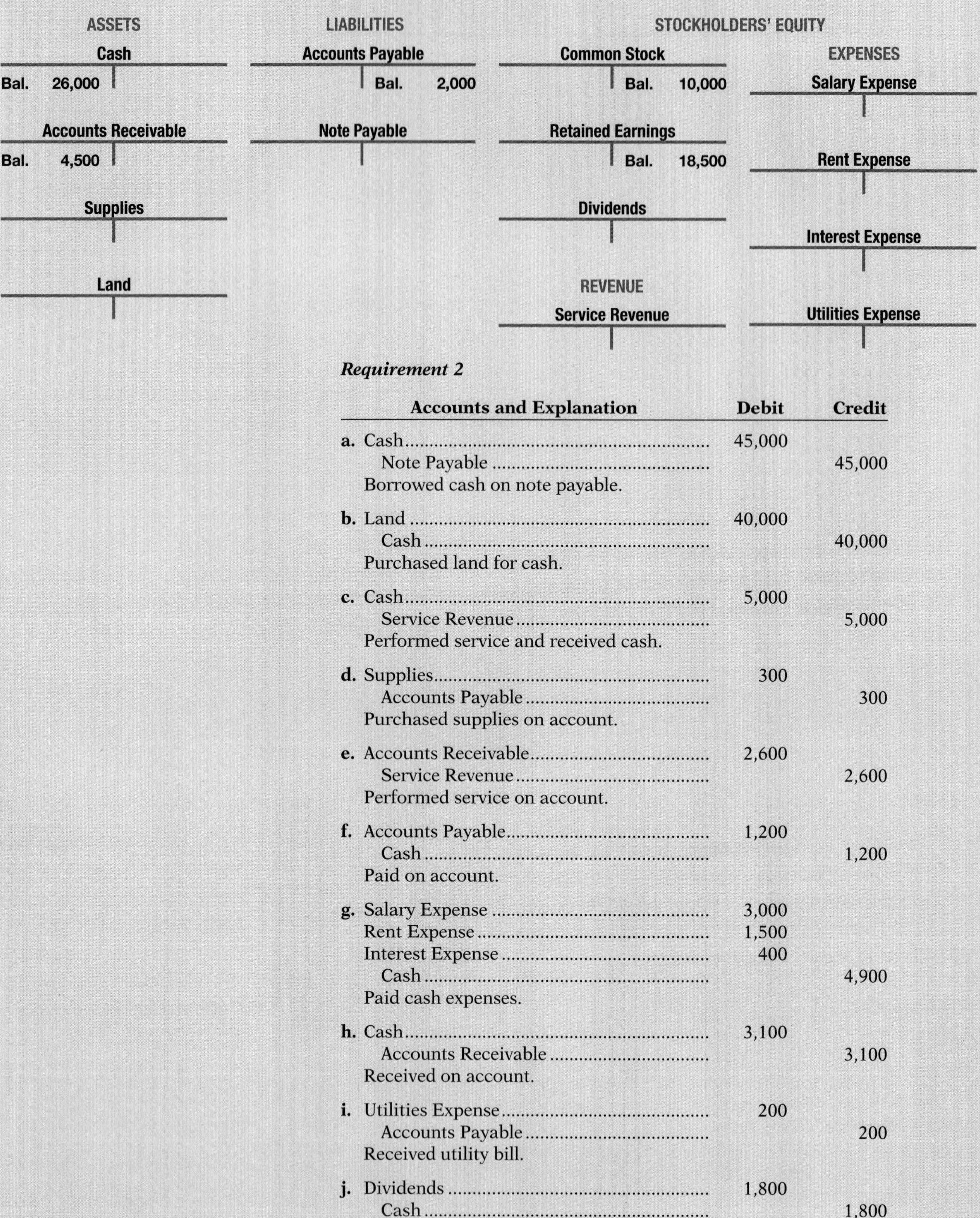

Requirement 2

Accounts and Explanation	Debit	Credit
a. Cash	45,000	
Note Payable		45,000
Borrowed cash on note payable.		
b. Land	40,000	
Cash		40,000
Purchased land for cash.		
c. Cash	5,000	
Service Revenue		5,000
Performed service and received cash.		
d. Supplies	300	
Accounts Payable		300
Purchased supplies on account.		
e. Accounts Receivable	2,600	
Service Revenue		2,600
Performed service on account.		
f. Accounts Payable	1,200	
Cash		1,200
Paid on account.		
g. Salary Expense	3,000	
Rent Expense	1,500	
Interest Expense	400	
Cash		4,900
Paid cash expenses.		
h. Cash	3,100	
Accounts Receivable		3,100
Received on account.		
i. Utilities Expense	200	
Accounts Payable		200
Received utility bill.		
j. Dividends	1,800	
Cash		1,800
Declared and paid dividends.		

Requirement 3

ASSETS

Cash

Bal.	26,000	(b)	40,000
(a)	45,000	(f)	1,200
(c)	5,000	(g)	4,900
(h)	3,100	(j)	1,800
Bal.	31,200		

Accounts Receivable

Bal.	4,500	(h)	3,100
(e)	2,600		
Bal.	4,000		

Supplies

(d)	300		
Bal.	300		

Land

(b)	40,000		
Bal.	40,000		

LIABILITIES

Accounts Payable

(f)	1,200	Bal.	2,000
		(d)	300
		(i)	200
		Bal.	1,300

Note Payable

		(a)	45,000
		Bal.	45,000

STOCKHOLDERS' EQUITY

Common Stock

		Bal.	10,000

Retained Earnings

		Bal.	18,500

Dividends

(j)	1,800		
Bal.	1,800		

REVENUE

Service Revenue

		(c)	5,000
		(e)	2,600
		Bal.	7,600

EXPENSES

Salary Expense

(g)	3,000		
Bal.	3,000		

Rent Expense

(g)	1,500		
Bal.	1,500		

Interest Expense

(g)	400		
Bal.	400		

Utilities Expense

(i)	200		
Bal.	200		

Requirement 4

CALDERON COMPUTER SERVICE CENTER, INC.
Trial Balance
March 31, 19X2

Account Title	Balance Debit	Balance Credit
Cash	$31,200	
Accounts receivable	4,000	
Supplies	300	
Land	40,000	
Accounts payable		$ 1,300
Note payable		45,000
Common stock		10,000
Retained earnings		18,500
Dividends	1,800	
Service revenue		7,600
Salary expense	3,000	
Rent expense	1,500	
Interest expense	400	
Utilities expense	200	
Total	$82,400	$82,400

Requirement 5

CALDERON COMPUTER SERVICE CENTER, INC. Income Statement Month Ended March 31, 19X2		
Revenue:		
Service revenue		$7,600
Expenses:		
Salary expense	$3,000	
Rent expense	1,500	
Interest expense	400	
Utilities expense	200	
Total expenses		5,100
Net income		$2,500

Requirement 6

A $5,000 investment in Calderon appears to be warranted because

a. The company earned net income of $2,500 on revenues of $7,600, so the business appears profitable.

b. Total assets of $75,500 ($31,200 + $4,000 + $300 + $40,000) far exceed total liabilities of $46,300 ($45,000 + $1,300), which suggests that Calderon can pay its debts and remain in business.

c. The existing owners have at least $10,000 of their own money invested in the business, as indicated by the balance of Common Stock. An investor can take comfort in the fact that the organizers are willing to risk their own money in the business.

d. Calderon is paying a dividend, so an investment in the stock may yield a quick return in the form of dividends.

SUMMARY OF LEARNING OBJECTIVES

1. *Define and use key accounting terms: account, asset, liability, stockholders' equity, revenue, and expense.* An *account* is the detailed record of the changes that have occurred in a particular asset, liability, or stockholders' equity during a period. *Assets* are the economic resources that benefit the business and will continue to do so in the future. *Liabilities* are debts payable to outsiders. *Stockholders' equity* (sometimes called *shareholders' equity* or simply *owners' equity*) are the owners' claims to the assets of a corporation. *Revenues* are increases in stockholders' equity created by delivering goods or services to customers. *Expenses* are the costs of doing business that decrease stockholders' equity.

2. *Use the accounting equation to analyze business transactions.* A *transaction* is any event that both affects the financial position of the business entity and can be reliably recorded. Analyzing business transactions involves determining each transaction's effects on the accounting equation: assets = liabilities + stockholders' equity. The summary of all the business's transactions over a period forms the basis for its financial statements.

3. *Understand how double-entry accounting works.* *Double-entry accounting* is an accounting system that uses debits and credits to record the dual effects of each business transaction. Every transaction involves both a debit and a credit, and the total amount debited must equal the total amount credited for each transaction. *Debits* are simply the left side of an account; *credits* are the right side of an account. Assets and expenses are increased by debits and decreased by credits. Liabilities, stockholders' equity, and revenues are increased by credits and decreased by debits.

4. *Record transactions in the journal, and post from the journal to the ledger.* Accountants record business transactions first in a *journal,* a chronological record of the entity's transactions. Each journal entry includes a date, the titles of the accounts debited and credited, the dollar amounts debited and credited, and a short explanation of the transaction. This information is then posted (transferred) to the *ledger,* a grouping of all the individual accounts and their balances. The balance of each account in the ledger may be taken after all posting is done.

5. *Prepare and use a trial balance.* A *trial balance* is a list of all accounts with their balances—assets first, followed by liabilities, stockholders' equity, revenues, and expenses. It provides an accuracy check by showing whether or not total debits equal total credits. If total debits do not equal total credits, an accounting error has occurred somewhere in journalizing or posting.

6. *Set up a chart of accounts for a business.* An organization's *chart of accounts* lists all its accounts and their account numbers. These account numbers make it easy to locate individual accounts in the ledger. Companies may start with a relatively small number of accounts, and add new accounts as the business grows.

7. *Analyze transactions without a journal.* Decision makers must often make decisions without a complete accounting system. With some basic accounting knowledge, one can analyze certain situations by going directly to the ledger, thus compressing transaction analysis, journalizing, and posting into one step.

ACCOUNTING VOCABULARY

account *(p. 52).*
chart of accounts *(p. 77).*
credit *(p. 64).*
debit *(p. 64).*
double-entry system *(p. 63).*
journal *(p. 66).*
ledger *(p. 69).*
posted *(p. 69).*
transaction *(p. 54).*
trial balance *(p. 74).*

QUESTIONS

1. Name the basic summary device of accounting. Which letter of the alphabet does it resemble? Name its two sides.
2. Is the following statement true or false? "Debit means decrease and credit means increase." Explain your answer.
3. What are the three *basic* types of accounts? Name two additional types of accounts. To which one of the three basic types are these two additional types of accounts most closely related?
4. What role do transactions play in accounting?
5. Briefly describe the flow of accounting information from the business transaction to the ledger.
6. Label each of the following transactions as increasing stockholders' equity (+), decreasing stockholders' equity (–), or having no effect on stockholders' equity (0). Write the appropriate symbol in the space provided.

   ___**a.** Investment by owner
   ___**b.** Revenue transaction
   ___**c.** Purchase of supplies on credit
   ___**d.** Expense transaction
   ___**e.** Cash payment on account
   ___**f.** Dividends
   ___**g.** Borrowing money on a note payable
   ___**h.** Sale of service on account

7. Rearrange the following accounts in their logical sequence in the ledger:

Notes Payable	Cash
Accounts Receivable	Common Stock
Sales Revenue	Salary Expense

8. What is the meaning of the following statement? "Accounts Payable has a credit balance of $1,700."
9. Jack Brown Campus Cleaners launders the shirts of customer Bobby Baylor, who has a charge account at the cleaners. When Bobby picks up his clothes and is short of cash, he asks Jack Brown if he can pay later in the month. When Bobby receives his monthly statement from the cleaners, he writes a check on Dear Old Dad's bank account and mails the check to Jack Brown. Identify the two business transactions described here. Which transaction increases the business's stockholders' equity? Which transaction increases the business's cash?
10. Why do accountants prepare a trial balance?
11. To what does the *normal balance* of an account refer?
12. Indicate the normal balance of the five types of accounts.

Account Type	Normal Balance
Assets	________
Liabilities	________
Stockholders' equity	________
Revenues	________
Expenses	________

13. The accountant for Bower Construction Company mistakenly recorded a $500 purchase of supplies on account as a $5,000 purchase. He debited Supplies and credited Accounts Payable for $5,000. Does this error cause the trial balance to be out of balance? Explain your answer.
14. What is the effect on total assets of collecting cash on account from customers?
15. What is the advantage of analyzing transactions without the use of a journal? Describe how this "journal-less" analysis works.

EXERCISES

E2-1 Your employer, Florida Resources, Inc., has just hired an office manager who does not understand accounting. The trial balance for Florida Resources lists Cash of $365,000. Write a short memo to the office manager, explaining the accounting process that produced this listing on the trial balance. Mention *debits, credits, journals, ledgers,* and *posting.*

Using accounting vocabulary
(Obj. 1)

Business transactions and the accounting equation ***(Obj. 2)***

E2-2 For each of the following items, give an example of a business transaction that has the described effect on the accounting equation:

a. Increase an asset and increase a liability.
b. Increase one asset and decrease another asset.
c. Decrease an asset and decrease owners' equity.
d. Decrease an asset and decrease a liability.
e. Increase an asset and increase owners' equity.

Transaction analysis ***(Obj. 2)***

E2-3 The following events were experienced by either Ravitch Manufacturing Company, a corporation, or Derrick Ravitch, the major stockholder. State whether each event (1) increased, (2) decreased, or (3) had no effect on the total assets of the business. Identify any specific asset affected.

a. Borrowed money from the bank.
b. Cash purchase of land for a future building site.
c. Ravitch increased his cash investment in the business, and the business issued additional stock to him.
d. Paid cash on accounts payable.
e. Purchased machinery and equipment for a manufacturing plant; signed a promissory note in payment.
f. Performed service for a customer on account.
g. The business paid Ravitch a cash dividend.
h. Received cash from a customer on account receivable.
i. Ravitch used personal funds to purchase a swimming pool for his home.
j. Sold land for a price equal to the cost of the land; received cash.

Transaction analysis; accounting equation ***(Obj. 2)***

E2-4 Anna Gittner opens a medical practice to specialize in gynecology. During the first month of operation (January), her practice, entitled Anna Gittner, Professional Corporation (P.C.), experienced the following events:

Jan. 6	Gittner invested $20,000 in the business, which in turn issued its common stock to her.
9	The business paid cash for land costing $15,000. Gittner plans to build an office building on the land.
12	The business purchased medical supplies for $2,000 on account.
15	Gittner, P.C., officially opened for business.
15–31	During the rest of the month, Gittner treated patients and earned service revenue of $8,000, receiving cash for half the revenue earned.
15–31	The business paid cash expenses: employee salaries, $1,400; office rent, $1,000; utilities, $300.
28	The business sold supplies to another physician for cost of $500.
30	The business borrowed $10,000, signing a note payable to the bank.
31	The business paid $1,500 on account.

Required

1. Analyze the effects of these events on the accounting equation of the medical practice of Anna Gittner, P.C. Use a format similar to that of Exhibit 2-1, Panel B, with headings for Cash, Accounts Receivable, Medical Supplies, Land, Accounts Payable, Note Payable, Common Stock, and Retained Earnings.

2. After completing the analysis, answer these questions about the business.
   a. How much does the business expect to collect from patients?
   b. How much does the business owe in total?
   c. How much net income or net loss did the business experience during its first month of operations?
   d. How much are total assets?

Journalizing transactions ***(Obj. 3, 4)***

E2-5 Refer to Exercise 2-4.
Record the transactions in the journal of Anna Gittner, Professional Corporation (P.C.). List the transactions by date, and give an explanation for each transaction.

Analyzing transactions and determining net income ***(Obj. 2)***

E2-6 The analysis of the transactions in which Mossimo Leasing Corporation engaged during its first month of operations follows in their order of occurrence. The company buys equipment that it leases out to earn revenue. Mossimo Leasing paid no dividends during the period.

	Cash	+	Accounts Receivable	+	Lease Equipment	=	Note Payable	+	Common Stock	+	Retained Earnings
(a)	+50,000								+50,000		
(b)					+100,000		+100,000				
(c)			+500								+ 500
(d)	− 750				+750						
(e)	+ 150		−150								
(f)	− 1,000										−1,000
(g)	+ 2,500										+2,500
(h)	−10,000						− 10,000				

Required

1. Describe each transaction.
2. If these transactions fully describe the operations of Mossimo Leasing during the month, what was the amount of net income or net loss?

E2-7 Brennan Consulting Service, Inc., engaged in the following transactions during March 19X3, its first month of operations:

Journalizing transactions (Obj. 3, 4)

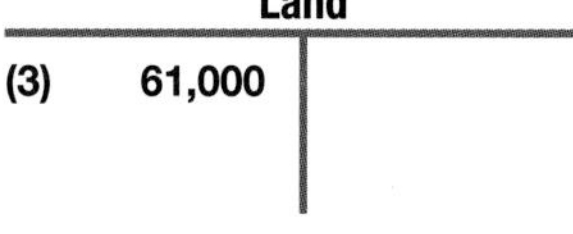

Mar. 1 Alex Brennan invested $60,000 of cash to start the business. The corporation issued common stock to Brennan.
2 Purchased $200 of office supplies on account.
4 Paid $40,000 cash for a building to use as a future office.
6 Performed service for customers and received cash, $2,000.
9 Paid $100 on accounts payable.
17 Performed service for customers on account, $1,200.
23 Received $1,200 cash from customers on account.
31 Paid the following expenses: salary, $1,000; rent, $500.

Required

1. Record the preceding transactions in the journal of Brennan Consulting Service, Inc. Key transactions by date and include an explanation for each entry, as illustrated in the chapter.
2. After these transactions, how much cash does Brennan Consulting Service have to work with?

E2-8 Refer to Exercise 2-7.

Posting to the ledger and preparing a trial balance (Obj. 4, 5)

Required

1. After journalizing the transactions of Exercise 2-7, post the entries to the ledger, using T-account format. Key transactions by date. Date the ending balance of each account Mar. 31.
2. Prepare the trial balance of Brennan Consulting Service, Inc., at March 31, 19X3.
3. How much are total assets, total liabilities, and total stockholders' equity on March 31?

E2-9 The first seven transactions of Sheshunoff Security Company have been posted to the company's accounts as follows:

Journalizing transactions (Obj. 3, 4)

Cash

(1)	60,000	(3)	42,000
(4)	100	(5)	6,000
(7)	7,000	(6)	2,300

Supplies

(2)	400	(4)	100

Equipment

(5)	6,000		

Land

(3)	61,000		

Accounts Payable

(6)	2,300	(2)	400

Note Payable

		(3)	19,000
		(7)	7,000

Common Stock

		(1)	60,000

Required

Prepare the journal entries that served as the sources for the seven transactions. Include an explanation for each entry as illustrated in the chapter.

E2-10 The accounts of Jefferson Sales Company appear at the top of page 88 with their normal balances at October 31, 19X4. The accounts are listed in no particular order.

Preparing a trial balance (Obj. 5)

Account	Balance	Account	Balance
Common stock	$48,800	Building	$75,000
Advertising expense	650	Rent expense	2,000
Accounts payable	4,300	Dividends	6,000
Sales commission revenue	22,000	Utilities expense	400
Land	29,000	Accounts receivable	5,500
Note payable	25,000	Supplies expense	300
Cash	15,000	Supplies	250
Salary expense	6,000	Retained earnings	?

Required

1. Prepare the company's trial balance at October 31, 19X4, listing accounts in proper sequence, as illustrated in the chapter. For example, Supplies comes before Building and Land. List the expense with the largest balance first, the expense with the next largest balance second, and so on.
2. Prepare the financial statement for the month ended October 31, 19X4, that will tell Jefferson's top managers the results of operations for the month.

Correcting errors in a trial balance ***(Obj. 5)***

E2-11 The trial balance of Vermont Maple Syrup, Inc., at February 28, 19X9, does not balance:

Cash	$ 4,200	
Accounts receivable	2,000	
Supplies	600	
Inventory	1,400	
Land	46,000	
Accounts payable		$ 3,000
Common stock		46,900
Sales revenue		9,700
Salary expense	1,700	
Rent expense	800	
Utilities expense	300	
Total	$57,000	$59,600

Investigation of the accounting records reveals the following errors:

a. Recorded a $400 cash revenue transaction by debiting Accounts Receivable. The credit entry was correct.
b. Posted a $1,000 credit to Accounts Payable as $100.
c. Did not record utilities expense or the related account payable in the amount of $200.
d. Understated Common Stock by $400.
e. Omitted Cost of Goods Sold, an expense of $3,900, from the trial balance.

Required

Prepare the correct trial balance at February 28, complete with a heading. Journal entries are not required.

Recording transactions without a journal ***(Obj. 7)***

E2-12 Open the following T-accounts: Cash, Accounts Receivable, Office Supplies, Office Furniture, Accounts Payable, Common Stock, Dividends, Service Revenue, Salary Expense, Rent Expense.

Record the following transactions directly in the T-accounts without using a journal. Use the letters to identify the transactions.

a. Jay Barlow opened an accounting firm by investing $6,200 cash and office furniture valued at $5,400. Organized as a professional corporation, the business issued common stock to Barlow.
b. Paid monthly rent of $1,500.
c. Purchased office supplies on account, $800.
d. Paid employees' salaries, $1,800.
e. Paid $400 of the account payable created in Transaction c.
f. Performed accounting service on account, $1,700.
g. Declared and paid dividends of $2,000.

Preparing a trial balance
(Obj. 5)

E2-13 Refer to Exercise 2-12.

1. After recording the transactions in Exercise 2-12, prepare the trial balance of Jay Barlow, CPA, P.C., at May 31, 19X7.
2. How well did the business perform during its first month? Give the basis for your answer.

SERIAL EXERCISE

Exercise 2-14 begins an accounting cycle that is completed in Chapter 3.

Recording transactions and preparing a trial balance
(Obj. 3, 4, 5)

E2-14 Dirk Olsen, Accountant, Professional Corporation (P.C.), completed these transactions during the first part of December:

Dec.	2	Received $12,000 cash from Olsen. Issued common stock to him.
	2	Paid monthly office rent, $500.
	3	Paid cash for a Gateway computer, $3,000. The computer is expected to remain in service for five years.
	4	Purchased office furniture on account, $3,600. The furniture should last for five years.
	5	Purchased supplies on account, $300.
	9	Performed tax service for a client and received cash for the full amount of $800.
	12	Paid utility expenses, $200.
	18	Performed consulting service for a client on account, $1,700.

Required

1. Open T-accounts in the ledger: Cash, Accounts Receivable, Supplies, Equipment, Furniture, Accounts Payable, Common Stock, Dividends, Service Revenue, Rent Expense, Utilities Expense, and Salary Expense.
2. Journalize the transactions. Explanations are not required.
3. Post to the T-accounts. Key all items by date, and denote an account balance on December 18 as Bal. Formal posting references are not required.
4. Prepare a trial balance at December 18. In the Serial Exercise of Chapter 3, we will add transactions for the remainder of December and will require a trial balance at December 31.

CHALLENGE EXERCISES

Identifying the accounts of a new business
(Obj. 6)

E2-15 Mike Majid asks your advice in setting up the accounting records for Studio Gallery, his new business, which he plans to organize as a corporation. Studio Gallery will be a photography studio and will operate in a rented building. Majid will need office equipment, cameras, tripods, lights, backdrops, and so on. The business will borrow money to buy the needed equipment and sign a note payable. The gallery will purchase on account photographic supplies (such as film, paper, and developing solution) and office supplies. Each asset needs its own expense account, some of which we have not yet discussed. For example, equipment wears out (depreciates) and thus needs a depreciation account. As supplies are used up, the business must record a supplies expense.

Majid owns the land on which the studio building stands. He will contribute the land to the business, which will then pay the property tax on the land. A gas station located on a corner of the property will start paying its monthly rent to the photography studio. The studio will need an office manager to arrange appointments, keep the books, design advertisements, and pay the rent and the insurance in advance and the utility bills as they come due. Majid anticipates paying this person a weekly salary of $300.

Majid will want to know which aspects of the business are the most, and the least, profitable, so he will account for each category of service revenue separately: portraits, school pictures, and weddings. He will let his better customers open accounts with the business and expects to collect cash over a three-month period. The studio will carry an inventory of picture frames for sale to customers—a separate category of revenue.

Required

List all the accounts the studio will need, starting with assets and ending with expenses. Indicate which accounts will be reported on the balance sheet and which will be on the income statement.

Determining financial statement amounts without a journal
(Obj. 7)

E2-16 The owner of AAdvantage Sales, Inc., is an engineer with little understanding of accounting. He needs to compute the following summary information from the accounting records:

a. Net income for the month of March.
b. Total cash paid during March.
c. Cash collections from customers during March.
d. Cash paid on a note payable during March.

The quickest way to compute these amounts is to analyze the following accounts:

Account	Balance Feb. 28	Balance Mar. 31	Additional Information for the Month of March
1. Retained Earnings	$9,200	$10,500	Dividends, $3,800
2. Cash	4,600	5,400	Cash receipts, $71,200
3. Accounts Receivable	24,300	26,700	Sales on account, $65,500
4. Note Payable	13,900	12,400	New borrowing, $6,300

The net income for March can be computed as follows:

Retained Earnings

March Dividends	3,800	Feb. 28 Bal.	9,200
		March Net Income x =	$5,100
		March 31	Bal. 10,500

Use a similar approach to compute the other three items.

Analyzing accounting errors ***(Obj. 3, 4, 5)***

E2-17 Klutz Accountant has trouble keeping his debits and credits equal. During a recent month, he made the following errors:

a. In journalizing a cash sale, Klutz correctly debited Cash for $300 but accidentally credited Accounts Receivable.

b. Klutz posted a $200 utility expense as $20. The credit posting to Cash was correct.

c. In preparing the trial balance, Klutz omitted a $20,000 note payable.

d. Klutz recorded a $120 purchase of supplies on account by debiting Supplies and crediting Accounts Payable for $210.

e. In recording a $500 payment on account, Klutz debited Supplies and credited Accounts Payable.

Required

1. For each of these errors, state whether the total debits equal total credits on the trial balance.

2. Identify any accounts with misstated balances, and indicate the amount and direction of the error (account balance too high or too low).

PROBLEMS

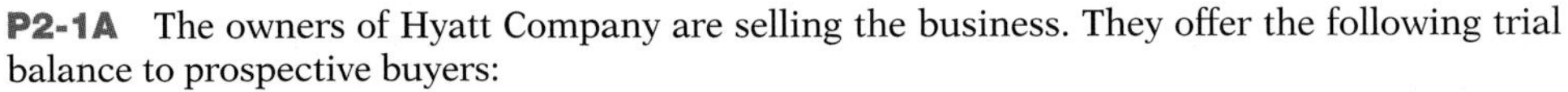

(GROUP A)

Analyzing a trial balance ***(Obj. 1)***

P2-1A The owners of Hyatt Company are selling the business. They offer the following trial balance to prospective buyers:

HYATT COMPANY
Trial Balance
December 31, 19XX

Account	Debit	Credit
Cash	$ 47,000	
Accounts receivable	11,000	
Prepaid expenses	4,000	
Land	231,000	
Accounts payable		$ 31,000
Note payable		120,000
Common stock		103,000
Retained earnings		40,000
Dividends	21,000	
Service revenue		77,000
Rent expense	14,000	
Advertising expense	3,000	
Wage expense	33,000	
Supplies expense	7,000	
	$371,000	$371,000

Your best friend is considering buying Hyatt Company. He seeks your advice in interpreting this information. Specifically, he asks whether this trial balance is the same as a balance sheet and an income statement. He also wonders whether Hyatt is a sound company. After all, the accounts are in balance.

Required

Write a short note to answer your friend's questions. To aid his decision, state how he can use the information on the trial balance to compute Hyatt's net income or net loss for the current period. State the amount of net income or net loss in your note.

Analyzing transactions using the accounting equation and preparing the financial statements
(Obj. 2)

P2-2A Glen Blake operates and is the major stockholder of an interior design studio called Blake Interiors, Inc. The following amounts summarize the financial position of the business on August 31, 19X2:

	Assets				=	Liabilities	+	Stockholders' Equity	
	Cash +	**Accounts Receivable** +	**Supplies** +	**Land**	=	**Accounts Payable**	+	**Common Stock** +	**Retained Earnings**
Bal.	1,250	1,500		12,000		8,000		4,000	2,750

During September 19X2, the following events occurred:

a. Blake inherited $20,000 and deposited the cash in the business bank account. The business issued common stock to Blake.
b. Performed services for a client and received cash of $700.
c. Paid off the beginning balance of accounts payable.
d. Purchased supplies on account, $1,000.
e. Collected cash from a customer on account, $500.
f. Received cash of $1,000 and issued common stock to Blake.
g. Consulted on the interior design of a major office building and billed the client for services rendered, $2,400.
h. Recorded the following business expenses for the month:
(1) Paid office rent—$900. **(2)** Paid advertising—$300.
i. Sold supplies to another business for $150 cash, which was the cost of the supplies.
j. Declared and paid a cash dividend of $1,800.

Required

1. Analyze the effects of the preceding transactions on the accounting equation of Blake Interiors, Inc. Adapt the format of Exhibit 2-1, Panel B.
2. Prepare the income statement of Blake Interiors, Inc., for the month ended September 30, 19X2. List expenses in decreasing order by amount.
3. Prepare the entity's statement of retained earnings for the month ended September 30, 19X2.
4. Prepare the balance sheet of Blake Interiors, Inc., at September 30, 19X2.
5. As the manager of Blake Interiors, how will you use the information from the income statement and the balance sheet to manage the business? Be specific.

Recording transactions, posting
(Obj. 3, 4)

P2-3A This problem should be used only in conjunction with Problem 2-2A. Refer to Problem 2-2A.

Required

1. Journalize the transactions of Blake Interiors, Inc. Explanations are not required.
2. Set up the following T-accounts: Cash, Accounts Receivable, Supplies, Land, Accounts Payable, Common Stock, Retained Earnings, Dividends, Service Revenue, Rent Expense, Advertising Expense. Insert in each account its balance as given (example: Cash $1,250). Post to the accounts. Posting references are not required.
3. Compute the balance in each account. For each asset account, each liability account, and for Common Stock, compare its balance to the ending balance you obtained in Problem 2-2A. Are the amounts the same or different? (In Chapter 3, we will complete the accounting process. There you will learn how the Retained Earnings, Dividends, Revenue, and Expense accounts work together in the processing of accounting information.)

Analyzing transactions using the accounting equation
(Obj. 2, 3)

P2-4A Ronald Richey practiced law with a large firm, a partnership, for five years after graduating from law school. Recently, he resigned his position to open his own law office, which he operates as a professional corporation. The name of the new entity is Ronald Richey, Attorney,

Professional Corporation (P.C.). Richey experienced the following events during the organizing phase of his new business and its first month of operations. Some of the events were personal and did not affect his law practice. Others were business transactions and should be accounted for by the business.

Feb. 4 Richey received $100,000 cash from his former partners in the law firm from which he resigned.

5 Richey deposited $50,000 cash in a new business bank account entitled Ronald Richey, Attorney, P.C. The business issued common stock to Richey.

6 The business paid $300 cash for letterhead stationery for the new law office.

7 The business purchased office furniture for his law office. The company paid cash of $10,000 and agreed to pay the account payable for the remainder, $7,000, within six months.

10 Richey sold 500 shares of IBM stock, which he and his wife had owned for several years, receiving $75,000 cash from his stockbroker.

11 Richey deposited the $75,000 cash from sale of the IBM stock in his personal bank account.

12 A representative of a large company telephoned Richey and told him of the company's intention to transfer its legal business to the new entity of Ronald Richey, Attorney, P.C.

18 Richey finished court hearings on behalf of a client and submitted his bill for legal services, $4,000. Richey expected to collect from this client within two weeks.

21 The business paid half its account payable for the furniture purchased on February 7.

25 The business paid office rent, $1,000.

28 The business declared and paid a cash dividend of $2,000.

Required

1. Classify each of the preceding events as one of the following:
   a. A business transaction to be accounted for by the business of Ronald Richey, Attorney, P.C.
   b. A business-related event but not a transaction to be accounted for by the business of Ronald Richey, Attorney, P.C.
   c. A personal transaction not to be accounted for by the business of Ronald Richey, Attorney, P.C.
2. Analyze the effects of the preceding events on the accounting equation of the business of Ronald Richey, Attorney, P.C. Use a format similar to that in Exhibit 2-1, Panel B.
3. At the end of the first month of operations, Richey has a number of questions about the financial standing of the business. Explain to him:
   a. How the business can have so much cash and so little in retained earnings.
   b. How much in total resources the business has, how much it owes, and what Richey's ownership interest is in the assets of the business.
4. Record the transactions of the business in its journal. Include an explanation for each entry.

Analyzing and journalizing transactions
(Obj. 3, 4)

P2-5A Sara Litton practices medicine under the business title Sara Litton, M.D., Professional Corporation (P.C.). During May, her medical practice engaged in the following transactions:

May 1 Litton deposited $16,000 cash in the business bank account. The business issued common stock to Litton.

5 Paid monthly rent on medical equipment, $700.

9 Paid $5,000 cash and signed a $25,000 note payable to purchase land for an office site.

10 Purchased supplies on account, $1,200.

19 Paid $1,000 on account.

22 Borrowed $10,000 from the bank for business use. Litton signed a note payable to the bank in the name of the business.

30 Revenues earned during the month included $6,000 cash and $5,000 on account.

30 Paid employees' salaries ($2,400), office rent ($1,500), and utilities ($400).

30 Declared and paid a cash dividend of $4,000.

Litton's business uses the following accounts: Cash, Accounts Receivable, Supplies, Land, Accounts Payable, Notes Payable, Common Stock, Dividends, Service Revenue, Salary Expense, Rent Expense, and Utilities Expense.

Required

1. Journalize each transaction of Sara Litton, M.D., P.C. Explanations are not required.
2. After these transactions, how much cash does the business have? How much in total does it owe?

P2-6A Dave Brindley opened a law office on January 2 of the current year. During the first month of operations, the business completed the following transactions:

Journalizing transactions, posting to T-accounts, and preparing a trial balance ***(Obj. 3, 4, 5)***

Jan. 2 Brindley deposited $28,000 cash in the business bank account Dave Brindley, Attorney, Professional Corporation (P.C.). The corporation issued common stock to Brindley.
3 Purchased supplies, $500, and furniture, $2,600, on account.
4 Performed legal service for a client and received cash, $1,500.
7 Paid cash to acquire land for a future office site, $22,000.
11 Defended a client in court and billed the client $800.
15 Paid secretary's salary, $650.
16 Paid for the furniture purchased January 3 on account.
17 Paid the telephone bill, $110.
18 Received partial payment from client on account, $400.
19 Prepared legal documents for a client on account, $900.
22 Paid the water and electricity bills, $130.
29 Received $1,800 cash for helping a client sell real estate.
31 Paid secretary's salary, $650.
31 Paid rent expense, $700.
31 Declared and paid dividends of $2,200.

Required

Open the following T-accounts: Cash, Accounts Receivable, Supplies, Furniture, Land, Accounts Payable, Common Stock, Dividends, Service Revenue, Salary Expense, Rent Expense, and Utilities Expense.

1. Record each transaction in the journal, using the account titles given. Key each transaction by date. Explanations are not required.
2. Post the transactions to the ledger, using transaction dates as posting references in the ledger. Label the ending balance of each account Bal., as shown in the chapter.
3. Prepare the trial balance of Dave Brindley, Attorney, P.C., at January 31 of the current year.
4. How will what you learned in this problem help you manage a business?

P2-7A The trial balance of the accounting practice of Larry Jaynes, CPA, Professional Corporation (P.C.), at November 15, 19X3, follows.

Journalizing transactions, posting to accounts in four-column format, and preparing a trial balance ***(Obj. 3, 4, 5)***

LARRY JAYNES, CPA, P.C.
Trial Balance
November 15, 19X3

Account Number	Account	Debit	Credit
11	Cash	$13,000	
12	Accounts receivable	8,000	
13	Supplies	1,200	
14	Land	35,000	
21	Accounts payable		$ 4,400
31	Common stock		18,000
32	Retained earnings		32,600
33	Dividends	2,100	
41	Service revenue		7,100
51	Salary expense	1,800	
52	Rent expense	700	
53	Utilities expense	300	
	Total	$62,100	$62,100

During the rest of November, the business completed the following transactions:

Nov. 16 Collected $4,000 cash from a client on account.
17 Performed tax service for a client on account, $1,700.
19 Paid utilities, $100.
21 Paid on account, $2,600.
22 Purchased supplies on account, $200.
23 Declared and paid dividends of $2,100.

Nov. 23 Used personal funds to pay for the renovation of private residence, $55,000.
24 Received $1,900 cash for audit work just completed.
30 Paid rent, $700.
30 Paid employees' salaries, $1,800.

Required

1. Record the transactions that occurred during November 16 through 30 on Page 6 of the journal. Include an explanation for each entry.
2. Open the ledger accounts listed in the trial balance together with their balances at November 15. Use the four-column account format (with a running balance) illustrated in the chapter. Enter Bal. (for previous balance) in the Item column, and place a check mark (✓) in the Journal Reference column for the November 15 balance of each account. Post the transactions to the ledger, using dates, account numbers, journal references, and posting references.
3. Prepare the trial balance of Larry Jaynes, CPA, P.C., at November 30, 19X3.

Correcting errors in a trial balance
(Obj. 5)

P2-8A The trial balance for Dole Transit Service does not balance. The following errors were detected:

a. The cash balance is understated by $400.
b. Maintenance expense of $200 is omitted from the trial balance.
c. Rent expense of $200 was posted as a credit rather than a debit.
d. The balance of Advertising Expense is $300, but it is listed as $400 on the trial balance.
e. A $600 debit to Accounts Receivable was posted as $60.
f. The balance of Utilities Expense is understated by $60.
g. A $1,300 debit to the Dividends account was posted as a debit to Common Stock.
h. A $100 purchase of supplies on account was neither journalized nor posted.
i. A $6,400 credit to Service Revenue was not posted.
j. Office furniture should be listed in the amount of $1,300.

DOLE TRANSIT SERVICE, INC.
Trial Balance
October 31, 19X1

Cash	$ 3,800	
Accounts receivable	2,000	
Supplies	500	
Office furniture	2,300	
Delivery equipment	46,000	
Accounts payable		$ 2,000
Note payable		18,300
Common stock		29,500
Dividends	3,700	
Service revenue		4,900
Salary expense	1,000	
Rent expense	600	
Advertising expense	400	
Utilities expense	200	
Property tax expense	100	
Total	$60,600	$54,700

Required

Prepare the correct trial balance at October 31. Journal entries are not required.

Recording transactions directly in the ledger and preparing a trial balance
(Obj. 5, 7)

P2-9A Sandy Saxe obtained a corporate charter from the state of Ohio and started Cable-Vision, Inc. During the first month of operations (January 19X7), the business completed the following selected transactions:

a. Saxe began the business with an investment of $10,000 cash and a building valued at $50,000. The corporation issued common stock to Saxe.
b. Borrowed $35,000 from the bank; signed a note payable.
c. Paid $32,000 for transmitting equipment.
d. Purchased office supplies on account, $400.
e. Paid employees' salaries, $1,300.

f. Received $500 for cable TV service performed for customers.
g. Sold cable service to customers on account, $1,800.
h. Paid $100 of the account payable created in Transaction d.
i. Received a $600 bill for utility expense that will be paid in the near future.
j. Received cash on account, $1,100.
k. Paid the following cash expenses:
   (1) Rent on land, $1,000.
   (2) Advertising, $800.
l. Declared and paid dividends of $2,600.

Required

1. Open the following T-accounts: Cash, Accounts Receivable, Office Supplies, Transmitting Equipment, Building, Accounts Payable, Note Payable, Common Stock, Dividends, Service Revenue, Salary Expense, Rent Expense, Advertising Expense, and Utilities Expense.
2. Record the foregoing transactions directly in the T-accounts without using a journal. Use the letters to identify the transactions.
3. Prepare the trial balance of CableVision, Inc., at January 31, 19X7.

(GROUP B)

Analyzing a trial balance
(Obj. 1)

P2-1B The owners of ReliaStar Financial Services are selling the business. They offer the following trial balance to prospective buyers.

Your best friend is considering buying ReliaStar. She seeks your advice in interpreting this information. Specifically, she asks whether this trial balance is the same as a balance sheet and an income statement. She also wonders whether ReliaStar is a sound company. After all, the accounts are in balance.

RELIASTAR FINANCIAL SERVICES
Trial Balance
December 31, 19XX

Cash	$ 12,000	
Accounts receivable	87,000	
Prepaid expenses	4,000	
Land	181,000	
Accounts payable		$ 85,000
Note payable		92,000
Common stock		10,000
Retained earnings		50,000
Dividends	18,000	
Service revenue		124,000
Rent expense	26,000	
Advertising expense	3,000	
Wage expense	23,000	
Supplies expense	7,000	
	$361,000	$361,000

Required

Write a memo to answer your friend's questions. To aid her decision, state how she can use the information on the trial balance to compute ReliaStar's net income or net loss for the current period. State the amount of net income or net loss in your note.

Analyzing transactions using the accounting equation and preparing the financial statements
(Obj. 2)

P2-2B Samir Abel operates and is the major stockholder of an interior design studio called Abel Designers, Inc. The following amounts summarize the financial position of the business on April 30, 19X5:

	Assets							=	Liabilities	+	Stockholders' Equity		
	Cash	+	Accounts Receivable	+	Supplies	+	Land	=	Accounts Payable	+	Common Stock	+	Retained Earnings
Bal.	1,720		2,240				24,100		5,400		10,000		12,660

During May 19X5, the following events occurred:

a. Abel received $12,000 as a gift and deposited the cash in the business bank account. The business issued common stock to Abel.

b. Paid off the beginning balance of accounts payable.

c. Performed services for a client and received cash of $1,100.

d. Collected cash from a customer on account, $750.

e. Purchased supplies on account, $720.

f. Consulted on the interior design of a major office building and billed the client for services rendered, $5,000.

g. Received cash of $1,700 and issued common stock to Abel.

h. Recorded the following business expenses for the month:

(1) Paid office rent—$1,200. **(2)** Paid advertising—$660.

i. Sold supplies to another interior designer for $80 cash, which was the cost of the supplies.

j. Declared and paid a cash dividend of $2,400.

Required

1. Analyze the effects of the preceding transactions on the accounting equation of Abel Designers, Inc. Adapt the format of Exhibit 2-1, Panel B.
2. Prepare the income statement of Abel Designers, Inc., for the month ended May 31, 19X5. List expenses in decreasing order by amount.
3. Prepare the statement of retained earnings of Abel Designers, Inc., for the month ended May 31, 19X5.
4. Prepare the balance sheet of Abel Designers, Inc., at May 31.
5. As the manager of Abel Designers, how will you use the information from the income statement and the balance sheet to manage the business? Be specific.

Recording transactions, posting
(Obj. 3, 4)

P2-3B This problem should be used only in conjunction with Problem 2-2B. Refer to Problem 2-2B.

Required

1. Journalize the transactions of Abel Designers, Inc. Explanations are not required.
2. Set up the following T-accounts: Cash, Accounts Receivable, Supplies, Land, Accounts Payable, Common Stock, Retained Earnings, Dividends, Service Revenue, Rent Expense, Advertising Expense. Insert in each account its balance as given (example: Cash $1,720). Post to the accounts. Posting references are not required.
3. Compute the balance in each account. For each asset account, each liability account, and for Common Stock, compare its balance to the ending balance you obtained in Problem 2-2B. Are the amounts the same or different? (In Chapter 3, we will complete the accounting process. There you will learn how the Retained Earnings, Dividends, Revenue, and Expense accounts work together in the processing of accounting information.)

Analyzing transactions using the accounting equation
(Obj. 2, 3)

P2-4B Felicia Blair practiced law with a large firm, a partnership, for ten years after graduating from law school. Recently, she resigned her position to open her own law office, which she operates as a professional corporation. The name of the new entity is Felicia Blair, Attorney and Counselor, Professional Corporation (P.C.). Blair experienced the following events during the organizing phase of her new business and its first month of operations. Some of the events were personal and did not affect the law practice. Others were business transactions and should be accounted for by the business.

July 1 Blair sold 1,000 shares of Eastman Kodak stock, which she had owned for several years, receiving $88,000 cash from her stockbroker.

2 Blair deposited in her personal bank account the $88,000 cash from sale of the Eastman Kodak stock.

3 Blair received $150,000 cash from her former partners in the law firm from which she resigned.

5 Blair deposited $140,000 cash in a new business bank account entitled Felicia Blair, Attorney and Counselor, P.C. The business issued common stock to Blair.

6 A representative of a large company telephoned Blair and told her of the company's intention to transfer its legal business to the new entity of Felicia Blair, Attorney and Counselor, P.C.

7 The business paid $550 cash for letterhead stationery for the law office.

9 The business purchased office furniture for the law office. Blair paid cash of $10,000 and agreed to pay the account payable for the remainder, $9,500, within three months.

July 23 Blair finished court hearings on behalf of a client and submitted her bill for legal services, $3,000. She expected to collect from this client within one month.
29 The business paid $5,000 of its account payable on the furniture purchased on July 9.
30 The business paid office rent, $1,900.
31 The business declared and paid a cash dividend of $500.

Required

1. Classify each of the preceding events as one of the following:
   - **a.** A business transaction to be accounted for by the business of Felicia Blair, Attorney and Counselor, P.C.
   - **b.** A business-related event but not a transaction to be accounted for by the business of Felicia Blair, Attorney and Counselor, P.C.
   - **c.** A personal transaction not to be accounted for by the business of Felicia Blair, Attorney and Counselor, P.C.
2. Analyze the effects of the above events on the accounting equation of the business of Felicia Blair, Attorney and Counselor, P.C. Use a format similar to Exhibit 2-1, Panel B.
3. At the end of the first month of operations, Blair has a number of questions about the financial standing of the business. Explain to her:
   - **a.** How the business can have so much cash and so little in retained earnings.
   - **b.** How much in total resources the business has, how much it owes, and what Blair's ownership interest is in the assets of the business.
4. Record the transactions of the business in its journal. Include an explanation for each entry.

Analyzing and journalizing transactions
(Obj. 3, 4)

P2-5B Casa Linda Theater Company owns movie theaters in the shopping centers of a major metropolitan area. The business engaged in the following business transactions:

Feb. 1 Received cash of $30,000 and issued common stock to the investor.
2 Paid $20,000 cash and signed a $30,000 note payable to purchase land for a theater site.
5 Borrowed $180,000 from the bank to finance the construction of the new theater. Signed a note payable to the bank.
7 Received $15,000 cash from ticket sales and deposited that amount in the bank. (Label the revenue as Sales Revenue.)
10 Purchased theater supplies on account, $1,700.
15 Paid employees' salaries, $2,800, and rent on a theater building, $1,800.
15 Paid property tax expense, $1,200.
16 Paid $800 on account.
17 Declared and paid a cash dividend of $3,000.

Casa Linda uses the following accounts: Cash, Supplies, Land, Accounts Payable, Notes Payable, Common Stock, Dividends, Sales Revenue, Salary Expense, Rent Expense, and Property Tax Expense.

Required

1. Journalize each transaction. Explanations are not required.
2. After these transactions, how much cash does the business have? How much does it owe in total?

Journalizing transactions, posting to T-accounts, and preparing a trial balance
(Obj. 3, 4, 5)

P2-6B Annie Todd opened a law office on September 3 of the current year. During the first month of operations, the business completed the following transactions:

Sep. 3 Todd transferred $20,000 cash from her personal bank account to a business account entitled Annie Todd, Attorney, Professional Corporation (P.C.). The corporation issued common stock to Todd.
4 Purchased supplies, $200, and furniture, $1,800, on account.
6 Performed legal services for a client and received $1,000 cash.
7 Paid $15,000 cash to acquire land for a future office site.
10 Defended a client in court, billed the client, and received his promise to pay the $600 within one week.
14 Paid for the furniture purchased September 4 on account.
15 Paid secretary's salary, $600.
16 Paid the telephone bill, $120.
17 Received partial payment from client on account, $500.
20 Prepared legal documents for a client on account, $800.
24 Paid the water and electricity bills, $110.
28 Received $1,500 cash for helping a client sell real estate.

Sep. 30 Paid secretary's salary, $600.
30 Paid rent expense, $500.
30 Declared and paid dividends of $2,400.

Required

Open the following T-accounts: Cash, Accounts Receivable, Supplies, Furniture, Land, Accounts Payable, Common Stock, Dividends, Service Revenue, Salary Expense, Rent Expense, and Utilities Expense.

1. Record each transaction in the journal, using the account titles given. Key each transaction by date. Explanations are not required.
2. Post the transactions to the ledger, using transaction dates as posting references in the ledger. Label the ending balance of each account Bal., as shown in the chapter.
3. Prepare the trial balance of Annie Todd, Attorney, P.C., at September 30 of the current year.
4. How will what you learned in this problem help you manage a business?

Journalizing transactions, posting to accounts in four-column format, and preparing a trial balance ***(Obj. 3, 4, 5)***

P2-7B The trial balance of the accounting practice of Stewart Brand, CPA, Professional Corporation (P.C.), is dated February 14, 19X3.

STEWART BRAND, CPA, P.C.
Trial Balance
February 14, 19X3

Account Number	Account	Debit	Credit
11	Cash	$12,000	
12	Accounts receivable	8,000	
13	Supplies	1,400	
14	Land	18,600	
21	Accounts payable		$ 3,000
31	Common stock		10,000
32	Retained earnings		25,600
33	Dividends	1,200	
41	Service revenue		7,200
51	Salary expense	3,600	
52	Rent expense	800	
53	Utilities expense	200	
	Total	$45,800	$45,800

During the rest of February, the business completed the following transactions:

Feb. 15 Collected $2,000 cash from a client on account.
16 Performed tax services for a client on account, $900.
18 Paid utilities, $300.
20 Paid on account, $1,000.
21 Purchased supplies on account, $100.
21 Declared and paid dividends of $1,200.
21 Paid for a swimming pool for private residence, using personal funds, $13,000.
22 Received cash of $2,100 for audit work just completed.
28 Paid rent, $800.
28 Paid employees' salaries, $1,600.

Required

1. Record the transactions that occurred during February 15 through 28 in Page 3 of the journal. Include an explanation for each entry.
2. Open the ledger accounts listed in the trial balance, together with their balances at February 14. Use the four-column account format (with a running balance) illustrated in the chapter. Enter Bal. (for previous balance) in the Item column, and place a check mark (✓) in the Journal Reference column for the February 14 balance in each account. Post the transactions to the ledger, using dates, account numbers, journal references, and posting references.
3. Prepare the trial balance of Stewart Brand, CPA, P.C., at February 28, 19X3.

P2-8B The following trial balance for Enrico Consulting Service, Inc., does not balance.

Correcting errors in a trial balance ***(Obj. 5)***

ENRICO CONSULTING SERVICE, INC.
Trial Balance
June 30, 19X2

Cash	$ 2,000	
Accounts receivable	10,000	
Supplies	900	
Office furniture	13,600	
Land	25,000	
Accounts payable		$ 4,000
Note payable		14,000
Common stock		10,000
Retained earnings		18,600
Dividends	2,000	
Service revenue		6,500
Salary expense	1,600	
Rent expense	1,000	
Advertising expense	500	
Utilities expense	300	
Property tax expense	100	
Total	$57,000	$53,100

The following errors were detected:

a. The cash balance is understated by $300.
b. Property tax expense of $500 was not recorded.
c. Land should be listed in the amount of $23,000.
d. A $200 purchase of supplies on account was neither journalized nor posted.
e. A $3,400 credit to Service Revenue was not posted.
f. Rent expense of $200 was posted as a credit rather than a debit.
g. The balance of Advertising Expense is $600, but it was listed as $500 on the trial balance.
h. A $300 debit to Accounts Receivable was posted as $30.
i. The balance of Utilities Expense is overstated by $70.
j. A $900 debit to the Dividends account was posted as a debit to Common Stock.

Required

Prepare the correct trial balance at June 30. Journal entries are not required.

P2-9B Cary Boswell obtained a corporate charter from the state of New York and started a counseling service. During the first month of operations (June 19X3), the business completed the following selected transactions.

Recording transactions directly in the ledger and preparing a trial balance ***(Obj. 5, 7)***

a. Boswell began the business with an investment of $3,000 cash and a building valued at $60,000. The corporation issued common stock to Boswell.
b. Borrowed $30,000 from the bank; signed a note payable.
c. Purchased office supplies on account, $1,300.
d. Paid $18,000 for office furniture.
e. Paid employees' salaries, $2,200.
f. Performed counseling service on account for a client, $2,100.
g. Paid $800 of the account payable created in Transaction c.
h. Received a $600 bill for advertising expense that will be paid in the near future.
i. Performed counseling service for clients and received cash, $1,100.
j. Received cash on account, $1,200.
k. Paid the following cash expenses:
(1) Rent on land, $700. **(2)** Utilities, $400.
l. Declared and paid dividends of $3,500.

Required

1. Open the following T-accounts: Cash, Accounts Receivable, Office Supplies, Office Furniture, Building, Accounts Payable, Note Payable, Common Stock, Dividends, Service Revenue, Salary Expense, Advertising Expense, Rent Expense, Utilities Expense.
2. Record each transaction directly in the T-accounts without using a journal. Use the letters to identify the transactions.
3. Prepare the trial balance of Boswell Counseling Service, Inc., at June 30, 19X3.

EXTENDING YOUR KNOWLEDGE

DECISION CASES

Recording transactions directly in the ledger, preparing a trial balance, and measuring net income or loss ***(Obj. 5, 7)***

Case 1. You have been requested by a friend named Don Hunter to give advice on the effects that certain business transactions will have on the entity he has started. Time is short, so you will not be able to do all the detailed procedures of journalizing and posting. Instead, you must analyze the transactions without the use of a journal. Hunter will continue the business only if it can be expected to earn monthly net income of $5,000. The following transactions have occurred this month:

a. Hunter deposited $1,000 cash in a business bank account, and the corporation issued common stock to Hunter.
b. Borrowed $4,000 cash from the bank and signed a note payable due within one year.
c. Paid $300 cash for supplies.
d. Purchased advertising in the local newspaper for cash, $800.
e. Purchased office furniture on account, $4,400.
f. Paid the following cash expenses for one month: secretary's salary, $1,400; office rent, $600; utilities, $300; interest, $50.
g. Earned revenue on account, $5,300.
h. Earned revenue and received $2,500 cash.
i. Collected cash from customers on account, $1,200.
j. Paid on account, $1,000.
k. Declared and paid dividends of $900.

Required

1. Open the following T-accounts: Cash, Accounts Receivable, Supplies, Furniture, Accounts Payable, Notes Payable, Common Stock, Dividends, Service Revenue, Salary Expense, Advertising Expense, Rent Expense, Utilities Expense, and Interest Expense.
2. Record the transactions directly in the accounts without using a journal. Key each transaction by letter.
3. Prepare a trial balance at the current date. List expenses with the largest amount first, the next largest amount second, and so on. The business name will be Hunter Profiles, Inc.
4. Compute the amount of net income or net loss for this first month of operations. Would you recommend that Hunter continue in business? Why or why not?

Analyzing unusual transactions ***(Obj. 7)***

Case 2 Campbell Camps, Inc., conducts summer camps for children with diabetes. Because of the nature of its business, Campbell experiences many unusual transactions. Evaluate each of the following transactions in terms of its effect on the business's income statement and balance sheet.

a. A camper suffered an injury that was not covered by insurance. Campbell paid $320 for the child's medical care. How does this transaction affect the income statement and the balance sheet?
b. Campbell sold land adjacent to the camp for cash of $190,000. When purchased five years earlier, the land cost Campbell $120,000. How should Campbell account for the sale of the land?
c. Some campers cannot pay their fees, so Campbell solicits donations for camp scholarships. Because the business is organized to earn a profit, donation receipts are treated as revenue. How should Campbell account for a donation receipt of a small building valued at $45,000?
d. One camper's mother is a physician. Campbell allows this child to attend camp in return for the mother's serving part-time in the camp infirmary for the two-week term. The standard fee for a camp term is $600. The physician's salary for this part-time work would be $600. How should Campbell account for this arrangement?
e. Camp counselors build playground equipment during their off-duty hours. If Campbell had purchased this equipment, it would have cost $2,000. But counselors are paid only

their room, board, and transportation to and from camp. Should this equipment be included in Campbell's financial statements? If so, where, and at what dollar amount?

Understanding debits and credits **(Obj. 3)**

Case 3. Although the following questions deal with the accounting equation, they are not related:

a. When you deposit money in your bank account, the bank credits your account. Is the bank misusing the word *credit* in this context? Why does the bank use the term *credit* to refer to your deposit, and not *debit?*

b. Your friend asks, "When revenues increase assets and expenses decrease assets, why are revenues credits and expenses debits and not the other way around?" Explain to your friend why revenues are credits and expenses are debits.

ETHICAL ISSUE

Caritas, a charitable organization in Tucson, Arizona, has a standing agreement with Phoenix State Bank. The agreement allows Caritas to overdraw its cash balance at the bank when donations are running low. In the past, Caritas managed funds wisely and rarely used this privilege. Alex Mann has been named president of Caritas. To expand operations, he is acquiring office equipment and spending a lot for fund-raising. During his presidency, Caritas has maintained a negative bank balance of about $3,000.

Required

What is the ethical issue in this situation? Do you approve or disapprove of Mann's management of Caritas's and Phoenix State Bank's funds? Why?

FINANCIAL STATEMENT CASES

Journalizing transactions **(Obj. 3, 4)**

Case 1. This problem helps to develop skill in recording transactions by using an actual company's account titles. Refer to the Lands' End, Inc., financial statements in Appendix A. Assume that Lands' End completed the following selected transactions during March 1998:

Mar. 5 Earned sales revenue on account, $130,000.
9 Borrowed $500,000 by signing a note payable (long-term debt).
12 Purchased equipment on account, $240,000.
17 Paid $100,000, a current maturity of a long-term debt, plus interest expense of $8,000.
19 Earned sales revenue of $80,000 and immediately received cash of $16,000.
22 Collected the cash on account that was earned on March 5.
24 Paid rent of $24,000 for three months in advance.
28 Received a home-office electricity bill for $1,000, which will be paid in April (this is a general and administrative expense).
30 Paid off half the account payable created on March 12.

Required

Journalize these transactions, using the following account titles taken from the financial statements of Lands' End, Inc.: Cash, Receivables, Prepaid Expenses, Equipment, Current Maturities of Long-Term Debt, Accounts Payable, Long-Term Debt, Sales Revenue, Selling, General and Administrative Expense, and Interest Expense. Explanations are not required.

Journalizing transactions, preparing a trial balance **(Obj. 4, 5)**

Case 2. Obtain the annual report of a company of your choice. Assume that the company completed the following selected transactions during May of the current year:

May 3 Borrowed $350,000 by signing a short-term note payable (may be called *short-term debt* or other account title).
5 Paid rent for six months in advance, $4,600.
9 Earned revenue on account, $74,000.
12 Purchased equipment on account, $33,000.
17 Paid a telephone bill, $300. (This is Selling Expense.)
19 Paid $90,000 of the money borrowed on May 3.
26 Collected half the cash on account from May 9.
30 Paid the account payable from May 12.

Required

1. Journalize these transactions, using the company's actual account titles taken from its annual report. Explanations are not required.
2. Open a ledger account for each account that you used in journalizing the transactions. (For clarity, insert no actual balances in the accounts.) Post the transaction amounts to the accounts, using the dates as posting references. Take the balance of each account.
3. Prepare a trial balance.

GROUP PROJECTS

Project 1. You are promoting a rock concert in your area. Your purpose is to earn a profit, so you will need to establish the business. Assume you organize as a corporation.

Required

1. Make a detailed list of ten factors you must consider as you establish the business.
2. Describe ten of the items your business must arrange in order to promote and stage the rock concert.
3. Identify the transactions that your business will undertake to organize, promote, and stage the concert. Journalize the transactions, and post to the relevant T-accounts. Set up the accounts you will need for your business's ledger. Refer to the chapter appendix if needed.
4. Prepare the income statement, statement of retained earnings, balance sheet, and statement of cash flows immediately after the rock concert—that is, before you have had time to pay all the business's bills and to collect all receivables.
5. Assume that you will continue to promote rock concerts if the venture is successful. If it is unsuccessful, you will terminate the business within three months after the concert. Discuss how you will evaluate the success of your venture and how you will decide whether to continue in business.

Project 2. Contact a local business and arrange with the owner to learn what accounts the business uses.

Required

1. Obtain a copy of the business's chart of accounts.
2. Prepare the company's financial statements for the most recent month, quarter, or year. You may use either made-up account balances or balances supplied by the owner.

If the business has a large number of accounts within a category, combine related accounts and report a single amount on the financial statements. For example, the company may have several cash accounts. Combine all cash amounts and report a single Cash amount on the balance sheet.

You will probably encounter numerous accounts that you have not yet learned. Deal with these as best you can. The charts of accounts given in the appendix to this chapter will be helpful.

INTERNET EXERCISE

MAKING SENSE OF THE FINANCIAL STATEMENTS: THE MOTLEY FOOL

Information is the grease that makes the stock market run smoothly, and much of that information is readily available from companies whose stock is publicly traded. However, sorting through the avalanche of data can be overwhelming. The Internet has hundreds of sites that help investors understand the marketplace.

One such site, The Motley Fool, is geared to the financial novice. This site, started by two English majors, explains the basics of financial reporting in a straightforward and witty manner. What began as an investment newsletter has blossomed into a very popular interactive financial advice column. Located here are many valuable resources, including the latest in market research and financial news.

Required

1. Go to **http://www.fool.com/.** There you will find the Motley Fool's home page and a group of friendly icons that map out the Web site.
2. Click on **The 13 Steps.** The 13 steps to Investing Foolishly (The Motley Fool Approach) are presented.
3. Read the 13 steps to get a better sense of financial statements.
   - **a.** How do you get financial reports from a company?
   - **b.** What reports should you request from the company?
   - **c.** How does the annual report differ from a 10-K?
   - **d.** What is a 10-Q?
   - **e.** Why does the Motley Fool rely on analysts' reports?
   - **f.** How much does all of this information cost you?
   - **g.** To what key elements do the Motley Fools recommend you pay attention when reading financial reports?

APPENDIX TO CHAPTER 2

Typical Charts of Accounts for Different Types of Businesses

A SIMPLE SERVICE CORPORATION

Assets

Cash
Accounts Receivable
Allowance for Uncollectible Accounts
Notes Receivable, Short-Term
Interest Receivable
Supplies
Prepaid Rent
Prepaid Insurance
Notes Receivable, Long-Term
Land
Furniture
Accumulated Depreciation—Furniture
Equipment
Accumulated Depreciation—Equipment
Building
Accumulated Depreciation—Building

Liabilities

Accounts Payable
Notes Payable, Short-Term
Salary Payable
Wage Payable
Employee Income Tax Payable
FICA Tax Payable
State Unemployment Tax Payable
Federal Unemployment Tax Payable
Employee Benefits Payable
Interest Payable
Unearned Service Revenue
Notes Payable, Long-Term

Stockholders' Equity

Common Stock
Retained Earnings
Dividends

Revenues and Gains

Service Revenue
Interest Revenue
Gain on Sale of Land (Furniture, Equipment, or Building)

Expenses and Losses

Salary Expense
Payroll Tax Expense
Insurance Expense for Employees
Rent Expense
Insurance Expense
Supplies Expense
Uncollectible Account Expense
Depreciation Expense—Furniture
Depreciation Expense—Equipment
Depreciation Expense—Building
Property Tax Expense
Interest Expense
Miscellaneous Expense
Loss on Sale (or Exchange) of Land (Furniture, Equipment, or Building)

SERVICE PARTNERSHIP

Same as service corporation, except for owners' equity:

Owners' Equity

Partner 1, Capital
Partner 2, Capital
⋮
Partner *N*, Capital

Partner 1, Drawing
Partner 2, Drawing
⋮
Partner *N*, Drawing

A COMPLEX MERCHANDISING CORPORATION

Assets

Cash
Short-Term Investments (Trading Securities)
Accounts Receivable
Allowance for Uncollectible Accounts
Notes Receivable, Short-Term
Interest Receivable
Inventory
Supplies
Prepaid Rent
Prepaid Insurance
Notes Receivable, Long-Term
Investments in Subsidiaries
Investments in Stock (Available-for-Sale Securities)
Investments in Bonds (Held-to-Maturity Securities)
Other Receivables, Long-Term
Land
Land Improvements
Furniture & Fixtures
Accumulated Depreciation—Furniture & Fixtures
Equipment
Accumulated Depreciation—Equipment
Buildings
Accumulated Depreciation—Buildings
Organization Cost
Franchises
Patents
Leaseholds
Goodwill

Liabilities

Accounts Payable
Notes Payable, Short-Term
Current Portion of Bonds Payable
Salary Payable
Wage Payable
Employee Income Tax Payable
FICA Tax Payable
State Unemployment Tax Payable
Federal Unemployment Tax Payable
Employee Benefits Payable
Interest Payable
Income Tax Payable
Unearned Sales Revenue
Notes Payable, Long-Term
Bonds Payable
Lease Liability
Minority Interest

Stockholder's Equity

Preferred Stock
Paid-in Capital in Excess of Par—Preferred
Common Stock
Paid-in Capital in Excess of Par—Common
Paid-in Capital from Treasury Stock Transactions
Paid-in Capital from Retirement of Stock
Retained Earnings
Foreign Currency Translation Adjustment
Treasury Stock

Revenues and Gains

Sales Revenue
Interest Revenue
Dividend Revenue
Equity-Method Investment Revenue
Unrealized Holding Gain on Trading Investments
Gain on Sale of Investments
Gain on Sale of Land (Furniture & Fixtures, Equipment, or Buildings)
Discontinued Operations—Gain
Extraordinary Gains

Expenses and Losses

Cost of Goods Sold
Salary Expense
Wage Expense
Commission Expense
Payroll Tax Expense
Insurance Expense for Employees
Rent Expense
Insurance Expense
Supplies Expense
Uncollectible Account Expense
Depreciation Expense—Land Improvements
Depreciation Expense—Furniture & Fixtures
Depreciation Expense—Equipment
Depreciation Expense—Buildings
Organization Expense
Amortization Expense—Franchises
Amortization Expense—Leaseholds
Amortization Expense—Goodwill
Income Tax Expense
Unrealized Holding Loss on Trading Investments
Loss on Sale of Investments
Loss on Sale (or Exchange) of Land (Furniture & Fixtures, Equipment, or Buildings)
Discontinued Operations—Loss
Extraordinary Losses

A MANUFACTURING CORPORATION

Same as merchandising corporation, except for Assets:

Assets

Inventories:
- Materials Inventory
- Work-in-Process Inventory
- Finished Goods Inventory

3

Accrual Accounting and the Financial Statements

Learning Objectives

After studying this chapter, you should be able to

1. Distinguish accrual-basis accounting from cash-basis accounting
2. Apply the revenue and matching principles
3. Make adjusting entries at the end of the accounting period and prepare an adjusted trial balance
4. Prepare the financial statements
5. Close the revenue, expense, and dividends accounts
6. Correct typical accounting errors
7. Use the current ratio and the debt ratio to evaluate a business

It's Just Lunch, Inc.
Income Statement
Year Ended December 31, 1996

Net revenues		$4,453,363
Expenses		
Payroll	$1,446,637	
Advertising/marketing	1,388,150	
Office	887,220	
Professional fees	119,179	
Insurance	85,080	
Depreciation	32,501	
Interest	20,579	
Miscellaneous	63,451	
Total expenses		4,042,797
Net income		$ 410,566

"None of my competitors had the low-tech, high level of personal service I was looking for."

—ANDREA MCGINTY, PRESIDENT AND FOUNDER, IT'S JUST LUNCH

Disappointed by blind dates, personal ads, and video dating services, Andrea McGinty started her own matchmaking firm and found a lucrative career.

In 1991, Andrea McGinty's fiancé walked out on her five weeks before the wedding. It was back to the singles scene for the 29-year-old Chicago-based marketing manager for a California jewelry firm.

One blind date threw a pizza against the wall when she got up to leave. Personal ads didn't do much, either. There *had* to be a more civilized and convenient way to meet potential partners, McGinty thought. Wouldn't it be nice if there were a dating service that arranged prescreened lunch dates for busy professionals like herself? "Lunch is over in an hour, and you don't have to kiss goodnight," she dreamed.

McGinty followed her dream. Her company, **It's Just Lunch,** now has 6,000 customers and chalked up $4.5 million in revenues in 1996. McGinty charges $675 for arranging eight dates. Lunch is extra, dutch treat. "These are people who spent their 20s in graduate school, then working long hours in fast-track careers. Now they need help with their social lives," says McGinty.

The business is a cash machine, netting $400,000 after taxes in 1996 on revenues of $4.5 million. McGinty has 21 employees, and her second biggest expense is advertising. She pays herself a $180,000 salary, double what she was making selling jewelry.

Source: *Adapted from Suzanne Oliver, "Yuppie Yenta,"* Forbes *(March 25, 1996), pp. 102–103.*

What do we mean when we say that It's Just Lunch *nets* $400,000 per year? The business earns net income, or profit, of more than $400,000 per year, as reported on its income statement. What are the business's revenues? Service revenue fees of $675 per client to arrange eight lunch dates. What are the business's expenses? Advertising, computer data searches, mailings to clients, and office expenses (such as employee salaries, rent, supplies, depreciation on office furniture, and computers and other office equipment). It's Just Lunch operates in much the same way as Air & Sea Travel, the travel agency we studied in Chapters 1 and 2.

Whether the business is It's Just Lunch, Air & Sea Travel, IBM, or Lands' End, the profit motive increases the owners' drive to start and carry on the business. As you study this chapter, consider how important net income is to a business and how the pursuit of profit affects people's behavior.

How does a business know whether it is profitable or not? By preparing its financial statements. This chapter completes the **accounting cycle,** the process that begins with recording transactions (which we studied in Chapter 2) and ends with the financial statements that help measure profits and losses.

The entity prepares its financial statements at the end of each accounting period. The period may be a month, three months, six months, or a full year. Whatever the length of the period, the end accounting product is the financial statements. And the most important amount reported in these statements is the net income or net loss (the profit or loss) for the period. Net income captures much information: total revenues minus total expenses for the period. In essence, net income (or net loss) measures the ability of the business to generate revenues from its outputs (products or services) that exceed the costs of its inputs (merchandise, employee labor, supplies, utilities, and so on). A business that consistently earns net income, like It's Just Lunch, increases the value of the business for its owners, its employees, its customers, and society. The business is able to pay its debts. Net income captures these important aspects of a business.

The trial balance, introduced in Chapter 2, page 74, lists the ledger accounts and their balances.

An important step in financial statement preparation is the trial balance. The account balances in the trial balance include the effects of the transactions that occurred during the period—cash collections, purchases of assets, payments of bills, sales of assets, and so on. To measure its income, however, a business must do some additional accounting at the end of the period to update its records before preparing the financial statements. This process is called *adjusting the books,* and it consists of making special entries, called *adjusting entries,* that are needed to measure business income and generate accurate financial statements. This chapter also covers the process of closing the books at the end of the period.

The accounting profession has concepts and principles to guide the measurement of business income. Chief among these are the concepts of accrual-basis accounting, the time-period concept, the revenue principle, and the matching principle. In this chapter, we apply these and other concepts and principles to measure the income and prepare the financial statements of Air & Sea Travel, Inc., for the month of April.

Accrual-Basis Accounting Versus Cash-Basis Accounting

Objective 1

Distinguish accrual-basis accounting from cash-basis accounting

There are two widely used bases of accounting: the accrual basis and the cash basis. In **accrual-basis accounting,** an accountant recognizes the impact of a business event as it occurs. When the business performs a service, makes a sale, or incurs an expense, the accountant enters the transaction into the books, whether or not cash has been received or paid. In **cash-basis accounting,** the accountant does not record a transaction until cash is received or paid. Cash receipts are treated as revenues, and cash payments are handled as expenses.

Four Seasons Hotels and Resorts, which operates nearly 40 luxury properties worldwide and serves 3.1 million guests a year, uses accrual-basis accounting.

Suppose a client paid the **Four Seasons Hotel** in New York City $15,000 on October 1, 1998, for a six-month stay to begin immediately. Exhibit 3-1 shows how the hotel would record this revenue over the six-month period from October 1, 1998, through March 31, 1999, by the two methods of accounting. In actuality, Four Seasons Hotels and Resorts, which operates nearly 40 luxury properties worldwide and serves 3.1 million guests a year, uses accrual-basis accounting.

GAAP requires that businesses use the accrual basis. This means that the business records revenues as they are *earned* and expenses as they are *incurred*—not necessarily when cash changes hands.

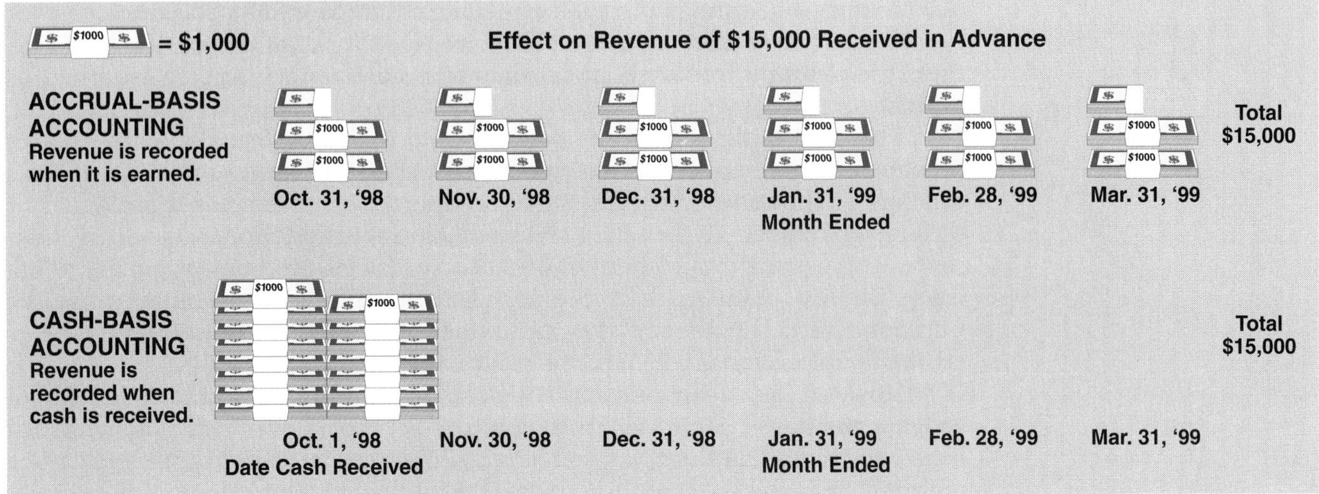

EXHIBIT 3-1
Accrual-Basis Accounting Versus Cash-Basis Accounting

Using accrual-basis accounting, It's Just Lunch would record revenue when it provides a list of dates to a client, not when it collects cash. Air & Sea Travel records revenue when the business performs services for a client on account. The travel agency has earned the revenue at that time because its efforts have generated an account receivable, a legal claim against the client for whom it did the work. In contrast, if Air & Sea used cash-basis accounting, it would not record revenue at the time the business performed the service. It would wait until it received cash.

Why do generally accepted accounting principles require use of the accrual basis? What advantage does accrual-basis accounting offer? Suppose Air & Sea's accounting period ends after it earned some revenue but before it has collected the money. If it used the cash-basis method, its financial statements would not include this revenue or the related account receivable. As a result, the financial statements would be misleading: Revenue and the asset Accounts Receivable would be understated, so the business would look less successful than it actually is. If Air & Sea needs a bank loan to expand, the understated revenue and asset figures might hurt its chances.

Using accrual-basis accounting, Air & Sea Travel also records expenses as they are incurred. For instance, salary expense includes amounts paid to employees plus any amount owed to employees but not yet paid. Air & Sea Travel's use of an employee's service, not the payment of cash to the employee, brings about the expense.

Under cash-basis accounting, a business records salary expense only when it actually pays the employee. Suppose Air & Sea owed a travel agent a salary, and the financial statements were drawn up before the business paid that salary. Expenses and liabilities would be understated, so Air & Sea would look more successful than it really is. This incomplete information would give potential creditors an inaccurate accounting.

As these examples show, accrual-basis accounting provides more complete information than cash-basis accounting does. This difference is important because the more complete the data, the better equipped decision makers are to reach conclusions about the firm's financial health and future prospects. Three concepts used in accrual-basis accounting are the time-period concept, the revenue principle, and the matching principle.

The Time-Period Concept

The only way for a business to know for certain how successfully it has operated is to close its doors, sell all its assets, pay the liabilities, and return any leftover cash to the owners. This process, called *liquidation,* means going out of business. Obviously, it is not practical for accountants to measure business income in this manner. Instead, businesses need periodic reports on their progress.

Accountants slice time into small segments and prepare financial statements for specific periods. Until a business sells all its assets for cash and pays all its liabilities, the amounts reported in its financial statements must be regarded as estimates.

The most basic accounting period is one year, and virtually all businesses prepare annual financial statements. For about 60% of large companies in a recent survey, the annual accounting period runs the calendar year from January 1 through December 31. Retailers are a notable exception. For instance, **JC Penney Company** and most other retailers use a fiscal year ending on January 31 because the low point in their business activity falls during January after the Christmas sales. JC Penney does more than 30% of its yearly sales during November and December but only 5% in January.

However, managers and investors cannot wait until the end of the year to gauge a company's progress. Thus, companies prepare financial statements for *interim* periods, which are less than a year. Publicly owned companies must issue quarterly financial statements. Managers want financial information more often, so monthly statements are common. A series of monthly statements can be combined for quarterly and semiannual periods. Most of the discussions in this text are based on an annual accounting period, but the procedures and statements can be applied to interim periods as well.

The **time-period concept** ensures that accounting information is reported at regular intervals. To measure income accurately, companies update the revenue and expense accounts immediately before the end of the accounting period. **Avon Products, Inc.,** the cosmetics company, provides an example of an expense accrual. At December 31, 1994, Avon recorded employee compensation of $100 million, which the company owed its workers for unpaid services performed before year end. The company's accrual entry was

1994			
Dec. 31	Salary and Wage Expense	100,000,000	
	Salary and Wage Payable...........		100,000,000

This entry serves two purposes. First, it assigns the expense to the proper period. Without the accrual entry at December 31, total expenses for 1994 would be understated, and as a result, net income would be overstated. The expense would incorrectly fall in 1995 when the company makes the next payroll disbursement. Second, the accrual entry also records the liability for reporting on the balance sheet at December 31, 1994. Without the accrual entry, total liabilities would be understated.

At the end of the accounting period, companies also accrue revenues that have been earned but not collected. We discuss these adjustments later in this chapter.

The Revenue Principle

Objective 2

Apply the revenue and matching principles

The **revenue principle** tells accountants (1) *when* to record revenue by making a journal entry, and (2) the *amount* of revenue to record. The act of "recording" (or recognizing) a transaction naturally leads to posting to the ledger accounts and preparing the trial balance and the financial statements. Although the financial statements are the end product of accounting and thus the documents that accountants and managers are most concerned about, our discussions often focus on recording the entry in the journal because that is where the accounting process starts.

Revenue, defined in Chapter 1, page 14, is the increase in retained earnings from delivering goods and services to customers in the course of operating a business.

The general principle guiding *when* to record revenue says to record revenue when it has been earned—but not before. In most cases, revenue is earned when the business has delivered a completed good or service to the customer. The business has done everything required by the agreement, and has transferred the good or service to the customer. Exhibit 3-2 shows two situations that provide guidance on when to record revenue. Situation 1 illustrates when *not* to record revenue.

EXHIBIT 3-2
Recording Revenue

Situation 2 illustrates when revenue should be recorded. If the client pays for Air & Sea Travel's service immediately, the business will debit Cash. If the service is performed on account, Air & Sea will debit Accounts Receivable. In either case, the travel agency should record revenue by crediting the Service Revenue account.

The general principle guiding the *amount* of revenue says to record revenue equal to the cash value of the goods or services transferred to the customer. Suppose that in order to obtain a new client, the Lyons perform travel service for the price of $500. Ordinarily, they would have charged $600 for this service. How much revenue should the business record? The answer is $500, the cash value of the transaction. Air & Sea Travel will not receive the full value of $600, so that is not the amount of revenue to record. The business will receive only $500 cash, which pinpoints the amount of revenue earned.

The Matching Principle

The **matching principle** is the basis for recording expenses. Recall that expenses, such as rent, utilities, and advertising, are the costs of operating a business. *Expenses* are the costs of assets that are used up in the earning of revenue. The matching principle directs accountants (1) to identify all expenses incurred during the accounting period, (2) to measure the expenses, and (3) to match the expenses against the revenues earned during that same period. To match expenses against revenues means to subtract the expenses from the revenues in order to compute net income or net loss for the period. Exhibit 3-3 illustrates the matching principle.

An expense, defined in Chapter 1, page 14, is a decrease in retained earnings that occurs in the course of operating a business.

There is a natural link between revenues and some types of expenses. Accountants follow the matching principle by first identifying a period's revenues and the expenses that can be linked to particular revenues. For example, a business that pays sales commissions to its sales personnel will have commission

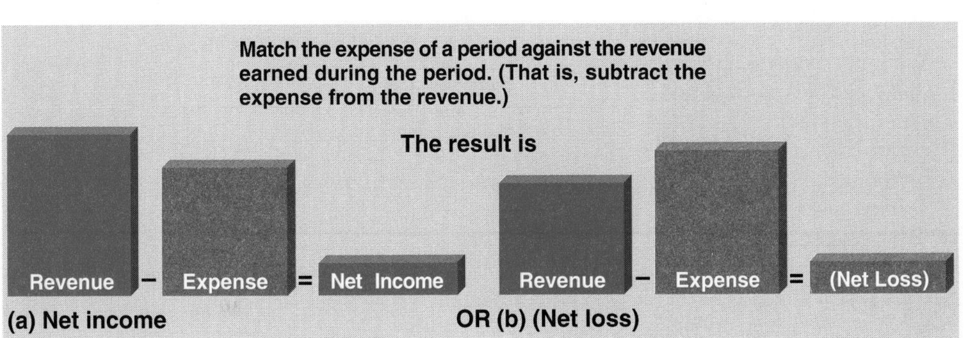

EXHIBIT 3-3
The Matching Principle

expense if the employees make sales. If they make no sales, the business has no commission expense. *Cost of goods sold* is another example. If there are no sales of women's suits, **Liz Claiborne, Inc.,** has no cost of goods sold.

Other expenses are not so easy to link with particular sales. Monthly rent expense occurs, for example, regardless of the revenues earned during the period. The matching principle directs accountants to identify these types of expenses with a particular time period, such as a month or a year. If Air & Sea Travel employs a secretary at a monthly salary of $1,900, the business will record salary expense of $1,900 at the end of each month.

STOP & THINK

1. A client pays Air & Sea $900 on March 15 for service to be performed April 1 to June 30. Has Air & Sea earned revenue on March 15?
2. Air & Sea Travel pays $4,500 on July 31 for office rent for the next three months. Has the company incurred an expense on July 31?

Answers

1. No. Air & Sea has received the cash but will not perform the service until later.
2. No. Air & Sea has paid cash, but the rent will not expire for three months. This prepaid rent is an asset because Air & Sea has the use of an office in the future.

Adjusting Entries

Objective 3

Make adjusting entries at the end of the accounting period

At the end of the period, the accountant prepares the financial statements. This end-of-period process begins with the trial balance, which lists the accounts and their balances after the period's transactions have been recorded in the journal and posted to the ledger. Exhibit 3-4 is the trial balance of Air & Sea Travel, Inc., at April 30, 19X1.

See Chapter 2, page 74, for a review of the trial balance.

This *unadjusted trial balance* includes some new accounts that we will explain here. It lists most, but not all, of the travel agency's revenue and expenses for the month of April. These trial balance amounts are incomplete because they omit certain revenue and expense transactions that affect more than one accounting period. This is why it is called an *unadjusted* trial balance. In most cases, however, we refer to it simply as the trial balance, without the label "unadjusted."

EXHIBIT 3-4
Unadjusted Trial Balance

AIR & SEA TRAVEL, INC.
Unadjusted Trial Balance
April 30, 19X1

Cash	$24,800	
Accounts receivable	2,250	
Supplies	700	
Prepaid rent	3,000	
Furniture	16,500	
Accounts payable		$13,100
Unearned service revenue		450
Common stock		20,000
Retained earnings		11,250
Dividends	3,200	
Service revenue		7,000
Salary expense	950	
Utilities expense	400	
Total	$51,800	$51,800

Under cash-basis accounting, there would be no need for adjustments to the accounts because all April cash transactions would have been recorded. The accrual basis requires adjusting entries at the end of the period to produce correct balances for the financial statements. To see why, consider the Supplies account in Exhibit 3-4.

Air & Sea Travel uses supplies in providing travel services for clients during the month. This use reduces the quantity of supplies on hand and thus constitutes an expense, just like salary expense or rent expense. Gary and Monica Lyon do not bother to record this expense daily, and it is not worth their while to record supplies expense more than once a month. It is time-consuming to make hourly, daily, or even weekly journal entries to record the expense for the use of supplies. So how does the business account for supplies expense?

By the end of the month, the Supplies balance is not correct. The amount on the trial balance represents the amount of supplies on hand at the start of the month plus any supplies purchased during the month. This balance fails to take into account the supplies used (supplies expense) during the accounting period. It is necessary to count the supplies on hand at the end of the period and, then, to adjust the supplies account to this amount. The resulting new adjusted balance measures the cost of supplies that are still on hand at April 30. This is the correct amount of supplies to report on the balance sheet. Adjusting the accounts in this way will bring the accounts up to date.

Adjusting entries assign revenues to the period in which they are earned and expenses to the period in which they are incurred. Adjusting entries also update the asset and liability accounts. They are needed (1) to measure properly the period's income, and (2) to bring related asset and liability accounts to correct balances for the financial statements. For example, an adjusting entry is needed to transfer the amount of supplies used during the period from the asset account Supplies to the expense account Supplies Expense. The adjusting entry updates both the Supplies asset account and the Supplies Expense account. This adjustment achieves accurate measures of assets and expenses. Adjusting entries, which are the key to accurate accrual-basic accounting, are made before the financial statements are prepared. The end-of-period process of updating the accounts is called *adjusting the accounts, making the adjusting entries,* or *adjusting the books.*

A large company would use accounting software to print out a trial balance. At **Occidental Petroleum (OXY),** a multidivisional oil and gas company, each division has its own accounting software that prints a monthly trial balance. The accountants then analyze the amounts on the trial balance, testing them for reasonableness and tracing the balances back to the ledger. If necessary, the accountants go back to the supporting documents that generated the transactions. This analysis results in the adjusting entries. Posting the adjusting entries updates the ledger accounts, and the new trial balance becomes the adjusted trial balance.

Adjusting entries can be divided into five categories:

1. Prepaid expenses
2. Depreciation of plant assets
3. Accrued expenses
4. Accrued revenues
5. Unearned revenues

Prepaid Expenses

Prepaid expenses, sometimes called **deferrals,** is a category of miscellaneous assets that typically expire or are used up in the near future. They are called "prepaid" expenses because they are expenses that are paid in advance. Prepaid rent and prepaid insurance are prepaid expenses. Salary expense and utilities expense, among others, are typically not prepaid expenses because they are not paid in advance. All companies, large and small, must make adjustments regarding prepaid expenses. For example, **McDonald's Corporation** must contend with such prepayments as rents, packaging supplies, and insurance.

LEARNING TIP Prepaid expenses are assets, not expenses.

PREPAID RENT Landlords usually require business tenants to pay rent in advance. This prepayment creates an asset for the renter because that business has purchased the future benefit of using the rented item. Suppose Air & Sea Travel prepays three months' rent on April 1, 19X1, after negotiating a lease for the business office. If the lease specifies a monthly rental amount of $1,000, the entry to record the payment for three months is a debit to the asset account, Prepaid Rent, as follows:

Apr. 1	Prepaid Rent ($1,000 × 3)	3,000	
	Cash		3,000
	Paid three months' rent in advance.		

ASSETS	=	LIABILITIES	+	STOCKHOLDERS' EQUITY
3,000 −3,000	=	0	+	0

After posting, Prepaid Rent appears as follows:

Prepaid Rent		
Apr. 1	3,000	

The trial balance at April 30, 19X1, lists Prepaid Rent as an asset with a debit balance of $3,000. Throughout April, the Prepaid Rent account maintains this beginning balance, as shown in Exhibit 3-4.

At April 30, Prepaid Rent should be adjusted to remove from its balance the amount of the asset that has expired, which is one month's worth of the prepayment. By definition, the amount of an asset that has expired is an *expense*. The adjusting entry transfers one-third, or $1,000 ($3,000 × ⅓), of the debit balance from Prepaid Rent to Rent Expense. The debit side of the entry records an increase in Rent Expense, and the credit records a decrease in the asset Prepaid Rent:

(Adjusting entry a)*

Apr. 30	Rent Expense ($3,000 × ⅓)	1,000	
	Prepaid Rent		1,000
	To record rent expense.		

ASSETS	=	LIABILITIES	+	STOCKHOLDERS' EQUITY	−	EXPENSES
−1,000	=	0			−	1,000

After posting, Prepaid Rent and Rent Expense appear as follows:

Prepaid Rent			
Apr. 1	3,000	Apr. 30	1,000
Bal.	2,000		

→

Rent Expense		
Apr. 30	1,000	
Bal.	1,000	

Correct asset amount: $2,000 → **Total accounted for: $3,000** ← **Correct expense amount: $1,000**

The full $3,000 has been accounted for: Two-thirds measure the asset, and one-third measures the expense. Recording this expense illustrates the matching

*See Exhibit 3-9, page 124, for a summary of all the adjustments a–g.

principle. The same analysis applies to a prepayment of three months' insurance premiums. The only difference is in the account titles, which would be Prepaid Insurance and Insurance Expense instead of Prepaid Rent and Rent Expense, respectively. In a computerized system, the adjusting entry crediting the prepaid account and debiting the expense account could be established to recur automatically in each subsequent accounting period until the prepaid account has a zero balance.

SUPPLIES Supplies are accounted for in the same way as prepaid expenses. On April 2, Air & Sea Travel paid cash of $700 for office supplies:

Apr. 2	Supplies	700	
	Cash		700
	Paid cash for supplies.		

ASSETS	=	LIABILITIES	+	STOCKHOLDERS' EQUITY
700 −700	=	0	+	0

Assume that the business purchased no additional supplies during April. The April 30 trial balance therefore lists Supplies with a $700 debit balance (Exhibit 3-4).

During April, Air & Sea Travel used supplies in performing services for clients. The cost of the supplies used is the measure of *supplies expense* for the month. To measure the business's supplies expense during April, the Lyons count the supplies on hand at the end of the month. This is the amount of the asset still available to the business. Assume that the count indicates that supplies costing $400 remain. Subtracting the entity's $400 supplies on hand at the end of April from the cost of supplies available during April ($700) measures supplies expense during the month ($300).

Cost of asset available during the period	−	**Cost of asset on hand at the end of the period**	=	**Cost of asset used (expense) during the period**
$700	−	**$400**	=	**$300**

The April 30 adjusting entry to update the Supplies account and to record the supplies expense for the month debits the expense and credits the asset:

Apr. 30	Supplies Expense ($700 – $400)	300		(Adjusting entry b)
	Supplies		300	
	To record supplies expense.			

ASSETS	=	LIABILITIES	+	STOCKHOLDERS' EQUITY	−	EXPENSES
−300	=	0			−	300

After posting, the Supplies and Supplies Expense accounts appear as follows:

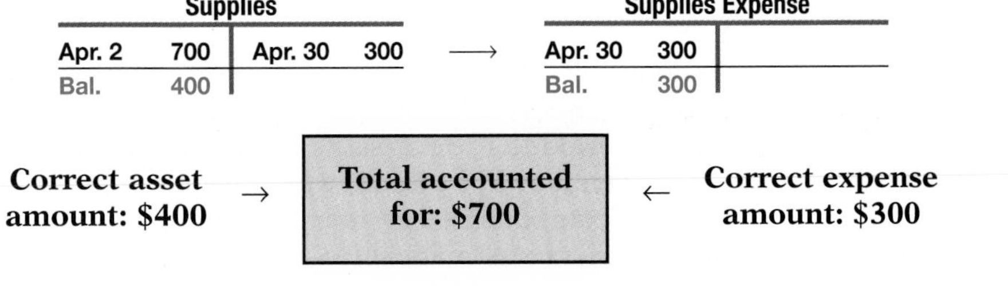

The Supplies account then enters the month of May with a $400 balance, and the adjustment process is repeated each month.

STOP & THINK At the beginning of the month, supplies were $5,000. During the month, $7,800 of supplies were purchased. At month's end, it was determined that $3,600 of supplies were still on hand. What are the adjusting entry and the ending balance in the Supplies account?

Answer

Supplies Expense ($5,000 + $7,800 – $3,600)	9,200	
Supplies		9,200

Ending balance of supplies = 3,600

Depreciation of Plant Assets

The logic behind accrual accounting is probably best illustrated by how businesses account for plant assets. **Plant assets** are long-lived tangible assets, such as land, buildings, furniture, machinery, and equipment used in the operations of the business. As one accountant said, "All assets but land are on a march to the junkyard." That is, all plant assets but land decline in usefulness as they age. This decline is an *expense* to the business. Accountants systematically spread the cost of each plant asset, except land, over the years of its useful life. This process of allocating cost to expense is called **depreciation.**

SIMILARITY TO PREPAID EXPENSES The concept underlying accounting for plant assets and depreciation expense is the same as for prepaid expenses. In a sense, plant assets are large prepaid expenses that expire over a number of periods. For both prepaid expenses and plant assets, the business purchases an asset that wears out or is used up. As the asset is used, more and more of its cost is transferred from the asset account to the expense account. The major difference between prepaid expenses and plant assets is the length of time it takes for the asset to lose its usefulness. Prepaid expenses usually expire within a year, while most plant assets remain useful for a number of years.

Consider Air & Sea Travel's operations. Suppose that on April 3 the business purchased furniture on account for $16,500:

Apr. 3	Furniture	16,500	
	Accounts Payable...		16,500
	Purchased office furniture on account.		

ASSETS	=	LIABILITIES	+	STOCKHOLDERS' EQUITY
16,500	=	16,500	+	0

After posting, the Furniture account appears as follows:

Furniture	
Apr. 3 16,500	

In accrual-basis accounting, an asset is recorded when the furniture is acquired. Then, a portion of the asset's cost is transferred from the asset account to Depreciation Expense each period that the asset is used. This method matches the asset's expense to the revenue of the period, which is an application of the matching principle. In many computerized systems, the adjusting entry for depreciation is programmed to occur automatically each month for the duration of the asset's life.

Gary and Monica Lyon believe the furniture will remain useful for five years and will be virtually worthless at the end of its life. One way to compute the amount of depreciation for each year is to divide the cost of the asset ($16,500 in our example) by its expected useful life (five years). This procedure—called the *straight-line method*—gives annual depreciation of $3,300 ($16,500/5 years = $3,300 per year). Depreciation for the month of April is $275 ($3,300/12 months = $275 per month). Chapter 7 covers depreciation and plant assets in more detail.

THE ACCUMULATED DEPRECIATION ACCOUNT Depreciation expense for April is recorded by the following entry:

Apr. 30	Depreciation Expense—Furniture	275		(Adjusting entry c)
	Accumulated Depreciation—Furniture		275	
	To record depreciation on furniture.			

ASSETS	=	LIABILITIES	+	STOCKHOLDERS' EQUITY	−	EXPENSES
−275	=	0			−	275

Accumulated Depreciation is credited instead of Furniture because the original cost of the plant asset (the furniture) is an objective measurement, and that amount remains in the original asset account as long as the business uses the asset. Accountants may refer to that account if they need to know how much the asset cost. This information may be useful in a decision about whether to replace the furniture and the amount to pay. The amount of depreciation, however, is an *estimate*. Accountants use the **Accumulated Depreciation** account to show the cumulative sum of all depreciation expense from the date of acquiring the asset. Therefore, the balance in this account increases over the life of the asset.

Accumulated Depreciation is a *contra asset* account, which means an asset account with a normal credit balance. A **contra account** has two distinguishing characteristics: (1) It always has a companion account, and (2) its normal balance is opposite that of the companion account. In this case, Accumulated Depreciation is the contra (companion) account to the asset account Furniture. It appears in the ledger directly after Furniture. Furniture has a debit balance, and therefore Accumulated Depreciation, a contra asset, has a credit balance. All contra asset accounts have credit balances. Note that in the accounting equation for this adjusting entry, we have *decreased* assets by $275, the amount credited to the contra asset account.

A business carries an accumulated depreciation account for each depreciable asset. If a business has a building and a machine, for example, it will carry the accounts Accumulated Depreciation—Building, and Accumulated Depreciation—Machine.

After the depreciation entry has been posted, the Furniture, Accumulated Depreciation, and Depreciation Expense accounts of Air & Sea Travel, Inc., are

Furniture

	Debit	Credit
Apr. 3	16,500	
Bal.	16,500	

Accumulated Depreciation—Furniture

Debit		Credit
	Apr. 30	275
	Bal.	275

Depreciation Expense—Furniture

	Debit	Credit
Apr. 30	275	
Bal.	275	

LEARNING TIP Use a separate Depreciation Expense account and Accumulated Depreciation account for each type of asset (Depreciation Expense—Furniture; Depreciation Expense—Buildings, and so on).

BOOK VALUE The net amount of a plant asset (cost minus accumulated depreciation) is called that asset's **book value,** *net book value,* or *carrying value,* as shown here for Air & Sea's Furniture account:

Plant Assets:	
Furniture	$16,500
Less Accumulated Depreciation	275
Book value	$16,225

Accumulated Depreciation is reported on the balance sheet with its companion account to determine the asset's book value.

Suppose the travel agency owns a building that cost $48,000 and on which annual depreciation is $2,400 ($48,000/20 years). The amount of depreciation for one month would be $200 ($2,400/12), and the following entry records depreciation for April:

Apr. 30	Depreciation Expense—Building	200	
	Accumulated Depreciation—Building		200
	To record depreciation on building.		

ASSETS	=	LIABILITIES	+	STOCKHOLDERS' EQUITY	−	EXPENSES
−200	=	0			−	200

The balance sheet, as shown in Exhibit 3-5, reports Air & Sea's plant assets at April 30.

STOP & THINK

1. What is the book value of Air & Sea Travel's furniture at the end of May?
2. Is that what the furniture could be sold for then?

Answers

1. $16,500 – $275 – $275 = $15,950.
2. Not necessarily. Book value represents the part of the asset's *cost* that has not yet been depreciated. Book value is not necessarily related to the amount that an asset can be sold for.

Exhibit 3-6 shows how **Johnson & Johnson**—makers of Band-Aids, Tylenol, and other health-care products—displayed Property, Plant, and Equipment in its annual report. Johnson & Johnson has real-estate holdings around the world; they are reported in line 1 of Exhibit 3-6. Line 2 includes the cost of buildings used for office space, manufacturing, and research as well as the air conditioners, elevators, plumbing, and so on in those buildings. The company's manufacturing machinery, office equipment, and furniture are given in line 3, and line 4 represents assets that are under construction. Line 5 reports the sum of the accumulated depreciation on all of Johnson & Johnson's plant assets. Line 6 gives the assets' book value of $4,115 million.

ACCRUED EXPENSES Businesses often incur expenses before they pay cash. Payment is not due until later. Consider an employee's salary. The employer's salary expense and salary payable grow as the employee works, so the liability is

EXHIBIT 3-5
Plant Assets on the Balance Sheet of Air & Sea Travel, Inc. (April 30)

PLANT ASSETS		
Furniture	$16,500	
Less Accumulated depreciation	275	$16,225
Building	$48,000	
Less Accumulated depreciation	200	47,800
Book value of plant assets		$64,025

1	Land and land improvements	$ 262
2	Buildings and building equipment	2,226
3	Machinery and equipment	3,143
4	Construction in progress	672
		6,303
5	Less Accumulated depreciation	2,188
6		$4,115

EXHIBIT 3-6
Johnson & Johnson's Reporting of Property, Plant, and Equipment (In millions)

said to *accrue.* Another example is interest expense on a note payable. Interest accrues as the clock ticks. The term **accrued expense** refers to a liability that arises from an expense that the business has incurred but has not yet paid.

It is time-consuming to make hourly, daily, or even weekly journal entries to record expenses. Consequently, the accountant waits until the end of the period. Then an adjusting entry brings each expense (and related liability) up to date just before the financial statements are prepared.

SALARY EXPENSE Most companies pay their employees at set times. Suppose Air & Sea Travel pays its employee a monthly salary of $1,900, half on the 15th and half on the last day of the month. Here is a calendar for April that has the paydays circled:

APRIL

Sun.	Mon.	Tue.	Wed.	Thur.	Fri.	Sat.
					1	2
3	4	5	6	7	8	9
10	11	12	13	14	(15)	16
17	18	19	20	21	22	23
24	25	26	27	28	29	(30)

Assume that if either payday falls on the weekend, Air & Sea Travel pays the employee on the following Monday. During April, the agency paid its employee's first half-month salary of $950 on Friday, April 15, and recorded the following entry:

Apr. 15	Salary Expense	950	
	Cash		950
	To pay salary.		

ASSETS	=	LIABILITIES	+	STOCKHOLDERS' EQUITY	−	EXPENSES
−950	=	0			−	950

After posting, the Salary Expense account is

Salary Expense		
Apr. 15	950	

The trial balance at April 30 (Exhibit 3-4, page 112) includes Salary Expense, with its debit balance of $950. Because April 30, the second payday of the month, falls on a Saturday, the second half-month amount of $950 will be paid on Monday, May 2. Without an adjusting entry, this second $950 amount is not included in the April 30 trial balance amount for Salary Expense. Therefore, at April 30, Air & Sea's accountant adjusts for additional *salary expense* and *salary payable* of $950 by recording an increase in each of those accounts as follows:

(Adjusting entry d)

		Debit	Credit
Apr. 30	Salary Expense	950	
	Salary Payable		950
	To accrue salary expense.		

ASSETS	=	LIABILITIES	+	STOCKHOLDERS' EQUITY	−	EXPENSES
0	=	950			−	950

After posting, the Salary Payable and Salary Expense accounts appear as follows:

Salary Payable

Debit		Credit	
		Apr. 30	950
		Bal.	950

Salary Expense

Debit		Credit
Apr. 15	950	
Apr. 30	950	
Bal.	1,900	

The accounts at April 30 now contain the complete salary information for the month. The expense account has a full month's salary, and the liability account shows the portion that the business still owes at April 30.

Air & Sea Travel will record the payment of this liability on May 2 by debiting Salary Payable and crediting Cash for $950. This payment entry will not affect April or May expenses because the April expense was recorded on April 15 and April 30. May expense will be recorded in a like manner. All accrued expenses are recorded with similar entries—a debit to the appropriate expense account and a credit to the related liability account.

Many computerized systems contain a payroll module, or functional unit. The adjusting entry for accrued salaries is automatically journalized and posted at the end of each accounting period.

STOP & THINK What is the adjusting entry at April 30 for this situation? Weekly salaries for a five-day week total $3,500, payable on Friday. April 30 falls on a Tuesday.

Answer: $3,500 × 2/5 = $1,400. The adjusting entry is

	Debit	Credit
Salary Expense	1,400	
Salary Payable		1,400
To accrue salary expense.		

Accrued Revenues

Businesses often earn revenue before they receive the cash because collection occurs later. A revenue that has been earned but not yet received in cash is called an **accrued revenue.** An accrued revenue creates a receivable, which is an asset. Assume that Guerrero Tours hires Air & Sea Travel on April 15 to perform services on a monthly basis. Under this agreement, Guerrero will pay the travel agency $500 monthly, with the first payment on May 15. During April, Air & Sea will earn half a month's fee, $250, for work performed April 15 through April 30. On April 30, Air & Sea's accountant makes the following adjusting entry to record increases in Accounts Receivable and Service Revenue:

(Adjusting entry e)

		Debit	Credit
Apr. 30	Accounts Receivable ($500 × ½)	250	
	Service Revenue		250
	To accrue service revenue.		

ASSETS	=	LIABILITIES	+	STOCKHOLDERS' EQUITY	+	REVENUES
250	=	0			+	250

Recall that Accounts Receivable has an unadjusted balance of $2,250, and the Service Revenue unadjusted balance is $7,000 (Exhibit 3-4, page 112). Posting this adjusting entry has the following effects on these two accounts:

Accounts Receivable		
	2,250	
Apr. 30	250	
Bal.	2,500	

Service Revenue		
		7,000
	Apr. 30	250
	Bal.	7,250

This adjusting entry illustrates accrual-basis accounting and the revenue principle in action. Without the adjustment, the travel agency's financial statements would be misleading—they would understate Accounts Receivable and Service Revenue by $250 each. All accrued revenues are accounted for similarly—by debiting a receivable and crediting a revenue.

STOP & THINK Suppose Air & Sea Travel held a note receivable from a client. At the end of April, $125 of interest revenue has been earned. Prepare the adjusting entry at April 30.

Answer

Interest Receivable	125	
Interest Revenue		125
To accrue interest revenue.		

Unearned Revenues

Some businesses collect cash from customers in advance of doing work for them. Doing so creates a liability called **unearned revenue,** which is an obligation arising from receiving cash in advance of providing a product or a service. Only when the job is completed will the business have earned the revenue. Suppose Baldwin Investment Bankers engages Air & Sea Travel's services, agreeing to pay the travel agency $450 monthly, beginning immediately. If Baldwin makes the first payment on April 20, Air & Sea records this increase in its assets and its liabilities as follows:

Apr. 20	Cash	450	
	Unearned Service Revenue		450
	Received revenue in advance.		

ASSETS	=	LIABILITIES	+	STOCKHOLDERS' EQUITY
450	=	450	+	0

After posting, the liability account appears as follows:

Unearned Service Revenue		
	Apr. 20	450

Unearned Service Revenue is a liability because it represents Air & Sea's obligation to perform service for the client. The April 30 unadjusted trial balance (Exhibit 3-4) lists this account with a $450 credit balance prior to the adjusting entries. During the last 10 days of the month—April 21 through April 30—the travel agency will have *earned* one-third (10 days divided by April's total 30 days) of the $450, or $150. Therefore, the accountant makes the following adjustment to decrease the liability, Unearned Service Revenue, and to record an increase in Service Revenue:

(Adjusting entry f)	Apr. 30	Unearned Service Revenue ($\$450 \times 1/3$)	150	
		Service Revenue		150
		To record unearned service revenue that has been earned.		

ASSETS	=	LIABILITIES	+	STOCKHOLDERS' EQUITY	+	REVENUES
0	=	−150			+	150

This adjusting entry shifts $150 of the total amount from the liability account to the revenue account. After posting, the balance of Unearned Service Revenue is reduced to $300, and the balance of Service Revenue is increased by $150.

Unearned Service Revenue

Apr. 30	150	Apr. 20	450
		Bal.	300

Service Revenue

			7,000
		Apr. 30	250
		Apr. 30	150
		Bal.	7,400

Correct liability amount: $300 → **Total accounted for: $450** ← **Correct revenue amount: $150**

All types of revenues that are collected in advance are accounted for similarly.

LEARNING TIP An unearned revenue is a liability, not a revenue.

An unearned revenue to one company can be a prepaid expense to the company that made the payment. For example, suppose that two months in advance, Xerox Corporation paid American Airlines $1,800 for the airfare of Xerox executives. To Xerox, the payment is Prepaid Travel Expense. To American Airlines, the receipt of cash creates Unearned Service Revenue. After the executives take the trip, American Airlines records the revenue.

Exhibit 3-7 diagrams the timing of prepaid- and accrual-type adjusting entries. Study prepaid expenses all the way across. Then study unearned revenues, and so on.

STOP & THINK Consider the tuition you pay. Assume that one semester's tuition costs $500 and that you make a single payment at the start of the term. Can you make the journal entries to record the tuition transactions on your own books and on the books of your college or university at the beginning and end of the semester?

Answer

	Your Entries			Your College's Entries		
Start of semester:	Prepaid Tuition	500		Cash	500	
	Cash		500	Unearned Tuition Revenue		500
	Paid semester tuition.			Received revenue in advance.		
End of semester:	Tuition Expense	500		Unearned Tuition Revenue	500	
	Prepaid Tuition		500	Tuition Revenue		500
	To record tuition expense.			To record unearned tuition revenue that has been earned.		

Summary of the Adjusting Process

One purpose of the adjusting process is to measure business income, so each adjusting entry affects at least one income statement account—a revenue or an expense. The other purpose of the adjusting process is to update the balance sheet

Concept Highlight

EXHIBIT 3-7
Prepaid- and Accrual-Type Adjustments

PREPAIDS—The cash transaction occurs initially.

	Initially				**Later**		
Prepaid expenses	Pay cash and record an asset:			→	Record an expense and decrease the asset:		
	Prepaid Expense	XXX			Expense	XXX	
	Cash		XXX		Prepaid Expense.........		XXX
Unearned revenues	Receive cash and record unearned revenue:			→	Record a revenue and decrease unearned revenue:		
	Cash	XXX			Unearned Revenue............	XXX	
	Unearned Revenue		XXX		Revenue		XXX

ACCRUALS—The cash transaction occurs later.

	Initially				**Later**		
Accrued expenses	Record (accrue) an expense and the related payable:			→	Pay cash and decrease the payable:		
	Expense	XXX			Payable	XXX	
	Payable..........		XXX		Cash		XXX
Accrued revenues	Record (accrue) a revenue and the related receivable:			→	Receive cash and decrease the receivable:		
	Receivable	XXX			Cash	XXX	
	Revenue		XXX		Receivable......		XXX

The authors thank Darrel Davis and Alfonso Oddo for suggesting this exhibit.

accounts. Therefore, the other side of each adjusting entry—a debit or a credit—affects an asset or a liability. No adjusting entry debits or credits Cash because the cash transactions are recorded at other times. The end-of-period adjustment process is reserved for the noncash transactions that are required by accrual-basis accounting. Exhibit 3-8 summarizes the adjusting entries.

Exhibit 3-9 on page 124 summarizes the adjusting entries of Air & Sea Travel, Inc., at April 30—the adjusting entries we've examined over the past few pages. Panel A briefly describes the data for each adjustment, Panel B gives the adjusting entries, and Panel C shows the accounts after the adjusting entries have been posted. ⇐ The adjustments are keyed by letter.

⇐⇐⇐ Recall from Chapter 2, page 69, that posting is the process of transferring amounts from the journal to the ledger.

Exhibit 3-9 includes an additional adjusting entry that we have not yet discussed: the accrual of income tax expense. Corporations are subject to income tax, as other taxpayers are. They typically accrue income tax expense and the

EXHIBIT 3-8
Summary of Adjusting Entries

Category of Adjusting Entry	**Type of Account** Debited	Credited
Prepaid expense	Expense	Asset
Depreciation	Expense	Contra asset
Accrued expense	Expense	Liability
Accrued revenue	Asset	Revenue
Unearned revenue	Liability	Revenue

Adapted from material provided by Beverly Terry.

EXHIBIT 3-9

Journalizing and Posting the Adjusting Entries of Air & Sea Travel, Inc.

PANEL A—Information for Adjustments at April 30, 19X1

(a) Prepaid rent expired, $1,000.
(b) Supplies on hand, $400.
(c) Depreciation on furniture, $275.
(d) Accrued salary expense, $950.
(e) Accrued service revenue, $250.
(f) Amount of unearned service revenue that has been earned, $150.
(g) Accrued income tax expense, $540.

PANEL B—Adjusting Entries

		Debit	Credit
(a)	Rent Expense	1,000	
	Prepaid Rent		1,000
	To record rent expense.		
(b)	Supplies Expense	300	
	Supplies		300
	To record supplies used.		
(c)	Depreciation Expense—Furniture	275	
	Accumulated Depreciation—Furniture		275
	To record depreciation on furniture.		
(d)	Salary Expense	950	
	Salary Payable		950
	To accrue salary expense.		
(e)	Accounts Receivable	250	
	Service Revenue		250
	To accrue service revenue.		
(f)	Unearned Service Revenue	150	
	Service Revenue		150
	To record unearned revenue that has been earned.		
(g)	Income Tax Expense	540	
	Income Tax Payable		540
	To accrue income tax expense.		

PANEL C—Ledger Accounts

ASSETS

Cash

Debit	Credit
Bal. 24,800	

Accounts Receivable

Debit	Credit
2,250	
(e) 250	
Bal. 2,500	

Supplies

Debit	Credit
700	(b) 300
Bal. 400	

Prepaid Rent

Debit	Credit
3,000	(a) 1,000
Bal. 2,000	

Furniture

Debit	Credit
Bal. 16,500	

Accumulated Depreciation—Furniture

Debit	Credit
	(c) 275
	Bal. 275

LIABILITIES

Accounts Payable

Debit	Credit
	Bal. 13,100

Salary Payable

Debit	Credit
	(d) 950
	Bal. 950

Unearned Service Revenue

Debit	Credit
(f) 150	450
	Bal. 300

Income Tax Payable

Debit	Credit
	(g) 540
	Bal. 540

STOCKHOLDERS' EQUITY

Common Stock

Debit	Credit
	Bal. 20,000

Retained Earnings

Debit	Credit
	Bal. 11,250

Dividends

Debit	Credit
Bal. 3,200	

REVENUE

Service Revenue

Debit	Credit
	7,000
	(e) 250
	(f) 150
	Bal. 7,400

EXPENSES

Rent Expense

Debit	Credit
(a) 1,000	
Bal. 1,000	

Salary Expense

Debit	Credit
950	
(d) 950	
Bal. 1,900	

Supplies Expense

Debit	Credit
(b) 300	
Bal. 300	

Depreciation Expense—Furniture

Debit	Credit
(c) 275	
Bal. 275	

Utilities Expense

Debit	Credit
Bal. 400	

Income Tax Expense

Debit	Credit
(g) 540	
Bal. 540	

AIR & SEA TRAVEL, INC.
Preparation of Adjusted Trial Balance
April 30, 19X1

Account Title	Trial Balance Debit	Trial Balance Credit	Adjustments Debit	Adjustments Credit	Adjusted Trial Balance Debit	Adjusted Trial Balance Credit
Cash	24,800				24,800	
Accounts receivable	2,250		(e) 250		2,500	
Supplies	700			(b) 300	400	
Prepaid rent	3,000			(a) 1,000	2,000	
Furniture	16,500				16,500	
Accumulated depreciation				(c) 275		275
Accounts payable		13,100				13,100
Salary payable				(d) 950		950
Unearned service revenue		450	(f) 150			300
Income tax payable				(g) 540		540
Common stock		20,000				20,000
Retained earnings		11,250				11,250
Dividends	3,200				3,200	
Service revenue		7,000		(e) 250 (f) 150		7,400
Rent expense			(a) 1,000		1,000	
Salary expense	950		(d) 950		1,900	
Supplies expense			(b) 300		300	
Depreciation expense			(c) 275		275	
Utilities expense	400				400	
Income tax expense			(g) 540		540	
	51,800	51,800	3,465	3,465	53,815	53,815

EXHIBIT 3-10
Adjusted Trial Balance

related income tax payable as the final adjusting entry of the period. Air & Sea Travel, Inc., accrues income tax expense with adjusting entry g, as follows:

Income Tax Expense............................	540		(Adjusting entry g)
Income Tax Payable.....................		540	
To accrue income tax expense.			

The Adjusted Trial Balance

This chapter began with the trial balance before any adjusting entries—the unadjusted trial balance (Exhibit 3-4). After the adjustments are journalized and posted, the accounts appear as shown in Exhibit 3-9, Panel C. A useful step in preparing the financial statements is to list the accounts, along with their adjusted balances, on an **adjusted trial balance.** This document has the advantage of listing all the accounts and their adjusted balances in a single place. Exhibit 3-10 shows the preparation of the adjusted trial balance.

Note how clearly this format presents the data. The information in the Account Title column and in the Trial Balance columns is drawn directly from the trial balance. The two Adjustments columns list the debit and credit adjustments directly across from the appropriate account title. Each adjusting debit is identified by a letter in parentheses that refers to the adjusting entry. For example, the debit labeled (e) on the work sheet refers to the debit adjusting entry of $250 to Accounts Receivable in Panel B of Exhibit 3-9. Likewise for adjusting credits, the corresponding credit—labeled (e)—refers to the $250 credit to Service Revenue.

The Adjusted Trial Balance columns give the adjusted account balances. Each amount on the adjusted trial balance of Exhibit 3-10 is computed by taking the amounts from the unadjusted trial balance and adding or subtracting the adjustments. For example, Accounts Receivable starts with a debit balance of

$2,250. Adding the $250 debit amount from adjusting entry (e) gives Accounts Receivable an adjusted balance of $2,500. Supplies begins with a debit balance of $700. After the $300 credit adjustment, its adjusted balance is $400. More than one entry may affect a single account, as is the case for Service Revenue. Accounts that are unaffected by the adjustments will show the same amount on both the unadjusted and the adjusted trial balances. Here, this will be the case for Cash, Furniture, Accounts Payable, Common Stock, Retained Earnings, Dividends, and Utilities Expense.

Preparing the Financial Statements from the Adjusted Trial Balance

Objective 4

Prepare the financial statements

The April financial statements of Air & Sea Travel, Inc., can be prepared from the adjusted trial balance. Exhibit 3-11 shows how the accounts are distributed from the adjusted trial balance to the financial statements. The income statement (Exhibit 3-12) comes from the revenue and expense accounts. The statement of retained earnings (Exhibit 3-13) shows the reasons for the change in retained earnings during the period. The balance sheet (Exhibit 3-14) reports the assets, liabilities, and stockholders' equity. The adjusting process does not affect cash, so we can temporarily ignore the statement of cash flows.

The financial statements are best prepared in the order shown: the income statement first, followed by the statement of retained earnings, and then the balance sheet. The essential features of all financial statements are (1) the name of the entity, (2) the title of the statement, (3) the date or the period covered by the statement, and (4) the body of the statement.

It is customary to list expenses in descending order by amount, as shown in Exhibit 3-12. However, Miscellaneous Expense, a catchall account for expenses that do not fit another category, is usually reported last regardless of its amount. Also, Income Tax Expense is usually reported after income before tax, as shown in the exhibit.

The chapter appendix discusses an accounting spreadsheet that can also be used to prepare the financial statements.

EXHIBIT 3-11
Preparing the Financial Statements of Air & Sea Travel, Inc., from the Adjusted Trial Balance

Account Title	Adjusted Trial Balance Debit	Adjusted Trial Balance Credit	
Cash	24,800		Balance Sheet (Exhibit 3-14)
Accounts receivable	2,500		
Supplies	400		
Prepaid rent	2,000		
Furniture	16,500		
Accumulated depreciation		275	
Accounts payable		13,100	
Salary payable		950	
Unearned service revenue		300	
Income tax payable		540	
Common stock		20,000	
Retained earnings		11,250	Statement of Retained Earnings (Exhibit 3-13)
Dividends	3,200		
Service revenue		7,400	Income Statement (Exhibit 3-12)
Rent expense	1,000		
Salary expense	1,900		
Supplies expense	300		
Depreciation expense	275		
Utilities expense	400		
Income tax expense	540		
	53,815	53,815	

EXHIBIT 3-12
Income Statement

AIR & SEA TRAVEL, INC. Income Statement For the Month Ended April 30, 19X1		
Revenue:		
Service revenue		$7,400
Expenses:		
Salary expense	$1,900	
Rent expense	1,000	
Utilities expense	400	
Supplies expense	300	
Depreciation expense	275	3,875
Income before tax		3,525
Income tax expense		540
Net income		$2,985

①

EXHIBIT 3-13
Statement of Retained Earnings

AIR & SEA TRAVEL, INC. Statement of Retained Earnings For the Month Ended April 30, 19X1	
Retained earnings, April 1, 19X1	$11,250
Add: Net income	2,985
	14,235
Less: Dividends	3,200
Retained earnings, April 30, 19X1	$11,035

EXHIBIT 3-14
Balance Sheet

②

AIR & SEA TRAVEL, INC. Balance Sheet April 30, 19X1				
Assets			**Liabilities**	
Cash		$24,800	Accounts payable	$13,100
Accounts receivable		2,500	Salary payable	950
Supplies		400	Unearned service revenue	300
Prepaid rent		2,000	Income tax payable	540
Furniture	$16,500		Total liabilities	14,890
Less Accumulated depreciation	275	16,225	**Stockholders' Equity**	
			Common stock	20,000
			Retained earnings	11,035
			Total stockholders' equity	31,035
Total assets		$45,925	Total liabilities and stockholders' equity	$45,925

Relationships Among the Financial Statements

The arrows in Exhibits 3-12, 3-13, and 3-14 illustrate the relationships among the income statement, the statement of retained earnings, and the balance sheet. Consider why the income statement is prepared first and the balance sheet last.

The relationships among the financial statements were introduced in Chapter 1, page 23.

1. The income statement reports net income or net loss, calculated by subtracting expenses from revenues. Because revenues and expenses affect stockholders' equity, their net amount is then transferred to the statement of retained earnings. Note that net income in Exhibit 3-12, $2,985, increases retained earnings in Exhibit 3-13. A net loss would decrease retained earnings.

2. Retained Earnings is a balance sheet account, so the ending balance in the statement of retained earnings is transferred to the balance sheet. This amount is the final balancing element of the balance sheet. To solidify your understanding of this relationship, trace the $11,035 retained earnings figure from Exhibit 3-13 to Exhibit 3-14.

You may be wondering why the total assets on the balance sheet ($45,925 in Exhibit 3-14) do not equal the total debits on the adjusted trial balance ($53,815 in Exhibit 3-11). Likewise, the total liabilities and stockholders' equity on the balance sheet do not equal the total credits on the adjusted trial balance. The reason for these differences? Accumulated Depreciation and Dividends are *subtracted* from their related accounts on the balance sheet but *added* in their respective columns on the adjusted trial balance.

STOP & THINK Examine Air & Sea Travel's financial statements on page 127. If the accountant forgot to record the $540 accrual of income tax expense at April 30, what net income would the travel agency have reported for April? What total assets, total liabilities, and total stockholders' equity would the balance sheet have reported at April 30?

Answer: Omission of the income tax accrual would produce these effects:

1. Net income would have been reported on the income statement (Exhibit 3-12) as $3,525 ($2,985 + $540).
2. Total assets would have been unaffected by the error—$45,925, as reported on the balance sheet (Exhibit 3-14).
3. Total liabilities would have been reported as $14,350 ($14,890 – $540) on the balance sheet (Exhibit 3-14).
4. Stockholders' equity (Common Stock plus Retained Earnings) would have been reported at $31,575 ($31,035 + $540) on the balance sheet (Exhibit 3-14).

This specific example addresses an accounting-error question. But the analysis needed to compute these amounts is important to marketing, finance, statistics, and management personnel in business—because everyone is affected by the amount of net income that a business reports.

Mid-Chapter SUMMARY PROBLEM FOR YOUR REVIEW

The trial balance of State Service Company on p. 129 pertains to December 31, 19X3, which is the end of its year-long accounting period. Data needed for the adjusting entries include

- **a.** Supplies on hand at year end, $2,000.
- **b.** Depreciation on furniture and fixtures, $20,000.
- **c.** Depreciation on building, $10,000.
- **d.** Salaries owed but not yet paid, $5,000.
- **e.** Accrued service revenue, $12,000.
- **f.** Of the $45,000 balance of unearned service revenue, $32,000 was earned during the year.
- **g.** Accrued income tax expense, $35,000.

Required

1. Open the ledger accounts with their unadjusted balances. Show dollar amounts in thousands, as shown for Accounts Receivable:

Accounts Receivable	
370	

2. Journalize State Service Company's adjusting entries at December 31, 19X3. Key entries by letter as in Exhibit 3-9.
3. Post the adjusting entries.
4. Write the trial balance on a work sheet, enter the adjusting entries, and prepare an adjusted trial balance, as shown in Exhibit 3-10.
5. Prepare the income statement, the statement of retained earnings, and the balance sheet. (At this stage, it is not necessary to classify assets or liabilities as current or long term.) Draw arrows linking these three financial statements.

STATE SERVICE COMPANY
Trial Balance
December 31, 19X3

Account	Debit	Credit
Cash	$ 198,000	
Accounts receivable	370,000	
Supplies	6,000	
Furniture and fixtures	100,000	
Accumulated depreciation—furniture and fixtures		$ 40,000
Building	250,000	
Accumulated depreciation—building		130,000
Accounts payable		380,000
Salary payable		
Unearned service revenue		45,000
Income tax payable		
Common stock		100,000
Retained earnings		193,000
Dividends	65,000	
Service revenue		286,000
Salary expense	172,000	
Supplies expense		
Depreciation expense—furniture and fixtures		
Depreciation expense—building		
Income tax expense		
Miscellaneous expense	13,000	
Total	$1,174,000	$1,174,000

ANSWERS

Requirements 1 and 3

ASSETS

Cash

	Debit		Credit
Bal.	198		

Accounts Receivable

	Debit		Credit
	370		
(e)	12		
Bal.	382		

Supplies

	Debit		Credit
	6	(a)	4
Bal.	2		

Furniture and Fixtures

	Debit		Credit
Bal.	100		

Accumulated Depreciation—Furniture and Fixtures

	Debit		Credit
			40
		(b)	20
		Bal.	60

Building

	Debit		Credit
Bal.	250		

Accumulated Depreciation—Building

	Debit		Credit
			130
		(c)	10
		Bal.	140

LIABILITIES

Accounts Payable

	Debit		Credit
		Bal.	380

Salary Payable

	Debit		Credit
		(d)	5
		Bal.	5

Unearned Service Revenue

	Debit		Credit
(f)	32		45
		Bal.	13

Income Tax Payable

	Debit		Credit
		(g)	35
		Bal.	35

STOCKHOLDERS' EQUITY

Common Stock

	Debit		Credit
		Bal.	100

Retained Earnings

	Debit		Credit
		Bal.	193

Dividends

	Debit		Credit
Bal.	65		

REVENUE

Service Revenue

	Debit		Credit
			286
		(e)	12
		(f)	32
		Bal.	330

EXPENSES

Salary Expense

	Debit		Credit
	172		
(d)	5		
Bal.	177		

Supplies Expense

	Debit		Credit
(a)	4		
Bal.	4		

Depreciation Expense—Furniture and Fixtures

	Debit		Credit
(b)	20		
Bal.	20		

Depreciation Expense—Building

	Debit		Credit
(c)	10		
Bal.	10		

Income Tax Expense

	Debit		Credit
(g)	35		
Bal.	35		

Miscellaneous Expense

	Debit		Credit
Bal.	13		

Requirement 2

	19X3			
(a)	Dec. 31	Supplies Expense ($6,000 – $2,000)	4,000	
		Supplies		4,000
		To record supplies used.		
(b)	31	Depreciation Expense—Furniture and Fixtures	20,000	
		Accumulated Depreciation—Furniture and Fixtures		20,000
		To record depreciation expense on furniture and fixtures.		
(c)	31	Depreciation Expense—Building	10,000	
		Accumulated Depreciation—Building		10,000
		To record depreciation expense on building.		
(d)	31	Salary Expense	5,000	
		Salary Payable		5,000
		To accrue salary expense.		
(e)	31	Accounts Receivable	12,000	
		Service Revenue		12,000
		To accrue service revenue.		
(f)	31	Unearned Service Revenue	32,000	
		Service Revenue		32,000
		To record unearned service revenue that has been earned.		
(g)	31	Income Tax Expense	35,000	
		Income Tax Payable		35,000
		To accrue income tax expense.		

Requirement 4

STATE SERVICE COMPANY
Preparation of Adjusted Trial Balance
December 31, 19X3
(Amounts in Thousands)

	Trial Balance		Adjustments		Adjusted Trial Balance	
	Debit	**Credit**	**Debit**	**Credit**	**Debit**	**Credit**
Cash	198				198	
Accounts receivable	370		(e) 12		382	
Supplies	6			(a) 4	2	
Furniture and fixtures	100				100	
Accumulated depreciation—furniture and fixtures		40		(b) 20		60
Building	250				250	
Accumulated depreciation—building		130		(c) 10		140
Accounts payable		380				380
Salary payable				(d) 5		5
Unearned service revenue		45	(f) 32			13
Income tax payable				(g) 35		35
Common stock		100				100
Retained earnings		193				193
Dividends	65				65	
Service revenue		286		(e) 12 (f) 32		330
Salary expense	172		(d) 5		177	
Supplies expense			(a) 4		4	
Depreciation expense—furniture and fixtures			(b) 20		20	
Depreciation expense—building			(c) 10		10	
Income tax expense			(g) 35		35	
Miscellaneous expense	13				13	
	1,174	1,174	118	118	1,256	1,256

Requirement 5

STATE SERVICE COMPANY
Income Statement
For the Year Ended December 31, 19X3
(Amounts in Thousands)

Revenue:		
Service revenue		$330
Expenses:		
Salary expense	$177	
Depreciation expense—furniture and fixtures	20	
Depreciation expense—building	10	
Supplies expense	4	
Miscellaneous expense	13	224
Income before tax		106
Income tax expense		35
Net income		$ 71

STATE SERVICE COMPANY
Statement of Retained Earnings
For the Year Ended December 31, 19X3
(Amounts in Thousands)

Retained earnings, January 1, 19X3	$193
Add: Net income	71
	264
Less: Dividends	65
Retained earnings, December 31, 19X3	$199

STATE SERVICE COMPANY
Balance Sheet
December 31, 19X3
(Amounts in Thousands)

Assets			**Liabilities**	
Cash		$198	Accounts payable	$380
Accounts receivable		382	Salary payable	5
Supplies		2	Unearned service revenue	13
Furniture and fixtures	$100		Income tax payable	35
Less Accumulated			Total liabilities	433
depreciation	60	40	**Stockholders' Equity**	
Building	$250			
Less Accumulated			Common stock	100
depreciation	140	110	Retained earnings	199
			Total stockholders' equity	299
			Total liabilities and	
Total assets		$732	stockholders' equity	$732

Ethical Issues in Accrual Accounting

Accrual accounting provides some ethical challenges that cash accounting can avoid. For example, suppose that in 1998, MajorCo prepays a $3 million advertising campaign to be conducted by Saatchi & Saatchi, a leading advertising agency. If the advertisements are scheduled to run during December, January, and February, MajorCo is buying an asset with a life of three months, and the company should record the expense over the three-month period. Suppose MajorCo pays for the advertisements on December 1 and the ads start running immediately. Major should record one-third of the expense ($1 million) during the year ended December 31, 1998, and two-thirds ($2 million) during 1999.

Suppose 1998 is a great year for Major; net income for the year is better than expected. Major's top managers believe that 1999 will not be as profitable. In this case, the company has a strong incentive to expense the full $3 million during 1998 in order to report all the expense in the 1998 income statement. This unethical action will keep $2 million of advertising expense off the 1999 income statement and make 1999's operating results look better.

We are not suggesting that companies follow this course of action. Most companies follow standard procedures to keep all aspects of their business dealings ethical, including their accounting. Thus, Major would expense $1 million in 1998 and $2 million in 1999, as required by generally accepted accounting principles. But violations of good accounting sometimes occur, and auditors—who must sign their names to their opinions of the financial statements they audit—are always on the lookout for these violations.

In cash-basis accounting, this particular ethical challenge could not arise. Under the cash basis, it would be appropriate for MajorCo to record the full $3 million as expense in December 1998 because the cash payment occurred during that month. But the cash basis is unacceptable because it distorts reported figures for assets, expenses, and net income. In this hypothetical example, MajorCo does in fact have a $2 million asset, prepaid advertising, at December 31, 1998. To expense the full $3 million in December denies the reality of the asset and overstates 1998's expenses. The main results? Assets and net income for 1998 are understated, and the company does not appear to be as successful as it really is.

Another ethical challenge in accrual accounting arises because it is easy to fail to record a liability at the end of the accounting period. Suppose it is now December 31, 1999, and—as expected—the year has not turned out very well for MajorCo. If top managers are unethical, the company can "manufacture" some net income by failing to accrue some of its expenses. For example, suppose the company owes $4 million in interest expense that it will pay in January 2000. At December 31, 1999, company accountants can "overlook" the $4 million interest expense accrual owed by the company at that date.

How will this unethical action affect the financial statements? MajorCo's balance sheet will fail to report a $4 million liability for interest payable. Perhaps more important is the understatement of interest expense on the income statement. As a direct result, net income will be overstated, and operating results for 1999 will paint an overly rosy picture of the company's operations.

This ethical challenge cannot arise under the cash basis. With no cash payment to make in 1999, there is no expense to record for that year. Because the payment is made in January 2000, the cash basis dictates the accounting for the entire interest expense in the later year. But, as before, the cash basis is deficient because it fails to report the company's interest expense correctly for 1999. This overstates reported profits for 1999. The cash basis also fails to report the interest payable liability at December 31, 1999. This is why generally accepted accounting principles require the accrual basis, despite the ethical temptations it poses for accountants and managers.

Objective 5

Close the revenue, expense, and dividends accounts

Closing the Accounts

The term **closing the accounts** refers to the end-of-period process of preparing the accounts to begin recording the next period's transactions. Closing the accounts consists of journalizing and posting the *closing entries,* which set the balances of the revenue and expense accounts back to zero in order to measure the next period's net income. The idea is the same as setting the score of an athletic contest back to zero after each game and before the next game starts. We want to know how each team performed in a particular game.

Closing is a clerical procedure that requires only accounting procedures that we've already covered. Recall that the income statement reports only one period's income. For example, net income for **Burger King, Inc.,** for 1998 relates exclusively to 1998. At December 31, 1998, Burger King's accountants close the company's revenue and expense accounts for that year. Because these account balances relate to a particular accounting period and are therefore closed at the end of the period, the revenue and expense accounts are called **temporary (nominal) accounts.** The Dividends account—although not a revenue or an expense—is also a temporary account because it measures the dividends declared during a specific period. The closing process applies only to temporary accounts.

At December 31, 1998, Burger King's accountants close the company's revenue and expense accounts for that year.

To understand better the closing process, contrast the nature of the temporary accounts with the nature of the **permanent (real) accounts**—the assets, liabilities, and stockholders' equity. The permanent accounts are *not* closed at the end of the period because their balances are not used to measure income. Consider Cash, Accounts Receivable, Supplies, Buildings, Accounts Payable, Notes Payable, Common Stock, and Retained Earnings. These accounts do not represent increases and decreases for a single period as do the revenues and expenses, which relate exclusively to only one accounting period. Instead, the permanent accounts represent assets, liabilities, and stockholders' equity that are on hand at a specific time. Their balances at the end of one accounting period carry over to become the beginning balances of the next period. For example, the Cash balance at December 31, 19X1, is also the beginning balance for 19X2.

Closing entries transfer the revenue, expense, and dividends balances from their respective accounts to the Retained Earnings account. As you know, revenues increase retained earnings, and expenses and dividends decrease retained earnings. It is when we post the closing entries that the Retained Earnings account absorbs the impact of the balances in the temporary accounts. As an intermediate step, however, the revenues and the expenses are transferred first to an account entitled **Income Summary,** which collects in one place the total debit amount for the sum of all expenses and the total credit amount for the sum of all revenues of the period. The Income Summary account is like a temporary "holding tank" that is used only in the closing process. The balance of Income Summary is then transferred to Retained Earnings.

LEARNING TIP There is no account for Net Income, which is the net result of all revenue and expense accounts. The Income Summary account combines all revenue and expense amounts into one account.

The steps in closing the accounts of a corporation such as Air & Sea Travel, Inc., follow: As you read, keep in mind the cardinal rule of double-entry accounting: Every debit entry must have an equal credit entry, and vice versa.

① Debit each revenue account for the amount of its credit balance. Credit Income Summary for the sum of the revenues. This entry transfers the sum of the revenues to the credit side of Income Summary.

② Credit each expense account for the amount of its debit balance. Debit Income Summary for the sum of the expenses. This entry transfers the sum of the expenses to the debit side of Income Summary.

③ Determine the balance of the Income Summary account. If the Income Summary has a credit balance, then debit Income Summary and credit Retained Earnings. If Income Summary has a debit balance, then credit Income Summary for this amount, and debit Retained Earnings. This entry transfers the net income or loss from Income Summary to Retained Earnings.

④ Credit the Dividends account for the amount of its debit balance. Debit the Retained Earnings account. This entry transfers the dividends amount to the debit side of the Retained Earnings account. Remember that dividends are not expenses and do not affect net income or net loss.

To illustrate, suppose Air & Sea Travel closes the books at the end of April. Exhibit 3-15 presents the complete closing process for the business. Panel A gives the closing journal entries, and Panel B shows the accounts after the closing entries have been posted. The amount in the debit side of each expense account is its adjusted balance. For example, Rent Expense has a $1,000 debit balance. Also note that Service Revenue has a credit balance of $7,400 before closing. (These amounts come directly from the adjusted trial balance in Exhibit 3-11.)

Closing entry ① in Panel A of Exhibit 3-15, denoted in the Service Revenue account in Panel B by Clo., transfers Service Revenue's balance to the Income Summary account. This entry zeroes out Service Revenue for April and places the revenue on the credit side of Income Summary. Closing entry ② zeroes out the expenses and moves their total ($4,415) to the debit side of Income Summary. At this point, Income Summary contains the impact of April's revenues and expenses; hence Income Summary's balance is the month's net income ($7,400 – $4,415 = $2,985). Closing entry ③ closes the Income Summary account by transferring net income to the credit side of Retained Earnings.[1] The last closing entry, entry ④, moves the dividends to the debit side of Retained Earnings, leaving a zero balance in the Dividends account.

After all the closing entries have been made, the revenue, expense, and Dividends accounts are set back to zero for use in the next period. The Retained Earnings account includes the full effects of the April revenues, expenses, and dividends. These amounts, combined with the beginning Retained Earnings balance, give Retained Earnings an ending balance of $11,035. This Retained Earnings balance agrees with the amount reported on the statement of retained earnings and on the balance sheet in Exhibits 3-13 and 3-14.

CLOSING A NET LOSS What would the closing entries be if Air & Sea Travel had suffered a net *loss* during April? Suppose April expenses totaled $7,700 and all other factors were unchanged. Only closing entries ② and ③ would be altered. Closing entry ② would transfer expenses of $7,7000 to the debit side of Income Summary, as follows:

Income Summary

	Debit		Credit	
② Clo.	7,700	Clo.	7,400	①
Bal.	300			

Closing entry ③ would then credit Income Summary to close its debit balance and to transfer the net loss to Retained Earnings:

		Debit	Credit
③ Apr. 30	Retained Earnings	300	
	Income Summary		300

After posting, these two accounts would appear as follows:

Income Summary

	Debit		Credit
Clo.	7,700	Clo.	7,400
Bal.	300	Clo.	300

Retained Earnings

	Debit	Credit
Clo.	300	11,250

[1]The Income Summary account is a convenience for combining the effects of the revenues and expenses before transferring their income effect to Retained Earnings. It is not necessary to use the Income Summary account in the closing process. Another way of closing the revenues and expenses makes no use of this account. In this alternative procedure, the revenues and expenses are closed directly to Retained Earnings.

EXHIBIT 3-15
Journalizing and Posting the Closing Entries

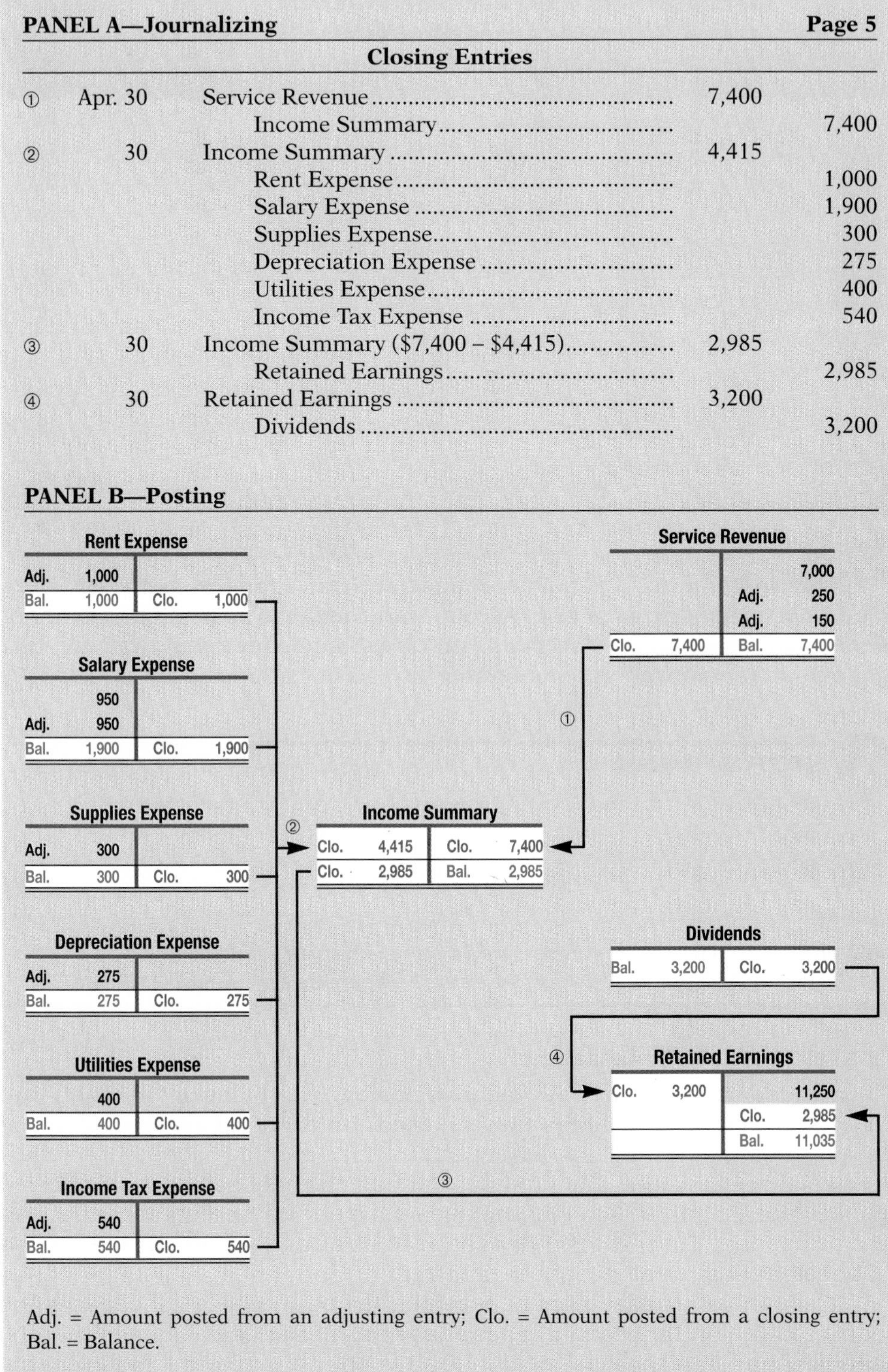

PANEL A—Journalizing **Page 5**

Closing Entries

	Date	Accounts	Debit	Credit
①	Apr. 30	Service Revenue	7,400	
		Income Summary		7,400
②	30	Income Summary	4,415	
		Rent Expense		1,000
		Salary Expense		1,900
		Supplies Expense		300
		Depreciation Expense		275
		Utilities Expense		400
		Income Tax Expense		540
③	30	Income Summary ($7,400 – $4,415)	2,985	
		Retained Earnings		2,985
④	30	Retained Earnings	3,200	
		Dividends		3,200

PANEL B—Posting

Adj. = Amount posted from an adjusting entry; Clo. = Amount posted from a closing entry; Bal. = Balance.

As arrow ② in Panel B shows, it is not necessary to make a separate closing entry for each expense. In one closing entry, record one debit to Income Summary and a separate credit to each expense account.

Finally, the Dividends balance would be closed to Retained Earnings, as before.

The double line in an account, as in Income Summary above, means that the account has a zero balance; nothing more will be posted to it in the current period. The double line is drawn immediately after the closing entry is posted. In the general ledger, the account has a zero balance.

EXHIBIT 3-16
Postclosing Trial Balance

AIR & SEA TRAVEL, INC. Postclosing Trial Balance April 30, 19X1		
Cash	$24,800	
Accounts receivable	2,500	
Supplies	400	
Prepaid rent	2,000	
Furniture	16,500	
Accumulated depreciation		$ 275
Accounts payable		13,100
Salary payable		950
Unearned service revenue		300
Income tax payable		540
Common stock		20,000
Retained earnings		11,035
Total	$46,200	$46,200

The closing process is fundamentally mechanical and is completely automated in a computerized system. Accounts are identified as either temporary or permanent. The temporary accounts are closed automatically by selecting that option from the software's menu. Posting also occurs automatically.

STOP & THINK

1. Would the Income Summary have a debit or a credit balance if the company suffers a net loss?
2. In the event of a loss, how is Income Summary closed?

Answers

1. Expenses would exceed revenues, and Income Summary would have a debit balance.
2. Income Summary is credited to close a loss, and Retained Earnings is debited.

Postclosing Trial Balance

The accounting cycle ends with the **postclosing trial balance** (Exhibit 3-16). The postclosing trial balance is the final check on the accuracy of journalizing and posting the adjusting and closing entries. Like the trial balance that begins the end-of-period process that produces the financial statements, the postclosing trial balance lists all the accounts and their balances for the start of the next accounting period. The postclosing trial balance is dated as of the end of the period for which the statements have been prepared.

The postclosing trial balance resembles the balance sheet. It contains the ending balances of the permanent accounts—the balance sheet accounts: assets, liabilities, and stockholders' equity. No temporary accounts—revenues, expenses, or dividends accounts—are included because their balances have been closed. The ledger is up-to-date and ready for the next period's transactions.

Objective 6

Correct typical accounting errors

Correcting Accounting Errors

In Chapter 2, we discussed errors that affect the trial balance: treating a debit as a credit (and vice versa), transpositions, and slides. Here we show how to correct errors in journal entries.

When a journal entry contains an error, the entry can be deleted and corrected—if the error is caught immediately. A computerized accounting system makes it easy to retrieve an incorrect entry. When you delete the original entry, the posting is also canceled. You can then record the correct entry, which is posted automatically.

If the error is detected after posting, the accountant makes a *correcting entry.* Suppose Air & Sea Travel paid $5,000 cash for furniture and erroneously debited Supplies as follows:

Incorrect Entry

May 13	Supplies	5,000	
	Cash		5,000
	Bought supplies.		

The debit to Supplies is incorrect, so it is necessary to make a correcting entry as follows:

Correcting Entry

May 15	Furniture	5,000	
	Supplies		5,000
	To correct May 13 entry.		

The credit to Supplies in the second entry offsets the incorrect debit of the first entry. The debit to Furniture in the correcting entry places the furniture's cost in the correct account. Now both Supplies and Furniture are correct. Cash was unaffected by the error because Cash was credited correctly in the original entry.

STOP & THINK

1. John Doe recorded the collection of a $1,000 receivable as a debit to Cash and a credit to Service Revenue for $1,000. Prepare Doe's correcting entry.
2. If Doe's net income before the correction was $26,000, how much is the corrected net income?

Answers

1. Service Revenue	1,000	
Accounts Receivable		1,000

2. $25,000 ($26,000 – $1,000)

Detailed Classification of Assets and Liabilities

On the balance sheet, assets and liabilities are classified as either *current* or *long-term* to indicate their relative liquidity. **Liquidity** is a measure of how quickly an item can be converted to cash. Cash is the most liquid asset. Accounts receivable is a relatively liquid asset because the business expects to collect the amount in cash in the near future. Supplies are less liquid than accounts receivable, and furniture and buildings are even less so.

Users of financial statements are interested in liquidity because business difficulties often arise from a shortage of cash. How quickly can the business convert an asset to cash and pay a debt? How soon must a liability be paid? These are questions of liquidity. Balance sheets list assets and liabilities in the order of their relative liquidity.

CURRENT ASSETS As we saw in Chapter 1, **current assets** are assets that are expected to be converted to cash, sold, or consumed during the next 12 months or within the business's normal operating cycle if longer than a year. The **operating cycle** is the time span during which (1) cash is used to acquire goods and services, and (2) these goods and services are sold to customers, from whom the business collects cash. For most businesses, the operating cycle is a few months. A few types of businesses have operating cycles longer than a year. Cash, Accounts Receivable, Notes Receivable due within a year or less, and Prepaid

Expenses are current assets. Merchandising entities such as **Kmart, Sears,** and **Motorola** have an additional current asset, Inventory. This account shows the cost of goods that are held for sale to customers.

LONG-TERM ASSETS **Long-term assets** are assets that are not current assets. They are not held for sale, but rather are used to operate the business. One category of long-term assets is plant assets, often labeled Property, Plant, and Equipment, as we saw earlier in the chapter. Land, Buildings, Furniture and Fixtures, and Equipment are plant assets. Of these, Air & Sea Travel has only Furniture. Other categories of long-term assets include Investments in Available-for-Sale Securities and Investments in Held-to-Maturity Securities and Other Assets (a catchall category for assets that are not classified more precisely).

Those who use financial statements (such as bankers and other creditors) are interested in the due dates of an entity's liabilities. The sooner a liability must be paid, the more current it is. Liabilities that must be paid on the earliest future date create the greatest strain on cash. Therefore, the balance sheet lists liabilities in the order in which they are due. Knowing how many of a borrower's liabilities are current and how many are long-term helps creditors assess the likelihood that the borrower can pay off a loan. Balance sheets usually have at least two liability classifications, *current liabilities* and *long-term liabilities.*

CURRENT LIABILITIES As we saw in Chapter 1, **current liabilities** are debts that are due to be paid within one year or within the entity's operating cycle if the cycle is longer than a year. Accounts Payable, Notes Payable due within one year, Salary Payable, Unearned Revenue, Interest Payable, and Income Tax Payable are current liabilities.

LONG-TERM LIABILITIES All liabilities that are not current are classified as **long-term liabilities.** Many notes payable are long-term. Other notes payable are paid in installments, with the first installment due within one year, the second installment due the second year, and so on. In this case, the first installment would be a current liability, and the remainder long-term liabilities.

Let's see how a real company reports these asset and liability categories on its balance sheet.

Analyzing the Financial Statements of Hawaiian Airlines, Inc.

Exhibit 3-17 (Panels A through C) shows the actual classified balance sheet, the income statement, and the statement of cash flows of **Hawaiian Airlines, Inc.,** which provides passenger and freight service among the Hawaiian Islands. A **classified balance sheet** shows the current assets separate from the long-term assets and the current liabilities separate from the long-term liabilities. Virtually all companies use a classified balance sheet to report their financial position. You should be familiar with most of Hawaiian Airlines' account titles.

The classified balance sheet of Hawaiian Airlines is shown here in *report format,* with the assets stacked at the top and the liabilities and the shareholders' equity beneath the assets. An alternative way to show the balance sheet, the *account format,* reports the assets on the left and the liabilities and stockholders' equity on the right. Exhibit 3-14, page 127, is an example of the account format of the balance sheet. Both formats are acceptable. (We discuss these formats in detail a bit later in this chapter.)

On the balance sheet, Panel A of Exhibit 3-17, leasehold improvements are listed as assets, along with ground equipment and buildings (line 8). *Leasehold improvements* are modifications that Hawaiian Airlines has made to customize airplanes and other assets leased by the airline. The leasehold improvements are assets because they represent future benefits to Hawaiian Airlines even though the company does not own the leased assets. Hawaiian Airlines also reports *accumulated depreciation and amortization* (line 9). Amortization is similar to depreciation, except that amortization usually applies to intangible assets (those assets with no physical form)—in this case, the leasehold improvements.

Among the liabilities are *capital lease obligations*—lease payments the company must pay in the future to lease the airplanes (line 20). Observe the *accumulated deficit* in shareholders' equity (line 24). For its entire life, Hawaiian Airlines' net losses have exceeded the company's net incomes, so the company has an accumulated deficit, which is the opposite of retained earnings.

The income statement—labeled the Statement of Operations in Panel B—shows why the company has an accumulated deficit. During 1995, the company's net loss (as shown by the "bottom line," line 21) exceeded $5.5 million. In fact, Hawaiian Airlines has been losing money for several years and almost went bankrupt because it could not pay its debts. In 1995, Hawaiian Airlines underwent a major reorganization. This explains why Exhibit 3-17 contains no comparative income statement for 1994. The reorganized company is "new" insofar as its operations (revenues and expenses) are concerned.

EXHIBIT 3-17
Financial Statements of Hawaiian Airlines, Inc.

HAWAIIAN AIRLINES, INC.
Classified Balance Sheet (Adapted)
December 31, 1995 and 1994

PANEL A

		(In thousands)	
		1995	**1994**
	ASSETS		
	Current Assets:		
1	Cash and cash equivalents	$ 5,389	$ 3,501
2	Accounts receivable	18,178	16,275
3	Inventories	7,648	6,234
4	Assets held for sale	1,344	1,594
5	Prepaid expenses	5,804	6,079
6	**Total current assets**	38,363	33,683
	PROPERTY AND EQUIPMENT		
7	Flight equipment	40,659	34,702
8	Ground equipment, buildings, and leasehold improvements	5,775	3,976
9	Accumulated depreciation and amortization	(5,043)	(922)
10	Property and equipment, net	41,391	37,756
11	**Other Assets**	81,886	91,862
12	**Total Assets**	$161,640	$163,301
	LIABILITIES AND SHAREHOLDERS' EQUITY		
	Current Liabilities:		
13	Current portion of long-term debt	$ 6,027	$ 6,394
14	Current portion of capital lease obligations	2,662	2,907
15	Accounts payable	35,182	17,529
16	Air traffic liability	30,461	40,382
17	Other accrued liabilities	15,730	12,298
18	**Total current liabilities**	90,062	79,510
19	**Long-Term Debt**	5,523	14,152
20	**Capital Lease Obligations**	10,102	12,764
21	**Other Liabilities**	26,775	23,026
	SHAREHOLDERS' EQUITY		
22	Common stock	41,287	40,000
23	Other	(452)	—
24	Accumulated deficit	(11,657)	(6,151)
25	**Shareholders' equity**	29,178	33,849
26	**Total Liabilities and Shareholders' Equity**	$161,640	$163,301

(Continued)

EXHIBIT 3-17 *(continued)*

HAWAIIAN AIRLINES, INC.
Statement of Operations (Adapted)
For the Year ended December 31, 1995

PANEL B

		(In thousands) 1995
	Operating Revenues:	
1	Passenger	$297,527
2	Charter	22,200
3	Cargo	18,169
4	Other	9,008
5	**Total**	346,904
	Operating Expenses:	
6	Flying operations	104,847
7	Maintenance	79,156
8	Passenger service	39,210
9	Aircraft and traffic servicing	54,616
10	Promotion and sales	43,162
11	General and administrative	18,377
12	Depreciation and amortization	7,437
13	Other	2,000
14	**Total**	348,805
15	**Operating Income (Loss)**	(1,901)
	Nonoperating Income (Expense):	
16	Interest expense	(4,341)
17	Interest income	762
18	Loss on disposition of equipment	(233)
19	Other, net	207
20	**Total**	(3,605)
21	**Net Income (Loss)**	$ (5,506)

PANEL C

		(In thousands) 1995
	Cash Flows from Operating Activities:	
1	**Net cash provided by operating activities**	$18,788
	Cash Flows from Investing Activities:	
2	Additions to property and equipment	$ (9,165)
3	Net proceeds from disposition of equipment	4,225
4	**Net cash provided by (used in) investing activities**	**(4,940)**
	Cash Flows from Financing Activities:	
5	Issuance of long-term debt	$ 1,591
6	Repayment of long-term debt	(10,644)
7	Repayment of capital lease obligations	(2,907)
8	**Net cash provided by (used in) financing activities**	**(11,960)**
9	**Net increase (decrease) in cash and cash equivalents**	$ 1,888
10	Cash and cash equivalents—Beginning of year	3,501
11	**Cash and cash equivalents—End of year**	**$ 5,389**

Hawaiian Airlines reports its revenues by category, with passengers generating the bulk of company revenues (line 1). During 1995, the company had total revenues of almost $347 million (line 5). In terms of expenses, flying operations—pilot and other salaries, fuel, and gate rentals at airports—consumed $105 million (line 6). Maintenance was the second largest expense, at $79 million (line 7). Hawaiian Airlines reports interest expense under the Nonoperating category along with interest income (same as interest revenue) and loss on disposition (sale) of equipment (lines 16–18). Not all companies report interest expense as a nonoperating item. Some companies consider interest expense—the cost of borrowing money—to be an operating expense.

Hawaiian Airlines reports its revenues by category, with passengers generating the bulk of company revenues

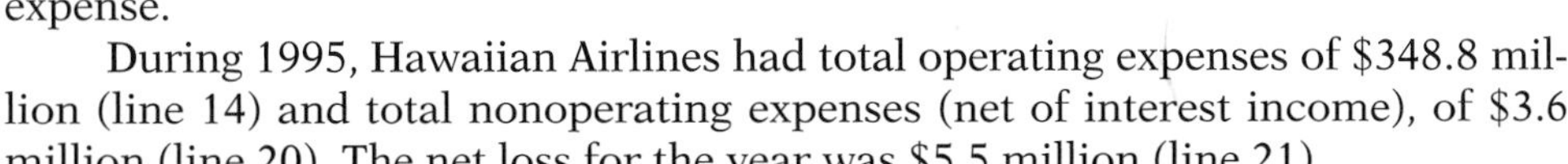

During 1995, Hawaiian Airlines had total operating expenses of $348.8 million (line 14) and total nonoperating expenses (net of interest income), of $3.6 million (line 20). The net loss for the year was $5.5 million (line 21).

The statement of cash flows, Panel C, indicates that operating activities were Hawaiian Airlines' main source of cash, bringing in $18.8 million (line 1). During 1995, the airline invested in new property and equipment and sold some older equipment (lines 2–3). Regarding financing, the company paid off much more long-term debt and lease obligations than it borrowed during the year (lines 5–7).

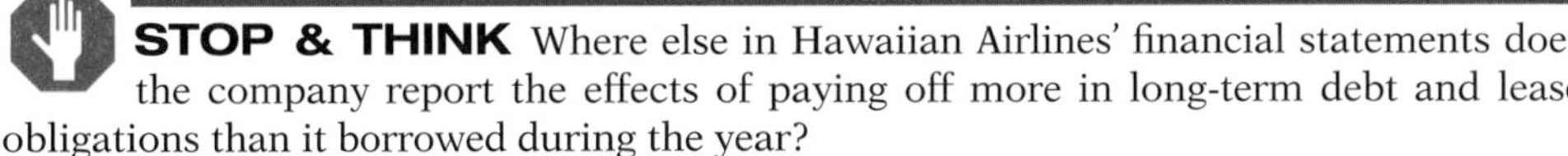

STOP & THINK Where else in Hawaiian Airlines' financial statements does the company report the effects of paying off more in long-term debt and lease obligations than it borrowed during the year?

Answer: The balance sheet (Panel A) also reports that long-term debt and capital lease obligations decreased during 1995 (see lines 19 and 20). You should be learning how to work back and forth among the financial statements in this manner—using the data on one statement to help explain the relationships in another statement.

Overall, Panel C shows that the company increased its cash by almost $1.9 million (line 9) and ended the year with cash of $5.4 million (line 11). In what two places does this information appear in Hawaiian Airlines' financial statements? Line 1 of the comparative balance sheet reports the beginning and ending balances of cash, and the statement of cash flows ends with this same information. Hawaiian Airlines is still experiencing financial difficulty, as shown by the accumulated deficit in retained earnings, the net loss on the income statement, and the small cash balance.

Let's now examine different formats for reporting the financial statements.

Different Formats for the Financial Statements

Companies can format their financial statements in different ways. Both the balance sheet and the income statement can be formatted in two basic ways.

Balance Sheet Formats

The balance sheet can be formatted in two different ways. The **account format** lists the assets at left and the liabilities and stockholders' equity at right in the same way that a T-account appears, with assets (debits) on the left and liabilities and equity (credits) on the right.

The **report format** lists the assets at the top, followed by the liabilities and stockholders' equity below. The balance sheet of Hawaiian Airlines in Exhibit 3-17 illustrates the report format. Either format is acceptable. The report format is more popular, with approximately 60% of large companies using the report format.

Income Statement Formats

There are two basic formats for the income statement. A **single-step income statement** lists all the revenues together under a heading such as Revenues or Revenues and Gains. The expenses appear in a separate category titled Expenses, Costs and Expenses, or perhaps Expenses and Losses. There is only one step, the subtraction of Expenses and Losses from the sum of Revenues and Gains, in arriving at net income.

A **multi-step income statement** contains a number of subtotals to highlight important relationships between revenues and expenses. For example, a merchandising company's multi-step income statement highlights gross margin (also called gross profit), income from operations, and other income and expense as follows (using assumed figures for illustrative purposes):

MULTI-STEP INCOME STATEMENT

Net sales revenue		$150,000
Cost of goods sold		80,000
Gross margin		70,000
Operating expenses		
(listed individually)		40,000
Income from operations		30,000
Other income (expense):		
Interest revenue	$2,000	
Interest expense	(9,000)	
Gain on sale of equipment	3,000	(4,000)
Income before income tax		26,000
Income tax expense		10,000
Net income		$ 16,000

Most actual companies' income statement do not conform to either a pure single-step format or a pure multi-step format. Business operations are too complex for all companies to conform to rigid reporting formats. For example, Hawaiian Airlines' income statement in Exhibit 3-17 appears in a modified single-step format. Hawaiian Airlines lists all *operating* revenues together and all *operating* expenses together, as in the single-step format. But Hawaiian Airlines reports *nonoperating* income (expense) in a separate category, which is more like the multi-step format. In practice, the multi-step format is more popular, with approximately 67% of large companies using it.

Use of Accounting Information in Decision Making: Accounting Ratios

Objective 7

Use the current ratio and the debt ratio to evaluate a business

As we've seen, the purpose of accounting is to provide information for decision making. Chief users of accounting information include managers, investors, and creditors. A creditor considering lending money must predict whether the borrower can repay the loan. If the borrower already has a lot of debt, the probability of repayment is lower than if the borrower has a small amount of liabilities.

To assess a company's financial position, decision makers use ratios computed from various items drawn from a company's financial statements.

Current Ratio

One of the most widely used financial ratios is the **current ratio,** which is the ratio of an entity's current assets to its current liabilities:

$$\textbf{Current ratio} = \frac{\textbf{Total current assets}}{\textbf{Total current liabilities}}$$

The current ratio measures the company's ability to pay current liabilities with current assets. A company prefers to have a high current ratio, which means that the business has plenty of current assets to pay current liabilities. An increasing current ratio from period to period indicates improvement in financial position.

A rule of thumb: A strong current ratio is 2.00, which indicates that the company has $2.00 in current assets for every $1.00 in current liabilities. A company with a current ratio of 2.00 would probably have little trouble paying its current liabilities. Most successful businesses operate with current ratios between 1.50 and 2.00. A current ratio of 1.00 is considered quite low. Lenders and investors would view a company with a current ratio of 1.50 or 2.00 as substantially less risky. Such a company could probably borrow money on better terms and also attract more investors. The Decision Guidelines feature on page 144 provides some tips for using the current ratio.

Debt Ratio

A second aid to decision making is the **debt ratio,** which is the ratio of total liabilities to total assets:

$$\textbf{Debt ratio} = \frac{\textbf{Total liabilities}}{\textbf{Total assets}}$$

The debt ratio indicates the proportion of a company's assets that is financed with debt. This ratio measures a business's ability to pay both current and long-term debts—total liabilities.

A low debt ratio is safer than a high debt ratio. Why? Because a company with a small amount of liabilities has low required payments. Such a company is unlikely to get into financial difficulty. By contrast, a business with a high debt ratio may have trouble paying its liabilities, especially when sales are low and cash is scarce. When a company fails to pay its debts, the creditors can take the business away from its owner. The largest retail bankruptcy in history, **Federated Department Stores** (parent company of **Bloomingdale's**), was due largely to high debt during a retail-industry recession. Federated was unable to weather the downturn and had to declare bankruptcy.

In general, a *high* current ratio is preferable to a low current ratio. *Increases* in the current ratio indicate improving financial position. By contrast, a *low* debt ratio is preferable to a high debt ratio. Improvement is indicated by a *decrease* in the debt ratio. The Decision Guidelines suggest how to use the debt ratio.

Financial ratios are an important aid to decision making. However, it is unwise to place too much confidence in a single ratio or in any group of ratios. For example, a company may have a high current ratio, which indicates financial strength. It may also have a high debt ratio, which suggests weakness. Which ratio gives the more reliable signal about the company? Experienced managers, lenders, and investors evaluate a company by examining a large number of ratios over several years to spot trends and turning points. They also consider other factors, such as the company's cash position and its trend in net income. No single ratio gives the whole picture about a company.

Decision Guidelines

Using the Current Ratio

Decision	Guidelines
How to measure a company's ability to pay current liabilities with current assets?	$\text{Current ratio} = \dfrac{\text{Total current assets}}{\text{Total current liabilities}}$
Who uses the current ratio for decision making?	*Creditors,* who must predict whether a borrower can pay its current liabilities *Stockholders,* who know that a company that cannot pay its debts is not a good investment because it may go bankrupt *Managers,* who must have enough cash to pay the company's current liabilities
What is a good value of the current ratio?	Depends on the company's industry: A company with strong cash flow can operate successfully with a low current ratio of, say, 1.10–1.20 A company with weak cash flow needs a higher current ratio of, say, 1.50–1.60 Traditionally, a current ratio of 2.00 was considered ideal. Recently, acceptable values have decreased as companies have been able to operate more efficiently.
What happens when the current ratio is low?	The company must pay a higher interest rate when it borrows money.
Can the current ratio be too high?	Yes, because most of the current assets (cash, short-term investments, receivables, and prepaid expenses) are low-earning assets. Also, it costs money to keep inventory on hand. Therefore, managers strive for a current ratio that is high enough to pay the bills but not so high that it hurts profits.

Using the Debt Ratio

Decision	Guidelines
How to measure a company's ability to pay total liabilities?	$\text{Debt ratio} = \dfrac{\text{Total liabilities}}{\text{Total assets}}$
Who uses the debt ratio for decision making?	*Creditors,* who must predict whether a borrower can pay its debts *Stockholders,* who know that a company that cannot pay its debts is not a good investment because it may go bankrupt *Managers,* who must have enough assets to pay the company's debts
What is a good value of the debt ratio?	Depends on the company's industry: A company with strong cash flow can operate successfully with a high debt ratio of, say, 0.80–0.90 A company with weak cash flow needs a lower debt ratio of, say, 0.60–0.70 Traditionally, a debt ratio of 0.50 was considered ideal. Recently, values have increased as companies have been able to operate more efficiently.
What happens when the debt ratio is high?	The company must pay a high interest rate when it borrows money.
Can the debt ratio be too low?	Yes and no. *Yes,* because a company with no long-term debt gives up some profits it could earn from borrowing at a lower rate and investing the money at a higher rate. But, *no,* because a company with no long-term debt rarely gets into trouble from inability to pay its (low) debts.

As you progress through the study of accounting, we will introduce key ratios used for decision making. Chapter 13 summarizes all the ratios discussed throughout this text and provides a good overview of the ratios used in decision making.

Application: Should a Bank Grant a Loan to Hawaiian Airlines?

Suppose Hawaiian Airlines, the company whose financial statements are reproduced in Exhibit 3-17, needs a bank loan to meet payroll and other expenses. How would a bank evaluate the company's financial position to decide whether to grant the loan? As we've just seen, a loan officer would consider both the company's current ratio and its debt ratio.

THE CURRENT RATIO The bank might look first at Hawaiian Airlines' current ratio to determine its ability to pay its current liabilities with current assets. The bank could use Hawaiian Airlines' balance sheet to calculate a current ratio of 0.426 at December 31, 1995:

$$\textbf{Current ratio} = \frac{\$38{,}363}{\$90{,}062} = 0.426$$

The extremely low value of this ratio indicates that Hawaiian Airlines could not pay its current liabilities with its current assets if all the current liabilities came due immediately. This is a very risky position and indicates financial distress. One year earlier, at December 31, 1994, Hawaiian Airlines' current ratio stood at 0.424 ($33,683/$79,510 = 0.424). The company's current ratio has not improved much during the past year.

THE DEBT RATIO The bank would want more information than just the current ratio before making a loan decision. It could also compute Hawaiian Airlines' debt ratio to measure the airline's ability to pay both current and long-term debts. From the balance sheet, Hawaiian Airlines' debt ratio is calculated to be 0.820 at December 31, 1995:

$$\textbf{Debt ratio} = \frac{\$90{,}062 + \$5{,}523 + \$10{,}102 + \$26{,}775}{\$161{,}640}$$

$$= \frac{\$132{,}462}{\$161{,}640} = 0.819$$

Hawaiian Airlines' debt ratio is quite high. It means that the company's creditors own 82% of the company's assets (the company's owners actually own just 18% of company assets). One year earlier, at December 31, 1994, Hawaiian Airlines' debt ratio was 0.793 [($79,510 + $14,152 + $12,764 + $23,026)/$163,301 = 0.793], so the debt ratio has deteriorated a bit during the past year.

THE FINAL DECISION What will the bank loan officer decide about Hawaiian Airlines' request for a loan? The low current ratio and the high debt ratio, coupled with the net loss on the income statement, would worry the loan officer because the company's ability to pay its debts is not clearly evident. If the bank were to make the loan, it would require a very high interest rate to compensate for the risk that Hawaiian Airlines may be unable to pay the debt. For example, if a normal interest rate were 8%, the bank might charge Hawaiian Airlines 12%.

Also, the bank would probably require the airline to pledge certain assets as collateral for the loan. If Hawaiian Airlines fails to pay the bank, the bank could take the pledged assets. The bank may also require Hawaiian Airlines to agree neither to pay any dividends to its stockholders nor to borrow any money from other lenders. These restrictions would increase the bank's likelihood of receiving its money from Hawaiian Airlines.

SUMMARY PROBLEM FOR YOUR REVIEW

Refer to the mid-chapter summary problem that begins on page 128.

Required

1. Make State Service Company's closing entries at December 31, 19X3. Explain what the closing entries accomplish and why they are necessary.
2. Post the closing entries to the Retained Earnings account and compare Retained Earnings's ending balance with the amount reported on the balance sheet on page 131. The two amounts should be the same.
3. Prepare State Service Company's classified balance sheet to identify the company's current assets and the company's current liabilities. (State has no long-term liabilities.) Then compute State Service Company's current ratio and debt ratio at December 31, 19X3.
4. The top management of State Service Company has asked you for a $500,000 loan to expand the business. State proposes to pay off the loan over a 10-year period. Recompute State's debt ratio assuming you make the loan. Use the company's financial statements plus the ratio values to decide whether to grant the loan at an interest rate of 8, 10, or 12 percent. State Service Company's cash flow is strong. Give the reasoning underlying your decision.

ANSWERS

Requirement 1

19X1		**(In thousands)**	
Dec. 31	Service Revenue	330	
	Income Summary		330
31	Income Summary	259	
	Salary Expense		177
	Depreciation Expense—Furniture and Fixtures		20
	Depreciation Expense—Building		10
	Supplies Expense		4
	Income Tax Expense		35
	Miscellaneous Expense		13
31	Income Summary ($330 – $259)	71	
	Retained Earnings		71
31	Retained Earnings	65	
	Dividends		65

Explanation of Closing Entries:

The closing entries set the balance of each revenue account, each expense account, and the Dividends account back to zero for the start of the next accounting period. It is necessary to close these accounts because their balances relate only to a particular accounting period.

Requirement 2

Retained Earnings			
Clo.	65		**193**
		Clo.	71
		Bal.	199

The balance in the Retained Earnings account agrees with the amount reported on the balance sheet, as it should.

Requirement 3

STATE SERVICE COMPANY
Balance Sheet
December 31, 19X3
(Amounts in Thousands)

Assets			**Liabilities**	
Current assets:			Current liabilities:	
Cash		$198	Accounts payable	$380
Accounts receivable		382	Salary payable	5
Supplies		2	Unearned service revenue	13
Total current assets		582	Income tax payable	35
Furniture and fixtures	$100		Total current liabilities	433
Less Accumulated depreciation	60	40	**Stockholders' Equity**	
Building	$250		Common stock	$100
Less Accumulated depreciation	140	110	Retained earnings	199
			Total stockholders' equity	299
Total assets		$732	Total liabilities and stockholders' equity	$732

$$\textbf{Current ratio} = \frac{\$582}{\$433} = 1.34 \qquad \textbf{Debt ratio} = \frac{\$433}{\$732} = 0.59$$

Requirement 4

$$\textbf{Debt ratio assuming the loan is made} = \frac{\$433 + \$500}{\$732 + \$500} = \frac{\$933}{\$1,232} = 0.76$$

Decision: Make the loan at 10 percent.

Reasoning: Prior to the loan, the company's financial position and cash flow are strong. The current ratio is in a middle range, and the debt ratio is not too high. Net income (from the income statement) is high in relation to total revenue. Therefore, the company should be able to repay the loan.

The loan will increase the company's debt ratio from 59% to 76%, which is more risky than the company's financial position at present. On this basis, a mid-range interest rate appears reasonable—at least as the starting point for the negotiation between State Service Company and the bank.

SUMMARY OF LEARNING OBJECTIVES

1. *Distinguish accrual-basis accounting from cash-basis accounting.* In *accrual-basis accounting,* an accountant recognizes the impact of a business event as it occurs, whether or not cash is received or paid. In *cash-basis accounting,* the accountant does not record a transaction unless cash changes hands. The cash basis omits important events such as purchases and sales on account and distorts the financial statements. For this reason, generally accepted accounting principles require the use of accrual-basis accounting.

2. *Apply the revenue and matching principles.* The *revenue principle* tells accountants (1) to record revenue when it has been earned, but not before, and (2) to record revenue equal to the cash value of the goods or services transferred to the customer. The *matching principle* directs accountants to identify all the expenses incurred during the accounting period, to measure those expenses, and to match the expenses against the revenues earned during that period.

3. *Make adjusting entries at the end of the accounting period and prepare an adjusted trial balance.* *Adjusting entries* assign revenues to the period in which they are earned and expenses to the period in which they are incurred. These entries, made at the end of the period, update the accounts for preparation of the financial statements. Adjusting entries fall into five categories: prepaid expenses, depreciation of plant assets, accrued expenses, accrued revenues, and unearned revenues.

Accountants prepare an adjusted trial balance by entering the adjusting entries next to the unadjusted trial balance and then computing each account's new balance.

4. *Prepare the financial statements.* Accountants use the adjusted trial balance to prepare three of the financial statements: the income statement, statement of retained earnings, and balance sheet. All financial statements should include the name of the entity, the title of the statement, the date or period covered by the statement, and the body of the statement. On the income statement, it is customary to list expenses in descending order, with Miscellaneous Expense appearing last and Income Tax Expense appearing after income before tax.

Income, shown on the *income statement,* increases retained earnings. This increase also appears on the *statement of retained earnings.* The ending balance of retained earnings appears on the *balance sheet.*

5. *Close the revenue, expense, and dividend accounts.* At the end of each accounting period, accountants must close the *temporary accounts*—that is, the revenue, expense, and dividend accounts. The purpose is to set each account back to zero so that the next period's income can be measured accurately. The *permanent accounts*—assets, liabilities, and stockholders' equity—are not closed. The final check on the accuracy of the closing entries is the *postclosing trial balance.*

6. *Correct typical accounting errors.* Errors in journalizing and posting are corrected by making a correcting entry in the relevant accounts.

7. *Use the current ratio and the debt ratio to evaluate a business.* The *current ratio,* which measures a company's ability to pay current liabilities with current assets, is equal to total current assets divided by total current liabilities. The higher the current ratio, the stronger the company's financial position. The *debt ratio,* which measures a company's ability to pay its debts, equals total liabilities divided by total assets. In general, the lower the debt ratio, the stronger the company's financial position.

ACCOUNTING VOCABULARY

account format *(p. 141).*
accounting cycle *(p. 108).*
accrual-basis accounting *(p. 108).*
accrued expense *(p. 119).*
accrued revenue *(p. 120).*
Accumulated Depreciation *(p. 117).*
adjusted trial balance *(p. 125).*
adjusting entry *(p. 113).*
book value (of a plant asset) *(p. 117).*
cash-basis accounting *(p. 108).*
classified balance sheet *(p. 138).*
closing the accounts *(p. 132).*
closing entries *(p. 133).*
contra account *(p. 117).*
current asset *(p. 137).*
current liability *(p. 138).*
current ratio *(p. 143).*
debt ratio *(p. 143).*
deferral *(p. 113).*
depreciation *(p. 116).*
Income Summary *(p. 133).*
liquidity *(p. 137).*
long-term asset *(p. 138).*
long-term liability *(p. 138).*
matching principle *(p. 111).*
multi-step income statement *(p. 142).*
nominal accounts *(p. 133).*
operating cycle *(p. 137).*
permanent accounts *(p. 133).*
plant asset *(p. 116).*
postclosing trial balance *(p. 136).*
prepaid expense *(p. 113).*
real accounts *(p. 133).*
report format *(p. 142).*
revenue principle *(p. 110).*
single-step income statement *(p. 142).*
temporary accounts *(p. 133).*
time-period concept *(p. 110).*
unearned revenue *(p. 121).*

QUESTIONS

1. Distinguish accrual-basis accounting from cash-basis accounting.
2. What two questions does the revenue principle help answer?
3. Briefly explain the matching principle.
4. Name five categories of adjusting entries, and give an example of each.
5. Do all adjusting entries affect the net income or net loss of the period? Include the definition of an adjusting entry.
6. Manning Supply Company pays $1,800 for an insurance policy that covers three years. At the end of the first year, the balance of its Prepaid Insurance account contains two elements. What are the two elements, and what is the correct amount of each?
7. The title Prepaid Expense suggests that this type of account is an expense. If it is, explain why. If it is not, what type of account is it?
8. The manager of a Quickie-Pickie convenience store presents his entity's balance sheet to a banker when applying for a loan. The balance sheet reports that the entity's plant assets have a book value of $135,000 and accumulated depreciation of $65,000. What does *book value* of a plant asset mean? What was the cost of the plant assets?
9. Why is an unearned revenue a liability? Give an example.
10. Identify the types of accounts (assets, liabilities, and so on) debited and credited for each of the five types of adjusting entries.

11. Explain the relationship among the income statement, the statement of retained earnings, and the balance sheet.
12. Bellevue Company failed to record the following adjusting entries at December 31, the end of its fiscal year: (a) accrued expenses, $500; (b) accrued revenues, $850; and (c) depreciation, $1,000. Did these omissions cause net income for the year to be understated or overstated, and by what overall amount?
13. Which types of accounts are closed? What purpose is served by closing the accounts?
14. Distinguish between permanent accounts and temporary accounts; indicate which type is closed at the end of the period. Give five examples of each type of account.
15. Why are assets classified as current or long-term? On what basis are they classified? Where do the classified amounts appear?
16. Indicate which of the following accounts are current assets and which are long-term assets: Prepaid Rent, Building, Furniture, Accounts Receivable, Merchandise Inventory, Cash, Note Receivable (due within one year), Note Receivable (due after one year).
17. Identify an outside party that would be interested in whether a liability is current or long-term. Why would this party be interested in this information?
18. A friend tells you that the difference between a current liability and a long-term liability is that they are payable to different types of creditors. Is your friend correct? Define these two categories of liabilities.
19. Show how to compute the current ratio and the debt ratio. Indicate what ability each ratio measures, and state whether a high value or a low value is safer for each.
20. Capp Company purchased supplies of $120 on account. The accountant debited Supplies and credited Cash for $120. A week later, after this entry has been posted to the ledger, the accountant discovers the error. How should she correct the error?

EXERCISES

Accrual basis of accounting (Obj. 1)

E3-1 Wal-Mart Stores, Inc., is the world's largest retailer, with over 2,600 stores in the United States. Adapted versions of Wal-Mart's income statement and balance sheet follow.

WAL-MART STORES, INC.
Statement of Income (Adapted)
Fiscal year ended January 31, 19X6

	(In billions)
Net sales and other revenue	$94.7
Costs and expenses:	
Cost of sales	74.6
Operating, selling, and general and administrative expenses	14.9
Interest expense	0.9
Income before income taxes	4.3
Income tax expense	1.6
Net income	$ 2.7

WAL-MART STORES, INC.
Balance Sheet (Adapted)
January 31, 19X6

	(In billions)
Current Assets:	
Cash	$ 0.1
Accounts receivable	0.8
Inventories	16.0
Prepaid expenses	0.4
Property, plant, and equipment, at cost	23.3
Less Accumulated depreciation	(4.4)
Other assets	1.3
Total assets	$37.5
Current Liabilities:	
Accounts payable	$ 6.4
Long-term debt due within one year	-0-
Other	5.1
Long-term liabilities	11.3
Shareholders' equity	14.7
Total liabilities & shareholders' equity	$37.5

Required

Identify every account (other than Inventories and Property, plant, and equipment) listed in the Wal-Mart statements that is direct evidence that the company uses the accrual basis of accounting. For each account you identify, specify a related Wal-Mart account (other than Cash) that is increased by the transaction that created the first account.

Applying accounting concepts and principles (Obj. 2)

E3-2 Identify the accounting concept or principle that gives the most direction on how to account for each of the following situations:

a. A physician states her intention to switch accountants. Should the new accountant record revenue based on this intention?
b. Expenses of the period total $6,100. This amount must be used to compute the period's income.

c. Expenses of $2,800 must be accrued at the end of the period to measure income properly.

d. March has been a particularly slow month, and the business will have a net loss for the first quarter of the year. Management is considering not following its customary practice of reporting quarterly earnings to the public. Investors depend on quarterly earnings reports to decide whether to buy, hold, or sell the company's stock.

e. A construction company is building a highway system, and construction may take three years. When should the company record the revenue it earns?

Applying accounting concepts ***(Obj. 2)***

E3-3 Write a short paragraph to explain in your own words the concept of depreciation as it is used in accounting.

Journalizing adjusting entries and analyzing their effects on net income; accrual versus cash basis ***(Obj. 1, 3)***

E3-4 An accountant made the following adjustments at December 31, the end of the accounting period.

a. Prepaid insurance expired, $600.

b. Interest revenue accrued, $4,100.

c. Unearned service revenue earned, $800.

d. Depreciation, $6,200.

e. Employees' salaries owed for two days of a five-day workweek; weekly payroll, $9,000.

f. Income tax expense accrued, $2,200.

Required

1. Journalize the adjusting entries.

2. Suppose the adjustments were not made. Compute the overall overstatement or understatement of net income as a result of the omission of these adjustments.

3. Explain why the cash basis of accounting avoids the need to make these adjusting entries.

Allocating prepaid expense to the asset and the expense ***(Obj. 2, 3)***

E3-5 Compute the amounts indicated by question marks for each of the following Prepaid Insurance situations. For situations 1 and 2, journalize the needed entry. Consider each situation separately.

	Situation			
	1	**2**	**3**	**4**
Beginning Prepaid Insurance	$ 600	$500	$ 200	$ 900
Payments for Prepaid Insurance during the year	1,100	?	?	1,100
Total amount to account for	?	?	1,300	2,000
Ending Prepaid Insurance	500	600	400	?
Insurance Expense	$?	$700	$ 900	$1,400

Journalizing adjusting entries ***(Obj. 3)***

E3-6 Journalize the adjusting entry needed at December 31 for each of the following independent situations.

a. The business will pay interest expense of $9,000 early in the next period. Of this amount, $6,700 is expense of the current year.

b. Interest revenue of $900 has been earned but not yet received. The business holds a $20,000 note receivable that it will collect, along with the interest, next year.

c. On July 1, when we collected $6,000 rent in advance, we debited Cash and credited Unearned Rent Revenue. The tenant was paying for two years' rent.

d. Salary expense is $1,000 per day—Monday through Friday—and the business pays employees each Friday. This year, December 31 falls on a Thursday.

e. The unadjusted balance of the Supplies account is $3,100. The total cost of supplies on hand is $800.

f. Equipment was purchased last year at a cost of $10,000. The equipment's useful life is four years. Record the year's depreciation.

g. On September 1, when we prepaid $1,800 for a one-year insurance policy, we debited Prepaid Insurance and credited Cash.

Recording adjustments in T-accounts ***(Obj. 3)***

E3-7 The accounting records of Sun City Art Supplies include the following unadjusted balances at May 31: Accounts Receivable, $1,200; Supplies, $700; Salary Payable, $0; Unearned Service Revenue, $400; Service Revenue, $4,700; Salary Expense, $1,200; Supplies Expense, $0. Sun City's accountant develops the following data for the May 31 adjusting entries:

a. Supplies on hand, $400.

b. Salary owed to employee, $700.

c. Service revenue accrued, $350.

d. Unearned service revenue that has been earned, $250.

Open the foregoing T-accounts and record the adjustments directly in the accounts, keying each adjustment amount by letter. Show each account's adjusted balance. Journal entries are not required.

E3-8 The adjusted trial balance of Ship-n-Go Service, Inc., is given.

Preparing the financial statements (Obj. 4)

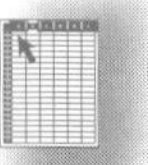

SHIP-N-GO SERVICE, INC.
Adjusted Trial Balance
June 30, 19X2

	Adjusted Trial Balance	
	Debit	**Credit**
Cash	3,000	
Accounts receivable	13,400	
Supplies	800	
Office furniture	29,300	
Accumulated depreciation—furniture		11,420
Salary payable		600
Unearned revenue		690
Income tax payable		2,100
Common stock		10,000
Retained earnings		16,340
Dividends	6,200	
Service revenue		18,940
Salary expense	3,290	
Rent expense	1,400	
Depreciation expense—furniture	360	
Supplies expense	240	
Income tax expense	2,100	
	60,090	60,090

Required

Prepare Ship-n-Go's income statement and statement of retained earnings for the three months ended June 30, 19X2, and its balance sheet on that date. Draw the arrows linking the three statements.

E3-9 The adjusted trial balances of PW Corporation at December 31, 19X6, and December 31, 19X5, include these amounts.

Computing financial statement amounts (Obj. 3)

	19X6	19X5
Supplies	$ 2,100	$ 1,500
Salary payable	3,100	3,700
Unearned service revenue	14,200	16,300

Analysis of the accounts at December 31, 19X6, reveals these transactions for 19X6.

Purchases of supplies	$ 9,100
Cash disbursements for salaries	81,600
Cash receipts for service revenue	301,200

Compute the amount of supplies expense, salary expense, and service revenue to report on the 19X6 income statement.

E3-10 Prepare the entity's closing entries from the following selected accounts that AAdvantage Delivery Service, Inc., reported in its September 30, 19X4, annual financial statements:

Closing the accounts (Obj. 5)

Unearned revenues	$ 1,350	Note payable	$50,000
Salary expense	42,500	Depreciation expense	1,200
Accumulated depreciation	35,000	Rent expense	5,900
Supplies expense	1,100	Dividends	40,000
Interest revenue	700	Income tax expense	9,000
Retained earnings	45,600	Interest expense	2,200
Service revenue	96,100	Income tax payable	9,000

Suppose AAdvantage owes you the $50,000 note payable. What about AAdvantage's dividends during the year would disturb you? Why?

Identifying and recording adjusting and closing entries ***(Obj. 3, 5)***

E3-11 The unadjusted trial balance and income statement amounts from the March adjusted trial balance of Dial Bonding Company are given.

Account Title	Unadjusted Trial Balance		From the Adjusted Trial Balance	
Cash	9,100			
Supplies	2,400			
Prepaid rent	1,100			
Office equipment	30,100			
Accumulated depreciation		6,200		
Accounts payable		4,600		
Salary payable				
Unearned service revenue		8,400		
Income tax payable				
Common stock		7,500		
Retained earnings		10,300		
Dividends	1,000			
Service revenue		11,700		18,100
Salary expense	3,000		3,800	
Rent expense	1,200		1,400	
Depreciation expense			300	
Supplies expense			400	
Utilities expense	800		800	
Income tax expense			1,600	
	48,700	48,700	8,300	18,100
Net income			9,800	
			18,100	18,100

Required

Journalize the adjusting and closing entries of Dial Bonding Company at March 31. There was only one adjustment to Service Revenue.

Preparing a classified balance sheet and using the ratios ***(Obj. 4, 7)***

E3-12 Refer to Exercise 3-11.

Required

1. After solving Exercise 3-11, use the data in that exercise to prepare Dial Bonding Company's classified balance sheet at March 31 of the current year. Use the report format.
2. Compute Dial's current ratio and debt ratio at March 31. One year ago, the current ratio was 1.20 and the debt ratio was 0.30. Indicate whether Dial's ability to pay its debts has improved or deteriorated during the current year.

Correcting accounting errors ***(Obj. 6)***

E3-13 Prepare a correcting entry for each of the following accounting errors:

a. Accrued interest revenue of $400 by a debit to Accounts Receivable and a credit to Interest Revenue.
b. Recorded a $600 cash purchase of supplies by debiting Supplies and crediting Accounts Payable.
c. Debited Supplies and credited Accounts Payable for a $6,000 purchase of office equipment on account.
d. Adjusted prepaid rent by debiting Prepaid Rent and crediting Rent Expense for $900. This adjusting entry should have debited Rent Expense and credited Prepaid Rent for $900.
e. Debited Salary Expense and credited Cash to accrue salary expense of $900.
f. Recorded the earning of $3,200 service revenue collected in advance by debiting Accounts Receivable and crediting Service Revenue.

SERIAL EXERCISE

Adjusting the accounts, preparing the financial statements, closing the accounts, and evaluating the business ***(Obj. 3, 4, 5, 7)***

Exercise 3-14 continues the Dirk Olsen, Accountant, P.C., situation begun in Exercise 2-14 of Chapter 2.

E3-14 Refer to Exercise 2-14 of Chapter 2. Start from the trial balance and the posted T-accounts that Dirk Olsen, Accountant, Professional Corporation (P.C.), prepared for his accounting practice at December 18. A professional corporation is not subject to income tax.

Later in December, the business completed these transactions:

Dec. 21	Received $900 in advance for tax work to be performed evenly over the next 30 days.
21	Hired a secretary to be paid $1,500 on the 20th day of each month.
26	Paid for the supplies purchased on December 5.
28	Collected $600 from the consulting client on December 18.
30	Declared and paid dividends of $1,600.

Required

1. Open these T-accounts: Accumulated Depreciation—Equipment, Accumulated Depreciation—Furniture, Salary Payable, Unearned Service Revenue, Retained Earnings, Depreciation Expense—Equipment, Depreciation Expense—Furniture, Supplies Expense, and Income Summary. Also, use the T-accounts opened for E2-14.
2. Journalize the transactions of December 21 through 30.
3. Post the December 21-30 transactions to the T-accounts, keying all items by date.
4. Prepare a trial balance at December 31. Also set up columns for the adjustments and for the adjusted trial balance, as illustrated in Exhibit 3-10.
5. At December 31, Olsen gathers the following information for the adjusting entries:
   - **a.** Accrued service revenue, $400.
   - **b.** Earned a portion of the service revenue collected in advance on December 21.
   - **c.** Supplies on hand, $100.
   - **d.** Depreciation expense—equipment, $50; furniture, $60.
   - **e.** Accrued expense for secretary's salary.

   Make these adjustments directly in the adjustments columns, and complete the adjusted trial balance at December 31.
6. Journalize and post the adjusting entries. Denote each adjusting amount as Adj. and an account balance as Bal.
7. Prepare the income statement and statement of retained earnings of Dirk Olsen, Accountant, P.C., for the month ended December 31, and the classified balance sheet at that date.
8. Journalize and post the closing entries at December 31. Denote each closing amount as Clo. and an account balance as Bal.
9. Compute the current ratio and the debt ratio of Olsen's accounting practice and evaluate these ratio values as indicative of a strong or weak financial position.

CHALLENGE EXERCISES

Computing revenue and cash amounts ***(Obj. 3)***

E3-15 Gao Enterprises aids Chinese students upon their arrival in the United States. Paid by the Chinese government, Haiyuan Gao collects some service revenue in advance. In other cases, he receives cash after performing relocation services. At the end of August—a particularly busy period—Gao's books show the following:

	August 31	July 31
Accounts receivable	$1,200	$2,200
Unearned service revenue	1,200	300

a. During August, Gao Enterprises received cash of $6,100 from the Chinese government. How much service revenue did the business earn during August? Show your computations.

b. Assume the service revenue of Gao is $5,700 during August. How much cash did the business collect from the Chinese government during August? Show your computations.

Computing financial statement amounts ***(Obj. 3, 4)***

E3-16 The unadjusted trial balance of ElsiMate Company follows:

Cash	$ 1,900	Unearned service revenue	$ 5,300
Accounts receivable	7,200	Note payable, long-term	6,000
Rent receivable		Common stock	10,000
Supplies	1,100	Retained earnings	50,100
Prepaid insurance	2,200	Dividends	16,200
Furniture	8,400	Service revenue	93,600
Accumulated depreciation—furniture	1,300	Rent revenue	1,900
Building	57,800	Salary expense	32,700
Accumulated depreciation—building	14,900	Depreciation expense—furniture	
Land	51,200	Depreciation expense—building	
Accounts payable	6,100	Supplies expense	
Salary payable		Insurance expense	
Interest payable		Interest expense	
Property tax payable		Advertising expense	7,800
		Property tax expense	
		Utilities expense	2,700

Adjusting data at the end of the year include:

a. Unearned service revenue that has been earned, $1,900.
b. Accrued rent revenue, $1,200.
c. Accrued property tax expense, $900.
d. Accrued service revenue, $1,700.
e. Supplies used in operations, $600.
f. Accrued salary expense, $1,400.
g. Insurance expense, $1,800.
h. Depreciation expense—furniture, $800; building, $2,100.
i. Accrued interest expense, $500.

Elsie Sharp, the principal stockholder, has received an offer to sell ElsiMate Company. She needs to know the following information within one hour:

a. Net income for the year covered by these data.
b. Total assets.
c. Total liabilities.
d. Total stockholders' equity.
e. Proof that total assets = total liabilities + total stockholders' equity after all items are updated.

Required

Without opening any accounts, making any journal entries, or using a work sheet, provide Elsie Sharp with the requested information. The business is not subject to income tax. Show all computations.

PROBLEMS

(GROUP A)

Cash basis versus accrual basis
(Obj. 1)

P3-1A Buzzard Billy's Armadillo Bar and Grill-O had the following selected transactions during May:

May	5	Paid electricity expenses, $700.
	9	Received cash for the day's sales, $1,400.
	14	Purchased two video games, $3,000.
	23	Served a banquet, receiving a note receivable, $1,200.
	31	Accrued salary expense, $900.
	31	Prepaid building rent for June, July, and August, $3,000.

Required

1. Show how each transaction would be handled using the cash basis and the accrual basis. Under each column, give the amount of revenue or expense for May. Journal entries are not required. Use the following format for your answer, and show your computations:

Buzzard Billy's—Amount of Revenue or Expense for May		
Date	**Cash Basis**	**Accrual Basis**

2. Compute income (loss) before tax for May under the two methods.
3. Which method better measures income and assets? Use the last transaction to explain.

Applying accounting principles
(Obj. 1, 2)

P3-2A Write a short memo to a new bookkeeper to explain the difference between the cash basis of accounting and the accrual basis. Mention the roles of the revenue principle and the matching principle in accrual-basis accounting.

Making accounting adjustments
(Obj. 3)

P3-3A Journalize the adjusting entry needed on December 31, end of the current accounting period, for each of the following independent cases affecting Potosi Painting Contractors, Inc.

a. Details of Prepaid Insurance are shown in the account:

Prepaid Insurance				
Jan.	1	Bal.	600	
Mar.	31		1,200	
Sept.	30		1,200	

Potosi prepays insurance semiannually on March 31 and September 30.

b. Potosi pays its employees each Friday. The amount of the weekly payroll is $3,000 for a five-day work week, and the daily salary amounts are equal. The current accounting period ends on Monday.

c. Potosi has loaned money, receiving notes receivable. During the current year, the entity has earned accrued interest revenue of $509 that it will receive next year.

d. The beginning balance of Supplies was $2,680. During the year, the entity purchased supplies costing $6,180, and at December 31 the cost of supplies on hand is $2,150.

e. Potosi is servicing the air-conditioning system in a large building, and the owner of the building paid Potosi $12,900 as the annual service fee. Potosi recorded this amount as Unearned Service Revenue. Mari Potosi, the general manager, estimates that the company has earned one-fourth the total fee during the current year.

f. Depreciation for the current year includes Office Furniture, $850; Equipment, $2,730; and Trucks, $10,320. Make a compound entry.

Analyzing and recording adjustments ***(Obj. 3)***

P3-4A AccuTrac Court Reporting Company's unadjusted and adjusted trial balances at April 30, 19X1, follow.

ACCUTRAC COURT REPORTING COMPANY
Adjusted Trial Balance
April 30, 19X1

	Trial Balance		Adjusted Trial Balance	
Account Title	**Debit**	**Credit**	**Debit**	**Credit**
Cash	8,180		8,180	
Accounts receivable	6,360		6,840	
Interest receivable			300	
Note receivable	4,100		4,100	
Supplies	980		290	
Prepaid rent	2,480		720	
Building	66,450		66,450	
Accumulated depreciation		16,010		17,110
Accounts payable		6,920		6,920
Wages payable				170
Unearned service revenue		670		110
Common stock		18,000		18,000
Retained earnings		42,790		42,790
Dividends	3,600		3,600	
Service revenue		9,940		10,980
Interest revenue				300
Wage expense	1,600		1,770	
Rent expense			1,760	
Depreciation expense			1,100	
Insurance expense	370		370	
Supplies expense			690	
Utilities expense	210		210	
	94,330	94,330	96,380	96,380

Required

Make the adjusting entries that account for the differences between the two trial balances. AccuTrac Court Reporting Company is not subject to income tax.

Preparing the financial statements and using the debt ratio ***(Obj. 4, 7)***

P3-5A The adjusted trial balance of Global Travel Designers, Inc., at December 31, 19X6, is given on page 156.

Required

1. Prepare Global's 19X6 income statement, statement of retained earnings, and balance sheet. List expenses (except for income tax) in decreasing order on the income statement and show total liabilities on the balance sheet. Draw arrows linking the three financial statements.
2. Global's lenders require that the company maintain a debt ratio no higher than 0.70. Compute Global's debt ratio at December 31, 19X6, to determine whether the company is in compliance with this debt restriction. If not, suggest an easy way that Global could have avoided this difficult situation by altering the amount of dividends.

GLOBAL TRAVEL DESIGNERS, INC.
Adjusted Trial Balance
December 31, 19X6

Cash	$ 1,320	
Accounts receivable	8,920	
Supplies	2,300	
Prepaid rent	1,600	
Office equipment	30,180	
Accumulated depreciation—office equipment		$14,350
Office furniture	17,710	
Accumulated depreciation—office furniture		4,870
Accounts payable		3,640
Property tax payable		1,100
Interest payable		830
Unearned service revenue		620
Income tax payable		7,100
Note payable		18,400
Common stock		5,000
Retained earnings		1,090
Dividends	44,000	
Service revenue		127,910
Depreciation expense—office equipment	6,680	
Depreciation expense—office furniture	2,370	
Salary expense	39,900	
Rent expense	10,300	
Interest expense	3,100	
Utilities expense	2,670	
Insurance expense	3,810	
Supplies expense	2,950	
Income tax expense	7,100	
Total	$184,910	$184,910

Preparing an adjusted trial balance and the financial statements; using the current ratio to evaluate the business ***(Obj. 3, 4, 7)***

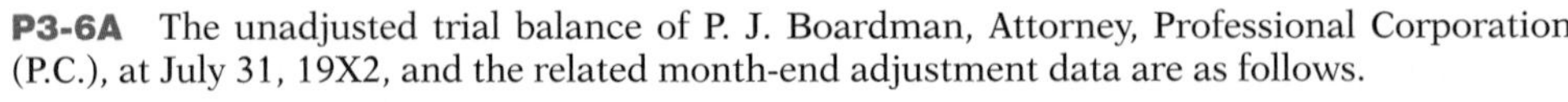

P3-6A The unadjusted trial balance of P. J. Boardman, Attorney, Professional Corporation (P.C.), at July 31, 19X2, and the related month-end adjustment data are as follows.

P. J. BOARDMAN, ATTORNEY, P.C.
Trial Balance
July 31, 19X2

Cash	$ 3,600	
Accounts receivable	11,600	
Prepaid rent	3,600	
Supplies	800	
Furniture	34,800	
Accumulated depreciation		$ 3,500
Accounts payable		10,450
Salary payable		
Common stock		25,000
Retained earnings		13,650
Dividends	4,000	
Legal service revenue		8,750
Salary expense	2,400	
Rent expense		
Utilities expense	550	
Depreciation expense		
Supplies expense		
Total	$61,350	$61,350

Adjustment data:

a. Accrued legal service revenue at July 31, $400.

b. Prepaid rent expired during the month. The unadjusted prepaid balance of $3,600 relates to the period July through October.

c. Supplies used during July, $600.

d. Depreciation on furniture for the month. The estimated useful life of the furniture is four years.

e. Accrued salary expense at July 31 for Wednesday through Friday. The five-day weekly payroll is $1,200.

Required

1. Using Exhibit 3-10 as an example, prepare the adjusted trial balance of P. J. Boardman, Attorney, P.C., at July 31, 19X2. Key each adjusting entry by letter. A professional corporation is not subject to income tax.
2. Prepare the income statement, the statement of retained earnings, and the classified balance sheet. Draw arrows linking the three financial statements.
3. **a.** Compare the business's net income for July to the amount of dividends paid to the owners. Suppose this trend continues each month for the remainder of 19X2. What will be the effect on the business's financial position, as shown by its accounting equation?

   b. Will the trend make it easier or more difficult to borrow money if the business gets in a bind and needs cash? Why?

   c. Does either the current ratio or the cash position suggest the need for immediate borrowing? Explain.

Preparing a classified balance sheet and using the ratios to evaluate the business ***(Obj. 4, 7)***

P3-7A The accounts of Bret Coody, CPA, Professional Corporation (P.C.), at March 31, 19X3, are listed in alphabetical order.

Account	Amount	Account	Amount
Accounts payable	$14,700	Insurance expense	$ 600
Accounts receivable	11,500	Interest payable	300
Accumulated depreciation—building	47,300	Interest receivable	900
Accumulated depreciation—furniture	7,700	Note payable, long-term	3,200
Advertising expense	900	Note receivable, long-term	6,900
Building	55,900	Other assets	2,300
Cash	3,400	Prepaid expenses	5,300
Common stock	9,100	Retained earnings, March 31, 19X2	30,800
Current portion of note payable	800	Salary expense	17,800
Depreciation expense	1,900	Salary payable	2,400
Dividends	31,200	Service revenue	71,100
Furniture	43,200	Supplies	3,800
		Supplies expense	4,600
		Unearned service revenue	2,800

Required

1. All adjustments have been journalized and posted, but the closing entries have not yet been made. Prepare the company's classified balance sheet at March 31, 19X3. Use captions for total assets, total liabilities, and total liabilities and stockholders' equity. A professional corporation is not subject to income tax.
2. Compute Coody's current ratio and debt ratio at March 31, 19X3. At March 31, 19X2, the current ratio was 1.28 and the debt ratio was 0.35. Did Coody's ability to pay debts improve or deteriorate during 19X3?

Analyzing and journalizing corrections, adjustments, and closing entries ***(Obj. 3, 5, 6)***

P3-8A The accountants of Salazar Septic Service, Inc., encountered the following situations while adjusting and closing the books at February 28. Consider each situation independently.

a. The $1,620 balance of Utilities Expense was entered as $16,200 on the trial balance.

   (1) What is this type of error called?

   (2) Assume that this is the only error in the trial balance. Which will be greater, the total debits or the total credits, and by how much?

   (3) How can this type of error be identified?

b. The company bookkeeper made the following entry to record a $950 credit purchase of supplies:

Date	Accounts	Debit	Credit
Feb. 26	Equipment	950	
	Accounts Payable		950

Prepare the correcting entry, dated February 28.

c. A $690 credit to Accounts Receivable was posted as $960.
 (1) At what stage of the accounting process will this error be detected?
 (2) Describe the technique for identifying the amount of the error.

d. The accountant failed to make the following adjusting entries at February 28:
 (1) Accrued service revenue, $900.
 (2) Insurance expense, $360.
 (3) Accrued interest revenue on a note receivable, $520.
 (4) Depreciation of equipment, $3,700.
 (5) Earned service revenue that had been collected in advance, $2,700.
 (6) Accrued income tax expense, $6,300.
 Compute the overall net income effect of these omissions.

e. Journalize each of the adjusting entries identified in item *d.*

f. The revenue and expense accounts after the adjusting entries had been posted were Service Revenue, $91,330; Wage Expense, $29,340; Depreciation Expense, $6,180; Interest Expense, $4,590; Utilities Expense, $1,620; Insurance Expense, $640; and Income Tax Expense, $6,300. Two balances prior to closing were Retained Earnings, $75,150, and Dividends, $44,000. Journalize the closing entries.

Analyzing financial ratios
(Obj. 7)

P3-9A This problem demonstrates the effects of transactions on the current ratio and the debt ratio of a well-known company. **Texaco, Inc.**, is a leading oil company, famous for its Texaco gas stations. Texaco's condensed balance sheet at December 31, 19X5, is given.

	(In millions)
Total current assets	$ 6,458
Properties, plant, equipment, and other assets	18,479
	$24,937
Total current liabilities	$ 5,206
Total long-term liabilities	10,212
Total stockholders' equity	9,519
	$24,937

Assume that during the first quarter of the following year, 19X6, Texaco completed the following transactions:

a. Paid half the current liabilities.

b. Borrowed $3 billion ($3,000 million) on long-term debt.

c. Earned service revenue, $2.5 billion ($2,500 million) on account.

d. Paid selling expense of $1 billion ($1,000 million).

e. Accrued general expense of $800 million. Credit General Expense Payable, a current liability.

f. Purchased equipment, paying cash of $1.4 billion ($1,400 million) and signing a long-term note payable for $2.8 billion ($2,800 million).

g. Recorded depreciation expense of $600 million.

Required

1. Compute Texaco's current ratio and debt ratio at December 31, 19X5.

2. Compute Texaco's current ratio and debt ratio after each transaction. Consider each transaction separately.

3. Compute Texaco's current ratio and debt ratio after the company has completed all the transactions. The following format will aid your analysis:

	Current Assets	+	Properties, Plant, Equipment, and Other Assets	=	Current Liabilities	+	Long-term Liabilities	+	Stockholders' Equity
Balance, Dec. 31, 19X5	$	+	$	=	$	+	$	+	$
(a)									
.									
.									
.									
(g)									
Balance after all the transactions	$	+	$	=	$	+	$	+	$

4. Based on your analysis, you should be able to readily identify the effects of certain transactions on the current ratio and the debt ratio. Test your understanding by completing these statements with either "increase" or "decrease":

   a. Revenues usually ________________ the current ratio.

   b. Revenues usually ________________ the debt ratio.

   c. Expenses usually ________________ the current ratio. (*Note:* Depreciation is an exception to this rule.)

   d. Expenses usually ________________ the debt ratio.

   e. If a company's current ratio is greater than 1.0, as it is for Texaco, paying off a current liability will always ________________ the current ratio.

   f. Borrowing money on long-term debt will always ________________ the current ratio and ________________ the debt ratio.

(GROUP B)

Cash basis versus accrual basis
(Obj. 1)

P3-1B Katz Counseling Service, Inc., had the following selected transactions in October:

Oct. 1	Prepaid insurance for October through December, $900.
4	Purchased office equipment for cash, $800.
5	Performed counseling service and received cash, $700.
8	Paid advertising expense, $300.
11	Performed counseling service on account, $1,800.
19	Purchased office furniture on account, $100.
24	Collected for the October 11 service.
26	Paid account payable from October 19.
29	Paid salary expense, $900.
31	Recorded adjusting entry for October insurance expense (see Oct. 1).
31	Debited unearned revenue and credited revenue to adjust the accounts, $600.

Required

1. Show how each transaction would be handled using the cash basis and the accrual basis. Under each column, give the amount of revenue or expense for October. Journal entries are not required. Use the following format for your answer, and show your computations:

Katz Counseling Service—Amount of Revenue or Expense for October		
Date	**Cash Basis**	**Accrual Basis**

2. Compute October income (loss) before tax under each method.
3. Indicate which measure of net income or net loss is preferable. Use the transactions on October 11 and 24 to explain.

Applying accounting principles
(Obj. 1, 2)

P3-2B As the controller of Auto Glass Masters Company, you have hired a new bookkeeper, whom you must train. He objects to making an adjusting entry for accrued salaries at the end of the period. He reasons, "We will pay the salaries soon. Why not wait until payment to record the expense? In the end, the result will be the same." Write a reply to explain to the bookkeeper why the adjusting entry for accrued salary expense is needed.

Making accounting adjustments
(Obj. 3)

P3-3B Journalize the adjusting entry needed on December 31, end of the current accounting period, for each of the following independent cases affecting Mercedes Engineering, Inc.

a. Each Friday, Mercedes pays its employees for the current week's work. The amount of the payroll is $3,500 for a five-day work week. The current accounting period ends on Monday.

b. Mercedes has received notes receivable from some clients for professional services. During the current year, Mercedes has earned accrued interest revenue of $2,640, which will be received next year.

c. The beginning balance of Engineering Supplies was $3,800. During the year, the entity purchased supplies costing $12,530, and at December 31, the inventory of supplies on hand is $2,970.

d. Mercedes is conducting tests of the strength of the steel to be used in a large building, and the client paid Mercedes $36,000 at the start of the project. Mercedes recorded this amount as Unearned Engineering Revenue. The tests will take several months to complete. Mercedes executives estimate that the company has earned three-fourths of the total fee during the current year.

e. Depreciation for the current year includes Office Furniture, $5,500; Engineering Equipment, $6,360; Building, $3,790. Make a compound entry.

f. Details of Prepaid Insurance are shown in the account:

Prepaid Insurance		
Jan. 1	Bal. 1,200	
Apr. 30	1,800	
Oct. 31	1,800	

Mercedes pays semiannual insurance premiums (the payment for insurance coverage is called a *premium*) on April 30 and October 31.

Analyzing and recording adjustments
(Obj. 3)

P3-4B Oriole Commission Company's unadjusted and adjusted trial balances at December 31, 19X7, is given.

ORIOLE COMMISSION COMPANY
Adjusted Trial Balance
December 31, 19X7

	Trial Balance		Adjusted Trial Balance	
Account Title	**Debit**	**Credit**	**Debit**	**Credit**
Cash	4,120		4,120	
Accounts receivable	11,260		12,090	
Supplies	1,090		780	
Prepaid insurance	2,600		910	
Office furniture	21,630		21,630	
Accumulated depreciation		8,220		10,500
Accounts payable		6,310		6,310
Salary payable				960
Interest payable				480
Note payable		12,000		12,000
Unearned commission revenue		1,840		1,160
Common stock		10,000		10,000
Retained earnings		3,510		3,510
Dividends	29,370		29,370	
Commission revenue		72,890		74,400
Depreciation expense			2,280	
Supplies expense			310	
Utilities expense	4,960		4,960	
Salary expense	26,660		27,620	
Rent expense	12,200		12,200	
Interest expense	880		1,360	
Insurance expense			1,690	
	114,770	114,770	119,320	119,320

Required

Make the adjusting entries that account for the difference between the two trial balances. Oriole Commission Company is not subject to income tax.

Preparing the financial statements and using the debt ratio
(Obj. 4, 7)

P3-5B The adjusted trial balance of McMullen Appliance Service, Inc., at December 31, 19X8, is given at the top of page 161.

Required

1. Prepare McMullen's 19X8 income statement, statement of retained earnings, and balance sheet. List expenses in decreasing order on the income statement and show total liabilities on the balance sheet. Draw arrows linking the three financial statements.
2. McMullen's lenders require that the company maintain a debt ratio no higher than 0.60. Compute McMullen's debt ratio at December 31, 19X8, to determine whether the company is in compliance with this debt restriction. If not, suggest an easy way that McMullen could have avoided this difficult situation by altering the amount of dividends.

MCMULLEN APPLIANCE SERVICE, INC. Adjusted Trial Balance December 31, 19X8		
Cash	$ 2,340	
Accounts receivable	41,490	
Prepaid rent	1,350	
Supplies	970	
Equipment	75,690	
Accumulated depreciation—equipment		$ 22,240
Office furniture	24,100	
Accumulated depreciation—office furniture		18,670
Accounts payable		13,600
Unearned service revenue		4,520
Interest payable		2,130
Salary payable		930
Income tax payable		8,800
Note payable		36,200
Common stock		12,000
Retained earnings		20,380
Dividends	48,000	
Service revenue		195,790
Depreciation expense—equipment	11,300	
Depreciation expense—office furniture	2,410	
Salary expense	94,000	
Rent expense	12,000	
Interest expense	4,200	
Utilities expense	3,770	
Insurance expense	3,150	
Supplies expense	1,690	
Income tax expense	8,800	
Total	$335,260	$335,260

Preparing an adjusted trial balance and the financial statements; using the current ratio to evaluate the business ***(Obj. 3, 4, 7)***

P3-6B Consider the unadjusted trial balance of Sandra Steiner, Speech Therapist, Professional Corporation (P.C.), at October 31, 19X2, and the related month-end adjustment data.

SANDRA STEINER, SPEECH THERAPIST, P.C. Trial Balance October 31, 19X2		
Cash	$ 1,300	
Accounts receivable	7,000	
Prepaid rent	4,000	
Supplies	600	
Furniture	36,000	
Accumulated depreciation		$ 3,000
Accounts payable		8,800
Salary payable		
Common stock		15,000
Retained earnings		21,000
Dividends	4,600	
Consulting service revenue		10,400
Salary expense	4,400	
Rent expense		
Utilities expense	300	
Depreciation expense		
Supplies expense		
Total	$58,200	$58,200

Adjustment data:

a. Accrued consulting service revenue at October 31, $2,000.

b. Prepaid rent expired during the month. The unadjusted prepaid balance of $4,000 relates to the period October 19X2 through January 19X3.

c. Supplies used during October, $200.

d. Depreciation on furniture for the month. The furniture's expected useful life is five years.

e. Accrued salary expense at October 31 for Tuesday through Friday. The five-day weekly payroll is $2,000.

Required

1. Using Exhibit 3-10 as an example, prepare the adjusted trial balance of Sandra Steiner, Speech Therapist, P.C., at October 31, 19X2. Key each adjusting entry by letter. A professional corporation is not subject to income tax.

2. Prepare the income statement, the statement of retained earnings, and the classified balance sheet. Draw arrows linking the three financial statements.

3. **a.** Compare the business's net income for October to the amount of dividends paid to the owners. Suppose this trend continues into 19X3. What will be the effect on the business's financial position, as shown by its accounting equation?

b. Will the trend make it easier or more difficult for Steiner to borrow money if the business gets in a bind and needs cash? Why?

c. Does either the current ratio or the cash position suggest the need for immediate borrowing? Explain.

Preparing a classified balance sheet and using the ratios to evaluate the business ***(Obj. 4, 7)***

P3-7B The accounts of Cookie Lapp Travel Agency, Inc., at December 31, 19X6, are listed in alphabetical order.

Accounts payable	$ 5,100	Insurance expense	$ 800
Accounts receivable	6,600	Interest payable	600
Accumulated depreciation—building	37,800	Interest receivable	200
Accumulated depreciation—furniture	11,600	Note payable, long-term	29,800
Advertising expense	2,200	Note receivable, long-term	4,000
Building	104,400	Other assets	3,600
Cash	6,500	Prepaid expenses	7,700
Commission revenue	93,500	Retained earnings, December 31, 19X5	35,300
Common stock	15,000	Salary expense	24,600
Current portion of note payable	2,200	Salary payable	3,900
Depreciation expense	1,300	Supplies	2,500
Dividends	47,400	Supplies expense	5,700
Furniture	22,700	Unearned commission revenue	5,400

Required

1. All adjustments have been journalized and posted, but the closing entries have not yet been made. Prepare the company's classified balance sheet in report format at December 31, 19X6. Use captions for total assets, total liabilities, and total liabilities and stockholders' equity. The travel agency is not subject to income tax.

2. Compute Lapp's current ratio and debt ratio at December 31, 19X6. At December 31, 19X5, the current ratio was 1.52, and the debt ratio was 0.45. Did Lapp's ability to pay debts improve or deteriorate during 19X6?

Analyzing and journalizing corrections, adjustments, and closing entries ***(Obj. 3, 5, 6)***

P3-8B Accountants for Bon Apetit Catering Service, Inc., encountered the following situations while adjusting and closing the books at December 31. Consider each situation independently.

a. The $39,000 balance of Equipment was entered as $3,900 on the trial balance.

(1) What is this type of error called?

(2) Assume that this is the only error in the trial balance. Which will be greater, the total debits or the total credits, and by how much?

(3) How can this type of error be identified?

b. The company bookkeeper made the following entry to record a $600 credit purchase of office equipment:

Nov. 12	Office Supplies	600	
	Accounts Payable		600

Prepare the correcting entry, dated December 31.

c. A $750 debit to Cash was posted as a credit.
   (1) At what stage of the accounting process will this error be detected?
   (2) Describe the technique for identifying the amount of the error.

d. The accountant failed to make the following adjusting entries at December 31:
   (1) Accrued property tax expense, $200.
   (2) Supplies expense, $1,090.
   (3) Accrued interest revenue on a note receivable, $650.
   (4) Depreciation of equipment, $4,000.
   (5) Earned service revenue that had been collected in advance, $5,100.
   (6) Accrued income tax expense, $2,100.
   Compute the overall net income effect of these omissions.

e. Journalize each of the adjusting entries identified in item *d*.

f. The revenue and expense accounts after the adjusting entries had been posted were Service Revenue, $41,900; Interest Revenue, $2,000; Salary Expense, $14,200; Rent Expense, $5,100; Depreciation Expense, $5,550; Supplies Expense, $1,530; Property Tax Expense, $1,190; and Income Tax Expense, $2,100. Two balances prior to closing were Retained Earnings, $58,600, and Dividends, $15,000. Journalize the closing entries.

Analyzing financial ratios ***(Obj. 7)***

P3-9B This problem demonstrates the effects of transactions on the current ratio and the debt ratio of a well-known company. **Unocal Corporation** is a leading oil company, famous for its 76 gas stations. Unocal's condensed balance sheet at December 31, 19X5, is given.

	(In millions)
Total current assets	$1,576
Properties, net, and other assets	8,315
	$9,891
Total current liabilities	$1,316
Total long-term liabilities	5,645
Total stockholders' equity	2,930
	$9,891

Assume that during the first quarter of the following year, 19X6, Unocal completed the following transactions.

a. Paid half the current liabilities.
b. Borrowed $3 billion ($3,000 million) on long-term debt.
c. Earned service revenue, $2.5 billion ($2,500 million) on account.
d. Paid selling expense of $1 billion ($1,000 million).
e. Accrued general expense of $800 million. Credit General Expense Payable, a current liability.
f. Purchased equipment, paying cash of $1.4 billion ($1,400 million) and signing a long-term note payable for $2.8 billion ($2,800 million).
g. Recorded depreciation expense of $600 million.

Required

1. Compute Unocal's current ratio and debt ratio at December 31, 19X5.
2. Compute Unocal's current ratio and debt ratio after each transaction. Consider each transaction separately.
3. Compute Unocal's current ratio and debt ratio after the company has completed all the transactions. The following format will aid your analysis:

	Current Assets	+	**Properties, Net, and Other Assets**	=	**Current Liabilities**	+	**Long-term Liabilities**	+	**Stockholders' Equity**
Balance, Dec. 31, 19X5	$	+	$	=	$	+	$	+	$
(a)									
.									
.									
.									
(g)									
Balance after all the transactions	$	+	$	=	$	+	$	+	$

4. Based on your analysis, you should be able to readily identify the effects of certain transactions on the current ratio and the debt ratio. Test your understanding by completing those statements with either "increase" or "decrease":
   a. Revenues usually _______________ the current ratio.
   b. Revenues usually _______________ the debt ratio.
   c. Expenses usually _______________ the current ratio. (*Note:* Depreciation is an exception to this rule.)
   d. Expenses usually _______________ the debt ratio.
   e. If a company's current ratio is greater than 1.0, as it is for Unocal, paying off a current liability will always _______________ the current ratio.
   f. Borrowing money on long-term debt will always _______________ the current ratio and _______________ the debt ratio.

EXTENDING YOUR KNOWLEDGE

DECISION CASES

Valuing a business on the basis of its net income ***(Obj. 3, 4)***

Case 1. Slade McQueen has owned and operated McQueen Biomedical Systems, Inc., a professional corporation for physicians, since its beginning ten years ago. From all appearances, the business has prospered. McQueen lives in the fast lane—flashy car, home located in an expensive suburb, frequent trips abroad, and other signs of wealth. In the past few years, you have become friends with him and his wife through weekly rounds of golf at the country club. Recently, he mentioned that he has lost his zest for the business and would consider selling it for the right price. He claims that his clientele is firmly established and that the business "runs itself." According to McQueen, the consulting procedures are fairly simple and anyone could perform the work.

Assume that you are interested in buying this business. You obtain its most recent monthly trial balance, which follows. Revenues and expenses vary little from month to month, and April is a typical month. Your investigation reveals that the trial balance does not include the effects of monthly revenues of $1,100 and expenses totaling $2,100. If you were to buy McQueen Biomedical Systems, you would hire a manager so you could devote your time to other duties. Assume that this person would require a monthly salary of $2,000.

MCQUEEN BIOMEDICAL SYSTEMS, INC., P.C.
Trial Balance
April 30, 19XX

Cash	$ 9,700	
Accounts receivable	4,900	
Prepaid expenses	2,600	
Plant assets	221,300	
Accumulated depreciation		$189,600
Land	158,000	
Accounts payable		13,800
Salary payable		
Unearned consulting revenue		56,700
Common stock		50,000
Retained earnings		87,400
Dividends	9,000	
Consulting revenue		12,300
Rent expense		
Salary expense	3,400	
Utilities expense	900	
Depreciation expense		
Supplies expense		
Total	$409,800	$409,800

Required

1. Assume that the most you would pay for the business is 30 times the monthly net income you could expect to earn from it. Compute this possible price.
2. McQueen states that the least he will take for the business is its stockholders' equity on April 30. Compute this amount.
3. Under these conditions, how much should you offer McQueen? Give your reason.

Case 2. One year ago, Shea Squires founded Squires Computing Service, Inc. The business has prospered. Squires, who remembers that you took an accounting course while in college, comes to you for advice. She wishes to know how much net income her business earned during the past year. She also wants to know what the entity's total assets, liabilities, and stockholders' equity are. Her accounting records consist of the T-accounts of her ledger, which were prepared by an accountant who moved to another city. The ledger at December 31 appears as follows:

Completing the accounting cycle to develop the information for a bank loan ***(Obj. 3, 5)***

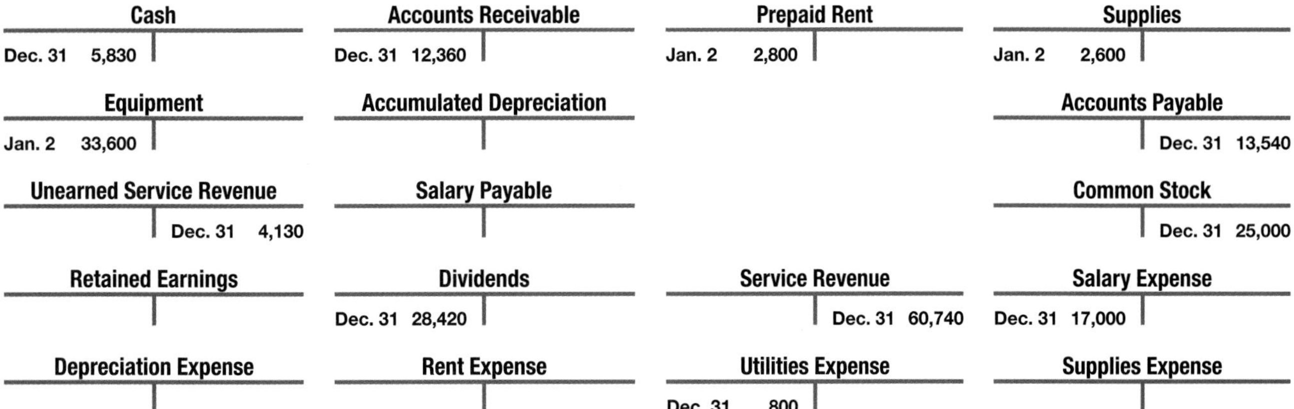

Squires indicates that at the year's end, customers owe her $1,600 accrued service revenue, which she expects to collect early next year. These revenues have not been recorded. During the year, she collected $4,130 service revenue in advance from customers, but she earned only $600 of that amount. Rent expense for the year was $2,400, and she used up $2,100 in supplies. Squires estimates that depreciation on her equipment was $5,900 for the year. At December 31, she owes her employee $1,200 accrued salary.

At the conclusion of your meeting, Squires expresses concern that dividends during the year might have exceeded net income. To get a loan to expand the business, Squires must show the bank that total stockholders' equity has grown from its original $25,000 balance. Has it? You and Squires agree that you will meet again in one week. You perform the analysis and prepare the financial statements to answer her questions.

ETHICAL ISSUES

Issue 1. Pastille Associates, a management consulting firm, is in its third year of operations. The company was initially financed by owners' equity as the three partners each invested $30,000. The first year's slim profits were expected because new businesses often start slowly. During the second year, Pastille landed a large contract with a paper mill, and referrals from that project brought in several other large jobs. To expand the business, Pastille borrowed $100,000 from First State Bank of Juneau, Alaska. As a condition for making this loan, the bank required that Pastille maintain a current ratio of at least 1.50 and a debt ratio of no more than 0.50.

Business during the third year has been good, but slightly below the target for the year. Expansion costs have brought the current ratio down to 1.47 and the debt ratio up to 0.51 at December 15. Jacques Pastille is considering the implication of reporting this current ratio to the bank. One course of action is to record in December of the third year some revenue on account that Pastille will earn in January of their fourth year of operations. The contract for this job has been signed, and Pastille will perform the management consulting service for the client during January.

Required

1. Journalize the revenue transaction, and indicate how recording this revenue in December would affect the current ratio and the debt ratio.
2. State whether it is ethical to record the revenue transaction in December. Identify the accounting principle relevant to this situation.
3. Propose for Pastille Associates a course of action that is ethical.

Issue 2. The net income of Loveman's, a department store, decreased sharply during 1998. Louis Loveman, owner of the store, anticipates the need for a bank loan in 1999. Late in 1998, he instructed the accountant to record a $10,200 sale of furniture to the Loveman family, even though the goods will not be shipped from the manufacturer until January 1999. Loveman also told the accountant not to make the following December 31, 1999, adjusting entries:

Salaries owed to employees	$1,800
Prepaid insurance that has expired	530

Required

1. Compute the overall effect of these transactions on the store's reported income for 1998. Is income overstated or understated?
2. Why did Loveman take these actions? Are they ethical? Give your reason, identifying the parties helped and the parties harmed by Loveman's action.
3. As a personal friend, what advice would you give the accountant?

FINANCIAL STATEMENT CASES

Journalizing and posting transactions and tracing account balances to the financial statements ***(Obj. 3, 7)***

Case 1. Lands' End, Inc.—like all other businesses—makes adjusting entries prior to year end in order to measure assets, liabilities, revenues, and expenses properly. Examine the Lands' End balance sheet in Appendix A, and pay particular attention to Prepaid Advertising, Accrued Profit Sharing (Payable) (a current liability similar to Salary Payable), and Current Maturities of Long-Term Debt. Assume that Salary Payable and Interest Payable are the only Accrued Liabilities.

Required

1. Open T-accounts for the first three accounts listed above. Insert the Lands' End balances (in thousands) at January 27, 1995 (example: Prepaid Advertising, $7,506).
2. Journalize the following for the current year, ended February 2, 1996. Key entries by letter. Explanations are not required.
   Cash transactions (amounts in thousands):
   a. Paid prepaid advertising, $21,382.
   b. Paid the January 27, 1995, accrued profit sharing.
   c. Paid the January 27, 1995, current maturity of long-term debt.
   Adjustments at February 2, 1996 (amounts in thousands):
   d. Prepaid advertising expired: $13,064. Debit Selling Expense.
   e. Accrued the profit sharing for the year. Debit General Expense.
3. After these entries are posted, show that the balances in Prepaid Advertising, Accrued Profit Sharing, and Current Maturities of Long-Term Debt agree with the corresponding amounts reported in the February 2, 1996, balance sheet. Performing this operation for an actual company should increase your understanding of the financial statements.
4. Compute the current ratios and debt ratios for Lands' End at February 2, 1996, and January 27, 1995. Did the ratio values improve, deteriorate, or hold steady during the fiscal year ended February 2, 1996? Refer to the income statement to explain your evaluation of the ratio values.

Adjusting the accounts of an actual company ***(Obj. 3)***

Case 2. Obtain the annual report of a company of your choosing. Assume that the company accountants *failed* to make four adjustments at the end of the current year. For illustrative purposes, we shall assume that the amounts reported in the company's balance sheet for the related assets and liabilities are *incorrect.*

Adjustments omitted:

a. Depreciation of equipment, $800,000.
b. Salaries owed to employees but not yet paid, $230,000.
c. Prepaid rent used up during the year, $100,000.
d. Accrued sales (or service) revenue, $140,000.

Required

1. Compute the correct amounts for the following balance sheet items:
   a. Book value of plant assets
   b. Total liabilities
   c. Prepaid expenses
   d. Accounts receivable
2. Compute the amount of net income or net loss that the company would have reported if the accountants had recorded these transactions properly. Ignore income tax.

GROUP PROJECT

Jack Roberts formed a lawn service company as a summer job. To start the business on May 1, he deposited $1,000 in a new bank account in the name of the corporation. The $1,000 consisted of a $600 loan from his father and $400 of his own money. The corporation issued 400 shares of common stock to Jack.

Jack rented lawn equipment, purchased supplies, and hired high-school students to mow and trim his customers' lawns.

At the end of each month, Jack mailed bills to his customers. On August 31, Jack was ready to dissolve the business and return to Baylor University for the fall semester. Because he had been so busy, he had kept few records other than his checkbook and a list of amounts owed to him by customers.

At August 31, Jack's checkbook shows a balance of $1,640, and his customers still owe him $500. During the summer, he collected $5,200 from customers. His checkbook lists payments for supplies totaling $400, and he still has gasoline, weedeater cord, and other supplies that cost a total of $50. He paid his employees $1,900, and he still owes them $200 for the final week of the summer. Jack rented some equipment from Ludwig Tool Company. On May 1, he signed a six-month lease on mowers and paid $600 for the full lease period. Ludwig will refund the unused portion of the prepayment if the equipment is in good shape. In order to get the refund, Jack has kept the mowers in excellent condition. In fact, he had to pay $300 to repair a mower that ran over a hidden tree stump. To transport employees and equipment to jobs, Jack used a trailer that he bought for $300. He figures that the summer's work used up one-third of the trailer's service potential. The business checkbook lists an expenditure of $460 for dividends paid to Jack during the summer. Jack paid his father back during the summer.

Required

1. Prepare the income statement of Roberts Lawn Service, Inc., for the four months May through August. The business is not subject to income tax.
2. Prepare the classified balance sheet of Roberts Lawn Service, Inc., at August 31.
3. Prepare the statement of cash flows for Roberts Lawn Service, Inc., for the four months May through August.

INTERNET EXERCISE

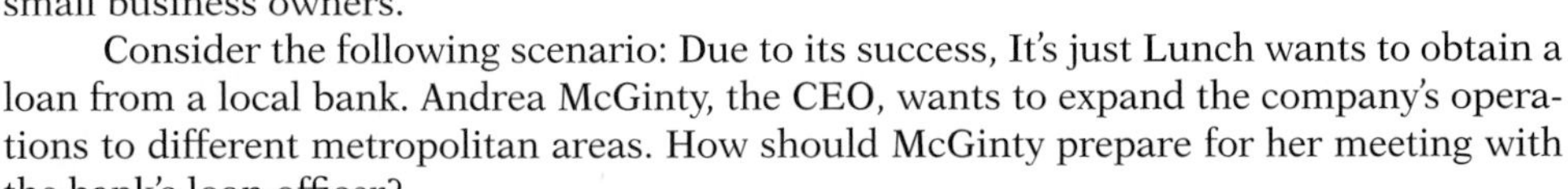

IT'S JUST LUNCH

Many companies provide detailed, insightful information on their Web sites. For example, Commerce Clearing House (CCH), a provider of reference materials to accountants, attorneys, and business owners, offers versions of their products on the Internet. One CCH product available on the Net is the SOHO (Small Office, Home Office) Guidebook for small business owners.

Consider the following scenario: Due to its success, It's just Lunch wants to obtain a loan from a local bank. Andrea McGinty, the CEO, wants to expand the company's operations to different metropolitan areas. How should McGinty prepare for her meeting with the bank's loan officer?

Required

1. To assist McGinty in expanding her business, you need a good understanding of the ins and outs of financing. Proceed as follows.
2. Go to **http://www.toolkit.cch.com.** This is CCH's "welcome page" and it lists the resources available to business owners.
3. Click on **The SOHO Guidebook.** Doing so takes you to the Guidebook's Table of Contents, a treasure trove of excellent and practical tips for small busines owners.
4. Click on **Getting Financing for Your Business.** This section of the guidebook helps you understand the choices available to small business owners in their quest for additional capital.
5. Because Ms. McGinty is interested in obtaining a business loan, click on the highlighted term **Debt Financing** to learn which issues the bankers will consider in evaluating her loan request (you may have to scroll down the page). Answer the following questions so that you can assist McGinty as she prepares for her meeting with the bank's loan officer.
   a. What is debt financing?
   b. Why is debt financing attractive?
   c. What are the different types of bank loans?
   d. Which loan type might be best for It's Just Lunch's expansion plans? Why?
   e. What documents should McGinty expect the bank to request in reviewing her loan application?
   f. Will the bank focus on the financial position and opportunities of It's Just Lunch? If not, what other factors will the bank consider in its review?
   g. Why do banks look beyond a company's financial statements in evaluating a loan request?

APPENDIX TO CHAPTER 3

Accounting Work Sheet

This appendix extends the adjusted trial balance given in Exhibit 3-10, page 125. Some accountants use a work sheet to summarize data for preparation of the financial statements. Exhibit 3A-1 is not part of the journal or the ledger, nor is it a financial statement. Therefore, it is not part of the formal accounting system. It exists merely for the accountant's convenience in preparing the financial statements.

The first three pairs of columns repeat the data on the adjusted trial balance in Exhibit 3-10. Following the adjusted trial balance are Income Statement columns for the revenues and expenses and to compute net income or net loss. For the month of April 19X1, Air & Sea Travel earned net income of $2,985, which appears as a debit on the spreadsheet to balance net income and total expenses (debits) with total revenues (credits).

The balance sheet columns show the assets, liabilities, and stockholders' equity amounts. Air & Sea Travel's net income of $2,985 for April also appears as a credit on the balance sheet. This entry parallels the closing of net income into Retained Earnings (a credit to Retained Earnings). Retained Earnings' amount on the work sheet ($11,250) is the beginning balance. Neither net income nor Dividends has been closed to Retained Earnings. Only the closing entries can bring Retained Earnings' balance to the correct amount for the balance sheet.

EXHIBIT 3A-1
Accounting Work Sheet

AIR & SEA TRAVEL, INC.
Accounting Work Sheet
For the Month Ended April 30, 19X1

	Trial Balance		Adjustments		Adjusted Trial Balance		Income Statement		Balance Sheet	
Account Title	**Debit**	**Credit**	**Debit**	**Credit**	**Debit**	**Credit**	**Debit**	**Credit**	**Debit**	**Credit**
Cash	24,800				24,800				24,800	
Accounts receivable	2,250		(e) 250		2,500				2,500	
Supplies	700			(b) 300	400				400	
Prepaid rent	3,000			(a) 1,000	2,000				2,000	
Furniture	16,500				16,500				16,500	
Accumulated depreciation				(c) 275		275				275
Accounts payable		13,100				13,100				13,100
Salary payable				(d) 950		950				950
Unearned service revenue		450	(f) 150			300				300
Income tax payable				(g) 540		540				540
Common stock		20,000				20,000				20,000
Retained earnings		11,250				11,250				11,250
Dividends	3,200				3,200				3,200	
Service revenue		7,000		(e) 250 (f) 150		7,400		7,400		
Rent expense			(a) 1,000		1,000		1,000			
Salary expense	950		(d) 950		1,900		1,900			
Supplies expense			(b) 300		300		300			
Depreciation expense			(c) 275		275		275			
Utilities expense	400				400		400			
Income tax expense			(g) 540		540		540			
	51,800	51,800	3,465	3,465	53,815	53,815	4,415	7,400	49,400	46,415
Net income							2,985			2,985
							7,400	7,400	49,400	49,400

4

Internal Control and Managing Cash

Learning Objectives

After studying this chapter, you should be able to

1. Identify the characteristics of an effective system of internal control
2. Use a bank reconciliation as a control device
3. Manage cash and account for cash transactions
4. Apply internal controls to cash receipts
5. Apply internal controls to cash disbursements
6. Use a budget to manage cash
7. Weigh ethical judgments in business

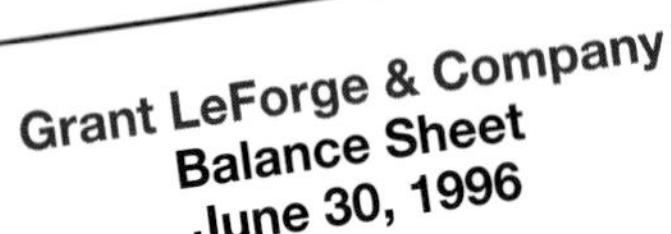

Grant LeForge & Company
Balance Sheet
June 30, 1996

Assets

Current assets:	
Cash	$1,710,934
Marketable securities	2,136,842
Receivables	859,763
Prepaid expenses	181,845
	4,889,384
Long-term investments	12,633,790
Property and equipment	5,436,211
Less accumulated depreciation	(1,707,946)
Other assets	663,582
	$21,915,021

BANK STATEMENT
June 30, 1996

Grant LeForge & Company
Idaho Tower Building, Suite 700
Boise, Idaho 83702

Balance $1,100,000

What happened to the $610,934?

"If all employees were always accurate and ethical, internal controls would not be necessary. Our ineffective internal control system gave one dishonest employee the opportunity to embezzle cash over several years' time. From now on, we're going to make it a lot harder to steal anything!"

BILL BAUER, OFFICE MANAGER OF GRANT LEFORGE & COMPANY

Steve Lane was a cashier at the Boise, Idaho, office of the brokerage firm **Grant LeForge & Company.** His problems began when an auto accident forced him to miss work and office manager Bill Bauer received complaints from customers who had not received credit for their deposits. Bauer uncovered an elaborate embezzlement scheme that Lane had begun five years earlier.

The court found that Lane had stolen a total of $610,934 in a "rob-Peter-to-pay-Paul scheme." He transferred customer deposits into his personal account and concealed the missing amounts with deposits from other customers. In this way, customer accounts always balanced as long as Lane was present to respond to customer inquiries. He simply explained that the account was temporarily out of balance. But while he was recovering in the hospital, his replacement was unable to explain the irregularities in customers' accounts. When all the evidence came to light, it pointed in the direction of Lane, who was later tried and convicted of embezzlement. Bauer then understood why Lane had never taken a vacation.

What went wrong at the Grant LeForge office? Steve Lane was able to control not only the cash received from customers, but also part of his company's accounting records. By manipulating the records, he was able to hide his theft for several years. Evidently, no one checked his work on a regular basis. Several procedures that we discuss in this chapter explain how the company could have prevented this embezzlement. Such *control systems* cannot prevent all employee misconduct, but they can help to detect unethical or illegal behavior and thereby limit its effects.

The need for laws requiring internal control procedures has received increased attention since the 1970s. At that time, some high-profile illegal payments, embezzlements, and other criminal business practices came to light. Concerned citizens wanted to know why the companies' internal controls had failed to alert management to these illegalities. "Where were the auditors?" people asked. To answer these growing worries, the U.S. Congress passed the Foreign Corrupt Practices Act in 1977. This act requires companies under SEC jurisdiction to maintain an appropriate system of internal control, whether or not they have foreign operations. The act also contains specific prohibitions against bribery and other corrupt practices.

This chapter discusses *internal control*—the organizational plan and integrated framework that managers use to keep the business under control and protect company assets. The chapter applies these control techniques mainly to the management of cash (the most liquid asset) and provides a framework for making ethical judgments in business. Later chapters discuss how managers control other assets.

Internal Control

A key responsibility of a business's managers is to control operations. The owners and the top managers set the entity's goals, the managers lead the way, and the employees carry out the plan. Good managers must decide where the organization is headed over the next several years. But unless they control operations today, the entity may not stay in business long enough for managers to put lofty plans into effect.

Internal control is the organizational plan and all the related measures that an entity adopts to

1. Safeguard assets,
2. Encourage adherence to company policies,
3. Promote operational efficiency, and
4. Ensure accurate and reliable accounting records.

Internal controls are most effective when employees at all levels adopt the goals, objectives, and ethical standards of the organization. Top managers should communicate these goals and standards to workers. Lee Iacocca, former president of **Chrysler Corporation,** instilled management's goals in Chrysler employees by getting out of the executive suite and spending time with assembly-line workers. (Japanese firms pioneered this style of participative management.) The result? Defects decreased dramatically, and Chrysler products became more competitive. Its sales of cars and trucks increased 14% in one year.

The only constant in business is that things are going to change. Companies take risks when they move into new industries. Although Grant LeForge & Company is in the investment brokerage business, it also serves as a banker for its clients. Perhaps Grant LeForge's lack of experience in the banking business contributed to the breakdown in internal controls that led to the embezzlement of $610,934. An effective system of internal control is designed to manage organizational change.

Exhibit 4-1 presents an excerpt from the Responsibility for Consolidated Financial Statements of **Lands' End, Inc.** The company's top managers take responsibility for the financial statements and for the related system of internal control. The second paragraph refers to a system of internal control, the protection of assets, and the prevention of fraudulent financial reporting. Let's examine in more detail how companies create an effective system of internal control.

Objective 1

Identify the characteristics of an effective system of internal control

Establishing an Effective System of Internal Control

Whether the business is Grant LeForge, Lands' End, or a local department store, an effective system of internal controls has the following characteristics.

Competent, Reliable, and Ethical Personnel Employees should be *competent, reliable,* and *ethical.* Paying top salaries to attract top-quality employees, training them to do their job well, and supervising their work all help a

EXHIBIT 4-1
Management Statement About Internal Controls—Lands' End, Inc.

LANDS' END, INC.—Responsibility for Consolidated Financial Statements

The management of Lands' End, Inc., and its subsidiaries has the responsibility for preparing the accompanying financial statements and for their integrity and objectivity. The statements were prepared in accordance with generally accepted accounting principles applied on a consistent basis. The consolidated financial statements include amounts that are based on management's best estimates and judgments. Management also prepared the other information in the annual report and is responsible for its accuracy and consistency with the consolidated financial statements.

Management of the company has established and maintains a system of internal control that provides for appropriate division of responsibility, reasonable assurance as to the integrity and reliability of the consolidated financial statements, the protection of assets from unauthorized use or disposition, and the prevention and detection of fraudulent financial reporting, and the maintenance of an active program of internal audits. Management believes that, as of February 2, 1996, the company's system of internal control is adequate to accomplish the objectives discussed herein.

Michael J. Smith
Chief Executive Officer

Stephen A. Orum
Chief Financial Officer

Source: Lands' End, Inc., *Annual Report 1996,* p. 20. Courtesy of Lands' End.

company build a competent staff. A business adds flexibility to its staffing by rotating employees through various jobs. If one employee is sick or on vacation, a second employee is trained to step in and do the job.

ASSIGNMENT OF RESPONSIBILITIES In a business with a good internal control system, no important duty is overlooked. Each employee is assigned certain responsibilities. A model of such *assignment of responsibilities* appears in the corporate organizational chart in Exhibit 4-2 on page 174. Notice that the corporation has a vice president of finance and accounting. Two other officers, the treasurer and the controller, report to that vice president. The treasurer is responsible for cash management. The **controller** is the chief accounting officer.

Within this organization, the controller may be responsible for approving invoices (bills) for payment, and the treasurer may actually sign the checks. Working under the controller, one accountant may be responsible for property taxes, another accountant for income taxes. In sum, all duties are clearly defined and assigned to individuals who bear responsibility for carrying them out.

PROPER AUTHORIZATION An organization generally has a written set of rules that outlines approved procedures. Any deviation from standard policy requires *proper authorization.* For example, managers or assistant managers of retail stores must approve customer checks for amounts above the store's usual limit. Likewise, deans or department chairs of colleges and universities must authorize a junior to enroll in courses restricted to seniors.

SEPARATION OF DUTIES Smart management divides the responsibilities for transactions between two or more people or departments. *Separation of duties* limits the chances for fraud and promotes the accuracy of the accounting records. The Lands' End responsibility statement (Exhibit 4-1) refers to a *division of responsibility.* This crucial component of the internal control system may be divided into four parts:

1. *Separation of operations from accounting.* The entire accounting function should be completely separate from operating departments, such as manufacturing

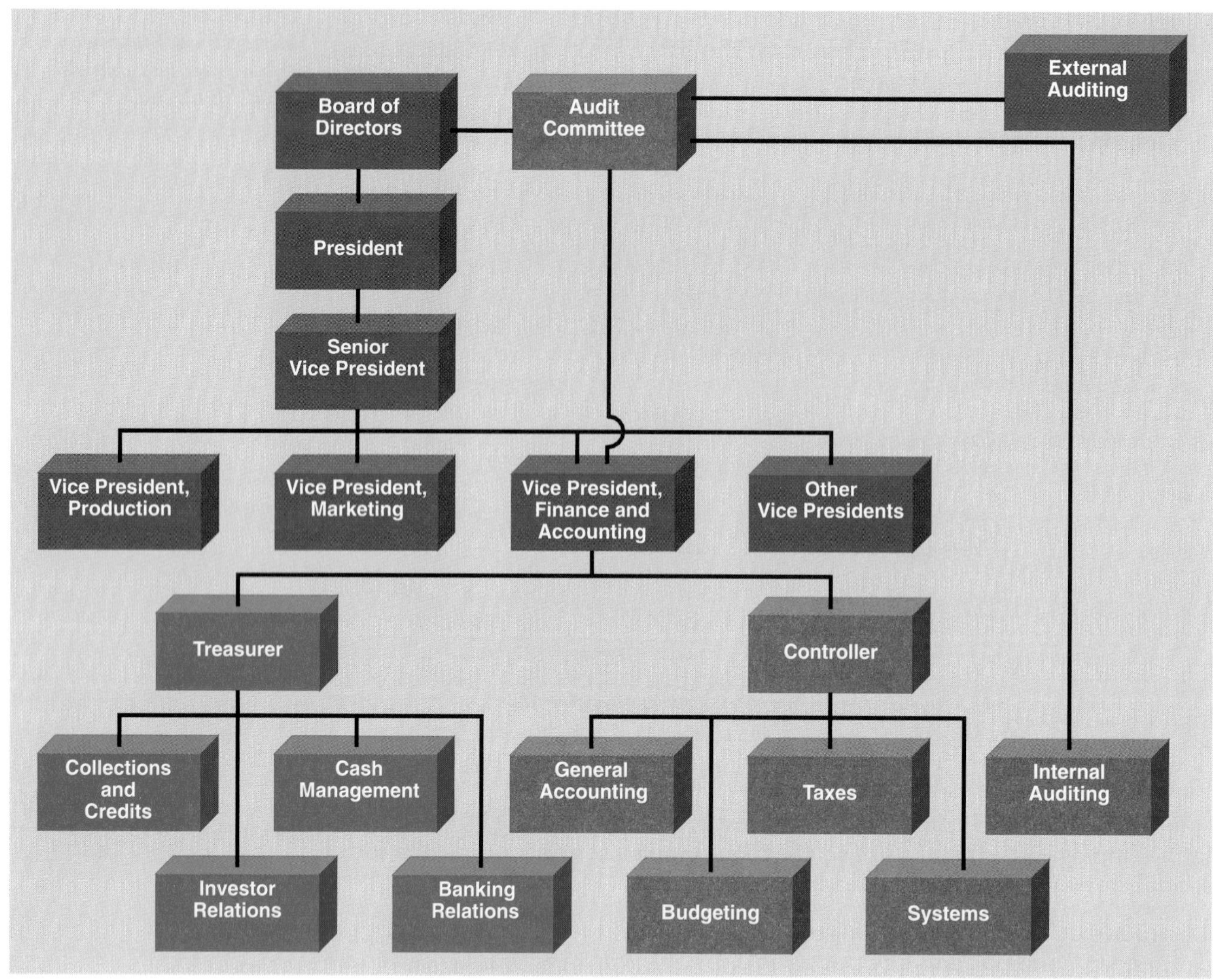

EXHIBIT 4-2
Organizational Chart of a Corporation

and sales, so that reliable records may be kept. For example, product inspectors, not machine operators, should count units produced by a manufacturing process. Accountants, not salespeople, should keep inventory records. Observe the separation of accounting from production and marketing in Exhibit 4-2.

2. *Separation of the custody of assets from accounting.* Temptation and fraud are reduced if accountants do not handle cash and if cashiers do not have access to the accounting records. If one employee has both cash-handling and accounting duties, that person can steal cash and conceal the theft by making a bogus entry on the books. We see this component of internal control in Exhibit 4-2. The treasurer has custody of the cash, and the controller accounts for the cash. Neither person has both responsibilities. Steve Lane was able to apply one customer's cash deposit to another customer's account at Grant LeForge. Apparently, Lane, the cashier, controlled some data entered into the accounting system. This is a serious violation of the separation of duties.

Warehouse employees with no accounting duties should handle inventory. If they were allowed to account for the inventory, they could steal it and write it off as obsolete. A *write-off* is an entry that credits an asset account. This write-off could be recorded by debiting Loss on Inventory Obsolescence and crediting Inventory. A person with custody of assets should not have access to the computer programs. Similarly, the programmer should not have access to tempting assets such as cash.

3. *Separation of the authorization of transactions from the custody of related assets.* If possible, persons who authorize transactions should not handle the related asset. For example, the same person should not authorize the payment of a supplier's invoice and also sign the check to pay the bill. With both duties, the person can authorize payments to him- or herself and then sign the checks. When these duties are separated, only legitimate bills are paid.

4. *Separation of duties within the accounting function.* Different people should perform the various phases of accounting to minimize errors and opportunities for fraud. For example, different accountants should be responsible for recording cash receipts and cash disbursements. The employee who processes accounts payable and check requests should have nothing to do with the approval process.

INTERNAL AND EXTERNAL AUDITS To guarantee the accuracy of their accounting records, most companies undergo periodic audits. An **audit** is an examination of the company's financial statements and the accounting systems, controls, and records that produced them.

It is not economically feasible for auditors to examine all the transactions during a period, so they must rely on the accounting system to produce accurate records. To gauge the reliability of the company's accounting system, auditors evaluate its system of internal controls. Auditors also spot the weaknesses in the system and recommend corrections. Auditors offer *objectivity* in their reports, while managers immersed in operations may overlook their own weaknesses.

Audits can be internal or external. Exhibit 4-2 shows *internal auditors* as employees of the business reporting directly to the audit committee. Some organizations have the internal auditors report directly to a vice president. Throughout the year, they audit various segments of the organization to ensure that employees adhere to company policies. *External auditors* are entirely independent of the business. They are hired by a company such as Lands' End to audit the entity as a whole. External auditors are concerned mainly with the financial statements and the factors affecting them. Both internal and external auditors are independent of the operations they examine.

An auditor may find that an employee has both cash-handling and cash-accounting duties or may learn that a cash shortage has resulted from lax efforts to collect accounts receivable. In such cases, the auditor suggests improvements. Auditors' recommendations help the business run more efficiently.

DOCUMENTS AND RECORDS Business *documents and records* vary considerably, from source documents such as invoices and purchase orders to special journals and subsidiary ledgers. Documents should be prenumbered. A gap in the numbered sequence calls attention to a missing document.

Prenumbering cash-sale receipts discourages theft by cashiers because the copies retained by the cashiers, which list the amount of the sale, can be checked against the actual amount of cash received. If the receipts are not prenumbered, the cashier can destroy the copy and pocket the cash-sale amount. However, if the receipts are prenumbered, the missing copy or copies can easily be identified. In a computerized system, a permanent record of the sale is stored electronically when the transaction is completed.

In a bowling alley, for example, a key document is the score sheet. The manager can check on cashiers by comparing the number of games scored with the amount of cash received. By multiplying the number of games by the price per game and comparing the result with each day's cash receipts, the manager can see whether the business is collecting all the bowling revenue. If cash on hand is low, the cashier might be stealing.

ELECTRONIC AND COMPUTER CONTROLS Businesses use electronic devices to meet their needs for control over assets and operations. For example, retailers such

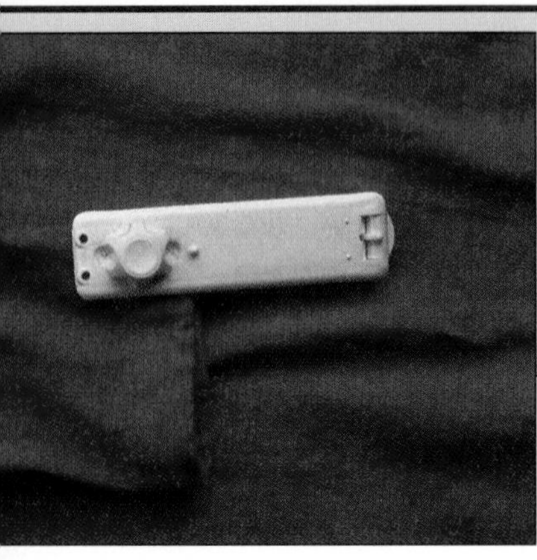

Target Stores, Bradlees, and Dillard's control their inventories by attaching an electronic sensor to merchandise. If a customer tries to remove from the store an item with the sensor attached, an alarm is activated.

as **Target Stores, Bradlees,** and **Dillard's** control their inventories by attaching an electronic sensor to merchandise. The cashier removes the sensor when a sale is made. If a customer tries to remove from the store an item with the sensor attached, an alarm is activated. According to Checkpoint Systems, which manufactures electronic sensors, these devices reduce loss due to theft by as much as 50 percent.

Accounting systems are relying less and less on documents and more and more on digital storage devices. Computers produce accurate records and enhance operational efficiency, but they do not automatically safeguard assets or encourage employees to behave in accordance with company policies. What computers have done is shift the internal controls to the people who write the programs. Programmers carry out the plans of managers and accountants. All the controls that apply to accountants apply to computer programmers as well.

Within a single company, each department may take steps to maintain control over its assets and accounting records. Consider a large company such as the retailer **Saks Fifth Avenue.** If the Saks system is well designed, each department can ensure that its transactions are processed correctly. Each department needs to maintain its own records. For example, the shoe department submits daily credit sales totals for computer processing. The shoe department expects a printout showing a total sales amount agreeing with the control total that it calculated *before* its documents went to the computer operators.

The accounts receivable department relies on computer operators to post correctly to thousands of customer accounts. Proper posting can be ensured by devising customer account numbers so that the last digit is a mathematical function of the previous digits (for example, 1359, where $1 + 3 + 5 = 9$). Any miskeying of a customer account number would trigger an error message to the keyboarder, and the computer would not accept the number. Many companies now employ electronic data processing (EDP) auditors to ensure the integrity of their computer databases.

OTHER CONTROLS Businesses of all types keep cash and important business documents such as contracts and titles to property in *fireproof vaults.* They use *burglar alarms* to protect buildings and other property.

Retailers receive most of their cash from customers on the spot. To safeguard cash, they use *point-of-sale terminals* that serve as a cash register and record each transaction as it is entered into the machine. Several times each day a supervisor removes the cash for deposit in the bank.

Employees who handle cash are in an especially tempting position. Many businesses purchase *fidelity bonds* on cashiers. The bond is an insurance policy that reimburses the company for any losses due to employee theft. Before issuing a fidelity bond, the insurance company investigates the employee's past to ensure a record of ethical conduct.

General Electric, Eastman Kodak, and other large companies move employees from job to job—often at six-month intervals. Knowing that someone else will be doing their job next month also keeps employees honest.

Mandatory vacations and *job rotation* require that employees be trained to do a variety of jobs. **General Electric, Eastman Kodak,** and other large companies move employees from job to job—often at six-month intervals. This practice enhances morale by giving employees a broad view of the business and helping them decide where they want to specialize. Knowing that someone else will be doing their job next month also keeps employees honest. If Grant LeForge had moved Steve Lane from job to job, and had required him to take a vacation, his embezzlement would probably have been detected much earlier.

STOP & THINK Ralph works the late movie at Big-Hit Theater. Occasionally, he must both sell the tickets and take them as customers enter the theater. Standard procedure requires that Ralph tear the tickets, give one-half to the customer, and keep the other half. To control cash receipts, the theater manager compares each night's cash receipts with the number of ticket stubs on hand.

What is the internal control weakness in this situation? What might a dishonest employee do to steal cash? What additional steps should the manager take to strengthen the control over cash receipts?

Answer: The internal control weakness is the lack of separation of duties. Ralph receives cash from customers and also controls the tickets. Good internal control would require that Ralph handle either cash or the tickets, but not both. If he were dishonest, he could occasionally fail to issue a ticket and then keep that customer's cash. To control that dishonest behavior, the manager could physically count the people watching a movie and compare that number with the number of ticket stubs collected. Or a dishonest employee could destroy some ticket stubs and keep the cash received from customers. To catch that dishonest behavior, the manager could account for all ticket stubs by serial number. Missing serial numbers would raise questions that would lead to investigation.

The Limitations of Internal Control

Unfortunately, most internal control measures can be overcome. Systems designed to thwart an individual employee's fraud can be beaten by two or more employees working as a team—*colluding*—to defraud the firm. Consider the Big-Hit Theater again. Ralph and a fellow employee could put together a scheme in which the ticket seller pockets the cash from ten customers and the ticket taker admits ten customers without tickets. To prevent this situation, the manager could take additional control measures, such as matching the number of people in the theater against the number of ticket stubs retained. But that would take time away from other duties. The stricter the internal control system, the more expensive it becomes.

A system of internal control that is too complex can strangle the business with red tape. Efficiency and control are hurt rather than helped. Just how tight should an internal control be? Managers must make sensible judgments. Investments in internal control must be judged in light of the costs and benefits.

Using the Bank Account as a Control Device

Cash is the most liquid asset because it is the medium of exchange. But cash is also intangible, often consisting of electronic impulses in a bank's accounting system with no accompanying paper checks or deposit slips. Cash is easy to conceal, easy to move, and relatively easy to steal. As a result, most businesses use an elaborate system of internal controls to safeguard and manage their cash.

Keeping cash in a *bank account* is an important part of internal control because banks have established practices for safeguarding cash. Banks also provide depositors with detailed records of cash transactions. To take full advantage of these control features, the business should deposit all cash receipts in the bank account and make all cash payments through it (except petty cash disbursements, which we look at later in this chapter).

The documents used to control a bank account include the signature card, the deposit ticket, the check, the bank statement, and the bank reconciliation.

SIGNATURE CARD Banks require each person authorized to transact business through an account in that bank to sign a *signature card.* The bank compares the signatures on documents against the signature card to protect the bank and the depositor against forgery.

DEPOSIT TICKET Banks supply standard forms such as *deposit tickets.* The customer fills in the dollar amount and the date of deposit. As proof of the transaction, the customer retains either (1) a duplicate copy of the deposit ticket, or (2) a deposit receipt, depending on the bank's practice.

CHECK To draw money from an account, the depositor writes a **check,** which is a document instructing the bank to pay the designated person or business a specified amount of money. There are three parties to a check: the *maker,* who signs the check; the *payee*, to whom the check is drawn; and the *bank* on which the check is drawn.

Most checks are serially numbered and preprinted with the name and address of the maker and the bank. The checks have places for the date, the name of the payee, the signature of the maker, and the amount. The bank name, bank identification number, and maker account number are usually imprinted in magnetic ink for machine processing.

Exhibit 4-3 shows a check drawn on the bank account of Business Research, Inc. The check has two parts, the check itself and the *remittance advice,* an optional attachment that tells the payee the reason for the payment. The maker (Business Research) retains a duplicate copy of the check for its recording in the check register (cash disbursements journal). Note that internal controls at Business Research require two signatures on checks.

BANK STATEMENT Most banks send monthly **bank statements** to their depositors. The statement shows the account's beginning and ending balance for the period and lists the month's transactions. Included with the statement are the maker's *canceled checks,* those checks that the bank has paid on behalf of the depositor. The bank statement also lists any deposits and other changes in the account. Deposits appear in chronological order and checks in a logical order (usually by check serial number), along with the date each check cleared the bank.

Exhibit 4-4 is the bank statement of Business Research, Inc., for the month ended January 31, 19X6. Many banks send some individual depositors their statements on the first of the month, some on the second, and so on. This spacing eliminates the clerical burden of supplying all the statements at one time. Most businesses—like Business Research—receive their bank statements at the end of each calendar month.

Electronic funds transfer (EFT) is a system that relies on electronic communications—not paper documents—to transfer cash. More and more businesses today rely on EFT for repetitive cash transactions. It is much cheaper for a company to pay employees by EFT (direct deposit) than by issuing hundreds of

EXHIBIT 4-3
Check with Remittance Advice

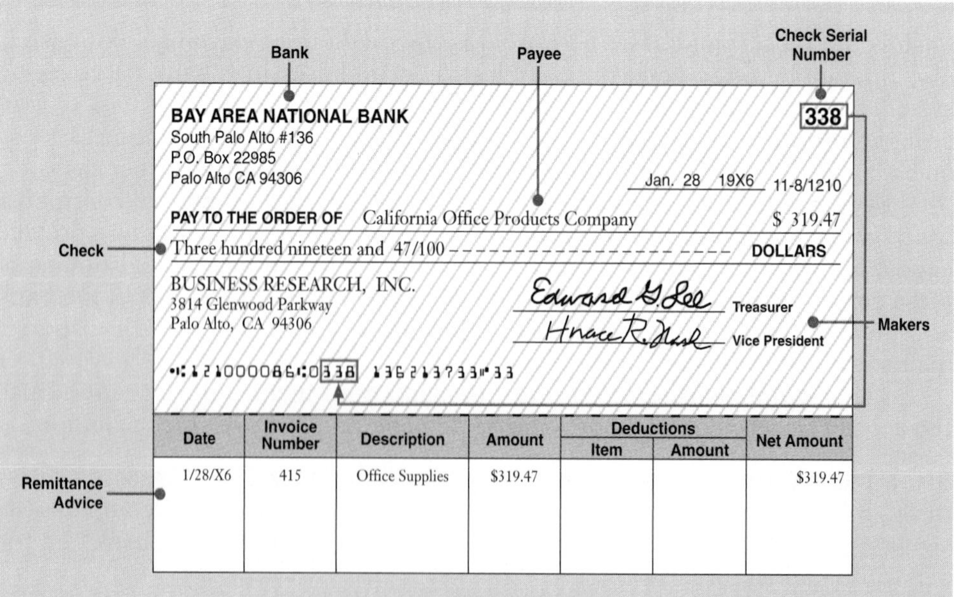
BAY AREA NATIONAL BANK
South Palo Alto #136
P.O. Box 22985
Palo Alto CA 94306

338

Jan. 28 19X6 11-8/1210

PAY TO THE ORDER OF California Office Products Company $ 319.47

Three hundred nineteen and 47/100 DOLLARS

BUSINESS RESEARCH, INC.
3814 Glenwood Parkway
Palo Alto, CA 94306

Edward G. Lee Treasurer
Horace R. Nash Vice President

Date	Invoice Number	Description	Amount	Deductions Item	Deductions Amount	Net Amount
1/28/X6	415	Office Supplies	$319.47			$319.47

ACCOUNT STATEMENT

Business Research, Inc.
3814 Glenwood Parkway
Palo Alto, CA 94306

CHECKING ACCOUNT 136–213733

CHECKING ACCOUNT SUMMARY AS OF 01/31/X6

BEGINNING BALANCE	TOTAL DEPOSITS	TOTAL WITHDRAWALS	SERVICE CHARGES	ENDING BALANCE
6,556.12	**4,352.64**	**4,963.00**	**14.25**	**5,931.51**

CHECKING ACCOUNT TRANSACTIONS

DEPOSITS	DATE	AMOUNT
Deposit	01/04	1,000.00
Deposit	01/04	112.00
Deposit	01/08	194.60
EFT—Collection of rent	01/17	904.03
Bank Collection	01/26	2,114.00
Interest	01/31	28.01

CHARGES	DATE	AMOUNT
Service Charge	01/31	14.25
Checks:		

CHECKS

Number	Date	Amount
332	01/12	3,000.00
656	01/06	100.00
333	01/12	150.00
334	01/10	100.00
335	01/06	100.00
336	01/31	1,100.00

BALANCES

Date	Balance	Date	Balance
12/31	6,556.12	01/17	5,264.75
01/04	7,616.12	01/20	4,903.75
01/06	7,416.12	01/26	7,017.75
01/08	7,610.72	01/31	5,931.51
01/12	4,360.72		

OTHER CHARGES	DATE	AMOUNT
NSF	01/04	52.00
EFT—Insurance	01/20	361.00

MONTHLY SUMMARY

Withdrawals: 8 Minimum Balance: 4,360.00 Average Balance: 6,091.00

EXHIBIT 4-4
Bank Statement

payroll checks. Also, many people make mortgage, rent, and insurance payments by prior arrangement with their bank and never write checks for those payments. The bank statement lists cash receipts by EFT among the deposits and cash payments by EFT among the checks and other bank charges.

The Bank Reconciliation

There are two records of a business's cash: (1) its Cash account in its own general ledger, and (2) the bank statement, which tells the actual amount of cash the business has in the bank. The balance in the business's Cash account rarely equals the balance shown on the bank statement.

The books and the bank statement may show different amounts, but both are correct. The difference arises because of a time lag in recording certain transactions. When a firm writes a check, it immediately credits its Cash account. The bank, however, will not subtract the amount of the check from the business's balance until it receives the check for payment. This step may take days, even weeks, if the payee waits to cash the check. Likewise, the business immediately debits Cash for all cash receipts, but it may take a day or so for the bank to add this amount to the business's bank balance.

To ensure accuracy of the financial records, the firm's accountant must explain the reasons for the difference between the firm's records and the bank statement figures on a certain date. The result of this process is a document called the **bank reconciliation.** Properly done, the bank reconciliation ensures that all cash transactions have been accounted for and that the bank and book records of cash are correct. Knowledge of where cash comes from, how it is spent, and the balance of cash available is vital to a business's success.

Here are some common items that cause differences between the bank balance and the book balance.

1. Items recorded by the company but not yet recorded by the *bank:*
   - **a. Deposits in transit** (outstanding deposits). The company has recorded these deposits, but the bank has not.
   - **b. Outstanding checks.** The company has issued these checks and recorded them on its books, but the bank has not yet paid them.
2. Items recorded by the bank but not yet recorded by the *company:*
   - **a. Bank collections.** Banks sometimes collect money on behalf of depositors. Many businesses have their customers pay directly to the company bank account. This practice, called a *lock-box system,* reduces the possibility of theft and also places the business's cash in circulation faster than if the cash had to be collected and deposited by company personnel. An example is a bank's collecting cash and interest on a note receivable for the depositor. The bank may notify the depositor of these bank collections on the bank's statement.
   - **b.** *Electronic funds transfers.* The bank may receive or pay cash on behalf of the depositor. The bank statement will list the EFTs and may serve to notify the depositor to record these transactions.
   - **c.** *Service charge.* This is the bank's fee for processing the depositor's transactions. Banks commonly base the service charge on the account balance. The depositor learns the amount of the service charge from the bank statement.
   - **d.** *Interest revenue on checking account.* Banks often pay interest to depositors who keep a large enough balance of cash in their account. This is especially true of business checking accounts. The bank notifies depositors of this interest on the bank statement.
   - **e. NSF (nonsufficient funds) checks** received from customers. To understand how NSF checks (*hot checks*) are handled, consider the route a check takes. The maker writes a check and gives the check to the payee, who deposits the check in his bank. The payee's bank adds the receipt amount to the payee's bank balance on the assumption that the check is good. A good check is returned to the maker's bank, which then deducts the check amount from the maker's bank balance.

     NSF checks are cash *receipts* that turn out to be worthless. If the maker's bank balance is insufficient to pay the check, the maker's bank refuses to pay the check and sends an NSF notice back to the payee's bank. The payee's bank then subtracts the receipt amount from the payee's bank balance and notifies the payee of this NSF action. The payee may learn of NSF checks through the bank statement, which lists the NSF check as a charge (subtraction), as shown near the bottom of Exhibit 4-4.
   - **f.** *Checks collected, deposited, and returned to payee by the bank for reasons other than NSF.* Banks return checks to the payee if (1) the maker's account has closed, (2) the date is stale (some checks state "void after 30 days"), (3) the signature is not authorized, (4) the check has been altered, or (5) the check form is improper (for example, a counterfeit). Accounting for all returned checks is the same as for NSF checks.
   - **g.** *The cost of printed checks.* This charge against the company's bank account balance is handled like a service charge.

3. Errors by either the company or the bank: For example, a bank may improperly charge (decrease) the bank balance of Business Research, Inc., for a check drawn by another company, perhaps Business Research Associates. Or a company may miscompute its bank balance on its own books. Computational errors are becoming less frequent with the widespread use of computers. Nevertheless, all errors must be corrected, and the corrections will be a part of the bank reconciliation.

Objective 2

Use a bank reconciliation as a control device

PREPARING THE BANK RECONCILIATION The steps in preparing the bank reconciliation are as follows:

1. Start with two figures, the balance shown on the bank statement *(balance per bank)* and the balance in the company's Cash account *(balance per books)*. These two amounts will probably disagree because of the differences discussed earlier.
2. Add to, or subtract from, the *bank* balance those items that appear on the books but not on the bank statement:
   a. Add *deposits in transit* to the bank balance. Deposits in transit are identified by comparing the deposits listed on the bank statement with the company's list of cash receipts. Deposits in transit show up as cash receipts on the books but not as deposits on the bank statement.
   b. Subtract *outstanding checks* from the bank balance. Outstanding checks are identified by comparing the canceled checks returned with the bank statement with the company's list of checks written for cash payments. Outstanding checks show up as cash payments on the books but not as paid checks on the bank statement. Outstanding checks are usually the most numerous items on a bank reconciliation.
3. Add to, or subtract from, the *book* balance those items that appear on the bank statement but not on the company books:
   a. Add to the book balance (1) *bank collections,* (2) *EFT cash receipts,* and (3) *interest revenue* earned on money in the bank. These items are identified by comparing the deposits listed on the bank statement with the company's list of cash receipts. They show up as cash receipts on the bank statement but not on the books.
   b. Subtract from the book balance (1) *EFT cash payments,* (2) *service charges,* (3) *cost of printed checks,* and (4) *other bank charges* (for example, charges for NSF or stale-date checks). These items are identified by comparing the other charges listed on the bank statement with the cash disbursements recorded on the company books. They show up as subtractions on the bank statement but not as cash payments on the books.
4. Compute the *adjusted bank balance* and the *adjusted book balance.* The two adjusted balances should be equal.
5. Journalize each item in step 3—that is, each item listed on the book portion of the bank reconciliation. These items must be recorded on the company books because they affect cash.
6. Correct all book errors and notify the bank of any errors it has made.

BANK RECONCILIATION ILLUSTRATED The bank statement in Exhibit 4-4 indicates that the January 31 bank balance of Business Research, Inc., is $5,931.51. However, the company's Cash account has a balance of $3,294.21. In following the steps outlined in the preceding section, the accountant finds these reconciling items:

1. The January 30 deposit of $1,591.63 does not appear on the bank statement.
2. The bank erroneously charged to the Business Research, Inc., account a $100 check—number 656—written by Business Research Associates.
3. Five company checks issued late in January and recorded in the cash disbursements journal have not been paid by the bank:

Check No.	Date	Amount
337	Jan. 27	$286.00
338	28	319.47
339	28	83.00
340	29	203.14
341	30	458.53

4. The bank received $904.03 by EFT on behalf of Business Research, Inc. The bank statement serves as initial notification of this receipt of monthly rent revenue on unused office space.
5. The bank collected on behalf of the company a note receivable, $2,114 (including interest revenue of $214). Business Research has not recorded this cash receipt.
6. The bank statement shows interest revenue of $28.01, which the company has earned on its cash balance.
7. Check number 333 for $150 paid to Brown Company on account was recorded as a cash payment of $510, creating a $360 understatement of the Cash balance in the books.
8. The bank service charge for the month was $14.25.
9. The bank statement shows an NSF check for $52, which was received from customer L. Ross.
10. Business Research pays insurance expense monthly by EFT. The company has not yet recorded this $361 payment.

Exhibit 4-5 is the bank reconciliation based on the preceding data. Panel A lists the reconciling items, which are keyed by number to the reconciliation in Panel B. After the reconciliation, the adjusted bank balance equals the adjusted book balance. This equality is an accuracy check.

Accounting for Transactions from the Reconciliation The bank reconciliation does not directly affect the journals or the ledgers. The reconciliation is an accountant's tool, separate from the company's books.

The bank reconciliation acts as a control device by signaling the company to record the transactions listed as reconciling items in the Books section of the reconciliation because the company has not yet recorded these items. For example, the bank collected the note receivable on behalf of the company, but the company has not yet recorded this cash receipt. In fact, the company learned of the cash receipt only when it received the bank statement.

STOP & THINK Why doesn't the company need to record the reconciling items on the Bank side of the reconciliation?

Answer: Those items have already been recorded on the company books.

On the basis of the reconciliation in Exhibit 4-5, Business Research, Inc., makes the following entries. They are dated January 31 to bring the Cash account to the correct balance on that date. Numbers in parentheses correspond to the reconciling items listed in Exhibit 4-5, Panel A.

EXHIBIT 4-5
Bank Reconciliation

PANEL A—Reconciling Items

1. Deposit in transit, $1,591.63.
2. Bank error, add $100 to bank balance.
3. Outstanding checks: no. 337, $286; no. 338, $319.47; no. 339, $83; no. 340, $203.14; no. 341, $458.53.
4. EFT receipt of rent revenue, $904.03.
5. Bank collection, $2,114, including interest revenue of $214.
6. Interest earned on bank balance, $28.01.
7. Book error, add $360 to book balance.
8. Bank service charge, $14.25.
9. NSF check from L. Ross, $52.
10. EFT payment of insurance expense, $361.00.

PANEL B—Bank Reconciliation

BUSINESS RESEARCH, INC.
Bank Reconciliation
January 31, 19X6

Bank			Books		
Balance, January 31		$5,931.51	Balance, January 31....................		$3,294.21
Add:			Add:		
1. Deposit of January 30 in transit		1,591.63	4. EFT receipt of rent revenue..		904.03
2. Correction of bank error—Business Research Associates check erroneously charged against company account.....................................		100.00	5. Bank collection of note receivable, including interest revenue of $214		2,114.00
		7,623.14	6. Interest revenue earned on bank balance........................		28.01
			7. Correction of book error—overstated amount of check no. 333		360.00
3. Less: Outstanding checks					6,700.25
No. 337	$286.00		Less:		
No. 338	319.47		8. Service charge.......	$ 14.25	
No. 339	83.00		9. NSF check............	52.00	
No. 340	203.14		10. EFT payment of		
No. 341	458.53	(1,350.14)	insurance expense	361.00	(427.25)
Adjusted bank balance		$6,273.00	Adjusted bank balance		$6,273.00

Amounts agree.

Each reconciling item is treated in the same way in every situation. Here is a summary.

Bank Balance—always

- *Add* deposits in transit
- *Subtract* outstanding checks

Book Balance—always

- *Add* bank collection items, interest revenue, and EFT receipts
- *Subtract* service charges, NSF checks, and EFT payments

Jan. 31	(4)	Cash	904.03	
		Rent Revenue		904.03
		Receipt of monthly rent.		

ASSETS	=	LIABILITIES	+	STOCKHOLDERS' EQUITY	+	REVENUES
904.03	=	0			+	904.03

Jan. 31 (5)	Cash	2,114.00	
	Notes Receivable		1,900.00
	Interest Revenue		214.00
	Note receivable collected by bank.		

ASSETS	=	LIABILITIES	+	STOCKHOLDERS' EQUITY	+	REVENUES
+2,114.00 −1,900.00	=	0			+	214.00

Jan. 31 (6)	Cash	28.01	
	Interest Revenue		28.01
	Interest earned on bank balance.		

ASSETS	=	LIABILITIES	+	STOCKHOLDERS' EQUITY	+	REVENUES
28.01	=	0			+	28.01

Jan. 31 (7)	Cash	360.00	
	Accounts Payable—Brown Co.		360.00
	Correction of check no. 333.		

ASSETS	=	LIABILITIES	+	STOCKHOLDERS' EQUITY
360.00	=	360.00	+	0

Jan. 31 (8)	Miscellaneous Expense[1]	14.25	
	Cash		14.25
	Bank service charge.		

ASSETS	=	LIABILITIES	+	STOCKHOLDERS' EQUITY	−	EXPENSES
−14.25	=	0			−	14.25

Jan. 31 (9)	Accounts Receivable—L. Ross	52.00	
	Cash		52.00
	NSF check returned by bank.		

ASSETS	=	LIABILITIES	+	STOCKHOLDERS' EQUITY
+52.00 −52.00	=	0	+	0

Jan. 31 (10)	Insurance Expense	361.00	
	Cash		361.00
	Payment of monthly insurance.		

ASSETS	=	LIABILITIES	+	STOCKHOLDERS' EQUITY	−	EXPENSES
−361.00	=	0			−	361.00

These entries bring the business's books up to date.

The entry for the NSF check (entry 9) needs explanation. Upon learning that L. Ross's $52 check was not good, Business Research credits Cash to

[1]Note: Miscellaneous Expense is debited for the bank service charge because the service charge pertains to no particular expense category.

bring the Cash account up to date. Since Business Research still has a receivable from Ross, it debits Accounts Receivable—L. Ross and pursues collection from him.

STOP & THINK The bank statement balance is $4,500 and shows a service charge of $15, interest earned of $5, and an NSF check for $300. Deposits in transit total $1,200; outstanding checks are $575. The bookkeeper recorded as $152 a check of $125 in payment of an account payable.

1. What is the adjusted bank balance?
2. What was the book balance of cash before the reconciliation?
3. Prepare the adjusting journal entry(ies).

Answers

1. $5,125 ($4,500 + $1,200 – $575).
2. $5,408 ($5,125 + $15 + $300 – $5 – $27). The adjusted book and bank balances are the same. The answer can be determined by working backward from the adjusted balance.
3. Cash 27

Cash	27	
Accounts Payable		27
Miscellaneous Expense	15	
Cash		15
Accounts Receivable	300	
Cash		300
Cash	5	
Interest Revenue		5

How Managers and Owners Use the Bank Reconciliation

The bank reconciliation becomes a powerful control device in the hands of a business manager or owner, as the following example illustrates.

Randy Vaughn is a CPA in Houston, Texas. He owns several small apartment complexes that are managed by his aunt. His accounting practice keeps him busy, so he has little time to devote to his apartment investments. His aunt signs up tenants, collects the monthly rent checks, arranges custodial and maintenance work, hires and fires employees, writes the checks, and performs the bank reconciliation. In short, she does it all. This concentration of duties in one person is terrible from an internal control standpoint. Vaughn's aunt could be stealing from him, and as a CPA he is aware of this possibility.

Vaughn trusts his aunt because she is a member of the family. Nevertheless, he exercises some loose controls over her management of his apartments. Vaughn periodically drops by his properties to see whether the custodial/maintenance staff is keeping them in good condition. He asks tenants whether appliances are working and if their requests are answered promptly. These measures establish a degree of control over the buildings and grounds.

To control cash, Vaughn uses the bank statement and the bank reconciliation. On an irregular basis, he examines the bank reconciliation that his aunt has performed. He matches every check that cleared the bank to the journal entry on the books. Vaughn would know immediately if his aunt is writing checks to herself. By examining each check, Vaughn establishes control over cash disbursements. If his aunt is stealing cash and concealing it by manipulating the bank reconciliation, this too would come to light. To keep his aunt on her toes, Vaughn lets her know that he periodically audits her work.

Vaughn has a simple method for controlling cash receipts. He knows the occupancy level of his apartments. He also knows the monthly rent he charges. He multiplies the number of apartments—say 20—by the monthly rent (which averages $500 per unit) to arrive at expected monthly rent revenue of $10,000. By tracing the $10,000 revenue to the bank statement, Vaughn can tell that his rent money went into his bank account.

Control activities such as these are critical in small businesses. There may be only a few employees in a small business, so a separation of duties may not be feasible. But the manager or owner must oversee and control the operations of the business, or the assets will slip away, as they did for Grant LeForge & Company in the chapter opening story.

Mid-Chapter SUMMARY PROBLEM FOR YOUR REVIEW

The Cash account of Bain Company at February 28, 19X3, is as follows:

Cash			
Feb. 1	Balance 3,995	Feb. 3	400
6	800	12	3,100
15	1,800	19	1,100
23	1,100	25	500
28	2,400	27	900
Feb. 28	Balance 4,095		

Bain Company receives this bank statement on February 28, 19X3 (as always, negative amounts are in parentheses):

Bank Statement for February 19X3

Beginning balance		$3,995
Deposits:		
Feb. 7	$ 800	
15	1,800	
24	1,100	3,700
Checks (total per day):		
Feb. 8	$ 400	
16	3,100	
23	1,100	(4,600)
Other items:		
Service charge		(10)
NFS check from M. E. Crown		(700)
Bank collection of note receivable for the company		1,000*
EFT—monthly rent expense		(330)
Interest on account balance		15
Ending balance		$3,070

*Includes interest of $119.

Additional data: Bain Company deposits all cash receipts in the bank and makes all cash disbursements by check.

Required

1. Prepare the bank reconciliation of Bain Company at February 28, 19X3.
2. Record the entries based on the bank reconciliation.

ANSWERS

Requirement 1

BAIN COMPANY
Bank Reconciliation
February 28, 19X3

Bank:		
Balance, February 28, 19X3		$3,070
Add: Deposit of February 28 in transit		2,400
		5,470
Less: Outstanding checks issued on Feb 25 ($500) and Feb. 27 ($900)		(1,400)
Adjusted bank balance, February 28, 19X3		$4,070
Books:		
Balance, February 28, 19X3		$4,095
Add: Bank collection of note receivable, including interest of $119		1,000
Interest earned on bank balance		15
		5,110
Less: Service charge	$ 10	
NSF check	700	
EFT—Rent expense	330	(1,040)
Adjusted book balance, February 28, 19X3		$4,070

Requirement 2

Feb. 28	Cash	1,000	
	Note Receivable ($1,000 – $119)		881
	Interest Revenue		119
	Note receivable collected by bank.		
28	Cash	15	
	Interest Revenue		15
	Interest earned on bank balance.		
28	Miscellaneous Expense	10	
	Cash		10
	Bank service charge.		
28	Accounts Receivable—M. E. Crown	700	
	Cash		700
	NSF check returned by bank.		
28	Rent Expense	330	
	Cash		330
	Monthly rent expense.		

The Operating Cycle of a Business

A company such as Lands' End or Macy's buys inventory, sells the goods to customers, and uses the cash to purchase more inventory to repeat the cycle. Exhibit 4-6 on page 188 diagrams the operating cycle for *cash sales* and for *sales on account*. For a cash sale, the cycle is from cash to inventory, which is purchased for resale, and back to cash. For a sale on account, the cycle is from cash to inventory to accounts receivable and back to cash. In all lines of business, managers strive to shorten the cycle in order to keep cash flowing as quickly as possible. The faster the sale of inventory and the collection of cash, the higher the company's profits.

EXHIBIT 4-6
Operating Cycle of a Business

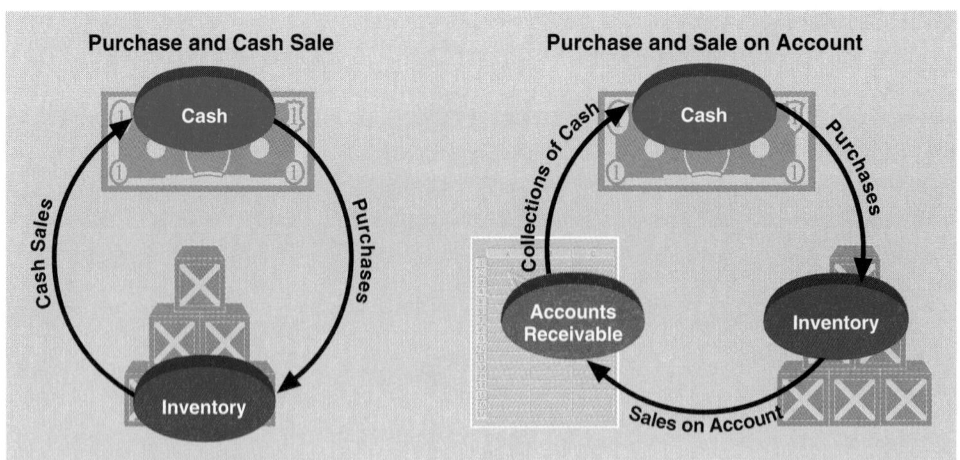

Managing Cash

Objective 3

Manage cash and account for cash transactions

Managing cash requires a balancing act. Lands' End, Toys "Я" Us, and Macy's must have enough cash to pay their bills, or the company will go bankrupt. But cash is a relatively low-earning asset. Toys "Я" Us earns far more income by investing in inventory than by keeping most of its money in bank deposits. Therefore, companies strive to keep their cash circulating, as shown in Exhibit 4-6.

Companies use numerous techniques to manage their cash. In this section, we discuss some of these techniques.

Speeding the Collection of Cash from Sales

When a retailer such as Macy's makes a cash sale, the Macy's clerk rings up the sale, receives cash from the customer, and places the money in the cash register. Timely collection is no problem here because the business receives cash with the transaction and can reinvest the money immediately. But cash sales are limited mainly to retail establishments such as Macy's, restaurants, grocery stores, and gas stations.

Manufacturers such as **Sony, Eastman Kodak,** and **Fisher-Price** (the toy maker) sell most of their goods on account to retail establishments. Consider a credit sale by Fisher-Price to Toys "Я" Us. Because Fisher-Price does not receive cash at the point of sale, Fisher-Price must do some additional accounting. To keep track of how much cash it expects from Toys "Я" Us, Fisher-Price keeps a subsidiary accounts receivable ledger with a separate account for each customer. The sum of the amounts receivable from all Fisher-Price customers equals the balance in the company's Accounts Receivable account in the general ledger, as shown in Exhibit 4-7.

EXHIBIT 4-7
Accounts Receivable Records for Fisher Price

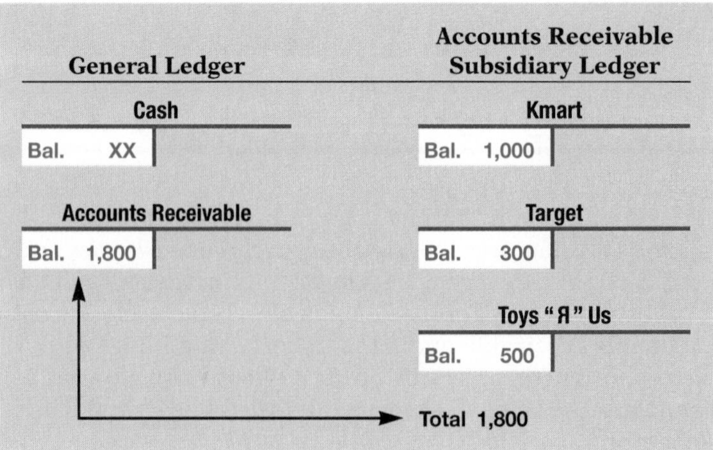

Like all companies, Fisher-Price uses the accounts receivable ledger to pursue collection from individual customers. For example, if Kmart fails to pay its account balance, Fisher-Price will follow up with additional billings.

To speed the collection of cash, companies offer *sales discounts* that motivate customers to pay within a specified period, usually ten days. Credit terms of "2/10 n/30" are common. This abbreviated discount formula means that the customer can take a 2% discount by paying within ten days of the date of sale. If not, the seller expects the buyer to pay the full amount within 30 days.

Suppose Fisher-Price makes a $50,000 sale to Toys "Я" Us on August 4. Assume credit terms of 2/10 n/30 and that Fisher-Price collects on August 14. Fisher-Price would record the sale and collection transactions with these journal entries:

Aug. 4	Accounts Receivable—Toys "Я" Us	50,000	
	Sales Revenue...		50,000
	Sale on account.		

ASSETS	=	LIABILITIES	+	STOCKHOLDERS' EQUITY	+	REVENUES
50,000	=	0			+	50,000

Aug. 14	Cash ($50,000 × .98)	49,000	
	Sales Discounts ($50,000 × .02)	1,000	
	Accounts Receivable—Toys "Я" Us............		50,000
	Collection on account.		

ASSETS	=	LIABILITIES	+	STOCKHOLDERS' EQUITY	−	CONTRA REVENUES
+49,000 −50,000	=	0			−	1,000

In this transaction, Fisher-Price received cash of $49,000 for a sale that it had recorded at $50,000. The customer took a $1,000 discount, which decreased the company's net sales revenue to $49,000. The discount is recorded as a debit to a separate account, Sales Discounts, which is a contra account to Sales Revenue. Sales Discounts, a contra revenue account, is subtracted from Sales Revenue to measure net sales revenue. Fisher-Price records the account receivable from Toys "Я" Us to keep track of the amount receivable from each customer. Computerized accounting systems ease the burden of keeping records on thousands of individual customer accounts.

The 2% discount within ten days works out to an annual interest rate of around 37%, high enough to motivate many customers to pay quickly. Why are companies such as Fisher-Price willing to offer this large discount? Because, as the saying goes, "A bird in the hand is worth two in the bush." By getting the cash immediately, the seller avoids a cash shortage and the resulting need to borrow, which is costly. The seller also avoids having to pursue collection later on. Chapter 5 discusses accounts receivable in more detail.

Internal Control over Cash Receipts

Internal control over cash receipts ensures that all cash receipts are deposited in the bank and that the company's accounting record is correct. Many businesses receive cash over the counter and through the mail. Each source of cash receipts calls for its own security measures.

Objective 4

Apply internal controls to cash receipts

CASH RECEIPTS OVER THE COUNTER The point-of-sale terminal (cash register) offers management control over the cash received in a store. Consider a Macy's store. First, the terminal should be positioned so that customers can see the amounts the cashier enters into the computer. No person willingly pays more than the marked price for an item, so the customer helps prevent the sales clerk from overcharging and pocketing the excess over actual prices. Also, company policy should require issuance of a receipt to make sure each sale is recorded by the cash register. Stores often give customers a bonus if the clerk fails to give them a receipt.

Second, the cash drawer opens only when the sales clerk enters an amount on the keypad, and a roll of tape locked inside the machine records each sale and cash transaction. At the end of the day, a manager proves the cash by comparing the total amount in the cash drawer against the tape's total. This step helps prevent outright theft by the clerk. For security reasons, the clerk should not have access to the tape.

Third, pricing merchandise at "uneven" amounts—say, \$3.95 instead of \$4.00—means that the clerk generally must make change, which in turn means having to get into the cash drawer. This requires entering the amount of the sale on the keypad and so onto the register tape—another way to prevent fraud.

At the end of the day, the cashier or other employee with cash-handling duties deposits the cash in the bank. The tape then goes to the accounting department as the basis for an entry in the accounting records. These security measures, coupled with periodic onsite inspection by a manager, discourage theft.

CASH RECEIPTS BY MAIL All incoming mail should be opened by a mailroom employee. This person should compare the amount of the check received with the attached remittance advice (the slip of paper that lists the amount of the check). If no advice was sent, the mailroom employee should prepare one and enter the amount of each receipt on a control tape. At the end of the day, this control tape is given to a responsible official, such as the controller, for verification. Cash receipts should be given to the cashier, who combines them with any cash received over the counter and prepares the bank deposit.

Having a mailroom employee be the first person to handle postal cash receipts is just another application of a good internal control procedure—in this case, separation of duties. If the accountants opened postal cash receipts, they could easily hide a theft.

The mailroom employee forwards the remittance advices to the accounting department. These provide the data for entries in the cash books and postings to customers' accounts in the accounts receivable ledger. As a final step, the controller compares the three records of the day's cash receipts: (1) the control tape total from the mailroom, (2) the bank deposit amount from the cashier, and (3) the debit to Cash from the accounting department.

Many companies use a *lock-box system* to separate cash duties and establish control over cash receipts. Customers send their checks directly to an address that is essentially a bank account. Internal control over the cash is enhanced because company personnel do not handle the cash. The lock-box system improves efficiency because the cash goes to work for the company immediately.

CASH SHORT AND OVER A difference often exists between actual cash receipts and the day's record of cash received. Usually, the difference is small and results from honest errors. When the recorded cash balance exceeds cash on hand, a *cash short* situation exists. When actual cash exceeds the recorded cash balance, there is a *cash over* situation. Suppose the cash register tapes of Macy's indicated sales revenue of \$25,000, but the cash received was \$24,980. To record the day's sales, the store would make this entry:

Cash	24,980	
Cash Short and Over	20	
Sales Revenue		25,000
Daily cash sales.		

ASSETS	=	LIABILITIES	+	STOCKHOLDERS' EQUITY	+	REVENUES	−	EXPENSES
24,980	=	0			+	25,000	−	20

As the entry shows, Cash Short and Over is debited when sales revenue exceeds cash receipts. This account is credited when cash receipts exceed sales. A debit balance in Cash Short and Over appears on the income statement as Miscellaneous Expense, a credit balance as Other Revenue.

The Cash Short and Over balance should be small. The debits and credits for cash shorts and overs collected over an accounting period tend to cancel each other. A large balance signals the accountant to investigate. For example, too large a debit balance may mean an employee is stealing. Cash Short and Over, then, also acts as an internal control device.

Exhibit 4-8 summarizes the controls over cash receipts.

STOP & THINK The bookkeeper in your company has stolen cash received from customers. The bookkeeper prepared fake documents to indicate that the customers had returned merchandise. What internal control feature could have prevented this theft?

Answer: The bookkeeper should not have had access to cash.

Concept Highlight

EXHIBIT 4-8
Internal Controls over Cash Receipts

Element of Internal Control	Internal Controls over Cash Receipts
Competent, reliable, ethical personnel	Companies carefully screen employees for undesirable personality traits. They also spend large sums for training programs.
Assignment of responsibilities	Specific employees are designated as cashiers, supervisors of cashiers, or accountants for cash receipts.
Proper authorization	Only designated employees, such as department managers, can grant exceptions for customers, approve check receipts above a certain amount, and allow customers to purchase on credit.
Separation of duties	Cashiers and mailroom employees who handle cash do not have access to the accounting records. Accountants who record cash receipts have no opportunity to handle cash.
Internal and external audits	Internal auditors examine company transactions for agreement with management policies. External auditors examine the internal controls over cash receipts to determine whether the accounting system produces accurate amounts for revenues, receivables, and other items related to cash receipts.
Documents and records	Customers receive receipts as transaction records. Bank statements list cash receipts for reconciliation with company records (deposit tickets). Customers who pay by mail include a remittance advice showing the amount of cash they sent to the company.
Electronic and computer controls	Cash registers serve as transaction records. Each day's receipts are matched with customer remittance advices and with the day's deposit ticket from the bank.
Other controls	Cashiers are bonded. Cash is stored in vaults and banks. Employees are rotated among jobs and are required to take vacations.

Internal Control over Cash Disbursements (Payments)

Objective 5

Apply internal controls to cash disbursements

Exercising control over cash disbursements (payments) is at least as important as controlling cash receipts.

Controls over Payment by Check

Payment by *check* is an important control over cash disbursements. First, the check acts as a source document. Second, to be valid, the check must be signed by an authorized official, so each payment by check draws the attention of management. Before signing the check, the manager should study the evidence supporting the payment.

To illustrate the internal control over cash disbursements, suppose the business is buying inventory for sale to customers. Let's examine the process leading up to the cash payment.

CONTROLS OVER PURCHASING The purchasing process—outlined in Exhibit 4-9—starts when the sales department identifies the need for merchandise and prepares a *purchase request* (or *requisition*). A separate purchasing department specializes in locating the best buys and mails a *purchase order* to the supplier, the outside company that sells the needed goods. When the supplier ships the goods to the requesting business, the supplier also mails the *invoice*, or bill, which is notification of the need to pay. As the goods arrive, the receiving department checks the goods for any damage and lists the merchandise received on a document called the *receiving report*. The accounting department combines all the foregoing documents, checks them for accuracy and agreement, and forwards this *disbursement packet* to designated officers for approval and payment. The packet includes the invoice, receiving report, purchase order, and purchase request, as shown in Exhibit 4-10.

EXHIBIT 4-9
Purchasing Process

Business Document	Prepared by	Sent to
Purchase request (requisition)	Sales department	Purchasing department
Purchase order	Purchasing department	Outside company that sells the needed merchandise (supplier or vendor)
Invoice (bill)	Outside company that sells the needed merchandise (supplier or vendor)	Accounting department
Receiving report	Receiving department	Accounting department
Disbursement packet	Accounting department	Officer who signs the check

EXHIBIT 4-10
Disbursement Packet

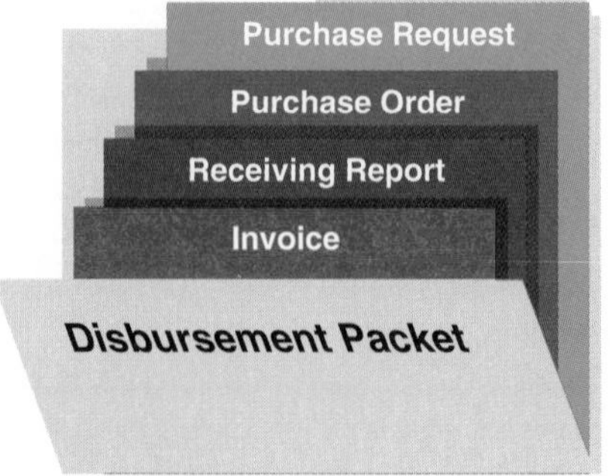

Controls over Approval of Payments Before approving the disbursement, the controller and the treasurer should examine a sample of transactions to determine that the accounting department has performed the following control steps:

1. The invoice is compared with a copy of the purchase order and purchase request to ensure that the business pays cash only for the goods that it ordered.
2. The invoice is compared with the receiving report to ensure that cash is paid only for the goods that were actually received.
3. The mathematical accuracy of the invoice is proved.

The use of *vouchers,* documents that authorize cash disbursements, improves the internal control over disbursements. As further security and control over disbursements, many firms require two signatures on a check, as we saw in Exhibit 4-3. To avoid document alteration, some firms also use machines that indelibly stamp the amount on the check. After payment, the check signer can punch a hole through the disbursement packet. This hole denotes that the invoice has been paid and discourages dishonest employees from running the documents through the system for a duplicate payment.

Information technology is streamlining cash disbursement procedures in many businesses. For example, the CPA firm of Deloitte & Touche is revamping the payment system of Bank of America. Exhibit 4-11 summarizes the internal controls over cash disbursements.

EXHIBIT 4-11
Internal Controls over Cash Disbursements

Element of Internal Control	Internal Controls over Cash Disbursements
Competent, reliable, ethical personnel	Cash disbursements are entrusted to high-level employees, with larger amounts paid by the treasurer or assistant treasurer.
Assignment of responsibilities	Specific employees approve purchase documents for payment. Executives examine approvals, then sign checks.
Proper authorization	Large expenditures must be authorized by the company owner or board of directors to ensure agreement with organizational goals.
Separation of duties	Computer operators and other employees who handle checks have no access to the accounting records. Accountants who record cash disbursements have no opportunity to handle cash.
Internal and external audits	Internal auditors examine company transactions for agreement with management policies. External auditors examine the internal controls over cash disbursements to determine whether the accounting system produces accurate amounts for expenses, assets, and other items related to cash disbursements.
Documents and records	Suppliers issue invoices that document the need to pay cash. Bank statements list cash payments (checks and EFT disbursements) for reconciliation with company records. Checks are prenumbered in sequence to account for payments.
Electronic, computer, and other controls	Blank checks are stored in a vault and controlled by a responsible official with no accounting duties. Machines stamp the amount on a check in indelible ink. Paid invoices are punched to avoid duplicate payment.

STOP & THINK Talon Computer Concepts processes payroll checks for small businesses. Clients give their employees' time cards to Talon each week, and Talon programmers write computer programs to meet the clients' payroll needs. Talon computer operators process and deliver the checks to the clients for distribution to employees. Identify two employee functions of Talon's cash disbursements system that should be separated. Give your reason.

Answer: The programmers should not also be computer operators. Any person who performs both functions could write the program to process checks to him- or herself or to a fictitious employee and then pocket the printed checks.

Controlling Petty Cash Disbursements

It would be uneconomical and time-consuming for a business to write separate checks for an executive's taxi fare, a box of pencils needed right away, or the delivery of a special message across town. Therefore, companies keep a small amount of cash on hand to pay for such minor amounts. This fund is called **petty cash.**

The petty cash fund is opened when management agrees to start a petty cash fund with a particular amount of cash. A check for that amount is then issued to Petty Cash. Assume that on February 28, the business decides to establish a petty cash fund of $200. The custodian of the petty cash fund cashes the check and places the currency and coin in the fund, which may be a cash box, safe, or other device. Starting the fund is recorded as follows:

Feb. 28	Petty Cash	200	
	Cash in Bank		200
	To open the petty cash fund.		

ASSETS	=	LIABILITIES	+	STOCKHOLDERS' EQUITY
+200 −200	=	0	+	0

For each petty cash disbursement, the custodian prepares a *petty cash ticket* like the one illustrated in Exhibit 4-12. Control is established by recording on the petty cash ticket the date and purpose of the disbursement, the name of the person who received the cash, the account to be debited, and the amount of the disbursement.

The sum of the cash in the petty cash fund plus the total of the ticket amounts should equal the opening balance at all times—in this case, $200. The Petty Cash account keeps its prescribed $200 balance at all times. Maintaining the Petty Cash account at this balance, supported by the fund (cash plus tickets), is characteristic of an **imprest system.** The control feature of an imprest system is that it clearly identifies the amount for which the custodian is responsible.

Disbursements reduce the amount of cash in the fund, so periodically the fund must be replenished. Suppose that on March 31, the fund has $118 in cash and $82 in tickets. A check for $82 is issued, made payable to Petty Cash. The fund custodian cashes this check for currency and coins and puts the money in

EXHIBIT 4-12
Petty Cash Ticket

PETTY CASH TICKET

Date Mar. 25, 19X4 No. 47
Amount $23.00
For Box of floppy diskettes
Debit Office Supplies, Acct. No. 145
Received by Lewis Wright Fund Custodian WAR

the fund to return its actual cash to $200. The petty cash tickets identify the accounts to be debited when the Petty Cash fund is replenished. The entry to record replenishment of the fund is

Mar. 31	Office Supplies	23	
	Delivery Expense	17	
	Miscellaneous Selling Expense	42	
	Cash in Bank		82
	To replenish the petty cash fund.		

ASSETS	=	LIABILITIES	+	STOCKHOLDERS' EQUITY	–	EXPENSES
+23	=	0			–	17
–82					–	42

LEARNING TIP No journal entries are made for petty cash disbursements until the fund is replenished. At that time, all petty cash payments are recorded as a credit to the Cash in Bank account. There is no debit to Petty Cash when the fund is replenished.

Using a Budget to Manage Cash

Objective 6

Use a budget to manage cash

Managers control their organizations with the help of budgets. A **budget** is a quantitative expression of a plan that helps managers coordinate the entity's activities. Cash receives the most attention in the budgeting process because all transactions ultimately affect cash. In this section we introduce *cash budgeting* as a way to manage this important asset. (The second accounting course goes into budgeting in more detail.)

How does MCI decide when to invest millions in new telecommunications equipment? How will the company decide how much to spend? Will borrowing be needed, or can MCI finance the purchase with internally generated cash? Similarly, by what process do you decide how much to spend on your education? On an automobile? On a house? All these decisions depend to some degree on the information that a cash budget provides.

A cash budget helps a company manage its cash by expressing the plan for the receipt and disbursement of cash during a future period. To prepare for the future, a company must determine how much cash it will need, then decide whether or not its operations will bring in the needed cash. To prepare for their future cash needs, managers proceed in four steps:

1. Start with the entity's cash balance at the beginning of the period. The beginning balance tells how much cash is left over from the preceding period.
2. Add the budgeted cash receipts and subtract the budgeted cash disbursements. This is the most challenging part of the budgeting process because managers must predict the cash effects of all transactions of the budget period, including:
   a. Revenue and expense transactions (operating activities from the income statement)
   b. Asset acquisition and sale transactions (investing activities from the statement of cash flows)
   c. Liability and stockholders' equity transactions (financing activities from the statement of cash flows)

   Because foresight is imperfect, the actual figure will not always turn out as expected. However, it is important to develop *realistic* estimates of the cash receipts and disbursements during the budget period. A realistic estimate is better than no estimate at all.

3. The beginning balance plus the expected receipts minus the expected disbursements equals the expected cash balance at the end of the period.
4. Compare the expected cash balance to the desired, or *budgeted,* cash balance at the end of the period. Managers know the minimum amount of cash they need (the budgeted balance) to keep the entity running. If there is excess cash, they can invest. If the expected cash balance falls below the budgeted balance, the company will need to obtain additional financing to reach the desired cash balance.

Let's consider the benefits of budgeting cash. Suppose MCI's cash budget reveals a cash shortage during June of the coming year. The budget gives MCI managers an early warning of the need for additional cash in June. Managers can arrange financing in advance and probably get a lower interest rate and better payment terms than if they are forced to borrow money under rushed conditions at the last minute. If the cash budget indicates an excess of cash in September, managers know in advance to look for promising investments during October and November. In short, the cash budget helps managers make decisions in an orderly manner. A budget serves the same purpose for individuals.

The budget period can span any length of time desired by managers. Large corporations use a daily cash budget because the amounts of money involved are so vast that a small mistake can cost millions of dollars in interest expense or lost interest revenue. Many organizations budget their cash at weekly or monthly intervals. The annual budget is simply the combination of all the daily, weekly, or monthly budgets for the year.

Exhibit 4-13 shows a hypothetical cash budget for The Gap, Inc., for the year ended January 31, 19X2. Study it carefully because at some point in your career or personal affairs you will use a cash budget.

Like the statement of cash flows, the cash budget has sections for cash receipts and cash disbursements. The budget, however, is prepared *before* the period's transactions, while the statement of cash flows reports on the effects of transactions *after* they have occurred. Also, the cash budget can take any form that helps managers make decisions. The cash budget is an internal document, used only by the managers of the business, so it is not bound by generally ac-

EXHIBIT 4-13
Cash Budget (Hypothetical)

THE GAP, INC.
Cash Budget
For the Year Ended January 31, 19X2

			(In millions)
(1)	Cash balance, February 1, 19X1		$ 202.6
	Estimated cash receipts:		
(2)	Collections from customers		2,858.3
(3)	Interest and dividends on investments		6.2
(4)	Sale of store fixtures		4.9
			3,072.0
	Estimated cash disbursements:		
(5)	Purchases of inventory	$1,906.2	
(6)	Operating expenses	561.0	
(7)	Expansions of existing stores	206.4	
(8)	Opening of new stores	344.6	
(9)	Payment of long-term debt	148.7	
(10)	Payment of dividends	219.0	3,385.9
(11)	Cash available (needed) before new financing		(313.9)
(12)	Budgeted cash balance, January 31, 19X2		(200.0)
(13)	Cash available for additional investments (New financing needed)		$ (513.9)

cepted accounting principles, which require the statement of cash flows to report operating, investing, and financing activities separately.

The Gap's hypothetical cash budget in Exhibit 4-13 begins with $202.6 million of cash (line 1)—$2.6 million above the company's desired minimum balance of $200 million (line 12). The effects of the budgeted cash receipts and disbursements are expected to leave the company with a need for additional financing during the year. Observe that the budget for expanding existing stores will require $206.4 million (line 7), and the opening of new stores is expected to cost the company $344.6 million (line 8). Without these investing transactions, The Gap would not have needed additional cash. But long-term investments such as new stores and store expansions are needed to remain competitive.

Assume that managers of The Gap wish to maintain a cash balance of at least $200 million (line 12). Because the year's activity is expected to leave the company with a negative cash balance of $313.9 million (line 11), The Gap's managers need to arrange $513.9 million of financing (line 13). Line 11 of the cash budget identifies the amount of cash available or needed. Line 12 lists the minimum cash balance to maintain at all times. *Add* lines 11 and 12 to arrive at the amount of new financing needed.

Because the year's activity is expected to leave the company $313.9 million short (line 11), The Gap's managers need to arrange $513.9 million of financing (line 13).

The cash budget provides information that should help The Gap's managers arrange the financing in an orderly manner. With the cash, The Gap can expand its stores and search out exciting new products that keep customers coming back. Without the cash needed to make these kinds of investments, The Gap cannot compete with The Limited, Macy's, and other stores.

Managers also use budgets to evaluate performance. As the year progresses, managers compare actual figures with the budgeted amounts. Suppose it is now March 15 of the new year, and sales and collections from customers are lagging behind expectations for the first quarter of the year. The company does not have the cash to expand a store as planned. Top managers of The Gap realize that the economy is in a recession, and people simply cannot afford expensive clothing.

The point is that the budget provides a signal that operations are not measuring up to expectations very well. Managers may have an idea that business is slow, but the budget provides concrete evidence that the cash balance is less than expected and that cash receipts are lagging. The budget thus prompts managers to take action where it is needed.

STOP & THINK Suppose that economists are predicting difficult times for the remainder of the year. As a manager of The Gap, what action would you take to protect the interests of the company?

Answer: One response might be to reduce prices and run a 20% off sale. If you think the recession will last a year or longer, you may instruct the company's buyers to purchase less expensive lines of merchandise.

Reporting Cash on the Balance Sheet

Cash is the first current asset listed on the balance sheet of most companies. Even small businesses have several bank accounts and one or more petty cash funds, but companies usually combine all cash amounts into a single total called "Cash and Cash Equivalents" on the balance sheet. Cash equivalents include liquid assets such as time deposits and certificates of deposit, which are interest-bearing accounts that can be withdrawn with no penalty after a short period of time. Although they are slightly less liquid than cash, they are sufficiently similar to be reported along with cash. For example, the balance sheet of **Intel Corporation,** maker of the Pentium© processor, recently reported the following:

INTEL CORP.
Consolidated Balance Sheet (Adapted)
December 31, 1995 and December 31, 1994

(In millions)	1995	1994
Assets		
Current assets:		
Cash and cash equivalents	$1,463	$1,180
Short-term investments	995	1,230
Accounts receivable	3,116	1,978
Inventories	2,004	1,169
Deferred tax assets	408	552
Other current assets	111	58
Total current assets	$8,097	$6,167

Source: Intel Corporation. *Annual Report 1995,* p. 15.

Intel's notes to the financial statements explain how the company accounts for cash equivalents and investments:

NOTES TO CONSOLIDATED FINANCIAL STATEMENTS

Investments. Highly liquid investments with insignificant interest rate risk and with original maturities of three months or less are classified as cash and cash equivalents. Investments with maturities greater than three months and less than one year are classified as short-term investments.

Ethics and Accounting

An article in the *Wall Street Journal* quoted a young entrepreneur in Russia as saying that he was getting ahead in business by breaking laws. He stated that "Older people have an ethics problem. By that I mean they *have* ethics." Conversely, Roger Smith, former chairman of **General Motors,** said, "Ethical practice is, quite simply, good business." Which perspective is valid? The latter.

There are at least two key differences between these competing perspectives. The Russian entrepreneur is operating in a country where legal, social, and ethical structures are in tremendous upheaval. In contrast, Smith's environment—the United States—is stable. Businesses in Russia are fledglings with little in the way of internal controls. Apparently, the young entrepreneur has not yet been caught (in Russia these days, this increasingly means shot). Smith, in contrast, has been in business long enough to see the danger in unethical behavior. Sooner or later, unethical conduct comes to light, as we saw in our chapter opening story.

Corporate and Professional Codes of Ethics

Most large companies have a code of ethics designed to encourage ethical and responsible behavior by their employees. However, a set of general guidelines may not be specific enough to identify misbehavior, and a list of dos and don'ts can lead to the false view that anything is okay if it's not specifically forbidden. There is no easy answer. But most businesses are intolerant of unethical conduct by employees. One executive has stated, "I cannot describe all unethical behavior, but I know it when I see it."

Accountants have additional incentives to behave ethically. As professionals, they are expected to maintain higher standards than society in general. Why? Their ability to attract business or remain employed depends entirely on their reputation. Most independent accountants are members of the American Institute of Certified Public Accountants and must abide by the *AICPA Code of Professional Conduct*. Accountants who are members of the Institute of Management Accountants are bound by the *Standards of Ethical Conduct for Management Accountants*. These documents set standards of conduct for members. Unacceptable actions can result in expulsion from the organization, which makes it difficult for the person to remain in the accounting profession.

Refer to Chapter 1, page 8, for further discussion of these topics.

Ethical Issues in Accounting

Objective 7

Weigh ethical judgments in business

In many situations the ethical choice is clearcut. For example, stealing cash is illegal and unethical. In our chapter opening story, the cashier's actions landed him in jail. In other cases, the choices are more difficult. In every instance, however, ethical judgments boil down to a personal decision: How should I behave in a given situation? Let's consider three ethical issues in accounting. The first two are easy to resolve. The third is more difficult.

SITUATION 1 Sonja Kleberg is preparing the income tax return of a client who has had a particularly good year—higher income than expected. On January 2, the client pays for newspaper advertising and asks Sonja to backdate the expense to the preceding year. The tax deduction would help the client more in the year just ended than in the current year. Backdating would increase expenses and decrease taxable income of the earlier year, and save the client a few dollars in tax payments. There is a difference of only two days between January 2 and December 31, and this client is important to Kleberg. What should she do? She should refuse the request because the transaction took place in January of the new year. What internal control device could prove that Kleberg behaved unethically if she backdated the transaction in the accounting records? An IRS audit and documents and records: The date of the cash payment could prove that the expense occurred in January rather than in December.

SITUATION 2 Jack Mellichamp's software company owes $40,000 to Bank of America. The loan agreement requires Mellichamp's company to maintain a current ratio (current assets divided by current liabilities) of 1.50 or higher. It is late in the year, and the bank will review Mellichamp's situation early next year. At present, the company's current ratio is 1.40. At this level, Mellichamp is in violation of his loan agreement. He can increase the current ratio to 1.53 by paying off some current liabilities right before year end. Is it ethical to do so? Yes, because the action is a real business transaction. But paying off the liabilities is only a delaying tactic. It will hold off the creditors for now, but time will tell whether the business can improve its underlying operations.

For a review of the current ratio, see Chapter 3, page 143.

SITUATION 3 Emilia Gomez, an accountant for the Democratic Party, discovers that her supervisor, Myles Packer, made several errors last year. Campaign contributions received from foreign citizens, which are illegal, were recorded as normal. It is not clear whether the errors were deliberate or accidental. Gomez is deciding what to do. She knows that Packer evaluates her job performance, and lately her work has been marginal. What should Gomez do? The answer is uncertain. To make her decision, Gomez could follow the framework outlined in the Decision Guidelines feature on page 200.

Decision Guidelines

Ethical Judgments

Weighing tough ethical judgments requires a decision framework. Consider these six steps as general guidelines. Then apply them to Emilia Gomez's situation.

Question	Decision Guidelines
1. What are the facts?	1. *Determine the facts.*
2. What is the ethical issue, if any?	2. *Identify the ethical issues.* The root word of ethical is *ethics,* which Webster's dictionary defines as "the discipline dealing with what is good and bad and with moral duty and obligation." Gomez's ethical dilemma is to decide what she should do with the information she has uncovered.
3. What are the options?	3. *Specify the alternatives.* For Emilia Gomez, three reasonable alternatives include (a) reporting the errors to Packer, (b) reporting the errors to Packer's boss, and (c) doing nothing.
4. Who is involved in the situation?	4. *Identify the people involved.* Individuals who could be affected include Gomez, Packer, the Democratic Party, and Gomez's co-workers who observe her behavior.
5. What are the possible consequences?	5. *Assess the possible outcomes.* (a) If Gomez reports the errors to Packer, he might penalize her, or he might reward her for careful work. Reporting the errors would preserve her integrity and probably would lead to return of the money to the donors. But the Democratic Party could suffer embarrassment if this situation were made public. (b) If Gomez reports to Packer's boss—going over Packer's head—her integrity would be preserved. Her relationship with Packer would surely be strained, and it might be difficult for them to work together in the future. Gomez might be rewarded for careful work. But if Packer's boss has colluded with Packer in recording the campaign contribution, Gomez could be penalized. If the error is corrected and outsiders notified, the Democratic Party would be embarrassed. Others observing this situation would be affected by the outcome. (c) If Gomez does nothing, she would avoid a confrontation with Packer or his boss. They might or might not discover the error. If they discover it, they might or might not correct it. All might criticize Gomez for not bringing the error to their attention. Fellow accountants might or might not learn of the situation.
6. What shall I do?	6. *Make the decision.* The best choice is unclear. Gomez must balance the likely effects on the various people against the dictates of her own conscience. Even though this framework does not provide an easy decision, it identifies the relevant factors. Reporting the error to Packer is preferable because he is Gomez's supervisor. Moreover, Gomez must protect her reputation and consider the interests of outsiders who depend on an honest accounting to preserve the integrity of political campaigns.

Ethics and External Controls

There is another dimension to most ethical issues: *external controls,* which refer to the discipline on business conduct placed by outsiders who interact with the company. In situation 1, for example, Sonja Kleberg could give in to the client's request to backdate the advertising expense. But this action would be both dishonest and illegal. These external controls arise from the business's interaction with the taxing authorities. An IRS audit of Kleberg's client could uncover her action.

In situation 2, the external controls arise from Jack Mellichamp's relationship with the bank that lent money to his software company. As long as the loan agreement is in effect, the company must maintain a current ratio of 1.50 or higher. Paying off current liabilities to improve the current ratio would be a short-term solution to Mellichamp's problem. Over the long run, his business must generate more current assets through operations. His business will almost certainly need to borrow in the future and will probably face similar loan restrictions. Managers are wise to focus on long-term solutions to their problems if they hope to succeed in business.

The primary external control in situation 3 results from the laws of the United States and their enforcement through the U.S. legal system governing campaign financing. Campaign contributions are public information, and sooner or later the public will learn that the Democratic Party received illegal campaign contributions.

It would be in the party's best interest to admit its mistake and correct the errors as quickly as possible—by returning the illegal contributions to the donors. The situation will probably lead to tighter party controls that will keep from repeating the mistake. This is why organizations have codes of conduct and why, as Roger Smith put it, "Ethical practice is . . . good business."

STOP & THINK Can you identify the external control in the chapter opening story? How did it impose discipline on the cashier?

Answer: The external control was the monthly statement that Grant LeForge sends each client. When customers saw their account balances underreported on the monthly statements, they called in to ask why. Steve Lane must have spent half his time explaining the out-of-balance conditions of clients' accounts. Sooner or later he was bound to get caught. That's how external controls work.

SUMMARY PROBLEM FOR YOUR REVIEW

Assume the following situation for PepsiCo, Inc.:

PepsiCo ended 19X3 with total assets of $24 billion ($24,000 million), which included cash of $230 million. At December 31, 19X3, PepsiCo owed $17 billion, of which it expected to pay $6,600 million during 19X4. At the end of 19X3, Bob Detmer, the Chief Financial Officer of PepsiCo, is preparing the budget for the next year.

During 19X4, Detmer expects PepsiCo to collect $26.4 billion from customers and an additional $90 million in interest that the company will earn on investments. PepsiCo expects to pay $12.5 billion for its inventories and $5.4 billion for operating expenses. To remain competitive, PepsiCo plans to spend $2.2 billion to upgrade the company's production facilities and an additional $320 million to acquire other companies. PepsiCo also plans to sell older assets for approximately $300 million and to collect $220 million of this amount in cash. PepsiCo certainly expects to earn a profit during 19X4 (approximately $1.8 billion), so the company is budgeting dividend payments of $550 million during the year. Finally, the company is scheduled to pay off $1.2 billion of long-term debt, in addition to the current liabilities left over from 19X3.

Because of the increased level of activity planned for 19X4, Detmer budgets the need for a minimum cash balance of $330 million.

Required

1. How much must PepsiCo borrow during 19X4 to keep its cash balance from falling below $330 million? Prepare the 19X4 cash budget to answer this important question.
2. Consider the company's need to borrow $2,160 million. PepsiCo can avoid the need to borrow money in 19X4 by delaying one particular cash payment until 19X5 or later. Identify the item, and state why it would be unwise to delay its payment.
3. To relate the cash budget to the statement of cash flows, suppose PepsiCo's transactions during 19X4 occurred as planned. Prepare PepsiCo's statement of cash flows for 19X4.

ANSWERS

Requirement 1

PEPSICO, INC.
Cash Budget
For the Year Ended December 31, 19X4

		(In millions)
Cash balance, December 31, 19X3		$ 230
Estimated cash receipts:		
Collections from customers		26,400
Receipt of interest		90
Sale of assets		220
		26,940
Estimated cash disbursements:		
Purchases of inventory	$12,500	
Payment of operating expenses	5,400	
Upgrading of production facilities	2,200	
Acquisition of other companies	320	
Payment of dividends	550	
Payment of long-term debt and other liabilities ($1,200 + $6,600)	7,800	(28,770)
Cash available (needed) before new financing		(1,830)
Budgeted cash balance, December 31, 19X4		(330)
Cash available for additional investments, or (New financing needed)		$(2,160)

Requirement 2

PepsiCo can eliminate the need for borrowing $2,160 million by delaying the $2,200 million payment to *upgrade the company's production facilities.* The delay would be unwise because PepsiCo needs the upgrading to remain competitive.

Requirement 3

PEPSICO, INC.
Statement of Cash Flows
For the Year Ended December 31, 19X4

	(In millions)	
Cash Flows from Operating Activities:		
Receipts:		
Collections from customers		$26,400
Receipt of interest		90
		26,490
Payments:		
Purchases of inventory	$(12,500)	
Payment of operating expenses	(5,400)	(17,900)
Net cash provided by operating activities		8,590
Cash Flows from Investing Activities:		
Upgrading of production facilities	$ (2,200)	
Acquisition of other companies	(320)	
Sale of assets	220	
Net cash used for investing activities		(2,300)
Cash Flows from Financing Activities:		
Borrowing	$ 2,160	
Payment of long-term debt and other liabilities	(7,800)	
Payment of dividends	(550)	
Net cash used for financing activities		(6,190)
Increase in cash		$ 100
Cash balance, beginning of year		230
Cash balance, end of year		$ 330

SUMMARY OF LEARNING OBJECTIVES

1. *Identify the characteristics of an effective system of internal control.* An effective internal control system includes these features: *competent, reliable, and ethical personnel; clear-cut assignment of responsibilities; proper authorization; separation of duties; internal and external audits; documents and records;* and *electronic and computer controls.* Many companies also make use of fireproof vaults, point-of-sale terminals, fidelity bonds, mandatory vacations, and job rotation. Effective computerized internal control systems must meet the same basic standards that good manual systems do.

2. *Use a bank reconciliation as a control device.* The *bank account* helps control and safeguard cash. Businesses use the *bank statement* and the *bank reconciliation* to account for cash and banking transactions, and to bring the books up to date.

3. *Manage cash and account for cash transactions.* Managers strive to keep cash flowing through their organization. To speed the collection of cash from sales, they offer sales discounts to people who pay within a specified period of time.

4. *Apply internal controls to cash receipts.* To control cash receipts over the counter, companies use point-of-sale terminals that customers can see, and require that cashiers provide customers with receipts. A tape inside the machine records each sale and cash transaction. Pricing with uneven amounts means that cashiers must open the drawer to make change, which requires the transaction to be recorded on tape.

To control cash receipts by mail, a mailroom employee should be charged with opening the mail, comparing the enclosed amount with the remittance advice, and preparing a control tape. This is an essential separation of duties—the accounting department should not open the mail. At the end of the day, the controller compares the three records of the day's cash receipts: the control tape total from the mailroom, the bank deposit amount from the cashier, and the debit to Cash from the accounting department.

5. *Apply internal controls to cash disbursements.* To control payments by check, checks should be issued and signed only when a *disbursement packet* including the purchase request, purchase order, invoice (bill), and receiving report (with all appropriate signatures) has been prepared. To control petty cash disbursements, the custodian of the fund should require a completed petty cash ticket for all disbursements.

6. *Use a budget to manage cash.* A budget is a quantitative expression of a plan that helps managers coordinate the entity's activities. To prepare for the future, a company must determine how much cash it will need, then decide whether its operations will bring in the needed cash. If not, then the company knows to arrange financing early. If operations will bring in an excess of cash, the company can be on the lookout for investment activities.

7. *Weigh ethical judgments in business*. To make ethical decisions, people should proceed in six steps: (1) Determine the facts. (2) Identify the ethical issues. (3) Specify the alternatives. (4) Identify the people involved. (5) Assess the possible outcomes. (6) Make the decision. Ethical business practice is simply good business.

ACCOUNTING VOCABULARY

audit *(p. 175).*
bank collection *(p. 180).*
bank reconciliation *(p. 180).*
bank statement *(p. 178).*
budget *(p. 195).*
check *(p. 178).*
controller *(p. 173).*
deposit in transit *(p. 180).*
electronic funds transfer (EFT) *(p. 178).*
imprest system *(p. 194).*
internal control *(p. 172).*
nonsufficient funds (NSF) check *(p. 180).*
outstanding check *(p. 180).*
petty cash *(p. 194).*

QUESTIONS

1. What is the most basic goal of internal control, and why is it so important?
2. Which federal act affects internal control procedures? What requirement does it place on management?
3. Identify the features of an effective system of internal control.
4. Separation of duties may be divided into four parts. What are they?
5. How can internal control systems be circumvented?
6. Are internal control systems designed to be foolproof and perfect? What is a fundamental constraint in planning and maintaining these systems?
7. Briefly state how each of the following serves as an internal control measure over cash: bank account, signature card, deposit ticket, and bank statement.
8. Each of the items in the following list must be accounted for in the bank reconciliation. Next to each item, enter the appropriate letter from these possible treatments: (a) bank side of reconciliation—add the item; (b) bank side of reconciliation—subtract the item; (c) book side of reconciliation—add the item; (d) book side of reconciliation—subtract the item.
   ________________ Outstanding check
   ________________ NSF check
   ________________ Bank service charge
   ________________ Cost of printed checks
   ________________ Bank error that decreased bank balance
   ________________ Deposit in transit
   ________________ Bank collection
   ________________ Customer check returned because of unauthorized signature
   ________________ Book error that increased balance of Cash account
9. What purpose does a bank reconciliation serve?
10. How do accounts receivable records help a company manage its cash? How does offering discounts speed the collection of cash?
11. What role does a cash register play in an internal control system?
12. Describe the internal control procedures for cash received by mail.
13. What documents make up the disbursement packet? Describe three procedures that use the disbursement packet to ensure that each payment is appropriate.
14. Describe how a budget helps a company manage its cash.
15. Suppose a company has six bank accounts, two petty cash funds, and three certificates of deposit that can be withdrawn on demand. How many cash amounts would this company likely report on its balance sheet?
16. "Our managers know that they are expected to meet budgeted profit figures. We don't want excuses. We want results." Discuss the ethical implications of this policy.

EXERCISES

Correcting an internal control weakness ***(Obj. 1)***

E4-1 Consider this excerpt from a *Wall Street Journal* article:

TOKYO—**Sumitomo Corp.,** the giant Japanese trading company, said unauthorized trades by its former head of copper trading over the past decade caused it huge losses that may total $1.8 billion.

If Sumitomo's estimate pans out, the trading loss would be the largest in corporate history—dwarfing even the $1.3 billion lost by Nick Leeson of Barings PLC and the $1.1 billion lost by a trader at Japan's Daiwa Bank Ltd. And the fiasco adds a new name to the roll of all-time rogue traders: the flamboyant Yasuo Hamanaka, who until recently was the world's most powerful copper trader—and the one most feared by other traders.

Sumitomo's loss could have been deep repercussions for the world copper market and for Sumitomo, one of the world's largest companies. . . . Sumitomo is the largest player in the world's copper market, and is believed to control as much as half of the 10 billion ton annual production.

Sumitomo said it learned of the damage last week, when Mr. Hamanaka called a superior and confessed to making unauthorized trades that led to the losses over a 10-year period. Mr. Hamanaka, according to a Sumitomo statement, admitted to concealing the losses by falsifying Sumitomo's books and records.

What internal control weakness at Sumitomo Corp. allowed this loss to grow so large? How could the company have avoided and/or limited the size of the loss?

Identifying internal control strengths and weaknesses ***(Obj. 1)***

E4-2 The following situations suggest either a strength or a weakness in internal control. Identify each as *strength* or *weakness,* and give the reason for your answer.

a. Top managers delegate all internal control measures to the accounting department.

b. The accounting department orders merchandise and approves invoices for payment.

c. The operator of a computer has no other accounting or cash-handling duties.

d. Cash received over the counter is controlled by the sales clerk, who rings up the sale and places the cash in the register. The sales clerk has access to the control tape stored in the register.

e. Cash received by mail goes straight to the accountant, who debits Cash and credits Accounts Receivable from the customer.

f. The vice president who signs checks assumes that the accounting department has matched the invoice with other supporting documents and therefore does not examine the disbursement packet.

Identifying internal controls ***(Obj. 1)***

E4-3 Identify the missing internal control characteristic in the following situations:

a. Business is slow at White Water Park on Tuesday, Wednesday, and Thursday nights. To reduce expenses, the owner decides not to use a ticket taker on those nights. The ticket seller (cashier) is told to keep the tickets as a record of the number sold.

b. The manager of a discount store wants to speed the flow of customers through check-out. She decides to reduce the time that cashiers spend making change, so she prices merchandise at round dollar amounts—such as $8.00 and $15.00—instead of the customary amounts—$7.95 and $14.95.

c. Grocery stores such as Kroger and Winn Dixie purchase large quantities of their merchandise from a few suppliers. At another grocery store, the manager decides to reduce paperwork. He eliminates the requirement that a receiving department employee prepare a receiving report, which lists the quantities of items received from the supplier.

d. When business is brisk, Stop-n-Shop and many other retail stores deposit cash in the bank several times during the day. The manager at another convenience store wants to reduce the time that employees spend delivering cash to the bank, so he starts a new policy. Cash will build up over Saturdays and Sundays, and the total two-day amount will be deposited on Sunday evening.

e. While reviewing the records of Pay Less Pharmacy, you find that the same employee orders merchandise and approves invoices for payment.

Explaining the role of internal control ***(Obj. 1)***

E4-4 The following questions are unrelated except that they all pertain to internal control.

1. Separation of duties is an important consideration if a system of internal control is to be effective. Why is this so?
2. Cash may be a relatively small item on the financial statements. Nevertheless, internal control over cash is very important. Why is this true?
3. Ling Ltd. requires that all documents supporting a check be canceled (stamped Paid) by the person who signs the check. Why do you think this practice is required? What might happen if it were not?
4. Many managers think that safeguarding assets is the most important objective of internal control systems, while auditors emphasize internal control's role in ensuring reliable accounting data. Explain why managers are more concerned about safeguarding assets and auditors are more concerned about the quality of the accounting records.

Classifying bank reconciliation items ***(Obj. 2)***

E4-5 The following items may appear on a bank reconciliation:

1. Service charge.
2. Deposits in transit.
3. NSF check.
4. Bank collection of a note receivable on our behalf.
5. Book error: We debited Cash for $200. The correct debit was $2,000.
6. Outstanding checks.
7. Bank error: The bank charged our account for a check written by another customer.

Classify each item as (a) an addition to the bank balance, (b) a subtraction from the bank balance, (c) an addition to the book balance, or (d) a subtraction from the book balance.

Preparing a bank reconciliation ***(Obj. 2)***

E4-6 D. J. Hunter's checkbook lists the following:

Date	Check No.	Item	Check	Deposit	Balance
9/1					$ 525
4	622	La Petite France Bakery	$ 19		506
9		Dividends		$ 116	622
13	623	General Tire Co.	43		579
14	624	Exxon Oil Co.	58		521
18	625	Cash	50		471
26	626	Fellowship Bible Church	25		446
28	627	Bent Tree Apartments	275		171
30		Paycheck		1,800	1,971

The September bank statement shows

Balance			$525
Add: Deposits			116
Deduct checks: No.	Amount		
622	$19		
623	43		
624	68*		
625	50		(180)
Other charges:			
Printed checks		$ 8	
Service charge		12	(20)
Balance			$441

*This is the correct amount for check number 624.

Required

Prepare Hunter's bank reconciliation at September 30.

Preparing a bank reconciliation ***(Obj. 2)***

E4-7 Louis Nicosia operates four 7-11 stores. He has just received the monthly bank statement at October 31 from City National Bank, and the statement shows an ending balance of $3,840. Listed on the statement are an EFT rent collection of $400, a service charge of $12, two NSF checks totaling $74, and a $9 charge for printed checks. In reviewing his cash records, Nicosia identifies outstanding checks totaling $467 and an October 31 deposit in transit of $1,788. During October, he recorded a $290 check for the salary of a part-time employee by debiting Salary Expense and crediting Cash for $29. Nicosia's Cash account shows an October 31 cash balance of $5,117. Prepare the bank reconciliation at October 31.

Making journal entries from a bank reconciliation ***(Obj. 2, 3)***

E4-8 Using the data from Exercise 4-7, make the journal entries that Nicosia should record on October 31. Include an explanation for each entry.

Applying internal controls to the bank reconciliation ***(Obj. 1, 2)***

E4-9 A grand jury indicted the manager of a Broken Spoke restaurant for stealing cash from the company. Over a three-year period, the manager allegedly took almost $100,000 and attempted to cover the theft by manipulating the bank reconciliation.

Required

What is the most likely way that a person would manipulate a bank reconciliation to cover a theft? Be specific. What internal control arrangement could have avoided this theft?

Evaluating internal control over cash receipts ***(Obj. 4)***

E4-10 A cash register is located in each department of a Saks Fifth Avenue store. The register display shows the amount of each sale, the cash received from the customer, and any change returned to the customer. The machine also produces a customer receipt but keeps no record of transactions. At the end of the day, the clerk counts the cash in the register and gives it to the cashier for deposit in the company bank account.

Required

Write a memo to convince the store manager that there is an internal control weakness over cash receipts. Identify the weakness that gives an employee the best opportunity to steal cash, and state how to prevent such a theft.

Accounting for petty cash
(Obj. 3, 5)

E4-11 The Sisters of Charity in San Diego created a $400 imprest petty cash fund. During the first month of use, the fund custodian authorized and signed petty cash tickets as follows:

Ticket No.	Item	Account Debited	Amount
1	Delivery of pledge cards to donors	Delivery Expense	$ 22.19
2	Mail package	Postage Expense	52.80
3	Newsletter	Supplies Expense	134.14
4	Key to closet	Miscellaneous Expense	2.85
5	Wastebasket	Miscellaneous Expense	13.78
6	Computer diskettes	Supplies Expense	85.37

Required

1. Make the general journal entries that first would create the petty cash fund and then would show its replenishment. Include explanations.
2. Describe the items in the fund immediately before replenishment.
3. Describe the items in the fund immediately after replenishment.

Preparing a cash budget
(Obj. 6)

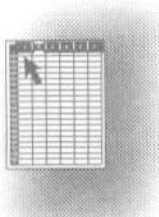

E4-12 Suppose **Sprint Corporation**, the long-distance telephone company, is preparing its cash budget for 19X4. The company ended 19X3 with $125.8 million, and top management foresees the need for a cash balance of at least $125 million to pay all bills as they come due in 19X4.

Collections from customers are expected to total $11,813.2 million during 19X4, and payments for the cost of services and products should reach $6,166 million. Operating expense payments are budgeted at $2,743.6 million.

During 19X4, Sprint expects to invest $1,825.7 million in new equipment, $275 million in the company's cellular division, and to sell older assets for $115.7 million. Debt payments scheduled for 19X4 will total $597.2 million. The company forecasts net income of $890.4 million for 19X4 and plans to pay dividends of $338 million.

Required

Prepare Sprint's cash budget for 19X4. Will the budgeted level of cash receipts leave Sprint with the desired ending cash balance of $125 million, or will the company need additional financing?

Evaluating the ethics of conduct by government legislators
(Obj. 7)

E4-13 Approximately 300 current and former members of the U.S. House of Representatives—on a regular basis—wrote $250,000 of checks without having the cash in their accounts. Later investigations revealed that no public funds were involved. The House bank was a free-standing institution that recirculated House members' cash. In effect, the delinquent check writers were borrowing money from each other on an interest-free, no-service-charge basis. Nevertheless, the House closed its bank after the events became public.

Required

Suppose you are a new congressional representative from your state. Apply the decision guidelines for ethical judgments outlined on page 200 to decide whether you would write NSF checks on a regular basis through the House bank.

CHALLENGE EXERCISES

Internal control over cash disbursements, ethical considerations
(Obj. 5, 7)

E4-14 Tracie Kenan, the owner of Tracie's Dress Shop, has delegated management of the business to Meg Grayson, a friend. Kenan drops by the business to meet customers and checks up on cash receipts, but Grayson buys the merchandise and handles cash disbursements. Business has been brisk lately, and cash receipts have kept pace with the apparent level of sales. However, for a year or so, the amount of cash on hand has been too low. When asked about this, Grayson explains that designers are charging more for dresses than in the past. During the past year, Grayson has taken two expensive vacations, and Kenan wonders how Grayson could afford these trips on her $35,000 annual salary and commissions.

Required

List at least three ways Grayson could be defrauding Kenan's business of cash. In each instance, also identify how Kenan can determine whether Grayson's actions are ethical. Limit your answers to the dress shop's cash disbursements. The business pays all suppliers by check (no EFTs).

Preparing and using a cash budget
(Obj. 6)

E4-15 Among its many products, **International Paper Company** makes paper for JC Penney shopping bags, the labels on Del Monte canned foods, and *Redbook* magazine. Marianne Parrs, the Chief Financial Officer, is responsible for International Paper's cash budget for 19X5. The budget will help Parrs determine the amount of long-term borrowing needed to end the year with a cash balance of $300 million. Parrs' assistants have assembled budget data for 19X5, which the computer printed in alphabetical order. Not all the data items, reproduced on page 208, are used in preparing the cash budget.

	(In millions)
Acquisition of other companies	$ 1,168
Actual cash balance, December 31, 19X4	270
Borrowing	?
Budgeted total assets before borrowing	23,977
Budgeted total current assets before borrowing	5,873
Budgeted total current liabilities before borrowing	4,863
Budgeted total liabilities before borrowing	16,180
Budgeted total stockholders' equity before borrowing	7,797
Collections from customers	19,467
Dividend payments	237
Issuance of stock	516
Net income	1,153
Other cash receipts	111
Payment of long-term and short-term debt	950
Payment of operating expenses	2,349
Purchases of inventory items	14,345
Purchase of property and equipment	1,518

Required

1. Prepare the cash budget to determine the amount of borrowing International Paper needs during 19X5.
2. Compute International Paper's expected current ratio and debt ratio at December 31, 19X5, both before and after borrowing on long-term debt. Based on these figures, and on the budgeted levels of assets and liabilities, would you lend the requested amount to International Paper? Give the reason for your decision.

PROBLEMS

(GROUP A)

Identifying the characteristics of an effective internal control system ***(Obj. 1)***

P4-1A Century One Real Estate Development Company prospered during the lengthy economic expansion of the 1980s. Business was so good that the company bothered with few internal controls. The decline in the local real estate market in the early 1990s, however, has caused Century One to experience a shortage of cash. Dave Campbell, the company owner, is looking for ways to save money.

Required

As a consultant for the company, write a memorandum to convince Campbell of the company's need for a system of internal control. Be specific in telling him how an internal control system could save the company money. Include the definition of internal control, and briefly discuss each characteristic of an effective internal control system, beginning with competent, reliable, and ethical personnel.

Identifying internal control weaknesses ***(Obj. 1, 4, 5)***

P4-2A Each of the following situations has an internal control weakness.

a. In evaluating the internal control over cash disbursements, an auditor learns that the purchasing agent is responsible for purchasing diamonds for use in the company's manufacturing process, approving the invoices for payment, and signing the checks. No supervisor reviews the purchasing agent's work.
b. Todd Wagoner owns a firm that performs engineering services. His staff consists of 12 professional engineers, and he manages the office. Often, his work requires him to travel to meet with clients. During the past six months, he has observed that when he returns from a business trip, the engineering jobs in the office have not progressed satisfactorily. He learns that when he is away, several of his senior employees take over office management and neglect their engineering duties. One employee could manage the office.
c. Amy Fariss has been an employee of Griffith's Shoe Store for many years. Because the business is relatively small, Fariss performs all accounting duties, including opening the mail, preparing the bank deposit, and preparing the bank reconciliation.
d. Most large companies have internal audit staffs that continuously evaluate the business's internal control. Part of the auditor's job is to evaluate how efficiently the company is running. For example, is the company purchasing inventory from the least expensive wholesaler? After a particularly bad year, Campbell Design Company eliminates its internal audit department to reduce expenses.
e. CPA firms, law firms, and other professional organizations use paraprofessional employees to perform routine tasks. For example, an accounting paraprofessional might examine documents to assist a CPA in conducting an audit. In the CPA firm of Dunham & Lee, Cecil Dunham, the senior partner, turns over a significant portion of his high-level audit work to his paraprofessional staff.

Required

1. Identify the missing internal control characteristic in each situation.
2. Identify the business's possible problem.
3. Propose a solution to the problem.
4. How will what you learned in this problem help you manage a business?

P4-3A The cash receipts and the cash disbursements of Fuddruckers for April 19X4 appear as follows:

Using the bank reconciliation as a control device ***(Obj. 2)***

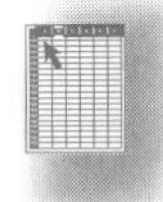

Cash Receipts (Posting reference is CR)		Cash Disbursements (Posting reference is CD)	
Date	**Cash Debit**	**Check No.**	**Cash Credit**
Apr. 2	$ 4,174	3113	$ 891
8	407	3114	147
10	559	3115	1,930
16	2,187	3116	664
22	1,854	3117	1,472
29	1,060	3118	1,000
30	337	3119	632
Total	$10,578	3120	1,675
		3121	100
		3122	2,413
		Total	$10,924

Assume that the Cash account of Fuddruckers shows the following information at April 30, 19X4:

Cash

Date	Item	Jrnl. Ref.	Debit	Credit	Balance
Apr. 1	Balance				7,911
30		CR. 6	10,578		18,489
30		CD. 11		10,924	7,565

Fuddruckers received the following bank statement on April 30, 19X4:

Bank Statement for April 19X4

Beginning balance		$ 7,911
Deposits and other Credits:		
Apr. 1	$ 326 EFT	
4	4,174	
9	407	
12	559	
17	2,187	
22	1,368 BC	
23	1,854	10,875
Checks and other Debits		
Apr. 7	$ 891	
13	1,390	
14	903 US	
15	147	
18	664	
21	219 EFT	
26	1,472	
30	1,000	
30	20 SC	(6,706)
Ending balance		$12,080

Explanation: EFT—electronic funds transfer, BC—bank collection, US—unauthorized signature, SC—service charge.

Additional data for the bank reconciliation include the following:

a. The EFT deposit was a receipt of monthly rent. The EFT debit was a monthly insurance payment.

b. The unauthorized signature check was received from S. M. Holt.

c. The $1,368 bank collection of a note receivable on April 22 included $185 interest revenue.

d. The correct amount of check number 3115, a payment on account, is $1,390. (Fuddruckers's accountant mistakenly recorded the check for $1,930.)

Required

1. Prepare the Fuddruckers bank reconciliation at April 30, 19X4.
2. Describe how a bank account and the bank reconciliation help the Fuddruckers managers control the business's cash.

Preparing a bank reconciliation and the related journal entries ***(Obj. 2)***

P4-4A The August 31 bank statement of Valu-D Company has just arrived from United Bank. To prepare the Valu-D bank reconciliation, you gather the following data:

a. Valu-D's Cash account shows a balance of $4,366.14 on August 31.

b. The bank statement includes two charges for returned checks from customers. One is a $395.00 check received from Shoreline Express and deposited on August 20, returned by Shoreline's bank with the imprint "Unauthorized Signature." The other is an NSF check in the amount of $146.67 received from Lipsey, Inc. This check had been deposited on August 17.

c. Valu-D pays rent ($750) and insurance ($290) each month by EFT.

d. The following Valu-D checks are outstanding at August 31:

Check No.	Amount
237	$ 46.10
288	141.00
291	578.05
293	11.87
294	609.51
295	8.88
296	101.63

e. The bank statement includes a deposit of $1,191.17, collected by the bank on behalf of Valu-D. Of the total, $1,011.81 is collection of a note receivable, and the remainder is interest revenue.

f. The bank statement shows that Valu-D earned $38.19 of interest on its bank balance during August. This amount was added to Valu-D's account by the bank.

g. The bank statement lists a $10.50 subtraction for the bank service charge.

h. On August 31, the Valu-D treasurer deposited $316.15, but this deposit does not appear on the bank statement.

i. The bank statement includes a $300.00 deposit that Valu-D did not make. The bank had erroneously credited the Valu-D account for another bank customer's deposit.

j. The August 31 bank balance is $5,484.22.

Required

1. Prepare the bank reconciliation for Valu-D Company at August 31.
2. Record the entries necessary to bring the book balance of Cash into agreement with the adjusted book balance on the reconciliation. Include an explanation for each entry.
3. How will what you learned in this problem help you manage a business?

Identifying internal control weakness ***(Obj. 4)***

P4-5A VisiCalc, Inc., makes all sales of its spreadsheet software on credit. Cash receipts arrive by mail, usually within 30 days of the sale. Lynn Tatum opens envelopes and separates the checks from the accompanying remittance advices. Tatum forwards the checks to another employee, who makes the daily bank deposit but has no access to the accounting records. Tatum sends the remittance advices, which show the amount of cash received, to the accounting department for entry in the accounts. Tatum's only other duty is to grant sales allowances to customers. (A *sales allowance* decreases the amount that the customer must pay.) When he receives a customer check for less than the full amount of the invoice, he records the sales allowance and forwards the document to the accounting department.

Required

You are a new employee of VisiCalc, Inc. Write a memo to the company president identifying the internal control weakness in this situation. State how to correct the weakness.

P4-6A Louis Lipschitz, Executive Vice President and Chief Financial Officer of **Toys "Я" Us, Inc.**, is responsible for the company's budgeting process. Suppose Lipschitz's staff is preparing the Toys "Я" Us cash budget for 19X7. A key input to the budgeting process is last year's statement of cash flows, reproduced in an adapted format as follows:

Preparing a cash budget and using cash-flow information ***(Obj. 6)***

TOYS "Я" US, INC., AND SUBSIDIARIES
Consolidated Statement of Cash Flows (Adapted)

(In millions)	19X6
Cash Flows from Operating Activities	
Collections from customers	$9,413.9
Interest received	17.4
Purchases of inventory	(6,749.7)
Operating expenses	(2,034.7)
Restructuring costs	(396.6)
Net cash provided by operating activities	250.3
Cash Flows from Investing Activities	
Capital expenditures	(467.5)
Purchases of other assets	(67.4)
Net cash used in investing activities	(534.9)
Cash Flows from Financing Activities	
Short-term borrowings	210.1
Long-term borrowings	82.2
Long-term debt repayments	(9.3)
Issuance of stock	16.2
Share repurchases	(200.2)
Net cash provided by financing activities	99.0
Effect of foreign-currency exchange rate changes on cash and cash equivalents	18.5
Cash and Cash Equivalents	
(Decrease)/increase during year	(167.1)
Beginning of year	369.8
End of year	$ 202.7

Required

1. Prepare the Toys "Я" Us cash budget for 19X7. Date the budget simply "19X7" and denote the beginning and ending cash balances as "beginning" and "ending." Assume the company expects 19X7 to be the same as 19X6, but with the following changes:
   a. In 19X7, the company expects a 12% increase in collections from customers and a 10% increase in purchases of inventory.
   b. The company expects to incur no restructuring costs in 19X7.
   c. The amount of any borrowings and issuances of stock needed in 19X7 will be determined as the result of the cash budget and thus are not causal factors for the preparation of the budget. (But scheduled long-term debt repayments and share repurchases should be the same in 19X7 as they were in 19X6.)
   d. Lipschitz plans to end the year with a cash balance of $500 million.

You will find these explanations helpful:

- "Capital expenditures" are purchases of property and equipment.
- Toys "Я" Us does not pay cash dividends. Instead, the company *repurchases* its stock from its stockholders. This is another way for a corporation to return cash to the stockholders.

2. Answer these questions about the company. Explain your reasoning for each answer.
   a. Does the company's cash budget for 19X7 suggest that Toys "Я" Us is growing, holding steady, or decreasing in size?
   b. Do the statement of cash flows for 19X6 and the cash budget for 19X7 suggest that operating activities are generating enough cash?

Making an ethical judgment
(Obj. 7)

P4-7A Jana Sauer is executive vice president of Global Loan Associates in Baton Rouge, Louisiana. Active in community affairs, Sauer serves on the board of directors of NAVPRESS Publishing Company. NAVPRESS is expanding rapidly and is considering relocating its plant. At a recent meeting, board members decided to try to buy 15 acres of land on the edge of town. The owner of the property is Kyle Lewie, a customer of Global Loan. Lewie is completing a bitter divorce, and Sauer knows that Lewie is eager to sell his property. In view of Lewie's difficult situation, Sauer believes he would accept almost any offer for the land. Realtors have appraised the property at $5 million.

Required

Apply the ethical judgment framework outlined in the chapter to help Sauer decide what her role should be in NAVPRESS's attempt to buy the land from Lewie.

(GROUP B)

Identifying the characteristics of an effective internal control system
(Obj. 1)

P4-1B An employee of Mirage Oil Company recently stole thousands of dollars of the company's cash. The company has decided to install a new system of internal controls.

Required

As a consultant for Mirage Oil Company, write a memo to the president explaining how a separation of duties helps to safeguard assets.

Identifying internal control weaknesses
(Obj. 1, 4, 5)

P4-2B Each of the following situations has an internal control weakness:

a. Luann Sorelle employs three professional interior designers in her design studio. She is located in an area with a lot of new construction, and her business is booming. Ordinarily, Sorelle does all the purchasing of furniture, draperies, carpets, fabrics, sewing services, and other materials and labor needed to complete jobs. During the summer, she takes a long vacation, and in her absence she allows each designer to purchase materials and labor. On her return, Sorelle reviews operations and notes that expenses are much higher and net income much lower than in the past.

b. Discount stores such as **Target** and **Sam's** receive a large portion of their sales revenue in cash, with the remainder in credit card sales. To reduce expenses, a store manager ceases purchasing fidelity bonds on the cashiers.

c. The office supply company from which Champs Sporting Goods purchases cash receipt forms recently notified Champs that the last shipped receipts were not prenumbered. Alex Champion, the owner, replied that he did not use the receipt numbers, so the omission is not important.

d. Flowers Computer Programs is a software company that specializes in programs with accounting applications. The company's most popular program prepares the journal, accounts receivable subsidiary ledger, and general ledger. In the company's early days, the owner and eight employees wrote the computer programs, lined up manufacturers to produce the diskettes, sold the products to stores such as ComputerLand and ComputerCraft, and performed the general management and accounting of the company. As the company has grown, the number of employees has increased dramatically. Recently, the development of a new software program stopped while the programmers redesigned Flowers's accounting system. Flowers's own accountants could have performed this task.

e. Lydia Pink, a widow with no known sources of outside income, has been a trusted employee of Stone Products Company for 15 years. She performs all cash-handling and accounting duties, including opening the mail, preparing the bank deposit, accounting for all aspects of cash and accounts receivable, and preparing the bank reconciliation. She has just purchased a new Lexus and a new home in an expensive suburb. Grant Chavez, the owner of the company, wonders how she can afford these luxuries on her salary.

Required

1. Identify the missing internal control characteristics in each situation.
2. Identify the business's possible problem.
3. Propose a solution to the problem.
4. How will what you learned in this problem help you manage a business?

P4-3B The cash receipts and the cash disbursements of Xircom Resources for March 19X5 are given.

Using the bank reconciliation as a control device ***(Obj. 2)***

Cash Receipts (Posting reference is CR)		Cash Disbursements (Posting reference is CD)	
Date	Cash Debit	Check No.	Cash Credit
Mar. 4	$2,716	1413	$ 1,465
9	544	1414	1,004
11	1,655	1415	450
14	896	1416	8
17	367	1417	775
25	890	1418	88
31	2,038	1419	4,126
Total	$9,106	1420	970
		1421	200
		1422	2,267
		Total	$11,353

The Cash account of Xircom Resources shows the following information on March 31, 19X5:

Cash

Date	Item	Jrnl. Ref.	Debit	Credit	Balance
Mar. 1	Balance				15,188
31		CR. 10	9,106		24,294
31		CD. 16		11,353	12,941

On March 31, 19X5, Xircom Resources received this bank statement:

Bank Statement for March 19X5

Beginning balance		$15,188
Deposits and other Credits:		
Mar. 1	$ 625 EFT	
5	2,716	
10	544	
11	1,655	
15	896	
18	367	
25	890	
31	1,000 BC	8,693
Checks and other Debits:		
Mar. 8	$ 441 NSF	
9	1,465	
13	1,004	
14	450	
15	8	
19	340 EFT	
22	775	
29	88	
31	4,216	
31	25 SC	(8,812)
Ending balance		$15,069

Explanation: BC—bank collection, EFT—electronic funds transfer, NSF—nonsufficient fund check, SC—service charge.

Additional data for the bank reconciliation:

a. The EFT deposit was a receipt of monthly rent. The EFT debit was payment of monthly insurance.

b. The NSF check was received late in February from Jay Andrews.

c. The $1,000 bank collection of a note receivable on March 31 included $122 interest revenue.

d. The correct amount of check number 1419, a payment on account, is $4,216. (The Xircom Resources accountant mistakenly recorded the check for $4,126.)

Required

1. Prepare the bank reconciliation of Xircom Resources at March 31, 19X5.
2. Describe how a bank account and the bank reconciliation help Xircom managers control the business's cash.

Preparing a bank reconciliation and the related journal entries
(Obj. 2)

P4-4B The May 31 bank statement of Merrill College has just arrived from Central Bank. To prepare the Merrill bank reconciliation, you gather the following data:

a. The May 31 bank balance is $19,530.82.

b. The bank statement includes two charges for returned checks from customers. One is an NSF check in the amount of $67.50 received from Harley Doherty, a student, recorded on the books by a debit to Cash, and deposited on May 19. The other is a $195.03 check received from Maria Shell and deposited on May 21. It was returned by Shell's bank with the imprint "Unauthorized Signature."

c. The following Merrill checks are outstanding at May 31:

Check No.	Amount
616	$403.00
802	74.25
806	36.60
809	161.38
810	229.05
811	48.91

d. A few students pay monthly fees by EFT. The May bank statement lists a $200 deposit for student fees.

e. The bank statement includes two special deposits: $899.14, which is the amount of dividend revenue the bank collected from General Electric Company on behalf of Merrill, and $16.86, the interest revenue the college earned on its bank balance during May.

f. The bank statement lists a $6.25 subtraction for the bank service charge.

g. On May 31 the Merrill treasurer deposited $381.14, but this deposit does not appear on the bank statement.

h. The bank statement includes a $410.00 deduction for a check drawn by Marimont Freight Company. Merrill promptly notified the bank of its error.

i. Merrill's Cash account shows a balance of $18,521.55 on May 31.

Required

1. Prepare the bank reconciliation for Merrill College at May 31.
2. Record the entries necessary to bring the book balance of Cash into agreement with the adjusted book balance on the reconciliation. Include an explanation for each entry.
3. How will what you learned in this problem help you manage a business?

Identifying internal control weakness
(Obj. 4)

P4-5B Long Island Lighting makes all sales on credit. Cash receipts arrive by mail, usually within 30 days of the sale. Brad Copeland opens envelopes and separates the checks from the accompanying remittance advices. Copeland forwards the checks to another employee, who makes the daily bank deposit but has no access to the accounting records. Copeland sends the remittance advices, which show the amount of cash received, to the accounting department for entry in the accounts. Copeland's only other duty is to grant sales allowances to customers. (A *sales allowance* decreases the amount that the customer must pay.) When he receives a customer check for less than the full amount of the invoice, he records the sales allowance and forwards the document to the accounting department.

Required

You are a new employee of Long Island Lighting. Write a memo to the company president identifying the internal control weakness in this situation. State how to correct the weakness.

P4-6B Louis Lipschitz, Executive Vice President and Chief Financial Officer of **Toys "Я" Us, Inc.**, is responsible for the company's budgeting process. Suppose Lipschitz's staff is preparing the Toys "Я" Us cash budget for 19X5. Assume the starting point is the statement of cash flows of the current year, 19X4, reproduced in an adapted format as follows:

Preparing a cash budget and using cash-flow information ***(Obj. 6)***

TOYS "Я" US, INC., AND SUBSIDIARIES
Consolidated Statement of Cash Flows (Adapted)

(In millions)	19X4
Cash Flows from Operating Activities	
Collections from customers	$8,089.2
Interest received	24.1
Purchases of inventory	(5,597.4)
Operating expenses	(1,858.8)
Net cash provided by operating activities	657.1
Cash Flows from Investing Activities	
Capital expenditures, net	(555.3)
Purchases of other assets	(58.3)
Net cash used in investing activities	(613.6)
Cash Flows from Financing Activities	
Short-term borrowings, net	119.1
Long-term borrowings	40.5
Long-term debt repayments	(1.3)
Issuance of stock	29.9
Share repurchases	(183.2)
Net cash provided by financing activities	5.0
Effect of foreign-currency exchange rate changes on cash and cash equivalents	(20.3)
Cash and Cash Equivalents	
(Decrease)/increase during year	28.2
Beginning of year	763.7
End of year	$ 791.9

Required

1. Prepare the Toys "Я" Us cash budget for 19X5. Date the budget simply "19X5" and denote the beginning and ending cash balances as "beginning" and "ending." Assume the company expects 19X5 to be the same as 19X4, but with the following changes:
   a. In 19X5, the company expects a 10% increase in collections from customers, an 8% increase in purchases of inventory, and a doubling of capital expenditures.
   b. The amount of borrowings and issuances of stock needed in 19X5 will be determined by the cash budget and thus does not appear on the cash budget. (But scheduled long-term debt repayments and share repurchases should be the same in 19X5 as they were in 19X4.)
   c. Lipschitz hopes to end the year with a cash balance of $500 million.

You will find these explanations helpful:

- "Capital expenditures" are purchases of property and equipment.
- Toys "Я" Us does not pay cash dividends. Instead the company *repurchases* its stock from its stockholders. This is another way for a corporation to return cash to the stockholders.

2. Answer these questions about the company. Explain your reasoning for each answer.
   a. Does the company's cash budget for 19X5 suggest that Toys "Я" Us is growing, holding steady, or decreasing in size?
   b. Do the statement of cash flows for 19X4 and the cash budget for 19X5 suggest that operating activities are generating enough cash?

Making an ethical judgment ***(Obj. 7)***

P4-7B Tri State Bank in Cairo, Illinois, has a loan receivable from Magellan Manufacturing Company. Magellan is six months late in making payments to the bank, and Lane Kidwell, a Tri State vice president, is assisting Magellan to restructure its debt. With unlimited access to Magellan's records, Kidwell learns that the company is depending on landing a manufacturing contract from Loew's Brothers, another Tri State Bank client. Kidwell also serves as Loew's loan officer at the bank. In this capacity, he is aware that Loew's is considering declaring bankruptcy. No one else outside Loew's Brothers knows this. Kidwell has been a great help to Magellan Manufacturing, and Magellan's owner is counting on his expertise in loan workouts to carry the company through this difficult process. To help the bank collect on this large loan, Kidwell has a strong motivation to help Magellan survive.

Required

Apply the ethical judgment framework outlined in the chapter to help Lane Kidwell plan his next action.

EXTENDING YOUR KNOWLEDGE

DECISION CASES

Correcting an internal control weakness ***(Obj. 1, 5)***

Case 1. This case is based on an actual situation experienced by one of the authors.

Alpha Construction Company, headquartered in Chattanooga, Tennessee, built a Roadway Inn Motel in Cleveland, 35 miles east of Chattanooga. The construction foreman, whose name was Slim, moved into Cleveland in March to hire the 40 workers needed to complete the project. Slim hired the construction workers, had them fill out the necessary tax forms, and sent the employment documents to the home office, which opened a payroll file for each employee.

Work on the motel began on April 1 and ended September 1. Each Thursday evening, Slim filled out a time card that listed the hours worked for each employee during the five-day work week ended at 5 P.M. on Thursday. Slim faxed the time sheets to the home office, which prepared the payroll checks on Friday morning. Slim drove to the home office after lunch on Friday, picked up the payroll checks, and returned to the construction site. At 5 P.M. on Friday, Slim distributed the payroll checks to the workers.

a. Describe in detail the internal control weakness in this situation. Specify what negative result could occur because of the internal control weakness.

b. Describe what you would do to correct the internal control weakness.

Using the bank reconciliation to detect a theft ***(Obj. 2)***

Case 2. First Union Company has poor internal control over its cash transactions. Recently Penelope Gann, the owner, has suspected the cashier of stealing. Here are some details of the business's cash position at September 30.

a. The Cash account shows a balance of $19,702. This amount includes a September 30 deposit of $3,794 that does not appear on the September 30 bank statement.

b. The September 30 bank statement shows a balance of $16,624. The bank statement lists a $200 credit for a bank collection, an $8 debit for the service charge, and a $36 debit for an NSF check. The First Union accountant has not recorded any of these items on the books.

c. At September 30, the following checks are outstanding:

Check No.	Amount
154	$116
256	150
278	353
291	190
292	206
293	145

d. The cashier handles all incoming cash and makes bank deposits. He also reconciles the monthly bank statement. Here is his September 30 reconciliation:

Balance per books, September 30		$19,702
Add: Outstanding checks		560
Bank collection		200
		20,462
Less: Deposits in transit	$3,794	
Service charge	8	
NSF check	36	3,838
Balance per bank, September 30		$16,624

Gann has requested that you determine whether the cashier has stolen cash from the business and, if so, how much. She also asks you to identify how the cashier has attempted to conceal the theft. To make this determination, you perform your own bank reconciliation using the format illustrated in the chapter. There are no bank or book errors. Gann also asks you to evaluate the internal controls and to recommend any changes needed to improve them.

ETHICAL ISSUE

Julie Fraser owns apartment buildings in Michigan and Ohio. Each property has a manager who collects rent, arranges for repairs, and runs advertisements in the local newspaper. The property managers transfer cash to Fraser monthly and prepare their own bank reconciliations. The manager in Detroit has been stealing large sums of money. To cover the theft, he understates the amount of the outstanding checks on the monthly bank reconciliation. As a result, each monthly bank reconciliation appears to balance. However, the balance sheet reports more cash than Fraser actually has in the bank. In negotiating the sale of the Detroit property, Fraser is showing the balance sheet to prospective investors.

Required

1. Identify two parties other than Fraser who can be harmed by this theft. In what ways can they be harmed?
2. Discuss the role accounting plays in this situation.

FINANCIAL STATEMENT CASES

Internal controls and cash ***(Obj. 1, 3)***

Case 1. Study the Lands' End responsibility statement and the audit opinion of the Lands' End, Inc., financial statements given at the end of Appendix A. Answer the following questions about the company's internal controls and cash position.

Required

1. What is the name of Lands' End's outside auditing firm? What office of this firm signed the audit report? How long after the Lands' End year end did the auditors issue their opinion?
2. Who bears primary responsibility for the financial statements? How can you tell?
3. Does it appear that the Land's End internal controls are adequate? How can you tell?
4. What standard of auditing did the outside auditors use in examining the Lands' End financial statements? By what accounting standards were the statements evaluated?
5. By how much did the company's cash position change during 1996? The statement of cash flows tells why this change occurred. Which type of activity—operating, investing, or financing—contributed to this change?

Audit opinion, management responsibility, internal controls, and cash ***(Obj. 1, 3)***

Case 2. Obtain the annual report of a company of your choosing. Study the audit opinion and the management statement of responsibility (if present) in conjunction with the financial statements. Then answer these questions.

Required

1. What is the name of the company's outside auditing firm? What office of this firm signed the audit report? How long after the company's year end did the auditors issue their opinion?
2. Who bears primary responsibility for the financial statements? How can you tell?
3. Does it appear that the company's internal controls are adequate? Give your reason.
4. What standard of auditing did the outside auditors use in examining the company's financial statements? By what accounting standards were the statements evaluated?
5. By how much did the company's cash position (including cash equivalents) change during the current year? The statement of cash flows tells why this increase or decrease occurred. Which type of activity—operating, investing, or financing—contributed most to the change in the cash balance?
6. Where is the balance of petty cash reported? Name the financial statement and the account, and identify the specific amount that includes petty cash.

GROUP PROJECT

You are promoting a rock concert in your area. Assume you organize as a corporation, with each member of your group purchasing $10,000 of the business's stock. Therefore, each of you is risking some hard-earned money on this venture. Assume it is April 1 and that the concert will be performed on June 30. Your promotional activities begin immediately, and ticket sales start on May 1. You expect to sell all the business's assets, pay all the liabilities, and distribute all remaining cash to the group members by July 31.

Required

Write an internal control manual that will help to safeguard the assets of the business. The manual should address the following aspects of internal control:

1. Assign responsibilities among the group members.
2. Authorize individuals, including group members and any outsiders that you need to hire, to perform specific jobs.
3. Separate duties among the group and any employees.
4. Describe all documents needed to account for and safeguard the business's assets.

INTERNET EXERCISE

KPMG'S BUSINESS ETHICS CENTER

Most companies have a business ethics program, whether stated in a formal policy or conveyed informally through the actions of top management. The values on which a firm is built affect its relationships with customers, owners, employees, suppliers, lenders, regulators, and taxing authorities.

KPMG Peat Marwick, one of the Big Six international accounting firms, recently created a Business Ethics Center to help firms identify, establish, and manage their business ethics policies. KPMG's Web site provides the visitor with a quick understanding of why ethics matter, not only at the individual level, but also at the corporate level.

Required

1. Go to **http://www.kpmg.ca/ethics/.** This is the "welcome page" for the KPMG offices in Canada.
2. A brief but good discussion of the importance of business ethics is located at **Business Ethics: An Overvew.** Click on the highlighted text.
   a. Why are ethics important in business?
   b. What are the components of an effective business ethics program?
3. Return to the welcome page by clicking on the "back one page" button on your Internet browser. Click on **KPMG's US Ethics Practice.** Doing so will take you to the U.S. KPMG business ethics Web site.
4. To gain an understanding of how ethics in our personal lives can be compared to ethics in the corporate world, click on the **Ethics Dilemma Archive.** Then select the **Heinz Ethics Dilemma.**
5. Read the case background along with the purpose of the case, then click **NEXT.** After you read the case scenario and the related questions, click on **click here.**
6. Use the framework presented in the text (page 200) to provide a response to each question. Click the appropriate "radio button" and then click the **Submit** button. The computer will provide an analysis of your responses. To relate this set of ethical issues to the business, click the highlighted text, **click here.**
   c. Write a summary of how you addressed the issues in this case. Use the textbook's framework as a guide.

5

Accounting for Short-Term Investments and Receivables

Learning Objectives

After studying this chapter, you should be able to

1. Account for short-term investments
2. Report short-term investments on the balance sheet and the related revenue on the income statement
3. Apply internal controls to receivables
4. Use the allowance method to account for uncollectible receivables
5. Account for notes receivable and the related interest revenue
6. Use the acid-test ratio and days' sales in receivables to evaluate a company's financial position
7. Report investment and receivables transactions on the statement of cash flows

Intel Corporation
Consolidated Balance Sheet (Assets Only)
December 31, 1995 and December 31, 1994

(In millions)	*1995*	*1994*
Assets		
Current assets:		
1 Cash and cash equivalents	$ 1,463	$ 1,180
2 Short-term investments	995	1,230
3 Accounts receivable, net of allowance for doubtful accounts of $57 ($32 in 1994)	3,116	1,978
4 Inventories	2,004	1,169
5 Deferred tax assets	408	552
6 Other current assets	111	58
7 **Total current assets**	8,097	6,167
Property, plant, and equipment:		
8 Land and buildings	3,145	2,292
9 Machinery and equipment	7,099	5,374
10 Construction in progress	1,548	850
11	11,792	8,516
12 Less accumulated depreciation	4,321	3,149
13 **Property, plant, and equipment, net**	7,471	5,367
14 **Long-term investments**	1,653	2,127
15 **Other assets**	283	155
16 **Total assets**	$17,504	$13,816

"The year's biggest success story is the market demand for [Intel's] Pentium© processor. The Pentium processor's ability to drive today's most exciting software, such as multimedia and communications applications, has made it the mainstream PC processor of choice. . . . At year's end, entry-level buyers could take home the flexibility of a 75-MHz Pentium processor-based PC for under $1,500, while power users had a new 133-MHz Pentium processor to run their high-performance systems. Never before has so much processing power been available at such low system prices—and consumers are responding."

INTEL CORPORATION, *1995 ANNUAL REPORT,* PP. 4, 15.

The success of the Pentium processor has dramatically increased **Intel Corporation's** sales. This success has also created a large amount of cash the company must invest. Indeed, at the end of 1995, Intel had almost 32% of its assets invested in the three most liquid assets: cash and cash equivalents, short-term investments, and accounts receivable. Observe these amounts on lines 1–3 of Intel's 1995 balance sheet, and compare Intel's liquid-asset percentage to those of other major companies in Exhibit 5-1 on page 222.

The differences shown in Exhibit 5-1 result from differing industry structures. They do not imply that companies with low percentages of liquid assets are in financial difficulty. For example, **Toys "Я" Us** is able to operate very well, and earn a very nice profit, with only 5% of its assets in liquid form. The amounts a company holds as liquid assets are affected by numerous factors, such as the need to make payments on debt. This is not the case for Intel Corporation, whose short- and long-term debt are very low.

It may be unhealthy for a company to be heavily invested in liquid assets, which typically pay no interest or only a very low interest rate. Does Intel's high percentage of liquid assets mean that the company is having trouble finding new investment opportunities in its own industry? Is the company's cash hoard temporary? Will Intel be able to continue introducing blockbuster high-tech products in the future? If not, where will the company be in five years? These are some of the questions investors raise when they see an unusually high percentage of liquid assets on a company's balance sheet. Nevertheless, too much cash is a much better "problem" than a cash shortage.

Intel's balance sheet shows that the company has invested its extra cash in short-term investments (line 2, $995 million at the end of 1995) and long-term investments (line 14, $1,653 million). This chapter continues the discussion of accounting for liquid assets that we began in Chapter 4. There we talked about accounting for and managing cash; here we examine short-term investments and receivables. Chapter 10 covers long-term investments.

EXHIBIT 5-1
Percentages of Total Assets Invested in Liquid Assets (Cash and Cash Equivalents, Short-Term Investments, and Current Receivables)

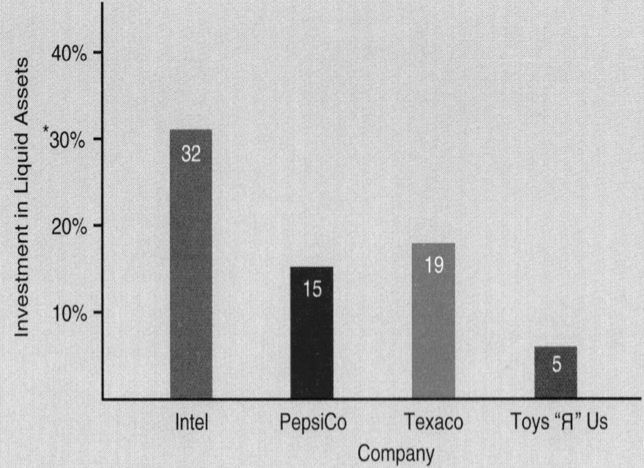

*Liquid assets = cash and cash equivalents, short-term investments, and current receivables

Some Basic Terminology

Before we examine the accounting for investments and receivables, it will be helpful to review and define some key terms.

creditor. The party to whom money is owed. The creditor has a receivable, which can also be called an *investment*.

debt instrument. A payable, usually some form of note or bond payable. The maker (issuer) of a debt instrument is the debtor. The holder of a debt instrument is the creditor (or investor) to whom the instrument is a receivable (or investment).

debtor. The party who has a debt. The debtor has a payable.

equity securities. Stock certificates that represent the investor's ownership of shares of stock in a corporation.

maturity. The date on which a debt instrument matures—that is, becomes payable.

securities. Notes payable or stock certificates that entitle the owner to the benefits of an investment.

term. The length of time until a debt instrument matures.

Short-Term Investments (Marketable Securities)

Objective 1

Account for short-term investments

Short-term investments, also called **marketable securities,** are investments that a company plans to hold for one year or less. These investments allow the company to "park" its cash temporarily and earn a modest return until the cash is needed. Short-term investments fall into three categories:

1. *Held-to-maturity securities,* which the investor expects to hold until the securities' maturity date and on which the investor earns interest revenue.
2. *Trading securities,* which the investor holds for the purpose of generating profits on short-term price movements.
3. *Available-for-sale securities,* which are all investments other than held-to-maturity securities and trading securities.

All trading securities are short-term investments because companies intend to hold them for only a few months or less. Held-to-maturity securities and available-for-sale securities may be either short- or long-term investments, depending on the length of time that management intends to hold them. In the sections that follow, we explain how companies account for short-term investments. The examples are designed to show how Intel Corporation might have arrived at the reported amounts of short-term investments on its 1994 balance sheet (line 2, $1,230 million) and its 1995 balance sheet ($995 million). As you work through the chapter, return to the Intel balance sheet on page 220 and check these amounts.

Held-to-Maturity Securities

Held-to-maturity securities are debt instruments that pay interest. Companies buy held-to-maturity securities to earn interest revenue, and they plan to hold these investments until their maturity date. Many held-to-maturity securities are virtually risk-free. Examples of risk-free securities include U.S. Treasury bills and the commercial paper (very short-term notes payable) of large corporations with excellent credit ratings. For example, Intel Corporation may have cash that it will not need for 90 days. Suppose that on December 1, 1994, Intel pays $1,200 million for General Electric Co. (GE) commercial paper that will mature at $1,290 million in 90 days. All investments are recorded initially at cost. On December 1, 1994, Intel would record the purchase of the investment in GE commercial paper as follows, with the investment account appearing at right:

1994		*(In millions)*	
Dec. 1	Short-Term Investment in GE Commercial Paper....	1,200	
	Cash		1,200
	Purchased investment.		

Short-Term Investment in GE Commercial Paper

1,200	

ASSETS	=	LIABILITIES	+	STOCKHOLDERS' EQUITY
+1,200 −1,200	=	0	+	0

Intel's accounting year ends on December 31, so at year end Intel would accrue 30 days' interest revenue that it has earned on the investment. With investments such as commercial paper and U.S. Treasury bills, the accrual of interest revenue increases the carrying (book) value of the investment (shown in the accompanying T-account), as follows:

1994		*(In millions)*	
Dec. 31	Short-Term Investment in GE Commercial Paper.........	30	
	Interest Revenue ($90 million × 30/90).................		30
	Accrued interest revenue earned on investment.		

Short-Term Investment in GE Commercial Paper

1,200	
30	

ASSETS	=	LIABILITIES	+	STOCKHOLDERS' EQUITY	+	REVENUES
30	=	0			+	30

REPORTING HELD-TO-MATURITY SECURITIES AT AMORTIZED COST ON THE BALANCE SHEET Held-to-maturity securities are reported on the balance sheet at *amortized cost,* which means cost plus accrued interest to date. At December 31, 1994, Intel's amortized cost of its investment in GE commercial paper is $1,230 million ($1,200 million cost + $30 million accrued interest to date).

Assuming this is Intel's only short-term investment at December 31, 1994, Intel would report short-term investments at $1,230 million, as shown on its balance sheet on page 220.

Suppose Intel collects the maturity amount of the GE commercial paper on March 1, 1995. On that day, Intel would record the transaction as follows:

Short-Term Investment in GE Commercial Paper	
1,200	1,230
30	

1995		*(In millions)*	
Mar. 1	Cash	1,290	
	Short-Term Investment in GE Commercial Paper......................		1,230
	Interest Revenue ($90 million × 60/90)		60
	Collected maturity value of investment.		

ASSETS	=	LIABILITIES	+	STOCKHOLDERS' EQUITY	+	REVENUES
+1,290 −1,230	=	0			+	60

STOP & THINK Intel needed to accrue interest revenue at December 31, 1994, to place the correct amount of interest revenue in each year: $30 million in 1994 and $60 million in 1995. Suppose Intel Corporation did not accrue the interest revenue at December 31, 1994.

1. How would this error affect the balance sheet at December 31, 1994?
2. How would the error affect the company's income statements for 1994 and 1995?

Answers

1. At December 31, 1994, short-term investments would be understated by $30 million.
2. The 1994 income statement would report $30 million too little interest revenue, and the 1995 income statement would report $30 million too much interest revenue.

Trading Securities

Trading securities can be either the stock of another company (*equity securities*) or debt instruments purchased as a short-term investment. Companies intend to hold trading investments for a very short period of time—a few months at most. The *market-value method* is used to account for all trading investments because they will be sold in the near term at their current market value on the date of sale. Cost is used only as the initial amount for recording trading investments.

Assume it is late 1995, and once again Intel has excess cash for short-term investing. To illustrate accounting for trading securities, suppose Intel buys Ford Motor Company stock for $80 million on October 23, 1995. Assume further that Intel's top management hopes to sell this stock within three months at a gain, so the investment is a trading security. The entry to record the investment is

Short-Term Investment in Ford Stock	
80	

1995		*(In millions)*	
Oct. 23	Short-Term Investment in Ford Stock	80	
	Cash		80
	Purchased investment.		

ASSETS	=	LIABILITIES	+	STOCKHOLDERS' EQUITY
+80 −80	=	0	+	0

Ford stock pays a cash dividend of $1.40 per share, so Intel would receive a dividend on the investment. Intel's entry to record receipt of a $1 million dividend on November 14, 1995, is

1995		*(In millions)*	
Nov. 14	Cash	1	
	Dividend Revenue...		1
	Received cash dividend.		

ASSETS	=	LIABILITIES	+	STOCKHOLDERS' EQUITY	+	REVENUES
1	=	0			+	1

Reporting Trading Investments at Market Value on the Balance Sheet Trading investments are reported on the balance sheet at current market value, not at their cost. This rule requires a year-end adjustment of the trading investments from their last carrying amount to current market value. Assume that the Ford stock has increased in value, and at December 31, 1995, Intel's investment in Ford stock is worth $90 million (which is $10 million more than the purchase price). At year end, Intel would make the following adjustment:

Objective 2

Report short-term investments on the balance sheet and the related revenue on the income statement

1995		*(In millions)*	
Dec. 31	Short-Term Investment in Ford Stock	10	
	Unrealized Gain on Investment.................		10
	Adjusted trading investment to market value.		

Short-Term Investment in Ford Stock

80	
10	

ASSETS	=	LIABILITIES	+	STOCKHOLDERS' EQUITY	+	GAINS
10	=	0			+	10

An *unrealized* gain (or loss) is one that is not the result of a sale transaction. If the market value of the stock had been less than $80 million, Intel would have debited Unrealized Loss on Investment and credited Short-Term Investment in Ford Stock.

Let's see how Intel would report its investment activity in 1995. Suppose it is now December 31, 1995, and Intel holds both the Ford Motor Company stock, a trading security, and U.S. Treasury bills as held-to-maturity securities with an amortized cost of $905 million. In our example, Intel's short-term investment portfolio consists of the following securities at December 31, 1995:

	(In millions)
Held-to-maturity securities:	
U.S. Treasury bills, at amortized cost	$905
Trading securities:	
Ford Motor Company stock, at current market value..........	90
Short-term investments, as reported on the balance sheet at December 31, 1995...	$995

The Intel balance sheet on page 220 reports short-term investments of $995 million at December 31, 1995.

A company that holds debt instruments (such as corporate bonds) as trading securities accounts for interest revenue in the same way we showed above for held-to-maturity securities. The investor reports the trading investments at market value on the balance sheet. The investor measures gains and losses as the difference between the securities' current market value and their amortized cost. Gains and losses appear on the income statement.

REPORTING INTEREST REVENUE, DIVIDEND REVENUE, AND INVESTMENT GAINS AND LOSSES ON THE INCOME STATEMENT We have seen how Intel reports short-term investments on its balance sheet. Intel could report its investment revenues, gains, and losses as Other Revenue and Expense on its income statement as follows:

INTEL CORPORATION
Income Statements (Adapted)
Years Ended December 31, 1995 and December 31, 1994

		1995	1994
1	Net revenues	$XXX	$XXX
2	Cost of sales	XX	XX
3	Research and development and other expenses	XX	XX
4	Operating income	XX	XX
5	Other revenue and (expense):		
6	Interest expense	(X)	(X)
7	Interest revenue (1995 amount assumed)	125	30
8	Dividend revenue	1	—
9	Unrealized gain on investment	10	—
10	Income before taxes	XX	XX
11	Income tax expense	X	X
12	Net income	$ X	$ X

Operating income (line 4) reports on Intel's success in its main operations. *Other revenue* (line 5) arises from activities other than the company's main operations, which are producing and selling high-tech products. When the individual amounts are small, companies like Intel combine the Other Revenues and Expenses and report the net amount as a single figure. For example, Intel could combine the dividend revenue and the unrealized gain (from lines 8 and 9) and report the total of $11 million as investment revenue.

GAIN AND LOSSES ON THE SALE OF TRADING SECURITIES When a company sells a trading investment, the gain or loss on the sale is the difference between the sale proceeds and the last carrying amount of the investment. For example, suppose Intel sells the Ford stock for $84 million on January 19, 1996. On that day, Intel would record the sale as follows:[1]

Short-Term Investment in Ford Stock

Debit	Credit
80	90
10	

1996		*(In millions)*	
Jan. 19	Cash	84	
	Loss on Sale of Investment	6	
	Short-Term Investment in Ford Stock		90
	Sold investment.		

ASSETS	=	LIABILITIES	+	STOCKHOLDERS' EQUITY	−	LOSSES
+84 −90	=	0			−	6

[1]Some accountants would record the sale by debiting Cash and crediting Short-Term Investments at the sale price of $84 million. This accounting would require a prior entry to record an unrealized loss of $6 million to write down Short-Term Investments from $90 million to the current market value of $84 million at the time of the sale.

Observe that this loss results from the sale of the investment. Because the loss was based on a transaction, the loss has been *realized*. We labeled the gain in 1995 as *unrealized* because Intel had not yet sold the Ford stock. For reporting on the income statement, Intel could combine all gains and losses on short-term investments—realized and unrealized—and report a single net amount under Other Revenue and Expense.

Available-for-Sale Securities

Available-for-sale securities are all investment securities not classified as held-to-maturity or trading. They are reported on the balance sheet at market value. Accounting for available-for-sale securities follows the same pattern we illustrated for trading securities with one exception. Unrealized gains and losses on available-for-sale securities are reported on the balance sheet as a separate element of stockholders' equity. These unrealized gains and losses are not reported on the income statement. We cover available-for-sale securities in more detail in Chapter 10.

Exhibit 5-2 summarizes the accounting for short-term investments.

EXHIBIT 5-2
Summary of Accounting for Short-Term Investments

	Category of Investment		
	Held-to-Maturity	**Trading**	**Available-for-Sale**
Accounting method	Amortized cost	Market value	Market value
Carrying amount on the balance sheet	Cost plus accrued interest to date	Current market value	Current market value
Unrealized gains and losses	Ignored	Report on the income statement	Report on the balance sheet

Mid-Chapter
SUMMARY PROBLEM FOR YOUR REVIEW

Humana, Inc., is one of the largest U.S. managed health-care companies. It provides a full array of health plans, including health maintenance organizations (HMOs) and administrative-services-only plans. The largest current asset on Humana's balance sheet is Marketable Securities (short-term investments). Note 4 to Humana's financial statements indicates that U.S. government securities, tax-exempt bonds, and corporate bonds make up the bulk of the company's marketable securities.

Assume Humana paid $1,136 million when it purchased the marketable securities in November 19X5. At December 31, 19X5, their amortized cost is $1,144 million, and their market value is $1,156 million.

Required

Test your understanding of accounting for short-term investments by answering these questions about Humana's marketable securities.

1. If Humana plans to hold the marketable securities until their maturity, will these securities be classified as held-to-maturity, trading, or available-for-sale? At what amount will Humana report the investment on the balance sheet at December 31, 19X5? What will Humana report on its income statement for 19X5?

2. If Humana holds the marketable securities in the hope of selling them at a profit within a few days or weeks, how will it classify the securities? At what amount will Humana report the investment on the balance sheet at December 31, 19X5? What will Humana report on its 19X5 income statement?

ANSWERS

Requirement 1

Held-to-maturity securities, reported as follows on the balance sheet:

	(In millions)
Current assets:	
Cash	$ XX
Marketable securities (or short-term investments), at amortized cost	1,144

Humana's income statement will report:

	(In millions)
Other revenue and expense:	
Interest revenue ($1,144 million – $1,136 million)	$ 8

Requirement 2

Trading securities, reported as follows on the balance sheet:

	(In millions)
Current assets:	
Cash	$ XX
Marketable securities (or short-term investments), at market value	1,156

Humana's income statement will report:

	(In millions)
Other revenue and expense:	
Interest revenue ($1,144 million – $1,136 million)	$ 8
Unrealized gain on investments ($1,156 million – $1,144 million)	12

Accounts and Notes Receivable

Receivables are the third most liquid asset—after cash (including cash equivalents) and short-term investments. Receivables are usually good for a company to have because they are claims to someone else's cash. But a receivable can be bad news if the business cannot collect the receivable. In the remainder of the chapter, we discuss how to control and manage the collection of receivables and how to account for these assets.

The Different Types of Receivables

Receivables are monetary claims against businesses and individuals. They are acquired mainly by selling goods and services and by lending money.

The two major types of receivables are accounts receivable and notes receivable. A business's *accounts receivable* are the amounts that its customers owe it. Accounts receivable, which are *current assets,* are sometimes called *trade receivables.*

The Accounts Receivable account in the general ledger serves as a *control account* that summarizes the total amounts receivable from all customers. Companies also keep a *subsidiary ledger* of accounts receivable with a separate account for each customer, illustrated as follows:

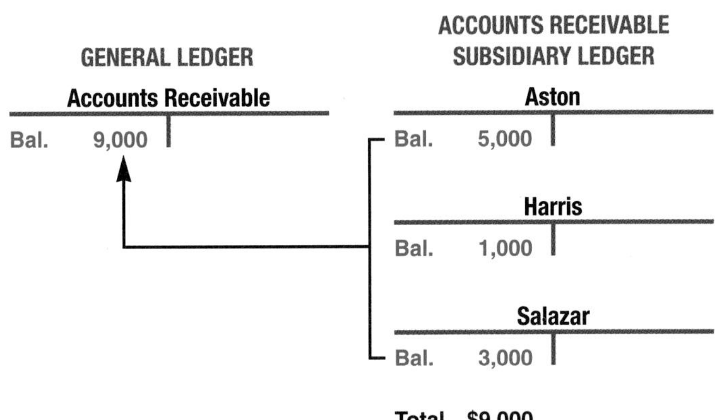

We discuss subsidiary ledgers in detail in Appendix F at the end of this book.

Notes receivable are more formal than accounts receivable. The debtor in a note receivable arrangement promises in writing to pay the creditor a definite sum at a specific future date—the *maturity* date. The terms of these notes usually extend for at least 60 days. A written document known as a *promissory note* serves as evidence of the receivable. The note may require the debtor to pledge *security* for the loan. This means that the borrower promises that the lender may claim certain assets if the borrower fails to pay the amount due at maturity.

Notes receivable due within one year or less are current assets. Those notes due beyond one year are *long-term receivables.* Some notes receivable are collected in periodic installments. The portion due within one year is a current asset, and the remaining amount a long-term asset. General Motors may hold a \$6,000 note receivable from you, but only the \$1,500 you owe on it this year is a current asset to GM.

Other receivables is a miscellaneous category that includes loans to employees and subsidiary companies. Usually, these are long-term receivables, but they are current assets if receivable within one year or less. Long-term notes receivable, and other receivables, are often reported on the balance sheet after current assets. Each type of receivable is a separate account in the general ledger and may be supported by a subsidiary ledger if needed.

The Decision Guidelines on page 230 feature identifies the main issues in controlling, managing, and accounting for receivables. These guidelines serve as a framework for the remainder of the chapter.

Establishing Internal Control over the Collection of Receivables

Objective 3

Apply internal controls to receivables

Businesses that sell on credit receive most of their cash receipts by mail. Internal control over collections of cash on account is an important part of the overall internal control system. Chapter 4 detailed control procedures over cash receipts, but a critical element of internal control deserves emphasis here—the separation of cash-handling and cash-accounting duties. Consider the following case.

> **Butler Supply Co.** is a small, family-owned business that takes pride in the loyalty of its workers. Most company employees have been with the Butlers for at least five years. The company makes 90% of its sales on account.

Decision Guidelines

Controlling, Managing, and Accounting for Receivables

It is easy to lose sight of the big picture—the main issues—in controlling, managing, and accounting for receivables. Most of the rest of this chapter relates to one or more of the following issues:

The main issues in *controlling* and *managing* the collection of receivables, along with a related plan of action, are

Issues	Plan of Action
1. Extending credit only to creditworthy customers, the ones most likely to pay us.	1. Run a credit check on prospective customers.
2. Separating cash-handling, credit, and accounting duties to keep employees from stealing the cash collected from customers.	2. Design the internal control system to separate duties.
3. Pursuing collection from customers to maximize cash flow.	3. Keep a close eye on collections from customers.

The main issues in *accounting* for receivables, and the related plans of action, are

Issues	Plan of Action
1. Measuring and reporting receivables on the balance sheet at their *net realizable value,* the amount we expect to collect. This is necessary to report assets accurately.	1. Report receivables at their net realizable value.
2. Measuring and reporting the expense associated with failure to collect receivables, which we call *uncollectible-account expense,* on the income statement. This helps to report net income at a reasonable amount.	2. Measure the expense of failure to collect from our customers.

The office staff consists of a bookkeeper and a supervisor. The bookkeeper maintains the general ledger and the accounts receivable subsidiary ledger. He also makes the daily bank deposit. The supervisor prepares monthly financial statements and any special reports the Butlers require. She also takes sales orders from customers and serves as office manager.

Can you identify the internal control weakness here? The bookkeeper has access to the general ledger, the accounts receivable subsidiary ledger, and the cash. The bookkeeper could take a customer check and write off the customer's account as uncollectible.[2] Unless the supervisor or some other manager reviews the bookkeeper's work regularly, the theft may go undetected. In small businesses like Butler Supply Co., such a review may not be performed routinely.

How can this control weakness be corrected? The supervisor could open incoming mail and make the daily bank deposit. The bookkeeper should not be allowed to handle cash. Only the remittance advices would be forwarded to the bookkeeper to indicate which customer accounts to credit. By removing cash-handling duties from the bookkeeper and keeping the accounts receivable subsidiary ledger away from the supervisor, the company would separate duties and strengthen internal control. These actions would reduce an employee's opportunity to steal cash and then cover it up with a false credit to a customer account.

Using a bank lock box would achieve the same separation of duties. Customers would send their payments directly to Butler Supply's bank, which would record and deposit the cash into the company's account. The bank would then forward the remittance advice to Butler Supply's bookkeeper to credit the appropriate customer accounts.

[2]The bookkeeper would need to forge the endorsements of the checks and deposit them in a bank account he controls.

Managing the Collection of Receivables: The Credit Department

A customer who uses a credit card to acquire goods or services is buying on account. This transaction creates a receivable for the seller. Most companies with a high proportion of sales on account have a separate credit department. This department evaluates customers who apply for credit cards by using standard formulas—which include the applicant's income and credit history, among other factors—for deciding which customers the store will sell to on account. The extension of credit requires a balancing act. The company wants to avoid losing sales to good customers who demand time to pay. It also wants to avoid losses from selling to deadbeats.

After approving a customer, the credit department monitors customer payment records. Customers with a history of paying on time may receive higher credit limits. Those who fail to pay on time have their limits reduced or eliminated. The goal is to collect from customers quickly enough to keep cash circulating. The credit department also assists the accounting department in measuring collection losses on customers who do not pay.

We examined techniques for speeding the collection of cash in Chapter 4, pages 188–189.

For good internal control over cash collections of receivables, it is critical that the credit department have no access to cash. For example, if a credit employee handles cash, he can pocket the money received from a customer. He can then label the customer's account as uncollectible, and the accounting department writes off the account receivable. The company stops billing the customer, and the credit employee has covered up the embezzlement. If the customer places another order with the company, the credit employee can reinstate the account, and repeat the cycle of theft.

Uncollectible Accounts (Bad Debts)

Selling on credit creates both a benefit and a cost. The benefit? Customers who are unwilling or unable to pay cash immediately may make a purchase on credit, and company revenues and profits rise as sales increase. The cost? The company will be unable to collect from some of its credit customers. Accountants label this cost **uncollectible-account expense, doubtful-account expense,** or **bad-debt expense.**

Bad debts cost Albany Ladder about $100,000 a year, or about 1 to 1½% of total sales.

The extent of uncollectible-account expense varies from company to company. In certain businesses, a six-month-old receivable of $1 is worth only 67 cents, and a five-year-old receivable of $1 is worth only 4 cents. Uncollectible-account expense depends on the credit risks that managers are willing to accept. At **Albany Ladder,** a $23 million construction-equipment and supply firm headquartered in Albany, New York, 85% of company sales are on account. Albany's receivables grow in proportion to sales. Bad debts cost Albany Ladder about $100,000 a year, or about 1 to 1½% of total sales, a figure that has remained fairly constant as a result of careful credit screening and rigorous collection activity. It takes Albany Ladder an average of 70 days to collect its receivables.

Many small retail businesses accept a higher level of risk than do large stores such as Sears. Why? To increase sales. Moreover, small businesses often have personal ties to customers, who are more likely to pay their accounts when they know the proprietor personally.

Measuring Uncollectible Accounts

For a firm that sells on credit, uncollectible-account expense is as much a part of doing business as salary expense and depreciation expense. Uncollectible-Account Expense—an operating expense—must be measured, recorded, and reported. To do so, accountants use the allowance method or, in certain limited cases, the direct write-off method (which we discuss on page 235).

ALLOWANCE METHOD To present the most accurate financial statements possible, accountants in firms with large credit sales use the **allowance method** of measuring bad debts. This method records collection losses on the basis of estimates instead of waiting to see which customers the business will not collect from.

Smart managers know that not every customer will pay in full. But at the time of sale, managers do not know which customers will not pay. If they did, they certainly wouldn't sell on credit to those customers!

Rather than try to guess which accounts will go bad, managers estimate the total bad-debt expense for the period on the basis of the company's collection experience. The business records Uncollectible-Account Expense for the estimated amount and sets up **Allowance for Uncollectible Accounts** (or **Allowance for Doubtful Accounts**), a contra account related to Accounts Receivable. This allowance account shows the amount of the receivables that the business expects *not* to collect.

Subtracting the uncollectible allowance amount from Accounts receivable yields the net amount that the company does expect to collect, as shown here (using assumed numbers):

Accounts receivable	$10,000
Less Allowance for uncollectible accounts	(900)
Accounts receivable, net	$ 9,100

Customers owe this company $10,000, of which it expects to collect $9,100. The company estimates that it will not collect $900 of its accounts receivable.

Another way to report these receivables follows the pattern used by Intel Corporation (see line 3 of its balance sheet), as follows:

Accounts receivable, net of allowance of $900	$9,100

STOP & THINK Examine Intel Corporation's balance sheet at the beginning of the chapter.

1. At December 31, 1995, how much did Intel expect to collect from customers?
2. How much of Intel's accounts receivable did the company expect *not* to collect?
3. In total, how much did customers owe Intel at December 31, 1995?
4. Suppose that Intel did not use the allowance method to account for uncollectibles. At what amount would Intel report its receivables on the balance sheet? Is this amount realistic? Why or why not?

Answers

1. $3,116 million.
2. $57 million.
3. $3,173 million ($3,116 million + $57 million).
4. $3,173 million is misleading because Intel does not expect to collect the full amount of the receivables.

Estimating Uncollectibles

Objective 4

Use the allowance method to account for uncollectible receivables

The more accurate the estimate of uncollectible accounts, the more reliable the information in the financial statements. How are bad-debt estimates made? The most logical way to estimate bad debts is to examine the business's past records. Both the *percentage of sales* method and the *aging of accounts receivable* method use the company's collection experience.

PERCENTAGE OF SALES A popular way to estimate uncollectibles, the **percentage of sales approach,** computes the expense as a percentage of net sales. This method is also called the *income statement approach* because it focuses on the amount of bad debt expense to be reported on the income statement.

Uncollectible-account expense is recorded as an adjusting entry at the end of the period. Assume it is December 31, 19X3 and the accounts have these balances *before the year-end adjustments:*

Accounts Receivable		Allowance for Uncollectible Accounts	
120,000			500

The $500 balance in the Allowance account is left over from the preceding period. Prior to any adjustments, the net receivable amount is $119,500 ($120,000 – $500), which is more than the business expects to collect from customers.

Basing its decision on prior experience, the credit department estimates that bad-debt expense is 1.5% of net credit sales, which were $500,000. The adjusting entry to record bad-debt expense for the year and to update the allowance is

19X3			
Dec. 31	Uncollectible-Account Expense ($500,000 × .015)	7,500	
	Allowance for Uncollectible Accounts		7,500
	Recorded expense for the year.		

ASSETS	=	LIABILITIES	+	STOCKHOLDERS' EQUITY	–	EXPENSES
–7,500	=	0			–	7,500

Now the accounts are ready for reporting in the 19X3 financial statements.

Accounts Receivable		Allowance for Uncollectible Accounts	
120,000			500
			7,500
			8,000

The balance sheet will report accounts receivable at the net amount of $112,000 ($120,000 – $8,000). The income statement will report the period's uncollectible-account expense of $7,500, along with salary expense, depreciation expense, and the other operating expenses for the period.

Aging of Accounts Receivable The second popular way to estimate bad debts is called **aging of accounts receivable.** This approach is also called the *balance sheet approach* because it focuses on accounts receivable. Individual accounts receivable are analyzed according to the length of time they have been receivable from the customer.

Computerized accounting packages prepare a report for aging accounts receivable. The computer accesses files of customer data and sorts accounts by customer number and date of invoice. The credit department of Schmidt Builders Supply groups its accounts receivable into 30-day periods, as Exhibit 5-3 on page 234 shows.

Schmidt's total balance of accounts receivable is $112,000. Of this amount, the aging schedule indicates that the company will not collect $3,769. *Prior to the year-end adjustment,* Schmidt's accounts appear as follows:

Accounts Receivable		Allowance for Uncollectible Accounts	
112,000			1,100

EXHIBIT 5-3
Aging the Accounts of Schmidt Builders Supply

	Age of Account				
Customer Name	**1–30 Days**	**31–60 Days**	**61–90 Days**	**Over 90 Days**	**Total Balance**
T-Bar-M Co.	$20,000				$ 20,000
Chicago Pneumatic Parts	10,000				10,000
Sarasota Pipe Corp.		$13,000	$10,000		23,000
Oneida, Inc.			3,000	$1,000	4,000
Other accounts*	39,000	12,000	2,000	2,000	55,000
Totals	$69,000	$25,000	$15,000	$3,000	$112,000
Estimated percentage uncollectible	0.1%	1%	5%	90%	
Allowance for Uncollectible Accounts balance	$69	$250	$750	$2,700	$3,769

*Each of the "Other accounts" would appear individually.

The aging method is designed to bring the balance of the allowance account to the needed amount ($3,769) determined by the aging schedule. To update the allowance, Schmidt makes this entry:

19X8			
Dec. 31	Uncollectible-Account Expense	2,669	
	Allowance for Uncollectible Accounts ($3,769 – $1,100)		2,669
	Recorded expense for the year.		

ASSETS	=	LIABILITIES	+	STOCKHOLDERS' EQUITY	–	EXPENSES
–2,669	=	0			–	2,669

Now the balance sheet can report the amount that Schmidt expects to collect from customers, $108,231 ($112,000 – $3,769).

Accounts Receivable	
112,000	

Allowance for Uncollectible Accounts	
	1,100
	2,669
	3,769

As with the allowance method, the income statement reports the uncollectible-account expense.

Writing Off Uncollectible Accounts

Early in 19X9, Schmidt Builders Supply collects on most of its $112,000 accounts receivable as follows:

19X9			
Jan.–Mar.	Cash	92,000	
	Accounts Receivable		92,000
	Collected on account.		

ASSETS	=	LIABILITIES	+	STOCKHOLDERS' EQUITY
+92,000 –92,000	=	0	+	0

However, the credit department determines that Schmidt cannot collect a total of $1,200 from customers Abbott and Smith. The accountant writes off their receivables with the following entry:

19X9			
Mar. 31	Allowance for Uncollectible Accounts	1,200	
	Accounts Receivable—Abbott		900
	Accounts Receivable—Smith		300
	Wrote off uncollectible accounts.		

ASSETS	=	LIABILITIES	+	STOCKHOLDERS' EQUITY
+1,200 −1,200	=	0	+	0

Observe that the write-off entry does not include an expense account. Therefore, writing off an uncollectible account does not affect net income. The write-off has no effect on net receivables either, as shown for Schmidt Builders Supply in Exhibit 5-4.

EXHIBIT 5-4

Net Receivables Before and After the Write-Off of Uncollectible Accounts Are the Same

	Before Write-Off		After Write-Off
Accounts receivable ($112,000 – $92,000)	$20,000	($20,000 – $1,200)	$18,800
Less Allowance for uncollectible accounts	(3,769)	($3,769 – $1,200)	(2,569)
Accounts receivable, net	$16,231 ◄──	same	──► $16,231

STOP & THINK

If the write-off of specific uncollectible accounts affects neither an expense account nor the net amount of receivables, then why go to the trouble of writing off the uncollectible accounts of specific customers?

Answer: We have decided the uncollectible accounts are worthless. It is appropriate to eliminate these accounts from our records. Getting rid of the specific customer accounts alerts the credit department not to waste time and money pursuing collections from these customers. The credit department stores their names in a database. If they apply for credit in the future, the credit department will think twice about extending credit to them.

Using the Percentage of Sales and the Aging Methods Together

In practice, companies use the percentage of sales and the aging of accounts methods together. For interim statements (monthly or quarterly), companies use the percentage of sales method because it is easier to apply. The percentage of sales method focuses on the amount of uncollectible-account *expense*. But that is not enough. At the end of the year, these companies use the aging method to ensure that Accounts Receivable is reported at expected realizable value—that is, the expected amount to be collected. The aging method focuses on the amount of the receivables—the *asset*—that is uncollectible. Using the two methods together provides good measures of both the expense and the asset. Exhibit 5-5 on page 236 summarizes and compares the two methods.

Concept Highlight

EXHIBIT 5-5
Comparing the Two Methods of Estimating Uncollectibles

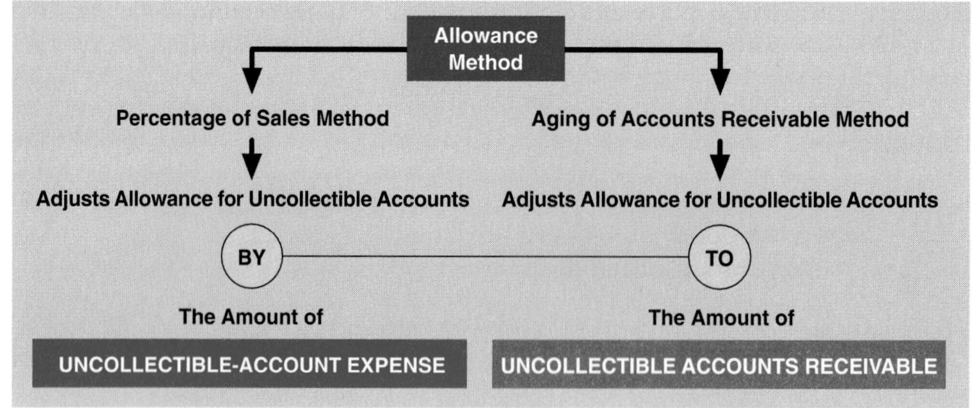

The Direct Write-Off Method

Under the **direct write-off method** of accounting for bad debts, the company waits until the credit department decides that a customer's account receivable is uncollectible. Then the accountant debits Uncollectible-Account Expense and credits the customer's Account Receivable to write off the account, as follows (using assumed data):

19X9			
Jan. 2	Uncollectible-Account Expense	2,000	
	Accounts Receivable—Jones		2,000
	Wrote off a bad account.		

ASSETS	=	LIABILITIES	+	STOCKHOLDERS' EQUITY	−	EXPENSES
−2,000	=	0			−	2,000

This method is defective for two reasons:

1. It does not set up an allowance for uncollectibles. As a result, it always reports the receivables at their full amount, which is more than the business expects to collect. Assets are overstated on the balance sheet.

2. It may not match the uncollectible-account expense against the revenue of the period in which the sale was made. In this example, the company made the sale to Jones in 19X1 and should have recorded the expense during 19X1 to measure net income properly. By recording the expense in 19X2, the company overstates net income in 19X1 and understates net income in 19X2.

According to the matching principle (Chapter 3, page 111), expenses incurred must be matched against revenue earned during the period. The direct write-off method is acceptable only when the amount of uncollectibles is so low that there is no material difference between bad-debt amounts determined by the allowance method and the direct write-off method.

Credit-Card Sales

Credit-card sales are common in retailing. **American Express, VISA, MasterCard,** and **Discover** are popular credit cards. Customers present credit cards as payment for purchases. The sales invoice is prepared in triplicate. The customer and the seller keep copies as receipts. The third copy goes to the credit-card company, which then pays the seller the transaction amount and bills the customer.

Credit cards offer customers the convenience of buying without having to pay the cash immediately. Consumers receive a monthly statement from the credit-card company, detailing each credit-card transaction. They can then write a single check to cover the entire month's credit-card purchases.

Retailers also benefit from credit-card sales. They do not have to check a customer's credit rating. The company that issued the card has already done so. Retailers do not have to keep an accounts receivable subsidiary ledger account for each customer, and they do not have to collect cash from customers. Further, retailers receive cash more quickly from the credit-card companies than they would from the customers themselves.

Of course, these services to the seller do not come free. The seller receives less than 100% of the face value of the invoice. The credit-card company takes a discount ranging between 1 and 5% on the sale to cover its services. Suppose a friend treats you to lunch at the Russian Tea Room (the seller) and pays the bill—$100—with a Discover card. The seller's entry to record the $100 Discover card sale, subject to the credit-card company's 2% discount, is

Accounts Receivable—Discover	98	
Credit-Card Discount Expense	2	
Sales Revenue		100
Recorded credit-card sales.		

ASSETS	=	LIABILITIES	+	STOCKHOLDERS' EQUITY	+	REVENUES	−	EXPENSES
98	=	0			+	100	−	2

On collection of the discounted value, the seller records:

Cash	98	
Accounts Receivable—Discover		98
Collected from Discover.		

ASSETS	=	LIABILITIES	+	STOCKHOLDERS' EQUITY
+98 −98	=	0	+	0

Notes Receivable

As we pointed out earlier, notes receivable are more formal arrangements than accounts receivable. There are two parties to a note. The **creditor** has a note receivable, and the **debtor** has a note payable. Often, the debtor signs a promissory note, which serves as evidence of the debt. Exhibit 5-6 is a typical promissory note.

Objective 5

Account for notes receivable and the related interest revenue

The **principal** amount of the note is the amount borrowed by the debtor, lent by the creditor. The term of the note runs from August 31, 19X7, to August 31, 19X8, when Lauren Holland (the maker) promises to pay Continental Bank (the payee) the principal of $1,000 plus 9% interest for the year. **Interest** is the borrower's cost of renting money from the lender. Interest is revenue for the lender, expense for the borrower.

EXHIBIT 5-6
A Promissory Note

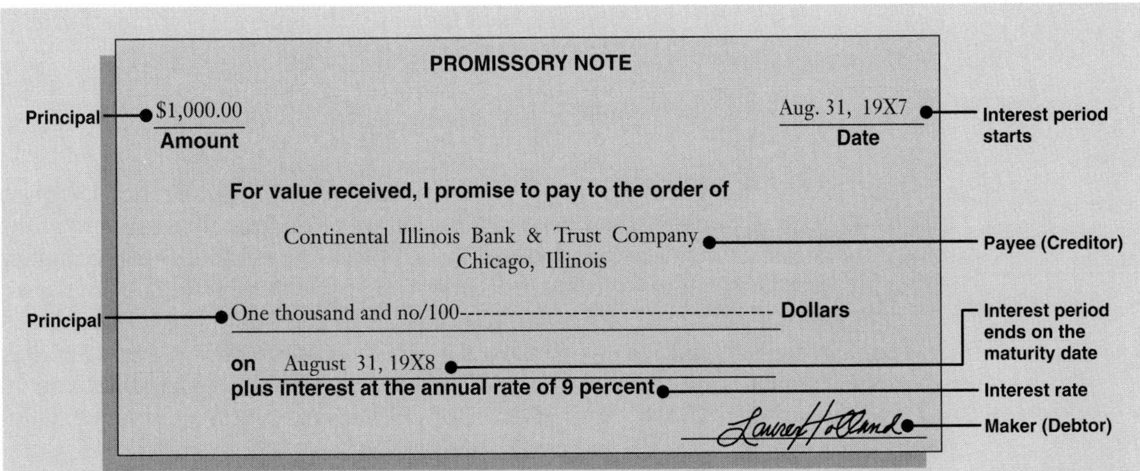
PROMISSORY NOTE

$1,000.00
Amount

Aug. 31, 19X7
Date

For value received, I promise to pay to the order of

Continental Illinois Bank & Trust Company
Chicago, Illinois

One thousand and no/100---------------------------------- Dollars

on August 31, 19X8
plus interest at the annual rate of 9 percent

Lauren Holland

Accounting for Notes Receivable

Consider the promissory note shown in Exhibit 5-6. After Lauren Holland signs the note, Continental Bank gives her $1,000 cash. At maturity, Holland pays the bank $1,090 ($1,000 principal plus $90 interest). The bank's entries are as follows, assuming a December 31 year end:

19X7			
Aug. 31	Note Receivable—L. Holland	1,000	
	Cash		1,000
	Made a loan.		

ASSETS	=	LIABILITIES	+	STOCKHOLDERS' EQUITY
+1,000 −1,000	=	0	+	0

Dec. 31	Interest Receivable ($1,000 × .09 × 4/12)	30	
	Interest Revenue		30
	Accrued interest revenue.		

ASSETS	=	LIABILITIES	+	STOCKHOLDERS' EQUITY	+	REVENUES
30	=	0			+	30

When Holland pays off the note on August 31, 19X8, the bank's entry is

19X8			
Aug. 31	Cash	1,090	
	Note Receivable—L. Holland		1,000
	Interest Receivable		30
	Interest Revenue ($1,000 × .09 × 8/12)		60
	Collected note at maturity.		

ASSETS	=	LIABILITIES	+	STOCKHOLDERS' EQUITY	+	REVENUES
+1,090 −1,000 − 30	=	0			+	60

Three aspects of these entries deserve mention:

1. Interest rates are always stated for an annual period unless they are specifically denoted otherwise. In this example, the annual interest rate is 9 percent. At December 31, 19X7, Continental Bank accrues interest revenue for the four months (4/12 of the year) the bank has held the note. The interest computation is

Principal	×	Interest rate	×	Time	=	Amount of Interest
$1,000	×	.09	×	4/12	=	$30

2. The December 31, 19X7, entry to accrue interest revenue includes a debit to Interest Receivable because the interest is in addition to the principal amount of the note. By contrast, some debt instruments, such as U.S. Treasury bills and commercial paper, include the interest in their maturity value. That is why we debited the Investment account for the accrual of interest revenue in our example on page 223.

3. Throughout this text we illustrate interest computations using a 360-day (12-month) year. This provides you with round numbers and enables you to focus on the concepts without the clutter of dollars and cents. In practice, computers eliminate the burden and use a 365-day year.

Some companies sell merchandise on notes receivable. This arrangement often occurs when the payment term extends beyond the customary accounts receivable period, which generally ranges from 30 to 60 days.

Suppose that on March 20, 19X3, General Electric sells household appliances for $15,000 to Dorman Builders. Dorman signs a 90-day promissory note at 10% annual interest. General Electric's entries to record the sale and collection from Dorman are as follows:

19X3			
Mar. 20	Note Receivable—Dorman Builders	15,000	
	Sales Revenue		15,000
	Made a sale, receiving a note.		

ASSETS	=	LIABILITIES	+	STOCKHOLDERS' EQUITY	+	REVENUES
15,000	=	0			+	15,000

June 18	Cash	15,375	
	Note Receivable—Dorman Builders.............		15,000
	Interest Revenue ($15,000 × 0.10 × 90/360) ..		375
	Collected note at maturity.		

ASSETS	=	LIABILITIES	+	STOCKHOLDERS' EQUITY	+	REVENUES
+15,375 −15,000	=	0			+	375

A company may accept a note receivable from a trade customer who fails to pay an account receivable within the customary 30 to 60 days. The customer signs a promissory note—that is, becomes the maker of the note—and gives it to the creditor, who becomes the payee.

Suppose Marlboro, Inc., sees that it will not be able to pay off its $2,400 account payable to Hoffman Supply that is due in 15 days. Hoffman may accept a one-year, $2,400 note receivable, with 9% interest, from Marlboro on October 1, 19X1. Hoffman's entry is

19X1			
Oct. 1	Note Receivable—Marlboro, Inc.	2,400	
	Accounts Receivable—Marlboro, Inc.		2,400
	Received a note on account from a customer.		

ASSETS	=	LIABILITIES	+	STOCKHOLDERS' EQUITY
+2,400 −2,400	=	0		0

Why does a company accept a note receivable instead of pressing the customer for payment of the account receivable? The company may pursue receipt and learn that its customer does not have the money. A note receivable gives the company written evidence of the maker's debt, which may aid any legal action for collection. Also, the note receivable may carry a maker's pledge that gives the payee certain assets if cash is not received by the due date. The company's reward for its patience is the interest revenue that it earns on the note receivable.

Using Receivables to Finance Operations

In the chapter-opening story we saw that Intel Corporation had much of its money tied up in liquid assets. We observed that this might not be a good strategy for some businesses. Specifically, accounts receivable earn no revenue. A company with a large amount of accounts receivable tries to collect the receivables as quickly as possible to keep its cash circulating. This is why companies have credit departments—to examine the credit histories of prospective customers before extending credit, and then to manage the receivables after credit sales are made.

Some industries are plagued with slow collections of receivables. Textile companies are an example. They sell to garment manufacturers, which are often small businesses that are short of cash. Most retailers are happy to let credit specialists, such as VISA, MasterCard, and American Express, take the credit risks. Other companies have financial divisions that handle the financing of their products. The automobile industry is an example. During 1995, **Ford Motor Company** earned more net income from financial services than from selling vehicles and automotive parts.

During 1995, Ford Motor Company earned more net income from financial services than from selling vehicles and automotive parts.

There are numerous financing arrangements. The simplest is the credit-card sale, as illustrated on pages 236–237. In another financing arrangement, companies sell their notes receivable to financial institutions, who then collect the notes and earn the interest. This practice is called *discounting notes receivable* because the seller receives a discounted price for the note. The seller is willing to take less money in order to receive cash immediately and to shift the credit risk to another party. The financial institutions that buy notes receivable then earn the interest revenue on the note.

A third arrangement, called *factoring accounts receivable,* is similar to discounting notes receivable. A company that does not want to bother collecting its receivables can sell them to a financial institution called a *factor.* The factor earns income by buying the receivables at one price—say, 80% of their face value—and collecting a larger amount from the debtor. If the sale of the receivables is *without recourse,* the factor cannot demand anything more from the seller if the receivables prove uncollectible. Sales of receivables without recourse are made at deep discounts to compensate the factor for bearing added risk. Factoring of receivables *with recourse* leaves the seller with the credit risk. If the receivables prove uncollectible, the factor can look back to the seller for additional compensation. Factoring with recourse leads to a smaller discount on the sale of the receivables.

Discounting notes receivable and factoring accounts receivable are essentially sale arrangements. Determining the amounts can be quite complex, but their accounting follows this pattern for the discounting of a $100,000 note receivable for $96,000:

Cash	96,000	
Interest Expense	4,000	
Note Receivable		100,000
Discounted a note receivable.		

ASSETS	=	LIABILITIES	+	STOCKHOLDERS' EQUITY	−	EXPENSES
+ 96,000 −100,000	=	0			−	4,000

The seller records interest expense because the cash received from selling the note is less than the note's carrying value on the books. Recording interest expense is explicit recognition that the sale of the note receivable is a financing arrangement.

A fourth arrangement is called *assigning accounts receivable.* Under an assignment arrangement, the company borrows money and assigns its accounts receivable as collateral for the loan. If the company cannot pay the loan, the creditor can take the accounts receivable as compensation.

Contingent Liabilities on Discounted Notes Receivable

A **contingent liability** is a potential liability that will become an actual liability only if a potential event occurs. Discounting a note receivable can create a contingent liability for the seller of the note. To illustrate, assume General Electric has a second note receivable from Dorman Builders. Suppose GE discounts, or sells, this note to a bank. If Dorman Builders fails to pay the maturity value to the new payee (the bank), then the original payee (GE) legally must pay the bank the amount due. Now we see why the liability is "potential." If Dorman pays the bank, then GE can forget the note. But if Dorman dishonors the note—fails to pay it—GE has an actual liability.

This contingent liability of GE exists from the time of the sale of the note to its maturity date. Contingent liabilities are not included with actual liabilities on the balance sheet. After all, they are not real debts. However, financial statement users should be alerted that the business has *potential* debts. Many businesses report contingent liabilities in a footnote to the financial statements. GE's end-of-period balance sheet might carry this note:

> As of December 31, 19X3, the Company is contingently liable on notes receivable discounted in the amount of $15,000.

Using Accounting Information for Decision Making

Objective 6

Use the acid-test ratio and days' sales in receivables to evaluate a company's financial position.

The balance sheet lists assets in the order of relative liquidity. Cash comes first because it is the medium of exchange and can be used to purchase any item or to pay any bill. Short-term investments come next because they can be sold for cash at the will of the owner. Current receivables are less liquid because receivables must be collected. Merchandise inventory is less liquid than receivables because the goods must first be sold; selling the goods creates a receivable that can be collected. Intel Corporation's balance sheet in the chapter-opening story shows the ordering of these accounts.

Acid-Test (or Quick) Ratio

In making decisions, owners and managers use some ratios based on the relative liquidity of assets. In Chapter 3, for example, we discussed the current ratio, which indicates the company's ability to pay current liabilities with current assets. A more stringent measure of the company's ability to pay current liabilities is the **acid-test** (or **quick**) **ratio:**

The acid-test ratio is similar to the current ratio introduced in Chapter 3 (page 143), but it excludes inventory and prepaid expenses from the numerator.

For Intel Corporation, 1995
(Dollar amounts in millions)

$$\textbf{Acid-test ratio} = \frac{\text{Cash} + \text{Short-term investments} + \text{Net current receivables}}{\text{Total current liabilities}} \qquad \frac{\$1{,}463 + \$995 + \$3{,}116}{\$3{,}619^*} = 1.54$$

*Taken from Intel Corporation's 1995 balance sheet. Courtesy of Intel Corporation.

The higher the acid-test ratio, the better the business is able to pay its current liabilities. Intel's acid-test ratio of 1.54 means that Intel has $1.54 of quick assets to pay each $1 of current liabilities—a comfortable position.

Inventory, although included in the computation of the current ratio, is excluded from the acid-test ratio because it may not be easy to sell the goods. A company may have an acceptable current ratio and a poor acid-test ratio because of a large amount of inventory.

What is an acceptable acid-test ratio value? The answer depends on the industry. Automobile dealers can operate smoothly with an acid-test ratio of 0.20. Several things make this possible: Car dealers have almost no current receivables. They receive cash from customers, who borrow from banks and other lenders. Dealers carry large inventories, and the manufacturers—**GM, Toyota, Mercedes-Benz,** for example—allow dealers to pay the cost of automobiles as they are sold at retail prices. In summary, car dealers need little in the way of liquid assets.

The acid-test ratio values for most department stores cluster about .80, while travel agencies average 1.10. In general, an acid-test ratio of 1.00 is considered safe. Intel Corporation's ratio of 1.54 is quite high, as is that of competitor **Texas Instruments,** whose quick ratio is 1.29.

STOP & THINK Compute the current ratio and the acid-test ratio for the following selected accounts and their balances at 12/31:

Equipment	$4,000
Supplies	500
Interest Payable	600
Accounts Receivable	2,600
Accounts Payable	3,400
Accumulated Depreciation	1,200
Inventory	1,600
Cash	1,300

Answer: Current ratio = 1.5 ($6,000*/$4,000†)
Acid-test ratio = 0.975 ($3,900‡/$4,000)

*($500 + $2,600 + $1,600 + $1,300 = $6,000)
†($600 + $3,400 = $4,000)
‡($2,600 + $1,300 = $3,900)

Days' Sales in Receivables

After a business makes a credit sale, the next critical event in the business cycle is collection of the receivable. Several financial ratios center on receivables. **Days' sales in receivables,** also called the *collection period,* indicates how many days it takes to collect the average level of receivables. The shorter the collection period, the more quickly the organization can use cash for operations. The longer the collection period, the less cash is available to pay bills and expand. Days' sales in receivables can be computed in two steps, as follows:

For Intel Corporation
(Dollar amounts in millions)

$$\textbf{1. One day's sales} = \frac{\textbf{Net sales}}{\textbf{365 days}} \qquad \frac{\$16{,}202^*}{365} = \$44.4 \text{ per day}$$

$$\textbf{2. Days' sales in average accounts receivable} = \frac{\textbf{Average net accounts receivable}}{\textbf{One day's sales}} = \frac{\left(\textbf{Beginning net receivables} + \textbf{Ending net receivables}\right) \div 2}{\textbf{One day's sales}} = \frac{(\$1{,}978 + \$3{,}116)/2}{\$44.4} = 57 \text{ days}$$

*Taken from Intel Corporation's 1995 income statement. Courtesy of Intel Corporation.

The length of the collection period depends on the credit terms of the company's sales. For example, sales on net 30 terms should be collected within approximately 30 days. When there is a discount, such as 2/10 net 30, the collection period may be shorter. Terms of net 45 or net 60 result in longer collection periods.

We discussed sales discounts in Chapter 4, page 189.

STOP & THINK Intel Corporation's collection period averaged 57 days during 1995. Which credit terms are more likely for Intel's sales: net 60, or 3/15 net 60? Why?

Answer: 3/15 net 60. Intel collects receivables in a little under 60 days, which suggests that the company offers a discount to customers who pay before 60 days.

Companies watch their collection period closely. Whenever the collection period lengthens, the business must find other sources of financing, such as borrowing or factoring their receivables. During recessions, customers pay more slowly, and a longer collection period may be unavoidable.

LEARNING TIP Investors and creditors do not evaluate a company on the basis of one or two ratios. Instead, they perform a thorough analysis of all the information available on a company. Then they stand back from the data and ask, "What is our overall impression of the strength of this business?"

Relating Short-Term Investments and Receivables to the Statement of Cash Flows

Objective 7

Report investment and receivables transactions on the statement of cash flows

Short-term investments and receivables are assets, which appear on the balance sheet. We saw these in Intel's balance sheet in the chapter-opening story, and we've also seen how to report the related revenues, gains, and losses on the income statement. As we've discussed, investment and receivables transactions affect cash, so their effects must also be reported on another financial statement, the statement of cash flows.

A sale on account creates a receivable, but the sale brings in no cash. Collections of receivables are the most important source of cash for a business that sells on credit. The sale that creates a receivable is an operating transaction, so collections from customers are cash receipts from *operating activities.*

The purchase of a U.S. Treasury bill requires a cash payment. This purchase is reported as an *investing activity* on the statement of cash flows. When Intel cashes in a Treasury bill, the cash receipt is an investing activity. Intel's purchase and sale of Ford Motor Company stock are also investing activities that must be reported on the statement of cash flows. Exhibit 5-7 on page 244 shows how the statement of cash flows can report the effects of short-term investment and receivables transactions.

Each amount listed on the cash-flow statement in Exhibit 5-7 is either a cash receipt, a positive amount, or a cash payment, a negative amount (denoted by parentheses). The largest amount is the cash receipt for collections from customers. This amount will differ from sales revenue (as reported on the income statement) if the business sells on account and has not collected all its receivables before year end.

For most companies, receipts of cash from interest and dividends are much smaller than collections from customers. Cash receipts of interest and dividends are related to interest revenue and dividend revenue, which are reported on the income statement. Thus, the receipts of interest and dividends are viewed as cash flows from operating activities. (Recall that the income statement is a summary of the firm's operating activities—revenues and expenses—over a period.)

EXHIBIT 5-7
Reporting the Effects of Short-Term Investment and Receivables Transactions on the Statement of Cash Flows

EXAMPLE COMPANY Statement of Cash Flows (Partial) Year Ended December 31, 19XX	
Cash flows from operating activities:	
Collections from customers	$15,000
Receipts of interest	350
Receipts of dividends	150
Net cash inflow from operating activities	15,500
Cash flows from investing activities:	
Purchases of short-term investments	$(1,400)
Sales of short-term investments	800
Loaned money on notes receivable	(500)
Collected notes receivable	200
Net cash outflow from investing activities	(900)

The investing activities section of the cash-flow statement lists purchases and sales of short-term investments. "Purchases of short-term investments . . . $(1,400)" means that the company paid $1,400 cash for investments during the year. The starting point in accounting for investments is cost—in this case, $1,400. "Sale of short-term investments . . . $800" means that the company sold some short-term investments for $800 cash during the year. These cash-flow amounts from investing activities are separate from the cash receipts of interest and dividends, which (as we saw) are reported under operating activities.

For most companies, loaning money is an investing activity because the business is investing in a note receivable. Collecting on the note receivable is also an investing activity. However, lending and collecting are *operating activities* for financial institutions because that is their main line of business. Exhibit 5-7 omits the financing-activities section of the cash-flow statement because investments and receivables relate more closely to operating and investing activities.

STOP & THINK

1. During its first year of operations, Glade Corporation made credit sales of $10,000. At the end of the year, Glade's accounts receivable total $800. How much cash did Glade collect from customers during the year?
2. Glade's sales in its second year were $15,000, and at year end, accounts receivable have grown to $1,700. How much did Glade collect from customers during the second year? Ignore uncollectibles.

Answers

1. $9,200. Sales were $10,000, but at year end, Glade had not collected the accounts receivable balance of $800. Therefore, Glade must have collected $9,200 ($10,000 – $800) from customers.
2. $14,100. Early in the year, Glade collected last year's receivable balance of $800. Sales during the second year were $15,000, but Glade had not collected the ending receivables of $1,700. Glade must have collected $13,300 ($15,000 – $1,700) of the second year's sales. In all, Glade collected $14,100 ($800 + $13,300) from customers during its second year.

Here is a shortcut computation—illustrated for the second year:

Cash collections = Sales for the period, $15,000 { **– an increase in accounts receivable, $900** or **+ a decrease in accounts receivable** }

= $14,100

The computations illustrated in the Stop & Think point to another way to report cash flows from operating activities. This alternative reporting method starts with net income and makes a series of adjustments to compute net cash flows from operating activities. We can use Intel's financial statements to illustrate. During 1995, Intel earned net income of $3,566 million. During the year, the company's accounts receivable increased from $1,978 million to $3,116 million—an increase of $1,138 million. Intel's 1995 statement of cash flows includes these items.

	(In millions)
Cash flows provided by operating activities:	
Net income	$3,566
Adjustments to reconcile net income to net cash provided by operating activities:	
(Increase) in accounts receivable	(1,138)

The $1,138 million increase in Intel's accounts receivable during 1995 means that cash collections from customers were less than the amount of sales that the company used to compute net income for the year. We explain this method of formatting cash flows from operating activities, called the *indirect approach,* more fully in Chapter 12.

You should now understand why an increase in a company's liquid assets may be good news or bad news. Such an increase is good news if investments earn high returns and both sales and collections are increasing, but bad news if the company cannot collect its receivables.

SUMMARY PROBLEM FOR YOUR REVIEW

CPC International, Inc., is the food-products company that produces Skippy peanut butter, Hellmann's mayonnaise, and Mazola corn oil. The company balance sheet at December 31, 19X7, reported:

	(In millions)
Notes and accounts receivable [total]	$549.9
Allowance for doubtful accounts	(12.5)

Required

1. How much of the December 31, 19X7, balance of notes and accounts receivable did CPC expect to collect? Stated differently, what was the expected realizable value of these receivables?
2. Journalize, without explanations, 19X8 entries for CPC International, assuming:
   a. Estimated Doubtful-Account Expense of $19.2 million, based on the percentage of sales method.
   b. Write-offs of uncollectible accounts receivable totaling $23.6 million.
   c. December 31, 19X8, aging of receivables, which indicates that $15.3 million of the total receivables of $582.7 million is uncollectible.
3. Show how CPC International's receivables and related allowance will appear on the December 31, 19X8, balance sheet.
4. Show what CPC International's income statement will report for the foregoing transactions.

ANSWERS

Requirement 1

	(In millions)
Expected realizable value of receivables ($549.9 – $12.5)	$537.4

Requirement 2

a. Doubtful-Account Expense...	19.2	
Allowance for Doubtful Accounts		19.2
b. Allowance for Doubtful Accounts...	23.6	
Accounts Receivable		23.6

Allowance for Doubtful Accounts

19X8 Write-offs	23.6	Dec. 31, 19X7	12.5
		19X8 Expense	19.2
		19X8 balance prior to December 31, 19X8	8.1

c. Doubtful-Account Expense ($15.3 – $8.1)	7.2	
Allowance for Doubtful Accounts		7.2

Allowance for Doubtful Accounts

	8.1
	7.2
	15.3

Requirement 3

	(In millions)
Notes and accounts receivable	$582.7
Allowance for doubtful accounts..	(15.3)

Requirement 4

	(In millions)
Expenses: Doubtful-account expense for 19X8 ($19.2 + $7.2).............	26.4

SUMMARY OF LEARNING OBJECTIVES

1. *Account for short-term investments.* Short-term investments, also called *marketable securities,* are investments that a company plans to hold for one year or less. There are three types of short-term investments: held-to-maturity securities, trading securities, and available-for-sale securities.

2. *Report short-term investments on the balance sheet and the related revenue on the income statement.* Held-to-maturity securities are reported on the balance sheet at *amortized cost* (cost plus interest accrued to date). Trading and available-for-sale securities are reported on the balance sheet at market value. Realized and unrealized gains and losses on trading securities are reported on the income statement; interest and dividend revenue from investments must also be reported on the income statement. Unrealized gains and losses on available-for-sale securities are reported on the balance sheet as a separate element of stockholders' equity.

3. *Apply internal controls to receivables.* Businesses that sell on credit receive most of their cash receipts by mail. To ensure internal control, cash-handling duties must be separated from cash-accounting duties. A bank lock box is often used to achieve this separation of duties.

4. *Use the allowance method to account for uncollectible receivables.* The most logical way to estimate bad debts is to examine the business's past records. In the *percentage of sales* method, uncollectible-account expense is estimated as a percentage of the company's net sales. This method adjusts Allowance for Uncollectible Accounts *by* the amount of uncollectible-account expense. Under the *aging of accounts receivable* method, individual accounts are analyzed according to the length of time they have been receivable from the customer. This method adjusts Allowance for Uncollectible Accounts *to* the proper amount of uncollectible accounts receivable.

5. *Account for notes receivable and the related interest revenue.* *Notes receivable* are formal receivable arrangements in which the debtor signs a promissory note, agreeing to pay back both the principal borrowed plus a stated amount of interest on a certain date. To increase their cash flow, companies may discount, factor, or assign their receivables.

6. *Use the acid-test ratio and days' sales in receivables to evaluate a company's financial position.* The *acid-test ratio* measures a company's ability to pay current liabilities with the most liquid current assets. *Days' sales in receivables* indicates how long it takes a company to collect its average level of receivables.

7. *Report investment and receivables transactions on the statement of cash flows.* Investment and receivables transactions affect cash, so their effects are reported on the statement of cash flows. Collections from customers are cash receipts from *operating activities,* as are receipts of dividend and interest revenue. Purchases and sales of investments are *investing activities.*

ACCOUNTING VOCABULARY

acid-test ratio *(p. 241).*
aging of accounts receivable *(p. 233).*
Allowance for Doubtful Accounts *(p. 232).*
Allowance for Uncollectible Accounts *(p. 232).*
allowance method *(p. 232).*
available-for-sale securities *(p. 227).*
bad-debt expense *(p. 231).*
contingent liability *(p. 241).*
creditor *(p. 237).*
days' sales in receivables *(p. 242).*
debt instrument *(p. 222).*
debtor *(p. 222).*
direct write-off method *(p. 236).*
doubtful-account expense *(p. 231).*
equity securities *(p. 222).*
held-to-maturity securities *(p. 223).*
interest *(p. 237).*
marketable securities *(p. 222).*
maturity *(p. 222).*
percentage of sales approach *(p. 232).*
principal *(p. 237).*
quick ratio *(p. 241).*
receivable *(p. 228).*
securities *(p. 222).*
short-term investments *(p. 222).*
term *(p. 222).*
trading securities *(p. 224).*
uncollectible-account expense *(p. 231).*

QUESTIONS

1. Suppose you are the president of Lands' End, Inc. In general, would you be most inclined to make large investments in U.S. Treasury bills, the stock of General Motors Corporation, or new lines of merchandise in your main line of business? Explain your choice.
2. Describe the three categories of short-term investments. Indicate the amount to report on the balance sheet for each investment category.
3. MFS Communication, Inc., purchases a corporate bond as a short-term investment. Show how MFS will report the investment on its balance sheet, including a description of the dollar amount to report, if
   a. MFS expects to hold the bond to its maturity in 120 days.
   b. MFS intends to sell the bond at a profit within a few weeks.
   Identify the category of assets in which the investment is reported and the accounts that come before and after the investment on the balance sheet.
4. Many businesses receive most of their cash on credit sales through the mail. Suppose you own a business so large that you must hire employees to handle cash receipts and perform the related accounting duties. What internal control feature should you use to ensure that the cash received from customers is not taken by a dishonest employee?
5. Which of the two methods of accounting for uncollectible accounts—the allowance method or the direct write-off method—is preferable? Why?
6. Identify the accounts debited and credited to account for uncollectibles under (a) the allowance method, and (b) the direct write-off method.
7. Identify and briefly describe the two ways to estimate bad-debt expense and uncollectible accounts under the allowance method.
8. Briefly describe how a company may use both the percentage of sales method and the aging method to account for uncollectibles.
9. For each of the following notes receivable, compute the amount of interest revenue earned during 19X6:

	Principal	Interest Rate	Interest Period	Maturity Date
a. Note 1	$ 10,000	9%	60 days	11/30/19X6
b. Note 2	50,000	10%	3 months	9/30/19X6
c. Note 3	100,000	8%	18 months	12/31/19X7
d. Note 4	15,000	12%	90 days	1/15/19X7

10. How does a contingent liability differ from an ordinary liability? How does discounting a note receivable create a contingent liability? When does the contingency cease to exist?

11. Why does the payee of a note receivable usually need to make adjusting entries for interest at the end of the accounting period?

12. Show two ways to report Accounts Receivable of $100,000 and Allowance for Uncollectible Accounts of $2,800 on the balance sheet or in the related notes.

13. Why is the acid-test ratio a more stringent measure of the ability to pay current liabilities than the current ratio?

14. Which measure of days' sales in receivables is preferable, 30 or 40? Give your reason.

EXERCISES

Accounting for a held-to-maturity investment
(Obj. 1, 2)

E5-1 Ford Motor Company holds over $1 billion of short-term investments. Suppose the following investment transactions were among Ford's many transactions during 19X7:

19X7	
Dec. 16	Purchased a 90-day U.S. Treasury bill for $228,000. The Treasury bill will mature at $240,000 on March 16, 19X8, when Ford plans to cash it in.
31	Accrued interest revenue. The market value of the Treasury bill is $227,000.
19X8	
Mar. 16	Received cash for the Treasury bill.

Required

1. Make the entries to record Ford's investment transactions. Explanations are not required.
2. Show how Ford would report this investment on its balance sheets at December 31, 19X7 and 19X8, and the related revenues, gains, and losses on the 19X7 and 19X8 income statements.
3. Identify any unused information, and explain why it is not used. In your explanation, state how Ford classifies the Treasury bill investment (held-to-maturity, trading, or available-for-sale). Describe the amount that Ford should report for the investment on the balance sheet.
4. Explain why Ford may have chosen to hold $1 billion in short-term investments rather than use the money in some other way.

Reporting a trading investment
(Obj. 2, 7)

E5-2 On November 16, a company paid $50,000 for a trading investment in the stock of Hewlett-Packard Company. On December 12, the company received a $400 cash dividend from Hewlett-Packard. It is now December 31, and the market value of the Hewlett-Packard stock is $48,000. Show what the company should report in its income statement, balance sheet, and statement of cash flows related to this investment.

Accounting for a trading investment in stock
(Obj. 1, 2)

E5-3 Curtiss-Wright Corporation developed the Wankel engine that thrust Mazda automobiles into prominence. Curtiss-Wright reports over $50 million of short-term investments on its balance sheet. Suppose Curtiss-Wright completed the following investment transactions during 19X8:

19X8	
Nov. 6	Purchased 1,000 shares of Titan Corporation stock for $69,000. Curtiss-Wright plans to sell the stock at a profit in the near future.
30	Received a quarterly cash dividend of $.85 per share on the Titan stock.
Dec. 31	Adjusted the investment in Titan stock. Current market value is $67,000, but Curtiss-Wright still plans to sell the stock at a profit early in 19X9.
19X9	
Jan. 11	The price of the Titan stock has started to move upward. The market value of Curtiss-Wright's investment is now $68,000.
14	Sold the Titan stock for $70,000.

Required

1. Make the entries to record Curtiss-Wright's investment transactions. Explanations are not required.

2. Show how Curtiss-Wright would report this investment on its balance sheets at December 31, 19X8 and 19X9, and the related revenues, gains, and losses on the 19X8 and 19X9 income statements.

Reporting available-for-sale investments ***(Obj. 2)***

E5-4 American General Corporation is one of the largest diversified financial services organizations in the United States. Founded in 1926 and headquartered in Houston, it is a leading provider of consumer loans and life insurance. American General's balance sheet (as adapted) at December 31, 19X5, reports the following under Assets:

Investments	**(In millions)**
Fixed maturity securities (amortized cost: $34,590)	$37,213
Loans on real estate............	3,041
Equity securities (cost: $138)............	186

Required

Answer these questions about American General's investments:

1. American General is holding the fixed maturity securities as available-for-sale securities. What does the $37,213 million amount represent? Give the basis for your answer. Has American General experienced a gain or loss on these investments? Give the amount. Is the gain or loss realized or unrealized? How can you tell?
2. Give another account title for "Loans on real estate." What does the $3,041 million represent?
3. American General holds the equity securities as available-for-sale securities. Give another account title for "Equity securities." What does the $186 million represent?
4. Does American General appear to be a successful investor or an unsuccessful investor? Why?

Controlling cash receipts from customers ***(Obj. 3)***

E5-5 As a recent college graduate, you land your first job in the customer collections department of Lowes & Kellogg, a partnership. Grant Kellogg, one of the owners, has asked you to propose a system to ensure that cash received by mail from customers is handled properly. Draft a short memorandum identifying the essential element in your proposed plan, and state why this element is important. Refer to Chapter 4 if necessary.

Using the allowance method for bad debts ***(Obj. 4)***

E5-6 On September 30, SaveTime Delivery Service had a $28,000 debit balance in Accounts Receivable. During October, the company had sales of $137,000, which included $90,000 in credit sales. October collections were $91,000, and write-offs of uncollectible receivables totaled $1,070. Other data include

- September 30 credit balance in Allowance for Uncollectible Accounts, $1,600.
- Uncollectible-account expense, estimated as 2% of credit sales.

Required

1. Prepare journal entries to record sales, collections, uncollectible-account expense by the allowance method (using the percentage of sales approach), and write-offs of uncollectibles during October.
2. Show the ending balances in Accounts Receivable, Allowance for Uncollectible Accounts, and *net* accounts receivable at October 31. How much does SaveTime expect to collect?
3. Show how SaveTime will report Accounts Receivable on its October 31 balance sheet. Use the Intel Corporation format.

Using the direct write-off method for bad debts ***(Obj. 4)***

E5-7 Refer to Exercise 5-6.

Required

1. Record uncollectible-account expense for October by the direct write-off method.
2. What amount of accounts receivable would SaveTime report on its October 31 balance sheet under the direct write-off method? Does SaveTime expect to collect the full amount?

Using the aging approach to estimate bad debts ***(Obj. 4)***

E5-8 At December 31, 19X7, the accounts receivable balance of First Arkansas Company is $269,000. The allowance for doubtful accounts has a $3,910 credit balance. Accountants for First Arkansas prepare the following aging schedule for its accounts receivable:

	Age of Accounts			
Total Balance	**1–30 Days**	**31–60 Days**	**61–90 Days**	**Over 90 Days**
$269,000	$107,000	$78,000	$69,000	$15,000
Estimated percentage uncollectible	0.3%	1.2%	6.0%	50%

Required

1. Journalize the adjusting entry for doubtful accounts on the basis of the aging schedule. Show the T-account for the allowance.
2. Show how First Arkansas will report Accounts Receivable on its December 31 balance sheet. Include the two accounts that come before receivables on the balance sheet, using assumed amounts.

Reporting bad debts by the allowance method ***(Obj. 4)***

E5-9 At December 31, 19X5, Gateway 5000, Inc., has an accounts receivable balance of $137,000. Sales revenue for 19X5 is $950,000, including credit sales of $600,000. For each of the following situations, prepare the year-end adjusting entry to record doubtful-account expense. Show how the accounts receivable and the allowance for doubtful accounts are reported on the balance sheet. Use the reporting format of Intel Corporation.

a. Allowance for Doubtful Accounts has a credit balance before adjustment of $1,600. Gateway estimates that doubtful-account expense for the year is ½ of 1% of credit sales.
b. Allowance for Doubtful Accounts has a debit balance before adjustment of $1,700. Gateway estimates that $3,900 of the accounts receivable will prove uncollectible.

Recording notes receivable and accruing interest revenue ***(Obj. 5)***

E5-10 Record the following transactions in the journal of Key Elements, Inc.

Nov. 1	Loaned $50,000 cash to Jay Merck on a one-year, 9% note.
Dec. 3	Sold goods to Baylor, Inc., receiving a 90-day, 12% note for $3,750.
16	Received a $2,000, six-month, 12% note on account from EMC Co.
31	Accrued interest revenue on all notes receivable.

Recording a note receivable and accruing interest revenue ***(Obj. 5)***

E5-11 Record the following transactions in Postino Company's journal:

19X6	
Apr. 1	Loaned $8,000 to Lee Franz on a one-year, 10% note.
Dec. 31	Accrued interest revenue on the Franz note.
19X7	
Apr. 1	Received the maturity value of the note from Franz.

Recording notes receivable, discounting a note, and reporting the contingent liability in a note ***(Obj. 5)***

E5-12 Rider Systems, Inc., sells on account. When customer accounts become three months old, Rider converts the accounts to notes receivable and immediately discounts the notes—with recourse—to a bank. During 19X4, Rider completed these transactions:

Aug. 29	Sold goods on account to V. Moyer, $3,900.
Dec. 1	Received a $3,900, 60-day, 10% note from V. Moyer in satisfaction of his past-due account receivable.
1	Sold the Moyer note by discounting it to a bank for $3,600.

Required

1. Record the transactions in Rider Systems' journal.
2. Write the note to the financial statements that will disclose the contingent liability at December 31.

Evaluating ratio data ***(Obj. 6)***

E5-13 Goldstein-Migel Co., a department store, reported the following amounts in its 19X6 financial statements. The 19X5 figures are given for comparison.

	19X6		19X5	
Current assets:				
Cash		$ 4,000		$ 9,000
Short-term investments		23,000		11,000
Accounts receivable	$80,000		$74,000	
Less Allowance for uncollectibles	7,000	73,000	6,000	68,000
Inventory		192,000		189,000
Prepaid insurance		2,000		2,000
Total current assets		294,000		279,000
Total current liabilities		$114,000		$107,000
Net sales		$703,000		$732,000

Required

1. Determine whether the acid-test ratio improved or deteriorated from 19X5 to 19X6. How does Goldstein-Migel's acid-test ratio compare with the industry average of .90?
2. Compare the days' sales in receivables measure for 19X6 with the company's credit terms of net 30. What action, if any, should Goldstein-Migel take?

E5-14 Wal-Mart Stores, Inc., is the largest retailer in the United States. Recently, Wal-Mart reported these figures in millions of dollars:

Analyzing a company's financial statements ***(Obj. 6)***

	19X9	19X8
Net sales	$43,887	$32,602
Receivables at end of year	419	305

The Wal-Mart financial statements include no uncollectible-account expense or allowance for uncollectibles.

Required

1. Compute Wal-Mart's average collection period on receivables during 19X9.
2. Why are Wal-Mart's receivables so low? How can Wal-Mart have $419 million of receivables at January 31, 19X9, and no significant allowance for uncollectibles?

Reporting investment and receivables transactions on the statement of cash flows ***(Obj. 7)***

E5-15 Arden, Inc., is a manufacturer of cosmetics, specializing in products for sensitive skin. During 19X7, Kmart and Target offered Arden products for the first time, so 19X7 was Arden's best year ever. Net income reached $80 million on sales of $430 million, and Arden collected $440 million from customers.

The increased volume of sales and collections left Arden with excess cash during the year, so the company invested $18 million in 90-day U.S. Treasury bills. These were the first short-term investments in the company's history. Arden cashed in $16 million of the T-bills during the year. At December 31, 19X7, Arden's interest revenue for the year totaled $1.3 million. Of this amount, Arden expects to collect $0.3 million early in 19X8 when the T-bills mature.

Required

Show what Arden, Inc., will report on its 19X7 cash flow statement as a result of these transactions.

CHALLENGE EXERCISE

E5-16 Crossroads Appliance Mart sells on store credit and manages its own receivables. Average experience for the past three years has been as follows:

Evaluating credit-card sales for profitability ***(Obj. 3)***

	Cash	Credit	Total
Sales	$200,000	$150,000	$350,000
Cost of goods sold	120,000	90,000	210,000
Uncollectible-account expense	—	4,000	4,000
Other expenses	34,000	27,000	61,000

Larry Salomon, the owner, is considering whether to accept bank credit cards (VISA, MasterCard). Typically, the availability of bank cards increases total sales by 10 percent. But VISA and MasterCard charge approximately 1% of sales. If Salomon switches to bank cards, he can save $2,000 on accounting and other expenses. He figures that cash customers will continue buying in the same volume regardless of the type of credit the store offers.

Required

Should Crossroads Appliance start selling on bank credit cards? Show the computations of net income under the present plan and under the bank credit-card plan.

PROBLEMS

(GROUP A)

P5-1A During the second half of 19X6, operations of Four Seasons, Inc., generated excess cash, which the company invested in securities, as follows:

Accounting for trading securities and held-to-maturity securities ***(Obj. 1, 2)***

July	3	Purchased 5,000 shares of common stock as a trading investment, paying $9.25 per share.
Aug.	14	Received semiannual cash dividend of $0.32 per share on the trading investment.
Sep.	15	Sold the trading investment for $10.50 per share.
Nov.	24	Purchased trading investments for $226,000.
Dec.	13	Purchased held-to-maturity investments for $106,000. The commercial paper will mature at $110,000 in 180 days.
	31	Accrued interest revenue, and adjusted the trading securities to their market value of $219,000.

Required

1. Record the transactions in the journal of Four Seasons. Explanations are not required.
2. Post to the Short-Term Investments accounts. Then show how to report the short-term investments on the Four Seasons balance sheet at December 31.

Reporting held-to-maturity investments and trading investments
(Obj. 2, 7)

P5-2A On September 12, 19X3, MIC Systems, Inc., purchased Microsoft commercial paper for $640,000. The paper will mature at $664,000 in 120 days (on January 10, 19X4), and MIC intends to hold the paper until its maturity.

MIC sold a trading investment in General Motors stock for $55,000 in October 19X3 after holding the stock for only one month. MIC had purchased the stock for $52,000.

Another cash excess developed in November 19X3, and MIC paid $112,000 for some notes receivable that it will hold in the hope of selling them at a profit early in January 19X4. The notes are scheduled to mature in August 19X4. At December 31, 19X3, the market value of these notes is $110,000, not including $1,000 of accrued interest that MIC has earned on the notes.

Required

Show what MIC Systems will report on its 19X3 income statement and statement of cash flows and on its December 31, 19X3, balance sheet for these transactions. Show all computations. Journal entries are not required.

Controlling cash receipts from customers
(Obj. 3)

P5-3A Dental Laboratory Service prepares crowns, dentures, and other dental appliances. All work is performed on account, with regular monthly billing to participating dentists. Melany Rank, accountant for Dental Laboratory Service, receives and opens the mail. Company procedure requires her to separate customer checks from the remittance slips, which list the amounts she posts as credits to customer accounts receivable. Rank deposits the checks in the bank. She computes each day's total amount posted to customer accounts and matches this total to the bank deposit slip. This procedure is intended to ensure that all receipts are deposited in the bank.

Required

As a consultant hired by Dental Laboratory Service, write a memo to management evaluating the company's internal controls over cash receipts from customers. If the system is effective, identify its strong features. If the system has flaws, propose a way to strengthen the controls.

Accounting for uncollectibles by the direct write-off and allowance methods
(Obj. 4)

P5-4A On May 31, Schlotzky, Inc., had a $219,000 debit balance in Accounts Receivable. During June, the company had sales revenue of $789,000, which included $640,000 in credit sales. Other data for June include

- Collections on accounts receivable, $581,400
- Write-offs of uncollectible receivables, $8,900

Required

1. Record uncollectible-account expense for June by the direct write-off method. Show all June activity in Accounts Receivable and Uncollectible-Account Expense.
2. Record uncollectible-account expense and write-offs of customer accounts for June by the allowance method. Show all June activity in Accounts Receivable, Allowance for Uncollectible Accounts, and Uncollectible-Account Expense. The May 31 unadjusted balance in Allowance for Uncollectible Accounts was $2,800 (credit), as the company closes its books at the end of each calendar quarter. Uncollectible-Account Expense was estimated at 2% of credit sales.
3. What amount of uncollectible-account expense would Schlotzky, Inc., report on its June income statement under the two methods? Which amount better matches expense with revenue? Give your reason.
4. What amount of *net* accounts receivable would Schlotzky, Inc., report on its June 30 balance sheet under the two methods? Which amount is more realistic? Give your reason.
5. How will what you have learned about uncollectible receivables help you manage a business?

Using the percentage of sales and aging approaches for uncollectibles
(Obj. 4)

P5-5A The June 30, 19X4, balance sheet of A-1 Healthcare, Inc., reports the following:

Accounts Receivable	$143,000
Allowance for Doubtful Accounts (credit balance)	3,200

At the end of each quarter, A-1 estimates doubtful-account expense to be 1½% of credit sales. At the end of the year, the company ages its accounts receivable and adjusts the balance in Allowance for Doubtful Accounts to correspond to the aging schedule. During the second half of 19X4, A-1 completes the following selected transactions:

Aug. 9	Made a compound entry to write off the following uncollectible accounts: Clif, Inc., $235; Matz Co., $188; and L. Norris, $706.
Sep. 30	Recorded doubtful-account expense based on credit sales of $130,000.
Oct. 18	Wrote off as uncollectible the $767 account receivable from Bliss Co. and the $430 account receivable from Micro Data.
Dec. 31	Recorded doubtful-account expense based on the following summary of the aging of accounts receivable.

Total Balance	Age of Accounts: 1–30 Days	31–60 Days	61–90 Days	Over 90 Days
$129,400	$74,600	$31,100	$14,000	$9,700
Estimated percentage uncollectible	0.1%	0.4%	5.0%	30.0%

Required

1. Record the transactions in the journal.
2. Open the Allowance for Doubtful Accounts, and post entries affecting that account. Keep a running balance.
3. Most companies report two-year comparative financial statements. If A-1's Accounts Receivable balance was $118,000 and the Allowance for Doubtful Accounts stood at $2,700 at December 31, 19X3, show how the company will report its accounts receivable on a comparative balance sheet for 19X4 and 19X3.

Uncollectibles, notes receivable, discounting notes, and accrued interest revenue ***(Obj. 4, 5)***

P5-6A Assume that **Del Monte Foods,** famous for its canned vegetables, completed the following selected transactions:

19X5

Nov. 1	Sold goods to Safeway Co., receiving a $24,000, three-month, 8% note.
Dec. 31	Made an adjusting entry to accrue interest on the Safeway note.
31	Made an adjusting entry to record doubtful-account expense based on an aging of accounts receivable. The aging analysis indicates that $197,400 of accounts receivable will not be collected. Prior to this adjustment, the credit balance in Allowance for Doubtful Accounts is $189,900.

19X6

Feb. 1	Collected the maturity value of the Safeway note.
23	Received a 90-day, 15%, $4,000 note from Bliss Co. on account.
Mar. 31	Discounted the Bliss Co. note to Lakewood Bank, receiving cash of $3,925.
June 23	Sold merchandise to Lear Corp., receiving a 60-day, 10% note for $9,000.
Aug. 22	Lear Corp. dishonored (failed to pay) its note at maturity; converted the maturity value of the note to an account receivable.
Nov. 16	Loaned $8,500 cash to McNeil, Inc., receiving a 90-day, 12% note.
Dec. 5	Collected in full from Lear Corp.
31	Accrued the interest on the McNeil, Inc., note.

Required

Record the transactions in the journal. Explanations are not required.

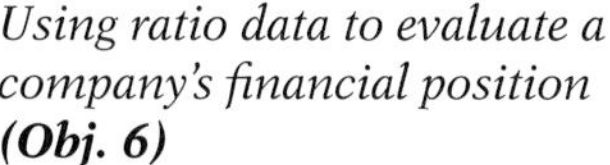

Using ratio data to evaluate a company's financial position ***(Obj. 6)***

P5-7A The comparative financial statements of Pinnacle East, Inc., for 19X9, 19X8, and 19X7 included the following selected data.

	19X9	19X8	19X7
		(In millions)	
Balance sheet:			
Current assets:			
Cash	$ 76	$ 80	$ 60
Short-term investments	140	174	122
Receivables, net of allowance for doubtful accounts of $6, $6, and $5, respectively	257	265	218
Inventories	429	341	302
Prepaid expenses	21	27	46
Total current assets	923	887	748
Total current liabilities	503	528	413
Income statement:			
Sales revenue	$5,189	$4,995	$4,206
Cost of sales	2,734	2,636	2,418

Required

1. Compute these ratios for 19X9 and 19X8:
   a. Current ratio
   b. Acid-test ratio
   c. Days' sales in receivables
2. Write a memo explaining to top management which ratio values showed improvement from 19X8 to 19X9 and which ratio values showed deterioration. Which item in the financial statements caused some ratio values to improve and others to deteriorate? Discuss whether this factor conveys a favorable or an unfavorable sign about the company.

(GROUP B)

Accounting for trading securities and held-to-maturity securities
(Obj. 1, 2)

P5-1B During the second half of 19X8, the operations of Picadilly, Inc., generated excess cash, which the company invested in securities, as follows:

July 2	Purchased 2,000 shares of common stock as a trading investment, paying $12.75 per share.
Aug. 21	Received semiannual cash dividend of $0.45 per share on the trading investment.
Sep. 16	Sold the trading investment for $13.50 per share.
Oct. 8	Purchased trading investments in stock for $136,000.
Nov. 11	Purchased held-to-maturity investments for $280,000. The commercial paper will mature in 150 days at $301,000.
Dec. 31	Accrued interest revenue, and adjusted the trading securities to their market value of $132,000.

Required

1. Record the transactions in the journal of Picadilly, Inc. Explanations are not required.
2. Post to the Short-Term Investments accounts, and show how to report the short-term investments on Picadilly's balance sheet at December 31.

Reporting held-to-maturity investments and trading investments
(Obj. 2, 7)

P5-2B In August 19X5, Oracle Corporation purchased as a trading investment some PepsiCo stock for $312,000. The stock headed down, and one month later, Oracle sold the stock for $309,000.

On November 16, 19X5, Oracle purchased a 90-day U.S. Treasury bill for $380,000. Oracle intends to collect the T-bill at its maturity value of $388,000.

Another cash excess developed in December, and Oracle paid $263,000 for some notes receivable that it will hold in the hope of selling them at a profit early in January 19X6. The notes are scheduled to mature in August 19X6. At December 31, 19X5, the market value of these notes is $262,000, not including $2,000 of accrued interest that Oracle has earned on the notes.

Required

Show what Oracle will report on its 19X5 income statement and statement of cash flows and on its December 31, 19X5, balance sheet for these transactions. Show all computations. Journal entries are not required.

Controlling cash receipts from customers
(Obj. 3)

P5-3B Oshman's Sporting Goods distributes merchandise to sporting goods stores. All sales are on credit, so virtually all cash receipts arrive in the mail. Menachem Fultz, the company president, has just returned from a trade association meeting with new ideas for the business. Among other things, Fultz plans to institute stronger internal controls over cash receipts from customers.

Required

Assume you are Menachem Fultz, the company president. Write a memo to employees outlining a set of procedures to ensure that all cash receipts are deposited in the bank and that the total amounts of each day's cash receipts are posted as credits to customer accounts receivable.

Accounting for uncollectibles by the direct write-off and allowance methods
(Obj. 4)

P5-4B On February 28, Dudley Curry Co. had a $75,000 debit balance in Accounts Receivable. During March, the company had sales revenue of $509,000, which included $445,000 in credit sales. Other data for March include

- Collections on accounts receivable, $431,600.
- Write-offs of uncollectible receivables, $3,500.

Required

1. Record uncollectible-account expense for March by the direct write-off method. Show all March activity in Accounts Receivable and Uncollectible-Account Expense.
2. Record uncollectible-account expense and write-offs of customer accounts for March by the allowance method. Show all March activity in Accounts Receivable, Allowance for Uncollectible Accounts, and Uncollectible-Account Expense. The February 28 unadjusted balance in Allowance for Uncollectible Accounts was $800 (debit), as the company closes

its books at the end of each calendar quarter. Uncollectible-Account Expense was estimated at 2% of credit sales.

3. What amount of uncollectible-account expense would Dudley Curry Co. report on its March income statement under the two methods? Which amount better matches expense with revenue? Give your reason.
4. What amount of *net* accounts receivable would Dudley Curry Co. report on its March 31 balance sheet under the two methods? Which amount is more realistic? Give your reason.
5. How will what you learned about uncollectible receivables help you manage a business?

Using the percentage of sales and aging approaches for uncollectibles ***(Obj. 4)***

P5-5B The June 30, 19X9, balance sheet of The Headliners Club, Inc., reports the following:

Accounts Receivable	$265,000
Allowance for Doubtful Accounts (credit balance)	7,100

At the end of each quarter, The Headliners Club estimates doubtful-account expense to be 2% of credit sales. At the end of the year, the company ages its accounts receivable and adjusts the balance in Allowance for Doubtful Accounts to correspond to the aging schedule. During the second half of 19X9, The Headliners Club completes the following selected transactions:

July 14	Made a compound entry to write off the following uncollectible accounts: C. H. Harris, $766; Graphics, Inc., $2,413; and B. McQueen, $134.
Sep. 30	Recorded doubtful-account expense based on credit sales of $141,400.
Nov. 22	Wrote off the following accounts receivable as uncollectible: Monet Corp., $1,345; Blocker, Inc., $2,109; and M Street Plaza, $755.
Dec. 31	Recorded doubtful-account expense based on the following summary of the aging of accounts receivable:

Total Balance	Age of Accounts: 1–30 Days	31–60 Days	61–90 Days	Over 90 Days
$296,600	$161,500	$86,000	$34,000	$15,100
Estimated percentage uncollectible	0.2%	0.5%	4.0%	50.0%

Required

1. Record the transactions in the journal.
2. Open the Allowance for Doubtful Accounts, and post entries affecting that account. Keep a running balance.
3. Most companies report two-year comparative financial statements. If The Headliners Club Accounts Receivable balance was $271,400 and the Allowance for Doubtful Accounts stood at $8,240 at December 31, 19X8, show how the company will report its accounts receivable in a comparative balance sheet for 19X9 and 19X8.

Uncollectibles, notes receivable, discounting notes, and accrued interest revenue ***(Obj. 4, 5)***

P5-6B Assume that Sherwin Williams, a major paint manufacturer, completed the following selected transactions:

19X4	
Dec. 1	Sold goods to Central Paint Co., receiving a $17,000, three-month, 10% note.
31	Made an adjusting entry to accrue interest on the Central Paint Co. note.
31	Made an adjusting entry to record doubtful-account expense based on an aging of accounts receivable. The aging analysis indicates that $355,800 of accounts receivable will not be collected. Prior to this adjustment, the credit balance in Allowance for Doubtful Accounts is $346,100.
19X5	
Feb. 18	Received a 90-day, 10%, $5,000 note from Altex Co. on account.
Mar. 1	Collected the maturity value of the Central Paint Co. note.
8	Discounted the Altex note to First State Bank, receiving cash of $4,894.
July 21	Sold merchandise to Logos, Inc., receiving a 60-day, 9% note for $4,000.
Sep. 19	Logos, Inc., dishonored (failed to pay) its note at maturity; converted the maturity value of the note to an account receivable.
Nov. 11	Loaned $40,000 cash to Consolidated, Inc., receiving a 90-day, 9% note.
Dec. 2	Collected in full from Logos, Inc.
31	Accrued the interest on the Consolidated, Inc., note.

Required

Record the transactions in the journal. Explanations are not required.

Using ratio data to evaluate a company's financial position ***(Obj. 6)***

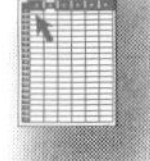

P5-7B The comparative financial statements of Mainline Sales Company for 19X8, 19X7, and 19X6 included the following selected data:

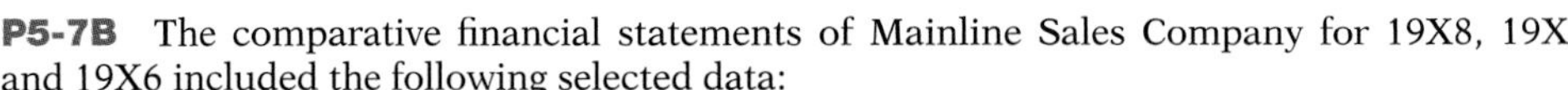

	19X8	19X7	19X6
		(In millions)	
Balance sheet:			
Current assets:			
Cash	$ 27	$ 26	$ 22
Short-term investments	93	101	69
Receivables, net of allowance for doubtful accounts of $7, $6, and $4, respectively	146	154	127
Inventories	438	383	341
Prepaid expenses	32	31	25
Total current assets	736	695	584
Total current liabilities	440	446	388
Income statement:			
Sales revenue	$2,671	$2,505	$1,944
Cost of sales	1,380	1,360	963

Required

1. Compute these ratios for 19X8 and 19X7:
   a. Current ratio
   b. Acid-test ratio
   c. Days' sales in receivables
2. Write a memo explaining to top management which ratio values showed improvement from 19X7 to 19X8 and which ratio values deteriorated. Which item in the financial statements caused some ratio values to improve and others to deteriorate? Discuss whether this factor conveys a favorable or an unfavorable sign about the company.

EXTENDING YOUR KNOWLEDGE

DECISION CASES

Uncollectible accounts and evaluating a business ***(Obj. 4, 5)***

Case 1. SunItaly Corporation performs service either for cash or on notes receivable. The business uses the direct write-off method to account for bad debts. Ann Adolfo, the owner, has prepared the company's financial statements. The most recent comparative income statements, for 19X8 and 19X7, are as follows:

	19X8	19X7
Total revenue	$220,000	$195,000
Total expenses	157,000	143,000
Net income	$ 63,000	$ 52,000

On the basis of the increase in net income, Adolfo seeks to expand operations. She asks you to invest $50,000 in the business. You and Adolfo have several meetings, at which you learn that notes receivable from customers were $200,000 at the end of 19X6 and $400,000 at the end of 19X7. Also, total revenues for 19X8 and 19X7 include interest at 15% on the year's beginning notes receivable balance. Total expenses include doubtful-account expense of $2,000 each year, based on the direct write-off basis. Adolfo estimates that doubtful-account expense would be 5% of sales revenue if the allowance method were used.

Required

1. Prepare for SunItaly Corporation a comparative single-step income statement that identifies service revenue, interest revenue, doubtful-account expense, and other expenses, all computed in accordance with generally accepted accounting principles.
2. Is SunItaly's future as promising as Adolfo's income statement makes it appear? Give the reason for your answer.

Case 2. Assume that you work in the corporate loan department of Bank of San Remo. Jake Butler, owner of Butler Builders, a manufacturer of mobile homes, has come to you seeking a loan for $1 million to expand operations. Butler proposes to use accounts receivable as collateral for the loan and has provided you with the following information from the most recent financial statements:

Estimating the collectibility of accounts receivable
(Obj. 4)

	19X9	19X8	19X7
		(In thousands)	
Sales	$1,475	$1,589	$1,502
Cost of goods sold	876	947	905
Gross profit	599	642	597
Other expenses	518	487	453
Net profit or (loss) before taxes	$ 81	$ 155	$ 144
Accounts receivable	$ 458	$ 387	$ 374
Allowance for doubtful accounts	23	31	29

Required

1. What analysis would you perform on the information Butler has provided? Would you grant the loan on the basis of this information? Give your reason.
2. What additional information would you request from Butler? Give your reason.
3. Assume that Butler provided you with the information requested in Requirement 2. What would make you change the decision you made in Requirement 1?

ETHICAL ISSUE

E-Z Finance Company is in the consumer loan business. It borrows from banks and loans out the money at higher interest rates. E-Z's bank requires E-Z to submit quarterly financial statements in order to keep its line of credit. E-Z's main asset is Notes Receivable. Therefore, Uncollectible-Account Expense and Allowance for Uncollectible Accounts are important accounts.

Alicia Johnston, the company's owner, likes net income to increase in a smooth pattern, rather than increase in some periods and decrease in other periods. To report smoothly increasing net income, Johnston underestimates Uncollectible-Account Expense in some periods. In other periods, Johnston overestimates the expense. She reasons that the income overstatements roughly offset the income understatements over time.

Required

Is E-Z's practice of smoothing income ethical? Why or why not?

FINANCIAL STATEMENT CASES

Case 1. Use data from the balance sheet and income statement of Lands' End, Inc., in Appendix A.

Accounts receivable and cash flows
(Obj. 7)

Required

a. Analyze the Receivables account to compute the amount of cash Lands' End collected from customers during the year ended February 2, 1996.
b. Open the Receivables account, and insert the balance at January 27, 1995. Record net sales (all on credit) and cash collections from customers for the year ended February 2, 1996. Post to the Receivables account, and compare its ending balance to the amount reported on the February 2, 1996, balance sheet.
c. Why is the Lands' End Receivables balance so low relative to net sales revenue?

Case 2. Obtain the annual report of a company of your choosing.

Accounts receivable, uncollectibles, and notes receivable
(Obj. 1, 5)

Required

a. How much did customers owe the company at the end of the current year? Of this amount, how much did the company expect to collect? How much did the company expect *not* to collect?
b. Assume that during the current year, the company recorded doubtful-account expense equal to 1% of net sales. Starting with the beginning balance, analyze the Allowance for Doubtful Accounts to determine the amount of the receivable write-offs during the current year.

c. If the company does not have notes receivable, you may skip this requirement. If notes receivable are present at the end of the current year, assume that their interest rate is 9%. Assume also that the company received no new notes receivable during the following year. Journalize these transactions, which took place during the following year:
    a. Received cash for 75% of the interest revenue earned during the year.
    b. Accrued the remaining portion of the interest revenue earned during the year.
    c. At year end, collected half the notes receivable.

GROUP PROJECT

Shannon Billings and Monica Salazar worked for several years as sales representatives for Xerox Corporation. During this time, they became close friends as they acquired expertise with the company's full range of copier equipment. Now they see an opportunity to put their experience to work and fulfill lifelong desires to establish their own business. Taft Community College, located in their city, is expanding, and there is no copy center within five miles of the campus. Business in the area is booming—office buildings and apartments are springing up, and the population of the Taft section of the city is growing.

Billings and Salazar want to open a copy center, similar to a Kinko's, near the Taft campus. A small shopping center across the street from the college has a vacancy that would fit their needs. Billings and Salazar each have $35,000 to invest in the business, but they forecast the need for $200,000 to renovate the store and purchase some of the equipment they will need. Xerox Corporation will lease two large copiers to them at a total monthly rental of $6,000. With enough cash to see them through the first six months of operation, they are confident they can make the business succeed. The two women work very well together, and both have excellent credit ratings. Billings and Salazar must borrow $130,000 to start the business, advertise its opening, and keep it running for its first six months.

Required

Assume two roles: (1) Billings and Salazar, the partners who will own Taft Copy Center; and (2) loan officers at Central National Bank.

1. As a group, visit a copy center to familiarize yourselves with its operations. If possible, interview the manager or another employee. Then write a loan request that Billings and Salazar will submit to Central National Bank with the intent of borrowing $130,000 to be paid back over three years. The loan will be a personal loan to the partnership of Billings and Salazar, not to Taft Copy Center. The request should specify all the details of Billings' and Salazar's plan that will motivate the bank to grant the loan. Include a budget for each of the first six months of operation.
2. As a group, interview a loan officer in a bank. Write Central National Bank's reply to the loan request. Specify all the details that the bank should require as conditions for making the loan.
3. If necessary, modify the loan request or the bank's reply in order to reach agreement between the two parties.

INTERNET EXERCISE

INTEL CORPORATION

The microprocessor is one of the greatest technological advancements in history. Commonly called the "computer chip," the microprocessor is the computer's "brain"—the place where all instructions are processed. The microchip has been responsible for the personal computer (PC) revolution. Indeed, from automobiles to toasters, the microchip has quickly become a part of our daily routine.

Intel Corporation, along with Texas Instruments, developed the first microchips. Today, over 80% of the world's PCs run on Intel chips.

Developing and enchancing microchips require a significant investment in both basic research and in chip manufacturing plants. Having the funds available to invest in these activities is crucial to helping Intel maintain its dominance in the microprocessor market. An examination of Intel's financial statements reveals that Intel holds huge amounts of cash and marketable securities.

Required

1. Go to Intel's home page at **http://www.intel.com/.**
2. Click on **Company Info** to learn more about Intel. This section has several interesting sites, including a listing of jobs available at Intel.
3. Click the highlighted text, **Investor Relations.** This area has many resources that allow investors to learn more about Intel.

4. Go to the financial statements by clicking the **Annual Report** icon.
   a. What were Intel's balances for the past two years for
      (i) Cash?
      (ii) Short-term Investments?
      (iii) Long-term Investments?
   b. What criteria does Intel use to classify its assets as:
      (i) Cash?
      (ii) Short-term Investments?
      (iii) Long-term Investments?
   c. What portion of Intel's Investments (Short-term and Long-term) are classified as
      (i) Trading securities?
      (ii) Available-for-sale securities?
      (iii) Held-to-maturity securities?
   d. How does Intel generate most of its cash—through operating, investing, or financing activities?
   e. Why does Intel maintain such a large portion of its assets as investments? Are Intel's investment strategy and accounting practices consistent with its stated objectives?
   f. Intel's major competitors, Cyrix and Advanced Micro Devices, hold 16% of their assets in cash and investments. How does this percentage compare to Intel's? Does Intel's cash and investment position relative to its competitors provide it with a competitive advantage? If so, how?

6

Accounting for Merchandise Inventory, Cost of Goods Sold, and the Gross Margin

Learning Objectives

After studying this chapter, you should be able to

1. Account for inventory by the periodic and perpetual systems
2. Apply the inventory costing methods: specific unit cost, weighted-average cost, FIFO, and LIFO
3. Identify the income effects and the tax effects of the inventory costing methods
4. Apply the lower-of-cost-or-market rule to inventory
5. Compute the effects of inventory errors on cost of goods sold and net income
6. Estimate inventory by the gross margin method
7. Use the gross margin percentage and the inventory turnover ratio to evaluate a business

Huntington Galleries, Inc.
Income Statement
For the Year Ended December 31, 1996
(In thousands)

Net sales		$165,900
Cost of goods sold		90,800
Gross margin		75,100
Operating expenses:		
Wage expense	$10,200	
Rent expense	8,400	
Insurance expense	1,000	
Depreciation expense	600	
Supplies expense	550	20,750
Operating income		54,350
Other revenue and (expense):		
Interest revenue	$ 1,000	
Interest expense	(1,500)	(500)
Income before tax		53,850
Income tax expense		18,750
Net income		$ 35,100

Huntington Galleries, Inc.
Balance Sheet
December 31, 1996
(In thousands)

Assets

Current:			
Cash		$ 2,850	
Short-term investments		1,600	
Note receivable		11,000	
Interest receivable		400	
Inventory		40,200	
Prepaid expenses		300	
Total current assets			56,350
Plant:			
Store fixtures and equipment	$33,200		
Less: Accumulated depreciation	3,000		30,200
Total assets			$86,550

Liabilities

Current:	
Accounts payable	$43,200
Unearned sales revenue	700
Wages payable	400
Interest payable	200
Income tax payable	3,800
Total current liabilities	48,300
Long term:	
Note payable	12,600
Total liabilities	60,900

Stockholders' Equity

Common stock	10,000
Retained earnings	15,650
Total stockholders' equity	25,650
Total liabilities and stockholders' equity	$86,550

"Over the past few years, we have been focusing on building net income, and our record-breaking 1996 profits show that our efforts have paid off. But when we took a hard look at our inventory costing method, we were amazed to find that we could eventually save millions of dollars in taxes just by switching methods."

—Brad Street, Controller of Huntington Galleries

Huntington Galleries, a Maryland-based furniture retailer, reported net income of $35.1 million for 1996, up 20% from the previous year. The reported figures continued the company's pattern of uninterrupted growth in profits. Wall Street responded favorably to the announcement, and Huntington's stock price rose $0.75.

Lori Huntington, chief executive officer of Huntington Galleries, attributed the strong performance to a demand for the company's high-end line of furniture during the second half of the year. In a report filed with the SEC, Huntington disclosed that the company switched from the *FIFO method* to the *LIFO method* of accounting for inventories. Brad Street, the controller of Huntington Galleries, explained that the company changed inventory methods to save on income taxes. He estimated that the switch in inventory methods will save Huntington Galleries $1.3 million over the next two years.

The experience of Huntington Galleries underscores the importance of *merchandise inventory.* Huntington is a **merchandising company**—a company that earns most of its revenue by selling products. As Huntington's balance sheet shows, inventory is the lifeblood of a merchandising entity—the entity's major current asset. What is the entity's major expense? It is **cost of goods sold** or **cost of sales,** the cost of the inventory that the business has sold to customers. For example, **Wal-Mart Stores, Inc.,** reported cost of goods sold at $74.6 billion and operating, selling, and administrative expenses at $15.0 billion in 1996. For many merchandising companies, cost of goods sold is greater than all other expenses combined. This is the case at Huntington Galleries, as the company's income statement shows.

If the business buys inventory that is in demand, it will be able to sell the goods at a profit. But there is much more to merchandising than buying and selling.

Accounting plays an important role in merchandising. The most obvious role is the recordkeeping required to stay abreast of quantities on hand in order to meet customer demand. Beyond that, there are several different methods of accounting for the cost of inventories. The chapter opening story refers to the FIFO and LIFO inventory methods, which you will learn about shortly. *FIFO* stands for "first-in, first-out." *LIFO* stands for "last-in, first-out." These popular methods have some distinct characteristics that managers, investors, and creditors need to understand. For example, FIFO and LIFO result in different amounts of reported income and different amounts of income tax. Huntington Galleries' switch from FIFO to LIFO will save the company $1.3 million in income taxes. In short, accounting for inventory goes far beyond recordkeeping.

We begin this chapter with the basic concept of accounting for inventories. Then we examine different inventory systems (perpetual and periodic), the different inventory methods (FIFO, LIFO, and average), and several related topics.

The Basic Concept of Inventory Accounting

The basic concept of accounting for inventory is simple. Huntington Galleries buys three chairs for $300 each, marks them up $200, and sells two chairs for the retail price of $500 each. Huntington's balance sheet and income statement report the following:

Balance Sheet (partial)	
Current assets:	
Cash	$XXX
Short-term investments	XXX
Accounts receivable	XXX
Inventory (1 chair @ $300)	300
Prepaid expenses	XXX

Income Statement (partial)	
Sales revenue	
(2 chairs @ $500)	$1,000
Cost of goods sold	
(2 chairs @ $300)	600
Gross margin	$ 400

Gross margin, also called **gross profit,** is the excess of sales revenue over cost of goods sold. It is called *gross* margin because operating expenses have not yet been subtracted. Gross margin minus all the operating expenses equals *net* income.

In practice, accounting for inventory is usually more complex than our simple example would suggest. Complexity arises from several sources. The following sections describe alternative ways to account for inventories.

Inventory Systems

Objective 1

Account for inventory by the periodic and perpetual systems

There are two main types of inventory accounting systems: the periodic system and the perpetual system. The **periodic inventory system** is used by businesses that sell relatively inexpensive goods. Convenience stores without optical-scanning cash registers do not keep a daily running record of every loaf of bread and every six pack of drinks they buy and sell. Instead, these stores count their inventory periodically—at least once a year—to determine the quantities on hand. The inventory amounts are used to prepare the annual financial statements. Businesses such as office supply outlets, restaurants, and small department stores also use the periodic inventory system.

LEARNING TIP Typically, a business counts its inventory when the quantity on hand is lowest, so that counting the inventory will be as simple as possible. For most retailers, such as Wal-Mart Stores, Inc., this is January 31.

Under the **perpetual inventory system,** the business maintains a running record of inventory on hand, usually on computer. This system achieves control over goods such as automobiles, jewelry, and furniture. The loss of one item would be significant, and this justifies the cost of a perpetual system. Because the cost of computers has come down, many small businesses are now using perpetual inventory systems for all types of goods.

Even under a perpetual system the business still counts the inventory on hand annually. The physical count establishes the correct amount of ending inventory and serves as a check on the perpetual records. The following chart compares the periodic and perpetual systems:

Periodic Inventory System	Perpetual Inventory System
• Does not keep a running record of all goods bought and sold.	• Keeps a running record of all goods bought and sold.
• Inventory counted at least once a year.	• Inventory counted once a year.
• Used for inexpensive goods.	• Used for all types of goods.

Perpetual Inventory System

Perpetual inventory records can be a computer printout like the Huntington Galleries record shown in Exhibit 6-1 on page 266. The quantities of goods on hand are updated daily, as inventory transactions occur. Many companies, such as Huntington Galleries, keep their perpetual records in terms of quantities only. We shall soon see how these data can be used to determine the cost of ending inventory and the cost of goods sold. Perpetual inventory records provide information for the following decisions:

1. When a customer asks how soon she can get six chairs, the salesperson can answer by referring to the perpetual inventory record. On November 5, the salesperson would reply that the company's stock ("quantity on hand") is low, and the customer may have to wait a few days. On November 7, the salesperson could offer immediate delivery.

2. The perpetual records alert the business to reorder when inventory becomes low. On November 5, the company would be wise to purchase inventory. Sales may be lost if Huntington cannot promise immediate delivery.

3. At November 30, Huntington prepares monthly financial statements. The perpetual inventory records show that the company's ending inventory of Early American chairs is 20 units. This information is used to prepare the financial statements.

Perpetual inventory systems are very sophisticated. For example, **Frito-Lay's** Decision Support System can print out the weekly sales of Ruffles potato chips by each route salesperson. In one case, Frito-Lay identified a drop in sales of tortilla chips by a particular chain of stores. Within two weeks, the company revised its marketing strategy and increased sales again. Without the perpetual system, this process would have taken three months.

Frito-Lay identified a drop in sales of tortilla chips by a particular chain of stores. Within two weeks, the company revised its marketing strategy and increased sales again.

ENTRIES UNDER THE PERPETUAL SYSTEM In the perpetual system, the business records purchases of inventory by debiting the Inventory account. When the business makes a sale, two entries are needed. The company records the sale in the usual manner—debits Cash or Accounts Receivable and credits Sales Revenue for the sale price of the goods. The company also debits Cost of Goods Sold (which is an expense account) and credits Inventory for cost. The debit to Inventory (for purchases) and the credit to Inventory (for sales) serve to keep an up-to-date record of the cost of inventory on hand. The Inventory account and the Cost of Goods Sold account carry a current balance during the period.

EXHIBIT 6-1
Perpetual Inventory Record—Quantities Only, Huntington Galleries

Item: Early American Chair			
Date	**Quantity Received**	**Quantity Sold**	**Quantity on Hand**
Nov 1			10
5		6	4
7	25		29
12		13	16
26	25		41
30		21	20
Totals	50	40	20

Exhibit 6-2 illustrates the accounting for inventory transactions in a perpetual system (and in a periodic system as well) at Huntington Galleries. Panel A gives the journal entries and the T-accounts, and Panel B presents the income statement and balance sheet effects. All amounts are assumed. Appendix A to this chapter, pages 309-315, illustrates the details of recording transactions in a perpetual inventory system.

In Exhibit 6-2, Panel A, the first entry to Inventory summarizes a lot of detail. The cost of the inventory, $560,000, is the *net* amount of the purchases, determined as follows (using assumed amounts):

Purchase price of the inventory from the seller	$600,000
– Purchase returns for damaged or otherwise unsuitable goods returned to the seller	(25,000)
– Purchase allowances granted by the seller	(5,000)
– Purchase discounts for early payment	(14,000)
+ Transportation cost to move the goods from the seller to the buyer (also called *freight in*)	4,000
= Net purchases of inventory	$560,000

A **purchase return** is a decrease in the cost of purchases because the buyer returned the goods to the seller. A **purchase allowance** is a decrease in the cost of purchases because the seller granted the buyer a subtraction (an allowance) from the amount owed. Because purchase returns and allowances both decrease the buyer's cost of merchandise purchases, they are often combined into a single account, Purchase Returns and Allowances. Throughout the remainder of the book, we often refer to net purchases simply as Purchases, as in Exhibit 6-2.

The cost of the goods purchased by Huntington Galleries during the year was $560,000. This is based on a general principle:

The cost of an asset = The sum of all the costs incurred to bring the asset to its intended purpose, net of all discounts

Therefore, the buyer's cost of transporting goods from the seller to the buyer is part of the purchase cost of the inventory. These transportation charges are *not* recorded as an expense.

Chapter appendix A gives additional details on accounting for transportation costs, purchase discounts, and purchase returns and allowances, as well as sales transactions.

Periodic Inventory System

In the periodic inventory system, the business does not keep a continuous record of the inventory on hand. Instead, at the end of the period, the business makes a physical count of the inventory on hand and applies the unit costs to determine

EXHIBIT 6-2
Recording and Reporting Inventory Transactions of Huntington Galleries—Perpetual and Periodic Systems (amounts assumed)

Perpetual System

PANEL A—Recording in the Journal and the T-accounts

1. Credit purchases of $560,000:

Inventory	560,000	
Accounts Payable..........		560,000

ASSETS	=	LIABILITIES	+	STOCKHOLDERS' EQUITY
+560,000	=	560,000	+	0

2. Credit sales of $900,000 (cost $540,000):

Accounts Receivable	900,000	
Sales Revenue..............		900,000

ASSETS	=	LIABILITIES	+	STOCKHOLDERS' EQUITY	+	REVENUES
+900,000	=	0			+	900,000

Cost of Goods Sold.................	540,000	
Inventory........................		540,000

ASSETS	=	LIABILITIES	+	STOCKHOLDERS' EQUITY	−	EXPENSES
−540,000	=	0			−	540,000

3. End-of-period entries:
No entries required. Both Inventory and Cost of Goods Sold are up to date.

INVENTORY AND COST OF GOODS SOLD ACCOUNTS

Inventory		Cost of Goods Sold	
100,000*	540,000	540,000	
560,000			
120,000			

*Beginning inventory was $100,000.

Periodic System

1. Credit purchases of $560,000:

Purchases..............................	560,000	
Accounts Payable..........		560,000

ASSETS	=	LIABILITIES	+	STOCKHOLDERS' EQUITY	−	EXPENSES
0	=	+560,000			−	560,000

2. Credit sales of $900,000:

Accounts Receivable	900,000	
Sales Revenue..............		900,000

ASSETS	=	LIABILITIES	+	STOCKHOLDERS' EQUITY	+	REVENUES
+900,000	=	0			+	900,000

3. End-of-period entries to update Inventory and record Cost of Goods Sold.
   a. Transfer the cost of beginning inventory ($100,000) to Cost of Goods Sold.

Cost of Goods Sold...........	100,000	
Inventory (beginning balance).....		100,000

   b. Record the cost of ending inventory ($120,000) based on a physical count.

Inventory (ending balance)	120,000	
Cost of Goods Sold ..		120,000

   c. Transfer the cost of purchases to Cost of Goods Sold.

Cost of Goods Sold..........	560,000	
Purchases		560,000

INVENTORY AND COST OF GOODS SOLD ACCOUNTS

Inventory		Cost of Goods Sold	
100,000*	100,000	100,000	120,000
120,000		560,000	
		540,000	

*Beginning inventory was $100,000.

(Continued)

the cost of ending inventory. This inventory figure appears on the balance sheet and is used to compute cost of goods sold.

The periodic system is also called the *physical system* because it relies on the actual physical count of inventory. To use the periodic system effectively, the company's owner must be able to control inventory by visual inspection. For example, when a customer inquires about quantities on hand, the owner or manager should be able to eyeball the goods in the store.

(Continued)

Perpetual System		Periodic System		
PANEL B—Reporting in the Financial Statements				
Income Statement (partial)				
Sales revenue	$900,000	Sales revenue		$900,000
Cost of goods sold	540,000	Cost of goods sold:		
Gross margin	$360,000	Beginning inventory	$100,000	
		Purchases	560,000	
		Ending inventory	(120,000)	
		Cost of goods sold		540,000
		Gross margin		$360,000
Ending Balance Sheet (partial)				
Current assets:		Current assets:		
Cash	$ XXX	Cash		$ XXX
Short-term investments	XXX	Short-term investments		XXX
Accounts receivable	XXX	Accounts receivable		XXX
Inventories	120,000	Inventories		120,000
Prepaid expenses	XXX	Prepaid expenses		XXX

ENTRIES UNDER THE PERIODIC SYSTEM In the periodic system, the business records purchases of inventory in the Purchases account (an expense account). Throughout the period, the Inventory account carries the beginning balance left over from the end of the preceding period. At the end of the period, the Inventory account must be updated for the financial statements. A journal entry removes the beginning balance, crediting Inventory and debiting Cost of Goods Sold. A second journal entry sets up the ending balance, based on the physical count. The debit is to Inventory, and the credit to Cost of Goods Sold. The final entry in this sequence transfers the amount of Purchases to Cost of Goods Sold. These end-of-period entries can be made during the closing process.

After the process is complete, Inventory has its correct balance of $120,000, and Cost of Goods Sold shows $540,000, regardless of which inventory system the company uses.

Compare the entries under both inventory systems in Exhibit 6-2 step by step. First study the perpetual system all the way through. On the income statement, the perpetual system reports cost of goods sold on a single line. Then study the periodic system, which reports a more detailed computation of cost of goods sold. Both inventory systems report the same amounts for inventory and cost of goods sold.

STOP & THINK Answer the following questions about various features of the perpetual inventory system and the periodic inventory system.

1. Do the perpetual and periodic inventory systems result in the same or different dollar amounts for Inventory and Cost of Goods Sold to be reported in the financial statements? Explain your answer.
2. a. Which inventory system records the cost of inventory purchased as an asset and then records the cost of inventory sold as expense?

   b. Which inventory system records the cost of inventory purchased as an expense (name the expense account) and then records the cost of inventory on hand at the end of the period as an asset?
3. Suppose your company produces microchips for use in manufacturing computer circuit boards. Technology is advancing rapidly, and you require monthly financial statements to remain competitive. Which inventory system should you use?

Answers

1. Both inventory systems result in the same amounts for Inventory and Cost of Goods Sold because the facts are the same regardless of the inventory system.

2. a. The *perpetual inventory system* records the cost of inventory purchased as an asset and then the cost of goods sold as an expense.

   b. The *periodic inventory system* records the cost of inventory purchased as an expense (the Purchases account) and then records the cost of inventory on hand at the end of the period as an asset.

3. You should use the *perpetual inventory system* because it gives up-to-date inventory information that can be used to prepare the financial statements at any time.

Cost of Goods Sold (Cost of Sales) and Gross Margin (Gross Profit)

Exhibit 6-2 illustrates the measurement of cost of goods sold (cost of sales) in the two inventory systems. In a perpetual system, cost of sales is simply the sum of all the amounts posted to the Cost of Goods Sold account throughout the period (see again Exhibit 6-2, Panel A). By contrast, the periodic system measures cost of sales only at the end of the period after a physical count of the inventory is done and the closing process is complete.

Using the periodic system, the cost-of-goods-sold computation from Exhibit 6-2 is as follows:

Cost of goods sold	
Beginning inventory	$100,000
+ Purchases (including transportation costs)	560,000
= Cost of goods available for sale	660,000
– Ending inventory	(120,000)
= Cost of goods sold	$540,000

The business began the period with $100,000 of inventory. During the period, it purchased goods costing $560,000. The sum of the beginning inventory plus the purchases equals the *cost of the goods available for sale* during the period, $660,000. Goods available are either in ending inventory, $120,000, or they were sold during the period. Cost of goods sold during the year was thus $660,000 – $120,000 = $540,000. Learn this model now because you will use it throughout your business career.

How Managers Use the Cost-of-Goods-Sold Model

Suppose you are the general manager of Huntington Galleries. You are planning for the next period and preparing a budget to guide your buying. You have examined the new lines of furniture offered by Drexel, Hickory, and Lane, your three main suppliers, and you've decided which sofas and chairs you wish to offer for the upcoming season. What is your next inventory decision? You must decide how much inventory to purchase. If you buy too much inventory, you may be unable to sell it and may even go bankrupt. If you buy too little, you will be unable to satisfy your customers, and they may take their business elsewhere. In short, your inventory buying decisions will eventually make or break the company.

How will you make the purchasing decision? The amount of inventory to purchase depends on three factors: budgeted cost of goods sold, budgeted ending inventory, and the beginning inventory with which you started the period. A rearrangement of the cost-of-goods-sold formula helps you budget purchases as follows (all budgeted amounts are assumed for the next period):

Cost of goods sold (based on the budget for the next period)	$600,000
+ Ending inventory (based on the budget for the next period)	150,000
= Cost of goods available for sale, as budgeted	750,000
– Beginning inventory (actual amount left over from the prior period)	(120,000)
= Purchases (how much inventory managers need to buy)	$630,000

Most managers use this formula to determine how much to spend on inventory, regardless of whether the business uses a perpetual or a periodic inventory system. The power of the cost-of-goods-sold model lies in the key information it captures: beginning and ending inventory levels, purchases, and cost of goods sold.

How Investors and Creditors Use the Cost-of-Goods-Sold Model

Investors and creditors analyze companies' financial statements to decide which stocks to buy and which companies they will lend money to. These outsiders must work with the company's financial statements, which do not reveal whether the company is using a perpetual or a periodic inventory system. To compare different companies, financial analysts convert companies' statements to a standard format. Appendix B to this chapter shows how investors and creditors can use the cost-of-goods-sold model to analyze a company's financial statements.

Gross Margin (Gross Profit)

As we saw earlier, *gross margin,* also called *gross profit,* is sales revenue minus cost of goods sold. A company's gross margin is one of its most important statistics. It reveals the company's success in selling its goods at a profit, before deducting operating expenses. "Gross" margin means *before operating expenses.* By contrast, "net" income means *after subtracting all expenses.* A humorous example illustrates the importance of earning a gross profit:

> Johnny and Susie operate a lemonade stand near a busy corner. Heading home from work on a hot day, Lee Jones, a neighbor, asks, "How much do you charge for a glass of lemonade?" "Ten cents," answers Johnny, whereupon Jones replies, "Pour me a big glass." While sipping the lemonade, Jones probes more deeply, "How much do you figure a glass of lemonade costs you?" "About a quarter," answers Susie. Jones thinks a minute and asks, "How do you expect to make any money selling lemonade for a dime if it costs you a quarter?" Johnny and Susie shoot back, "Volume. We'll make a profit if we have enough volume."

Businesses must sell their merchandise at a profit, or they will go bankrupt. For this reason, managers keep a close eye on the business's gross margin. Investors and creditors watch gross margin too. An increase in a company's gross margin means higher net income. A sharp downturn in the gross margin is cause for alarm.

Computing the Cost of Inventory

The Huntington Galleries inventory record in Exhibit 6-1 follows the common practice of recording quantities only. The company can multiply the quantity of 20 chairs on hand at November 30 by the unit cost of each chair to compute the value of the ending inventory for the balance sheet, as follows:

Quantity of Inventory on Hand × **Unit Cost** = **Cost of Inventory on Hand**

DETERMINING THE QUANTITY OF INVENTORY Many businesses—even those that use the perpetual system—physically count their inventory on the last day of the fiscal year. If you have worked at a grocery store or some other type of retail business, you will recall the process of "taking inventory." Some entities shut the business down to get a good count of inventory on hand.

Complications may arise in determining the inventory quantity. Suppose the business has purchased some goods that are in transit when the inventory is counted. Even though these items are not physically present, they should be included in the inventory count if title to the goods has passed to the purchaser. When title passes from seller to purchaser, the purchaser becomes the legal owner of the goods.

Another complication in counting inventory arises from consigned goods. In a **consignment** arrangement, the owner of the inventory (the *consignor*) transfers the goods to another business (the *consignee*). For a fee, the consignee sells the inventory on the owner's behalf. The consignee does *not* take title to the consigned goods and therefore should not include them in its own inventory. Consignments are common in retailing. Suppose Huntington Galleries is the consignee for a line of beds in its stores. Should Huntington include this consigned merchandise in its inventory count? No, because Huntington Galleries does not own the beds. Instead, the bed manufacturer—the consignor—includes the consigned goods in its inventory. A rule of thumb is to include in inventory only what the business owns.

DETERMINING THE UNIT COST OF INVENTORY As we've seen, *inventory cost* is the price the business pays to acquire the inventory—not the selling price of the goods. Suppose Huntington Galleries purchases furniture polish for $10 and offers it for sale at $15. The inventory is reported at its cost of $10 per unit, multiplied by the number of units owned, not at its selling price of $15.

Inventory cost includes invoice price, less any purchase discount, plus sales tax, tariffs, transportation charges, insurance while in transit, and all other costs incurred to make the goods ready for sale. *Net purchases* means the net cost of inventory acquired for resale, after subtracting any purchase discounts and purchase returns for goods sent back to the seller. In this chapter we use the terms *purchases* and *net purchases* interchangeably. Appendix A to this chapter gives more details on accounting for purchase discounts and purchase returns.

Inventory Costing Methods

Determining the unit cost of inventory is easy when the unit cost remains constant during the period. But the unit cost often changes. For example, during times of inflation, prices rise. The chair that cost Huntington Galleries $300 in January may cost $315 in June and $322 in October. Suppose Huntington sells 40 chairs in November. How many of them cost $300, how many cost $315, and how many cost $322? To compute the cost of goods sold and cost of inventory on hand, the accountant must have some way to assign the business's cost to each item sold. The four costing methods that GAAP allows are

1. Specific unit cost
2. Weighted-average cost
3. First-in, first-out (FIFO) cost
4. Last-in, first-out (LIFO) cost

A company can use any of these methods. Many companies use different methods for different categories of inventory. Here we use the periodic inventory system to illustrate the four inventory costing methods. We illustrate the methods under the perpetual method later in this chapter.

Objective 2

Apply the inventory costing methods: specific unit cost, weighted-average cost, FIFO, and LIFO

SPECIFIC UNIT COST Some businesses deal in inventory items that may be identified individually, such as automobiles, jewels, and real estate. These businesses usually cost their inventory at the specific unit cost of the particular unit. For instance, a Chevrolet dealer may have two vehicles in the showroom—a "stripped-down" model that cost $14,000 and a "loaded" model that cost $17,000. If the dealer sells the loaded model for $19,700, cost of goods sold is $17,000, the cost of the specific unit. The gross margin on this sale is $2,700 ($19,700 – $17,000). If the stripped-down auto is the only unit left in inventory at the end of the period, ending inventory is $14,000, the dealer's cost of the specific unit on hand.

The **specific-unit-cost method** is also called the *specific identification* method. This method is not practical for inventory items that have common characteristics, such as bushels of wheat, gallons of paint, or boxes of laundry detergent.

The weighted-average cost, FIFO (first-in, first-out) cost, and LIFO (last-in, first-out) cost methods are fundamentally different from the specific-unit-cost method. These methods do not assign to inventory the specific cost of particular units. Instead, they assume different flows of costs into and out of inventory.

WEIGHTED-AVERAGE COST The **weighted-average cost method,** often called the *average-cost method,* is based on the weighted-average cost of inventory during the period. Weighted-average cost is determined as follows: Divide the cost of goods available for sale (beginning inventory plus purchases) by the number of units available for sale (beginning inventory plus purchases). Compute the ending inventory and cost of goods sold by multiplying the number of units by the weighted-average cost per unit.

Suppose the business has 60 units of inventory available for sale during the period. Ending inventory consists of 20 units, and cost of goods sold is based on 40 units. Panel A of Exhibit 6-3 gives the data for computing ending inventory and cost of goods sold. Panel B shows the weighted-average cost computations.

EXHIBIT 6-3
Inventory and Cost of Goods Sold under Weighted-Average, FIFO, and LIFO Inventory Costing Methods

PANEL A—Illustrative Data

Beginning inventory (10 units @ $1,000 per unit)		$10,000
Purchases:		
No. 1 (25 units @ $1,400 per unit)	$35,000	
No. 2 (25 units @ $1,800 per unit)	45,000	
Total purchases		80,000
Cost of goods available for sale (60 units)		90,000
Ending inventory (20 units @ $? per unit)		?
Cost of goods sold (40 units @ $? per unit)		$?

PANEL B—Ending Inventory and Cost of Goods Sold

Weighted-Average Cost Method

Cost of goods available for sale—see Panel A (60 units @ average cost of $1,500* per unit)		$90,000
Ending inventory (20 units @ $1,500 per unit)		(30,000)
Cost of goods sold (40 units @ $1,500 per unit)		$60,000

$$^*\frac{\text{Cost of goods available for sale, \$90,000}}{\text{Number of units available for sale, 60}} = \text{Average cost per unit, \$1,500}$$

FIFO Cost Method

Cost of goods available for sale (60 units—see Panel A)		$90,000
Ending inventory (cost of the *last* 20 units available):		
20 units @ $1,800 per unit (from purchase No. 2)		(36,000)
Cost of goods sold (cost of the *first* 40 units available):		
10 units @ $1,000 per unit (all of beginning inventory)	$10,000	
25 units @ $1,400 per unit (all of purchase No. 1)	35,000	
5 units @ $1,800 per unit (from purchase No. 2)	9,000	
Cost of goods sold		$54,000

LIFO Cost Method

Cost of goods available for sale (60 units—see Panel A)		$90,000
Ending inventory (cost of the *first* 20 units available):		
10 units @ $1,000 per unit (all of beginning inventory)	$10,000	
10 units @ $1,400 per unit (from purchase No. 1)	14,000	
Ending inventory		(24,000)
Cost of goods sold (cost of the *last* 40 units available):		
25 units @ $1,800 per unit (all of purchase No. 2)	$45,000	
15 units @ $1,400 per unit (from purchase No. 1)	21,000	
Cost of goods sold		$66,000

		FIFO		LIFO		Weighted-Average
Sales revenue (assumed)		$100,000		$100,000		$100,000
Cost of goods sold:						
Goods available for sale (assumed)	$90,000		$90,000		$90,000	
Ending inventory	36,000		24,000		30,000	
Cost of goods sold		54,000		66,000		60,000
Gross margin		$ 46,000		$ 34,000		$ 40,000

Summary of Income Effects—When inventory unit costs are increasing

FIFO	LIFO	Weighted-average
FIFO—Highest ending inventory Lowest cost of goods sold Highest gross margin	LIFO—Lowest ending inventory Highest cost of goods sold Lowest gross margin	Weighted-average—Results fall between the extremes of FIFO and LIFO

Summary of Income Effects—When inventory unit costs are decreasing

FIFO	LIFO	Weighted-average
FIFO—Lowest ending inventory Highest cost of goods sold Lowest gross margin	LIFO—Highest ending inventory Lowest cost of goods sold Highest gross margin	Weighted-average—Results fall between the extremes of FIFO and LIFO

EXHIBIT 6-4
Income Effects of FIFO, LIFO, and Weighted-Average Inventory Methods

FIRST-IN, FIRST-OUT (FIFO) COST Under the **first-in, first-out (FIFO) method,** the company must keep a record of the cost of each inventory unit purchased. The unit costs used in computing the ending inventory may then be different from the unit costs used in computing the cost of goods sold. Under FIFO, the first costs into inventory are the first costs out to cost of goods sold—hence the name *first-in, first-out.* Ending inventory is based on the costs of the most recent purchases. In our example in Exhibit 6-3, the FIFO cost of ending inventory is $36,000. Cost of goods sold is $54,000. Panel A gives the data, and Panel B shows the FIFO computations.

LAST-IN, FIRST-OUT (LIFO) COST The **last-in, first-out (LIFO) method** also depends on the costs of particular inventory purchases. LIFO is the opposite of FIFO. Under LIFO, the last costs into inventory are the first costs out to cost of goods sold. This method leaves the oldest costs—those of beginning inventory and plus the earliest purchases of the period—in ending inventory. In our example in Exhibit 6-3, the LIFO cost of ending inventory is $24,000. Cost of goods sold is $66,000. Again, Panel A gives the data, and Panel B shows the LIFO computations.

Income Effects of FIFO, LIFO, and Weighted-Average Cost

In our discussion and examples, the cost of inventory rose during the accounting period. When inventory unit costs change, the different costing methods produce different cost of goods sold and ending inventory figures, as Exhibit 6-3 shows. When inventory unit costs are increasing, FIFO ending inventory is *highest* because it is priced at the most recent costs, which are the highest. LIFO ending inventory is *lowest* because it is priced at the oldest costs, which are the lowest. When inventory unit costs are decreasing, FIFO ending inventory is lowest, and LIFO is highest.

Exhibit 6-4 summarizes the income effects of the three inventory methods, using the data from Exhibit 6-3. Study the exhibit carefully, focusing on ending inventory, cost of goods sold, and gross margin.

The Income Tax Advantage of LIFO

Objective 3

Identify the income effects and the tax effects of the inventory costing methods

When prices are rising, applying the LIFO method results in the *lowest taxable income* and thus the *lowest income taxes.* Let's use the gross margin data of Exhibit 6-4.

	FIFO	LIFO	Weighted-Average
Gross margin	$46,000	$34,000	$40,000
Operating expenses (assumed)	26,000	26,000	26,000
Income before income tax	$20,000	$ 8,000	$14,000
Income tax expense (40%)	$ 8,000	$ 3,200	$ 5,600

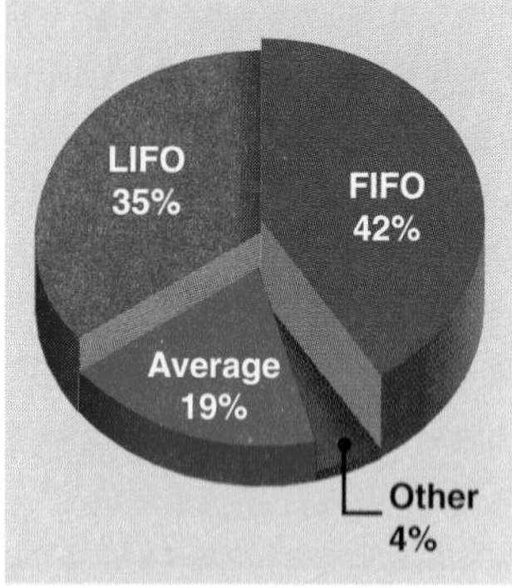

EXHIBIT 6-5
Use of the Various Inventory Methods

Income tax expense is lowest under LIFO ($3,200) and highest under FIFO ($8,000). The most attractive feature of LIFO is reduced income tax payments, which is why Huntington Galleries in our chapter opening story switched from the FIFO to the LIFO method.

The 1970s and early 1980s were marked by high inflation, so many companies changed to LIFO for its tax advantage. Exhibit 6-5, based on an American Institute of Certified Public Accountants (AICPA) survey of 600 companies, indicates that FIFO and LIFO are the most popular inventory costing methods.

GAAP and Practical Considerations: A Comparison of Inventory Methods

We may ask three questions to judge the three major inventory costing methods.

1. How well does each method match inventory expense—the cost of goods sold—to sales revenue on the income statement?
2. Which method reports the most up-to-date inventory amount on the balance sheet?
3. What effects do the methods have on income taxes?

LIFO better matches the current value of cost of goods sold with current revenue by assigning to this expense the most recent inventory costs. Therefore, LIFO produces the cost of goods sold figure that is closest to what it would cost the company to replace the goods that were sold. In this sense, LIFO produces the best measure of net income. In contrast, FIFO matches the oldest inventory costs against the period's revenue—a poor matching of current expense with current revenue.

FIFO reports the most current inventory costs on the balance sheet. LIFO can result in misleading inventory costs on the balance sheet because the oldest prices are left in ending inventory.

As shown earlier, LIFO results in the lowest income tax payments when prices are rising. Tax payments are highest under FIFO. When inventory prices are decreasing, tax payments are highest under LIFO and lowest under FIFO. The weighted-average cost method produces amounts between the extremes of LIFO and FIFO.

FIFO Produces Inventory Profits FIFO is sometimes criticized because it overstates income by so-called inventory profit during periods of inflation. Briefly, **inventory profit** is the difference between gross margin figured on the FIFO basis and gross margin figured on the LIFO basis. Exhibit 6-4 illustrates inventory profit. The $12,000 difference between FIFO and LIFO gross margins ($46,000 − $34,000) results from the difference in cost of goods sold. This

$12,000 amount is called *FIFO inventory profit, phantom profit,* or *illusory profit.* Why? Because to stay in business, the company must replace the inventory it has sold. The replacement cost of the merchandise is more closely approximated by the cost of goods sold under LIFO ($66,000) than by the FIFO amount ($54,000).

LIFO ALLOWS MANAGERS TO MANAGE REPORTED INCOME—UP OR DOWN LIFO is often criticized because it allows managers to manage net income. When inventory prices are rising rapidly and a company wants to show less income for the year (in order to pay less in taxes), managers can buy a large amount of inventory near the end of the year. Under LIFO, these high inventory costs immediately become expense—as cost of goods sold. As a result, the income statement reports a lower net income. Conversely, if the business is having a bad year, management may wish to increase reported income. To do so, managers can delay a large purchase of high-cost inventory until the next period. This high-cost inventory is not expensed as cost of goods sold in the current year. Thus, management avoids decreasing the current year's reported income. In the process, the company draws down inventory quantities, a practice known as *inventory liquidation.*

LIFO LIQUIDATION When the LIFO method is used and inventory quantities fall below the level of the previous period, the situation is called *LIFO liquidation.* To compute cost of goods sold, the company must dip into older layers of inventory cost. Under LIFO and during a period of rising inventory costs, that action shifts older, lower costs into cost of goods sold. The result is higher net income than the company would have reported if no LIFO liquidation had occurred. Managers try to avoid LIFO liquidation because it increases reported income and income taxes. **Owens-Corning,** the world's leading supplier of glass fiber materials, reported that LIFO liquidations added $2.7 million to its net income.

Owens-Corning, the world's leading supplier of glass fiber materials, reported that LIFO liquidations added $2.7 million to its net income.

INTERNATIONAL PERSPECTIVE Many companies manufacture their inventory in foreign countries, and companies that value inventory by the LIFO method often must use another accounting method for their inventories in foreign countries. Why? LIFO is allowed in the United States, but other countries are not bound by U.S. accounting practices. Australia and the United Kingdom, for example, do not permit the use of LIFO. Virtually all countries permit FIFO and the weighted-average cost method. Exhibit 6-6 lists a sampling of countries and whether or not they permit LIFO.

HIGHER INCOME OR LOWER TAXES? A company may want to report the highest income, and (as we've seen) FIFO meets this need when prices are rising. But the company also pays the highest income taxes under FIFO. When prices are falling, LIFO reports the highest income.

EXHIBIT 6-6
LIFO Use by Country

Country	LIFO Permitted?	Country	LIFO Permitted?
Australia	No	Netherlands	Yes
Brazil	Yes	Nigeria	No
Canada	Yes	Singapore	No
France	Yes	South Africa	Yes
Germany	Yes	Sweden	No
Hong Kong	No	Switzerland	No
Japan	Yes	United Kingdom	No
Mexico	Yes	United States	Yes

Which inventory method is better—LIFO or FIFO? There is no single answer to this question. Different companies have different motives for the inventory method they choose. **Polaroid Corporation** uses FIFO, **JC Penney Company** uses LIFO, and **Motorola, Inc.,** uses weighted-average cost. Still other companies use more than one method. The **Black & Decker Corporation,** best known for its power tools and small appliances, uses both LIFO and FIFO. The following excerpt is from a Black & Decker annual report (amount in millions):

Inventories $390

Notes to Consolidated Financial Statements

Note 1: Summary of Accounting Policies

Inventories: The cost of United States inventories is based on the last-in, first-out (LIFO) method; all other inventories are based on the first-in, first-out (FIFO) method. The cost of . . . inventories stated under the LIFO method represents approximately 40% of the value of total inventories.

Mid-Chapter SUMMARY PROBLEM FOR YOUR REVIEW

Suppose a division of IBM Corporation that handles computer components has these inventory records for January 19X6:

Date	Item	Quantity	Unit Cost	Sale Price
Jan. 1	Beginning inventory	100 units	$ 8	
6	Purchase	60 units	9	
13	Sale	70 units		$20
21	Purchase	150 units	9	
24	Sale	210 units		22
27	Purchase	90 units	10	
30	Sale	30 units		25

Company accounting records reveal that operating expense for January was $1,900.

Required

1. Prepare the January income statement, showing amounts for FIFO, LIFO, and weighted-average cost. Label the bottom line "Operating income." (Round figures to whole-dollar amounts.) Show your computations, and use the model on page 269 to compute cost of goods sold.
2. Suppose you are the financial vice president of IBM. Which inventory method will you use if your motive is to
   - **a.** Minimize income taxes?
   - **b.** Report the highest operating income?
   - **c.** Report operating income between the extremes of FIFO and LIFO?
   - **d.** Report inventory to balance at the most current cost?
   - **e.** Attain the best measure of net income for the income statement?

State the reason for each of your answers.

ANSWERS

Requirement 1

IBM CORPORATION
Income Statement for Component
Month Ended January 31, 19X6

	FIFO		LIFO		Weighted-Average	
Sales revenue		$6,770		$6,770		$6,770
Cost of goods sold:						
Beginning inventory	$ 800		$ 800		$ 800	
Net purchases	2,790		2,790		2,790	
Cost of goods available for sale	3,590		3,590		3,590	
Ending inventory	900		720		808	
Cost of goods sold		2,690		2,870		2,782
Gross margin		4,080		3,900		3,988
Operating expenses		1,900		1,900		1,900
Operating income		$2,180		$2,000		$2,088

Computations

Sales revenue:	(70 × $20) + (210 × $22) + (30 × $25) = $6,770
Beginning inventory:	100 × $8 = $800
Purchases:	(60 × $9) + (150 × $9) + (90 × $10) = $2,790
Ending inventory—FIFO:	90* × $10 = $900
LIFO:	90 × $8 = $720
Weighted-average:	90 × $8.975** = $808 (rounded from $807.75)

*Number of units in ending inventory = 100 + 60 − 70 + 150 − 210 + 90 − 30 = 90
**$3,590/400 units† = $8.975 per unit
†Number of units available = 100 + 60 + 150 + 90 = 400

Requirement 2

a. Use LIFO to minimize income taxes. Operating income under LIFO is lowest when inventory unit costs are increasing, as they are in this case (from $8 to $10). (If inventory costs were decreasing, income under FIFO would be lowest.)

b. Use FIFO to report the highest operating income. Income under FIFO is highest when inventory unit costs are increasing, as in this situation.

c. Use weighted-average cost to report an operating income amount between the FIFO and LIFO extremes. This is true in this situation and in others when inventory unit costs are increasing or decreasing.

d. Use FIFO to report inventory on the balance sheet at the most current cost. The oldest inventory costs are expensed as cost of goods sold, leaving in ending inventory the most recent (most current) costs of the period.

e. Use LIFO to attain the best measure of net income. LIFO produces the best matching of current expense with current revenue. The most recent (most current) inventory costs are expensed as cost of goods sold.

Perpetual Inventory Records Under FIFO, LIFO, and Weighted-Average Costing

Many companies keep their perpetual inventory records in quantities only, as illustrated in Exhibit 6-1. Other companies keep perpetual records in both quantities and dollar costs.

Huntington Galleries									
Item: Early American Chairs									
	Received			**Sold**			**Balance**		
Date	**Qty.**	**Unit Cost**	**Total**	**Qty.**	**Unit Cost**	**Total**	**Qty.**	**Unit Cost**	**Total**
Nov. 1							10	$300	$3,000
5				6	$300	$ 1,800	4	300	1,200
7	25	$310	$ 7,750				4	300	1,200
							25	310	7,750
12				4	300	1,200			
				9	310	2,790	16	310	4,960
26	25	320	8,000				16	310	4,960
							25	320	8,000
30				16	310	4,960			
				5	320	1,600	20	320	6,400
Totals	50		$15,750	40		$12,350	20		$6,400

EXHIBIT 6-7
Perpetual Inventory Record—FIFO Cost

FIFO Huntington Galleries uses the FIFO inventory method. Exhibit 6-7 shows Huntington's perpetual inventory record for the Early American chairs—in both quantities and dollar costs for the month of November.

To prepare financial statements at November 30, Huntington can take the ending inventory cost ($6,400) straight to the balance sheet. Cost of goods sold for the November income statement is $12,350. Here is Huntington's computation of cost of goods sold during November, with data taken from the perpetual record in Exhibit 6-7:

Cost of Goods Sold (Early American Chairs)—November	
Beginning inventory	$ 3,000
+ Purchases	15,750
= Cost of goods available for sale	18,750
– Ending inventory	(6,400)
= Cost of goods sold	$12,350

Some companies combine elements of the perpetual and periodic inventory systems—the perpetual system for control and preparation of the financial statements, and the periodic system for analysis.

LIFO Few companies keep perpetual inventory records at LIFO cost. The recordkeeping is expensive, and LIFO liquidations can occur during the year. To avoid these problems, LIFO companies can keep perpetual inventory records in terms of quantities only, as illustrated in Exhibit 6-1. For financial statements, they can apply LIFO costs at the end of the period. Other companies maintain perpetual inventory records at FIFO cost and then convert the FIFO amounts to LIFO costs for the financial statements. **Wal-Mart** and other companies make this adjustment through the LIFO reserve account illustrated on page 316. This topic is covered in intermediate accounting courses.

WEIGHTED-AVERAGE COST Perpetual inventory records can be kept at weighted-average cost. Most companies that use this method compute the weighted-average cost for the entire period. They apply this cost to both ending inventory and cost of goods sold. These procedures parallel those used in the periodic inventory system (Exhibit 6-2).

The use of computer software to account for inventory eases the computation of the average cost per unit each time additional goods are purchased. The new average unit cost is then applied to each subsequent sale until more goods are purchased, at which time another new average cost is computed.

STOP & THINK Examine Exhibit 6-7. What was Huntington Galleries' weighted-average unit cost during November? How much were ending inventory and cost of goods sold at weighted-average unit cost? What was the cost of goods available for sale?

Answers

$$\textbf{Weighted-average unit cost} = \frac{\$3{,}000 + \$15{,}750}{10 \text{ units} + 50 \text{ units}} = \frac{\$18{,}750}{60 \text{ units}} = \$312.50$$

Ending inventory = 20 units × $312.50	=	**$ 6,250**
Cost of goods sold = 40 units × $312.50	=	**12,500**
Cost of goods available for sale	=	**$18,750**

Accounting Principles and Their Relevance to Inventories

Several of the generally accepted accounting principles have special relevance to inventories. Among these principles are the consistency principle, the disclosure principle, the materiality concept, and accounting conservatism.

Consistency Principle

The **consistency principle** states that businesses should use the same accounting methods and procedures from period to period. Consistency makes it possible to compare a company's financial statements from one period to the next.

Suppose you are analyzing a company's net income pattern over a two-year period. The company switched from LIFO to FIFO during that time. Its net income increased dramatically but only as a result of the change in inventory method. If you did not know of the change, you might believe that the company's income increased because of improved operations, which is not the case.

The consistency principle does not require that all companies within an industry use the same accounting method. Nor does it mean that a company may *never* change its accounting methods. However, a company making an accounting change must disclose the effect of the change on net income. **Sun Company, Inc.**, an oil company, disclosed the following in a note to its annual report:

> EXCERPT FROM NOTE 6 OF THE SUN COMPANY FINANCIAL STATEMENTS
> . . . Sun changed its method of accounting for the cost of crude oil and refined product inventories . . . from the FIFO method to the LIFO method. Sun believes that the use of the LIFO method better matches current costs with current revenues. . . . The change decreased the 19X1 net loss . . . by $3 million. . . .

Disclosure Principle

The **disclosure principle** holds that a company's financial statements should report enough information for outsiders to make knowledgeable decisions about the company. In short, the company should report *relevant, reliable,* and *comparable* information about its economic affairs. With respect to inventories, the disclosure principle means disclosing the method or methods in use. Without knowledge of the inventory method, a banker could gain an unrealistic impression of a company and make an unwise lending decision. For example, suppose the banker is comparing two companies—one using LIFO and the other, FIFO. The FIFO company reports higher net income, but only because it uses a particular inventory method. Without knowledge of the accounting methods the companies are using, the banker could loan money to the wrong business or could refuse a loan to a promising customer. Appendix B to this chapter shows how the banker can convert the LIFO company's net income to the FIFO basis in order to compare the two companies.

Materiality Concept

The **materiality concept** states that a company must perform strictly proper accounting *only* for items and transactions that are significant to the business's financial statements. Information is significant—or, in accounting terminology, *material*—when its inclusion and correct presentation in the financial statements would cause a statement user to change a decision because of that information. Immaterial—nonsignificant—items justify less-than-perfect accounting. The inclusion and proper presentation of *immaterial* items would not affect a statement user's decision. The materiality concept frees accountants from having to compute and report every last item in strict accordance with GAAP. Thus, the materiality concept reduces the cost of recording accounting information.

How does a business decide where to draw the line between the material and the immaterial? This decision rests to a great degree on how large the business is. The fast-food chain **Wendy's,** for example, has close to $500 million in assets. Management would likely treat as immaterial a $100 loss of inventory due to spoilage. A loss of this amount is immaterial to Wendy's total assets and net income, so company accountants may not report the loss separately. Will this accounting treatment affect anyone's decision about Wendy's? Probably not, so it doesn't matter whether the loss is reported separately or simply imbedded in cost of goods sold.

Accounting Conservatism

Conservatism in accounting means reporting items in the financial statements at amounts that lead to the gloomiest immediate financial results. Conservatism comes into play when there are alternative ways to account for an item. What advantage does conservatism give a business? Management often looks on the brighter side of operations and may overstate a company's income and asset values. Many accountants regard conservatism as a counterbalance to management's optimistic tendencies. The goal is for financial statements to present realistic figures.

Conservatism appears in accounting guidelines such as "anticipate no gains, but provide for all probable losses" and "if in doubt, record an asset at the lowest reasonable amount and a liability at the highest reasonable amount."

Conservatism directs accountants to decrease the accounting value of an asset if it appears unrealistically high—even if no transaction occurs. Assume that a company paid $35,000 for inventory that has become obsolete and whose current value is only $12,000. Conservatism dictates that the inventory be *written down* (that is, decreased) to $12,000.

Lower-of-Cost-or-Market Rule

Objective 4

Apply the lower-of-cost-or-market rule to inventory

The **lower-of-cost-or-market rule** (abbreviated as LCM) shows accounting conservatism in action. LCM requires that inventory be reported in the financial statements at whichever is lower—its historical cost or its market value. Applied to inventories, *market value* generally means *current replacement cost* (that is, how much the business would have to pay now to purchase the amount of inventory that it has on hand). If the replacement cost of inventory falls below its historical cost, the business must write down the value of its goods because of the likelihood of incurring a loss on the inventory. GAAP requires this departure from historical cost accounting. The business reports ending inventory at its LCM value on the balance sheet. All this can be done automatically by a computerized accounting system. How is the write-down accomplished?

Suppose a business paid $3,000 for inventory on September 26. By December 31, its value has fallen. The inventory can now be replaced for $2,200. Market value is below cost, and the December 31 balance sheet reports this inventory at its LCM value of $2,200. Usually, the market value of inventory is higher than historical cost, so inventory's accounting value is cost for most companies. Exhibit 6-8 presents the effects of LCM on the income statement and the balance

EXHIBIT 6-8
Lower-of-Cost-or-Market (LCM) Effects

Balance Sheet

Current assets:		
Cash	$ XXX	
Short-term investments	XXX	
Accounts receivable	XXX	
Inventories, at market (which is lower than $3,000 cost)	**2,200**	
Prepaid expenses	XXX	
Total current assets	$X,XXX	

Income Statement

Sales revenue		$20,000
Cost of goods sold:		
Beginning inventory (LCM = Cost)	**$ 2,800**	
Net purchases	11,000	
Cost of goods available for sale	13,800	
Ending inventory—		
Cost = $3,000		
Replacement cost (market value) = $2,200		
LCM = Market	**2,200**	
Cost of goods sold		11,600
Gross margin		$ 8,400

sheet. The exhibit shows that the lower of (a) cost or (b) market value—the replacement cost—is the relevant amount for valuing inventory on the balance sheet.

Examine the income statement in Exhibit 6-8. What expense absorbs the impact of the $800 inventory write-down? Cost of goods sold is increased by $800 because ending inventory is $800 less at market ($2,200) than at cost ($3,000).

	Ending Inventory at		
	Cost	LCM	
Cost of goods available for sale	$13,800	$13,800	
Ending inventory:			
Cost	3,000		$800 lower
Replacement cost (market value)		2,200	at LCM
Cost of goods sold	$10,800	$11,600	$800 higher at LCM

Companies often disclose LCM in notes to their financial statements, as shown here for **CBS, Inc.**, the television broadcasting conglomerate:

> NOTE 1: STATEMENT OF SIGNIFICANT ACCOUNTING POLICIES
> *Inventories.* Inventories are stated at the *lower of cost* (principally based on average cost) *or market value.* [Emphasis added.]

Effects of Inventory Errors

Objective 5

Compute the effects of inventory errors on cost of goods sold and net income

Businesses count their inventories at the end of the period. In the process of counting the items, applying unit costs, and computing amounts, errors may arise. As the period 1 segment of Exhibit 6-9 on page 282 shows, an error in the ending inventory amount creates errors in the amounts for cost of goods sold and gross margin. Compare period 1, when ending inventory is overstated and cost of goods sold is understated, each by $5,000, with period 3, which is correct. Period 1 should look exactly like period 3.

	Period 1		Period 2		Period 3	
	Ending Inventory Overstated by $5,000		Beginning Inventory Overstated by $5,000		Correct	
Sales revenue		$100,000		$100,000		$100,000
Cost of goods sold:						
Beginning inventory	$10,000		$15,000		$10,000	
Net purchases	50,000		50,000		50,000	
Cost of goods available for sale	60,000		65,000		60,000	
Ending inventory	15,000		10,000		10,000	
Cost of goods sold		45,000		55,000		50,000
Gross margin		$ 55,000		$ 45,000		$ 50,000
			$100,000			

Source: The authors thank Carl High for this example.

EXHIBIT 6-9
Inventory Errors: An Example

Recall that one period's ending inventory is the next period's beginning inventory. Thus, the error in ending inventory carries over into the next period; note the amounts in color in Exhibit 6-9.

Because ending inventory is *subtracted* in computing cost of goods sold in one period and the same amount is *added* as beginning inventory to compute next period's cost of goods sold, the error's effect cancels out at the end of the second period. The overstatement of cost of goods sold in period 2 counterbalances the understatement in cost of goods sold in period 1. Thus, the total gross margin amount for the two periods is the correct $100,000 figure whether or not an error entered into the computation. These effects are summarized in Exhibit 6-10.

Inventory errors cannot be ignored simply because they counterbalance, however. Suppose you are analyzing trends in the business's operations. Exhibit 6-9 shows a drop in gross margin from period 1 to period 2, followed by an increase in period 3. But that picture of operations is untrue because of the accounting error. The correct gross margin is $50,000 for each period. Providing accurate information for decision making requires that all inventory errors be corrected.

Ethical Issues in Inventory Accounting

No area of accounting has a deeper ethical dimension than inventory. Managers of companies whose profits do not meet stockholder expectations are sometimes tempted to "cook the books" to increase reported income. The increase in reported income may lead investors and creditors into thinking the business is more successful than it really is.

What do managers hope to gain from the fraudulent accounting? In some cases, they are trying to keep their jobs. In other cases, their bonuses are tied to

EXHIBIT 6-10
Effects of Inventory Errors

	Period 1		Period 2	
Inventory Error	Cost of Goods Sold	Gross Margin and Net Income	Cost of Goods Sold	Gross Margin and Net Income
Period 1 Ending inventory overstated	Understated	Overstated	Overstated	Understated
Period 1 Ending inventory understated	Overstated	Understated	Understated	Overstated

reported income: the higher the company's net income, the higher the managers' bonuses. In still other cases, the business may need a loan. Financial statements that report high profits and large inventory values are more likely to impress lenders than low net income and inventory amounts.

There are two main schemes for cooking the books. The easiest, and the most obvious, is simply to overstate ending inventory. In the preceding section on the effects of inventory errors, we saw how an error in ending inventory affects net income. A company can intentionally overstate its ending inventory. Such an error understates cost of goods sold and overstates net income and retained earnings, as shown in the accounting equation. The upward-pointing arrows indicate an overstatement—reporting more assets and equity than are actually present:

ASSETS	=	LIABILITIES	+	STOCKHOLDERS' EQUITY
↑	=	0	+	↑

Remember that an inventory error has an offsetting effect in the next period. This means that managers who misstate ending inventory can only hope to "buy some time" by hyping reported income in the short term. Next period's net income will be lower as a result of this period's error. As with all other deceptions, an inventory misstatement comes back to haunt the business.

The second way of using inventory to cook the books involves sales. Sales schemes are more complex than simple inventory overstatements. **Datapoint Corporation** and **MiniScribe,** both computer-related concerns, were charged with creating fictitious sales to boost their reported profits.

Datapoint is alleged to have hired drivers to transport its inventory around San Antonio so that the goods could not *be physically counted.*

Datapoint is alleged to have hired drivers to transport its inventory around San Antonio so that the goods could *not* be physically counted. Datapoint's logic seemed to be that excluding the goods from ending inventory would imply that the goods had been sold. The faulty reasoning broke down when the trucks returned the goods to Datapoint's warehouse. Datapoint had far too much in sales returns. What would you think of a company with $10 million in sales and $4 million worth of the goods were returned by customers?

MiniScribe is alleged to have cooked its books by shipping boxes of bricks labeled as computer parts to its distributors right before year end. The accounting equations show how the scheme affected MiniScribe's reported figures (assuming sales of $10 million and cost of goods sold of $6 million):

	ASSETS	=	LIABILITIES	+	STOCKHOLDERS' EQUITY
Sales	10	=	0	+	10
Cost of goods sold	− 6	=	0	−	6
Net effect	4	=	0	+	4

The bogus transactions increased the company's assets and stockholders' equity by $4 million—but only temporarily.

The distributors refused to accept the goods and returned them to MiniScribe—but in the next accounting period. In the earlier period, MiniScribe recorded sales revenue and temporarily reported millions of dollars of sales and income that did not exist. Again, the scheme boomeranged in the next period when MiniScribe had to record the sales returns. In virtually every area, accounting imposes a discipline that should keep every business honest in its financial reporting.

EXHIBIT 6-11
Estimating Ending Inventory

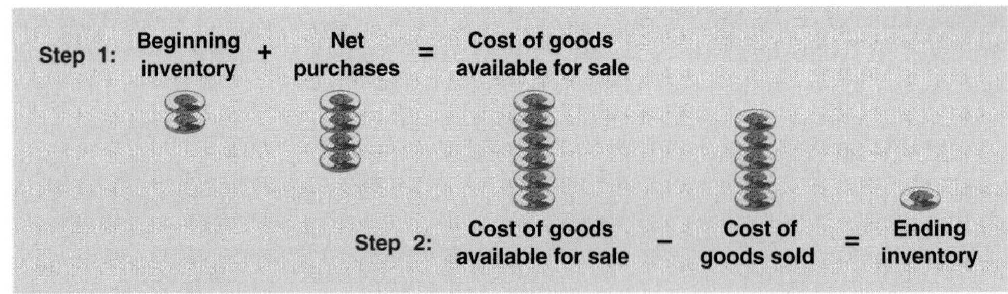

Estimating Inventory

> *Objective 6*
> Estimate inventory by the gross margin method

Often a business must *estimate* the value of its inventory. Because of cost and inconvenience, few companies physically count their inventories at the end of each month, yet they may need monthly financial statements. Suppose the company does not use the perpetual inventory system and thus cannot determine ending inventory by looking at the Inventory account.

A fire may destroy inventory, and to file an insurance claim, the business must estimate the value of its loss. In this case, the business needs to know the value of ending inventory but cannot count it. A widely used method for estimating ending inventory is the *gross margin method.*

Gross Margin (Gross Profit) Method

The **gross margin method,** also known as the *gross profit method,* is a way of estimating inventory on the basis of the familiar cost-of-goods-sold model.

	Beginning inventory
+	**Net purchases**
=	**Cost of goods available for sale**
−	**Ending inventory**
=	**Cost of goods sold**

Rearranging *ending inventory* and *cost of goods sold* makes the model useful for estimating ending inventory and is illustrated in the following equations and in Exhibit 6-11:

	Beginning inventory
+	**Net purchases**
=	**Cost of goods available for sale**
−	**Cost of goods sold**
=	**Ending inventory**

Suppose a fire destroys your business's inventory. To collect insurance, you must estimate the cost of the ending inventory. Beginning inventory and net purchases amounts may be taken directly from the accounting records. Sales Revenue less Sales Returns and Allowances and Sales Discounts indicates net sales up to the date of the fire. Using the entity's normal *gross margin rate* (that is, gross margin divided by net sales revenue), you can estimate cost of goods sold. The last step is to subtract cost of goods sold from goods available to estimate ending inventory. Exhibit 6-12 illustrates the gross margin method.

EXHIBIT 6-12
Gross Margin Method of Estimating Inventory
(amounts assumed)

Beginning inventory		$14,000
Net purchases		66,000
Cost of goods available for sale		80,000
Cost of goods sold:		
Net sales revenue	$100,000	
Less estimated gross margin of 40%	40,000	
Estimated cost of goods sold		60,000
Estimated cost of *ending inventory*		$20,000

Accountants, managers, and auditors use the gross margin method to test the overall reasonableness of an ending inventory amount that has been determined by a physical count. This method helps to detect large errors.

STOP & THINK Beginning inventory is $70,000, net purchases total $292,000, and net sales are $480,000. With a normal gross margin rate of 40% of sales, how much is ending inventory?

Answer: $74,000 = [$70,000 + $292,000 – (0.60 × $480,000)]

Analyzing Financial Statements—Use of Accounting Information in Decision Making

Objective 7

Use the gross margin percentage and the inventory turnover ratio to evaluate a business

To manage the firm, owners and managers focus on the best way to sell the company's inventory. They use several ratios to evaluate operations.

Gross Margin Percentage

A key decision-making tool for a merchandiser is based on gross margin, which we've seen equals sales revenue minus cost of goods sold. Merchandisers strive to increase their **gross margin percentage,** which is computed as follows for Huntington Galleries, Inc.:

$$\textbf{Gross margin percentage} = \frac{\textbf{Gross margin*}}{\textbf{Net sales revenue}} = \frac{\$75{,}100}{\$165{,}900} = 0.453$$

$$= 45.3\%$$

The gross margin (or gross profit) percentage is one of the most carefully watched measures of profitability. A 45% gross margin means that each dollar of sales generates 45 cents of gross profit. On average, the goods cost the seller 55 cents. For most firms, the gross margin percentage changes little from year to year. A small downturn may signal an important drop in income. A small change in the gross margin percentage usually indicates a sizable shift in profitability.

Huntington Galleries' gross margin percentage of 45.3% compares very favorably with the industry average for furniture retailers, which is 40.4 percent. By contrast, the average gross margin percentage is 14.1% for automobile dealers, 22.8% for grocery stores, and 55.7% for restaurants, according to Robert Morris Associates' *Annual Statement Studies.* Exhibit 6-13 compares Huntington Galleries' gross margin to that of **Wal-Mart.**

EXHIBIT 6-13
Gross Margin on $1.00 of Sales for Two Merchandisers

Inventory Turnover

Owners and managers strive to sell inventory as quickly as possible because it generates no profit until it is sold. The faster the sales occur, the higher the company's income. The slower the sales, the lower the company's income. Ideally, a business could operate with zero inventory. Most businesses, however, including retailers such as Huntington Galleries, must keep display goods on hand for customers. **Inventory turnover,** the ratio of cost of goods sold to average inventory, indicates how rapidly inventory is sold. Its computation for Huntington Galleries, Inc., is as follows:

$$\textbf{Inventory turnover} = \frac{\textbf{Cost of goods sold*}}{\textbf{Average inventory}} = \frac{\textbf{Cost of goods sold}}{\left(\textbf{Beginning inventory} + \textbf{Ending inventory*}\right) \div 2}$$

$$= \frac{\$90{,}800}{(\$38{,}600^{**} + \$40{,}200)/2} = \text{2.3 times per year (about every 159 days)}$$

*These numbers are taken from the income statement on page 262.
**This amount is assumed.

EXHIBIT 6-14
Rate of Inventory Turnover for Two Retailers

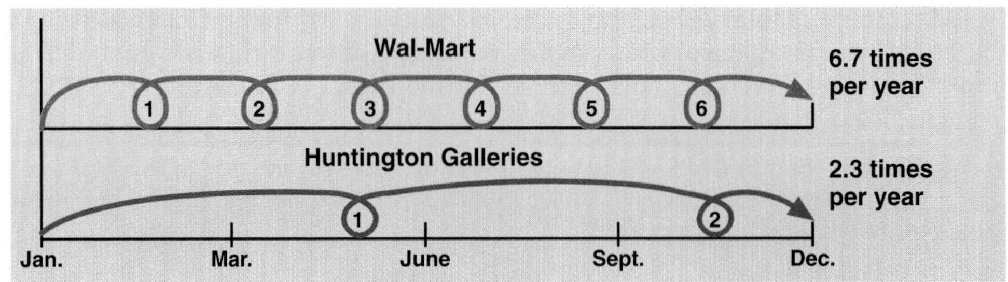

Inventory turnover is usually computed for an annual period, and the relevant cost of goods sold figure is the amount for the entire year. Average inventory is computed from the beginning and ending inventory amounts. (The Huntington Galleries beginning inventory would be taken from the company's balance sheet at the end of the preceding year; the other figures we need can be found in Huntington's financial statements on page 262.) The resulting inventory turnover statistic shows how many times the average level of inventory was sold (or turned over) during the year. A high rate of turnover is preferable to a low rate because an increase in turnover usually means higher profits.

Inventory turnover varies from industry to industry. Grocery stores, for example, turn their goods over faster than automobile dealers do. Drug stores have higher turnover than furniture stores do. Retailers of furniture, such as Huntington Galleries, have an average turnover of 3 times per year. Huntington's turnover rate of 2.3 times per year suggests that Huntington is not very successful. The lower one-fourth of furniture retailers average a turnover rate of 2.6, so Huntington's turnover of 2.3 looks rather bad. Exhibit 6-14 compares the inventory turnover rate of Huntington Galleries and Wal-Mart Stores, Inc.

Exhibits 6-13 and 6-14 tell an interesting story. **Wal-Mart** sells a lot of inventory at a relatively low gross profit margin. Wal-Mart turns its inventory over rapidly. Huntington Galleries, a much smaller company, prices inventory to earn a higher gross margin on each dollar of sales. As a result, Huntington cannot sell its merchandise as rapidly as Wal-Mart can. When analyzed together, gross margin percentage and rate of inventory turnover tell a lot about a retailer's merchandising strategy.

STOP & THINK Calculate inventory turnover from the following data:

Beginning inventory	$ 2,350
Ending inventory	1,980
Purchases	14,550

Answer

$$\text{Inventory turnover} = \frac{\text{Cost of goods sold*}}{\text{Average inventory**}} = \frac{\$14{,}920}{\$2{,}165} = \text{7 times per year}$$

---

*$2,350 + $14,550 − $1,980 = $14,920
**($2,350 + $1,980) ÷ 2 = $2,165

The Decision Guidelines feature offers some tips on using the gross margin percentage and the rate of inventory turnover to manage gross margin.

Internal Control over Inventory

Internal control over inventory is important because inventory is such an important asset. Successful companies take great care to protect their inventory. Elements of good internal control over inventory include

Decision Guidelines

Using the Gross Margin Percentage and the Rate of Inventory Turnover to Manage Gross Margin (Gross Profit)

Decision	Guidelines
How to increase the gross margin (gross profit) on sales?	1. Conduct market research to pinpoint which products sell the best to particular groups of customers. Research will reveal which merchandise can be sold at a price that will bring in the desired gross margin. 2. Increase advertising to help boost sales. 3. Increase the selling price of the products. This plan is risky because it may decrease the rate of inventory turnover and result in a lower gross margin. 4. Cut the cost of inventory purchases. a. Take all purchase discounts offered if it is economical to do so. b. Buy in large quantities to get quantity discounts. c. Use the most economical shipper to transport the merchandise to the various locations.
How to increase the rate of inventory turnover?	1. Same as 1 above. 2. Decrease the selling price of the products. This plan is risky because it may result in a lower gross margin.
How to manage the conflict between the gross margin percentage and the rate of inventory turnover?	1. Measure gross profits often to ensure that the company is not earning lower gross margins while selling more goods. 2. Several years ago PepsiCo, Inc., drastically cut the prices of the products sold by one of its subsidiaries, Taco Bell. PepsiCo was willing to accept a lower gross margin percentage in order to turn inventory over more rapidly. The desired result? Higher gross profits. Thus far, the strategy has been successful. This is also the marketing strategy of discounters such as Wal-Mart, Kmart, and Target: Low gross margin percentage × Fast turnover = High gross margins. This strategy has worked better for some companies than for others.

1. Physically counting inventory at least once each year regardless of which inventory accounting system is used
2. Storing inventory to protect it against theft, damage, and decay
3. Allowing access to inventory only to personnel who do *not* have access to the accounting records
4. Keeping perpetual inventory records for high-unit-cost merchandise
5. Keeping enough inventory on hand to prevent shortage situations, which lead to lost sales
6. Not keeping too large an inventory stockpiled, thus avoiding the expense of tying up money in unneeded items
7. Purchasing inventory in economical quantities

The annual physical count of inventory (item 1) is necessary because the only way to be certain of the amount of inventory on hand is to count it. Errors arise in even the best accounting systems, and the count is needed to establish the correct value of the inventory. When an error is detected, the records are brought into agreement with the physical count.

Keeping inventory handlers away from the accounting records (item 3) is an essential separation of duties, discussed in Chapter 4. An employee with access to both inventory and the accounting records can steal the goods and make an entry to conceal the theft. For example, the employee could increase the amount of an inventory write-down to make it appear that goods became obsolete when in fact they were stolen.

Computerized inventory systems allow companies to minimize both the amount of inventory on hand and the chances of running out of stock (items 5 and 6). In an increasingly competitive business environment, companies cannot afford to have cash tied up in too much inventory. Many manufacturing companies use *just-in-time (JIT) inventory systems,* which require suppliers to deliver materials just in time to be used in the production process. Just-in-time systems help minimize the amount of money a company has tied up in inventory.

Reporting Inventory Transactions on the Statement of Cash Flows

Let's return once again to the Huntington Galleries example. In addition to the income statement and the balance sheet, Huntington budgets cash flows and then publishes a statement of cash flows at the end of the year. As we have seen throughout this chapter, a company's inventory transactions are among its most important activities. And huge amounts of cash are involved in inventory transactions.

Examine the Huntington Galleries income statement and balance sheet on page 262. The income statement shows Huntington's revenues, expenses, and net income—the company's operating results for 1996. The balance sheet reports the company's assets, liabilities, and stockholders' equity—financial position—at the end of the year.

But how much cash did Huntington spend on inventory during the year? And how much cash did the company collect from customers? Did operations provide a net cash inflow, as they should for a successful company? Or were operating activities a drain on cash? Only the statement of cash flows answers these questions. Exhibit 6-15 highlights Huntington's inventory-related transactions on its statement of cash flows for 1996.

Inventory-related transactions are *operating activities* because the purchase and sale of merchandise are at the very core of a company's operations. Huntington Galleries is no exception. Collections from customers and payments for inventory are its two largest operating cash flows. As we saw in Chapter 5, collections from customers are related to receivables.

The cash-flow statement reports that Huntington collected $164.1 million from customers and paid $91.6 million for inventory during the year. These figures combine with Huntington's other operating activities to report that operations provided a net total of $30.1 million of cash during 1996. Overall, the company's operating cash flows look strong. We will reexamine the reporting of cash flows in Chapter 12.

Decision Guidelines

This chapter has discussed various aspects of controlling and accounting for inventory, cost of goods sold, and gross margin. The Decision Guidelines feature on page 289 summarizes some basic decision guidelines that are helpful in managing a business's inventory operations.

EXHIBIT 6-15
Statement of Cash Flows for Huntington Galleries

HUNTINGTON GALLERIES, INC.
Statement of Cash Flows (partial)
For the Year Ended December 31, 1996

Cash flows from operating activities:	**(Amounts in Thousands)**
Collections from customers	$164,100
Receipts of interest	800
Payments for inventory	(91,600)
Payments to other suppliers	(21,700)
Payments of interest	(2,200)
Payments of income tax	(19,300)
Cash provided by operating activities	$ 30,100

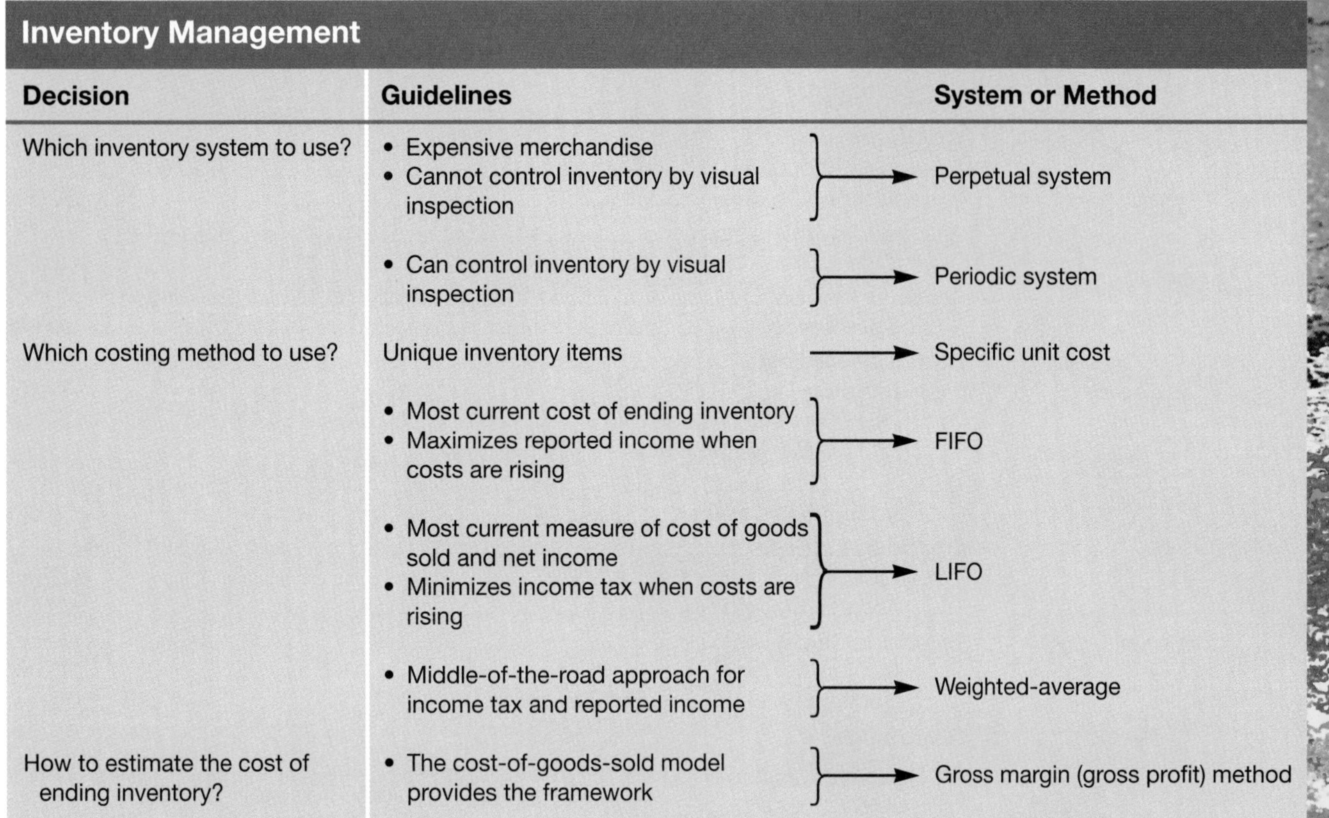

Decision Guidelines

Inventory Management

Decision	Guidelines	System or Method
Which inventory system to use?	• Expensive merchandise • Cannot control inventory by visual inspection	Perpetual system
	• Can control inventory by visual inspection	Periodic system
Which costing method to use?	Unique inventory items	Specific unit cost
	• Most current cost of ending inventory • Maximizes reported income when costs are rising	FIFO
	• Most current measure of cost of goods sold and net income • Minimizes income tax when costs are rising	LIFO
	• Middle-of-the-road approach for income tax and reported income	Weighted-average
How to estimate the cost of ending inventory?	• The cost-of-goods-sold model provides the framework	Gross margin (gross profit) method

SUMMARY PROBLEM FOR YOUR REVIEW

Mesa Hardware Company began 19X8 with 60,000 units of inventory that cost $36,000. During 19X8, Mesa purchased merchandise on account for $352,500 as follows:

Purchase No. 1 (100,000 units costing)	$ 65,000
Purchase No. 2 (270,000 units costing)	175,500
Purchase No. 3 (160,000 units costing)	112,000

Cash payments on account totaled $326,000 during the year.

Mesa's sales during 19X8 consisted of 520,000 units of inventory for $660,000, all on account. The company uses the FIFO inventory method.

Cash collections from customers were $630,000. Operating expenses totaled $240,500, of which Mesa paid $211,000 in cash. Mesa credited Accrued Liabilities for the remainder. At December 31, Mesa accrued income tax expense at the rate of 35% of income before tax.

Required

1. Make summary journal entries to record Mesa Hardware's transactions for the year, assuming the company uses a perpetual inventory system.
2. Determine the FIFO cost of Mesa's ending inventory at December 31, 19X8, two ways:
   a. Use a T-account.
   b. Multiply the number of units by the unit cost.
3. Show how Mesa would compute cost of goods sold for 19X8 if the company used the periodic inventory system.
4. Prepare Mesa Hardware's income statement for 19X8. Show totals for the gross margin and income before tax.

5. Determine Mesa's gross profit percentage, rate of inventory turnover, and net income as a percentage of sales for the year. In the hardware industry, a gross profit percentage of 40%, an inventory turnover of six times per year, and a net income percentage of 7% are considered excellent. How well does Mesa compare to these industry averages?

ANSWERS

Requirement 1

Inventory ($65,000 + $175,500 + $112,000)	352,500	
Accounts Payable		352,500
Accounts Payable	326,000	
Cash		326,000
Accounts Receivable	660,000	
Sales Revenue		660,000
Cost of Goods Sold	339,500	
Inventory		339,500
[$36,000 + $65,000 + $175,500 + $63,000 (90,000 units × $0.70)]		
($112,000 ÷ 160,000 units = $0.70 per unit)		
Cash	630,000	
Accounts Receivable		630,000
Operating Expenses	240,500	
Cash		211,000
Accrued Liabilities		29,500
Income Tax Expense	28,000	
Income Tax Payable		28,000
($660,000 − $339,500 − $240,500) × .35 = $28,000		

Requirement 2

a.

Inventory	
36,000	339,500
352,500	
49,000	

b.

Number of units in ending inventory (60,000 + 100,000 + 270,000 + 160,000 − 520,000)	70,000
Unit cost of ending inventory at FIFO ($112,000 ÷ 160,000)	× $ 0.70
FIFO cost of ending inventory	$49,000

Requirement 3

Cost of goods sold:	
Beginning inventory	$ 36,000
Purchases	352,500
Cost of goods available for sale	388,500
Ending inventory	(49,000)
Cost of goods sold	$339,500

Requirement 4

MESA HARDWARE COMPANY
Income Statement
For the Year Ended December 31, 19X8

Sales revenue	$660,000
Cost of goods sold	339,500
Gross margin	320,500
Operating expenses	240,500
Income before tax	80,000
Income tax expense	28,000
Net income	$ 52,000

Requirement 5

Gross profit percentage: $320,500 ÷ $660,000 = 48.6%

Inventory turnover: $\dfrac{\$339{,}500}{(\$36{,}000 + \$49{,}000)/2}$ **= 8 times**

Net income as a percentage of sales: $52,000 ÷ $660,000 = 7.9%

Mesa's statistics are better than the industry averages.

SUMMARY OF LEARNING OBJECTIVES

1. *Account for inventory by the periodic and perpetual systems.* Accounting for inventory plays an important part in merchandisers' accounting systems because selling inventory is the heart of their business. Inventory is generally the largest current asset on their balance sheet, and inventory expense—called *cost of goods sold*—is usually the largest expense on the income statement.

Merchandisers can choose between two inventory systems. In a *periodic inventory system,* the business does not keep a running record of the inventory on hand. Instead, at the end of the period, the business counts the inventory on hand and then updates its records. In a *perpetual inventory system,* the business keeps a continuous record for each inventory item to show the inventory on hand at all times. A physical count of inventory is needed in both systems for control purposes.

2. *Apply the inventory costing methods: specific unit cost, weighted-average cost, FIFO, and LIFO.* Businesses multiply the quantity of inventory items by their unit cost to determine inventory cost. There are four inventory costing methods: *specific unit cost; weighted-average cost; first-in, first out (FIFO) cost;* and *last-in, first-out (LIFO) cost.* Only businesses that sell items that may be identified individually, such as automobiles and jewels, use the specific identification method. Most other companies use the other methods. FIFO reports ending inventory at the most current cost. LIFO reports cost of goods sold at the most current cost.

3. *Identify the income effects and the tax effects of the inventory costing methods.* When inventory costs are increasing, LIFO produces the highest cost of goods sold and the lowest income, thus minimizing income taxes. FIFO results in the highest income. The weighted-average cost method gives results between the extremes of FIFO and LIFO.

4. *Apply the lower-of-cost-or-market rule to inventory.* The *lower-of-cost-or-market (LCM) rule*—an example of accounting *conservatism*—requires that businesses report inventory on the balance sheet at the lower of its cost or current replacement value. Companies can disclose LCM in notes to their financial statements.

5. *Compute the effects of inventory errors on the cost of goods sold and net income.* Although inventory overstatements in one period are counterbalanced by inventory understatements in the next period, effective decision making depends on accurate inventory information.

6. *Estimate inventory by the gross margin method.* The *gross margin method* is a technique for estimating the cost of inventory. It comes in handy for preparing interim financial statements and for estimating the cost of inventory destroyed by fire or other casualties.

7. *Use the gross margin percentage and the inventory turnover ratio to evaluate a business.* Two key decision aids for merchandising companies are (1) the *gross margin percentage* (gross margin divided by net sales revenue), which measures the percentage of gross profit on each dollar of sales, and (2) *inventory turnover* (cost of goods sold divided by average inventory), which indicates how rapidly the company is selling its inventory. Increases in these measures usually signal an increase in profits.

ACCOUNTING VOCABULARY

conservatism *(p. 280).*
consignment *(p. 271).*
consistency principle *(p. 279).*
cost of goods sold *(p. 263).*
cost of sales *(p. 263).*
disclosure principle *(p. 279).*
first-in, first-out (FIFO) method *(p. 273).*
gross margin *(p. 264).*
gross margin method *(p. 284).*
gross margin percentage *(p. 285).*
gross profit *(p. 264).*
inventory profit *(p. 274).*
inventory turnover *(p. 285).*
last-in, first-out (LIFO) method *(p. 273).*
LIFO Reserve *(p. 316).*
lower-of-cost-or-market (LCM) rule *(p. 280).*
materiality concept *(p. 280).*
merchandising company *(p. 263).*
periodic inventory system *(p. 264).*
perpetual inventory system *(p. 265).*
purchase allowance *(p. 266).*
purchase return *(p. 266).*
specific-unit-cost method *(p. 271).*
weighted-average cost method *(p. 272).*

QUESTIONS

1. Suppose your company deals in expensive jewelry. Which inventory system should you use to achieve good internal control over the inventory? If your business is a hardware store that sells low-cost goods, which inventory system would you be likely to use? Why would you choose this system?
2. What is the role of the physical count of inventory in (a) the periodic inventory system, and (b) the perpetual inventory system?
3. **a.** If beginning inventory is $10,000, purchases total $85,000, and ending inventory is $12,700, how much is cost of goods sold?
   b. If beginning inventory is $32,000, purchases total $119,000, and cost of goods sold is $127,000, how much is ending inventory?
4. Briefly describe the four generally accepted inventory cost methods. During a period of rising prices, which method produces the highest reported income? Which produces the lowest reported income?
5. Which inventory costing method produces the ending inventory valued at the most current cost? Which method produces the cost-of-goods-sold amount valued at the most current cost?

6. What is the most attractive feature of LIFO? Does LIFO have this advantage during periods of increasing prices or during periods of decreasing prices? Why has LIFO had this advantage recently?
7. What is inventory profit? Which method produces it?
8. Identify the chief criticism of LIFO.
9. How does the consistency principle affect accounting for inventory?
10. Briefly describe the influence that the concept of conservatism has on accounting for inventory.
11. Manley Company's inventory has a cost of $48,000 at the end of the year, and the current replacement cost of the inventory is $51,000. At which amount should the company report the inventory on its balance sheet? Suppose the current replacement cost of the inventory is $45,000 instead of $51,000. At which amount should Manley report the inventory? What rule governs your answers to these questions?
12. Gabriel Company accidentally overstated its ending inventory by $10,000 at the end of period 1. Is gross margin of period 1 overstated or understated? Is gross margin of period 2 overstated, understated, or unaffected by the period 1 error? Is total gross margin for the two periods overstated, understated, or correct? Give the reason for your answers.
13. Identify an important method of estimating inventory amounts. What familiar model underlies this estimation method?
14. A fire destroyed the inventory of Olivera Company, but the accounting records were saved. The beginning inventory was $22,000, purchases for the period were $71,000, and sales were $140,000. Olivera's customary gross margin is 45% of sales. Use the gross margin method to estimate the cost of the inventory destroyed by the fire.
15. True or false? A company that sells inventory of low unit cost needs no internal controls over the goods. Any inventory loss would probably be small.

EXERCISES

Accounting for inventory under the perpetual and periodic systems
(Obj. 1)

E6-1 Accounting records for Big Gap, Inc., yield the following data for the year ended December 31, 19X5 (amounts in thousands):

Inventory, December 31, 19X4	$ 370,638
Purchases of inventory (on account)	2,933,392
Sales of inventory—80% on account; 20% for cash (cost $2,821,455)	4,395,253
Inventory at the lower of FIFO cost or market, December 31, 19X5	?

Required

1. Journalize Big Gap's inventory transactions for the year—first under the perpetual system, then under the periodic system. Show all amounts in thousands. Use Exhibit 6-2 as a model.
2. Report ending inventory, sales, cost of goods sold, and gross margin on the appropriate financial statement (amounts in thousands). Show the computation of cost of goods sold in the periodic system.

Budgeting inventory purchases
(Obj. 1)

E6-2 Toys "Я" Us is budgeting for the fiscal year ended January 31, 1997. During the preceding year ended January 31, 1996, sales totaled $9,427 million and cost of goods sold was $6,592 million. Inventory stood at $1,752 million at January 31, 1995; and at January 31, 1996, inventory stood at $1,999 million.

During the upcoming 1997 year, suppose Toys "Я" Us expects sales and cost of goods sold to increase by 8 percent. The company budgets next year's ending inventory at $2,110 million.

Required

How much inventory should Toys "Я" Us purchase during the upcoming year in order to reach its budgeted figures? Round to the nearest $1 million.

Determining ending inventory and cost of goods sold by four methods
(Obj. 2)

E6-3 Abba Medical Supply's inventory records for industrial switches indicate the following at October 31:

Oct. 1	Beginning inventory	7 units @ $160
8	Purchase	4 units @ 160
15	Purchase	11 units @ 170
26	Purchase	5 units @ 176

The physical count of inventory at October 31 indicates that eight units are on hand, and there are no consignment goods.

Required

Compute ending inventory and cost of goods sold, using each of the following methods:

1. Specific unit cost, assuming five $170 units and three $160 units are on hand
2. Weighted-average cost
3. First-in, first-out
4. Last-in, first-out

E6-4 Use the data in Exercise 6-3 to journalize the following, first for the perpetual inventory system, then for the periodic system:

Recording inventory transactions ***(Obj. 1, 2)***

1. Total October purchases in one summary entry. All purchases were on credit.
2. Total October sales in a summary entry. Assume that the selling price was $300 per unit and that all sales were on credit. Abba Medical Supply uses LIFO.
3. October 31 entries for inventory. Abba Medical Supply uses LIFO. For the periodic inventory system, post to the Cost of Goods Sold T-account to show how this amount is determined. Label each item in the account. How does the balance for Cost of Goods Sold compare to the Cost of Goods Sold amount recorded under the perpetual system?

E6-5 Use the data in Exercise 6-3 to illustrate the income tax advantage of LIFO over FIFO, assuming that sales revenue is $8,000, operating expenses are $1,100, and the income tax rate is 30 percent. How much in taxes would Abba Medical Supply save by using the LIFO method?

Computing the tax advantage of LIFO over FIFO ***(Obj. 3)***

E6-6 Supply the missing income statement amounts for each of the following companies:

Determining amounts for the income statement ***(Obj. 1)***

Company	Net Sales	Beginning Inventory	Net Purchases	Ending Inventory	Cost of Goods Sold	Gross Margin
A	$92,800	$12,500	$62,700	$19,400	(a)	$37,000
B	(b)	27,450	93,000	(c)	$94,100	51,200
C	94,700	(d)	54,900	22,600	59,400	(e)
D	98,600	10,700	(f)	8,200	(g)	47,100

Prepare the income statement for company D, which uses the periodic inventory system. Company D's operating expenses for the year were $32,100, and its income tax rate is 30 percent.

Note: Exercise 6-15 builds on Exercise 6-6 with a profitability analysis of companies A–D.

E6-7 Piazza Music World carries a large inventory of guitars, keyboards, and other musical instruments. Because each item is expensive, Piazza uses a perpetual inventory system. Company records indicate the following for a particular line of Casio keyboards:

Determining ending inventory and cost of goods sold in a perpetual system ***(Obj. 1, 2)***

Date	Item	Quantity	Unit Cost
May 1	Balance	5	$90
6	Sale	3	
8	Purchase	11	95
17	Sale	4	
30	Sale	1	

Required

Determine the amounts that Piazza should report for ending inventory and cost of goods sold by the FIFO method. Prepare the perpetual inventory record for Casio keyboards. Use Exhibit 6-7 as a model.

E6-8 Magna Enterprises is considering a change from the LIFO inventory method to the FIFO method. Managers are concerned about the effect of this change on income tax expense and reported net income. If the change is made, it will become effective on March 1. Inventory on hand at February 28 is $63,000. During March, Magna managers expect sales of $260,000, net purchases between $159,000 and $182,000, and operating expenses, excluding income tax, of $83,000. The income tax rate is 30 percent. Inventories at March 31 are budgeted as follows: FIFO, $85,000; LIFO, $78,000.

Change from LIFO to FIFO ***(Obj. 3)***

Required

Create a spreadsheet model to compute estimated net income for March under FIFO and LIFO. Format your answer as shown at the top of page 294.

A	B	C	D	E
	MAGNA ENTERPRISES			
	Estimated Income under FIFO and LIFO			
	March 19XX			
	FIFO	**LIFO**	**FIFO**	**LIFO**
Sales	$260,000	$260,000	$260,000	$260,000
Cost of goods sold				
Beginning inventory	63,000	63,000	63,000	63,000
Net purchases	159,000	159,000	182,000	182,000
Cost of goods available				
Ending inventory	85,000	78,000	85,000	78,000
Cost of goods sold				
Gross margin				
Operating expenses	83,000	83,000	83,000	83,000
Income from operations				
Income tax expense				
Net income	$	$	$	$

Managing income taxes under the LIFO method ***(Obj. 3)***

E6-9 Deitrick Enterprises is nearing the end of its best year ever. With three weeks until year end, it appears that net income for the year will have increased by 70% over last year. Jim Deitrick, the principal stockholder and president, is pleased with the year's success but unhappy about the huge increase in income taxes that the business will have to pay.

He asks you, the financial vice president, to come up with a way to decrease the business's income tax burden. Inventory quantities are a little lower than normal because sales have been especially strong during the last few months. Deitrick Enterprises uses the LIFO inventory method, and inventory costs have risen dramatically during the latter part of the year.

Required

Write a memorandum to Jim Deitrick to explain how Deitrick Enterprises can decrease its income taxes for the current year. Deitrick is a man of integrity, so your plan must be completely honest.

Identifying income, tax, and other effects of the inventory methods ***(Obj. 3)***

E6-10 This exercise tests your understanding of the various inventory methods. In the space provided, write the name of the inventory method that best fits the description. Assume that the cost of inventory is rising.

______________ 1. Maximizes reported income.
______________ 2. Enables a company to buy high-cost inventory at year end and thereby decrease reported income.
______________ 3. Enables a company to keep reported income from dropping lower by liquidating older layers of inventory.
______________ 4. Matches the most current cost of goods sold against sales revenue.
______________ 5. Results in an old measure of the cost of ending inventory.
______________ 6. Generally associated with saving income taxes.
______________ 7. Results in a cost of ending inventory that is close to the current cost of replacing the inventory.
______________ 8. Used to account for automobiles, jewelry, and art objects.
______________ 9. Associated with inventory profits.
______________ 10. Provides a middle-ground measure of ending inventory and cost of goods sold.

Applying the lower-of-cost-or-market rule to inventories; perpetual system ***(Obj. 1, 4)***

E6-11 Hillis Corporation, which uses a perpetual inventory system, has these account balances at December 31, 19X7, prior to releasing the financial statements for the year:

Inventory			Cost of Goods Sold			Sales Revenue	
Beg. bal.	12,489						
End. bal.	18,028		Bal.	110,161		Bal.	225,000

A year ago, when Hillis prepared its 19X6 financial statements, the replacement cost of ending inventory was $13,051. Hillis has determined that the replacement cost of the December 31, 19X7, ending inventory is $16,840.

Required

Prepare Hillis Corporation's 19X7 income statement through gross margin to show how Hillis would apply the lower-of-cost-or-market rule to its inventories.

Applying the lower-of-cost-or-market rule to inventories; periodic system ***(Obj. 1, 4)***

E6-12 Brunswick Tool Company uses a periodic inventory system and reports inventory at the lower of FIFO cost or market. Prior to releasing its March 19X4 financial statements, Brunswick's preliminary income statement appears as follows:

Income Statement (partial)

Sales revenue		$89,000
Cost of goods sold:		
Beginning inventory	$17,200	
Net purchases	51,700	
Cost of goods available for sale	68,900	
Ending inventory	23,800	
Cost of goods sold		45,100
Gross margin		$43,900

Brunswick has determined that the current replacement cost of ending inventory is $19,800. Adjust the preceding data to apply the lower-of-cost-or market rule to Brunswick's inventory. The replacement cost of Brunswick's beginning inventory was $18,600.

Correcting an inventory error ***(Obj. 5)***

E6-13 Malzone Auto Supply reported the following comparative income statement for the years ended September 30, 19X9 and 19X8:

MALZONE AUTO SUPPLY
Income Statements
For the Years Ended September 30, 19X9 and 19X8

	19X9		19X8	
Sales revenue		$137,300		$121,700
Cost of goods sold:				
Beginning inventory	$14,000		$12,800	
Net purchases	72,000		66,000	
Cost of goods available	86,000		78,800	
Ending inventory	16,600		14,000	
Cost of goods sold		69,400		64,800
Gross margin		67,900		56,900
Operating expenses		30,300		26,100
Net income		$ 37,600		$ 30,800

During 19X9, accountants for the company discovered that ending 19X8 inventory was overstated by $2,000. Prepare the corrected comparative income statement for the two-year period. What was the effect of the error on net income for the two years combined? Explain your answer.

Estimating inventory by the gross margin method ***(Obj. 6)***

E6-14 Gobel Aviation Supply began January with inventory of $42,000. The business made net purchases of $37,600 and had net sales of $60,000 before a fire destroyed the company's inventory. For the past several years, Gobel's gross margin on sales has been 40 percent. Estimate the cost of the inventory destroyed by the fire. Identify another reason managers use the gross margin method to estimate inventory cost on a regular basis.

Measuring profitability ***(Obj. 7)***

E6-15 Refer to the data in Exercise 6-6. Which company is likely to be the most profitable, based on its gross margin percentage and rate of inventory turnover? Why should the company with the fastest inventory turnover have the lowest operating expenses?

Suppose you are a financial analyst, and a client has asked you to recommend an investment in one of these companies. Write a memo outlining which company you recommend, and explain your reasoning.

CHALLENGE EXERCISES

Inventory policy decisions
(Obj. 2, 3)

E6-16 For each of the following situations, identify the inventory method that you would use, or, given the use of a particular method, state the strategy that you would follow to accomplish your goal.

a. Company management, like that of IBM, prefers a middle-of-the-road inventory policy that avoids extremes.

b. Your inventory turns over *very* rapidly, and the company uses a perpetual inventory system. Inventory costs are increasing, and the company prefers to report high income.

c. Suppliers of your inventory are threatening a labor strike, and it may be difficult for your company to obtain inventory. This situation could increase your income taxes.

d. Inventory costs are decreasing, and your company's board of directors wants to minimize income taxes.

e. Inventory costs are increasing. Your company uses LIFO and is having an unexpectedly good year. It is near year end, and you need to keep net income from increasing too much.

f. Inventory costs have been stable for several years, and you expect costs to remain stable for the indefinite future. (Give the reason for your choice of method.)

LIFO liquidation
(Obj. 2)

E6-17 Whirlpool Corporation, the world's leading manufacturer of major home appliances, reported these figures for 19X1 (in millions of dollars):

Income Statement (adapted)	
Net revenues	$6,757
Cost of products sold	4,967
Operating expenses	1,397
Other expense (net)	93
Earnings before income taxes	300
Income taxes	130
Net earnings	$ 170

Note 4 of the financial statements disclosed:
Liquidation of prior years' LIFO inventory layers increased net earnings $8 million.

Required

1. Explain what the LIFO liquidation means and why it affects net earnings.
2. Would Whirlpool management be pleased or displeased at the increase in income due to the LIFO liquidation? Give your reason.
3. Prepare a revised income statement for Whirlpool Corporation if no LIFO liquidation had occurred. The income tax rate was 43.33 percent.

Evaluating a company's profitability
(Obj. 7)

E6-18 Pharmacy Management Services, Inc. (PMSI), is a leading provider of products for workers' compensation insurance purposes. The company recently reported these figures.

PHARMACY MANAGEMENT SERVICES, INC., AND SUBSIDIARIES
Consolidated Statements of Operations
For the Years Ended July 31, 19X2 and 19X1

	19X2	19X1
Sales	$106,115,984	$81,685,715
Cost of sales	76,424,328	60,981,847
Gross margin	29,691,656	20,703,868
Cost and expenses		
Selling, general and administrative	21,801,737	16,576,484
Depreciation and amortization	2,169,196	918,693
Restructuring charges	7,096,774	—
	31,067,707	17,495,177
Operating income (loss)	(1,376,051)	3,208,691
Other items (summarized)	(635,153)	(1,315,490)
Net income (loss)	$ (2,011,204)	$ 1,893,201

Required

Evaluate PMSI's operations during 19X2 in comparison with 19X1. Consider sales, gross margin, operating income, and net income. Track the gross margin percentage and inventory turnover in both years. PMSI's inventories at December 31, 19X2, 19X1, and 19X0, were $7,766,322, $12,163,053, and $10,176,722, respectively. In the annual report, PMSI's management describes the restructuring charges in 19X2 as a one-time event. How does this additional information affect your evaluation?

Note: Exercise 6-19 relates to Appendix B at the end of this chapter.

E6-19 Harland Business Forms, Inc., reported:

Converting LIFO financial statements to the FIFO basis ***(Appendix B to Chapter 6)***

	19X5	19X4
Balance Sheet:		
Inventories—note 4	$ 67,800	$ 60,300
Income Statement:		
Cost of goods sold	399,600	381,400
Net income	72,100	66,700
Income tax rate	35%	34%

Note 4. The company determines inventory cost by the last-in, first-out method. If the first-in, first-out method were used, inventories would be $7,100 higher at year end 19X5 and $2,500 higher at year end 19X4.

Required

Show the cost-of-goods-sold computations for 19X5 under LIFO and FIFO. Then compute Harland's net income for 19X5 if the company had used FIFO.

PROBLEMS

(GROUP A)

P6-1A Toys "Я" Us purchases inventory in crates of merchandise, so each unit of inventory is a crate of toys. Assume you are dealing with a single Toys "Я" Us store in Knoxville, Tennessee. The fiscal year of Toys "Я" Us ends each January 31.

Accounting for inventory in a perpetual system ***(Obj. 1, 2)***

Assume the Knoxville Toys "Я" Us store began fiscal year 19X5 with an inventory of 20,000 units that cost a total of $1,200,000. During the year, the store purchased merchandise on account as follows:

April (30,000 units @ $65)	$ 1,950,000
August (50,000 units @ $65)	3,250,000
November (90,000 units @ $70)	6,300,000
Total purchases	$11,500,000

Cash payments on account during the year totaled $11,390,000.

During fiscal year 19X5, the store sold 180,000 units of merchandise for $16,400,000, of which $5,300,000 was for cash and the balance was on account. Toys "Я" Us uses the LIFO method for inventories.

Operating expenses for the year were $3,630,000. The store paid two-thirds in cash and accrued the rest. The store accrued income tax at the rate of 40 percent.

Required

1. Make summary journal entries to record the store's transactions for the year ended January 31, 19X5. Toys "Я" Us uses a perpetual inventory system.
2. Determine the LIFO cost of the store's ending inventory at January 31, 19X5. Use a T-account.
3. Prepare the store's income statement for the year ended January 31, 19X5. Show totals for the gross margin, income before tax, and net income.

P6-2A Condensed versions of a Texaco convenience store's most recent income statement and balance sheet reported the figures at the top of page 298. The business is organized as a proprietorship, so it pays no corporate income tax. It uses a periodic inventory system.

Using the cost-of-goods-sold model to budget operations ***(Obj. 1)***

TEXACO CONVENIENCE STORE Income Statement Year Ended December 31, 19X4	
Sales	$800,000
Cost of sales	660,000
Gross margin	140,000
Operating expenses	80,000
Net income	$ 60,000

TEXACO CONVENIENCE STORE Balance Sheet December 31, 19X4			
Assets		**Liabilities and Capital**	
Cash	$ 70,000	Accounts payable	$ 35,000
Inventories	35,000	Note payable	280,000
Land and buildings, net	360,000	Total liabilities	315,000
		Owner, capital	150,000
Total assets	$465,000	Total liabilities and capital	$465,000

The owner is budgeting for 19X5. He expects sales to increase by 10% and the gross margin *percentage* to remain unchanged. To meet customer demand for the increase in sales, ending inventory will need to be $40,000 at December 31, 19X5. The owner can lower operating expenses by doing some of the work himself. He hopes to earn a net income of $80,000 next year.

Required

1. A key variable the owner can control is the amount of inventory he purchases. Show how to determine the amount of purchases he should make in 19X5.
2. Prepare the store's budgeted income statement for 19X5 to reach the target net income of $80,000.

Using the perpetual and periodic inventory systems ***(Obj. 1, 2)***

P6-3A An American Tourister outlet store began August 19X8 with 50 units of inventory that cost $40 each. The sale price of these units was $70. During August, the store completed these inventory transactions:

		Units	Unit Cost	Unit Sale Price
Aug. 3	Sale	16	$40	$70
8	Purchase	80	41	72
11	Sale	34	40	70
19	Sale	9	41	72
24	Sale	35	41	72
30	Purchase	18	42	73
31	Sale	6	41	72

Required

1. The preceding data are taken from the store's perpetual inventory records. Which cost method does the store use?
2. Determine the store's cost of goods sold for August under the
   a. Perpetual inventory system **b.** Periodic inventory system
3. Compute gross margin for August.

Computing inventory by three methods ***(Obj. 2, 3)***

P6-4A BullsEye Electric Co. began March with 73 units of inventory that cost $23 each. During the month, BullsEye made the following purchases:

March 4	113 @ $27
12	81 @ 29
19	167 @ 32
25	44 @ 35

The company uses the periodic inventory system, and the physical count at March 31 indicates that ending inventory consists of 51 units.

Required

1. Determine the ending inventory and cost-of-goods-sold amounts for March under (1) weighted-average cost, (2) FIFO cost, and (3) LIFO cost. Round weighted-average cost per unit to the nearest cent, and round all other amounts to the nearest dollar.
2. How much income tax would BullsEye Electric save during the month by using LIFO versus FIFO? The income tax rate is 40 percent.

Preparing an income statement directly from the accounts ***(Obj. 2, 3)***

P6-5A The records of Ridgewood Golf Shop include the following accounts at December 31 of the current year.

Inventory

Jan. 1	Balance {700 units @ $7.00}	4,900	

Purchases

Jan. 6	300 units @ $7.05	2,115	
Mar. 19	1,100 units @ 7.35	8,085	
June 22	8,400 units @ 7.50	63,000	
Oct. 4	500 units @ 8.50	4,250	
Dec. 31	Balance	77,450	

Sales Revenue

	Feb. 5	1,000 units @ $12.00	12,000
	Apr. 10	700 units @ 12.10	8,470
	July 31	1,800 units @ 13.25	23,850
	Sep. 4	3,500 units @ 13.50	47,250
	Nov. 27	3,100 units @ 15.00	46,500
	Dec. 31	Balance	138,070

Required

1. Prepare a partial income statement through gross margin under the weighted-average cost, FIFO cost, and LIFO cost methods. Ridgewood uses a periodic inventory system.
2. Which inventory method would you use to minimize income tax?

Applying the lower-of-cost-or-market rule to inventories ***(Obj. 4)***

P6-6A Hypermart has recently been plagued with lackluster sales. The rate of inventory turnover has dropped, and some of the company's merchandise is gathering dust. At the same time, competition has forced Hypermart's suppliers to lower the prices that Hypermart will pay when it replaces its inventory. It is now December 31, 19X9, and the current replacement cost of Hypermart's ending inventory is $800,000 below what Hypermart actually paid for the goods, which was $4,900,000. Before any adjustments at the end of the period, Hypermart's Cost of Goods Sold account has a balance of $29,600,000.

What action should Hypermart take in this situation, if any? Give any journal entry required. At what amount should Hypermart report Inventory on the balance sheet? At what amount should the company report Cost of Goods Sold on the income statement? Discuss the accounting principle or concept that is most relevant to this situation.

Correcting inventory errors over a three-year period ***(Obj. 5)***

P6-7A The Schlecte Glass Company books show these data (in thousands):

	19X6		19X5		19X4	
Net sales revenue		$360		$285		$244
Cost of goods sold:						
Beginning inventory	$ 65		$ 55		$ 70	
Net purchases	195		135		130	
Cost of goods available	260		190		200	
Less ending inventory	70		65		55	
Cost of goods sold		190		125		145
Gross margin		170		160		99
Operating expenses		113		109		76
Net income		$ 57		$ 51		$ 23

In early 19X7, a team of internal auditors discovered that the ending inventory for 19X4 had been overstated by $5 thousand and that the ending inventory for 19X6 had been understated by $6 thousand. The ending inventory at December 31, 19X5, was correct.

Required

1. Show corrected income statements for the three years.
2. State whether each year's net income and owners' equity amounts are understated or overstated. Ignore income tax because Schlecte is a proprietorship. For each incorrect figure, indicate the amount of the understatement or overstatement.

Estimating inventory by the gross margin method; preparing the income statement ***(Obj. 6)***

P6-8A Rolex Quartz Company estimates its inventory by the gross margin method when preparing monthly financial statements. For the past two years, the gross margin has averaged 40% of net sales. The company's inventory records reveal the following data:

Inventory, July 1	$ 367,000
Transactions during July:	
Purchases	3,789,000
Purchase discounts	26,000
Purchase returns	12,000
Sales	6,430,000
Sales returns	25,000

Note: Sales returns are decreases in net sales revenue due to a customer's return of merchandise to the seller. *Purchase discounts* and *purchase returns* are decreases in arriving at net purchases.

Required

1. Estimate the July 31 inventory, using the gross margin method.
2. Prepare the July income statement through gross margin for the Rolex Quartz Company.

Using the gross margin percentage and the inventory turnover ratio to evaluate two retailers ***(Obj. 7)***

P6-9A Wal-Mart Stores, Inc., the world's largest retailer, recently reported these figures:

WAL-MART STORES, INC.
Consolidated Statement of Income

	Fiscal Years Ended January 31	
(Amounts in millions)	**1996**	**1995**
Revenues:		
Net sales	$93,627	$82,494
Other income—net	1,122	918
	94,749	83,412
Costs and Expenses:		
Cost of sales	74,564	65,586
Operating, selling, and general and administrative expenses	14,951	12,858

WAL-MART STORES, INC.
Consolidated Balance Sheet

	January 31	
(Amounts in millions)	**1996**	**1995**
Assets		
Current Assets:		
Cash and cash equivalents	$ 83	$ 45
Receivables	853	900
Inventories	15,989	14,064
Prepaid expenses and other	406	329
Total Current Assets	17,331	15,338

For the same year ended January 31, 1996, **The May Department Stores Company,** which owns over 300 upscale Lord & Taylor, Hecht's, Foley's, Robinson-May, Kaufmanns, Filene's Basement, and other stores, reported the following:

THE MAY DEPARTMENT STORES COMPANY
Consolidated Statement of Earnings

(Dollars in millions)	Fiscal Year 1996	1995
Net Retail Sales	$10,507	$ 9,759
Other revenues	445	348
Cost of sales	7,461	6,879
Selling, general and administrative expenses	2,081	1,916
Interest expense, net	250	233
Total cost of sales and expenses	9,792	9,028
Earnings from continuing operations before income taxes	1,160	1,079
Provision for income taxes	460	429
Net Earnings from Continuing Operations	700	650

THE MAY DEPARTMENT STORES COMPANY
Consolidated Balance Sheet

(Dollars in millions)	Fiscal Year End February 3, 1996	January 28, 1995
Assets		
Current Assets:		
Cash	$ 12	$ 8
Cash equivalents	147	40
Accounts receivable, net	2,403	2,432
Merchandise inventories	2,134	1,813
Other current assets	169	182
Net current assets of discontinued operation	232	243
Total Current Assets	$5,097	$4,718

Required

1. Compute both companies' gross margin percentage and inventory turnover ratio during 1996.
2. What do these statistics reveal about Wal-Mart's and May's marketing strategies? Which company is clearly the discount merchandiser? Which company depends on higher markups to earn a profit?

Note: Problem 6-10A relates to Appendix B at the end of this chapter.

Converting a company's reported income from the LIFO basis to the FIFO basis ***(Appendix B to Chapter 6)***

P6-10A Colgate-Palmolive Company uses the LIFO method for inventories. In a recent annual report, the company reported these amounts on the balance sheet (in millions):

	December 31, 19X9	19X8
Inventories..................	$676	$692

A note to the financial statements indicated that if current cost (approximate FIFO) had been used, inventories would have been higher by $30 million at the end of 19X9 and higher by $28 million at the end of 19X8. The income statement reported sales revenue of $6,060 million and cost of goods sold of $3,296 million for 19X9.

Required

1. Show the computation of Colgate-Palmolive's gross margin for 19X9 by the LIFO method as actually reported.
2. Compute Colgate-Palmolive's cost of goods sold and gross margin for 19X9 by the FIFO method.
3. Which method makes the company look better in 19X9? Give your reason. If Colgate-Palmolive used the FIFO method, what would be the amount of inventory profit for 19X9?
4. Assume an income tax rate of 35 percent. How much in taxes did Colgate-Palmolive save during 19X9 by using LIFO?
5. How will what you learned in this problem help you (a) evaluate an investment, and (b) manage a business?

(GROUP B)

Accounting for inventory in a perpetual system (Obj. 1, 2)

P6-1B The May Department Stores Company operates 346 department stores in the United States, including Lord & Taylor, Hecht's, Foleys, Robinson-May, Kaufmanns, and Filene's Basement. Assume you are dealing with a single Lord & Taylor store in Washington, D.C. The company's fiscal year ends each January 31. Also assume the Lord & Taylor store in Washington, D.C., began fiscal year 19X6 with an inventory of 50,000 units that cost $1,500,000. During the year, the store purchased merchandise on account as follows:

March (60,000 units @ $32)	$1,920,000
August (40,000 units @ $34)	1,360,000
October (180,000 units @ $35)	6,300,000
Total purchases	$9,580,000

Cash payments on account during the year totaled $9,110,000.

During fiscal year 19X6, the store sold 300,000 units of merchandise for $13,400,000, of which $4,700,000 was for cash and the balance was on account. The May Company uses the LIFO method for inventories.

Operating expenses for the year were $2,430,000. The store paid two-thirds in cash and accrued the rest. The store accrued income tax at the rate of 40 percent.

Required

1. Make summary journal entries to record the Lord & Taylor store's transactions for the year ended January 31, 19X6. The company uses a perpetual inventory system.
2. Determine the LIFO cost of the store's ending inventory at January 31, 19X6. Use a T-account.
3. Prepare the Lord & Taylor store's income statement for the year ended January 31, 19X6. Show totals for the gross margin, income before tax, and net income.

Using the cost-of-goods-sold model to budget operations (Obj. 1)

P6-2B Condensed versions of an Exxon convenience store's most recent income statement and balance sheet reported the following figures. The business is organized as a proprietorship, so it pays no corporate income tax. It uses a periodic inventory system.

EXXON CONVENIENCE STORE
Income Statement
Year Ended December 31, 19X7

Sales	$900,000
Cost of sales	720,000
Gross margin	180,000
Operating expenses	90,000
Net income	$ 90,000

EXXON CONVENIENCE STORE
Balance Sheet
December 31, 19X7

Assets		Liabilities and Capital	
Cash	$ 40,000	Accounts payable	$ 30,000
Inventories	70,000	Note payable	190,000
Land and buildings net	270,000	Total liabilities	220,000
		Owner, capital	160,000
Total assets	$380,000	Total liabilities and capital	$380,000

The owner is budgeting for 19X8. He expects sales to increase by 5% and the gross margin percentage to remain unchanged. To meet customer demand for the increase in sales, ending inventory will need to be $80,000 at December 31, 19X8. The owner can lower operating expenses by doing some of the work himself. He hopes to earn a net income of $100,000 next year.

Required

1. A key variable the owner can control is the amount of inventory he purchases. Show how to determine the amount of purchases the owner should make in 19X8.

2. Prepare the store's budgeted income statement for 19X8 to reach the target net income of $100,000.

Using the periodic and perpetual inventory systems ***(Obj. 1, 2)***

P6-3B Kendrick Tire Co. began March with 50 units of inventory that cost $19 each. The sale price of each was $36. During March, Kendrick completed these inventory transactions:

			Units	Unit Cost	Unit Sale Price
March	2	Purchase......	12	$20	$37
	8	Sale..............	27	19	36
	13	Sale..............	23	19	36
		....	1	20	37
	17	Purchase......	24	20	37
	22	Sale..............	31	20	37
	29	Purchase......	24	21	39

Required

1. The preceding data are taken from Kendrick's perpetual inventory records. Which cost method does Kendrick use?
2. Determine Kendrick's cost of goods sold for March under the
   a. Perpetual inventory system **b.** Periodic inventory system
3. Compute gross margin for March.

Computing inventory by three methods ***(Obj. 2, 3)***

P6-4B An AT&T Phone Center began December with 140 units of inventory that cost $79 each. During December, the store made the following purchases:

Dec.	3	217 @ $81
	12	95 @ 82
	18	210 @ 84
	24	248 @ 87

The store uses the periodic inventory system, and the physical count at December 31 indicates that ending inventory consists of 229 units.

Required

1. Determine the ending inventory and cost-of-goods-sold amounts under the weighted-average, FIFO, and LIFO cost methods. Round weighted-average cost per unit to the nearest cent, and round all other amounts to the nearest dollar.
2. How much income tax would AT&T save during December for this one store by using LIFO versus FIFO? The income tax rate is 40 percent.

Preparing an income statement directly from the accounts ***(Obj. 2, 3)***

P6-5B The records of Sav-On Office Supply include the following accounts for one of its products at December 31 of the current year:

Inventory

Date		Description	Debit	Credit
Jan. 1	Balance	300 units @ $3.00 100 units @ 3.15	1,215	

Purchases

Date	Description	Debit	Credit
Feb. 6	800 units @ $3.15	2,520	
May 19	600 units @ 3.35	2,010	
Aug. 12	460 units @ 3.50	1,610	
Oct. 4	800 units @ 3.70	2,960	
Dec. 31	Balance	9,100	

Sales Revenue

Debit	Date	Description	Credit
	Mar. 12	500 units @ $4.10	2,050
	June 9	1,100 units @ 4.20	4,620
	Aug. 21	300 units @ 4.50	1,350
	Nov. 2	600 units @ 4.50	2,700
	Dec. 18	100 units @ 4.80	480
	Dec. 31	Balance	11,200

Required

1. Prepare a partial income statement through gross margin under the weighted-average, FIFO, and LIFO cost methods. Round weighted-average cost to the nearest cent and all other amounts to the nearest dollar. Sav-On uses a periodic inventory system.
2. Which inventory method would you use to report the highest net income?

Applying the lower-of-cost-or-market rule to inventories ***(Obj. 4)***

P6-6B Kmart has recently been plagued with lackluster sales. The rate of inventory turnover has dropped, and some of the company's merchandise is gathering dust. At the same time, competition has forced some of Kmart's suppliers to lower the prices that Kmart will pay when it replaces its inventory. It is now December 31, 19X9. Assume the current replacement cost of a Kmart store's ending inventory is $500,000 below what Kmart paid for the goods, which was $3,900,000. Before any adjustments at the end of the period, assume the store's Cost of Goods Sold account has a balance of $22,400,000.

What action should Kmart take in this situation, if any? Give any journal entry required. At what amount should Kmart report Inventory on the balance sheet? At what amount should the company report Cost of Goods Sold on the income statement? Discuss the accounting principle or concept that is most relevant to this situation.

Correcting inventory errors over a three-year period ***(Obj. 5)***

P6-7B The accounting records of Heitmiller Steak House show these data (in thousands):

	19X3		19X2		19X1	
Net sales revenue		$210		$165		$170
Cost of goods sold:						
Beginning inventory	$ 15		$ 25		$ 40	
Net purchases	135		100		90	
Cost of goods available	150		125		130	
Less ending inventory	30		15		25	
Cost of goods sold		120		110		105
Gross margin		90		55		65
Operating expenses		74		38		46
Net income		$ 16		$ 17		$ 19

In early 19X4, a team of internal auditors discovered that the ending inventory for 19X1 had been understated by $4 thousand and that the ending inventory for 19X3 had been overstated by $3 thousand. The ending inventory at December 31, 19X2, was correct.

Required

1. Show corrected income statements for the three years.
2. State whether each year's net income as reported here and the related owners' equity amounts are understated or overstated. Ignore income tax because Heitmiller is organized as a proprietorship. For each incorrect figure, indicate the amount of the understatement or overstatement.

Estimating inventory by the gross margin method; preparing the income statement ***(Obj. 6)***

P6-8B Canon Color Labs estimates its inventory by the gross margin method when preparing monthly financial statements. For the past two years, gross margin has averaged 25% of net sales. Assume further that the company's inventory records for stores in the southeastern region reveal the following data:

Inventory, March 1	$ 292,000
Transactions during March:	
Purchases	6,585,000
Purchase discounts	149,000
Purchase returns	8,000
Sales	8,657,000
Sales returns	17,000

Note: Sales returns are decreases in net sales revenue due to a customer's return of merchandise to the seller. *Purchase discounts* and *purchase returns* are decreases in arriving at net purchases.

Required

1. Estimate the March 31 inventory using the gross margin method.
2. Prepare the March income statement through gross margin for the Canon Color Labs stores in the southeastern region.

P6-9B General Motors Corporation is the world's largest automobile manufacturer and one of the largest companies in the world. General Motors reported these figures:

Using the gross margin percentage and the inventory turnover ratio to evaluate two auto makers ***(Obj. 7)***

GENERAL MOTORS CORPORATION
Consolidated Statement of Income

(Dollars in millions)	Years Ended December 31, 1995	1994
Net Sales and Revenues		
Manufactured products	$143,666.1	$134,759.8
Financial services	11,664.0	9,418.8
Computer systems services	8,531.0	6,412.9
Other income	4,967.5	4,359.7
Total Net Sales and Revenues	168,828.6	154,951.2
Costs and Expenses		
Cost of sales	126,535.3	117,220.5
Selling, general, and administrative expenses	13,514.7	12,233.7

GENERAL MOTORS CORPORATION
Consolidated Balance Sheet

(Dollars in millions)	December 31, 1995	1994
Assets		
Cash and cash equivalents	$11,044.3	$10,939.0
Other marketable securities	5,598.6	5,136.6
Total cash and marketable securities	16,642.9	16,075.6
Finance receivables—net	58,732.0	54,077.3
Accounts and notes receivable (less allowances)	9,988.4	8,977.8
Inventories (less allowances)	11,529.5	10,127.8

For the same years, Ford Motor Company, the second largest automaker in the United States, reported the following:

FORD MOTOR COMPANY
Consolidated Statement of Income

(In millions)	Years Ended December 31, 1995	1994
AUTOMOTIVE		
Sales	$110,496	$107,137
Costs and expenses		
Costs of sales	101,171	95,887
Selling, administrative, and other expenses	6,044	5,424
Total costs and expenses	107,215	101,311
Operating income	3,281	5,826

FORD MOTOR COMPANY
Consolidated Balance Sheet

(In millions)	December 31, 1995	1994
ASSETS		
Automotive		
Cash and cash equivalents	$ 5,750	$ 4,481
Marketable securities	6,656	7,602
Total cash, cash equivalents, and marketable securities	12,406	12,083
Receivables	3,321	2,548
Inventories	7,162	6,487
Deferred income taxes	2,709	3,062
Other current assets	1,483	2,006
Net current receivable from Financial Services	200	677
Total current assets	27,281	26,863

Required

1. Compute both companies' gross margin percentage on the sales of automotive and other manufactured products, and their inventory turnover ratio during 1995.
2. Can you tell from these statistics which company should be more profitable? Why? What important category of expenses do the gross margin percentage and the inventory turnover ratio fail to consider?

Note: Problem 6-10B relates to Appendix B at the end of this chapter.

Converting a company's reported income from the LIFO basis to the FIFO basis ***(Appendix B to Chapter 6)***

P6-10B **JC Penney, Inc.,** uses the LIFO method for inventories. In a recent annual report, the company reported these amounts on the balance sheet (in millions):

	End of Fiscal Year 19X6	19X5
Merchandise inventories	$2,657	$2,613

A note to the financial statements indicated that if another method (assume FIFO) had been used, inventories would have been higher by $405 million at the end of the fiscal year 19X6 and higher by $356 million at the end of 19X5. The income statement reported sales revenue of $16,365 million and cost of goods sold of $10,969 million for 19X6.

Required

1. Show the computation of Penney's gross margin for fiscal year 19X6 by the LIFO method as actually reported.
2. Compute Penney's cost of goods sold and gross margin for 19X6 by the FIFO method.
3. Which method makes the company look better in 19X6? Give your reason. If Penney used the FIFO method, what would be the amount of inventory profit for 19X6?
4. Assume an income tax rate of 35 percent. How much did Penney save in taxes during 19X6 by using LIFO?
5. How will what you learned in this problem help you (a) evaluate an investment, and (b) manage a business?

EXTENDING YOUR KNOWLEDGE

DECISION CASES

Assessing the impact of a year-end purchase of inventory ***(Obj. 2, 3)***

Case 1. Whitewater Sporting Goods is nearing the end of its first year of operations. The company made inventory purchases of $745,000 during the year, as follows:

January	1,000	units @	$100.00	=	$100,000
July	4,000		121.25		485,000
November	1,000		160.00		160,000
Totals	6,000				$745,000

Sales for the year will be 5,000 units for $1,200,000 revenue. Expenses other than cost of goods sold and income taxes will be $200,000. The president of the company is undecided about whether to adopt the FIFO method or the LIFO method for inventories.

The company has storage capacity for 5,000 additional units of inventory. Inventory prices are expected to stay at $160 per unit for the next few months. The president is considering purchasing 1,000 additional units of inventory at $160 each before the end of the year. He wishes to know how the purchase would affect net income under both FIFO and LIFO. The income tax rate is 40 percent.

Required

1. To aid company decision making, prepare income statements under FIFO and under LIFO, both without and with the year-end purchase of 1,000 units of inventory at $160 per unit.
2. Compare net income under FIFO without and with the year-end purchase. Make the same comparison under LIFO. Under which method does the year-end purchase have the greater effect on net income?
3. Under which method can a year-end purchase be made in order to manage net income?

Assessing the impact of the inventory costing method on the financial statements ***(Obj. 2, 3, 4)***

Case 2. The inventory costing method a company chooses can affect the financial statements and thus the decisions of the people who use those statements.

Required

1. A leading accounting researcher stated that one inventory costing method reports the most recent costs in the income statement, while another method reports the most recent costs in the balance sheet. In this person's opinion, the result is that one or the other of the statements is "inaccurate" when prices are rising. What did the researcher mean?
2. Conservatism is an accepted accounting concept. Would you want management to be conservative in accounting for inventory if you were (a) a shareholder, or (b) a prospective shareholder? Give your reason.
3. Elgin Ltd. follows conservative accounting and writes the value of its inventory of bicycles down to market, which has declined below cost. The following year, an unexpected cycling craze results in a demand for bicycles that far exceeds supply, and the market price increases above the previous cost. What effect will conservatism have on the income of Elgin over the two years?

ETHICAL ISSUE

During 19X6, Arrow Carpet Company changed to the LIFO method of accounting for inventory. Suppose that during 19X7, Arrow changes back to the FIFO method and the following year switches back to LIFO again.

Required

1. What would you think of a company's ethics if it changed accounting methods every year?
2. What accounting principle would changing methods every year violate?
3. Who can be harmed when a company changes its accounting methods too often? How?

FINANCIAL STATEMENT CASES

Case 1. (Note: To complete requirement 4, you must first read Appendix B to this chapter.)

Inventories ***(Obj. 2, 3, Appendix B to Chapter 6)***

The notes are an important part of a company's financial statements, giving valuable details that would clutter the tabular data presented in the statements. This case will help you learn to use a company's inventory notes. Refer to the Lands' End, Inc., statements and related notes in Appendix A at the end of the book and answer the following questions.

1. How much was the Lands' End merchandise inventory at February 2, 1996? At January 27, 1995?
2. How does Lands' End value its inventories? Which cost method does the company use?
3. By rearranging the cost-of-goods-sold formula, you can determine purchases, which are not disclosed in the Lands' End statements. How much were the company's inventory purchases during the year ended February 2, 1996?
4. Compute the amounts of cost of sales and gross margin that Lands' End would have reported for fiscal 1996 if the company had used the FIFO method for inventory. The Inventory note gives relevant information on the difference between LIFO and FIFO costs of beginning and ending inventory. You are a top manager at Lands' End. Which inventory method would you select if your motive were to report the maximum acceptable gross margin? Which method would you select to minimize income tax?

Analyzing inventories ***(Obj. 2, 3, Appendix B to Chapter 6)***

Case 2. Obtain the annual report of a company. Make sure that *Inventories* are included among its current assets. Answer these questions about the company.

1. How much were the company's total inventories at the end of the current year? At the end of the preceding year?
2. How does the company value its inventories? Which cost method or methods does the company use?
3. Depending on the nature of the company's business, would you expect the company to use a periodic inventory system or a perpetual system? Give your reason.
4. By rearranging the cost-of-goods-sold formula, you can solve for net purchases, which are not disclosed. Show how to compute the company's net purchases during the current year. Examine the company's note titled *Inventories, Merchandise Inventories,* or a similar term. If the company discloses several categories of inventories, including a title similar to Finished Goods, use the beginning and ending balances of Finished Goods for the computation of net purchases. If only one category of Inventories is disclosed, use these beginning and ending balances.
5. (Note: If the company does not use the LIFO method for inventories, you can omit this requirement.) If the company uses LIFO, convert gross margin from the LIFO basis, as reported, to the FIFO basis, which approximates current cost. For this computation, assume that the entire amount of the excess of FIFO (or current) cost over LIFO cost applies to Finished Goods inventories. If your motive were to maximize reported income, would you prefer LIFO or FIFO? If your goal were to minimize income tax, which method would be preferable?

GROUP PROJECT

Comparing companies' inventory turnover ratios ***(Obj. 7)***

Obtain the annual reports of ten companies, two from each of five different industries.

1. Compute each company's gross margin percentage and rate of inventory turnover for the most recent two years. If annual reports are unavailable or do not provide enough data for multiple-year computations, you can gather financial statement data from *Moody's Industrial Manual.*
2. For the industries of the companies you are analyzing, obtain the industry averages for gross margin percentage and inventory turnover from Robert Morris Associates, *Annual Statement Studies;* Dun and Bradstreet, *Industry Norms and Key Business Ratios;* or Leo Troy, *Almanac of Business and Industrial Financial Ratios.*
3. How well does each of your companies compare to the other company in its industry? How well do your companies compare to the average for their industry? What insight about your companies can you glean from these ratios?
4. Write a memo to summarize your findings, stating whether your group would invest in each of the companies it has analyzed.

INTERNET EXERCISE

APPLE COMPUTER

The computer industry poses some interesting inventory-management challenges. As technology improves the computer's internal components, the market value of existing computer inventory drops significantly. This is quite a different situation than that encountered in many industries, where inventory prices tend to increase.

Over the past ten years, Apple Computer—one of the first personal computer companies and a leader in computer innovation—has seen its market share drop from more than 20% to less than 10 percent. This loss of market share is reflected in the company's financial performance. An examination of Apple Computer's financial statements reveals some disturbing trends.

Required

1. Go to **http://www.apple.com/,** the home page for Apple Computer. The company's home page design and content reflect its status as an industry leader.
2. To find Apple's financial statements, click on the highlighted text, **About Apple.** This section provides information regarding Apple's corporate strategy, community outreach programs, history, and financial statements. To go to the financial statements, click on **Investors** under the Investor's Information heading.
3. In the Investor's Information section, scroll down past the recent press releases, quarterly statements, and employment opportunities to the company's most recent annual report. Click on the highlighted text, **annual report.** Answer the following questions regarding Apple Computer's inventory methods.
   a. What inventory valuation method does Apple Computer use?

b. If inventory prices are declining over time and inventory levels are constant, what effect would the LIFO inventory method have on cost of goods sold? Explain.
c. What portion of Apple's assets is tied up in inventory? What elements comprise inventory on the balance sheet?
d. Compute Apple Computer's gross margin and inventory turnover ratios for the past five years. Comment on these trends.
e. What is management's explanation for the changes in gross margin?
f. What is Apple's corporate strategy for the future regarding its gross margins?

APPENDIX A TO CHAPTER 6
Details of Recording Inventory Transactions in a Perpetual Accounting System

The Purchase Invoice: A Basic Business Document

Business documents are the tangible evidence of transactions. In this appendix we will trace the steps that **Austin Sound Stereo Center, Inc.**, a merchandising business in Austin, Texas, takes in ordering, receiving, and paying for inventory. In the process, we will point out the roles that documents play in carrying on business.

1. Suppose Austin Sound wants to stock JVC brand CD players, cassette decks, and speakers. Austin Sound prepares a *purchase order* and mails it to JVC.
2. On receipt of the purchase order, JVC scans its warehouse for the inventory that Austin Sound ordered. JVC ships the equipment and sends an invoice to Austin the same day. The *invoice* is the seller's request for payment from the purchaser. It is also called the *bill.*
3. Often, the purchaser receives the invoice before the inventory arrives. Austin Sound does not pay immediately. Instead, Austin waits until the inventory arrives in order to ensure that it is the correct type and the correct quantity ordered, and that it has arrived in good condition. After the inventory is inspected and approved, Austin Sound pays JVC the invoice amount.

Exhibit 6A-1 on page 310 is an updated copy of an actual invoice from JVC to Austin Sound Stereo Center. From Austin Sound's perspective, this document is a *purchase invoice* (it is being used to purchase goods). To JVC, it is a *sales invoice* (it is being used to sell goods).

Discounts from Purchase Prices

There are two major types of discounts from purchase prices: quantity discounts and cash discounts (called purchase discounts).

QUANTITY DISCOUNTS A *quantity discount,* which is a type of *trade discount,* works this way: The larger the quantity purchased, the lower the price per item. For example, JVC may offer no discount for the purchase of only one or two CD players and charge the *list price*—the full price—of $200 per unit. However, JVC may offer the following quantity discount terms to persuade customers to buy more CD players.

Quantity	Quantity Discount	Net Price Per Unit
Buy minimum quantity, 3 CD players	5%	$190 [$200 – 0.05($200)]
Buy 4–9 CD players	10%	$180 [$200 – 0.10($200)]
Buy more than 9 CD players..........	20%	$160 [$200 – 0.20($200)]

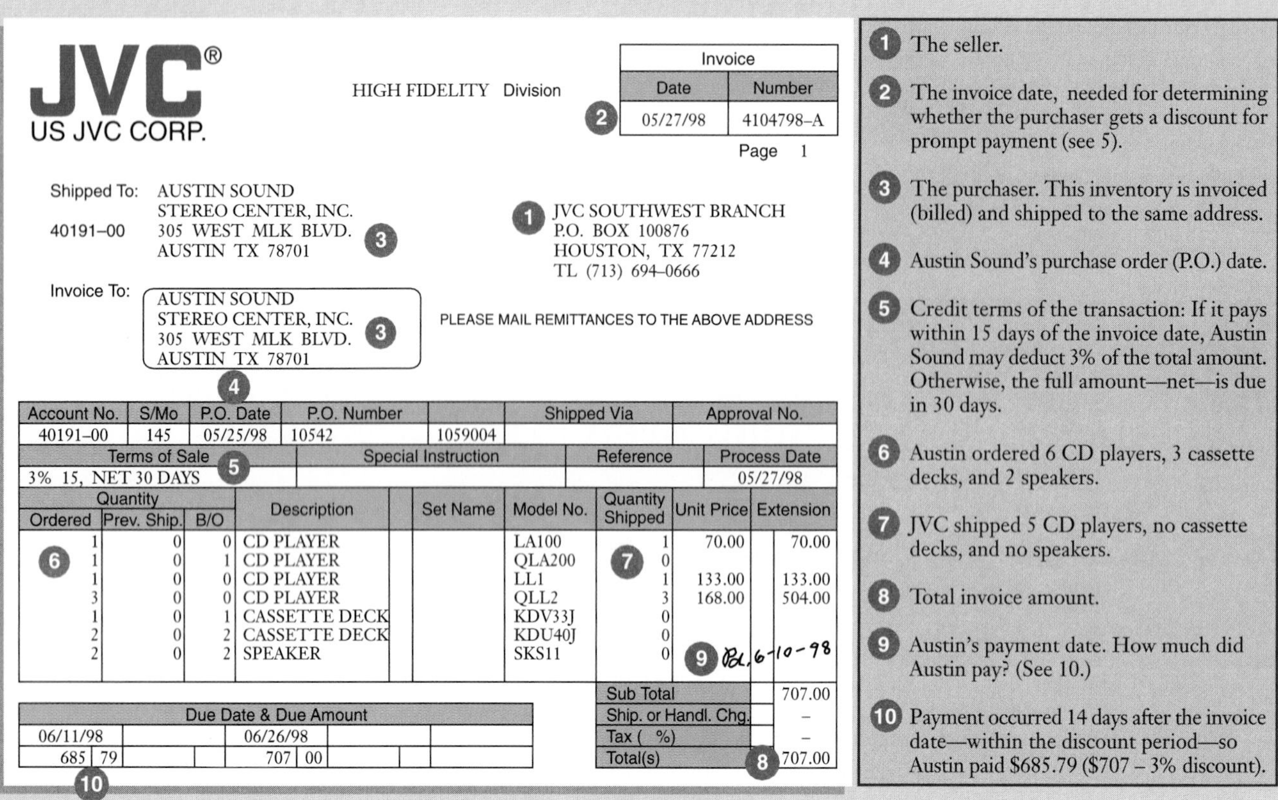

JVC®
US JVC CORP.

HIGH FIDELITY Division

Invoice	
Date	Number
05/27/98	4104798-A

Page 1

Shipped To: AUSTIN SOUND
STEREO CENTER, INC.
40191–00 305 WEST MLK BLVD.
AUSTIN TX 78701

JVC SOUTHWEST BRANCH
P.O. BOX 100876
HOUSTON, TX 77212
TL (713) 694–0666

Invoice To: AUSTIN SOUND
STEREO CENTER, INC.
305 WEST MLK BLVD.
AUSTIN TX 78701

PLEASE MAIL REMITTANCES TO THE ABOVE ADDRESS

Account No.	S/Mo	P.O. Date	P.O. Number		Shipped Via	Approval No.
40191–00	145	05/25/98	10542	1059004		

Terms of Sale	Special Instruction	Reference	Process Date
3% 15, NET 30 DAYS			05/27/98

Quantity Ordered	Quantity Prev. Ship.	Quantity B/O	Description	Set Name	Model No.	Quantity Shipped	Unit Price	Extension
1	0	0	CD PLAYER		LA100	1	70.00	70.00
1	0	1	CD PLAYER		QLA200	0		
1	0	0	CD PLAYER		LL1	1	133.00	133.00
3	0	0	CD PLAYER		QLL2	3	168.00	504.00
1	0	1	CASSETTE DECK		KDV33J	0		
2	0	2	CASSETTE DECK		KDU40J	0		
2	0	2	SPEAKER		SKS11	0	Pd. 6-10-98	
						Sub Total		707.00
						Ship. or Handl. Chg.		–
						Tax (%)		–
						Total(s)		707.00

Due Date & Due Amount	
06/11/98	06/26/98
685 79	707 00

1. The seller.
2. The invoice date, needed for determining whether the purchaser gets a discount for prompt payment (see 5).
3. The purchaser. This inventory is invoiced (billed) and shipped to the same address.
4. Austin Sound's purchase order (P.O.) date.
5. Credit terms of the transaction: If it pays within 15 days of the invoice date, Austin Sound may deduct 3% of the total amount. Otherwise, the full amount—net—is due in 30 days.
6. Austin ordered 6 CD players, 3 cassette decks, and 2 speakers.
7. JVC shipped 5 CD players, no cassette decks, and no speakers.
8. Total invoice amount.
9. Austin's payment date. How much did Austin pay? (See 10.)
10. Payment occurred 14 days after the invoice date—within the discount period—so Austin paid $685.79 ($707 – 3% discount).

EXHIBIT 6A-1
An Invoice

Suppose that Austin Sound purchases five CD players from JVC. The cost of each CD player is therefore $180. Purchase of five units on account would be recorded by debiting Inventory and crediting Accounts Payable for the total price of $900 ($180 × 5).

There is no Quantity Discount account, and there is no special accounting entry for a quantity discount. Instead, all accounting entries are based on the net price of a purchase after the quantity discount has been subtracted.

PURCHASE DISCOUNTS Many businesses also offer *purchase discounts* to their customers as a reward for prompt payment. If a quantity discount is also offered, the purchase discount is computed on the net purchase amount after the quantity discount has been subtracted, further reducing the cost of the inventory.

JVC's credit terms of 3% 15, NET 30 DAYS can also be expressed as 3/15 n/30. This means that Austin Sound may deduct 3% of the total amount due if it pays within 15 days of the invoice date. Otherwise, the full amount—net—is due in 30 days. Terms of simply n/30 indicate that no discount is offered and that payment is due 30 days after the invoice date. Terms of *eom* usually mean that payment is due at the *e*nd *o*f the current *m*onth. However, a purchase after the 25th of the current month on terms of *eom* can be paid at the end of the next month.

Let's use the Exhibit 6A-1 transaction to illustrate accounting for a purchase discount. Austin Sound records this purchase on account as follows:

May 27	Inventory	707.00	
	Accounts Payable		707.00
	Purchased inventory on account.		

Austin Sound paid within the discount period, so its cash payment entry is

June 10	Accounts Payable	707.00	
	Cash ($707.00 × 0.97)		685.79
	Inventory ($707.00 × 0.03)		21.21
	Paid on account within discount period.		

In effect, this inventory cost Austin Sound $685.79 ($707.00 – $21.21), as shown in the following Inventory account:

Inventory			
May 27	707.00	June 10	21.21
Bal.	685.79		

Accounts Payable			
June 10	707.00	May 27	707.00

The account payable to JVC is zero after the invoice is paid.

Alternatively, if Austin Sound pays this invoice after the discount period, it must pay the full invoice amount. In that case, the payment entry is

June 29	Accounts Payable	707.00	
	Cash		707.00
	Paid on account after discount period.		

Without the discount, Austin Sound's cost of the inventory is the full amount of $707, as shown in the following T-account:

Inventory			
May 27	707.00		

Purchase Returns and Allowances

Most businesses allow their customers to return merchandise that is defective, damaged in shipment, or otherwise unsuitable. Or if the buyer chooses to keep damaged goods, the seller may deduct an *allowance* from the amount the buyer owes. Because returns and allowances decrease the cost of inventory, they are recorded by crediting the Inventory account.

Suppose the $70 CD player purchased by Austin Sound (Exhibit 6A-1) was not the CD player ordered. Austin returns the merchandise to the seller and records the purchase return as follows:

June 3	Accounts Payable	70.00	
	Inventory		70.00
	Returned inventory to seller.		

Now assume that one of the CD players was damaged in shipment to Austin Sound. The damage is minor, and Austin decides to keep the CD player in exchange for a $10 allowance from JVC. To record this purchase allowance, Austin Sound makes this entry:

June 4	Accounts Payable	10.00	
	Inventory		10.00
	Received a purchase allowance.		

The return and the allowance had two effects: (1) They decreased Austin Sound's liability, which is why we debit Accounts Payable. (2) They decreased the net cost of the inventory, which is why we credit Inventory.

Assume that Austin Sound has not paid its debt to JVC. After these return and allowance transactions are posted, Austin Sound's accounts will show these balances:

Inventory			
May 27	707.00	June 3	70.00
		June 4	10.00
Bal.	627.00		

Accounts Payable			
June 3	70.00	May 27	707.00
June 4	10.00		
		Bal.	627.00

Transportation Costs

The transportation cost of moving inventory from seller to buyer can be significant. The purchase agreement specifies *FOB terms* to indicate who pays the shipping charges. The term *FOB* stands for *free on board* and governs when the legal title to—ownership of—the goods passes from seller to buyer. When *FOB shipping point* terms are in effect, title passes when the inventory leaves the seller's place of business—the shipping point. The buyer owns the goods while they are in transit and therefore pays the transportation cost. Under *FOB destination* terms, title passes when the goods reach the destination, so the seller pays transportation cost. Exhibit 6A-2 summarizes FOB terms.

FOB shipping point terms are most common, so the buyer generally bears the shipping cost. A freight cost that the buyer pays on an inventory purchase is called *freight in*. In accounting, the cost of an asset includes all costs incurred to bring the asset to its intended use. For inventory, cost includes the net cost after all discounts taken, plus any transportation charges paid. To record the payment for freight in, the buyer debits Inventory and credits Cash or Accounts Payable for the amount. Suppose Austin Sound receives a $60 shipping bill directly from the freight company. Austin Sound's entry to record payment of the freight charge is

June 1	Inventory	60	
	Cash..		60
	Paid a freight bill.		

The freight charge increases the cost of the inventory as follows:

Inventory			
May 27	**707.00**	**June 3**	**70.00**
June 1	**60.00**	**June 4**	**10.00**
Bal.	687.00		

After the returns, allowances, and transportation costs are considered, this inventory has a cost of $687. Any discounts would be computed only on the account payable to the seller, not on the transportation costs, because the freight company offers no discount.

Under FOB shipping point terms, the seller sometimes prepays the transportation cost as a convenience and lists this cost on the invoice. The buyer can then debit Inventory for the combined cost of the inventory and the shipping cost because both costs apply to the merchandise. A $5,000 purchase of goods on account, coupled with a related freight charge of $400, would be recorded as follows:

March 12	Inventory..	5,400	
	Accounts Payable..		5,400
	Purchased inventory on account plus freight.		

If the buyer pays within the discount period, the discount will be computed on the $5,000 merchandise cost, not on the $5,400. No discount is offered on transportation cost.

Freight out is the cost of freight charges paid to ship goods sold to customers. It is paid by the seller, not by the purchaser. Freight out, which is also

EXHIBIT 6A-2
FOB Terms

	FOB Shipping Point	FOB Destination
When does the title pass to the buyer?	Shipping point	Destination
Who pays the transportation cost?	Buyer	Seller

called *delivery expense,* is an operating expense for the seller. It is debited to an account such as Delivery Expense.

Alternative Procedures for Purchase Discounts, Returns and Allowances, and Transportation Costs

Some businesses may want to keep a detailed record of purchase discounts, returns and allowances, and transportation costs. For example, Austin Sound may receive too many defective CD players from an off-brand manufacturer. In recording purchase returns, Austin Sound could credit a special account, Purchase Returns and Allowances, that would serve as a running record of the defective merchandise. The Purchase Returns and Allowances account would carry a credit balance and be treated as a contra account to Inventory. Freight In would be debited for transportation costs. Then, for reporting on the financial statements, these accounts could be combined with the Inventory account as follows (amounts assumed):

Inventory		$35,000
Less: Purchase discounts	$700	
Purchase returns and allowances	800	1,500
Net purchases of inventory		33,500
Freight in		2,100
Total cost of inventory		$35,600

Sale of Inventory and Cost of Goods Sold

Sales of inventory are usually made for cash or on account.

CASH SALE Sales of retailers such as grocery stores, drug stores, gift shops, and restaurants are often for cash. A $3,000 cash sale is recorded by debiting Cash and crediting the revenue account, Sales Revenue, as follows:

Jan. 9	Cash	3,000	
	Sales Revenue		3,000
	Cash sale.		

To update the inventory records, the business also must decrease the Inventory balance. Suppose these goods cost the seller $1,900. An accompanying entry is needed to transfer the $1,900 cost of the goods—not their selling price of $3,000—from the Inventory account (an asset) to Cost of Goods Sold (an expense) as follows:

Jan. 9	Cost of Goods Sold	1,900	
	Inventory		1,900
	Recorded the cost of goods sold.		

As we saw in the chapter, *cost of goods sold* (also called *cost of sales*) is the largest single expense of most businesses that sell merchandise, such as Sony and Austin Sound. It is the cost of the inventory that the business has sold to customers. The Cost of Goods Sold account keeps a current balance as transactions are journalized and posted.

After posting, the Cost of Goods Sold account holds the cost of the merchandise sold (amounts assumed):

Inventory				Cost of Goods Sold	
Purchases	50,000	Jan. 9	1,900	Jan. 9	1,900

The recording of Cost of Goods Sold along with Sales Revenue is an example of the matching principle (Chapter 3, page 111)—matching expense against revenue to measure net income.

The computer automatically records this entry when the cashier keys in the code number of the inventory that is sold. Optical scanners perform this task in most stores.

SALE ON ACCOUNT Most sales by wholesalers, manufacturers, and retailers are made on account (on credit). A $5,000 sale on account is recorded by a debit to Accounts Receivable and a credit to Sales Revenue, as follows:

Jan. 11	Accounts Receivable	5,000	
	Sales Revenue		5,000
	Sale on account.		

If we assume that these goods cost the seller $2,900, the accompanying inventory entry is

Jan. 11	Cost of Goods Sold	2,900	
	Inventory		2,900
	Recorded the cost of goods sold.		

After the recording of the January 9 and 11 transactions, sales revenue is $8,000 ($3,000 + $5,000). Cost of goods sold totals $4,800 ($1,900 + $2,900).

The related cash receipt on account is journalized as follows:

Jan. 19	Cash	5,000	
	Accounts Receivable		5,000
	Collection on account.		

STOP & THINK Why is there no January 19 entry to Sales Revenue, Cost of Goods Sold, or Inventory?

Answer: On January 19, the seller merely receives one asset—Cash—in place of another asset—Accounts Receivable. The sales revenue, the related cost of goods sold, and the decrease in inventory for the goods sold were recorded on January 11.

Sales Discounts and Sales Returns and Allowances

Just as purchase discounts and purchase returns and allowances decrease the cost of inventory purchases, *sales discounts* and *sales returns and allowances,* which are contra accounts to Sales Revenue, decrease the revenue earned on sales. Companies keep close watch on their customers' paying habits and on their own sales of defective and unsuitable merchandise. They maintain separate accounts for Sales Discounts and Sales Returns and Allowances. Let's examine a sequence of the sale transactions of JVC.

On July 7, JVC sells stereo components for $7,200 on credit terms of 2/10 n/30. These goods cost JVC $4,700. JVC's entries to record this credit sale and the cost of the goods sold are as follows:

July 7	Accounts Receivable	7,200	
	Sales Revenue		7,200
	Sale on account.		
July 7	Cost of Goods Sold	4,700	
	Inventory		4,700
	Recorded the cost of goods sold.		

Assume that the buyer returns goods that sold for $600. JVC's cost of this inventory was $400. JVC records the sales return and the related decrease in Accounts Receivable as follows:

July 12	Sales Returns and Allowances	600	
	Accounts Receivable		600
	Received returned goods.		

JVC would also update the inventory records to include the goods returned by the customer and to decrease cost of goods sold as follows:

July 12	Inventory	400	
	Cost of Goods Sold		400
	Returned goods to inventory.		

JVC grants a $100 sales allowance for damaged goods. JVC journalizes this transaction by debiting Sales Returns and Allowances and crediting Accounts Receivable as follows:

July 15	Sales Returns and Allowances	100	
	Accounts Receivable		100
	Granted a sales allowance for damaged goods.		

No inventory entry is needed for a sales allowance transaction because the seller receives no returned goods from the customer. Instead, JVC will receive less cash from the customer.

After the preceding entries are posted, all the accounts have up-to-date balances. Accounts Receivable has a $6,500 debit balance, as follows:

Accounts Receivable

July 7	**7,200**	**July 12**	**600**
		15	**100**
Bal.	6,500		

On July 17, the last day of the discount period, JVC collects half ($3,250) of this receivable ($6,500 × 1/2 = $3,250). The cash receipt is $3,185 [$3,250 – ($3,250 × 0.02)], and the collection entry is

July 17	Cash	3,185	
	Sales Discounts ($3,250 × 0.02)	65	
	Accounts Receivable		3,250
	Cash collection within the discount period.		

Suppose that JVC collects the remainder, $3,250, on July 28. That date is after the discount period, so there is no sales discount. To record this collection on account, JVC debits Cash and credits Accounts Receivable for the $3,250 received, as follows:

July 28	Cash	3,250	
	Accounts Receivable		3,250
	Cash collection after the discount period.		

Net sales is computed by subtracting the contra accounts as follows:

Sales Revenue (*credit* balance account)
– Sales Discounts (*debit* balance account)
– Sales Returns and Allowances (*debit* balance account)
= Net sales (a *credit* subtotal, not a separate account)

Most companies, such as JVC Corp., report to the public only the net sales figure. But JVC managers use the return and allowance data to track customer satisfaction and product quality.

APPENDIX B TO CHAPTER 6

Analyzing Financial Statements—Converting a LIFO Company's Income to the FIFO Basis

Suppose you are a financial analyst, and it is your job to recommend stocks for your clients to purchase as investments. You have narrowed your choice to **Wal-Mart Stores, Inc.**, and **The Gap, Inc.**, the clothing retailer. In your analysis, you observe that Wal-Mart uses the LIFO method for inventories and The Gap uses FIFO. The two companies' net incomes are not comparable because they use different inventory methods. To compare the two companies, you need to place them on the same footing.

The Internal Revenue Service allows companies to use LIFO for income-tax purposes only if they use LIFO for financial reporting. But companies may also report an alternative inventory amount in the financial statements. Doing so presents a rare opportunity to convert a company's net income from the LIFO basis to what the income would have been if the business had used FIFO. Fortunately, you can convert Wal-Mart's income from the LIFO basis, as reported in the company's financial statements, to the FIFO basis. Then you can compare Wal-Mart and The Gap.

Like many other companies that use LIFO, Wal-Mart reports the FIFO cost, a LIFO Reserve, and the LIFO cost of ending inventory. The **LIFO Reserve**[1] is the difference between the LIFO cost of an inventory and what the cost of that inventory would be under FIFO. Wal-Mart reported the following amounts:

WAL-MART USES LIFO:

	(In millions)	
	19X2	**19X1**
From the Wal-Mart balance sheet:		
Inventories (approximate FIFO cost)	$ 7,856	$6,207
Less LIFO reserve	(472)	(399)
LIFO cost	7,384	5,808
From the Wal-Mart income statement:		
Cost of goods sold	$34,786	
Net income	1,608	
Income tax rate	37%	

Converting Wal-Mart's 19X2 net income to the FIFO basis focuses on the LIFO Reserve because the reserve captures the difference between Wal-Mart's ending inventory costed at LIFO and at FIFO. Observe that during each year, the FIFO cost of ending inventory exceeded the LIFO cost. During 19X2, the LIFO Reserve increased by $73 million ($472 million – $399 million). *The LIFO Reserve can increase only when inventory costs are rising.* Recall that during a period of rising costs, LIFO produces the highest cost of goods sold and the lowest net income. Therefore, for 19X2, Wal-Mart's cost of goods sold would have been lower if the company had used the FIFO method for inventories. Wal-Mart's net income would have been higher, as the following computations show:

[1]The LIFO Reserve account is widely used in practice even though the term *reserve* is poor terminology.

IF WAL-MART HAD USED FIFO IN 19X2:

		(In millions)
Cost of goods sold, as reported under LIFO		$34,786
– Increase in LIFO Reserve ($472 – $399)		(73)
= Cost of goods sold, if Wal-Mart had used FIFO		$34,713
Lower Cost of goods sold →	Higher pretax income by	$ 73
	Minus income taxes (37%)	(27)
	Higher net income under FIFO	46
	Actual net income under LIFO	1,608
	Net income Wal-Mart would have reported for 19X2 if using FIFO	$ 1,654

Finally, you can compare Wal-Mart's net income with that of The Gap. All the ratios used for the analysis—current ratio, inventory turnover, and so on—can be compared between the two companies as though they both used the FIFO inventory method.

STOP & THINK How much in income taxes did Wal-Mart save during 19X2 by using LIFO?

Answer: $27 million, which can be used to open new stores.

7

Accounting for Plant Assets, Intangible Assets, and Related Expenses

Learning Objectives

After studying this chapter, you should be able to

1. Determine the cost of a plant asset
2. Account for depreciation
3. Select the best depreciation method for income tax purposes
4. Analyze the effect of a plant asset disposal
5. Account for natural resource assets and depletion
6. Account for intangible assets and amortization
7. Report plant asset transactions on the statement of cash flows

Consolidated Balance Sheet (Assets Only)
The Home Depot, Inc., and Subsidiaries
Amounts in Thousands

		January 28, 1996	*January 29, 1995*
	Assets		
	Current Assets:		
1	Cash and Cash Equivalents	$ 53,269	$ 1,154
2	Short-Term Investments, including current maturities of long-term investments	54,756	56,712
3	Receivables, Net	325,384	272,225
4	Merchandise Inventories	2,180,318	1,749,312
5	Other Current Assets	58,242	53,560
6	Total Current Assets	2,671,969	2,132,963
	Property and Equipment, at cost:		
7	Land (Plant Assets)	1,510,619	1,167,063
8	Buildings (Plant Assets)	1,885,742	1,311,806
9	Furniture, Fixtures and Equipment (Plant Assets)	857,082	634,173
10	Leasehold Improvements (Plant Assets)	314,933	273,015
11	Construction in Progress (Plant Assets)	308,365	289,157
12	Capital Leases (Plant Assets)	92,154	72,054
13		4,968,895	3,747,268
14	Less Accumulated Depreciation and Amortization	507,871	350,031
15	Net Property and Equipment	4,461,024	3,397,237
16	Long-Term Investments	25,436	98,022
17	Notes Receivable	54,715	32,528
18	Cost in Excess of the Fair Value of Net Assets Acquired, net of accumulated amortization of $10,536 at January 28, 1996 and $8,064 at January 29, 1995	87,238	88,513
19	Other	53,651	28,778
20	Total Assets	$7,354,033	$5,778,041

"The Home Depot is one of the really great retailing companies of all time, and it is still in a very powerful growth mode."

—CS FIRST BOSTON/OCTOBER 19, 1995

Founded in 1978 in Atlanta, Georgia, **The Home Depot®** is the world's largest home improvement retailer and ranks among the ten largest retailers in the United States. The company has experienced major growth in the last decade, and the company plans to continue expanding. An excerpt from the annual report makes The Home Depot's strategy clear:

> In keeping with our philosophy that market penetration is one key to our success, we advanced across the United States and Canada in fiscal 1995, opening 83 new stores and relocating five existing stores. That represented a total of approximately 9.2 million square feet of new selling space, a 26% increase over fiscal 1994. By year-end we were operating a total of 423 stores in North America—404 in 31 states and 19 in three Canadian provinces.
>
> We plan to open 90 to 95 new stores in 1996, including 17 in large and medium markets, bringing our total store count to over 500.

Source: The Home Depot® 1995 Annual Report, *Inside Cover, p. 6.*

How did The Home Depot develop the reputation for being in a "very powerful growth mode"? By opening new stores at a rapid pace, as its annual report describes. The Home Depot's balance sheet shows the effect of the company's growth. During the most recent year, total assets increased from \$5.8 billion to \$7.4 billion (line 20)—an increase of 27 percent. The bulk of the growth in assets shows up in Property and Equipment, collectively labeled *plant assets,* which we examine in this chapter.

In this chapter we also cover *intangible assets,* those assets without physical form, such as Cost in Excess of the Fair Value of Net Assets Acquired—better known as *goodwill.* This is the next-to-last asset reported on Home Depot's balance sheet (line 18). Finally, we discuss natural resource assets (such as oil, gas, timber, and gravel) and the expenses that relate to plant assets, natural resources, and intangible assets: depreciation, depletion, and amortization.

Chapter 7 concludes our coverage of asset topics, except for long-term investments, which we discuss in Chapter 10. By the time you complete this chapter, you should feel comfortable with your understanding of the various assets of a business and how companies manage, control, and account for them.

Types of Assets

Long-lived assets used in the operation of a business and not held for sale as investments can be divided into two categories: plant assets and intangible assets. **Plant assets,** or *fixed assets,* are long-lived assets that are tangible—for instance, land, buildings, and equipment. Their physical form provides their usefulness. The expense associated with plant assets is called *depreciation.* Of the plant assets, land is unique. Its cost is *not* depreciated—expensed over time—because its usefulness does not decrease as does that of other assets. Most companies report plant assets under the heading Property, plant, and equipment on the balance sheet.

We introduced the concept of depreciation in Chapter 3, page 116.

Intangible assets are useful not because of their physical characteristics, but because of the special rights they carry. Patents, copyrights, and trademarks are intangible assets. Accounting for intangibles is similar to accounting for plant assets that have a physical form.

Accounting for intangibles has its own terminology. Different names apply to the individual plant assets and their corresponding expense accounts, as shown in Exhibit 7-1.

In the first half of the chapter we illustrate how to identify the cost of a plant asset and how to expense its cost. In the second half we discuss the disposal of plant assets and how to account for natural resources, intangible assets, and capital expenditures. Unless stated otherwise, we describe accounting in accordance with generally accepted accounting principles for financial statement reporting, as distinguished from reporting to the IRS for income tax purposes.

Measuring the Cost of Plant Assets

Objective 1

Determine the cost of a plant asset

The *cost principle* directs a business to carry an asset on the balance sheet at the amount paid for the asset. The *cost of a plant asset* is the purchase price, applicable taxes, purchase commissions, and all other amounts paid to acquire the asset and to ready it for its intended use. In Chapter 6, we applied this principle to determine the cost of inventory. Because the types of costs differ for various categories of plant assets, we discuss the major groups individually.

Refer to Chapter 1, page 12, for a discussion of the cost principle.

EXHIBIT 7-1
Terminology Used in Accounting for Plant Assets and Intangible Assets

Asset Account on the Balance Sheet	Related Expense Account on the Income Statement
Plant Assets	
Land	None
Buildings, Machinery and Equipment, Furniture and Fixtures, and Land Improvements	Depreciation
Natural Resources	Depletion
Intangibles	Amortization

Land

The cost of land includes its purchase price (cash plus any note payable given), brokerage commission, survey fees, legal fees, and any back property taxes that the purchaser pays. Land cost also includes any expenditures for grading and clearing the land and for demolishing or removing any unwanted buildings.

The cost of land does *not* include the cost of fencing, paving, sprinkler systems, and lighting. These separate plant assets—called *land improvements*—are subject to depreciation.

Suppose The Home Depot signs a $300,000 note payable to purchase 20 acres of land for a new store site. Home Depot also pays $10,000 in back property tax, $8,000 in transfer taxes, $5,000 for removal of an old building, a $1,000 survey fee, and $260,000 to pave the parking lot, all in cash. What is the cost of this land?

Purchase price of land		$300,000
Add related costs:		
Back property tax	$10,000	
Transfer taxes	8,000	
Removal of building	5,000	
Survey fee	1,000	
Total related costs		24,000
Total cost of land		$324,000

Note that the cost of paving the lot, $260,000, is *not* included, because the pavement is a land improvement. The Home Depot's entry to record purchase of the land is

Land	324,000	
Note Payable		300,000
Cash		24,000

ASSETS	=	LIABILITIES	+	STOCKHOLDERS' EQUITY
+324,000 −24,000	=	+300,000	+	0

Buildings

The cost of constructing a building includes architectural fees, building permits, contractors' charges, and payments for material, labor, and overhead. The time between the first expenditure for a new building and its completion can be many months, even years, and the number of separate expenditures numerous. If the company constructs its own assets, the cost of the building may also include the cost of interest on money borrowed to finance the construction. (We discuss this topic in the next section of this chapter.) Computers keep track of these details efficiently and assist in monitoring costs as they accumulate.

When an existing building (new or old) is purchased, its cost includes the purchase price, brokerage commission, sales and other taxes, and cash or credit expenditures for repairing and renovating the building for its intended purpose.

Machinery and Equipment

The cost of machinery and equipment includes its purchase price (less any discounts), transportation charges, insurance while in transit, sales and other taxes, purchase commission, installation costs, and any expenditures to test the asset before it is placed in service. After the asset is up and running, insurance, taxes, and maintenance costs are recorded as expenses.

Land and Leasehold Improvements

For a Home Depot store, the cost to pave a parking lot ($260,000) is not part of the cost of the land. Instead, the $260,000 would be recorded in a separate account entitled Land Improvements. This account includes costs for such other items as driveways, signs, fences, and sprinkler systems. Although these assets are located on the land, they are subject to decay, and therefore their cost should be depreciated. Also, the cost of a new building constructed on the land is a debit to the asset account Building.

The Home Depot leases some of its store buildings, warehouses, and vehicles. The company also customizes some of these assets to meet its special needs. For example, The Home Depot may paint its logo on a rental truck and install a special lift on the truck. These improvements are assets of The Home Depot even though the company does not own the truck. The cost of improvements to leased assets appear on the company's balance sheet as *leasehold improvements* (see, for example, line 10 of Home Depot's balance sheet on page 320). The cost of leasehold improvements should be depreciated over the term of the lease. Some companies refer to the depreciation on leasehold improvements as *amortization,* which is the same basic concept as depreciation.

Construction in Progress and Capital Leases

The Home Depot's balance sheet includes two additional categories of plant assets: Construction in Progress (line 11) and Capital Leases (line 12).

For The Home Depot, construction in progress is a plant asset because the company expects to use the assets in its operations.

Construction in Progress *Construction in Progress* is an asset, such as a warehouse, that the company is constructing for its own use. On the balance sheet date, the construction is incomplete and the warehouse is not ready for use. However, the construction costs are assets because The Home Depot expects the warehouse, when completed, to render future benefits for the company. For The Home Depot, construction in progress is a plant asset because the company expects to use the asset in its operations.

Capital Leases A *capital lease* is a lease arrangement similar to an installment purchase of the leased asset. Companies report assets rented through capital leases as assets even though they do not own the assets. Why? Because their lease payments secure the use of the asset over the term of the lease. For example, The Home Depot has long-term capital leases on some of its store buildings. The Home Depot could report the cost of these assets either under Buildings or under Capital Leases. Either way, the asset shows up on the balance sheet as a plant asset. Chapter 8 on long-term liabilities goes into capital leases in more detail.

A capital lease is different from an *operating lease,* which is an ordinary rental agreement, such as an apartment lease or the rental of a Hertz automobile. The lessee (the renter) records an operating lease as Rent Expense.

Capitalizing the Cost of Interest

The Home Depot constructs some of its plant assets and finances part of the construction with borrowed money, on which The Home Depot must pay interest. A company should generally include its interest cost as part of the cost of a self-constructed asset, such as a building or equipment that takes a long time to build. The practice of including interest as part of an asset's cost is called *capitalizing interest.* To **capitalize** a cost means to include it as part of an asset's cost. In accounting, we debit a capitalized cost to an asset (versus an expense) account.

Capitalizing interest cost is an exception to the normal practice of recording interest as an expense. Ordinarily, a company that borrows money records interest expense. But on assets that the business builds for its own use, the company should capitalize some of its interest cost. The logic goes like this: If The Home Depot buys a building from a construction company, the price of the building will include the builder's interest cost to finance the construction. To place self-constructed assets on the same footing, it makes sense to capitalize any interest incurred to finance the construction.

The amount of interest to capitalize is based on the average accumulated construction expenditures for the asset. The interest to capitalize should not exceed the company's actual interest cost. The following equation shows the amount of interest to capitalize:

Interest cost to capitalize = **The lesser of** {
Interest cost based on the average accumulated construction expenditures
or
Actual interest cost on borrowed money during the period
}

Suppose on January 2, 19X7, The Home Depot borrows $1,000,000 on a one-year, 10% note payable to build a warehouse. The company spends the money on construction during 19X7. Total interest for the year is $1,000,000 × .10 = $100,000. Assume The Home Depot's average accumulated expenditures on the construction project during 19X7 are $600,000. The company should capitalize $60,000 ($600,000 × .10) of its total $100,000 interest as part of the building's cost. The Home Depot's full sequence of entries to borrow the money, incur the construction cost, and accrue the interest at year end follows this pattern.

19X7			
Jan. 2	Cash	1,000,000	
	Note Payable		1,000,000
	Borrowed money for construction of building.		

ASSETS	=	LIABILITIES	+	STOCKHOLDERS' EQUITY
+1,000,000	=	+1,000,000	+	0

19X7			
Jan. – Dec.	Building	1,000,000	
	Cash		1,000,000
	Incurred construction cost.		

ASSETS	=	LIABILITIES	+	STOCKHOLDERS' EQUITY
+1,000,000 −1,000,000	=	0	+	0

19X7			
Dec. 31	Building ($600,000 × .10)	60,000	
	Interest Expense	40,000	
	Interest Payable ($1,000,000 × .10)		100,000
	Accrued interest on construction loan.		

ASSETS	=	LIABILITIES	+	STOCKHOLDERS' EQUITY	−	EXPENSES
+60,000	=	+100,000			−	40,000

The last entry capitalizes $60,000 of interest as part of the cost of the building. The remaining $40,000 of interest is expensed as usual. In January 19X8, The Home Depot will pay off the note and the interest payable.

What is The Home Depot's cost of the building? For accounting purposes, the building's cost is $1,060,000, the construction cost ($1,000,000) plus the capitalized amount of interest ($60,000). The Home Depot will then depreciate the asset's total cost of $1,060,000.

STOP & THINK How much interest expense would The Home Depot report on its income statement for 19X7?

Answer: $40,000, the amount recorded as interest expense.

Lump-Sum (or Basket) Purchases of Assets

Businesses often purchase several assets as a group, or in a "basket," for a single lump-sum amount. For example, a company may pay one price for land and an office building. The company must identify the cost of each asset. The total cost is divided among the assets according to their relative sales (or market) values. This allocation technique is called the *relative-sales-value method.*

Suppose Xerox Corporation purchases land and a building in Kansas City for a midwestern sales office. The building sits on two acres of land, and the combined purchase price of land and building is $2,800,000. An appraisal indicates that the land's market (sales) value is $300,000 and that the building's market (sales) value is $2,700,000.

An accountant first figures the ratio of each asset's market value to the total market value. Total appraised value is $2,700,000 + $300,000 = $3,000,000. Thus, the land, valued at $300,000, is 10% of the total market value. The building's appraised value is 90% of the total:

Asset	Market (Sales) Value		Total Market Value		Percentage
Land	$ 300,000	÷	$3,000,000	=	10%
Building	2,700,000	÷	3,000,000	=	90%
Total	$3,000,000				100%

The percentage for each asset is then multiplied by the total purchase price to determine its cost in the purchase:

Asset	Total Purchase Price		Percentage		Allocated Cost
Land	$2,800,000	×	0.10	=	$ 280,000
Building	$2,800,000	×	0.90	=	2,520,000
Total			1.00		$2,800,000

If Xerox pays cash, the entry to record the purchase of the land and building is

Land	280,000	
Building	2,520,000	
Cash		2,800,000

ASSETS	=	LIABILITIES	+	STOCKHOLDERS' EQUITY
+280,000 +2,520,000 −2,800,000	=	0	+	0

STOP & THINK How would a business divide a $120,000 lump-sum purchase price for land, building, and equipment with estimated market values of $40,000, $95,000, and $15,000, respectively?

Answer

	Estimated Market Value	Percentage of Total
Land	$ 40,000	26.7%
Building	95,000	63.3%
Equipment	15,000	10.0%
	$150,000	100.0%

	Allocation of Purchase Price
Land ($120,000 × .267)	$ 32,040
Building ($120,000 × .633)	75,960
Equipment ($120,000 × .10)	12,000
	$120,000

Measuring the Depreciation of Plant Assets

The allocation of a plant asset's cost to expense over the period the asset is used is called *depreciation.* This allocation is designed to match the asset's expense against the revenue generated over the asset's life, as the matching principle directs. Exhibit 7-2 shows the depreciation process for the purchase of a Boeing 737 jet by United Airlines. The primary purpose of depreciation accounting is to measure income accurately. Of less importance is the need to account for the asset's decline in usefulness.

See Chapter 3, page 111, for a discussion of the matching principle.

Suppose The Home Depot buys a computer for use in its accounting system. Home Depot believes it will get four years of service from the computer, which will then be worthless. Using the straight-line depreciation method (which we discuss later in this chapter), The Home Depot expenses one-quarter of the asset's cost in each of its four years of use.

Let's contrast what depreciation accounting is with what it is *not.*

1. *Depreciation is not a process of valuation.* Businesses do not record depreciation based on appraisals of their plant assets made at the end of each period. Instead, businesses allocate the asset's cost to the periods of its useful life based on a specific depreciation method. (We discuss these methods later in this chapter.)

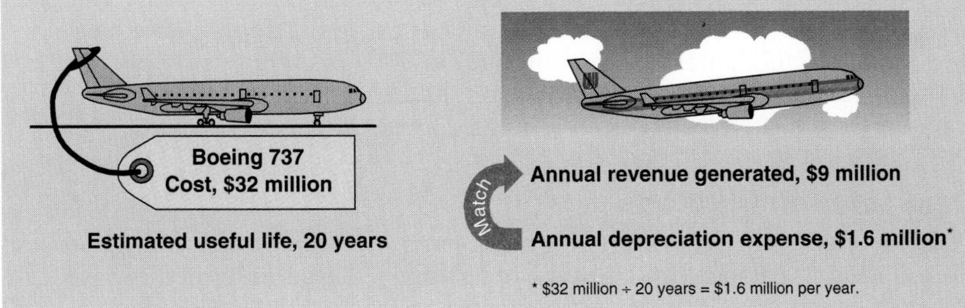

EXHIBIT 7-2
Depreciation and the Matching of Expense with Revenue

2. *Depreciation does not mean that the business sets aside cash to replace assets as they become fully depreciated.* Establishing such a cash fund is a decision entirely separate from depreciation. *Accumulated depreciation* is that portion of the plant asset's cost that has already been recorded as an expense. Accumulated depreciation does not represent a growing amount of cash.

We learned in Chapter 3 (p. 117) that *accumulated depreciation* is the sum of all depreciation expense from the date a plant asset was acquired. *Depreciation expense* is the depreciation amount for the current period only.

The Causes of Depreciation

No asset (other than land) has an unlimited useful life. For some plant assets, physical *wear and tear* from operations and from the elements is the primary cause of depreciation. For example, physical deterioration takes its toll on the usefulness of trucks that move Home Depot merchandise from warehouses to the company's stores. The store fixtures used to display merchandise are also subject to physical wear and tear.

Assets such as computers, other electronic equipment, and airplanes may be *obsolete* before they physically deteriorate. An asset is obsolete when another asset can do the job better or more efficiently. Thus, an asset's useful life may be much shorter than its physical life. Accountants usually depreciate computers over a short period of time—perhaps four years—even though they know the computers will remain in working condition much longer. Whether wear and tear or obsolescence causes depreciation, the asset's cost is depreciated over its expected useful life.

Measuring Depreciation

To measure depreciation for a plant asset, we must know the asset's

1. Cost
2. Estimated useful life
3. Estimated residual value

We have already discussed cost, the purchase price of the asset, which is a known amount. The other two factors must be estimated.

Estimated useful life is the length of service the business expects to get from the asset—an estimate of how long the asset will be useful. Useful life may be expressed in years, units of output, miles, or another measure. For example, the useful life of a building is stated in years. The useful life of a bookbinding machine may be stated as the number of books the machine is expected to bind—that is, its expected units of output. A reasonable measure of a delivery truck's useful life is the total number of miles the truck is expected to travel. Companies base such estimates on past experience and information from industry magazines and government publications.

Estimated residual value—also called *scrap value* or *salvage value*—is the expected cash value of an asset at the end of its useful life. For example, a business may believe that a machine's useful life will be seven years. After that time, the company expects to sell the machine as scrap metal. The amount the business believes it can get for the machine is the estimated residual value. In computations of depreciation, estimated residual value is *not* depreciated because the business expects to receive this amount from disposing of the asset. The full cost of a plant asset is depreciated if the asset is expected to have no residual value. The plant asset's cost minus its estimated residual value is called the **depreciable cost.**

Of the factors entering the computation of depreciation, only one factor is known—cost. The other two factors—useful life and residual value—must be estimated. Depreciation, then, is an estimated amount.

Objective 2

Account for depreciation

Depreciation Methods

Four methods exist for computing depreciation: straight-line, units-of-production, declining-balance, and sum-of-years'-digits. These four methods allocate different amounts of depreciation expense to each period. However, they all result in the same total amount of depreciation, the asset's depreciable cost over

EXHIBIT 7-3
Data for Depreciation Computations for a Home Depot Truck

Data Item	Amount
Cost of truck	$41,000
Estimated residual value	1,000
Depreciable cost	$40,000
Estimated useful life:	
Years	5 years
Units of production	100,000 units [miles]

the life of the asset. Exhibit 7-3 presents the data we will use to illustrate depreciation computations by the three most widely used methods for a Home Depot truck. We omit the sum-of-years'-digits method because so few companies use it.

STRAIGHT-LINE METHOD In the **straight-line (SL) method,** an equal amount of depreciation expense is assigned to each year (or period) of asset use. Depreciable cost is divided by useful life in years to determine the annual depreciation expense. The equation for SL depreciation, applied to the Home Depot truck data from Exhibit 7-3, is

$$\textbf{Straight-line depreciation per year} = \frac{\textbf{Cost} - \textbf{Residual value}}{\textbf{Useful life, in years}} = \frac{\$41{,}000 - \$1{,}000}{5} = \$8{,}000$$

The entry to record this depreciation is

Depreciation Expense	8,000	
Accumulated Depreciation		8,000

ASSETS	=	LIABILITIES	+	STOCKHOLDERS' EQUITY	–	EXPENSES
−8,000	=	0			–	8,000

Assume that the truck was purchased on January 1, 19X1, and that Home Depot's fiscal year ends on December 31. A *straight-line depreciation schedule* is presented in Exhibit 7-4. The final column in Exhibit 7-4 shows the asset's *book value,* which is its cost less accumulated depreciation. Book value is also called *carrying amount* or *carrying value.*

We introduced the concept of book value/carrying value in Chapter 3, page 117.

As an asset is used, accumulated depreciation increases, and the book value decreases. (Compare the Accumulated Depreciation column and the Book Value column.) An asset's final book value is its *residual value* ($1,000 in Exhibit 7-4). At the end of its useful life, the asset is said to be *fully depreciated.*

EXHIBIT 7-4
Straight-Line Depreciation Schedule for a Home Depot Truck

		Depreciation for the Year						
Date	Asset Cost	Depreciation Rate		Depreciable Cost		Depreciation Expense	Accumulated Depreciation	Asset Book Value
1- 1-19X1	$41,000							$41,000
12-31-19X1		0.20*	×	$40,000	=	$8,000	$ 8,000	33,000
12-31-19X2		0.20	×	40,000	=	8,000	16,000	25,000
12-31-19X3		0.20	×	40,000	=	8,000	24,000	17,000
12-31-19X4		0.20	×	40,000	=	8,000	32,000	9,000
12-31-19X5		0.20	×	40,000	=	8,000	40,000	1,000

*1/5 years = 0.20 per year.

Date	Asset Cost	Depreciation for the Year: Depreciation Per Unit		Number of Units		Depreciation Expense	Accumulated Depreciation	Asset Book Value
1- 1-19X1	$41,000							$41,000
12-31-19X1		$0.40	×	20,000	=	$ 8,000	$ 8,000	33,000
12-31-19X2		0.40	×	30,000	=	12,000	20,000	21,000
12-31-19X3		0.40	×	25,000	=	10,000	30,000	11,000
12-31-19X4		0.40	×	15,000	=	6,000	36,000	5,000
12-31-19X5		0.40	×	10,000	=	4,000	40,000	1,000

EXHIBIT 7-5
Units-of-Production Depreciation Schedule for a Home Depot Truck

STOP & THINK An asset with cost of $10,000, useful life of five years, and residual value of $2,000 was purchased on 1/1. What was SL depreciation for the first year?

Answer: $1,600 = ($10,000 – $2,000)/5

UNITS-OF-PRODUCTION METHOD In the **units-of-production (UOP) method,** a fixed amount of depreciation is assigned to each *unit of output,* or service, produced by the plant asset. Depreciable cost is divided by useful life, in units of production, to determine this amount. This per-unit depreciation expense is then multiplied by the number of units produced each period to compute depreciation for the period. The UOP depreciation equation for the Home Depot truck data in Exhibit 7-3, in which the units are miles, is

$$\textbf{Units-of-production depreciation per unit of output} = \frac{\textbf{Cost} - \textbf{Residual value}}{\textbf{Useful life, in units of production}} = \frac{\$41{,}000 - \$1{,}000}{100{,}000 \text{ miles}} = \$0.40 \text{ per mile}$$

Assume that the truck is expected to be driven 20,000 miles during the first year, 30,000 during the second, 25,000 during the third, 15,000 during the fourth, and 10,000 during the fifth. The UOP depreciation schedule for this asset is shown in Exhibit 7-5.

The amount of UOP depreciation each period varies with the number of units the asset produces. In our example, the total number of units produced is 100,000, the measure of this asset's useful life. Therefore, UOP depreciation does not depend directly on time as do the other methods.

STOP & THINK The asset in the preceding Stop & Think produced 3,000 units in the first year, 4,000 in the second, 4,500 in the third, 2,500 in the fourth, and 2,000 units in the last year. Its estimated useful life is 16,000 miles. What was UOP depreciation for each year?

Answers

Depreciation per unit ($10,000 – $2,000)/16,000 = $0.50
- Yr. 1: $1,500 (3,000 × $0.50)
- Yr. 2: $2,000 (4,000 × $0.50)
- Yr. 3: $2,250 (4,500 × $0.50)
- Yr. 4: $1,250 (2,500 × $0.50)
- Yr. 5: $1,000 (2,000 × $0.50)

DOUBLE-DECLINING-BALANCE METHOD An **accelerated depreciation method** writes off a relatively larger amount of the asset's cost nearer the start of its useful life than the straight-line method does. *Double-declining-balance* is one

Date	Asset Cost	DDB Rate		Depreciation for the Year: Asset Book Value		Depreciation Expense	Accumulated Depreciation	Asset Book Value
1- 1-19X1	$41,000							$41,000
12-31-19X1		0.40	×	$41,000	=	$16,400	$16,400	24,600
12-31-19X2		0.40	×	24,600	=	9,840	26,240	14,760
12-31-19X3		0.40	×	14,760	=	5,904	32,144	8,856
12-31-19X4		0.40	×	8,856	=	3,542	35,686	5,314
12-31-19X5						4,314*	40,000	1,000

*Last-year depreciation is the amount needed to reduce asset book value to the residual value ($5,314 – $1,000 = $4,314).

EXHIBIT 7-6
Double-Declining-Balance Depreciation Schedule for a Home Depot Truck

of the accelerated depreciation methods. **Double-declining-balance (DDB) depreciation** computes annual depreciation by multiplying the asset's book value by a constant percentage, which is 2 times the straight-line depreciation rate. DDB amounts are computed as follows.

First, compute the straight-line depreciation rate per year. For example, a five-year truck has a straight-line depreciation rate of 1/5, or 20 percent. A ten-year asset has a straight-line rate of 1/10, or 10%, and so on.

Second, multiply the straight-line rate by 2 to compute the DDB rate. The DDB rate for a ten-year asset is 20% per year (10% × 2 = 20%). For a five-year asset, such as the Home Depot truck in Exhibit 7-3, the DDB rate is 40% (20% × 2 = 40%).

Third, multiply the DDB rate by the period's beginning asset book value (cost less accumulated depreciation). Ignore the residual value of the asset in computing depreciation by the DDB method, except during the last year. The DDB rate for the truck in Exhibit 7-3 is:

$$\textbf{DDB depreciation rate per year} = \frac{1}{\textbf{Useful life, in years}} \times 2$$

$$= \frac{1}{\textbf{5 years}} \times 2$$

$$= \textbf{20\%} \times 2 = \textbf{40\%}$$

Fourth, determine the final year's depreciation amount, the amount needed to reduce the asset's book value to its residual value. In the DDB depreciation schedule in Exhibit 7-6, the fifth and final year's depreciation is $4,314—the $5,314 book value less the $1,000 residual value. The residual value should not be depreciated but should remain on the books until the asset's disposal.

Many companies change to the straight-line method during the next-to-last year of the asset's life. Under this plan, annual depreciation for 19X4 and 19X5 is $3,928. Look at Exhibit 7-6. Depreciable cost at the end of 19X3 is $7,856 (book value of $8,856 less residual value of $1,000). Depreciable cost can be spread evenly over the last two years of the asset's life ($7,856 ÷ 2 remaining years = $3,928 per year).

The DDB method differs from the other methods in two ways. (1) The asset's residual value is ignored initially. In the first year, depreciation is computed on the asset's full cost. (2) The final year's calculation is changed in order to bring the asset's book value to the residual value.

LEARNING TIP Depreciation expense in the final year is whatever amount is needed to reduce the asset's book value to the residual value.

STOP & THINK What is the DDB depreciation of the asset in the Stop & Think at the top of page 330 for each year?

Answers

Yr. 1: $4,000 ($10,000 × 40%)
Yr. 2: $2,400 ($6,000 × 40%)
Yr. 3: $1,440 ($3,600 × 40%)
Yr. 4: $160 ($10,000 – $4,000 – $2,400 – $1,440 – $2,000)*

*The asset is not depreciated below residual value.

Comparing the Depreciation Methods

Let's compare the three methods we've just discussed in terms of the yearly amount of depreciation:

	Amount of Depreciation Per Year		
			Accelerated Method
Year	Straight-Line	Units-of-Production	Double-Declining-Balance
1	$ 8,000	$ 8,000	$16,400
2	8,000	12,000	9,840
3	8,000	10,000	5,904
4	8,000	6,000	3,542
5	8,000	4,000	4,314
Total	$40,000	$40,000	$40,000

The yearly amount of depreciation varies by method, but the total $40,000 depreciable cost is the same under all the methods.

Generally accepted accounting principles (GAAP) direct a business to match an asset's expense against the revenue that asset produces. For a plant asset that generates revenue evenly over time, the straight-line method best meets the matching principle. During each period the asset is used, an equal amount of depreciation is recorded.

The units-of-production method best fits those assets that wear out because of physical use, not obsolescence. Depreciation is recorded only when the asset is used, and the more units the asset generates in a given year, the greater the depreciation expense.

The accelerated method (DDB) applies best to those assets that generate greater revenue earlier in their useful lives. The greater expense recorded under the accelerated methods in the earlier periods is matched against those periods' greater revenue.

Exhibit 7-7 graphs annual depreciation amounts for the straight-line, units-of-production, and accelerated depreciation (DDB) methods. The graph of straight-line depreciation is flat because annual depreciation is the same in all

EXHIBIT 7-7
Depreciation Patterns Through Time

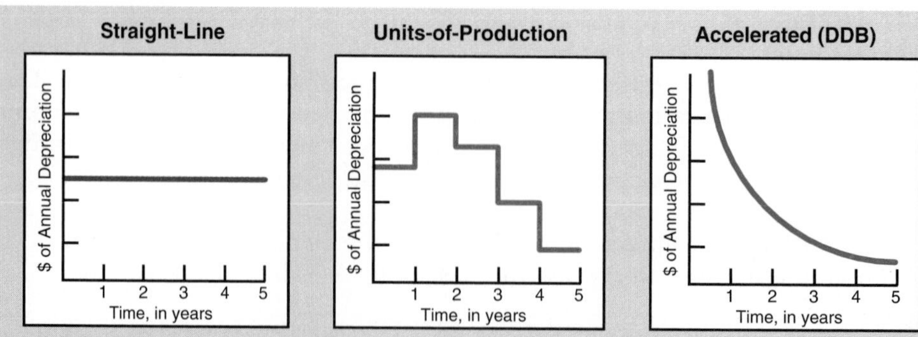

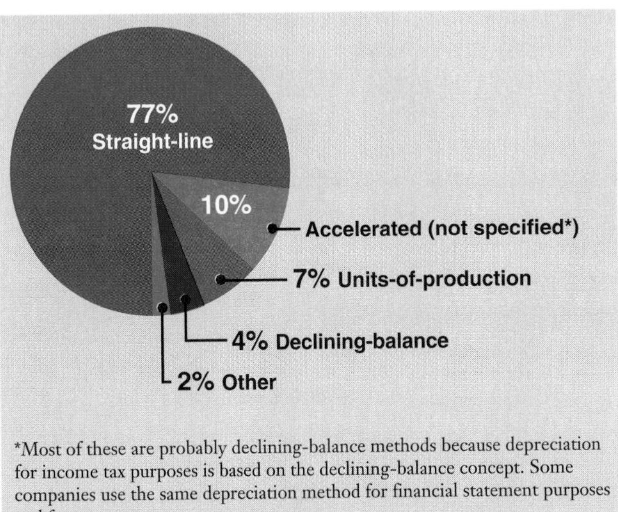

EXHIBIT 7-8
Use of the Depreciation Methods by 600 Companies

periods. Units-of-production depreciation follows no particular pattern because annual depreciation depends on the use of the asset. The greater the use, the greater the amount of depreciation. Accelerated depreciation is greatest in the asset's first year and less in the later years.

A recent survey of 600 companies, conducted by the American Institute of CPAs, indicated that the straight-line method is most popular. Exhibit 7-8 shows the percentages of companies that use each of the depreciation methods.

Mid-Chapter SUMMARY PROBLEM FOR YOUR REVIEW

Hubbard Company purchased equipment on January 1, 19X5, for $44,000. The expected useful life of the equipment is ten years or 100,000 units of production, and its residual value is $4,000. Under three depreciation methods, the annual depreciation expense and the balance of accumulated depreciation at the end of 19X5 and 19X6 are as follows:

	Method A		Method B		Method C	
Year	Annual Depreciation Expense	Accumulated Depreciation	Annual Depreciation Expense	Accumulated Depreciation	Annual Depreciation Expense	Accumulated Depreciation
19X5	$4,000	$4,000	$8,800	$ 8,800	$1,200	$1,200
19X6	4,000	8,000	7,040	15,840	5,600	6,800

Required

1. Identify the depreciation method used in each instance, and show the equation and computation for each. (Round off to the nearest dollar.)
2. Assume continued use of the same method through year 19X7. Determine the annual depreciation expense, accumulated depreciation, and book value of the equipment for 19X5 through 19X7 under each method, assuming 12,000 units of production in 19X7.

ANSWERS

Requirement 1

Method A: Straight-line

Depreciable cost = $40,000 ($44,000 − $4,000)

Each year: $40,000/10 years = $4,000

Method B: Double-declining-balance

$$\text{Rate} = \frac{1}{10 \text{ years}} \times 2 = 10\% \times 2 = 20\%$$

19X5: 0.20 × \$44,000 = \$8,800

19X6: 0.20 × (\$44,000 − \$8,800) = \$7,040

Method C: Units-of-production

$$\text{Depreciation per unit} = \frac{\$44,000 - \$4,000}{100,000 \text{ units}} = \$0.40$$

19X5: \$0.40 × 3,000 units = \$1,200

19X6: \$0.40 × 14,000 units = \$5,600

Requirement 2

	Method A: Straight-Line		
Year	Annual Depreciation Expense	Accumulated Depreciation	Book Value
Start			\$44,000
19X5	\$4,000	\$ 4,000	40,000
19X6	4,000	8,000	36,000
19X7	4,000	12,000	32,000

	Method B: Double-Declining-Balance		
Year	Annual Depreciation Expense	Accumulated Depreciation	Book Value
Start			\$44,000
19X5	\$8,800	\$ 8,800	35,200
19X6	7,040	15,840	28,160
19X7	5,632	21,472	22,528

	Method C: Units-of-Production		
Year	Annual Depreciation Expense	Accumulated Depreciation	Book Value
Start			\$44,000
19X5	\$1,200	\$ 1,200	42,800
19X6	5,600	6,800	37,200
19X7	4,800	11,600	32,400

Computations for 19X7:

Straight-line	\$40,000/10 years	=	\$4,000
Double-declining-balance	0.20 × \$28,160	=	\$5,632
Units-of-production	\$0.40 × 12,000 units	=	\$4,800

Objective 3

Select the best depreciation method for income tax purposes

The Relationship Between Depreciation and Income Taxes

Most companies use the straight-line depreciation method for reporting to their stockholders and creditors on their financial statements. But companies keep a separate set of depreciation records for computing their income taxes. For income tax purposes, most companies use an accelerated depreciation method.

Suppose you are a business manager. The IRS allows an accelerated depreciation method, which most managers prefer to straight-line depreciation. Why? Because it provides the most depreciation expense as quickly as possible, thus decreasing your immediate tax payments. You can then apply the cash you save to fit your business needs. This is the strategy most businesses follow.

To understand the relationships between cash flow (cash provided by operations), depreciation, and income tax, recall our earlier depreciation example for a Home Depot truck: First-year depreciation is $8,000 under straight-line and $16,400 under double-declining-balance. Now for illustrative purposes, let's assume that DDB is permitted for income tax reporting. Let's apply this to a Home Depot store that has a truck with the same depreciation schedule as before. This store has $400,000 in cash sales and $300,000 in cash operating expenses during the truck's first year and an income tax rate of 30 percent. The cash flow analysis appears in Exhibit 7-9.

Exhibit 7-9 highlights several important business relationships. Compare the amount of cash provided by operations before income tax. Both columns show $100,000. If there were no income taxes, the total cash provided by operations would be the same regardless of the depreciation method used. Depreciation is a noncash expense (an expense that requires no outlay of cash) and thus does not affect cash from operations.

Depreciation, however, is a tax-deductible expense. The higher the depreciation expense, the lower the before-tax income and thus the lower the income tax payment. Therefore, accelerated depreciation helps conserve cash for use in the business. Exhibit 7-9 indicates that the business will have $2,520 more cash at the end of the first year if it uses accelerated depreciation instead of SL ($74,920 versus $72,400). If the company invests this money to earn a return of 10% during the second year, it will be better off by $252 ($2,520 × 10% = $252). The cash advantage of using the accelerated method is the $252 additional revenue.

The Tax Reform Act of 1986 created a special depreciation method—used only for income tax purposes—called the Modified Accelerated Cost Recovery System (MACRS). Under this method, assets are grouped into one of eight classes identified by asset life, as shown in Exhibit 7-10 on page 336. Depreciation for the first four classes is computed by the double-declining-balance method. Depreciation for 15-year assets and 20-year assets is computed by the 150%-declining-balance method. Under this method, the annual depreciation rate is computed by multiplying the straight-line rate by 1.50 (rather than by 2.00, as for DDB). For a 20-year asset, the straight-line rate is 0.05 (1/20 = 0.05), so the annual MACRS depreciation rate is 0.075 (0.05 × 1.50 = 0.075). Most real estate is depreciated by the straight-line method.

EXHIBIT 7-9
Cash-Flow Advantage of Accelerated Depreciation over Straight-Line Depreciation for Income Tax Purposes

	Income Tax Rate (30%)	
	SL	**Accelerated**
Cash revenues	$400,000	$400,000
Cash operating expenses	300,000	300,000
Cash provided by operations before income tax	100,000	100,000
Depreciation expense (a noncash expense)	8,000	16,400
Income before income tax	92,000	83,600
Income tax expense (30%)	27,600	25,080
Net income	$ 64,400	$ 58,520
Cash-flow analysis:		
Cash provided by operations before income tax	$100,000	$100,000
Income tax expense	27,600	25,080
Cash provided by operations	$ 72,400	$ 74,920
Extra cash available for investment if DDB is used ($74,920 – $72,400)		$2,520
Assumed earnings rate on investment of extra cash		× 0.10
Cash advantage of using DDB over SL		$ 252

EXHIBIT 7-10
Details of the Modified Accelerated Cost Recovery System (MACRS) Depreciation Method

Class Identified by Asset Life (years)	Representative Assets	Depreciation Method
3	Race horses	DDB
5	Automobiles, light trucks	DDB
7	Equipment	DDB
10	Equipment	DDB
15	Sewage-treatment plants	150% DB
20	Certain real estate	150% DB
27½	Residential rental property	SL
39	Nonresidential rental property	SL

Depreciation for Partial Years

Companies purchase plant assets as needed. They do not wait until the beginning of a year or a month. Therefore, companies must develop policies to compute *depreciation for partial years.* Suppose the **County Line Bar-B-Q Restaurant** in Denver purchases a building on April 1 for $500,000. The building's estimated life is 20 years, and its estimated residual value is $80,000. The restaurant company's fiscal year ends on December 31. Let's consider how the company computes depreciation for the year ended December 31.

Many companies compute partial-year depreciation by first computing a full year's depreciation. They then multiply that amount by the fraction of the year that they held the asset. Assuming the straight-line method, the year's depreciation for the restaurant building is $15,750, computed as follows:

$$\textbf{Full-year depreciation} \quad \frac{\$500{,}000 - \$80{,}000}{20} = \$21{,}000$$

$$\textbf{Partial year depreciation} \quad \$21{,}000 \times 9/12 = \$15{,}750$$

What if the company bought the asset on April 18? A widely used policy directs businesses to record no depreciation on assets purchased after the 15th of the month and to record a full month's depreciation on an asset bought on or before the 15th. Thus, the company would record no depreciation for April on an April 18 purchase. In that case, the year's depreciation would be $14,000 ($21,000 × 8/12).

How is partial-year depreciation computed under the other depreciation methods? Suppose County Line Bar-B-Q acquires the building on October 4 and uses the double-declining-balance method. For a 20-year asset, the DDB rate is 10% (1/20 = 5%; 5% × 2 = 10%). The annual depreciation computations for 19X1, 19X2, and 19X3 are shown in Exhibit 7-11.

Most companies use computerized systems to account for fixed assets. They identify each asset with a unique identification number and indicate the asset's cost, estimated life, residual value, and depreciation method. The system will automatically calculate the depreciation expense for each period. Both Accumulated Depreciation and book value are automatically updated.

EXHIBIT 7-11
Annual DDB Depreciation for Partial Years

		Depreciation for the Year								
Date	Asset Cost	DDB Rate		Asset Book Value, Beginning		Fraction of the Year		Depreciation Expense	Accumulated Depreciation	Asset Book Value, Ending
10- 4-19X1	$500,000									$500,000
12-31-19X1		1/20 × 2 = 0.10	×	$500,000	×	3/12	=	$12,500	$ 12,500	487,500
12-31-19X2		0.10	×	487,500	×	12/12	=	48,750	61,250	438,750
12-31-19X3		0.10	×	438,750	×	12/12	=	43,875	105,125	394,875

Changing the Useful Life of a Depreciable Asset

> *The Walt Disney Company made a change in accounting estimate, to recalculate depreciation on the basis of revised useful lives of several of its theme park assets.*

As we've discussed, a business must estimate the useful life of a plant asset to compute depreciation on that asset. This prediction is the most difficult part of accounting for depreciation. After the asset is put into use, the business may refine its estimate on the basis of experience and new information. The **Walt Disney Company** made such a change, called a *change in accounting estimate.* Disney recalculated depreciation on the basis of revised useful lives of several of its theme park assets. The following note in Walt Disney's financial statements reports this change in accounting estimate:

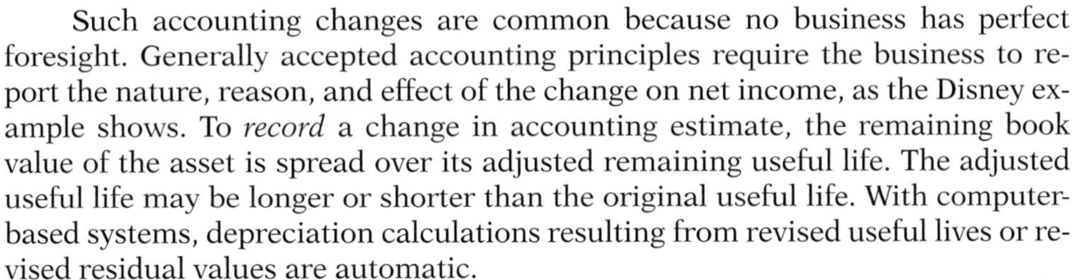

Note 5

. . . [T]he Company extended the estimated useful lives of certain theme park ride and attraction assets based upon historical data and engineering studies. The effect of this change was to decrease depreciation by approximately $8 million (an increase in net income of approximately $4.2 million . . .).

Such accounting changes are common because no business has perfect foresight. Generally accepted accounting principles require the business to report the nature, reason, and effect of the change on net income, as the Disney example shows. To *record* a change in accounting estimate, the remaining book value of the asset is spread over its adjusted remaining useful life. The adjusted useful life may be longer or shorter than the original useful life. With computer-based systems, depreciation calculations resulting from revised useful lives or revised residual values are automatic.

Assume that Disney's hot dog stand cost $40,000 and that the company originally believed the asset had an eight-year useful life with no residual value. Using the straight-line method, the company would record $5,000 depreciation each year ($40,000/8 years = $5,000). Suppose Disney used the asset for two years. Accumulated depreciation reached $10,000, leaving a remaining depreciable book value (cost *less* accumulated depreciation *less* residual value) of $30,000 ($40,000 – $10,000). From its experience with the asset during the first two years, management believes the asset will remain useful for an additional ten years. The company would compute a revised annual depreciation amount and record it as follows:

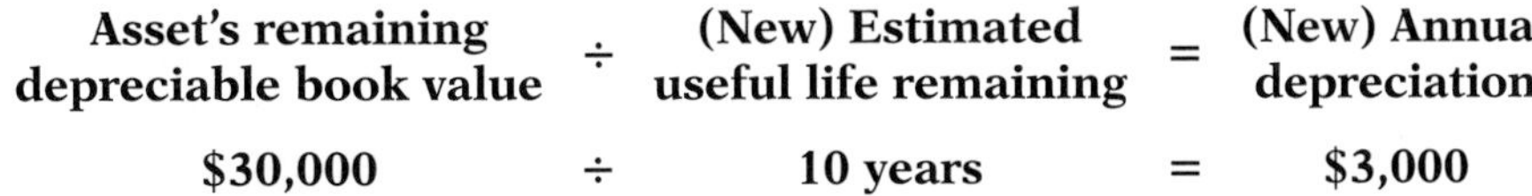

Asset's remaining depreciable book value	÷	(New) Estimated useful life remaining	=	(New) Annual depreciation
$30,000	÷	**10 years**	=	**$3,000**

The yearly depreciation entry based on the new estimated useful life is

Depreciation Expense—Hot Dog Stand	3,000	
Accumulated Depreciation—Hot Dog Stand		3,000

ASSETS	=	LIABILITIES	+	STOCKHOLDERS' EQUITY	−	EXPENSES
−3,000	=	0			−	3,000

STOP & THINK

1. Suppose The Home Depot was having a bad year—net income below expectations and lower than last year's income. For depreciation purposes, Home Depot extended the estimated useful lives of its depreciable assets. How would this accounting

change affect Home Depot's (a) depreciation expense, (b) net income, and (c) owners' equity?

2. Suppose that The Home Depot's accounting change turned a loss year into a profitable year. Without the accounting change, the company would have reported a net loss for the year. But the accounting change enabled The Home Depot to report net income. Under GAAP, Home Depot's annual report must disclose the accounting change and its effect on net income. Would investors evaluate The Home Depot as better or worse in response to these disclosures?

Answers

1. An accounting change that lengthens the estimated useful lives of depreciable assets (a) decreases depreciation expense and (b, c) increases net income and owners' equity.
2. Investors' reactions are not always predictable. There is evidence, however, that companies cannot fool investors. If investors have enough information—such as the knowledge of an accounting change disclosed in the annual report—they can process the information correctly. In this case, investment advisers would *probably* subtract from Home Depot's reported net income the amount caused by the accounting change. Investors could then use the remaining net *loss* figure to evaluate Home Depot's lack of progress during the year. Investors would probably view The Home Depot as worse for having made this accounting change. For this reason, and because the ethics behind such an accounting change are questionable, The Home Depot's managers would not engage in this type of activity.

Using Fully Depreciated Assets

A *fully depreciated asset* is an asset that has reached the end of its *estimated* useful life. No more depreciation is recorded for the asset. If the asset is no longer suitable for its purpose, it is disposed of, as discussed in the next section. However, the company may be in a cash bind and unable to replace the asset. Or the asset's useful life may have been underestimated at the outset. Foresight is not perfect. In any event, companies sometimes continue using fully depreciated assets. The asset account and its related accumulated depreciation account remain in the ledger even though no additional depreciation is recorded for the asset.

LEARNING TIP The total amount of depreciation recorded on an asset cannot exceed its depreciable cost. An asset *can* be used after it is fully depreciated.

Disposal of Plant Assets

Objective 4

Analyze the effect of a plant asset disposal

Eventually, a plant asset ceases to serve a company's needs. The asset may have become worn out, obsolete, or for some other reason no longer useful to the business. In general, a company disposes of a plant asset by selling it or exchanging it. If the asset cannot be sold or exchanged, then the asset is junked. Whatever the method of disposal, the business should bring depreciation up to date to measure the asset's final book value properly.

To account for disposal, credit the asset account and debit its related accumulated depreciation account. Suppose the final year's depreciation expense has just been recorded for a machine that cost $6,000 and is estimated to have zero residual value. The machine's accumulated depreciation thus totals $6,000. Assuming that this asset cannot be sold or exchanged, the entry to record its disposal is

Accumulated Depreciation—Machinery	6,000	
Machinery		6,000
To dispose of fully depreciated machine.		

ASSETS	=	LIABILITIES	+	STOCKHOLDERS' EQUITY
+6,000 −6,000	=	0	+	0

If assets are junked before being fully depreciated, the company records a loss equal to the asset's book value. Suppose Wal-Mart store fixtures that cost $4,000 are disposed of in this manner. Accumulated depreciation is $3,000, and book value is therefore $1,000. Disposal of these store fixtures is recorded as follows:

Accumulated Depreciation—Store Fixtures	3,000	
Loss on Disposal of Store Fixtures	1,000	
Store Fixtures..		4,000
To dispose of store fixtures.		

ASSETS	=	LIABILITIES	+	STOCKHOLDERS' EQUITY	−	LOSSES
+3,000 −4,000	=	0			−	1,000

Note that the $3,000 debit to Accumulated Depreciation represents a $3,000 increase in assets. This is the case because we are *decreasing* a contra asset account, which is the same as *increasing* an asset account.

Loss accounts such as Loss on Disposal of Store Fixtures decrease net income. Losses are reported on the income statement.

Selling a Plant Asset

Suppose a business sells furniture on September 30, 19X4, for $5,000 cash. The furniture cost $10,000 when purchased on January 1, 19X1, and has been depreciated on a straight-line basis. Managers estimated a ten-year useful life and no residual value. Prior to recording the sale of the furniture, accountants must update depreciation. Since the business uses the calendar year as its accounting period, partial-year depreciation must be recorded for the asset's expense from January 1, 19X4, to the sale date. The straight-line depreciation entry at September 30, 19X4, is

Sep. 30	Depreciation Expense ($10,000/10 years × 9/12)	750	
	Accumulated Depreciation—Furniture		750
	To update depreciation.		

ASSETS	=	LIABILITIES	+	STOCKHOLDERS' EQUITY	−	EXPENSES
−750	=	0			−	750

After this entry is posted, the Furniture account and the Accumulated Depreciation—Furniture account appear as follows. The furniture book value is $6,250 ($10,000 − $3,750).

Furniture

Jan. 1, 19X1	10,000	

Accumulated Depreciation—Furniture

	Dec. 31, 19X1	1,000
	Dec. 31, 19X2	1,000
	Dec. 31, 19X3	1,000
	Sep. 30, 19X4	750
	Balance	3,750

Suppose the business sells the furniture for $5,000 cash. The loss on the sale is $1,250, determined as follows:

Cash received from sale of the asset		$5,000
Book value of asset sold:		
Cost	$10,000	
Accumulated depreciation up to date of sale	3,750	6,250
Gain (loss) on sale of the asset		($1,250)

The entry to record sale of the furniture for $5,000 cash is

Sep. 30	Cash	5,000	
	Accumulated Depreciation—Furniture	3,750	
	Loss on Sale of Furniture	1,250	
	Furniture		10,000
	To sell furniture.		

ASSETS	=	LIABILITIES	+	STOCKHOLDERS' EQUITY	−	LOSSES
+5,000						
+3,750	=	0			−	1,250
−10,000						

When recording the sale of a plant asset, the business must remove the balances in the asset account (Furniture, in this case) and its related accumulated depreciation account and also record a gain or a loss if the amount of cash received differs from the asset's book value. In our example, cash of $5,000 is less than the book value of the furniture, $6,250. The result is a loss of $1,250.

If the sale price had been $7,000, the business would have had a gain of $750 (Cash, $7,000 – asset book value, $6,250). The entry to record this transaction would be

Sep. 30	Cash	7,000	
	Accumulated Depreciation—Furniture	3,750	
	Furniture		10,000
	Gain on Sale of Furniture		750
	To sell furniture.		

ASSETS	=	LIABILITIES	+	STOCKHOLDERS' EQUITY	+	GAINS
+7,000						
+3,750	=	0			+	750
−10,000						

A gain is recorded when an asset is sold for a price greater than the asset's book value. A loss is recorded when the sale price is less than book value. Gains increase net income. Gains and losses are reported on the income statement, as shown for Wal-Mart Stores, Inc., in the following Stop & Think.

STOP & THINK Suppose Wal-Mart's comparative income statement for two years included these items:

	(In billions) 19X2	19X1
Net sales	$42.0	$40.0
Income from operations	$ 0.2	$ 1.0
Gain on sale of store facilities	1.2	
Income before income taxes	$ 1.4	$ 1.0

Which was a better year for Wal-Mart—19X2 or 19X1?

Answer: From a *sales* standpoint, 19X2 was better because sales were higher. But from an *income* standpoint, 19X1 was the better year. In 19X1, merchandising operations—Wal-Mart's main business—generated $1 billion of income before taxes. In 19X2, merchandising produced only $0.2 billion of pre-tax income. Most of the company's income in 19X2 came from selling store facilities. A business cannot hope to continue on this path very long. This example illustrates why investors and creditors are interested in the sources of a company's profits, not just the final amount of net income.

Exchanging Plant Assets

Businesses often exchange (trade in) their old plant assets for similar assets that are newer and more efficient. For example, Domino's pizzeria may decide to trade in a five-year-old delivery car for a newer model. To record the exchange, the business must remove from the books the balances for the asset being exchanged and its related accumulated depreciation account.

In many cases, the business simply carries forward the book value of the old asset plus any cash payment as the cost of the new asset. For example, assume the pizzeria's old delivery car cost $9,000 and has accumulated depreciation of $8,000. The car's book value is $1,000. If the pizzeria trades in the old automobile and pays cash of $10,000, the cost of the new delivery car is $11,000. The pizzeria records the exchange transaction as follows:

Delivery Auto (new)	11,000	
Accumulated Depreciation (old)	8,000	
Delivery Auto (old)		9,000
Cash		10,000
Traded in old delivery car for new auto.		

ASSETS	=	LIABILITIES	+	STOCKHOLDERS' EQUITY
+11,000				
+8,000	=	0	+	0
−9,000				
−10,000				

Under certain conditions, the business can have a loss on an exchange. Gains on the exchange of assets are not as common because accounting conservatism favors losses but not gains.

Internal Control of Plant Assets

Internal control of plant assets includes provisions for safeguarding the assets and an adequate accounting system. To see the need for controlling plant assets, consider the following situation. The home office and top managers of **Symington Wayne Corporation** are in New Jersey. The company manufactures gas pumps in Canada, then sells them in Europe. The company's top managers and owners rarely see the manufacturing plant and therefore cannot control plant assets by on-the-spot management. What features does their internal control system need?

Recall from Chapter 4 the importance of a strong system of internal controls within a business.

Safeguarding plant assets includes

1. Assigning responsibility for custody of the assets.
2. Separating custody of assets from accounting for the assets. (This separation of duties is a cornerstone of internal control in almost every area.)
3. Setting up security measures—for instance, armed guards and restricted access to plant assets—to prevent theft.
4. Protecting assets from the elements (rain, snow, and so on).
5. Having adequate insurance against fire, storm, and other casualty losses.

EXHIBIT 7-12
Plant Asset Control Record

Asset Display racks **Location** Paint
Employee responsible for the asset Department manager

Cost $190,000 **Purchased From** Industrial Furniture Co.
Depreciation Method SL
Useful Life 10 years **Residual Value** $10,000
General Ledger Account Store Fixtures

Date	Explanation	Asset			Accumulated Depreciation		
		Dr.	Cr.	Bal.	Dr.	Cr.	Bal.
Jul. 3, 19X4	Purchase	190,000		190,000			
Dec. 31, 19X4	Depreciation					9,000	9,000
Dec. 31, 19X5	Depreciation					18,000	27,000
Dec. 31, 19X6	Depreciation					18,000	45,000

6. Training operating personnel in the proper use of the assets.
7. Keeping a regular maintenance schedule.

Plant assets are controlled in much the same way that high-priced inventory is controlled—with the help of subsidiary records. For plant assets, companies use a plant asset ledger. Each plant asset is represented by a control record describing the asset and listing its location and the employee responsibile for it. These details aid in safeguarding the asset. The control record also shows the asset's cost, useful life, and other accounting data. Exhibit 7-12 could be an example for the display racks in a Home Depot store.

The control record provides the data for computing depreciation on the asset. It serves as a subsidiary record of accumulated depreciation. The asset balance ($190,000) and accumulated depreciation amount ($45,000) agree with the balances in the respective general ledger accounts (Store Fixtures and Accumulated Depreciation—Store Fixtures).

Accounting for Natural Resources and Depletion

Objective 5

Account for natural resource assets and depletion

Natural resources such as iron ore, petroleum (oil), natural gas, and timber are plant assets of a special type. An investment in natural resources could be described as an investment in inventories in the ground (oil) or on top of the ground (timber). As plant assets (such as machines) are expensed through depreciation, so natural resource assets are expensed through depletion. **Depletion expense** is that portion of the cost of natural resources that is used up in a particular period. Depletion expense is computed in the same way as units-of-production depreciation.

An oil well may cost $100,000 and contain an estimated 10,000 barrels of oil. The depletion rate would be $10 per barrel ($100,000/10,000 barrels). If 3,000 barrels are extracted during the year, depletion expense is $30,000 (3,000 barrels × $10 per barrel). The depletion entry for the year is

Depletion Expense (3,000 barrels × $10)	30,000	
Accumulated Depletion—Oil		30,000

ASSETS	=	LIABILITIES	+	STOCKHOLDERS' EQUITY	−	EXPENSES
−30,000	=	0			−	30,000

If 4,500 barrels are removed the next year, that period's depletion is $45,000 (4,500 barrels × $10 per barrel). Accumulated Depletion is a contra account similar to Accumulated Depreciation.

Natural resource assets can be reported on the balance sheet as follows:

Property, Plant, and Equipment:		
Land		$ 120,000
Buildings	$ 800,000	
Equipment	160,000	
	960,000	
Less: Accumulated depreciation	410,000	550,000
Oil	**$340,000**	
Less: Accumulated depletion	**75,000**	**265,000**
Total property, plant, and equipment		$ 935,000

STOP & THINK Pulp Products pays $500,000 for land that contains an estimated 500,000 board feet of timber. The land can be sold for $100,000 after the timber has been cut. If Pulp harvests 200,000 board feet in the year of purchase, how much depletion should be recorded?

Answer: ($500,000 – $100,000) ÷ 500,000 = $0.80 per foot × 200,000 = $160,000

Accounting for Intangible Assets and Amortization

Objective 6

Account for intangible assets and amortization

As we saw earlier in the chapter, *intangible assets* are long-lived assets that are not physical in nature. Instead, these assets are special rights to current and expected future benefits from patents, copyrights, trademarks, franchises, leaseholds, and goodwill.

The acquisition cost of an intangible asset is debited to an asset account. The intangible is expensed through **amortization,** the systematic reduction of a lump-sum amount. Amortization applies to intangible assets in the same way depreciation applies to plant assets and depletion applies to natural resources. All three methods of expensing assets are conceptually the same.

Amortization is generally computed on a straight-line basis over the asset's estimated useful life—up to a maximum of 40 years, according to GAAP. But obsolescence often cuts an intangible asset's useful life shorter than its legal life. Amortization expense for an intangible asset is written off directly against the asset account rather than held in an accumulated amortization account. The residual value of most intangible assets is zero.

Assume that a business purchases a patent on a special manufacturing process. Legally, the patent may run for 17 years. The business realizes, however, that new technologies will limit the patented process's life to four years. If the patent cost $80,000, each year's amortization expense is $20,000 ($80,000/4). The balance sheet reports the patent at its acquisition cost less amortization expense to date. After one year, the patent has a $60,000 balance ($80,000 – $20,000), after two years a $40,000 balance, and so on.

A brief discussion of specific intangible assets follows.

- **Patents** are federal government grants giving the holder the exclusive right for 17 years to produce and sell an invention. The invention may be a product or a process—for example, **Sony** compact disk players and the **Dolby** noise-reduction process. Like any other asset, a patent may be purchased. Suppose a company pays $170,000 to acquire a patent on January 1, and the business believes the expected useful life of the patent is only five years.

Amortization expense is $34,000 per year ($170,000/5 years). The company's acquisition and amortization entries for this patent are

Jan. 1	Patents	170,000	
	Cash		170,000
	To acquire a patent.		

ASSETS	=	LIABILITIES	+	STOCKHOLDERS' EQUITY
+170,000 −170,000	=	0	+	0

Dec. 31	Amortization Expense—Patents ($170,000/5)	34,000	
	Patents		34,000
	To amortize the cost of a patent.		

ASSETS	=	LIABILITIES	+	STOCKHOLDERS' EQUITY	−	EXPENSES
−34,000	=	0			−	34,000

- **Copyrights** are exclusive rights to reproduce and sell a book, musical composition, film, or other work of art. Copyrights also protect computer software programs, such as **Microsoft's** Windows and **Lotus's** 1-2-3 spreadsheet. Issued by the federal government, copyrights extend 50 years beyond the author's (composer's, artist's, or programmer's) life. The cost of obtaining a copyright from the government is low, but a company may pay a large sum to purchase an existing copyright from the owner. For example, a publisher may pay the author of a popular novel $1 million or more for the book's copyright. The useful life of a copyright is usually no longer than two or three years, so each period's amortization amount is a high proportion of the copyright's cost.
- **Trademarks** and **trade names** (or **brand names**) are distinctive identifications of products or services. The "eye" symbol that flashes across our television screens is the trademark that identifies the **CBS** television network. You are probably also familiar with **NBC's** peacock trademark. Seven-Up, Pepsi, Egg McMuffin, and Rice-a-Roni are everyday trade names. Advertising slogans that are legally protected include **United Airlines'** "Fly the friendly skies" and **Avis Rental Car's** "We try harder."

  The cost of a trademark or trade name is amortized over its useful life, not to exceed 40 years. The cost of advertising and promotions that use the trademark or trade name is not a part of the asset's cost, but rather a debit to the Advertising Expense account.
- **Franchises** and **licenses** are privileges granted by a private business or a government to sell a product or service in accordance with specified conditions. The **Dallas Cowboys** football organization is a franchise granted to its owner, Jerry Jones, by the National Football League. **McDonald's** restaurants and **Holiday Inns** are popular franchises. **Consolidated Edison Company (ConEd)** holds a New York City franchise right to provide electricity to residents. The acquisition costs of franchises and licenses are amortized over their useful lives rather than over legal lives, subject to the 40-year maximum.

The Dallas Cowboys football organization is a franchise granted to its owner, Jerry Jones, by the National Football League.

- A **leasehold** is a prepayment of rent that a lessee (renter) makes to secure the use of an asset from a lessor (landlord). For example, Wal-Mart leases many of its store buildings from other entities. Often, leases require the lessee to make this prepayment in addition to monthly rental payments. The lessee debits the monthly lease payments to the Rent Expense account. The prepayment, however, is prepaid rent recorded in an intangible asset account titled Leaseholds. This amount is amortized over the life of the lease by debiting Rent Expense and crediting Leaseholds.

Refer to the discussion of The Home Depot's balance sheet on page 324.

- The term *goodwill* in accounting has a rather different meaning than the everyday term, "goodwill among men." In accounting, **goodwill** is defined as the excess of the cost of an acquired company over the sum of the market values of its net assets (assets minus liabilities). Recently, Wal-Mart Stores, Inc., has been expanding into Mexico. Suppose Wal-Mart acquires Mexana Company at a cost of \$10 million. The sum of the market values of Mexana's assets is \$9 million, and its liabilities total \$1 million. In this case, Wal-Mart paid \$2 million for goodwill, computed as follows:

Purchase price paid for Mexana Company....................		\$10 million
Sum of the market values of Mexana		
Company's assets	\$9 million	
Less: Mexana Company's liabilities..............................	1 million	
Market value of Mexana Company's net assets		8 million
Excess is called *goodwill*		\$ 2 million

Wal-Mart's entry to record the acquisition of Mexana Company, including its goodwill, would be

Assets (Cash, Receivables, Inventories, Plant Assets, all at market value)....................	9,000,000	
Goodwill	2,000,000	
Liabilities		1,000,000
Cash		10,000,000

ASSETS	=	LIABILITIES	+	STOCKHOLDERS' EQUITY
+9,000,000 +2,000,000 −10,000,000	=	+1,000,000	+	0

Note that Wal-Mart has acquired both Mexana's assets *and* its liabilities.

Goodwill has special features, which include the following points:

1. Goodwill is recorded, at its cost, only when it is purchased in the acquisition of another company. Even though a favorable location, a superior product, or an outstanding reputation may create goodwill for a company, that entity never records goodwill for its own business. Instead, goodwill is recorded *only* by the acquiring company. A purchase transaction provides objective evidence of the value of the goodwill.

2. According to generally accepted accounting principles, goodwill is amortized over a period not to exceed 40 years. In reality, the goodwill of many entities increases in value. Nevertheless, the Accounting Principles Board specified in *Opinion No. 17* that the cost of all intangible assets must be amortized as expense. The Opinion prohibits a lump-sum write-off of the cost of goodwill upon acquisition.

RESEARCH AND DEVELOPMENT COSTS Accounting for research and development (R&D) costs is one of the most difficult issues the accounting profession has faced. R&D is the lifeblood of companies such as Procter & Gamble, General Electric, Intel, and Boeing. At these and many other companies, R&D is vital to the development of new products and processes. Thus, it can be argued that the cost of R&D activities is one of these companies' most valuable (intangible) assets. But, in general, they do not report R&D assets on their balance sheets.

GAAP requires companies to expense R&D costs as they incur the costs. Only in limited circumstances may the company capitalize the R&D cost as an asset. For example, assume that a company incurs R&D costs under a contract guaranteeing that the company will recover the costs from a customer. In this case, it is clear that the R&D cost is an asset, and the company records an intangible R&D asset when it incurs the cost. But this is the exception to the general rule.

In other situations, it is often unclear whether the R&D cost is an asset (with future benefit) or an expense (with no future benefit). The Financial Accounting Standards Board (FASB) could have let each company make the decision whether to capitalize or expense its R&D costs. Instead, the FASB decided to standardize accounting practice by requiring that R&D costs be expensed as incurred.

INTERNATIONAL ACCOUNTING Companies in The Netherlands (such as **Royal Dutch Shell** and **Phillips**), in Great Britain (such as **British Petroleum** and **British Airways**), and in other European nations do not have to record goodwill when they purchase another business. Instead, they may record the cost of goodwill as a decrease in owners' equity. These companies never have to amortize the cost of goodwill, so their net income is higher than a U.S. company's would be. Not surprisingly, U.S. companies often cry "foul" when bidding against a European firm to acquire another business. Why? Americans claim the Europeans can pay higher prices because their income never takes a hit for amortization expense.

STOP & THINK How could companies around the world be placed on the same accounting basis?

Answer: If all companies worldwide followed the same accounting rules, they would be reporting income and other amounts computed similarly. But this is not the case. Companies must follow the accounting rules of their own nation, and there are differences, as the goodwill situation illustrates. This is why international investors keep abreast of accounting methods used in different nations—for much the same reason that U.S. investors care whether a company uses LIFO or FIFO for inventories. An international body, the International Accounting Standards Committee, has a set of accounting standards, but the organization has no enforcement power.

Capital Expenditures Versus Revenue Expenditures

When a company makes a plant asset expenditure, it must decide whether to debit an asset account or an expense account. In this context, *expenditure* refers to either a cash purchase or a credit purchase of goods or services related to the asset. Examples of these expenditures range from General Motors' purchase of robots to be used in an auto assembly plant to a motorist's replacing the windshield wipers on an automobile.

Expenditures that increase the asset's capacity or efficiency or extend its useful life are called **capital expenditures.** For example, the cost of a major overhaul that extends a taxi's useful life is a capital expenditure. Repair work that generates a capital expenditure is called an **extraordinary repair.** The amount of the capital expenditure, said to be capitalized, is a debit to an asset account. For an extraordinary repair on a taxi, we would debit the asset account Automobile.

Other expenditures do not extend the asset's capacity or efficiency. Expenditures that merely maintain the asset or restore the asset to working order are called **revenue expenditures** because these costs are matched against revenue. Examples include the costs of repainting a taxi, repairing a dented fender, and

Debit an Asset Account for Capital Expenditures	Debit Repair and Maintenance Expense for Revenue Expenditures
Extraordinary repairs:	Ordinary repairs:
Major engine overhaul	Repair of transmission or other mechanism
Modification of body for new use of truck	Oil change, lubrication, and so on
Addition to storage capacity of truck	Replacement tires, windshield, and the like
	Paint job

EXHIBIT 7-13
Delivery-Truck Expenditures

replacing tires. Revenue expenditures are debited to an expense account. For the **ordinary repairs,** or betterments, on the taxi, we would debit Repair Expense.

Costs associated with intangible assets and natural resource assets also must be identified as either capital expenditures or revenue expenditures. For example, a license fee paid to the state of Arkansas to mine bauxite is a capital expenditure. This cost should be debited to the Bauxite Mineral Asset account. The cost of selling the ore—sales commission paid to a salesperson, for example—is a revenue expenditure and should be debited to an expense account.

The distinction between capital and revenue expenditures is often a matter of opinion. Does the cost extend the life of the asset, or does it only maintain the asset in good order? When doubt exists, companies tend to debit an expense, for two reasons. First, many expenditures are minor in amount, and most companies have a policy of debiting expense for all expenditures below a specific minimum, such as $1,000. Second, the income-tax motive favors debiting all borderline expenditures to expense in order to create an immediate tax deduction. Capital expenditures are not immediate tax deductions.

Exhibit 7-13 illustrates the distinction between capital expenditures and revenue expenditures (expense) for several delivery-truck expenditures. Note also the difference between extraordinary and ordinary repairs.

Treating a capital expenditure as a revenue expenditure, or vice versa, creates errors in the financial statements. Suppose a company makes an extraordinary repair to equipment and erroneously expenses this cost. This is a capital expenditure that should have been debited to an asset account. This accounting error overstates expenses and understates net income on the income statement. On the balance sheet, the equipment account is understated, and so is owners' (or stockholders') equity. Capitalizing the cost of an ordinary repair creates the opposite error. Expenses are then understated and net income is overstated on the income statement. And the balance sheet reports overstated amounts for assets and for owners' equity.

Ethical Issues in Accounting for Plant Assets and Intangibles

The main ethical issue in accounting for plant assets and intangibles is whether to capitalize or expense a particular cost. In this area, companies have split personalities. On the one hand, they all want to save on taxes. This motivates companies to expense all the costs they can in order to decrease their taxable income. On the other hand, most companies also want their financial statements to look as good as they can, with high net income and high reported amounts for assets.

In most cases, a cost that is capitalized or expensed for tax purposes must be treated the same way for reporting to stockholders and creditors in the financial statements. What, then, is the ethical path? Accountants should follow the

Decision Guidelines

Plant Assets and Related Expenses

Decision	Guidelines
Capitalize or expense a cost?	General rule: Capitalize all costs that provide *future* benefit for the business. Expense all costs that provide *no future* benefit.
Capitalize or expense:	
• Cost associated with a new asset?	Capitalize all costs that bring the asset to its intended use.
• Cost associated with an existing asset?	Capitalize only those costs that add to the asset's usefulness or its useful life. Expense all other costs as maintenance or repairs.
• Interest cost incurred to finance the asset's acquisition?	Capitalize interest cost only on assets constructed by the business for its own use. Expense all other interest cost.
Which depreciation method to use:	
• For financial reporting?	Use the method that best matches depreciation expense against the revenues produced by the asset.
• For income tax?	Use the method that produces the fastest tax deductions (MACRS). A company can use different depreciation methods for financial reporting and for income tax purposes. In the United States, this practice is considered perfectly legal and ethical.

general guidelines for capitalizing a cost: Capitalize all costs that provide a future benefit for the business, and expense all other costs, as outlined in the Decision Guidelines feature.

Many companies have gotten into trouble by capitalizing costs they should have expensed. They made their financial statements look better than the facts warranted. But there are very few cases of companies getting into trouble by following the general guidelines, or even by erring on the side of expensing questionable costs. This is another example of accounting conservatism in action. It works.

We discussed accounting conservatism in Chapter 6, page 280.

Reporting Plant Asset Transactions on the Statement of Cash Flows

Objective 7

Report plant asset transactions on the statement of cash flows

Three main types of plant asset transactions appear on the statement of cash flows: acquisitions, sales, and depreciation (including amortization and depletion). Acquisitions and sales are *investing* activities. A company invests in plant assets by paying cash or by incurring a liability. The cash payments for plant and equipment are investing activities that appear on the statement of cash flows. The sale of plant assets results in a cash receipt, as illustrated in Exhibit 7-14, which excerpts data from the cash-flow statement of The Home Depot, Inc. The acquisitions, sales, and depreciation of plant assets are denoted in color.

Let's examine the investing activities first. During the fiscal year ended January 28, 1996, The Home Depot paid $1,278.1 million for plant assets. The cash-flow statement reports this cash payment as Capital Expenditures, a common description (line 5). During the year, the company sold property and equipment, receiving cash of $29.4 million. The Home Depot labels the cash received as Proceeds from Sales of Property and Equipment, also a common reporting practice (line 6). The $29.4 million is the amount of cash received from the sale of plant

EXHIBIT 7-14
Reporting Plant Asset Transactions on the Statement of Cash Flows

THE HOME DEPOT, INC.
Statement of Cash Flows (partial)
Fiscal Year Ended January 28, 1996

		(In millions)
	Cash Provided From Operations:	
1	Net Earnings	$ 731.5
	Reconciliation of Net Earnings to Net Cash Provided by Operations:	
2	Depreciation and Amortization	181.2
3	Other items (summarized)	(199.7)
4	Net Cash Provided by Operations	713.0
	Cash Flows From Investing Activities:	
5	Capital Expenditures	(1,278.1)
6	Proceeds from Sales of Property and Equipment	29.4
7	Other items (summarized)	71.7
8	Net Cash Used in Investing Activities	(1,177.0)
	Cash Flows From Financing Activities:	
9	Net Cash Provided by Financing Activities	515.7
10	Other items	.4
11	Increase in Cash and Cash Equivalents	52.1
12	Cash and Cash Equivalents at Beginning of Year	1.2
13	Cash and Cash Equivalents at End of Year	$ 53.3

assets. It is neither the cost nor the book value of the assets sold. If the cash received from the sale differs from the asset's book value, the company reports a gain or a loss on the sale in the income statement.

The Home Depot's statement of cash flows reports Depreciation and Amortization in the operating activities section (line 2). Observe that Depreciation and Amortization is listed as a positive item under Reconciliation of Net Earnings to Net Cash Provided by Operations. You may be wondering why depreciation appears on the cash-flow statement. After all, depreciation does not affect cash. The entry to record depreciation debits the expense and credits Accumulated Depreciation, not Cash.

In this particular statement format, the operating activities section of the cash-flow statement starts with net income (line 1) and reconciles to net cash provided by operating activities (line 4). Because depreciation decreases net income like all other expenses do, but has no effect on cash, depreciation is added back to net income in determining cash flow from operations. In effect, the add-back of depreciation to net income offsets the earlier subtraction of the expense. The sum of net income plus depreciation helps to reconcile net income (which is on the accrual basis) to cash flow from operations (which is a cash-basis amount). We revisit this topic in the full context of the statement of cash flows in Chapter 12.

STOP & THINK

Test your ability to use the cash-flow statement.

1. Make an entry in the journal to record The Home Depot's capital expenditures during the year.
2. Suppose the book value of the property and equipment that The Home Depot sold was $31.5 million. The assets' cost was $52.7 million and their accumulated depreciation was $21.2 million. Record the company's transaction to sell the property and equipment. Also write a sentence to explain why the sale transaction resulted in a loss for The Home Depot.

Answers

	(In millions)	
1. Property and Equipment	1,278.1	
Cash		1,278.1
Made capital expenditures.		
2. Cash	29.4	
Accumulated Depreciation	21.2	
Loss on Sale of Property and Equipment	2.1	
Property and Equipment		52.7
Sold property and equipment.		

The company sold for $29.4 million assets that had book value of $31.5 million. The result of the sale was a loss of $2.1 million ($31.5 million – $29.4 million).

SUMMARY PROBLEMS FOR YOUR REVIEW

PROBLEM 1

The figures that follow appear in the *Answers to the Mid-Chapter Summary Problem,* Requirement 2, on page 334.

	Method A: Straight-Line			Method B: Double-Declining-Balance		
Year	**Annual Depreciation Expense**	**Accumulated Depreciation**	**Book Value**	**Annual Depreciation Expense**	**Accumulated Depreciation**	**Book Value**
Start			$44,000			$44,000
19X5	$4,000	$ 4,000	40,000	$8,800	$ 8,800	35,200
19X6	4,000	8,000	36,000	7,040	15,840	28,160
19X7	4,000	12,000	32,000	5,632	21,472	22,528

Required

Suppose the income tax authorities permitted a choice between these two depreciation methods. Which method would you select for income tax purposes? Why?

PROBLEM 2

A corporation purchased the equipment above on January 1, 19X5. Management has depreciated the equipment by using the double-declining-balance method. On July 1, 19X7, the company sold the equipment for $27,000 cash.

Required

Record depreciation for 19X7 and the sale of the equipment on July 1, 19X7.

ANSWERS

PROBLEM 1

For tax purposes, most companies select the accelerated method because it results in the most depreciation in the earliest years of the equipment's life. Accelerated depreciation minimizes taxable income and income tax payments in the early years of the asset's life, thereby maximizing the business's cash at the earliest possible time.

PROBLEM 2

To record depreciation to date of sale and sale of the equipment:

19X7			
July 1	Depreciation Expense—Equipment ($5,632 × ½ year)	2,816	
	Accumulated Depreciation—Equipment		2,816
	To update depreciation.		
July 1	Cash	27,000	
	Accumulated Depreciation—Equipment ($15,840 + $2,816)	18,656	
	Equipment		44,000
	Gain on Sale of Equipment		1,656
	To record sale of equipment.		

SUMMARY OF LEARNING OBJECTIVES

1. *Determine the cost of a plant asset.* Plant assets are long-lived tangible assets, such as land, buildings, and equipment, used in the operation of a business. The cost of a plant asset is the purchase price plus applicable taxes, purchase commissions, and all other amounts paid to acquire the asset and to prepare it for its intended use.

2. *Account for depreciation.* Businesses may account for depreciation (the allocation of a plant asset's cost to expense over its useful life) by four methods: the *straight-line method,* the *units-of-production method,* the *double-declining-balance method,* or the *sum-of-the-years'-digits method.* (In practice, the last method is not used much.) All these methods require accountants to estimate the asset's useful life and residual value.

3. *Select the best depreciation method for income tax purposes.* Most companies use an accelerated depreciation method for income tax purposes. Accelerated depreciation results in higher expenses, lower taxable income, and lower tax payments early in the asset's life.

4. *Analyze the effect of a plant asset disposal.* Before disposing of, selling, or trading in a plant asset, the company must update the asset's depreciation. Disposal is then recorded by removing the book balances from both the asset account and its related accumulated depreciation account. Sales often result in a gain or loss, which is reported on the income statement. When exchanging a plant asset, the company often carries forward the book value of the old asset plus any cash payment as the cost of the new asset and thus records no gain or loss on the exchange.

5. *Account for natural resource assets and depletion.* The cost of natural resources, a special category of long-lived assets, is expensed through *depletion.* Depletion is computed on a units-of-production basis. Accumulated Depletion is a contra account similar to Accumulated Depreciation.

6. *Account for intangible assets and amortization.* *Intangible assets* are assets that have no physical form. They give their owners a special right to current and expected future benefits. The major types of intangible assets are patents, copyrights, trademarks, franchises and licenses, leaseholds, and goodwill.

The cost of intangibles is expensed through *amortization,* which is the same concept as depreciation. Amortization on intangibles is computed on a straight-line basis over a maximum of 40 years. However, the useful life of an intangible is often shorter than its legal life.

7. *Report plant asset transactions on the statement of cash flows.* Three main types of plant asset transactions appear on the statement of cash flows. Acquisitions and sales of plant assets appear in the investing activities section of the statement. Depreciation, depletion, and amortization appear in the statement's operating activities section as addbacks to net income.

ACCOUNTING VOCABULARY

accelerated depreciation method *(p. 330).*
amortization *(p. 343).*
brand name *(p. 344).*
capital expenditure *(p. 346).*
capitalize *(p. 324).*
copyright *(p. 344).*
depletion expense *(p. 342).*
depreciable cost *(p. 328).*
double-declining-balance (DDB) method *(p. 331).*
estimated residual value *(p. 328).*
estimated useful life *(p. 328).*
extraordinary repair *(p. 346).*
franchises and licenses *(p. 344).*
goodwill *(p. 345).*
intangible asset *(p. 322).*
leasehold *(p. 344).*
ordinary repair *(p. 347).*
patent *(p. 343).*
plant asset *(p. 322).*
revenue expenditure *(p. 346).*
straight-line (SL) method *(p. 329).*
trademark, trade name *(p. 344).*
units-of-production (UOP) method *(p. 330).*

QUESTIONS

1. To what types of long-lived assets do the following expenses apply: depreciation, depletion, and amortization?
2. Describe how to measure the cost of a plant asset. Would an ordinary cost of repairing the asset after it is placed in service be included in the asset's cost?
3. When assets are purchased as a group for a single price and no individual asset cost is given, how is each asset's cost determined?
4. Define depreciation. Present the common misconceptions about depreciation.

5. Explain the concept of accelerated depreciation. Which other depreciation method is used in the definition of double-declining-balance depreciation? Which of the depreciation methods results in the most depreciation in the first year of the asset's life?
6. The level of business activity fluctuates widely for Harwood Delivery Service, reaching its peak around Christmas each year. At other times, business is slow. Which depreciation method is most appropriate for the company's fleet of Ford Aerostar minivans?
7. Magnum Service Center uses the most advanced computers available to keep a competitive edge over other service centers. To maintain this advantage, Magnum replaces its computers before they are worn out. Describe the major factors affecting the useful life of a plant asset, and indicate which factor seems most relevant to Magnum's computers.
8. Which type of depreciation method is best from an income tax standpoint? Why? How does depreciation affect income taxes? How does depreciation affect cash provided by operations?
9. Identify seven elements of internal control designed to safeguard plant assets.
10. What expense applies to natural resources? By which depreciation method is this expense computed?
11. How do intangible assets differ from most other assets? Why are they assets at all? What type of expense applies to intangible assets?
12. Why is the cost of patents and other intangible assets often expensed over a shorter period than the legal life of the asset?
13. Your company has just purchased another company for $400,000. The market value of the other company's net assets is $325,000. What is the $75,000 excess called? What type of asset is it? What is the maximum period over which its cost is amortized under generally accepted accounting principles?
14. IBM Corporation is recognized as a world leader in the manufacture and sale of computers. The company's past success created vast amounts of business goodwill. Would you expect to see this goodwill reported on IBM's financial statements? Why or why not?
15. Distinguish a capital expenditure from a revenue expenditure. Explain the title "revenue expenditure," which is curious in that a revenue expenditure is a debit to an expense account.
16. Describe the three types of plant asset transactions reported on a statement of cash flows. Indicate where and how each type of transaction appears on the statement.

EXERCISES

Determining the cost of plant assets
(Obj. 1)

E7-1 Shannon Miller, Inc., purchased land, paying $90,000 cash as a down payment and signing a $120,000 note payable for the balance. In addition, Miller paid delinquent property tax of $2,000, title insurance costing $2,500, and a $5,400 charge for leveling the land and removing an unwanted building. The company constructed an office building on the land at a cost of $810,000. It also paid $63,000 for a fence around the boundary of the property, $10,400 for the company sign near the entrance to the property, and $6,000 for special lighting of the grounds. Determine the cost of the company's land, land improvements, and building.

Measuring the cost of an asset; capitalizing interest
(Obj. 1)

E7-2 Garcia Brick Co. manufactures brick and other building materials in Reynosa, Arizona. During 19X7, Garcia constructed its own factory building with financing from Maricopa Bank of Reynosa. The 11% loan was for $1,300,000. During the year, Garcia spent $980,000 on construction of the building, expecting to complete construction during January 19X8. Garcia's average accumulated expenditures during 19X7 were $640,000. At year end, Garcia accrued the interest for one year.

Required

1. How much should Garcia record as the cost of the building in 19X7? What other account could Garcia use in place of the Factory Building account while the building is being constructed?
2. Record all of Garcia's transactions during 19X7.

Allocating cost to assets acquired in a lump-sum purchase
(Obj. 1)

E7-3 Advantage Leasing Company bought three used machines in a $40,000 lump-sum purchase. An independent appraiser valued the machines as follows:

Machine No.	Appraised Value
1	$14,000
2	18,000
3	16,000

Advantage paid half in cash and signed a note payable for the remainder. Record the purchase in the journal, identifying each machine's individual cost in a separate Machine account. Round decimals to three places.

Explaining the concept of depreciation
(Obj. 2)

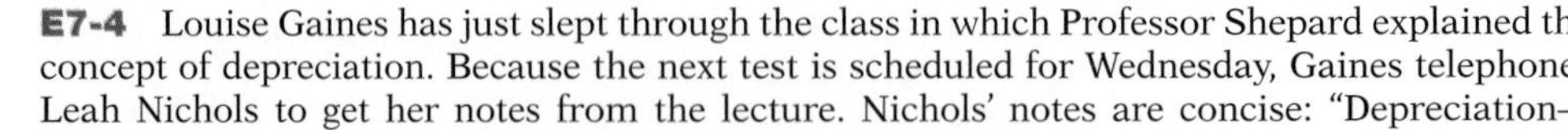

E7-4 Louise Gaines has just slept through the class in which Professor Shepard explained the concept of depreciation. Because the next test is scheduled for Wednesday, Gaines telephones Leah Nichols to get her notes from the lecture. Nichols' notes are concise: "Depreciation—

Sounds like Greek to me." Gaines next tries Ray Mellichamp, who says he thinks depreciation is what happens when an asset wears out. Sally Bower is confident that depreciation is the process of building up a cash fund to replace an asset at the end of its useful life. Explain the concept of depreciation for Gaines. Evaluate the explanations of Mellichamp and Bower. Be specific.

Determining depreciation amounts by three methods ***(Obj. 2, 3)***

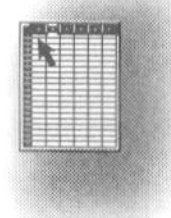

E7-5 Lancer Furniture bought a delivery truck on January 2, 19X1, for $13,000. The truck was expected to remain in service four years and to last 100,000 miles. At the end of its useful life, Lancer officials estimated that the truck's residual value would be $3,000. The truck traveled 34,000 miles the first year, 28,000 the second year, 18,000 the third year, and 20,000 in the fourth year. Prepare a schedule of *depreciation expense* per year for the truck under the three depreciation methods. After two years under the double-declining-balance method, the company switches to the straight-line method. Show your computations.

Which method tracks the wear and tear on the truck most closely? Which method would Lancer prefer to use for income tax purposes? Explain in detail why Lancer prefers this method.

Selecting the best depreciation method for income-tax purposes ***(Obj. 3)***

E7-6 Beth Spencer Co. paid $140,000 for equipment that is expected to have a seven-year life. In this industry, the residual value of equipment is approximately 10% of the asset's cost.

Select the appropriate MACRS depreciation method for income tax purposes. Then determine the extra amount of cash that Spencer Co. can invest by using MACRS depreciation, versus straight-line, during the first two years of the equipment's life. Ignore any interest Spencer can earn by investing the extra cash.

Changing a plant asset's useful life ***(Obj. 2)***

E7-7 Manhattan Shirt Co. purchased a building for $900,000 and depreciated it on a straight-line basis over a 40-year period. The estimated residual value was $100,000. After using the building for 15 years, Manhattan realized that wear and tear on the building would force the company to replace it before 40 years. Starting with the sixteenth year, Manhattan began depreciating the building over a revised total life of 30 years, and increasing the estimated residual value to $200,000. Record depreciation expense on the building for years 15 and 16.

Analyzing the effect of a sale of a plant asset; DDB depreciation ***(Obj. 4)***

E7-8 On January 2, 19X7, Gulf Coast Products purchased store fixtures for $8,700 cash, expecting the fixtures to remain in service five years. Gulf Coast has depreciated the fixtures on a double-declining-balance basis, with $1,000 estimated residual value. On September 30, 19X8, Gulf Coast sold the fixtures for $4,950 cash. Record both the depreciation expense on the fixtures for 19X8, and the sale of the fixtures.

Measuring a plant asset's cost, using UOP depreciation, and trading in a used asset ***(Obj. 1, 2, 4)***

E7-9 **Granite Shoals Corporation,** based in Branson, Missouri, is a large trucking company that operates throughout the midwestern United States. Granite Shoals uses the units-of-production (UOP) method to depreciate its trucks because its managers believe UOP depreciation best measures the wear and tear on the trucks.

Granite Shoals trades in used trucks often to keep driver morale high and to maximize fuel efficiency. Consider these facts about one Mack truck in the company's fleet:

When acquired in 19X6, the tractor/trailer rig cost $285,000 and was expected to remain in service for ten years, or 1,000,000 miles. Estimated residual value was $85,000. During 19X6, the truck was driven 75,000 miles; during 19X7, 120,000 miles; and during 19X8, 210,000 miles. After 40,000 miles in 19X9, the company traded in the Mack truck for a less-expensive Freightliner rig. Granite Shoals paid cash of $80,000. Determine Granite Shoals' cost of the new truck. Journal entries are not required.

Recording natural resource assets and depletion ***(Obj. 5)***

E7-10 Grand Teton Mines paid $298,500 for the right to extract ore from a 200,000-ton mineral deposit. In addition to the purchase price, Grand Teton also paid a $500 filing fee, a $1,000 license fee to the state of Wyoming, and $60,000 for a geological survey of the property. Because the company purchased the rights to the minerals only, the company expected the asset to have zero residual value when fully depleted. During the first year of production, Grand Teton removed 35,000 tons of ore. Make general journal entries to record (a) purchase of the mineral rights (debit Mineral Asset), (b) payment of fees and other costs, and (c) depletion for first-year production.

Recording intangibles, amortization, and a change in the asset's useful life ***(Obj. 6)***

E7-11 ***Part 1.*** Karolyi Corporation, which manufactures high-speed printers, has recently purchased for $1.52 million a patent for the design for a new laser printer. Although it gives legal protection for 20 years, the patent is expected to provide Karolyi with a competitive advantage for only eight years. Assuming the straight-line method of amortization, use journal entries to record (a) the purchase of the patent, and (b) amortization for year 1.

Part 2. After using the patent for four years, Karolyi learns at an industry trade show that another company is designing a more efficient printer. On the basis of this new information, Karolyi decides, starting with year 5, to amortize the remaining cost of the patent over two additional years, giving the patent a total useful life of six years. Record amortization for year 5.

Measuring goodwill ***(Obj. 6)***

E7-12 **Campbell Soup Company's** 1995 statement of cash flows includes the following:

	1995
Cash Flows from Investing Activities:	Millions
Businesses acquired......................................	$(1,255)

Campbell's "Note 15. Intangible Assets," includes this:

	1995	1994
	Millions	
Purchase price in excess of net assets of businesses acquired	$1,716	$542
Less: Accumulated amortization	(133)	(90)

Required

Answer these questions related to Campbell Soup Company's goodwill.

1. What title does Campbell Soup Company use to describe its goodwill? How well does Campbell's title agree with the text definition of goodwill?
2. How much did Campbell Soup Company pay to acquire other businesses during 1995? How much of the purchase price was for goodwill? How much did Campbell pay for other assets? What other assets besides goodwill was Campbell Soup Company acquiring?

Measuring and recording goodwill
(Obj. 6)

E7-13 PepsiCo, Inc., has aggressively acquired other companies, such as Kentucky Fried Chicken, Frito-Lay, Pizza Hut, and Taco Bell. Assume that PepsiCo, Inc., purchased Chip-O Company for $12 million cash. The market value of Chip-O's assets is $14 million, and Chip-O Company has liabilities of $11 million.

Required

1. Compute the cost of the goodwill purchased by PepsiCo.
2. Record the purchase by PepsiCo.
3. Record amortization of goodwill for year 1, assuming the straight-line method and a useful life of ten years.

Distinguishing capital expenditures from expenses
(Obj. 1)

E7-14 Classify each of the following expenditures as a capital expenditure or a revenue expenditure (expense) related to machinery: (a) purchase price, (b) sales tax paid on the purchase price, (c) transportation and insurance while machinery is in transit from seller to buyer, (d) installation, (e) training of personnel for initial operation of the machinery, (f) special reinforcement to the machinery platform, (g) income tax paid on income earned from the sale of products manufactured by the machinery, (h) major overhaul to extend useful life by three years, (i) ordinary recurring repairs to keep the machinery in good working order, (j) lubrication of the machinery before it is placed in service, (k) periodic lubrication after the machinery is placed in service.

Interpreting a cash-flow statement
(Obj. 7)

E7-15 Prior to its purchase by Boeing, McDonnell Douglas was one of the world's largest makers of commercial and military aircraft. The following items are excerpted from the company's 19X4 annual report:

MCDONNELL DOUGLAS
Consolidated Statement of Cash Flows

Year Ended December 31 (Millions of dollars)	19X4
Operating Activities	
Net earnings	$598
Adjustments to reconcile net earnings to net cash provided by operating activities:	
Depreciation of property, plant and equipment	213
Amortization of intangible and other assets	15
Investing Activities	
Property, plant and equipment acquired	(112)
Proceeds from sale of assets	24
Other, including discontinued operations	62

Required

Answer these questions.

1. Why are depreciation and amortization listed on the statement of cash flows?
2. Explain in detail each investing activity.

CHALLENGE EXERCISES

Capitalizing versus expensing; measuring the effect of an error ***(Obj. 1)***

E7-16 Mirage Sportswear is a catalog merchant in France—similar to L. L. Bean and Lands' End in the United States. The company's assets consist mainly of inventory, a warehouse, and automated shipping equipment. Assume that early in year 1, Mirage purchased equipment at a cost of 3 million francs (F 3 million). Management expects the equipment to remain in service five years. Because the equipment is so specialized, estimated residual value is negligible. Mirage uses the straight-line depreciation method. *Through an accounting error, Mirage accidentally expensed the entire cost of the equipment at the time of purchase.* The company is family-owned and operated as a partnership, so it pays no income tax.

Required

Prepare a schedule to show the overstatement or understatement in the following items at the end of each year over the five-year life of the equipment.

1. Total current assets
2. Equipment, net
3. Net income
4. Owners' equity

Reconstructing transactions from the financial statements ***(Obj. 2, 4)***

E7-17 **Ford Motor Company's** comparative balance sheet reported these amounts (in millions of dollars):

	December 31, 19X1	December 31, 19X0
Property:		
Land, plant, and equipment	$35,726.3	$34,825.1
Less accumulated depreciation	(19,422.0)	(18,486.8)
Net land, plant, and equipment	16,304.3	16,338.3
Unamortized special tools	6,218.0	5,869.5
Net property	$22,522.3	$22,207.8

Ford's income statement for 19X1 reported the following expenses (in millions):

Depreciation	$2,455.8
Amortization of special tools	1,822.1

Unamortized special tools refers to the remaining asset balance after amortization expense has been subtracted. Ford does not use an accumulated amortization account for special tools.

Required

1. There were no disposals of special tools during 19X1. Compute the cost of new acquisitions of special tools.
2. Assume that during 19X1 Ford sold land, plant, and equipment for $92 million and that this transaction produced a gain of $9 million. What was the book value of the assets sold?
3. Use the answer to Requirement 2 to compute the cost of land, plant, and equipment acquired during 19X1. For convenience, work with net land, plant, and equipment.

PROBLEMS

(GROUP A)

Identifying the elements of a plant asset's cost ***(Obj. 1, 2)***

P7-1A Alameda Construction Company incurred the following costs in acquiring land, making land improvements, and constructing and furnishing its own sales building.

a. Purchase price of four acres of land, including an old building that will be used for a garage (land market value is $280,000; building market value is $40,000)	$300,000
b. Landscaping (additional dirt and earth moving)	8,100
c. Fence around the boundary of the land	17,650
d. Attorney fee for title search on the land	600
e. Delinquent real estate taxes on the land to be paid by Alameda	5,900

f. Company signs at front of the company property .... $ 1,800
g. Building permit for the sales building 350
h. Architect fee for the design of the sales building 19,800
i. Masonry, carpentry, roofing, and other labor to construct the sales building 709,000
j. Concrete, wood, and other materials used in the construction of the sales building 214,000
k. Renovation of the garage building 41,800
l. Interest cost on construction loan for sales building, based on average accumulated expenditures 9,000
m. Landscaping (trees and shrubs) 6,400
n. Parking lot and concrete walks on the property 29,750
o. Lights for the parking lot, walkways, and company signs 7,300
p. Supervisory salary of construction supervisor (85% to sales building; 9% to fencing, parking lot, and concrete walks; and 6% to garage building renovation) 40,000
q. Office furniture for the sales building 107,100
r. Transportation and installation of furniture 1,800

Alameda depreciates buildings over 40 years, land improvements over 20 years, and furniture over 8 years, all on a straight-line basis with zero residual value.

Required

1. Set up columns for Land, Land Improvements, Sales Building, Garage Building, and Furniture. Show how to account for each of Alameda's costs by listing the cost under the correct account. Determine the total cost of each asset.
2. Assuming that all construction was complete and the assets were placed in service on May 4, record depreciation for the year ended December 31. Round figures to the nearest dollar.
3. How will what you learned in this problem help you manage a business?

Recording plant asset transactions, exchanges, changes in useful life
(Obj. 1, 2, 4)

P7-2A Central Forwarding provides local freight service in Des Moines, Iowa. The company's balance sheet includes the following assets under Property, Plant, and Equipment: Land, Buildings, and Motor-Carrier Equipment. Central has a separate accumulated depreciation account for each of these assets except land. Assume that Central Forwarding completed the following transactions:

Jan. 5 — Traded in motor-carrier equipment with book value of $47,000 (cost of $130,000) for similar new equipment with a cash cost of $176,000. Central received a trade-in allowance of $70,000 on the old equipment and paid the remainder in cash.

July 2 — Sold a building that had cost $550,000 and had accumulated depreciation of $247,500 through December 31 of the preceding year. Depreciation is computed on a straight-line basis. The building has a 30-year useful life and a residual value of $55,000. Central received $100,000 cash and a $600,000 note receivable.

Oct. 26 — Purchased land and a building for a single price of $300,000. An independent appraisal valued the land at $115,000 and the building at $230,000.

Dec. 31 — Recorded depreciation as follows:

Motor-carrier equipment has an expected useful life of five years and an estimated residual value of 5% of cost. Depreciation is computed on the double-declining-balance method.

Depreciation on buildings is computed by the straight-line method. The company had assigned to its older buildings, which cost $4,000,000, an estimated useful life of 30 years with a residual value equal to 10% of the asset cost. However, management has come to believe that the buildings will remain useful for a total of 40 years. Residual value remains unchanged. The company has used all its buildings, except for the one purchased on October 26, for 10 years. The new building carries a 40-year useful life and a residual value equal to 10% of its cost. Make separate entries for depreciation on the building acquired on October 26 and the other buildings purchased in earlier years.

Required

Record the transactions in Central Forwarding's journal.

Explaining the concept of depreciation
(Obj. 2)

P7-3A The board of directors of Ultramar Corporation is reviewing the 19X8 annual report. A new board member—a professor with little business experience—questions the company accountant about the depreciation amounts. The professor wonders why depreciation expense has decreased from $200,000 in 19X6 to $184,000 in 19X7 to $172,000 in 19X8. She states that she could understand the decreasing annual amounts if the company had been disposing of properties each year, but that has not occurred. Further, she notes that growth in the city is increasing the values of company properties. Why is the company recording depreciation when the property values are increasing?

Required

Write a paragraph or two to explain the concept of depreciation to the professor and to answer her questions.

Computing depreciation by three methods and the cash-flow advantage of accelerated depreciation for tax purposes ***(Obj. 2, 3)***

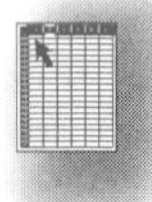

P7-4A On January 3, 19X1, Zivley Corporation paid $224,000 for equipment used in manufacturing automotive supplies. In addition to the basic purchase price, the company paid $700 transportation charges, $100 insurance for the goods in transit, $12,100 sales tax, and $3,100 for a special platform on which to place the equipment in the plant. Zivley management estimates that the equipment will remain in service five years and have a residual value of $20,000. The equipment will produce 50,000 units the first year, with annual production decreasing by 5,000 units during each of the next four years (that is, 45,000 units in year 2; 40,000 units in year 3; and so on). In trying to decide which depreciation method to use, Martha Zivley has requested a depreciation schedule for each of three depreciation methods (straight-line, units-of-production, and double-declining-balance).

Required

1. For each of the generally accepted depreciation methods, prepare a depreciation schedule showing asset cost, depreciation expense, accumulated depreciation, and asset book value.
2. Zivley reports to stockholders and creditors in the financial statements using the depreciation method that maximizes reported income in the early years of asset use. For income tax purposes, however, the company uses the depreciation method that minimizes income tax payments in those early years. Consider the first year Zivley uses the equipment. Identify the depreciation methods that meet Zivley's objectives, assuming the income tax authorities would permit the use of any of the methods.
3. Assume that cash provided by operations before income tax is $180,000 for the equipment's first year. The combined federal and state income tax rate is 40 percent. For the two depreciation methods identified in Requirement 2, compare the net income and cash provided by operations (cash flow). Show which method gives the net-income advantage and which method gives the cash-flow advantage. Ignore the earnings rate in the cash-flow analysis.

Analyzing plant asset transactions from a company's financial statements ***(Obj. 2, 4, 7)***

P7-5A IBM is the world's largest computer company. After a few lean years, Big Blue, as the company is called, has rebounded strongly with some new products and improving profits. The following excerpts come from IBM's 1995 financial statements:

INTERNATIONAL BUSINESS MACHINES CORPORATION AND SUBSIDIARY COMPANIES
Consolidated Statement of Financial Position

(Dollars in millions) **At December 31:**	**1995**	**1994**
Assets		
Current assets:		
Cash	$ 1,746	$ 1,240
Cash equivalents	5,513	6,682
Marketable securities	442	2,632
Notes and accounts receivable—trade, net of allowances	16,450	14,018
Sales-type leases receivable	5,961	6,351
Other accounts receivable	991	1,164
Inventories	6,323	6,334
Prepaid expenses and other current assets	3,265	2,917
Total current assets	40,691	41,338
Plant, rental machines, and other property	43,981	44,820
Less: Accumulated depreciation	27,402	28,156
Plant, rental machines, and other property—net	16,579	16,664
Software, less accumulated amortization (1995, $11,276; 1994, $10,793)	2,419	2,963
Investments and sundry assets	20,603	20,126
Total assets	$80,292	$81,091

INTERNATIONAL BUSINESS MACHINES CORPORATION AND SUBSIDIARY COMPANIES
Consolidated Statement of Cash Flows

(Dollars in millions) For the year ended December 31:	1995	1994
Cash flow from operating activities:		
Net earnings	$4,178	$3,021
Adjustments to reconcile net earnings to cash provided from operating activities:		
Depreciation	3,955	4,197
Amortization of software	1,647	2,098
Cash flow from investing activities:		
Payments for plant, rental machines, and other property	(4,744)	(3,078)
Proceeds from disposition of plant, rental machines, and other property	1,561	900

Required

Answer these questions about IBM's plant assets.

1. At December 31, 1995, what was IBM's cost of its plant assets? What was the amount of accumulated depreciation? What percentage of the cost has been used up? Are IBM's plant assets at the end of 1995 relatively new, of middle age, or relatively old? How can you tell?
2. How much was IBM's depreciation expense for 1995? Why is the amount of depreciation expense so different from accumulated depreciation at December 31, 1995?
3. How much did IBM pay for plant assets during 1995? Prepare a T-account for Plant Assets at cost to determine whether IBM bought or sold more plant assets during the year.
4. How much cash did IBM receive for the sale of plant assets during 1995? If the plant assets that IBM sold had a book value of $1,222 million, did IBM have a gain or a loss on the sale of plant assets? How much was the gain or loss?
5. IBM's balance sheet reports Software. What category of asset is software? How much of the cost of software did IBM amortize during 1995? Is IBM's software relatively new or mostly used up? How can you tell?

Accounting for natural resources, intangibles, and the related expenses ***(Obj. 5, 6)***

P7-6A ***Part 1.*** **Georgia-Pacific Corporation** is one of the world's largest forest products companies. The company's balance sheet includes the assets Natural Gas, Oil, and Coal.

Suppose Georgia-Pacific paid $2.8 million cash for a lease giving the firm the right to work a mine that contained an estimated 100,000 tons of coal. Assume that the company paid $60,000 to remove unwanted buildings from the land and $45,000 to prepare the surface for mining. Further assume that Georgia-Pacific signed a $30,000 note payable to a landscaping company to return the land surface to its original condition after the lease ends. During the first year, Georgia-Pacific removed 35,000 tons of coal, which it sold on account for $37 per ton. Operating expenses for the first year totaled $240,000, all paid in cash. In addition, the company accrued income tax at the tax rate of 40 percent.

Required

1. Record all of Georgia-Pacific's transactions for the year.
2. Prepare the company's income statement for its coal operations for the first year. Evaluate the profitability of the coal operations.

Part 2. **Collins Foods International, Inc.,** is the majority owner of Sizzler Restaurants. The company's balance sheet reports the asset Cost in Excess of Net Assets of Purchased Businesses. Assume that Collins purchased this asset as part of the acquisition of another company, which carried these figures:

Book value of assets	$2.4 million
Market value of assets	3.1 million
Liabilities	2.2 million

Required

1. What is another title for the asset Cost in Excess of Net Assets of Purchased Businesses?
2. Make the journal entry to record Collins's purchase of the other company for $2.7 million cash.
3. Assuming Collins amortizes Cost in Excess of Net Assets of Purchased Businesses over 20 years, record the straight-line amortization for one year.

P7-7A At the end of 1995, The Coca-Cola Company had total assets of $15.0 billion and total liabilities of $9.6 billion. Included among the assets were property, plant, and equipment with a cost of $6.7 billion and accumulated depreciation of $2.3 billion.

Reporting plant asset transactions on the statement of cash flows ***(Obj. 7)***

Assume that Coca-Cola completed the following selected transactions during 1996:

The company earned total revenues of $19.1 billion and incurred total expenses of $15.2 billion, which included depreciation of $0.5 billion. During the year, Coca-Cola paid $1.1 billion for new property, plant, and equipment and sold old plant assets for $0.2 billion. The cost of the assets sold was $0.6 billion, and their accumulated depreciation was $0.4 billion.

Required

1. Show how Coca-Cola would report property, plant, and equipment on the balance sheet at December 31, 1996. What was the book value of property, plant, and equipment?
2. Show how Coca-Cola would report operating activities and investing activities on its statement of cash flows for 1996. The company's cash-flow statement starts with net income.
3. Explain how to determine whether Coca-Cola had a gain or loss on the sale of old plant assets during the year. What was the amount of the gain or loss, if any?

(GROUP B)

P7-1B Potomac Electric Company incurred the following costs in acquiring land and a garage, making land improvements, and constructing and furnishing a district office building.

Identifying the elements of a plant asset's cost ***(Obj. 1, 2)***

a. Purchase price of 3½ acres of land, including an old building that will be used as a garage for company vehicles (land market value is $700,000; building market value is $100,000)	$640,000
b. Delinquent real estate taxes on the land to be paid by Potomac Electric	3,700
c. Landscaping (additional dirt and earth moving)	3,550
d. Title insurance on the land acquisition	1,000
e. Fence around the boundary of the land	44,100
f. Building permit for the office building	200
g. Architect fee for the design of the office building	45,000
h. Company signs near front and rear approaches to the company property	23,550
i. Renovation of the garage	23,800
j. Concrete, wood, and other materials used in the construction of the office building	814,000
k. Masonry, carpentry, roofing, and other labor to construct a district office building	734,000
l. Interest cost on construction loan for office building, based on average accumulated expenditures	3,400
m. Parking lots and concrete walks on the property	17,450
n. Lights for the parking lot, walkways, and company signs	8,900
o. Supervisory salary of construction supervisor (90% to office building; 6% to fencing, parking lot, and concrete walks; and 4% to garage renovation)	55,000
p. Office furniture for the office building	123,500
q. Transportation of furniture from seller to the office building	1,300
r. Landscaping (trees and shrubs)	9,100

Potomac Electric depreciates buildings over 40 years, land improvements over 20 years, and furniture over 8 years, all on a straight-line basis with zero residual value.

Required

1. Set up columns for Land, Land Improvements, District Office Building, Garage, and Furniture. Show how to account for each of Potomac's costs by listing the cost under the correct account. Determine the total cost of each asset.
2. Assuming that all construction was complete and the assets were placed in service on March 19, record depreciation for the year ended December 31. Round figures to the nearest dollar.
3. How will what you learned in this problem help you manage a business?

Recording plant asset transactions, exchanges, changes in useful life ***(Obj. 1, 2, 4)***

P7-2B Boyd & Yankovitz surveys American television viewing trends. The company's balance sheet reports the following assets under Property and Equipment: Land, Buildings, Office Furniture, Communication Equipment, and Televideo Equipment. The company has a separate

accumulated depreciation account for each of these assets except land. Assume that Boyd & Yankovitz completed the following transactions:

Jan. 4	Traded in communication equipment with book value of $11,000 (cost of $96,000) for similar new equipment with a cash cost of $88,000. The seller gave Boyd & Yankovitz a trade-in allowance of $20,000 on the old equipment, and Boyd & Yankovitz paid the remainder in cash.
Aug. 29	Sold a building that had cost $475,000 and had accumulated depreciation of $353,500 through December 31 of the preceding year. Depreciation is computed on a straight-line basis. The building has a 30-year useful life and a residual value of $47,500. Boyd & Yankovitz received $150,000 cash and a $450,000 note receivable.
Nov. 10	Purchased used communication and televideo equipment from the Gallup polling organization. Total cost was $80,000 paid in cash. An independent appraisal valued the communication equipment at $75,000 and the televideo equipment at $25,000.
Dec. 31	Recorded depreciation as follows: Equipment is depreciated by the double-declining-balance method over a five-year life with zero residual value. Record depreciation on the equipment purchased on January 4 and on November 10 separately Depreciation on buildings is computed by the straight-line method. The company had assigned buildings an estimated useful life of 30 years and a residual value that is 10% of cost. After using the buildings for 20 years, the company has come to believe that their total useful life will be 35 years. Residual value remains unchanged. The buildings cost $96,000,000.

Required

Record the transactions in the journal of Boyd & Yankovitz.

Explaining the concept of depreciation
(Obj. 2)

P7-3B The board of directors of High Tumblers Gymnastics Center is having its regular quarterly meeting. Accounting policies are on the agenda, and depreciation is being discussed. A new board member, an attorney, has some strong opinions about two aspects of depreciation policy. Bryce Dodson argues that depreciation must be coupled with a fund to replace company assets. Otherwise, there is no substance to depreciation, he argues. He also challenges the five-year estimated life over which High Tumblers is depreciating company computers. He notes that the computers will last much longer and should be depreciated over at least ten years.

Required

Write a paragraph or two to explain the concept of depreciation to Bryce Dodson and to answer his arguments.

Computing depreciation by three methods and the cash-flow advantage of accelerated depreciation for tax purposes
(Obj. 2, 3)

P7-4B On January 2, 19X1, Quantum Construction Company purchased a used dump truck at a cost of $63,000. Before placing the truck in service, the company spent $2,200 painting it, $800 replacing tires, and $4,000 overhauling the engine. Quantum management estimates that the truck will remain in service for six years and have a residual value of $16,000. The truck's annual mileage is expected to be 18,000 miles in each of the first four years and 14,000 miles in each of the next two years. In trying to decide which depreciation method to use, George Farouk, the general manager, requests a depreciation schedule for each of the depreciation methods (straight-line, units-of-production, and double-declining-balance).

Required

1. Prepare a depreciation schedule for each of the depreciation methods, showing asset cost, depreciation expense, accumulated depreciation, and asset book value.
2. Quantum reports to creditors in the financial statements using the depreciation method that maximizes reported income in the early years of asset use. For income tax purposes, however, the company uses the depreciation method that minimizes income tax payments in those early years. Consider the first year that Quantum uses the truck. Identify the depreciation methods that meet the general manager's objectives, assuming the income tax authorities would permit the use of any of the methods.
3. Cash provided by operations before income tax is $150,000 for the truck's first year. The combined federal and state income tax rate is 40 percent. For the two depreciation methods identified in Requirement 2, compare the net income and cash provided by operations (cash flow). Show which method gives the net-income advantage and which method gives the cash-flow advantage. Ignore the earnings rate in the cash-flow analysis.

P7-5B **Curtiss-Wright Corporation** is a medium-sized maker of high-tech parts used in commercial and military aircraft. The following excerpts come from Curtiss-Wright's 1995 financial statements:

Analyzing plant asset transactions from a company's financial statements
(Obj. 2, 4, 7)

CURTISS-WRIGHT CORPORATION AND SUBSIDIARIES
Consolidated Balance Sheet

	December 31,	
(In thousands)	**1995**	**1994**
Assets		
Current assets:		
Cash and cash equivalents	$ 8,865	$ 4,245
Short-term investments	69,898	72,200
Receivables, net	36,277	32,467
Deferred tax assets (prepaid income tax expense)	7,149	8,204
Inventories	29,111	24,889
Other current assets	2,325	2,338
Total current assets	153,625	144,343
Property, plant and equipment, at cost:		
Land	4,504	4,655
Buildings and improvements	79,352	78,680
Machinery, equipment and other	114,195	119,653
	198,051	202,988
Less, accumulated depreciation	141,782	142,550
Property, plant and equipment, net	56,269	60,438
Prepaid pension costs	31,128	28,092
Other assets	5,179	5,821
Total assets	$246,201	$238,694

CURTISS-WRIGHT CORPORATION AND SUBSIDIARIES
Consolidated Statements of Cash Flows

	For the Years Ended December 31,	
(In thousands)	**1995**	**1994**
Cash flows from operating activities:		
Net earnings	$18,169	$19,303
Adjustments to reconcile net earnings to net cash provided by operating activities:		
Depreciation	9,512	10,883
Cash flows from investing activities:		
Proceeds from sales and disposals of plant assets	3,290	1,326
Additions to property, plant and equipment	(6,985)	(4,609)

Required

Answer these questions about Curtiss-Wright's plant assets.

1. At December 31, 1995, what was Curtiss-Wright's cost of its plant assets? What was the amount of accumulated depreciation? What was the book value of the plant assets? Does book value measure how much Curtiss-Wright could sell the assets for? Why or why not?
2. How much was Curtiss-Wright's depreciation expense for 1995? Why is the amount of depreciation expense so different from accumulated depreciation at December 31, 1995?
3. How much did Curtiss-Wright pay for plant assets during 1995? Prepare a T-account for Plant Assets at cost to determine whether Curtiss-Wright bought or sold more plant assets during the year.
4. How much cash did Curtiss-Wright receive for the sale of plant assets during 1995? If the plant assets sold by the company had a book value of $3,071,000, did Curtiss-Wright experience a gain or a loss on the sale of plant assets? How much was the gain or loss?

Accounting for natural resources, intangibles, and the related expenses
(Obj. 5, 6)

P7-6B ***Part 1.*** **Continental Pipeline Company** operates a pipeline that provides natural gas to Atlanta; Washington, D.C.; Philadelphia; and New York City. The company's balance sheet includes the asset Oil Properties.

Suppose Continental paid $7 million cash for oil and gas reserves that contained an estimated 500,000 barrels of oil. Assume that the company paid $350,000 for additional geological tests of the property and $110,000 to prepare the surface for drilling. Prior to production, the company signed a $65,000 note payable to have a building constructed on the property. Because the building provides on-site headquarters for the drilling effort and will be abandoned when the oil is depleted, its cost is debited to the Oil Properties account and included in depletion charges. During the first year of production, Continental removed 82,000 barrels of oil, which it sold on credit for $19 per barrel. Operating expenses related to this project totaled $185,000 for the first year, all paid in cash. In addition, Continental accrued income tax at the rate of 40 percent.

Required

1. Record all of Continental's transactions for the year.
2. Prepare the company's income statement for this oil and gas project for the first year. Evaluate the profitability of the project.

Part 2. **United Telecommunications, Inc.** (United Telecom) provides communication services in Florida, North Carolina, New Jersey, Texas, and other states. The company's balance sheet reports the asset Cost of Acquisitions in Excess of the Fair Market Value of the Net Assets of Subsidiaries. Assume that United Telecom purchased this asset as part of the acquisition of another company, which carried these figures:

Book value of assets..................	$640,000
Market value of assets	920,000
Liabilities	405,000

Required

1. What is another title for the asset Cost of Acquisitions in Excess of the Fair Market Value of the Net Assets of Subsidiaries?
2. Make the journal entry recording United Telecom's purchase of the other company for $1,650,000 cash.
3. Assuming United Telecom amortizes Cost of Acquisitions in Excess of the Fair Market Value of the Net Assets of Subsidiaries over 20 years, record the straight-line amortization for one year.

Reporting plant asset transactions on the statement of cash flows
(Obj. 7)

P7-7B At the end of 1995, **Sprint Corporation**, the telecommunications company, had total assets of $15.2 billion and total liabilities of $10.5 billion. Included among the assets were property, plant, and equipment with a cost of $19.9 billion and accumulated depreciation of $10.2 billion.

Assume that Sprint completed the following selected transactions during 1996:

The company earned total revenues of $13.9 billion and incurred total expenses of $13.2 billion, which included depreciation of $1.5 billion. During the year Sprint paid $2.1 billion for new property, plant, and equipment and sold old plant assets for $0.2 billion. The cost of the assets sold was $0.6 billion, and their accumulated depreciation was $0.4 billion.

Required

1. Show how Sprint Corporation would report property, plant, and equipment on the balance sheet at December 31, 1996.
2. Show how Sprint would report operating activities and investing activities on its statement of cash flows for 1996. The company's cash-flow statement starts with net income.
3. Explain how to determine whether Sprint had a gain or a loss on the sale of old plant assets. What was the amount of the gain or loss, if any?

EXTENDING YOUR KNOWLEDGE

DECISION CASES

Measuring profitability based on different inventory and depreciation methods
(Obj. 2, 3)

Case 1. Suppose you are considering investing in two businesses, Waldorf, Inc., and Seattle Supply Company. The two companies are virtually identical, and both began operations at the beginning of the current year. During the year, each company purchased inventory as follows:

Jan. 4	10,000 units at $4 =	$ 40,000
Apr. 6	5,000 units at 5 =	25,000
Aug. 9	7,000 units at 6 =	42,000
Nov. 27	10,000 units at 7 =	70,000
Totals	32,000	$177,000

During the first year, both companies sold 25,000 units of inventory.

In early January, both companies purchased equipment costing $150,000 that had a ten-year estimated useful life and a $20,000 residual value. Waldorf uses the inventory and depreciation methods that maximize reported income. By contrast, Seattle Supply uses the inventory and depreciation methods that minimize income tax payments. Both companies' trial balances at December 31 included the following:

Sales revenue	$370,000
Operating expenses	80,000

The income tax rate is 40 percent.

Required

1. Prepare both companies' income statements.
2. Write an investment newsletter to address the following questions for your clients: Which company appears to be more profitable? Which company has more cash to invest in promising projects? If prices continue rising in both companies' industries over the long term, which company would you prefer to invest in? Why?

Plant assets and intangible assets
(Obj. 1, 6)

Case 2. The following questions are unrelated except that they all apply to fixed assets and intangible assets:

a. The manager of Garden Ridge Corporation regularly buys plant assets and debits the cost to Repairs and Maintenance Expense. Why would he do that, since he knows this action violates GAAP?

b. The manager of Onassis Company regularly debits the cost of repairs and maintenance of plant assets to Plant and Equipment. Why would she do that, since she knows she is violating GAAP?

c. It has been suggested that, since many intangible assets have no value except to the company that owns them, they should be valued at $1.00 or zero on the balance sheet. Many accountants disagree with this view. Which view do you support? Why?

ETHICAL ISSUE

Village Oak Apartments purchased land and a building for the lump sum of $2.2 million. To get the maximum tax deduction, Village Oak managers allocated 90% of the purchase price to the building and only 10% to the land. A more realistic allocation would have been 70% to the building and 30% to the land.

Required

1. Explain the tax advantage of allocating too much to the building and too little to the land.
2. Was Village Oak's allocation ethical? If so, state why. If not, why not? Identify who was harmed.

FINANCIAL STATEMENT CASES

Plant assets and intangible assets
(Obj. 2, 3, 6, 7)

Case 1. Refer to the Lands' End, Inc., financial statements in Appendix A at the end of the book, and answer the following questions.

a. Which depreciation method does Lands' End use for reporting to stockholders and creditors in the financial statements? What type of depreciation method does the company probably use for income tax purposes? Why is this method preferable for tax purposes?

b. Depreciation expense is embedded in the expense amounts listed on the income statement. The statement of cash flows gives the amount of depreciation and amortization expense. During the year ended February 2, 1996 (fiscal year 1996), Lands' End made no acquisitions of other companies and thus purchased no new goodwill. You can determine the amortization of intangibles from the information on the balance sheet. Compute amortization of intangibles, and then use that figure to determine Lands' End's depreciation expense for fiscal year 1996.

c. Explain why Lands' End adds depreciation and amortization expenses back to net income in the computation of net cash flows from operating activities.

d. Explain both of Lands' End's investing activities on the statement of cash flows.

Plant assets and intangible assets
(Obj. 2, 6, 7)

Case 2. Obtain the annual report of a company of your choosing. Answer these questions about the company. Concentrate on the current year in the annual report you select.

a. Which depreciation method or methods does the company use for reporting to stockholders and creditors in the financial statements? Does the company disclose the estimated useful lives of plant assets for depreciation purposes? If so, identify the useful lives.

b. Depreciation and amortization expenses are often combined because they are similar. Many income statements embed depreciation and amortization in other expense amounts. To learn the amounts of these expenses, it is often necessary to examine the statement of cash flows. Where does your company report depreciation and amortization? What were these expenses for the current year? (*Note:* The company you selected may have no amortization—only depreciation.)

c. How much did the company spend to acquire plant assets during the current year? Journalize the acquisitions in a single entry.

d. How much did the company receive on the sale of plant assets? Assume a particular cost and accumulated depreciation of the plant assets sold. Journalize the sale of the plant assets, assuming that the sale resulted in a $700,000 loss.

e. What categories of intangible assets does the company report? What is their reported amount?

GROUP PROJECT

Visit a local business.

Required

1. List all its plant assets.
2. If possible, interview the manager. Gain as much information as you can about the business's plant assets. For example, try to determine the assets' costs, the depreciation method the company is using, and the estimated useful life of each asset category. If an interview is impossible, then develop your own estimates of the assets' costs, useful lives, and book values, assuming an appropriate depreciation method.
3. Determine whether the business has any intangible assets. If so, list them and gain as much information as possible about their nature, cost, and estimated useful lives.
4. Write a detailed report of your findings and be prepared to present your results to the class.

INTERNET EXERCISE

THE HOME DEPOT

The Home Depot has become a retailing innovator by combining the economies of warehouse-format stores with a high level of customer service. Today, The Home Depot is the largest do-it-yourself retailer in the United States and is continuing to grow. As a consequence of its success, The Home Depot needs to acquire more buildings, equipment, and land.

The Home Depot Web site is an excellent information source for understanding the company's objectives, its approach to business, and its perspective on community and environmental responsibility. The site is also a repository of data useful to investors, including the company's financial statements.

Required

1. Go to **http://www.homedepot.com/.** There you will find The Home Depot's home page and meet Homer, your helpful Home Depot guide.
2. Check out some of The Home Depot's various pages, then examine The Home Depot's financial success by clicking on the highlighted text, **Annual Stockholder Report.**
3. The annual report's table of contents appears. Capturing the elements of the printed annual report, this section presents links to the company's ten-year financial review, the CEO and president's letter to the stockholders, and explanations of The Home Depot's marketing and operating strategies.
4. To learn how The Home Depot accounts for, manages, and controls its plant assets, intangible assets, and related expenses, answer the following questions.
   a. The Home Depot describes the home-improvement market and the company's role within that market. What are the company's strengths?
   b. Briefly explain The Home Depot's marketing strategy.
   c. Review the financial statements, along with Management's Discussion and Analysis.
   (i) What are The Home Depot's accounting policies for depreciation?
   (ii) Why is the estimated useful life of "Furniture, fixtures, and equipment" less than that of "Buildings"?
   (iii) What were The Home Depot's cash expenditures for new plant assets during the last fiscal year? Are these expenditures consistent with the company's marketing strategy?
   (iv) The Home Depot's name, customer goodwill, and its blaring orange logo are all valuable intangible assets. Are they located in the financial statements? Why or why not?

8

Accounting for Current and Long-Term Liabilities

Learning Objectives

After studying this chapter, you should be able to

1. Account for current liabilities
2. Identify and report contingent liabilities
3. Account for basic bonds payable transactions
4. Measure interest expense; amortize bond discount and premium by the effective-interest method
5. Explain the advantages and disadvantages of borrowing
6. Account for lease transactions
7. Report liabilities on the balance sheet

AMR Corporation
(parent company of American Airlines)
Balance Sheet (partial)

	(In millions, except shares and par value)	*December 31,* 1995	1994
	Liabilities and Stockholders' Equity		
	Current Liabilities		
1	Accounts payable	$ 817	$ 920
2	Accrued salaries and wages	729	619
3	Accrued liabilities	1,331	1,004
4	Air traffic liability	1,466	1,473
5	Current maturities of long-term debt	228	590
6	Current obligations under capital leases	122	128
7	Total current liabilities	4,693	4,734
8	Long-Term Debt, Less Current Maturities	4,983	5,603
9	Obligations Under Capital Leases, Less Current Obligations	2,069	2,275
	Other Liabilities and Credits		
10	Deferred income taxes	446	279
11	Deferred gains	696	733
12	Postretirement benefits	1,439	1,254
13	Other liabilities and deferred credits	1,510	1,228
		4,091	3,494
	Commitments, Leases, and Contingencies		
	Stockholders' Equity		
14	Convertible preferred stock:* 20,000,000 shares authorized; 159,000 shares issued and outstanding	78	78
15	Common stock—$1 par value;* shares authorized: 150,000,000; shares issued and outstanding: 1995—76,400,000; 1994—75,900,000	76	76
16	Additional paid-in capital	2,239	2,212
17	Other	(91)	(242)
18	Retained earnings	1,418	1,256
		3,720	3,380
19	Total Liabilities and Stockholders' Equity	$19,556	$19,486

**We explain preferred stock and par value in Chapter 9. For a review of common stock and paid-in capital, see Chapter 1.*

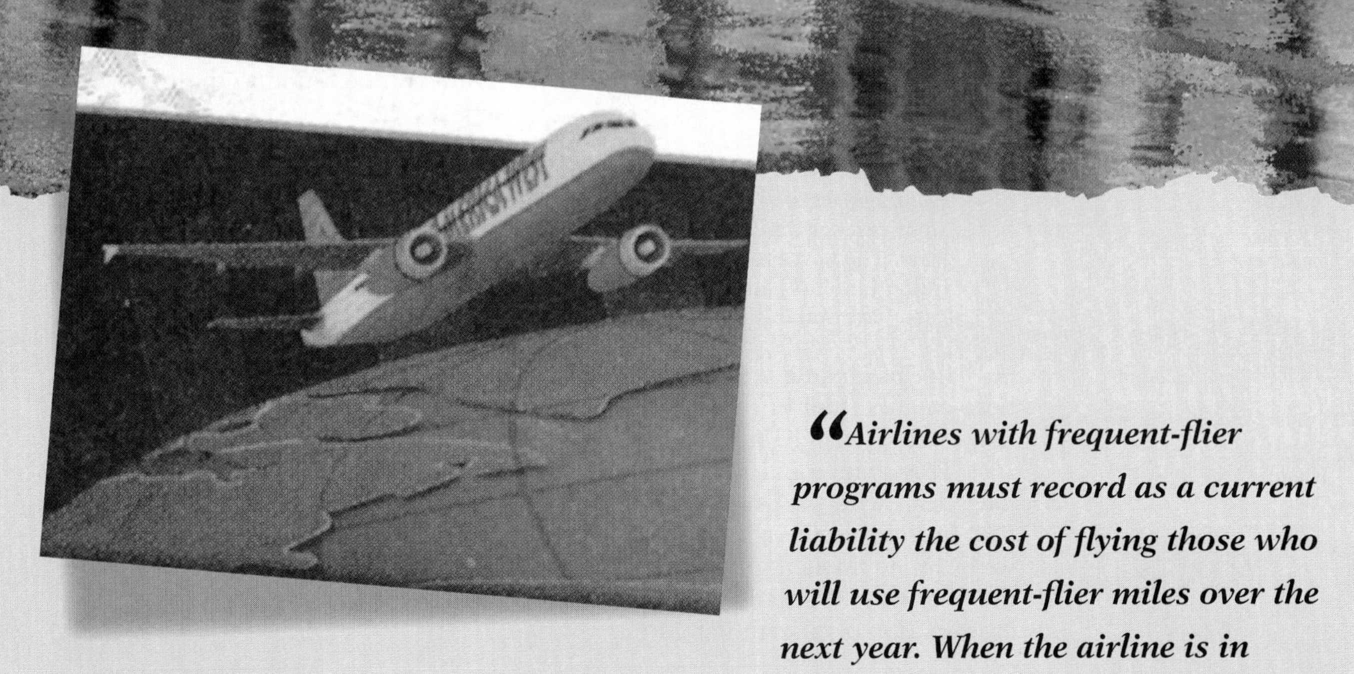

"Airlines with frequent-flier programs must record as a current liability the cost of flying those who will use frequent-flier miles over the next year. When the airline is in partnership with another organization (such as a hotel chain), the problem of determining the current liability becomes more complex."

—Joseph D. Wesselkamper, CPA, President of Joseph D. Wesselkamper & Associates, Inc.

First came the airlines' frequent-flier programs: Fly so many miles on a particular airline, and receive a free ticket to the destination of your choice. Now some hotels—first Marriotts, then Holiday Inns and Sheratons—are offering their guests free *airline* mileage on such carriers as American, United, and Delta.

For example, **Holiday Inn Worldwide** offers its guests 2.5 frequent-flier miles per dollar spent on Holiday Inn rooms. Why would Holiday Inn make such an offer? To encourage travelers to stay at one of its hotels. To the hotel company, the cost is promotion expense. Why would an airline like **American Airlines** allow the hotels to make this offer? To generate revenue: The airlines charge the hotels approximately $0.015 per mile credited to a customer's account.

The arrangement between Holiday Inn and the airlines illustrates the challenge of accounting for liabilities. In this case, the airlines have an obligation to provide travel that the hotels have paid for in advance. To the airline, receiving cash in advance creates an obligation to provide future transportation—a current liability. **AMR Corporation** (the parent company of American Airlines) reports this obligation as Air Traffic Liability, one of the current liabilities shown on its balance sheet (see line 4).

More information on how AMR Corporation accounts for the liabilities and revenues arising from its frequent-flier program can be found in the company's annual report:

> ***Frequent Flier Program*** The estimated incremental cost of providing free travel awards is accrued [as expense and a liability] when such award levels are reached. American sells mileage credits to participating companies in its frequent flier program. The portion of such revenues that relates to transportation is deferred [as Air Traffic Liability] and recognized [as revenue] over a period approximating the time transportation is provided.

In this chapter we explain how to account for current and long-term liabilities. The first half of the chapter concentrates on current liabilities, the second half on long-term liabilities.

This chapter marks a turning point in this text. The four preceding chapters have dealt with the assets of a business. Assets relate to a firm's *investing* activities. In this and the next chapter we shift our focus to *financing* activities. First, we examine financing the business with liabilities. Then, in Chapter 9, we cover the financing of operations with stockholders' equity. Let's turn now to a closer examination of current liabilities.

Current Liabilities of Known Amount

Objective 1

Account for current liabilities

Recall that *current liabilities* are obligations due within one year or within the company's normal operating cycle if it is longer than one year. Obligations due beyond that period of time are classified as *long-term liabilities.*

Current liabilities fall into one of two categories: liabilities of a known amount and those whose amount must be estimated. We look first at current liabilities of known amount.

Current liabilities and long-term liabilities were discussed in Chapter 3, page 138.

Accounts Payable

Amounts owed to suppliers for products or services purchased on open account are *accounts payable.* We have seen many accounts payable examples in preceding chapters. For example, a business may purchase inventories and office supplies on an account payable. AMR Corporation reported Accounts Payable of $817 million at December 31, 1995 (see line 1 of the balance sheet on page 366).

Current liabilities arising from many similar transactions are well suited to computerized accounting. One of a merchandiser's most common transactions is the credit purchase of inventory. A computer makes it easy to integrate the accounts payable and perpetual inventory systems. When merchandise dips below a predetermined level, the computer automatically prepares a purchase request. After the order is placed and the goods are received, clerks enter inventory and accounts payable data into the system. The computer then increases Inventory and Accounts Payable to account for the purchase. For payments, the computer decreases Accounts Payable and Cash. The program may also update account balances and print journals, ledger accounts, and the financial statements.

Recall from Chapter 3, page 119, that all adjusting entries for accrued expenses require a debit to an expense and a credit to a payable.

Short-Term Notes Payable

Short-term notes payable, a common form of financing, are notes payable due within one year. Companies often issue short-term notes payable to borrow cash or to purchase inventory or plant assets. In addition to recording the note payable and its eventual payment, the business must also accrue interest expense and interest payable at the end of the period. The following entries are typical of this liability:

19X1			
Sep. 30	Inventory	8,000	
	Note Payable, Short-Term		8,000
	Purchase of inventory by issuing a one-year 10% note payable.		

ASSETS	=	LIABILITIES	+	STOCKHOLDERS' EQUITY
8,000	=	8,000	+	0

Dec. 31	Interest Expense ($8,000 × 0.10 × 3/12)	200	
	Interest Payable		200
	Adjusting entry to accrue interest expense at year end.		

ASSETS	=	LIABILITIES	+	STOCKHOLDERS' EQUITY	–	EXPENSES
0	=	200			–	200

The balance sheet at December 31, 19X1, will report the Note Payable of $8,000 and the related Interest Payable of $200 as current liabilities. The 19X1 income statement will report interest expense of $200.

The following entry records the note's payment:

19X2			
Sep. 30	Note Payable, Short-Term	8,000	
	Interest Payable	200	
	Interest Expense ($8,000 × 0.10 × 9/12)	600	
	Cash [$8,000 + ($8,000 × 0.10)]		8,800
	Payment of a note payable and interest at maturity.		

ASSETS	=	LIABILITIES	+	STOCKHOLDERS' EQUITY	–	EXPENSES
–8,800	=	–8,000 – 200			–	600

The cash payment entry must separate the total interest on the note between the portion accrued at the end of the previous period ($200) and the current period's expense ($600).

The face amount of notes payable and their interest rates and payment dates can be stored for electronic data processing. Computer programs calculate interest, print the interest checks, journalize the transactions, and update account balances.

Short-Term Notes Payable Issued at a Discount

In another common borrowing arrangement, a company may **discount a note payable** at the bank. The bank subtracts the interest amount from the note's face value, and the borrower receives the net amount. In effect, the borrower prepays the interest, which is computed on the note's principal.

Suppose Procter & Gamble discounts a $100,000, 60-day note payable to its bank at 12 percent. The company will receive $98,000—that is, the $100,000 face value less interest of $2,000 ($100,000 × 0.12 × 60/360). Assume that this transaction occurs on November 25, 19X1. Procter & Gamble's entries to record discounting the note would be as follows:

19X1			
Nov. 25	Cash ($100,000 – $2,000)	98,000	
	Discount on Note Payable ($100,000 × 0.12 × 60/360)	2,000	
	Note Payable, Short-Term		100,000
	Discounted a $100,000, 60-day, 12% note payable to borrow cash.		

ASSETS	=	LIABILITIES	+	STOCKHOLDERS' EQUITY
+98,000	=	− 2,000 +100,000	+	0

Discount on Note Payable is a contra account to the liability Note Payable, Short-Term. For this reason, it is journalized as a *debit* against the liability's normal *credit* balance. A balance sheet prepared immediately after this transaction would report the note payable at its net amount of $98,000, as follows:

Current liabilities:	
Note payable, short-term	$100,000
Less: Discount on note payable	(2,000)
Note payable, short-term, net	$ 98,000

STOP & THINK How much did Procter & Gamble (P&G) borrow from the bank—$98,000 or $100,000? How much will P&G pay back? How much interest expense will P&G record for the borrowing arrangement?

Answers: P&G borrowed $98,000, the amount of cash the company received.
P&G will pay back $100,000 at maturity.
P&G's interest expense will be $2,000 ($100,000 paid back – $98,000 borrowed).

The accrued interest at year end still must be recorded, as it would for any note payable. The adjusting entry at December 31 records interest for 36 days as follows:

19X1			
Dec. 31	Interest Expense ($100,000 × 0.12 × 36/360)	1,200	
	Discount on Note Payable		1,200
	Adjusting entry to accrue interest expense at year end.		

ASSETS	=	LIABILITIES	+	STOCKHOLDERS' EQUITY	−	EXPENSES
0	=	1,200			−	1,200

This entry credits the Discount account instead of Interest Payable. Why? Because the Discount balance represents future interest expense, and the accrual of interest records the current-period portion of the expense. Thus, the Discount account must be decreased by the amount of current-period expense. This is accomplished by *crediting* the Discount contra account, which has a normal debit balance. Crediting the Discount account reduces the contra account's balance and increases the net amount of the note payable. After the adjusting entry, only $800 of the Discount remains, and the carrying amount of the note payable increases to $99,200, as follows:

Current liabilities:	
Note payable, short-term	$100,000
Less: Discount on note payable ($200,000 – $1,200)	(800)
Note payable, short-term, net	$ 99,200

At maturity, the business records the final amount of interest expense and the payment of the note:

19X2			
Jan. 24	Interest Expense ($100,000 × 0.12 × 24/360) ...	800	
	Discount on Note Payable........................		800
	To record interest expense.		

ASSETS	=	LIABILITIES	+	STOCKHOLDERS' EQUITY	–	EXPENSES
0	=	800			–	800

Jan. 24	Note Payable, Short-Term	100,000	
	Cash..		100,000
	To pay note payable at maturity.		

ASSETS	=	LIABILITIES	+	STOCKHOLDERS' EQUITY
–100,000	=	–100,000	+	0

After these entries, the balances in the Note Payable and Discount accounts are zero. Each period's income statement reports the appropriate amount of interest expense.

Sales Tax Payable

Every state except Delaware, Montana, New Hampshire, and Oregon levies a sales tax on retail sales. Retailers charge their customers the sales tax in addition to the price of the item sold. Because the retailers owe the state the sales tax collected, the account Sales Tax Payable is a current liability. For example, **ShowBiz Pizza Time, Inc.** (known for its family restaurant/entertainment centers, such as Chuck E. Cheese), recently reported sales tax payable of $737,712 as a current liability.

ShowBiz Pizza Time, Inc. (known for its family restaurant/entertainment centers, such as Chuck E. Cheese), recently reported sales tax payable of $737,712 as a current liability.

States do not levy sales tax on the sales of manufacturers, such as Procter & Gamble and General Motors. Such companies sell their products to wholesalers and retailers rather than to final consumers. Therefore, manufacturers have no sales tax liability.

Suppose one Saturday's sales at a ShowBiz Pizza Time totaled $10,000. The business collected an additional 5% in sales tax, which would equal $500 ($10,000 × 0.05). The business would record that day's sales as follows:

Cash ($10,000 × 1.05)..	10,500	
Sales Revenue		10,000
Sales Tax Payable ($10,000 × 0.05)................................		500
To record cash sales and the related sales tax.		

ASSETS	=	LIABILITIES	+	STOCKHOLDERS' EQUITY	+	REVENUES
10,500	=	500			+	10,000

Companies forward the collected sales tax to the taxing authority at regular intervals, at which time they debit Sales Tax Payable and credit Cash. Observe that Sales Tax Payable does *not* correspond to any sales tax expense that the business is incurring. Nor does this liability arise from the purchase of any asset. Rather, the obligation arises because the business is collecting money for the government.

Many companies consider it inefficient to credit Sales Tax Payable when recording sales. Rather, they record the sales in an amount that includes the tax. Then, prior to paying tax to the state, they make a single entry for the entire period's transactions to bring Sales Revenue and Sales Tax Payable to their correct balances.

Suppose a company made July sales of \$100,000, subject to a tax of 6 percent. Its summary entry to record the month's sales could be as follows:

July 31	Cash (\$100,000 × 1.06)......................................	106,000	
	Sales Revenue		106,000
	To record sales for the month.		

ASSETS	=	LIABILITIES	+	STOCKHOLDERS' EQUITY	+	REVENUES
106,000	=	0			+	106,000

The entry to adjust Sales Revenue and Sales Tax Payable to their correct balances would then be

July 31	Sales Revenue [\$106,000 – (\$106,000 ÷ 1.06)]........	6,000	
	Sales Tax Payable..		6,000
	To record sales tax.		

ASSETS	=	LIABILITIES	+	STOCKHOLDERS' EQUITY	+	REVENUES
0	=	6,000			–	6,000

Companies that follow this procedure need to make an adjusting entry at the end of the period in order to report the correct amounts of revenue and sales tax liability on their financial statements.

Current Portion of Long-Term Debt

Some long-term notes payable and long-term bonds payable must be paid in installments. The **current portion of long-term debt,** or *current maturity,* is the amount of the principal that is payable within one year. At the end of each year, a company reclassifies (from long-term debt to a current liability) the amount of its long-term debt that must be paid during the upcoming year.

AMR's balance sheet (page 366) reports Current maturities of long-term debt, the next-to-last current liability (line 5). AMR reports Long-Term Debt, Less Current Maturities immediately after total current liabilities (line 8). *Long-term debt* refers to the notes payable and bonds payable that we cover in the second half of this chapter.

STOP & THINK Study AMR's balance sheet and answer these questions about the company's current and long-term debt:

1. At December 31, 1995, how much in total did AMR owe on current and long-term debt?
2. How much of the long-term debt did AMR expect to pay during 1996? How much was the company scheduled to pay during 1997 or later?

Answers

1. AMR owed a total of \$5,211 million on current and long-term debt (\$228 million + \$4,983 million).
2. AMR expected to pay the current maturities of \$228 million during 1996. AMR expected to pay the remainder (\$4,983 million) during 1997 or later.

The liabilities for the current portion of long-term debt (line 5) and for the long-term portion (line 8) do *not* include any accrued interest payable. The two accounts, Current Portion of Long-Term Debt and Long-Term Debt, represent only the principal amounts owed. Interest Payable is a separate account for a different liability—the interest that must be paid. AMR includes interest payable under the current liability caption Accrued liabilities (line 3).

AMR Corporation reports Current obligations under capital leases as its last current liability (line 6). This liability, which is similar to current maturities of long-term debt, is next year's lease payment on leases that AMR has capitalized as an asset. (AMR also reports a long-term liability for Obligations Under Capital Leases, Less Current Obligations—line 9.) We cover capital leases in more detail in the second half of the chapter.

Accrued Expenses (Accrued Liabilities)

An **accrued expense** is an expense incurred but not yet paid by the company. Therefore, it is also a liability, which explains why accrued expenses are sometimes called **accrued liabilities.** Accrued expenses typically occur with the passage of time, such as AMR Corporation's interest payable on its long-term debt. By contrast, an account payable results from a particular transaction in which the company purchased a good or a service.

American Airlines' obligations under its frequent-flier program are reported as Air Traffic Liability.

Like most other companies, AMR Corporation reports several categories of accrued expenses on its balance sheet: Accrued Salaries and Wages (line 2); Accrued Liabilities (line 3); and Air Traffic Liability (line 4). Accrued Salaries and Wages are the company's liabilities for salaries and wages payable at the end of the period. This caption also includes other payroll-related liabilities, such as taxes withheld from employee paychecks. Accrued Liabilities includes the company's current liabilities for such items as interest payable and income tax payable. (Many companies report Income Tax Payable as a separate liability on the balance sheet.) Air Traffic Liability is the sum of the company's current liabilities that are unique to its airline operations. For example, American Airlines' obligations under its frequent-flier program are reported as Air Traffic Liability.

Payroll Liabilities

Payroll, also called *employee compensation,* is a major expense of many businesses. For service organizations—such as CPA firms, real estate brokers, and travel agents—payroll is *the* major expense of conducting business. Service organizations sell their personnel's services, so employee compensation is their primary cost of doing business, just as cost of goods sold is the largest expense in a merchandising company.

Employee compensation takes different forms. Some employees collect a *salary,* which is pay stated at a yearly, monthly, or weekly rate. Other employees work for *wages,* which are stated at an hourly figure. Sales employees often receive a *commission,* which is a percentage of the sales the employee has made. Some companies reward excellent performance with a *bonus,* an amount over and above regular compensation. Accounting for all these forms of compensation follows the same pattern, which is illustrated in Exhibit 8-1 on page 374 (using assumed figures).

Salary (or other payroll) expense, which represents employees' *gross pay* (that is, pay before subtractions for taxes and other deductions), creates several liabilities for the company. Salary payable to employees, which is their *net* (take-home) *pay,* is the largest payroll liability. *Employee Income Tax Payable* is the employees' income tax that has been withheld from their paychecks. *FICA Tax Payable* is the employees' Social Security tax, which also is withheld from paychecks. (FICA stands for the Federal Insurance Contributions Act, which created the Social Security tax.) The company owes these liabilities to the U.S.

EXHIBIT 8-1
Accounting for Payroll Expenses and Liabilities

Salary Expense (or Wage Expense or Commission Expense)	10,000	
Employee Income Tax Payable		1,200
FICA Tax Payable		800
Employee Union Dues Payable		140
Salary Payable to Employees [take-home pay]		7,860
To record salary expense.		

ASSETS	=	LIABILITIES	+	STOCKHOLDERS' EQUITY	−	EXPENSES
		+1,200				
0	=	+ 800			−	10,000
		+ 140				
		+7,860				

government. In our example in Exhibit 8-1, employees have authorized the company to withhold union dues, which are payable to the union.

In addition to salaries and wages, companies must pay some employer payroll taxes and expenses for employee fringe benefits. Accounting for these expenses is similar to the illustration in Exhibit 8-1.

Unearned Revenues

Unearned revenues are also called *deferred revenues, revenues collected in advance,* and *customer prepayments.* All these account titles indicate that the business has received cash from its customers before it has earned the revenue. The company has an obligation to provide goods or services to the customer. The chapter opening story provides one illustration. Let's consider another example.

As we saw in Chapter 3, page 121, an unearned revenue is a liability because it represents an obligation to provide a good or service.

The **Dun & Bradstreet (D&B) Corporation** provides credit evaluation services to businesses that subscribe to the D&B reports. When finance companies pay in advance to have D&B investigate the credit histories of potential customers, D&B incurs a liability to provide future service. The liability account is called Unearned Subscription Revenue (which could also be titled Unearned Subscription Income).

Assume that D&B charges $150 for a finance company's three-year subscription. D&B's entries would be as follows:

19X1			
Jan. 1	Cash	150	
	Unearned Subscription Revenue		150
	To record receipt of cash at start of the three-year subscription agreement.		

ASSETS	=	LIABILITIES	+	STOCKHOLDERS' EQUITY
150	=	150	+	0

19X1, 19X2, 19X3			
Dec. 31	Unearned Subscription Revenue	50	
	Subscription Revenue ($150/3)		50
	To record subscription revenue earned at the end of each of three years.		

YEAR	ASSETS	=	LIABILITIES	+	STOCKHOLDERS' EQUITY	+	REVENUES
19X1	0	=	−50			+	50
19X2	0	=	−50			+	50
19X3	0	=	−50			+	50

D&B's financial statements would report the following:

Balance Sheet	Year 1	December 31, Year 2	Year 3
Current liabilities			
Unearned subscription revenue	$50	$50	$-0-
Long-term liabilities			
Unearned subscription revenue	$50	-0-	-0-
Income Statement	**Year 1**	**Year 2**	**Year 3**
Revenues			
Subscription revenue	$50	$50	$50

Current Liabilities That Must Be Estimated

A business may know that a liability exists but not know the exact amount. The liability may not simply be ignored. The unknown amount of a liability must be estimated, recorded in the accounts, and reported on the balance sheet.

Estimated current liabilities vary among companies. As a first example, let's look at Estimated Warranty Payable, a liability account common among merchandisers.

Estimated Warranty Payable

Many merchandising companies guarantee their products against defects under *warranty* agreements. The warranty period may extend for any length of time. Ninety-day warranties and one-year warranties are common. The automobile companies—**BMW, General Motors,** and **Toyota,** for example—accrue liabilities for their four- or five-year, 60,000-mile warranties.

Whatever the warranty's lifetime, the matching principle demands that the company record the *warranty expense* in the same period that the business recognizes sales revenue. After all, offering the warranty—and incurring any possible expense through the warranty agreement—is a part of generating revenue through sales. At the time of the sale, however, the company does not know which products are defective. The exact amount of warranty expense cannot be known with certainty, so the business must estimate its warranty expense and the related liability.

For a review of the matching principle, see Chapter 3, page 111.

Assume that Whirlpool Corporation, which manufactures appliances for Sears and other companies, made sales of $200,000,000, subject to product warranties. If, in past years, between 2% and 4% of products proved defective, Whirlpool management could estimate that 3% of the products it sells this year will require repair or replacement during the one-year warranty period. The company would record warranty expense of $6,000,000 ($200,000,000 × 0.03) for the period:

Warranty Expense	6,000,000	
Estimated Warranty Payable		6,000,000
To accrue warranty expense.		

ASSETS	=	LIABILITIES	+	STOCKHOLDERS' EQUITY	−	EXPENSES
0	=	6,000,000			−	6,000,000

Assume that defective merchandise totals $5,800,000. Whirlpool may either repair or replace it. Corresponding entries follow:

Estimated Warranty Payable	5,800,000	
Cash		5,800,000
To *repair* defective products sold under warranty.		

ASSETS	=	LIABILITIES	+	STOCKHOLDERS' EQUITY
−5,800,000	=	−5,800,000	+	0

Estimated Warranty Payable	5,800,000	
Inventory		5,800,000
To *replace* defective products sold under warranty.		

ASSETS	=	LIABILITIES	+	STOCKHOLDERS' EQUITY
−5,800,000	=	−5,800,000	+	0

Whirlpool's expense is $6,000,000 on the income statement no matter what the cash payment or the cost of the replacement inventory. In future periods, Whirlpool may debit the liability Estimated Warranty Payable for the remaining $200,000. However, *when* the company repairs or replaces defective merchandise has no bearing on when the company records warranty expense. Whirlpool records warranty expense in the same period as the sale. The company reports its estimated warranty payable on the balance sheet under the current-liability caption Accrued expenses.

Estimated Vacation Pay Liability

Most companies grant paid vacations to their employees. The employees receive this benefit when they take their vacation, but they earn the benefit by working the other days of the year. Two-week vacations are common. To match expense with revenue properly, the company accrues the vacation pay expense and liability for each of the 50 work weeks of the year. Then, the company records payment during the two-week vacation period. Employee turnover, terminations, and ineligibility force companies to estimate their vacation pay liability.

Suppose a company's January payroll is $100,000 and vacation pay adds 4% (2 weeks of annual vacation divided by 50 work weeks each year). Experience indicates that only 90% of the available vacations will be taken, so the January vacation pay estimate is $3,600 ($100,000 × 0.04 × 0.90). In January, the company records vacation pay as follows:

Jan. 31	Vacation Pay Expense	3,600	
	Estimated Vacation Pay Liability		3,600

ASSETS	=	LIABILITIES	+	STOCKHOLDERS' EQUITY	−	EXPENSES
0	=	3,600			−	3,600

Each month thereafter, the company makes a similar entry.

If an employee takes a two-week vacation during August, his or her $2,000 salary is recorded as follows:

Aug. 31	Estimated Vacation Pay Liability	2,000	
	Cash		2,000

ASSETS	=	LIABILITIES	+	STOCKHOLDERS' EQUITY
−2,000	=	−2,000	+	0

Contingent Liabilities

A *contingent liability* is not an actual liability. Instead, it is a potential liability that depends on a *future* event arising out of past events. For example, AMR Corporation, the parent company of American Airlines, faces a possible loss if its pilots walk off the job in a threatened labor strike. The future event is the negotiation between the airline and the pilots' labor union. The airline thus faces a contingent liability, which may or may not become an actual loss.

Objective 2

Identify and report contingent liabilities

We introduced contingent liabilities in Chapter 5, page 241.

It would be unethical for the airline to withhold knowledge of the labor negotiations from its creditors and from anyone considering investing in the business. A person or business could be misled into thinking the company is stronger financially than it really is. The *disclosure principle* (see Chapter 6) requires a company to report any information deemed relevant to outsiders. The goal is to give people relevant, reliable information for decision making. The Financial Accounting Standards Board (FASB) separates contingencies into two categories:

1. Contingent losses and related liabilities
2. Contingent gains and related assets

Businesses do not record contingent gains and their related assets. Accountants record only actual gains. But accountants record some contingent losses as though they had already occurred.

The FASB provides these guidelines to account for contingent losses (or expenses) and their related liabilities:

1. Record a liability if it is *probable*—likely—that the loss (or expense) will occur and the *amount can be reasonably estimated.* Warranty expense and vacation pay expense are examples.

2. Report the contingency in a financial statement note if it is *reasonably possible* that a loss (or expense) will occur. The remainder of this section discusses contingencies of this type.

3. There is no need to report a contingent loss that is *remote*—unlikely to occur. Instead, wait until an actual transaction clears up the situation. For example, suppose Del Monte Foods conducts business in Nicaragua, and the Nicaraguan government issues a mild threat to confiscate the assets of all foreign companies. Del Monte will neither record a loss nor report the contingency if the probability of a loss is considered remote.

Sometimes, the contingent liability has a definite amount. Recall from Chapter 5 that the payee of a discounted note receivable has a contingent liability. If the maker of the note pays at maturity, the contingent liability ceases to exist. If the maker defaults, however, the payee, who sold the note, must pay its maturity value to the purchaser. In this case, the payee knows the note's maturity value, which is the amount of the contingent liability.

Another contingent liability of known amount arises from company A's guaranteeing that company B will pay a note payable owed to company C. This practice, called *cosigning a note,* obligates the guarantor (company A) to pay the note and interest if, and only if, the primary debtor (company B) fails to pay. Thus, the guarantor has a contingent liability until the note becomes due. If the primary debtor pays off the note, the contingent liability ceases to exist. If the primary debtor fails to pay, the guarantor's contingent liability becomes actual.

The amount of a contingent liability may be hard to determine. For example, companies face lawsuits, which may cause possible obligations of amounts to be determined by the courts.

Contingent liabilities may be reported in two ways. In what is called a **short presentation,** the contingent liability appears in the body of the balance sheet, after total liabilities, but with no amounts given. In general, an explanatory note accompanies a short presentation. **Sears, Roebuck and Company** reported contingent liabilities this way:

	Millions
Total liabilities	$27,830.7
Contingent liabilities (note 10)	—

Note 10: Various legal actions and governmental proceedings are pending against Sears, Roebuck and Co. and its subsidiaries. The consequences of these matters are not presently determinable but, in the opinion of management, the ultimate liability resulting, if any, will not have a material effect on the company.

AMR Corporation's balance sheet on page 366 includes a short presentation of contingencies.

Many companies use a second method of reporting, presenting the footnote only. International Business Machines Corporation (IBM) mentions its contingent liabilities in a half-page supplementary note labeled *litigation.*

International Business Machines Corporation (IBM) mentions its contingent liabilities in a half-page supplementary note labeled **litigation.**

FASB Guidelines The line between a contingent liability and a real liability may be hard to draw. As a practical guide, the FASB says to record an actual liability if (1) it is probable that the business has suffered a loss, and (2) its amount can be reasonably estimated. If both of these conditions are met, the FASB reasons that the obligation has passed from contingent to real, even if its amount must be estimated. Suppose that at the balance sheet date, a hospital has lost a court case for uninsured malpractice, but the amount of damages is uncertain. The hospital estimates that the liability will fall between $1.0 and $2.5 million. In this case, the hospital must record a loss or expense and a liability for $1.0 million. The income statement will report the loss, and the balance sheet the liability. Also, the hospital must disclose in a note the possibility of an additional $1.5 million loss.

Mid-Chapter SUMMARY PROBLEM FOR YOUR REVIEW

This problem consists of three independent parts.

Required

1. A Wendy's hamburger restaurant made cash sales of $4,000 subject to a 5% sales tax. Record the sales and the related sales tax. Also record Wendy's payment of the tax to the state government.
2. At April 30, 19X2, H. J. Heinz Company reported its 6% long-term debt as follows:

Current Liabilities (in part)	
Portion of long-term debt due within one year	$ 14,000,000
Interest payable ($200,000,000 × 0.06 × 5/12)	5,000,000
Long-Term Debt and Other Liabilities (in part)	
Long-term debt	$186,000,000

The company pays interest on its long-term debt on November 30 each year.

Show how Heinz Company would report its liabilities on the year-end balance sheet at April 30, 19X3. Assume that the current maturity of its long-term debt is $16 million.

3. What distinguishes a contingent liability from an actual liability?

ANSWERS

1. Cash ($4,000 × 1.05)	4,200	
Sales Revenue		4,000
Sales Tax Payable ($4,000 × 0.05)		200
To record cash sales and related sales tax.		

Sales Tax Payable	200	
Cash		200
To pay sales tax to the state government.		

2. H. J. Heinz Company balance sheet at April 30, 19X3:

Current Liabilities (in part)	
Portion of long-term debt due within one year	$ 16,000,000
Interest payable ($186,000,000 × 0.06 × 5/12)	4,650,000
Long-Term Debt and Other Liabilities (in part)	
Long-term debt	$170,000,000

3. A contingent liability is a *potential* liability, which may or may not become an actual liability.

Financing Operations with Long-Term Debt

Large companies such as **Chrysler Corporation** cannot borrow billions from a single lender because no lender will risk that much money on a single company. Banks and other lenders diversify their risk by loaning smaller amounts to numerous customers. This way, if a borrower cannot repay, the lender is not devastated.

How do large corporations borrow a huge amount? They issue (sell) bonds to the public. **Bonds payable** are groups of notes payable issued to multiple lenders, called *bondholders*. The idea is that Chrysler can borrow large amounts by issuing bonds to thousands of individual investors, each buying a modest amount of Chrysler bonds. Chrysler receives the amount it needs, and each investor limits his or her risk by diversifying investments—not putting all the "eggs in one basket."

In the pages that follow, we treat bonds payable and long-term notes payable together because their accounting is the same.

Bonds: An Introduction

To gain access to large amounts of cash, a company may issue bonds. Each bond is, in effect, a long-term note payable that pays interest. Bonds are debts of the company for the amounts borrowed from the investors.

Purchasers of bonds receive a bond certificate, which carries the issuing company's name. The certificate also states the *principal,* the amount that the company has borrowed from the bondholder. This figure, typically stated in units of $1,000, is also called the bond's *face value, maturity value,* or *par value.* The bond obligates the issuing company to pay the holder the principal amount at a specific future date called the *maturity date.* This date also appears on the bond certificate.

Bondholders loan their money to companies for a price: interest on the principal. The bond certificate states the interest rate that the issuer will pay the holder and the dates that the interest payments are due (generally twice a year). Some bond certificates name the bondholder (the investor). When the company pays back the principal, the holder returns the certificate, which the company retires (or cancels). Exhibit 8-2 on page 380 shows an actual bond certificate.

The board of directors may authorize a bond issue. In some companies, the stockholders—as owners—may also have to vote their approval. Issuing bonds usually requires the services of a securities firm, such as **Merrill Lynch,** to act as

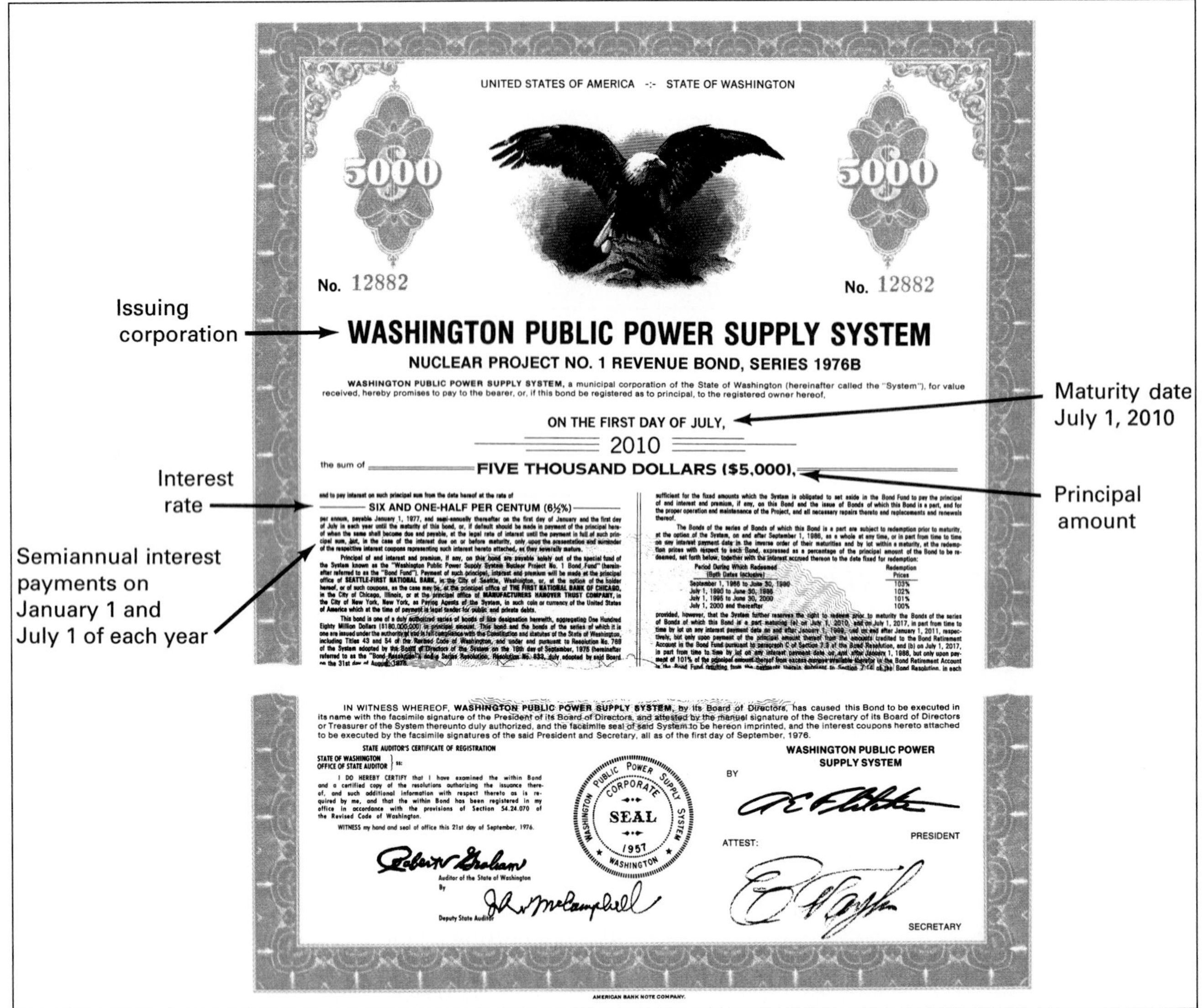

UNITED STATES OF AMERICA -:- STATE OF WASHINGTON

5000 5000

No. 12882 No. 12882

WASHINGTON PUBLIC POWER SUPPLY SYSTEM

NUCLEAR PROJECT NO. 1 REVENUE BOND, SERIES 1976B

WASHINGTON PUBLIC POWER SUPPLY SYSTEM, a municipal corporation of the State of Washington (hereinafter called the "System"), for value received, hereby promises to pay to the bearer, or, if this bond be registered as to principal, to the registered owner hereof,

ON THE FIRST DAY OF JULY,

2010

the sum of FIVE THOUSAND DOLLARS ($5,000),

SIX AND ONE-HALF PER CENTUM (6½%)

IN WITNESS WHEREOF, WASHINGTON PUBLIC POWER SUPPLY SYSTEM, by its Board of Directors, has caused this Bond to be executed in its name with the facsimile signature of the President of its Board of Directors, and attested by the manual signature of the Secretary of its Board of Directors or Treasurer of the System thereunto duly authorized, and the facsimile seal of said System to be hereon imprinted, and the interest coupons hereto attached to be executed by the facsimile signatures of the said President and Secretary, all as of the first day of September, 1976.

WASHINGTON PUBLIC POWER SUPPLY SYSTEM

BY

PRESIDENT

ATTEST:

SECRETARY

SEAL 1957

AMERICAN BANK NOTE COMPANY

EXHIBIT 8-2
Bond (Note) Certificate

the underwriter of the bond issue. The **underwriter** purchases the bonds from the issuing company and resells them to its clients, or it may sell the bonds in return for a commission from the issuer, agreeing to buy all unsold bonds.

Types of Bonds

All the bonds in a particular issue may mature at a specified time (**term bonds**), or they may mature in installments over a period of time (**serial bonds**). By issuing serial bonds, the company spreads its principal payments over time and avoids repaying the entire principal at one time. Serial bonds are like installment notes payable.

Secured, or *mortgage, bonds* give the bondholder the right to take specified assets of the issuer if the company *defaults*—that is, fails to pay interest or principal. *Unsecured bonds,* called **debentures,** are backed only by the good faith of the borrower. Debentures usually carry a higher rate of interest than secured bonds because debentures are a riskier investment.

Bond Prices

Investors may transfer bond ownership through bond markets. The most famous bond market is the New York Exchange, which lists several thousand bonds. Bond prices are quoted at a percentage of their maturity value. For example, a $1,000 bond quoted at 100 is bought or sold for $1,000, which is 100% of its face value. The same bond quoted at 101½ has a market price of $1,015 (101.5% of

Bonds	Volume	High	Low	Close	Net Change
OhEd 9½ 06	12	79½	78½	79½	+2

EXHIBIT 8-3
Bond Price Information for Ohio Edison Company (OhEd)

face value, or $1,000 × 1.015). Prices are quoted to one-eighth of 1 percent. A $1,000 bond quoted at 88⅜ is priced at $883.75 ($1,000 × 0.88375).

Exhibit 8-3 contains actual price information for the bonds of **Ohio Edison Company,** taken from the *Wall Street Journal.* On this particular day, 12 of Ohio Edison's 9½%, $1,000 face value bonds maturing in the year 2006 (indicated by 06) were traded. The bonds' highest price on this day was $795 ($1,000 × 0.795). The lowest price of the day was $785 ($1,000 × 0.785). The closing price (last sale price of the day) was $795. This price was 2 points higher than the closing price of the preceding day. What was the bonds' closing price the preceding day? It was 77½ (79½ – 2).

The length of time until the bond matures is one factor that affects the bond's market price. The earlier the maturity date, the more attractive the bond, and the more an investor is willing to pay for it. Also, the bonds issued by a company with a proven ability to meet all payments commands a higher price than an issue from a company with a poor record.

A bond issued at a price above its face (par) value is said to be issued at a **premium,** and a bond issued at a price below face (par) value has a **discount.** As a bond nears maturity, its market price moves toward par value. On the maturity date, a bond's market value exactly equals its par value because the company that issued the bond pays that amount to retire the bond.

Present Value

A dollar received today is worth more than a dollar received in the future. You may invest today's dollar and earn income from it. Likewise, deferring any payment gives your money a longer period to grow. Money earns income over time, a fact called the *time value of money.* Let's examine how the time value of money affects the pricing of bonds.

Assume that a bond with a face value of $1,000 reaches maturity three years from today and carries no interest. Would you pay $1,000 to purchase the bond? No, because the payment of $1,000 today to receive the same amount in the future provides you with no income on the investment. You would not be taking advantage of the time value of money. Just how much would you pay today to receive $1,000 at the end of three years? The answer is some amount *less* than $1,000. Let's suppose that you feel $750 is a good price. By investing $750 now to receive $1,000 later, you earn $250 interest revenue over the three years. The issuing company sees the transaction this way: It pays you $250 interest for the use of your $750 for three years.

The amount that a person would invest *at the present time* to receive a greater amount at a future date is called the **present value** of a future amount. In our example, $750 is the present value of the $1,000 amount to be received three years later.

Our $750 bond price is a reasonable estimate. The exact present value of any future amount depends on (1) the amount of the future payment (or receipt), (2) the length of time from the investment to the date when the future amount is to be paid (or received), and (3) the interest rate during the period. Present value is always less than the future amount. We discuss how present value is computed in Appendix B at the end of the book (page 720). We need to be aware of the present-value concept, however, in the discussion of bond prices that follows.

LEARNING TIP Present value is always less than future value. You should be able to invest today's money (present value) so that it will increase (future value). The difference between present value and future value is interest.

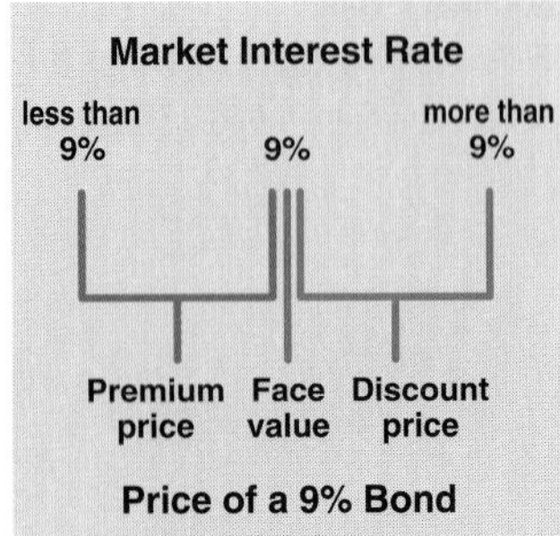

EXHIBIT 8-4
Price of a 9% Bond Under Different Market Interest Rates

Bond Interest Rates

Bonds are sold at market price, which is the amount that investors are willing to pay at any given time. Market price is the bond's present value, which equals the present value of the principal payment plus the present value of the cash interest payments (which are made semiannually [that is, twice a year], annually, or quarterly over the term of the bond).

Two interest rates work to set the price of a bond. The **contract interest rate,** or **stated interest rate,** is the interest rate that determines the amount of cash interest the borrower pays—and the investor receives—each year. For example, Chrysler Corporation's 9% bonds have a contract interest rate of 9 percent. Thus, Chrysler pays $9,000 of interest annually on each $100,000 bond. Each semiannual interest payment is $4,500 ($100,000 × 0.09 × 1/2).

The **market interest rate,** or **effective interest rate,** is the rate that investors demand for loaning their money. The market rate varies, sometimes daily. A company may issue bonds with a contract interest rate that differs from the prevailing market interest rate. Chrysler may issue its 9% bonds when the market rate has risen to 10 percent. Will the Chrysler bonds attract investors in this market? No, because investors can earn 10% on other bonds of similar risk. Therefore, investors will purchase Chrysler bonds only at a price less than par value. The difference between the lower price and face value is a *discount* (Exhibit 8-4). Conversely, if the market interest rate is 8%, Chrysler's 9% bonds will be so attractive that investors will pay more than face value for them. The difference between the higher price and face value is a *premium.* At this point, you should study Appendix B at the end of the book, which discusses the time value of money.

Exhibit 8-5 summarizes the effects of various factors on bond prices.

Issuing Bonds Payable to Borrow Money

Objective 3
Account for basic bonds payable transactions

Suppose Chrysler Corporation has $50 million in 9% bonds that mature in five years. Assume that Chrysler issues these bonds at par on January 1, 1998. The issuance entry is

1998			
Jan. 1	Cash	50,000,000	
	Bonds Payable		50,000,000
	To issue 9%, 5-year bonds at par.		

ASSETS	=	LIABILITIES	+	STOCKHOLDERS' EQUITY
50,000,000	=	50,000,000	+	0

Chrysler, the borrower, makes only a one-time entry to record the receipt of cash and the issuance of bonds. Afterward, investors buy and sell the bonds through the bond markets. The buy-and-sell transactions between investors do

EXHIBIT 8-5
Factors Affecting Bond Prices

Factor	Effects on Bond Price	
Risk of the issuing corporation	High-risk company →	Low price
	Low-risk company →	High price
Length of time to maturity	Long time to maturity →	Low price
	Short time to maturity →	High price
Contract interest rate paid by the bond	High contract interest rate →	High price
	Low contract interest rate →	Low price
Market interest rate when the bonds are issued	High market interest rate →	Low price
	Low market interest rate →	High price

not involve the corporation that issued the bonds. Thus, Chrysler keeps no records of these transactions, except for the names and addresses of the bondholders. It needs this information to mail the interest and principal payments.

Interest payments occur each January 1 and July 1. Chrysler's entry to record the first semiannual interest payment is

1998			
July 1	Interest Expense		
	($50,000,000 × 0.09 × 6/12)	2,250,000	
	Cash		2,250,000
	To pay semiannual interest.		

ASSETS	=	LIABILITIES	+	STOCKHOLDERS' EQUITY	–	EXPENSES
−2,250,000	=	0			–	2,250,000

At year end, Chrysler must accrue interest expense and interest payable for six months (July through December), as follows:

1998			
Dec. 31	Interest Expense		
	($50,000,000 × 0.09 × 6/12)	2,250,000	
	Interest Payable		2,250,000
	To accrue interest.		

ASSETS	=	LIABILITIES	+	STOCKHOLDERS' EQUITY	–	EXPENSES
0	=	2,250,000			–	2,250,000

At maturity, Chrysler will record payment of the bonds as follows:

2003			
Jan. 1	Bonds Payable	50,000,000	
	Cash		50,000,000
	To pay bonds payable at maturity.		

ASSETS	=	LIABILITIES	+	STOCKHOLDERS' EQUITY
−50,000,000	=	−50,000,000	+	0

Issuing Bonds and Notes Payable Between Interest Dates

The foregoing entries to record Chrysler's bond transactions are straightforward because the company issued the bonds on an interest payment date (January 1). However, corporations often issue bonds between interest dates.

Assume that MGM Grand, Inc., which runs the MGM Grand Hotel and Theme Park in Las Vegas, has issued $230 million of 12% notes payable due in the year 2007. Assume further that these notes were dated June 15, 1997, and carry the price "100 plus accrued interest from date of original issue." An investor purchasing the MGM Grand, Inc., notes after the issue date must pay market value *plus accrued interest*. The issuing company will then pay the full semiannual interest amount to the bondholder at the next interest payment date. Companies do not split semiannual interest payments among two or more investors who happen to hold the same bonds during a particular six-month interest period.

Now assume that MGM Grand, Inc., sold $100 million of its notes on July 15, 1997, one month after the date of original issue on June 15. The market price of the notes on July 15 is their face value. MGM Grand receives one month's accrued interest in addition to the notes' face value when MGM issues the bonds on July 15. MGM Grand's entry to record issuance of the notes payable is as follows:

1997			
July 15	Cash	101,000,000	
	Notes Payable		100,000,000
	Interest Payable		
	($100,000,000 × 0.12 × 1/12)...		1,000,000
	To issue 12%, 10-year notes at par, one month after the original issue date.		

ASSETS	=	LIABILITIES	+	STOCKHOLDERS' EQUITY
101,000,000	=	100,000,000 + 1,000,000	+	0

MGM Grand's entry to record the first semiannual interest payment is

1997			
Dec. 15	Interest Expense		
	($100,000,000 × 0.12 × 5/12)	5,000,000	
	Interest Payable	1,000,000	
	Cash ($100,000,000 × 0.12 × 6/12)....		6,000,000
	To pay semiannual interest on notes payable.		

ASSETS	=	LIABILITIES	+	STOCKHOLDERS' EQUITY	–	EXPENSES
−6,000,000	=	−1,000,000			–	5,000,000

The debit to Interest Payable eliminates the credit balance in that account (from July 15). MGM Grand, Inc., has now paid off that liability.

Note that MGM Grand, Inc., pays a full six months' interest on December 15. After subtracting the one month's accrued interest received at the time of issuing the note, MGM Grand has recorded interest expense for five months ($5,000,000). This interest expense is the correct amount for the five months the notes have been outstanding.

Selling bonds and notes between interest dates at market value plus accrued interest simplifies the borrower's accounting. MGM Grand, Inc., pays the same amount of interest on each note regardless of the length of time the investor has held the note. MGM Grand need not compute each noteholder's interest payment on an individual basis.

Suppose you hold MGM Grand, Inc., notes as an investment for two months of a semiannual interest period and sell the notes to another investor before you receive your interest. The person who buys the notes will receive your two months of interest on the next specified interest date. Business practice dictates that you must collect your share of the interest from the buyer when you sell your investment. For this reason, all bond or note transactions are "plus accrued interest."

Issuing Bonds Payable at a Discount

We know that market conditions may force the issuing corporation to accept a discount price for its bonds. Suppose Chrysler Corporation issues $100,000 of its 9%, five-year bonds when the market interest rate is 10 percent. The market price of the bonds drops below $100,000, and Chrysler receives $96,149[1] at issuance. The entry is

[1]Appendix B at the end of the book shows how to determine the price of this bond.

1998			
Jan. 1	Cash	96,149	
	Discount on Bonds Payable	3,851	
	Bonds Payable		100,000
	To issue 9%, 5-year bonds at a discount.		

ASSETS	=	LIABILITIES	+	STOCKHOLDERS' EQUITY
+96,149	=	− 3,851 +100,000		

After posting, the bond accounts have the following balances:

Bonds Payable		Discount on Bonds Payable	
	100,000	3,851	

Chrysler's balance sheet immediately after issuance of the bonds would report the following:

Total current liabilities		$ XXX
Long-term liabilities:		
Bonds payable, 9%, due 2003	$100,000	
Less: Discount on bonds payable	3,851	96,149

Discount on Bonds Payable is a contra account to Bonds Payable, a decrease in the company's liabilities. Subtracting its balance from Bonds Payable yields the *carrying amount* of the bonds. The relationship between Bonds Payable and the Discount account is similar to the relationships between Equipment and Accumulated Depreciation and between Accounts Receivable and Allowance for Uncollectible Accounts. Thus, Chrysler's liability is $96,149, which is the amount the company borrowed. If Chrysler were to pay off the bonds immediately (an unlikely occurrence), Chrysler's required outlay would be $96,149 because the market price of the bonds is $96,149.

Effective-Interest Method of Debt Amortization

Objective 4

Measure interest expense; amortize bond discount and premium by the effective-interest method

Chrysler Corporation pays interest on its bonds semiannually, which is common for corporate bonds. Each semiannual interest payment is the same amount over the life of the bonds, $4,500 ($100,000 × 0.09 × 6/12) because the payment amount is fixed by the bond contract. But Chrysler's interest expense varies from period to period as the bonds march toward maturity. For bonds issued at a discount, the amount of interest expense each period increases as the bonds' carrying amount increases.

Panel A of Exhibit 8-6 on page 386 repeats the Chrysler bond data we've been using so far. Panel B provides an amortization table that is useful for determining the periodic amounts of the company's interest payments and interest expense. It also shows the bond carrying amount. Study the exhibit carefully because the amounts we will be using come directly from the amortization table. This exhibit is an example of the *effective-interest method of amortization.*

Recall from Chapter 7, page 343, that *amortization* is the systematic reduction of a particular amount—in this case, the Discount on Bonds Payable.

INTEREST EXPENSE ON BONDS ISSUED AT A DISCOUNT—AMORTIZING DISCOUNT ON BONDS PAYABLE In Exhibit 8-6, Chrysler Corporation borrows $96,149 cash but must pay $100,000 when the bonds mature. What happens to the $3,851 balance of the discount account over the life of the bond issue?

The $3,851 discount is really additional interest expense to the issuing company. That amount is a cost—beyond the stated interest rate—that Chrysler pays

PANEL A—Bond Data

Issue date—January 1, 1998
Maturity (face, or par) value—$100,000
Contract interest rate—9%
Interest paid—4½% semiannually, $4,500 = $100,000 × 0.045
Market interest rate at time of issue—10% annually, 5% semiannually
Issue price—$96,149
Maturity date—January 1, 2003

PANEL B—Amortization Table

	A	B	C	D	E
Semiannual Interest Date	**Interest *Payment* (4½% of Maturity Value)**	**Interest *Expense* (5% of Preceding Bond Carrying Amount)**	**Discount Amortization (B – A)**	**Discount Account Balance (D – C)**	**Bond Carrying Amount ($100,000 – D)**
Jan. 1, 1998				$3,851	$ 96,149
July 1	$4,500	$4,807	$307	3,544	96,456
Jan. 1, 1999	4,500	4,823	323	3,221	96,779
July 1	4,500	4,839	339	2,882	97,118
Jan. 1, 2000	4,500	4,856	356	2,526	97,474
July 1	4,500	4,874	374	2,152	97,848
Jan. 1, 2001	4,500	4,892	392	1,760	98,240
July 1	4,500	4,912	412	1,348	98,652
Jan. 1, 2002	4,500	4,933	433	915	99,085
July 1	4,500	4,954	454	461	99,539
Jan. 1, 2003	4,500	4,961*	461	-0-	100,000

*Adjusted for effect of rounding.

Notes

- Column A The semiannual interest payments are constant—fixed by the bond contract.
- Column B The interest expense each period = the preceding bond carrying amount × the market interest rate. The amount of interest each period increases as the market interest rate, a constant, is applied to the increasing bond carrying amount (E).
- Column C The excess of each interest expense amount (B) over each interest payment amount (A) is the discount amortization for the period.
- Column D The discount balance decreases by the amount of amortization for the period (C).
- Column E The bond carrying amount increases from $96,149 at issuance to $100,000 at maturity.

EXHIBIT 8-6
Debt Amortization for a Bond Discount

for using the investors' money. Exhibit 8-7 graphs the data from Exhibit 8-6: the interest expense (column B), the interest payment (column A), and the amortization of bond discount (column C).

Observe that the semiannual interest payment—by contract—is fixed at $4,500. But the amount of interest expense increases each period as the bond carrying amount is amortized upward toward maturity value.

The discount is interest expense that is not paid until the bonds are paid off at maturity. The discount is allocated to interest expense through amortization each period over the term of the bonds. Exhibit 8-8 illustrates the amortization of the bond discount from its beginning balance of $3,851 to its ending balance of $0. These amounts come from Exhibit 8-6, column D.

Chrysler issues its bonds on January 1, 1998. On July 1, Chrysler makes the first $4,500 semiannual interest payment. On that date, Chrysler also amortizes (decreases) the bond discount because its balance must be reduced to zero over the term of the bonds. Chrysler's journal entry to record the interest payment and amortization of the bond discount is as follows (with all amounts taken from Exhibit 8-6):

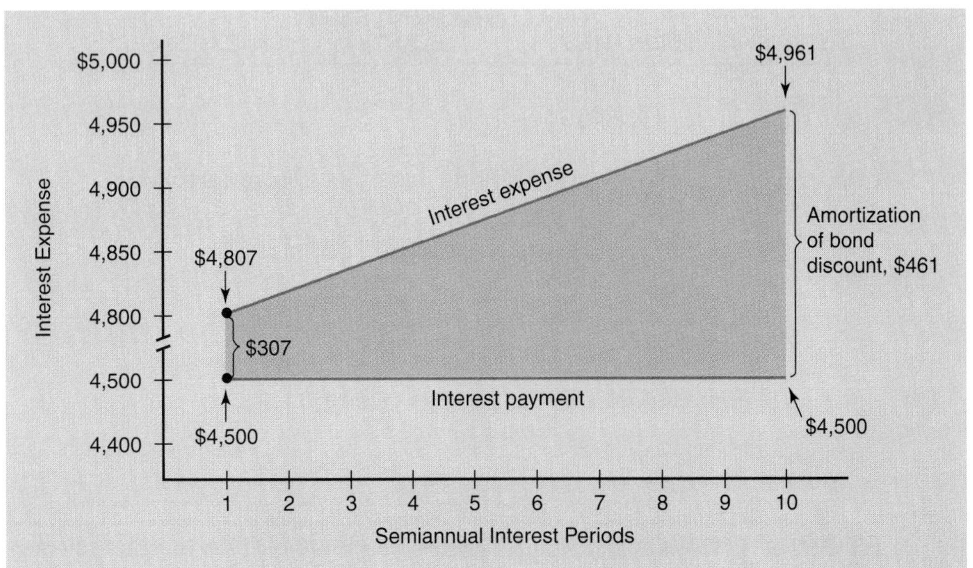

EXHIBIT 8-7
Interest Expense on Bonds Payable Issued at a Discount

1998			
July 1	Interest Expense	4,807	
	Discount on Bonds Payable		307
	Cash		4,500
	To pay semiannual interest and amortize bond discount.		

ASSETS	=	LIABILITIES	+	STOCKHOLDERS' EQUITY	−	EXPENSES
−4,500	=	+307			−	4,807

At December 31, 1998, Chrysler accrues interest and amortizes the bond discount for July through December with this entry (amounts from Exhibit 8-6):

1998			
Dec. 31	Interest Expense	4,823	
	Discount on Bonds Payable		323
	Interest Payable		4,500
	To accrue semiannual interest and amortize bond discount.		

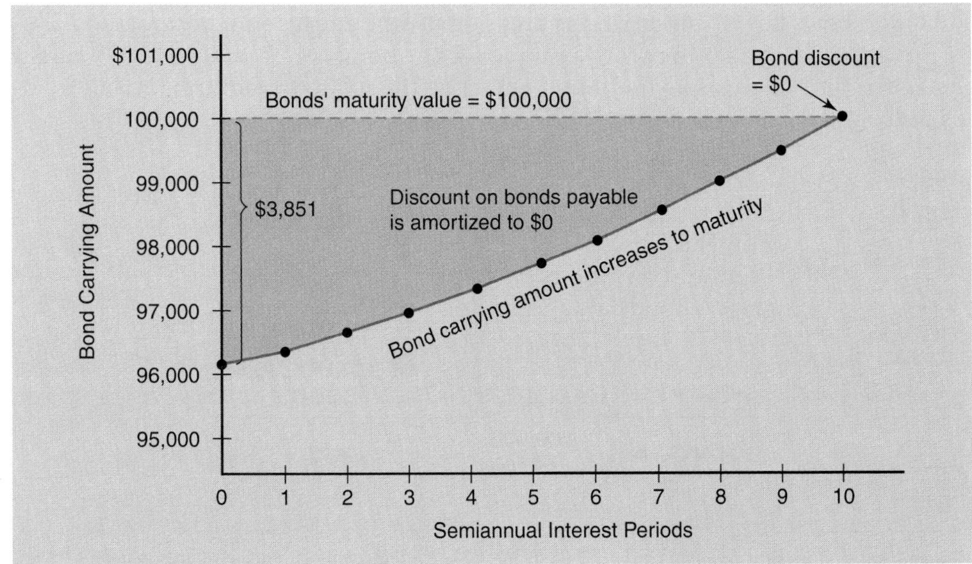

EXHIBIT 8-8
Amortizing Discount on Bonds Payable

ASSETS	=	LIABILITIES	+	STOCKHOLDERS' EQUITY	–	EXPENSES
0	=	+ 323 +4,500			–	4,823

At December 31, 1998, Chrysler's bond accounts appear as follows:

Bonds Payable		Discount on Bonds Payable	
	100,000	3,851	307
			323
		Bal. 3,221	

Bond carrying amount, $96,779 = ($100,000 – $3,221) from Exhibit 8-6

STOP & THINK What would Chrysler Corporation's 1998 income statement and year-end balance sheet report for these bonds?

Answer

Income statement		
Interest expense ($4,807 + $4,823)		$ 9,630
Balance sheet		
Current liabilities:		
Interest payable		$ 4,500
Long-term liabilities:		
Bonds payable	$100,000	
Less: Discount on bonds payable	3,221	96,779

At the bonds' maturity on January 1, 2003, the discount will have been amortized to zero, and the bonds' carrying amount will be $100,000. Chrysler will retire the bonds by making a $100,000 payment.

Issuing Bonds Payable at a Premium

Let's modify the Chrysler bond example to illustrate issuance of the bonds at a premium. Assume that Chrysler Corporation issues $100,000 of five-year, 9% bonds that pay interest semiannually. If the bonds are issued when the market interest rate is 8%, their issue price is $104,100.[2] The premium on these bonds is $4,100, and Exhibit 8-9 shows how to amortize the premium by the effective-interest method.

Chrysler's entries to record issuance of the bonds on January 1, 1998, and to make the first interest payment and amortize the related premium on July 1, are as follows:

1998			
Jan. 1	Cash	104,100	
	Bonds Payable		100,000
	Premium on Bonds Payable		4,100
	To issue 9% bonds at a premium.		

ASSETS	=	LIABILITIES	+	STOCKHOLDERS' EQUITY
104,100	=	100,000 + 4,100	+	0

[2]Again, Apppendix B at the end of the book shows how to determine the price of this bond.

PANEL A—Bond Data

Issue date—January 1, 1998
Maturity (face, or par) value—$100,000
Contract interest rate—9%
Interest paid—4 1/2% semiannually, $4,500 = $100,000 × 0.045
Market interest rate at time of issue—8% annually, 4% semiannually
Issue price—$104,100
Maturity date—January 1, 2003

PANEL B—Amortization Table

	A	B	C	D	E
Semiannual Interest Date	**Interest *Payment* (4½% of Maturity Value)**	**Interest *Expense* (4% of Preceding Bond Carrying Amount)**	**Premium Amortization (A – B)**	**Premium Account Balance (D – C)**	**Bond Carrying Amount ($100,000 + D)**
Jan. 1, 1998				$4,100	$104,100
July 1	$4,500	$4,164	$336	3,764	103,764
Jan. 1, 1999	4,500	4,151	349	3,415	103,415
July 1	4,500	4,137	363	3,052	103,052
Jan. 1, 2000	4,500	4,122	378	2,674	102,674
July 1	4,500	4,107	393	2,281	102,281
Jan. 1, 2001	4,500	4,091	409	1,872	101,872
July 1	4,500	4,075	425	1,447	101,447
Jan. 1, 2002	4,500	4,058	442	1,005	101,005
July 1	4,500	4,040	460	545	100,545
Jan. 1, 2003	4,500	3,955*	545	-0-	100,000

*Adjusted for effect of rounding.

Notes

- Column A The semiannual interest payments are constant—fixed by the bond contract.
- Column B The interest expense each period = the preceding bond carrying amount × the market interest rate. The amount of interest decreases each period as the bond carrying amount decreases.
- Column C The excess of each interest payment (A) over the period's interest expense (B) is the premium amortization for the period.
- Column D The premium balance decreases by the amount of amortization for the period (C).
- Column E The bond carrying amount decreases from $104,100 at issuance to $100,000 at maturity.

EXHIBIT 8-9
Debt Amortization for a Bond Premium

1998			
July 1	Interest Expense	4,164	
	Premium on Bonds Payable	336	
	Cash		4,500
	To pay semiannual interest and amortize bond premium.		

ASSETS	=	LIABILITIES	+	STOCKHOLDERS' EQUITY	–	EXPENSES
–4,500	=	–336			–	4,164

Immediately after issuing the bonds at a premium on January 1, 1998, Chrysler would report the bonds payable on the balance sheet as follows:

Total current liabilities		$ XXX
Long-term liabilities:		
Bonds payable	$100,000	
Premium on bonds payable	4,100	104,100

Note that the premium on bonds payable is *added* to the balance of bonds payable to determine the bonds' carrying amount.

EXHIBIT 8-10
Interest Expense on Bonds Payable Issued at a Premium

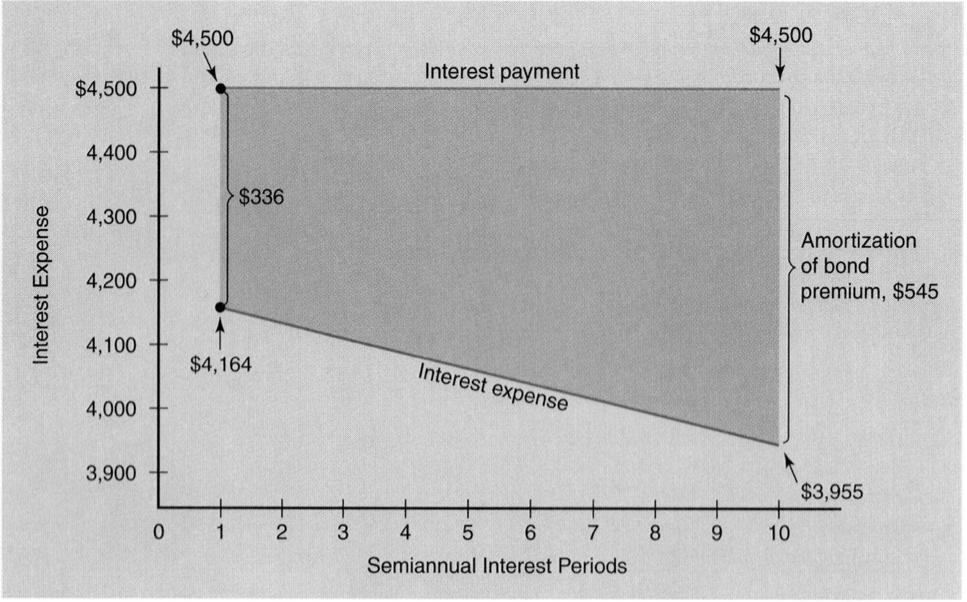

INTEREST EXPENSE ON BONDS ISSUED AT A PREMIUM—AMORTIZING PREMIUM ON BONDS PAYABLE In Exhibit 8-9, Chrysler Corporation borrows $104,100 cash but must pay only $100,000 at maturity. The $4,100 premium on the bonds is a reduction in Chrysler's interest expense over the term of the bonds. Exhibit 8-10 graphs Chrysler's interest expense (column B from Exhibit 8-9), interest payments (column A), and the amortization of bond premium (column C).

Observe that the semiannual interest payment is fixed—by contract—at $4,500. The amount of interest expense each period decreases as the bond carrying amount is amortized downward toward maturity value.

The premium is allocated as a subtraction of interest expense through amortization each period over the term of the bonds. Exhibit 8-11 diagrams the amortization of the bond premium from its beginning balance of $4,100 to its ending balance of $0. All amounts are taken from Exhibit 8-9.

Straight-Line Amortization of Bond Discount and Bond Premium

The tables in Exhibits 8-6 and 8-9 show the best way to amortize bond discounts and premiums (the effective-interest method). A less precise method is used for developing estimates and performing quick analyses that do not require a perfect

EXHIBIT 8-11
Amortizing Premium on Bonds Payable

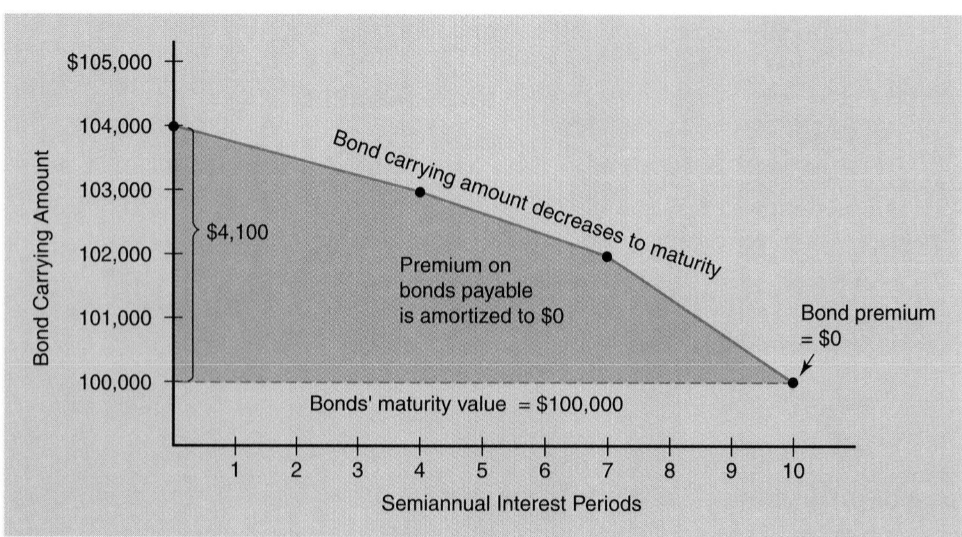

measure of interest expense on a bond. Called the *straight-line amortization method,* it divides a bond discount (or premium) into equal periodic amounts over the bond's term. The amount of interest expense is thus the same for each interest period.

Let's apply the straight-line amortization method to the Chrysler Corporation bonds issued at a discount and illustrated in Exhibit 8-6. Suppose Chrysler's financial vice president is considering issuance of the 9% bonds at $96,149. To estimate semiannual interest expense on the bonds, the executive can use the straight-line amortization method for the bond discount. Estimated semiannual interest expense is

Semiannual cash interest payment ($100,000 × 0.09 × 6/12)	$4,500
+ Semiannual amortization of discount ($3,851 ÷ 10)	385
= Estimated semiannual interest expense	$4,885

Chrysler's entry to record each semiannual interest payment and amortization of the discount under the straight-line amortization method would be

1998			
July 1	Interest Expense	4,885	
	Discount on Bonds Payable		385
	Cash		4,500
	To pay semiannual interest and amortize bond discount.		

ASSETS	=	LIABILITIES	+	STOCKHOLDERS' EQUITY	−	EXPENSES
−4,500	=	385			−	4,885

GAAP permits the straight-line amortization method only when its amounts differ insignificantly from the amounts determined by the effective-interest method.

Early Retirement of Bonds Payable

Normally, companies wait until maturity to pay off, or *retire,* their bonds payable. All bond discount or premium has been amortized, and the retirement entry debits Bonds Payable and credits Cash for the bonds' maturity value. But companies sometimes retire their bonds payable prior to maturity. The main reason for retiring bonds early is to relieve the pressure of making interest payments. Interest rates fluctuate. The company may be able to borrow at a lower interest rate and then use the proceeds from new bonds to pay off the old bonds, which bear a higher interest rate.

Some bonds are **callable,** which means that the bonds' issuer may *call,* or pay off, those bonds at a specified price whenever the issuer so chooses. The call price is usually a few percentage points above the par value, perhaps 104 or 105. Callable bonds give the issuer the benefit of being able to take advantage of low interest rates by paying off the bonds whenever it is most favorable to do so. An alternative to calling the bonds is to purchase them in the open market at their current market price. Whether the bonds are called or purchased in the open market, the journal entry is the same.

Air Products and Chemicals, Inc., a producer of industrial gases and chemicals, has $70 million of debentures outstanding with unamortized discount of $350,000. Lower interest rates in the market may convince management to pay off these bonds now. Assume that the bonds are callable at 103. If the market price of the bonds is 99¼, will Air Products and Chemicals call the bonds or purchase them in the open market? The market price is lower than the call price, so market price is the better choice. Retiring the bonds at 99¼ results in a gain of $175,000, computed as follows:

Par value of bonds being retired	$70,000,000
Unamortized discount	350,000
Carrying amount of the bonds	69,650,000
Market price ($70,000,000 × 0.9925)	69,475,000
Gain on retirement	$ 175,000

The following entry records retirement of the bonds, immediately after an interest date:

June 30	Bonds Payable	70,000,000	
	Discount on Bonds Payable		350,000
	Cash ($70,000,000 × 0.9925)		69,475,000
	Extraordinary Gain on Retirement of Bonds Payable		175,000
	To retire bonds payable before maturity.		

ASSETS	=	LIABILITIES	+	STOCKHOLDERS' EQUITY	+	GAINS
−69,475,000	=	−70,000,000 + 350,000			+	175,000

The entry removes the bonds payable and the related discount from the accounts and records a gain on retirement. Any existing premium would be removed with a debit. If Air Products and Chemicals retired only half these bonds, the accountant would remove half the discount or premium. Likewise, if the price paid to retire the bonds exceeded their carrying amount, the retirement entry would record a loss with a debit to the account Extraordinary Loss on Retirement of Bonds. GAAP identifies gains and losses on early retirement of debts as *extraordinary,* and they are reported separately on the income statement, net of tax.

STOP & THINK Quill Corp. has sold $300,000 of ten-year bonds at a discount. Interest has just been paid, and the remaining carrying value of the bonds is $299,000. Half the bonds are retired by paying the market price of 96½. What entry is required?

Answer

Bonds Payable	150,000*	
Discount on Bonds Payable		500†
Cash		144,750‡
Extraordinary Gain on Retirement of Bonds Payable		4,750§

*$300,000 par value × 1/2 = $150,000
†$1,000 unamortized discount × 1/2 = $500
‡$150,000 × 0.965 = $144,750
§($150,000 − $500) − $144,750 = $4,750 gain

Convertible Bonds and Notes

For a review of common stock, see Chapter 1, page 14.

Many corporate bonds and notes payable may be converted into the issuing company's common stock at the investor's option. These bonds and notes, called **convertible bonds** (or **notes**), combine the safety of assured interest receipts and receipt of principal on the bonds with the opportunity for large gains on the stock. The conversion feature is so attractive that investors usually accept a lower contract, or stated, interest rate than they would on nonconvertible bonds. The lower cash interest payments benefit the issuer. Convertible bonds are recorded like any other debt at issuance.

If the market price of the issuing company's stock gets high enough, the bondholders will convert the bonds into stock. The corporation records conversion by debiting the bond accounts and crediting the stockholders' equity accounts. The carrying amount of the bonds becomes the book value of the newly issued stock. No gain or loss is recorded.

Prime Western, Inc., which operates hotels, had convertible notes outstanding carried on the books at $12.5 million. Assume that the maturity value of the notes was $13 million. Also assume that Prime Western's stock rose significantly so that noteholders converted the notes into 400,000 shares of the company's $1 par common stock. Prime Western's entry to record conversion is as follows:

May 14	Notes Payable	13,000,000	
	Discount on Notes Payable		500,000
	Common Stock (400,000 × $1 par)..		400,000
	Paid-in Capital in Excess of Par—Common..........................		12,100,000
	To record conversion of notes payable.		

ASSETS	=	LIABILITIES	+	STOCKHOLDERS' EQUITY
0	=	−13,000,000	+	400,000
		+ 500,000		12,100,000

The carrying amount of the notes ($13,000,000 – $500,000) becomes the amount of increase in stockholders' equity ($400,000 + $12,100,000). The entry closes the notes (or bonds) payable account and its related discount or premium account.

Common Stock is recorded at its *par value,* which is a dollar amount assigned to each share of stock. In this case, the credit to Common Stock is $400,000 (400,000 shares × $1 par value per share). Any extra amount of the notes (or bonds) payable carrying amount is credited to another stockholders' equity account, Paid in Capital in Excess of Par—Common. In effect, the carrying amount of the notes (or bonds) is transferred from a liability to stockholders' equity.

Advantages of Financing Operations with Bonds Versus Stock

Objective 5

Explain the advantages and disadvantages of borrowing

Businesses have different ways to acquire assets. Management may decide to purchase equipment or lease equipment. The money to obtain the asset may be financed by the business's retained earnings, a stock issue, a note payable, or a bond issue. Each financing strategy has its advantages:

Advantages of Financing Operations By

Issuing Stock	Issuing Notes or Bonds Payable
• Creates no liabilities or interest expense, which must be paid even during bad years. Less risky to the issuing corporation.	• Does not dilute stock ownership or control of the corporation. • Results in higher earnings per share because interest expense is tax deductible and ownership is not diluted.

Exhibit 8-12 on page 394 shows the earnings-per-share advantage of borrowing. **Earnings per share (EPS)** is the amount of a company's net income for each share of its stock. EPS is perhaps the single most important statistic used to evaluate companies because it is a standard measure of operating performance that can be used to compare companies of different sizes and from different industries.

		Plan 1 Borrow $500,000 at 10%		Plan 2 Issue $500,000 of Common Stock
Net income before expansion		$300,000		$300,000
Project income before interest and income tax	$200,000		$200,000	
Less interest expense ($500,000 × 0.10)	50,000		-0-	
Project income before income tax	150,000		200,000	
Less income tax expense (40%)	60,000		80,000	
Project net income		90,000		120,000
Total company net income		$390,000		$420,000
Earnings per share after expansion:				
Plan 1 ($390,000/100,000 shares)		$3.90		
Plan 2 ($420,000/150,000 shares)				$2.80

EXHIBIT 8-12
Earnings-Per-Share Advantage of Borrowing

Suppose that a corporation with net income of $300,000 and 100,000 shares of common stock outstanding needs $500,000 for expansion. Management is considering two financing plans. Plan 1 is to issue $500,000 of 10% bonds payable, and plan 2 is to issue 50,000 shares of common stock for $500,000. Management believes the new cash can be invested in operations to earn income of $200,000 before interest and taxes.

As Exhibit 8-12 shows, the earnings-per-share amount is higher if the company borrows by issuing bonds. The business earns more on the investment ($90,000) than the interest it pays on the bonds ($50,000). Earning more income on borrowed money than the related interest expense increases the earnings for common stockholders and is called **trading on the equity.** It is widely used in business to increase earnings per share of common stock.

Borrowing has its disadvantages, however. Interest expense may be high enough to eliminate net income and lead to a cash crisis or even bankruptcy. Also, borrowing creates liabilities that accrue during bad years as well as during good years. In contrast, a company that issues stock can omit its dividends during a bad year. The Decision Guidelines feature provides some guidelines to help decide how to finance a company's operations.

Computer spreadsheets are useful in evaluating financing alternatives: issuing common stock or bonds. This assessment is often called "what if" analysis—for instance, "what if we finance with common stock?" The answers to "what if" questions can be modeled on a spreadsheet to project the company's financial statements over the next few years.

Lease Liabilities

Objective 6

Account for lease transactions

A **lease** is a rental agreement in which the tenant (**lessee**) agrees to make rent payments to the property owner (**lessor**) in exchange for the use of the asset. Leasing allows the lessee to acquire the use of a needed asset without having to make the large initial cash down payment that purchase agreements require. Accountants distinguish between two types of leases: operating and capital.

Operating Leases

Operating leases are often short-term or cancelable. Many apartment leases and most car-rental agreements are for a year or less. These operating leases give the lessee the right to use the asset but provide the lessee with no continuing rights to the asset. The lessor retains the usual risks and rewards of owning the leased asset. To account for an operating lease, the lessee debits Rent Expense

Decision Guidelines

Financing with Debt or with Stock

Decision	Guidelines
How will you finance your business's operations?	Your financing plan depends on several factors, including the ability of the business's operations to generate cash flow, your willingness to give up some control of the business, the amount of financing risk you are willing to take, and the business's credit rating.
Do the business's operations generate enough cash to meet all its financing needs?	If yes, the business needs little outside financing. There is no need for debt. If no, the business will need to issue additional stock or borrow the money it needs.
Are you willing to give up some of your control of the business?	If yes, then issue stock to other stockholders, who can vote their shares to elect the company's directors. If no, then borrow from bondholders, who have no vote in the management of the company.
How much financing risk are you willing to take?	If much, then borrow as much as you can. This will increase the business's debt ratio and the risk of being unable to pay its debts. If little, then borrow sparingly. This will hold the debt ratio down and reduce the risk of default on borrowing agreements.
How good is the business's credit rating?	The better the credit rating, the easier it is to borrow on favorable terms. A good credit rating also makes it easier to issue stock. Neither stockholders nor creditors will entrust their money to a company with a bad credit rating.

(or Lease Expense) and credits Cash for the amount of the lease payment. The lessee's books do not report the leased asset or any lease liability (except perhaps a prepaid rent amount or a rent accrual at the end of the period).

Capital Leases

Most businesses use capital leasing to finance the acquisition of some assets. A **capital lease** is a long-term and noncancelable financing obligation that is a form of debt. How do you distinguish a capital lease from an operating lease? *FASB Statement No. 13* provides the guidelines. To be classified as a capital lease, a particular lease agreement must meet any *one* of the following criteria:

1. The lease transfers title of the leased asset to the lessee at the end of the lease term. Thus, the lessee becomes the legal owner of the leased asset.
2. The lease contains a *bargain purchase option.* The lessee can be expected to purchase the leased asset and become its legal owner.
3. The lease term is 75% or more of the estimated useful life of the leased asset. The lessee uses up most of the leased asset's service potential.
4. The present value of the lease payments is 90% or more of the market value of the leased asset. In effect, the lease payments operate as installment payments for the leased asset.

Only those leases that fail to meet any of these criteria may be accounted for as operating leases.

Accounting for a Capital Lease Accounting for a capital lease is much like accounting for a purchase by the lessee and a sale by the lessor. The lessee enters the asset into its own accounts and records a lease liability at the beginning of the lease term. Thus, the lessee capitalizes the asset in its own financial statements even though the lessee may never take legal title to the property. The lessor removes the asset from its books.

Most companies lease some of their plant assets rather than buy them. A recent survey of 600 companies indicates that they have more leases than any other type of long-term debt.

Walgreen Co. operates drug stores in buildings that it leases from other companies.

Walgreen Co. operates drug stores in buildings that it leases from other companies. Suppose that Walgreen leases a building, agreeing to pay \$10,000 annually for a 20-year period, with the first payment due immediately. This arrangement is similar to purchasing the building on an installment plan. In an installment purchase, Walgreen would debit Building and credit Cash and Installment Note Payable. The company would then pay interest and principal on the note payable and record depreciation on the building. Accounting for a capital lease follows the same pattern.

In a capital leasing arrangement, Walgreen records the building at cost, which is the sum of the \$10,000 initial payment plus the present value of the 19 future lease payments of \$10,000 each. The company credits Cash for the initial payment and credits Lease Liability for the present value of the total future lease payments. Assume that the interest rate on Walgreen's lease is 10% and that the present value (PV) of the future lease payments is \$83,650.[3] At the beginning of the lease term, Walgreen makes the following entry:

19X1			
Jan. 2	Building (\$10,000 + \$83,650)................................	93,650	
	Cash..		10,000
	Lease Liability (PV of future lease payments)..		83,650
	To acquire a building and make the first annual lease payment on a capital lease.		

ASSETS	=	LIABILITIES	+	STOCKHOLDERS' EQUITY
+93,650 −10,000	=	83,650	+	0

Because Walgreen Co. has capitalized the building, the company records depreciation. Assume that the building has an expected life of 25 years. It is depreciated over the lease term of 20 years because the lessee has the use of the building only for that period. No residual value enters into the depreciation computation because the lessee will have no residual asset when the lessee returns the building to the lessor at the expiration of the lease. Therefore, the annual depreciation entry is as follows:

19X1			
Dec. 31	Depreciation Expense (\$93,650/20)	4,683	
	Accumulated Depreciation—Building		4,683
	To record depreciation on leased building.		

ASSETS	=	LIABILITIES	+	STOCKHOLDERS' EQUITY	−	EXPENSES
−4,683	=	0			−	4,683

[3]The formula for this computation appears in Appendix B at the end of the book.

At year end, Walgreen must also accrue interest expense on the lease liability the same way it would accrue interest expense on bonds payable. Interest expense is computed by multiplying the lease liability by the interest rate on the lease. The entry to accrue interest expense credits Lease Liability (not Interest Payable) for this interest accrual:

19X1			
Dec. 31	Interest Expense ($83,650 × 0.10)	8,365	
	Lease Liability		8,365
	To accrue interest on the lease liability.		

ASSETS	=	LIABILITIES	+	STOCKHOLDERS' EQUITY	−	EXPENSES
0	=	8,365			−	8,365

The balance sheet at December 31, 19X1 reports the following:

Assets		
Plant assets:		
Building	$93,650	
Less: Accumulated depreciation	4,683	$88,967
Liabilities		
Current liabilities:		
Lease liability (next payment due on Jan. 2, 19X2)		$10,000
Long-term liabilities:		
Lease liability [beginning balance ($83,650) + interest accrual ($8,365) − current portion ($10,000)]		82,015

The lease liability is split into current and long-term portions because the next payment ($10,000) is a current liability and the remainder is long-term.

The January 2, 19X2, lease payment is recorded as follows:

19X2			
Jan. 2	Lease Liability	10,000	
	Cash		10,000
	To make second annual lease payment on building.		

ASSETS	=	LIABILITIES	+	STOCKHOLDERS' EQUITY
−10,000	=	−10,000	+	0

Off-Balance-Sheet Financing

An important part of business is obtaining the funds needed to acquire assets. To finance operations, a company may issue stock, borrow money, or retain earnings in the business. All three of these financing plans affect the right-hand side of the balance sheet. Issuing stock affects the stock accounts. Borrowing creates notes or bonds payable. Internal funds come from profitable operations (represented by retained earnings) that generate cash.

Off-balance-sheet financing is the acquisition of assets or services with debt that is not reported on the balance sheet. A prime example is an operating lease. The lessee has the use of the leased asset, but neither the asset nor any lease liability is reported on the balance sheet. In the past, most leases were accounted for by the operating method. However, *FASB Statement No. 13* has required businesses to account for an increasing number of leases by the capital lease method. Also, *FASB Statement No. 13* has brought about detailed reporting of operating lease payments in the notes to the financial statements. Much useful information is reported only in the notes. Experienced investors study them carefully.

Pension Liabilities

Most companies have a pension plan for their employees. A **pension** is employee compensation that will be received during retirement. Employees earn the pensions by their service, so the company records pension expense while employees work for the company. To record the company's payment into a pension plan, the company debits Pension Expense and credits Cash. Insurance companies and pension trusts manage pension plans. They receive the employer payments and any employee contributions, then invest those amounts for the employees' future benefit. The goal is to have the funds available to meet any obligations to retirees.

Pensions are perhaps the most complex area of accounting. As employees earn their pensions and the company pays into the pension plan, the plan's assets grow. The obligation for future pension payments to employees also accumulates. At the end of each period, the company compares the fair market value of the assets in the pension plan—cash and investments—with the plan's accumulated benefit obligation. The *accumulated benefit obligation* is the present value of promised future pension payments to retirees. If the plan assets exceed the accumulated benefit obligation, the plan is said to be *overfunded.* In this case, the asset and obligation amounts need to be reported only in the notes to the financial statements. However, if the accumulated benefit obligation exceeds plan assets, the plan is *underfunded,* and the company must report the excess liability amount as a long-term pension liability on the balance sheet.

Suppose that the pension plan of Mainstream Manufacturing & Sales, Inc., has assets with a fair market value of $3 million on December 31, 19X0. On this date, the accumulated pension benefit obligation to employees is $4 million. Mainstream's balance sheet will report Long-Term Pension Liability of $1 million. This liability will be listed, in no particular order, along with Bonds Payable, Long-Term Notes Payable, Lease Liabilities, and other long-term liabilities. In this case Mainstream will also report the $1 million as a negative component of other comprehensive income. *Comprehensive income* is the company's change in total stockholders' equity from all sources other than from the owners of the business. One such change in equity is the difference between the pension plan's accumulated benefit obligation and the market value of the pension plan assets.

Postretirement Benefits Liabilities

In 1993, the FASB began requiring accrual-basis accounting for the expense and liability of providing benefits, mainly for health care, to retirees. The concept is the same as for pensions. As employees work, the company accrues the expense and the liability of providing health benefits during retirement. This practice satisfies the matching principle. Before *FASB Statement No. 106,* many companies accounted for these costs on a pay-as-you-go basis. Under that system, companies reported no liability. The long-term liability for postretirement benefits other than pensions can be substantial, as these figures (in millions) show for several well-known companies:

Company	Liability for Postretirement Benefits Other Than Pensions	Total Stockholders' Equity
IBM	$6,074	$22,423
Texaco, Inc.	804	9,519
The Coca-Cola Company	273	5,392

IBM's liability is over 25% of total stockholders' equity. Texaco's and Coca-Cola's nonpension liabilities are a smaller percentage of stockholders' equity.

Reporting Current and Long-Term Liabilities on the Balance Sheet

Objective 7

Report liabilities on the balance sheet

This chapter began with the liabilities reported on the balance sheet of AMR Corporation, the parent company of American Airlines. Your study of this chapter should have increased your confidence that you can understand the liabilities reported on any company's balance sheet. As a review of the material covered in this chapter, Exhibit 8-13 repeats the liabilities section of AMR's balance sheet. You should be familiar with all the current liabilities and most of AMR's long-term liabilities.

You now have the tools to understand the two new categories of long-term liabilities listed under "Other Liabilities and Credits." *Deferred income taxes* (line 10) are what the name implies: income tax liabilities that the company can defer and pay later. In effect, deferred income taxes reported as liabilities are long-term income taxes payable. We will examine accounting for income taxes in more detail in Chapter 11. *Deferred gains* (line 11) are simply long-term unearned revenues. Deferred credits (line 13) are similar to deferred gains.

AMR reports Commitments, Leases, and Contingencies (line 14) "short"—that is, with no dollar amounts because these are not real liabilities. *Commitments* refer to future payments that AMR will make when the conditions materialize. The following note from AMR's 1995 annual report explains.

> **3. Commitments and Contingencies**
> The Company has on order four Boeing 757-200 jet aircraft scheduled for delivery in 1996. Remaining payments for these aircraft and related equipment will be approximately $100 million in 1996. In addition to these commitments for aircraft, the Company has authorized expenditures of approximately $850 million for aircraft modifications, renovations of, and additions to, airport and office facilities and various other equipment and assets. AMR expects to spend approximately $350 million of this amount in 1996.

EXHIBIT 8-13
Liabilities Section of the Balance Sheet, AMR Corporation

AMR CORPORATION
(parent company of American Airlines)
Balance Sheet (partial)

	(In millions, except shares and par value)	December 31, 1995	December 31, 1994
	Liabilities and Stockholders' Equity		
	Current Liabilities		
1	Accounts payable	$ 817	$ 920
2	Accrued salaries and wages	729	619
3	Accrued liabilities	1,331	1,004
4	Air traffic liability	1,466	1,473
5	Current maturities of long-term debt	228	590
6	Current obligations under capital leases	122	128
7	Total current liabilities	4,693	4,734
8	**Long-Term Debt, Less Current Maturities**	4,983	5,603
9	**Obligations Under Capital Leases, Less Current Obligations**	2,069	2,275
	Other Liabilities and Credits		
10	Deferred income taxes	446	279
11	Deferred gains	696	733
12	Postretirement benefits	1,439	1,254
13	Other liabilities and deferred credits	1,510	1,228
		4,091	3,494
14	**Commitments, Leases and Contingencies**		

STOP & THINK Why would AMR Corporation report a commitment to purchase airplanes in the future? After all, the company will conduct a lot of other business in future years. Why single out this commitment for special mention in the company's annual report?

Answer: The purchase of airplanes is critical for an airline, and the expected future payment amounts are significant. AMR Corporation's stockholders and creditors (and, indeed, the public at large) are vitally interested in American Airlines' maintaining a safe, modern fleet of aircraft. The *disclosure principle* is the theoretical basis for reporting this information.

The leases referred to in the short presentation are *operating leases.* As discussed earlier in the chapter, a company does not report assets or liabilities for operating leases, as it does for capital leases. Nevertheless, AMR is obligated to make the operating lease payments, as reported in the following note (excerpted):

> **4. Leases**
> AMR's subsidiaries lease various types of equipment and property, including aircraft, passenger terminals, equipment, and various other facilities. The future minimum lease payments required under [. . .] operating leases that have initial or remaining non-cancelable lease terms in excess of one year as of December 31, 1995, were (in millions):

Years Ending December 31,	Operating Leases
1996	$ 879
1997	919
1998	926
1999	918
2000	874
2001 and subsequent	14,402
	$18,918

Reporting Financing Activities on the Statement of Cash Flows

AMR's balance sheet shows that the company finances most of its operations with debt. In fact, the company's debt ratio is 81% (total liabilities of $15,836 million ÷ total assets of $19,556 million). Let's examine AMR's financing activities as reported on its statement of cash flows. Exhibit 8-14 is an excerpt from AMR's cash-flow statement.

During 1995, AMR received cash of $184 million from issuing long-term debt (such as notes payable and bonds payable; see line 3). Another way for AMR to describe these financing activities would be: "Borrowings . . . $184 million." During the year, AMR paid $1,401 million on its long-term debt and capital lease obligations (line 6). The last financing activity of 1995, Other, net, brought in $21 million (line 8).

During 1995, AMR paid cash dividends of $5 million to its preferred stockholders (line 7). (We explain preferred stock in detail in Chapter 9.) Dividends are *financing activities* because the company is paying its stockholders for financing the company. AMR Corporation also pays interest to its creditors for the use of their money. Unlike dividends, interest is an expense, which appears on the income statement. Operating activities focus on the impact of income-statement items (revenues and expenses) on cash flows. Therefore, interest payments are reported as *operating activities,* and AMR's interest payments are included in Net cash provided by operating activities, $2,185 million (line 1). During 1995, financing activities used

EXHIBIT 8-14
Statement of Cash Flows (adapted) for AMR Corporation

AMR CORPORATION
(parent company of American Airlines)
Consolidated Statement of Cash Flows

	(In millions)	Year Ended December 31, 1995	1994
	Cash Flow from Operating Activities:		
1	Net cash provided by operating activities	$ 2,185	$ 1,609
	Cash Flow from Investing Activities:		
2	Net cash used for investing activities	(925)	(1,463)
	Cash Flow from Financing Activities:		
3	Proceeds from issuance of long-term debt	184	146
4	Other short-term borrowings	—	200
5	Payments on other short-term borrowings	—	(200)
6	Payments on long-term debt and capital lease obligations	(1,401)	(549)
7	Payment of preferred stock dividends	(5)	(66)
8	Other, net	21	283
9	Net cash provided by (used for) financing activities	(1,201)	(186)
10	Net increase (decrease) in cash	59	(40)
11	Cash at beginning of year	23	63
12	Cash at end of year	$ 82	$ 23

$1,201 million of AMR Corporation's cash (line 9). Overall, the company's cash increased by $59 million during the year (line 10), and at December 31, 1995, AMR had $82 million in its various cash accounts (line 12).

SUMMARY PROBLEM FOR YOUR REVIEW

The Cessna Aircraft Company has outstanding an issue of 8% convertible bonds that mature in 2018. Suppose the bonds are dated October 1, 1998, and pay interest each April 1 and October 1.

Required

1. Complete the following effective-interest amortization table through October 1, 2000:

   Bond Data

   Maturity value—$100,000
   Contract interest rate—8%
   Interest paid—4% semiannually, $4,000 ($100,000 × 0.04)
   Market interest rate at the time of issue—9% annually, 4½% semiannually
   Issue price—90¾

   Amortization Table

	A	B	C	D	E
Semiannual Interest Date	**Interest Payment (4% of Maturity Amount)**	**Interest Expense (4½% of Preceding Bond Carrying Amount)**	**Discount Amortization (B − A)**	**Discount Account Balance (D − C)**	**Bond Carrying Amount ($100,000 − D)**
10-1-98					
4-1-99					
10-1-99					
4-1-00					
10-1-00					

2. Using the amortization table, record the following transactions:
   a. Issuance of the bonds on October 1, 1998.
   b. Accrual of interest and amortization of discount on December 31, 1998.
   c. Payment of interest and amortization of discount on April 1, 1999.
   d. Conversion of one-third of the bonds payable into no-par stock on October 2, 2000. For no-par stock, transfer the bond carrying amount into the Common Stock account. There is no Additional Paid-in Capital.
   e. Retirement of two-thirds of the bonds payable on October 2, 2000. Purchase price of the bonds was based on their market value of 102.

ANSWERS

Requirement 1

	A	B	C	D	E
Semiannual Interest Date	**Interest Payment (4% of Maturity Amount)**	**Interest Expense (4½% of Preceding Bond Carrying Amount)**	**Discount Amortization (B − A)**	**Discount Account Balance (D − C)**	**Bond Carrying Amount ($100,000 − D)**
10-1-98				$9,250	$90,750
4-1-99	$4,000	$4,084	$84	9,166	90,834
10-1-99	4,000	4,088	88	9,078	90,922
4-1-00	4,000	4,091	91	8,987	91,013
10-1-00	4,000	4,096	96	8,891	91,109

Requirement 2

Date	Accounts	Debit	Credit
1998			
a. Oct. 1	Cash ($100,000 × 0.9075)	90,750	
	Discount on Bonds Payable	9,250	
	Bonds Payable		100,000
	To issue 8%, 20-year bonds at a discount.		
b. Dec. 31	Interest Expense ($4,084 × 3/6)	2,042	
	Discount on Bonds Payable ($84 × 3/6)		42
	Interest Payable ($4,000 × 3/6)		2,000
	To accrue interest and amortize bond discount for three months.		
1999			
c. Apr. 1	Interest Expense	2,042	
	Interest Payable	2,000	
	Discount on Bonds Payable ($84 × 3/6)		42
	Cash		4,000
	To pay semiannual interest, part of which was accrued, and amortize three months' discount on bonds payable.		
2000			
d. Oct. 2	Bonds Payable ($100,000 × 1/3)	33,333	
	Discount on Bonds Payable ($8,891 × 1/3)		2,964
	Common Stock ($91,109 × 1/3)		30,369
	To record conversion of bonds payable.		
e. Oct. 2	Bonds Payable ($100,000 × 2/3)	66,667	
	Extraordinary Loss on Retirement of Bonds	7,260	
	Discount on Bonds Payable ($8,891 × 2/3)		5,927
	Cash ($100,000 × 2/3 × 1.02)		68,000
	To retire bonds payable before maturity.		

SUMMARY OF LEARNING OBJECTIVES

1. *Account for current liabilities.* *Current liabilities* are obligations due within one year or within the company's normal operating cycle if it is longer than one year. Obligations beyond that term are classified as *long-term liabilities.*

Current liabilities fall into two categories: those whose amounts are known (accounts payable, short-term notes payable, sales tax payable, current portion of long-term debt, some accrued expenses payable, payroll liabilities, and unearned revenues) and those that must be estimated (estimated warranty payable, estimated vacation pay liability).

2. *Identify and report contingent liabilities.* *Contingent liabilities* are not actual liabilities but rather potential liabilities that depend on a future event arising out of a past transaction. Contingent liabilities may be of known or indefinite amounts. Companies must report a liability if it is *probable* that the loss or expense will occur and the amount can be reasonably estimated. Contingencies should be reported in financial statement notes if it is *reasonably possible* that they will occur. There is no need to report contingent losses that are *remote possibilities.*

3. *Account for basic bonds payable transactions.* Corporations may borrow by issuing long-term notes and/or bonds payable. A bond contract specifies the *maturity value* of the bonds, the *principal* (amount borrowed from the lender), a *contract interest rate,* and dates for the payment of interest and principal. Bonds issued above par are issued at a *premium,* and bonds issued below par are issued at a *discount. Market interest rates* fluctuate and may differ from the contract rate on a bond.

Money earns income over time, a fact that gives rise to the *time-value-of-money concept.* An investor will pay a price for a bond equal to the present value of the bond principal plus the present value of the bond interest. The cash paid for a bond purchased on a date after an interest date is market value plus accrued interest.

4. *Measure interest expense; amortize bond discount and premium by the effective-interest method.* When a bond's contract interest rate differs from the market interest rate, the company's interest expense differs from period to period. For bonds issued at a discount, the amount of interest expense each period increases as the bond carrying amount increases. For bonds issued at a premium, the amount of interest expense each period decreases as the bond carrying amount decreases.

To amortize a bond discount or premium over the life of the bond and calculate interest expense accurately, accountants use the *effective-interest method of amortization.* A less precise method is the *straight-line amortization method,* which divides a bond discount or premium into equal periodic amounts over the bond's term.

5. *Explain the advantages and disadvantages of borrowing.* A key advantage of raising money by selling bonds versus issuing stock is that interest expense on debt is tax-deductible. Thus, selling bonds is less costly than issuing stock. Bonds also lead to a higher earnings per share than stock issues do. The key disadvantage of borrowing: The company must repay the loan and interest, in good times and in bad.

6. *Account for lease transactions.* A *lease* is a rental agreement between a property owner *(lessor)* and a tenant *(lessee). Operating leases* are often short-term or cancelable, and are accounted for by debiting expense and crediting cash. *Capital leases* are long-term and noncancelable, and are similar to installment purchases of the leased asset. With capital leases, the lessee capitalizes the leased asset and reports a lease liability. The lessee also records depreciation on the leased asset and interest expense on the lease liability.

7. *Report liabilities on the balance sheet.* Many companies report additional categories of liabilities on the balance sheet. *Deferred income taxes* are income tax liabilities that the company has deferred and will pay later. *Deferred gains* and *deferred credits* are long-term unearned revenues.

ACCOUNTING VOCABULARY

accrued expense *(p. 373).*
accrued liability *(p. 373).*
bonds payable *(p. 379).*
callable bonds *(p. 391).*
capital lease *(p. 395).*
contract interest rate *(p. 382).*
convertible bonds (*or* **notes**) *(p. 392).*
current portion of long-term debt *(p. 372).*
debentures *(p. 380).*
discount (on a bond) *(p. 381).*
discounting a note payable *(p. 369).*
earnings per share (EPS) *(p. 393).*
effective interest rate *(p. 382).*
lease *(p. 394).*
lessee *(p. 394).*
lessor *(p. 394).*
market interest rate *(p. 382).*
off-balance-sheet financing *(p. 397).*
operating lease *(p. 394).*
payroll *(p. 373).*
pension *(p. 398).*
premium (on a bond) *(p. 381).*
present value *(p. 381).*
serial bonds *(p. 380).*
short presentation *(p. 377).*
short-term note payable *(p. 368).*
stated interest rate *(p. 382).*
term bonds *(p. 380).*
trading on the equity *(p. 394).*
underwriter *(p. 380).*

QUESTIONS

1. What distinguishes a current liability from a long-term liability? What distinguishes a contingent liability from an actual liability?
2. A company purchases a machine by signing a $21,000, 10%, one-year note payable on July 31. Interest is to be paid at maturity. What two current liabilities related to this purchase does the company report on its December 31 balance sheet? What is the amount of each current liability?
3. At the beginning of the school term, what type of account is the tuition that your college or university collects from students? What type of account is the tuition at the end of the school term?
4. Patton Company warrants its products against defects for three years from date of sale. During the current year, the company made sales of $300,000.

Store management estimated that warranty costs on those sales would total $18,000 over the three-year warranty period. Ultimately, the company paid $22,000 cash on warranties. What was the company's warranty expense for the year? What accounting principle governs this answer?

5. Identify two contingent liabilities of a definite amount and two contingent liabilities of an indefinite amount.
6. Compute the price to the nearest dollar for the following bonds with a face value of $10,000:
   a. 93
   b. 88¾
   c. 101⅜
   d. 122½
   e. 100
7. In which of the following situations will bonds sell at par? At a premium? At a discount?
   a. 9% bonds sold when the market rate is 9%
   b. 9% bonds sold when the market rate is 10%
   c. 9% bonds sold when the market rate is 8%
8. Why are bonds sold for a price "plus accrued interest"? What happens to accrued interest when the bonds are sold by an individual?
9. A company retires ten-year bonds payable of $100,000 after five years. The business issued the bonds at 104 and called them at 103. Compute the amount of gain or loss on retirement. How is this gain or loss reported on the income statement?
10. Why are convertible bonds attractive to investors? Why are they popular with borrowers?
11. Contrast the effects on a company of issuing bonds versus issuing stock.
12. What characteristics distinguish a capital lease from an operating lease?
13. What is off-balance-sheet financing? Give two examples.
14. Distinguish an overfunded pension plan from an underfunded plan. Which situation requires the company to report a pension liability on the balance sheet? How is this liability computed?

EXERCISES

Accounting for warranty expense and the related liability
(Obj. 1)

E8-1 The accounting records of Delta Corporation, a manufacturer of household appliances, included the following balances at the end of the period:

Estimated Warranty Payable		Sales Revenue		Warranty Expense	
	Beg. bal 8,100		161,000		

In the past, Delta's warranty expense has been 7% of sales. During the current period, the business paid $10,430 to satisfy the warranty claims of customers.

Required

1. Record Delta Corporation's warranty expense for the period and the company's cash payments during the period to satisfy warranty claims. Explanations are not required.
2. Show what Delta will report on its income statement and balance sheet for this situation.

Recording note payable transactions
(Obj. 1)

E8-2 Record the following note payable transactions of Polymer Plastics, Inc., in the company's journal. Explanations are not required.

19X2	
May 1	Purchased equipment costing $21,000 by issuing a one-year, 8% note payable.
Dec. 31	Accrued interest on the note payable.
19X3	
May 1	Paid the note payable at maturity.

Discounting a note payable
(Obj. 1)

E8-3 On November 1, 19X4, Sharp Electronics discounted a six-month, $12,000 note payable to the bank at 7 percent.

Required

1. How much in total liabilities will Sharp report for this situation on its December 31, 19X4, balance sheet?
2. How much interest expense will Sharp report on its 19X4 income statement? On its 19X5 income statement?

Accounting for income tax
(Obj. 1)

E8-4 At December 31, 1994, **Campbell Soup Company** reported a current liability for income tax payable of $117 million. During 1995, Campbell Soup earned income of $1,042 million before income tax. The company's income tax rate during 1995 was 33 percent. Also during 1995, Campbell Soup paid income taxes of $341 million.

How much income tax payable did Campbell Soup Company report on its balance sheet at December 31, 1995? How much income tax expense did Campbell Soup report on its 1995 income statement?

Analyzing liabilities
(Obj. 1, 7)

E8-5 **Temple-Inland, Inc.**, is a large holding company with major interests in paper, packaging, building products, and timber resources. Temple-Inland's 1995 revenues totaled $2,794 million, and at December 31, 1995, the company had $653 million in current assets. The December 31, 1995, balance sheet reported the following:

At year end *(in millions)*	1995	1994
Liabilities and Shareholders' Equity		
Current Liabilities		
Accounts payable	$ 138	$ 176
Accrued expenses	157	178
Employee compensation and benefits	37	25
Current portion of long-term debt	5	14
Total Current Liabilities	337	393
Long-Term Debt	1,489	1,316
Deferred Income Taxes	259	229
Postretirement Benefits	132	126
Other Liabilities	21	17
Shareholders' Equity	1,975	1,783
Total Liabilities And Shareholders' Equity	$4,213	$3,864

Required

1. Describe each of Temple-Inland's liabilities, and state how the liability arose.
2. How much were Temple-Inland's total assets at December 31, 1995? Was the company's debt ratio high, low, or in a middle range?

Reporting a contingent liability ***(Obj. 2)***

E8-6 Magnetic Imaging, Inc., is a defendant in lawsuits brought against the marketing and distribution of its products. Damages of $6.3 million are claimed against Magnetic Imaging, but the company denies the charges and is vigorously defending itself. In a recent press conference, the president of the company stated that he could not predict the outcome of the lawsuits. Nevertheless, he said management does not believe that any actual liabilities resulting from the lawsuits will significantly affect the company's financial position.

Required

1. Prepare a partial balance sheet to show how Magnetic Imaging would report this contingent liability in a short presentation. Total actual liabilities are $10.2 million. Also, write the disclosure note to describe the contingency.
2. Suppose Magnetic Imaging's attorneys believe it is probable that a judgment of $1.5 million will be rendered against the company. Describe how to report this situation in the Magnetic Imaging financial statements. Journalize any entry required under GAAP. Explanations are not required.

Reporting current liabilities ***(Obj. 1)***

E8-7 The top management of High Flier, Inc., examines the following company accounting records at December 29, immediately before the end of the year:

Total current assets	$ 480,000
Noncurrent assets	1,240,000
	$1,720,000
Total current liabilities	$ 250,000
Noncurrent liabilities	810,000
Owners' equity	660,000
	$1,720,000

High Flier's borrowing agreements with creditors require the company to keep a current ratio of 2.0 or better. How much in current liabilities should the company pay off within the next two days in order to comply with its borrowing agreements?

Reporting current and long-term liabilities ***(Obj. 1, 7)***

E8-8 Assume that Wilson Sporting Goods completed these selected transactions during December 19X6:

a. Sport Spectrum, a chain of sporting goods stores, ordered $50,000 of tennis and golf equipment. With its order, Sport Spectrum sent a check for $50,000. Wilson will ship the goods on January 3, 19X7.
b. The December payroll of $195,000 is subject to employee withheld income tax of 9% and FICA tax of 8 percent. On December 31, Wilson pays employees but accrues all tax amounts.
c. Sales of $2,000,000 are subject to estimated warranty cost of 1.4 percent.
d. On December 1, Wilson signed a $100,000 note payable that requires annual payments of $20,000 plus 9% interest on the unpaid balance each December 1.

Required

Classify each liability as current or long-term, and report the amount that would appear for these items on the Wilson Sporting Goods balance sheet at December 31, 19X6.

Issuing bonds payable, paying and accruing interest, and amortizing discount by the straight-line method
(Obj. 3)

E8-9

1. On February 1, Memorix Corporation issues 20-year, 8% bonds payable with a face value of $1,000,000. The bonds sell at 98 and pay interest on January 31 and July 31. Memorix amortizes bond discount by the straight-line method. Record (a) issuance of the bonds on February 1, (b) the semiannual interest payment on July 31, and (c) the interest accrual on December 31.
2. If Memorix issued the bonds payable on May 31, how much cash would the company receive upon issuance of the bonds?

Issuing bonds payable; recording interest payments and the related discount amortization
(Obj. 3, 4)

E8-10 Toblerone Chocolate Co. is authorized to issue $500,000 of 7%, ten-year bonds payable. On January 1, 19X4, when the market interest rate is 8%, the company issues $400,000 of the bonds and receives cash of $372,660. Toblerone amortizes bond discount by the effective-interest method. The semiannual interest dates are June 30 and December 31.

Required

1. Prepare an amortization table for the first four semiannual interest periods.
2. Record the first semiannual interest payment on June 30, 19X4, and the second payment on December 31, 19X4.

Issuing bonds payable; recording interest accrual and payment and the related premium amortization
(Obj. 3, 4)

E8-11 On September 30, 1998, the market interest rate is 7 percent. Template Software, Inc., issues $300,000 of 8%, 20-year bonds payable at 110⅝. The bonds pay interest on March 31 and September 30. Template amortizes bond premium by the effective-interest method.

Required

1. Prepare an amortization table for the first four semiannual interest periods.
2. Record issuance of the bonds on September 30, 1998, the accrual of interest at December 31, 1998, and the semiannual interest payment on March 31, 1999.

Debt payment and discount amortization schedule
(Obj. 4)

E8-12 Atlas Airlines, Inc., issued $600,000 of 8⅜% (0.08375), five-year bonds payable on January 1, 19X1, when the market interest rate was 9½% (0.095). Atlas pays interest annually at year end. The issue price of the bonds was $574,082.

Required

Create a spreadsheet model to prepare a schedule to amortize the discount on these bonds. Use the effective-interest method of amortization. Round to the nearest dollar, and format your answer as follows:

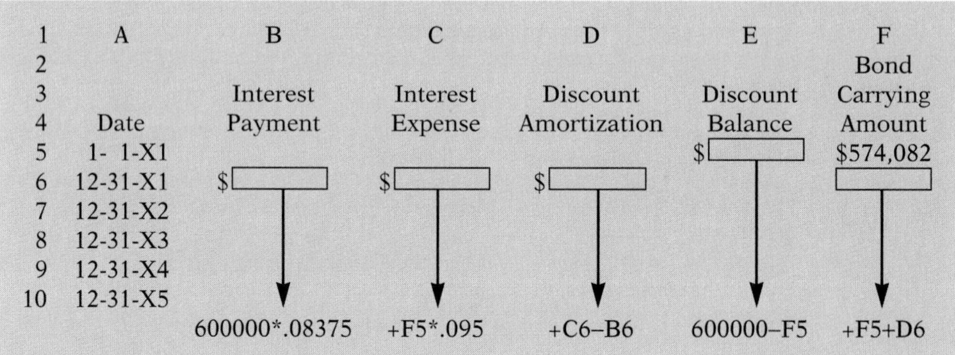

Recording conversion of bonds payable
(Obj. 3)

E8-13 Skytell Communications issued $400,000 of 8½% bonds payable on July 1, 19X4, at a price of 98½. After five years, the bonds may be converted into the company's common stock. Each $1,000 face amount of bonds is convertible into 35 shares of $20 par stock. The bonds' term to maturity is 15 years. On December 31, 19X9, bondholders exercised their right to convert the bonds into common stock.

Required

1. What would cause the bondholders to convert their bonds into common stock?
2. Without making journal entries, compute the carrying amount of the bonds payable at December 31, 19X9, immediately before the conversion. Skytell uses the straight-line method to amortize bond premium and discount.
3. All amortization has been recorded properly. Journalize the conversion transaction at December 31, 19X9.

Recording early retirement and conversion of bonds payable
(Obj. 3)

E8-14 Riviera Industries reported the following at September 30:

Long-term liabilities:		
Convertible bonds payable, 9%, 8 years to maturity	$300,000	
Discount on bonds payable	6,000	$294,000

Required

1. Record retirement of half the bonds on October 1 at the call price of 102.
2. Record conversion of one-fourth of the bonds into 4,000 shares of Riviera's $10-par common stock on October 1. What would cause the bondholders to convert their bonds into stock?

Analyzing alternative plans for raising money ***(Obj. 5)***

E8-15 Gulfstream Avionics Company is considering two plans for raising $1,000,000 to expand operations. Plan A is to borrow at 9%, and plan B is to issue 100,000 shares of common stock. Before any new financing, Gulfstream has net income of $600,000 and 100,000 shares of common stock outstanding. Assume you own most of Gulfstream's existing stock. Management believes the company can use the new funds to earn additional income of $420,000 before interest and taxes. The income tax rate is 40 percent.

Required

1. Analyze Gulfstream's situation to determine which plan will result in higher earnings per share. Use Exhibit 8-12 as a model.
2. Which plan allows you to retain control of the company? Which plan creates more financial risk for the company? Which plan do you prefer? Why? Present your conclusion in a memo to Gulfstream's board of directors.

Journalizing capital lease and operating lease transactions ***(Obj. 6)***

E8-16 A capital lease agreement for equipment requires ten annual payments of $9,000, with the first payment due on January 2, 19X5. The present value of the nine future lease payments at 10% is $51,831.

Required

1. Journalize the following lessee transactions:

19X5	
Jan. 2	Beginning of lease term and first annual payment.
Dec. 31	Depreciation of equipment.
31	Interest expense on lease liability.
19X6	
Jan. 2	Second annual lease payment.

2. On the 19X5 income statement and the balance sheet at December 31, 19X5, show how to report all accounts (but Cash) that are affected by the 19X5 capital lease transactions.
3. Journalize the January 2, 19X5, lease payment if this is an operating lease.

Reporting long-term debt and pension liability on the balance sheet ***(Obj. 7)***

E8-17 Consider the following situations.

a. A note to the financial statements of Mapco, Inc., reported (in thousands):

Note 5: Long-Term Debt	
Total	$537,888
Less—Current portion	22,085
Unamortized discount	1,391
Long-term debt	$514,412

Assume that none of the unamortized discount is related to the current portion of long-term debt. Show how Mapco's classified balance sheet would report these liabilities.

b. WynStone Incorporated's pension plan has assets with a market value of $700,000. The plan's accumulated benefit obligation is $770,000. What amount of long-term pension liability, if any, will WynStone report on its balance sheet?

CHALLENGE EXERCISES

Analyzing bond transactions ***(Obj. 3, 4)***

E8-18 This (updated) advertisement appeared in the *Wall Street Journal.*

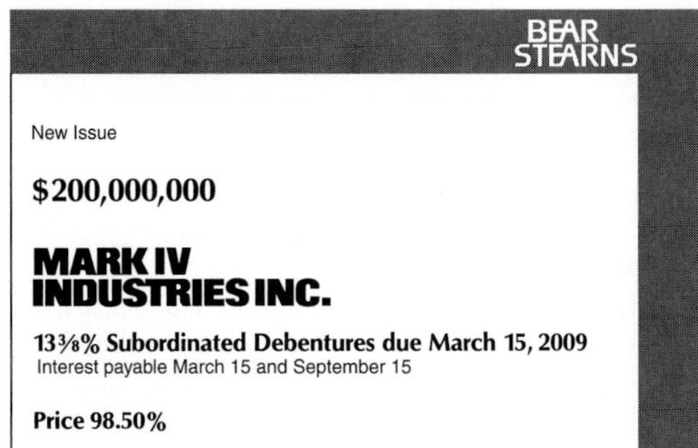

Note: A *subordinated debenture* is one whose rights are subordinated to the rights of other bondholders.

Required

Answer these questions.

1. Suppose investors purchased these securities at their offering price on March 15, 1999. Describe the transaction in detail, indicating who received cash, who paid cash, and how much.
2. Why is the contract interest rate on these bonds so high?
3. Compute the annual cash interest payment on the bonds.
4. Compute the annual interest expense under the straight-line amortization method.
5. Compute both the first-year (from March 15, 1999, to March 15, 2000) and the second-year interest expense (March 15, 2000, to March 15, 2001) under the effective-interest amortization method. The market rate of interest at the date of issuance was approximately 13.65 percent.
6. Suppose you purchased $500,000 of these bonds on March 15, 1999. How much cash did you pay? If you had purchased $500,000 of these bonds on March 31, 1999, how much cash would you have paid?

Using the balance sheet and the statement of cash flows to explain long-term debt transactions
(Obj. 7)

E8-19 The Coca-Cola Company reported the following on its December 31, 1995, balance sheet:

THE COCA-COLA COMPANY AND SUBSIDIARIES
Consolidated Balance Sheet

(In millions)	December 31, 1995	1994
Liabilities and Share-Owners' Equity		
Current		
Accounts payable and accrued expenses	$2,894	$2,564
Loans and notes payable	2,371	2,048
Current maturities of long-term debt	552	35
Accrued taxes	1,531	1,530
Total Current Liabilities	7,348	6,177
Long-Term Debt	1,141	1,426

Coca-Cola's statement of cash flows for 1995 reported the following:

THE COCA-COLA COMPANY AND SUBSIDIARIES
Consolidated Statement of Cash Flows

(In millions)	Year Ended Decmber 31, 1995	1994
Operating Activities		
Net cash provided by operating activities	$3,115	$3,183
Investing Activities		
Net cash used in investing activities	(1,013)	(1,037)
Net cash provided by operations after reinvestment	2,102	2,146
Financing Activities		
Issuances of debt	754	491
Payments of debt	(212)	(154)

Required

1. Combine Loans and notes payable, Current maturities of long-term debt, and Long-Term Debt from the balance sheet, and determine by how much Coca-Cola's total amount of debt increased or decreased during 1995.
2. Determine from the statement of cash flows whether The Coca-Cola Company issued more new debt or paid off more old debt during 1995. Compute the amount of difference.
3. Compare the amount of new debt issued with the amount of increase or decrease in total debt determined for Requirement 1. What is the most likely explanation for the difference? Did this transaction result in a gain or a loss for Coca-Cola? How much was the gain or loss? Two journal entries—one for the issuance of new debt, the other for the payment of old debt—will aid your analysis. You may use a Total Debt account for the combination of the three accounts.

PROBLEMS

(GROUP A)

Measuring current liabilities ***(Obj. 1)***

P8-1A Following are six pertinent facts about events during the current year at Muñoz Tool Company.

a. On August 31, Muñoz signed a six-month, 7% note payable to purchase a machine costing $40,000. The note requires payment of principal and interest at maturity.

b. On October 31, Muñoz received rent of $2,400 in advance for a lease on a building. This rent will be earned evenly over six months.

c. On November 30, Muñoz discounted a $10,000 note payable to borrow money from Inter-Bank Savings. The interest rate on the one-year note is 8 percent.

d. December sales totaled $104,000 and Muñoz collected sales tax of 9 percent. This amount will be sent to the state of Washington early in January.

e. Muñoz owes $75,000 on a long-term note payable. At December 31, 6% interest for the year plus $25,000 of this principal are payable within one year.

f. Sales of $909,000 were covered by Muñoz's product warranty. At January 1, estimated warranty payable was $11,300. During the year, Muñoz recorded warranty expense of $27,900 and paid warranty claims of $28,100.

Required

For each item, indicate the account and the related amount to be reported as a current liability on Muñoz's December 31 balance sheet.

Recording liability-related transactions ***(Obj. 1)***

P8-2A The following transactions of Island Recording Company occurred during 19X2 and 19X3.

19X2	
Feb. 3	Purchased a machine for $10,200, signing a six-month, 8% note payable.
Apr. 30	Borrowed $100,000 on a 9% note payable that calls for annual installment payments of $25,000 principal plus interest. Record the short-term note payable in a separate account from the long-term note payable.
Aug. 3	Paid the six-month, 8% note at maturity.
Sep. 14	Discounted a $6,000, 7%, 60-day note payable to the bank, receiving cash for the net amount borrowed after interest was deducted from the note's maturity value.
Nov. 13	Recognized interest on the 7% discounted note and paid off the note at maturity.
30	Purchased inventory at a cost of $7,200, signing a 9%, three-month note payable for that amount.
Dec. 31	Accrued warranty expense, which is estimated at 3% of sales of $145,000.
31	Accrued interest on all outstanding notes payable. Made a separate interest accrual entry for each note payable.
19X3	
Feb. 28	Paid off the 9% inventory note, plus interest, at maturity.
Apr. 30	Paid the first installment and interest for one year on the long-term note payable.

Required

Record the transactions in the company's journal. Explanations are not required.

Identifying contingent liabilities ***(Obj. 2)***

P8-3A Bent Tree Farm provides riding lessons for girls ages 8 through 15. Most students are beginners, and none of the girls owns her own horse. Lisa Peder, the owner of Bent Tree Farm, uses horses stabled at her farm and owned by the Kultgens. Most of the horses are for sale, but the economy has been bad for several years and horse sales have been slow. The Kultgens are happy that Peder uses their horses in exchange for rooming and boarding them. Because of a recent financial setback, Peder cannot afford insurance. She seeks your advice about her business's exposure to liabilities.

Required

Write a memorandum to inform Peder of specific contingent liabilities arising from the business. It will be necessary to define a contingent liability because she is a professional horse trainer, not a businessperson. Propose a way for Peder to limit her exposure to these liabilities.

Recording bond transactions (at par) and reporting bonds payable on the balance sheet ***(Obj. 3)***

P8-4A The board of directors of NetCore Communications authorizes the issue of $3 million of 7%, ten-year bonds payable. The semiannual interest dates are May 31 and November 30. The bonds are issued through an underwriter on July 31, 19X5, at par plus accrued interest.

Required

1. Journalize the following transactions:

  a. Issuance of the bonds on July 31, 19X5.

  b. Payment of interest on November 30, 19X5.

c. Accrual of interest on December 31, 19X5.
d. Payment of interest on May 31, 19X6.

2. Report interest payable and bonds payable as they would appear on the NetCore balance sheet at December 31, 19X5.

Issuing bonds at a discount, amortizing by the straight-line method, and reporting bonds payable on the balance sheet
(Obj. 3, 7)

P8-5A On March 1, 19X4, Univar Corp. issues 8½%, 20-year bonds payable with a face value of $500,000. The bonds pay interest on February 28 and August 31. Univar amortizes premium and discount by the straight-line method.

Required

1. If the market interest rate is 7⅜% when Univar issues its bonds, will the bonds be priced at par, at a premium, or at a discount? Explain.
2. If the market interest rate is 8⅞% when Univar issues its bonds, will the bonds be priced at par, at a premium, or at a discount? Explain.
3. Assume that the issue price of the bonds is 97. Journalize the following bond transactions.
   - **a.** Issuance of the bonds on March 1, 19X4.
   - **b.** Payment of interest and amortization of discount on August 31, 19X4.
   - **c.** Accrual of interest and amortization of discount on December 31, 19X4.
   - **d.** Payment of interest and amortization of discount on February 28, 19X5.
4. Report interest payable and bonds payable as they would appear on the Univar balance sheet at December 31, 19X4.

Analyzing a company's long-term debt and reporting long-term debt on the balance sheet
(Obj. 3, 4, 7)

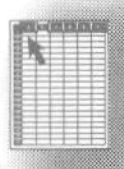

P8-6A The notes to Van Kemp Trust Corp.'s financial statements recently reported the following data on September 30, Year 1 (the end of the fiscal year):

Note 4. Indebtedness

Long-Term debt at September 30, Year 1, included the following:	
6.00% debentures due Year 20 with an effective-interest rate of 9.66%, net of unamortized discount of $58,695,000	$166,305,000
Other indebtedness with an interest rate of 8.30%, due $12,108,000 in Year 5 and $19,257,000 in Year 6	31,365,000

Van Kemp amortizes discount by the effective-interest method.

Required

1. Answer the following questions about Van Kemp's long-term liabilities:
   - **a.** What is the maturity value of the 6.00% debenture bonds?
   - **b.** What are Van Kemp's annual cash interest payments on the 6.00% debenture bonds?
   - **c.** What is the carrying amount of the 6.00% debenture bonds at September 30, Year 1?
2. Prepare an amortization table through September 30, Year 4, for the 6.00% debenture bonds. Round all amounts to the nearest thousand dollars, and assume that Van Kemp pays interest annually on September 30. How much is Van Kemp's interest expense for the year ended September 30, Year 4? Round interest to the nearest thousand dollars.
3. Show how Van Kemp would report the debenture bonds payable and other indebtedness at September 30, Year 4.

Issuing convertible bonds at a discount, amortizing by the effective-interest method, retiring bonds early, converting bonds, and reporting the bonds payable on the balance sheet
(Obj. 3, 4, 7)

P8-7A On December 31, 19X1, Visioneer Corp. issues 8%, ten-year convertible bonds with a maturity value of $500,000. The semiannual interest dates are June 30 and December 31. The market interest rate is 9%, and the issue price of the bonds is 94. Visioneer amortizes bond premium and discount by the effective-interest method.

Required

1. Prepare an effective-interest method amortization table for the first four semiannual interest periods.
2. Journalize the following transactions:
   - **a.** Issuance of the bonds on December 31, 19X1. Credit Convertible Bonds Payable.
   - **b.** Payment of interest and amortization of discount on June 30, 19X2.
   - **c.** Payment of interest and amortization of discount on December 31, 19X2.
   - **d.** Retirement of bonds with face value of $200,000 July 1, 19X3. Visioneer purchases the bonds at 96 in the open market.
   - **e.** Conversion by the bondholders on July 1, 19X3, of bonds with face value of $200,000 into 50,000 shares of Visioneer's $1-par common stock.
3. Show how Visioneer would report the remaining bonds payable on its balance sheet at December 31, 19X3.

Accounting for bonds payable and capital lease transactions
(Obj. 3, 6)

P8-8A Journalize the following transactions of Outré Cosmetics, Inc.:

1998		
Jan.	1	Issued $1,000,000 of 8%, ten-year bonds payable at 97.
	1	Signed a five-year capital lease on machinery. The agreement requires annual lease payments of $16,000, with the first payment due immediately. At 12%, assume the present value of the four future lease payments is $48,590.
July	1	Paid semiannual interest and amortized discount by the straight-line method on our 8% bonds payable.
Dec.	31	Accrued semiannual interest expense and amortized discount by the straight-line method on our 8% bonds payable.
	31	Recorded depreciation on leased machinery.
	31	Accrued interest expense on the lease liability.
2008		
Jan.	1	Paid the 8% bonds at maturity.

At December 31, 1998, after all year-end adjustments, determine the carrying amount of Outré's:

a. Bonds payable, net **b.** Lease liability **c.** Machinery, net

Financing operations with debt or with stock
(Obj. 5)

P8-9A Marketing studies have shown that consumers prefer upscale restaurants, and recent trends in industry sales have supported the research. To capitalize on this trend, Samurai Steak House, Inc., is embarking on a massive expansion. Plans call for opening 20 new restaurants during the next two years. Each restaurant is scheduled to be 30% larger than the company's existing locations, furnished more elaborately, and with upgraded menus. Management estimates that company operations will provide $3 million of the cash needed for expansion. Samurai must raise the remaining $1.5 million from outsiders. The board of directors is considering obtaining the $1.5 million either through borrowing or by issuing common stock.

Required

1. Write a memo to company management discussing the advantages and disadvantages of borrowing and of issuing common stock to raise the needed cash. Which method of raising the funds would you recommend?
2. How will what you learned in this problem help you manage a business?

Reporting liabilities on the balance sheet
(Obj. 7)

P8-10A The accounting records of Pinelli Tire Co. include the following items at December 31, 19X5:

Capital lease liability, long-term	$ 81,000	Accumulated depreciation, equipment	$ 46,000
Discount on bonds payable (all long-term)	7,000	Capital lease liability, current	18,000
Interest revenue	5,000	Mortgage note payable, current	16,000
Equipment acquired under capital lease	137,000	Accumulated pension benefit obligation	419,000
Pension plan assets (market value)	382,000	Bonds payable, long-term	300,000
Interest payable	9,000	Mortgage note payable, long-term	82,000
Interest expense	57,000	Bonds payable, current portion	75,000

Required

1. Show how these items would be reported on the Pinelli Tire Co. classified balance sheet, including headings and totals for current liabilities, long-term liabilities, and so on. Note disclosures are not required.
2. Answer the following questions about Pinelli's financial position at December 31, 19X5:
   a. What is the carrying amount of the bonds payable?
   b. When will Pinelli make the last payment on the bonds?
   c. How can the cost of the equipment be so much more than the amount of lease liability?
   d. Why is the interest payable amount so much less than the amount of interest expense?

(GROUP B)

Measuring current liabilities
(Obj. 1)

P8-1B Following are six pertinent facts about events during the current year at Custom Plastics, Inc.

a. On September 30, Custom Plastics signed a six-month, 9% note payable to purchase equipment costing $12,000. The note requires payment of principal and interest at maturity.

b. On September 30, Custom Plastics discounted a $50,000 note payable to borrow money from Lake Air National Bank. The interest rate on the one-year note is 8 percent.

c. On November 30, Custom Plastics received rent of $5,400 in advance for a lease on a building. This rent will be earned evenly over three months.

d. December sales totaled $38,000, and Custom Plastics collected an additional state sales tax of 7 percent. This amount will be sent to the state of Ohio early in January.

e. Custom Plastics owes $100,000 on a long-term note payable. At December 31, 6% interest since July 31 and $20,000 of this principal are payable within one year.

f. Sales of $430,000 were covered by Custom Plastics's product warranty. At January 1, estimated warranty payable was $8,100. During the year, Custom Plastics recorded warranty expense of $22,300 and paid warranty claims of $20,600.

Required

For each item, indicate the account and the related amount to be reported as a current liability on the Custom Plastics December 31 balance sheet.

Journalizing liability-related transactions
(Obj. 1)

P8-2B The following transactions of Puebla Paper Company occurred during 19X4 and 19X5.

Required

Record the transactions in the company's journal. Explanations are not required.

19X4	
Jan. 9	Purchased a machine at a cost of $14,000, signing an 8%, six-month note payable for that amount.
Feb. 28	Borrowed $200,000 on a 9% note payable that calls for annual installment payments of $50,000 principal plus interest. Record the short-term note payable in a separate account from the long-term note payable.
July 9	Paid the six-month, 8% note at maturity.
Oct. 22	Discounted a $5,000, 7%, 90-day note payable to the bank, receiving cash for the net amount borrowed after interest was deducted from the note's maturity value.
Nov. 30	Purchased inventory for $3,100, signing a six-month, 10% note payable.
Dec. 31	Accrued warranty expense, which is estimated at 3% of sales of $650,000.
31	Recorded interest on all outstanding notes payable. Made a separate interest accrual entry for each note payable.
19X5	
Jan. 20	Paid off the 7% discounted note payable. Made a separate entry for the interest.
Feb. 28	Paid the first installment and interest for one year on the long-term note payable.
May 31	Paid off the 10% note plus interest on maturity.

Identifying contingent liabilities
(Obj. 2)

P8-3B Sewell Motor Company is the largest Cadillac dealer in the United States. The dealership sells new and used cars and operates a body shop and a service department. Grant Sewell, the general manager, is considering changing insurance companies because of a disagreement with Doug Stillwell, agent for the Travelers Insurance Company. Travelers is doubling Sewell's liability insurance cost for the next year. In discussing insurance coverage with you, a trusted business associate, Stillwell brings up the subject of contingent liabilities.

Required

Write a memorandum to inform Sewell Motor Company of specific contingent liabilities arising from the business. In your discussion, define a contingent liability.

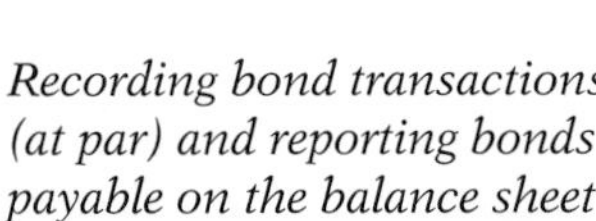

Recording bond transactions (at par) and reporting bonds payable on the balance sheet
(Obj. 3)

P8-4B The board of directors of Xena Production Company authorizes the issue of $2 million of 8%, 20-year bonds payable. The semiannual interest dates are March 31 and September 30. The bonds are issued through an underwriter on May 31, 19X7, at par plus accrued interest.

Required

1. Journalize the following transactions:
   - **a.** Issuance of the bonds on May 31, 19X7.
   - **b.** Payment of interest on September 30, 19X7.
   - **c.** Accrual of interest on December 31, 19X7.
   - **d.** Payment of interest on March 31, 19X8.
2. Report interest payable and bonds payable as they would appear on the Xena Production Company balance sheet at December 31, 19X7.

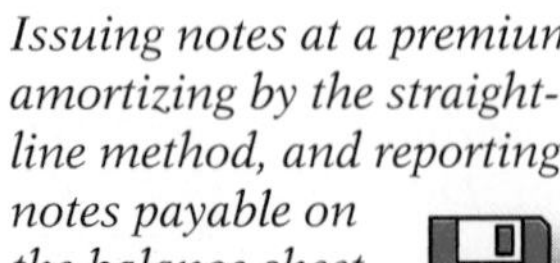

Issuing notes at a premium, amortizing by the straight-line method, and reporting notes payable on the balance sheet
(Obj. 3, 7)

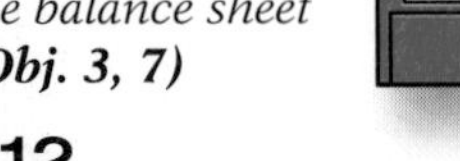

P8-5B On March 1, 19X6, AMC Trade Mart, Inc., issues 7¾%, ten-year notes payable with a face value of $300,000. The notes pay interest on February 28 and August 31, and AMC amortizes premium and discount by the straight-line method.

Required

1. If the market interest rate is 8½% when AMC issues its notes, will the notes be priced at par, at a premium, or at a discount? Explain.

2. If the market interest rate is 7% when AMC issues its notes, will the notes be priced at par, at a premium, or at a discount? Explain.
3. Assume that the issue price of the notes is 102. Journalize the following note payable transactions:
   a. Issuance of the notes on March 1, 19X6.
   b. Payment of interest and amortization of premium on August 31, 19X6.
   c. Accrual of interest and amortization of premium on December 31, 19X6.
   d. Payment of interest and amortization of premium on February 28, 19X7.
4. Report interest payable and notes payable as they would appear on the AMC balance sheet at December 31, 19X6.

Analyzing a company's long-term debt and reporting the long-term debt on the balance sheet
(Obj. 3, 4, 7)

P8-6B The notes to the Aston Staffing Services, Inc., financial statements reported the following data on September 30, Year 1 (the end of the fiscal year):

Note E—Long-Term Debt

5% debentures due Year 14, net of unamortized discount of $31,645,000 (effective interest rate of 7.50%)	$119,855,000
Notes payable, interest rate of 8.67%, principal due in annual amounts of $22,840,000 in Years 5 through 16	274,080,000

Aston amortizes discount by the effective-interest method.

Required

1. Answer the following questions about Aston's long-term liabilities:
   a. What is the maturity value of the 5% debenture bonds?
   b. What are Aston's annual cash interest payments on the 5% debenture bonds?
   c. What is the carrying amount of the 5% debenture bonds at September 30, Year 1?
2. Prepare an amortization table through September 30, Year 4, for the 5% debenture bonds. Round all amounts to the nearest thousand dollars, and assume that Aston pays interest annually on September 30. How much is Aston's interest expense for the year ended September 30, Year 4?
3. Show how Aston would report the debenture bonds payable and notes payable at September 30, Year 4.

Issuing convertible bonds at a premium, amortizing by the effective-interest method, retiring bonds early, converting bonds, and reporting the bonds payable on the balance sheet
(Obj. 3, 4, 7)

P8-7B On December 31, 19X1, Marquis, Inc., issues 9%, ten-year convertible bonds with a maturity value of $300,000. The semiannual interest dates are June 30 and December 31. The market interest rate is 8%, and the issue price of the bonds is 106. Marquis amortizes bond premium and discount by the effective-interest method.

Required

1. Prepare an effective-interest method amortization table for the first four semiannual interest periods.
2. Journalize the following transactions:
   a. Issuance of the bonds on December 31, 19X1. Credit Convertible Bonds Payable.
   b. Payment of interest and amortization of premium on June 30, 19X2.
   c. Payment of interest and amortization of premium on December 31, 19X2.
   d. Retirement of bonds with face value of $100,000 on July 1, 19X3. Marquis pays the call price of 101.
   e. Conversion by the bondholders on July 1, 19X3, of bonds with face value of $50,000 into 10,000 shares of Marquis' $1-par common stock.
3. Show how Marquis would report the remaining bonds payable on its balance sheet at December 31, 19X3.

Accounting for bonds payable and capital lease transactions
(Obj. 3, 6)

P8-8B Journalize the following transactions of Lincoln Properties, Inc.:

1998	
Jan. 1	Issued $500,000 of 8%, ten-year bonds payable at 94.
1	Signed a five-year capital lease on equipment. The agreement requires annual lease payments of $20,000, with the first payment due immediately. Assume that at 12%, the present value of the four future lease payments is $60,750.
July 1	Paid semiannual interest and amortized discount by the straight-line method on our 8% bonds payable.
Dec. 31	Accrued semiannual interest expense, and amortized discount by the straight-line method on our 8% bonds payable.
31	Recorded depreciation on leased equipment.
31	Accrued interest expense on the lease liability.
2008	
Jan. 1	Paid the 8% bonds at maturity.

At December 31, 1998, after all year-end adjustments, determine the carrying amount of Lincoln's:

a. Bonds payable, net **b.** Lease liability **c** Leased equipment, net

Financing operations with debt or with stock
(Obj. 5)

P8-9B Two businesses must consider how to raise $10 million.

Oshkosh Corporation is in the midst of its most successful period since it began operations in 1952. For each of the past 10 years, net income and earnings per share have increased by 15 percent. The outlook for the future is equally bright, with new markets opening up and competitors unable to manufacture products of Oshkosh's quality. Oshkosh Corporation is planning a large-scale expansion.

Fond du Lac Company has fallen on hard times. Net income has remained flat for five of the last six years, even falling by 10% from last year's level of profits, and cash flow also took a nose dive. Top management has experienced some turnover and has stabilized only recently. To become competitive again, Fond du Lac Company needs $10 million for expansion.

Required

1. Propose a plan for each company to raise the needed cash. Which company should borrow? Which company should issue stock? Consider the advantages and the disadvantages of raising money by borrowing and by issuing stock, and discuss them in your answer.
2. How will what you learned in this problem help you manage a business?

Reporting liabilities on the balance sheet
(Obj. 7)

P8-10B The accounting records of Fleet Rentals, Inc., include the following items at December 31, 19X0:

Bonds payable, long-term	$180,000	Interest expense	$ 47,000
Premium on bonds payable (all long-term)	13,000	Pension plan assets (market value)	402,000
Interest payable	6,200	Bonds payable, current portion	20,000
Interest revenue	5,300	Accumulated depreciation, building	88,000
Capital lease liability, long-term	73,000	Mortgage note payable, long term	67,000
Accumulated pension benefit obligation	436,000		
Building acquired under capital lease	190,000		

Required

1. Show how these items would be reported on Fleet Rentals's classified balance sheet, including headings and totals for current liabilities, long-term liabilities, and so on. Disclosures are not required.
2. Answer the following questions about the financial position of Fleet Rentals at December 31, 19X0:
   a. What is the carrying amount of the bonds payable?
   b. When will Fleet Rentals make its final payment on the bonds?
   c. How can the cost of the building be so much more than the amount of the lease liability?
   d. Why is the interest payable amount so much less than the amount of interest expense?

EXTENDING YOUR KNOWLEDGE

DECISION CASES

Analyzing alternative ways of raising $5 million
(Obj. 5)

Case 1. Business is going well for Trinitron Robotics Corporation. The board of directors of this family-owned company believes that Trinitron could earn an additional $1,500,000 income before interest and taxes by expanding into new markets. However, the $5 million that the business needs for growth cannot be raised within the family. The directors, who strongly wish to retain family control of the company must consider issuing securities to outsiders. They are considering three financing plans.

Plan A is to borrow at 8 percent. Plan B is to issue 100,000 shares of common stock. Plan C is to issue 100,000 shares of nonvoting, $3.75 preferred stock ($3.75 is the annual dividend paid on each share of preferred stock).* Trinitron presently has net income of $6,000,000 and 1,000,000 shares of common stock outstanding. The company's income tax rate is 40 percent.

*For a discussion of preferred stock, see Chapter 9.

Required

1. Prepare an analysis to determine which plan will result in the highest earnings per share of common stock.
2. Recommend one plan to the board of directors. Give your reasons.

Questions about long-term debt
(Obj. 6 and Appendix B at end of the book)

Case 2. The following questions are not related.

a. Why do you think corporations prefer operating leases over capital leases? How do you think a wise shareholder would view an operating lease?

b. Companies like to borrow for longer terms when interest rates are low and for shorter terms when interest rates are high. Why is this statement true?

c. If you were to win $2 million from a Canadian lottery, you would receive the $2 million at once, but if you won $2 million in a U.S. lottery, you would receive 20 annual payments of $100,000. Are the prizes equivalent? If not, why not?

ETHICAL ISSUE 1

The Boeing Company, manufacturer of jet aircraft, is the defendant in numerous lawsuits claiming unfair trade practices. Boeing has strong incentives not to disclose these contingent liabilities. However, GAAP requires that companies report their contingent liabilities.

Required

1. Why would a company prefer not to disclose its contingent liabilities?
2. Describe how a bank could be harmed if a company seeking a loan did not disclose its contingent liabilities.
3. What is the ethical tightrope that companies must walk when they report their contingent liabilities?

ETHICAL ISSUE 2

Ling-Temco-Vought, Inc. (LTV), manufacturer of aircraft and aircraft-related electronic devices, borrowed heavily during the 1970s to exploit the advantage of financing operations with debt. At first, LTV was able to earn operating income much higher than its interest expense and was therefore quite profitable. However, when the business cycle turned down, LTV's debt burden pushed the company to the brink of bankruptcy. Operating income was less than interest expense.

Required

Is it unethical for managers to saddle a company with a high level of debt? Or is it just risky? Who could be hurt by a company's taking on too much debt? Discuss.

FINANCIAL STATEMENT CASES

Long-term debt
(Obj. 3, 7)

Case 1. The Lands' End, Inc., income statement, balance sheet, and statement of cash flows in Appendix A at the end of the book provide details about the company's long-term debt. Use those data to answer the following questions.

1. How much cash did Lands' End borrow during the year ended February 2, 1996? What account on the balance sheet shows the effect of the new borrowing? Record the borrowing transaction.
2. How much long-term debt did Lands' End pay off during the year ended February 2, 1996? Record this transaction.
3. How much long-term debt do you expect Lands' End to pay off during the year ended January 31, 1997? Give your reason.
4. Record the Lands' End interest expense for the year ended February 2, 1996. Interest paid is reported at the bottom of the statement of cash flows.

Long-term debt
(Obj. 3, 7)

Case 2. Obtain the annual report of a company of your choosing. Answer the following questions about the company. Concentrate on the current year in the annual report you select.

1. Examine the statement of cash flows. How much long-term debt did the company pay off during the current year? How much new long-term debt did the company incur during the year? Journalize these transactions, using the company's actual account balances.
2. Prepare a T-account for the Long-Term Debt account to show the beginning and ending balances and all activity in the account during the year. If there is a discrepancy, insert this amount in the appropriate place. (*Note:* Don't expect to be able to explain all details in real financial statements!)
3. Study the notes to the financial statements. Is any of the company's retained earnings balance restricted as a result of borrowings? If so, indicate the amount of the retained

earnings balance that is restricted and the amount that is unrestricted. How will the restriction affect the company's dividend payments in the future?

4. Journalize in a single entry the company's interest expense for the current year. If the company discloses the amount of amortization of premium or discount on long-term debt, use the real figures. If not, assume the amortization of discount totaled $700,000 for the year.

GROUP PROJECTS

Project 1. Consider three different businesses:

1. A bank
2. A magazine publisher
3. A department store

For each business, list all of its liabilities—both current and long-term. Then compare the three lists to identify the liabilities that the three businesses have in common. Also identify the liabilities that are unique to each type of business.

Project 2. Alcenon Corporation leases the majority of the assets that it uses in operations. Alcenon prefers operating leases (versus capital leases) in order to keep the lease liability off its balance sheet and maintain a low debt ratio.

Alcenon is negotiating a ten-year lease on an asset with an expected useful life of 15 years. The lease requires Alcenon to make ten annual lease payments of $20,000 each, with the first payment due at the beginning of the lease term. The leased asset has a market value of $135,180. The lease agreement specifies no transfer of title to the lessee and includes no bargain purchase option.

Write a report for Alcenon's management to explain what condition must be present for Alcenon to be able to account for this lease as an operating lease.

INTERNET EXERCISE

AMERICA WEST AIRLINES

America West is a fast-growing airline. From its humble beginnings in 1983, the airline now earns over $1 billion in passenger revenues annually and has approximately 100 airplanes. Fueling the company's growth takes an aggressive management plan and a significant amount of capital. How to finance the growth in personnel and airplanes is a critical decision.

America West's Web site has limited financial data, but with an understanding of financial accounting, we can see how the company is financing its growth.

Required

1. Go to **http://www.americawest.com/,** America West's home page. From this page you can book flights, inquire about flights, get frequent-flyer information, and check out the latest sales.
2. The corporate information is tucked away at the bottom of the page at **AWA Inc.** Click on the highlighted text.
3. Examine the links to America West's **Annual Report Excerpts** and recent **Press Releases,** and answer the following questions.
   a. Look at the **Chairman/CEO's Message** under the **Annual Report Excerpts.** What are America West's future expansion plans and needs for aircraft?
   b. Examine the **Financial Highlights** under the **Annual Report Excerpts.** What does EBITDAR stand for? Why is this financial measure preferred to Operating Income? What is America West's ratio of Operating Income to Operating Revenues? Is this number substantially different from EBITDAR?
   c. Look at a recent **Press Release** detailing America West's quarterly financial performance. Here detailed financial statement data are presented. Describe the specific differences between EBITDAR and Operating Income. Based on your observations, do you believe that America West purchases or leases the majority of its aircraft? Why?

9

Measuring and Reporting Stockholders' Equity

Learning Objectives

After studying this chapter, you should be able to

1. Explain the advantages and disadvantages of a corporation
2. Measure the effect of issuing stock on a company's financial position
3. Describe how treasury stock transactions affect a company
4. Account for dividends and measure their impact on a company
5. Use different stock values in decision making
6. Evaluate a company's return on assets and return on stockholders' equity
7. Report stockholders' equity transactions on the statement of cash flows

IHOP Corp.
Consolidated Balance Sheet

	(In thousands)	December 31, 1995	1994
	Assets		
	Current assets		
1	Cash and cash equivalents	$ 3,860	$ 2,036
2	Receivables	21,476	16,802
3	Reacquired franchises and equipment held for sale, net	1,157	854
4	Inventories	792	817
5	Prepaid expenses	233	668
6	Total current assets	27,518	21,177
7	Long-term receivables	115,800	92,122
8	Property and equipment, net	87,795	69,550
9	Reacquired franchises and equipment held for sale, net	6,553	4,837
10	Excess of costs over net assets acquired, net	13,336	13,762
11	Other assets	1,055	1,105
12	**Total assets**	**$252,057**	**$202,553**
	Liabilities and Shareholders' Equity		
	Current liabilities		
13	Current maturities of long-term debt	$ 4,672	$ 122
14	Accounts payable	15,979	10,733
15	Accrued employee compensation and benefits	1,562	2,321
16	Other accrued expenses	2,349	1,872
17	Deferred income taxes	3,436	1,443
18	Capital lease obligations	719	749
19	**Total current liabilities**	**28,717**	**17,240**
20	Long-term debt	30,584	34,855
21	Deferred income taxes	21,495	17,698
22	Capital lease obligations and other	62,964	44,461
23	Shareholders' equity		
23a.	Preferred stock, $1 par value, 10,000,000 shares authorized; issued and outstanding: 1995 and 1994, no shares	—	—
23b.	Common stock, $.01 par value, 40,000,000 shares authorized; shares issued and outstanding: 1995, 9,375,515 shares; 1994, 9,183,327 shares	94	92
24	Additional paid-in capital	46,363	42,621
25	Retained earnings	60,640	44,486
26	Contribution to employee stock ownership plan	1,200	1,100
27	**Total shareholders' equity**	**108,297**	**88,299**
28	**Total liabilities and shareholders' equity**	**$252,057**	**$202,553**

"Going public is a good way for a company to raise needed capital. Being publicly traded gets the company more attention in the financial pages and in brokerage-firm research reports. This allows the company, when it's doing well, to raise money more easily and cheaply. These benefits come at the cost of intense scrutiny from stockholders, who expect the company to continue to do well."

—MALCOLM P. APPELBAUM, PRIVATE EQUITY INVESTOR, WAND PARTNERS, INC.

Based in Glendale, California, **IHOP Corp.** develops, franchises, and operates International House of Pancakes family restaurants. There are almost 600 IHOPs in 35 states, Canada, and Japan—with large concentrations of IHOP restaurants in California, New York, New Jersey, Florida, and Texas.

IHOP serves up stacks of great pancakes, but you can buy the stock as well. When IHOP Corp. went public, the company offered 6.2 million shares at $10 each. The shares got off to a strong start and have performed well. IHOP's stock lately has traded at about $25 per share. "For people who bought this [IHOP Corp. stock] at the offering," said Sandy Mehta, a vice president with Ariel Capital Management, "this has been a really good investment."

What does it mean to "go public," as IHOP did? A corporation *goes public* when it sells its stock to the general public. A common reason for going public is to raise money for expansion. By offering its stock to the public, a company can raise more money than if the stockholders remain a small group. The IHOP Corp. balance sheet (lines 23b and 24) indicates that through the end of 1995, the company had received a little over $46 million (the sum of common stock and additional paid-in capital) from its stockholders. (For a review of common stock, see Chapter 1, page 14.)

Chapters 4–8 discussed accounting for the assets and the liabilities of a company. By this time, you should be familiar with all the assets and liabilities listed on IHOP's balance sheet. Let's focus now on the last part of the balance sheet—IHOP's stockholders' equity, which the company labels as *shareholders' equity.* In this chapter we discuss the elements of stockholders' equity in detail. First, however, let's review what a corporation is and how it is organized.

Corporations: An Overview

Objective 1

Explain the advantages and disadvantages of a corporation

The corporation is the dominant form of business organization in the United States. International House of Pancakes is an example. Although proprietorships and partnerships are more numerous, corporations transact more business and are larger in terms of total assets, sales revenue, and number of employees. Most well-known companies, such as **Lands' End, CBS, General Motors,** and **IBM,** are corporations. Their full names include *Corporation* or *Incorporated* (abbreviated *Corp.* and *Inc.*) to indicate that they are corporations—for example, CBS, Inc., and General Motors Corporation.

Characteristics of a Corporation

Why is the corporate form of business so attractive? We now look at the features that distinguish corporations from proprietorships and partnerships, and some of the advantages and disadvantages of corporations.

SEPARATE LEGAL ENTITY A corporation is a business entity formed under state law. The state grants a **charter,** which is a document that gives a business the state's permission to form a corporation. Neither a proprietorship nor a partnership requires state approval to do business, because in the eyes of the law the business is the same as the owner(s).

From a legal perspective, a corporation is a distinct entity, an artificial person that exists apart from its owners, who are called **stockholders** or **shareholders.** The corporation has many of the rights that a person has. For example, a corporation may buy, own, and sell property. Assets and liabilities in the business belong to the corporation rather than to its owners. The corporation may enter into contracts, sue, and be sued.

The owners' equity of a corporation is divided into shares of **stock.** The corporate charter specifies how much stock the corporation can issue (sell).

CONTINUOUS LIFE AND TRANSFERABILITY OF OWNERSHIP Most corporations have *continuous lives* regardless of changes in the ownership of their stock. The stockholders of IHOP or any corporation may transfer stock as they wish. They may sell or trade the stock to another person, give it away, bequeath it in a will, or dispose of it in any other way. The transfer of the stock does not affect the continuity of the corporation. In contrast, proprietorships and partnerships terminate when their ownership changes.

NO MUTUAL AGENCY *Mutual agency* is an arrangement whereby all owners act as agents of the business. A contract signed by one owner is binding for the whole company. Mutual agency operates in partnerships but *not* in corporations. A stockholder of IHOP Corp. cannot commit the corporation to a contract (unless he or she is also an officer in the business). For this reason, a stockholder need not exercise the care that partners must in selecting co-owners of the business.

LIMITED LIABILITY OF STOCKHOLDERS Stockholders have **limited liability** for corporation debts. That is, they have no personal obligation for corporation liabilities. The most that a stockholder can lose on an investment in a corporation's stock is the cost of the investment. In contrast, proprietors and partners are personally liable for all the debts of their businesses.

The combination of limited liability and no mutual agency means that persons can invest limited amounts in a corporation without fear of losing all their personal wealth if the business fails. This feature enables a corporation to raise more capital from a wider group of investors than proprietorships and partnerships can.

SEPARATION OF OWNERSHIP AND MANAGEMENT Stockholders own the business, but a *board of directors*—elected by the stockholders—appoints corporate officers to manage the business. Thus, stockholders may invest $1,000 or $1 million in the corporation without having to manage the business or disrupt their personal affairs.

Management's goal is to maximize the firm's value for the stockholders' benefit. However, the separation between owners—stockholders—and management may create problems. Corporate officers may decide to run the business for their own benefit and not to the stockholders' advantage. Stockholders may find it difficult to lodge an effective protest against management policy because of the distance between them and management.

CORPORATE TAXATION Corporations are separate taxable entities. They pay a variety of taxes not borne by proprietorships or partnerships, including an annual franchise tax levied by the state. The franchise tax is paid to keep the corporate charter in force and enables the corporation to continue in business. Corporations also pay federal and state income taxes.

Corporate earnings are subject to **double taxation.** First, corporations pay income taxes on corporate income. Then, stockholders pay personal income tax on the cash dividends (distributions) that they receive from corporations. Proprietorships and partnerships pay no business income tax. Instead, the tax falls solely on the owners.

GOVERNMENT REGULATION Because stockholders have only limited liability for corporation debts, outsiders doing business with the corporation can look no further than the corporation itself for any claims that may arise against the business. To protect persons who loan money to a corporation or who invest in its stock, both federal agencies and the states monitor the affairs of corporations. This *government regulation* consists mainly of ensuring that corporations disclose the information that investors and creditors need to make informed decisions. For many corporations, government regulation is expensive.

Exhibit 9-1 summarizes the advantages and disadvantages of the corporate form of business organization.

Organization of a Corporation

The process of creating a corporation begins when its organizers, called the **incorporators,** obtain a charter from the state. The charter includes the authorization for the corporation to issue a certain number of shares of stock, which are shares of ownership in the corporation. The incorporators pay fees, sign the charter, and file required documents with the state. The corporation then comes into existence. The incorporators agree to a set of **bylaws,** which act as the constitution for governing the corporation.

The ultimate control of the corporation rests with the stockholders. The stockholders elect the members of the **board of directors,** which sets policy for

Concept Highlight

EXHIBIT 9-1
Advantages and Disadvantages of a Corporation

Advantages	Disadvantages
1. Can raise more capital than a proprietorship or partnership can	1. Separation of ownership and management
2. Continuous life	2. Corporate taxation
3. Ease of transferring ownership	3. Government regulation
4. No mutual agency of stockholders	
5. Limited liability of stockholders	

the corporation and appoints the officers. The board elects a **chairperson,** who usually is the most powerful person in the corporation. The board also designates the **president,** who is the chief operating officer in charge of day-to-day operations. Most corporations also have vice presidents in charge of sales, manufacturing, accounting and finance, and other key areas. Often, the president and one or more vice presidents are also elected to the board of directors. Exhibit 9-2 shows the authority structure in a corporation.

Most corporations have an annual meeting at which the stockholders elect directors and make other stockholder decisions. Stockholders unable to attend this meeting may vote on corporation matters by use of a *proxy,* which is a legal document that expresses the stockholder's preference and appoints another person to cast the vote.

Stockholders' Rights

The ownership of stock entitles stockholders to four basic rights, unless specific rights are withheld by agreement with the stockholders:

1. *Vote.* The right to participate in management by voting on matters that come before the stockholders. This is the stockholder's sole right to a voice in the management of the corporation. A stockholder is entitled to one vote for each share of stock owned.
2. *Dividends.* The right to receive a proportionate part of any dividend. Each share of stock in a particular class receives an equal dividend.
3. *Liquidation.* The right to receive a proportionate share (based on number of shares held) of any assets remaining after the corporation pays its liabilities in liquidation. *Liquidation* means to go out of business, sell the entity's assets, pay its liabilities, and distribute any remaining cash to the owners of the business.
4. *Preemption.* The right to maintain one's proportionate ownership in the corporation. Suppose you own 5% of a corporation's stock. If the corporation issues 100,000 new shares of stock, it must offer you the opportunity to buy 5% (5,000) of the new shares. This right, called the *preemptive right,* is usually withheld from the stockholders.

Stockholders' Equity: Paid-In Capital and Retained Earnings

As we saw in Chapter 1, **stockholders' equity** represents the stockholders' ownership interest in the assets of a corporation. Stockholders' equity is divided into two main parts:

EXHIBIT 9-2
Authority Structure in a Corporation

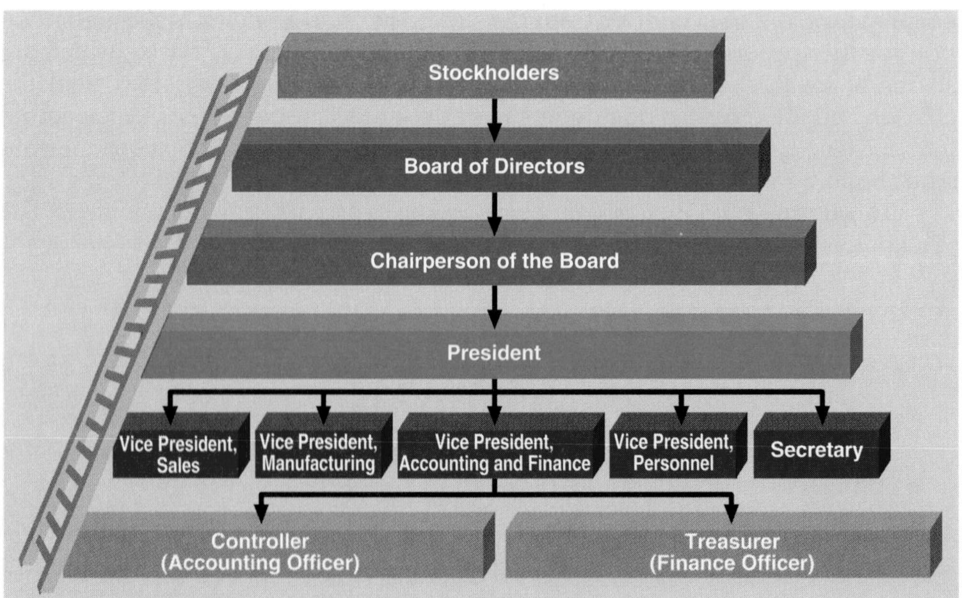

EXHIBIT 9-3
Stock Certificate

1. **Paid-in capital,** also called **contributed capital,** is the amount of stockholders' equity that the stockholders have contributed to the corporation. Paid-in capital includes the stock accounts and any additional paid-in capital.
2. **Retained earnings** is the amount of stockholders' equity that the corporation has earned through profitable operations and has not given back to the stockholders—hence the term *retained* earnings.

Companies report each element of their stockholders' equity by source. They report paid-in capital separately from retained earnings because most states have laws prohibiting the declaration of cash dividends from paid-in capital. This means that cash dividends are declared from retained earnings, not from paid-in capital. For example, a company with paid-in capital of $40 million and retained earnings of $0 could declare no cash dividends regardless of the amount of cash the company has. Reporting retained earnings separately from paid-in capital alerts stockholders to the possibility of receiving cash dividends from their company.

CAPITAL STOCK A corporation issues *stock certificates* to its owners in exchange for their investments in the business. Because stock represents the corporation's capital, it is often called *capital stock.* The basic unit of capital stock is called a *share.* A corporation may issue a stock certificate for any number of shares it wishes—one share, 100 shares, or any other number—but the total number of *authorized* shares is limited by charter. Exhibit 9-3 depicts an actual stock certificate for 288 shares of **Central Jersey Bancorp** common stock. The certificate shows the company name, the stockholder name, the number of shares, and the par value of the stock (discussed later in this chapter).

Stock in the hands of a stockholder is said to be **outstanding.** The total number of shares of stock outstanding at any time represents 100% ownership of the corporation.

Classes of Stock

Corporations issue different types of stock to appeal to a variety of investors. The stock of a corporation may be either common or preferred and par or no-par.

Common and Preferred Stock

Every corporation issues **common stock,** the most basic form of capital stock. Unless designated otherwise, the word *stock* is understood to mean "common stock." Common stockholders have the four basic rights of stock ownership, unless a right is specifically withheld. For example, some companies issue Class A common stock, which usually carries the right to vote, and Class B common stock, which may be nonvoting. (Classes of common stock may also be designated Series A, Series B, and so on.) The ledger has a separate account for each class of common stock. In describing a corporation, we would say the common stockholders are the owners of the business.

Investors who buy common stock take the ultimate risk with a corporation. If the corporation succeeds, it will pay dividends to its stockholders, but if net income and cash are too low, the stockholders may receive no dividends. The stock of successful corporations increases in value, and investors enjoy the benefit of selling the stock at a gain. But stock prices can decrease, leaving the investors holding worthless stock certificates. Because common stockholders take a risky investment position, they demand increases in stock prices, high dividends, or both. If the corporation does not deliver, the stockholders sell the stock, and its market price falls. Short of bankruptcy, this is one of the worst things that can happen to a corporation because it means that the company cannot raise capital as needed.

Preferred stock gives its owners certain advantages over common stockholders. Preferred stockholders receive dividends before the common stockholders and receive assets before the common stockholders if the corporation liquidates. Because of the preferred stockholders' rights, common stock represents the *residual ownership* in the corporation's assets after the liabilities and the claims of preferred stockholders have been subtracted. Owners of preferred stock also have the four basic stockholder rights, unless a right is specifically denied. Often, the right to vote is withheld from preferred stockholders. Companies may issue different classes of preferred stock (Class A and Class B or Series A and Series B, for example). Each class is recorded in a separate account.

Investors who buy preferred stock take less risk than common stockholders do. Why? Because corporations pay a fixed amount of dividends on preferred stock. Investors usually buy preferred stock to earn those dividends. A large increase in the market value of preferred stock is less likely than a large increase in the market value of common stock because preferred-stock values do not fluctuate much.

Preferred stock operates as a hybrid between common stock and long-term debt. Like debt, preferred stock pays a fixed dividend amount to the investor. But like stock, the dividend becomes a liability only after the board of directors has declared the dividend. Also, companies must repay their debt but have no obligation to pay back true preferred stock. Preferred stock that must be redeemed (paid back) by the corporation is a liability masquerading as a stock. Experienced investors treat mandatorily redeemable preferred stock as part of total liabilities, not as part of owners' equity. Preferred stock that must be redeemed is rare.

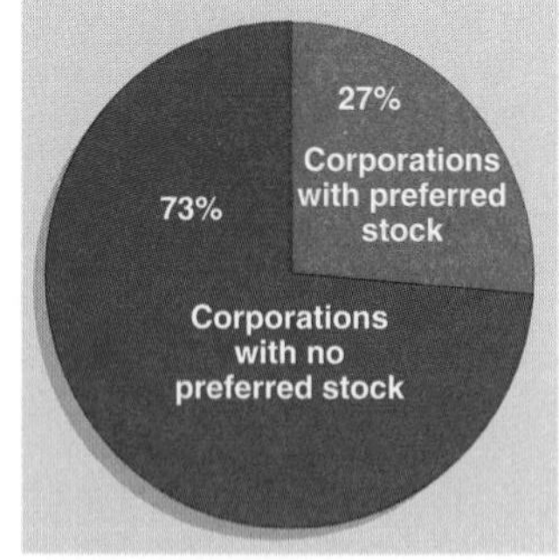

EXHIBIT 9-4
Preferred Stock

Preferred stock is rarer than you might think. A recent survey of 600 corporations revealed that only 160 of them (only 27%) had some preferred stock outstanding (Exhibit 9-4). All corporations have common stock. The balance sheet of IHOP Corp. (page 418) shows that IHOP is authorized to issue preferred stock. To date, however, IHOP has issued none of the preferred stock.

Preferred stock is unpopular mainly because dividend payments are not tax deductible. **Dividends** are a distribution of assets created by earnings. Dividends are *not* an expense. If companies are going to commit to pay a fixed amount (of preferred dividends) each year, they want a tax deduction for the payment. Therefore, most companies would rather borrow money and get a tax deduction for the interest expense. Exhibit 9-5 summarizes the similarities and differences among common stock, preferred stock, and long-term debt.

Par Value and No-Par Stock

Stock may be par value stock or no-par stock. **Par value** is an arbitrary amount assigned by a company to a share of its stock. Most companies set the par value of their common stock quite low to avoid legal difficulties from issuing their stock below par. Most states require companies to maintain a minimum amount of stockholders' equity for the protection of creditors, and this minimum is often called the corporation's legal capital. For corporations with par-value stock, **legal capital** is the par value of the shares issued.

The common stock par value of Kimberly Clark, best known for its Kleenex tissues, is $1.25 per share.

The common stock par value of **Kimberly Clark,** best known for its Kleenex tissues, is $1.25 per share. Of 600 million shares of stock, Kimberly Clark has issued 282.3 million shares. **JC Penney's** common stock par value is 50¢ per share, and **Bethlehem Steel's** common stock par value is $1 per share. Par value of preferred stock is often higher; $100 per share is typical, but some preferred stocks have par values of $25 and $10. Par value is used to compute dividends on preferred stock, as we shall see.

No-par stock does not have par value. Kimberly Clark has 20 million shares of preferred stock authorized with no par value. But some no-par stock has a **stated value,** which makes it similar to par value stock. The stated value is an arbitrary amount that accountants treat as though it were par value.

Issuing Stock

Objective 2

Measure the effect of issuing stock on a company's financial position

Large corporations such as **Coca-Cola, Xerox,** and **British Petroleum** need huge quantities of money to operate. They cannot expect to finance all their operations through borrowing. They need capital that they raise by issuing stock. The charter that the incorporators receive from the state includes an **authorization of stock**—that is, a provision giving the state's permission for the business to issue (to sell) a certain number of shares of stock. Corporations may sell the stock directly to the stockholders or use the service of an *underwriter,* such as the brokerage firms **Merrill Lynch** and **Dean Witter.** An underwriter agrees to buy all the stock it cannot sell to its clients.

The corporation need not issue all the stock that the state authorizes. Management may hold some stock back and issue it later if the need for additional capital arises. The stock that the corporation issues to stockholders is called *issued stock.* Only by issuing stock—not by receiving authorization—does the corporation increase the asset and stockholders' equity amounts on its balance sheet.

EXHIBIT 9-5
Comparison of Common Stock, Preferred Stock, and Long-Term Debt

	Common Stock	Preferred Stock	Long-Term Debt
Investment risk	High	Medium	Low
Corporate obligation to repay principal	No	No	Yes
Dividends/interest	Dividends	Dividends	Tax-deductible interest expense
Corporate obligation to pay dividends/ interest	Only after declaration	Only after declaration	At fixed dates
Fluctuations in market value under normal conditions	High	Medium	Low

LEARNING TIP Owners invest in a corporation by buying its stock. Receiving assets and issuing stock increases the corporation's assets and stockholders' equity.

The price that the stockholder pays to acquire stock from the corporation is called the *issue price*. Often, the issue price far exceeds the stock's par value because the par value was intentionally set quite low. A combination of market factors—including the company's earnings record, financial position, prospects for success, and general business conditions—determines issue price. Investors will not pay more than market value for the stock. In the following sections we show how companies account for the issuance of stock.

Issuing Common Stock

Companies often advertise the issuance of their stock to attract investors. The *Wall Street Journal* is the most popular medium for the advertisements, which are also called *tombstones*. Exhibit 9-6 is a reproduction of IHOP's tombstone, which appeared in the *Wall Street Journal*, with the data given in the chapter opening story.

The lead underwriter of IHOP's public offering was **The First Boston Corporation.** Twenty-one other domestic brokerage firms and investment bankers sold IHOP's stock to their clients. Outside the United States, six investment bankers assisted with the offering. Altogether, IHOP hoped to raise approximately \$62 million of capital. As it turned out, IHOP issued only 3.2 million of the shares and received cash of approximately \$32 million.

ISSUING COMMON STOCK AT PAR Suppose IHOP's common stock carried a par value of \$10 per share. The stock issuance entry of 3.2 million shares would be

Jan. 8	Cash (3,200,000 × \$10)	32,000,000	
	Common Stock		32,000,000
	To issue common stock at par.		

ASSETS	=	LIABILITIES	+	STOCKHOLDERS' EQUITY
32,000,000	=	0	+	32,000,000

The amount invested in the corporation, \$32 million in this case, is paid-in capital, or contributed capital, of IHOP. The credit to Common Stock records an increase in the corporation's paid-in capital.

ISSUING COMMON STOCK AT A PREMIUM Many corporations set par value at a low amount, then issue common stock for a price above par value. The amount above par is called a *premium*. IHOP's common stock has a par value of \$0.01 (1 cent) per share. The \$9.99 difference between issue price (\$10) and par value (\$0.01) is a premium. This sale of stock increases the corporation's paid-in capital by the full \$10, the total issue price of the stock. Both the par value of the stock and the premium are part of paid-in capital.

A premium on the sale of stock is not gain, income, or profit to the corporation, because the entity is dealing with its own stockholders. This situation illustrates one of the fundamentals of accounting: *A company neither earns a profit nor incurs a loss when it sells its stock to, or buys its stock from, its own stockholders.*

With a par value of \$0.01, IHOP's entry to record the issuance of the stock is

July 23	Cash (3,200,000 × \$10)	32,000,000	
	Common Stock (3,200,000 × \$0.01)		32,000
	Paid-in Capital in Excess of Par—Common (3,200,000 × \$9.99)		31,968,000
	To issue common stock at a premium.		

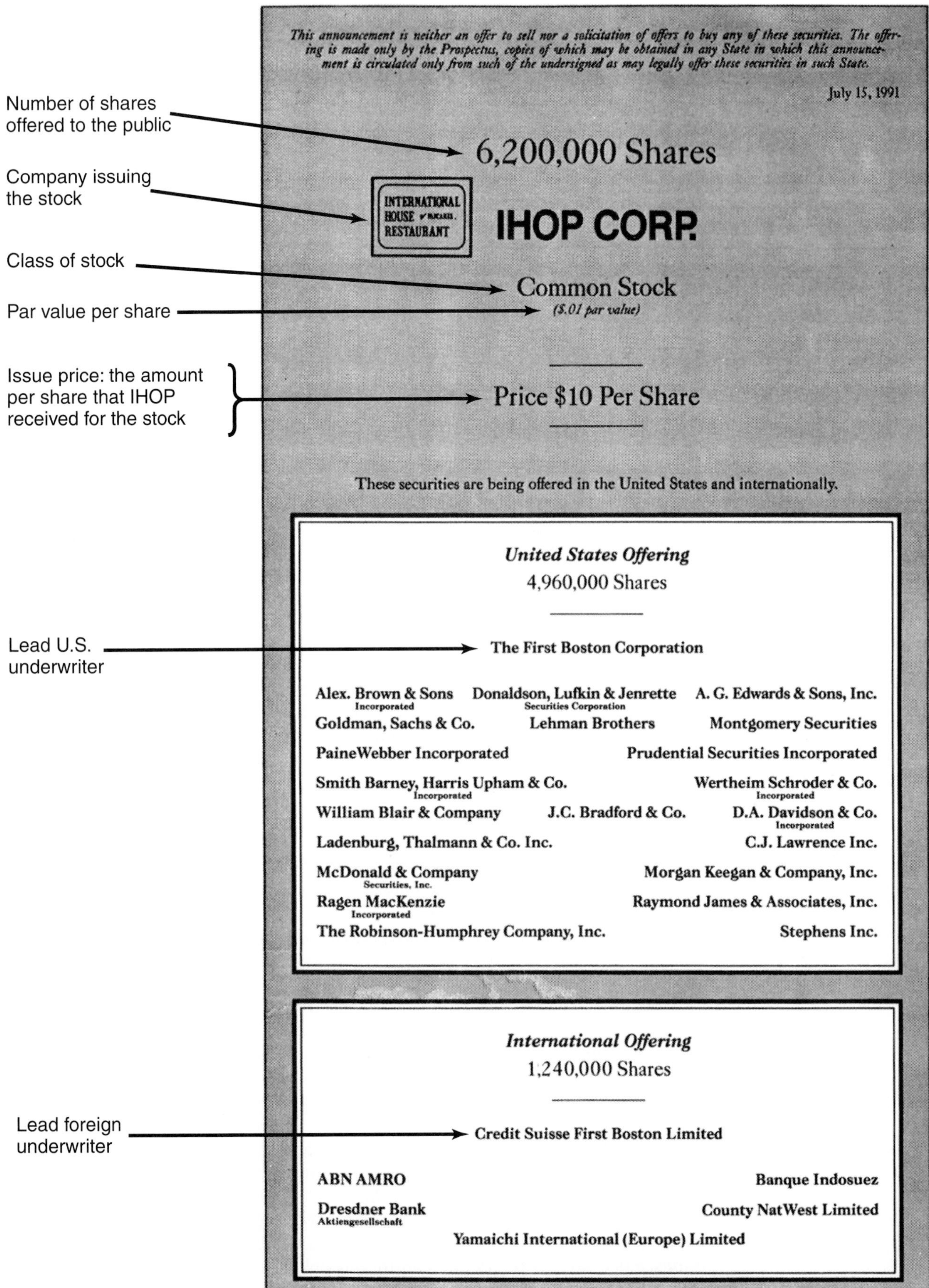

EXHIBIT 9-6
Announcement of Public Offering of IHOP Stock

ASSETS	=	LIABILITIES	+	STOCKHOLDERS' EQUITY
32,000,000	=	0		+32,000 +31,968,000

Account titles that could be used in place of Paid-in Capital in Excess of Par—Common are Additional Paid-in Capital—Common and Premium on Common Stock. Since both par value and premium amounts increase the corporation's capital, they appear in the stockholders' equity section of the balance sheet.

At the end of the year, IHOP Corp. would report stockholders' equity on its balance sheet as follows, assuming that the corporate charter authorizes 40,000,000 shares of common stock and the balance of retained earnings is $26,000,000.

Stockholders' Equity	
Common stock, $0.01 par, 40 million shares authorized, 3.2 million shares issued	$ 32,000
Paid-in capital in excess of par	31,968,000
Total paid-in capital	32,000,000
Retained earnings	26,000,000
Total stockholders' equity	$58,000,000

We determine the dollar amount reported for common stock by multiplying the total number of shares *issued* (3.2 million) by the par value per share. The *authorization* reports the maximum number of shares the company may issue under its charter.

All of the transactions recorded in this section include a receipt of cash by the corporation as it issues new stock to its stockholders. These transactions are different from the vast majority of stock transactions reported each day in the financial press. In those transactions, one stockholder sells his or her stock to another investor, as the corporation makes no formal journal entry.

STOP & THINK Examine IHOP's balance sheet at December 31, 1995, given at the beginning of the chapter (page 418). Answer these questions:

1. What was IHOP's total paid-in capital at December 31, 1995?
2. What is the total amount of profits that IHOP has retained for use in the business through the end of 1995?
3. What is the fundamental difference between paid-in capital and retained earnings?

Answers

1. Total paid-in capital: $46,457,000 ($94,000 + $46,363,000).
2. Retained earnings: $60,640,000.
3. Paid-in capital comes from investments that the stockholders have made in the company. Retained earnings come from profits that the company has earned from customers.

ISSUING NO-PAR COMMON STOCK When a company issues stock that has no par value, there can be no premium. A recent survey of 600 companies revealed that they had 69 issues of no-par stock.

When a company issues no-par stock, it debits the asset received and credits the stock account. Glenwood Corporation, which manufactures skateboards, issues 3,000 shares of no-par common stock for $20 per share. The stock issuance entry is

Aug. 14	Cash (3,000 × $20)	60,000	
	Common Stock		60,000
	To issue no-par common stock.		

ASSETS	=	LIABILITIES	+	STOCKHOLDERS' EQUITY
60,000	=	0	+	60,000

Regardless of the stock's price, Cash is debited and Common Stock is credited for the amount of cash received. There is no Paid-in Capital in Excess of Par for true no-par stock.

Glenwood Corporation's charter authorizes Glenwood to issue 10,000 shares of no-par stock, and the company has $46,000 in retained earnings. The corporation reports stockholders' equity on the balance sheet as follows:

Stockholders' Equity	
Common stock, no par, 10,000 shares authorized, 3,000 shares issued	$ 60,000
Retained earnings	46,000
Total stockholders' equity	$106,000

ISSUING NO-PAR COMMON STOCK WITH A STATED VALUE Accounting for no-par stock with a stated value is identical to accounting for par value stock. The premium account for no-par common stock with a stated value is entitled Paid-in Capital in Excess of Stated Value—Common.

ISSUING COMMON STOCK FOR ASSETS OTHER THAN CASH When a corporation issues stock in exchange for assets other than cash, it records the assets received at their current market value and credits the capital accounts accordingly. The assets' prior book value does not matter because the stockholder will demand stock equal to the market value of the asset given. Kahn Corporation issued 15,000 shares of its $1 par common stock for equipment worth $4,000 and a building worth $120,000. Kahn's entry is

Nov. 12	Equipment	4,000	
	Building	120,000	
	Common Stock (15,000 × $1)		15,000
	Paid-in Capital in Excess of Par—Common ($124,000 – $15,000)		109,000
	To issue common stock in exchange for equipment and a building.		

ASSETS	=	LIABILITIES	+	STOCKHOLDERS' EQUITY
+ 4,000 +120,000	=	0		+15,000 +109,000

STOP & THINK How did this transaction affect Kahn Corporation's cash? Total assets? Paid-in capital? Retained earnings? Total stockholders' equity?

Answer

	Cash	Total Assets	Paid-in Capital	Retained Earnings	Total Stockholders' Equity
Effect:	None	Increase $124,000	Increase $124,000	None	Increase $124,000

Issuing Preferred Stock

Accounting for preferred stock follows the pattern we illustrated for common stock. The charter of Brown-Forman Corporation, a distilling company, authorizes issuance of 1,177,948 shares of 4%, $10 par preferred stock. [The 4% refers to the annual cash dividend rate on the stock. Each Brown-Forman preferred stockholder receives an annual cash dividend of $0.40 ($10 par × .04). Note that the dividend is paid on the *par value.*] Assume that on July 31 the company issued all the shares at a price equal to the par value. The issuance entry is

July 31	Cash..	11,779,480	
	Preferred Stock (1,177,948 × $10)...		11,779,480
	To issue preferred stock at par.		

ASSETS	=	LIABILITIES	+	STOCKHOLDERS' EQUITY
+11,779,480	=	0	+	11,779,480

If Brown-Forman had issued the preferred stock at a premium, the entry would have also credited an account titled Paid-in Capital in Excess of Par—Preferred. A corporation lists separate accounts for Paid-in Capital in Excess of Par on Preferred Stock and on Common Stock to differentiate the two classes of equity.

Accounting for no-par preferred stock follows the pattern we illustrated for no-par common stock. When reporting stockholders' equity on the balance sheet, a corporation lists preferred stock, common stock, and retained earnings—in that order.

Accounting for Preferred Stock Conversions

If they choose, preferred stockholders may exchange **convertible preferred stock** for another class of stock in the corporation. For example, suppose that Pine Industries, Inc., issued preferred stock that may be converted into the company's common stock. A note to Pine's balance sheet describes the conversion terms as follows:

> The . . . preferred stock is convertible at the rate of 6.51 shares of common stock for each share of preferred stock outstanding.

If you owned 100 shares of Pine's convertible preferred stock, you could convert it into 651 (100 × 6.51) shares of Pine common stock. Under what condition would you exercise the conversion privilege? You would do so if the market value of the common stock that you could receive from conversion exceeds the market value of the preferred stock that you presently hold.

Pine Industries' preferred stock has par value of $100 per share, and the par value of Pine's common stock is $1. The company would thus record conversion of 100 shares of preferred stock, issued previously at par, into 651 shares of common stock as follows:

Mar. 7	Preferred Stock (100 × $100)................................	10,000	
	Common Stock (651 × $1)...........................		651
	Paid-in Capital in Excess of Par—Common		9,349
	Conversion of preferred stock into common.		

ASSETS	=	LIABILITIES	+	STOCKHOLDERS' EQUITY
				−10,000
0	=	0		+651
				+9,349

If the preferred stock was issued at a premium, Paid-in Capital in Excess of Par—Preferred must also be debited to remove its balance from the books.

The accounting-equation analysis shows that neither assets nor liabilities nor total stockholders' equity is affected by conversion of a company's preferred stock into its common stock. Only the composition of stockholders' equity changes—an increase in common equity, a decrease in preferred equity.

Ethical Considerations in Accounting for the Issuance of Stock

Issuance of stock for *cash* poses no serious ethical challenge. The company simply receives cash and issues the stock to the shareholders, giving them stock certificates as evidence of their purchase.

Issuing stock for assets other than cash can pose an ethical challenge, however. The company issuing the stock often wishes to record a large amount for the noncash asset received (such as land or a building) and for the stock that it is issuing. Why? Because large asset and stockholders' equity amounts on the balance sheet make the business look more prosperous and more creditworthy. The motivation to look good can inject a subtle bias into the amount recorded for stock issued in return for assets other than cash.

As we discussed on page 429, a company is supposed to record an asset received at its current market value. But one person's perception of a particular asset's market value can differ from another person's perception. One person may appraise land at a market value of $400,000. Another may honestly believe the land is worth only $300,000. A company receiving land in exchange for its stock must decide whether to record the land received and the stock issued at $300,000, at $400,000, or at some amount in between.

The ethical course of action is to record the asset at its current fair market value, as determined by a good-faith estimate of market value from independent appraisers. It is rare for a public corporation to be found guilty of *understating* the asset values on its balance sheet, but companies have been embarrassed by *overstating* their asset values. Investors who rely on the financial statements may be able to prove that an overstatement of asset values caused them to pay too much for the company's stock. In this case, a court of law may render a judgment against the company. For this reason, companies often tend to value assets conservatively in order to avoid an overstatement of their book value.

Donations Received by a Corporation

Corporations occasionally receive gifts, or *donations*. For example, city council members may offer a company free land to encourage it to locate in their city. Cities in the southern United States have lured some companies away from the North with such offers. The free land is a donation. For example, **JCPenney Co.** and **American Airlines** moved corporate headquarters from New York City to the Dallas–Fort Worth area because of concessions granted by the Texas cities. Also, a stockholder may make a donation to the corporation in the form of cash, land or other assets, or stock.

A donation increases the corporation's assets, but the donor (giver) receives no ownership interest in the company in return. A donation increases the corporation's revenue and thus affects income and retained earnings. The corporation records a donation by debiting the asset received at its current market value and by crediting Revenue from Donations, which is reported as Other Revenue on the income statement. But a donation received from a government entity is recorded as a credit to Donated Capital. For example, American Airlines would credit Donated Capital for the value of any land it receives from a city or county government.[1] Donated capital is a separate category of paid-in capital. The Lands' End balance sheet in Appendix A at the end of the book lists Donated Capital after Common Stock. This is a common method of reporting donated capital.

[1] FASB, *Statement of Financial Accounting Standards No. 116, Accounting for Contributions Received and Contributions Made* (June 1993).

Mid-Chapter

SUMMARY PROBLEMS FOR YOUR REVIEW

1. Test your understanding of the first half of this chapter by deciding whether each of the following statements is true or false.
   a. A stockholder may bind the corporation to a contract.
   b. The policy-making body in a corporation is called the board of directors.
   c. The owner of 100 shares of preferred stock has greater voting rights than the owner of 100 shares of common stock.
   d. Par value stock is worth more than no-par stock.
   e. Issuance of 1,000 shares of $5 par value stock at $12 increases contributed capital by $12,000.
   f. The issuance of no-par stock with a stated value is fundamentally different from issuing par value stock.
   g. A corporation issues its preferred stock in exchange for land and a building with a combined market value of $200,000. This transaction increases the corporation's owners' equity by $200,000 regardless of the assets' prior book values.
   h. Preferred stock is a riskier investment than common stock.
2. The brewery **Adolph Coors Company** has two classes of common stock. Only the Class A common stockholders are entitled to vote. The company's balance sheet included the following presentation:

Shareholders' Equity	
Capital stock	
Class A common stock, voting, $1 par value,	
authorized and issued 1,260,000 shares	$ 1,260,000
Class B common stock, nonvoting, no par value,	
authorized and issued 46,200,000 shares	11,000,000
	12,260,000
Additional paid-in capital	2,011,000
Retained earnings	872,403,000
	$886,674,000

Required

a. Record the issuance of the Class A common stock. Use the Coors account titles.
b. Record the issuance of the Class B common stock. Use the Coors account titles.
c. How much of Coors's stockholders' equity was contributed by the stockholders? How much was provided by profitable operations? Does this division of equity suggest that the company has been successful? Why or why not?
d. Write a sentence to describe what Coors's stockholders' equity means.

ANSWERS

1. a. False b. True c. False d. False e. True
   f. False g. True h. False

2.

		Debit	Credit
a.	Cash	3,271,000	
	Class A Common Stock		1,260,000
	Additional Paid-in capital		2,011,000
	To record issuance of Class A common stock.		
b.	Cash	11,000,000	
	Class B Common Stock		11,000,000
	To record issuance of Class B common stock.		

c. Contributed by the stockholders: $14,271,000 ($12,260,000 + $2,011,000).
Provided by profitable operations: $872,403,000.
This division suggests that the company has been very successful because most of its stockholders' equity has come from profitable operations.

d. Coors's stockholders' equity of $886,674,000 means that the company's stockholders own $886,674,000 of the business's assets.

Treasury Stock

Objective 3

Describe how treasury stock transactions affect a company

Stock that a corporation has issued and later reacquired is called **treasury stock.**[2] In effect, the corporation holds the stock in its treasury. Corporations may purchase their own stock for several reasons:

1. The company has issued all its authorized stock and needs the stock for distributions to officers and employees under bonus plans or stock purchase plans.
2. The purchase helps support the stock's current market price by decreasing the supply of stock available to the public.
3. The business is trying to increase net assets by buying its shares low and hoping to sell them for a higher price later.
4. Management wants to avoid a takeover by an outside party.

Treasury stock is like unissued stock: Neither category of stock is outstanding in the hands of shareholders. The company does not receive cash dividends on its treasury stock, and treasury stock does not entitle the company to vote or to receive assets in liquidation. The difference between unissued stock and treasury stock is that treasury stock has been issued and bought back by the company itself. Unissued stock has never been issued.

The purchase of treasury stock decreases the company's assets and its stockholders' equity. The size of the company literally decreases, as shown on its balance sheet. Purchasing treasury stock is consistent with a corporate strategy of downsizing.

The Treasury Stock account has a debit balance, which is the opposite of the other owners' equity accounts. Therefore, *Treasury Stock is a contra stockholders' equity account.*

Purchase of Treasury Stock

We record the purchase of treasury stock by debiting Treasury Stock and crediting the asset given in exchange—usually Cash. Suppose that Jupiter Drilling Company had the following stockholders' equity before purchasing treasury stock:

Stockholders' Equity [*Before* Purchase of Treasury Stock]	
Common stock, $1 par, 10,000 shares authorized, 8,000 shares issued	$ 8,000
Paid-in capital in excess of par—common	12,000
Retained earnings	14,600
Total stockholders' equity	$34,600

On November 22, Jupiter purchases 1,000 shares of its $1 par common as treasury stock, paying cash of $7.50 per share. Jupiter records the purchase of treasury stock as follows:

Nov. 22	Treasury Stock, Common (1,000 × $7.50)	7,500	
	Cash		7,500
	Purchased 1,000 shares of treasury stock at $7.50 per share.		

ASSETS	=	LIABILITIES	+	STOCKHOLDERS' EQUITY
−7,500	=	0	−	7,500

Treasury stock is recorded at cost, without reference to the stock's par value. The Treasury Stock account is often reported beneath Retained Earnings on the balance sheet. Treasury Stock has a debit balance, which makes it a

[2]In this text we illustrate the *cost* method of accounting for treasury stock because it is used most widely. Other methods are presented in intermediate accounting courses.

contra stockholders' equity account, so its balance is subtracted from the sum of total paid-in capital and retained earnings, as follows:

Stockholders' Equity [*After* Purchase of Treasury Stock]	
Common stock, $1 par, 10,000 shares authorized, 8,000 shares issued, 7,000 shares outstanding	$ 8,000
Paid-in capital in excess of par—common	12,000
Retained earnings	14,600
Subtotal	34,600
Less treasury stock, 1,000 shares at cost	(7,500)
Total stockholders' equity	$27,100

The purchase of treasury stock does not decrease the number of shares issued. The Common Stock, Paid-in Capital in Excess of Par, and Retained Earnings accounts remain unchanged. However, total stockholders' equity decreases by the cost of the treasury stock. Also, shares of stock *outstanding* decrease from 8,000 to 7,000. To compute the number of outstanding shares, subtract the treasury shares (1,000) from the shares issued (8,000). Although the number of *outstanding shares* is not required to be reported on the balance sheet, this figure is important. Only outstanding shares have voting rights, receive cash dividends, and share in assets if the corporation liquidates.

STOP & THINK *Ethical Issue:* Treasury stock transactions have a serious ethical and legal dimension. A company buying its own shares as treasury stock must be extremely careful that its disclosures of information are complete and accurate. Otherwise, a stockholder who sold shares back to the company may claim that he or she was deceived into selling the stock at too low a price. What would happen if a company purchased treasury stock at $17 per share and one day later announced a technological breakthrough that would generate millions of dollars in new business?

Answer: The stock price would likely increase in response to the new information. If it could be proved that management withheld the information, a shareholder selling stock back to the company may file a lawsuit to gain the difference per share. The stockholder would claim that with knowledge of the technological advance, he or she would have held the stock until after the price increase.

Sale of Treasury Stock

A company may sell its treasury stock at a variety of prices.

SALE OF TREASURY STOCK AT COST The company may sell its treasury stock at any price agreeable to the corporation and the purchaser. If the stock is sold for the same price that the corporation paid to reacquire it, the entry is a debit to Cash and a credit to Treasury Stock for the same amount.

SALE OF TREASURY STOCK ABOVE COST If the sale price of treasury stock is greater than its reacquisition cost, the difference is credited to the account Paid-in Capital from Treasury Stock Transactions because the excess came from the company's stockholders. Suppose Jupiter Drilling Company resold 200 of its treasury shares for $9 per share (cost was $7.50 per share). The entry is

Dec. 7	Cash (200 × $9)	1,800	
	Treasury Stock, Common (200 × $7.50—the purchase cost per share)		1,500
	Paid-in Capital from Treasury Stock Transactions		300
	To sell 200 shares of treasury stock at $9 per share.		

ASSETS	=	LIABILITIES	+	STOCKHOLDERS' EQUITY
+1,800	=	0		+1,500 +300

Paid-in Capital from Treasury Stock Transactions is reported with the other paid-in capital accounts on the balance sheet, beneath the Common Stock and Capital in Excess of Par accounts. Its balance can be combined as part of Additional Paid-in Capital, as shown for IHOP Corp. on page 418 (line 24).

SALE OF TREASURY STOCK BELOW COST At times the resale price of treasury stock is less than cost. The difference between these two amounts is debited to Paid-in Capital from Treasury Stock Transactions if this account has a credit balance, as in our example. If the difference between resale price and cost is greater than the credit balance in Paid-in Capital from Treasury Stock Transactions, or if Paid-in Capital from Treasury Stock Transactions has a zero balance, then the company debits Retained Earnings for the remaining amount. For example, Jupiter Drilling records the sale of 400 shares of treasury stock at $5 per share in the following entry:

Dec. 23	Cash (400 × $5)..	2,000	
	Paid-in Capital from Treasury Stock Transactions (from Dec. 7 entry on page 434).........................	300	
	Retained Earnings	700	
	Treasury Stock, Common (400 × $7.50—the purchase cost per share)......................		3,000
	To sell 400 shares of treasury stock at $5 per share.		

ASSETS	=	LIABILITIES	+	STOCKHOLDERS' EQUITY
+2,000	=	0		−300 −700 +3,000

STOP & THINK

1. Examine the preceding entry to record Jupiter Drilling's sale of treasury stock at a price below its cost. What effect did the sale of the treasury stock have on Jupiter's assets? On its stockholders' equity?
2. Now assume that Jupiter Drilling sold for $2,000 an investment that Jupiter held in Texaco stock. Assume further that Jupiter's carrying value of the Texaco investment was $3,000. What effect would this sale have on Jupiter's assets? On its stockholders' equity?
3. Explain why your answers to Questions 1 and 2 differ.

Answers

1. The accounting equation shows that the sale of the treasury stock increased Jupiter's assets and its stockholders' equity by $2,000, the amount of cash received.
2. The accounting equation provides the analysis as follows:

ASSETS	=	LIABILITIES	+	STOCKHOLDERS' EQUITY	−	LOSSES
+2,000 −3,000	=	0			−	1,000

3. Selling treasury stock is fundamentally different from selling an asset. The sale of treasury stock always increases assets and stockholders' equity by the amount of cash received. There is no gain or loss to record. The sale of an asset at more or less than the asset's carrying value requires the recording of a gain or a loss, which is reported on the income statement.

Treasury Stock Transactions: A Summary

Neither the purchase nor the sale of treasury stock creates a gain or a loss, and thus neither has an effect on net income. Sale of treasury stock above cost is an increase in paid-in capital, not an element of income. Likewise, sale of treasury stock below cost is a decrease in paid-in capital or retained earnings, not a loss. Treasury stock transactions take place between the business and its owners, the stockholders.

EXHIBIT 9-7
Effects of a Purchase and Resale of Treasury Stock

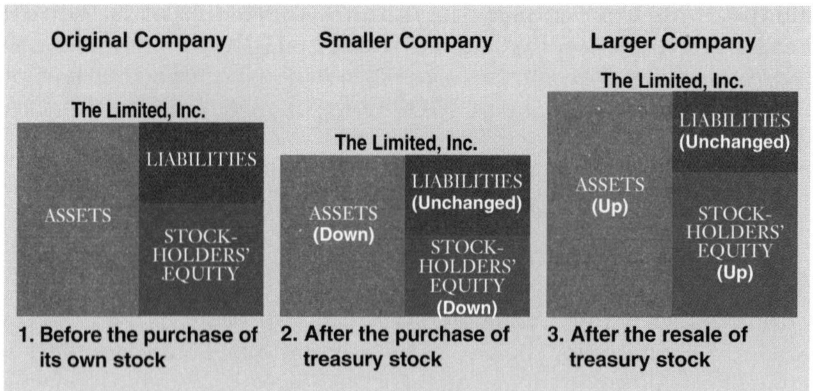

Because a company cannot earn a profit in dealing in its own stock with its owners, we credit Paid-in Capital from Treasury Stock Transactions for sale above cost and debit that account (and, if necessary, Retained Earnings) for a sale below cost. These accounts appear on the balance sheet, not on the income statement.

The Limited, Inc., purchased $500 million of its own stock.

Does this mean that a company cannot increase its net assets by buying treasury stock low and selling it high? Not at all. Management often buys treasury stock because it believes that the market price of its stock is too low. For example, **The Limited, Inc.**, purchased $500 million of its own stock. Suppose The Limited holds the stock as the market price rises and resells the stock for $600 million. Net assets of the company increase by $100 million. This increase is reported as paid-in capital, not as income. Exhibit 9-7 summarizes The Limited's financial position before and after the sale of treasury stock.

Retirement of Stock

A corporation may purchase its own common stock or preferred stock and *retire* it by canceling the stock certificates. Retirements of preferred stock occur more often than retirements of common stock, as companies seek to avoid having to pay dividends on the preferred stock. The retired stock cannot be reissued. Retiring stock, like purchasing treasury stock, decreases the corporation's outstanding stock. Unlike a treasury stock purchase, stock retirement decreases the number of shares issued. In retiring stock, the corporation removes the balances from all paid-in capital accounts related to the retired shares, such as Capital in Excess of Par.

A corporation may repurchase shares for retirement for a price that is below the stock's issue price (par value plus any capital in excess of par). This difference between repurchase price and issue price increases Paid-in Capital from Retirement of Stock. This new layer of paid-in capital created by a retirement of stock (preferred or common) belongs to the common stockholders. If the corporation must pay more than the stock's issue price, the excess decreases Retained Earnings.

Retiring stock, like purchasing treasury stock, is a transaction that does not affect net income. No gain or loss arises from stock retirement because the company is doing business with its owners. Stock retirement affects the balance sheet, not the income statement.

Retained Earnings and Dividends

We have seen that the equity section on the corporation balance sheet is called stockholders' equity or shareholders' equity. The paid-in capital accounts and retained earnings make up the stockholders' equity section.

Retained Earnings is the corporation account that carries the balance of the business's net income less its net losses from operations and less any declared dividends accumulated over the corporation's lifetime. *Retained* means "held onto." Retained Earnings is the shareholders' claim against total assets arising from accumulated income. Successful companies grow by reinvesting the assets they generate through profitable operations. IHOP Corp. is an example; the majority of its equity comes from retained earnings.

A credit balance in Retained Earnings is normal, indicating that the corporation's lifetime earnings exceed its lifetime losses and dividends. A debit balance in Retained Earnings arises when a corporation's lifetime losses and dividends exceed its lifetime earnings. Called a **deficit,** this amount is subtracted from the sum of the other equity accounts on the balance sheet to determine total stockholders' equity. In a recent survey, 94 of 600 companies (15.7%) had a retained earnings deficit (Exhibit 9-8).

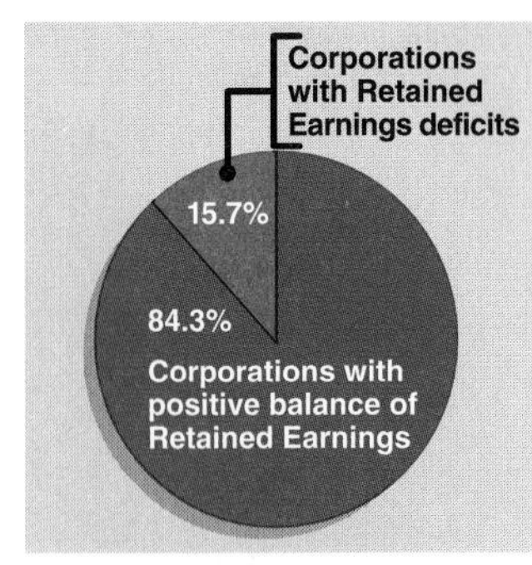

EXHIBIT 9-8
Retained Earnings of the Accounting Trends & Techniques *600 Companies*

At the end of each accounting period, the Income Summary account—which carries the balance of net income for the period—is closed to the Retained Earnings account. Assume that the following amounts are drawn from a corporation's temporary accounts:

We introduced the Income Summary account in Chapter 3, page 133.

Income Summary

Dec. 31, 19X6	Expenses	750,000	Dec. 31, 19X6	Revenues	850,000
			Dec. 31, 19X6	Bal.	100,000

This final closing entry transfers net income from Income Summary to Retained Earnings:

19X6			
Dec. 31	Income Summary	100,000	
	Retained Earnings		100,000
	To close net income to Retained Earnings.		

STOP & THINK Assume that the beginning balance of Retained Earnings was $680,000. What will Retained Earnings's balance be after this year's net income of $100,000?

Answer

Retained Earnings

	Jan. 1, 19X6	Bal.	680,000
	Dec. 31, 19X6	Net inc.	100,000
	Dec. 31, 19X6	Bal.	780,000

Remember that the account title includes the word *earnings. Credits to the Retained Earnings account arise only from net income.* When we examine a corporation's financial statements and want to learn how much net income the corporation has earned and retained in the business, we turn to Retained Earnings.

The Retained Earnings account is not a reservoir of cash waiting for the board of directors to pay dividends to the stockholders. Instead, Retained Earnings is an owners' equity account representing a claim on all assets in general and not on any asset in particular. Its balance is the cumulative lifetime earnings of the company less its cumulative losses and dividends. In fact, the corporation may have a large balance in Retained Earnings but not have the cash to pay a dividend. Why? Because, for example, the company may have used its cash to purchase a building. To *declare* a dividend, the company must have an adequate balance in Retained Earnings. To *pay* the dividend, it must have the cash. Cash and Retained Earnings are two separate accounts with no particular relationship.

LEARNING TIP Retained Earnings is *not* a bank account. A $500,000 balance in Retained Earnings simply means that $500,000 of owners' equity has been created by profits reinvested in the business. It says nothing about the company's Cash balance.

Dividends and Dividend Dates

A dividend is a corporation's return to its stockholders of some of the benefits of previous earnings, most commonly in the form of cash payments to the stockholders. A corporation must declare a dividend before paying it. Only the board of directors has the authority to declare a dividend. The corporation has no obligation to pay a dividend until the board declares one, but once declared, the dividend becomes a legal liability of the corporation. Three relevant dates for dividends are

1. *Declaration date.* On the declaration date, the board of directors announces the intention to pay the dividend. The declaration creates a liability for the corporation. Declaration is recorded by debiting Retained Earnings and crediting Dividends Payable.

2. *Date of record.* As part of the declaration, the corporation announces the record date, which follows the declaration date by a few weeks. The corporation makes no journal entry on the date of record because no transaction occurs. Nevertheless, much work takes place behind the scenes to identify the stockholders of record on this date because the stock is traded continuously. Only the people who own the stock on the date of record receive the dividend.

3. *Payment date.* Payment of the dividend usually follows the record date by two to four weeks. Payment is recorded by debiting Dividends Payable and crediting Cash.

Dividends on Preferred and Common Stock

Objective 4

Account for dividends and measure their impact on a company

Declaration of a $50,000 cash dividend is recorded by debiting Retained Earnings and crediting Dividends Payable, as follows:[3]

June 19	Retained Earnings	50,000	
	Dividends Payable....................................		50,000
	To declare a cash dividend.		

ASSETS	=	LIABILITIES	+	STOCKHOLDERS' EQUITY
0	=	50,000	−	50,000

Payment of the dividend, which usually follows declaration by a few weeks, is recorded by debiting Dividends Payable and crediting Cash:

July 2	Dividends Payable	50,000	
	Cash		50,000
	To pay a cash dividend.		

ASSETS	=	LIABILITIES	+	STOCKHOLDERS' EQUITY
−50,000	=	−50,000	+	0

Dividends Payable is a current liability. When a company has issued both preferred and common stock, the preferred stockholders receive their dividends first. The common stockholders receive dividends only if the total declared dividend is large enough to pay the preferred stockholders first.

[3]In Chapters 1–8, we debited the Dividends account, which is closed to Retained Earnings. Many businesses debit Retained Earnings directly, as shown here.

In addition to its common stock, Pine Industries, Inc., a furniture manufacturer, has 90,000 shares of preferred stock outstanding. Preferred dividends are paid at the annual rate of $1.75 per share. Assume that in 19X4, Pine Industries declares an annual dividend of $1,500,000. The allocation to preferred and common stockholders is as follows:

Preferred dividend (90,000 shares × $1.75 per share)	$ 157,500
Common dividend (remainder: $1,500,000 – $157,500)	1,342,500
Total dividend	$1,500,000

If Pine declares only a $200,000 dividend, preferred stockholders receive $157,500, and the common stockholders receive the remainder, $42,500 ($200,000 – $157,500).

This example illustrates an important relationship between preferred stock and common stock. To an investor, preferred stock is safer because it receives dividends first. For example, if Pine Industries earns only enough net income to pay the preferred stockholders' dividends, the owners of common stock receive no dividends. However, the earnings potential from an investment in common stock is much greater than the earnings potential of an investment in preferred stock. Preferred dividends are usually limited to the specified amount, but there is no upper limit on the amount of common dividends.

We noted that preferred stockholders have priority over common stockholders in receiving dividends. The dividend preference is stated as a percentage rate or a dollar amount. For example, preferred stock may be "6% preferred," which means that owners of the preferred stock receive an annual dividend of 6% of the stock's par value. If par value is $100 per share, preferred stockholders receive an annual cash dividend of $6 per share (6% of $100). The preferred stock may be "$3 preferred," which means that stockholders receive an annual dividend of $3 per share regardless of the preferred stock's par value. The dividend rate on no-par preferred stock is stated in a dollar amount per share.

STOP & THINK During 1995, Ford Motor Company declared and paid cash dividends of $1.5 billion. Prior to the dividend, Ford had total assets of $244.8 billion and total liabilities of $218.7 billion. What effect did Ford's dividend payment have on the size of the company? Use the accounting equation to answer.

Answer: The declaration and payment of cash dividends always reduce the size of a company because both total assets and total stockholders' equity decrease, as shown by the following analysis (amounts in billions):

	Assets	=	Liabilities	+	Stockholders' Equity
Before dividend	**$244.8**	=	**$218.7**	+	**$26.1**
Dividend	– 1.5	=		–	1.5
After dividend	**$243.3**	=	**$218.7**	+	**$24.6**

Dividends on Cumulative and Noncumulative Preferred Stock

The allocation of dividends may be complex if the preferred stock is *cumulative.* Corporations sometimes fail to pay a dividend to their preferred stockholders. This occurrence is called *passing the dividend,* and the passed dividends are said to be *in arrears.* The owners of **cumulative preferred stock** must receive all dividends in arrears plus the current year's dividend before the corporation can pay dividends to the common stockholders.

The preferred stock of Pine Industries is cumulative. Suppose the company passed the 19X4 preferred dividend of $157,500. Before paying dividends to its common stockholders in 19X5, the company must first pay preferred dividends of $157,500 for both 19X4 and 19X5, a total of $315,000. *The law considers preferred stock cumulative unless it is specifically labeled as noncumulative.*

Assume that Pine Industries passes its 19X4 preferred dividend. In 19X5, the company declares a $500,000 dividend. The entry to record the declaration is

Sep. 6	Retained Earnings	500,000	
	Dividends Payable, Preferred ($157,500 × 2)		315,000
	Dividends Payable, Common ($500,000 – $315,000)		185,000
	To declare a cash dividend.		

ASSETS	=	LIABILITIES	+	STOCKHOLDERS' EQUITY
0	=	315,000 185,000	–	500,000

If the preferred stock is *noncumulative,* the corporation is not obligated to pay dividends in arrears. Suppose that the Pine Industries preferred stock was noncumulative and the company passed the 19X4 preferred dividend of $157,500. The preferred stockholders would lose the 19X4 dividend forever. Of course, the common stockholders would not receive a 19X4 dividend either. Before paying any common dividends in 19X5, the company would have to pay the 19X5 preferred dividend of $157,500.

Having dividends in arrears on cumulative preferred stock is *not* a liability to the corporation. (A liability for dividends arises only when the board of directors declares the dividend.) Nevertheless, a corporation must report cumulative preferred dividends in arrears—usually in a note to the financial statements. This information alerts common stockholders as to how much in cumulative preferred dividends must be paid before any dividends will be paid on the common stock. This information gives the common stockholders an idea about the likelihood of receiving dividends and satisfies the disclosure principle.

For a review of the disclosure principle, see Chapter 6, page 279.

Stock Dividends

A **stock dividend** is a proportional distribution by a corporation of its own stock to its stockholders. Stock dividends are fundamentally different from cash dividends because stock dividends do not transfer the corporation's assets to the stockholders. Stock dividends increase the stock account and decrease Retained Earnings. Because both these accounts are elements of stockholders' equity, total stockholders' equity is unchanged. There is merely a transfer from one stockholders' equity account to another, and no asset or liability is affected by a stock dividend.

The corporation distributes stock dividends to stockholders in proportion to the number of shares they already own. For example, suppose you own 300 shares of Xerox Corporation common stock. If Xerox distributed a 10% common stock dividend, you would receive 30 (300 × 0.10) additional shares. You would then own 330 shares of the stock. All other Xerox stockholders would receive additional shares equal to 10% of their prior holdings. You would all be in the same relative position after the dividend as you were before.

Reasons for Stock Dividends

In distributing a stock dividend, the corporation gives up no assets. Why, then, do companies issue stock dividends? A corporation may choose to distribute stock dividends for these reasons:

1. *To continue dividends but conserve cash.* A company may want to keep cash in the business in order to expand, buy inventory, pay off debts, and so on. Yet the company may wish to continue dividends in some form. To do so, the corporation may distribute a stock dividend. Stockholders pay tax on cash dividends but not on stock dividends.

2. *To reduce the market price of its stock.* Distribution of a stock dividend may cause the market price of a share of the company's stock to decrease because of the increased supply of the stock. Suppose the market price of a share of stock is $50. Doubling the number of shares of stock outstanding by issuing a stock dividend would drop the stock's market price by approximately half, to $25 per share. The objective is to make the stock less expensive and thus more attractive to a wider range of investors.

Recording Stock Dividends

The board of directors announces stock dividends on the declaration date. The date of record and the payment date follow. (This is the same sequence of dates used for a cash dividend.) The declaration of a stock dividend does *not* create a liability because the corporation is not obligated to pay assets. (Recall that a liability is a claim on *assets.*) Instead, the corporation has declared its intention to distribute its stock. Assume that Louisiana Lumber Corporation has the following stockholders' equity prior to a stock dividend:

Stockholders' Equity	
Common stock, $10 par, 50,000 shares authorized, 20,000 shares issued	$200,000
Paid-in capital in excess of par—common	70,000
Retained earnings	85,000
Total stockholders' equity	$355,000

The entry to record a stock dividend depends on its size. Generally accepted accounting principles distinguish between *small stock dividends* (less than 25% of the corporation's issued stock) and *large stock dividends* (25% or more of issued stock). Stock dividends between 20% and 25% are rare.

SMALL STOCK DIVIDEND—LESS THAN 25% Assume that Louisiana Lumber Corporation declares a 10% (*small*) common stock dividend on November 17. The company will distribute 2,000 (20,000 × 0.10) shares in the dividend. On November 17, the market value of its common stock is $16 per share. GAAP requires small stock dividends to be accounted for at market value. Therefore, Retained Earnings is debited for the market value of the 2,000 dividend shares. Common Stock Dividend Distributable is credited for par value, and Paid-in Capital in Excess of Par—Common is credited for the remainder. Louisiana Lumber makes the following entry on the declaration date:

Date	Account	Debit	Credit
Nov. 17	Retained Earnings (20,000 × 0.10 × $16)	32,000	
	Common Stock Dividend Distributable (20,000 × 0.10 × $10)		20,000
	Paid-in Capital in Excess of Par—Common		12,000
	To declare a 10% common stock dividend.		

ASSETS	=	LIABILITIES	+	STOCKHOLDERS' EQUITY
0	=	0		−32,000 +20,000 +12,000

On the distribution (payment) date, the company records issuance of the dividend shares as follows:

Dec. 12	Common Stock Dividend Distributable............	20,000	
	Common Stock		20,000
	To issue common stock in a stock dividend.		

ASSETS	=	LIABILITIES	+	STOCKHOLDERS' EQUITY
0	=	0		−20,000 +20,000

Common Stock Dividend Distributable is an owners' equity account. If the company prepares financial statements after the declaration of the stock dividend but before the dividend has been issued, Common Stock Dividend Distributable is reported in the stockholders' equity section of the balance sheet immediately after Common Stock and before Paid-in Capital in Excess of Par—Common. However, the Common Stock Dividend Distributable account holds the par value of the dividend shares only from the declaration date to the date of distribution.

The following tabulation shows the changes in the stockholders' equity of Louisiana Lumber caused by the stock dividend:

Stockholders' Equity	Before the Dividend	After the Dividend	Change
Paid-in capital:			
Common stock, $10 par,			
50,000 shares authorized,			
20,000 shares issued	$200,000		
22,000 shares issued		$220,000	Up by $20,000
Paid-in capital in excess of par—			
common	70,000	82,000	Up by $12,000
Total paid-in capital	270,000	302,000	Up by $32,000
Retained earnings..........................	85,000	53,000	Down by $32,000
Total stockholders' equity	$355,000	$355,000	Unchanged

Compare total stockholders' equity before and after the stock dividend. Observe the increase in the balances of Common Stock and Paid-in Capital in Excess of Par—Common and the decrease in Retained Earnings. Also observe that total stockholders' equity is unchanged from $355,000.

LARGE STOCK DIVIDEND—25% OR MORE A *large* stock dividend significantly increases the number of shares available in the market and thus is likely to decrease the stock price significantly. Because of the drop in market price per share, a large stock dividend is not likely to be perceived as a dividend. GAAP does not require that large stock dividends be accounted for at a specific amount. A common practice is to use the par value of the dividend shares.

Suppose Louisiana Lumber declares a 50% common stock dividend. The declaration entry is as follows:

Dec. 7	Retained Earnings (20,000 × 0.50 × $10 par)....	100,000	
	Common Stock Dividend Distributable ...		100,000
	To declare a 50% common stock dividend.		

ASSETS	=	LIABILITIES	+	STOCKHOLDERS' EQUITY
0	=	0		−100,000 +100,000

The company records issuance of the dividend shares on the payment date by this entry:

Dec. 22	Common Stock Dividend Distributable	100,000	
	Common Stock		100,000
	To issue common stock in a stock dividend.		

ASSETS	=	LIABILITIES	+	STOCKHOLDERS' EQUITY
0	=	0		−100,000 +100,000

Once again, total stockholders' equity is unchanged. For a large stock dividend, the increase in Common Stock is exactly offset by the decrease in Retained Earnings.

STOP & THINK A corporation issued 1,000 shares of its $15-par common stock as a stock dividend when the stock's market price was $25 per share. Record the declaration and distribution. Assume that the 1,000 shares issued are (1) 10% of the outstanding shares, and (2) 100% of the outstanding shares.

Answer

(1) *Date of declaration (small stock dividend):*		
Retained Earnings (1,000 × $25)	25,000	
Common Stock Dividend Distributable (1,000 × $15)...		15,000
Paid-in Capital in Excess of Par—Common		10,000
Date of distribution:		
Common Stock Dividend Distributable	15,000	
Common Stock		15,000
(2) *Date of declaration (large stock dividend):*		
Retained Earnings (1,000 × $15)	15,000	
Common Stock Dividend Distributable.......................		15,000
Date of distribution:		
Common Stock Dividend Distributable	15,000	
Common Stock		15,000

Stock Splits

A large stock dividend may decrease the market price of the stock. A stock *split* also decreases the market price of stock—with the intention of making the stock more attractive. A **stock split** is an increase in the number of authorized, issued, and outstanding shares of stock, coupled with a proportionate reduction in the stock's par value. For example, if the company splits its stock 2 for 1, the number of outstanding shares is doubled and each share's par value is halved. Most leading companies in the United States—**IBM, Ford Motor Company, Giant Food, Inc.,** and others—have split their stock. **Honeywell, Inc.,** which makes electronic controls, split its stock 2 for 1 twice in a three-year period.

Most leading companies in the United States—IBM, Ford Motor Company, Giant Food, Inc., and others—have split their stock. Honeywell, Inc., split its stock 2 for 1 twice in a three-year period.

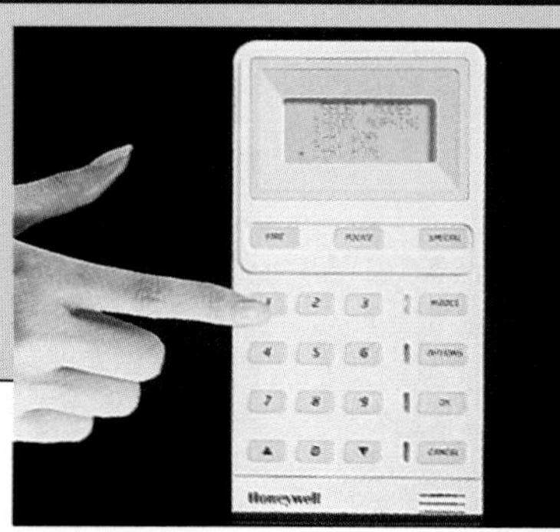

The market price of a share of IBM common stock has been approximately $100. Assume that the company wishes to decrease the market price to approximately $25. IBM decides to split the common stock 4 for 1 to reduce the stock's market price from $100 to $25. A 4-for-1 stock split means that the company would have four times as many shares of stock outstanding after the split as it had before and that each share's par value would be quartered. Assume that IBM had 140 million shares of $5 par common stock issued and outstanding before the split:

IBM Stockholders' Equity (Adapted):

Before 4-for-1 Stock Split:	(In millions)	After 4-for-1 Stock Split	(In millions)
Common stock, $5 par, 187.5 million shares authorized, 140 million shares issued	$ 700	Common stock, $1.25 par, 750 million shares authorized, 560 million shares issued	$ 700
Capital in excess of par	6,800	Capital in excess of par	6,800
Retained earnings	11,630	Retained earnings	11,630
Other	3,293	Other	3,293
Total stockholders' equity	$22,423	Total stockholders' equity	$22,423

After the 4-for-1 stock split, IBM would have 750 million shares authorized and 560 million shares (140 million shares × 4) of $1.25 par ($5/4) common stock issued and outstanding. Total stockholders' equity would be exactly as before the stock split. Indeed, the balance in the Common Stock account does not even change. Only the par value of the stock and the number of shares authorized, issued, and outstanding change. Compare the figures in blue in the preceding stockholders' equity presentations for IBM.

Because the stock split affects no account balances, no formal journal entry is necessary. Instead, the split is recorded in a memorandum entry such as the following:

Aug. 19	Called in the outstanding $5 par common stock and distributed four shares of $1.25 par common stock for each old share previously outstanding.

A company may engage in a reverse split to decrease the number of shares of stock outstanding. For example, IBM could split its stock 1 for 4. After the split, par value would be $20 ($5 × 4), shares authorized would be 46.875 million (187.5 million/4), and shares issued and outstanding would be 35 million (140 million/4). Reverse splits are unusual.

Similarities and Differences Between Stock Dividends and Stock Splits

Both stock dividends and stock splits increase the number of shares of stock owned per stockholder. Also, neither stock dividends nor stock splits change the investor's total cost of the stock owned or the company's total stockholders' equity.

Consider **Avon Products, Inc.**, whose beauty products are sold in 119 countries primarily by independent sales representatives. Assume that you paid $3,000 to acquire 150 shares of Avon common stock. If Avon distributes a 100% stock dividend, your 150 shares increase to 300, but your total cost is still $3,000. Likewise, if Avon distributes a 2-for-1 stock split, your shares increase in number to 300, but your total cost is unchanged. Neither type of stock action creates taxable income for the investor.

Both stock dividends and stock splits increase the corporation's number of shares of stock issued and outstanding. For example, a 100% stock dividend and a 2-for-1 stock split both double the number of outstanding shares and cut the stock's market price per share in half. They differ in that a stock *dividend* shifts an amount from retained earnings to paid-in capital, leaving the par value per share unchanged. A stock *split* affects no account balances whatsoever. Instead, a stock split changes the par value of the stock. It also increases the number of shares of stock authorized, issued, and outstanding.

Exhibit 9-9 summarizes the effects of dividends and stock splits on total stockholders' equity.

Objective 5

Use different stock values in decision making

Different Values of Stock

The business community refers to several different *stock values* in addition to par value. These values include market value, redemption value, liquidation value, and book value.

EXHIBIT 9-9
Effects of Dividends and Stock Splits on Total Stockholders' Equity

Event	Effect on Total Stockholders' Equity
Declaration of cash dividend	Decrease
Payment of cash dividend	No effect
Declaration of stock dividend	No effect
Distribution of stock dividend	No effect
Stock split	No effect

Source: Adapted from material provided by Beverly Terry.

Market Value

A stock's **market value,** or *market price,* is the price for which a person could buy or sell a share of the stock. The issuing corporation's net income, financial position, and future prospects and the general economic conditions determine market value. Daily newspapers report the market price of many stocks. Corporate annual reports report the high and the low market values of the company's common stock for each quarter of the year. *In almost all cases, stockholders are more concerned about the market value of a stock than about any of the other values discussed next.* In the chapter opening story, IHOP's most recent stock price was quoted at 25, which means that the stock could be sold for, or bought for, $25 per share. The purchase of 100 shares of IHOP stock would cost $2,500 ($25.00 × 100), plus a commission. If you were selling 100 shares of IHOP stock, you would receive cash of $2,500 less a commission. The commission is the fee an investor pays to a stockbroker for buying or selling the stock. The price of a share of IHOP stock has fluctuated from $10 at issuance to a recent high of $26.50.

LEARNING TIP If you buy stock in IBM from another investor, IBM gets no cash. The transaction is a sale between investors. IBM records only the change in stockholder name.

Redemption Value

Preferred stock that requires the company to redeem (pay to retire) the stock at a set price is called *redeemable preferred stock.* The company is *obligated* to redeem the preferred stock. The price the corporation agrees to pay for the stock, which is set when the stock is issued, is called the *redemption value.* Some preferred stock is *callable,* which means that the company may call (pay to retire) the stock if it wishes.

The preferred stock of Pine Industries, Inc., is "callable at the option of the Company at $25 per share." Beginning in 1999, Pine is "required to redeem annually 6,765 shares of the preferred stock ($169,125 annually)." Pine's annual redemption payment to the preferred stockholders will include this redemption value plus any dividends in arrears.

STOP & THINK Suppose you are a financial analyst who follows Pine Industries as a potential investment. In computing Pine's debt ratio, how will you treat the preferred stock at December 31, 1998, and beyond? Give your reason.

Answer: At December 31, 1998, and beyond, you should treat Pine Industries' preferred stock as a liability because starting in 1999, the company is *required* to pay the stockholders to redeem the stock.

Liquidation Value

The *liquidation value,* which applies only to preferred stock, is the amount the corporation agrees to pay the preferred stockholder per share if the company liquidates. Dividends in arrears are added to liquidation value in determining the payment to the preferred stockholders if the company liquidates. Consider the **BF Goodrich Company,** which makes chemicals and aerospace components and sells tires under the Michelin label. BF Goodrich has 2.2 million shares of convertible preferred stock that is stated at "a liquidation value of $50 per share." The balance in BF Goodrich's preferred stock account is thus $110 million (2.2 million shares × $50).

Book Value

The **book value** of a stock is the amount of owners' equity on the company's books for each share of its stock. Corporations often report this amount in their annual reports. If the company has only common stock outstanding, its book value is computed by dividing total stockholders' equity by the number of shares *outstanding.* A company with stockholders' equity of $180,000 and 5,000 shares of common stock outstanding has a book value of $36 per share ($180,000/5,000 shares).

If the company has both preferred and common stock outstanding, the preferred stockholders have the first claim to owners' equity. Ordinarily, preferred stock has a specified liquidation or redemption value. The book value of preferred stock is its redemption value plus any cumulative dividends in arrears on the stock. Its book value *per share* equals the sum of redemption value and any cumulative dividends in arrears divided by the number of preferred shares *outstanding.* After the corporation figures the book value of the preferred shares, it computes the common stock book value per share. The corporation divides the common equity (total stockholders' equity minus preferred equity) by the number of common shares outstanding.

Assume that the company balance sheet reports the following amounts:

Stockholders' Equity	
Preferred stock, 6%, $100 par, 5,000 shares authorized, 400 shares issued	$ 40,000
Paid-in capital in excess of par—preferred	4,000
Common stock, $10 par, 20,000 shares authorized, 5,500 shares issued	55,000
Paid-in capital in excess of par—common	72,000
Retained earnings	85,000
Treasury stock—common, 500 shares at cost	(15,000)
Total stockholders' equity	$241,000

Suppose that four years' (including the current year) cumulative preferred dividends are in arrears and that preferred stock has a redemption value of $130 per share. The book-value-per-share computations for this corporation are as follows:

Preferred:	
Redemption value (400 shares × $130)	$ 52,000
Cumulative dividends ($40,000 × 0.06 × 4)	9,600
Stockholders' equity allocated to preferred	$ 61,600
Book value per share ($61,600/400 shares)	$ 154.00

Common:	
Total stockholders' equity	$241,000
Less stockholders' equity allocated to preferred	(61,600)
Stockholders' equity allocated to common	$179,400
Book value per share [$179,400/5,000 shares outstanding (5,500 shares issued minus 500 treasury shares)]	$ 35.88

BOOK VALUE AND DECISION MAKING How is book value per share used in decision making? Companies negotiating the purchase of a corporation may wish to know the book value of its stock. The book value of stockholders' equity may figure into the negotiated purchase price. Corporations—especially those whose stock is not publicly traded—may buy out a retiring executive, agreeing to pay the book value of the person's stock in the company.

EXHIBIT 9-10
Book Value and Market Value for Three Companies

	Year-End Book Value	Fourth-Quarter Market-Value Range
IHOP Corp.	$11.55	$22.50 – $30.25
Toys "Я" Us................	12.57	$20.50 – $24.38
IBM	40.47	$67.38 – $76.38

Some investors have traditionally compared the book value of a share of a company's stock with the stock's market value. The idea was that a stock selling below its book value was underpriced and thus a good buy. The relationship between book value and market value is far from clear, however, as some investors believe that a company whose stock sells at a price below book value must be experiencing financial difficulty.

Book value is a product of the accounting system, which is based on historical costs. Market value, conversely, depends on investors' subjective outlook for dividends and increases in the stock's value. Exhibit 9-10 contrasts the book values and ranges of market values for the common stocks of three well-known companies. For all three companies, the market value of stock exceeds its book value—a mark of success.

Evaluating Operations: Rate of Return on Total Assets and Rate of Return on Common Stockholders' Equity

Objective 6

Evaluate a company's return on assets and return on stockholders' equity

Investors and creditors are constantly evaluating managers' ability to earn profits. Investors search for companies whose stocks are likely to increase in value. Creditors are interested in profitable companies that can pay their debts. Investment and credit decisions often include a comparison of companies. But a comparison of IHOP Corp.'s net income with the net income of a new company in the restaurant industry simply is not meaningful. IHOP's profits may run into the millions of dollars, which far exceed a new company's net income. Does this fact automatically make IHOP a better investment? Not necessarily. To make relevant comparisons among companies different in size, scope of operations, or any other measure, investors, creditors, and managers use some standard profitability measures, including rate of return on total assets and rate of return on stockholders' equity.

Return on Assets

The **rate of return on total assets,** or simply **return on assets,** measures a company's success in using its assets to earn income for the persons who are financing the business. Creditors have loaned money to the corporation and thus earn interest. Stockholders have invested in the corporation's stock and expect the company to earn net income. The sum of interest expense and net income is the return to the two groups that have financed the corporation's activities, and this is the numerator of the return-on-assets ratio. The denominator is average total assets. Return on assets is computed as follows, using actual data from the 1995 annual report of IHOP Corp. (dollar amounts in thousands of dollars):

$$\text{Rate of return on total assets} = \frac{\text{Net income} + \text{Interest expense}}{\text{Average total assets}}$$

$$= \frac{\$16{,}154 + \$6{,}918}{(\$202{,}553 + \$252{,}057)/2} = \frac{\$23{,}072}{\$227{,}305} = 0.102$$

Net income and interest expense are taken from the income statement. Average total assets is computed from the beginning and ending balance sheets.

Investors use return on assets to compare companies in terms of how well their management earns a return for the people who finance the corporation. By relating the sum of net income and interest expense to average total assets, they have a standard measure that describes the profitability of all types of companies. Brokerage companies such as **Merrill Lynch** and **Paine Webber** often single out particular industries as likely sources of good investments. For example, brokerage analysts may believe that the health-care industry is in a growth phase. These analysts would identify specific health-care companies whose profitabilities are likely to lead the industry and so be sound investments. Return on assets is one measure of profitability.

What is a good rate of return on total assets? There is no single answer to this question because rates of return vary widely by industry. For example, high technology companies earn much higher returns than do utility companies, groceries, and manufacturers of consumer goods such as toothpaste. The Decision Guidelines feature offers some tips for investors on buying the stocks that most fit their needs.

Return on Equity

Rate of return on common stockholders' equity, often called **return on equity,** shows the relationship between net income and average common stockholders' equity. The numerator is net income minus preferred dividends, information taken from the income statement. The denominator is average *common stockholders' equity*—total stockholders' equity minus preferred equity. IHOP Corp.'s rate of return on common stockholders' equity for 1995 is computed as follows (dollar amounts in thousands of dollars):

$$\textbf{Rate of return on common stockholders' equity} = \frac{\textbf{Net income} - \textbf{Preferred dividends}}{\textbf{Average common stockholders' equity}}$$

$$= \frac{\$16{,}154 - \$0}{(\$88{,}299 + \$108{,}297)/2} = \frac{\$16{,}154}{\$98{,}298} = 0.164$$

IHOP Corp. has no preferred stock, so preferred dividends are zero. With no preferred stock outstanding, average *common* stockholders' equity is the same as average *total* equity—the average of the beginning and ending amounts.

IHOP's return on equity (16.4%) is higher than its return on assets (10.2%). This difference results from the interest-expense component of return on assets. Companies such as IHOP borrow at one rate (say, 7%) and invest the funds to earn a higher rate (say, 16%). Borrowing at a lower rate than the return on investments is called *using leverage.* During good times, leverage produces high returns for stockholders. However, too much leverage can make it difficult to pay the interest on the debt. The company's creditors are guaranteed a fixed rate of return on their loans. However, the stockholders have no guarantee that the corporation will earn net income, so their investments are riskier. Consequently, stockholders demand a higher rate of return than do creditors, which explains why return on equity should exceed return on assets. If return on assets is higher than return on equity, the company is in trouble. Interest expense should always be lower than the amount the company earns on its investments.

Investors and creditors use return on common stockholders' equity in much the same way they use return on total assets—to compare companies. The higher the rate of return, the more successful the company. IHOP's 16.4% return on common stockholders' equity would be considered quite good in most industries. Investors also compare a company's return on stockholders' equity with interest rates available in the market. If interest rates are almost as high as return on equity, many investors will lend their money to earn interest. They choose to forgo the extra risk of investing in stock when the rate of return on equity is too low.

Decision Guidelines

Investing in Stock

Investor Decision	Guidelines
Which category of stock to buy for:	
• A safe investment?	Preferred stock is safer than common, but for even more safety, invest in high-grade corporate bonds or government securities.
• Steady dividends?	Cumulative preferred stock. However, the company is not obligated to declare preferred dividends, and the dividends are unlikely to increase.
• Increasing dividends?	Common stock, as long as the company's net income is increasing and the company has adequate cash flow to pay a dividend after meeting all obligations and other cash demands.
• Increasing stock price?	Common stock, but again only if the company's net income and cash flow are increasing.
How to identify a good stock to buy?	There are many ways to pick stock investments. One strategy that works reasonably well is to invest in companies that consistently earn higher rates of return on assets and on equity than competing firms in the same industry. Also, select industries that are expected to grow.

Reporting Stockholders' Equity Transactions on the Statement of Cash Flows

Objective 7

Report stockholders' equity transactions on the statement of cash flows

Many of the transactions discussed in this chapter are reported on the statement of cash flows. Stockholders' equity transactions are *financing activities* because the company is dealing with its owners, the stockholders—the most basic group of people who finance the company. The financing transactions that affect stockholders' equity and cash (and thus appear on the statement of cash flows) fall into three main categories: issuances of stock, repurchases of stock, and dividends.

1. *Issuances of stock* include basic transactions in which a company issues its stock for cash. Most companies, including IHOP Corp., have employee stock ownership plans (ESOPs). In an ESOP, a company issues its stock to employees to increase their stake in the company because employees who own part of a company work hard to help it succeed. Most companies also have executive stock option plans that allow top managers to buy the company's stock at below-market prices. In both ESOPs and executive stock option plans, the transaction is essentially the same as a basic issuance of stock. The company receives cash and issues stock.

2. As we discussed earlier in the chapter, a company can repurchase its stock as treasury stock, or it can buy the stock and retire it. In both cases, the company pays cash to repurchase its own stock. A sale of treasury stock, like issuances of stock, increases the company's cash.

3. Most companies pay cash dividends to their stockholders. Dividend payments are a type of financing transaction because the company is paying its stockholders for the use of their money. In contrast, stock dividends are not reported on the statement of cash flows because the company receives no cash in a stock dividend. Recall that a stock dividend affects no assets or liabilities; it merely rearranges the composition of stockholders' equity.

It is difficult to find any one company that reports all types of financing transactions on its statement of cash flows. The following excerpts are taken from the cash-flow statements of **IHOP Corporation, Campbell Soup Company, Sprint Corporation, Intel Corporation,** and **International Paper Company.** Cash receipts appear as positive amounts and cash payments as negative amounts, denoted by parentheses.

Cash Flows from Financing Activities	
	(In millions)
Proceeds from common stock issued	$ 16.9
Exercise of stock options (sale of stock to executives)	2.6
Proceeds from issuance of stock to employees	38.8
Treasury stock issued (sale of treasury stock)	37.0
Treasury stock purchases	(24.0)
Repurchase and retirement of common stock	(1,034.0)
Dividends paid	(351.5)
Net cash used by financing activities	$(1,314.2)

SUMMARY PROBLEM FOR YOUR REVIEW

1. Use the following accounts and related balances to prepare the classified balance sheet of Whitehall, Inc., at September 30, 19X4. Use the account format of the balance sheet.

Common stock, $1 par, 50,000 shares authorized, 20,000 shares issued	$ 20,000	Long-term note payable	$ 80,000
Dividends payable	4,000	Inventory	85,000
Cash	9,000	Property, plant, and equipment, net	226,000
Accounts payable	28,000	Revenue from donations	18,000
Retained earnings	75,000	Accounts receivable, net	23,000
Paid-in capital in excess of par—common	115,000	Preferred stock, $3.75, no-par, 10,000 shares authorized, 2,000 shares issued	24,000
Treasury stock, common, 1,000 shares at cost	6,000	Accrued liabilities	3,000

2. The balance sheet of Trendline Corporation reported the following at March 31, 19X6, the end of its fiscal year.

Stockholders' Equity	
Preferred stock, 4%, $10 par, 10,000 shares authorized and issued (redemption value, $110,000)	$100,000
Common stock, no-par, $5 stated value, 100,000 shares authorized	250,000
Paid-in capital in excess of par or stated value:	
Common stock	231,500
Retained earnings	395,000
Total stockholders' equity	$976,500

Required

a. Is the preferred stock cumulative or noncumulative? How can you tell?

b. What is the total amount of the annual preferred dividend?

c. How many shares of common stock has the company issued?

d. Compute the book value per share of the preferred and the common stock. No prior-year preferred dividends are in arrears, and Trendline has not yet declared the current-year dividend.

ANSWERS

1.

WHITEHALL, INC.
Balance Sheet
September 30, 19X4

Assets		Liabilities		
Current:		Current:		
Cash	$ 9,000	Accounts payable		$ 28,000
Accounts receivable, net	23,000	Dividends payable		4,000
Inventory	85,000	Accrued liabilities		3,000
Total current assets	117,000	Total current liabilities		35,000
Property, plant and equipment, net	226,000	Long-term note payable		80,000
		Total liabilities		115,000
		Stockholders' Equity		
		Preferred stock, $3.75, no-par, 10,000 shares authorized, 2,000 shares issued	$ 24,000	
		Common stock, $1 par, 50,000 shares authorized, 20,000 shares issued	20,000	
		Paid-in capital in excess of par—common	115,000	
		Retained earnings	75,000	
		Treasury stock, common, 1,000 shares at cost	(6,000)	
		Total stockholders' equity		228,000
Total assets	$343,000	Total liabilities and stockholders' equity		$343,000

2. **a.** The preferred stock is cumulative because it is not specifically labeled otherwise.
   b. Total annual preferred dividend: $4,000 ($100,000 × 0.04).
   c. Common stock issued: 50,000 shares ($250,000/$5 stated value).
   d. Book values per share of preferred and common stock:

Preferred:	
Redemption value	$110,000
Cumulative dividend for current year ($100,000 × 0.04)	4,000
Stockholders' equity allocated to preferred	$114,000
Book value per share ($114,000/10,000 shares)	$ 11.40
Common:	
Total stockholders' equity	$976,500
Less stockholders' equity allocated to preferred	(114,000)
Stockholders' equity allocated to common	$862,500
Book value per share ($862,500/49,000 shares)	$ 17.60

SUMMARY OF LEARNING OBJECTIVES

1. *Explain the advantages and disadvantages of a corporation.* The corporation is the dominant form of business in the United States. Corporations are separate legal entities that exist apart from their owners. The advantages of corporations are their ability to raise capital, continuous life, transferability of ownership, lack of mutual agency, and limited liability of stockholders. The disadvantages of corporations are the separation of ownership from management, double taxation, and government regulation.

2. *Measure the effect of issuing stock on a company's financial position.* Corporations receive the authorization to sell (issue) a certain number of shares of stock. They may issue common or preferred stock, or par or no-par stock. Stock issued above its par value is sold at a *premium;* stock is not issued at a price below its par value.

3. *Describe how treasury stock transactions affect a company.* *Treasury stock* is stock that a corporation has issued and later reacquired. Treasury stock has the same effect as unissued stock: Neither category of stock is outstanding in the hands of shareholders. The purchase of treasury stock decreases the company's assets and stockholders' equity. The sale of treasury stock increases the company's assets and stockholders' equity. Treasury stock is reported on the balance sheet as a contra element of stockholders' equity, often following Retained Earnings.

4. *Account for dividends and measure their impact on a company.* Companies may issue dividends in either cash or stock. Once cash dividends have been *declared,* the company incurs a liability. That liability is paid off when the company pays the cash dividend. Preferred stock has priority over common stock when dividends are declared. The preferred dividend amount may be stated as a dollar value or as a percentage of the preferred stock's par value. In addition, the owners of *cumulative* preferred stock must receive all dividends in arrears before the corporation can pay dividends to the common stockholders.

A *stock dividend* is a proportional distribution by a corporation of its own stock to its stockholders. Stock dividends increase the stock account and decrease Retained Earnings. Because both these accounts are elements of stockholders' equity, total stockholders' equity is unchanged by a stock dividend. A *stock split* is an increase in the number of authorized, issued, and outstanding shares of stock, coupled with a proportionate reduction in the stock's par value. A stock split affects no account balances and therefore leaves total stockholders' equity unchanged.

5. *Use different stock values in decision making.* A stock's *market value* is the price for which a person could buy or sell a share of the stock. The price a company agrees to pay for a stock when buying it back is the stock's *redemption value. Liquidation value,* which applies only to preferred stock, is the amount the corporation agrees to pay the preferred stockholders per share if the corporation liquidates. A stock's *book value* is the amount of owners' equity on the company's books for each share of its preferred stock or common stock.

6. *Evaluate a company's return on assets and return on stockholders' equity.* Return on assets and return on stockholders' equity are two measures of a corporation's profitability. *Return on assets* measures a company's success in using its assets to earn income for all parties who finance the business. *Return on equity* shows the relationship between net income and average common stockholders' equity to measure the company's ability to earn net income for the common stockholders. A healthy company's return on equity will exceed its return on assets.

7. *Report stockholders' equity transactions on the statement of cash flows.* Three main financing categories that affect stockholders' equity, and thus appear on the statement of cash flows, are (1) issuances of stock, (2) repurchases of stock, and (3) dividends.

ACCOUNTING VOCABULARY

authorization of stock *(p. 425).*
board of directors *(p. 421).*
book value (of a stock) *(p. 446).*
bylaws *(p. 421).*
chairperson *(p. 422).*
charter *(p. 420).*
common stock *(p. 424).*
contributed capital *(p. 423).*
convertible preferred stock *(p. 430).*
cumulative preferred stock *(p. 439).*
deficit *(p. 437).*
dividends *(p. 424).*
double taxation *(p. 421).*
incorporators *(p. 421).*
legal capital *(p. 425).*
limited liability *(p. 420).*
market value (of a stock) *(p. 445).*
outstanding stock *(p. 423).*
paid-in capital *(p. 423).*
par value *(p. 425).*
preferred stock *(p. 424).*
president *(p. 422).*
rate of return on common stockholders' equity *(p. 448).*
rate of return on total assets *(p. 447).*
retained earnings *(p. 423).*
return on assets *(p. 447).*
return on equity *(p. 448).*
shareholder *(p. 420).*
stated value *(p. 425).*
stock *(p. 420).*
stock dividend *(p. 440).*
stockholder *(p. 420).*
stockholders' equity *(p. 422).*
stock split *(p. 443).*
treasury stock *(p. 433).*

QUESTIONS

1. Why is a corporation called a "creature of the state"? Briefly outline the steps in the organization of a corporation.
2. Identify the characteristics of a corporation, and explain why corporations face a tax disadvantage.
3. Suppose H. J. Heinz Company issued 1,000 shares of its 3.65%, $100-par preferred stock for $120 per share. How much would this transaction increase the company's paid-in capital? How much would it increase Heinz's retained earnings? How much would it increase Heinz's annual cash dividend payments?
4. Rank the following accounts in the order they would appear on the balance sheet: Common Stock, Equipment, Preferred Stock, Retained Earnings, Dividends Payable. Also, give each account's balance sheet classification.
5. Briefly discuss the three important dates for a dividend.
6. As a preferred stockholder, would you rather own cumulative or noncumulative preferred? If all other factors are the same, would the corporation rather the preferred stock be cumulative or noncumulative? Give your reason.

7. Distinguish between the market value of stock and the book value of stock. Which is more important to investors?
8. Why should a healthy company's rate of return on stockholders' equity exceed its rate of return on total assets?
9. Ametek, Inc., reported a cash balance of $73 million and a retained earnings balance of $162.5 million. Explain how Ametek can have so much more retained earnings than cash. In your answer, identify the nature of retained earnings and state how it ties to cash.
10. A friend of yours receives a stock dividend on an investment. He believes that stock dividends are the same as cash dividends. Explain why the two are not the same.
11. What is the difference between a small stock dividend and a large stock dividend? What is the main difference in accounting for small and large stock dividends?
12. What effect does the purchase of treasury stock have on the (a) assets, (b) issued stock, and (c) outstanding stock of the corporation?
13. What is the normal balance of the Treasury Stock account? What type of account is Treasury Stock? Where is Treasury Stock reported on the balance sheet?
14. What effect does the purchase and retirement of common stock have on the (a) assets, (b) issued stock, and (c) outstanding stock of the corporation?

EXERCISES

Organizing a corporation **(Obj. 1)**

E9-1 Cathy Whittle and Angela Lane are opening a limousine service to be named W&A Transportation Enterprises. They need outside capital, so they plan to organize the business as a corporation. Because your office is in the same building, they come to you for advice. Write a memorandum informing them of the steps in forming a corporation. Identify specific documents used in this process, and name the different parties involved in the ownership and management of a corporation.

Issuing stock and measuring paid-in capital **(Obj. 2)**

E9-2 Exhibition Software made the following stock issuance transactions:

Feb. 19	Issued 1,000 shares of $1.50 par common stock for cash of $10.50 per share.
Mar. 3	Sold 300 shares of $4.50, no-par Class A preferred stock for $12,000 cash.
11	Received inventory valued at $23,000 and equipment with market value of $11,000 for 3,300 shares of the $1.50 par common stock.
15	Issued 1,000 shares of 5%, no-par Class B preferred stock with stated value of $50 per share. The issue price was cash of $60 per share.

Required

1. Journalize the transactions. Explanations are not required.
2. How much paid-in capital did these transactions generate for Exhibition Software?

Recording issuance of stock **(Obj. 2)**

E9-3 The balance sheet of Gulf Resources & Chemical Corporation (as adapted) reported the following stockholders' equity. Gulf has two separate classes of preferred stock, labeled Series A and Series B. All dollar amounts, except for per-share amounts, are given in thousands.

GULF RESOURCES & CHEMICAL CORPORATION
Stockholders' Investment
[same as Stockholders' Equity]

Preferred stock, $1 par, authorized 4,000,000 shares (Note 7)	
Series A	$ 58
Series B	376
Common stock, $0.10 par, authorized 20,000,000, [issued and] outstanding 9,130,000 shares	913
Capital in excess of par	75,542

Note 7. Preferred Stock:

	Shares [Issued and] Outstanding
Series A	58,000
Series B	376,000

Required

Assume that the Series A preferred stock was issued for $5 cash per share, the Series B preferred was issued for $10 cash per share, and the common was issued for cash of $72,839. Make the summary journal entries to record issuance of all the Gulf Resources stock. Explanations are not required. After you record these entries, what are the balances in the three stock accounts? What is the balance of Capital in Excess of Par?

Stockholders' equity section of a balance sheet ***(Obj. 2)***

E9-4 The charter of Aladdin Corporation authorizes the issuance of 5,000 shares of Class A preferred stock, 1,000 shares of Class B preferred stock, and 10,000 shares of common stock. During a two-month period, Aladdin completed these stock-issuance transactions:

June 23	Issued 1,000 shares of $1 par common stock for cash of $12.50 per share.
July 2	Sold 300 shares of $4.50, no-par Class A preferred stock for $20,000 cash.
12	Received inventory valued at $25,000 and equipment with market value of $16,000 for 3,300 shares of the $1 par common stock.
17	Issued 1,000 shares of 5%, no-par Class B preferred stock with stated value of $50 per share. The issue price was cash of $60 per share.

Required

Prepare the stockholders' equity section of the Aladdin balance sheet for the transactions given in this exercise. Retained earnings has a balance of $172,000.

Measuring the paid-in capital of a corporation ***(Obj. 2)***

E9-5 Miranda Corp. was recently organized. The company issued common stock to an attorney who gave Lee Miranda legal services of $5,000 to help him organize the corporation. It issued common stock to another person in exchange for his patent with a market value of $40,000. In addition, Miranda Corp. received cash both for 1,000 shares of its preferred stock at $110 per share and for 26,000 shares of its common stock at $15 per share. The city of Columbus donated 50 acres of land to the company as a plant site. The market value of the land was $600,000. During the first year of operations, Miranda Corp. earned net income of $85,000 and declared a cash dividend of $26,000. Without making journal entries, determine the total paid-in capital created by these transactions.

Stockholders' equity section of a balance sheet ***(Obj. 2, 3)***

E9-6 Pay-n-Sav, Inc., has the following selected account balances at June 30, 19X7. Prepare the stockholders' equity section of the company's balance sheet.

Inventory	$112,000	Common stock, no-par with $1 stated value, 500,000 shares authorized, 120,000 shares issued	$120,000
Machinery and equipment, net	109,000	Accumulated depreciation—machinery and equipment	62,000
Preferred stock, 5%, $20 par, 20,000 shares authorized, 11,000 shares issued	220,000	Retained earnings	119,000
Paid-in capital in excess of par—common stock	88,000	Accounts receivable, net	43,000
Treasury stock, common, 2,200 shares at cost	5,000	Revenue from donations	81,000

Recording treasury stock transactions and measuring their effects on stockholders' equity ***(Obj. 3)***

E9-7 Journalize the following transactions of Larry's Shoes, a regional chain of discount shoe stores:

May 19	Issued 20,000 shares of no-par common stock at $15 per share.
Aug. 22	Purchased 900 shares of treasury stock at $14 per share.
Dec. 11	Sold 200 shares of treasury stock at $16 per share.
Dec. 28	Sold 100 shares of treasury stock at $13 per share.

What was the overall effect of the two December transactions on the company's stockholders' equity?

Inferring transactions from a company's stockholders' equity ***(Obj. 2, 3, 4, 5)***

E9-8 **Chrysler Corporation** recently reported the following shareholders' equity section on its balance sheet.

(Dollars and shares in millions) **Shareholders' Equity**	**December 31** **19X5**	**19X4**
Preferred stock—$1 per share par value; authorized 20.0 shares; Series A Convertible Preferred Stock; issued and outstanding: 1995 and 1994—0.1 and 1.7 shares, respectively (aggregate liquidation preference $68 million and $863 million, respectively)	$ *	$ 2
Common stock—$1 per share par value; authorized 1,000.0 shares; issued: 1995 and 1994—408.2 and 364.1 shares, respectively	408	364
Additional paid-in capital	5,506	5,536
Retained earnings	6,280	5,006
Treasury stock, common—at cost: 1995—29.9 shares; 1994—9.0 shares	(1,235)	(214)
Total Shareholders' Equity	10,959	10,694
Total Liabilities and Shareholders' Equity	$53,756	$49,539

*Less than $1 million

Required

1. Identify two likely transactions that caused Chrysler's preferred stock to decrease during 19X5.
2. Identify two likely transactions that caused Chrysler's common stock to increase during 19X5.
3. How many shares of Chrysler common stock were outstanding at December 31, 19X5?
4. Assume that during 19X5, Chrysler sold no treasury stock. What average price per share did Chrysler pay for the treasury stock the company purchased during the year? During 19X5, the market price of Chrysler's common stock ranged from a low of $38.25 to a high of $58.13. Compare the average price Chrysler paid for its treasury stock during 19X5 to the range of market prices during the year.
5. Chrysler's net income during 19X5 was $2,025 million. How much were dividends and other adjustments to retained earnings during the year?

Computing dividends on preferred and common stock ***(Obj. 4)***

E9-9 The following elements of stockholders' equity are adapted from the balance sheet of **Gulf Resources & Chemical Corporation.** All dollar amounts, except the dividends per share, are given in thousands.

GULF RESOURCES & CHEMICAL CORPORATION
Stockholders' Equity

Preferred stock, cumulative and nonparticipating, $1 par (Note 7)	
Series A, 58,000 shares issued	$ 58
Series B, 376,000 shares issued	376
Common stock, $0.10 par, 9,130,000 shares issued	913

Note 7. Preferred Stock:

	Designated Annual Cash Dividend per Share
Series A	$0.20
Series B	1.30

Assume that the Series A preferred has preference over the Series B preferred and that the company has paid all preferred dividends through 19X4.

Required

Compute the dividends to both series of preferred and to common for 19X5 and 19X6 if total dividends are $0 in 19X5 and $1,100,000 in 19X6. Round to the nearest dollar.

Recording dividends and reporting stockholders' equity ***(Obj. 4)***

E9-10 Groesbeck, Inc., is authorized to issue 100,000 shares of $1 par common stock. The company issued 50,000 shares at $4 per share, and all 50,000 shares are outstanding. When the retained earnings balance was $150,000, Groesbeck declared and distributed a 50% stock dividend. Later, Groesbeck declared and paid a $0.30 per share cash dividend.

Required

1. Journalize the declaration and distribution of the stock dividend.
2. Journalize the declaration and payment of the cash dividend.
3. Prepare the stockholders' equity section of the balance sheet after both dividends.
4. Which dividend decreased total stockholders' equity? By how much? Use the accounting equation to answer this question. Groesbeck's total assets prior to the dividends stood at $900,000, paid-in capital was $200,000, and retained earnings were $150,000.

Recording a stock dividend and reporting stockholders' equity ***(Obj. 4)***

E9-11 The stockholders' equity for Cohen Jewelry Corporation on September 30, 19X4—end of the company's fiscal year—is as follows:

Stockholders' Equity	
Common stock, $10 par, 100,000 shares authorized, 50,000 shares issued	$500,000
Paid-in capital in excess of par—common	50,000
Retained earnings	340,000
Total stockholders' equity	$890,000

On November 16, the market price of Cohen's common stock was $16 per share, and the company declared a 10% stock dividend. Cohen issued the dividend shares on November 30.

Required

1. Journalize the declaration and distribution of the stock dividend.
2. Prepare the stockholders' equity section of the balance sheet after the issuance of the stock dividend.
3. Why is total stockholders' equity unchanged by the stock dividend?

Measuring the effects of stock issuance, dividends, and treasury stock transactions ***(Obj. 2, 3, 4)***

E9-12 Identify the effects of these transactions on total stockholders' equity. Each transaction is independent.

a. Issuance of 50,000 shares of $10 par common at $16.50.

b. 10% stock dividend. Before the dividend, 500,000 shares of $1 par common stock were outstanding; market value was $7.625 at the time of the dividend.

c. Sale of 600 shares of $5 par treasury stock for $9.00 per share. Cost of the treasury stock was $6.00 per share.

d. A 3-for-1 stock split. Prior to the split, 60,000 shares of $4.50 par common were outstanding.

e. Purchase of 1,500 shares of treasury stock (par value $0.50) at $4.25 per share.

f. A 50% stock dividend. Before the dividend, 1,000,000 shares of $2 par common stock were outstanding; market value was $13.75 at the time of the dividend.

Reporting stockholders' equity after a stock split ***(Obj. 4)***

E9-13 Mad Dog Showbiz, Inc., had the following stockholders' equity at May 31:

Common stock, $2 par, 200,000 shares authorized, 50,000 shares issued	$100,000
Paid-in capital in excess of par	180,000
Retained earnings	210,000
Total stockholders' equity	$490,000

On June 7, Mad Dog Showbiz split its $2 par common stock 2 for 1. Make the memorandum entry to record the stock split, and prepare the stockholders' equity section of the balance sheet immediately after the split.

Measuring the book value per share of preferred and common stock ***(Obj. 5)***

E9-14 The balance sheet of Grudnitski Corporation reported the following, with all amounts, including shares, in thousands:

Redeemable preferred stock; redemption value $6,362	$ 4,860
Common stockholders' equity, 11,120 shares issued and outstanding	216,788
Total stockholders' equity	$221,648

Assume that Grudnitski has paid preferred dividends for the current year and all prior years (no dividends in arrears) and that the company has 100 shares of preferred stock outstanding.

Required

1. Compute the book value per share of the preferred stock and the common stock.
2. Compute the book value per share of the preferred stock and the common stock, assuming that three years' preferred dividends (including dividends for the current year) are in arrears. The preferred stock dividend rate is 6 percent.
3. Grudnitski Corporation's common stock recently traded at market value of $17.87. Discuss two ways of interpreting the relationship between the stock's book value and market value.

Evaluating profitability ***(Obj. 6)***

E9-15 Stratton, Inc., reported these figures for 19X7 and 19X6:

	19X7	19X6
Income statement:		
Interest expense	$ 9,400,000	$ 7,100,000
Net income	22,000,000	18,700,000
Balance sheet:		
Total assets	351,000,000	317,000,000
Preferred stock, $2.30, no-par, 100,000 shares issued and outstanding	2,500,000	2,500,000
Common stockholders' equity	164,000,000	151,000,000
Total stockholders' equity	166,500,000	153,500,000

Compute Stratton's rate of return on total assets and rate of return on common stockholders' equity for 19X7. Do these rates of return suggest strength or weakness? Give your reason.

Reporting investing and financing transactions on the statement of cash flows ***(Obj. 7)***

E9-16 **General Motors Corporation** included the following items on its statement of cash flows for 19X5 (amounts in millions):

Cash dividends paid to stockholders	$ 1,328
Decrease in long-term debt	9,636
Expenditures for real estate, plants, and equipment	6,351
Expenditures for special tools	3,726
Increase in long-term debt	12,130
Investment in [other] companies	616
Net increase in short-term loans payable	6,088

Proceeds from disposals of real estate, plants, and equipment	$ 541
Proceeds from issuing common stock	505
Proceeds from the sale of various assets	183
Repurchases of common and preferred stocks	1,681

Required

1. Show how General Motors reported each of these items on its 19X5 statement of cash flows—as a cash flow from investing activities or as a cash flow from financing activities. Report cash payments in parentheses, and list items in order of decreasing amounts.
2. Write a brief description of the three largest financing cash flows in your own words.

CHALLENGE EXERCISES

Analyzing the effects of stockholders' equity transactions ***(Obj. 2, 4)***

E9-17 Wal-Mart Stores, Inc., reported these comparative stockholders' equity data (amounts in thousands except par value per share):

	January 31, 19X2	19X1
Common stock ($0.10-par value per share)	$ 114,903	$ 114,228
Capital in excess of par value	625,669	415,586
Retained earnings	6,249,138	4,835,710

During 19X2, Wal-Mart completed these transactions and events:

a. Net income, $1,608,476.
b. Cash dividends, $195,048.
c. Issuance of stock for cash, 914 shares, $21,025.
d. Issuance of stock to purchase other companies (Wal-Mart debited the Investments account), 5,842 shares, $189,733.

Required

Without making journal entries, show how Wal-Mart's 19X2 transactions and events accounted for the changes in the stockholders' equity accounts. For each stockholders' equity account, start with the January 31, 19X1, balance and work toward the balance at January 31, 19X2.

Analyzing the effects of a stock dividend and a stock split ***(Obj. 2, 4)***

E9-18 Van Kamp Engineering Associates began 19X8 with 3 million shares of $1 par common stock issued and outstanding. Beginning capital in excess of par was $6.4 million, and retained earnings were $9.7 million. In March 19X8, Van Kamp issued 50,000 shares of stock at $50 per share. 19X8 was an exceptional year for Van Kamp. The company's stock price reached an all-time high of $95 late in October. Van Kamp split the stock 2 for 1. Then in December, when the stock's market price was $45 per share, the board of directors declared a 2% stock dividend, distributable in January 19X9.

Required

Without making journal entries, show the balance in each stockholders' equity account at December 31, 19X8. Use the following format for your answer, and show all computations.

	Common Stock	Common Stock Dividend Distributable	Capital in Excess of Par	Retained Earnings	Total Stockholders' Equity
Balance Dec. 31, 19X7	$3,000,000	$ —	$6,400,000	$9,700,000	$19,100,000
Issuance of stock					
Stock split					
Stock dividend					
Balance Dec. 31, 19X8	$	$	$	$	$21,600,000

PROBLEMS

(GROUP A)

Explaining the features of a corporation's stock ***(Obj. 1)***

P9-1A Answer the following questions about a company's stockholders' equity.

1. Why are capital stock and retained earnings shown separately in the shareholders' equity section of the balance sheet?

2. Lynn Liu, major shareholder of L-S, Inc., proposes to give some land she owns to the company in exchange for common shares in L-S. What challenge does L-S, Inc., face in recording the transaction?
3. Preferred shares generally are preferred with respect to dividends and on liquidation. Why would investors buy common stock when preferred stock is available?
4. What does it mean if the liquidation value of a company's preferred stock is greater than its market value?
5. Suppose you own 100 shares of stock in Carta Corporation and someone offers to buy your shares for their book value. Under what circumstances would you accept the offer? Under what circumstances would you *not* accept the offer?

Recording corporate transactions and preparing the stockholders' equity section of the balance sheet
(Obj. 2)

P9-2A The partners who own Barcus & Nixon wished to avoid the unlimited personal liability of the partnership form of business, so they incorporated as B&N Exploration, Inc. The charter from the state of Oklahoma authorizes the corporation to issue 10,000 shares of 6%, $100 par preferred stock and 250,000 shares of no-par common stock with a stated value of $5 per share. In its first month, B&N Exploration completed the following transactions:

Dec.	3	Issued 500 shares of common stock to the promoter for assistance with issuance of the common stock. The promotional fee was $5,000. Debit the asset account Organization Cost.
	3	Issued 5,100 shares of common stock to Barcus and 3,800 shares to Nixon in return for cash.
	7	Received land valued at $160,000 as a donation from the city of McAlester.
	12	Issued 1,000 shares of preferred stock to acquire a patent with a market value of $110,000.
	22	Issued 1,500 shares of common stock for $10 cash per share.

Required

1. Record the transactions in the journal.
2. Prepare the stockholders' equity section of the B&N Exploration, Inc., balance sheet at December 31. The ending balance of Retained Earnings is $31,300.

Preparing the stockholders' equity section of the balance sheet
(Obj. 2, 4)

P9-3A The following is stockholders' equity information for Human Touch, Incorporated:

Human Touch's charter authorizes the company to issue 10,000 shares of $2.50 preferred stock with par value of $100 and 120,000 shares of no-par common stock. The company issued 1,000 shares of the preferred stock at $104 per share. It issued 40,000 shares of the common stock for a total of $220,000. The company's retained earnings balance at the beginning of 19X3 was $41,000, and net income for the year was $90,000. During 19X3, Human Touch declared the specified dividend on preferred and a $0.50 per share dividend on common. Preferred dividends for 19X2 were in arrears.

Required

Prepare the stockholders' equity section of Human Touch, Incorporated's balance sheet at December 31, 19X3. Show the computation of all amounts. Entries are not required.

Purchasing treasury stock to fight off a takeover of the corporation
(Obj. 3)

P9-4A Nogales Corporation is positioned ideally in its line of business. Located in Yuma, Arizona, Nogales is the only company between Texas and California with reliable sources for its imported gifts. The company does a brisk business with specialty stores such as Pier 1 Imports. Nogales's recent success has made the company a prime target for a takeover. An investment group from Toronto is attempting to buy 51% of Nogales's outstanding stock against the wishes of Nogales's board of directors. Board members are convinced that the Toronto investors would sell the most desirable pieces of the business and leave little of value.

At the most recent board meeting, several suggestions were advanced to fight off the hostile takeover bid. The suggestion with the most promise is to purchase a huge quantity of treasury stock. Nogales has the cash to carry out this plan.

Required

1. Suppose you are a significant stockholder of Nogales Corporation. Write a memorandum to explain for the board how the purchase of treasury stock would make it more difficult for the Toronto group to take over Nogales. Include in your memo a discussion of the effect that purchasing treasury stock would have on stock outstanding and on the size of the corporation.
2. Suppose Nogales management is successful in fighting off the takeover bid and later sells the treasury stock at prices greater than the purchase price. Explain what effect these sales will have on assets, stockholders' equity, and net income.

Measuring the effects of stock issuance, treasury stock, and dividend transactions on stockholders' equity
(Obj. 2, 3, 4)

P9-5A The corporate charter of McNamara Associates, Inc., granted by the state of New Jersey, authorizes the company to issue 1,000,000 shares of $1 par common stock and 100,000 shares of $50 par preferred stock.

In its initial public offering during 19X2, McNamara Associates, Inc., issued 500,000 shares of its $1 par common stock for $6.50 per share. Over the next five years, McNamara's common stock price increased in value, and the company issued 200,000 more shares at prices ranging from $7 to $11. The average issue price of these shares was $9.25.

During 19X4, the price of McNamara's common stock dropped to $8, and McNamara purchased 30,000 shares of its common stock for the treasury. After the market price of the common stock increased in 19X5, McNamara sold 20,000 shares of the treasury stock for $9 per share.

During the five years 19X2–19X6, McNamara earned net income of $295,000 and declared and paid cash dividends of $119,000. Stock dividends of $110,000 were distributed to the stockholders in 19X3, with $14,000 transferred to common stock and $96,000 transferred to additional paid-in capital. At December 31, 19X6, total assets of the company are $8,240,000, and liabilities add up to $3,024,000.

Required

Show the computation of McNamara's total stockholders' equity at December 31, 19X6. Present detailed computations of each element of stockholders' equity.

Analyzing the stockholders' equity and dividends of a corporation ***(Obj. 2, 4)***

P9-6A The purpose of this problem is to familiarize you with the information in the financial statement of a real company, in this case, **U and I Group.** U and I, which makes food products and livestock feeds, included the following stockholders' equity on its year-end balance sheet at February 28:

Stockholders' Equity	(In thousands)
Voting Preferred stock, 5.5% cumulative—par value $23 per share; authorized 100,000 shares in each class:	
Class A—issued 75,473 shares	$ 1,736
Class B—issued 92,172 shares	2,120
Common stock—par value $5 per share; authorized 5,000,000 shares; issued 2,870,950 shares	14,355
[Additional] Paid-in Capital	5,548
Retained earnings	8,336
	$32,095

Required

1. Identify the different issues of stock U and I has outstanding.
2. Give the summary entries to record issuance of all the U and I stock. Assume that all the stock was issued for cash and that the additional paid-in capital applies to the common stock. Explanations are not required.
3. Suppose U and I passed its preferred dividends for one year. Would the company have to pay those dividends in arrears before paying dividends to the common stockholders? Give your reason.
4. What amount of preferred dividends must U and I declare and pay each year to avoid having preferred dividends in arrears?
5. Assume that preferred dividends are in arrears for 19X8.
   a. Write Note 5 of the February 28, 19X8, financial statements to disclose the dividends in arrears.
   b. Record the declaration of a $450,000 dividend in the year ended February 28, 19X9. An explanation is not required.

Measuring the effects of dividend and treasury stock transactions on a company ***(Obj. 3, 4)***

P9-7A Crystal Fresh, Inc., completed the following selected transactions during 19X6:

Jan. 21	Split common stock 3 for 1 by calling in the 10,000 shares of $15 par common and issuing new stock in its place.
Feb. 6	Declared a cash dividend on the 10,000 shares of $2.25, no-par preferred stock. Declared a $0.20 per share dividend on the common stock outstanding. The date of record was February 27, and the payment date was March 20.
Mar. 20	Paid the cash dividends.
Apr. 18	Declared a 50% stock dividend on the common stock to holders of record on April 30, with distribution set for May 30. The market value of the common stock was $15 per share.
May 30	Issued the stock dividend shares.
June 18	Purchased 2,000 shares of the company's own common stock at $12 per share.
Nov. 14	Sold 800 shares of treasury common stock for $10 per share.
Dec. 22	Sold 700 shares of treasury common stock for $16 per share.

Required

Analyze each transaction in terms of its effect on the accounting equation of Crystal Fresh, Inc.

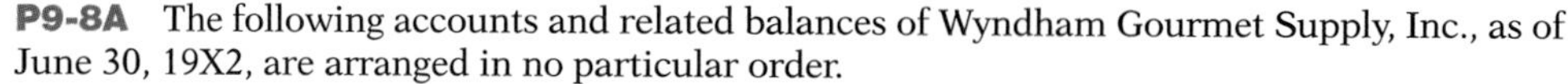

Preparing a corporation balance sheet; measuring profitability
(Obj. 3, 6)

P9-8A The following accounts and related balances of Wyndham Gourmet Supply, Inc., as of June 30, 19X2, are arranged in no particular order.

Cash	$ 13,000	Interest expense	$ 6,100
Accounts receivable, net	24,000	Property, plant, and equipment, net	247,000
Paid-in capital in excess of par—common	19,000	Common stock, $1 par, 500,000 shares authorized, 236,000 shares issued	236,000
Accrued liabilities	26,000	Prepaid expenses	10,000
Long-term note payable	72,000	Revenue from donation	6,000
Inventory	139,000	Common stockholders' equity, June 30, 19X1	322,000
Dividends payable	9,000	Net income	31,000
Retained earnings	?	Total assets, June 30, 19X1	504,000
Accounts payable	31,000	Treasury stock, common 18,000 shares at cost	22,000
Trademark, net	9,000	Goodwill, net	14,000
Preferred stock, $0.20, no-par, 10,000 shares authorized and issued	27,000		

Required

1. Prepare the company's classified balance sheet in the account format at June 30, 19X2.
2. Compute rate of return on total assets and rate of return on common stockholders' equity for the year ended June 30, 19X2.
3. Do these rates of return suggest strength or weakness? Give your reason.
4. How will what you learned in this problem help you evaluate an investment?

Analyzing the statement of cash flows
(Obj. 7)

P9-9A The statement of cash flows of **Ford Motor Company** reported the following for the year ended December 31, 19X5:

Cash flows from financing activities—amounts in millions:	
Cash dividends [declared and paid]	$(1,559)
Issuance of common stock	601
Changes in short-term debt	6,297
Proceeds from issuance of other debt	24,154
Principal payments on debt	(11,664)
Redemption of preferred stock	(1,875)

Required

1. Make the journal entry that Ford used to record each of these transactions.
2. From these transactions, would you expect Ford's total assets, total liabilities, and total stockholders' equity to have grown or shrunk during 19X5? Ford's net income for 19X5 was $4,139 million. State the reasoning behind your answer.

(GROUP B)

Explaining the features of a corporation's stock
(Obj. 1)

P9-1B Answer the following questions about a corporation's stockholders' equity.

1. Why do so many businesses organize as corporations if they have to pay an additional layer of income tax?
2. How is preferred stock similar to common stock? How is preferred stock similar to debt?
3. What makes convertible preferred stock more valuable than nonconvertible preferred stock? Name two economic benefits that an investor hopes to gain by purchasing convertible preferred stock.
4. MR Designs purchased treasury stock for $50,000 and a year later sold it for $65,000. Explain to the manager of MR Designs why the $15,000 excess is not profit to be reported on the company's income statement.
5. As an investor, would you prefer to receive cash dividends or stock dividends? Explain your reasoning.

Recording corporate transactions and preparing the stockholders' equity section of the balance sheet
(Obj. 2)

P9-2B The partnership of Chiu and Bong needed additional capital to expand into new markets, so the business incorporated as CB, Inc. The charter from the state of Oregon authorizes CB, Inc., to issue 50,000 shares of 6%, $100 par preferred stock and 100,000 shares of no-par common stock with a stated value of $5 per share. In its first month, CB, Inc., completed the following transactions:

Dec. 2 Issued 300 shares of common stock to the promoter for assistance with issuance of the common stock. The promotional fee was $1,800. Debit the asset account Organization Cost.

Dec.	2	Issued 9,000 shares of common stock to Chiu and 12,000 shares to Bong in return for cash.
	8	Received a parcel of land valued at $92,000 as a donation from the city of Portland.
	10	Issued 400 shares of preferred stock to acquire a patent with a market value of $50,000.
	16	Issued 2,000 shares of common stock for cash of $12,000.

Required

1. Record the transactions in the journal.
2. Prepare the stockholders' equity section of the CB, Inc., balance sheet at December 31. The ending balance of Retained Earnings is $33,100.

Preparing the stockholders' equity section of the balance sheet
(Obj. 2, 4)

P9-3B The following summary provides the information needed to prepare the stockholders' equity section of the Business Pro, Inc., balance sheet.

Business Pro's charter authorizes the company to issue 5,000 shares of 5%, $100 par preferred stock and 500,000 shares of no-par common stock. Business Pro issued 1,000 shares of the preferred stock at $105 per share. It issued 100,000 shares of the common stock for $400,000. The company's retained earnings balance at the beginning of 19X4 was $73,000. Net income for 19X4 was $80,000, and the company declared a 5% cash dividend on preferred stock for 19X4. Preferred dividends for 19X3 were in arrears.

Required

Prepare the stockholders' equity section of Business Pro's balance sheet at December 31, 19X4. Show the computation of all amounts. Entries are not required.

Using stock dividends to fight off a takeover of the corporation
(Obj. 4)

P9-4B Weberg Corporation is positioned ideally in the clothing business. Located in Scranton, Pennsylvania, Weberg is the only company with a distribution network for its imported goods. The company does a brisk business with specialty stores such as Bloomingdale's, I. Magnin, and Bonwit Teller. Weberg's recent success has made the company a prime target for a takeover. Against the wishes of Weberg's board of directors, an investment group from Boston is attempting to buy 51% of Weberg's outstanding stock. Board members are convinced that the Boston investors would sell off the most desirable pieces of the business and leave little of value.

At the most recent board meeting, several suggestions were advanced to fight off the hostile takeover bid. One suggestion is to increase the stock outstanding by distributing a 100% stock dividend.

Required

Suppose you are a significant stockholder of Weberg Corporation. Write a short memo explaining to the board whether distributing the stock dividend would make it more difficult or less difficult for the investor group to take over Weberg Corporation. Include in your memo a discussion of the effect the stock dividend would have on assets, liabilities, and total stockholders' equity—that is, the dividend's effect on the size of the corporation.

Measuring the effects of stock issuance, treasury stock, and dividend transactions on stockholders' equity
(Obj. 2, 3, 4)

P9-5B The corporate charter of U.S. Ribbon Company, granted by the state of New York, authorizes the company to issue 5,000,000 shares of $1 par common stock and 50,000 shares of $50 par preferred stock.

In its initial public offering during 19X1, U.S. Ribbon issued 1,000,000 shares of its $1 par common stock for $4.50 per share. Over the next five years, U.S. Ribbon's stock price increased in value and the company issued 400,000 more shares at prices ranging from $6 to $10.75. The average issue price of these shares was $8.50.

During 19X3, the price of U.S. Ribbon's common stock dropped to $7, and the company purchased 60,000 shares of its common stock for the treasury. After the market price of the common stock increased in 19X4, U.S. Ribbon sold 40,000 shares of the treasury stock for $8 per share.

During the five years 19X1–19X5, U.S. Ribbon earned net income of $1,590,000 and declared and paid cash dividends of $640,000. Stock dividends of $220,000 were distributed to the stockholders in 19X4, with $35,000 transferred to common stock and $185,000 transferred to additional paid-in capital. At December 31, 19X5, the company has total assets of $15,100,000 and total liabilities of $6,350,000.

Required

Show the computation of U.S. Ribbon's total stockholders' equity at December 31, 19X5. Present detailed computations of each element of stockholders' equity.

Analyzing the stockholders' equity of a corporation
(Obj. 2, 4)

P9-6B The purpose of this problem is to familiarize you with the information contained in the financial statements of a real company. **Bethlehem Steel Corporation** is one of the nation's largest steel companies. Bethlehem included the following stockholders' equity on its balance sheet:

Stockholders' Equity	($ Millions)
Preferred stock—	
Authorized 20,000,000 shares in each class; issued:	
$5.00 Cumulative Convertible Preferred Stock, at $50.00 stated value, 2,500,000 shares	$ 125
$2.50 Cumulative Convertible Preferred Stock, at $25.00 stated value, 4,000,000 shares	100
Common stock—$8 par value— Authorized 80,000,000 shares; issued 48,308,516 shares	621
Retained earnings	529
	$1,375

Observe that Bethlehem reports no Paid-in Capital in Excess of Par or Stated Value. Instead, the company reports those items in the stock accounts.

Required

1. Identify the different issues of stock Bethlehem has outstanding.
2. Which class of stock did Bethlehem issue at par or stated value, and which class did it issue above par or stated value?
3. Suppose Bethlehem passed its preferred dividends for one year. Would the company have to pay these dividends in arrears before paying dividends to the common stockholders? Give your reason.
4. What amount of preferred dividends must Bethlehem declare and pay each year to avoid having preferred dividends in arrears?
5. Assume preferred dividends are in arrears for 19X5.
   - **a.** Write Note 6 of the December 31, 19X5, financial statements to disclose the dividends in arrears.
   - **b.** Journalize the declaration of a $60 million dividend for 19X6. An explanation is not required.

Measuring the effects of dividend and treasury stock transactions on a company ***(Obj. 3, 4)***

P9-7B Assume that IHOP Corp. completed the following selected transactions during the current year:

Feb. 10	Split common stock 2 for 1 by calling in the 100,000 shares of $10 par common and issuing new stock in its place.
April 18	Declared a cash dividend on the 5%, $100 par preferred stock (1,000 shares outstanding). Declared a $0.20 per share dividend on the common stock outstanding. The date of record was May 2, and the payment date was May 23.
May 23	Paid the cash dividends.
July 30	Declared a 10% stock dividend on the common stock to holders of record August 21, with distribution set for September 11. The market value of the common stock was $15 per share.
Sep. 11	Issued the stock dividend shares.
Oct. 26	Purchased 2,500 shares of the company's own common stock at $14 per share.
Nov. 8	Sold 1,000 shares of treasury common stock for $17 per share.
Dec. 13	Sold 500 shares of treasury common stock for $13 per share.

Required

Analyze each transaction in terms of its effect on the accounting equation of IHOP.

Preparing a corporation's balance sheet; measuring profitability ***(Obj. 3, 6)***

P9-8B The following accounts and related balances of Adventure Films, Inc., are arranged in no particular order.

Dividends payable	$ 3,000	Accounts Payable	$ 31,000
Total assets, November 30, 19X6	781,000	Retained earnings	?
Net income	36,200	Common stock, $5-par, 100,000 shares authorized, 42,000 shares issued	210,000
Common stockholders' equity, November 30, 19X6	483,000	Inventory	170,000
Interest expense	12,800	Property, plant, and equipment, net	378,000
Treasury stock, common, 1,600 shares at cost	11,000	Goodwill, net	6,000

Prepaid expenses	$ 13,000	Preferred stock, 4%, $10 par, 25,000 shares authorized, 3,700 shares issued	$ 37,000
Patent, net	31,000	Cash	32,000
Accrued liabilities	17,000	Additional paid-in capital—common	140,000
Long-term note payable	104,000		
Accounts receivable, net	102,000		

Required

1. Prepare the company's classified balance sheet in the account format at November 30, 19X7.
2. Compute rate of return on total assets and rate of return on common stockholders' equity for the year ended November 30, 19X7.
3. Do these rates of return suggest strength or weakness? Give your reason.
4. How will what you learned in this problem help you evaluate an investment?

Analyzing the statement of cash flows
(Obj. 7)

P9-9B The statement of cash flows of **Ford Motor Company** reported the following for the year ended December 31, 19X4:

Cash flows from financing activities—amounts in millions:	
Cash dividends [declared and paid]	$(1,205)
Issuance of common stock	715
Changes in short-term debt	9,519
Proceeds from issuance of other debt	22,043
Principal payments on debt	(14,163)
Issuance of preferred stock	417

Required

1. Make the journal entry that Ford used to record each of these transactions.
2. From these transactions, would you expect Ford's total assets, total liabilities, and total stockholders' equity to have grown or shrunk during 19X4? Ford's net income for 19X4 was $5,308 million. State the reasoning behind your answer.

EXTENDING YOUR KNOWLEDGE

DECISION CASES

Evaluating alternative ways of raising capital
(Obj. 2)

Case 1. Rashad Khalik and Dan Collins have written a computer program for a video game that they believe will rival Nintendo and SegaGenesis. They need additional capital to market the product, and they plan to incorporate their partnership. They are considering alternative capital structures for the corporation. Their primary goal is to raise as much capital as possible without giving up control of the business. The partners plan to receive 110,000 shares of the corporation's common stock in return for the net assets of the partnership. After the partnership books are closed and the assets adjusted to current market value, Khalik's capital balance will be $60,000, and Collins's balance will be $50,000.

The corporation's plans for a charter include an authorization to issue 5,000 shares of preferred stock and 500,000 shares of $1 par common stock. Khalik and Collins are uncertain about the most desirable features for the preferred stock. Prior to incorporating, the partners are discussing their plans with two investment groups. The corporation can obtain capital from outside investors under either of the following plans:

Plan 1. Group 1 will invest $105,000 to acquire 1,000 shares of $5, no-par preferred stock and $70,000 to acquire 70,000 shares of common stock. Each preferred share receives 50 votes on matters that come before the stockholders.

Plan 2. Group 2 will invest $160,000 to acquire 1,400 shares of 6%, $100 par nonvoting, noncumulative preferred stock.

Required

Assume that the corporation is chartered.

1. Journalize the issuance of common stock to Khalik and Collins. Debit each partner's capital account for its balance. Credit Common Stock.
2. Journalize the issuance of stock to the outsiders under both plans.
3. Assume that net income for the first year is $150,000 and total dividends are $19,100. Prepare the stockholders' equity section of the corporation's balance sheet under both plans.
4. Recommend one of the plans to Khalik and Collins. Give your reasons.

Analyzing cash dividends and stock dividends
(Obj. 4)

Case 2. Startex Products, Inc., had the following stockholders' equity amounts on June 30 of the current year:

Common stock, no-par, 100,000 shares issued	$ 750,000
Retained earnings	830,000
Total stockholders' equity	$1,580,000

In the past, Startex has paid an annual cash dividend of $1.50 per share. Last year, despite the large retained earnings balance, the board of directors wished to conserve cash for expansion. The board delayed the payment of cash dividends by one month and in the meantime distributed a 10% stock dividend. This year, the company's cash position improved. The board declared and paid a cash dividend of $1.364 per share.

Suppose you own 10,000 shares of Startex common stock, acquired three years ago, prior to the 10% stock dividend. The market price of the stock was $30 per share before any of the above dividends.

Required

1. How does the stock dividend affect your proportionate ownership in Startex Products, Inc.? Explain.
2. What amount of cash dividends did you receive last year? What amount of cash dividends will you receive after the above dividend action?
3. Immediately after the stock dividend was distributed, the market value of Startex stock decreased from $30 per share to $27.273 per share. Does this decrease represent a loss to you? Explain.
4. Suppose Startex announces at the time of the stock dividend that the company will continue to pay the annual $1.50 cash dividend per share, even after the stock dividend. Would you expect the market price of the stock to decrease to $27.273 per share as in Requirement 3? Explain.

ETHICAL ISSUE 1

Note: This case is based on a real situation.

George Campbell paid $50,000 for a franchise that entitled him to market Success Associates software programs in the countries of the European Union. Campbell intended to sell individual franchises for the major language groups of western Europe—German, French, English, Spanish, and Italian. Naturally, investors considering buying a franchise from Campbell asked to see the financial statements of his business.

Believing the value of the franchise to be greater than $50,000, Campbell sought to capitalize his own franchise at $500,000. The law firm of McDonald & LaDue helped Campbell form a corporation chartered to issue 500,000 shares of common stock with par value of $1 per share. Attorneys suggested the following chain of transactions:

a. A third party borrows $500,000 and purchases the franchise from Campbell.
b. Campbell pays the corporation $500,000 to acquire all its stock.
c. The corporation buys the franchise from the third party, who repays the loan.

In the final analysis, the third party is debt-free and out of the picture. Campbell owns all the corporation's stock, and the corporation owns the franchise. The corporation balance sheet lists a franchise acquired at a cost of $500,000. This balance sheet is Campbell's most valuable marketing tool.

Required

1. What is unethical about this situation?
2. Who can be harmed? How can they be harmed? What role does accounting play here?

ETHICAL ISSUE 2

Anadarko Petroleum Company is an independent oil producer in Anadarko, Oklahoma. In February, company geologists discovered a pool of oil that tripled the company's proven reserves. Prior to disclosing the new oil to the public, Anadarko quietly bought most of its stock as treasury stock. After the discovery was announced, Anadarko's stock price increased from $13 to $40.

Required

1. Did Anadarko managers behave ethically? Explain your answer.
2. Identify the accounting principle relevant to this situation.
3. Who was helped and who was harmed by management's action?

FINANCIAL STATEMENT CASES

Analyzing stockholders' equity
(Obj. 2, 3)

Case 1. The Lands' End, Inc., financial statements appear in Appendix A at the end of the book. Answer the following questions about the company's common stock.

1. What does Lands' End call its stockholders' equity?
2. Solely on the basis of the balance sheet, how much common stock did Lands' End issue during the year ended February 2, 1996? Give your reason.
3. An investor or creditor should not jump to a premature conclusion in analyzing a company's financial statements. It is often necessary to analyze different parts of the statements to reach a correct conclusion. Refer to the statement of shareholders' investment for the year ended February 2, 1996 (the top two panels of the statement), and answer Question 2 again. Give your reason.
4. On the basis of the balance sheet, what is the par value per share of Lands' End common stock? Read note 2 to confirm your answer.
5. The company's Donated Capital arose prior to the FASB statement that requires companies to report donations as revenues. The asset donated to Lands' End was a recreation center for company employees. The founder of the company made the donation. How does donated capital differ from the other paid-in capital?

Analyzing treasury stock and retained earnings
(Obj. 3, 5)

Case 2. Use the Lands' End, Inc., financial statements in Appendix A at the end of the book to answer the following questions.

1. Lands' End reports stock *issued* on the balance sheet and gives details in the statement of shareholders' investment. At February 2, 1996, how many shares of common stock had Lands' End issued? How many shares were in the treasury? How many shares were outstanding at February 2, 1996?
2. Examine the Lands' End balance sheet. Did the company purchase any treasury stock during the year ended February 2, 1996? Explain. Now refer to the statement of shareholders' investment, and journalize the purchase of treasury stock and the issuance (sale) of treasury stock. How can you tell that the sale of treasury stock neither created nor used up paid-in capital from treasury stock transactions?
3. Prepare a T-account for Retained Earnings to show the beginning and ending balances and all activity in the account during the year ended February 2, 1996.

Analyzing treasury stock and retained earnings
(Obj. 3, 5)

Case 3. Obtain the annual report of a company of your choosing. Answer the following questions about the company. Concentrate on the current year in the annual report you select.

1. How many shares of common stock had the company issued through the end of the current year? How many shares were in the treasury? How many shares were outstanding on the date of the current balance sheet?
2. Compute average cost per share of treasury stock (common). Compare this figure to book value per share of common stock. Does it appear that the company was able to purchase treasury stock at book value?
   Note: This question can be answered only if the company reports the cost of treasury stock.
3. Prepare a T-account for Retained Earnings to show the beginning and ending balances and all activity in the account during the current year.

GROUP PROJECT

Competitive pressures are the norm in business. **Lexus** automobiles (made in Japan) have cut into the sales of **Mercedes-Benz** (a German company), **Jaguar Motors** (a British company), **General Motors' Cadillac Division,** and **Ford's Lincoln Division** (both U.S. companies). **Dell, Gateway,** and **Compaq** computers have siphoned business away from **Apple** and **IBM.** Foreign steelmakers have reduced the once-massive U.S. steel industry to a fraction of its former size.

Indeed, corporate downsizing has occurred on a massive scale. During the past few years, each company or industry mentioned here has pared down plant and equipment, laid off employees, or restructured operations.

Required

1. Identify all the stakeholders of a corporation. A *stakeholder* is a person or a group who has an interest (that is, a stake) in the success of the organization.
2. Identify several measures by which a company may be considered deficient and in need of downsizing. How can downsizing help to solve this problem?
3. Debate the downsizing issue. One group of students takes the perspective of the company and its stockholders, and another group of students takes the perspective of other stakeholders of the company.

INTERNET EXERCISE

SPRING STREET BREWING CO.

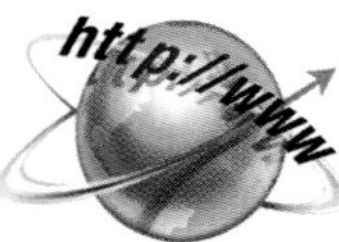

Andrew Klein, a Harvard-educated lawyer, quit his law practice in 1993 to start Spring Street Brewing Co., a small microbrewery. After some initial success, Spring Street sought to acquire more capital, but it did not want to give up control to private investors or pay the hefty fees charged by underwriters. So Klein decided to offer Spring Street's common stock over the Internet directly to potential investors. After some discussion, the Securities and Exchange Commission approved the first-ever Internet initial public offering (IPO).

To "go public," a company must disclose all material and relevant information to investors through a prospectus. The prospectus must include not only the financial statements, but also information on all aspects of the company, including its markets, management, risks, and plans for the IPO proceeds. The Spring Street Brewing Co. has its current prospectus on its Web site.

Required

1. Go to **http://plaza.interport.net/witbeer/,** the home page of the Spring Street Brewing Company.
2. You can find information regarding the current stock offering by clicking the highlighted text, **Friendly Links.** Here you can surf Spring Street and its related company, Wit Capital.
3. After exploring the site, answer the following questions.
   - **a.** What is Spring Street's business? What does "Wit" mean?
   - **b.** How does Spring Street's niche fit within the U.S. beer market?
   - **c.** Describe Spring Street's current strategy.
   - **d.** What does Spring Street plan to do with the monies from the issuance of common stock?
   - **e.** How much beer brewing or retailing experience does Spring Street's senior management have?
   - **f.** What are the major risks that investors should consider?
   - **g.** Has Spring Street been profitable since its inception?
   - **h.** What is the primary source of cash to Spring Street?
   - **i.** Investors are typically compensated for their risks by either dividends or stock-price appreciation. What is Spring Street's dividend policy? Are there limitations or restrictions on selling Spring Street stock?
   - **j.** What recommendation would you make to a potential investor based on the information on the Web site?

10

Accounting for Long-Term Investments and International Operations

Learning Objectives

After studying this chapter, you should be able to

1. Account for available-for-sale investments
2. Use the equity method for investments
3. Consolidate parent and subsidiary balance sheets
4. Account for long-term investments in bonds
5. Account for transactions stated in a foreign currency
6. Compute and interpret a foreign-currency translation adjustment
7. Report investing transactions on the statement of cash flows

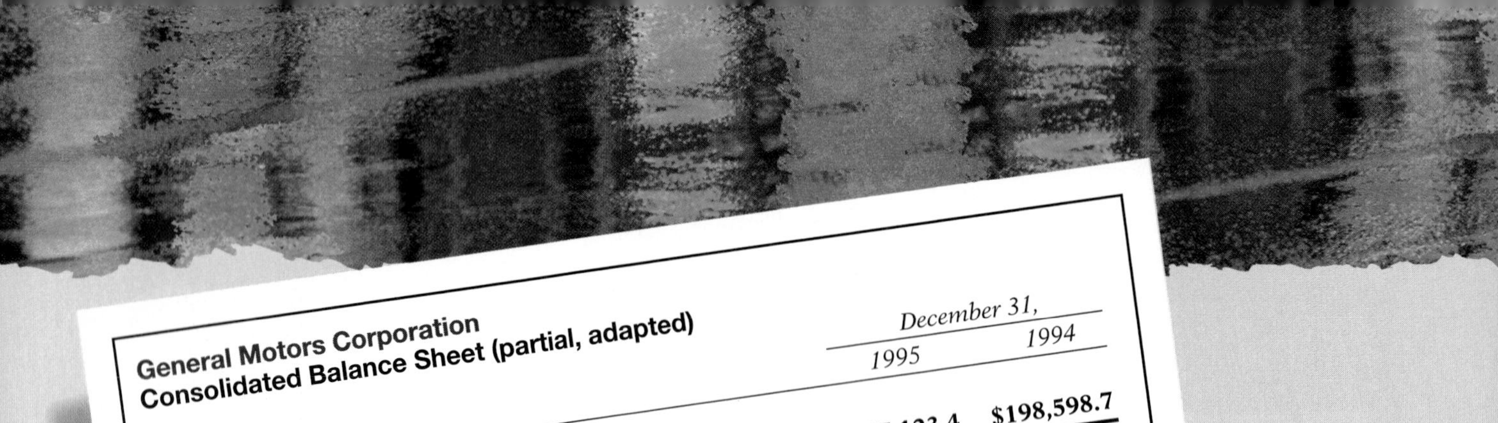

General Motors Corporation
Consolidated Balance Sheet (partial, adapted)

(Dollars in Millions)	*December 31,* 1995	1994
Assets		
1 **Total Assets**	**$217,123.4**	**$198,598.7**
Liabilities and Stockholders' Equity		
Liabilities		
2 **Total Liabilities**	**$193,777.9**	**$185,774.9**
Stockholders' Equity		
3 Preference stocks	$ 1.2	$ 2.4
Common stocks		
4 $1⅔ par value (issued, 753,008,273 and 754,345,782 shares)	1,255.0	1,257.2
5 Class E (issued, 442,812,166 and 268,125,255 shares)	44.3	26.8
6 Class H (issued, 97,152,014 and 78,720,022 shares)	9.7	7.9
7 Capital surplus (principally additional paid-in capital)	18,870.9	13,149.4
8 Net income retained for use in the business	7,185.4	1,785.8
9 Subtotal	27,366.5	16,229.5
10 Other	(4,736.3)	(3,548.4)
11 Accumulated foreign-currency translation adjustments	222.5	(100.4)
12 Net unrealized gains on investments in certain debt and equity securities	492.8	243.1
13 Total Stockholders' Equity	23,345.5	12,823.8
14 Total Liabilities and Stockholders' Equity	**$217,123.4**	**$198,598.7**

> ***"Over a third of General Motors' assets are employed outside the United States, and the company earns more than half its profits outside the United States."***
>
> —GENERAL MOTORS ANNUAL REPORT, 1996

General Motors Corporation (GM) is the world's largest business entity, with annual revenues of $168 billion and assets totaling $217 billion, as shown on the company's 1995 balance sheet. The GM organization includes hundreds of individual corporations whose financial statements are combined and reported under the General Motors name. For example, **Libbey-Owens-Ford** makes the glass for GM cars, **Fisher Body** makes the auto chassis, and **Delco** makes the batteries. GM's financial statements are called *consolidated* financial statements because they combine the reports of various GM companies. For example, GM's balance sheet is labeled the Consolidated Balance Sheet. In this chapter we explain how a company such as General Motors prepares its consolidated statements.

Many of the companies that GM owns are located in foreign countries. In fact, over a third of GM's assets are employed outside the United States, and the company earns more than half its profits in other countries. A direct result of GM's foreign operations is *Accumulated foreign-currency translation adjustments,* which appear on the balance sheet as the next-to-last item in stockholders' equity (line 11). We explain the foreign-currency translation adjustment in this chapter. As international operations increase in importance, companies must deal with the foreign-currency translation adjustment.

General Motors also holds investments. The last item on GM's balance sheet is labeled *Net unrealized gains on investments in certain debt and equity securities* (line 12). This item relates directly to GM's investments. It reports that on December 31, 1995, the current market value of GM's investments was $492.8 million more than GM paid for the investments. In this chapter we will examine the source of this net unrealized gain.

Throughout this course, you have become increasingly familiar with the financial statements of companies such as **Lands' End, Intel,** and **IHOP.** You have seen most of the items you will encounter in a set of financial statements. Only a few items remain. This chapter, which discusses long-term investments and international operations, continues your education in the financial statements and how to use them.

Accounting for Long-Term Investments

Investments come in all sizes and shapes—from the acquisition of an entire company, to the purchase of a few shares of a company's stock, to an investment in bonds. In earlier chapters we discussed stocks and bonds from the perspective of the company that issued the securities. In Chapter 5, we covered *short-term* investments that companies make to put their idle cash to work. In this chapter we examine *long-term* investments in stocks and bonds.

Why do individuals and corporations make long-term investments in stocks? You as an individual would probably make an investment to earn dividends and to sell the stock at a higher price than you paid for it. Investment companies such as brokerage firms, mutual funds, insurance companies, and bank trust departments buy stocks and bonds for this same reason.

Most other companies invest in stocks for a second reason: to influence or to control the other company. The purchase of an entire company raises questions about how the parent company should account for its investment. We address these questions later in this chapter. First, however, let's review how investment transactions take place.

Stock Investments: A Review

Stock Prices

Investors buy more stock in transactions among themselves than from the issuing company. Each share of stock is issued only once, but it may be traded among investors many times thereafter. Individuals and businesses buy and sell stocks from each other in markets, such as the New York Stock Exchange and the American Stock Exchange. Brokers such as **Merrill Lynch** and **Prudential Securities, Inc.** handle stock transactions for a commission.

Brokers such as Merrill Lynch and Prudential Securities, Inc. handle stock transactions for a commission.

A broker may "quote a stock price," which means to state the current market price per share. The financial community quotes stock prices in dollars and one-eighth fractions. A stock selling at 32⅛ costs $32.125 per share. A stock listed at 55¾ sells at $55.75. Financial publications and many newspapers carry daily information on the stock issues of thousands of corporations. These one-line summaries carry information as of the close of trading on the previous day.

Exhibit 10-1 presents information for the common stock of **The Boeing Company,** a large aircraft manufacturer, just as this information appeared in newspaper listings. During the previous 52 weeks, Boeing common stock reached a high price of $114.50 and a low price of $74.125 per share. The annual cash dividend is $1.12 per share. During the previous day, 1,059,800 (10,598 × 100) shares of Boeing common stock were traded. The prices of these transactions ranged from a high of $109.875 to a low of $108.75 per share. The day's closing price of $109.125 was $0.50 lower than the closing price of the preceding day.

What causes a change in a stock's price? The development of new products, favorable court rulings, and increasing earnings drive a stock's price up. Business failures and bad economic news pull it down. The market sets the price at which a stock changes hands.

52 weeks								
High	Low	Stock	Dividend	Sales 100s	High	Low	Close	Net Change
114½	74⅛	Boeing	1.12	10598	109⅞	108¾	109⅛	−½

EXHIBIT 10-1
Stock Price Information for The Boeing Company

Investors and Investees

To move further into our discussion of investments in stock, we need to define two key terms. The person or company that owns stock in a corporation is the *investor.* The corporation that issued the stock is the *investee.* If you own shares of Boeing common stock, you are an investor and Boeing is the investee.

A business may purchase another corporation's stock simply to put extra cash to work in the hope of earning dividends and gains on the sale of the stock. Such investments are rare, however. Most entities prefer to invest in inventory, employees, and plant assets in their own line of business. Most of the time, the entity makes long-term investments to gain a degree of control over the investee's operation. An investor holding 25% of the investee's outstanding stock owns one-fourth of the business. This one-quarter voice in electing the directors of the corporation is likely to give the investor a lot of say in how the investee conducts its business. An investor holding more than 50% of the outstanding shares controls the investee.

Let's consider why one corporation might want a say in another corporation's business. The investor may want to exert some control over the level of dividends paid by the investee. Or perhaps the investee has products closely linked to the investor's own line of business. This is the case with **General Motors** and **Delco.** By influencing the investee's business, the investor may be able to exert some control over product distribution, product-line improvements, pricing strategies, and other important business considerations. General Motors can control its supply of auto batteries by holding a controlling interest in Delco.

Classifying Stock Investments

Investments in stock are assets to the investor. The investments may be short-term or long-term. **Short-term investments**—sometimes called **marketable securities**—are current assets. To be listed on the balance sheet as short-term, investments must be liquid (readily convertible to cash). Also, the investor must intend either to convert the investments to cash within one year or to use them to pay a current liability. We saw how to account for short-term investments in Chapter 5.

Investments not meeting the two requirements of short-term investments are classified on the balance sheet as **long-term investments,** a category of noncurrent assets. Long-term investments include stocks and bonds that the investor expects to hold longer than one year or that are not readily marketable—for instance, real estate not used in the operations of the business. Exhibit 10-2 shows the positions of short-term and long-term investments on the balance sheet. For the remainder of this chapter we focus on long-term investments.

Current Assets		
Cash	$X	
Short-term investments	X	
Accounts receivable	X	
Inventories	X	
Prepaid expenses	X	
Total current assets		$X
Long-term investments [or simply Investments]		X
Property, plant, and equipment		X
Intangible assets		X
Other assets		X

EXHIBIT 10-2
Reporting Investments on the Balance Sheet

We report assets in the order of their liquidity. Cash is the most liquid asset, followed by Short-Term Investments, Accounts Receivable, and so on. Long-Term Investments are less liquid than Current Assets but more liquid than

Property, Plant, and Equipment. However, many companies report their long-term investments after property, plant, and equipment.

Stock Investments

We begin our discussion of stock investments with those situations in which the investor holds less than a 20% interest in the investee company. These investments in stock are classified as either trading securities or as available-for-sale securities. **Trading securities** are stock investments that are to be sold in the very near future—days, weeks, or only a few months—with the intent of generating profits on price changes. Trading securities are therefore classified as *current assets* (see short-term investments in Exhibit 10-2).

Available-for-sale securities are all stock investments other than trading securities. They are classified as current assets if the business expects to sell the investments within the next year or within the business's normal operating cycle if longer than a year. All other available-for-sale securities are classified as long-term investments (Exhibit 10-2).

After classifying an investment as a trading security or as an available-for-sale security, the investor accounts for the two categories separately. We begin by illustrating the accounting for available-for-sale investments.

Accounting for Available-for-Sale Investments

Objective 1

Account for available-for-sale investments

The **market value method** is used to account for all available-for-sale investments in stock because the company expects to resell the stock at its market value. *Cost* is used only as the initial amount for recording the investments. These investments are reported on the balance sheet at their current *market* value.

Suppose that Dade, Inc., purchases 1,000 shares of Hewlett-Packard Company common stock at the market price of 35¾. Dade intends to hold this investment for longer than a year and therefore classifies it as an available-for-sale investment. Dade's entry to record the investment is

19X1			
Feb. 23	Long-Term Investment (1,000 × $35.75)	35,750	
	Cash		35,750
	Purchased investment.		

ASSETS	=	LIABILITIES	+	STOCKHOLDERS' EQUITY
+35,750 −35,750	=	0	+	0

Assume that Dade receives a $0.22 per share cash dividend on the Hewlett-Packard stock. Dade's entry to record receipt of the dividend is

19X1			
July 14	Cash (1,000 × $0.22)..	220	
	Dividend Revenue..		220
	Received cash dividend.		

ASSETS	=	LIABILITIES	+	STOCKHOLDERS EQUITY	+	REVENUES
+220	=	0			+	220

Unlike interest, dividends do not accrue with the passage of time. In this example, Hewlett-Packard has no liability for dividends until the dividends are declared. An investor makes no accrual entry for dividend revenue at year end in anticipation of a dividend declaration.

For a review of stock dividends, see Chapter 9, page 440.

Receipt of a *stock* dividend is different from receipt of a cash dividend. For a stock dividend, the investor records no dividend revenue. Instead, the investor makes a memorandum entry in the accounting records to denote the new number of shares of stock held as an investment. Because the number of shares of stock held has increased, the investor's cost per share of the stock decreases. For example, suppose Dade, Inc., receives a 5% stock dividend from Hewlett-Packard Company. Dade would receive 50 shares (5% of 1,000 shares previously held) and make this memorandum entry in its accounting records:

MEMORANDUM—Receipt of stock dividend: Received 50 shares of Hewlett-Packard common stock in 5% stock dividend. New cost per share is $34.05 (cost of $35,750 ÷ 1,050 shares).

In all of Dade's future transactions that use Dade's cost of the Hewlett-Packard investment, Dade will use the new cost per share of $34.05.

Reporting Available-for-Sale Investments at Current Market Value

Because of the relevance of market values for decision making, available-for-sale investments in stock are reported on the balance sheet at their market value. This reporting requires an adjustment of the investments from their last carrying amount to current market value. Assume that the market value of Dade's investment in Hewlett-Packard's common stock is $36,400 on December 31, 19X1. In this case, Dade, Inc., the investor, makes the following adjustment:

19X1			
Dec. 31	Allowance to Adjust Investment to Market ($36,400 – $35,750)	650	
	Unrealized Gain on Investment		650
	Adjusted investment to market value.		

ASSETS	=	LIABILITIES	+	STOCKHOLDERS' EQUITY
+650	=	0	+	650

Allowance to Adjust Investment to Market is a companion account that is used in conjunction with the Long-Term Investment account to bring the investment's carrying amount to current market value. In this case, the investment's cost ($35,750) plus the Allowance ($650) equals the investment carrying amount ($36,400).

Long-Term Investment		Allowance to Adjust Investment to Market	
35,750		650	

Investment carrying amount = Market value of $36,400

Here the Allowance has a debit balance because the market value of the investment increased. If the investment's market value declines, the Allowance is credited, and the investment carrying amount is its cost minus the Allowance.

The other side of the adjustment entry is a credit to Unrealized Gain on Investment. If the market value of the investment declines, the company debits Unrealized Loss on Investment. Recall that an *unrealized* gain or loss results from a change in the investment's market value, not from the sale of the investment. For available-for-sale investments, the Unrealized Gain account or the Unrealized Loss account is reported in two places in the financial statements:

- Other comprehensive income, which can be reported on the income statement in a separate section below net income, or in a separate statement of comprehensive income.
- Accumulated other comprehensive income, which is a separate section of stockholders' equity, below retained earnings, on the balance sheet.

The following display shows how Dade, Inc. reported its investment and the related unrealized gain in its financial statements at the end of 19X1 (all other figures are assumed for illustration in context):

Income statement:		
Revenues		$10,000
Expenses, including income tax		6,000
Net income		$ 4,000
Other comprehensive income:		
Unrealized gain on investments	$650	
Less income tax (40%)	260	390
Comprehensive income		$ 4,390

Balance sheet:	
Assets:	
Total current assets	$ XXX
Long-term investments—at market value ($35,750 + $650)	36,400
Property, plant, and equipment, net	XXX
Stockholders' equity:	
Common stock	$ 1,000
Retained earnings	2,000
Accumulated other comprehensive income:	
Unrealized gain on investment	390
Total stockholders' equity	$ 3,390

The unrealized gain appears on the income statement as part of comprehensive income but not as part of net income. The unrealized gain is reported at its net-of-tax amount ($390) because it comes after net income, which also is an after-tax figure. The investments appear on the balance sheet at current market value. The balance sheet also reports the unrealized gain in a separate section of stockholders' equity, Accumulated other comprehensive income, which comes after Retained Earnings.

Selling an Available-for-Sale Investment

The sale of an available-for-sale investment can result in a *realized* gain or loss. Realized gains and losses measure the difference between the amount received from the sale of the investment and the cost of the investment.

Suppose Dade, Inc., sells its investment in Hewlett-Packard stock for $34,000 during 19X2. Dade would record the sale as follows:

19X2			
May 19	Cash	34,000	
	Loss on Sale of Investment	1,750	
	Long-Term Investment (cost)		35,750
	Sold investment.		

ASSETS	=	LIABILITIES	+	STOCKHOLDERS' EQUITY	−	LOSSES
+34,000 −35,750	=	0			−	1,750

Dade would report the Loss on Sale of Investments as an "Other" item on the income statement. At December 31, 19X2, Dade must update the Allowance to Adjust Investment to Market and the Unrealized Gain on Investment accounts to their current balance. These adjustments are covered in intermediate accounting courses.

STOP & THINK Suppose Xenon Corporation holds the following available-for-sale securities as long-term investments at December 31, 19X8:

Stock	Cost	Current Market Value
The Coca-Cola Company	$ 85,000	$ 71,000
Eastman Kodak Company	16,000	12,000
$101,000	$ 93,000	

Show how Xenon Corporation will report long-term investments on its December 31, 19X8, balance sheet.

Answer

Assets	
Long-term investments, at market value	$93,000

Accounting for Equity-Method Investments

Objective 2

Use the equity method for investments

An investor who holds less than 20% of the investee's voting stock usually plays no important role in the investee's operations. However, an investor with a larger stock holding—between 20 and 50% of the investee's voting stock—may *significantly influence* how the investee operates the business. Such an investor can likely affect the investee's decisions on dividend policy, product lines, sources of supply, and other important matters.

For this reason, investments in the range of 20–50% of another company's stock are common. For example, **General Motors** owns nearly 40% of **Isuzu Motors Overseas Distribution Corporation.** Similarly, **Chrysler Corporation** owns 50% of a partnership with **Renault** of France. Because the investor has a voice in shaping business policy and operations, accountants believe that some measure of the investee's success and failure should be included in accounting for the investment. We use the **equity method** to account for investments in which the investor owns 20–50% of the investee's stock and thus can significantly influence the investee's decisions. A recent survey of 600 companies by *Accounting Trends & Techniques* indicated that 252 (42%) of the corporations held investments that they accounted for by the equity method. These investee companies are often referred to as *affiliates.*

Investments accounted for by the equity method are recorded initially at cost. Suppose Phillips Petroleum Company pays $400,000 for 30% of the common stock of White Rock Corporation. Phillips may refer to White Rock Corporation as an *affiliated company.* Phillips's entry to record the purchase of this investment is as follows:

Jan. 6	Long-Term Investment	400,000	
	Cash..		400,000
	To purchase equity-method investment.		

ASSETS	=	LIABILITIES	+	STOCKHOLDERS' EQUITY
+400,000 −400,000	=	0	+	0

Under the equity method, Phillips, as the investor, applies its percentage of ownership—30%, in our example—in recording its share of the investee's net income and dividends. If White Rock reports net income of $250,000 for the year, Phillips records 30% of this amount as an increase in the investment account and as equity-method investment revenue, as follows:

Dec. 31	Long-Term Investment ($250,000 × 0.30)	75,000	
	Equity-Method Investment Revenue		75,000
	To record investment revenue.		

ASSETS	=	LIABILITIES	+	STOCKHOLDERS' EQUITY	+	REVENUES
+75,000	=	0			+	75,000

The Investment Revenue account carries the Equity-Method label to identify its source. This labeling is similar to distinguishing Sales Revenue from Service Revenue.

The investor increases the Investment account and records Investment Revenue when the investee reports income because of the close relationship between the two companies. As the investee's (affiliate's) owners' equity increases, so does the Investment account on the investor's books.

Phillips records its proportionate part of cash dividends received from White Rock. Assuming that White Rock declares and pays a cash dividend of $100,000, Phillips receives 30% of this dividend, recorded by Phillips as follows:

Dec. 31	Cash ($100,000 × 0.30)..	30,000	
	Long-Term Investment		30,000
	To record receipt of cash dividend on equity-method investment.		

ASSETS	=	LIABILITIES	+	STOCKHOLDERS' EQUITY
+30,000 −30,000	=	0	+	0

The Investment account is credited for the receipt of a dividend on an equity-method investment. Why? Because the dividend decreases the investee's owners' equity, and so it also reduces the investor's investment. The investor received cash for this portion of the investment and reduced the investor's claim against the investee.

After the preceding entries are posted, Phillips's Investment account reflects its equity in the net assets of White Rock:

Long-Term Investment

19X1			**19X2**		
Jan. 6	**Purchase**	**400,000**	**Jan. 17**	**Dividends**	**30,000**
Dec. 31	**Net income**	**75,000**			
19X2					
Jan. 17	Balance	445,000			

Phillips would report the long-term investment on the balance sheet and the equity-method investment revenue on the income statement as follows:

Balance sheet (partial):	
Assets	
Total current assets	$ XXX
Long-term investments, at equity..	445,000
Property, plant, and equipment, net..	XXX
Income statement (partial):	
Income from operations..	$ XXX
Other revenue:	
Equity-method investment revenue	75,000
Net income..	$ XXX

Gain or loss on the sale of an equity-method investment is measured as the difference between the sale proceeds and the carrying amount of the investment. For example, sale of one-tenth of the White Rock common stock for $41,000 would be recorded as follows:

Feb. 13	Cash	41,000	
	Loss on Sale of Investment	3,500	
	Long-Term Investment ($445,000 × 1/10)....		44,500
	Sold one-tenth of investment.		

ASSETS	=	LIABILITIES	+	STOCKHOLDERS' EQUITY	−	LOSSES
+41,000 −44,500	=	0			−	3,500

As we've seen, companies with investments accounted for by the equity method often refer to the investee as an *affiliated company.* The account title Investment in Affiliated Companies refers to investments that are accounted for by the equity method. Consider **Whirlpool Corporation,** manufacturer of refrigerators, washing machines, and other appliances. Whirlpool reported a $13 million equity-method loss on its investments in Brazilian and Mexican affiliated companies, which include Brastemp S.A., Consul S.A., (both in Brazil) and Vitromatic S.A. (in Mexico). Whirlpool recorded the transaction as follows:

	($ Millions)	
Equity-Method Investment Loss	13	
Investment in Brazilian and Mexican Companies....................		13

ASSETS	=	LIABILITIES	+	STOCKHOLDERS' EQUITY	−	LOSSES
−13,000,000	=	0			−	13,000,000

LEARNING TIP The T-account illustrates how to account for equity-method investments:

Equity Method	
Original Cost	Share of losses
Share of income	Share of dividends

Joint Ventures—Accounted for by the Equity Method

A *joint venture* is a separate entity or project owned and operated by a small group of businesses. Joint ventures are common in risky endeavors such as oil exploration in the petroleum industry and the construction of nuclear power plants. For example, Aramco, which stands for Arabian American Oil Company, is a joint venture half owned by Saudi Arabia. Several multinational oil companies (Exxon, Chevron, and others) own the remaining 50 percent. Despite the risks of operating in the volatile Middle East, Aramco's partners have enjoyed big profits.

A joint venturer such as Exxon accounts for its investment in a joint venture by the equity method even when the investor owns less than 20% of the venture. The equity method is used for accounting purposes because a joint venturer is presumed to have a significant influence on the investee company.

Accounting for Consolidated Subsidiaries

Objective 3

Consolidate parent and subsidiary balance sheets

Most large corporations own controlling interests in other corporations. A **controlling** (or **majority**) **interest** is the ownership of more than 50% of the investee's voting stock. Such an investment enables the investor to elect a majority of the investee's board of directors and so control the investee. The investor is called the **parent company,** and the investee company is called the **subsidiary.** For example, Saturn Corporation is a subsidiary of General Motors, the parent, so the stockholders of GM control Saturn, as diagrammed in Exhibit 10-3.

Saturn Corporation is a subsidiary of General Motors, the parent, so the stockholders of GM control Saturn.

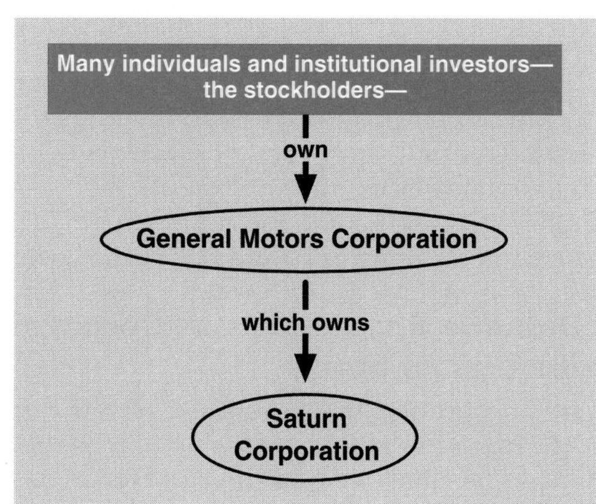

EXHIBIT 10-3
Ownership Structure of General Motors Corporation and Saturn Corporation

EXHIBIT 10-4
Selected Subsidiaries of the "Big Three" U.S. Automobile Manufacturers

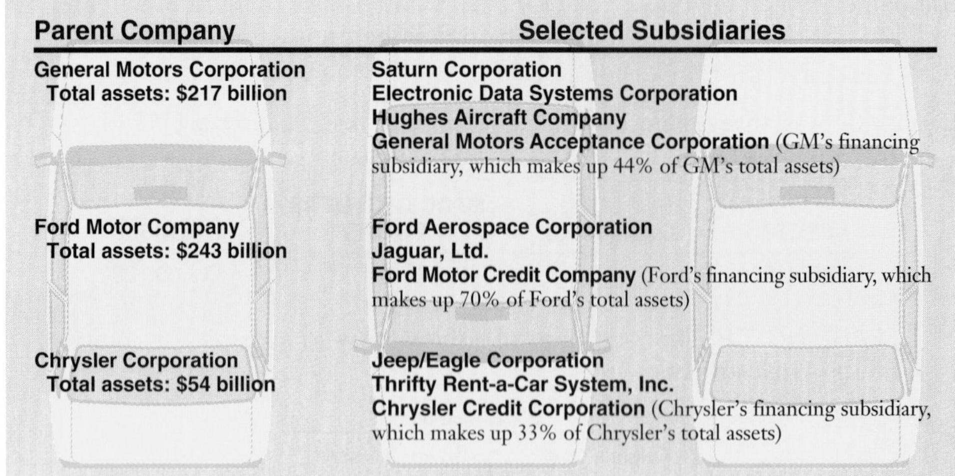

Parent Company	Selected Subsidiaries
General Motors Corporation **Total assets: $217 billion**	**Saturn Corporation** **Electronic Data Systems Corporation** **Hughes Aircraft Company** **General Motors Acceptance Corporation** (GM's financing subsidiary, which makes up 44% of GM's total assets)
Ford Motor Company **Total assets: $243 billion**	**Ford Aerospace Corporation** **Jaguar, Ltd.** **Ford Motor Credit Company** (Ford's financing subsidiary, which makes up 70% of Ford's total assets)
Chrysler Corporation **Total assets: $54 billion**	**Jeep/Eagle Corporation** **Thrifty Rent-a-Car System, Inc.** **Chrysler Credit Corporation** (Chrysler's financing subsidiary, which makes up 33% of Chrysler's total assets)

Why have subsidiaries? Why not have the corporation take the form of a single legal entity? Subsidiaries may enable the parent to save on income taxes, may limit the parent's liabilities in a risky venture, and may ease expansion into foreign countries. For example, **IBM** finds it more feasible to operate in France through a French-based subsidiary company than through the U.S. parent company. Exhibit 10-4 shows some of the more interesting subsidiaries of the "Big Three" U.S. automakers.

Consolidation accounting is a method of combining the financial statements of two or more companies that are controlled by the same owners. This method implements the entity concept by reporting a single set of financial statements for the consolidated entity, which carries the name of the parent company. Exhibit 10-5 illustrates the accounting method that should be used for stock investments according to the percentage of the investor's ownership in the investee company.

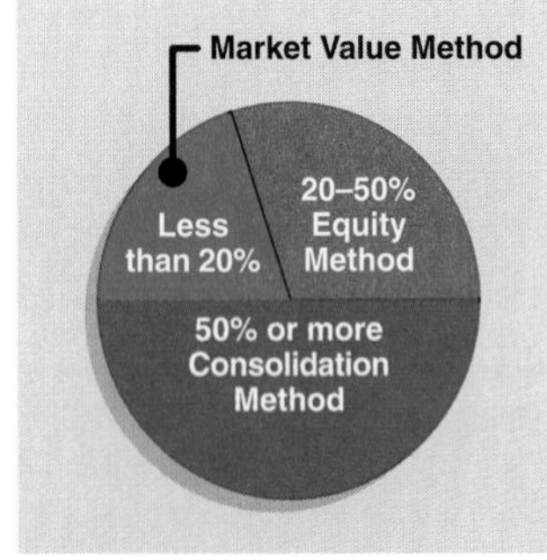

EXHIBIT 10-5
Accounting Methods for Stock Investment by Percentage of Ownership

Almost all published financial reports include consolidated statements. To understand the statements you are likely to encounter, you need to know the basic concepts underlying consolidation accounting. **Consolidated statements** combine the balance sheets, income statements, and other financial statements of the parent company with those of majority-owned subsidiaries into an overall set of statements as if the parent and its subsidiaries were a single entity. The goal is to provide a better perspective on total operations than could be obtained by examining the separate reports of each individual company. The assets, liabilities, revenues, and expenses of each subsidiary are added to the parent's accounts. The consolidated financial statements present the combined account balances. For example, the balance in the Cash account of Saturn Corporation is added to the balance in the General Motors Cash account, and the sum of the two amounts is presented as a single amount in the consolidated balance sheet of General Motors Corporation. Each account balance of a subsidiary loses its identity in the consolidated statements. The annual report may list the subsidiary companies' names. Exhibit 10-6 diagrams a corporate structure whose parent corporation owns controlling interests in five subsidiary companies and an equity-method investment in another investee company.

The sections that follow discuss the *purchase* method of accounting for consolidations. The purchase method is used most often in practice. Another method, called *pooling of interests* accounting, is covered in advanced accounting courses.

Consolidated Balance Sheet—Parent Corporation Owns All of Subsidiary's Stock

Suppose that Parent Corporation has purchased all the outstanding common stock of Subsidiary Corporation at its book value of $150,000. In addition, Parent Corporation loaned Subsidiary Corporation $80,000. The $150,000 is paid to

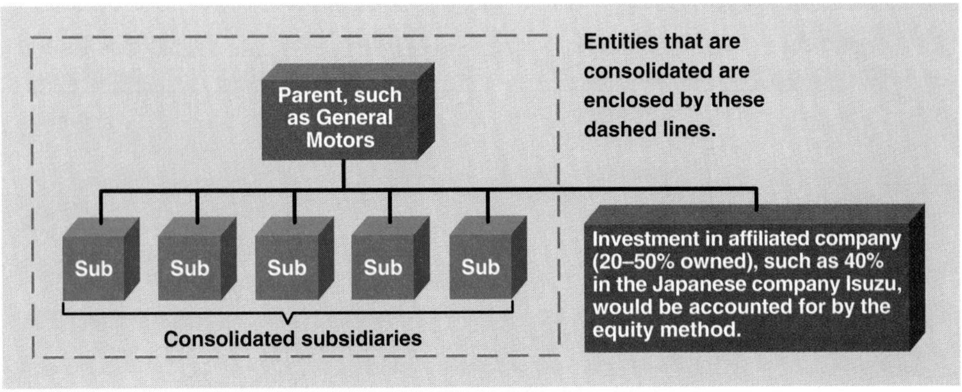

EXHIBIT 10-6
Parent Company with Consolidated Subsidiaries and an Equity-Method Investment

Entities that are consolidated are enclosed by these dashed lines.

Parent, such as General Motors

Sub | Sub | Sub | Sub | Sub

Consolidated subsidiaries

Investment in affiliated company (20–50% owned), such as 40% in the Japanese company Isuzu, would be accounted for by the equity method.

the *former owners* of Subsidiary Corporation as private investors. The $150,000 is *not* an addition to the existing assets and stockholders' equity of Subsidiary Corporation. That is, *the books of Subsidiary Corporation are completely unaffected by Parent Corporation's initial investment and Parent's subsequent accounting for that investment. Subsidiary Corporation is not dissolved. It lives on as a separate legal entity but with a new owner, Parent Corporation.*

Parent Corporation Books[1]			Subsidiary Corporation Books		
Investment in Subsidiary Corporation	150,000		No entry		
Cash		150,000			
Note Receivable from Subsidiary...........................	80,000		Cash	80,000	
Cash		80,000	Note Payable to Parent..		80,000

Each legal entity has its individual set of books. The consolidated entity does not keep a separate set of books. Instead, a work sheet is used to prepare the consolidated statements. (We will see two of these work sheets shortly.) A major concern in consolidation accounting is this: *Do not double-count—that is, do not include the same item twice.*

Companies may prepare a consolidated balance sheet immediately after the acquisition. The consolidated balance sheet shows all the assets and liabilities of both the parent and the subsidiary. The Investment in Subsidiary Corporation account on the parent's books represents all the assets and liabilities of Subsidiary. The consolidated statements cannot show both the investment amount *plus* the amounts for the subsidiary's assets and liabilities. Doing so would count the same resources twice.

Explanation of Elimination Entry (a) Exhibit 10-7 on page 480 shows the work sheet for consolidating the balance sheet. Consider the elimination entry for the parent-subsidiary ownership accounts. Entry (a) credits the parent Investment account to eliminate its debit balance. It also eliminates the subsidiary stockholder's equity accounts by debiting Common Stock for $100,000 and Retained Earnings for $50,000. Without this elimination, the consolidated financial statements would include both the parent company's investment in the subsidiary and the subsidiary company's equity. Because these accounts represent the same thing—Subsidiary's equity—they must be eliminated from the consolidated totals. If they weren't, the same item would be counted twice.

[1]The parent company may use either the cost method or the equity method for entries to the Investment account. Regardless of the method used, the consolidated statements are the same. Advanced accounting courses deal with this topic.

Assets	Parent Corporation	Subsidiary Corporation	Eliminations Debit	Eliminations Credit	Consolidated Amounts
Cash	12,000	18,000			30,000
Notes receivable from Subsidiary	80,000	—		(b) 80,000	—
Inventory	104,000	91,000			195,000
Investment in Subsidiary	150,000	—		(a) 150,000	—
Other assets	218,000	138,000			356,000
Total	564,000	247,000			581,000
Liabilities and Stockholders' Equity					
Accounts payable	43,000	17,000			60,000
Notes payable	190,000	80,000	(b) 80,000		190,000
Common stock	176,000	100,000	(a) 100,000		176,000
Retained earnings	155,000	50,000	(a) 50,000		155,000
Total	564,000	247,000	230,000	230,000	581,000

EXHIBIT 10-7
Work Sheet for Consolidated Balance Sheet—Parent Corporation Owns All of Subsidiary's Stock

The resulting consolidated balance sheet reports no Investment in Subsidiary account, and the consolidated totals for Common Stock and Retained Earnings are those of Parent Corporation only. The consolidated amounts appear in the final column of the consolidation work sheet.

EXPLANATION OF ELIMINATION ENTRY (B) Parent Corporation loaned $80,000 to Subsidiary Corporation, and Subsidiary signed a note payable to Parent. Therefore, Parent's balance sheet includes an $80,000 note receivable, and Subsidiary's balance sheet reports a note payable, for the same amount. The parent's receivable and the subsidiary's payable represent the same resources (all entirely within the consolidated entity) and so must be eliminated. Entry (b) accomplishes this. The $80,000 credit in the elimination column of the work sheet offsets Parent's Notes Receivable from Subsidiary. After this work sheet entry, the consolidated amount for notes receivable is zero. The $80,000 debit in the elimination column offsets the Subsidiary's Notes Payable, and the resulting consolidated amount for notes payable is the amount owed to creditors outside the consolidated entity, which is appropriate.

STOP & THINK Examine Exhibit 10-7. Why does the consolidated stockholders' equity ($176,000 + $155,000) exclude the equity of Subsidiary Corporation?

Answer: Because the stockholders' equity of the consolidated entity is that of the parent only. Also, the subsidiary's equity and the parent company's investment balance represent the same resources. Therefore, including them both would amount to double counting.

Parent Corporation Buys Subsidiary's Stock and Pays for Goodwill

A company may acquire a subsidiary by paying a price in excess of the market value of the subsidiary's net assets (assets minus liabilities). By definition, this excess is *goodwill.* What drives a company's market value up? The company may create goodwill through its superior products, service, or location.

In Chapter 7, page 345, we defined *goodwill* as the excess of the cost of an acquired company over the sum of the market values of its net assets.

The subsidiary does not record goodwill. The goodwill is identified in the process of consolidating the parent and subsidiary financial statements.

Suppose Parent Corporation paid $450,000 to acquire 100% of the common stock of Subsidiary Corporation, which had Common Stock of $200,000 and Retained Earnings of $180,000. Parent's payment included $70,000 for goodwill

($450,000 – $200,000 – $180,000 = $70,000).[2] The following entry eliminates Parent's Investment account against Subsidiary's equity accounts:

Dec. 31	Common Stock, Subsidiary	200,000	
	Retained Earnings, Subsidiary	180,000	
	Goodwill	70,000	
	Investment in Subsidiary		450,000
	To eliminate cost of Investment in Subsidiary against Subsidiary's equity balances and to recognize Subsidiary's unrecorded goodwill.		

In practice, this entry would be made only on the consolidation work sheet. Here we show it in journal form for instructional purposes.

The asset goodwill is reported on the consolidated balance sheet among the intangible assets, after plant assets. For example, the last asset on **Coca-Cola's** consolidated balance sheet is Goodwill and Other Intangible Assets. Goodwill is amortized to expense over its useful life but not to exceed 40 years.

Consolidated Balance Sheet—Parent Company Owns Less Than 100% of Subsidiary's Stock

When a parent company owns more than 50% (a majority) of the subsidiary's stock but less than 100% of it, a new category of owners' equity, called *minority interest,* must appear on the consolidated balance sheet. Suppose Parent Company buys 75% of Subsidiary's common stock. **Minority interest** is the subsidiary's equity that is held by stockholders other than the parent company. Thus, minority interest in this example is the remaining 25% of Subsidiary's equity. Most companies report minority interest as a liability, while a few show it as a separate element of stockholders' equity. To be consistent with actual practice, in this book we list minority interest as a liability. Exhibit 10-8 is the consolidation work sheet. Again, focus on the Eliminations columns and the Consolidated Amounts.

Entry (a) in Exhibit 10-8 eliminates P Company's Investment balance of $120,000 against the $160,000 owners' equity (common stock plus retained earnings) of S Company. All of S's equity is eliminated even though P holds only 75% of S's stock. The outside 25% interest in S's equity is credited to Minority Interest ($160,000 × 0.25 = $40,000). Thus, entry (a) reclassifies 25% of S Company's equity

EXHIBIT 10-8
Work Sheet for Consolidated Balance Sheet—Parent Company Owns Less Than 100% of Subsidiary's Stock (There will be a minority interest.)

			Eliminations		Consolidated
Assets	**P Company**	**S Company**	**Debit**	**Credit**	**Amounts**
Cash	33,000	18,000			51,000
Notes receivable from P	—	50,000		(b) 50,000	—
Accounts receivable, net	54,000	39,000			93,000
Inventory	92,000	66,000			158,000
Investment in S	120,000	—		(a) 120,000	—
Plant and equipment, net	230,000	123,000			353,000
Total	529,000	296,000			655,000
Liabilities and Stockholders' Equity					
Accounts payable	141,000	94,000			235,000
Notes payable	50,000	42,000	(b) 50,000		42,000
Minority interest	—	—		(a) 40,000	40,000
Common stock	170,000	100,000	(a) 100,000		170,000
Retained earnings	168,000	60,000	(a) 60,000		168,000
Total	529,000	296,000	210,000	210,000	655,000

[2]For simplicity, we are assuming that the fair market value of the subsidiary's net assets (assets minus liabilities) equals the book value of the company's owners' equity. Advanced courses consider other situations.

EXHIBIT 10-9
Consolidated Balance Sheet of P Company

P COMPANY AND CONSOLIDATED SUBSIDIARY
Consolidated Balance Sheet
December 31, 19XX

Assets	
Cash	$ 51,000
Accounts receivable, net	93,000
Inventory	158,000
Plant and equipment, net	353,000
Total assets	$655,000
Liabilities and Stockholders' Equity	
Accounts payable	$235,000
Notes payable	42,000
Minority interest	40,000
Common stock	170,000
Retained earnings	168,000
Total liabilities and stockholders' equity	$655,000

as minority interest. Entry (b) in Exhibit 10-8 eliminates S Company's $50,000 note receivable against P's note payable of the same amount. The consolidated amount of notes payable ($42,000) is the amount that S Company owes to outsiders.

The consolidated balance sheet of P Company in Exhibit 10-9 is based on the work sheet of Exhibit 10-8. The consolidated balance sheet reveals that ownership of P Company and its consolidated subsidiary is divided between P's stockholders (common stock and retained earnings totaling $338,000) and the minority interest of S Company ($40,000).

LEARNING TIP The elimination entry requires, at most, five steps:

1. Eliminate intercompany receivables and payables.
2. Eliminate the stockholders' equity accounts of the subsidiary.
3. Eliminate the Investment in Subsidiary account.
4. Record any goodwill.
5. Record any minority interest.

Income of a Consolidated Entity

The income of a consolidated entity is the net income of the parent plus the parent's proportion of the subsidiaries' net income. Suppose Parent Company owns all the stock of Subsidiary S-1 and 60% of the stock of Subsidiary S-2. During the year just ended, Parent earned net income of $330,000, S-1 earned $150,000, and S-2 had a net loss of $100,000. Parent Company would report net income of $420,000, computed as follows:

	Net Income (Net Loss)		Parent Stockholders' Ownership		Parent's Consolidated Net Income (Net Loss)
Parent Company	$ 330,000	×	100%	=	$330,000
Subsidiary S-1	150,000	×	100%	=	150,000
Subsidiary S-2	(100,000)	×	60%	=	(60,000)
Consolidated net income					$420,000

STOP & THINK Answer these questions about consolidated financial statements:

1. Whose name appears on the consolidated statements—the parent company, the subsidiary company, or both?
2. Company A owns 90% of Company B. What is the remaining 10% of Company B's stock called, and where does it appear, if at all, in Company A's financial statements?
3. Company C paid $1 million to acquire Company D, whose stockholders' equity (same as net assets) totaled $700,000. What is the $300,000 excess called? Which company reports the excess? Where in the financial statements is the excess reported?

Answers

1. Parent Company only.
2. Minority Interest—reported on (Parent) Company A's balance sheet among the liabilities.
3. Goodwill—reported on (Parent) Company C's balance sheet as an intangible asset.

Computers and Consolidations

Consider diversified companies such as W. R. Grace & Co., the world's largest specialty chemicals company. Grace includes nearly 30 subsidiary firms, with more than 100 different product lines—from food packaging to construction materials to health-care products. A company such as Grace can prepare its consolidated financial statements automatically with a fully integrated accounting information system. But many wholly-owned subsidiaries retain their own accounting systems. If the subsidiaries have adopted the parent company's standard chart of accounts, a supplementary system can automatically combine the accounts of the parent and subsidiary companies and prepare the consolidated statements.

Long-Term Investments in Bonds and Notes

Objective 4

Account for long-term investments in bonds

Industrial and commercial companies invest far more in stocks than they invest in bonds. The major investors in bonds are financial institutions, such as pension plans, bank trust departments, mutual funds, and insurance companies. The relationship between the issuing corporation and the investor (bondholder) may be diagrammed as follows:

Issuing Corporation		Investor (Bondholder)
Bonds payable	←——→	Investment in bonds
Interest expense	←——→	Interest revenue

The dollar amount of a bond transaction is the same for issuer and investor, but the accounts debited and credited differ. For example, the issuing corporation's interest expense is the investor's interest revenue.

An investment in bonds is classified either as short-term (a current asset) or as long-term. Short-term investments in bonds are rare. Here, we focus on long-term investments in bonds and notes that the investor intends to hold until the bonds mature. These are called **held-to-maturity investments.**

We first encountered held-to-maturity investments in Chapter 5, page 223.

Accounting for Held-to-Maturity Investments— The Amortized Cost Method

Bond investments are recorded at cost. At maturity, the investor will receive the bonds' face value. For held-to-maturity investments, discount or premium is amortized to account more precisely for interest revenue over the period the bonds will be held. The amortization of discount or premium on a bond investment affects both Interest Revenue for the investor and the carrying amount of the bonds for the company that issued the bonds. Held-to-maturity investments in bonds are reported at their *amortized cost,* which determines the carrying amount.

For a review of the amortized-cost method, see Chapter 5, pages 223–224. *Amortized cost* means cost plus accrued interest to date.

Suppose an investor purchases $10,000 of 6% CBS bonds at a price of 95.2 on April 1, 19X2. The investor intends to hold the bonds as a long-term investment until their maturity. Interest dates are April 1 and October 1. These bonds mature on April 1, 19X6, so they will be outstanding for 48 months. Assume amortization of the discount by the straight-line method. The following are the entries for this long-term investment:

Straight-line amortization of premium or discount on a bond investment is calculated the same way as it is calculated for bonds payable (see Chapter 8, pages 390–391).

Date	Accounts	Debit	Credit
Apr. 1	Long-Term Investment in Bonds ($10,000 × 0.952)..	9,520	
	Cash		9,520
	To purchase bond investment.		
Oct. 1	Cash ($10,000 × 0.06 × 6/12)........	300	
	Interest Revenue........		300
	To receive semiannual interest.		
Oct. 1	Long-Term Investment in Bonds		
	[($10,000 – $9,520)/48] × 6	60	
	Interest Revenue........		60
	To amortize discount on bond investment for six months.		

At December 31, the year-end adjustments are

Date	Accounts	Debit	Credit
Dec. 31	Interest Receivable ($10,000 × 0.06 × 3/12)........	150	
	Interest Revenue		150
	To accrue interest revenue for three months.		
Dec. 31	Long-Term Investment in Bonds		
	[($10,000 – $9,520)/48] × 3	30	
	Interest Revenue		30
	To amortize discount on bond investment for three months.		

This amortization entry has two effects: (1) It increases the Long-Term Investment account on its march toward maturity value, and (2) it records the related interest revenue that the investor has earned as a result of the increase in the carrying amount of the investment.

The financial statements at December 31, 19X2, report the following effects of this investment in bonds (assume that the bonds' market price is 102):

Balance sheet at December 31, 19X2:

Current assets:	
Interest receivable	$ 150
Total current assets	X,XXX
Long-term investments in bonds ($9,520 + $60 + $30)—Note 6	9,610
Property, plant, and equipment........	X,XXX

Note 6: Long-term investments:
Bond investments that will be held-to-maturity are reported at *amortized cost*. At December 31, 19X2, the market value of long-term investments in bonds was $10,200 ($10,000 × 1.02).

Income statement (multiple-step) for the year ended December 31, 19X2:

Other revenues:	
Interest revenue ($300 + $60 + $150 + $30)........	$ 540

Decision Guidelines

Accounting Method to Use for Each Type of Long-Term Investment

Type of Long-Term Investment	Accounting Method
Investor owns less than 20% of investee stock (Available-for-sale investment classified as noncurrent asset)	Market value
Investor owns between 20 and 50% of investee/affiliate stock	Equity
Investment in a joint venture	Equity
Investor owns more than 50% of investee stock	Consolidation
Long-term investment in bonds (Held-to-maturity investment)	Amortized cost

Summary of Accounting Methods

This chapter has illustrated how to account for various types of long-term investments. The Decision Guidelines feature shows which accounting method to use for each type of long-term investment.

Mid-Chapter SUMMARY PROBLEMS FOR YOUR REVIEW

1. Identify the appropriate accounting method for each of the following situations:
   a. Investment in 25% of investee's stock
   b. Available-for-sale investment in stock
   c. Investment in more than 50% of investee's stock

2. At what amount should the following available-for-sale investment portfolio be reported on the December 31 balance sheet? All the investments are less than 5% of the investee's stock.

Stock	Investment Cost	Current Market Value
DuPont	$ 5,000	$ 5,500
Exxon	61,200	53,000
Procter & Gamble	3,680	6,230

   Journalize any adjusting entry required by these data.

3. Investor paid $67,900 to acquire a 40% equity-method investment in the common stock of Investee. At the end of the first year, Investee's net income was $80,000, and Investee declared and paid cash dividends of $55,000. Journalize Investor's (a) purchase of the investment, (b) share of Investee's net income, (c) receipt of dividends from Investee, and (d) sale of Investee stock for $80,100.

4. Parent Company paid $100,000 for all the common stock of Subsidiary Company, and Parent owes Subsidiary $20,000 on a note payable. Complete the consolidation work sheet at the top of page 486.

Assets	Parent Company	Subsidiary Company	Eliminations Debit	Eliminations Credit	Consolidated Amounts
Cash	7,000	4,000			
Note receivable from Parent	—	20,000			
Investment in Subsidiary	100,000	—			
Goodwill	—	—			
Other assets	108,000	99,000			
Total	215,000	123,000			
Liabilities and Stockholders' Equity					
Accounts payable	15,000	8,000			
Notes payable	20,000	30,000			
Common stock	135,000	60,000			
Retained earnings	45,000	25,000			
Total	215,000	123,000			

ANSWERS

1. (a) Equity (b) Market value (c) Consolidation

2. Report the investments at market value, $64,730.

Stock	Investment Cost	Current Market Value
DuPont	$ 5,000	$ 5,500
Exxon	61,200	53,000
Procter & Gamble	3,680	6,230
Totals	$69,880	$64,730

Adjusting entry:

	Debit	Credit
Unrealized Loss on Investments ($69,880 – $64,730)	5,150	
Allowance to Adjust Investment to Market		5,150
To adjust investments to current market value.		

3.

	Debit	Credit
a. Long-Term Investment	67,900	
Cash		67,900
To purchase equity-method investment.		
b. Long-Term Investment ($80,000 × 0.40)	32,000	
Equity-Method Investment Revenue		32,000
To record investment revenue.		
c. Cash ($55,000 × 0.40)	22,000	
Long-Term Investment		22,000
To record receipt of cash dividend on equity-method investment.		
d. Cash	80,100	
Long-Term Investment ($67,900 + $32,000 – $22,000)		77,900
Gain on Sale of Investment		2,200
Sold investment.		

4. Consolidation work sheet:

Assets	Parent Company	Subsidiary Company	Eliminations Debit	Eliminations Credit	Consolidated Amounts
Cash	7,000	4,000			11,000
Note receivable from Parent	—	20,000		(a) 20,000	—
Investment in Subsidiary	100,000	—		(b) 100,000	—
Goodwill	—	—	(b) 15,000*		15,000
Other assets	108,000	99,000			207,000
Total	215,000	123,000			233,000
Liabilities and Stockholders' Equity					
Accounts payable	15,000	8,000			23,000
Notes payable	20,000	30,000	(a) 20,000		30,000
Common stock	135,000	60,000	(b) 60,000		135,000
Retained earnings	45,000	25,000	(b) 25,000		45,000
Total	215,000	123,000	120,000	120,000	233,000

*Computation of goodwill:

Cost of investment in Subsidiary	$100,000
– Subsidiary's stockholder equity ($60,000 + $25,000)	(85,000)
= Goodwill	$ 15,000

Accounting for International Operations

Did you know that Exxon and Bank of America earn most of their revenue outside the United States? It is common for U.S. companies to do a large part of their business abroad. Coca-Cola, IBM, Johnson & Johnson, Bristol-Myers Squibb, and Campbell Soup, among many others, are very active in other countries. Exhibit 10-10 shows the percentages of international sales and operating income for these companies.

Accounting for business activities across national boundaries makes up the field of *international accounting.* As communications and transportation improve and trade barriers fall, global integration makes international accounting more important. This section starts with economic structures and their impact on international accounting and then shows several applications to specific areas.

EXHIBIT 10-10
Extent of International Business

Company	Percent of International Sales	Percent of International Operating Income or Net Income
Coca-Cola	71%	82%
IBM	60	86
Johnson & Johnson	51	48
Bristol-Myers Squibb	44	31
Campell Soup	32	20

Economic Structures and Their Impact on International Accounting

The business environment varies widely across the globe. New York reflects the diversity of the market-driven economy of the United States. Japan's economy is similar to that of the United States, although Japanese business activity focuses more on imports and exports. The central government controls the economy of China, so private business decisions are only beginning to take root there. In Brazil, high rates of inflation have made historical-cost amounts meaningless. Accounting amounts are altered periodically to measure changes in the purchasing power of the cruzeiro, Brazil's monetary unit. International accounting deals with such differences in economic structures.

Foreign Currencies and Foreign-Currency Exchange Rates

Each country uses its own national currency. If Boeing, a U.S.-owned company, sells a 747 jet to Air France, will Boeing receive U.S. dollars or French francs? If the transaction takes place in dollars, Air France must exchange its francs for dollars to pay Boeing in U.S. currency. If the transaction takes place in francs, Boeing will receive francs, which it must exchange for dollars. In either case, a step has been added to the transaction: One company must convert domestic currency into foreign currency, or the other company must convert foreign currency into domestic currency.

The price of one nation's currency may be stated in terms of another country's monetary unit. This measure of one currency against another currency is called the **foreign-currency exchange rate.** In Exhibit 10-11, the dollar value of a French franc is \$0.19. This means that one French franc can be bought for 19 cents. Other currencies, such as the pound and the yen (also listed in Exhibit 10-11), are similarly bought and sold.

We use the exchange rate to convert the cost of an item given in one currency to its cost in a second currency. We call this conversion a *translation.* Suppose an item costs 200 French francs. To compute its cost in dollars, we multiply the amount in francs by the conversion rate: 200 French francs × \$0.19 = \$38.

To aid the flow of international business, a market exists for foreign currencies. Traders buy and sell U.S. dollars, French francs, and other currencies in the same way that they buy and sell other commodities such as beef, cotton, and automobiles. And just as supply and demand cause the prices of these other commodities to shift, so supply and demand for a particular currency cause exchange rates to fluctuate daily. When the demand for a nation's currency exceeds the supply of that currency, its exchange rate rises. When supply exceeds demand, the currency's exchange rate falls.

Two main factors determine the supply and demand for a particular currency: (1) the ratio of a country's imports to its exports, and (2) the rate of return available in the country's capital markets.

THE IMPORT/EXPORT RATIO Japanese exports far surpass Japan's imports. Customers of Japanese companies must buy yen (the Japanese unit of currency) in the international currency market to pay for their purchases. This strong demand drives up the price—the foreign exchange rate—of the yen. In contrast, France imports more goods than it exports. French businesses must sell francs to buy the foreign currencies needed to acquire the foreign goods. The supply of the French franc increases, and so its price decreases.

EXHIBIT 10-11
Foreign-Currency Exchange Rates

Country	Monetary Unit	Dollar Value	Country	Monetary Unit	Dollar Value
Canada	Dollar	\$0.73	Great Britain	Pound	\$1.55
European Common Market	European currency unit	1.25	Italy	Lira	0.0006
			Japan	Yen	0.0091
France	Franc	0.19	Mexico	Peso	0.133
Germany	Mark	0.66			

Source: The *Wall Street Journal,* September 20, 1996, p. C15.

The Rate of Return The rate of return available in a country's capital markets affects the amount of investment funds flowing into the country. When rates of return are high in a politically stable country such as the United States, international investors buy stocks, bonds, and real estate in that country. This activity increases the demand for the nation's currency and drives up its exchange rate.

Currencies are often described as "strong" or "weak." The exchange rate of a **strong currency** is rising relative to other nations' currencies. The exchange rate of a **weak currency** is falling relative to other currencies.

Suppose the *Wall Street Journal* listed the exchange rate for the British pound as \$1.55 on October 14. On October 15, that rate has changed to \$1.53. We would say that the dollar has risen against—is stronger than—the British pound because the pound has become less expensive, and so the dollar now buys more pounds. A stronger dollar would make travel to England more attractive to Americans.

Assume that the *Wall Street Journal* reports a rise in the exchange rate of the Japanese yen from \$0.0091 to \$0.0099. This change indicates that the yen is stronger than the dollar. Japanese automobiles, cameras, and electronic products are more expensive because each dollar buys fewer yen.

Managing Cash in International Transactions

Objective 5

Account for transactions stated in a foreign currency

As international transactions become more and more common, more companies are understanding the need to manage cash transactions conducted in foreign currencies. **D. E. Shipp Belting,** a small family-owned company in Waco, Texas, provides an example. Shipp makes conveyor belts that are used in a variety of industries. For example, **M&M Mars,** which makes Snickers candy bars in Waco, is an important customer of Shipp Belting. Farmers in the Rio Grande Valley along the Texas-Mexico border use Shipp conveyor belts to process vegetables. Some of these customers are on the Mexican side of the border, so Shipp Belting conducts some of its business in pesos, the Mexican monetary unit.

M&M Mars, which makes Snickers candy bars in Waco, is an important customer of Shipp Belting.

The Swiss have developed some of the leading technologies for manufacturing high-grade conveyor belts, and competitive pressure forces Shipp to stay on the cutting edge of the industry. Greg Ogden, one of Shipp Belting's owners, purchases inventory from the Swiss companies and pays a fee to use their patented processes. Some of these transactions are conducted in Swiss francs.

Cash Receipts in a Foreign Currency Consider Shipp Belting's sale of conveyor belts to Artes de Mexico, a vegetable grower in Matamoros, Mexico. The sale can be conducted either in dollars or in pesos. If Artes de Mexico agrees to pay in dollars, Shipp avoids the complication of dealing in a foreign currency, and the transaction is the same as selling to M&M Mars across town. But suppose that Artes de Mexico orders 1 million pesos (approximately \$130,000) worth of conveyor belts from Shipp. This large sale would be very important to Shipp Belting. Further suppose that Artes demands to pay in pesos and that Shipp reluctantly agrees to receive pesos instead of dollars.

Shipp will need to convert the pesos to dollars, so the transaction poses a challenge. What if the peso loses value—weakens as it takes more pesos to obtain each dollar—before Shipp collects from Artes? In this case, Shipp will not earn as much as expected on the sale. The following example shows how to account for international transactions that result in the receipt of a foreign currency. It also shows how to measure the effects of such transactions on a company's cash position and profits.

Shipp Belting sells goods to Artes de Mexico for a price of 1 million pesos on June 2. On that date, a peso was worth \$0.1316, as quoted in exchange rate tables of the *Wall Street Journal.* One month later, on July 2, the peso has weakened against the dollar and a peso is worth only $0.1266. Shipp receives 1 million pesos from Artes on July 2, but the dollar value of Shipp's cash receipt is $5,000 less than expected, so Shipp ends up earning less than hoped for on the transaction. The following journal entries show how Shipp Belting would account for these transactions:

June 2	Accounts Receivable—Artes (1,000,000 pesos × $0.1316)	131,600	
	Sales Revenue		131,600
	Sale on account.		

ASSETS	=	LIABILITIES	+	STOCKHOLDERS' EQUITY	+	REVENUES
131,600	=	0			+	131,600

July 2	Cash (1,000,000 pesos × $0.1266)	126,600	
	Foreign-Currency Transaction Loss	5,000	
	Accounts Receivable—Artes		131,600
	Collection on account.		

ASSETS	=	LIABILITIES	+	STOCKHOLDERS' EQUITY	−	LOSSES
+126,600 −131,600	=	0			−	5,000

If Shipp had required Artes to pay at the time of the sale, Shipp would have received pesos worth $131,600. But by waiting the normal 30-day collection period to receive cash, Shipp exposed itself to *foreign-currency exchange risk,* the risk of loss in an international transaction. In this case, Shipp experienced a $5,000 foreign-currency transaction loss and received $5,000 less cash than expected, as shown in the collection entry.

If the peso had increased in value, Shipp would have experienced a foreign-currency transaction gain. When a company holds a receivable denominated in a foreign currency, it wants the foreign currency to remain strong so that it can be converted into more dollars. Unfortunately, this did not occur for Shipp Belting. One way of managing foreign-currency exchange risk is for the seller to simply quote a higher price for its goods in foreign markets. If the buyer accepts, the seller has protected itself against the risk of loss.

CASH DISBURSEMENTS IN A FOREIGN CURRENCY Purchasing from a foreign company may also expose a company to foreign-currency exchange risk. To illustrate, assume Shipp Belting buys inventory from Gesellschaft Ltd., a Swiss company. After lengthy negotiations, the two companies decide on a price of 20,000 Swiss francs. On August 10, when Shipp receives the goods, the Swiss franc is quoted in international currency markets at $0.7999. When Shipp pays two weeks later, on August 24, the Swiss franc has weakened against the dollar—decreased in value to $0.7810. Shipp would record the purchase and payment as follows:

Aug. 10	Inventory (20,000 Swiss francs × $0.7999)	15,998	
	Accounts Payable—Gesellschaft Ltd		15,998
	Purchase on account.		

ASSETS	=	LIABILITIES	+	STOCKHOLDERS' EQUITY
15,998	=	15,998	+	0

Aug. 24	Accounts Payable—Gesellschaft Ltd. (20,000 × $0.7999)	15,998	
	Foreign-Currency Transaction Gain		378
	Cash (20,000 Swiss francs × $0.7810)		15,620
	Payment on account.		

ASSETS	=	LIABILITIES	+	STOCKHOLDERS' EQUITY	+	GAINS
−15,620	=	−15,998			+	378

The Swiss franc could have strengthened against the dollar, in which case Shipp would have had a foreign-currency transaction loss. A company with a payable denominated in a foreign currency hopes that the dollar gets stronger. When the payment date arrives, the company can use fewer dollars to purchase the foreign currency and thereby reduce its cost.

REPORTING FOREIGN-CURRENCY TRANSACTION GAINS AND LOSSES ON THE INCOME STATEMENT The Foreign-Currency Transaction Gain account is the record of the gains on transactions settled in a currency other than the dollar. Likewise, the Foreign-Currency Transaction Loss account shows the amount of the losses on transactions conducted in foreign currencies. The company reports the *net amount* of these two accounts on the income statement as Other Revenues and Gains, or Other Expenses and Losses, as the case may be. For example, Shipp Belting would combine the $5,000 foreign-currency loss and the $378 gain and report the net loss of $4,622 on the income statement as follows:

Other Expenses and Losses:	
Foreign-currency transaction loss, net	$4,622

These gains and losses fall into the "Other" category because they arise from buying and selling foreign currencies, not from the main line of the company's business (in the case of D. E. Shipp Belting, selling conveyor belts).

Managers examine these gains and losses to see how well the company is faring in foreign-currency transactions. The gains and losses may offset each other, and the net gain or loss may be small. But if losses exceed gains and the net loss reaches a critical level, managers may take action to shield themselves against the risk of further loss. One such action is hedging, which we discuss next.

HEDGING—A STRATEGY TO AVOID FOREIGN-CURRENCY TRANSACTION LOSSES One way for U.S. companies to avoid foreign-currency transaction losses is to insist that international transactions be settled in dollars. This requirement puts the burden of currency translation on the foreign party. However, such a strategy may alienate customers and decrease sales, or it may cause customers to demand unreasonable credit terms. Another way for a company to protect itself from the effects of fluctuating foreign-currency exchange rates is by hedging.

Hedging means to protect oneself from losing money in one transaction by engaging in a counterbalancing transaction. A U.S. company selling goods to be collected in Mexican pesos expects to receive a fixed number of pesos in the future. If the peso is losing value, the U.S. company would expect the pesos to be worth fewer dollars than the amount of the receivable—an expected loss situation, as we saw for Shipp Belting.

The U.S. company may have accumulated payables stated in a foreign currency in the normal course of its business, such as the amount payable by Shipp to the Swiss company. Losses on the receipt of pesos may be approximately offset by gains on the payment of Swiss francs to Gesellschaft Ltd. Most companies do not have equal amounts of receivables and payables in foreign currency, so offsetting receivables and payables is imprecise. To obtain a more precise hedge, some companies buy *futures contracts,* which are contracts for foreign currencies to be received in the future. Futures contracts can effectively create a payable to exactly offset a receivable, and vice versa. Many companies that do business internationally use hedging techniques.

Consolidation of Foreign Subsidiaries

Objective 6

Compute and interpret a foreign-currency translation adjustment

A U.S. company with a foreign subsidiary must consolidate the subsidiary's financial statements into its own statements for reporting to the public. The consolidation of a foreign subsidiary poses two special challenges. Many countries outside the United States specify accounting treatments that differ from American accounting principles. For the purpose of reporting to the American public, accountants for the parent company must first bring the subsidiary's statements into conformity with American GAAP.

The second accounting challenge arises when the subsidiary statements are expressed in a foreign currency. A preliminary step in the consolidation process is to translate the subsidiary statements into dollars. Then the dollar-value statements of the subsidiary can be combined with the parent's statements in the usual manner, as illustrated in the first part of this chapter.

The process of translating a foreign subsidiary's financial statements into dollars usually creates a *foreign-currency translation adjustment.* This item appears in the financial statements of most multinational companies and is reported as part of other comprehensive income on the income statement and as part of stockholders' equity on the consolidated balance sheet. A translation adjustment arises due to changes in the foreign exchange rate over time. In general, *assets* and *liabilities* in the foreign subsidiaries' financial statements are translated into dollars at the exchange rate in effect on the date of the statements. However, *stockholders' equity* is translated into dollars at older, historical exchange rates. This difference in exchange rates creates an out-of-balance condition on the balance sheet. The translation adjustment amount brings the balance sheet back into balance.

U.S. Express Corporation owns Italian Imports, Inc., whose financial statements are expressed in lire (the Italian currency). U.S. Express consolidates the Italian subsidiary's financial statements into its own statements. When U.S. Express acquired Italian Imports in 19X1, a lira was worth $0.00070. When Italian Imports earned its retained income during 19X1—19X6, the average exchange rate was $0.00067. On the balance sheet date in 19X6, a lira is worth only $0.00060. Exhibit 10-12 shows how to translate Italian Imports' balance sheet into dollars and shows how the translation adjustment arises.

The **foreign-currency translation adjustment** is the balancing amount that brings the dollar amount of the total liabilities and stockholders' equity of a foreign subsidiary into agreement with the dollar amount of its total assets (in Exhibit 10-12, total assets equal $480,000). Only after the translation adjustment of $24,000 do total liabilities and stockholders' equity equal total assets stated in

EXHIBIT 10-12
Translation of a Foreign-Currency Balance Sheet into Dollars

Italian Imports, Inc., Amounts	Lire	Exchange Rate	Dollars
Assets	800,000,000	$0.00060	$480,000
Liabilities	500,000,000	0.00060	$300,000
Stockholders' equity:			
Common stock	100,000,000	0.00070	70,000
Retained earnings	200,000,000	0.00067	134,000
Accumulated other comprehensive income:			
Translation adjustment	—		(24,000)
	800,000,000		$480,000

dollars. In this case, the translation adjustment is negative, and total stockholders' equity becomes $180,000 ($70,000 + $134,000 – $24,000).

What in the economic environment caused the negative translation adjustment? A weakening of the lira since the acquisition of Italian Imports brought about the need for this adjustment. When U.S. Express acquired the foreign subsidiary in 19X1, a lira was worth $0.00070. When Italian Imports earned its retained income during 19X1 through 19X6, the average exchange rate was $0.00067. On the balance sheet date in 19X6, a lira is worth only $0.00060, so Italian Imports' net assets (assets minus liabilities) are translated into only $180,000 ($480,000 – $300,000).

To bring stockholders' equity to $180,000 requires a $24,000 negative amount. In a sense, a negative translation adjustment is like a loss. But it is reported as a contra item in the stockholders' equity section of the balance sheet, not on the income statement. The interpretation of a negative translation adjustment is this: Measured in today's dollars, the book value of U.S. Express Corporation's investment in Italian Imports, Inc., is less than the amount U.S. Express invested to acquire the company.

The Italian Imports dollar figures in Exhibit 10-12 are the amounts that U.S. Express Corporation would include in its consolidated balance sheet. The consolidation procedures would follow those illustrated beginning on page 477.

The translation adjustment can be positive—a gain—as well as negative, depending on the movement of foreign currency exchange rates. Consider **Campbell Soup Company.** The following adapted excerpt from Campbell Soup's balance sheet shows a positive translation adjustment:

Shareowners' Equity	(In millions) 1995	1994
Preferred stock	$ —	$ —
Capital (common) stock	20	20
Capital surplus (Additional paid-in capital)	165	155
Earnings retained in the business	2,755	2,359
Capital stock in treasury	(550)	(559)
Accumulated other comprehensive income:		
Foreign-currency translation adjustments	78	14
Total shareowners' equity	$2,468	$1,989

In a recent survey of 600 companies, 395 (65%) reported a translation adjustment on their balance sheet.

STOP & THINK At the end of 1995, Campbell Soup Company's cumulative translation adjustment was $78 million, a positive amount. The 1995 translation adjustment exceeded the amount of the translation adjustment reported at the end of 1994.

1. State in your own words the meaning of Campbell Soup's translation adjustment at the end of 1995.
2. Does the positive translation adjustment at the end of 1995 indicate a strong dollar or a weak dollar? Explain your answer.
3. Did the dollar strengthen or weaken during 1995 relative to the currencies of Campbell Soup's foreign subsidiaries? Explain your answer.

Answers

1. At the end of 1995, the book value of Campbell Soup's investment in foreign subsidiaries, measured in current 1995 dollars, exceeds the amount Campbell Soup invested to acquire its foreign subsidiaries. This can be interpreted as a gain.
2. The positive translation adjustment indicates a *weak dollar.* The currencies of the countries in which Campbell Soup's foreign subsidiaries are located have risen in value relative to the dollar. The foreign currencies have been stronger than the dollar.

When translated into dollars, the foreign subsidiaries' net assets carry higher book amounts.

3. During 1995, the dollar weakened relative to the currencies of Campbell Soup's foreign subsidiaries. The foreign currencies strengthened. The increase in the dollar value of Campbell's foreign investments rose during 1995 from $14 million to $78 million, and such an increase can happen only when the foreign currencies have risen in value relative to the dollar.

International Accounting Standards

In this text we focus on the principles of accounting that are generally accepted in the United States. Most of the methods of accounting are consistent throughout the world. Double-entry accounting, the accrual system, and the basic financial statements are used worldwide. Differences, however, do exist among countries, as shown in Exhibit 10-13.

In discussing depreciation (Chapter 7), we emphasized that in the United States the methods used for reporting to tax authorities differ from the methods used for reporting to shareholders. However, tax reporting and shareholder reporting are identical in many countries. For example, France has a "Plan Compatible" that specifies that a National Uniform Chart of Accounts be used for both tax returns and reporting to shareholders. German financial reporting is also determined primarily by tax laws. In Japan, certain principles are allowed for tax purposes only if they are also used for shareholder reporting.

For inventory, goodwill, and research and development costs, German accounting practices are more similar to those of the United States than to those of other countries. Despite the common heritage of the United States and the United Kingdom, U.S. and British accounting practices vary widely.

A company that sells its stock through a foreign stock exchange must follow the accounting principles of the foreign country. For example, **British Petroleum (BP)** stock is available through the New York Stock Exchange, so BP financial statements issued in the United States follow American GAAP.

A significant difference among countries is the extent to which the financial statements account for inflation. The FASB has experimented with requiring supplementary disclosure of inflation-adjusted numbers, but there is no requirement for such supplementary disclosure in the United States. In contrast, some countries have full or partial adjustments for inflation as part of their reporting to both investors and tax authorities. For example, Argentina and Brazil, which have experienced very high inflation rates, require all statements to be adjusted for changes in the general price level.

The globalization of business enterprises and capital markets is creating much interest in establishing common, worldwide accounting standards. There

EXHIBIT 10-13
Some International Accounting Differences

Country	Inventories	Goodwill	Research and Development Costs
United States	Specific unit cost, FIFO, LIFO, weighted-average.	Amortized over period not to exceed 40 years.	Expensed as incurred
Germany	Similar to U.S.	Amortized over 5 years.	Expensed as incurred.
Japan	Similar to U.S.	Amortized over 5 years.	May be capitalized and amortized over 5 years.
United Kingdom	LIFO is unacceptable for tax purposes and is not widely used.	Amortized over useful life or not amortized if life is indefinite.*	Expense research costs. Some development costs may be capitalized.

*Proposal being considered.

are probably too many cultural, social, and political differences to expect complete worldwide standardization of financial reporting in the near future. However, the number of differences is decreasing.

Several organizations are working to achieve worldwide harmony of accounting standards. Chief among these is the *International Accounting Standards Committee (IASC).* Headquartered in London, the IASC operates much as the Financial Accounting Standards Board in the United States. It has the support of the accounting professions in the United States, most of the British Commonwealth countries, Japan, France, Germany, the Netherlands, and Mexico. However, the IASC has no authority to require compliance with its accounting standards. It must rely on cooperation by the various national accounting professions. Since its creation in 1973, the IASC has succeeded in narrowing some differences in international accounting standards.

Using the Statement of Cash Flows to Interpret a Company's Investing Activities

Objective 7

Report investing transactions on the statement of cash flows

Investing activities include many types of transactions. In Chapter 7, we covered investing transactions in which companies purchase and sell long-term assets such as plant and equipment. Because the purchase of equipment is a type of long-term investment, it follows that the sale of equipment is also an investing activity. As we have seen in this chapter, there is another type of investing activity that actually carries the name *investment.* The purchase and sale of investments in the stocks and bonds of other companies are also investing activities that are reported on the cash-flow statement.

Investing activities are usually reported on the statement of cash flows as the second category, after operating activities and before financing activities. This ordering is by design. Many business people view investing activities as the second most important thing a company does—less important than operating activities but more important than financing activities. Here is the logic:

1. What a company does with its cash (operating activities) is the major factor in business success or failure.
2. The assets in which a company invests (investing activities) shape the direction of the company's operations.
3. How a company finances its operations and its investments (financing activities) is less important than what the business buys and how it operates.

These are not hard-and-fast rules, and there are exceptions. Nevertheless, a company's investing transactions are vital to its ability to earn profits and provide jobs for its work force. Exhibit 10-14 on page 496 provides excerpts from **Campbell Soup Company's** statement of cash flows. During 1995, Campbell Soup spent $1.255 billion to acquire other companies (line 4). Campbell Soup sold other companies for a total of $12 million (line 5). In terms of its investing activities, Campbell Soup Company is definitely growing: The company is making far more new investments than it is selling off old investments.

During 1995, Campbell Soup spent $1.255 billion to acquire other companies. Campbell Soup sold other companies for a total of $12 million. In terms of its investing activities, Campbell Soup Company is definitely growing: The company is making far more new investments than it is selling off old investments.

How did Campbell Soup finance the acquisitions of the other businesses? The cash-flow statement gives the answer. Campbell's operating activities provided

EXHIBIT 10-14
Campbell Soup Company's Consolidated Statement of Cash Flows

CAMPBELL SOUP CO.
Consolidated Statement of Cash Flows

	(In millions)	1995	1994
	Cash Flows from Operating Activities:		
1	Net cash provided by operating activities	**$1,185**	$968
	Cash Flows from Investing Activities:		
2	Purchases of plant assets	**(391)**	(421)
3	Sales of plant assets	**21**	42
4	Businesses acquired	**(1,255)**	(14)
5	Sales of businesses	**12**	27
6	Net change in other assets and liabilities	**(45)**	(41)
7	Net cash used in investing activities	**(1,658)**	(407)
	Cash Flows from Financing Activities:		
8	Long-term borrowings	**312**	115
9	Repayments of long-term borrowings	**(29)**	(117)
10	Short-term borrowings	**1,087**	(50)
11	Repayments of short-term borrowings	**(662)**	(87)
12	Dividends paid	**(295)**	(266)
13	Treasury stock purchases	**(24)**	(145)
14	Treasury stock issued	**37**	16
15	Net cash provided by (used in) financing activities	**426**	(534)
16	Effect of exchange rate changes on cash	**4**	6
17	**Net Change in Cash and Cash Equivalents**	**(43)**	33
18	Cash and cash equivalents at beginning of year	**96**	63
19	**Cash and Cash Equivalents at End of Year**	**$ 53**	$ 96

cash of $1.185 billion during 1995 (line 1). This amount alone covered most of the cost of acquiring the other companies—a sign of Campbell Soup's financial strength.

The financing-activities section of the cash-flow statement indicates that long-term borrowings provided cash of $312 million (line 8), with an additional $1.087 billion coming from short-term borrowing (line 10). Moreover, these amounts far exceeded Campbell Soup's repayments of borrowings (lines 9 and 11), which means that the company had the cash to expand. For additional insight into Campbell Soup's financial situation, let's examine the company's balance sheet and income statement in Exhibit 10-15.

Campbell Soup's balance sheet at year end 1995 reveals a debt ratio (total liabilities divided by total assets) of .61 ($3,847/$6,315) *after the new financing.* A debt ratio of .61 is considered fairly low—unlikely to put the company in a squeeze and therefore quite safe from a lender's perspective. Campbell Soup Company should have little trouble borrowing money on favorable terms. The income statements for 1995 and 1994 reports steadily rising profits—net earnings increased from $630 million in 1994 to $698 million in 1995. Overall, Campbell Soup Company's financial position and operating results look very strong.

We introduced the debt ratio in Chapter 3, page 143.

The statement of cash flows, along with the balance sheet and the income statement, reveal how Campbell Soup financed its $1.255 billion acquisitions of other companies—through profitable operations and a modest amount of borrowing. This example illustrates how to use the financial statements to analyze a company. This is what financial analysis is all about: understanding and explaining what a company is doing, and using that information to make decisions.

EXHIBIT 10-15
Campbell Soup Company's Balance Sheet and Income Statement

CAMPBELL SOUP COMPANY Consolidated Balance Sheet (Adapted)		
(In millions)	**July 30, 1995**	**July 31, 1994**
Total assets	**$6,315**	$4,992
Total liabilities	**$3,847**	$3,003
Shareowners' Equity		
Preferred stock: authorized 40 shares; none issued	—	—
Capital stock, $.075 par value; authorized 280 shares; issued 271 shares	**20**	20
Capital surplus	**165**	155
Earnings retained in the business	**2,755**	2,359
Capital stock in treasury, 22 shares in 1995 and 23 shares in 1994, at cost	**(550)**	(559)
Cumulative translation adjustments	**78**	14
Total shareowners' equity	**2,468**	1,989
Total liabilities and shareowners' equity	**$6,315**	$4,992

CAMPBELL SOUP COMPANY Consolidated Statement of Earnings (Adapted)		
(In millions)	**1995**	**1994**
Net Sales	**$7,278**	$6,690
Total costs and expenses	**6,580**	6,060
Net Earnings	**$ 698**	$ 630

SUMMARY PROBLEM FOR YOUR REVIEW

Translate the balance sheet of the Spanish subsidiary of Wrangler Corp., a U.S. company, into dollars. When Wrangler acquired this subsidiary, the exchange rate of the peseta was $0.0101. The average exchange rate applicable to retained earnings is $0.0108. The peseta's current exchange rate is $0.0111.

Before performing the translation, predict whether the translation adjustment will be positive or negative. Does this situation generate a translation gain or a translation loss? Give your reasons.

	Pesetas
Assets	200,000,000
Liabilities	110,000,000
Stockholders' equity:	
Common stock	20,000,000
Retained earnings	70,000,000
	200,000,000

ANSWERS

Translation of foreign-currency balance sheet:

This situation will generate a *positive* translation adjustment, which is like a gain. The gain occurs because the peseta's current exchange rate, which is used to translate net assets (assets minus liabilities), exceeds the historical exchange rates used for stockholders' equity.

The calculation appears at the top of page 498.

	Pesetas	Exchange Rate	Dollars
Assets	200,000,000	$0.0111	$2,220,000
Liabilities	110,000,000	0.0111	$1,221,000
Stockholders' equity:			
Common stock	20,000,000	0.0101	202,000
Retained earnings	70,000,000	0.0108	756,000
Translation adjustment	—		41,000
	200,000,000		$2,220,000

SUMMARY OF LEARNING OBJECTIVES

1. *Account for available-for-sale investments.* *Available-for-sale securities* are all stock investments other than trading securities. They are classified as current assets if the business expects to sell them within a year or during the business's normal operating cycle if longer than a year. All other available-for-sale securities are classified as long-term investments. Available-for-sale investments are reported at current market value on the balance sheet. Unrealized gains or losses on available-for-sale investments are reported as other comprehensive income on the income statement and as accumulated other comprehensive income within stockholders' equity on the balance sheet. Realized gains or losses on the sale of investments are reported as an "Other" item on the income statement.

2. *Use the equity method for investments.* The *equity method* is used when an investor owns 20–50% of the stock of an investee. The investor applies its percentage of ownership in recording its share of the investee's net income and dividends. Equity-method investment revenue is reported under Other revenues on the income statement.

3. *Consolidate parent and subsidiary balance sheets.* Ownership of more than 50% of a company's voting stock creates a *parent-subsidiary* relationship, and the parent company must use the *consolidation method* to account for its subsidiaries. Because the parent has control over the subsidiary, the subsidiary's financial statements are included in the parent's consolidated financial statements. To avoid double counting, the consolidated statements must (1) eliminate intercompany receivables and payables, (2) eliminate the stockholders' equity accounts of the subsidiary, (3) eliminate the Investment in Subsidiary account, (4) record goodwill when necessary, and (5) record minority interest when necessary.

4. *Account for long-term investments in bonds.* *Held-to-maturity investments* are bonds and notes that the investor intends to hold until maturity. The *amortized-cost method* is used to account for held-to-maturity investments. An important part of this method is accruing interest receivable and amortizing any bond discount or premium over the life of the bond. Long-term bonds are presented on the balance sheet after current assets; interest revenue from bond investments appears on the income statement under Other revenues.

5. *Account for transactions stated in a foreign currency.* When two or more currencies are involved in a transaction, each company may incur a gain or loss on foreign-currency exchanges. These gains and losses are reported on the income statement under the category Other gains and losses. To protect themselves against foreign-currency transaction losses, some companies engage in *hedging*—they protect themselves from losing money on one transaction by engaging in a counterbalancing transaction.

6. *Compute and interpret a foreign-currency translation adjustment.* Consolidating a foreign subsidiary's financial statements into the parent company's statements requires adjusting the subsidiary statements to U.S. accounting principles, then translating the foreign-company statements into U.S. dollars. The translation process often creates a *translation adjustment,* which is needed to bring the dollar amount of the subsidiary's total liabilities and stockholders' equity into agreement with the dollar amount of total assets. A negative translation adjustment is like a loss—the book value of the investee company in dollars is less than the amount the parent company paid to acquire it. A positive translation adjustment is like a gain.

7. *Report investing transactions on the statement of cash flows.* Investing activities are the second major category of transactions reported on the statement of cash flows (after operating activities and before financing activities). The cash-flow statement, along with the balance sheet and income statement, provides vital information regarding a company's sources and uses of cash for investing activities.

ACCOUNTING VOCABULARY

available-for-sale securities *(p. 472).*
consolidated statements *(p. 478).*
controlling interest *(p. 477).*
equity method for investments *(p. 475).*
foreign-currency exchange rate *(p. 488).*
foreign-currency translation adjustment *(p. 492).*
hedging *(p. 491).*
held-to-maturity investments *(p. 483).*
long-term investment *(p. 471).*
majority interest *(p. 477).*
marketable security *(p. 471).*

market value method of accounting (for investments) *(p. 472)*.
minority interest *(p. 481)*.
parent company *(p. 477)*.
short-term investment *(p. 471)*.
strong currency *(p. 489)*.
subsidiary company *(p. 477)*.
trading securities *(p. 472)*.
weak currency *(p. 489)*.

QUESTIONS

1. How are stock prices quoted in the securities market? What is the investor's cost of 1,000 shares of Ford Motor Company stock at 55¾, with a brokerage commission of $1,350?
2. Show the positions of short-term investments and long-term investments on the balance sheet.
3. Outline the accounting methods for the different types of investments.
4. How does an investor record the receipt of a cash dividend on an available-for-sale investment? How does this investor record receipt of a stock dividend?
5. An investor paid $11,000 for 1,000 shares of stock—a trading investment—and later received a 10% stock dividend. At December 31, the investment's market value is $11,800. Compute the unrealized gain or loss on the investment.
6. When is an investment accounted for by the equity method? Outline how to apply the equity method. Mention how to record the purchase of the investment, the investor's proportion of the investee's net income, and receipt of a cash dividend from the investee. Describe how to measure gain or loss on sale of this investment.
7. Identify three transactions that cause increases or decreases to an equity-method investment account.
8. What two actions must accountants take when using the consolidation method for investments? That is, what must they do to prepare the consolidated financial statements?
9. Why are intercompany items eliminated from consolidated financial statements? Name two intercompany items that are eliminated.
10. Name the account that expresses the excess of the cost of an investment over the market value of the subsidiary's owners' equity. What type of account is this, and where in the financial statements is it reported?
11. When a parent company buys more than 50% but less than 100% of a subsidiary's stock, a new category of owners' equity must appear on the balance sheet. What is this category called, and under what heading do most companies report it?
12. How would you measure the net income of a parent company with three subsidiaries? Assume that two subsidiaries are wholly (100%) owned and that the parent owns 60% of the third subsidiary.
13. McVey, Inc., acquired a foreign subsidiary when the foreign currency's exchange rate was $0.32. Over the years, the foreign currency has steadily risen against the dollar. Will McVey's balance sheet report a positive or a negative foreign-currency translation adjustment?
14. Describe the computation of a foreign-currency translation adjustment.

EXERCISES

Journalizing transactions for an available-for-sale investment
(Obj. 1)

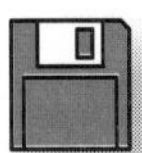

E10-1 Journalize the following long-term available-for-sale investment transactions of McDermott, Inc.:

a. Purchased 400 shares (8%) of Vehicle Safety Corporation common stock at $44 per share, with the intent of holding the stock for the indefinite future.

b. Received cash dividend of $1 per share on the Vehicle Safety investment.

c. At year end, adjusted the investment account to current market value of $45 per share.

d. Sold the Vehicle Safety stock for the market price of $49 per share.

Accounting for long-term investment transactions
(Obj. 1)

E10-2 Late in the current year, Travel Consumer Corporation bought 3,000 shares of Boeing common stock at $37.375, 600 shares of Anheuser-Busch stock at $46.75, and 1,400 shares of Hitachi stock at $79—all as available-for-sale investments. At December 31, the *Wall Street Journal* reports Boeing stock at $39.125, Anheuser-Busch at $48.50, and Hitachi at $68.25.

Required

1. Determine the cost and the market value of the long-term investment portfolio at December 31.
2. Record any adjusting entry needed at December 31.
3. What would Travel Consumer Corporation report on its balance sheet and income statement for the information given? Make the necessary disclosures. Income tax rate is 30%.

Accounting for transactions under the equity method
(Obj. 2)

E10-3 **Sears, Roebuck and Co.** owns equity-method investments in several companies. Suppose Sears paid $2 million to acquire a 25% investment in Thai Imports Company. Assume that Thai Imports Company reported net income of $640,000 for the first year and declared and paid cash dividends of $420,000. Record the following in Sears's journal: (a) purchase of the investment, (b) Sears's proportion of Thai Imports' net income, and (c) receipt of the cash dividends.

Measuring gain or loss on the sale of an equity-method investment
(Obj. 2)

E10-4 Without making journal entries, record the transactions of Exercise 10-3 directly in the Sears account, Long-Term Investment in Thai Imports. Assume that after all the noted

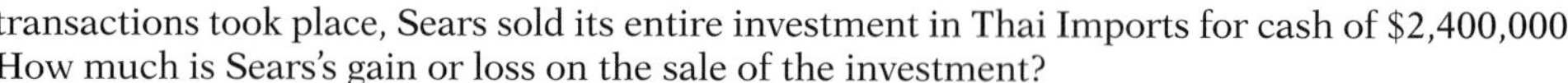

transactions took place, Sears sold its entire investment in Thai Imports for cash of $2,400,000. How much is Sears's gain or loss on the sale of the investment?

Applying the appropriate accounting method for investments ***(Obj. 2)***

E10-5 Analog Measurement Corporation paid $160,000 for a 40% investment in the common stock of Kahn, Inc. For the first year, Kahn reported net income of $84,000 and at year end declared and paid cash dividends of $16,000. On the balance sheet date, the market value of Analog's investment in Kahn stock was $134,000.

Required

1. Which method is appropriate for Analog to use in accounting for its investment in Kahn? Why?
2. Show everything that Analog would report for the investment and any investment revenue in its year-end financial statements.
3. What role does the market value of the investment play in this situation?

Preparing a consolidated balance sheet with minority interest ***(Obj. 3)***

E10-6 Legend Corp. owns a 90% interest in Kemp, Inc. The two companies' individual balance sheets are as follows:

Assets	**Legend Corp.**	**Kemp, Inc.**
Cash	$ 49,000	$ 14,000
Accounts receivable, net	82,000	53,000
Note receivable from Legend	—	12,000
Inventory	114,000	77,000
Investment in Kemp	90,000	—
Plant assets, net	186,000	129,000
Other assets	22,000	8,000
Total	$543,000	$293,000
Liabilities and Stockholders' Equity		
Accounts payable	$ 44,000	$ 26,000
Notes payable	47,000	36,000
Other liabilities	82,000	131,000
Minority interest	—	—
Common stock	210,000	80,000
Retained earnings	160,000	20,000
Total	$543,000	$293,000

Required

1. Prepare the consolidated balance sheet of Legend Corp. It is sufficient to complete the consolidation work sheet.
2. What is the amount of stockholders' equity of the consolidated entity?
3. Determine the least amount for Legend Corp. to have invested in Kemp, Inc., stock for the consolidated balance sheet to have reported goodwill.

Recording bond investment transactions ***(Obj. 4)***

E10-7 On March 31, 19X3, Crusader Corporation paid 92¼ for 7% bonds of Mattson Financial Services as a long-term held-to-maturity investment. The maturity value of the bonds will be $20,000 on September 30, 19X7. The bonds pay interest on March 31 and September 30. At December 31, the bonds' market value is 93.

Required

1. What method should Crusader Corporation use to account for its investment in the Mattson bonds?
2. Using the straight-line method of amortizing the discount, journalize all of Crusader Corporation's transactions on the bonds for 19X3.
3. Show how Crusader would report the bond investment on its balance sheet at December 31, 19X3.

Managing and accounting for foreign-currency transactions ***(Obj. 5)***

E10-8 Record the following foreign-currency transactions:

Nov. 17	Purchased inventory on account from a Japanese company. The price was 200,000 yen, and the exchange rate of the yen was $0.0090.
Dec. 16	Paid the Japanese supplier when the exchange rate was $0.0091.
19	Sold merchandise on account to a French company at a price of 60,000 French francs. The exchange rate was $0.16.
30	Collected from the French company when the exchange rate was $0.17.

On November 18, immediately after your purchase, and on December 20, immediately after your sale, which currencies did you want to strengthen? Which currencies did in fact strengthen? Explain your reasoning in detail.

E10-9 Translate into dollars the balance sheet of Pasta Systems Company's Italian subsidiary. When Pasta Systems acquired the foreign subsidiary, an Italian lira was worth $0.00080. The current exchange rate is $0.00085. During the period when retained earnings were earned, the average exchange rate was $0.00088.

Translating a foreign-currency balance sheet into dollars
(Obj. 6)

	Lire
Assets	500,000,000
Liabilities	300,000,000
Stockholders' equity:	
Common stock	50,000,000
Retained earnings	150,000,000
	500,000,000

During the period covered by this situation, which currency was stronger, the dollar or the lira?

E10-10 During fiscal year 1995, **The Home Depot,** which operates over 400 home improvement centers throughout the United States, reported net income of $604 million and paid $162 million to acquire other businesses. Home Depot made capital expenditures of $1,103 million to open new stores and sold property, plant, and equipment for $50 million. The company purchased long-term investments in stocks and bonds at a cost of $94 million and sold other long-term investments for $454 million. During the year, the company also cashed in short-term investments for $96 million.

Preparing and using the statement of cash flows
(Obj. 7)

Financing included $100 million of short-term borrowing and the issuance of common stock for $78 million. During the year, Home Depot paid off $2 million of long-term debt and also paid cash dividends of $68 million to its stockholders.

Required

Prepare the investing activities section of The Home Depot's statement of cash flows. Based solely on The Home Depot's investing activities, does it appear that the company is growing or shrinking? How can you tell?

E10-11 **Chrysler Corporation** earns approximately 15% of its net income from financial services through its wholly-owned subsidiary, **Chrysler Financial Corporation.** As a result, Finance Receivables is the largest single long-term asset on Chrysler's balance sheet. At the end of a recent year, Chrysler's statement of cash flows reported the following for investing activities:

Using the statement of cash flows
(Obj. 7)

CHRYSLER CORPORATION AND CONSOLIDATED SUBSIDIARIES
Consolidated Statement of Cash Flows (Partial)

	(In millions)
Cash Flows from Investing Activities	
Purchases of marketable securities	$ (4,700)
Sales and maturities of marketable securities	4,937
Finance receivables acquired	(16,809)
Finance receivables collected	9,616
Proceeds from sales of finance receivables*	7,846
Proceeds from sales of [intangible] assets	2,375
Proceeds from sales of automotive assets ($300) and investments ($161)	461
Expenditures for property and equipment	(1,761)
Expenditures for special tools	(1,234)
Other	446
Net Cash (Used in) Provided by Investing Activities	$ 1,177

**Note:* A finance receivable is similar to an account receivable, note receivable, or any other receivable. Finance receivables are long-term.

Required

1. For each item listed (except for the "Other" category), make the journal entry that placed the item on Chrysler's statement of cash flows. Assume each asset that Chrysler sold had a book value equal to its sale price, so there were no gains or losses on the sale.

2. Indicate where in Chrysler's financial statements (besides cash) you would expect to see each account that you recorded in your journal entries. Identify the financial statement and the section of that statement where the account should appear.

Examples: Balance sheet—Current assets;
Income statement—Revenues

What is the common element in all your answers? (*Hint:* Which category of accounts in the financial statements is affected by all investing activities?)

CHALLENGE EXERCISES

Analyzing available-for-sale investments and the cumulative translation adjustment
(Obj. 1, 6)

E10-12 AMP Incorporated, a world leader in the manufacture of electronic connection devices, reported the following stockholders' equity on its balance sheet at December 31:

AMP INCORPORATED
Balance Sheet (Partial)

	(In thousands)	
	1994	**1993**
Shareholders' Equity:		
Common stock, without par value—		
Authorized 700,000,000 shares,		
issued 224,640,000 shares	$ 12,480	$ 12,480
Other capital	82,379	81,400
Cumulative translation adjustments	131,711	68,367
Net unrealized investment gains	21,585	—
Retained earnings	2,329,691	2,131,436
Treasury stock, at cost	(243,431)	(237,328)
Total shareholders' equity	2,334,415	2,056,355

Required

1. How does the cumulative translation adjustment find its way onto AMP's balance sheet? Is AMP's cumulative translation adjustment for 1994 a gain or a loss? How can you tell?
2. AMP's balance sheet also reports available-for-sale investments at $287,898,000 ($287,898 thousand). What was AMP's cost of the investments? What was the market value of the investments on December 31, 1994?
3. Suppose AMP sold its available-for-sale investments in 1995 for $259,000,000 ($259,000 thousand). Determine the gain or loss on sale of the investments.

Analyzing equity-method investments
(Obj. 2)

E10-13 Whirlpool Corporation is a leading manufacturer of household appliances. In Brazil and Mexico, Whirlpool operates through affiliated companies, whose stock Whirlpool owns in various percentages between 20 and 50 percent. Whirlpool's financial statements reported these items:

	(In millions)	
	19X8	**19X7**
Balance Sheet (Adapted)		
Investment in affiliated companies	$286	$296
Statement of Cash Flows		
Increase in investment in affiliated companies	12	2
Statement of Earnings		
Equity in net earnings (losses) of affiliated companies	(13)	4

Whirlpool's financial statements reported no sales of investments in affiliated companies during 19X8 or 19X7.

Required

Prepare a T-account for Investment in Affiliated Companies to determine the amount of dividends Whirlpool Corporation received from affiliated companies during 19X8. Show your work.

E10-14 **Whirlpool Corporation** reported the following stockholders' equity:

Interpreting the cumulative translation adjustment ***(Obj. 6)***

	(In millions)	
	19X2	19X1
Stockholders' Equity		
Capital stock	$ 76	$ 75
Paid-in capital	47	37
Retained earnings	1,721	1,593
Other	(18)	(12)
Cumulative translation adjustments	(49)	(1)
Treasury stock—at cost	(177)	(177)
	$1,600	$1,515

Whirlpool owns controlling interests in several subsidiary companies that are incorporated in foreign countries, mainly in Europe. During 19X2, did the U.S. dollar strengthen or weaken relative to the monetary currencies of these European countries? Explain your answer.

PROBLEMS

(GROUP A)

P10-1A Manhattan Company owns numerous investments in the stock of other companies. Assume that Manhattan completed the following long-term investment transactions:

Reporting investments on the balance sheet and the related revenue on the income statement ***(Obj. 1, 2)***

19X2

Feb. 12	Purchased 20,000 shares, which exceeds 20%, of the common stock of Agribusiness, Inc., at total cost of $715,000.
July 1	Purchased 8,000 additional shares of Agribusiness common stock at cost of $300,000.
Aug. 9	Received annual cash dividend of $0.90 per share on the Agribusiness investment.
Oct. 16	Purchased 800 shares of Apex Company common stock as an available-for-sale investment, paying $41½ per share.
Nov. 30	Received semiannual cash dividend of $0.60 per share on the Apex investment.
Dec. 31	Received annual report from Agribusiness, Inc. Net income for the year was $510,000. Of this amount, Manhattan's proportion is 35 percent.

The current market value of the Apex stock is $34,100. The market value of the Agribusiness stock is $967,000.

Required

1. For which investment is current market value used in the accounting? Why is market value used for one investment and not the other?
2. Show what Manhattan Company would report on its year-end balance sheet and income statement for these investment transactions. It is helpful to use a T-account for the investment in Agribusiness stock. Ignore income tax.

P10-2A The beginning balance sheet of Nation Online Incorporated included the following:

Long–Term Investments in Affiliates (equity-method investments) $344,000

Accounting for available-for-sale and equity-method investments ***(Obj. 1, 2)***

The company completed the following investment transactions during the year:

Mar. 2	Purchased 2,000 shares of ATI, Inc., common stock as a long-term available-for-sale investment, paying $12¼ per share.
5	Purchased new long-term investment in affiliate at cost of $540,000.
Apr. 21	Received cash dividend of $0.75 per share on the ATI investment.
May 17	Received cash dividend of $47,000 from affiliated company.
Oct. 8	Purchased long-term available-for-sale investment in Bell Corp. stock for $136,000.
17	Received cash dividend of $49,000 from affiliated company.
Dec. 31	Received annual reports from affiliated companies. Their total net income for the year was $550,000. Of this amount, Nation Online's proportion is 22 percent. The market values of Nation Online's investments are ATI, $29,800; Bell, $132,400; Affiliated company, $800,000.

Required

1. Record the transactions in the journal of Nation Online Incorporated.
2. Post entries to the Long-Term Investments in Affiliates T-account, and determine its balance at December 31. Do likewise for the Long-Term Available-for-Sale Investments T-account and the Allowance to Adjust Investments to Market T-account.

3. Show how to report the Long-Term Available-for-Sale Investments and the Long-Term Investments in Affiliates accounts on Nation Online's balance sheet at December 31.

Analyzing consolidated financial statements ***(Obj. 3)***

P10-3A This problem demonstrates the dramatic effect that consolidation accounting can have on a company's ratios. **Ford Motor Company** (Ford) owns 100% of **Ford Motor Credit Corporation** (FMCC), its financing subsidiary. Ford's main operations consist of manufacturing automotive products. FMCC mainly helps people finance the purchase of automobiles from Ford and its dealers. The two companies' individual balance sheets are adapted and summarized as follows:

	Ford (Parent)	FMCC (Subsidiary)
Total assets	$89.6	$170.5
Total liabilities	$65.1	$156.9
Total stockholders' equity	24.5	13.6
Total liabilities and equity	$89.6	$170.5

Assume that FMCC's liabilities include $3.2 billion owed to Ford, the parent company.

Required

1. Compute the debt ratio of Ford Motor Company considered alone.
2. Determine the consolidated total assets, total liabilities, and stockholders' equity of Ford Motor Company after consolidating the financial statements of FMCC into the totals of Ford, the parent company.
3. Recompute the debt ratio of the consolidated entity. Explain why it took an FASB statement to get companies to consolidate their financing subsidiaries into their own financial statements.

Consolidating a wholly-owned subsidiary ***(Obj. 3)***

P10-4A Ben Silver Corp. paid $266,000 to acquire all the common stock of Massada, Inc., and Massada owes Ben Silver $81,000 on a note payable. Immediately after the purchase on June 30, 19X3, the two companies' balance sheets were as follows:

Assets	**Ben Silver Corp.**	**Massada, Inc.**
Cash	$ 24,000	$ 20,000
Accounts receivable, net	91,000	42,000
Note receivable from Massada	81,000	—
Inventory	145,000	214,000
Investment in Massada	266,000	—
Plant assets, net	178,000	219,000
Total	$785,000	$495,000
Liabilities and Stockholders' Equity		
Accounts payable	$ 57,000	$ 49,000
Notes payable	177,000	149,000
Other liabilities	129,000	31,000
Common stock	274,000	118,000
Retained earnings	148,000	148,000
Total	$785,000	$495,000

Required

1. Prepare the consolidated balance sheet for Ben Silver Corp. (It is sufficient to complete a consolidation work sheet.)
2. Why aren't total assets of the consolidated entity equal to the sum of total assets for both companies combined? Why isn't consolidated equity equal to the sum of the two companies' stockholders' equity amounts?

Using a consolidated balance sheet with minority interest ***(Obj. 3)***

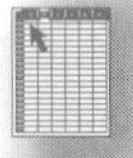

P10-5A On March 22, 19X4, Viking Travel Corp. paid $280,000 to purchase 80% of the common stock of Seaboard Cruise Line, and Seaboard owes Viking $67,000 on a note payable. Immediately after the purchase, the two companies' balance sheets were as follows:

Assets	Viking Travel Corp.	Seaboard Cruise Line
Cash	$ 41,000	$ 43,000
Accounts receivable, net	86,000	75,000
Note receivable from Seaboard	67,000	—
Inventory	128,000	36,000
Investment in Seaboard	280,000	—
Plant assets, net	277,000	338,000
Total	$879,000	$492,000
Liabilities and Stockholders' Equity		
Accounts payable	$ 72,000	$ 65,000
Notes payable	301,000	67,000
Other liabilities	11,000	10,000
Minority interest	—	—
Common stock	141,000	160,000
Retained earnings	354,000	190,000
Total	$879,000	$492,000

Required

1. Prepare Viking Travel's consolidated balance sheet. (It is sufficient to complete a consolidation work sheet.)
2. Answer these questions about Viking Travel Corp.:
   a. How much in total assets does Viking Travel control?
   b. If Viking decides to increase its investment in Seaboard, from whom will the management of Viking buy the remaining Seaboard stock? What item on the consolidated balance sheet helps answer this question?
   c. During the most recent year, Viking earned net income of $86,000, and Seaboard's net income was $41,000. Suppose you are an investor considering the purchase of Viking stock. What was Viking's rate of return on stockholders' equity for the year? Assume stockholders' equity changed very little during the year. Did Viking reach its goal of a 20% return on equity?

Accounting for a bond investment purchased at a premium ***(Obj. 4)***

P10-6A Financial institutions such as insurance companies and pension plans hold large quantities of bond investments. Suppose Ostway Insurance Co. purchases $600,000 of 9% bonds of Royal Corporation for 103 on March 1, 19X1. These bonds pay interest on March 1 and September 1 each year. They mature on March 1, 19X8. At December 31, 19X1, the market price of the bonds is 103½.

Required

1. Journalize Ostway's purchase of the bonds as a long-term investment on March 1, 19X1 (to be held to maturity), receipt of cash interest, and amortization of premium at December 31, 19X1. The straight-line method is appropriate for amortizing premium.
2. Show all financial statement effects of this long-term bond investment on Ostway Insurance Co.'s balance sheet and income statement at December 31, 19X1.

Note: Problem 10-7A is based on Appendix B at the end of the book.

Computing the cost of a bond investment to be held to maturity and journalizing its transactions ***(Obj. 4)***

P10-7A On December 31, 19X1, when the market interest is 8%, an investor purchases $500,000 of Bali Corp. six-year, 7.4% bonds at issuance. Determine the cost (present value) of this long-term bond investment, which the investor expects to hold to maturity. Journalize the purchase on December 31, 19X1, the first semiannual interest receipt on June 30, 19X2, and the year-end interest receipt on December 31, 19X2. The investor uses the effective-interest amortization method. Prepare a schedule for amortizing the discount on bond investment through December 31, 19X2. If necessary, refer to Appendix B at the end of the book.

Recording foreign-currency transactions and reporting the transaction gain or loss ***(Obj. 5)***

P10-8A Suppose United Rubber Corporation completed the following transactions:

May 1 Sold inventory on account to Pirelli Tire Company for $19,000. The exchange rate of the Italian lira is $0.0007, and Pirelli agrees to pay in dollars.

10 Purchased supplies on account from a Canadian company at a price of Canadian $50,000. The exchange rate of the Canadian dollar is $0.80, and payment will be in Canadian dollars.

17 Sold inventory on account to an English firm for 100,000 British pounds. Payment will be in pounds, and the exchange rate of the pound is $1.50.

22 Collected from Pirelli.

June 18 Paid the Canadian company. The exchange rate of the Canadian dollar is $0.77.
24 Collected from the English firm. The exchange rate of the British pound is $1.47.

Required

1. Record these transactions in United's journal, and show how to report the transaction gain or loss on the income statement.
2. How will what you learned in this problem help you structure international transactions?

Measuring and explaining the foreign-currency translation adjustment ***(Obj. 6)***

P10-9A Cunard, Inc., has a subsidiary company based in Japan.

Required

1. Translate into dollars the foreign-currency balance sheet of the Japanese subsidiary of Cunard, Inc. When Cunard acquired this subsidiary, the Japanese yen was worth $0.0064. The current exchange rate is $0.0093. During the period when the subsidiary earned its income, the average exchange rate was $0.0089 per yen.

	Yen
Assets	300,000,000
Liabilities	80,000,000
Stockholders' equity:	
Common stock	20,000,000
Retained earnings	200,000,000
	300,000,000

Before you perform the translation calculations, indicate whether Cunard has experienced a positive or a negative translation adjustment. State whether the adjustment is a gain or a loss, and show where it is reported in the financial statements.

2. To which company does the translation adjustment "belong"? In which company's financial statements will the translation adjustment be reported? How does the translation adjustment find its way into these financial statements?
3. How will what you learned in this problem help you understand published financial statements?

Using a cash-flow statement ***(Obj. 7)***

P10-10A Excerpts from **Intel Corporation's** statement of cash flows, as adapted, appear as follows:

INTEL CORPORATION
Consolidated Statement of Cash Flows (Partial)
Three Years Ended December 30,1995

(In millions)	1995	1994	1993
Cash and cash equivalents, beginning of year	**$ 1,180**	$ 1,659	$ 1,843
Net cash provided by operating activities	**4,026**	2,981	2,801
Cash flows provided by (used for) investing activities:			
Additions to property, plant, and equipment	**(3,550)**	(2,441)	(1,933)
Purchases of long-term, available-for-sale investments	**(129)**	(975)	(1,165)
Sales of long-term, available-for-sale investments	**114**	10	5
Maturities [of] available-for-sale investments	**878**	503	(244)
Net cash (used for) investing activities	**(2,687)**	(2,903)	(3,337)
Cash flows provided by (used for) financing activities:			
(Decrease) increase in short-term debt, net	**(179)**	(63)	197
Additions to long-term debt	—	128	148
Retirement of long-term debt	**(4)**	(98)	—
Proceeds from sales of shares through employee stock plans and other	**192**	150	133
Proceeds from sale of Step-Up Warrants, net	—	—	287
Proceeds from sales of put warrants,* net of repurchases	**85**	76	62
Repurchase and retirement of Common Stock	**(1,034)**	(658)	(391)
Payment of dividends to stockholders	**(116)**	(92)	(84)
Net cash (used for) provided by financing activities	**(1,056)**	(557)	352
Net increase (decrease) in cash and cash equivalents	**283**	(479)	(184)
Cash and cash equivalents, end of year	**$ 1,463**	$ 1,180	$ 1,659

**Note:* A *put warrant* is a contract that entitles a company to sell a stock at a stipulated price.

Required

As the chief executive officer of Intel Corporation, your duty is to write the management letter to your stockholders to explain Intel's investing activities during 1995. Compare the company's level of investment with preceding years, and indicate the major way the company financed its investments during 1995. Net income for 1995 was $3,566 million.

(GROUP B)

Reporting investments on the balance sheet and the related revenue on the income statement
(Obj. 1, 2)

P10-1B Sterling Chemical Company owns numerous investments in the stock of other companies. Assume that Sterling completed the following long-term investment transactions:

19X4	
May 1	Purchased 8,000 shares, which exceeds 20%, of the common stock of MIC Company at total cost of $720,000.
July 1	Purchased 1,600 additional shares of MIC Company common stock at cost of $140,000.
Sep. 15	Received semiannual cash dividend of $1.40 per share on the MIC investment.
Oct. 12	Purchased 1,000 shares of JAX Corporation common stock as an available-for-sale investment paying $22½ per share.
Dec. 14	Received semiannual cash dividend of $0.75 per share on the JAX investment.
Dec. 31	Received annual report from MIC Company. Net income for the year was $350,000. Of this amount, Sterling's proportion is 21.25 percent.

The current market value of the JAX stock is $20,700. The market value of the MIC stock is $865,000.

Required

1. For which investment is current market value used in the accounting? Why is market value used for one investment and not the other?
2. Show what Sterling Chemical Company would report on its year-end balance sheet and income statement for these investment transactions. (It is helpful to use a T-account for the investment in MIC stock.) Ignore income tax.

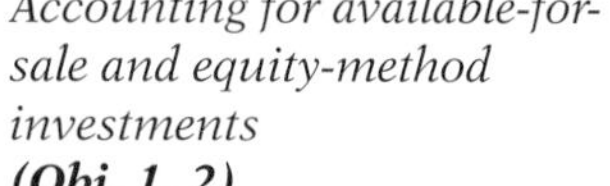

Accounting for available-for-sale and equity-method investments
(Obj. 1, 2)

P10-2B The beginning balance sheet of Lions, Inc., included the following:

Long-Term Investments in Affiliates (equity-method investments)................ $657,000

The company completed the following investment transactions during the year:

Mar. 3	Purchased 5,000 shares of BCM Software common stock as a long-term available-for-sale investment, paying $9¼ per share.
4	Purchased new long-term investment in affiliate at cost of $408,000.
May 14	Received cash dividend of $0.82 per share on the BCM investment.
June 15	Received cash dividend of $27,000 from affiliated company.
Oct. 24	Purchased long-term available-for-sale investment in Northern Communication stock for $226,000.
Dec. 15	Received cash dividend of $29,000 from affiliated company.
31	Received annual reports from affiliated companies. Their total net income for the year was $620,000. Of this amount, Lions' proportion is 30 percent.

The market values of Lions' investments are BCM, $48,100; Northern, $219,000; Affiliated companies, $947,000.

Required

1. Record the transactions in the journal of Lions, Inc.
2. Post entries to the Long-Term Investments in Affiliates T-account, and determine its balance at December 31. Do likewise for the Long-Term Available-for-Sale Investments T-account and the Allowance to Adjust Investments to Market T-account.
3. Show how to report the Long-Term Available-for-Sale Investments and the Long-Term Investments in Affiliates on Lions, Inc.'s balance sheet at December 31.

Analyzing consolidated financial statements
(Obj. 3)

P10-3B This problem demonstrates the dramatic effect that consolidation accounting can have on a company's ratios. **General Motors Corporation** (GM) owns 100% of **General Motors Acceptance Corporation** (GMAC), its financing subsidiary. GM's main operations consist of manufacturing automotive products. GMAC mainly helps people finance the purchase of automobiles from GM and its dealers. The two companies' individual balance sheets are summarized as follows:

	General Motors (Parent)	GMAC (Subsidiary)
Total assets..................................	$132.6	$94.6
Total liabilities..............................	$109.3	$86.3
Total stockholders' equity............	23.3	8.3
Total liabilities and equity...........	$132.6	$94.6

Included among GMAC's liabilities is $1.8 billion owed to General Motors, the parent company.

Required

1. Compute the debt ratio of General Motors Corporation considered alone.
2. Determine the consolidated total assets, total liabilities, and stockholders' equity of General Motors Corporation after consolidating the financial statements of GMAC into the totals of GM, the parent company.
3. Recompute the debt ratio of the consolidated entity. Explain why it took an FASB statement to get companies to consolidate their financing subsidiaries into their own financial statements.

Consolidating a wholly-owned subsidiary
(Obj. 3)

P10-4B Vitek Corporation paid $179,000 to acquire all the common stock of Ritz, Inc., and Ritz owes Vitek $55,000 on a note payable. Immediately after the purchase on May 31, 19X7, the two companies' balance sheets were as follows:

Assets	**Vitek Corporation**	**Ritz, Inc.**
Cash	$ 18,000	$ 32,000
Accounts receivable, net	64,000	43,000
Note receivable from Ritz	55,000	—
Inventory	93,000	153,000
Investment in Ritz	179,000	—
Plant assets, net	205,000	138,000
Total	$614,000	$366,000
Liabilities and Stockholders' Equity		
Accounts payable	$ 76,000	$ 37,000
Notes payable	118,000	123,000
Other liabilities	44,000	27,000
Common stock	282,000	90,000
Retained earnings	94,000	89,000
Total	$614,000	$366,000

Required

1. Prepare Vitek Corporation's consolidated balance sheet. (It is sufficient to complete a consolidation work sheet.)
2. Why aren't total assets of the consolidated entity equal to the sum of total assets for both companies combined? Why isn't consolidated equity equal to the sum of the two companies' stockholders' equity combined?

Using a consolidated balance sheet with goodwill
(Obj. 3)

P10-5B On August 17, 19X8, Kenyata Printing Corp. paid $229,000 to purchase all the common stock of Travelers, Inc., and Travelers owes Kenyata Printing $42,000 on a note payable. Immediately after the purchase, the two companies' balance sheets were as follows:

Assets	**Kenyata Printing Corp.**	**Travelers, Inc.**
Cash	$ 23,000	$ 37,000
Accounts receivable, net	71,000	54,000
Note receivable from Travelers	42,000	—
Inventory	213,000	170,000
Investment in Travelers	229,000	—
Plant assets, net	197,000	175,000
Goodwill	—	—
Total	$775,000	$436,000
Liabilities and Stockholders' Equity		
Accounts payable	$119,000	$ 77,000
Notes payable	190,000	71,000
Other liabilities	33,000	88,000
Common stock	219,000	113,000
Retained earnings	214,000	87,000
Total	$775,000	$436,000

Required

1. Prepare the consolidated balance sheet for Kenyata Printing (It is sufficient to complete a consolidation work sheet.)
2. Answer these questions about the two companies:
   a. How much goodwill did Kenyata Printing buy as part of the price paid for Travelers, Inc.? Show your computation of goodwill.
   b. Which company developed the goodwill? On which company's financial statements does the goodwill appear?
   c. Why is goodwill recorded only when it is purchased? Why don't generally accepted accounting principles permit companies to record goodwill as they develop it?

Accounting for a bond investment purchased at a discount ***(Obj. 4)***

P10-6B Financial institutions such as insurance companies and pension plans hold large quantities of bond investments. Suppose Prudential Bache, Inc., purchases $500,000 of 8% bonds of General Motors Corporation for 92 on January 31, 19X0. These bonds pay interest on January 31 and July 31 each year. They mature on July 31, 19X8. At December 31, 19X0, the market price of the bonds is 93.

Required

1. Journalize Prudential Bache's purchase of the bonds as a long-term investment on January 31, 19X0 (to be held to maturity), receipt of cash interest and amortization of discount on July 31, 19X0, and accrual of interest revenue and amortization of discount at December 31, 19X0. The straight-line method is appropriate for amortizing discount.
2. Show all financial statement effects of this long-term bond investment on Prudential Bache's balance sheet and income statement at December 31, 19X0.

Note: Problem 10-7B is based on Appendix B at the end of the book.

Computing the cost of a bond investment and journalizing its transactions ***(Obj. 4)***

P10-7B On December 31, 19X1, when the market interest rate is 10%, an investor purchases $400,000 of Tepotzlan, Inc., ten-year, 9.5% bonds at issuance. Determine the cost (present value) of this bond investment, which the investor expects to hold to maturity. Journalize the purchase on December 31, 19X1, the first semiannual interest receipt on June 30, 19X2, and the year-end interest receipt on December 31, 19X2. The investor uses the effective-interest amortization method. Prepare a schedule for amortizing the discount on the bond investment through December 31, 19X2. If necessary, refer to Appendix B at the end of the book.

Recording foreign-currency transactions and reporting the transaction gain or loss ***(Obj. 5)***

P10-8B Suppose PepsiCo, Inc., completed the following transactions:

May 4	Sold soft-drink syrup on account to a Mexican company for $71,000. The exchange rate of the Mexican peso is $0.141, and the customer agrees to pay in dollars.
13	Purchased inventory on account from a Canadian company at a price of Canadian $100,000. The exchange rate of the Canadian dollar is $0.75, and payment will be in Canadian dollars.
20	Sold goods on account to an English firm for 70,000 British pounds. Payment will be in pounds, and the exchange rate of the pound is $1.50.
27	Collected from the Mexican company.
June 21	Paid the Canadian company. The exchange rate of the Canadian dollar is $0.72.
July 17	Collected from the English firm. The exchange rate of the British pound is $1.47.

Required

1. Record these transactions in PepsiCo's journal, and show how to report the transaction gain or loss on the income statement.
2. How will what you learned in this problem help you structure international transactions?

Measuring and explaining the foreign-currency translation adjustment ***(Obj. 6)***

P10-9B Alaskan, Inc., owns a subsidiary based in Denmark.

Required

1. Translate the foreign-currency balance sheet of the Danish subsidiary of Alaskan, Inc., into dollars. When Alaskan acquired this subsidiary, the Danish krone was worth $0.17. The current exchange rate is $0.16. During the period when the subsidiary earned its income, the average exchange rate was $0.18 per krone.

	Kroner
Assets	3,000,000
Liabilities	1,000,000
Stockholders' equity:	
Common stock	300,000
Retained earnings	1,700,000
	3,000,000

Before you perform the translation calculation, indicate whether Alaskan, Inc., has experienced a positive or a negative translation adjustment. State whether the adjustment is a gain or loss, and show where it is reported in the financial statements.

2. To which company does the translation adjustment "belong"? In which company's financial statements will the translation adjustment be reported? How does the translation adjustment find its way into these financial statements?
3. How will what you learned in this problem help you understand published financial statements?

Using a cash-flow statement ***(Obj. 7)***

P10-10B Excerpts from **The Coca-Cola Company's** statement of cash flows, as adapted, appear as follows:

THE COCA-COLA COMPANY AND SUBSIDIARIES
Consolidated Statements of Cash Flows

(In millions)	Years Ended December 31, 1995	1994	1993
Operating Activities			
Net cash provided by operating activities	**$3,115**	$3,183	$2,508
Investing Activities			
Additions to finance subsidiary receivables	**(144)**	(94)	(177)
Collections of finance subsidiary receivables	**46**	50	44
Acquisitions and investments, principally bottling companies	**(338)**	(311)	(611)
Purchases of securities	**(190)**	(201)	(245)
Proceeds from disposals of investments	**580**	299	690
Purchases of property, plant, and equipment	**(937)**	(878)	(800)
Proceeds from disposals of property, plant, and equipment	**44**	109	312
Other investing activities	**(74)**	(11)	(98)
Net cash used in investing activities	**(1,013)**	(1,037)	(885)
Net cash provided by operations after reinvestment	**2,102**	2,146	1,623
Financing Activities			
Issuances of debt	**754**	491	445
Payments of debt	**(212)**	(154)	(567)
Issuances of stock	**86**	69	145
Purchases of stock for treasury	**(1,796)**	(1,192)	(680)
Dividends	**(1,110)**	(1,006)	(883)
Net cash used in financing activities	**(2,278)**	(1,792)	(1,540)
Effect of Exchange Rate Changes on Cash and Cash Equivalents	**(43)**	34	(41)
Cash and Cash Equivalents			
Net increase (decrease) during the year	**(219)**	388	42
Balance at beginning of year	**1,386**	998	956
Balance at end of year	**$1,167**	$1,386	$998

Required

As the chief executive officer of The Coca-Cola Company, your duty is to write the management letter to your stockholders explaining Coca-Cola's individual investing activities during 1995. Compare the company's level of investment with previous years, and indicate how the company financed its investments during 1995. Net income for 1995 was $2,986 million.

EXTENDING YOUR KNOWLEDGE

DECISION CASES

Explaining the market value and equity methods of accounting for investments ***(Obj. 1, 2)***

Case 1. Sarah Ringo is the manager of Avanti Corp., whose year end is December 31. The company made two investments during the first week of January 19X7. Both investments are to be held for the indefinite future. Information about the investments follows:

a. Avanti purchased 30% of the common stock of Rotary Motor Co. for its book value of $200,000. During the year ended December 31, 19X7, Rotary earned $106,000 and paid a total dividend of $53,000. At year end, the market value of the Rotary investment is $261,000.

b. One thousand shares of the common stock of Oxford Medical Corporation were purchased as an available-for-sale investment for $95,000. During the year ended December 31, 19X7, Oxford paid Avanti a dividend of $3,000. Oxford earned a profit of $317,000 for that period, and at year end, the market value of Avanti's investment in Oxford stock was $107,000.

Ringo has come to you to ask how to account for the investments. Avanti has never had such investments before. Explain the proper accounting to her by indicating that different accounting methods apply to different situations.

Required

Help Ringo understand by writing a memo to

1. Describe the methods of accounting applicable to these investments.
2. Identify which method should be used to account for the investments in Rotary Motor Co. and Oxford Medical Corporation. Also indicate the dollar amount to report for each investment on the year-end balance sheet.

Understanding the consolidation method for investments and for international accounting ***(Obj. 3, 5)***

Case 2. Prudyat Sen inherited some investments, and he has received the annual reports of the companies in which the funds are invested. The financial statements of the companies are puzzling to Sen, and he asks you the following questions:

a. The companies label their financial statements as *consolidated* balance sheet, *consolidated* income statement, and so on. What are consolidated financial statements?

b. Notes to the statements indicate that "certain intercompany transactions, loans, and other accounts have been eliminated in preparing the consolidated financial statements." Why does a company eliminate transactions, loans, and accounts? Sen states that he thought a transaction was a transaction and that a loan obligated a company to pay real money. He wonders if the company is juggling the books to defraud the IRS.

c. The balance sheet lists the asset Goodwill. What is goodwill? Does the presence of goodwill mean that the company's stock has increased in value?

d. The stockholders' equity section of the balance sheet reports Translation Adjustments. Sen asks what is being translated and why this item is negative.

Required

Write a memo to respond to each of Sen's questions.

ETHICAL ISSUE

Citizen Utilities owns 18% of the voting stock of Mohawk Electric Power Company. The remainder of the Mohawk stock is held by numerous investors with small holdings. Monica Kurtz, president of Citizen Utilities and a member of Mohawk's board of directors, heavily influences Mohawk Electric Power Company's policies.

Under the market value method of accounting for investments, Citizen's net income increases as it receives dividend revenue from Mohawk Power. Citizen Utilities pays President Kurtz a bonus computed as a percentage of Citizen's net income. Therefore, Kurtz can control her personal bonus to a certain extent by influencing Mohawk's dividends.

A recession occurs in 19X0, and Citizen Utilities' income is low. Kurtz uses her power to have Mohawk Electric Power pay a large cash dividend. The action requires Mohawk to borrow in order to pay the dividend.

Required

1. In getting Mohawk to pay the large cash dividend, is Kurtz acting within her authority as a member of the Mohawk board of directors? Are Kurtz's actions ethical? Whom can her actions harm?
2. Discuss how using the equity method of accounting for investments would decrease Kurtz's potential for manipulating her bonus.

FINANCIAL STATEMENT CASES

Investments in stock ***(Obj. 3, 5)***

Case 1. Use the Lands' End, Inc., financial statements in Appendix A at the end of the book to answer the following questions about the company's investments in the stock of other companies.

Required

1. The last asset on the Land's End balance sheet is Intangibles, Net (of Accumulated Amortization). Note 1 states that goodwill is the company's main intangible asset. Explain the nature of Lands' End's goodwill, and explain how the goodwill arose during the year ended January 27, 1995. Note 8 gives additional details.

2. During the year ended February 2, 1996, Lands' End's intangibles decreased. Assume for this requirement that goodwill is the company's only intangible asset. What is the most likely explanation for the decrease in goodwill? Is it likely that Lands' End acquired other companies at premium prices during the year ended February 2, 1996? Give the reason for your answer.
3. Lands' End reports no Minority Interest on its balance sheet. What does the absence of Minority Interest tell you about Lands' End's investments in consolidated subsidiaries?
4. During the year ended February 2, 1996, Lands' End's translation adjustment grew from $284,000 to $360,000. Are these amounts more like gains or more like losses? Was the dollar strong or weak relative to the currencies of the countries in which Lands' End's foreign subsidiaries are located? Explain.

Investments in stocks
(Obj. 1, 2, 3)

Case 2. Obtain the annual report of a company of your choosing. Answer the following questions about the company. Concentrate on the current year in the annual report you select.

Required

1. Many companies refer to other companies in which they own equity-method investments as *affiliated companies.* This signifies the close relationship between the two entities even though the investor does not own a controlling interest.

   Does the company have equity-method investments? Cite the evidence. If present, what were the balances in the investment account at the beginning and the end of the current year? If the company had no equity-method investments, skip the next question.
2. Scan the income statement. If equity-method investments are present, what amount of revenue (or income) did the company earn on the investments during the current year? Scan the statement of cash flows. What amount of dividends did the company receive during the current year from companies in which it held equity-method investments? *Note:* The amount of dividends received may not be disclosed. If not, you can still compute the amount of dividends received from the following T-account:

Investments, at Equity

Beg. bal. (from balance sheet	**W**		
Equity-method revenue (from income statement)	**X**	**Dividends received (unknown; must compute)**	**Y**
End. bal. (from balance sheet)	**Z**		

3. The company probably owns some consolidated subsidiaries. You can tell whether the parent company owns 100% or less of the subsidiaries. Examine the income statement and the balance sheet to determine whether there are any minority interests. If so, what does that fact indicate?
4. The stockholders' equity section of most balance sheets lists Foreign-Currency Translation Adjustment or a similar account title. A positive amount signifies a gain, and a negative amount indicates a loss. The change in this account balance from the beginning of the year to the end of the year signals whether the U.S. dollar was strong or weak during the year in comparison to the foreign currencies. For the company you are analyzing, was the dollar strong or weak during the current year?

GROUP PROJECT

Pick a stock from the *Wall Street Journal* or other database or publication. Assume that your group purchases 1,000 shares of the stock as a long-term investment and that your 1,000 shares are less than 20% of the company's outstanding stock. Research the stock in *Value Line, Moody's Investor Record,* or other source to determine whether the company pays cash dividends and, if so, how much and at what intervals.

Required

1. Track the stock for a period assigned by your professor. Over the specified period, keep a daily record of the price of the stock to see how well your investment has performed. Each day, search the Corporate Dividend News in the *Wall Street Journal* to keep a record of any dividends you've received. End the period of your analysis with a month end, such as September 30 or December 31.
2. Journalize all transactions that you have experienced, including the stock purchase, dividends received (both cash dividends and stock dividends), and any year-end adjustment required by the accounting method that is appropriate for your situation. Assume you will prepare financial statements on the ending date of your study.
3. Show what you will report on your company's balance sheet, income statement, and statement of cash flows as a result of your investment transactions.

INTERNET EXERCISE

GENERAL MOTORS

General Motors (GM) is a truly global company. Some of its automobiles were, in part, designed in Australia, assembled in Mexico using raw materials from South Africa, and ultimately sold in the United States. One of the largest companies in the world, General Motors employs hundreds of thousands of people across 50 countries and must manage its operations with a worldwide perspective.

GM's financial statements reflect this international orientation. The company's results are subdivided by geographic sales regions or by subsidiaries. This organization provides investors with a strong understanding of the sources behind GM's success.

Required

1. Go to **http://www.gm.com/index.cgi,** the General Motors home page. Here you can preview GM's lineup of cars and trucks, arrange financing, find a local dealer, and explore the concept cars of the future.
2. The excerpts from GM's annual report are located in **Invest in GM** section, highlighted at the top of the home page and down in the text near the bottom.
3. The **Annual Report Digest** contains highlights from the most recent annual report. Although this is an abbreviated version, the essence of the full financial statements is presented. From the various sources within the annual report, answer the following questions:
   - **a.** How does General Motors plan to operate as a global company? What are the three key regions outside GM's North American operations?
   - **b.** For the most recent year, what portion of GM automotive sales were from North American operations? From its international operations?
   - **c.** Estimate whether or not GM's shares of the North American and international automotive markets are increasing.
   - **d.** Much of GM's business is conducted outside the United States. What impact did foreign-currency translations have on GM's international operations? Where in the financial statements does this result appear?

11

Using the Income Statement and the Financial Statement Notes: Additional Corporate Reporting Issues

Learning Objectives

After studying this chapter, you should be able to

1. Analyze and use the elements of a complex income statement
2. Account for a corporation's income tax
3. Analyze a statement of stockholders' equity
4. Interpret notes to the financial statements
5. Use segment and interim financial data for decision making
6. Understand managers' and auditors' responsibilities for the financial statements

The May Department Stores Company
Consolidated Statement of Earnings (partial; adapted)

(In millions, except per share)	*1995*	*1994*	*1993*
	Fiscal Year		
1 **Net Retail Sales**	**$10,507**	**$ 9,759**	**$9,020**
2 Total revenues	$ 10,952	$10,107	$ 9,562
3 Cost of sales	7,461	6,879	6,537
4 Selling, general, and administrative expenses	2,081	1,916	1,824
5 Interest expense, net	250	233	244
6 Total cost of sales and expenses	9,792	9,028	8,605
7 **Earnings from continuing operations before income taxes**	**1,160**	**1,079**	**957**
8 Provision for income taxes	460	429	379
9 **Net Earnings from Continuing Operations**	**700**	**650**	**578**
10 Net earnings from discontinued operation	55	132	133
11 Net earnings before extraordinary loss	755	782	711
12 Extraordinary loss related to early extinguishment of debt, net of income taxes	(3)	—	—
13 **Net earnings**	**$ 752**	**$ 782**	**$ 711**
Earnings per Share:			
14 Continuing operations	$ 2.73	$ 2.53	$ 2.24
15 Discontinued operation	0.22	0.53	0.53
16 Net earnings before extraordinary loss	2.95	3.06	2.77
17 Extraordinary loss	(0.01)	—	—
18 Earnings per Share	$ 2.94	$ 3.06	$ 2.77

Notes:

Discontinued Operation

[During fiscal year 1995] the company announced its intention to spin off Payless, its chain of self-service family shoe stores, in May 1996. The company's financial statements presented herein have been restated to reflect Payless as a discontinued operation. The consolidated statement of earnings includes the results of Payless as a discontinued operation through [the end of 1995].

Long-Term Debt

During the 1995 fourth quarter, the company recorded an extraordinary after-tax loss of $3 million ($5 million pretax) as it executed a binding contract to call $112 million, 9.25% debentures due to mature March 1, 2016.

"Our investors are interested in the level of income a company can expect to earn in the future. Therefore, we are most likely to base our recommendations on our review of a company's income from continuing operations rather than its net income."

—Murray Weintraub, Business Analyst, Sledd & Co. Investment Bankers

The **May Department Stores Company** is one of the country's leading department store companies, operating 346 quality department stores (including Lord & Taylor, Hecht's, Foley's, Robinsons-May, Filene's, and Meier & Frank) through eight regional divisions. Each division holds a leading position in its region. The company's total annual sales are $10.5 billion. May's operating results for 1995 are reported on the income statement reproduced on page 516.

Murray Weintraub, chief financial analyst for Sledd & Co. Investment Bankers, is pricing May Department Stores' common stock. Net earnings for 1995 are down from 1994, but net earnings from continuing operations have grown steadily from 1993 to 1994 and from 1994 to 1995. Which 1995 income figure—net earnings of $752 million (line 13) or net earnings of $700 million from continuing operations (line 9)—should Weintraub use to help decide whether May's stock at $46.25 per share is underpriced, overpriced, or priced about right? His decision will govern whether Sledd & Co. makes a "buy," "hold," or "sell" recommendation to its investment clients.

Investment analysts such as Murray Weintraub use the financial statements and other data to predict the future net income and cash flows of companies, including May's. But the financial statements are also used by other groups of people with different perspectives. Banks and other lenders use the financial statements to decide whether to grant a loan to the company. Governmental bodies such as the Federal Trade Commission may examine a corporation's financial statements to help determine whether the company is exercising monopoly power. Trade unions may look for "excessive" profits that they urge the company to share with its employees.

Given these different perspectives, let's return to the question posed earlier: Which income figure should investors use to evaluate a company's operating results? The answer depends on the decision you will make. If you want to measure how well the company has performed in light of all its activities, then you want to look at net income (line 13). But if you want to predict the level of income the company can expect to earn in the future, you should consider only those aspects of its operations that it can repeat from year to year. Murray Weintraub and his staff are probably more interested in income from continuing operations than in net income. Most sophisticated investors and lenders concentrate their analysis on income from continuing operations, which can be expected to generate income for the company in the future.

In this chapter we discuss continuing operations, discontinued operations, and other operating activities reported on the corporate income statement. We explain various special items—those gains and losses that also affect net income but differ from basic revenues and operating expenses—that appear on corporate income statements. We also cover a range of other topics that will enhance your understanding of corporate reporting and your ability to analyze financial statements.

Quality of Earnings—Analyzing a Corporate Income Statement

Objective 1

Analyze and use the elements of a complex income statement

A corporation's net income (revenues plus gains minus expenses and losses) receives more attention than any other item in the financial statements. In fact, net income is probably the most important piece of information about a company. Net income measures the business's ability to earn a profit and indicates how successfully the company has managed its operations. To stockholders, the larger the corporation's profit, the greater the likelihood of dividends. To creditors, the larger the corporation's profit, the better it is able to pay its debts. Net income builds up a company's assets and owners' equity. It also helps to attract capital from new investors who hope to receive dividends from future successful operations.

Suppose you are considering investing in the stock of two manufacturing companies. In reading their annual reports and examining their past records, you learn that the companies showed the same net income figure for last year and that each company has increased its net income by 15% annually over the last five years.

The two companies, however, have generated income in different ways. Company A's income has resulted from the successful management of its central operations (manufacturing). Company B's manufacturing operations have been flat for two years. Its growth in net income has resulted from selling off segments of its business at a profit. In which company would you invest?

Company A holds the promise of better future earnings. This corporation earns profits from continuing operations. We may reasonably expect the business to match its past earnings in the future. Company B shows no growth from operations. Its net income results from one-time transactions, the selling off of its operating assets. Sooner or later, Company B will have sold off the last of its assets used in operations. When that occurs, the business will have no means of generating income. On the basis of this reasoning, your decision is to invest in the stock of Company A. Investors would say that Company A's earnings are of *higher quality* than Company B's earnings.

This example points to two important investment considerations: the *trend* of a company's earnings and the *makeup* of its net income. Consider the May Department Stores income statement in the chapter opening story (page 516). May's trend of income from continuing operations (which May sets in boldface type and labels as Net Earnings from Continuing Operations, line 9) is up during both 1994 and 1995. The trend of net income (which May labels as Net earnings, line 13) is up to $782 million in 1994, then down to $752 million in 1995. May also reports a third income figure, net earnings before extraordinary loss (line

16). To explore the makeup of net income, let's examine the various types of income in detail. Exhibit 11-1 provides a comprehensive example that we will use in the following discussions. It is the income statement of **Allied Electronics Corporation,** a small manufacturer of precision instruments.

Continuing Operations

We have seen that income from a business's continuing operations helps investors make predictions about the business's future earnings. In the income statement of Exhibit 11-1, the topmost section reports income from continuing operations. This part of the business is expected to continue from period to period. We may use this information to predict that Allied Electronics Corporation will earn income of approximately $54,000 next year.

The continuing operations of Allied Electronics include three items deserving explanation. First, during 19X5, the company restructured operations at a loss of $10,000. Restructuring costs include severance pay to laid-off workers, moving expenses for employees transferred to other locations, and environmental cleanup expenses. The restructuring loss is part of continuing operations because Allied Electronics is remaining in the same line of business. But the restructuring loss is highlighted as an "other" item on the income statement because its cause—restructuring—falls outside Allied Electronics' main business endeavor, which is selling electronics products.

Second, Allied also had a gain on the sale of machinery, which is outside the company's core business activity. This explains why the gain is reported separately from Allied's sales revenue, cost of goods sold, and gross margin.

For a review of these terms, see Chapter 6.

EXHIBIT 11-1
Allied Corporation Income Statement

ALLIED ELECTRONICS CORPORATION
Income Statement
For the Year Ended December 31, 19X5

Sales revenue		$500,000
Cost of goods sold		240,000
Gross margin		260,000
Operating expenses (detailed)		181,000
Operating income		79,000
Other gains (losses):		
Loss on restructuring operations		(10,000)
Gain on sale of machinery		21,000
Income from continuing operations before income tax		90,000
Income tax expense		36,000
Income from continuing operations		54,000
Discontinued operations:		
Operating income, $30,000, less income tax of $12,000	$18,000	
Gain on disposal, $5,000, less income tax of $2,000	3,000	21,000
Income before extraordinary item and cumulative effect of change in depreciation method		75,000
Extraordinary flood loss, $20,000, less income tax saving of $8,000		(12,000)
Cumulative effect of change in depreciation method, $10,000, less income tax of $4,000		6,000
Net income		$ 69,000
Earnings per share of common stock (20,000 shares outstanding):		
Income from continuing operations		$2.70
Income from discontinued operations		1.05
Income before extraordinary item and cumulative effect of change in depreciation method		3.75
Extraordinary loss		(0.60)
Cumulative effect of change in depreciation method		0.30
Net income		$3.45

Third, income tax expense has been deducted in arriving at income from continuing operations. The tax that corporations pay on their income is a significant expense. The current maximum federal income tax rate for corporations is 35 percent. State income taxes run about 5% in many states. Thus, we use an income tax rate of 40% in our illustrations. The $36,000 income tax expense in Exhibit 11-1 equals the pretax income from continuing operations multiplied by the tax rate ($90,000 × 0.40 = $36,000).

STOP & THINK How much was Allied Electronics' *total* income tax expense during 19X5?

Answer

$46,000 = ($36,000 + $12,000 + $2,000 − $8,000 + $4,000)

Observe in Exhibit 11-1 that income tax is reported along with each separate category of income or loss:

Category of Income or Loss	Income Tax Expense (Saving)
Income from continuing operations	$36,000
Discontinued operations ($12,000 + $2,000)	14,000
Extraordinary gains and losses	(8,000)
Cumulative effect of accounting change	4,000
Total income tax expense for 19X5	$46,000

Note that $36,000 is the company's income tax expense from continuing operations; $46,000 is *total* income tax expense.

USING INCOME FROM CONTINUING OPERATIONS IN INVESTMENT ANALYSIS How is income from continuing operations used in investment analysis? Suppose Murray Weintraub is estimating the value of Allied Electronics' common stock. Weintraub and his staff may believe that Allied Electronics can earn annual income of $54,000 each year for the indefinite future, based on Allied's 19X5 income from continuing operations.

To estimate the value of Allied's common stock, financial analysts determine the present value (present value means *today*) of Allied's stream of future income. Weintraub must use some interest rate to compute the present value. Assume that an appropriate interest rate (i) for the computation is 12 percent. This rate is determined subjectively, based on the risk that Allied might not be able to earn annual income of $54,000 for the indefinite future. The rate is also called the **investment capitalization rate** because it is used to estimate the value of an investment in the capital stock of another company. The higher the risk, the higher the rate, and vice versa. The computation is

See Chapter 8 and Appendix B for a review of present value.

$$\textbf{Estimated value of Allied Electronics common stock} = \frac{\textbf{Estimated annual income in the future}}{\textbf{Investment capitalization rate}} = \frac{\$54{,}000}{.12} = \$450{,}000^{1}$$

[1]This valuation model has many forms, which are covered in finance classes. Here we introduce the most basic form of a widely used valuation model to illustrate how accounting income can be used in actual practice.

Another way to estimate the value of a company's stock uses the price/earnings (P/E) ratio, which is roughly equal to the reciprocal of the investment capitalization rate. In the P/E formulation of company value, the analyst multiplies net income by the P/E ratio. The computation for Allied Electronics is net income ($54,000), multiplied by the P/E ratio (8.33), which equals the estimated value of $450,000.

Weintraub thus estimates that Allied Electronics Corporation is worth \$450,000. He would then compare this estimate to the current market value of Allied Electronics' stock, which is \$513,000. To determine the company's current market value, we need information from both the company's financial statements and the financial press. Allied Electronics' balance sheet reports that Allied has 108,000 shares of common stock outstanding, and the *Wall Street Journal* reports that Allied common stock is selling for \$4.75 per share. The current market value of Allied Stock is thus

Current market value of the company	=	Number of shares of common stock outstanding	×	Current market price per share
\$513,000	=	**108,000**	×	**\$4.75**

The investment decision rule may take this form:

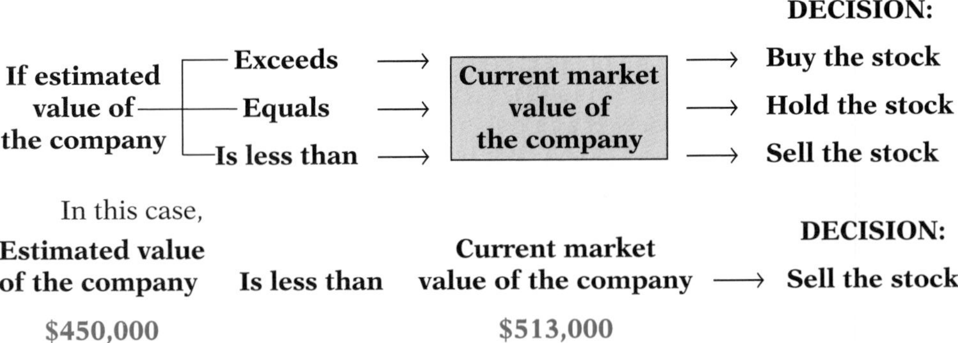

Sledd & Co. Investment Bankers would recommend that investors holding Allied Electronics stock sell it. Sledd believes the stock price should fall below its current market value of \$513,000 to somewhere in a range near \$450,000. Sledd believes that Allied's stock would be more fairly priced at \$450,000, based largely on its income from continuing operations.

Investors often make their decisions based on the value of a single share of stock. They can estimate the value of one share of stock with a variation of the valuation computation that uses earnings per share (EPS) of common stock, as follows:

$$\textbf{Estimated value of one share of common stock} = \frac{\textbf{Estimated annual earnings per share}}{\textbf{Investment capitalization rate}}$$

The analysis based on one share of stock follows the pattern illustrated for the company as a whole.

SUMMARY OF THE INVESTMENT DECISION PROCESS Let's summarize the investment-decision process. It begins with an income figure that experienced people—in this case, financial analysts who follow Allied stock—believe that Allied can earn annually for the indefinite future, an amount that most analysts base on *income from continuing operations.* Some analysts also use *cash flows from operating activities* to estimate the value of an investment. Many analysts use both income from continuing operations and cash flows from operating activities. Chapter 12 covers cash-flow analysis in detail.

Suppose Murray Weintraub's investment team fears that Allied Electronics cannot earn \$54,000 annually for the indefinite future. They may take a more conservative view—say, that Allied Electronics' income stream may be predictable for only 20 years into the future. In that case, analysts' estimate of the value of Allied's stock would be

Estimated value of Allied Electronics common stock	=	Estimated annual income in the future	×	Present value of annuity $n = 20$ periods; $i = 12\%$ (Appendix B, Table B-7, page 726)
	=	$ 54,000	×	7.469
	=	$403,326		

Based on this estimate, analysts would believe even more strongly that Allied's stock is overpriced at $513,000 ($4.75 per share).

Discontinued Operations

Most large corporations engage in several lines of business. For example, **General Mills, Inc.,** best known for its food products, also has retailing and restaurant operations. In addition to its retail stores, **Sears, Roebuck & Co.,** has a real estate development company (Homart) and an insurance company (Allstate). We call each identifiable division of a company a **segment of the business.**

A company may sell a segment of its business. For example, May Department Stores, sold Payless, its chain of shoe stores. Such a sale is not a regular source of income because a company cannot keep selling its segments indefinitely. The sale of a business segment is viewed as a one-time transaction. The income statement carries information on the segment that has been disposed of under the heading Discontinued Operations. This section of the income statement is divided into two components: (1) operating income or (loss) on the segment that is disposed of, and (2) any gain (or loss) on the disposal. Income and gain are taxed at the 40% rate and reported by Allied Electronics Corporation as follows:

Discontinued operations:		
Operating income, $30,000, less income tax, $12,000	$18,000	
Gain on disposal, $5,000, less income tax, $2,000	3,000	$21,000

Trace this presentation to Exhibit 11-1.

In the normal course of business, companies dispose of old plant and equipment as they acquire new, more productive assets. Gains and losses on these asset dispositions are *not* reported as discontinued operations because they don't relate to a segment of the business that is being discontinued. Gains and losses on normal asset dispositions can be reported along with operating revenues and expenses or highlighted in an "Other" section of the income statement.

It is necessary to separate discontinued operations into these two components because the company may operate the discontinued segment for part of the year. This is the operating income (or loss) component. Then, the disposal of the segment results in a gain (or loss).

Financial analysts typically do not include income or loss on discontinued operations in predictions of future corporate income. The discontinued segments will not generate income for the company in the future.

RJR Nabisco sold Kentucky Fried Chicken to PepsiCo, Inc., because of disappointing returns.

Discontinued operations are common in business. **RJR Nabisco** sold **Kentucky Fried Chicken** to **PepsiCo, Inc.,** because of disappointing returns. The **Black and Decker Manufacturing Company** disposed of its gasoline chain-saw business, and **Purolator, Inc.,** sold its armored-car segment. Each of these items was disclosed as discontinued operations in the company's income statement.

USING THE NOTES TO FINANCIAL STATEMENTS The notes to financial statements provide valuable information that would clutter the income statement or balance sheet. May Department Stores gives a good example.

The May Department Stores Company had net earnings of $55 million from discontinued operations during 1995 (see line 10 of the income statement, page 516). These earnings are explained in the Discontinued Operation note shown below the income statement. During 1995, May announced its intention to dispose of (spin off) **Payless Shoes.** Because Payless Shoes will cease to be part of May Department Stores, Payless's income is reported as a discontinued operation. In 1996, when May completes the disposition of Payless, May will report a gain or loss on disposition of the discontinued operation.

Extraordinary Gains and Losses (Extraordinary Items)

Extraordinary gains and losses, also called **extraordinary items,** are both unusual for the company and infrequent. Losses from natural disasters (such as earthquakes, floods, and tornadoes), and the taking of company assets by a foreign government (expropriation), are extraordinary. Gains and losses on the early retirement of debt are also extraordinary items.

Extraordinary items are reported along with their income tax effect. During 19X5, Allied Electronics Corporation lost $20,000 of inventory in a flood. This flood loss, which reduced income, also reduced Allied's income tax. The tax effect of the loss is computed by multiplying the amount of the loss by the tax rate. The tax effect decreases the net amount of the loss in the same way that the income tax reduces the amount of net income. An extraordinary loss can be reported along with its tax effect on the income statement as follows:

Extraordinary flood loss	$(20,000)
Less income tax saving	8,000
Extraordinary flood loss, net of tax	(12,000)

Trace this item to the income statement in Exhibit 11-1. An extraordinary gain is reported in the same way, net of the income tax on the gain.

Gains and losses due to employee strikes, the settlement of lawsuits, discontinued operations, and the sale of plant assets are *not* extraordinary items. They are considered normal business occurrences. However, because they are outside the business's central operations, they are reported on the income statement as other gains and losses. Examples include the gain on sale of machinery and the restructuring loss in the Other gains (losses) section of Exhibit 11-1.

USING THE NOTES TO FINANCIAL STATEMENTS During 1995, May Department Stores had an extraordinary loss due to the early extinguishment of its long-term debt (line 12). The Long-Term Debt note reports the details. On the transaction, May incurred a $5 million loss before taxes. Income tax savings of $2 million reduced the net amount of the extraordinary loss to $3 million.

Cumulative Effect of a Change in Accounting Principle

Companies sometimes change from one accounting method to another, such as from double-declining-balance (DDB) to straight-line depreciation, or from first-in, first-out (FIFO) to weighted-average cost for inventory. An accounting change makes it difficult to compare one period's financial statements with the statements of preceding periods. Without detailed information, investors and creditors can be misled into thinking that the current year is better or worse than the preceding year when in fact the only difference is a change in accounting method. To help investors separate the effects of regular business operations from those effects generated by a change in accounting method, companies report the effect of the accounting change in a special section of the income statement. This section usually appears after extraordinary items.

For a review of depreciation methods, see Chapter 7. For a review of inventory accounting methods, see Chapter 6.

We need to know what cumulative effect an accounting change would have had on net income of prior years. GAAP requires companies that change accounting methods to disclose the difference between net income actually reported under the old method and the net income that the company would have experienced if it had used the new method all along.

Suppose Allied Electronics Corporation changes from DDB to straight-line depreciation at the beginning of 19X5. How will this change in depreciation method affect the 19X5 financial statements? First, it will decrease depreciation expense for 19X5 and thereby increase 19X5 income from continuing operations. Second, the change will affect cumulative amounts from previous years. If the company had been using straight-line depreciation every year, depreciation expense would have been less, and net income would have been $6,000 higher ($10,000 minus the additional income tax of $4,000). Exhibit 11-1 reports the cumulative effect of this accounting change. A change from straight-line to double-declining-balance usually produces a negative cumulative effect.

The company generally reports changes in inventory methods and changes in revenue methods in this same manner. Numerous exceptions make changes in accounting principle—usually a change in accounting method—a complicated area. Details are covered in later accounting courses.

Earnings per Share

The final segment of a corporation income statement presents the company's earnings per share, abbreviated as EPS. In fact, GAAP requires that corporations disclose EPS figures on the income statement. **Earnings per share** is the amount of a company's net income per share of its outstanding *common* stock. EPS is a key measure of a business's success:

$$\textbf{Earnings per share} = \frac{\textbf{Net income}}{\textbf{Shares of common stock outstanding}}$$

Just as the corporation lists its different sources of income separately—from continuing operations, discontinued operations, and so on—it also lists the EPS figure based on different income sources separately. Consider the following EPS calculations for Allied Electronics Corporation:

Earnings per share of common stock (20,000 shares outstanding):	
Income from continuing operations ($54,000/20,000)	$2.70
Income from discontinued operations ($21,000/20,000)	1.05
Income before extraordinary item and cumulative effect of change in depreciation method ($75,000/20,000)	3.75
Extraordinary loss ($12,000/20,000)	(0.60)
Cumulative effect of change in depreciation method ($6,000/20,000)	0.30
Net income ($69,000/20,000)	$3.45

The final section of Exhibit 11-1 shows how the EPS figures are reported on the income statement.

WEIGHTED-AVERAGE SHARES OF COMMON STOCK OUTSTANDING Computing EPS is straightforward if the number of common shares outstanding does not change over the entire accounting period. For many corporations, however, this figure varies over the course of the year. Consider a corporation that had 100,000 shares outstanding from January through November, then purchased 60,000 shares as treasury stock. This company's EPS would be misleadingly high if computed using 40,000 (100,000 – 60,000) shares. To make EPS as meaningful as possible, corporations use the weighted-average number of common shares outstanding during the period.

Let's assume the following figures for Diskette Demo Corporation. From January through May, the company had 240,000 shares of common stock outstanding; from June through August, 200,000 shares; and from September through December, 210,000 shares. We compute the weighted average by considering the outstanding shares per month as a fraction of the year:

Number of Common Shares Outstanding	×	Fraction of Year		=	Weighted-Average Number of Common Shares Outstanding
240,000	×	5/12	(January through May)	=	100,000
200,000	×	3/12	(June through August)	=	50,000
210,000	×	4/12	(September through December)	=	70,000
			Weighted-average number of common shares outstanding during the year		220,000

The 220,000 weighted average number of shares of stock would be divided into net income to compute the corporation's EPS.

PREFERRED DIVIDENDS Throughout our EPS discussion thus far, we have used only the number of shares of common stock outstanding. Holders of preferred stock have no claim to the business's income beyond the stated preferred dividend. But preferred dividends do affect the EPS figure. Recall that EPS is earnings per share of *common* stock. Recall also that dividends on preferred stock are paid first. Therefore, preferred dividends must be subtracted from income subtotals (income from continuing operations, income before extraordinary items and cumulative effect of accounting change, and net income) in the computation of EPS. Preferred dividends are not subtracted from income or loss from discontinued operations, and they are not subtracted from extraordinary gains and losses.

Chapter 9, pages 429–430, provides detailed information on preferred stock.

If Allied Electronics Corporation had 10,000 shares of preferred stock outstanding, each with a $1.50 dividend, the annual preferred dividend would be $15,000 (10,000 × $1.50). The $15,000 would be subtracted from each of the different income subtotals, resulting in the following EPS computations for the company:

Earnings per share of common stock (20,000 shares outstanding):	
Income from continuing operations ($54,000 – $15,000)/20,000	$1.95
Income from discontinued operations ($21,000/20,000)	1.05
Income before extraordinary item and cumulative effect of change in depreciation method ($75,000 – $15,000)/20,000	3.00
Extraordinary loss ($12,000/20,000)	(0.60)
Cumulative effect of change in depreciation method ($6,000/20,000)	0.30
Net income ($69,000 – $15,000)/20,000	$2.70

DILUTION Some corporations make their preferred stock more attractive to investors by offering convertible preferred stock. Holders of convertible preferred may exchange the preferred stock for common stock. When preferred stock is converted to common stock, the EPS is *diluted*—reduced—because more common stock shares are divided into net income. Because convertible preferred can be traded in for common stock, the common stockholders want to know the amount of the decrease in EPS if the preferred stock is converted into common. To provide this information, corporations with complex capital structures present two sets of EPS amounts: EPS based on outstanding common shares (*basic* EPS) and EPS based on outstanding common shares plus the number of additional common shares that would arise from conversion of the preferred stock into common (*diluted* EPS). The May Department Stores Company reports basic earnings per share in line 18 of its 1995 income statement in the chapter opening story.

EPS is the most widely used accounting figure. Many income statement users place top priority on EPS. Also, a stock's market price is related to the company's EPS. By dividing the market price of a company's stock by its EPS, we compute a statistic called the *price-to-earnings* ratio. The *Wall Street Journal* reports the price/earnings ratio (abbreviated as P/E) daily for more than 3,000 companies.

The following excerpt was adapted from the *Wall Street Journal.* Note that Allied Electronics' stock had a price/earnings ratio of 8.

					Stock Exchange						
52 Weeks					Yld		Vol				Net
Hi	Lo	Stock	Sym	Div	%	PE	100s	Hi	Lo	Close	Chg
31⅛	20¼	AlliedElec	ADE	.20	.8	8	85	24½	24⅜	24½	+ ⅛
69	42⅛	AlliedSgnl	ALD	.90	1.3	20	15259	70⅛	68⅝	70⅛	+ 1½
34⅜	24⅜	AllmericaFnl	AFC	.20	.6	9	1449	31⅞	31½	31½	− ½

STOP & THINK What makes earnings per share so useful as a business statistic?

Answer: Earnings per share is useful because it relates a company's income to one share of stock. Stock prices are quoted at an amount per share, and investors usually consider how much they must pay for a certain number of shares. Earnings per share and cash flow per share are used to help determine the value of a share of stock.

Reporting Comprehensive Income

As we have seen throughout this book, all companies report net income or net loss on their income statement. Companies with certain gains and losses are also required by FASB Statement 130 to report another income figure. **Comprehensive income** is the company's change in total stockholders' equity from all sources other than from the owners of the business. Comprehensive income includes net income plus some specific gains and losses. In Chapter 10 we saw two new components of comprehensive income:

- Unrealized gains or losses on available-for-sale investments
- Foreign-currency translation adjustments

These items do not enter into the determination of net income but instead are reported as other comprehensive income as shown in Exhibit 11-2. Assumed figures are used for all items.

EXHIBIT 11-2
Reporting Comprehensive Income

NATIONAL EXPRESS COMPANY
Income Statement
Year Ended December 31, 19X9

Revenues			$10,000
Expenses (including income tax)			6,000
Net income			4,000
Other comprehensive income:			
Unrealized gain on investment	$650		
Less income tax (40%)	260	$390	
Foreign-currency translation adjustment (loss)	$(900)		
Less income tax (40%)	360	(540)	
Other comprehensive income			(150)
Comprehensive income			$3,850

Earnings per share applies only to net income and its components. Earnings per share is not reported for other comprehensive income.

Investors and creditors who believe net income is the best measure of performance can use net income to evaluate the company. Others who view comprehensive income as the best measure of the company's progress can use comprehensive income in their evaluations.

Objective 2

Account for a corporation's income tax

Accounting for the Income Tax of a Corporation

Corporations pay taxes on their income in the same way that individuals do. Corporate and personal tax rates differ, however. At this writing, the federal tax rate on most corporate income is 35 percent. In addition, most states also levy income taxes on corporations.

Income Tax Expense is based on income before tax, or **pretax accounting income,** from the income statement. In contrast, Income Tax Payable is based on the company's **taxable income** as reported on the tax return filed with the Internal Revenue Service. The income statement and the tax return are entirely separate documents. Taxable income is the basis for computing the amount of tax to pay the government. Pretax accounting income and taxable income are rarely the same amount.

Income tax expense	=	Pretax accounting income (from income statement)	×	Income tax rate
Income tax payable	=	Taxable income (from tax return)	×	Income tax rate

In practice, accounting for income tax is extremely complex. Additional complexities are covered in intermediate, advanced, and tax accounting courses.

Some revenues and expenses become a part of accounting income before or after they become a part of taxable income. Over a period of several years, total pretax accounting income may equal total taxable income, but for any one year the two income amounts are likely to differ.

A difference between pretax accounting income and taxable income usually occurs when a corporation uses the straight-line method to compute depreciation for the financial statements and a different depreciation method for its tax return and the payment of taxes. The special tax depreciation method is called the *modified accelerated cost recovery system,* abbreviated as MACRS. For any one year, MACRS depreciation listed on the tax return may differ from accounting depreciation on the income statement.

We learned in Chapter 7, pages 335–336, that the MACRS depreciation method is used only for income tax purposes. It groups assets into classes by years of asset life.

Suppose IHOP Corp. has pretax accounting income of $12,200,000 in each of two years. The accounting issue is, What is the correct amount of income tax expense for the two years? By answering this question, we can complete IHOP's income statement:

IHOP CORP.
Income Statement (partial)

	19X1	19X2
Income before income tax	$12,200,000	$12,200,000
Income tax expense	?	?
Net income	$?	$?

IHOP's income tax expense for both years is $4,270,000 ($12,200,000 × 0.35). IHOP uses straight-line depreciation to compute income for the income statement. On the tax return, IHOP and most other corporations use MACRS depreciation, so the company's tax returns report taxable income of $12,000,000 in 19X1 and $12,400,000 in 19X2. Exhibit 11-3 on page 528 gives IHOP's entries to record income tax during 19X1 and 19X2.

Total *taxable* income for the two years combined—$24,400,000—is the same as total *pretax accounting* income for the two years. However, each year shows a difference between taxable income and pretax accounting income. With a 35% tax rate, income tax payable to the government is $4,200,000 ($12,000,000 × 0.35) in 19X1 and $4,340,000 ($12,400,000 × 0.35) in 19X2.

Exhibit 11-4 shows IHOP's partial comparative financial statements for 19X1 and 19X2. Income Tax Expense, Income Tax Payable, and Deferred Tax Liability come directly from the entries recorded in Exhibit 11-3.

Income Tax Payable and Deferred Tax Liability are reported as liabilities on the balance sheet. Income Tax Payable is a current liability because it must be paid within a few months. Deferred Tax Liability is usually a long-term liability,

EXHIBIT 11-3
Income Tax Entries for IHOP Corp.

19X1	Income Tax Expense ($12,200,000 × 0.35)	4,270,000	
	Income Tax Payable ($12,000,000 × 0.35)		4,200,000
	Deferred Tax Liability ($200,000 × 0.35)		70,000

ASSETS	=	LIABILITIES	+	STOCKHOLDERS' EQUITY	−	EXPENSES
0	=	+4,200,000 + 70,000			−	4,270,000

19X2	Income Tax Expense ($12,200,000 × 0.35)	4,270,000	
	Deferred Tax Liability ($200,000 × 0.35)	70,000	
	Income Tax Payable ($12,400,000 × 0.35)		4,340,000

ASSETS	=	LIABILITIES	+	STOCKHOLDERS' EQUITY	−	EXPENSES
0	=	+4,340,000 − 70,000			−	4,270,000

as it is for IHOP Corp. Why long-term? Because the asset that caused the deferred tax (depreciable property) is classified as long-term.

Study the entries in Exhibit 11-3. Observe that the $70,000 Deferred Tax Liability amount for 19X1 was eliminated in 19X2. This is why Deferred Tax Liability has a zero balance in the 19X2 balance sheet in Exhibit 11-4.

May Department Stores provide another example of corporate reporting of income tax. May's 1995 income statement at the beginning of the chapter reports Provision for income taxes of $460 million (line 8). Provision for income taxes is another name for income tax expense.

May reports its income tax liabilities in much the same way as IHOP Corp. May's fiscal 1995 balance sheet reported the amounts shown in Exhibit 11-5.

EXHIBIT 11-4
Income Tax on Corporate Financial Statements

IHOP CORP.
Partial Income Statement
For the Years Ended December 31, 19X1 and 19X2

	19X1	19X2
Income before income tax	$12,200,000	$12,200,000
Income tax expense ($12,200,000 × 0.35 both years)	4,270,000	4,270,000
Net income	$ 7,930,000	$ 7,930,000

IHOP CORP.
Partial Balance Sheet
December 31, 19X1 and 19X2

Liabilities	19X1	19X2
Current:		
Income tax payable	$4,200,000	$4,340,000
Long-term:		
Deferred tax liability	70,000	—

EXHIBIT 11-5
May's Consolidated Balance Sheet

THE MAY DEPARTMENT STORES COMPANY
Consolidated Balance Sheet (partial, adapted)

(In millions)	Fiscal Year End 1995
Liabilities	
Current Liabilities:	
Current maturities of long-term debt	$ 132
Accounts payable	692
Accrued expenses	650
Income taxes payable	128
Total Current Liabilities	1,602
Long-term Debt	3,333
Deferred Tax Liability	378
Other Liabilities	204

STOP & THINK At the end of fiscal year 1995, how much income tax did May Department Stores owe that the company expected to pay within one year or less? How much income tax did May expect to pay after a year? What was May's total income tax liability?

Answers

	(In millions)
Payable within one year	$128
Payable after a year	378
Total income tax liability	$506

Prior-Period Adjustments

What happens when a company makes an error in recording revenues or expenses? Detecting the error in the period in which it occurs allows the company to correct the mistake before that period's financial statements have been prepared. But failure to detect the error until a later period means that the business will have reported an incorrect amount of income on its income statement. After the revenue and expense accounts are closed, the company's Retained Earnings account will absorb the effect of the error. The balance of Retained Earnings will be wrong until the error is corrected.

Corrections to the beginning balance of Retained Earnings for errors of an earlier period are called **prior-period adjustments.** The correcting entry includes a debit or credit to Retained Earnings for the error amount and a credit or debit to the asset or liability account that was misstated. The prior-period adjustment appears on the corporation's statement of retained earnings to indicate the amount and the nature of the change in the Retained Earnings balance.

Assume that De Graff Corporation recorded income tax expense for 19X4 as $30,000. The correct amount was $40,000. This error resulted in understating 19X4 expenses by $10,000 and overstating net income by $10,000. A bill from the government in 19X5 for the additional $10,000 in taxes alerted De Graff's management to the mistake. The entry to record this prior-period adjustment in 19X5 is

19X5			
June 19	Retained Earnings	10,000	
	Income Tax Payable		10,000
	Prior-period adjustment to correct error in recording income tax expense of 19X4.		

EXHIBIT 11-6
Reporting a Prior-Period Adjustment

DE GRAFF CORPORATION Statement of Retained Earnings For the Year Ended December 31, 19X5	
Retained earnings balance, December 31, 19X4, as originally reported	$390,000
Prior-period adjustment—debit to correct error in recording income tax expense of 19X4	**(10,000)**
Retained earnings balance, December 31, 19X4, as adjusted	380,000
Net income for 19X5	114,000
	494,000
Dividends for 19X5	(41,000)
Retained earnings balance, December 31, 19X5	$453,000

The debit to Retained Earnings keeps the error correction from being reported on the income statement of 19X5. Recall the matching principle. If Income Tax Expense is debited when the prior-period adjustment is recorded in 19X5, then this $10,000 in taxes will appear on the 19X5 income statement. Its appearance there would not be proper, because the income tax expense arose from 19X4 operations, not 19X5 operations.

This prior-period adjustment would appear on the statement of retained earnings, as shown in Exhibit 11-6.

Restrictions on Retained Earnings

For a review of treasury stock transactions and retirements of stock, see Chapter 9, pages 433–436.

Dividends, purchases of treasury stock, and retirements of stock require payments by the corporation to its stockholders. In fact, treasury stock purchases and stock retirements are returns of paid-in capital to the stockholders. These outlays decrease the corporation's assets, so fewer assets are available to pay liabilities. Therefore, a company's creditors seek to restrict a corporation's dividend payments and treasury stock purchases. For example, a bank may agree to loan $500,000 only if the borrowing corporation limits dividend payments and purchases of treasury stock.

To ensure that corporations maintain a minimum level of stockholders' equity for the protection of creditors, state laws restrict the amount of its own stock that a corporation may purchase. The maximum amount a corporation can pay its stockholders without decreasing paid-in capital is its balance of retained earnings. Therefore, restrictions on dividends and stock purchases focus on the balance of retained earnings.

Companies usually report their retained earnings restrictions in notes to the financial statements. The following disclosure by **RTE Corporation,** a manufacturer of electronic transformers, is typical:

> ***Notes to Consolidated Financial Statements***
>
> *Note F—Long-Term Debt*
>
> The . . . Company's loan agreements . . . restrict cash dividends and similar payments to shareholders. Under the most restrictive of these provisions, retained earnings of $4,300,000 were unrestricted as of December 31, 19X3.

Alberto-Culver Company—maker of Molly McButter butter substitute, Static Guard antistatic spray, and Alberto VO5 hair products—had restrictions on retained earnings.

Alberto-Culver Company—maker of Molly McButter butter substitute, Static Guard antistatic spray, and Alberto VO5 hair products—also had restrictions on retained earnings. These restrictions are indicated in Alberto-Culver's Note 3, part of which appears at the top of page 531.

Notes to Consolidated Financial Statements

Note 3: Long-Term Debt

Various borrowing arrangements impose restrictions on such items as total debt, working capital [current assets minus current liabilities], dividend payments, treasury stock purchases, and interest expense. At September 30, 19X3, the company was in compliance with these arrangements, and $73 million of consolidated retained earnings was not restricted as to the payment of dividends and purchases of treasury stock.

STOP & THINK Why would a borrower such as Alberto-Culver Company agree to restrict dividends as a condition for receiving a loan?

Answer: To get a lower interest rate. Other things being equal, the greater the borrower's concessions, the more favorable the terms offered by the lender.

Mid-Chapter SUMMARY PROBLEM FOR YOUR REVIEW

The following information was taken from the ledger of Kraft Corporation:

Loss on sale of discontinued operations	$ 5,000
Prior-period adjustments—credit to Retained Earnings	5,000
Gain on sale of plant assets	21,000
Cost of goods sold	380,000
Income tax expense (saving):	
Continuing operations	32,000
Discontinued operations:	
Operating income	10,000
Loss on sale	(2,000)
Extraordinary gain	10,000
Cumulative effect of change in inventory method	(4,000)
Preferred stock, 8%, $100 par, 500 shares issued	50,000
Paid-in capital in excess of par—preferred	$ 7,000
Treasury stock, common (5,000 shares at cost)	25,000
Dividends	16,000
Selling expenses	78,000
Common stock, no par, 45,000 shares issued	180,000
Sales revenue	620,000
Interest expense	30,000
Extraordinary gain	26,000
Operating income, discontinued operations	25,000
Loss due to lawsuit	11,000
General expenses	62,000
Retained earnings, beginning, as originally reported	103,000
Cumulative effect of change in inventory method (debit)	(10,000)

Required

Prepare a single-step income statement (with all revenues grouped together) and a statement of retained earnings for Kraft Corporation for the current year ended December 31. Include the earnings-per-share presentation and show computations. Assume no changes in the stock accounts during the year.

ANSWERS

KRAFT CORPORATION
Income Statement
For the Year Ended December 31, 19XX

Revenue and gains:		
Sales revenue		$620,000
Gain on sale of plant assets		21,000
Total revenues and gains		641,000
Expenses and losses:		
Cost of goods sold	$380,000	
Selling expenses	78,000	
General expenses	62,000	
Interest expense	30,000	
Loss due to lawsuit	11,000	
Income tax expense	32,000	
Total expenses and losses		593,000
Income from continuing operations		48,000
Discontinued operations:		
Operating income, $25,000, less income tax, $10,000	15,000	
Loss on sale of discontinued operations, $5,000, less income tax saving, $2,000	(3,000)	12,000
Income before extraordinary item and cumulative effect of change in inventory method		60,000
Extraordinary gain, $26,000, less income tax, $10,000		16,000
Cumulative effect of change in inventory method, $10,000, less income tax saving, $4,000		(6,000)
Net income		$ 70,000
Earnings per share:*		
Income from continuing operations [($48,000 – $4,000)/40,000 shares]		$1.10
Income from discontinued operations ($12,000/40,000 shares)		0.30
Income before extraordinary item and cumulative effect of change in inventory method [($60,000 – $4,000)/40,000 shares]		1.40
Extraordinary gain ($16,000/40,000 shares)		0.40
Cumulative effect of change in inventory method ($6,000/40,000)		(0.15)
Net income [($70,000 – $4,000)/40,000 shares]		$1.65

*Computations:

$$EPS = \frac{\text{Income} - \text{Preferred dividends}}{\text{Common shares outstanding}}$$

Preferred dividends: $50,000 × 0.08 = $4,000

Common shares outstanding:

45,000 shares issued – 5,000 treasury shares = 40,000 shares outstanding

KRAFT CORPORATION
Statement of Retained Earnings
For the Year Ended December 31, 19XX

Retained earnings balance, beginning, as originally reported	$103,000
Prior-period adjustment—credit	5,000
Retained earnings balance, beginning, as adjusted	108,000
Net income for current year	70,000
	178,000
Dividends for current year	(16,000)
Retained earnings balance, ending	$162,000

Analyzing the Statement of Stockholders' Equity

Objective 3

Analyze a statement of stockholders' equity

Many companies report a statement of stockholders' equity, which is more comprehensive than a statement of retained earnings. The statement of stockholders' equity (often shortened to "statement of equity") is formatted in a manner similar to a statement of retained earnings but with columns for each element of stockholders' equity. The **statement of stockholders' equity** thus reports the *changes* in all categories of equity during the period.

Exhibit 11-7 is the statement of stockholders' equity for Allied Electronics for 19X5. Study its format. There is a column for each element of equity, with the far right column reporting total stockholders' equity. The top row reports the beginning balance of each element, taken directly from last period's ending balance sheet. Each row of the statement reports the effect of a different category of transactions, starting with Issuance of stock. After explaining all the changes in stockholders' equity, the statement ends with the December 31, 19X5, balances, which appear on the ending balance sheet, given in Exhibit 11-8 on page 534.

Explaining the Items Reported on a Statement of Stockholders' Equity

The statement of stockholders' equity provides information about a company's transactions, such as

1. Net income from the income statement
2. Details about the company's issuance of stock
3. Declaration of cash dividends
4. Distribution of stock dividends
5. Purchase and sale of treasury stock
6. Accumulated other comprehensive income:
   a. Unrealized gains and losses on available-for-sale investments
   b. Foreign-currency translation adjustment

Let's delve more deeply into the transactions that affected Allied Electronics' stockholders' equity during 19X5. The purpose of this analysis is to understand the company's activities during the year. Only after we understand what the business did can we decide whether we approve or disapprove. Let's use Exhibit 11-7 to explain each category of transactions that changed Allied Electronics' stockholders' equity during 19X5.

ISSUANCE OF STOCK During 19X5, Allied issued common stock for $85,000—the total increase in stockholders' equity for the issuance of stock, which is

EXHIBIT 11-7
Statement of Stockholders' Equity

ALLIED ELECTRONICS CORPORATION
Statement of Stockholders' Equity
For the Year Ended December 31, 19X5

					Accumulated Other Comprehensive Income		
	Common Stock, $1 Par	Additional Paid-in Capital	Retained Earnings	Treasury Stock	Unrealized Gain (Loss) on Investments	Foreign-Currency Translation Adjustment	Total Stockholders' Equity
Balance, December 31, 19X4	$ 80,000	$160,000	$130,000	$(25,000)	$6,000	$(10,000)	$341,000
Issuance of stock	20,000	65,000					85,000
Net income			69,000				69,000
Cash dividends			(21,000)				(21,000)
Stock dividends—8%	8,000	26,000	(34,000)				-0-
Purchase of treasury stock				(9,000)			(9,000)
Sale of treasury stock		7,000		4,000			11,000
Unrealized gain					1,000		1,000
Translation adjustment						2,000	2,000
Balance, December 31, 19X5	$108,000	$258,000	$144,000	$(30,000)	$7,000	$ (8,000)	$479,000

EXHIBIT 11-8
Stockholders' Equity Section of the Balance Sheet

ALLIED ELECTRONICS CORPORATION Balance Sheet (partial) December 31, 19X5 and 19X4		
	19X5	**19X4**
Total assets	$939,000	$886,000
Total liabilities	$460,000	$545,000
Stockholders' Equity		
Common stock, $1 par,		
shares issued—108,000 and 80,000, respectively	108,000	80,000
Additional paid-in capital	258,000	160,000
Retained earnings	144,000	130,000
Treasury stock	(30,000)	(25,000)
Accumulated other comprehensive income:		
Unrealized gain on investments	7,000	6,000
Foreign-currency translation adjustment	(8,000)	(10,000)
Total stockholders' equity	479,000	341,000
Total liabilities and stockholders' equity	$939,000	$886,000

shown in the far right column of Exhibit 11-7. Of this total, $20,000 went into the Common Stock account, and $65,000 increased Additional Paid-in Capital. The issuance of stock increased Allied's total stockholders' equity by $85,000. Allied Electronics' creditors would be pleased to see this increase in equity because it decreased Allied's debt ratio and increased the security of the creditors' positions. As a corporation's stockholders' equity goes up, its debt ratio decreases, and so does its financial risk.

NET INCOME During 19X5, Allied Electronics earned net income of $69,000, which increased the Retained Earnings account. The net income figure is the "bottom line" of Allied's income statement (Exhibit 11-1). Trace net income from the income statement, where it originates, to the Retained Earnings column of the statement of stockholders' equity (Exhibit 11-7). Then trace the beginning and ending amounts of Retained Earnings to the balance sheet in Exhibit 11-8. Moving back and forth among the financial statements is an important part of financial analysis.

DECLARATION OF CASH DIVIDENDS The statement of stockholders' equity reports the amount of cash dividends the company declared during the year. Allied Electronics' cash dividends were $21,000, approximately one-third of net income. Exhibit 11-7 reports the decrease in retained earnings from the declaration of the cash dividends. Dividend *payments* may differ from dividends *declared.* The statement of cash flows (discussed in Chapter 12) reports the amount of cash dividends Allied *paid* during the year. The statement of stockholders' equity reports dividends *declared.*

See Chapter 9, page 438, for a review.

DISTRIBUTION OF STOCK DIVIDENDS During 19X5, Allied Electronics distributed to its stockholders stock dividends recorded at $34,000. This was a "small" stock dividend—8%, to be exact. Study the Common Stock column in Exhibit 11-7.

Prior to the stock dividend, Allied Electronics' common stock account had a balance of $100,000 (beginning balance of $80,000 + new issue of $20,000). The 8% stock dividend then added 8,000 shares of $1-par common stock, or $8,000, to the Common Stock account. But there was more to this stock dividend. Because the stock dividend was small—below 20–25% (recall from Chapter 9 the difference between "small" and "large" stock dividends)—Allied Electronics decreased (debited) Retained Earnings for the market value of the new shares issued in the stock dividend. This market value, $34,000, is reported under Retained Earnings in Exhibit 11-7. The difference between the market value of the dividend ($34,000) and the par value of the stock dividend ($8,000) was credited to Additional Paid-in Capital ($26,000).

As we saw in Chapter 9, a stock dividend has no effect on the total amount of stockholders' equity. This is clear from the zero effect of the stock dividend on total stockholders' equity in Exhibit 11-7.

PURCHASE AND SALE OF TREASURY STOCK The statement of stockholders' equity reports the purchases and sales of treasury stock. Recall from Chapter 9 that treasury stock is recorded at its cost. During 19X5, Allied Electronics paid $9,000 to buy treasury stock. This transaction decreased stockholders' equity by $9,000. Allied also sold some treasury stock during the year. The sale of treasury stock brought in $11,000 cash and increased total stockholders' equity by $11,000. The treasury stock that Allied sold had cost the company $4,000, and the extra $7,000 was added to additional Paid-in Capital. At year end, Allied still had treasury stock that had cost the company $30,000 when it was purchased. The parentheses around the treasury stock figures in Exhibit 11-7 mean that treasury stock is a negative element of stockholders' equity.

ACCUMULATED OTHER COMPREHENSIVE INCOME Two categories of other comprehensive income are unrealized gains and losses on available-for-sale investments and the foreign-currency translation adjustment.

UNREALIZED GAINS AND LOSSES ON AVAILABLE-FOR-SALE INVESTMENTS In Chapter 10, we saw that available-for-sale investments are reported on the balance sheet at their *current market value.* The statement of stockholders' equity reports any unrealized gains and losses on these investments under the heading Accumulated Other Comprehensive Income (Exhibit 11-7). *Unrealized* means that the gain or loss did *not* result from the sale of the investments, but rather from a change in the investments' market value.

At December 31, 19X4, Allied Electronics held available-for-sale investments that were worth $6,000 more than Allied paid for them. This explains the $6,000 beginning balance in Exhibit 11-7. Then, during 19X5, the market value of the investments increased by another $1,000. At December 31, 19X5, Allied's portfolio of available-for-sale investments had a market value that exceeded Allied's cost by the accumulated amount of $7,000. An unrealized loss on investments would appear on the statement of stockholders' equity as a negative amount.

FOREIGN-CURRENCY TRANSLATION ADJUSTMENT In Chapter 10, we discussed the foreign-currency translation adjustment that arises from consolidating the financial statements of a foreign subsidiary with a parent company. The foreign-currency translation adjustment, which can be either positive or negative, is like an unrealized gain or loss. At December 31, 19X4, Allied had a negative translation adjustment of $10,000 (see the beginning balance). During 19X5, the foreign currency strengthened against the dollar and decreased the negative amount of the translation adjustment by $2,000. At December 31, 19X5, Allied's cumulative foreign-currency translation adjustment stood at $8,000—a negative amount that resembles an unrealized loss. Like the unrealized gains and losses on investments, the foreign-currency translation adjustment is reported under Accumulated Other Comprehensive Income in Exhibit 11-7.

STOP & THINK Examine Exhibit 11-7. Consider the cash dividends, the purchase of treasury stock, and the sale of treasury stock. Which of Allied's other financial statements will also report these transactions? In what section of the statement will these transactions be reported? What amounts will be reported?

Answer: The statement of cash flows, under Cash flows from financing activities, will report the following:

Cash dividends paid	$(21,000)
Purchase of treasury stock	(9,000)
Sale of treasury stock	11,000

Interpreting Notes to the Financial Statements

Objective 4

Interpret notes to the financial statements

Because the financial statements must be clear and concise, it is important that they do not become overloaded with details. But the details are important. The balance sheet cannot report all the methods the company uses to account for its assets or the details of its long-term debt. These data are best reported in notes to the statements.

Published financial statements have been criticized for being so summarized that their usefulness is limited. For example, the 1995 income statement of **The Boeing Company**, the world's leading aircraft manufacturer, contains only 11 lines of information, yet it takes 15 pages of notes for Boeing to explain the various items in the financial statements. **Intel Corporation's** income statement includes only 13 lines of data, and its financial statement notes span 10 pages. These examples testify to the importance of the explanatory notes, which are an important part of the financial statements, not simply an add-on that can be avoided. For example, the income statement of The May Department Stores Company that appears in the chapter opening story includes the standard directive: "See Notes to Consolidated Financial Statements." Let's explore some of the information commonly reported in the notes.

Summary of Significant Accounting Policies

The first note to most companies' financial statements is a summary of the significant accounting policies used by the company. This note describes the accounting foundation underlying the statements and reports details such as the following:

1. CONSOLIDATION POLICY. As we saw in Chapter 10, companies use the consolidation method to account for subsidiary companies in which they own a controlling (greater than 50%) interest. They use the equity method to account for 20–50% investments in other companies. The Consolidation Policy explains how the company came up with the consolidated totals in its financial statements.

2. REVENUES. This note tells how the company accounts for its revenue. In its Summary of Significant Accounting Policies, The May Department Stores Company reports the following:

> Sales include sales of merchandise and services and [the] sales of leased and licensed departments. Sales [of $10,507 million] are net of returns and exclude sales tax. Total revenues [of $10,952 million] include finance charge revenues and all sales from all stores operating during the period.

It is common for department stores to lease out part of a store to another entity, such as a shoe department that is operated by another company. They also license other companies to carry and sell their merchandise. For example, **Ralph Lauren** licenses other companies to sell its Polo brand of merchandise. May Department Stores Company includes the sales of these leased and licensed departments in its total revenues.

STOP & THINK What is the "finance charge revenue" that May Department Stores is referring to? How much finance charge revenue did the company earn during the year?

Answer: Finance charge revenue is interest revenue that May earns on its customer charge accounts (receivables from customers). May earned $445 million ($10,952 million – $10,507 million) of finance revenue during the year.

3. EXPENSES. In its note on advertising expense, May Department Stores states, "Advertising and sales promotion costs are expensed at the time the advertising takes place." **The Gap, Inc.**, and **Lands' End** both follow the same policy, which matches the advertising expense against the revenue that the ads generate. An alternative accounting treatment would be to record advertising expense when the company *pays* for the advertising or promotional campaign. That treatment would be inappropriate because it would not match the advertising expense against the revenue the ads generate. May's policy therefore agrees with GAAP.

May Department Stores Company includes the sales of leased and licensed departments in its total revenues.

4. EARNINGS PER SHARE. As we saw earlier in this chapter, earnings per share (EPS) are computed by dividing net income minus preferred dividends by the weighted-average number of shares of common stock outstanding during the period. This note explains how the company computed its EPS. The note is standard fare in most companies' financial statements.

5. INVENTORY. GAAP requires companies to disclose which inventory method they use. May and **Lands' End** both use the last-in, first-out (LIFO) method to account for inventory and cost of goods sold. **The Gap** uses the first-in, first-out (FIFO) method. **Toys 'Я' Us** uses LIFO for 61% of its inventory and FIFO for the remaining 39 percent.

After measuring inventory cost by the FIFO, LIFO, or average-cost method, the company determines the market value of the inventory. GAAP requires companies to report inventory at the lower of its cost or market value. In most cases, cost is lower than market, so most companies report their inventory at cost.

We studied the lower-of-cost-or-market (LCM) rule in Chapter 6, pages 280–281.

As we saw in Appendix B to Chapter 6 (pages 316–317), companies that use the LIFO method also disclose enough information to enable investors to convert the company's net income over to the FIFO basis. This conversion allows investors to compare two companies, because income and inventory figures must be calculated on the same basis to be comparable.

6. DEPRECIATION. GAAP requires disclosure of the depreciation method used by the company. Most companies use the straight-line method to prepare their financial statements and accelerated depreciation to prepare their income tax returns, which they file with the Internal Revenue Service. As we saw earlier in this chapter, the straight-line/accelerated depreciation difference causes the deferred income taxes that companies report on their balance sheets.

7. CAPITALIZATION OF COSTS. Companies follow different policies for capitalizing some of their costs. (Recall from Chapter 7 that *capitalizing* a cost means recording the cost as an asset. The alternative accounting treatment is to record the cost as expense immediately.) Both May Department Stores and The Gap follow the conservative accounting policy of expensing the pre-opening costs (for example, rent and payrolls) associated with the opening or remodeling of stores. A more liberal accounting policy would be to capitalize pre-opening costs and then amortize them to expense over a future period. How a company treats certain costs—as assets or as expenses—says a lot about the company. Investors usually favor companies that follow conservative accounting policies over companies that follow more liberal policies.

For a discussion of the conservatism principle, see Chapter 6, page 280.

STOP & THINK Company A (which is conservative in the accounting sense) purposely avoids overstating its asset and income amounts. Company B (which is more liberal) selects accounting methods that make it look as good as possible. Other things being equal, Company B will report higher asset and income amounts than Company A. GAAP requires companies to disclose the accounting methods they use, so investors can decide which company's policies they prefer. In which company would you rather invest your life savings?

Answer: In general, Company B is more likely to provide negative surprises than Company A, so most, but not all, investors would favor Company A as an investment. It would appear that Company A is trying to hide less bad news than Company B.

Acquisitions and Dispositions

The statement of cash flows reports the amount of cash a company paid to acquire another company. But one line on the cash-flow statement cannot give investors enough information to evaluate the acquisition. Investors want to know the name of the company purchased, when the transaction occurred, and how the buyer financed the acquisition. Notes to the financial statements report these details. For example, May's 1995 financial statements include this note:

ACQUISITION
Effective August 28, 1995, the company purchased 14 John Wanamaker stores . . . and three Woodward & Lothrop stores . . . for approximately $412 million . . . . The acquisition was funded principally with long-term debt.

Investors can use this information to decide whether they believe the acquisition was good or bad for the company.

Pensions

Most companies have pension plans for their employees. Pension-plan details include the accumulated benefit obligations (ABO) the company has promised to retired employees and the fair market value of the pension plan's assets. As we saw in Chapter 8, the balance sheet reports a pension liability only when the ABO exceeds the plan assets. Companies report their pension-plan details in notes to the financial statements. The following is adapted from the notes to May's 1995 annual report:

	(In millions)
Accumulated benefit obligations to retired employees	$289
Plan assets at fair market value	290
Pension plan over (under) funded	$ 1

Overfunded or Underfunded? May's pension plan is overfunded—by only $1 million—so the company reported no pension liability on its balance sheet. If the pension plan assets had been less than the accumulated benefit obligation, May would have reported the difference as a long-term pension liability on its balance sheet.

Long-Term Debt

Most companies have some long-term debt. Large companies have a dozen or more long-term notes payable or separate issues of bonds payable. Each individual note or bond has its own principal amount, interest rate, and maturity date. Companies often group their debt issues and report them in summarized form in the notes, as May Department Stores has done:

The May Department Stores Company
Long-Term Debt
Long-term debt and capital lease obligations were:

(In millions)	February 3, 1996	January 28, 1995
5.7% to 10.75% unsecured notes and . . . debentures due 1997–2035	$3,341	$2,902
3.0% to 10.0% mortgage notes and bonds due 1996–2012	65	69
Total debt	3,406	2,971
Capital lease obligations	59	61
	3,465	3,032
Less current maturities	132	168
Total	$3,333	$2,864

The annual maturities of long-term debt . . . are $132 million, $234 million, $242 million, $81 million and $254 million for 1996 through 2000, respectively.

May's grouping of 5.7–10.75% unsecured notes and debentures due 1997–2035 can be criticized. The amount of debt involved, $3,341 million, is the bulk of the company's long-term debt, and details on the individual amounts of debt due each year, the interest rates, and maturity dates are lacking. Investors would find it hard to figure out what May's interest expense is likely to be each year in the future. It would be hard to perform meaningful analysis on such summarized data.

The Coca-Cola Company's long-term debt note is more helpful:

The Coca-Cola Company and Subsidiaries
Note 8. Long-Term Debt

Long-term debt consists of the following (in millions):

December 31,	1995	1994
7¾% U.S. dollar notes due 1996	**$ 250**	$ 250
5¾% Japanese yen notes due 1996	**292**	301
5¾% German mark notes due 1998	**175**	161
7⅞% U.S. dollar notes due 1998	**250**	250
6% U.S. dollar notes due 2000	**252**	—
6⅝% U.S. dollar notes due 2002	**149**	149
6% U.S. dollar notes due 2003	**150**	150
7⅜% U.S. dollar notes due 2093	**116**	116
Other, due 1996 to 2013	**59**	84
	1,693	1,461
Less current portion	**552**	35
	$1,141	$1,426

Maturities of long-term debt for the five years succeeding December 31, 1995, are as follows (in millions):

1996	1997	1998	1999	2000
$552	$10	$435	$8	$255

Coca-Cola's note shows the dollar amount, the interest rate, and the maturity date of each segment of its long-term debt. Investors can thus predict Coca-Cola's future interest expense and debt payments. Observe that both companies report their upcoming debt payments for the next five years, as required by GAAP. Again, Coke's data are easier to interpret.

BORROWING AGREEMENTS Borrowing agreements sometimes restrict the amount of dividends that a company is allowed to pay. These agreements may also require a company to maintain a certain level of the current ratio or the debt ratio. Such restrictions are reported in the Long-Term Debt note. Coca-Cola is such a blue-chip company that it appears to have no such restrictions.

See our discussion of the historical-cost principle in Chapter 1, page 12.

FAIR VALUE OF LONG-TERM DEBT As we have seen throughout this book, accounting is anchored to historical costs. However, there is a steady movement toward current-market-value accounting. We saw this when we studied accounting for long-term investments in Chapter 10. Trading investments and available-for-sale investments are reported on the balance sheet at their current market value, also called *fair market value* or simply *fair value*.

Companies still account for their long-term debt at historical-cost amounts: the amounts they actually borrowed, and the amounts due at maturity. In addition, the financial statement notes must report the fair value of long-term debt as a supplement to the basic historical-cost figures. The fair value of a debt is the amount the company would have to pay if the liability came due on the balance sheet date.

Reporting on the Different Segments of a Business

Objective 5

Use segment and interim financial data for decision making

Most large companies have several different segments. As we saw earlier in this chapter, a *business segment* is a clearly defined division of a company. For example, **PepsiCo's** segments are

- Restaurants: Pizza Hut, Taco Bell, and Kentucky Fried Chicken
- Beverages: Pepsi-Cola North America and Pepsi-Cola International
- Snack Foods: Frito-Lay and PepsiCo Foods International

A business segment is an entity within an entity, a part of the business that management and investors want to evaluate separately. For example, when the sales of Frito-Lay products were lagging behind expectations, PepsiCo installed a new president to bolster sales. How did top management know to make the change? PepsiCo's segment data reported the results of each division of the business (including Frito-Lay) to top managers. Segment data are important because they indicate which parts of the overall organization are most successful and which parts need improvement. If only companywide data were available, managers and investors would have less information for decision making.

Companies are fairly guarded about the segment data they report to the public because they don't want competitors to know their inner workings. Nevertheless, they report revenues and earnings by segment. Exhibit 11-9 is an excerpt from the 1995 annual report of **Campbell Soup Company.**

Management discusses the results of operations in a special section of the annual report entitled *Management Discussion and Analysis (MD&A).* Excerpts from Campbell Soup's MD&A are given in Exhibit 11-10.

Let's examine Campbell Soup's Supplemental Schedule of Sales and Earnings in Exhibit 11-9. The U.S.A. Division, which produces and sells Campbell soups, contributes the most to sales and earnings. The graphs in Exhibit 11-10 tell the same story. Compare the two graphs closely. Observe that the U.S.A. Division generates only around 60% of sales but almost 75% of earnings. The U.S.A. Division is the company's most profitable segment both in dollars and in percentages.

In the Overview section of the MD&A, Campbell reports that sales rose 9% during 1995, and net earnings increased by 11 percent. The company's stockholders should have been happy about those results, and indeed they were. Elsewhere in the annual report, Campbell reveals that its stock price as quoted on the

EXHIBIT 11-9
Segment Reporting

CAMPBELL SOUP COMPANY—Supplemental Schedule of Sales and Earnings (partial)

	1995		1994		1993	
(In millions)	**Sales**	**Earnings**	**Sales**	**Earnings**	**Sales**	**Earnings**
Contributions by Division:						
U.S.A.	**$4,295**	**$ 885**	$3,961	$ 783	$4,078	$605
Bakery & Confectionery	**1,628**	**182**	1,510	169	1,267	110
International Grocery	**1,412**	**135**	1,279	120	1,312	(71)
Interdivision	**(57)**		(60)		(71)	
Total Sales	**$7,278**		$6,690		$6,586	
Total operating earnings		**$1,202**		$1,072		$644

CAMPBELL SOUP COMPANY
Management's Discussion and Analysis of Results of Operations (partial)

Overview

Net sales rose 9% to $7.28 billion compared to $6.69 billion in the prior year, with strategic acquisitions contributing a third of the company's sales growth. Net earnings climbed 11% to $698 million versus $630 million last year. Earnings per share were $2.80, [. . .] up 12% over $2.51 for the previous year.

All three operating divisions—U.S.A., Bakery & Confectionery and International Grocery—delivered record-breaking sales and earnings in 1995.

Cash generated from operations climbed 22% to a record $1,185 million with a major contribution coming from reductions in working capital, particularly inventories which declined $63 million.

1995 COMPARED TO 1994

Results by Division

U.S.A.—[This Division includes Campbell Soups, Pace Foods, and Swanson frozen foods.] Net sales increased 8% to $4.3 billion in 1995 compared to $3.96 billion last year, with acquisitions contributing 50% of the sales growth. Operating earnings rose 13% to $885 million.

Bakery & Confectionery—This division consists of Pepperidge Farm in the U.S., Arnotts Limited in Australia, Delacre and Lamy Lutti in Europe, and Godiva Chocolatier worldwide.

Net sales grew 8% in fiscal 1995 to $1.63 billion, from $1.51 billion last year. Operating earnings increased 8% to $182 million, led by Pepperidge Farm and the confectionery businesses.

International Grocery—International Grocery consists of soup, sauces, juices and frozen businesses outside the U.S.

Net sales were $1.41 billion in fiscal 1995, up 10% from $1.28 billion last year. The . . . acquisition in the United Kingdom contributed 30% of the sales growth. Operating earnings were $135 million, 12% over the prior year. The devaluation of the Mexican peso reduced earnings by $4 million for the year.

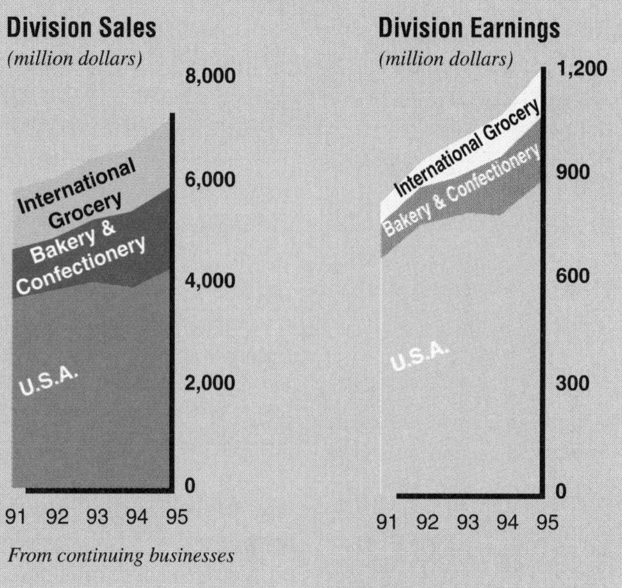

From continuing businesses

EXHIBIT 11-10
Management Discussion and Analysis

New York Stock Exchange rose during the year. The average ranges of its stock price during the four quarters of 1995 were

	Average Stock Price of the High-Low Range
First quarter	$39.13
Second quarter	43.32
Third quarter	46.82
Fourth quarter	48.32

By this measure, the average stock price rose by $9.19 (from $39.13 to $48.32) during 1995. Campbell also paid its stockholders $1.21 in cash dividends per share during the year. The change in the stock price (increase or decrease), plus the dividends received, make up an **investor's total return on an investment** in Campbell Soup stock, which is determined as follows:

$$\textbf{Total return on a stock investment} = \frac{\textbf{Stock price change + Dividends}}{\textbf{Beginning stock price}} = \frac{\$9.19 + \$1.21}{\$39.13} = 26.6\%$$

For people who invested in Campbell Soup stock, 1995 was a very good year. In the final paragraph of the Overview in Exhibit 11-10, Campbell reports that cash generated by operations (another name for cash flows from operating activities) climbed 22% during the year. Interestingly, the investment return of 26.6% more closely parallels the company's cash flow increase of 22% than its net income increase of 11 percent. Campbell's investors seem to be more interested in cash flows than in net income. This is common. The main reason for the increase in cash flows from operations was a decrease in inventories.

STOP & THINK How can a decrease in inventories contribute to an increase in cash flow from operations?

Answer: For a profitable company such as Campbell Soup, a decrease in inventories means that sales were robust. Inventory moved into and out of the company quickly, as measured by the rate of inventory turnover (see Chapter 6). Brisk sales enabled Campbell Soup to keep its inventory quantities low, which in turn decreased the cost of storing, insuring, and handling the goods. Cost reductions free up cash for reinvestment in the company. The result? Higher profits, increasing cash flows, and rising stock prices. Campbell Soup provides a clear example of how to manage a company. The company's financial statements show why Campbell Soup is considered a blue-chip company.

One final note about the results of Campbell's International Grocery Division in Exhibit 11-10: The acquisition of a British company contributed to the international division's growth. Earlier in this chapter we saw how companies report their acquisitions of other companies in the notes to the financial statements. Also during 1995, the devaluation of the Mexican peso hurt the earnings of Campbell's International Division. In Chapter 10, we studied the consolidation of foreign subsidiaries and learned how to analyze the effects of changes in foreign currencies.

Reporting for Interim Periods (Shorter Than One Year)

Investment decisions are made continuously. Therefore, investors cannot wait for audited financial statements after the end of the year to make their investment decisions. However, it is not feasible for companies to publish financial statements daily, weekly, or even monthly. To address the need for timely information, companies release financial data on an interim basis, which means more frequently than once a year. The most common **interim reporting** period is quarterly (that is, every three months). The quarterly statements are not audited by independent CPAs, so their form varies from company to company. Some companies also release quarterly balance sheets. Very few report cash flows or a full set of financial statement notes on an interim basis.

Exhibit 11-11 is an excerpt from a quarterly report issued by **Storage USA, Inc.**, which manages, develops, and constructs self-storage facilities from California to Massachusetts, primarily in the southern half of the United States. Storage USA's quarterly report includes income statements and abbreviated balance sheet data. The consolidated income statement, which Storage USA labels as *unaudited,* compares amounts for the three months ended June 30, 1996, with amounts for the three months ended June 30, 1995. Also included are current-year figures for the first six months of the year in comparison with year-earlier amounts. The report shows that Storage USA's Total property revenues, Income from property operations, and Net income are growing rapidly. Investors can use these data to help decide whether they wish to invest in Storage USA stock.

The interim balance sheet data are limited to the company's investment in storage facilities (assets), its mortgage and other notes payable (liabilities), and shareholders' equity. These quarterly figures suggest that Storage USA's debt is low in comparison to its stockholders' equity. Because the data are incomplete and unaudited, however, it is difficult to draw a firm conclusion about the company's total assets and its level of debt. In real-estate-related industries, the level of debt is a concern as many companies have failed because of a heavy debt load. This is probably why Storage USA reports these balance sheet figures quarterly—to reassure shareholders about the company's debt burden.

STORAGE USA, INC.
Consolidated Statements of Operations
(unaudited)

(In thousands, except per share data)	Three months ended June 30, 1996	Three months ended June 30, 1995	Six months ended June 30, 1996	Six months ended June 30, 1995
Property revenues:				
Rental income	$23,770	$15,834	$44,590	$27,806
Management income	206	199	446	443
Other income	380	200	654	347
Total property revenues	24,356	16,233	45,690	28,596
Property expenses:				
Cost of property operations & maintenance	6,376	4,621	12,113	7,911
Real estate taxes	2,051	1,094	3,744	1,900
General & administrative	969	597	1,749	1,109
Depreciation & amortization	2,762	1,835	5,433	3,404
Total property expenses	12,158	8,147	23,039	14,324
Income from property operations	12,198	8,086	22,651	14,272
Other income (expense)				
Interest expense	(1,558)	(1,063)	(3,223)	(1,220)
Interest income	175	22	330	37
Income before minority interest	10,815	7,045	19,758	13,089
Minority interest	(670)	(385)	(1,225)	(617)
Net income	$10,145	$ 6,660	$18,533	$12,472
Net income per share	$ 0.52	$ 0.47	$ 0.99	$ 0.90
Weighted-average shares outstanding	19,553	14,316	18,690	13,810

Balance Sheet Data

	As of June 30, 1996	As of June 30, 1995
Investment in storage facilities, at cost	$642,650	$410,464
Mortgage and other notes payable	$161,039	$ 10,351
Shareholders' equity	$416,308	$359,296

EXHIBIT 11-11
Interim Report (partial)—Storage USA, Inc.

For a more complete picture of Storage USA's finances, we must examine the company's annual financial statements, which are audited by independent CPAs. Storage USA's 1995 audited balance sheet reports total assets of $510 million, of which 97% is the company's storage facilities. Total liabilities at the end of 1995 were $151 million, so the company's debt ratio was only 29.6% ($151 million/$510 million), which is very low.

Management Responsibility for the Financial Statements

Objective 6

Understand managers' and auditors' responsibilities for the financial statements

The top managers of a corporation are responsible for the company's financial statements. Management issues a *statement of responsibility* along with the company's financial statements. Exhibit 11-12 on page 544 is the statement of management's responsibility included in the 1995 annual report of The May Department Stores Company.

In the first paragraph, management declares its responsibility for the preparation, integrity, and objectivity of the financial statements. Management indicates that the financial statements conform to generally accepted accounting principles (GAAP) on a consistent basis. As we've seen throughout this book,

EXHIBIT 11-12
Statement of Management Responsibility for the Financial Statements—The May Department Stores Company

Management's Responsibility

Report of Management. Management is responsible for the preparation, integrity, and objectivity of the financial information included in this annual report. The financial statements have been prepared in conformity with generally accepted accounting principles applied on a consistent basis. The preparation of financial statements in conformity with generally accepted accounting principles requires management to make estimates and assumptions that affect the reported amounts. Although the financial statements reflect all available information and management's judgement and estimates of current conditions and circumstances, prepared with the assistance of specialists within and outside the company, actual results could differ from those estimates.

Management has established and maintains a system of accounting and controls to provide reasonable assurance that assets are safeguarded against loss from unauthorized use or disposition, that the accounting records provide a reliable basis for the preparation of financial statements, and that such financial statements are not misstated due to material fraud or error. The system of controls includes the careful selection of associates, the proper segregation of duties and the communication and application of formal policies and procedures that are consistent with high standards of accounting and administrative practices. An important element of this system is a comprehensive internal audit program. Management continually reviews, modifies and improves its systems of accounting and controls in response to changes in business conditions and operations and in response to recommendations in the reports prepared by the independent public accountants and internal auditors.

Management believes that it is essential for the company to conduct its business affairs in accordance with the highest ethical standards and in conformity with the law. This standard is described in the company's policies on business conduct, which are publicized throughout the company.

Audit Committee of the Board of Directors. The Board of Directors, through the activities of its Audit Committee, participates in the reporting of financial information by the company. The committee meets regularly with management, the internal auditors and the independent public accountants. The committee met four times during 1995 and reviewed the scope, timing and fees for the annual audit and the results of audit examinations completed by the internal auditors and independent public accountants, including the recommendations to improve certain internal controls and the follow-up reports prepared by management. The independent public accountants and internal auditors have free access to the committee and the Board of Directors and attend each meeting of the committee.

The members of the Audit Committee are Russell E. Palmer (chairman), Edward H. Meyer, Michael R. Quinlan, William P. Stiritz, Robert D. Storey, and Murray L. Weidenbaum.

The Audit Committee reports the results of its activities to the full Board of Directors.

GAAP is the standard for preparing the financial statements, and is designed to produce relevant, reliable, and useful information for making investment and credit decisions. *Consistency* means that the company is not switching accounting methods back and forth to make itself look as good as possible.

This is the consistency principle in action. See Chapter 6, page 279.

Management further states that preparation of the financial statements requires the company to make estimates and certain assumptions. As you have seen, accounting is not as exact as you might have imagined before taking this introductory course in financial accounting.

Paragraph 2 of Exhibit 11-12 mentions the company's internal controls, which are designed to safeguard May's assets and produce reliable accounting records and financial statements. In paragraph 3, management declares its intention to use the highest ethical standards in conducting the company's business.

We explored internal control systems and ethical accounting practices in detail in Chapter 4.

Paragraph 4 describes the activities of the Audit Committee of the company's Board of Directors. The Audit Committee interacts with the outside auditors who examine May's financial statements to ensure they meet GAAP standards.

Auditor's Report on the Financial Statements

The Securities Exchange Act of 1934 requires most companies that issue their stock publicly to file audited financial statements with the Securities and Exchange Commission (SEC), a governmental agency. To comply with this requirement, companies engage outside auditors who are certified public accountants to examine their statements. The independent auditors decide whether the company's financial statements comply with GAAP and then issue an audit report. Exhibit 11-13 is the audit report on the fiscal year 1995 financial statements of The May Department Stores Company.

The audit report is addressed to the Board of Directors and Shareowners of the company. The auditors sign their name, in this case the St. Louis office of Arthur Andersen LLP (LLP is the abbreviation for limited liability partnership). The date of Andersen's audit report is February 26, 1996, shortly after the end of the company's 1995 fiscal year.

The audit report typically contains three paragraphs. The first paragraph reiterates that the management of May Department Stores bears primary responsibility for the company's financial statements. The auditor's responsibility is merely to express a professional opinion on the statements. The first paragraph in Exhibit 11-13 also indicates that the CPAs audited the financial statements for the three years in question.

The second paragraph describes how the audit was performed, mentioning that generally accepted auditing standards are the benchmark for evaluating the audit's quality. In the final sentence of the second paragraph, Arthur Andersen states its belief that the audit provides a reasonable basis for expressing a professional opinion on May's financial statements.

EXHIBIT 11-13
Audit Report on the Financial Statements of The May Department Stores Company

Report of
Independent Public Accountants

To the Board of Directors and Shareowners of
The May Department Stores Company:

We have audited the accompanying consolidated balance sheet of The May Department Stores Company (a New York corporation) and subsidiaries as of February 3, 1996, and January 28, 1995, and the related consolidated statements of earnings, shareowners' equity and cash flows for each of the three fiscal years in the period ended February 3, 1996. These financial statements are the responsibility of the company's management. Our responsibility is to express an opinion on these financial statements based on our audits.

We conducted our audits in accordance with generally accepted auditing standards. Those standards require that we plan and perform the audit to obtain reasonable assurance about whether the financial statements are free of material misstatement. An audit includes examining, on a test basis, evidence supporting the amounts and disclosures in the financial statements. An audit also includes assessing the accounting principles used and significant estimates made by management, as well as evaluating the overall financial statement presentation. We believe that our audits provide a reasonable basis for our opinion.

In our opinion, the financial statements referred to above present fairly, in all material respects, the financial position of The May Department Stores Company and subsidiaries as of February 3, 1996, and January 28, 1995, and the results of their operations and their cash flows for each of the three fiscal years in the period ended February 3, 1996, in conformity with generally accepted accounting principles.

Arthur Andersen LLP
1010 Market Street
St. Louis, Missouri 63101-2089
February 26, 1996

Decision Guidelines

Using the Income Statement and the Related Notes in Investment Analysis

Decision	Factors to Consider		Decision Variable or Model
Which measure of profitability to use for investment analysis?	Are you interested in accounting income? →	Income including all revenues, expenses, gains, and losses? →	Net income (bottom line)
	→	Income that can be expected to repeat from year to year? →	Income from continuing operations
	Are you interested in cash flows? →		Cash flows from operating activities (Chapter 12)
Note: A conservative strategy may use both income and cash flows and compare the two sets of results.			
What is the estimated value of the stock?	If you believe the company can earn the income (or cash flow) indefinitely →		$\text{Estimated value} = \dfrac{\text{Annual income}}{\text{Investment capitalization rate}}$
	If you believe the company can earn the income (or cash flow) for a finite number of years →		$\text{Estimated value} = \text{Annual income} \times$ Present value of annuity (See Appendix B, page 726)
How does risk affect the value of the stock?	If the investment is high-risk →		Increase the investment capitalization rate
	If the investment is low-risk →		Decrease the investment capitalization rate

The third paragraph gives Andersen's opinion. The words "present fairly, in all material respects" express the auditors' belief that May's financial statements conform to GAAP and that people can rely on the financial statements for decision making. May's audit report contains a *clean* opinion, more properly called an *unqualified* opinion. Audit reports usually fall into one of four categories:

1. **Unqualified (clean).** The statements are reliable.
2. **Qualified.** The statements are reliable, except for one or more items for which the opinion is said to be qualified.
3. **Adverse.** The statements are unreliable.
4. **Disclaimer.** The auditor was unable to reach a professional opinion.

Of what value is the audit? To answer this question, it is helpful to consider what we might expect in financial statements without an independent audit. The format of the statements would probably differ from company to company as each organization tried to put its best foot forward. The statements would be more likely to reflect the bias of the company's management. In many cases, the statements would probably make the company look more successful than it really is.

The independent audit adds credibility to the financial statements. It is no accident that financial reporting and auditing are more advanced in the United States and Canada than anywhere else in the world, and that these two countries' capital markets are the envy of the world. In addition, these two nations enjoy two of the highest living standards in the world.

The Decision Guidelines feature revisits the decision setting in which investors use accounting information for investment analysis. Study the guidelines to review the essence of this chapter.

SUMMARY PROBLEM FOR YOUR REVIEW

This problem is based on excerpts from the financial statements of **The Dow Chemical Company**, a world leader in the manufacture of chlorine, polymers, plastics, adhesives, sealants, and coatings.

Begin by familiarizing yourself with Dow's statements and notes, reproduced on pages 548–552. Then answer the following questions. You may have to refer to a preceding chapter. If so, the index at the end of the book will serve as a useful guide for finding what you need. Answering these questions should increase your confidence in your ability to perform some aspects of financial analysis.

Required

1. The 1993 and 1994 headings on Dow's income statement indicate that the results of operations for those years have been restated. This means that the 1994 and 1993 amounts reported here differ from the 1994 and 1993 amounts reported during those earlier years. Note A, under the heading "Principles of Consolidation," tells why Dow restated the amounts for the earlier years. What was the reason? As an investor in Dow, why would the restated amounts be important to you?
2. How important were discontinued operations to Dow's net income for 1995? Has the discontinued segment of the business been sold yet? How can you tell?
3. Is Minority Interests' Share in Income an addition or a subtraction in arriving at Dow's net income? Why? If necessary, review the discussion of consolidation in Chapter 10.
4. Evaluate the trend of income from continuing operations from 1993 to 1994 and from 1994 to 1995. Compute the percentage increase for 1994 and 1995. Is the trend favorable?
5. Use the balance sheet to compute the number of shares of common stock that Dow had outstanding (shares issued minus shares held as treasury stock) at the end of 1995 and at the beginning of 1995. Round to the nearest million shares. What caused shares outstanding to change during the year? The statement of stockholders' equity and balance sheet provide insight.
6. The annual report reveals that the market price of a share of Dow stock was $70.38 at December 31, 1995. Multiply this market price per share by the number of shares of common stock outstanding at December 31, 1995, to determine the total market value of the company's stock at year end. Then plug income from continuing operations for 1995 into the following formula to show how investors might have determined the company's value:

   $$\textbf{Market value of the company's stock} = \frac{\textbf{Income from continuing operations}}{\textbf{Investment capitalization rate}}$$

   Round all figures, except market price per share, to the nearest million.

   What investment capitalization rate did the market use to value Dow's stock? A capitalization rate for Dow Chemical Company between 8% and 15% was realistic in 1995, with 8% indicating lower risk and 15% suggesting a riskier investment. Evaluate the investment risk of Dow stock at this time.
7. Examine Dow's reporting of long-term debt *both* on the balance sheet and in Note I.
   a. Does the balance sheet provide enough detail for an investor to determine when the company must pay its various notes payable and bonds payable, or are the data too condensed for meaningful analysis? Does Note I provide sufficient detail? State your reason.
   b. How much of the principal amount of long-term debt must the company pay in 1996? Where can an investor or a creditor find this information?
   c. How much *interest* will Dow pay during 1996 on the 5.75% note payable scheduled to mature in 1997? (See the table in Note I, third promissory note from the top.)

THE DOW CHEMICAL COMPANY
Consolidated Statement of Income

(In millions, except for per share amounts)		1995	1994 Restated	1993 Restated
Net Sales		$20,200	$16,742	$15,052
Operating Costs and Expenses	Cost of sales	13,337	12,131	11,370
	Insurance and finance company operations, pretax income	(61)	(40)	(98)
	Research and development expenses	808	783	786
	Promotion and advertising expenses	416	411	367
	Selling and administrative expenses	1,771	1,594	1,485
	Amortization of intangibles	38	43	68
	Total operating costs and expenses	16,309	14,922	13,978
Operating Income		3,891	1,820	1,074
Other Income (Expense)	Equity in earnings (losses) of 20–50% owned companies	70	29	(127)
	Interest expense and amortization of debt discount	(434)	(362)	(413)
	Interest income and foreign exchange—net	289	98	140
	Net gain (loss) on investments	(330)	(42)	592
	Sundry income (expense)—net	43	83	(8)
	Total other income (expense)	(362)	(194)	184
Income before Provision for Taxes on Income and Minority Interests		3,529	1,626	1,258
Provision for Taxes on Income		1,442	654	514
Minority Interests' Share in Income		196	200	171
Preferred Stock Dividends		7	7	7
Income from Continuing Operations		1,884	765	566
Discontinued Operations	Income from pharmaceutical businesses, net of taxes on income	18	166	71
	Gain on sale of pharmaceutical businesses, net of taxes on income	169	—	—
Net Income Available for Common Stockholders		$ 2,071	$ 931	$ 637
Average Common Shares Outstanding		268.2	276.1	273.6
Earnings per Common Share from Continuing Operations		$ 7.03	$ 2.77	$ 2.07
Earnings per Common Share		$ 7.72	$ 3.37	$ 2.33
Common Stock Dividends Declared per Share		$ 2.90	$ 2.60	$ 2.60

See Notes to Financial Statements.

THE DOW CHEMICAL COMPANY
Consolidated Balance Sheet

(In millions)		December 31, 1995	1994
	Assets		
Current Assets	Cash and cash equivalents	$ 2,839	$ 569
	Marketable securities and interest-bearing deposits	611	565
	Accounts and notes receivable:		
	Trade (less allowance for doubtful receivables—1995, $53; 1994, $104)	2,729	3,359
	Other	1,380	1,099
	Inventories:		
	Finished and work in process	2,197	2,079
	Materials and supplies	551	633
	Deferred income tax assets—current	247	389
	Total current assets	10,554	8,693
Investments	[Investments in] capital stock at cost plus equity in accumulated earnings of 20–50% owned companies	848	931
	Other investments	1,558	1,529
	Noncurrent receivables	314	330
	Total investments	2,720	2,790
Plant Properties	Plant properties	23,218	23,210
	Less accumulated depreciation	15,105	14,484
	Net plant properties	8,113	8,726
Other Assets	Goodwill (net of accumulated amortization—1995, $177; 1994, $676)	658	4,365
	Deferred income tax assets—noncurrent	779	1,132
	Deferred charges and other assets	758	839
	Total other assets	2,195	6,336
Total Assets		$23,582	$26,545

See Notes to Financial Statements.

THE DOW CHEMICAL COMPANY
Consolidated Balance Sheet

(In millions, except for share amounts)		December 31, 1995	December 31, 1994
	Liabilities and Stockholders' Equity		
Current Liabilities	Notes payable	$ 323	$ 741
	Long-term debt due within one year	375	534
	Accounts payable:		
	Trade	1,529	1,928
	Other	717	634
	Income taxes payable	791	664
	Deferred income tax liabilities—current	55	56
	Dividends payable	192	202
	Accrued and other current liabilities	1,619	1,859
	Total current liabilities	5,601	6,618
Long-Term Debt		4,705	5,303
Other Noncurrent Liabilities	Deferred income tax liabilities—noncurrent	659	644
	Pension and other postretirement benefits—noncurrent	1,880	1,987
	Other noncurrent obligations	1,260	1,253
	Total other liabilities	3,799	3,884
Minority Interest in Subsidiary Companies		1,775	2,506
Temporary Equity	Temporary equity—other	313	—
	Preferred stock (authorized 250,000,000 shares of $1.00-par value each; issued Series A—1995: 1,521,175; 1994: 1,549,014) at redemption value	131	133
	Guaranteed ESOP obligation	(103)	(111)
	Total temporary equity	341	22
Stockholders' Equity	Common stock (authorized 500,000,000 shares of $2.50-par value each; issued 1995 and 1994: 327,125,854)	818	818
	Additional paid-in capital	315	326
	Retained earnings	10,159	8,857
	Unrealized gains (losses) on investments	62	(21)
	Cumulative translation adjustments	(349)	(330)
	Treasury stock, at cost (shares 1995: 76,168,614; 1994: 50,002,967)	(3,644)	(1,438)
	Net stockholders' equity	7,361	8,212
Total Liabilities and Stockholders' Equity		$23,582	$26,545

See Notes to Financial Statements.

THE DOW CHEMICAL COMPANY
Consolidated Statement of Stockholders' Equity (adapted)

(In millions)		1995	1994	1993
Common Stock	Balance at beginning and end of year	$ 818	$ 818	$ 818
Additional Paid-in Capital	Balance at beginning of year	326	366	350
	Tax benefit of contingent value rights	—	—	34
	Issuance of treasury stock at less than cost	(11)	(40)	(18)
	Balance at end of year	315	326	366
Retained Earnings	Balance at beginning of year	8,857	8,645	8,720
	Net income	2,078	938	644
	Preferred stock dividends declared	(7)	(7)	(7)
	Common stock dividends declared	(769)	(719)	(712)
	Balance at end of year	10,159	8,857	8,645
Unrealized Gains (Losses) on Investments	Balance at beginning of year	(21)	105	(2)
	Unrealized gains (losses)	83	(126)	107
	Balance at end of year	62	(21)	105
Cumulative Translation Adjustments	Balance at beginning of year	(330)	(304)	(107)
	Translation adjustments	(19)	(26)	(197)
	Balance at end of year	(349)	(330)	(304)
Treasury Stock	Balance at beginning of year	(1,438)	(1,596)	(1,715)
	Purchases	(2,115)	(38)	(17)
	Reclassification	(313)	—	—
	Issuance to employees and employee plans	222	196	136
	Balance at end of year	(3,644)	(1,438)	(1,596)
Net Stockholders' Equity		$ 7,361	$ 8,212	$ 8,034

See Notes to Financial Statements.

Notes to Financial Statements

In millions, except for share amounts

A Summary of Significant Accounting Policies

Principles of Consolidation and Basis of Presentation
The accompanying consolidated financial statements of The Dow Chemical Company and its subsidiaries (the Company) include the assets, liabilities, revenues and expenses of all majority-owned subsidiaries. Intercompany transactions and balances are eliminated in consolidation. Investments in companies 20%–50% owned (related companies) are accounted for on the equity basis.

The Company's consolidated statements of income and cash flows have been restated to reflect the pharmaceutical businesses as discontinued operations (see Note C [not included here]). Certain reclassifications of prior years' amounts have been made to conform to the presentation adopted for 1995.

I Notes Payable, Long-Term Debt and Available Credit Facilities

The average interest rate on long-term debt was 6.73 percent in 1995 compared to 6.64 percent in 1994. Annual installments on long-term debt for the next five years are as follows: 1996, $375; 1997, $610; 1998, $308; 1999, $201; 2000, $175.

(Continued)

Promissory Notes and Debentures at December 31	1995	1994
4.63%, final maturity 1995	$ —	$ 150
8.25%, final maturity 1996	150	150
5.75%, final maturity 1997	197	200
5.75%, final maturity 2001	—	15
7.38%, final maturity 2002	145	150
9.35%, final maturity 2002	194	200
7.13%, final maturity 2003	148	150
8.63%, final maturity 2006	187	200
8.55%, final maturity 2009	140	150
9.00%, final maturity 2010	125	150
9.20%, final maturity 2010	193	200
6.85%, final maturity 2013	138	150
7.13%, final maturity 2015	—	24
9.00%, final maturity 2021	219	300
8.85%, final maturity 2021	188	200
8.70%, final maturity 2022	96	138
7.38%, final maturity 2023	150	150
Subtotal	$2,270	$2,677

ANSWERS

Requirement 1

During 1995, Dow sold its pharmaceutical businesses, which then became discontinued operations to Dow. The revenues, expenses, and net income of Dow's pharmaceutical businesses were reported as part of continuing operations back in 1994 and 1993. Now that Dow has disposed of the discontinued segment, the pharmaceutical businesses' results should be removed from 1994's and 1993's continuing operations for comparison with 1995.

The restated amounts for 1994 and 1993 are important to investors who want to compare Dow's operating results for 1995, 1994, and 1993. The restated amounts are comparable for the three years and allow investors to analyze the company's income over a period of time.

Requirement 2

Discontinued operations contributed $187 million ($18 million + $169 million) to net income for 1995. This amount made up 9% of net income available to common stockholders ($187 million/$2,071 million = .090).

Dow sold the discontinued segment during 1995, as indicated by the Gain on sale of pharmaceutical businesses.

Requirement 3

Minority Interests' Share in Income is a *subtraction* in arriving at Dow's net income because the minority-interest part of Dow's net income belongs to the minority stockholders of some of Dow's subsidiary companies.

Requirement 4

Income from continuing operations is up in both 1994 and 1995. Income from continuing operations increased by $765 – $566 = $199 million (35%) in 1994 and by $1,884 – $765 = $1,119 million (146%) in 1995. This trend is very favorable.

Requirement 5

	December 31, 1995	December 31, 1994
Shares of common stock issued	327	327
Less: Shares of common held as treasury stock	(76)	(50)
Shares of common stock outstanding	251	277

Shares outstanding decreased during 1995 because the company purchased additional treasury stock. This is clear from the balance sheet and from the Treasury Stock section of the statement of stockholders' equity.

Requirement 6

(In millions except for market price per share)	
Shares of common stock outstanding at December 31, 1995 (from Requirement 5)	251
Market price per share of common stock..........................	× \$70.38
Total market price of Dow common stock	\$17,665

$$\textbf{Total market price of Dow common stock} = \frac{\textbf{Income from continuing operations}}{\textbf{Investment capitalization rate}}$$

Let X represent investment capitalization rate (dollar amounts in millions):

$$\$17{,}665 = \frac{\$1{,}884}{X}$$

$$= \frac{\$1{,}884}{\$17{,}665} = 10.7\%$$

Dow's stock doesn't look very risky because 10.7% falls in the lower end of the range of 8–15 percent.

Requirement 7

a. The balance sheet merely reports Long-Term Debt as a single amount. This information does *not* provide enough information to determine when Dow must pay its long-term debt.

Note I, entitled "Notes Payable, Long-Term Debt and Available Credit Facilities" gives the date when each note must be paid.

b. In 1996, Dow must pay \$375 million principal amount of its long-term debt. This amount appears in two places:

(1) Balance sheet, under Current Liabilities, as follows:

	(In millions)
Long-term debt due within one year	\$375

(2) Note I: The second sentence states, "Annual installments on long-term debt for the next [year are]: 1996, \$375 [million]."

c. Interest to pay during 1996 on the 5.75% note payable due in 1997:

\$197 million × .0575 = \$11.3 million

SUMMARY OF LEARNING OBJECTIVES

1. ***Analyze and use the elements of a complex income statement.*** A company's income statement reports on (1) continuing operations, (2) discontinued operations, (3) extraordinary gains and losses, and (4) the cumulative effect of accounting changes. It also reports income tax expense and earnings per share (EPS) for each of these categories.

2. ***Account for a corporation's income tax.*** Corporations pay income tax and must account for both income tax expense and income tax payable. *Income tax expense* is based on pretax accounting income. *Income tax payable* is based on taxable income. A difference between the expense and the payable creates another account, Deferred Tax Asset or Deferred Tax Liability.

3. ***Analyze a statement of stockholders' equity.*** A *statement of stockholders' equity* reports the changes in all categories of a company's equity during a period, including details about the company's (1) issuance of stock, (2) declaration of cash dividends, (3) distribution of stock dividends, (4) purchase and sale of treasury stock, (5) unrealized gains and losses on available-for-sale investments, and (6) the cumulative foreign-currency translation adjustment.

4. ***Interpret notes to the financial statements.*** The notes that accompany the financial statements are an integral part of the statements. The Summary of Significant Accounting Policies reports on such details as consolidation policy, revenues, expenses, earnings per share, inventory, depreciation, and capitalization of costs. Other notes report on acquisitions and dispositions, pensions, and long-term debt.

5. ***Use segment and interim financial data for decision making.*** A business *segment* is a clearly defined division of a company. Companies collect and report segment data to keep track of each division's performance and profitability.

To address the need for timely information, companies release financial data more frequently than once a year. The most common *interim* reporting period is three months (a quarter). Interim statements are not audited by independent CPAs, so their form varies from company to company.

6. *Understand managers' and auditor's responsibilities for the financial statements.* The top managers of a company are responsible for the preparation and integrity of the company's financial statements. Independent CPAs audit the financial statements, then offer an objective opinion on whether the statements meet GAAP standards.

ACCOUNTING VOCABULARY

adverse opinion *(p. 546).*
clean opinion *(p. 546).*
comprehensive income *(p. 526).*
disclaimer *(p. 546).*
earnings per share (EPS) *(p. 524).*
extraordinary gain or loss *(p. 523).*
extraordinary item *(p. 523).*
interim reporting *(p. 542).*
investment capitalization rate *(p. 520).*
investor's total return on investment *(p. 541).*
pretax accounting income *(p. 527).*
prior-period adjustment *(p. 529).*
qualified opinion *(p. 546).*
segment of the business *(p. 522).*
statement of stockholders' equity *(p. 533).*
taxable income *(p. 527).*
unqualified (clean) opinion *(p. 546).*

QUESTIONS

1. Why is it important for a corporation to report income from continuing operations separately from discontinued operations and extraordinary items?
2. Explain how an investor can use income from continuing operations to estimate the value of a stock. Give the equation using amounts of your own choosing.
3. Give two examples of extraordinary gains and losses and four examples of gains and losses that are *not* extraordinary.
4. Why is it important for companies to report the effects of their changes in accounting principles (accounting methods)? What appears on the income statement to alert investors that the company has made an accounting change?
5. What is the most widely used of all accounting statistics? What is the price-to-earnings ratio? Compute the price-to-earnings ratio for a company with EPS of $2 and market price of $12 per share of common stock.
6. What is the earnings per share of a company with net income of $5,500, issued common stock of 12,000 shares, and treasury common stock of 1,000 shares?
7. Identify three subtotals on the income statement that generate income tax expense. What is an income tax saving, and how does it arise?
8. Explain the difference between the income tax expense and the income tax payable of a corporation. How is the amount of each item determined, and where does each item appear in the financial statements?
9. Why do creditors wish to restrict a corporation's payment of cash dividends and purchases of treasury stock?
10. What information does the statement of stockholders' equity report? Identify which other financial statement (besides the balance sheet and the notes) reports on the transactions that appear on the statement of stockholders' equity.
11. Outline the major components of the Summary of Significant Accounting Policies note that is included in a set of financial statements. Why is this information so important? What information is reported in the other financial statement notes? What important information does each note give investors?
12. Who bears primary responsibility for the financial statements? What role do the independent auditors play? Of what value is the audit?
13. What is a *segment* of a business? Who is interested in segment data, and how do these persons use the data?
14. What is an interim period? How much data do companies report on an interim basis? Why are interim reports important? Are interim reports as reliable as the annual report? Why or why not?

EXERCISES

Preparing and using a complex income statement ***(Obj. 1)***

E11-1 **Texaco, Inc.,** the giant oil company, has reported a number of special items on its income statement. The following data, listed in no particular order, were adapted from Texaco's financial statements (amounts in millions):

Discontinued operations:	
Net loss from operations	$ 19
Net loss on disposal	223
Dividends paid	947
Total operating expenses	35,801
Preferred stock	300
Total revenues	36,787
Cumulative translation adjustment	61
Cumulative effect of accounting change—credit	147
Income tax expense (saving):	
Continuing operations	$ 258
Discontinued operations:	
Net loss from operations	(2)
Net loss on disposal	(49)
Cumulative effect of accounting change	26
Unrealized net gain on investments	62
Short-term investments	35
Retained earnings	7,186

Required

1. Show how the Texaco, Inc., income statement for 19X5 should appear. Omit earnings per share.
2. Although 19X5 was a bad year for Texaco, financial analysts believe that Texaco can easily earn its current level of income for the indefinite future. Therefore, they apply a 6% investment capitalization rate in estimating the value of Texaco stock. What is analysts' estimate of the market value of Texaco, Inc.? How can analysts use this figure to make an investment decision?

E11-2 Graz Corporation's accounting records contain the following information for 19X4 operations:

Preparing and using a complex income statement ***(Obj. 1)***

Cost of goods sold	$ 45,000
Loss on discontinued operations	50,000
Income tax expense—extraordinary gain	4,800
Income tax saving—change in depreciation method	2,000
Income tax saving—loss on discontinued operations	20,000
Extraordinary gain	12,000
Sales revenue	130,000
Operating expenses (including income tax)	43,000
Cumulative effect of change in depreciation method (debit)	(6,000)

Required

Prepare Graz Corporation's income statement for 19X4. Omit earnings per share. Was 19X4 a good year or a bad year for Graz Corporation? Explain your answer in terms of the outlook for 19X5.

E11-3 McDonnell Douglas, the manufacturer of the DC line of commercial aircraft, reported the following income statement for 19X2:

Using an income statement ***(Obj. 1)***

MCDONNELL DOUGLAS
Consolidated Statement of Operations

Year Ended December 31 (*In millions, except for share data*)	**19X2**
Revenues	$17,365
Costs and expenses:	
Cost of products, services and rentals	15,567
General and administrative expenses	825
Research and development	509
Postretirement benefits	(1,090)
Interest expense:	
Aerospace segments	309
Financial services and other segment	159
Total Costs and Expenses	16,279
Earnings From Continuing Operations Before Income Taxes and Cumulative Effect Of Accounting Change	1,086
Income taxes	388
Earnings From Continuing Operations Before Cumulative Effect Of Accounting Change	698
Discontinued operations, net of income taxes	57
Earnings Before Cumulative Effect Of Accounting Change	755
Cumulative effect of initial application of new accounting standard for postretirement benefits	(1,536)
Net Earnings (Loss)	$ (781)
Earnings (Loss) Per Share:	
Continuing operations	$ 5.99
Discontinued operations	.49
Cumulative effect of accounting change	(13.18)
	$ (6.70)
Dividends Declared Per Share	$ .47

Required

1. Evaluate the results of operations for 19X2. Give the reasoning underlying your evaluation.
2. 19X2 was a loss year for McDonnell Douglas. Do you think the company's stock price dropped to near zero as a result of the net loss? Give your reason.
3. How could McDonnell Douglas afford to declare cash dividends during a loss year? How could the company afford to pay cash dividends during the year?

Using income data for investment analysis ***(Obj. 1)***

E11-4 During 19X4, **PepsiCo, Inc.,** had sales of $28.5 billion, income from continuing operations of $1.8 billion, and net income of $1.7 billion. Earnings per share figures were $2.22 for continuing operations and $2.18 for net income. At December 31, 19X4, the market price of a share of PepsiCo's common stock closed at $36.25 on the New York Stock Exchange.

What investment capitalization rate did investors appear to be using to determine the value of one share of PepsiCo stock? The formula for the value of one share of stock uses earnings per share (EPS) in the calculation. Does this capitalization rate suggest high risk or low risk? What about PepsiCo's line of business is consistent with your evaluation of the company's risk?

Computing earnings per share ***(Obj. 1)***

E11-5 Swingline Corporation earned net income of $56,000 for the second quarter of 19X6. The ledger reveals the following figures:

Preferred stock, $1.75 per year, no par, 1,600 shares issued and outstanding	$ 70,000
Common stock, $10 par, 52,000 shares issued	520,000
Treasury stock, common, 2,000 shares at cost	36,000

Required

Compute EPS for the quarter, assuming no changes in the stock accounts during the quarter.

Computing earnings per share ***(Obj. 1)***

E11-6 Connecticut Supply had 40,000 shares of common stock and 10,000 shares of $10 par, 5% preferred stock outstanding on December 31, 19X8. On April 30, 19X9, the company issued 9,000 additional common shares and ended 19X9 with 49,000 shares of common stock outstanding. Income from continuing operations of 19X9 was $115,400, and loss on discontinued operations (net of income tax) was $8,280. The company had an extraordinary loss (net of tax) of $55,200.

Required

Compute Connecticut Supply's EPS amounts for 19X9, starting with income from continuing operations.

Accounting for income tax by a corporation ***(Obj. 2)***

E11-7 Krisler Manufacturing Company has pretax accounting income (on the income statement) of $420,000 in 19X6 and $470,000 in 19X7. Taxable income (on the tax return filed with the Internal Revenue Service) is $380,000 in 19X6 and $510,000 in 19X7. The federal income tax rate is 35 percent. Record Krisler's income taxes for both years. What is the balance in the Deferred Tax Liability account at the end of each year? Show what Krisler will report on its 19X6 and 19X7 income statement and balance sheet for this situation. Start the income statement with income before tax, and recall that a company pays each year's income tax payable early in the next year.

Analyzing income tax liabilities ***(Obj. 2)***

E11-8 **The Boeing Company**, the aircraft manufacturer, reported its liabilities, adapted as follows:

	December 31,	
(In millions)	**1995**	**1994**
Liabilities		
Accounts payable and other liabilities	$6,245	$6,267
Advances in excess of related costs	510	273
Income taxes payable	389	281
Current portion of long-term debt	271	6
Total current liabilities	7,415	6,827
Deferred tax [liability]	—	51
Accrued retiree health care	2,441	2,282
Long-term debt	2,344	2,603

Required

1. Give two explanations for the change in Deferred tax liability during 1995.
2. What is the most likely explanation for the increase in Income taxes payable during 1995?

E11-9 Big Red, Inc., a soft-drink company, reported a prior-period adjustment in 19X9. An accounting error caused net income of prior years to be overstated by $3.8 million. Retained earnings at January 1, 19X9, as previously reported, stood at $395.3 million. Net income for 19X9 was $92.1 million, and dividends were $39.8 million.

Reporting a prior-period adjustment on the statement of retained earnings ***(Obj. 3)***

Required

Prepare the company's statement of retained earnings for the year ended December 31, 19X9.

E11-10 The agreement under which Yung Corporation issued its long-term debt requires the restriction of $250,000 of the company's retained earnings balance. Total retained earnings is $270,000, and total paid-in capital is $820,000.

Reporting a retained earnings restriction ***(Obj. 3)***

Required

a. Show how to report stockholders' equity on Yung's balance sheet, assuming Yung discloses the retained earnings restriction in a note. Write the note.

b. Yung's cash balance is $85,000. What is the maximum amount of dividends Yung can declare?

E11-11 The Kroger Company, a large grocery company, had retained earnings of $792.6 million at the beginning of 19X7. The company showed these figures at December 31, 19X7:

Preparing a statement of retained earnings ***(Obj. 3)***

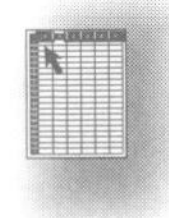

	(In millions)
Increases in retained earnings:	
Net income	$127.1
Decreases in retained earnings:	
Cash dividends—preferred	2.3
common	85.2
Debit to retained earnings due to retirement of preferred stock	11.3

Required

Prepare a statement of retained earnings for The Kroger Company for 19X7. Explain the transaction that caused the $11.3 million debit to Retained Earnings. The cash payment to retire the preferred stock was $81.6 million. The journal entry that recorded the retirement of preferred stock will help you understand the transaction.

E11-12 At December 31, 19X5, NOVA Corp. of Melbourne, Florida, reported this stockholders' equity:

Preparing a statement of stockholders' equity ***(Obj. 3)***

Common stock, $5 par, 200,000 shares authorized, 120,000 shares issued	$ 600,000
Additional paid-in capital	3,100,000
Retained earnings	1,700,000
Treasury stock, 2,500 shares at cost	(78,000)
	$5,322,000

During 19X6, NOVA completed these transactions and events (listed in chronological order):

a. Declared and issued a 50% stock dividend. At the time, NOVA's stock was quoted at a market price of $31 per share.

b. Sold 1,000 shares of treasury stock for $36 per share (cost was $31).

c. Issued 500 shares of common stock to employees at the price of $28 per share.

d. Net income for the year, $340,000.

e. Declared cash dividends of $180,000, to be paid early in 19X7.

Required

Prepare NOVA Corp.'s statement of stockholders' equity for 19X6, using the format of Exhibit 11-7 as a model. Then use the statement you prepared to answer the following questions:

1. Did NOVA's retained earnings increase or decrease during 19X6? What caused retained earnings to change during the year?
2. How did the stock dividend affect total stockholders' equity? How did it affect total assets? Total liabilities?
3. How would creditors feel about NOVA's sale of treasury stock? NOVA's issuance of common stock? Why?

Analyzing a statement of stockholders' equity
(Obj. 3)

E11-13 **The Coca-Cola Company** reported the following statement of stockholders' equity (adapted) for 1995:

THE COCA-COLA COMPANY
Consolidated Statement of Share-Owners' Equity (adapted)

Year Ended December 31, 1995	Number of Common Shares Outstanding	Common Stock	Capital Surplus (Additional Paid-in Capital)	Reinvested Earnings	Outstanding Restricted Stock	Accumulated Other Comprehensive Income: Foreign Currency Translation	Accumulated Other Comprehensive Income: Unrealized Gain on Securities	Treasury Stock
(In millions except per share data)								
Balance December 31, 1994	1,276	$427	$1,173	$11,006	$(74)	$(272)	$48	$(7,073)
Stock issued to employees exercising stock options	4	1	85	—	—	—	—	—
Tax benefit from employees' stock option and restricted stock plans	—	—	26	—	—	—	—	—
Stock issued under restricted stock plans	—	—	7	—	6	—	—	—
Translation adjustments	—	—	—	—	—	(152)	—	—
Net change in unrealized gain on securities, net of deferred taxes	—	—	—	—	—	—	34	—
Purchases of stock for treasury	(29)	—	—	—	—	—	—	(1,796)
Treasury stock issued in connection with an acquisition	1	—	—	—	—	—	—	70
Net income	—	—	—	2,986	—	—	—	—
Dividends (per share—$.88)	—	—	—	(1,110)	—	—	—	—
Balance December 31, 1995	1,252	$428	$1,291	$12,882	$(68)	$(424)	$82	$(8,799)

You should be able to understand all the stockholders' equity transactions reported on this statement, except for the "Tax benefit . . .," which is beyond the scope of this introductory course. Ignore the tax benefit as you answer the following questions about The Coca-Cola Company.

Required

1. What were Coca-Cola's retained earnings balances at year end 1994 and 1995? Where else in the financial statements did Coca-Cola report these amounts? Was 1995 a profitable year? How profitable?
2. Coca-Cola issued stock to employees who exercised their stock options and bought the stock at a below-market price. How much cash did Coca-Cola receive? Where else in the financial statements could you find this amount?
3. Was the U.S. dollar strong or weak during 1995 in comparison to the foreign currencies of Coca-Cola's foreign subsidiaries? How can you tell?
4. Did the market value of Coca-Cola's available-for-sale investments increase or decrease during 1995? By how much?

Exercises 11-14 through 11-18 and 11-20 are based on the financial statements and related notes of **Ford Motor Company,** reproduced on pages 559–565. By working through these exercises you will learn a great deal about Ford Motor Company and about accounting. Begin by scanning Ford's income statement and balance sheet. Then locate the notes, the statement of management responsibility, and the report of Ford's independent auditors.

To answer some of these exercises you may have to refer to preceding chapters. If necessary, you can use the index at the back of the book to locate what you need.

FORD MOTOR COMPANY
Consolidated Statement of Income
For the Years Ended December 31, 1995, 1994, and 1993

(In millions, except amounts per share)	1995	1994	1993
AUTOMOTIVE			
Sales (Note 1)	**$110,496**	$107,137	$91,568
Costs and expenses (Note 1)			
Costs of sales	**101,171**	95,887	85,280
Selling, administrative, and other expenses	**6,044**	5,424	4,856
Total costs and expenses	**107,215**	101,311	90,136
Operating income	**3,281**	5,826	1,432
Interest income	**800**	665	563
Interest expense	**622**	721	807
Net interest income/(expense)	**178**	(56)	(244)
Equity in net (loss)/income of affiliated companies (Note 1)	**(154)**	271	127
Net expense from transactions with Financial Services	**(139)**	(44)	(24)
Income before income taxes—Automotive	**3,166**	5,997	1,291
FINANCIAL SERVICES			
Revenues (Note 1)	**26,641**	21,302	16,953
Costs and expenses (Note 1)			
Interest expense	**9,424**	7,023	6,482
Depreciation	**6,500**	4,910	3,064
Operating and other expenses	**5,499**	4,607	3,196
Provision for credit and insurance losses	**1,818**	1,539	1,523
Loss on disposition of Granite Savings Bank (formerly First Nationwide Bank)	—	475	—
Total costs and expenses	**23,241**	18,554	14,265
Net revenue from transactions with Automotive	**139**	44	24
Income before income taxes—Financial Services	**3,539**	2,792	2,712
TOTAL COMPANY			
Income before income taxes	**6,705**	8,789	4,003
Provision for income taxes	**2,379**	3,329	1,350
Income before minority interests	**4,326**	5,460	2,653
Minority interests in net income of subsidiaries	**187**	152	124
Net income	**$ 4,139**	$ 5,308	$ 2,529
Income attributable to Common and Class B Stock after preferred stock dividends	**$ 3,839**	$ 5,021	$ 2,241
Average number of shares of Common and Class B Stock outstanding	**1,071**	1,010	986
Amounts per share of common and Class B Stock			
Income	**$ 3.58**	$ 4.97	$ 2.27
Cash dividends	**$ 1.23**	$ 0.91	$ 0.80

The accompanying notes (pages 561–565) are part of the financial statements.

FORD MOTOR COMPANY
Consolidated Balance Sheet (Adapted)

(In millions)	December 31, 1995	December 31, 1994
ASSETS		
Automotive		
Cash and cash equivalents	$ 5,750	$ 4,481
Marketable securities	6,656	7,602
Total cash, cash equivalents, and marketable securities	12,406	12,083
Receivables	3,321	2,548
Inventories (Note 4)	7,162	6,487
Deferred income taxes	2,709	3,062
Other current assets	1,483	2,006
Net current receivable from Financial Services	200	677
Total current assets	27,281	26,863
Equity in net assets of affiliated companies (Note 1)	2,248	3,554
Net property (Note 5)	31,273	27,048
Deferred income taxes	4,802	4,414
Other assets (Notes 1 and 8)	7,168	6,760
Total Automotive assets	72,772	68,639
Financial Services		
Cash and cash equivalents	2,690	1,739
Investments in securities	4,553	6,105
Net receivables and lease investments	149,694	130,356
Other assets (Note 1)	13,574	12,783
Total Financial Services assets	170,511	150,983
Total assets	$243,283	$219,622
LIABILITIES AND STOCKHOLDERS' EQUITY		
Automotive		
Trade payables	$ 11,260	$ 10,777
Other payables	1,976	2,280
Accrued liabilities	13,392	11,943
Income taxes payable	316	316
Debt payable within one year (Note 9)	1,832	155
Total current liabilities	28,776	25,471
Long-term debt (Note 9)	5,475	7,103
Other liabilities	25,677	24,920
Deferred income taxes	1,186	1,216
Total Automotive liabilities	61,114	58,710
Financial Services		
Payables	5,476	2,361
Debt (Note 9)	141,317	123,713
Deferred tax liability	3,831	2,958
Other liabilities and deferred income	6,116	7,669
Net payable to Automotive	200	677
Total Financial Services liabilities	156,940	137,378
Company-obligated mandatorily redeemable preferred securities of a subsidiary trust (aggregate principal amount of $632 million)	682	—
Preferred stockholders' equity in a subsidiary company	—	1,875

Stockholders' equity		
Capital stock		
Preferred Stock, par value $1.00 per share (aggregate liquidation preference of $1 billion and $3.4 billion)	*	*
Common Stock, par value $1.00 per share (1,089 and 952 million shares issued)	**1,089**	952
Class B Stock, par value $1.00 per share (71 million shares issued)	**71**	71
Capital in excess of par value of stock	**5,105**	5,273
Foreign-currency translation adjustments and other	**594**	189
Earnings retained for use in business	**17,688**	15,174
Total stockholders' equity	**24,547**	21,659
Total liabilities and stockholders' equity	**$243,283**	$219,622

*Less than $1 million
The accompanying notes (pages 561–565) are part of the financial statements.

Notes to Financial Statements (excerpts)

NOTE 1. ACCOUNTING POLICIES

Principles of Consolidation

The consolidated financial statements include all significant majority owned subsidiaries and reflect the operating results, assets, liabilities and cash flows for two business segments: Automotive and Financial Services. The assets and liabilities of the Automotive segment are classified as current or noncurrent, and those of the Financial Services segment are unclassified. Affiliates that are 20% to 50% owned, principally Mazda Motor Corporation and AutoAlliance International Inc., and subsidiaries where control is expected to be temporary, principally investments in certain dealerships, are generally accounted for on an equity basis. For purposes of Notes to Financial Statements, "Ford" or "the company" means Ford Motor Company and its majority owned consolidated subsidiaries unless the context requires otherwise.

Use of estimates and assumptions as determined by management is required in the preparation of consolidated financial statements in conformity with generally accepted accounting principles. Actual results could differ from those estimates and assumptions. Certain amounts for prior periods have been reclassified to conform with 1995 presentations.

Nature of Operations

The company operates in two principal business segments: Automotive and Financial Services. The Automotive segment consists of the design, manufacture, assembly and sale of cars, trucks and related parts and accessories. The Financial Services segment consists primarily of financing operations, insurance operations, and vehicle and equipment leasing operations.

Intersegment transactions represent principally transactions occurring in the ordinary course of business, borrowings and related transactions between entities in the Financial Services and Automotive segments, and interest and other support under special vehicle financing programs. These arrangements are reflected in the respective business segments.

Revenue Recognition—Automotive

Sales are recorded by the company when products are shipped to dealers. . . . Estimated costs for sales incentive programs approved [after] the related sales are [recorded as expense] when the programs are approved.

[S]ales through dealers to certain daily rental companies where the daily rental company has an option to require the company to repurchase vehicles, subject to certain conditions, are recognized over the period of daily rental service. . . .

Revenue Recognition—Financial Services

Revenue from finance receivables is recognized over the term of the receivable using the [effective] interest method.

Other Costs

Advertising and sales promotion costs are expensed as incurred. Advertising costs were $2,024 million in 1995, $1,823 million in 1994 and $1,610 million in 1993. Estimated costs related to product warranty are accrued at the time of sale. Research and development costs are expensed as incurred and were $6,509 million in 1995, $5,811 million in 1994, and $5,618 million in 1993.

Goodwill

Goodwill represents the excess of the purchase price over the fair value of the net assets of acquired companies and is amortized using the straight-line method principally over 40 years. Total goodwill included in Automotive and Financial Services other assets at December 31, 1995, was $2.3 billion and $3.2 billion, respectively.

NOTE 4. INVENTORIES—AUTOMOTIVE

Inventories at December 31 were as follows (in millions):

	December 31, 1995	December 31, 1994
Raw materials, work in process and supplies	**$3,717**	$3,192
Finished products	**3,445**	3,295
Total inventories	**$7,162**	$6,487
U.S. inventories	**$2,662**	$2,917

Inventories are stated at the lower of cost or market. The cost of most U.S. inventories is determined by the last-in, first-out ("LIFO") method. The cost of the remaining inventories is determined primarily by the first-in, first-out ("FIFO") method.

If the FIFO method had been used instead of the LIFO method, inventories would have been higher by $1,406 million and $1,383 million at December 31, 1995 and 1994, respectively.

NOTE 9. DEBT

Automotive

Debt at December 31 was as follows (in millions):

	Maturity	Weighted-Average Interest Rate 1995	Weighted-Average Interest Rate 1994	Book Value 1995	Book Value 1994
Debt payable within one year					
Short-term debt		**6.6%**	10.0%	**$ 872**	$ 112
Long-term debt payable within one year				**960**	43
Total debt payable within one year				**1,832**	155
Long-term debt	1997–2043	**9.2%**	9.0%	**5,475**	7,103
Total debt				**$7,307**	$7,258
Fair value				**$8,160**	$7,492

Long-term debt at December 31, 1995 included maturities as follows (in millions): 1996 - $960 (included in current liabilities); 1997 - $580; 1998 - $351; 1999 - $53; 2000 - $1,003; thereafter - $3,488.

Financial Services

Debt at December 31 was as follows (in millions):

	Maturity	Weighted-Average Interest Rate 1995	1994	Book Value 1995	1994
Debt payable within one year					
Unsecured short-term debt				**$ 3,032**	$ 2,990
Commercial paper				**56,002**	51,008
Other short-term debt				**1,927**	2,301
Total short-term debt		**5.7%**	5.9%	**60,961**	56,299
Long-term debt payable within one year				**12,097**	9,310
Total debt payable within one year				**73,058**	65,609
Long-term debt					
Secured indebtedness	1997–2005	**7.7%**	6.7%	**89**	98
Unsecured senior indebtedness					
Notes and bank debt	1997–2048	**6.9%**	7.1%	**64,810**	54,248
Debentures	1997–2010	**7.4%**	7.8%	**591**	560
Unamortized (discount)				**(5)**	(61)
Total unsecured senior indebtedness				**65,396**	54,747
Unsecured subordinated indebtedness					
Notes	1997–2021	**8.8%**	9.2%	**2,665**	3,159
Debentures	1997–2009	**8.1%**	8.1%	**141**	141
Unamortized (discount)				**(32)**	(41)
Total unsecured subordinated indebtedness				**2,774**	3,259
Total long-term debt				**68,259**	58,104
Total debt				**$141,317**	$123,713
Fair value				**$144,730**	$122,252

NOTE 17. SEGMENT INFORMATION

Financial information segregated by major geographic area is as follows (in millions):

Automotive	1995	1994	1993
Sales to unaffiliated customers			
United States	**$ 73,870**	$ 73,759	$ 62,108
Europe	**26,132**	22,623	19,468
All other	**10,494**	10,755	9,992
Total	**$110,496**	$107,137	$ 91,568
Net income/(loss)			
United States	**$ 1,843**	$ 3,002	$ 1,442
Europe	**116**	128	(873)
All other	**97**	783	439
Total	**$ 2,056**	$ 3,913	$ 1,008
Assets at December 31			
United States	**$ 45,841**	$ 45,889	$ 39,959
Europe	**17,010**	16,880	16,210
All other	**18,842**	16,798	15,197
Net receivables from Financial Services	**200**	677	910
Elimination of intercompany receivables	**(9,121)**	(11,605)	(10,539)
Total	**$ 72,772**	$ 68,639	$ 61,737

(Continued)

(Continued)

Financial Services	1995	1994	1993
Revenues			
United States	**$ 21,383**	$ 17,356	$ 14,102
Europe	**3,144**	2,336	1,673
All other	**2,114**	1,610	1,178
Total	**$ 26,641**	$ 21,302	$ 16,953
Net income			
United States	**$ 1,718**	$ 1,119	$ 1,340
Europe	**321**	218	140
All other	**44**	58	41
Total	**$ 2,083**	$ 1,395	$ 1,521
Assets at December 31			
United States	**$137,154**	$124,120	$117,290
Europe	**20,237**	16,507	12,132
All other	**13,120**	10,356	7,779
Total	**$170,511**	$150,983	$137,201

SUPPLEMENTARY DISCLOSURES
Summary Quarterly Financial Data (unaudited)

	1995				1994			
(In millions, except amounts per share)	First Quarter	Second Quarter	Third Quarter	Fourth Quarter	First Quarter	Second Quarter	Third Quarter	Fourth Quarter
Automotive								
Sales	**$28,601**	**$29,861**	**$24,437**	**$27,597**	$26,070	$28,375	$24,926	$27,766
Operating income/(loss)	**1,782**	**1,774**	**(204)**	**(71)**	1,559	1,966	989	1,312
Financial Services								
Revenues	**6,182**	**6,528**	**6,981**	**6,950**	4,332	5,397	5,696	5,877
Income before income taxes	**759**	**885**	**978**	**917**	196	911	896	789
Total Company								
Net income	**$ 1,550**	**$ 1,572**	**$ 357**	**$ 660**	$ 904	$ 1,711	$ 1,124	$ 1,569

MANAGEMENT'S FINANCIAL RESPONSIBILITY

Management is responsible for the preparation of the company's financial statements and the other financial information in this report. This responsibility includes maintaining the integrity and objectivity of financial records and the presentation of the company's financial statements in conformity with generally accepted accounting principles.

The company maintains an internal control structure intended to provide, among other things, reasonable assurance that its records include the transactions of its operations in all material respects and to provide protection against significant misuse or loss of company assets. The internal control structure is supported by careful selection and training of qualified personnel, written policies and procedures that communicate details of the internal control structure to the company's worldwide activities, and by a staff of internal auditors who employ thorough auditing programs.

The company's financial statements have been audited by Coopers & Lybrand L.L.P., independent certified public accountants. Their audit was conducted in accordance with generally accepted auditing standards which included consideration of the company's internal control structure. The Report of Independent Accountants appears below.

The Board of Directors, acting through its Audit Committee composed solely of directors who are not employees of the company, is responsible for determining that management fulfills its responsibilities in the financial control of operations and the preparation of financial statements. The Audit Committee appoints the independent accountants, subject to ratification by the stockholders. It meets regularly with management, internal auditors, and independent accountants. The independent accountants and internal auditors have full and free access to the Audit Committee and meet with it to discuss their audit work, the company's internal controls, and financial reporting matters.

Alex Trotman
Chairman of the Board

John M. Devine
Chief Financial Officer

REPORT OF INDEPENDENT ACCOUNTANTS

Coopers & Lybrand

Coopers & Lybrand L.L.P.

a professional services firm

To the Board of Directors and Stockholders
Ford Motor Company

We have audited the consolidated balance sheet of Ford Motor Company and Subsidiaries at December 31, 1995 and 1994, and the related consolidated statements of income, stockholders' equity and cash flows for each of the three years in the period ended December 31, 1995. These financial statements are the responsibility of the company's management. Our responsibility is to express an opinion on these financial statements based on our audits.

We conducted our audits in accordance with generally accepted auditing standards. Those standards require that we plan and perform the audit to obtain reasonable assurance about whether the financial statements are free of material misstatement. An audit includes examining, on a test basis, evidence supporting the amounts and disclosures in the financial statements. An audit also includes assessing the accounting principles used and significant estimates made by management, as well as evaluating the overall financial statement presentation. We believe that our audits provide a reasonable basis for our opinion.

In our opinion, the financial statements referred to above present fairly, in all material respects, the consolidated financial position of Ford Motor Company and Subsidiaries at December 31, 1995 and 1994, and the consolidated results of their operations and their cash flows for each of the three years in the period ended December 31, 1995, in conformity with generally accepted accounting principles.

Coopers & Lybrand LLP

400 Renaissance Center
Detroit, Michigan 48243
January 26, 1996

Using the financial statement notes: investments
(Obj. 4)

E11-14 Ford's Note 1. Accounting Policies, under Principles of Consolidation (page 561), describes how Ford Motor Company accounts for its significant investments in other companies.

Required

1. The note refers to "[a]ffiliates that are 20% to 50% owned, principally Mazda Motor Corporation . . . ." How well did Ford's affiliated companies perform during 1995? The income statement offers a clue.
2. Assume that Ford owns a 25% investment in its affiliated companies. How much net income did Ford's affiliates earn, or how much net loss did they incur, during 1995?
3. What is a majority-owned subsidiary? How does Ford account for its investments in majority-owned subsidiaries? Name the accounting method that Ford uses and describe how the method works. Is this method perfectly accurate, or must Ford management make estimates and assumptions?

Using the financial statement notes: revenues and expenses ***(Obj. 4)***

E11-15 Ford's Note 1. Accounting Policies, under the subheadings Revenue Recognition—Automotive and Financial Services (pages 561–562), describes when Ford records revenue.

Required

1. In general, when does Ford record revenue on its sales of automobiles—at the time it ships cars to its dealers, or when the dealers sell the cars to consumers? Does this policy seem reasonable, too conservative, or too liberal? Explain your answer.
2. When auto sales are lagging, Ford and General Motors offer sales incentives (rebates). You may have seen a related advertising campaign, such as "FORD OFFERING $1,000 REBATE ON THE TAURUS." What item on the income statement includes this expense? What was the total amount of this expense for 1995?
3. According to the note, Ford makes "sales through dealers to certain daily rental companies . . . ." Name several of these rental companies. Does Ford record this sales revenue at the time it ships autos to its dealers, or later? Why?
4. When does Ford record the revenue it earns on its finance receivables (that is, the revenues of its Financial Services Division)? What is another name for this revenue? What was its amount for 1995? What was the largest expense of Ford's Financial Services segment during 1995? How does this expense relate to Financial Services Revenues?

Using the financial statement notes: inventory ***(Obj. 4)***

E11-16 Examine Ford's Note 4. Inventories—Automotive (page 562).

Required

1. What is Ford's main inventory costing method? What other costing method does Ford also use to account for inventories? (Lower-of-cost-or-market is not a costing method.)
2. What are the two categories of Ford's inventories? Give the breakdown of the total cost of Ford's inventories at December 31, 1995.

   How much of Ford's inventories did the company hold in the United States? Outside the United States? (Assume the market value of Ford's inventories exceeds their cost, and thus that the reported figures represent cost.)
3. If Ford had used the FIFO method to account for all of its inventory, what amount would Ford have reported for inventory on its balance sheet at December 31, 1995? Does the difference between the LIFO and FIFO amounts suggest that Ford's inventory costs are increasing or decreasing? Why?
4. Use only finished products inventory to compute Ford's rate of inventory turnover during 1995. Then determine approximately how many days Ford held its average level of finished product inventory during the year. Do these data suggest that a completed Ford (or Mercury or Lincoln) sits at a Ford assembly plant very long?

Using the financial statement notes: debt ***(Obj. 4)***

E11-17 Study Ford's Note 9. Debt (pages 562–563), and trace Ford's Total debt figures—both Automotive and Financial Services—to the balance sheet.

Required

1. Determine Ford's total short-term and long-term debt—both Automotive and Financial Services—at December 31, 1995, as follows:
   - **a.** Total amount of debt payable during 1996
   - **b.** Total amount of debt payable after 1996

   State why some of these amounts cannot be taken directly from Ford's balance sheet at December 31, 1995.
2. Who would care about the breakdown of debts payable next year and the debts payable after one year? Why would these persons care? Identify two ratios that depend on the level of current liabilities. Give the formulas for computing the ratios.
3. Suppose Ford decided to pay off all its Debt at December 31, 1995, and assume that Ford could afford to do so. How much would Ford pay?

Examining management's and auditors' responsibilities for the financial statements ***(Obj. 6)***

E11-18 Study Ford's statement of Management's Financial Responsibility and Report of Independent Accountants (pages 564–565).

Required

1. The statement of Management's Responsibility goes rather deeply into Ford's internal control structure. Review the definition of internal control in Chapter 4. Then relate the definition to Ford's statement of responsibility for the company's internal controls.
2. Why is it important that members of the Audit Committee of Ford's Board of Directors not also serve as employees of the company? The statement of Management's Responsibility offers a clue.
3. Which accounting firm serves as Ford's independent auditors? Which office of the firm performed the audit? Are these auditors employees of Ford? What does *independent* mean in this context?
4. What did the accounting firm audit, Ford Motor Company or Ford's financial statements? What type of opinion did the auditors express? What difference does the audit opinion make to investors and creditors who might consider investing in Ford Motor Company?

CHALLENGE EXERCISES

Accounting for income tax by a corporation ***(Obj. 2)***

E11-19 **Case A**—The income statement of Hewitt Corp. reports the following:

	19X1	19X2
Income before income tax..............	$25,000	$30,000

The combined federal and state income tax rate is 40 percent.

1. How much net income will Hewitt Corp. report each year?
2. Compute the amount of income tax payable from each year's operations.

Case B—Keep all facts as they are in Case A, except that Hewitt uses straight-line depreciation for accounting purposes and MACRS depreciation for income tax purposes. During 19X1, MACRS depreciation exceeds straight-line depreciation by $6,000. In 19X2, MACRS depreciation exceeds straight-line by $4,000.

1. How much net income will Hewitt Corp. report each year?
2. Compute the amount of income tax payable from each year's operations.
3. Assume that Hewitt began operations in 19X1. What will be the balance of Deferred Tax Liability at the end of 19X1 and at the end of 19X2? Explain the desirable feature of the deferred tax liability.

Using segment data ***(Obj. 5)***

E11-20 Use Ford Motor Company's Note 17. Segment Information (pages 563–564), to answer the following questions about the company and its operations during 1995. Give amounts to support each answer.

1. Which segment of Ford Motor Company
   - **a.** Generates more revenue?
   - **b.** Is more profitable?
   - **c.** Has more assets?

   Which segment uses revenues more profitably?
   Which segment uses assets more profitably?
2. What percentage of its 1995 net income did Ford earn
   - **a.** In the United States from
     - **(1)** automotive sales?
     - **(2)** financial services?
   - **b.** In foreign countries from
     - **(1)** automotive sales?
     - **(2)** financial services?

Based on this analysis, which part of the business would you least like to keep? Why? Why do you think Ford keeps this part of the business?

PROBLEMS

(GROUP A)

Preparing a complex income statement and reporting stockholders' equity on the balance sheet ***(Obj. 1)***

P11-1A The following information was taken from the records of Mainframe Manufacturing Corporation at June 30, 19X5. Mainframe Manufacturing hopes to gain a foothold in the computer peripherals area.

General expenses	$ 71,000	Sales discounts..............................	$ 7,000
Loss on sale of discontinued segment.....................................	8,000	Extraordinary gain........................	27,000
Prior-period adjustment—debit to Retained Earnings.......	4,000	Loss on sale of plant assets	10,000
Cost of goods sold.........................	319,000	Operating income, discontinued segment.....................................	9,000
Income tax expense (saving):		Dividends on preferred stock	?
Continuing operations	28,000	Preferred stock, 6%, $25 par, 20,000 shares authorized, 4,000 shares issued....................	100,000
Discontinued segment:			
Operating income	3,600	Cumulative effect of change in depreciation method (credit).........................	7,000
Loss on sale............................	(3,200)		
Extraordinary gain....................	10,800	Dividends on common stock........	12,000
Cumulative effect of change in depreciation method.........	3,000	Sales revenue................................	589,000
Interest expense	23,000	Retained earnings, beginning, as originally reported................	63,000
Gain on settlement of lawsuit	8,000	Selling expenses	87,000
Sales returns.................................	15,000	Common stock, no par, 22,000 shares authorized and issued	350,000
Paid-in capital from retirement of preferred stock	16,000		
Dividend revenue	11,000		
Treasury stock, common (2,000 shares at cost)	28,000		

Required

1. Prepare Mainframe Manufacturing's single-step income statement, which lists all revenues together and all expenses together, for the fiscal year ended June 30, 19X5. Include earnings per share data.
2. Evaluate income for the year ended June 30, 19X5, in terms of the outlook for 19X6. 19X5 was a typical year, and Mainframe's top managers hoped to earn income from continuing operations equal to 10% of net sales.
3. Prepare the stockholders' equity section of the balance sheet. It will be helpful to prepare a statement of retained earnings.
4. How will what you learned in this problem help you evaluate an investment?

Using income data to make an investment decision ***(Obj. 1)***

P11-2A Mainframe Manufacturing Corporation in the preceding problem holds significant promise for carving a niche in the computer peripherals industry, and a group of Canadian investors is considering purchasing Mainframe Manufacturing. Mainframe's common stock is currently selling for $52 per share.

Forbes magazine recently carried a story that Mainframe's income is bound to grow. It appears that the company can earn at least its current level of income for the indefinite future. Based on this information, the investors think that an appropriate investment capitalization rate for estimating the value of Mainframe's common stock is 5 percent. Any capitalization rate below 5% would overvalue the stock. How much will this belief lead them to offer for Mainframe Manufacturing? Will the existing stockholders of Mainframe be likely to accept this offer? Explain your answers.

Computing earnings per share and estimating the price of a stock ***(Obj. 1)***

P11-3A Pellegrini Construction's capital structure at December 31, 19X2, included 5,000 shares of $2.50 preferred stock and 130,000 shares of common stock. Common shares outstanding during 19X3 were 130,000 January through February; 119,000 during March; 121,000 April through October; and 128,000 during November and December. Income from continuing operations during 19X3 was $371,885. The company discontinued a segment of the business at a gain of $69,160, and an extraordinary item generated a gain of $49,510. The board of directors of Pellegrini Construction has restricted $280,000 of retained earnings for expansion of the company's office facilities.

Required

1. Compute Pellegrini's earnings per share. Start with income from continuing operations. Income and loss amounts are net of income tax.
2. Analysts believe Pellegrini can earn its current level of income for the indefinite future. Estimate the market price of a share of Pellegrini common stock at investment capitalization rates of 8, 10, and 12 percent. The formula for estimating the value of one share of stock uses earnings per share. Which estimate presumes an investment in Pellegrini is the most risky? How can you tell?

Preparing a corrected income statement, including comprehensive income ***(Obj. 1)***

P11-4A Justin Gilbert, accountant for The Software Connection, Inc., was injured in a baseball accident. Another employee prepared the following income statement for the fiscal year ended June 30, 19X4:

THE SOFTWARE CONNECTION, INC.
Income Statement
June 30, 19X4

Revenues and gains:		
Sales		$733,000
Foreign-currency translation adjustment—gain		11,000
Paid-in capital in excess of par—common		100,000
Total revenues and gains		844,000
Expenses and losses:		
Cost of goods sold	$383,000	
Selling expenses	103,000	
General expenses	74,000	
Sales returns	22,000	
Unrealized loss on available-for-sale investments	4,000	
Dividends paid	15,000	
Sales discounts	10,000	
Income tax expense	56,400	
Total expenses and losses		667,400
Income from operations		176,600

(*Continued*)

Other gains and losses:		
Extraordinary gain	$ 30,000	
Operating income on discontinued segment	25,000	
Loss on sale of discontinued operations	(40,000)	
Total other gains		15,000
Net income		$191,600
Earnings per share		$ 9.58

The individual amounts listed on the income statement are correct. However, some accounts are reported incorrectly, and one does not belong on the income statement at all. Also, income tax (40%) has not been applied to all appropriate figures. The Software Connection, Inc., issued 24,000 shares of common stock in 19X1 and held 4,000 shares as treasury stock during the fiscal year 19X4.

Required

Prepare a corrected statement of income (single-step, which lists all revenues together and all expenses together), including comprehensive income, for fiscal year 19X4; include earnings per share.

Accounting for a corporation's income tax ***(Obj. 2)***

P11-5A The accounting (not the income tax) records of Waterhouse Microfilms, Inc., provide the comparative income statement for 19X3 and 19X4:

	19X3	19X4
Total revenue	$680,000	$720,000
Expenses:		
Cost of goods sold	$290,000	$310,000
Operating expenses	180,000	190,000
Total expenses before tax	470,000	500,000
Pretax accounting income	$210,000	$220,000

Total revenue of 19X4 includes rent of $10,000 that was received late in 19X3. This rent is included in 19X4 total revenue because the rent was earned in 19X4. However, rent revenue that is collected in advance is included in taxable income when the cash is received. In calculating taxable income on the tax return, this rent revenue belongs in 19X3.

Also, the operating expenses of each year include depreciation of $40,000 computed under the straight-line method. In calculating taxable income on the tax return, Waterhouse uses the modified accelerated cost recovery system (MACRS). MACRS depreciation was $60,000 for 19X3 and $20,000 for 19X4.

Required

The corporate income tax rate is 35 percent.

1. Compute Waterhouse Microfilms' taxable income for each year.
2. Journalize the corporation's income taxes for each year.
3. Prepare the corporation's income statement for each year.

Using a statement of stockholders' equity ***(Obj. 3)***

P11-6A Shedlester, Inc., reported the following statement of stockholders' equity for the year ended June 30, 19X6:

SHEDLESTER, INC.
Statement of Stockholders' Equity
Year Ended June 30, 19X6

(In millions)	Common Stock	Additional Paid-in Capital	Retained Earnings	Treasury Stock	Total
Balance, July 1, 19X5	$173	$2,118	$1,706	$(18)	$3,979
Net income			520		520
Cash dividends			(117)		(117)
Issuance of stock (5,000,000 shares)	3	46			49
Stock dividend	18	272	(290)		—
Sale of treasury stock		5		11	16
Balance, June 30, 19X6	$194	$2,441	$1,819	$ (7)	$4,447

Required

Answer these questions about Shedlester's stockholders' equity transactions.

1. The income tax rate is 35 percent. How much income before income tax did Shedlester report on the income statement?
2. What is the par value of the company's common stock?
3. At what price per share did Shedlester issue its common stock during the year?
4. What was the cost of treasury stock sold during the year? What was the selling price of the treasury stock sold? What was the increase in total stockholders' equity?
5. Shedlester's statement of stockholders' equity lists the stock transactions in the order in which they occurred. What was the percentage of the stock dividend? Round to the nearest percentage.

Using the financial statement notes, segment data, and the audit report ***(Obj. 4, 5, 6)***

P11-7A This problem uses the financial statements and excerpts from the related notes of **Clayton Homes, Inc.,** which manufactures low-cost homes across the southern half of the United States. These statements are reproduced on pages 570–575. Working through this problem will increase your confidence in your ability to perform financial analysis. You may have to refer to preceding chapters to answer some of the questions. If so, the index at the end of the book will help you locate what you need.

Required

Using the financial statements and related notes of Clayton Homes, Inc., answer the following questions about the company and its operations during the year ended June 30, 1996 (fiscal year 1996):

CLAYTON HOMES, INC., AND SUBSIDIARIES
Consolidated Balance Sheets

(In thousands)	For the fiscal years ended June 30, 1996	1995
Assets		
Cash and cash equivalents	**$ 47,400**	$ 49,394
Receivables, principally installment contracts and residual interests, net of reserves for credit losses of $4,787 and $8,329, respectively and unamortized discount of $4,359 and $9,001, respectively	**402,039**	343,408
Inventories	**124,280**	88,455
Securities held-to-maturity, approximate market value of $19,774 and $20,193	**20,361**	20,361
Restricted cash and investments	**70,403**	66,214
Property, plant and equipment, net	**184,271**	166,048
Other assets	**37,596**	27,271
Total assets	**$886,350**	$761,151
Liabilities and Shareholders' Equity		
Accounts payable and accrued liabilities	**$ 91,064**	$ 63,949
Long-term debt	**30,290**	48,737
Deferred tax liability	**5,680**	9,382
Other liabilities	**109,127**	94,896
Total liabilities	**236,161**	216,964
Shareholders' equity		
Preferred stock, $.10 par value, authorized 1,000 shares, none issued	—	—
Common stock, $.10 par value, authorized 200,000 shares; issued 95,091 at June 30, 1996 and 94,463 at June 30, 1995	**9,509**	9,446
Additional paid-in capital	**174,642**	168,280
Retained earnings	**466,038**	366,461
Total shareholders' equity	**650,189**	544,187
Total liabilities and shareholders' equity	**$886,350**	$761,151

The accompanying notes (pages 572–575) are an integral part of these consolidated financial statements.

1. Note 1—Summary of Significant Accounting Policies—describes Clayton's receivables under two headings: Income Recognition and Installment Contract Receivables. Each sale of a Clayton home generates revenue of several thousand dollars. Clayton's receivables are installment contracts receivable that Clayton expects to collect over a period of years. What does Clayton do with its receivables? At June 30, 1996, how much cash did Clayton expect to collect on its installment contract receivables during the upcoming year? The answer is not $402,039,000.
2. What methods does Clayton use to determine the amounts to report for the three categories of Investment Securities: Held-to-maturity; Trading; and Available-for-Sale? Review Chapter 10 to determine whether Clayton is following GAAP in accounting for investments. At June 30, 1996, what was the amortized cost of Clayton's held-to-maturity securities? What was the market value of these securities?
3. Clayton's balance sheet reports only the net amount of Property, plant, and equipment. What were the cost, accumulated depreciation, and book value of Clayton's plant assets at June 30, 1996?
4. Study Note 5—Long-Term Debt. Journalize Clayton's 1996 payment of the 10% note payable that was due on June 1, 1998. There was no gain or loss on this transaction.
5. Note 5 indicates that Clayton's borrowing agreements place some restrictions on the company. The note indicates that Clayton must maintain a minimum "tangible net worth," which is another term for stockholders' equity. Why would lenders want a borrower to keep a certain minimum level of net worth?
6. Examine Note 11—Industry Segment Information. Compare the relationships between operating income and identifiable assets for the Manufactured Housing segment and for the Financial Services segment. Which segment looks more profitable on a percentage basis? Why do you think Clayton Homes keeps the other segment?
7. Who bears primary responsibility for Clayton Homes' financial statements? Which accounting firm audits the financial statements of Clayton Homes, Inc.? What responsibility do the auditors take for the financial statements? Does the audit include an examination of all of Clayton Homes' transactions? How can you tell?

Report of Independent Accountants

We have audited the accompanying consolidated balance sheets of Clayton Homes, Inc. and Subsidiaries as of June 30, 1996 and 1995, and the related consolidated statements of income, changes in shareholders' equity, and cash flows for each of the three years in the period ended June 30, 1996. These financial statements are the responsibility of the Company's management. Our responsibility is to express an opinion on these financial statements based on our audits.

We conducted our audits in accordance with generally accepted auditing standards. Those standards require that we plan and perform the audit to obtain reasonable assurance about whether the financial statements are free of material misstatement. An audit includes examining, on a test basis, evidence supporting the amounts and disclosures in the financial statements. An audit also includes assessing the accounting principles used and significant estimates made by management, as well as evaluating the overall financial statement presentation. We believe that our audits provide a reasonable basis for our opinion.

In our opinion, the financial statements referred to above present fairly, in all material respects, the consolidated financial position of Clayton Homes, Inc. and Subsidiaries as of June 30, 1996 and 1995, and the consolidated results of their operations and their cash flows for each of the three years in the period ended June 30, 1996 in conformity with generally accepted accounting principles.

As discussed in Note 1 to the consolidated financial statements, the Company changed its methods of accounting for securities and income taxes in 1995 and 1994, respectively.

Coopers & Lybrand LLP

Coopers & Lybrand L.L.P.
Knoxville, Tennessee
August 5, 1996

CLAYTON HOMES, INC., AND SUBSIDIARIES
Consolidated Statement of Income

(In thousands, except per share data)	For the fiscal years ended June 30, 1996	1995	1994
Revenues:			
Net sales	**$762,396**	$621,351	$510,153
Financial services	**115,987**	102,108	95,198
Other income	**50,358**	34,633	22,885
	928,741	758,092	628,236
Costs and expenses:			
Cost of sales	**521,200**	431,826	357,698
Selling, general and administrative	**236,188**	188,835	153,698
Financial services interest	**3,649**	5,533	8,196
	761,037	626,194	519,592
Operating income	**167,704**	131,898	108,644
Interest income (expense), net	**4,596**	3,902	(359)
Income before income taxes and cumulative effect of change in method of accounting	**172,300**	135,800	108,285
Provision for income taxes	**(65,500)**	(48,800)	(39,000)
Income before change in method of accounting	**106,800**	87,000	69,285
Change in method of accounting for income taxes	**—**	—	3,000
Net income	**$106,800**	$ 87,000	$ 72,285
Income per common share before change in method of accounting:			
Primary	**$ 1.12**	$ .92	$ .75
Fully diluted	**$ 1.12**	$ .92	$ .74
Cumulative effect of change in method of accounting per common share:			
Primary	**$ —**	$ —	$ .03
Fully diluted	**$ —**	$ —	$ .03
Net income per common share:			
Primary	**$ 1.12**	$ .92	$ .78
Fully diluted	**$ 1.12**	$ .92	$ .77
Average shares outstanding:			
Primary	**95,477**	94,903	92,061
Fully diluted	**95,477**	94,903	95,920

NOTE 1—SUMMARY OF SIGNIFICANT ACCOUNTING POLICIES

Consolidated Financial Statements

The consolidated financial statements include the accounts of Clayton Homes, Inc. (CHI) and its wholly-owned subsidiaries. CHI and its subsidiaries are collectively referred to as the Company. Clayton Homes, Inc. is a vertically-integrated manufactured housing company headquartered in Knoxville, Tennessee. Employing more than 5,400 people and operating in 28 states, the Company builds, sells, finances and insures manufactured homes, as well as owns and operates residential manufactured housing communities. Significant intercompany accounts and transactions have been eliminated in the financial statements. See Note 11 for information related to the Company's business segments.

Income Recognition

Sales to independent retailers of homes produced by CHI are recognized as revenue upon shipment. Retail sales are recognized when cash payment is received or, in the case of credit sales, which represent the majority of retail sales, when a down payment is received and the customer enters into an installment sales contract.

Most of these installment sales contracts, which are normally [collectible] over 36 to 180 months, are financed by Vanderbilt Mortgage and Finance, Inc. (VMF), the Company's mortgage banking subsidiary.

Installment Contract Receivables

Installment contract receivables originated or purchased by VMF are sold to investors or pledged as collateral to long-term lenders.

Installment contract receivables held for sale of $225,951,000 and $154,356,000 in 1996 and 1995, respectively, are included in Receivables and are carried at the lower of aggregate cost or market.

Estimated principal receipts under installment contract receivables for each of the five fiscal years subsequent to 1996 are as follows:

1997	$154,270,000
1998	18,412,000
1999	18,965,000
2000	17,395,000
2001	17,525,000

Most of the installment contract receivables are with borrowers in the east, south, and southwest portions of the United States and are collateralized by manufactured homes.

Interest income on installment contract receivables is recognized by a method which approximates the [effective] interest method. Service fee income is recognized as the service is performed.

Investment Securities

Investments in certain debt and equity securities are classified as either Held-to-Maturity (reported at amortized cost), Trading (reported at fair value with unrealized gains and losses included in earnings), or Available-for-Sale (reported at fair value with unrealized gains and losses excluded from earnings and reported as a separate component of shareholders' equity).

Inventories

New homes and raw materials are valued at the lower of cost, using the last-in, first-out (LIFO) method of inventory valuation, or market. Previously owned manufactured homes are valued at estimated wholesale prices, which are not in excess of net realizable value.

Property, Plant, and Equipment

Land and improvements, buildings, and furniture and equipment are valued at cost. Major renewals and improvements are capitalized while replacements, maintenance and repairs, which do not improve or extend the life of the respective assets, are expensed currently. When depreciable assets are sold or retired, the cost and related accumulated depreciation are removed from the accounts, and any gain or loss is included in earnings for the period. Depreciation is computed primarily by the straight-line method over the estimated useful lives of the respective assets.

NOTE 4—PROPERTY, PLANT, AND EQUIPMENT

Property, plant, and equipment at June 30, 1996, and 1995 are as follows:

(In thousands)	**1996**	**1995**
Land and improvements	**$115,647**	$108,968
Buildings	**88,749**	71,292
Furniture and equipment	**24,445**	19,679
	228,841	199,939
Less: accumulated depreciation and amortization	**(44,570)**	(33,891)
	$184,271	$166,048

Depreciation . . . was $11,163,000, $8,296,000, and $6,679,000 for each of the years ended June 30, 1996, 1995, and 1994, respectively.

NOTE 5—LONG-TERM DEBT

Long-term debt at June 30, 1996, and 1995 are summarized as follows:

(In thousands)	1996	1995
CHI		
10% note payable due June 1, 1998, extinguished in June 1996	—	$ 4,866
Other notes payable	**$ 153**	231
	153	5,097
VMF		
Debt collateralized by installment contract receivables:		
Demand note payable to Clayton Employees Savings Plan at prime, extinguished in 1996	—	3,000
Maturing in fiscal years through:		
1997 to 2004: weighted-average rate of 10.07% at June 30, 1996	**27,380**	33,264
1996 to 2005: 9.4% REMIC trust senior certificates	—	2,855
1997 to 2002: adjustable rates, weighted-average rate of 10.18% at June 30, 1996, weighted-average maximum rate 13.83% at June 30, 1996	**1,091**	2,147
1998 to 2001: adjustable rates, average rate of 7.79% at June 30, 1996, no maximum rate	**1,666**	2,374
	30,137	43,640
Total	**$30,290**	$48,737

Certain of the long-term debt have various covenants, which among other things, require a minimum tangible net worth and the maintenance of certain financial ratios.

NOTE 10—COMMITMENTS AND CONTINGENCIES

Leases

Certain operating properties are rented under non-cancelable operating leases that expire at various dates through 2009. Total rental expense under operating leases was $2,722,000 in 1996, $2,721,000 in 1995, and $2,159,000 in 1994. The following is a schedule of minimum rental commitments under non-cancelable operating leases, primarily for retail centers, in effect at June 30, 1996:

1997	$2,551,000
1998	2,080,000
1999	1,583,000
2000	1,098,000
2001	760,000
2002 and thereafter	1,754,000

NOTE 11—INDUSTRY SEGMENT INFORMATION

The Company operates in three major business segments: Manufactured Housing, Financial Services, and Communities. The Manufactured Housing segment is engaged in the production, wholesale, and retail sale of manufactured homes. Financial Services includes retail financing of manufactured homes and . . . insurance policies. Communities is engaged in marketing and management of manufactured housing communities.

Information concerning operations by industry segment follows:

(In thousands)	Manufactured Housing	Financial Services	Communities	Corporate	Total
1996					
Revenues	**$761,111**	**$ 99,443**	**$ 68,187**	**$ —**	**$928,741**
Intersegment income	**7,436**	**103**	**94**	**(7,633)**	**—**
Operating income	**89,504**	**62,600**	**15,600**	**—**	**167,704**
Identifiable assets	**197,938**	**493,622**	**142,331**	**52,459**	**886,350**
Depreciation and amortization	**6,671**	**—**	**4,492**	**—**	**11,163**
Capital expenditures	**16,483**	**—**	**24,346**	**—**	**40,829**

(Continued)

(In thousands)	Manufactured Housing	Financial Services	Communities	Corporate	Total
1995					
Revenues	$ 621,474	$ 88,749	$ 47,869	$ —	$ 758,092
Intersegment income	11,406	274	1,194	(12,874)	—
Operating income	67,898	54,800	9,200	—	131,898
Identifiable assets	176,632	413,072	122,408	49,039	761,151
Depreciation and amortization	5,132	—	3,164	—	8,296
Capital expenditures	21,933	—	22,529	—	44,462
1994					
Revenues	$ 510,329	$ 80,741	$ 37,166	$ —	$ 628,236
Intersegment income	19,630	—	1,224	(20,854)	—
Operating income	48,183	53,620	6,841	—	108,644
Identifiable assets	122,101	440,690	99,032	39,325	701,148
Depreciation and amortization	4,005	—	2,674	—	6,679

(GROUP B)

P11-1B The following information was taken from the records of CPI Manufacturing, Inc., at September 30, 19X6. CPI is a subcontractor that manufactures electronic control devices for elevators.

Preparing a complex income statement and reporting stockholders' equity on the balance sheet
(Obj. 1)

Cost of goods sold	$424,000	General expenses	$113,000
Cumulative effect of change in depreciation method (debit)	(3,000)	Preferred stock—5%, $40 par, 10,000 shares authorized, 5,000 shares issued	200,000
Loss on sales of plant assets	8,000		
Sales returns	9,000	Paid-in capital in excess of par—common	20,000
Income tax expense (saving):			
Continuing operations	72,000	Retained earnings, beginning, as originally reported	88,000
Discontinued segment:			
Operating loss	(6,000)	Selling expenses	136,000
Gain on sale	8,000	Common stock, $10 par, 25,000 shares authorized and issued	250,000
Extraordinary loss	(12,000)		
Cumulative effect of change in depreciation method	(1,000)	Sales revenue	860,000
Gain on sale of discontinued segment	20,000	Treasury stock, common (1,000 shares at cost)	11,000
Prior-period adjustment—debit to Retained Earnings	6,000	Dividends	35,000
		Interest revenue	4,000
Contributed capital from treasury stock transactions	7,000	Extraordinary loss	30,000
Sales discounts	18,000	Operating loss, discontinued segment	15,000
Interest expense	11,000	Loss on insurance settlement	12,000

Required

1. Prepare CPI Manufacturing's single-step income statement, which lists all revenues together and all expenses together, for the fiscal year ended September 30, 19X6. Include earnings per share data.
2. Evaluate income for the year ended September 30, 19X6, in terms of the outlook for 19X7. 19X6 was a typical year, and CPI's top managers hoped to earn income from continuing operations equal to 10% of net sales.
3. Prepare the stockholders' equity section of the balance sheet. It will be helpful to prepare a statement of retained earnings.
4. How will what you learned in this problem help you evaluate an investment?

P11-2B CPI Manufacturing, Inc., in the preceding problem holds significant promise for carving a niche in the electronic control device industry, and a group of Swiss investors is considering purchasing the company. CPI's common stock is currently selling for $41.50 per share.

Using income data to make an investment decision
(Obj. 1)

Business Week magazine recently carried a story that CPI's income is bound to grow. It appears that the company can earn at least its current level of income for the indefinite future. Based on this information, the investors think that an appropriate investment capitalization rate for estimating the value of CPI's common stock is 7 percent. Any capitalization rate below 7% would overvalue the stock. How much will this belief lead them to offer for CPI Manufacturing? Will the existing stockholders of CPI be likely to accept this offer? Explain your answers.

Computing earnings per share and estimating the price of a stock
(Obj. 1)

P11-3B The capital structure of Priest Air Conditioning, Inc., at December 31, 19X6, included 20,000 shares of $1.25 preferred stock and 44,000 shares of common stock. Common shares outstanding during 19X7 were 44,000 January through May, 50,000 June through August, and 60,500 September through December. Income from continuing operations during 19X7 was $81,100. The company discontinued a segment of the business at a gain of $6,630, and an extraordinary item generated a loss of $33,660. Priest's board of directors restricts $80,000 of retained earnings for contingencies.

Required

1. Compute Priest's earnings per share. Start with income from continuing operations. Income and loss amounts are net of income tax.
2. Analysts believe Priest can earn its current level of income for the indefinite future. Estimate the market price of a share of Priest common stock at investment capitalization rates of 8, 10, and 12 percent. The formula for estimating the value of one share of stock uses earnings per share. Which estimate presumes an investment in Priest stock is the most risky? How can you tell?

Preparing a corrected income statement, including comprehensive income
(Obj. 1)

P11-4B Mike Cassell, accountant for Santa Rosa Book Distributors, was injured in a skiing accident. Another employee prepared the accompanying income statement for the fiscal year ended December 31, 19X3.

The individual amounts listed on the income statement are correct. However, some accounts are reported incorrectly, and one does not belong on the income statement at all. Also, income tax (40%) has not been applied to all appropriate figures. Santa Rosa issued 52,000 shares of common stock in 19X1 and held 2,000 shares as treasury stock during 19X3.

SANTA ROSA BOOK DISTRIBUTORS
Income Statement
19X3

Revenue and gains:		
Sales		$362,000
Unrealized gain on available-for-sale investments		10,000
Paid-in capital in excess of par—common		80,000
Total revenues and gains		452,000
Expenses and losses:		
Cost of goods sold	$103,000	
Selling expenses	56,000	
General expenses	61,000	
Sales returns	11,000	
Dividends paid	7,000	
Sales discounts	6,000	
Income tax expense	50,000	
Total expenses and losses		294,000
Income from operations		158,000
Other gains and losses:		
Gain on sale of discontinued operations	$ 10,000	
Extraordinary flood loss	(20,000)	
Operating loss on discontinued segment	(13,000)	
Foreign-currency translation adjustment (loss)	(15,000)	
Total other losses		(38,000)
Net income		$120,000
Earnings per share		$ 2.40

Required

Prepare a corrected statement of income (single-step, which lists all revenues together and all expenses together), including comprehensive income, for 19X3; include earnings per share.

P11-5B The accounting (not the income tax) records of Vista Petroleum Corporation provide the following comparative income statement for 19X7 and 19X8:

Accounting for a corporation's income tax ***(Obj. 2)***

	19X7	19X8
Total revenue	$930,000	$990,000
Expenses:		
Cost of goods sold	$430,000	$460,000
Operating expenses	270,000	280,000
Total expenses before tax	700,000	740,000
Pretax accounting income	$230,000	$250,000

Total revenue of 19X8 includes revenue of $15,000 that was received late in 19X7. This revenue is included in 19X8 total revenue because it was earned in 19X8. However, revenue collected in advance is included in the taxable income of the year when the cash is received. In calculating taxable income on the tax return, this revenue belongs in 19X7.

Also, the operating expenses of each year include depreciation of $50,000 computed on the straight-line method. In calculating taxable income on the tax return, Vista uses the modified accelerated cost recovery system (MACRS). MACRS depreciation was $80,000 for 19X7 and $20,000 for 19X8.

Required

The corporate income tax rate is 35 percent.

1. Compute Vista Petroleum Corporation's taxable income for each year.
2. Journalize the corporation's income taxes for each year.
3. Prepare the corporation's income statement for each year.

P11-6B DenHerder, Inc., reported the following statement of stockholders' equity for the year ended October 31, 19X4:

Using a statement of stockholders' equity ***(Obj. 3)***

DENHERDER, INC.
Statement of Stockholders' Equity
Year Ended October 31, 19X4

(In millions)	Common Stock	Additional Paid-in Capital	Retained Earnings	Treasury Stock	Total
Balance, Nov. 1, 19X3	$427	$1,622	$904	$(117)	$2,836
Net income			336		336
Cash dividends			(194)		(194)
Issuance of stock (10,000,000 shares)	8	41			49
Stock dividend	22	113	(135)		—
Sale of treasury stock		9		19	28
Balance, Oct. 31, 19X4	$457	$1,785	$911	$ (98)	$3,055

Required

Answer these questions about DenHerder's stockholders' equity transactions.

1. The income tax rate is 40 percent. How much income before income tax did DenHerder, Inc., report on the income statement?
2. What is the par value of the company's common stock?
3. At what price per share did DenHerder issue its common stock during the year?
4. What was the cost of treasury stock sold during the year? What was the selling price of the treasury stock sold? What was the increase in total stockholders' equity?
5. DenHerder's statement lists the stock transactions in the order they occurred. What was the percentage of the stock dividends? Round to the nearest percentage.

P11-7B This problem uses the financial statements and excerpts from the related notes of **Clayton Homes, Inc.,** which appear on pages 570–575. Clayton Homes manufactures low-cost homes across the southern half of the United States. Working through this problem will increase your confidence in your ability to perform financial analysis. You may have to refer to preceding chapters to answer some of the questions. If so, the index at the end of the book will help you locate what you need.

Using the financial statement notes, segment data, and the audit report ***(Obj. 4, 5, 6)***

Required

After familiarizing yourself with the financial statements and related notes of Clayton Homes, Inc., answer the following questions about the company and its operations during the year ended June 30, 1996 (fiscal year 1996):

1. Note 1—Summary of Significant Accounting Policies—describes Clayton's receivables under two headings: Income Recognition and Installment Contract Receivables. Each sale of a Clayton home generates revenue of several thousand dollars. Clayton's receivables are installment contracts receivable that Clayton expects to collect over a period of years. How many years? What revenue on the income statement is the direct result of Clayton's Receivables? What is the standard name of this revenue? How much of this revenue did Clayton Homes earn during fiscal year 1996?
2. Can you tell by examining the income statement how much depreciation expense Clayton recorded during fiscal year 1996? Now examine Note 4, and you can answer the question. What expense on the income statement includes Clayton's depreciation?
3. Study Note 5—Long-Term Debt. During fiscal year 1996, Clayton paid off a 10% note payable that was scheduled to come due in 1998. Approximately how much annual interest expense for fiscal 1997 did Clayton avoid by paying off the note early?
4. Note 5 indicates that Clayton's borrowing agreements place some restrictions on the company. The note indicates that Clayton must maintain certain financial ratios. Name two such ratios and explain why lenders place these restrictions on borrowers.
5. Examine Note 10—Commitments and Contingencies. Clayton rents some properties under operating leases, which means that Clayton records no asset or liability under the rental agreement. (Review the Lease topic in Chapter 8 if necessary.) How much rent expense did Clayton record during fiscal year 1996? At June 30, 1996, how much in rent payments did Clayton expect to pay during the upcoming fiscal year?
6. Examine Note 11—Industry Segment Information. Compare the relationships between operating income and revenues for the Manufactured Housing segment and for the Financial Services segment. Which segment looks more profitable on a percentage basis? Why do you think Clayton Homes keeps the other segment of the business?
7. Which accounting firm audits the financial statements of Clayton Homes, Inc.? By what standard did the accountants perform the audit? By what standard did the auditors evaluate Clayton's accounting? Do the auditors believe Clayton Homes' financial statements can be relied upon? How can you tell?

EXTENDING YOUR KNOWLEDGE

DECISION CASE

Using the financial statement notes in investment analysis ***(Obj. 4)***

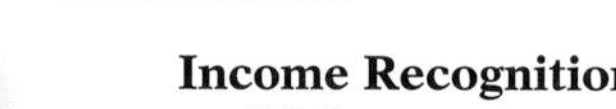

Clayton Homes, Inc., manufactures and sells houses across the southern part of the United States. Clayton's 1996 annual report includes Note 1—Summary of Significant Accounting Policies as follows:

> **Income Recognition**
>
> [S]ales are recognized when cash payment is received or, in the case of credit sales, which represent the majority of . . . sales, when a down payment is received and the customer enters into an installment sales contract. Most of these installment sales contracts . . . are normally [collectible] over 36 to 180 months . . . .
>
> Premium [revenue] from . . . insurance policies [sold to customers] are recognized as income over the terms of the contracts. [E]xpenses are matched to recognize profits over the life of the contracts.

Magnuson Home Builders, Inc., a competitor of Clayton, includes the following note in its 1996 Summary of Significant Accounting Policies:

> **Accounting Policies for Revenues**
>
> Sales are recognized when cash payment is received or, in the case of credit sales, which represent the majority of . . . sales, when the customer enters into an installment sales contract. Customer down payments on credit sales are rare. Most of these installment sales contracts are normally [collectible] over 36 to 180 months . . . .
>
> Premium revenue from insurance policies sold to customers are recognized when the customer signs an insurance contract. Expenses are recognized over the life of the insurance contracts.

Suppose you have decided to invest in the stock of a home builder and you've narrowed your choices to Clayton and Magnuson. Which company's policies of accounting for revenues do you favor? Why? Will their accounting policies affect your investment decision? If so, how? Mention specific accounts in the financial statements that will differ between the two companies.

ETHICAL ISSUE

The income statement of **General Cinema Corporation** reported the following results of operations for 19X2:

Earnings before income taxes, extraordinary gain, and cumulative effect of accounting change	$187,046
Income tax expense	72,947
Earnings before extraordinary gain and cumulative effect of accounting change	114,099
Extraordinary gain on elimination of debt, net	419,557
Cumulative effect of change in accounting for postretirement healthcare benefits, net	(39,196)
Net earnings	$494,460

Suppose General Cinema's management had reported the company's results of operations for 19X2 in this manner:

Earnings before income taxes and cumulative effect of accounting change	$886,307
Income tax expense	352,651
Earnings before cumulative effect of accounting change	533,656
Cumulative effect of change in accounting for postretirement healthcare benefits, net	(39,196)
Net earnings	$494,460

Required

1. Does it really matter how a company reports its operating results? Why? Who could be helped by management's action? Who could be hurt?
2. Suppose General Cinema's management has decided to report its operating results in the second manner. Evaluate the ethics of this decision.

FINANCIAL STATEMENT CASE

Using the financial statement notes for investment analysis ***(Obj. 1, 4, 5)***

The Lands' End financial statements and related notes, which appear in Appendix A at the end of the book, contain a wealth of information that is useful for evaluating Lands' End common stock as a potential investment.

Required

1. Track Lands' End's net sales, gross profit, income from operations, and net income for the three years presented on the income statement. Are the trends up or down? What factor explains the difference in the trends? As an investor, which trend do you regard as most important?
2. Examine Note 10—Consolidated Quarterly Analysis. Did Lands' End stock prices during fiscal years 1995 and 1996 follow the path of the company's sales or the path of its net income?
3. Estimate the year-end market price of a share of Lands' End stock by taking an average of the market high price and the market low price for the fourth quarter of fiscal year 1996. The formula for estimating the value (price) of one share of stock uses earnings per share. Assume it is reasonable to predict that Lands' End can earn its current level of net income for the indefinite future. What investment capitalization rate does the market seem to be using in pricing a share of Lands' End stock (use net income)? At its current level of income, does this rate suggest that analysts view Lands' End as a high-risk investment or a low-risk investment?
4. Suppose you purchased Lands' End stock at its lowest price during the first quarter of fiscal year 1995. Assume it is now the end of fiscal year 1996, and the market price of Lands' End stock is the high for the fourth quarter. What is your total return on your stock investment? How does this investment return correspond to the trend of Lands' End net income during this same period?

GROUP PROJECT

Select a company and research its business. Search the business press for articles about this company. Obtain its annual report by requesting it directly from the company or by using a copy from your college library or from *Moody's Industrial Manual* (the exercise will be most meaningful if you obtain copies from the company).

Required

1. Based on your group's analysis, come to class prepared to instruct the class on six interesting facts about the company that can be found in its financial statements and the related notes. Your group can mention only the obvious, such as net sales or total revenue, net income, total assets, total liabilities, total stockholders' equity, and dividends, in conjunction with other items. Once you use an obvious item, you may not use that item again.
2. The group should prepare a paper discussing the facts that it has uncovered. Limit the paper to two double-spaced, word-processed pages.

INTERNET EXERCISE

MAY DEPARTMENT STORES

Every industry has unique practices that are reflected in its financial statements. For example, the computer industry copes with declining inventory prices, and agribusiness has strong seasonal fluctuations. The retailing industry is no exception. A careful examination of a company's financial statements reveals the nature of the activities unique to that industry.

The May Department Stores operate in the highly competitive retailing market in which consumer tastes can change quickly. A close examination of May's financial statements reveals how the company is performing and how it is positioned for the future.

Required

1. Go to **http://www.maycompany.com/,** the home page for May Department Stores. This Web site provides a brief look at the stores that comprise May Department Stores, a college recruiting center, and financial information about the company.
2. Financial information is found in **Information About May** and **Current News Releases.** Answer the following questions about May's financial position and operating performance.
   a. Why does May's fiscal year end on a date other than December 31?
   b. What items are included in May's income statement (statement of operations) following Income From Continuing Operations?
   c. In evaluating May's performance, would you prefer to focus on Net Income or on Income From Continuing Operations? Why?
   d. Did May's sales growth come from opening new stores or from increasing store-to-store sales?
   e. What are the three largest assets on May's balance sheet? How do these assets relate to the retailing industry?
   f. Examine May's quarterly income statements. Are the company's sales seasonal? How can you tell?

12

Preparing and Using the Statement of Cash Flows

Learning Objectives

After studying this chapter, you should be able to

1. Identify the purposes of the statement of cash flows
2. Distinguish among operating, investing, and financing activities
3. Prepare a statement of cash flows by the direct method
4. Use the financial statements to compute the cash effects of a wide variety of business transactions
5. Prepare a statement of cash flows by the indirect method

W. T. Grant Company
Statements of Cash Flows
Years Ended January 31,

	(In thousands) 19X3	19X2
Cash flows from operating activities:		
1 Cash receipts from customers	$1,579,320	$1,317,218
2 Cash receipts from other revenues	10,057	8,924
3 Cash payments to suppliers and employees	(1,683,760)	(1,336,428)
4 Cash payments for interest	(21,127)	(16,452)
5 Cash payments for taxes	(8,459)	(8,143)
6 Other, net	9,704	7,964
7 Net cash inflow (outflow) from operating activities	(114,265)	(26,917)
Cash flows from investing activities:		
8 Acquisition of property, plant, and equipment	$ (26,250)	$ (25,918)
9 Investments in securities	(2,040)	(5,951)
10 Other, net	2,149	(46)
11 Net cash inflow (outflow) from investing activities	(26,141)	(31,915)
Cash flows from financing activities:		
12 New borrowing	$ 152,451	$ 100,000
13 Issuance of common stock	3,666	9,944
14 Retirement of debt	(1,760)	(13,823)
15 Payment of dividends	(21,141)	(21,139)
16 Purchase of treasury stock	(11,466)	—
17 Retirement of preferred stock	(252)	(308)
18 Net cash inflow (outflow) from financing activities	121,498	74,674
19 Increase (decrease) in cash	$ (18,908)	$ 15,842
20 Cash balance, beginning of year	49,851	34,009
21 Cash balance, end of year	$ 30,943	$ 49,851

"The bankruptcy of W. T. Grant Company forever changed the way investors analyze accounting data—and the information that companies report to the public."

—TODD STEPHENS, FINANCIAL EDITOR

The classic case of **W. T. Grant Company** forever changed the way investors analyze accounting data—and the information that companies report to the public. W. T. Grant was once one of the leading retailers in the United States, a serious rival to **Kmart, Target,** and other discount chains. Grant's income statement reported rising profits as the company slid into bankruptcy. What went wrong? Despite the company's profitability, Grant's operations simply did not generate enough cash to pay the bills. If anyone had analyzed Grant's cash flows, the cash shortage would have been crystal clear.

Examine the company's statements of cash flows on page 582, which have been reconstructed for 19X2 and 19X3. Notice the downward trend of cash flows from operating activities—a net cash *outflow* of $114 million in 19X3 (line 7). Cash receipts from customers (line 1) were not even as high as cash payments to suppliers and employees (line 3). Grant's situation was like a lemonade stand losing 10 cents on every glass of lemonade and hoping to make up the difference with high sales volume. The cash-flow statement shows that W. T. Grant's sales were draining cash, little by little. The only thing keeping the company afloat was borrowing (see cash flows from financing activities, line 12). Borrowing of such magnitude can continue only so long. Sooner or later, the company would go bankrupt, and it did.

Prior to W. T. Grant's bankruptcy, companies were not required to include a statement of cash flows in the annual report. Grant's failure rippled through the business community, with the result that cash-flow analysis has taken on new importance. Investors, creditors, and the accounting profession realized that net income is *not* the only measure of success in business. After all, a company does not pay the bills with net income—it pays bills with cash. And now, as we've seen throughout this text, the statement of cash flows is a basic financial statement on a par with the income statement and the balance sheet.

In preceding chapters we have included cash-flow analysis as it related to the topics covered: receivables, inventory, plant assets, long-term debt, and so on. But we have not yet discussed the statement of cash flows in its entirety. We do so in this chapter. Our goals are to round out your introduction to cash-flow analysis and to show how to prepare the statement of cash flows. We begin by explaining the statement format preferred by the Financial Accounting Standards Board. It is very clear and is thus called the *direct approach.* We end the chapter with the more common format of the statement of cash flows, the *indirect approach.* By the time you have worked through this chapter, you will feel more confident in your ability to analyze the cash flows of any company you might encounter.

We learned in Chapter 1 (Exhibit 1-11) that the statement of cash flows is one of the four required financial statements.

The statement of cash flows, a required financial statement, reports where cash came from and how it was spent. Like the other two major financial reports—the income statement and the balance sheet—the statement of cash flows enables investors and creditors to make informed decisions about a company. The income statement of W. T. Grant Company presented one picture of the company: relatively high net income. The cash-flow statement gave a different view: not enough cash. This example underscores the challenge of financial analysis—that a company's signals may point in different directions. Astute investors and creditors know what to look for; increasingly, they are focusing on cash flows.

The Statement of Cash Flows: Basic Concepts

The balance sheet reports the company's cash balance at the end of the period. By examining balance sheets from two consecutive periods, you can tell whether cash increased or decreased during the period. However, the balance sheet does not indicate *why* the cash balance changed. The income statement reports revenues, expenses, and net income—clues about the sources and uses of cash—but it does not tell *why* cash increased or decreased.

The **statement of cash flows** reports the entity's **cash flows** (cash receipts and cash payments) during the period—where cash came from and how it was spent. It explains the *causes* of the change in the cash balance. This information cannot be learned solely from other financial statements. The statement of cash flows covers a span of time and therefore is dated "For the Year Ended XXX" or "For the Month Ended XXX." Exhibit 12-1 illustrates the timing of the statements.

EXHIBIT 12-1
Timing of the Financial Statements

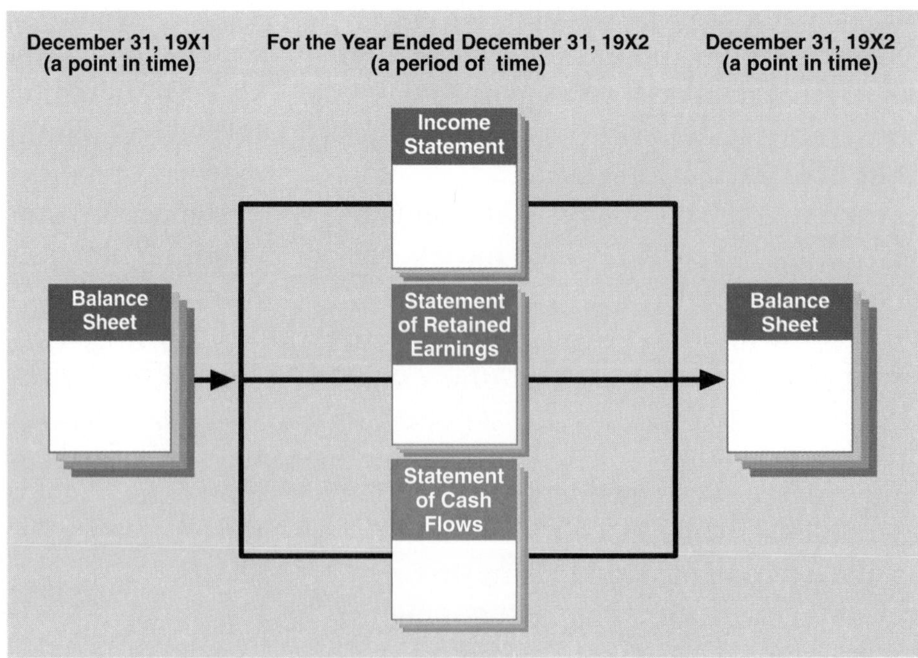

Overview of the Statement of Cash Flows

Objective 1

Identify the purposes of the statement of cash flows

The statement of cash flows is designed to fulfill the following purposes:

1. *To predict future cash flows.* Cash, not reported accounting income, pays the bills. The experience of W. T. Grant Company illustrates this fact. In many cases, past cash receipts and disbursements are a reasonably good predictor of future cash receipts and disbursements.

2. *To evaluate management decisions.* If managers make wise investment decisions, their businesses prosper. If they make unwise investments, the businesses suffer. The statement of cash flows reports the company's investment in plant assets and thus gives investors and creditors cash-flow information for evaluating managers' decisions. A classic example is **Montgomery Ward's** decision shortly after World War II *not* to expand the business. Montgomery Ward's top management expected a recession and decided to play it safe and conserve cash until the U.S. economy settled down after the war. In contrast, **Sears, Roebuck** predicted a strong economy and went full speed ahead. Sears invested heavily in new stores, and Montgomery Ward fell significantly behind Sears. Investors can analyze cash-flow statements to see which businesses are expanding and which are cutting back. It is clear from W. T. Grant's statement of cash flows (page 582) that the company was investing much less in new facilities (line 8, $26 million in 19X3) than it was borrowing (line 12, $152 million).

3. *To determine the company's ability to pay dividends to stockholders and interest and principal to creditors.* Stockholders are interested in receiving dividends on their investments. Creditors want to receive their interest and principal amounts on time. The statement of cash flows helps investors and creditors predict whether the business can make these payments.

4. *To show the relationship of net income to changes in the business's cash.* Usually, cash and net income move together. High levels of income tend to lead to increases in cash, and vice versa. However, a company's cash balance can decrease when net income is high, and cash can increase when income is low. The failures of companies such as W. T. Grant, which was earning net income but had insufficient cash, have pointed to the need for cash-flow information.

Cash and Cash Equivalents

On a statement of cash flows, *Cash* has a broader meaning than just cash on hand and cash in the bank. It includes **cash equivalents,** which are highly liquid short-term investments that can be converted into cash with little delay. Because their liquidity is one reason for holding these investments, they are treated as cash. Examples of cash equivalents are money-market investments and investments in U.S. Government Treasury bills. Businesses invest their extra cash in these types of liquid assets rather than let cash remain idle. Throughout this chapter, the term *cash* refers to cash and cash equivalents.

Operating, Investing, and Financing Activities

Objective 2

Distinguish among operating, investing, and financing activities

A business may be evaluated in terms of three types of business activities. After the business is up and running, *operations* are the most important activity, followed by *investing activities* and *financing activities.* Investing activities are generally more important than financing activities because *what* a company invests in is usually more important than *how* the company finances the acquisition.

The statement of cash flows in Exhibit 12-2 on page 586 shows how cash receipts and disbursements are divided into operating activities, investing activities, and financing activities for **Anchor Corporation,** a small manufacturer of glass products. As Exhibit 12-2 illustrates, each set of activities includes both cash inflows (receipts) and cash outflows (payments). Outflows are shown in parentheses to indicate that payments must be subtracted. Each section of the statement reports a net cash inflow or a net cash outflow.

Operating activities create revenues and expenses in the entity's major line of business. Therefore, operating activities affect the income statement, which reports the accrual-basis effects of operating activities. The statement of cash flows reports their impact on cash. The largest cash inflow from operations is the collection of cash from customers. Smaller inflows are receipts of interest on loans and dividends on stock investments. The operating cash outflows include payments to suppliers and to employees and payments for interest and taxes. Exhibit 12-2 shows that Anchor's net cash inflow from operating activities is $68,000. A large positive operating cash flow is a good sign. *In the long run, operations must be the main source of a business's cash.*

Operating Activities Are Related to the Transactions That Make Up Net Income.[1]

Cash flows from operating activities require analysis of each revenue and expense on the income statement, along with the related current asset or current liability from the balance sheet.

EXHIBIT 12-2
Statement of Cash Flows (Direct Method for Operating Activities)

ANCHOR CORPORATION
Statement of Cash Flows
For the Year Ended December 31, 19X2

	(In thousands)	
Cash flows from operating activities:		
Receipts:		
Collections from customers	$ 271	
Interest received on notes receivable	10	
Dividends received on investments in stock	9	
Total cash receipts		$290
Payments:		
To suppliers	$(133)	
To employees	(58)	
For interest	(16)	
For income tax	(15)	
Total cash payments		(222)
Net cash inflow from operating activities		68
Cash flows from investing activities:		
Acquisition of plant assets	$(306)	
Loan to another company	(11)	
Proceeds from sale of plant assets	62	
Net cash outflow from investing activities		(255)
Cash flows from financing activities:		
Proceeds from issuance of common stock	$ 101	
Proceeds from issuance of long-term debt	94	
Payment of long-term debt	(11)	
Payment of dividends	(17)	
Net cash inflow from financing activities		167
Net decrease in cash		**$(20)**
Cash balance, December 31, 19X1		42
Cash balance, December 31, 19X2		$ 22

[1]The authors thank Alfonso Oddo for suggesting this display.

Investing activities increase and decrease the long-term assets available to the business. A purchase or sale of a plant asset such as land, a building, or equipment is an investing activity, as is the purchase or sale of an investment in the stock or bonds of another company. Investing activities on the statement of cash flows include more than the buying and selling of assets that are classified as investments on the balance sheet. Making a loan is an investing activity because the loan creates a receivable for the lender, and collecting on the loan is also reported as an investing activity on the statement of cash flows. The acquisition of plant assets dominates Anchor Corporation's investing activities, which produce a net cash outflow of $255,000.

Investing Activities Require Analysis of the Long-Term Asset Accounts.

Investments in plant assets lay the foundation for future operations. A company that invests in plant and equipment appears stronger than one that is selling off its plant assets. Why? The latter company may have to sell income-producing assets to pay the bills. Its outlook is bleak.

Financing activities obtain from investors and creditors the cash needed to launch and sustain the business. Financing activities include issuing stock, borrowing money by issuing notes and bonds payable, buying or selling treasury stock, and making payments to the stockholders—dividends and purchases of treasury stock. Payments to the creditors include *principal* payments only. The payment of *interest* is an operating activity. Financing activities of Anchor Corporation brought in net cash of $167,000. One thing to watch among financing activities is whether the business is borrowing heavily. Excessive borrowing has been the downfall of many companies.

Financing Activities Require Analysis of the Long-Term Liability Accounts and the Owners' Equity Accounts.

Overall, Anchor's cash decreased by $20,000 during 19X2. The company began the year with cash of $42,000 and ended with $22,000. Each of these categories of activities includes both cash receipts and cash disbursements, as shown in Exhibit 12-3 on page 588. The exhibit lists the more common cash receipts and cash disbursements that appear on the statement of cash flows.

STOP & THINK Examine W. T. Grant's statement of cash flows on page 582, and reread the chapter opening story. Which of the following statements explains W. T. Grant's cash outflow from operations? Give your reason.

- **a.** W. T. Grant's cash drain resulted from investing too heavily in new properties.
- **b.** Payments to suppliers and employees exceeded cash receipts from customers.
- **c.** W. T. Grant did not borrow enough money to finance operations during the year.
- **d.** Net income was too low.

Answer: The statement of cash flows reports that for both 19X3 and 19X2, cash payments to suppliers employees exceeded cash receipts from customers, so the answer is b.

Interest and Dividends

You may be puzzled by the listing of receipts of interest and dividends as operating activities. After all, these cash receipts result from investing activities. Interest comes from investments in loans, and dividends come from investments in stock. Equally puzzling is listing the payment of interest as part of operations. Interest expense results from borrowing money—a financing activity. After much debate, the FASB decided to include all these items as part of operations. Why? Mainly because they affect the computation of net income. Interest revenue and

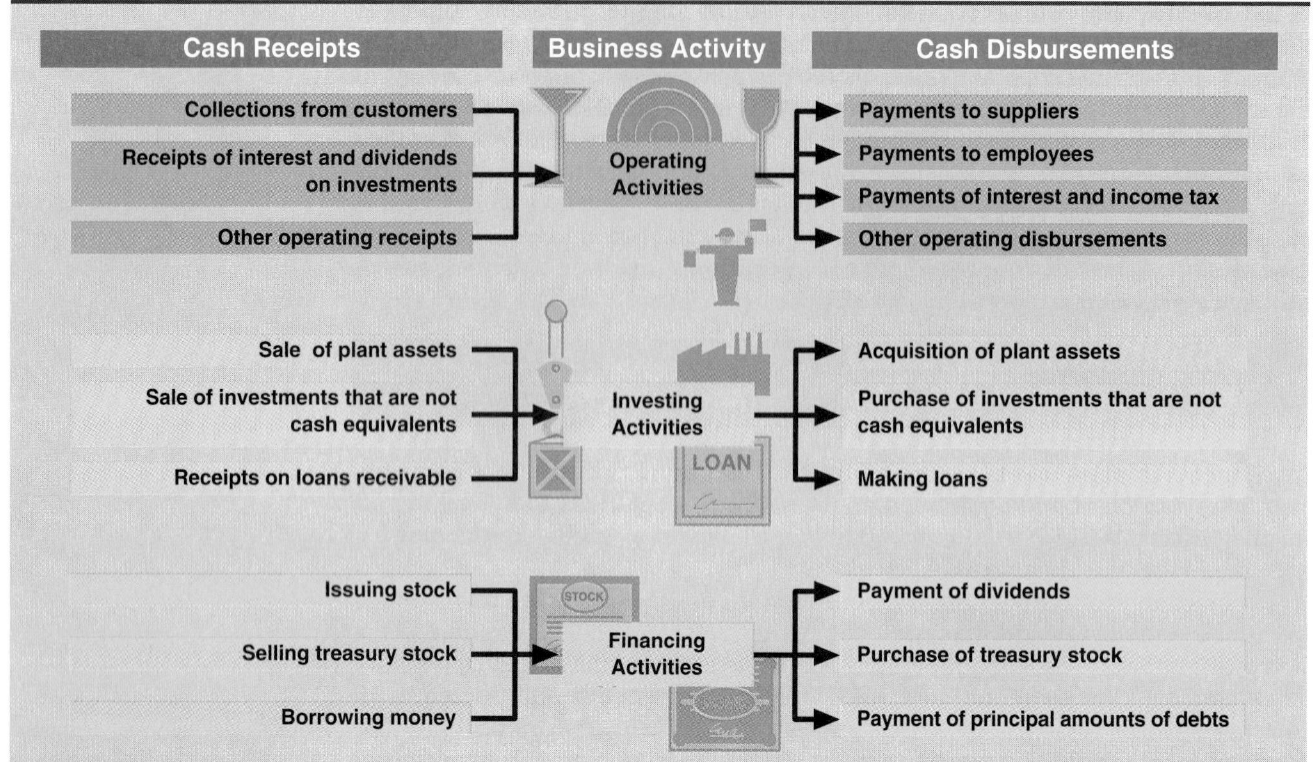

EXHIBIT 12-3
Cash Receipts and Disbursements on the Statement of Cash Flows

dividend revenue increase net income, and interest expense decreases income. Therefore, cash receipts of interest and dividends and cash payments of interest are reported as operating activities on the cash-flow statement.

In contrast, dividend payments are not listed among the operating activities of Exhibit 12-3. Why? Because they do not enter the computation of income. Dividend payments are reported in the financing activities section of the cash-flow statement because they go to the entity's owners, who finance the business by holding its stock.

Format of the Statement of Cash Flows

In *FASB Statement No. 95* (1987), the FASB approved two formats for reporting cash flows from operating activities. The **direct method,** illustrated in Exhibit 12-2, lists cash receipts from specific operating activities and cash payments for each major operating activity. *FASB Statement No. 95* expresses a clear preference for the direct method because it reports where cash came from and how it was spent on operating activities. The direct method is required for some insurance companies, and most governmental entities use the direct method.

In keeping with GAAP, companies' accounting systems are designed for accrual, rather than cash-basis, accounting. These systems make it easy for companies to compute cash flows from operating activities by a shortcut method. The **indirect method** starts with net income and reconciles to cash flows from operating activities. Exhibit 12-4 gives an overview of the process of converting from accrual-basis income to the cash basis for the statement of cash flows.

The direct method is easier to understand, it provides more information for decision making, and the FASB prefers it. By learning how to compute the cash-flow amounts for the direct method, you will be learning something far more important: how to determine the cash effects of business transactions. This is a critical skill for analyzing financial statements because accrual-basis accounting often hides cash effects. Then, after you have a firm foundation in cash-flow

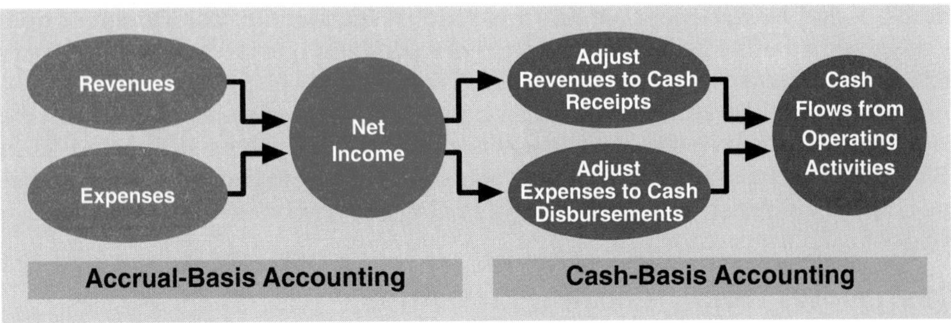

EXHIBIT 12-4
Converting from the Accrual Basis to the Cash Basis for the Statement of Cash Flows

analysis, it is easier to learn the indirect method. But if your instructor chooses to focus solely on the indirect method, you can study that method, which begins on page 605, with a minimum of references to earlier sections of this chapter.

The two basic ways of presenting the statement of cash flows arrive at the same subtotals for operating activities, investing activities, financing activities, and the net change in cash for the period. They differ only in the manner of showing the cash flows from *operating activities.*

Preparing the Statement of Cash Flows: The Direct Method

Objective 3

Prepare a statement of cash flows by the direct method

Let's see how to prepare the statement of cash flows by the direct method illustrated in Exhibit 12-2. (This is the format of the statement of cash flows that we have presented for W. T. Grant Company on page 582.) Suppose Anchor Corporation has assembled the summary of 19X2 transactions in Exhibit 12-5. These summary transactions give the data for both the income statement and the statement of cash flows. Some transactions affect one statement, some the other. For example, sales are reported on the income statement, but cash collections appear

EXHIBIT 12-5
Summary of Anchor Corporation's 19X2 Transactions

Operating Activities:
1. Sales on credit, $284,000
*2. Collections from customers, $271,000
3. Interest revenue on notes receivable, $12,000
*4. Collection of interest receivable, $10,000
*5. Cash receipt of dividend revenue on investments in stock, $9,000
6. Cost of goods sold, $150,000
7. Purchases of inventory on credit, $147,000
*8. Payments to suppliers, $133,000
9. Salary and wage expense, $56,000
*10. Payments of salary and wages, $58,000
11. Depreciation expense, $18,000
12. Other operating expense, $17,000
*13. Interest expense and payments, $16,000
*14. Income tax expense and payments, $15,000

Investing Activities:
*15. Cash payments to acquire plant assets, $306,000
*16. Loan to another company, $11,000
*17. Proceeds from sale of plant assets, $62,000, including $8,000 gain

Financing Activities:
*18. Proceeds from issuance of common stock, $101,000
*19. Proceeds from issuance of long-term debt, $94,000
*20. Payment of long-term debt, $11,000
*21. Declaration and payment of cash dividends, $17,000

*Indicates a cash-flow transaction to be reported on the statement of cash flows.

on the cash-flow statement. Other transactions, such as the cash receipt of dividend revenue, affect both. *The statement of cash flows reports only those transactions with cash effects* (those with an asterisk in Exhibit 12-5).

To prepare the statement of cash flows, follow these steps: (1) Identify the activities that increased cash or decreased cash—those items with asterisks in Exhibit 12-5; (2) classify each cash increase and each cash decrease as an operating activity, an investing activity, or a financing activity; and (3) identify the cash effect of each transaction.

Cash Flows from Operating Activities

Operating cash flows are listed first because they are the largest and most important source of cash for most businesses. The failure of a company's operations to generate the bulk of its cash inflows for an extended period may signal trouble. Exhibit 12-2 shows that Anchor is sound; its operating activities were the largest source of cash receipts, $290,000.

Cash Collections from Customers Cash sales bring in cash immediately. However, credit sales increase Accounts Receivable but not Cash. Receipts of cash on account are a separate transaction, and only cash receipts are reported on the statement of cash flows. "Collections from customers" in Exhibit 12-2 include both cash sales and collections of accounts receivable from credit sales—$271,000.

Cash Receipts of Interest Interest revenue is earned on notes receivable. The income statement reports interest revenue. As the clock ticks, interest accrues, but cash interest is received only on specific dates. Only the cash receipts of interest appear on the statement of cash flows—$10,000 in Exhibit 12-2.

Cash Receipts of Dividends Dividends are earned on investments in stock. Dividend revenue is ordinarily recorded as an income-statement item when cash is received. This cash receipt is reported on the statement of cash flows—$9,000 in Exhibit 12-2. (Dividends *received* are part of operating activities, but dividends *paid* are a financing activity.)

Payments to Suppliers Payments to suppliers include all cash disbursements for inventory and operating expenses except employee compensation, interest, and income taxes. *Suppliers* are those entities that provide the business with its inventory and essential services. For example, a clothing store's payments to Levi Strauss, Liz Claiborne, and Reebok are listed as payments to suppliers. A grocery store makes payments to suppliers such as Nabisco, Campbell's Soup, and Coca-Cola. Other suppliers provide advertising, utility, and other services that are classified as operating expenses. The payments to suppliers category *excludes* payments to employees, payments for interest, and payments for income taxes because these are separate categories of operating cash payments. In Exhibit 12-2, Anchor Corporation reports payments to suppliers of $133,000.

Payments to Employees This category includes disbursements for salaries, wages, commissions, and other forms of employee compensation. Accrued amounts are excluded because they have not yet been paid. The income statement reports the expense, including accrued amounts. The statement of cash flows in Exhibit 12-2 reports only the cash payments ($58,000).

Payments for Interest Expense and Income Tax Expense These cash payments are reported separately from the other expenses. Interest payments show the cash cost of borrowing money. Excessive borrowing can lead to a large amount of interest payments that could result in financial trouble. **Macy's** and **Donald Trump's** casinos are examples of businesses that have faced problems because of too much borrowing. Income tax payments also deserve emphasis because of their significant amount. In the Anchor Corporation example, interest and income tax expenses equal the cash payments. Therefore, the same amount appears on the income statement and the statement of cash flows. In practice, this is rarely the case. Year-end accruals and other transactions usually cause the expense and cash payment amounts to differ. The cash-flow statement reports the cash payments for interest ($16,000) and income tax ($15,000).

Macy's and Donald Trump's casinos are examples of businesses that have faced problems because of too much borrowing.

Depreciation, Depletion, and Amortization Expense These expenses are *not* listed on the statement of cash flows in Exhibit 12-2 because they do not affect cash. For example, depreciation is recorded by debiting the expense and crediting Accumulated Depreciation. No debit or credit to the Cash account occurs.

Cash Flows from Investing Activities

Many analysts regard investing as a critical activity because a company's investments determine its future course. Large purchases of plant assets signal expansion, which is usually a good sign. Low levels of investing activities over a lengthy period indicate that the business is not replenishing its capital assets. Knowing these cash flows helps investors and creditors evaluate the direction that managers are charting for the business.

Cash Payments to Acquire Plant Assets and Investments, and Loans to Other Companies These cash payments are similar because they acquire a noncash asset. The first investing activity reported by Anchor Corporation on its statement of cash flows in Exhibit 12-2 is the purchase of plant assets, such as land, buildings, and equipment ($306,000). In the second transaction, Anchor makes an $11,000 loan and obtains a note receivable. These are investing activities because the company is investing in assets for use in the business rather than for resale. These transactions have no effect on revenues or expenses and thus are not reported on the income statement. Another transaction in this category—not shown in Exhibit 12-2—is a purchase of an investment in the stocks or bonds of another company.

Proceeds from the Sale of Plant Assets and Investments, and the Collections of Loans These transactions are the opposites of acquisitions of plant assets and investments, and making loans. They are cash receipts from investment transactions.

The sale of the plant assets needs explanation. The statement of cash flows in Exhibit 12-2 reports that Anchor Corporation received $62,000 cash on the sale of plant assets. The income statement shows an $8,000 gain on this transaction. What is the appropriate amount to show on the cash-flow statement? It is $62,000, the cash proceeds from the sale. If we assume that Anchor sold equipment that cost $64,000 and had accumulated depreciation of $10,000, the following journal entry would record the sale:

Cash	62,000	
Accumulated Depreciation	10,000	
Equipment		64,000
Gain on Sale of Plant Assets (from income statement)		8,000

The analysis indicates that the book value of the equipment was $54,000 ($64,000 – $10,000). However, the book value of the asset sold is not reported on the statement of cash flows. Only the cash proceeds of $62,000 are reported on the statement. For the income statement, only the gain is reported. Because a gain occurred, you may wonder why this cash receipt is not reported as part of operations. Operations consist of buying and selling merchandise or rendering services to earn revenue. Investing activities are the acquisition and disposition of assets used in operations. Therefore, the FASB views the sale of plant assets and the sale of investments as cash inflows from investing activities.

STOP & THINK Suppose Scott Paper Company sold timber land at a $35 million gain. The land cost Scott Paper $9 million when it was purchased in 1969. What amount will Scott Paper Company report as an investing activity on the statement of cash flows?

Answer: Cash receipt of $44 million (cost of $9 million plus the gain of $35 million).

Investors and creditors are often critical of a company that sells large amounts of its plant assets. Such sales may signal an emergency. Because of budget cuts in the defense industry, the defense contractor **Grumman Corp.** recently shed almost one-third of its facilities worldwide. The closing of Grumman's aircraft manufacturing plant on Long Island, laboratories, and other facilities—plus massive employee layoffs—promised to save the company $600 million in operating expenses. Despite the downsizing, Grumman could no longer compete and was taken over by **Martin Marietta.**

Because of budget cuts in the defense industry, the defense contractor Grumman Corp. recently shed almost one-third of its facilities worldwide.

In other situations, selling off fixed assets may be good news about the company if it is getting rid of an unprofitable division. Whether sales of plant assets are good news or bad news should be evaluated in light of a company's operating and financing characteristics.

Cash Flows from Financing Activities

Cash flows from financing activities include the following:

PROCEEDS FROM ISSUANCE OF STOCK AND DEBT Readers of financial statements want to know how the entity obtains its financing. Issuing stock (preferred and common) and debt are two common ways to finance operations. In Exhibit 12-2, Anchor Corporation reports that it issued common stock for cash of $101,000 and long-term debt for $94,000.

PAYMENT OF DEBT AND PURCHASES OF THE COMPANY'S OWN STOCK The payment of debt decreases Cash, which is the opposite effect of borrowing money. Anchor Corporation reports long-term debt payments of $11,000. Other transactions in this category are purchases of treasury stock and payments to retire the company's stock.

PAYMENT OF CASH DIVIDENDS The payment of cash dividends decreases Cash and is therefore reported as a cash payment, as illustrated by Anchor's $17,000 payment in Exhibit 12-2. A dividend in another form—a stock dividend, for example—has no effect on Cash and is *not* reported on the cash-flow statement.

When the statement of cash flows became a required financial statement, computerized accounting systems were programmed to generate this statement as easily as they do the balance sheet and the income statement. Consider the direct method for preparing the statement of cash flows. The amounts for the operating section can be obtained by drawing cash inflows and outflows (grouped by related revenue and expense category) from the posted accounts. Specifically, the cash receipts postings to Accounts Receivable provide the information necessary to show Cash Collections from Customers. The computer adds the monthly postings to reach the yearly total. All other cash flows for operating activities, as well as cash flows for financing and investing activities, are handled similarly.

Mid-Chapter

SUMMARY PROBLEM FOR YOUR REVIEW

Drexel Corporation's accounting records include the following information for the year ended June 30, 19X8:

a. Salary expense, $104,000
b. Interest revenue, $8,000
c. Proceeds from issuance of common stock, $31,000
d. Declaration and payment of cash dividends, $22,000
e. Collection of interest receivable, $7,000
f. Payments of salaries, $110,000
g. Credit sales, $358,000
h. Loan to another company, $42,000
i. Proceeds from sale of plant assets, $18,000, including $1,000 loss
j. Collections from customers, $369,000
k. Cash receipt of dividend revenue on stock investments, $3,000
l. Payments to suppliers, $319,000
m. Cash sales, $92,000
n. Depreciation expense, $32,000
o. Proceeds from issuance of short-term debt, $38,000
p. Payments of long-term debt, $57,000
q. Interest expense and payments, $11,000
r. Loan collections, $51,000
s. Proceeds from sale of investments, $22,000, including $13,000 gain
t. Amortization expense, $5,000
u. Purchases of inventory on credit, $297,000
v. Income tax expense and payments, $16,000
w. Cash payments to acquire plant assets, $83,000
x. Cost of goods sold, $284,000
y. Cash balance: June 30, 19X7—$83,000
June 30, 19X8—$54,000

Required

Prepare Drexel Corporation's income statement and statement of cash flows for the year ended June 30, 19X8. Follow the cash-flow statement format of Exhibit 12-2 and the single-step format for the income statement (grouping all revenues together and all expenses together, as shown in Exhibit 12-5).

ANSWER

DREXEL CORPORATION
Income Statement
For the Year Ended June 30, 19X8

Item (Reference Letter)		(In thousands)	
	Revenue and gains:		
(g, m)	Sales revenue ($358 + $92)	$450	
(s)	Gain on sale of investments	13	
(b)	Interest revenue	8	
(k)	Dividend revenue	3	
	Total revenues and gains		$474
	Expenses and losses:		
(x)	Cost of goods sold	$284	
(a)	Salary expense	104	
(n)	Depreciation expense	32	
(v)	Income tax expense	16	
(q)	Interest expense	11	
(t)	Amortization expense	5	
(i)	Loss on sale of plant assets	1	
	Total expenses		453
	Net income		$ 21

Item (Reference Letter)	DREXEL CORPORATION Statement of Cash Flows For the Year Ended June 30, 19X8	(In thousands)	
	Cash flows from operating activities:		
	Receipts:		
(j, m)	Collections from customers ($369 + $92)	$ 461	
(e)	Interest received on notes receivable	7	
(k)	Dividends received on investments in stock	3	
	Total cash receipts		$ 471
	Payments:		
(l)	To suppliers	$ (319)	
(f)	To employees	(110)	
(q)	For interest	(11)	
(v)	For income tax	(16)	
	Total cash payments		(456)
	Net cash inflow from operating activities		15
	Cash flows from investing activities:		
(w)	Acquisition of plant assets	$ (83)	
(h)	Loan to another company	(42)	
(s)	Proceeds from sale of investments	22	
(i)	Proceeds from sale of plant assets	18	
(r)	Collection of loans	51	
	Net cash outflow from investing activities		(34)
	Cash flows from financing activities:		
(o)	Proceeds from issuance of short-term debt	$ 38	
(c)	Proceeds from issuance of common stock	31	
(p)	Payments of long-term debt	(57)	
(d)	Dividends declared and paid	(22)	
	Net cash outflow from financing activities		(10)
	Net decrease in cash		$ (29)
(y)	Cash balance, June 30, 19X7		83
(y)	Cash balance, June 30, 19X8		$ 54

Computing Individual Amounts for the Statement of Cash Flows

Objective 4

Use the financial statements to compute the cash effects of a wide variety of business transactions

How do accountants compute the amounts for the statement of cash flows? Many accountants prepare the statement of cash flows from the income statement amounts and from *changes* in the related balance sheet accounts. For the *operating* cash-flow amounts, the adjustment process follows this basic approach:

Revenue or expense from the income statement → **Adjustment for the change in the related balance sheet account(s)** → **Amount for the statement of cash flows**

Accountants label this the T-account approach.[2] Learning to analyze T-accounts in this manner is one of the most useful accounting skills you will acquire. It will enable you to identify the cash effects of a wide variety of transactions. It will also strengthen your grasp of accrual-basis accounting.

[2]The chapter appendix covers the work sheet approach to preparing the statement of cash flows.

The following discussions use Anchor Corporation's income statement in Exhibit 12-6 and comparative balance sheet in Exhibit 12-7, as well as the cash-flow statement in Exhibit 12-2. For continuity, trace the $22,000 and $42,000 cash amounts on the balance sheet in Exhibit 12-7 to the bottom part of the cash-flow statement in Exhibit 12-2.

EXHIBIT 12-6
Income Statement

ANCHOR CORPORATION
Income Statement
For the Year Ended December 31, 19X2

	(In thousands)	
Revenues and gains:		
Sales revenue	$284	
Interest revenue	12	
Dividend revenue	9	
Gain on sale of plant assets	8	
Total revenues and gains		$313
Expenses:		
Cost of goods sold	$150	
Salary and wage expense	56	
Depreciation expense	18	
Other operating expense	17	
Interest expense	16	
Income tax expense	15	
Total expenses		272
Net income		$ 41

EXHIBIT 12-7
Comparative Balance Sheet

ANCHOR CORPORATION
Comparative Balance Sheet
December 31, 19X2 and 19X1

(In thousands)	19X2	19X1	Increase (Decrease)	
Assets				
Current:				
Cash	$ 22	$ 42	$ (20)	
Accounts receivable	93	80	13	Changes in current assets—**Operating**
Interest receivable	3	1	2	
Inventory	135	138	(3)	
Prepaid expenses	8	7	1	
Long-term receivable from another company	11	—	11	Changes in noncurrent assets—**Investing**
Plant assets, net of depreciation	453	219	234	
Total	$725	$487	$238	
Liabilities				
Current:				
Accounts payable	$ 91	$ 57	$ 34	Changes in current liabilities—**Operating**
Salary and wage payable	4	6	(2)	
Accrued liabilities	1	3	(2)	
Long-term debt	160	77	83	Changes in long-term liabilities and paid-in capital accounts—**Financing**
Stockholders' Equity				
Common stock	359	258	101	
Retained earnings	110	86	24	Change due to net income—**Operating** and change due to dividends—**Financing**
Total	$725	$487	$238	

Computing the Cash Amounts of Operating Activities

COMPUTING CASH COLLECTIONS FROM CUSTOMERS Collections can be computed by converting sales revenue (an accrual-basis amount) to the cash basis. Anchor Corporation's income statement (Exhibit 12-6) reports sales of $284,000. Exhibit 12-7 shows that Accounts Receivable increased from $80,000 at the beginning of the year to $93,000 at year end, a $13,000 increase. Based on those amounts, Cash Collections equals $271,000, as shown in the Accounts Receivable T-account:

Accounts Receivable

Beginning balance	80,000		
Sales	284,000	Collections	271,000
Ending balance	93,000		

Accounts Receivable

Beginning balance	+	Sales	−	Collections	=	Ending balance				
$80,000	+	$284,000	−	X	=	$93,000				
				−X	=	$93,000	−	$80,000	−	$284,000
				X	=	$271,000				

Another explanation: Because Accounts Receivable increased by $13,000, we can say that Anchor Corporation received $13,000 less cash than sales revenue for the period. A decrease in Accounts Receivable would mean that the company received more cash than the amount of sales revenue. This computation is summarized as the first item in Exhibit 12-8.

All collections of receivables are computed in the same way. In our example, Anchor Corporation's income statement, Exhibit 12-6, reports interest revenue of $12,000. Interest Receivable's balance in Exhibit 12-7 increased $2,000. Cash receipts of interest must be $10,000 (Interest Revenue of $12,000 minus the $2,000 increase in Interest Receivable). Exhibit 12-8 summarizes this computation.

COMPUTING PAYMENTS TO SUPPLIERS This computation includes two parts, payments for inventory and payments for expenses other than interest and income tax.

Payments for inventory are computed by converting cost of goods sold to the cash basis. We accomplish this by analyzing Cost of Goods Sold from the income statement and Accounts Payable from the balance sheet. Many companies also purchase inventory on short-term notes payable. In that case, we would analyze Short-Term Notes Payable in the same manner as Accounts Payable. The computation of Anchor Corporation's cash payments for inventory is given by this analysis of the T-accounts (again, we are using Exhibits 12-6 and 12-7 for our numbers):

Cost of Goods Sold

Beg. inventory	138,000	End. inventory	135,000
Purchases	147,000		
Cost of goods sold	150,000		

Accounts Payable

Payments for inventory	113,000	Beg. bal.	57,000
		Purchases	147,000
		End bal.	91,000

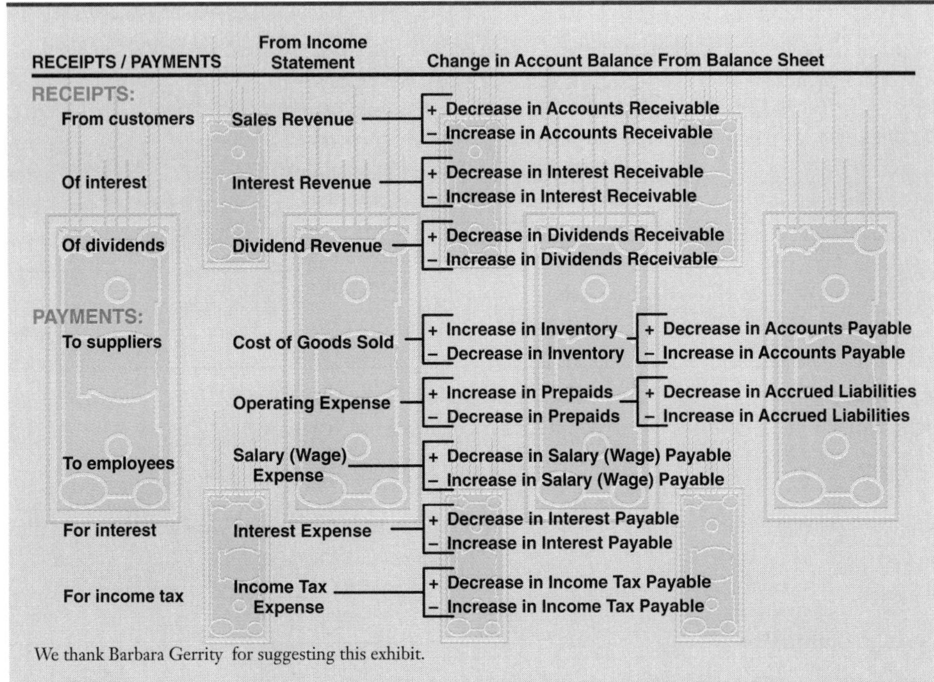

Concept Highlight

EXHIBIT 12-8
Direct Method of Determining Cash Flows from Operating Activities

Cost of Goods Sold

Beginning inventory	+	Purchases	−	Ending inventory	=	Cost of goods sold
$138,000	+	X	−	$135,000	=	$150,000
		X			=	$150,000 − $138,000 + $135,000
		X			=	$147,000

Now we can insert the figure for purchases into Accounts Payable to determine the amount of cash paid for inventory, as follows:

Accounts Payable

Beginning balance	+	Purchases	−	Payments for inventory	=	Ending balance
$57,000	+	$147,000	−	X	=	$91,000
				−X	=	$91,000 − $57,000 − $147,000
				X	=	$113,000

Beginning and ending inventory amounts are taken from the balance sheet, and Cost of Goods Sold from the income statement. We must solve for purchases, which affect both Cost of Goods Sold and Accounts Payable. *Payments for inventory* show up as a debit to Accounts Payable.

By another explanation, payments for inventory appear in the Accounts Payable account. But we must first work through Cost of Goods Sold and the change in the Inventory account, as summarized in Exhibit 12-8 under Payments to Suppliers.

Payments to suppliers ($133,000 in Exhibit 12-2) equal the sum of payments for inventory ($113,000) plus payments for operating expenses ($20,000), as explained next.

Computing Payments for Operating Expenses Payments for operating expenses other than interest and income tax can be computed as plug figures by analyzing Prepaid Expenses and Accrued Liabilities, as follows for Anchor Corporation (again, all numbers are taken from Exhibits 12-6 and 12-7):

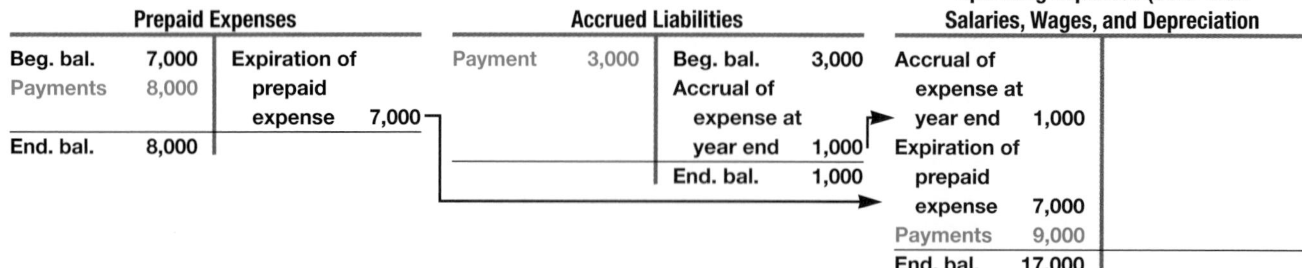

Prepaid Expenses			
Beg. bal.	7,000	Expiration of prepaid expense	7,000
Payments	8,000		
End. bal.	8,000		

Accrued Liabilities			
Payment	3,000	Beg. bal.	3,000
		Accrual of expense at year end	1,000
		End. bal.	1,000

Operating Expenses (other than Salaries, Wages, and Depreciation		
Accrual of expense at year end	1,000	
Expiration of prepaid expense	7,000	
Payments	9,000	
End. bal.	17,000	

Prepaid Expenses

Beginning balance	+ Payments	−	Expiration of prepaid expense	=	Ending balance
$7,000	+ X	−	$7,000	=	$8,000
	X			=	$8,000 − $7,000 + $7,000
	X			=	$8,000

Accrued Liabilities

Beginning balance	+	Accrual of expense at year end	−	Payments	=	Ending balance
$3,000	+	$1,000	−	X	=	$1,000
				−X	=	$1,000 − $3,000 − $1,000
				X	=	$3,000

Operating Expenses

Accrual of expense at year end	+	Expiration of prepaid expense	+	Payments	=	Ending balance
$1,000	+	7,000	+	X	=	$17,000
				X	=	$17,000 − $1,000 − $7,000
				X	=	$9,000

Total payments for operating expenses = $20,000
$8,000 + $3,000 + $9,000 = $20,000

By another explanation: Increases in prepaid expenses require cash payments, and decreases indicate that payments were less than expenses. Decreases in accrued liabilities can occur only from cash payments, and increases mean that cash was *not* paid. Exhibit 12-8 shows a streamlined version of this computation.

COMPUTING PAYMENTS TO EMPLOYEES The company may have separate accounts for salaries, wages, and other forms of cash compensation to employees. Payments to employees can be computed conveniently by combining them into one account. Anchor's calculation adjusts Salary and Wage Expense for the change in Salary and Wage Payable, as shown in the Salary and Wage Payable T-account:

Salary and Wage Payable			
		Beginning balance	6,000
Payments to employees	58,000	Salary and wage expense	56,000
		Ending balance	4,000

Salary and Wage Payable

Beginning balance	+	Salary and wage expense	−	Payments	=	Ending balance				
$6,000	+	$56,000	−	X	=	$4,000				
				−X	=	$4,000	−	$6,000	−	$56,000
				X	=	$58,000				

Exhibit 12-8 summarizes this computation under Payments to Employees.

Computing Payments of Interest and Income Taxes In our example, the expense and payment amounts are the same for each expense. Therefore, no analysis is required to determine the payment amount. If the expense and the payment differ, the payment can be computed by analyzing the related liability account. The payment computation follows the pattern illustrated for payments to employees; Exhibit 12-8 summarizes the procedure.

Computing the Cash Amounts of Investing Activities

Investing activities affect asset accounts, such as Plant Assets, Investments, and Notes Receivable. The cash amounts of investing activities can be identified by analyzing those accounts. Most data for the computations are taken directly from the income statement and the beginning and ending balance sheets. Other amounts come from analysis of accounts in the ledger.

Computing Acquisitions and Sales of Plant Assets Most companies have separate accounts for Land, Buildings, Equipment, and other plant assets. It is helpful to combine these accounts into a single summary for computing the cash flows from acquisitions and sales of these assets. Also, we subtract accumulated depreciation from the assets' cost and get a net figure for plant assets. This approach allows us to work with a single plant asset account as opposed to a large number of plant asset and related accumulated depreciation accounts.

To illustrate, observe that Anchor Corporation's balance sheet (Exhibit 12-7) reports beginning plant assets, net of depreciation, of $219,000 and an ending net amount of $453,000. The income statement (Exhibit 12-6) shows depreciation expense of $18,000 and an $8,000 gain on sale of plant assets. Further, the acquisitions of plant assets total $306,000 (see Exhibit 12-2). How much are the proceeds from the sale of plant assets? First, we must determine the book value of plant assets sold from the Plant Assets T-account, as follows:

Plant Assets (net)

Beginning balance	219,000	Depreciation	18,000
Acquisitions	306,000	Book value of assets sold	54,000
Ending balance	453,000		

Plant Assets (net)

Beginning balance	+	Acquisitions	−	Depreciation	−	Book value of assets sold	=	Ending balance
$219,000	+	$306,000	−	$18,000	−	X	=	$453,000
						−X	=	$453,000 − $219,000 − $306,000 + $18,000
						X	=	$54,000

Now we can compute the sale proceeds as follows:

Book value of assets sold	+	Gain	−	Loss	=	Sale proceeds
$54,000	+	$8,000	−	$0	=	$62,000

Trace the sale proceeds of $62,000 to the statement of cash flows in Exhibit 12-2. If the sale resulted in a loss of $3,000, the sale proceeds would be $51,000 ($54,000 – $3,000), and the statement would report $51,000 as a cash receipt from this investing activity.

LEARNING TIP Proceeds from the sale of an asset need not equal the asset's book value. Remember:

Book value + Gain = Proceeds

Book value – Loss = Proceeds

The book-value information comes from the balance sheet; the gain or loss comes from the income statement.

COMPUTING ACQUISITIONS AND SALES OF ASSETS CLASSIFIED AS INVESTMENTS, AND LOANS AND THEIR COLLECTIONS Accountants use a separate category of assets for investments in stocks, bonds, and other types of assets. The cash amounts of transactions involving these assets can be computed in the manner illustrated for plant assets. Investments are easier to analyze, however, because there is no depreciation to account for, as shown in the following T-account:

Investments

Beginning balance*	XXX		
Purchases**	XXX	Cost of investments sold	XXX
Ending balance*	XXX		

*From balance sheet.
**From statement of cash flows.

Investments (amounts assumed for illustration only):

Beginning balance	+ Purchases	– Cost of investments sold	= Ending balance
$100,000	+ $50,000	– X	= $140,000
		–X	= $140,000 – $100,000 – $50,000
		X	= $10,000

Loan transactions follow the pattern described on page 596 for collections from customers. New loans cause a debit to a receivable and an outflow of cash. Collections increase cash and cause a credit to the receivable:

Loans and Notes Receivable

Beginning balance*	XXX		
New loans made**	XXX	Collections	XXX
Ending balance*	XXX		

*From balance sheet.
**From statement of cash flows.

Loans and Notes Receivable (amounts assumed for illustration only):

Beginning balance	+ New loans made	– Collections	= Ending balance
$90,000	+ $10,000	– X	= $30,000
		–X	= $30,000 – $90,000 – $10,000
		X	= $70,000

RECEIPTS

From sale of plant assets	Beginning plant assets (net) + Acquisition cost − Depreciation − Book value of assets sold = Ending plant assets (net)
	Cash received = Book values of assets sold + Gain on sale or − Loss on sale
From sale of investments	Beginning investments + Purchase cost of investments − Cost of investments sold = Ending investments
	Cash received = Cost of investments sold + Gain on sale or − Loss on sale
From collection of loans and notes receivable	Beginning loans or notes receivable + New loans made − Collections = Ending loans or notes receivable

PAYMENTS

For acquisition of plant assets	Beginning plant assets (net) + Acquisition cost − Depreciation − Book value of assets sold = Ending plant assets (net)
For purchase of investments	Beginning investments + Purchase cost of investments − Cost of investments sold = Ending investments
For new loans made	Beginning loans or notes receivable + New loans made − Collections = Ending loans or notes receivable

EXHIBIT 12-9
Computation of Cash Flows from Investing Activities

Exhibit 12-9 summarizes the computation of cash flows from investing activities. We must solve for the dollar amount of each item highlighted in color. For example, to determine the amount of cash received from the sale of plant assets, we must first solve for the book value of the assets sold. Then, the book value of the assets sold, plus a gain or minus a loss on the sale, equals the amount of cash received from the sale of the assets.

Computing the Cash Amounts of Financing Activities

Financing activities affect liability and stockholders' equity accounts, such as Notes Payable, Bonds Payable, Long-Term Debt, Common Stock, Paid-in Capital in Excess of Par, and Retained Earnings. The cash amounts of financing activities can be computed by analyzing these accounts.

COMPUTING ISSUANCES AND PAYMENTS OF LONG-TERM DEBT The beginning and ending balances of Long-Term Debt, Notes Payable, or Bonds Payable are taken from the balance sheet. If either the amount of new issuances or the amount of the payments is known, the other amount can be computed. New debt issuances total $94,000 (see Exhibit 12-2). The computation of debt payments follows from analysis of the Long-Term Debt T-account, using amounts from Anchor Corporation's balance sheet, Exhibit 12-7:

Long-Term Debt

		Beginning balance	77,000
Payments	11,000	Issuance of new debt	94,000
		Ending balance	160,000

Long-Term Debt

Beginning balance	+	Issuance of new debt	−	Payments of debt	=	Ending balance				
$77,000	+	$94,000	−	X	=	$160,000				
				−X	=	$160,000	−	$77,000	−	$94,000
				X	=	$11,000				

COMPUTING ISSUANCES AND RETIREMENTS OF STOCK AND PURCHASES AND SALES OF TREASURY STOCK The cash effects of these financing activities can be determined by analyzing the various stock accounts. For example, the amount of a new issuance of common stock is determined by combining the Common Stock and any related Capital in Excess of Par account. It is convenient to work with a single summary account for stock as we do for plant assets. Using data from Exhibits 12-2 and 12-7, we have

Common Stock

		Beginning balance	258,000
Retirements of stock	0	Issuance of new stock	101,000
		Ending balance	359,000

Common Stock

Beginning balance	+	Issuance of new stock	−	Retirements of stock	=	Ending balance				
$258,000	+	$101,000	−	X	=	$359,000				
				−X	=	$359,000	−	$258,000	−	$101,000
				X	=	0				

Cash flows affecting Treasury Stock, a debit balance account, can be analyzed by using the Treasury Stock T-account:

Treasury Stock

Beginning balance	XXX		
Purchases of treasury stock	XXX	Cost of treasury stock sold	XXX
Ending balance	XXX		

Treasury Stock (amounts assumed for illustration only)

Beginning balance	+	Purchase of treasury stock	−	Cost of treasury stock sold	=	Ending balance				
$16,000	+	$3,000	−	X	=	$5,000				
				−X	=	$5,000	−	$16,000	−	$3,000
				X	=	$14,000				

If either the purchase amount or the cost of treasury stock sold is known, the other amount can be computed. For a sale of treasury stock, the amount to report on the cash-flow statement is the sale proceeds. Suppose a sale brought in cash that was $2,000 less than the $14,000 cost of the treasury stock sold. In this case, the statement of cash flows would report a cash receipt of $12,000 ($14,000 – $2,000).

COMPUTING DIVIDEND PAYMENTS If the amount of the dividends is not given elsewhere (for example, in a statement of retained earnings), it can be computed as follows:

Retained Earnings

Dividend		Beg. bal.	86,000
declarations	17,000	Net income	41,000
		End. bal.	110,000

Dividends Payable

		Beg. bal. (assumed)	0
Dividend payments	17,000	Dividend declarations	17,000
		End. bal. (assumed)	0

First, we compute dividend declarations by analyzing the Retained Earnings T-account. Then we solve for dividend payments with the Dividends Payable

RECEIPTS	
From issuance of long-term debt	Beginning long-term debt + Cash received from issuance of long-term debt − Payment of debt = Ending long-term debt
From issuance of stock	Beginning stock + Cash received from issuance of new stock − Payments to retire stock = Ending stock
From sale of treasury stock	Beginning treasury stock + Purchase cost of treasury stock − Cost of treasury stock sold = Ending treasury stock
	Cash received = Cost of treasury stock sold + Extra amount of sale above cost or – amount of cost in excess of sale amount
PAYMENTS	
Of long-term debt	Beginning long-term debt + Cash received from issuance of long-term debt − Payment of debt = Ending long-term debt
To retire stock	Beginning stock + Cash received from issuance of new stock − Payments to retire stock = Ending stock
To purchase treasury stock	Beginning treasury stock + Purchase cost of treasury stock − Cost of treasury stock sold = Ending treasury stock
For dividends	Beginning retained earnings + Net income − Dividend declarations = Ending retained earnings
	Beginning dividends payable + Dividend declarations − Dividend payments = Ending dividends payable

Concept Highlight

EXHIBIT 12-10
Computation of Cash Flows from Financing Activities

T-account. Anchor Corporation has no Dividends Payable account, so dividend payments are the same as declarations. The following computations show how to determine the amount of Anchor Corporation's dividend payments.

Retained Earnings

Beginning balance	+	**Net income**	−	**Dividend declarations**	=	**Ending balance**
$86,000	+	**$41,000**	−	**X**	=	**$110,000**
				−X	=	**$110,000 − $86,000 − $41,000**
				X	=	$17,000

Dividends Payable

Beginning balance	+	**Dividend declarations**	−	**Dividend payments**	=	**Ending balance**
$0	+	**$17,000**	−	**X**	=	**$0**
				−X	=	**$0 − $17,000 − $0**
				X	=	$17,000

Exhibit 12-10 summarizes the computation of cash flows from financing activities. The color highlights indicate amounts that must be computed. For example, cash receipts from issuance of long-term debt can be computed from the equation given.

Noncash Investing and Financing Activities

Companies make investments that do not require cash. They also obtain financing other than cash. Our examples thus far have included none of these transactions. Now suppose that Anchor Corporation issued no-par common stock valued at $320,000 to acquire a warehouse. Anchor would journalize this transaction as follows:

Warehouse Building	320,000	
Common Stock		320,000

This transaction would not be reported on the cash-flow statement because Anchor paid no cash. But the importance of the investment in the warehouse and the financing aspect of issuing stock require that the transaction be reported. Noncash investing and financing activities like this transaction are reported in a separate schedule that accompanies the statement of cash flows. Exhibit 12-11 illustrates how to report noncash investing and financing activities (all amounts are assumed). This information is required in a schedule immediately after any cash-flow statement or in a note.

EXHIBIT 12-11
Noncash Investing and Financing Activities (in thousands; all amounts assumed for illustration only)

Noncash Investing and Financing Activities:	
Acquisition of building by issuing common stock	$320
Acquisition of land by issuing note payable	72
Payment of long-term debt by transferring investments to the creditor	104
Acquisition of equipment by issuing short-term note payable	37
Total noncash investing and financing activities	$533

Reconciling Net Income to Net Cash Flow from Operating Activities

The FASB requires companies that format operating activities by the direct method to report a reconciliation from net income to net cash inflow (or outflow) from operating activities. The reconciliation shows how the company's net income is related to net cash flow from operating activities. Exhibit 12-12 shows the reconciliation for Anchor Corporation.

The end result—net cash inflow from operating activities of $68,000—is the same as the result we derived earlier under the *direct* method (see Exhibit 12-2). The reconciliation is also the same as the *indirect* method of computing operating cash flows. We now turn to the indirect method.

EXHIBIT 12-12
Reconciliation of Net Income to Net Cash Inflow from Operating Activities

ANCHOR CORPORATION
Reconciliation of Net Income to Net Cash Inflow from Operating Activities

		(In thousands)
Net income		$41
Add (subtract) items that affect net income and cash flow differently:		
Depreciation	$ 18	
Gain on sale of plant assets	(8)	
Increase in accounts receivable	(13)	
Increase in interest receivable	(2)	
Decrease in inventory	3	
Increase in prepaid expenses	(1)	
Increase in accounts payable	34	
Decrease in salary and wage payable	(2)	
Decrease in accrued liabilities	(2)	27
Net cash inflow from operating activities		$68

Preparing the Statement of Cash Flows: The Indirect Method

Objective 5

Prepare a statement of cash flows by the indirect method

An alternative to the direct method of computing cash flows from *operating* activities is the *indirect method,* or the **reconciliation method,** as shown in Exhibit 12-12. This method starts with net income and shows the reconciliation from net income to operating cash flows. For example, the consolidated cash-flow statement of the **Washington Post Company** lists first "Net income" and then "Adjustments to reconcile net income to net cash provided by operating activities." The indirect method shows the link between net income and cash flow from operations better than the direct method. That is why the Washington Post Company, which publishes the *Washington Post* and *Newsweek* and owns several television stations, chooses the indirect method over the direct method. In fact, 585 companies (97.5%) of a 600-firm survey *(Accounting Trends and Techniques, 1996)* use the indirect method even though the FASB recommends the direct method. The main drawback of the indirect method is that it does not report the detailed operating cash flows—collections from customers and other cash receipts, payments to suppliers, payments to employees, and payments for interest and taxes.

These two methods (direct and indirect) of preparing the cash-flow statement affect only the operating activities section of the statement. No difference exists in the reporting of investing activities or financing activities.

Exhibit 12-13 is Anchor Corporation's cash-flow statement prepared by the indirect method. Only the operating section of the statement differs from the

EXHIBIT 12-13
Statement of Cash Flows—Indirect Method for Operating Activities

ANCHOR CORPORATION
Statement of Cash Flows
For the Year Ended December 31, 19X2

			(In thousands)	
	Cash flows from operating activities:			
	Net income			$ 41
	Add (subtract) items that affect net income and cash flow differently:			
Ⓐ	Depreciation		$ 18	
Ⓑ	Gain on sale of plant assets		(8)	
Ⓒ	Increase in accounts receivable		(13)	
Ⓒ	Increase in interest receivable		(2)	
Ⓒ	Decrease in inventory		3	
Ⓒ	Increase in prepaid expenses		(1)	
Ⓒ	Increase in accounts payable		34	
Ⓒ	Decrease in salary and wage payable		(2)	
Ⓒ	Decrease in accrued liabilities		(2)	27
	Net cash inflow from operating activities			$ 68
From Exhibit 12-2	**Cash flows from investing activities:**			
	Acquisition of plant assets		$(306)	
	Loan to another company		(11)	
	Proceeds from sale of plant assets		62	
	Net cash outflow from investing activities			$(255)
	Cash flows from financing activities:			
	Proceeds from issuance of common stock		$ 101	
	Proceeds from issuance of long-term debt		94	
	Payment of long-term debt		(11)	
	Payment of dividends		(17)	
	Net cash inflow from financing activities			167
	Net decrease in cash			$ (20)
	Cash balance, December 31, 19X1			42
	Cash balance, December 31, 19X2			$ 22

direct method format in Exhibit 12-2. The new items are keyed to their explanations, which are discussed in the following text. One reason companies prefer the indirect method is its ease of preparation from the income statement and the beginning and ending balance sheets. For ease of reference, we repeat Anchor Corporation's income statement and balance sheet here as Exhibits 12-14 and 12-15.

EXHIBIT 12-14
Income Statement (repeated from Exhibit 12-6)

ANCHOR CORPORATION
Income Statement
For the Year Ended December 31, 19X2

	(In thousands)	
Revenues and gains:		
Sales revenue	$284	
Interest revenue	12	
Dividend revenue	9	
Gain on sale of plant assets	8	
Total revenues and gains		$313
Expenses:		
Cost of goods sold	$150	
Salary and wage expense	56	
Depreciation expense	18	
Other operating expense	17	
Interest expense	16	
Income tax expense	15	
Total expenses		272
Net income		$ 41

EXHIBIT 12-15
Comparative Balance Sheet (repeated from Exhibit 12-7)

ANCHOR CORPORATION
Comparative Balance Sheet
December 31, 19X2 and 19X1

(In thousands)	19X2	19X1	Increase (Decrease)
Assets			
Current:			
Cash	$ 22	$ 42	$(20)
Accounts receivable	93	80	13
Interest receivable	3	1	2
Inventory	135	138	(3)
Prepaid expenses	8	7	1
Long-term receivable from another company	11	—	11
Plant assets, net of depreciation	453	219	234
Total	$725	$487	$238
Liabilities			
Current:			
Accounts payable	$ 91	$ 57	$ 34
Salary and wage payable	4	6	(2)
Accrued liabilities	1	3	(2)
Long-term debt	160	77	83
Stockholders' Equity:			
Common stock	359	258	101
Retained earnings	110	86	24
Total	$725	$487	$238

Logic Behind the Indirect Method

The operating section of the cash-flow statement begins with net income, taken from the income statement. Additions and subtractions follow. These are labeled "Add (subtract) items that affect net income and cash flow differently." We discuss these items in the following sections.

Depreciation, Depletion, and Amortization Expenses These expenses are added back to net income when we go from net income to cash flow from operations. Let's see why.

Depreciation(A) is recorded as follows:

Depreciation Expense	18,000	
Accumulated Depreciation.............		18,000

This entry contains no debit or credit to Cash, so depreciation expense has no cash effect. However, depreciation expense is deducted from revenues in the computation of income. Therefore, in going from net income to cash flows from operations, we add depreciation back to net income. The addback cancels the earlier deduction. The following example should help clarify this practice: Suppose a company had only two transactions during the period, a $1,000 cash sale and depreciation expense of $300. Net income is $700 ($1,000 – $300). Cash flow from operations is $1,000. To show how net income ($700) is related to cash flow ($1,000), we must add back the depreciation amount of $300.

All expenses with no cash effects are added back to net income on the indirect form of the cash-flow statement.

Depletion and amortization are also added back.

Likewise, revenues that do not provide cash are subtracted from net income.

An example is equity-method investment revenue.

Gains and Losses on the Sale of Assets(B) Sales of plant assets are investing activities on the cash-flow statement. A gain or loss on the sale is an adjustment to income. Exhibit 12-13 includes an adjustment for a gain. Recall that Anchor sold equipment with a book value of $54,000 for $62,000, producing a gain of $8,000.

The $8,000 gain is reported on the income statement and is therefore included in net income. However, the cash receipt from the sale is $62,000, which includes the gain. To avoid counting the gain twice, we need to remove its effect from income and report the cash receipt of $62,000 in the investing activities section of the statement. Starting with net income, we subtract the gain. This deduction removes the gain's earlier effect on income. The sale of plant assets is reported as a $62,000 cash receipt from an investing activity, as shown in Exhibits 12-2 and 12-13.

A loss on the sale of plant assets is also an adjustment to net income on the statement of cash flows. However, a loss is *added back* to income to compute cash flow from operations. The proceeds from selling the plant assets are reported under investing activities.

Changes in the Current Asset and Current Liability Accounts(C) Most current assets and current liabilities result from operating activities. Changes in the current accounts are reported as adjustments to net income on the cash-flow statement. The following rules apply:

1. An *increase* in a current asset other than cash is subtracted from net income to compute cash flow from operations. Suppose a company makes a sale. Income is increased by the sale amount. However, collection of less than the full amount increases Accounts Receivable. For example, Exhibit 12-15 reports that Anchor Corporation's Accounts Receivable increased by $13,000 during 19X2. To compute the impact of revenue on Anchor's cash-flow amount,

Concept Highlight

EXHIBIT 12-16
Indirect Method of Determining Cash Flows from Operating Activities

	Net Income
Add (subtract) items that affect net income and cash flow differently	+ Depreciation
	+ Depletion
	+ Amortization
	+ Loss on disposal or exchange of long-term asset or early extinguishment of debt
	– Gain on disposal of long-term asset or early extinguishment of debt
	+ Decrease in current asset other than cash
	– Increase in current asset other than cash
	+ Increase in current liability*
	– Decrease in current liability*
	Net cash inflow (or outflow) from operating activities

*Short-term notes payable for general borrowing, and current portion of long-term notes payable, are related to *financing* activities, not to operating activities.

We thank Barbara Gerrity and Jean Marie Hudson for suggesting this exhibit.

we must subtract the $13,000 increase in Accounts Receivable from net income in Exhibit 12-13. The reason is this: We have *not* collected this $13,000 in cash. The same logic applies to the other current assets. If they increase during the period, subtract the increase from net income.

2. A *decrease* in a current asset other than cash is added to net income. Suppose Anchor's Accounts Receivable balance decreased by $4,000 during the period. Cash receipts cause the Accounts Receivable balance to decrease and cash to increase, so decreases in Accounts Receivable and the other current assets are *added* to net income.

3. A *decrease* in a current liability is subtracted from net income. The payment of a current liability causes both cash and the current liability to decrease, so decreases in current liabilities are subtracted from net income. For example, in Exhibit 12-13, the $2,000 decrease in Accrued Liabilities is *subtracted* from net income to compute net cash inflow from operating activities.

4. An *increase* in a current liability is added to net income. Anchor's Accounts Payable increased during the year. This increase can occur only if cash is not spent to pay this liability, which means that cash payments are less than the related expense and we have more cash on hand. Thus, increases in current liabilities are *added* to net income.

Computing net cash inflow or net cash outflow from *operating* activities by the indirect method takes a path that is very different from the direct-method computation. However, both methods arrive at the same amount of net cash flow from operating activities, as shown in Exhibits 12-2 and 12-13, both of which report a net cash inflow of $68,000.

Exhibit 12-16 summarizes the adjustments needed to convert net income to net cash inflow (or net cash outflow) from operating activities by the indirect method.

If you are studying *only* the indirect method for operating cash flows, please turn to page 599 for coverage of investing and financing activities.

Nike's Statement of Cash Flows for Operating Activities—An Application of the Indirect Method

Nike, Inc., is a well-known maker of athletic shoes and clothing. As Exhibit 12-17 shows, Nike uses the indirect method to report cash flows from operating activities. We've discussed most of the items in Nike's statement of cash flows earlier, but three need clarification. First, deferred income taxes are added back to net income in the operating section. These taxes do not require current cash payments and are therefore similar to accrued liabilities. Second, financing activities include

EXHIBIT 12-17
Nike, Inc., Statement of Cash Flows—Indirect Method

NIKE, INC. Statement of Cash Flows (Indirect Method for Operating Activities) For the Year Ended May 31, 19X7	(In thousands)
Cash provided (used) by operations:	
Net income	$ 35,879
Income charges (credits) not affecting cash:	
Depreciation	12,078
Deferred income taxes	8,486
Other	2,494
Changes in [current accounts]:	
Decrease in inventory	59,542
Decrease in accounts receivable	1,174
Decrease in other current assets	4,331
Increase in accounts payable, accrued liabilities, and income taxes payable	8,462
Cash provided by operations	132,446
Cash provided (used) by investing activities:	
Additions to property, plant, and equipment	(11,874)
Disposals of property, plant, and equipment	1,728
Additions to other assets	(930)
Cash used by investing activities	(11,076)
Cash provided (used) by financing activities:	
Additions to long-term debt	30,332
Reductions in long-term debt including current portion	(10,678)
Decrease in notes payable to banks	(18,489)
Proceeds from exercise of options	1,911
Dividends—common and preferred	(15,188)
Cash used by financing activities	(12,112)
Effect of exchange-rate changes on cash	(529)
Net increase (decrease) in cash	108,729
Cash and equivalents, beginning of year	18,138
Cash and equivalents, end of year	$126,867

proceeds from the exercise of options. This is the amount of cash received from issuance of stock to executives. Third, changes in exchange rates show the cash effect of fluctuations in foreign currencies.

Nike uses the indirect method to report cash flows from operating activities.

EVALUATION OF NIKE'S 19X7 CASH-FLOW RESULTS Nike's cash flows for 19X7 look very strong. Cash increased from $18 million to almost $127 million. Virtually all the cash increase came from operations—a sign of strength. During 19X7, Nike invested in new plant and equipment ($11.9 million) and paid off more than $29 million ($10.7 million + $18.5 million) of debt. The company issued only $30 million of new debt. Nike's board of directors was so confident of the future that the board paid $15 million of dividends, almost half of net income.

STOP & THINK Examine Anchor Corporation's statement of cash flows, Exhibit 12-13.

a. Does Anchor Corporation appear to be growing or shrinking? How can you tell?

b. Where did Anchor's cash for expansion come from?

c. Suppose Accounts Receivable increased by $40,000 (instead of $13,000) during the current year. What would this increase signal about the company?

Answers

a. This is an *INVESTING* question. Anchor appears to be growing. The company acquired more plant assets ($306,000) than it sold during the year.

b. This is a *FINANCING* question. The cash for expansion came from the issuance of common stock ($101,000) and from borrowing ($94,000).

c. This an *OPERATING* question. If accounts receivable had increased by $40,000, Anchor Corporation would have $27,000 less cash ($40,000 minus $13,000). A large increase in accounts receivable may signal difficulty in collecting cash from customers or a sharp increase in sales. A manager, stockholder, or creditor of Anchor Corporation should compare current-year sales with sales revenue for the preceding year. If sales are up, higher accounts receivable are good news. If sales are down, higher receivables may signal a cash shortage.

Computers and the Indirect Method of Generating the Statement of Cash Flows

The computer can easily generate the statement of cash flows by the indirect method. After the income statement is prepared, the computer picks up net income, depreciation, and the other noncash expenses. Changes in the current assets and the current liabilities and the data for the investing and financing activities are obtained from the specific account balances in the general ledger.

The statement of cash flows created from a computer's general ledger files is not automatically correct from a GAAP point of view. For example, noncash financing and investing activities of a large corporation, such as **Abbott Laboratories** (a manufacturer of pharmaceuticals), might be incorrectly combined with the company's cash flows. The computerized system must be sophisticated enough to distinguish among the various categories of cash activities. Most important, accountants must analyze the information fed into the computer and check that its output adheres to generally accepted accounting principles. Revisions to a company's computer accounting system are common.

Using Cash-Flow Information in Investment and Credit Analysis

The chapter opening story of W. T. Grant Company's bankruptcy makes it very clear that cash flows are important to a company's survival. A cash shortage is usually the most pressing problem of a struggling organization. Abundant cash allows a company to expand, invest in research and development, and hire the best employees. How, then, do investors (and their representatives, financial analysts) and creditors use cash-flow information to aid in decision making?

Neither cash-flow data, net-income information, balance sheet figures, nor the financial statement notes tell investors all they need to know about a company. Investor decision making is much more complex than plugging a few amounts into simple formulas. Investors analyze the financial statements, articles in the financial press, data about the company's industry, and predictions about the world economy to decide whether to invest in a company's stock. To evaluate a loan request, a bank loan officer will interview a company's top management to decide whether they are trustworthy. Both investors and creditors are interested mainly in where a company is headed. They want to make predictions about a company's net income and future cash flows.

It has been said that cash-flow data help to spot losers better than they help to spot winners. This is often true. When a company's business is booming, profits are high, and the financial position is improving. As the case of W. T. Grant Company vividly illustrates, a negative cash flow from operations warrants investigation. A cash downturn in a single year is not necessarily a danger signal. But negative cash flows for two consecutive years may hurt a company. This is especially true if operating activities generate negative cash flows for two or more years. Without cash coming in from basic operations, a business simply cannot survive.

Decision Guidelines

Investors' and Creditors' Use of Cash-Flow and Related Information

Investors

Question	Factors to Consider*	Financial Statement Predictor/Decision Model*
1. How much in dividends can I expect to receive from an investment in stock?	Expected future net income	Income from continuing operations**
	Expected future cash balance	Net cash flows from (in order) • operating activities • investing activities • financing activities
	Future dividend policy	Current and past dividend policy
2. Is the stock price likely to increase or decrease?	Expected future net income	Income from continuing operations**
	Expected future cash flows from operating activities	Income from continuing operations** Net cash flow from operating activities
3. What is the future stock price likely to be?	Expected future income from • continuing operations, *and* • net cash flow from operating activities	$\text{Expected future price of a share of stock} = \dfrac{\text{Expected future earnings per share}^{**}}{\text{Investment capitalization rate}}$ *or* $\text{Expected future price of a share of stock} = \dfrac{\text{Net cash flow from operations per share}}{\text{Investment capitalization rate}}$

Creditors

Question	Factors to Consider	Financial Statement Predictor
Can the company pay the interest and principal at the maturity of a loan?	Expected future net cash flow from operating activities	Income from continuing operations** —Net cash flow from • operating activities • investing activities

*There are many other factors to consider for making these decisions. These are some of the more common.
**See Chapter 11.

You may ask, "Can't the business raise money by issuing stock or by borrowing?" The answer is no, because if operations cannot generate enough cash, then stockholders will not find the company's stock very attractive. Bankers will not lend money to an organization whose operations do not provide enough cash; lenders are well aware that companies need cash to pay off their loans. Over the long run, if a company cannot generate cash from operations, it is doomed.

The Decision Guidelines feature provides investors and creditors with a few suggestions on how to use cash-flow information for their decision making. In several cases, income from continuing operations is listed as the predictor of a future amount. The predictor is often a historical amount because past figures are used to predict future amounts. Income from continuing operations serves as a reasonable predictor both of future income and of future cash flow because income tends not to vary widely from period to period. However, there are many other predictors. We list those in the Decision Guidelines merely as examples.

Measuring Cash Adequacy—Free Cash Flow

Throughout this chapter we have focused on cash flows from operating, investing, and financing activities. Some investors, creditors, and managers make a further distinction. They seek to measure the amount of cash flow that a company can "free up" for opportunities that arise unexpectedly. The business world changes so quickly that new possibilities arise almost daily. The company with the most free cash flow is best able to respond to new opportunities. **Free cash flow** is the amount of cash available from operations after paying for planned investments in plant, equipment, and other long-term assets. Free cash flow can be computed as follows:

Free cash flow = Net cash flow from operating activities − Cash outflow earmarked for investments in plant, equipment, and other long-term assets

PepsiCo, Inc., is one company that uses free cash flow to manage the business. Suppose PepsiCo expects net cash inflow of $2.3 billion from operations. Assume PepsiCo plans to spend $1.9 billion to upgrade its Pizza Hut and Taco Bell restaurants. In this case, PepsiCo's free cash flow would be $0.4 billion ($2.3 billion − $1.9 billion). If a smaller restaurant chain becomes available, PepsiCo should have $0.4 billion to invest in the other company. The managers of **Shell Oil Company, AT&T,** and **Briggs & Stratton** also use free cash flow analysis to manage their businesses.

Measuring the adequacy of free cash flow does not follow a specific formula. A large amount of free cash flow is preferable because it means that a lot of cash is available for new investments. But it can also mean that the company does not plan its long-term investments carefully. For example, if operating cash flows total $100 million and there is no plan for long-term investments, free cash flow is $100 million. Successful companies plan their investing activities in advance.

Planning long-term investments takes on added importance in industries whose investments take several years to implement. Public utilities construct large power-generating plants that require huge expenditures over a period of several years. The automakers (**General Motors, Toyota,** and **Mercedes-Benz**) plan their capital expenditures years in advance, as do aircraft manufacturers **Boeing** and **Airbus Industries.** With such long planning horizons, these companies may neither generate nor need huge amounts of free cash flow.

High-tech software companies such as **Intel, Microsoft,** and **Peachtree** depend on technological breakthroughs for their competitive edge. These companies certainly plan for the future, but their investment opportunities may arise more quickly than those of older companies like **General Motors** and **Consolidated Edison,** the electric utility. For Intel, Microsoft, and Peachtree, free cash flow may be more important.

SUMMARY PROBLEM FOR YOUR REVIEW

Prepare the 19X3 statement of cash flows for Robins Corporation, using the indirect method to report cash flows from operating activities. In a separate schedule, report Robin's noncash investing and financing activities.

	December 31, 19X3	December 31, 19X2
Current Assets:		
Cash and cash equivalents	$19,000	$ 3,000
Accounts receivable	22,000	23,000
Inventories	34,000	31,000
Prepaid expenses	1,000	3,000

	December 31, 19X3	19X2
Current Liabilities:		
Notes payable (for inventory purchases)	$11,000	$ 7,000
Accounts payable	24,000	19,000
Accrued liabilities	7,000	9,000
Income tax payable	10,000	10,000

Transaction Data for 19X3:

Purchase of equipment	$98,000	Depreciation expense	$ 7,000
Payment of cash dividends	18,000	Issuance of long-term note payable to borrow cash	7,000
Net income	26,000	Issuance of common stock for cash	19,000
Issuance of common stock to retire bonds payable	13,000	Sale of building	74,000
Purchase of long-term investment	8,000	Amortization expense	3,000
Issuance of long-term note payable to purchase patent	37,000	Purchase of treasury stock	5,000
		Loss on sale of building	2,000

ANSWER

ROBINS CORPORATION
Statement of Cash Flows
Year Ended December 31, 19X3

Cash flows from operating activities:		
Net income		$26,000
Add (subtract) items that affect net income and cash flow differently:		
Depreciation	$ 7,000	
Amortization	3,000	
Loss on sale of building	2,000	
Decrease in accounts receivable	1,000	
Increase in inventories	(3,000)	
Decrease in prepaid expenses	2,000	
Increase in notes payable, short-term	4,000	
Increase in accounts payable	5,000	
Decrease in accrued liabilities	(2,000)	19,000
Net cash inflow from operating activities		45,000
Cash flows from investing activities:		
Purchase of equipment	$(98,000)	
Sale of building	74,000	
Purchase of long-term investment	(8,000)	
Net cash outflow from investing activities		(32,000)
Cash flows from financing activities:		
Issuance of common stock	$ 19,000	
Payment of cash dividends	(18,000)	
Issuance of long-term note payable	7,000	
Purchase of treasury stock	(5,000)	
Net cash inflow from financing activities		3,000
Net increase in cash and cash equivalents		$16,000
Noncash investing and financing activities:		
Issuance of long-term note payable to purchase patent		$37,000
Issuance of common stock to retire bonds payable		13,000
Total noncash investing and financing activities		$50,000

SUMMARY OF LEARNING OBJECTIVES

1. *Identify the purposes of the statement of cash flows.* The *statement of cash flows* reports a business's cash receipts, cash disbursements, and net change in cash for the accounting period. It shows *why* cash increased or decreased during the period. A required financial statement, it gives a different view of the business from that given by accrual-basis statements. The cash-flow statement helps financial statement users predict the future cash flows of the entity. It also allows investors to evaluate management decisions, determine the company's ability to pay dividends to stockholders and interest and principal to creditors, and ascertain the relationship of net income to changes in the business's cash. Cash includes cash on hand, cash in bank, and *cash equivalents* such as liquid short-term investments.

2. *Distinguish among operating, investing, and financing activities.* The cash-flow statement is divided into *operating activities, investing activities,* and *financing activities.* Operating activities create revenues and expenses in the entity's major line of business. Investing activities increase and decrease the long-term assets available to the business. Financing activities obtain from investors and creditors the cash needed to launch and sustain the business. Each section of the statement includes cash receipts and cash payments and concludes with a net cash increase or decrease. In addition, *noncash investing and financing activities* are reported in an accompanying schedule.

3. *Prepare a statement of cash flows by the direct method.* Two formats are used to report operating activities—the direct method and the indirect method. The *direct method* lists the major categories of operating cash receipts (collections from customers and receipts of interest and dividends) and cash disbursements (payments to suppliers, payments to employees, and payments for interest and income taxes).

4. *Use the financial statements to compute the cash effects of a wide variety of business transactions.* The analysis of T-accounts aids the computation of the cash effects of business transactions. Much of the information needed to compute these amounts comes from the balance sheet, the income statement, and the related accounts.

5. *Prepare a statement of cash flows by the indirect method.* The *indirect method* starts with net income and reconciles to cash flow from operations. Although the FASB permits both the indirect and the direct methods, it prefers the direct method. However, the indirect method is more widely used.

ACCOUNTING VOCABULARY

cash equivalents *(p. 585).*
cash flows *(p. 584).*
direct method *(p. 588).*
financing activity *(p. 587).*
free cash flow *(p. 612).*
indirect method *(p. 588).*
investing activity *(p. 587).*
operating activity *(p. 586).*
reconciliation method *(p. 605).*
statement of cash flows *(p. 584).*

QUESTIONS

1. What information does the statement of cash flows report that is not shown on the balance sheet, the income statement, or the statement of retained earnings?
2. Identify four purposes of the statement of cash flows.
3. Identify and briefly describe the three types of activities that are reported on the statement of cash flows.
4. How is the statement of cash flows dated, and why?
5. What is the check figure for the statement of cash flows? (In other words, which figure do you check to make sure you've done your work correctly?) Where is it obtained, and how is it used?
6. What is the most important source of cash for most successful companies?
7. How can cash decrease during a year when income is high? How can cash increase during a year when income is low? How can investors and creditors learn these facts about the company?
8. DeBerg, Inc., prepares its statement of cash flows by the *direct* method for operating activities. Identify the section of DeBerg's statement of cash flows where each of the following transactions will appear. If the transaction does not appear on the cash-flow statement, give the reason.

a. Cash	14,000	
Note Payable, Long-Term		14,000
b. Salary Expense	7,300	
Cash		7,300
c. Cash	28,400	
Sales Revenue		28,400
d. Amortization Expense	6,500	
Goodwill		6,500
e. Accounts Payable	1,400	
Cash		1,400

9. Why are depreciation, depletion, and amortization expenses *not* reported on a cash-flow statement that reports operating activities by the direct method? Why and how are these expenses reported on a statement prepared by the indirect method?
10. Mainline Distributing Company collected cash of $92,000 from customers and $6,000 interest on notes receivable. Cash payments included $24,000 to employees, $13,000 to suppliers, $6,000 as dividends to stockholders, and $5,000 as a loan to another company. How much was Mainline's net cash inflow from operating activities?
11. Summarize the major cash receipts and cash disbursements in the three categories of activities that appear on the cash-flow statement.
12. Kirchner, Inc., recorded salary expense of $51,000 during a year when the balance of Salary Payable decreased from $10,000 to $2,000. How much cash did Kirchner pay to employees during the year? Where on the statement of cash flows should Kirchner report this item?
13. Marshall Corp.'s beginning plant asset balance, net of accumulated depreciation, was $193,000, and the ending amount was $176,000. Marshall recorded depreciation of $37,000 and sold plant assets with a book value of $9,000. How much cash did Marshall pay to purchase plant assets during the period? Where on the statement of cash flows should Marshall report this item?
14. How should issuance of a note payable to purchase land be reported in the financial statements? Identify three other transactions that fall in this same category.
15. Which format of the cash-flow statement gives a clearer description of the individual cash flows from operating activities? Which format better shows the relationship between net income and operating cash flow?
16. An investment that cost $65,000 was sold for $80,000, resulting in a $15,000 gain. Show how to report this transaction on a statement of cash flows prepared by the indirect method.
17. Identify the cash effects of increases and decreases in current assets other than cash. What are the cash effects of increases and decreases in current liabilities?
18. Milano Corporation earned net income of $38,000 and had depreciation expense of $22,000. Also, noncash current assets decreased $13,000, and current liabilities decreased $9,000. What was Milano's net cash flow from operating activities?
19. What is the difference between the direct and indirect methods of reporting investing activities and financing activities?
20. Milgrom Company reports operating activities by the direct method. Does this method show the relationship between net income and cash flow from operations? If so, state how. If not, how can Milgrom satisfy this purpose of the cash-flow statement?
21. What is free cash flow?

EXERCISES

Identifying the purposes of the statement of cash flows ***(Obj. 1)***

E12-1 Prime Hotel Properties, a real estate partnership, has experienced an unbroken string of 10 years of growth in net income. Nevertheless, the business is facing bankruptcy! Creditors are calling all of Prime's outstanding loans for immediate payment, and the cash is simply not available. Attempts to explain where Prime went wrong make it clear that managers placed undue emphasis on net income and gave too little attention to cash flows.

Required

Write a brief memo, in your own words, to explain to the managers of Prime Hotel Properties the purposes of the statement of cash flows.

Identifying activities for the statement of cash flows ***(Obj. 2)***

E12-2 Identify each of the following transactions as an operating activity (O), an investing activity (I), a financing activity (F), a noncash investing and financing activity (NIF), or a transaction that is not reported on the statement of cash flows (N). Assume that the direct method is used to report cash flows from operating activities.

____ **a.** Payment of account payable
____ **b.** Issuance of preferred stock for cash
____ **c.** Payment of cash dividend
____ **d.** Sale of long-term investment
____ **e.** Amortization of bond discount
____ **f.** Collection of account receivable
____ **g.** Issuance of long-term note payable to borrow cash
____ **h.** Depreciation of equipment
____ **i.** Purchase of treasury stock
____ **j.** Issuance of common stock for cash
____ **k.** Purchase of long-term investment
____ **l.** Payment of wages to employees
____ **m.** Collection of cash interest
____ **n.** Cash sale of land
____ **o.** Distribution of stock dividend
____ **p.** Acquisition of equipment by issuance of note payable
____ **q.** Payment of long-term debt
____ **r.** Acquisition of building by issuance of common stock
____ **s.** Accrual of salary expense

Classifying transactions for the statement of cash flows ***(Obj. 2)***

E12-3 Indicate where, if at all, each of the following transactions would be reported on a statement of cash flows prepared by the *direct* method and the accompanying schedule of non-cash investing and financing activities.

a.	Salary Expense	4,300	
	Cash		4,300
b.	Equipment	18,000	
	Cash		18,000
c.	Cash	7,200	
	Long-Term Investment		7,200
d.	Bonds Payable	45,000	
	Cash		45,000
e.	Building	164,000	
	Note Payable, Long-Term		164,000
f.	Cash	1,400	
	Accounts Receivable		1,400
g.	Dividends Payable	16,500	
	Cash		16,500
h.	Furniture and Fixtures	22,100	
	Note Payable, Short-Term		22,100
i.	Accounts Payable	8,300	
	Cash		8,300
j.	Cash	81,000	
	Common Stock		12,000
	Paid-in Capital in Excess of Par—Common		69,000
k.	Treasury Stock	13,000	
	Cash		13,000
l.	Retained Earnings	36,000	
	Common Stock		36,000
m.	Cash	2,000	
	Interest Revenue		2,000
n.	Land	87,700	
	Cash		87,700

Computing cash flows from operating activities—direct method ***(Obj. 3)***

E12-4 Analysis of the accounting records of Beaufain Corporation reveals the following:

Cash sales	$ 9,000	Increase in current assets other than cash	$17,000
Loss on sale of land	5,000	Payment of dividends	7,000
Acquisition of land	37,000	Collection of accounts receivable	93,000
Payment of accounts payable	48,000	Payment of salaries and wages	34,000
Net income	21,000	Depreciation	12,000
Payment of income tax	13,000	Decrease in current liabilities	23,000
Collection of dividend revenue	7,000		
Payment of interest	16,000		

Required

Compute cash flows from operating activities by the direct method. Use the format of the operating section of Exhibit 12-2. Evaluate the operating cash flow of Beaufain Corporation. Give the reason for your evaluation.

Identifying items for the statement of cash flows—direct method ***(Obj. 3)***

E12-5 Selected accounts of Indigo Investments, Inc., show

Dividends Receivable

Beginning balance	9,000	Cash receipts of dividends	38,000
Dividend revenue	40,000		
Ending balance	11,000		

Investment in Land

Beginning balance	90,000	Cost of investments sold	109,000
Acquisitions	127,000		
Ending balance	108,000		

Long-Term Debt

Payments	69,000	Beginning balance	273,000
		Issuance of debt for cash	83,000
		Ending balance	287,000

Required

For each account, identify the item or items that should appear on a statement of cash flows prepared by the direct method. State where to report the item.

E12-6 The income statement and additional data of Nebraska Milling Company follow.

Preparing the statement of cash flows—direct method ***(Obj. 3)***

NEBRASKA MILLING COMPANY
Income Statement
Year Ended September 30, 19X2

Revenues:		
Sales revenue	$229,000	
Dividend revenue	8,000	$237,000
Expenses:		
Cost of goods sold	103,000	
Salary expense	45,000	
Depreciation expense	29,000	
Advertising expense	11,000	
Interest expense	2,000	
Income tax expense	9,000	199,000
Net income		$ 38,000

Additional data:

a. Collections from customers are $7,000 more than sales.
b. Payments to suppliers are $9,000 less than the sum of cost of goods sold plus advertising expense.
c. Payments to employees are $1,000 more than salary expense.
d. Dividend revenue, interest expense, and income tax expense equal their cash amounts.
e. Acquisition of plant assets is $116,000. Of this amount, $101,000 is paid in cash, $15,000 by signing a note payable.
f. Proceeds from sale of land, $14,000.
g. Proceeds from issuance of common stock, $30,000.
h. Payment of long-term note payable, $15,000.
i. Payment of dividends, $11,000.
j. Change in cash balance, $?

Required

1. Prepare Nebraska Milling Company's statement of cash flows and accompanying schedule of noncash investing and financing activities. Report operating activities by the *direct* method.
2. Evaluate Nebraska Milling Company's cash flows for the year. In your evaluation, mention all three categories of cash flows, and give the reason for your evaluation.

E12-7 Compute the following items for the statement of cash flows:

Computing amounts for the statement of cash flows ***(Obj. 3, 4)***

a. Cost of goods sold is $82,000. Beginning Inventory balance is $25,000, and ending Inventory balance is $21,000. Beginning and ending Accounts Payable are $11,000 and $8,000, respectively. How much are cash payments for inventory?
b. Beginning and ending Accounts Receivable are $22,000 and $26,000, respectively. Credit sales for the period total $81,000. How much are cash collections?

E12-8 Compute the following items for the statement of cash flows:

Computing investing and financing amounts for the statement of cash flows ***(Obj. 4)***

a. Beginning and ending Plant Assets, net, are $103,000 and $107,000, respectively. Depreciation for the period is $16,000, and acquisitions of new plant assets are $27,000. Plant assets were sold at a $1,000 gain. What were the cash proceeds of the sale?
b. Beginning and ending Retained Earnings are $45,000 and $73,000, respectively. Net income for the period is $62,000, and stock dividends are $22,000. How much are cash dividend payments?

E12-9 The accounting records of Beaufain Corporation reveal the following:

Computing cash flows from operating activities—indirect method ***(Obj. 5)***

Cash sales	$ 9,000	Payment of accounts payable	$48,000
Loss on sale of land	5,000	Net income	21,000
Acquisition of land	37,000	Payment of income tax	13,000
Collection of dividend revenue	7,000	Collection of accounts receivable	93,000
Payment of interest	16,000	Payment of salaries and wages	34,000
Increase in current assets other than cash	17,000	Depreciation	12,000
Payment of dividends	7,000	Decrease in current liabilities	23,000

Required

Compute cash flows from operating activities by the indirect method. Use the format of the operating section of Exhibit 12-13. Then evaluate Beaufain's operating cash flows as strong or weak.

Classifying transactions for the statement of cash flows ***(Obj. 3, 5)***

E12-10 Two transactions of Battery Amusement Co. are recorded as follows:

a. Cash	59,000	
Accumulated Depreciation	83,000	
Equipment		135,000
Gain on Sale of Equipment		7,000
b. Land	290,000	
Cash		130,000
Note Payable		160,000

Required

1. Indicate where, how, and in what amount to report these transactions on the statement of cash flows and accompanying schedule of noncash investing and financing activities. Battery Amusement Co. reports cash flows from operating activities by the *direct* method.
2. Repeat Requirement 1, assuming that Battery reports cash flows from operating activities by the *indirect* method.

Preparing the statement of cash flows by the indirect method ***(Obj. 5)***

E12-11 Use the income statement of Nebraska Milling Company in Exercise 12-6, plus these additional data.

a. Collections from customers are $7,000 more than sales.
b. Payments to suppliers are $9,000 less than the sum of cost of goods sold plus advertising expense.
c. Payments to employees are $1,000 more than salary expense.
d. Dividend revenue, interest expense, and income tax expense equal their cash amounts.
e. Acquisition of plant assets is $116,000. Of this amount, $101,000 is paid in cash, $15,000 by signing a note payable.
f. Proceeds from sale of land, $14,000.
g. Proceeds from issuance of common stock, $30,000.
h. Payment of long-term note payable, $15,000.
i. Payment of dividends, $11,000.
j. Change in cash balance, $?
k. From the balance sheet:

	September 30, 19X2	19X1
Current Assets:		
Accounts receivable	$51,000	$58,000
Inventory	83,000	77,000
Prepaid expenses	9,000	8,000
Current Liabilities:		
Notes payable (for inventory purchases)	$20,000	$20,000
Accounts payable	35,000	22,000
Accrued liabilities	23,000	21,000

Required

1. Prepare Nebraska Milling Company's statement of cash flows for the year ended September 30, 19X2, using the indirect method.
2. Evaluate Nebraska Milling Company's cash flows for the year. In your evaluation, mention all three categories of cash flows, and give the reason for your evaluation.

Computing cash flows from operating activities—indirect method ***(Obj. 5)***

E12-12 The accounting records of Chen Restaurant Supply include these accounts:

Cash			
Mar. 1	5,000		
Receipts	47,000	Payments	48,000
Mar. 31	4,000		

Accounts Receivable			
Mar. 1	18,000		
Sales	43,000	Collections	47,000
Mar. 31	14,000		

Inventory			
Mar. 1	19,000		
Purchases	37,000	Cost of sales	35,000
Mar. 31	21,000		

Equipment			
Mar. 1	93,000		
Acquisition	6,000		
Mar. 31	99,000		

Accumulated Depreciation—Equipment			
		Mar. 1	52,000
		Depreciation	3,000
		Mar. 31	55,000

Accounts Payable			
		Mar. 1	14,000
Payments	32,000	Purchases	37,000
		Mar. 31	19,000

Accrued Liabilities			
		Mar. 1	9,000
Payments	14,000	Expenses	11,000
		Mar. 31	6,000

Retained Earnings			
		Mar. 1	64,000
Quarterly dividend	18,000	Net income	19,000
		Mar. 31	65,000

Compute Chen's net cash inflow or outflow from operating activities during March. Use the indirect method. Does Chen have trouble collecting receivables or selling inventory? How can you tell?

Interpreting a cash-flow statement—indirect method ***(Obj. 5)***

E12-13 Consider three independent cases for the cash-flow data of Prime Motor Company:

	Case A	Case B	Case C
Cash flows from operating activities:			
Net income	$ 30,000	$ 30,000	$ 30,000
Depreciation and amortization	11,000	11,000	11,000
Increase in current assets	(19,000)	(7,000)	(1,000)
Decrease in current liabilities	(6,000)	(8,000)	-0-
	$ 16,000	$ 26,000	$ 40,000
Cash flows from investing activities:			
Acquisition of plant assets	$(91,000)	$ (91,000)	$(91,000)
Sales of plant assets	97,000	4,000	8,000
	$ 6,000	$ (87,000)	$(83,000)
Cash flows from financing activities:			
New borrowing	$ 16,000	$104,000	$ 50,000
Payment of debt	(21,000)	(29,000)	(9,000)
	$ (5,000)	$ 75,000	$ 41,000
Net increase (decrease) in cash	$ 17,000	$ 14,000	$ (2,000)

For each case, identify from the cash-flow statement how Prime generated the cash to acquire new plant assets.

CHALLENGE EXERCISE

Analyzing an actual company's statement of cash flows ***(Obj. 5)***

E12-14 PepsiCo's statement of cash flows for 19X2 is reproduced on page 620.

Required

1. Which format does PepsiCo use for reporting cash flows from operating activities?
2. What was PepsiCo's largest source of cash during 19X2? 19X1? 19X0?
3. The operating activities section of the statement lists (in millions):

Accounts and notes receivable	($45.7)
Accounts payable	($102.0)

   Did these accounts' balances increase or decrease during 19X2? How can you tell?
4. During 19X2, PepsiCo sold property, plant, and equipment. The gain or loss on this transaction is included in "Other noncash charges and credits, net" of $315.6 million. Assume that the book value of the plant assets that PepsiCo sold during 19X2 was $104.3 million. Journalize the sale of the property, plant, and equipment.
5. During the three-year period 19X0 through 19X2, PepsiCo engaged in much activity with its long-term debt and short-term borrowings. On the basis of this activity, does PepsiCo appear to be growing or shrinking? Also consider the company's trends of income from continuing operations, cash provided by operations, and investing activities.

PEPSICO, INC., AND SUBSIDIARIES
Consolidated Statement of Cash Flows
Fifty-two weeks ended December 26, 19X2, December 28, 19X1 and December 29, 19X0

(In millions)	19X2	19X1	19X0
Cash Flows—Continuing Operations:			
Income from continuing operations before cumulative effect of accounting changes	$ 1,301.7	$ 1,080.2	$ 1,090.6
Adjustments to reconcile income from continuing operations before cumulative effect of accounting changes to net cash provided by continuing operations:			
Depreciation and amortization	1,214.9	1,034.5	884.0
Deferred income taxes	(52.0)	98.0	86.4
Gain on joint venture stock offering	—	—	(118.2)
Other noncash charges and credits, net	315.6	227.2	120.3
Changes in [current accounts] excluding effect of acquisitions:			
Accounts and notes receivable	(45.7)	(55.9)	(124.8)
Inventories	(11.8)	(54.8)	(20.9)
Prepaid expenses, taxes and other current assets	(27.4)	(75.6)	(41.9)
Accounts payable	(102.0)	57.8	25.4
Income taxes payable	(16.9)	(3.4)	136.3
Other current liabilities	135.2	122.3	72.8
Net change in operating working capital	(68.6)	(9.6)	46.9
Net Cash Provided by Continuing Operations	2,711.6	2,430.3	2,110.0
Cash Flows—Investing Activities:			
Acquisitions and investments in affiliates	(1,209.7)	(640.9)	(630.6)
Purchases of property, plant, and equipment	(1,549.6)	(1,457.8)	(1,180.1)
Proceeds from sales of property, plant, and equipment	89.0	69.6	45.3
Short-term investments, by original maturity:			
More than three months—purchases	(1,174.8)	(1,849.2)	(2,093.2)
More than three months—sales	1,371.8	1,873.2	2,139.4
Three months or less, net	(249.4)	(164.9)	(228.0)
Proceeds from joint venture stock offering	—	—	129.6
Other, net	(30.8)	(105.8)	(119.7)
Net Cash Used for Investing Activities	(2,753.5)	(2,275.8)	(1,937.3)
Cash Flows—Financing Activities:			
Proceeds from issuances of long-term debt	1,092.7	2,799.6	777.3
Payments of long-term debt	(616.3)	(1,348.5)	(298.0)
Short-term borrowings, by original maturity:			
More than three months—proceeds	911.2	2,551.9	4,041.9
More than three months—payments	(2,062.6)	(3,097.4)	(2,647.4)
Three months or less, net	1,075.3	(467.1)	(1,480.7)
Cash dividends paid	(395.5)	(343.2)	(293.9)
Purchases of treasury stock	(32.0)	(195.2)	(147.7)
Proceeds from exercises of stock options	82.8	15.8	9.3
Other, net	(30.9)	(47.0)	(37.9)
Net Cash Provided by (Used for) Financing Activities	24.7	(131.1)	(77.1)
Effect of Exchange Rate Changes on Cash and Cash Equivalents	0.4	(7.5)	(1.0)
Net Increase (Decrease) in Cash and Cash Equivalents	(16.8)	15.9	94.6
Cash and Cash Equivalents—Beginning of Year	186.7	170.8	76.2
Cash and Cash Equivalents—End of Year	$ 169.9	$ 186.7	$ 170.8

PROBLEMS

(GROUP A)

Using cash-flow information to evaluate performance ***(Obj. 1)***

P12-1A Top managers of Charter Flight Service, Inc., are reviewing company performance for 19X7. The income statement reports a 20% increase in net income over 19X6. However, most of the increase resulted from an extraordinary gain on insurance proceeds from storm damage to a building. The balance sheet shows a large increase in receivables. The cash-flow statement, in summarized form, reports the following:

Net cash outflow from operating activities	$(80,000)
Net cash inflow from investing activities	40,000
Net cash inflow from financing activities	50,000
Increase in cash during 19X7	$ 10,000

Required

Write a memo giving Charter managers your assessment of 19X7 operations and your outlook for the future. Focus on the information content of the cash-flow data.

Preparing the statement of cash flows—direct method ***(Obj. 2, 3)***

P12-2A Accountants for Pueblo Contractors, Inc., have developed the following data from the company's accounting records for the year ended April 30, 19X5:

a. Credit sales, $583,900
b. Loan to another company, $12,500
c. Cash payments to acquire plant assets, $59,400
d. Cost of goods sold, $382,600
e. Proceeds from issuance of common stock, $8,000
f. Payment of cash dividends, $48,400
g. Collection of interest, $4,400
h. Acquisition of equipment by issuing short-term note payable, $16,400
i. Payments of salaries, $93,600
j. Proceeds from sale of plant assets, $22,400, including $6,800 loss
k. Collections on accounts receivable, $462,600
l. Interest revenue, $3,800
m. Cash receipt of dividend revenue on stock investments, $4,100
n. Payments to suppliers, $368,500
o. Cash sales, $171,900
p. Depreciation expense, $59,900
q. Proceeds from issuance of short-term debt, $19,600
r. Payments of long-term debt, $50,000
s. Interest expense and payments, $13,300
t. Salary expense, $95,300
u. Loan collections, $12,800
v. Proceeds from sale of investments, $9,100, including $2,000 gain
w. Payment of short-term note payable by issuing long-term note payable, $63,000
x. Amortization expense, $2,900
y. Income tax expense and payments, $37,900
z. Cash balance: April 30, 19X4—$39,300
April 30, 19X5—$?

Required

1. Prepare Pueblo's statement of cash flows for the year ended April 30, 19X5. Follow the format of Exhibit 12-2, but do *not* show amounts in thousands. Include an accompanying schedule of noncash investing and financing activities.
2. Evaluate 19X5 from a cash-flow standpoint. Give your reasons.

Preparing the statement of cash flows—direct method ***(Obj. 2, 3, 4)***

P12-3A The 19X5 comparative balance sheet and income statement of Loco Taco Corp. follow.

LOCO TACO CORP.
Comparative Balance Sheet

	December 31, 19X5	December 31, 19X4	Increase (Decrease)
Current assets:			
Cash and cash equivalents	$ 7,200	$ 5,300	$ 1,900
Accounts receivable	28,600	26,900	1,700
Interest receivable	1,900	700	1,200
Inventories	83,600	87,200	(3,600)
Prepaid expenses	2,500	1,900	600
Plant assets:			
Land	89,000	60,000	29,000
Equipment, net	53,500	49,400	4,100
Total assets	$266,300	$231,400	$ 34,900
Current liabilities:			
Accounts payable	$ 31,400	$ 28,800	$ 2,600
Interest payable	4,400	4,900	(500)
Salary payable	3,100	6,600	(3,500)
Other accrued liabilities	13,700	16,000	(2,300)
Income tax payable	8,900	7,700	1,200
Long-term liabilities:			
Notes payable	75,000	100,000	(25,000)
Stockholders' equity:			
Common stock, no-par	88,300	64,700	23,600
Retained earnings	41,500	2,700	38,800
Total liabilities and stockholders' equity	$266,300	$231,400	$ 34,900

LOCO TACO CORP. Income Statement for 19X5		
Revenues:		
Sales revenue		$213,000
Interest revenue		8,600
Total revenues		221,600
Expenses:		
Cost of goods sold	$70,600	
Salary expense	27,800	
Depreciation expense	4,000	
Other operating expense	10,500	
Interest expense	11,600	
Income tax expense	29,100	
Total expenses		153,600
Net income		$ 68,000

Loco Taco had no noncash investing and financing transactions during 19X5. During the year, there were no sales of land or equipment, no issuances of notes payable, no retirements of stock, and no treasury stock transactions.

Required

1. Prepare the 19X5 statement of cash flows, formating operating activities by the direct method.
2. How will what you learned in this problem help you evaluate an investment?

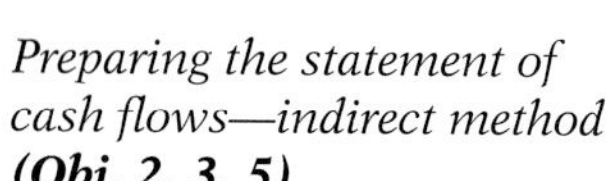

Preparing the statement of cash flows—indirect method ***(Obj. 2, 3, 5)***

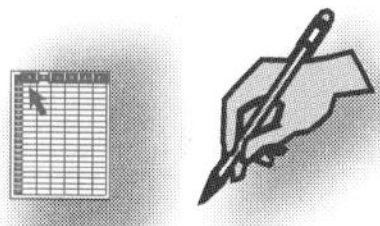

P12-4A Use the Loco Taco Corp. data from Problem 12-3A.

Required

1. Prepare the 19X5 statement of cash flows by the indirect method. If your instructor also assigned Problem 12-3A, prepare only the operating activities section of the statement.
2. How will what you learned in this problem help you evaluate an investment?

Preparing the statement of cash flows—indirect method ***(Obj. 2, 5)***

P12-5A NavStar Corporation accountants have assembled the following data for the year ended December 31, 19X7:

	December 31, 19X7	December 31, 19X6
Current Accounts (All Result from Operations):		
Current assets:		
Cash and cash equivalents	$55,700	$22,700
Accounts receivable	69,700	64,200
Inventories	88,600	83,000
Prepaid expenses	5,300	4,100
Current liabilities:		
Notes payable (for inventory purchases)	$22,600	$18,300
Accounts payable	52,900	55,800
Income tax payable	18,600	16,700
Accrued liabilities	15,500	27,200

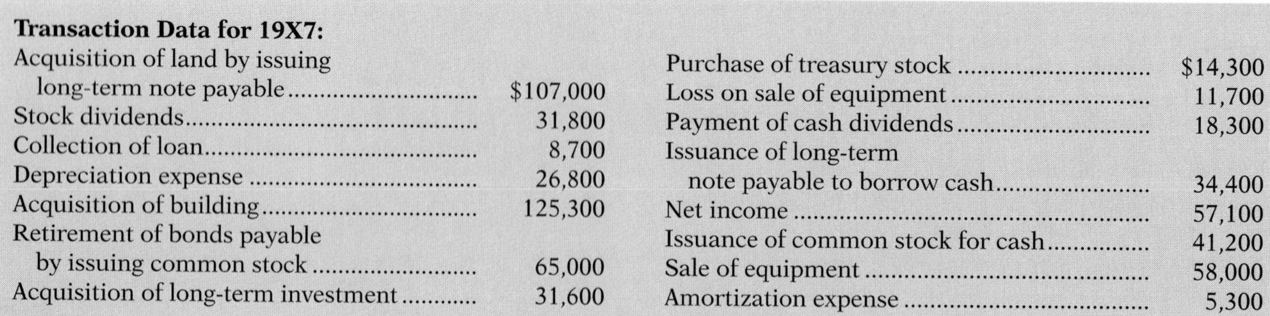

Transaction Data for 19X7:			
Acquisition of land by issuing long-term note payable	$107,000	Purchase of treasury stock	$14,300
Stock dividends	31,800	Loss on sale of equipment	11,700
Collection of loan	8,700	Payment of cash dividends	18,300
Depreciation expense	26,800	Issuance of long-term note payable to borrow cash	34,400
Acquisition of building	125,300	Net income	57,100
Retirement of bonds payable by issuing common stock	65,000	Issuance of common stock for cash	41,200
Acquisition of long-term investment	31,600	Sale of equipment	58,000
		Amortization expense	5,300

Required

Prepare NavStar Corporation's statement of cash flows, using the *indirect* method to report operating activities. Include an accompanying schedule of noncash investing and financing activities.

Preparing the statement of cash flows—indirect method ***(Obj. 2, 5)***

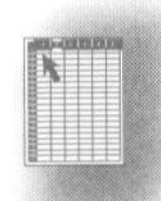

P12-6A The comparative balance sheet of Caterpillar Company at March 31, 19X7, reported the following:

	March 31, 19X7	March 31, 19X6
Current Assets:		
Cash and cash equivalents	$13,600	$ 4,000
Accounts receivable	14,900	21,700
Inventories	63,200	60,600
Prepaid expenses	1,900	1,700
Current Liabilities:		
Notes payable (for inventory purchases)	$ 4,000	$ 4,000
Accounts payable	30,300	27,600
Accrued liabilities	10,700	11,100
Income tax payable	8,000	4,700

Caterpillar's transactions during the year ended March 31, 19X7, included the following:

Acquisition of land by issuing note payable	$76,000	Sale of long-term investment	$13,700
Amortization expense	2,000	Depreciation expense	9,000
Payment of cash dividend	30,000	Cash acquisition of building	47,000
Cash acquisition of equipment	78,700	Net income	70,000
Issuance of long-term note payable to borrow cash	50,000	Issuance of common stock for cash	11,000
		Stock dividend	18,000

Required

1. Prepare Caterpillar's statement of cash flows for the year ended March 31, 19X7, using the *indirect* method to report cash flows from operating activities. Report noncash investing and financing activities in an accompanying schedule.
2. Evaluate Caterpillar's cash flows for the year. Mention all three categories of cash flows, and give the reason for your evaluation.

Preparing the statement of cash flows—direct and indirect methods ***(Obj. 3, 5)***

P12-7A To prepare the statement of cash flows, accountants for Pentech, Inc., have summarized 19X3 activity in two accounts as follows:

Cash

Beginning balance	53,600	Payment on accounts payable	399,100
Collection of loan	13,000	Payments of dividends	27,200
Sale of investment	8,200	Payments of salaries and wages	143,800
Receipts of interest	12,600	Payments of interest	26,900
Collections from customers	678,700	Purchase of equipment	31,400
Issuance of common stock	47,300	Payments of operating expenses	34,300
Receipts of dividends	4,500	Payment of long-term debt	41,300
		Purchase of treasury stock	26,400
		Payment of income tax	18,900
Ending balance	68,600		

Common Stock

		Beginning balance	84,400
		Issuance for cash	47,300
		Issuance to acquire land	80,100
		Issuance to retire long-term debt	19,000
		Ending balance	230,800

Required

1. Prepare the statement of cash flows of Pentech, Inc., for the year ended December 31, 19X3, using the *direct* method to report operating activities. Also prepare the accompanying schedule of noncash investing and financing activities.

2. Use the following data from Pentech's 19X3 income statement and (selected) balance sheet to prepare a supplementary schedule showing cash flows from operating activities by the *indirect* method. All activity in the current accounts results from operations.

PENTECH, INC.
Income Statement
For the Year Ended December 31, 19X3

Revenues:		
Sales revenue		$706,300
Interest revenue		12,600
Dividend revenue		4,500
Total revenues		723,400
Expenses and losses:		
Cost of goods sold	$402,600	
Salary and wage expense	150,800	
Depreciation expense	24,300	
Other operating expense	44,100	
Interest expense	28,800	
Income tax expense	16,200	
Loss on sale of investments	1,100	
Total expenses		667,900
Net income		$ 55,500

PENTECH, INC.
Balance Sheet Data
December 31, 19X3

	Increase (Decrease)
Current assets:	
Cash and cash equivalents	$?
Accounts receivable	27,600
Inventories	(11,800)
Prepaid expenses	600
Loan receivable	(13,000)
Long-term investments	(9,300)
Equipment, net	7,100
Land	80,100
Current liabilities:	
Accounts payable	$ (8,300)
Interest payable	1,900
Salary payable	7,000
Other accrued liabilities	10,400
Income tax payable	(2,700)
Long-term debt	(60,300)
Common stock, no-par	146,400
Retained earnings	28,300
Treasury stock	26,400

P12-8A The comparative balance sheet of Bosco Bolt Co. at June 30, 19X7, included the following balances:

Preparing the statement of cash flows—indirect and direct methods ***(Obj. 3, 4, 5)***

BOSCO BOLT CO.
Balance Sheet
June 30, 19X7 and 19X6

	19X7	19X6	Increase (Decrease)
Current assets:			
Cash	$ 16,500	$ 8,600	$ 7,900
Accounts receivable	45,900	48,300	(2,400)
Interest receivable	2,900	3,600	(700)
Inventories	68,600	60,200	8,400
Prepaid expenses	3,700	2,800	900
Long-term investment	10,100	5,200	4,900
Equipment, net	82,500	73,600	8,900
Land	42,400	96,000	(53,600)
	$272,600	$298,300	$(25,700)
Current liabilities:			
Notes payable, short-term (for general borrowing)	$ 13,400	$ 18,100	$ (4,700)
Accounts payable	42,400	40,300	2,100
Income tax payable	13,800	14,500	(700)
Accrued liabilities	8,200	9,700	(1,500)
Interest payable	3,700	2,900	800
Salary payable	900	2,600	(1,700)
Long-term note payable	47,400	94,100	(46,700)
Common stock	59,800	51,200	8,600
Retained earnings	83,000	64,900	18,100
	$272,600	$298,300	$(25,700)

Transaction data for the year ended June 30, 19X7:

a. Net income, $56,200.
b. Depreciation expense on equipment, $5,400.
c. Purchased long-term investment, $4,900.
d. Sold land for $46,900, including $6,700 loss.
e. Acquired equipment by issuing long-term note payable, $14,300.
f. Paid long-term note payable, $61,000.
g. Received cash for issuance of common stock, $3,900.
h. Paid cash dividends, $38,100.
i. Paid short-term note payable by issuing common stock, $4,700.

Required

1. Prepare the statement of cash flows of Bosco Bolt Co. for the year ended June 30, 19X7, using the *indirect* method to report operating activities. Also prepare the accompanying schedule of noncash investing and financing activities. All current accounts except short-term notes payable result from operating transactions.
2. Prepare a supplementary schedule showing cash flows from operations by the *direct* method. The income statement reports the following: sales, $237,300; interest revenue, $10,600; cost of goods sold, $82,800; salary expense, $38,800; other operating expenses, $42,000; depreciation expense, $5,400; income tax expense, $9,900; loss on sale of land, $6,700; interest expense, $6,100.

(GROUP B)

P12-1B Top managers of LTV Broadcasting, Inc., are reviewing company performance for 19X4. The income statement reports a 15% increase in net income, the fifth consecutive year with an income increase above 10 percent. The income statement includes a nonrecurring loss without which net income would have increased by 16 percent. The balance sheet shows modest increases in assets, liabilities, and stockholders' equity. The assets posting the largest increases are plant and equipment because the company is halfway through a five-year expansion program. No other assets and no liabilities are increasing dramatically. A summarized version of the cash-flow statement reports the following:

Using cash-flow information to evaluate performance ***(Obj. 1)***

Net cash inflow from operating activities	$ 310,000
Net cash outflow from investing activities	(290,000)
Net cash inflow from financing activities	70,000
Increase in cash during 19X4	$ 90,000

Required

Write a memo giving top managers of LTV Broadcasting your assessment of 19X4 and your outlook for the future. Focus on the information content of the cash-flow data.

Preparing the statement of cash flows—direct method ***(Obj. 2, 3)***

P12-2B Outback Outfitters, Inc., accountants have developed the following data from the company's accounting records for the year ended July 31, 19X9:

a. Salary expense, $105,300
b. Cash payments to purchase plant assets, $181,000
c. Proceeds from issuance of short-term debt, $44,100
d. Payments of long-term debt, $18,800
e. Proceeds from sale of plant assets, $59,700, including $10,600 gain
f. Interest revenue, $12,100
g. Cash receipt of dividend revenue on stock investments, $2,700
h. Payments to suppliers, $673,300
i. Interest expense and payments, $37,800
j. Cost of goods sold, $481,100
k. Collection of interest revenue, $11,700
l. Acquisition of equipment by issuing short-term note payable, $35,500
m. Payments of salaries, $104,000
n. Credit sales, $608,100
o. Loan to another company, $35,000
p. Income tax expense and payments, $56,400
q. Depreciation expense, $27,700
r. Collections on accounts receivable, $673,100
s. Loan collections, $74,400
t. Proceeds from sale of investments, $34,700, including $3,800 loss
u. Payment of long-term debt by issuing preferred stock, $107,300
v. Amortization expense, $23,900
w. Cash sales, $146,000
x. Proceeds from issuance of common stock, $116,900
y. Payment of cash dividends, $50,500
z. Cash balance: July 31, 19X8—$53,800
July 31, 19X9—$?

Required

1. Prepare Outback's statement of cash flows for the year ended July 31, 19X9. Follow the format of Exhibit 12-2, but do *not* show amounts in thousands. Include an accompanying schedule of noncash investing and financing activities.
2. Evaluate 19X9 in terms of cash flow. Give your reasons.

Preparing the statement of cash flows—direct method ***(Obj. 2, 3, 4)***

P12-3B The 19X3 comparative balance sheet and income statement of Silverado, Inc., follow:

SILVERADO, INC.
Comparative Balance Sheet

	December 31, 19X3	19X2	Increase (Decrease)
Current assets:			
Cash and cash equivalents	$ 13,700	$ 15,600	$ (1,900)
Accounts receivable	41,500	43,100	(1,600)
Interest receivable	600	900	(300)
Inventories	94,300	89,900	4,400
Prepaid expenses	1,700	2,200	(500)
Plant assets:			
Land	35,100	10,000	25,100
Equipment, net	100,900	93,700	7,200
Total assets	$287,800	$255,400	$ 32,400
Current liabilities:			
Accounts payable	$ 16,400	$ 17,900	$ (1,500)
Interest payable	6,300	6,700	(400)
Salary payable	2,100	1,400	700
Other accrued liabilities	18,100	18,700	(600)
Income tax payable	6,300	3,800	2,500
Long-term liabilities:			
Notes payable	55,000	65,000	(10,000)
Stockholders' equity:			
Common stock, no-par	131,100	122,300	8,800
Retained earnings	52,500	19,600	32,900
Total liabilities and stockholders' equity	$287,800	$255,400	$ 32,400

SILVERADO, INC. Income Statement for 19X3		
Revenues:		
Sales revenue		$438,000
Interest revenue		11,700
Total revenues		449,700
Expenses:		
Cost of goods sold	$205,200	
Salary expense	76,400	
Depreciation expense	15,300	
Other operating expense	49,700	
Interest expense	24,600	
Income tax expense	16,900	
Total expenses		388,100
Net income		$ 61,600

Silverado had no noncash investing and financing transactions during 19X3. During the year, there were no sales of land or equipment, no issuances of notes payable, no retirements of stock, and no treasury stock transactions.

Required

1. Prepare the 19X3 statement of cash flows, formating operating activities by the direct method.
2. How will what you learned in this problem help you evaluate an investment?

Preparing the statement of cash flows—indirect method ***(Obj. 2, 3, 5)***

P12-4B Use the Silverado data from Problem 12-3B.

Required

1. Prepare the 19X3 statement of cash flows by the indirect method. If your instructor also assigned Problem 12-3B, prepare only the operating activities section.
2. How will what you learned in this problem help you evaluate an investment?

Preparing the statement of cash flows—indirect method ***(Obj. 2, 5)***

P12-5B Accountants for Maplewood Manufacturing have assembled the following data for the year ended December 31, 19X4:

	December 31, 19X4	19X3
Current Accounts (All Result from Operations):		
Current assets:		
Cash and cash equivalents	$38,600	$34,800
Accounts receivable	70,100	73,700
Inventories	90,600	96,500
Prepaid expenses	3,200	2,100
Current liabilities:		
Notes payable (for inventory purchases)	$36,300	$36,800
Accounts payable	72,100	67,500
Income tax payable	5,900	6,800
Accrued liabilities	28,300	23,200

Transaction Data for 19X4:

Stock dividends	$ 12,600	Payment of cash dividends	$ 48,300
Collection of loan	10,300	Issuance of long-term debt to borrow cash	71,000
Depreciation expense	19,200	Net income	50,500
Acquisition of equipment	69,000	Issuance of preferred stock for cash	36,200
Payment of long-term debt by issuing common stock	89,400	Sale of long-term investment	12,200
Acquisition of long-term investment	44,800	Amortization expense	1,100
Acquisition of building by issuing long-term note payable	118,000	Payment of long-term debt	47,800
		Gain on sale of investment	3,500

Required

Prepare Maplewood Manufacturing's statement of cash flows, using the *indirect* method to report operating activities. Include an accompanying schedule of noncash investing and financing activities.

Preparing the statement of cash flows—indirect method ***(Obj. 2, 5)***

P12-6B The comparative balance sheet of Sumter Enterprises, Inc., at December 31, 19X5, reported the following:

	December 31, 19X5	December 31, 19X4
Current Assets:		
Cash and cash equivalents	$10,600	$12,500
Accounts receivable	28,600	29,300
Inventories	51,600	53,000
Prepaid expenses	4,200	3,700
Current Liabilities:		
Notes payable (for inventory purchases)	$ 9,200	$ -0-
Accounts payable	21,900	28,000
Accrued liabilities	14,300	16,800
Income tax payable	11,000	14,300

Sumter's transactions during 19X5 included the following:

Amortization expense	$ 5,000	Cash acquisition of building	$124,000
Payment of cash dividends	17,000	Net income	31,600
Cash acquisition of equipment	55,000	Issuance of common stock for cash	105,600
Issuance of long-term note payable to borrow cash	32,000	Stock dividend	13,000
Retirement of bonds payable by issuing common stock	55,000	Sale of long-term investment	6,000
		Depreciation expense	15,000

Required

1. Prepare the statement of cash flows of Sumter Enterprises for the year ended December 31, 19X5. Use the *indirect* method to report cash flows from operating activities. Report noncash investing and financing activities in an accompanying schedule.
2. Evaluate Sumter's cash flows for the year. Mention all three categories of cash flows, and give the reason for your evaluation.

Preparing the statement of cash flows—direct and indirect methods ***(Obj. 3, 5)***

P12-7B To prepare the statement of cash flows, accountants for Ball State Corp. have summarized 19X8 activity in two accounts as follows:

Cash

Beginning balance	87,100	Payments of operating expenses	46,100
Issuance of common stock	34,600	Payment of long-term debt	78,900
Receipts of dividends	1,900	Purchase of treasury stock	10,400
Collection of loan	18,500	Payment of income tax	8,000
Sale of investments	9,900	Payments on accounts payable	101,600
Receipts of interest	12,200	Payment of dividends	1,800
Collections from customers	298,100	Payments of salaries and wages	67,500
Sale of treasury stock	26,200	Payments of interest	21,800
		Purchase of equipment	79,900
Ending balance	72,500		

Common Stock

		Beginning balance	103,500
		Issuance for cash	34,600
		Issuance to acquire land	62,100
		Issuance to retire long-term debt	21,100
		Ending balance	221,300

Required

1. Prepare Ball State's statement of cash flows for the year ended December 31, 19X8, using the *direct* method to report operating activities. Also prepare the accompanying schedule of noncash investing and financing activities. Ball State's 19X8 income statement and selected balance sheet data follow.

BALL STATE CORP.
Income Statement
For the Year Ended December 31, 19X8

Revenues and gains:		
Sales revenue		$281,800
Interest revenue		12,200
Dividend revenue		1,900
Gain on sale of investments		700
Total revenues and gains		296,600
Expenses:		
Cost of goods sold	$103,600	
Salary and wage expense	66,800	
Depreciation expense	10,900	
Other operating expense	44,700	
Interest expense	24,100	
Income tax expense	2,600	
Total expenses		252,700
Net income		$ 43,900

BALL STATE CORP.
Balance Sheet Data

	19X8 Increase (Decrease)
Current assets:	
Cash and cash equivalents	$?
Accounts receivable	(16,300)
Inventories	5,700
Prepaid expenses	(1,900)
Loan receivable	(18,500)
Investments	(9,200)
Equipment, net	69,000
Land	62,100
Current liabilities:	
Accounts payable	$ 7,700
Interest payable	2,300
Salary payable	(700)
Other accrued liabilities	(3,300)
Income tax payable	(5,400)
Long-term debt	(100,000)
Common stock	117,800
Retained earnings	42,100
Treasury stock	(15,800)

2. Use these data to prepare a supplementary schedule showing cash flows from operating activities by the *indirect* method. All activity in the current accounts results from operations.

Preparing the statement of cash flows—indirect and direct methods
(Obj. 3, 4, 5)

P12-8B Seaman-Young Corporation's comparative balance sheet at September 30, 19X4, included the following balances:

SEAMAN-YOUNG CORPORATION
Balance Sheet
September 30, 19X4 and 19X3

	19X4	19X3	Increase (Decrease)
Current assets:			
Cash	$ 48,700	$ 17,600	$ 31,100
Accounts receivable	41,900	44,000	(2,100)
Interest receivable	4,100	2,800	1,300
Inventories	121,700	116,900	4,800
Prepaid expenses	8,600	9,300	(700)
Long-term investments	51,100	13,800	37,300
Equipment, net	131,900	92,100	39,800
Land	47,100	74,300	(27,200)
	$455,100	$370,800	$ 84,300
Current liabilities:			
Notes payable, short-term	$ 22,000	$ -0-	$ 22,000
Accounts payable	61,800	70,300	(8,500)
Income tax payable	21,800	24,600	(2,800)
Accrued liabilities	17,900	29,100	(11,200)
Interest payable	4,500	3,200	1,300
Salary payable	1,500	1,100	400
Long-term note payable	123,000	121,400	1,600
Common stock	113,900	62,000	51,900
Retained earnings	88,700	59,100	29,600
	$455,100	$370,800	$ 84,300

Transaction data for the year ended September 30, 19X4:

a. Net income, $93,900.
b. Depreciation expense on equipment, $8,500.
c. Acquired long-term investments, $37,300.
d. Sold land for $38,100, including $10,900 gain.
e. Acquired equipment by issuing long-term note payable, $26,300.
f. Paid long-term note payable, $24,700.
g. Received cash of $51,900 for issuance of common stock.
h. Paid cash dividends, $64,300.
i. Acquired equipment by issuing short-term note payable, $22,000.

Required

1. Prepare Seaman-Young's statement of cash flows for the year ended September 30, 19X4, using the *indirect* method to report operating activities. Also prepare the accompanying schedule of noncash investing and financing activities. All current accounts except short-term notes payable result from operating transactions.
2. Prepare a supplementary schedule showing cash flows from operations by the *direct* method. The income statement reports the following: sales, $370,600; gain on sale of land, $10,900; interest revenue, $7,300; cost of goods sold, $161,500; salary expense, $63,400; other operating expenses, $29,600; income tax expense, $18,400; interest expense, $13,500; depreciation expense, $8,500.

EXTENDING YOUR KNOWLEDGE

DECISION CASES

Preparing and using the statement of cash flows to evaluate operations
(Obj. 4, 5)

Case 1. The 19X6 comparative income statement and the 19X6 comparative balance sheet of Navasota, Inc., have just been distributed at a meeting of the company's board of directors. The members of the board of directors raise a fundamental question: Why is the cash balance so low? This question is especially troublesome to the board members because 19X6 showed record profits. As the controller of the company, you must answer the question.

NAVASOTA, INC.
Comparative Income Statement
Years Ended December 31, 19X6 and 19X5

(In thousands)	19X6	19X5
Revenues and gains:		
Sales revenue	$444	$310
Gain on sale of of equipment (sale price, $33)	—	18
Totals	$444	$328
Expenses and losses:		
Cost of goods sold	$221	$162
Salary expense	48	28
Depreciation expense	46	22
Interest expense	13	20
Amortization expense on patent	11	11
Loss on sale of land (sale price, $61)	—	35
Total expenses and losses	339	278
Net income	$105	$ 50

NAVASOTA, INC.
Comparative Balance Sheet
December 31, 19X6 and 19X5

(In thousands)	19X6	19X5
Assets		
Cash	$ 33	$ 63
Accounts receivable, net	72	61
Inventories	194	181
Long-term investments	31	-0-
Property, plant, and equipment	361	259
Accumulated depreciation	(244)	(198)
Patents	177	188
Totals	$624	$554
Liabilities and Owners' Equity		
Notes payable, short-term (for general borrowing)	$ 32	$101
Accounts payable	63	56
Accrued liabilities	12	17
Notes payable, long-term	147	163
Common stock, no-par	149	61
Retained earnings	221	156
Totals	$624	$554

Required

1. Prepare a statement of cash flows for 19X6 in the format that best shows the relationship between net income and operating cash flow. The company sold no plant assets or long-term investments and issued no notes payable during 19X6. The changes in all current accounts except short-term notes payable arose from operations. There were *no* noncash investing and financing transactions during the year. Show all amounts in thousands.
2. Answer the board members' question: Why is the cash balance so low? In explaining the business's cash flows, identify two significant cash receipts that occurred during 19X5 but not in 19X6. Also point out the two largest cash disbursements during 19X6.
3. Considering net income and the company's cash flows during 19X6, was it a good year or a bad year? Give your reasons.

Using cash-flow data to evaluate an investment ***(Obj. 1, 2)***

Case 2. Magna Corp. and Altex, Inc., are asking you to recommend their stock to your clients. Magna and Altex earn about the same net income and have similar financial positions, so your decision depends on their cash-flow statements, summarized as follows:

	Magna Corp.		Altex, Inc.	
Net cash inflows from operating activities		$ 70,000		$ 30,000
Net cash inflows (outflows) from investing activities:				
Purchase of plant assets	$(100,000)		$(20,000)	
Sale of plant assets	10,000	(90,000)	40,000	20,000
Net cash inflows (outflows) from financing activities:				
Issuance of common stock		30,000		—
Paying off long-term debt		—		(40,000)
Net increase in cash		$ 10,000		$ 10,000

Based on their cash flows, which company looks better? Give your reasons.

ETHICAL ISSUE

Jarvis Travel Agency is having a bad year. Net income is only $65,000. Also, two important clients are falling behind in their payments to Jarvis, and the agency's accounts receivable are ballooning. The company desperately needs a loan. The Jarvis board of directors is considering ways to put the best face on the company's financial statements. The agency's bank closely examines cash flow from operations. Gwen Morris, Jarvis's controller, suggests reclassifying as long-term the receivables from the slow-paying clients. She explains to the board that removing the $30,000 rise in accounts receivable will increase net cash inflow from operations. This approach will increase the company's cash balance and may help Jarvis get the loan.

Required

1. Using only the amounts given, compute net cash inflow from operations both with and without the reclassification of the receivables. Which reporting makes Jarvis look better?
2. Where else in the agency's cash-flow statement will the reclassification of the receivable be reported? What cash-flow effect will this item report? What effect would the reclassification have on *overall* cash flow from all activities?
3. Under what condition would the reclassification of the receivables be ethical? Unethical?

FINANCIAL STATEMENT CASES

Using the statement of cash flows ***(Obj. 1, 2, 3, 4, 5)***

Case 1. Use the Lands' End, Inc., statement of cash flows along with the company's other financial statements, all in Appendix A at the end of the book, to answer the following questions.

Required

1. By which method does Lands' End report net cash flows from *operating* activities? How can you tell?
2. Suppose Lands' End reported net cash flows from operating activities by the direct method. Compute these amounts for the year ended February 2, 1966:
   a. Collections from customers.
   b. Payments into employees' profit sharing plan. Assume that all transactions affecting the company's retirement plan for employees affect the Accrued Profit Sharing account. Note 7 provides some relevant information.
   c. Payments for inventory.
3. Evaluate the year ended February 2, 1996, in terms of net income, cash flows, balance sheet position, and overall results. Be specific.

Computing cash-flow amounts and using cash-flow data for analysis ***(Obj. 1, 2, 3, 4, 5)***

Case 2. Obtain the annual report of a company of your choosing. Answer the following questions about the company. Concentrate on the current year in the report.

Required

1. By which method does the company report net cash flows from *operating activities?* How can you tell?
2. Suppose the company reported net cash flows from operating activities by the direct method. Compute these amounts for the current year:
   a. Collections from customers.
   b. Payments to employees. Assume that the sum of Salary Expense, Wage Expense, and other payroll expenses for the current year make up 60% of Selling, General, and Administrative Expenses (or expense of similar title).
   c. Payments for inventory. d. Payments for income tax.
3. Evaluate the current year in terms of net income (or net loss), cash flows, balance sheet position, and overall results. Be specific.

GROUP PROJECTS

Project 1 Select a company and obtain its annual report, including all the financial statements. Focus on the statement of cash flows and the cash flows from operating activities in particular. Identify whether the company uses the direct method or the indirect method to report operating cash flows. Use the other financial statements (income statement, balance sheet, and statement of stockholders' equity) and the notes, if necessary, to prepare the company's cash flows from operating activities by the *other* method.

Project 2 Each member of the group should obtain the annual report of a different company. Select companies in different industries. Evaluate each company's trend of cash flows for the most recent two years. In your evaluation of the companies' cash flows, you may use any other information that is publicly available—for example, the other financial statements (income statement, balance sheet, statement of stockholders' equity, and the related notes) and news stories from magazines and newspapers. Rank the companies' cash flows from best to worst, and write a two-page report on your findings.

INTERNET EXERCISE

NETSCAPE CORP.

Netscape, the popular Internet browser, was developed on the University of Illinois campus by a graduate student, Marc Andreesen, to help scientists more easily navigate the cumbersome Internet. Today, Netscape is the leading provider of Internet browsers.

How does a 20-something graduate student take a great idea and transform it into a company valued at more than $5 billion? The Netscape Web site gives you a better understanding of the company and the direction the Internet is taking.

Required

1. Go to **http://www.netscape.com/,** the home page for Netscape. Here you will find a page replete with numerous places to visit. Learn about Netscape's current activities, download the latest browser software or plug-ins, check out the future plans for the Internet, jump to the Netscape list of favorite Web sites, or visit the various departments within Netscape.
2. Scroll down the page until you find the highlighted text, **Company & Products.** In this section, click on the highlighted text, **Investor Relations.** This page describes the products and services available from Netscape. At the bottom of the page are links to the company's financial information.
3. Click on the most recent **Annual Report** at the top of the page. Answer the following questions regarding Netscape.
   a. What does Netscape do?
   b. Netscape gives its browser away. How, then, does it make money?
   c. Examine the financial statements. Does Netscape make a profit? Are cash flows from operating activities positive or negative? Comment on the relation between these two results.
   d. How does the company define "cash and cash equivalents" for its Statement of Cash Flows?
   e. According to the Statement of Cash Flows, what was the greatest outflow of cash during 1995? What do you suspect was the source of those funds?

APPENDIX TO CHAPTER 12
The Work Sheet Approach to Preparing the Statement of Cash Flows

The body of this chapter discusses the uses of the statement of cash flows in decision making and shows how to prepare the statement by using T-accounts. The T-account approach works well as a learning device, especially for simple situations. In practice, however, most companies face complex situations. In these cases, a work sheet can help accountants prepare the statement of cash flows. This appendix shows how to prepare that statement using a specially designed work sheet.

ANCHOR CORPORATION Work Sheet for Statement of Cash Flows For the Year Ended December 31, 19X2				
	Balances	Transaction Analysis		Balances
	Dec. 31, 19X1	Debit	Credit	Dec. 31, 19X2
PANEL A—Account Titles				
Cash				
Accounts receivable				
PANEL B—Statement of Cash Flows				
Cash flows from operating activities:				
Cash flows from investing activities:				
Cash flows from financing activities:				
Net increase (decrease) in cash				

EXHIBIT 12A-1
Work Sheet for Preparing the Statement of Cash Flows

The basic task in preparing the statement of cash flows is to account for all the cash effects of transactions that took the business from its beginning financial position to its ending financial position. Like the T-account approach, the work sheet approach helps accountants identify the cash effects of all the period's transactions. The work sheet starts with the beginning balance sheet and concludes with the ending balance sheet. Two middle columns—one for debit amounts and the other for credit amounts—complete the work sheet. These columns, labeled Transaction Analysis, contain the data for the statement of cash flows. Exhibit 12A-1 presents the basic framework of the work sheet. Accountants can prepare the statement directly from the lower part of the work sheet (Panel B in Exhibit 12A-1). The advantage of the work sheet is that it organizes all relevant data for the statement's preparation in one place. All the exhibits in this appendix are based on the Anchor Corporation data presented earlier in the chapter.

The work sheet can be used with either the direct method or the indirect method for operating activities. As with the T-account approach, cash flows from investing activities and cash flows from financing activities are unaffected by the method used for operating activities.

Preparing the Work Sheet—Direct Method for Operating Activities

Objective A1

Prepare a work sheet for the statement of cash flows—direct method

The direct method separates operating activities into cash receipts and cash payments. Exhibit 12A-2 is the work sheet for preparing the statement of cash flows by the direct method. The work sheet can be prepared by following these steps:

Step 1: In Panel A, insert the beginning and ending balances for Cash, Accounts Receivable, and all other balance sheet accounts through Retained Earnings. The amounts are taken directly from the beginning and ending balance sheets in Exhibit 12-7.

Step 2: In Panel B, lay out the framework of the statement of cash flows as shown in Exhibit 12A-1—that is, enter the headings for cash flows from operating activities, investing activities, and financing activities. Exhibit 12A-2 is based on the direct method and splits operating activities into Receipts and Payments.

Step 3: At the bottom of the work sheet, write Net Increase in Cash or Net Decrease in Cash, as the case may be. This final amount on the work sheet is

ANCHOR CORPORATION Work Sheet for Statement of Cash Flows (Direct Method) For the Year Ended December 31, 19X2				
	(In thousands)			
	Balances	Transaction Analysis		Balances
	Dec. 31, 19X1	Debit	Credit	Dec. 31, 19X2
PANEL A—Account Titles				
Cash	42		(v) 20	22
Accounts receivable	80	(a) 284	(b) 271	93
Interest receivable	1	(c) 12	(d) 10	3
Inventory	138	(g) 147	(f) 150	135
Prepaid expenses	7	(h3) 1		8
Long-term receivable from another company	—	(p) 11		11
Plant assets, net	219	(o) 306	(k) 18	
			(q) 54	453
Totals	487			725
Accounts payable	57	(h1) 113	(g) 147	91
Salary and wage payable	6	(j) 58	(i) 56	4
Accrued liabilities	3	(h2) 19	(l) 17	1
Long-term debt	77	(t) 11	(s) 94	160
Common stock	258		(r) 101	359
Retained earnings	86	(f) 150	(a) 284	110
		(l) 17	(c) 12	
		(i) 56	(e) 9	
		(k) 18	(q) 8	
		(m) 16		
		(n) 15		
		(u) 17		
Totals	487	1,251	1,251	725
PANEL B—Statement of Cash Flows				
Cash flows from operating activities:				
Receipts:				
Collections from customers		(b) 271		
Interest received		(d) 10		
Dividends received		(e) 9		
Payments:				
To suppliers			(h1) 113	
			(h2) 19	
			(h3) 1	
To employees			(j) 58	
For interest			(m) 16	
For income tax			(n) 15	
Cash flows from investing activities:				
Acquisition of plant assets			(o) 306	
Proceeds from sale of plant		(q) 62		
Loan to another company			(p) 11	
Cash flows from financing activities:				
Proceeds from issuance of common stock		(r) 101		
Proceeds from issuance of long-term debt		(s) 94		
Payment of long-term debt			(t) 11	
Payment of dividends			(u) 17	
		547	567	
Net decrease in cash		(v) 20		
Totals		567	567	

EXHIBIT 12A-2 *Work Sheet for Statement of Cash Flows—Direct Method*

the difference between ending cash and beginning cash, as reported on the balance sheet. Fundamentally, the statement of cash flows is designed to explain why this change in cash occurred during the period.

Step 4: Analyze the period's transactions in the middle columns of the work sheet. Transaction analysis is the most challenging part of preparing the work sheet. The remainder of this appendix explains this crucial step.

Step 5: Prepare the statement of cash flows directly from Panel B of the work sheet.

Transaction Analysis on the Work Sheet

For your convenience, we repeat the Anchor Corporation transaction data from Exhibit 12-5. *Transactions with cash effects are denoted by an asterisk.*

Operating Activities:

(a) Sales on credit, $284,000
*(b) Collections from customers, $271,000
(c) Interest revenue earned, $12,000
*(d) Collection of interest receivable, $10,000
*(e) Cash receipt of dividend revenue, $9,000
(f) Cost of goods sold, $150,000
(g) Purchases of inventory on credit, $147,000
*(h) Payments to suppliers, $133,000
(i) Salary and wage expense, $56,000
*(j) Payments of salary and wages, $58,000
(k) Depreciation expense, $18,000
(l) Other operating expense, $17,000
*(m) Interest expense and payments, $16,000
*(n) Income tax expense and payments, $15,000

Investing Activities:

*(o) Cash payments to acquire plant assets, $306,000
*(p) Loan to another company, $11,000
*(q) Proceeds from sale of plant assets, $62,000, including $8,000 gain

Financing Activities:

*(r) Proceeds from issuance of common stock, $101,000
*(s) Proceeds from issuance of long-term debt, $94,000
*(t) Payment of long-term debt, $11,000
*(u) Declaration and payment of cash dividends, $17,000

The transaction analysis on the work sheet appears in the form of journal entries. Only balance sheet accounts appear on the work sheet. There are no income statement accounts. Therefore, revenue transactions are entered on the work sheet as credits to Retained Earnings. For example, in transaction (a), sales on account are entered on the work sheet by debiting Accounts Receivable and crediting Retained Earnings. Cash is neither debited nor credited because credit sales do not affect cash. Nevertheless, all transactions should be entered on the work sheet to identify all the cash effects of the period's transactions. In transaction (c), the earning of interest revenue is entered by debiting Interest Receivable and crediting Retained Earnings. The revenue transactions that generate cash are also recorded by crediting Retained Earnings.

Expense transactions are entered on the work sheet as debits to Retained Earnings. In transaction (f), cost of goods sold is entered by debiting Retained Earnings and crediting Inventory. Transaction (m) is a cash payment of interest expense. The work sheet entry debits Retained Earnings and credits Payments for Interest under operating activities. The remaining expense transactions follow a similar pattern.

NET INCREASE (DECREASE) IN CASH The net increase or net decrease in cash for the period is the balancing amount needed to equate the total debits and total credits ($567,000) on the statement of cash flows. In Exhibit 12A-2, Anchor Corporation experienced a $20,000 decrease in cash. This amount is entered as a credit to Cash, transaction (v), at the top of the work sheet and a debit to Net Decrease in Cash at the bottom. Totaling the columns completes the work sheet.

Preparing the Statement of Cash Flows from the Work Sheet

To prepare the statement of cash flows, Exhibit 12-2 in the text, the accountant has only to rewrite Panel B of the work sheet and add subtotals for the three categories of activities. It is also possible to use a computer-generated work sheet to prepare the statement of cash flows.

Preparing the Work Sheet—Indirect Method for Operating Activities

Objective A2

Prepare a work sheet for the statement of cash flows—indirect method

The indirect method shows the reconciliation from net income to net cash inflow (or net cash outflow) from operating activities. Exhibit 12A-3 on page 638 is the work sheet for preparing the statement of cash flows by the indirect method.

The steps in completing the work sheet by the indirect method are the same as those taken in the direct method. The analysis of investing activities and financing activities uses the information presented in Exhibit 12-5 and given on page 636 of this appendix. As mentioned previously, there is no difference for investing activities or financing activities between the direct- and the indirect-method work sheets. Therefore, the analysis that follows focuses on cash flows from operating activities. The Anchor Corporation data come from the income statement (Exhibit 12-6) and the comparative balance sheet (Exhibit 12-7).

Transaction Analysis Under the Indirect Method

Net income, transaction (a), is the first operating cash inflow.* Net income is entered on the work sheet as a debit to Net Income under cash flows from operating activities and a credit to Retained Earnings. Next come the additions to, and subtractions from, net income, starting with depreciation—transaction (b)—which is debited to Depreciation on the work sheet and credited to Plant Assets, Net. Transaction (c) is the sale of plant assets. The $8,000 gain on the sale is entered as a credit to Gain on Sale of Plant Assets under operating cash flows—a subtraction from net income. This credit removes the $8,000 amount of the gain from cash flow from operations because the cash proceeds from the sale were not $8,000. The cash proceeds were $62,000, so this amount is entered on the work sheet as a debit under investing activities. Entry (c) is completed by crediting the plant assets' book value of $54,000 ($62,000 – $8,000) to the Plant Assets, Net account.

Entries (d) through (j) reconcile net income to cash flows from operations for increases and decreases in the current assets other than Cash and for increases and decreases in the current liabilities. Entry (d) debits Accounts Receivable for its $13,000 increase during the year. This decrease in cash flows is credited to Increase in Accounts Receivable under operating cash flows. Entries (e) and (g) are similar for Interest Receivable and Prepaid Expenses.

The final item in Exhibit 12A-3 is the Net Decrease in Cash—transaction (q) on the work sheet—a credit to Cash and a debit to Net Decrease in Cash, exactly as in Exhibit 12A-2. To prepare the statement of cash flows from the work sheet, the accountant merely rewrites Panel B of the statement, adding subtotals for the three categories of activities.

NONCASH INVESTING AND FINANCING ACTIVITIES ON THE WORK SHEET Noncash investing and financing activities can also be analyzed on the work sheet. Because these types of transaction include both an investing activity and a financing activity, they require two work sheet entries. For example, suppose

*Note that we are now using the *indirect* method. The transactions we analyze here are *not* the same as those listed on page 636.

ANCHOR CORPORATION
Work Sheet for Statement of Cash Flows (Indirect Method)
For the Year Ended December 31, 19X2

	(In thousands)					
	Balances	Transaction Analysis				Balances
	Dec. 31, 19X1	Debit		Credit		Dec. 31, 19X2
PANEL A—Account Titles						
Cash	42			(q)	20	22
Accounts receivable	80	(d)	13			93
Interest receivable	1	(e)	2			3
Inventory	138			(f)	3	135
Prepaid expenses	7	(g)	1			8
Long-term receivable from another company	—	(l)	11			11
Plant assets, net	219	(k)	306	(b)	18	
				(c)	54	453
Totals	487					725
Accounts payable	57			(h)	34	91
Salary and wage payable	6	(i)	2			4
Accrued liabilities	3	(j)	2			1
Long-term debt	77	(o)	11	(n)	94	160
Common stock	258			(m)	101	359
Retained earnings	86	(p)	17	(a)	41	110
Totals	487		365		365	725
PANEL B—Statement of Cash Flows						
Cash flows from operating activities:						
Net income		(a)	41			
Add (subtract) items that affect net income and cash flow differently:						
Depreciation		(b)	18			
Gain on sale of plant assets				(c)	8	
Increase in accounts receivable				(d)	13	
Increase in interest receivable				(e)	2	
Decrease in inventory		(f)	3			
Increase in prepaid expenses				(g)	1	
Increase in accounts payable		(h)	34			
Decrease in salary and wage payable				(i)	2	
Decrease in accrued liabilities				(j)	2	
Cash flows from investing activities:						
Acquisition of plant assets				(k)	306	
Proceeds from sale of plant assets		(c)	62			
Loan to another company				(l)	11	
Cash flows from financing activities:						
Proceeds from issuance of common stock		(m)	101			
Proceeds from issuance of long-term debt		(n)	94			
Payment of long-term debt				(o)	11	
Payment of dividends				(p)	17	
			353		373	
Net decrease in cash		(q)	20			
Totals			373		373	

EXHIBIT 12A-3
Work Sheet for Statement of Cash Flows—Indirect Method

Anchor Corporation purchased a building by issuing common stock of $320,000. Exhibit 12A-4 illustrates the transaction analysis of this noncash investing and financing activity. Cash is unaffected.

Work sheet entry (t1) records the purchase of the building, and entry (t2) records the issuance of the stock. The order of these entries is unimportant.

ANCHOR CORPORATION Work Sheet for Statement of Cash Flows For the Year Ended December 31, 19X2				
	Balances	Transaction Analysis		Balances
	Dec. 31, 19X1	Debit	Credit	Dec. 31, 19X2
PANEL A—Account Titles				
Cash				
Accounts receivable				
Building	650,000	(t1) 320,000		970,000
Common stock	890,000		(t2) 320,000	1,210,000
PANEL B—Statement of Cash Flows				
Cash flows from operating activities:				
Net increase (decrease) in cash				
Noncash investing and financing transactions:				
Purchase of building by issuance of common stock		(t2) 320,000	(t1) 320,000	

EXHIBIT 12A-4
Noncash Investing and Financing Activities on the Work Sheet

APPENDIX PROBLEMS

Preparing the work sheet for the statement of cash flows—direct method
(Obj. A1)

P12A-1 The 19X3 comparative balance sheet and income statement of Silverado, Inc., follow. Silverado had no noncash investing and financing transactions during 19X3.

SILVERADO, INC. Comparative Balance Sheet			
	December 31,		Increase
	19X3	19X2	(Decrease)
Current assets:			
Cash and cash equivalents	$ 13,700	$ 15,600	$ (1,900)
Accounts receivable	41,500	43,100	(1,600)
Interest receivable	600	900	(300)
Inventories	94,300	89,900	4,400
Prepaid expenses	1,700	2,200	(500)
Plant assets:			
Land	35,100	10,000	25,100
Equipment, net	100,900	93,700	7,200
Total assets	$287,800	$255,400	$ 32,400
Current liabilities:			
Accounts payable	$ 16,400	$ 17,900	$ (1,500)
Interest payable	6,300	6,700	(400)
Salary payable	2,100	1,400	700
Other accrued liabilities	18,100	18,700	(600)
Income tax payable	6,300	3,800	2,500
Long-term liabilities:			
Notes payable	55,000	65,000	(10,000)
Stockholders' equity:			
Common stock, no-par	131,100	122,300	8,800
Retained earnings	52,500	19,600	32,900
Total liabilities and stockholders' equity	$287,800	$255,400	$ 32,400

SILVERADO, INC.
Income Statement for 19X3

Revenues:		
Sales revenue		$438,000
Interest revenue		11,700
Total revenues		449,700
Expenses:		
Cost of goods sold	$205,200	
Salary expense	76,400	
Depreciation expense	15,300	
Other operating expense	49,700	
Interest expense	24,600	
Income tax expense	16,900	
Total expenses		388,100
Net income		$ 61,600

Required

Prepare the work sheet for the 19X3 statement of cash flows. Format cash flows from operating activities by the *direct* method.

Preparing the work sheet for the statement of cash flows—indirect method ***(Obj. A2)***

P12A-2 Using the Silverado, Inc., data from Problem 12A-1, prepare the work sheet for Silverado's 19X3 statement of cash flows. Format cash flows from operating activities by the *indirect* method.

Preparing the work sheet for the statement of cash flows—indirect method ***(Obj. A2)***

P12A-3 Seaman-Young Corporation's comparative balance sheet at September 30, 19X4, follows.

SEAMAN-YOUNG CORPORATION
Balance Sheet
September 30, 19X4 and 19X3

	19X4	19X3	Increase (Decrease)
Current assets:			
Cash	$ 48,700	$ 17,600	$ 31,100
Accounts receivable	41,900	44,000	(2,100)
Interest receivable	4,100	2,800	1,300
Inventories	121,700	116,900	4,800
Prepaid expenses	8,600	9,300	(700)
Long-term investments	55,400	18,100	37,300
Plant assets:			
Land	65,800	93,000	(27,200)
Equipment, net	89,500	49,700	39,800
Total assets	$435,700	$351,400	$ 84,300
Current liabilities:			
Notes payable, short-term	$ 22,000	$ -0-	$ 22,000
Accounts payable	61,800	70,300	(8,500)
Income tax payable	21,800	24,600	(2,800)
Accrued liabilities	17,900	29,100	(11,200)
Interest payable	4,500	3,200	1,300
Salary payable	1,500	1,100	400
Note payable, long-term	62,900	61,300	1,600
Stockholders' equity:			
Common stock	142,100	90,200	51,900
Retained earnings	101,200	71,600	29,600
Total liability and stockholders' equity	$435,700	$351,400	$ 84,300

Transaction data for the year ended September 30, 19X4, are as follows:

a. Net income, $93,900.

b. Depreciation expense on equipment, $8,500.

c. Acquired long-term investments, $37,300.

d. Sold land for $38,100, including $10,900 gain.

e. Acquired equipment by issuing long-term note payable, $26,300.

f. Paid long-term note payable, $24,700.

g. Received cash of $51,900 for issuance of common stock.

h. Paid cash dividends, $64,300.

i. Acquired equipment by issuing short-term note payable, $22,000.

Required

Prepare Seaman-Young's work sheet for the statement of cash flows for the year ended September 30, 19X4, using the *indirect* method to report operating activities. Include on the work sheet the noncash investing and financing activities.

Preparing the work sheet for the statement of cash flows—direct method ***(Obj. A1)***

P12A-4 Refer to the data of Problem 12A-3.

Required

Prepare Seaman-Young's work sheet for the statement of cash flows for the year ended September 30, 19X4, using the *direct* method for operating activities. The income statement reports the following: sales, $370,600; gain on sale of land, $10,900; interest revenue, $7,300; cost of goods sold, $161,500; salary expense, $63,400; other operating expenses, $29,600; income tax expense, $18,400; interest expense, $13,500; depreciation expense, $8,500. Include on the work sheet the noncash investing and financing activities.

13

Financial Statement Analysis for Decision Making

Learning Objectives

After studying this chapter, you should be able to

1. Perform a horizontal analysis of comparative financial statements
2. Perform a vertical analysis of financial statements
3. Prepare common-size financial statements for benchmarking against the industry average and key competitors
4. Use the statement of cash flows in decision making
5. Compute the standard financial ratios used for decision making
6. Use ratios in decision making
7. Measure economic value added by a company's operations

Bristol-Myers Squibb Company
Consolidated Statement of Earnings

(In millions)	Year Ended December 31, 1995
Earnings	
1 **Net Sales**	**$13,767**
2 **Expenses:**	
3 Cost of products sold	3,637
4 Marketing, selling and administrative	3,670
5 Advertising and product promotion	1,646
6 Research and development	1,199
7 Special charge	950
8 Provision for restructuring	310
9 Other	(47)
10	11,365
11 **Earnings Before Income Taxes**	**2,402**
12 Provision for income taxes	590
13 **Net Earnings**	**$ 1,812**

The Procter & Gamble Company
Consolidated Statement of Earnings

(In millions)	Year Ended June 30, 1995
1 Net sales	$33,482
2 Cost of products sold	19,561
3 Marketing, research, and administrative expenses	9,677
4 Operating income	4,244
5 Interest expense	488
6 Other income, net	244
7 Earnings Before Income Taxes	4,000
8 Income taxes	1,355
9 Net Earnings	$ 2,645

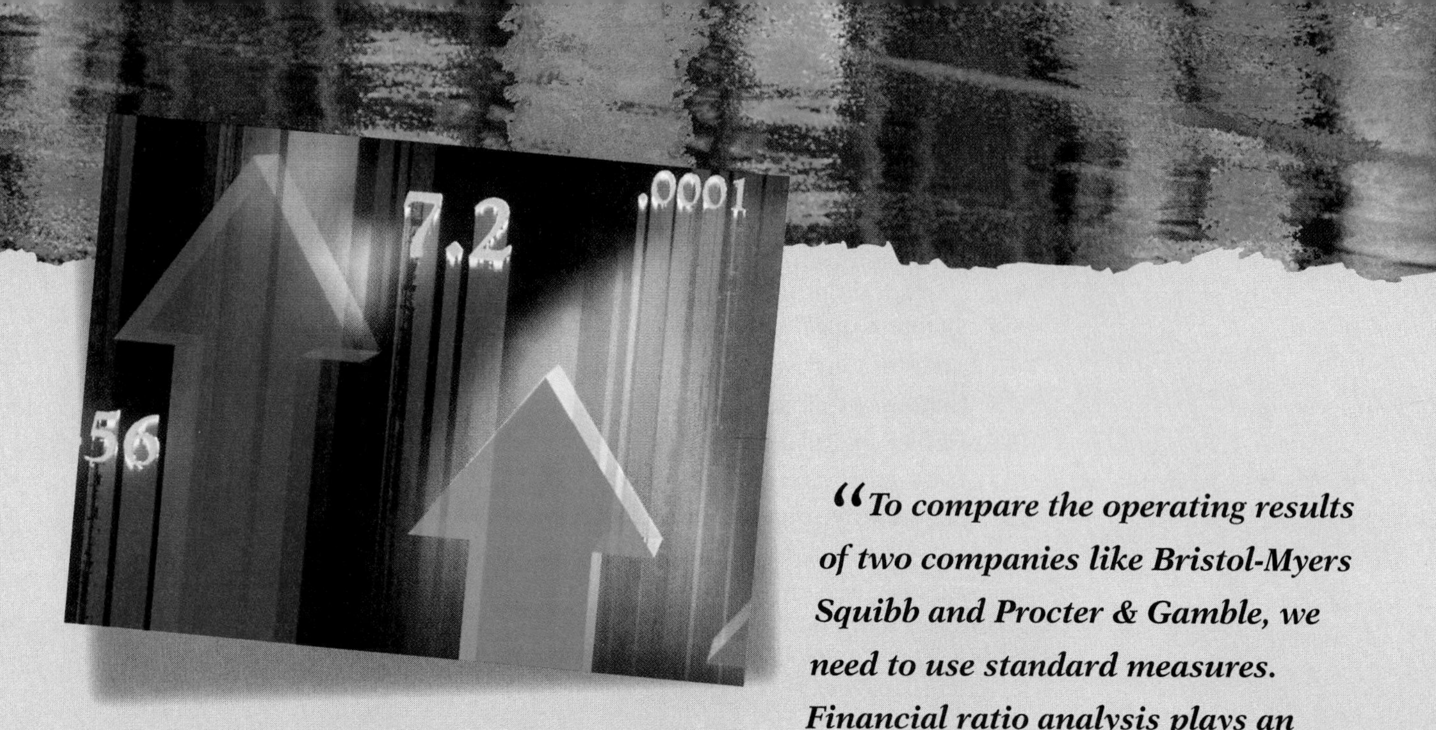

"To compare the operating results of two companies like Bristol-Myers Squibb and Procter & Gamble, we need to use standard measures. Financial ratio analysis plays an important part in the recommendations we make to our clients regarding which companies' stock to buy."

—ANGELA LANE, SENIOR ANALYST, BAER & FOSTER

Analysts at Baer & Foster, an investment banking firm, have identified health-care and consumer products as growth areas and will be recommending these companies' stocks to their clients. Angela Lane heads a team of analysts who are focusing on two companies: **Bristol-Myers Squibb** and **Procter & Gamble.** Bristol-Myers is best known for Clairol hair products, Ban deodorant, and Excedrin pain medicine. Some of Procter & Gamble's key products are Crest toothpaste, Tide detergent, Pampers diapers, and Pringles chips.

Lane and her team wish to compare the performance of Bristol-Myers and Procter & Gamble. However, the two companies differ greatly in size. Procter & Gamble has sales of $33 billion, compared to $14 billion for Bristol-Myers Squibb. Procter & Gamble's total assets of $28 billion are more than double Bristol-Myers' assets of $13 billion. How can Lane's team compare two companies of such different size?

Investors and creditors face similar challenges every day. The way to compare companies of different size is to use *standard* measures. Throughout this book we have discussed several financial ratios, such as the current ratio, the debt ratio, inventory turnover, and return on stockholders' equity. These ratios are standard measures that enable analysts to compare companies of different size or companies that operate in different industries. Managers use the ratios to monitor operations and help make business decisions, and they use the financial statements to calculate most of these ratios. In this chapter we discuss most of the basic ratios and related measures that managers use to run a company and investors and lenders use in their search for good investments and strong loan prospects. The extensive informational value of these ratios is one reason accounting is called the "language of business."

Financial Statement Analysis

Financial statement analysis focuses on the techniques used by internal managers and by analysts external to the organization. Outside analysts rely on publicly available information. A major source of such information is the annual report. In addition to the financial statements (income statement, balance sheet, and statement of cash flows), annual reports usually contain the following:

1. Notes to the financial statements
2. A summary of the accounting methods used
3. Management's discussion and analysis of the financial results
4. The auditor's report
5. Comparative financial data for a series of years

Items 1–4 are covered in Chapter 11.

Management's discussion and analysis (MD&A) of financial results is especially important because top management is in the best position to know how well or how poorly the company is performing. The SEC requires the MD&A from public corporations. For example, the 1995 annual report of **Bristol-Myers Squibb Company** includes six pages of MD&A. The report's Financial Review begins as follows:

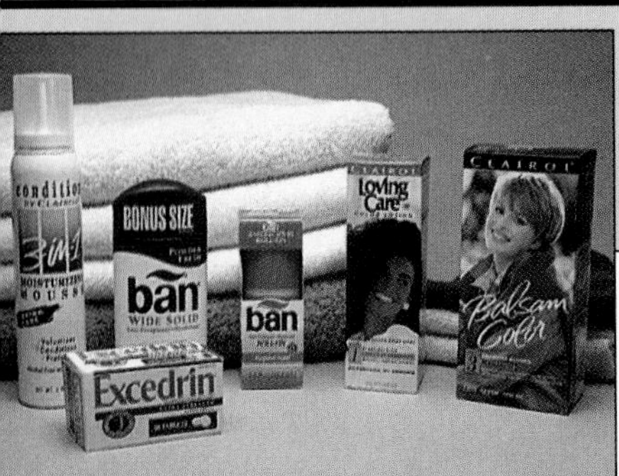

In 1995, Bristol-Myers Squibb achieved record sales, with all four of the company's segments reporting sales increases.

> In 1995, Bristol-Myers Squibb achieved record sales, with all four of the company's segments reporting sales increases. Sales increased 15% over the prior year to \$13.8 billion. Domestic sales increased 10% to \$7.7 billion, while international sales increased 22% to \$6.1 billion.

Bristol-Myers Squibb management also discusses its sales and profits in various industry segments—pharmaceuticals, medical devices, toiletries, and beauty aids. Each discussion is accompanied by graphical representation of important financial data, such as the graphs in Exhibit 13-1.

How relevant are these facts and predictions for making decisions about a company such as Bristol-Myers Squibb or Procter & Gamble? They are very relevant because they help managers, investors, and creditors interpret the financial statements. The balance sheet, income statement, and statement of cash flows are based on historical data. The MD&A offers glimpses into the company's future from the viewpoint of people in the know—top management. Investors and creditors are, after all, primarily interested in where the business is headed.

The Objectives of Financial Statement Analysis

Investors who purchase a company's stock expect that they will receive dividends and that the stock's value will increase. Creditors make loans with the expectation of receiving interest and principal. Both groups bear the risk that they will not receive their expected returns. They use financial statement analysis to (1) predict the amount of expected returns, and (2) assess the risks associated with those returns.

EXHIBIT 13-1
Representative Financial Data of Bristol-Myers Squibb Company

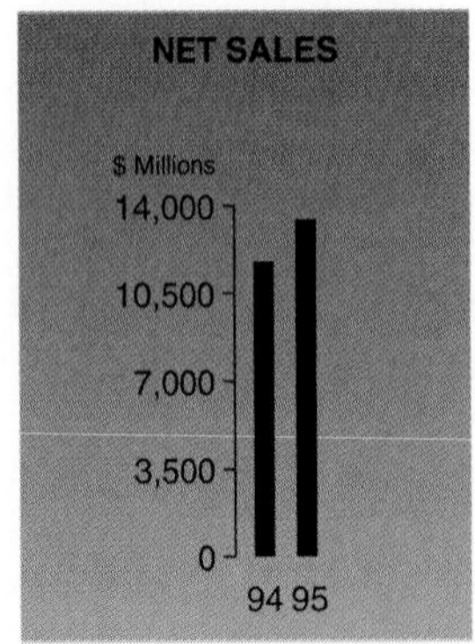

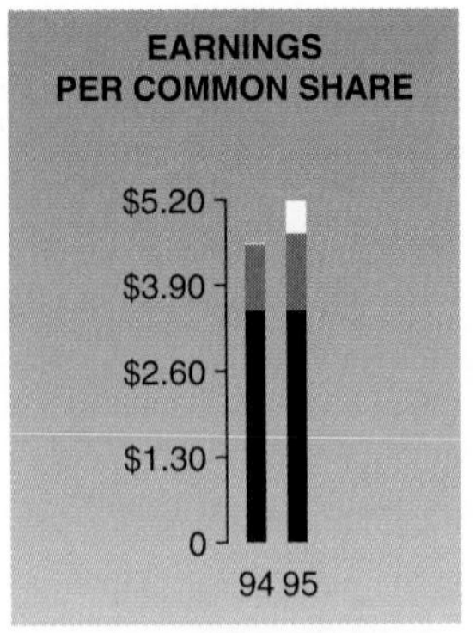

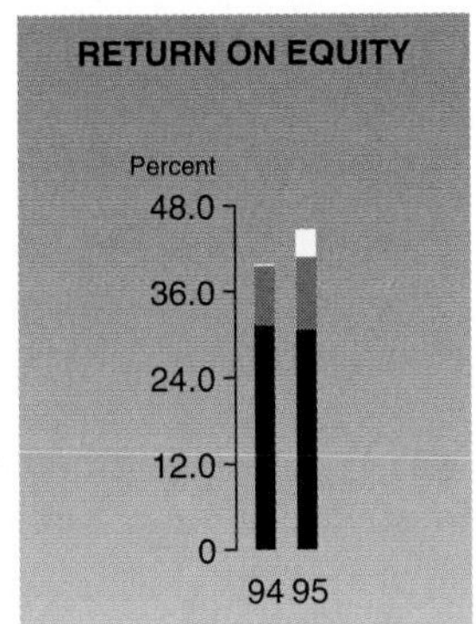

☐ Provision for Restructuring ■ Special Charge for Product Liability

Creditors generally expect to receive specific fixed amounts and have the first claim on a company's assets, so they are most concerned with assessing short-term liquidity and long-term solvency. **Short-term liquidity** is an organization's ability to meet current payments as they become due. **Long-term solvency** is the ability to generate enough cash to pay long-term debts as they mature.

In contrast, *investors* are more concerned with profitability, dividends, and future security prices. Why? Because dividend payments depend on profitable operations, and stock-price appreciation depends on the market's assessment of the company's prospects. Creditors also assess profitability because profitable operations are the company's main source of cash to repay loans.

The tools and techniques that the business community uses in evaluating financial statement information can be divided into three broad categories: horizontal analysis, vertical analysis, and ratio analysis.

Horizontal Analysis

Objective 1

Perform a horizontal analysis of comparative financial statements

Many managerial decisions hinge on whether the numbers—in sales, income, expenses, and so on—are increasing or decreasing over time. Has the sales figure risen from last year? From two years ago? By how much? We may find that the net sales figure has risen by $20,000. This fact may be interesting, but considered alone it is not very useful for decision making. An analysis of the *percentage change* in the net sales figure over time improves our ability to make decisions. It is more useful to know that sales have increased by 20% than to know that the increase in sales is $20,000.

The study of percentage changes in comparative statements is called **horizontal analysis.** Computing a percentage change in comparative statements requires two steps:

1. Compute the dollar amount of the change from the base (earlier) period to the later period.
2. Divide the dollar amount of change by the base-period amount.

Horizontal analysis is illustrated for Bristol-Myers Squibb as follows (dollar amounts in millions):

			Increase (Decrease)	
	1995	**1994**	**Amount**	**Percent**
Sales	$13,767	$11,984	$1,783	14.9%
Net income	1,812	1,842	(30)	(1.6%)

The percentage change in Bristol-Myers Squibb's sales during 1995 is computed as follows:

Step 1. Compute the dollar amount of change in sales from 19X4 to 19X5:

1995		1994		Increase
$13,767	–	**$11,984**	=	**$1,783**

Step 2. Divide the dollar amount of change by the base-period amount to compute the percentage change during the later period:

$$\text{Percentage change} = \frac{\text{Dollar amount of change}}{\text{Base-year amount}}$$

$$= \frac{\$1{,}783}{\$11{,}984} = 14.9\%$$

During 1995, Bristol-Myers Squibb's sales increased by 14.9 percent.

BRISTOL-MYERS SQUIBB COMPANY Statement of Earnings (Adapted) Years Ended December 31, 1995 and 1994				
			Increase (Decrease)	
(Dollar amounts in millions)	**1995**	**1994**	**Amount**	**Percent**
Net sales	$13,767	$11,984	$1,783	14.9%
Cost of products sold	3,637	3,122	515	16.5
Gross profit	10,130	8,862	1,268	14.3
Operating expenses:				
Marketing, selling, and administrative	3,670	3,166	504	15.9
Advertising and product promotion	1,646	1,367	279	20.4
Research and development	1,199	1,108	91	8.2
Special charge	950	750	200	26.7
Provision for restructuring	310	—	310	100.0*
Other	(47)	(84)	(37)	(44.0)
Earnings before income taxes	2,402	2,555	(153)	(6.0)
Provision for income taxes	590	713	(123)	(17.3)
Net earnings	$ 1,812	$ 1,842	$ (30)	(1.6)

*An increase from zero to any positive number is treated as an increase of 100 percent.

EXHIBIT 13-2
Comparative Income Statement—Horizontal Analysis

Detailed horizontal analyses of comparative income statements and comparative balance sheets are shown in the two right-hand columns of Exhibits 13-2 and 13-3, the financial statements of Bristol-Myers Squibb Company. The income statements (statements of earnings) reveal that net sales increased by 14.9% during 1995. But cost of goods sold and the two largest operating expenses grew even more. As a result, net income decreased slightly—a bad sign.

Other analysts would take a different view of Bristol-Myers Squibb's operations during 1995. The provision for restructuring—a one-time expense that is not expected to repeat from year to year—was the main reason that net income decreased in 1995. Without the restructuring expense, 1995 would have been a better year than 1994.

The comparative balance sheet in Exhibit 13-3 shows that 1995 was a year of expansion for Bristol-Myers Squibb. Total assets increased by $1,019 million, or 7.9 percent. The bulk of this growth occurred as a result of increases in current assets, other assets, and goodwill. Total liabilities increased by 12.5%, and total stockholders' equity grew by 2.1 percent.

STOP & THINK Identify the item on Bristol-Myers Squibb's 1995 income statement that experienced the largest percentage increase from 1994. As Bristol-Myers Squibb moves into 1996 and beyond, which is more important to the company, the percentage increase from 1994 to 1995 or the nature of this item? Explain.

Answer: The provision for restructuring increased by 100% from 1994 to 1995, from zero to $310 million. The nature of this item is more important than the percentage increase because the restructuring should pave the way for the company to make progress in the future.

Trend Percentages

Trend percentages are a form of horizontal analysis. Trends are important indicators of the direction a business is taking. How have sales changed over a five-year period? What trend does gross profit show? These questions can be answered by an analysis of trend percentages over a representative period, such as the most recent five or ten years. To gain a realistic view of the company, we often must examine more than just a two- or three-year period.

BRISTOL-MYERS SQUIBB COMPANY
Balance Sheet
December 31, 1995 and 1994

(Dollar amounts in millions)	1995	1994	Increase (Decrease) Amount	Percent
Assets				
Current Assets:				
Cash and cash equivalents	$ 1,645	$ 1,642	$ 3	0.2%
Time deposits and marketable securities	533	781	(248)	(31.8)
Receivables, net of allowances	2,356	2,043	313	15.3
Inventories	1,451	1,397	54	3.9
Prepaid expenses	1,033	847	186	22.0
Total Current Assets	7,018	6,710	308	4.6
Property, Plant, and Equipment—net	3,760	3,666	94	2.6
Insurance Recoverable	959	968	(9)	(0.9)
Other Assets	973	627	346	55.2
Excess of cost over net tangible assets received in business acquisitions [Goodwill]	1,219	939	280	29.8
	$13,929	$12,910	$1,019	7.9%
Liabilities				
Current Liabilities:				
Short-term borrowings	$ 575	$ 725	$ (150)	(20.7)%
Accounts payable	848	693	155	22.4
Accrued expenses [payable]	1,939	1,481	458	30.9
U.S. and foreign income taxes payable	744	740	4	0.5
Product liability*	700	635	65	10.2
Total Current Liabilities	4,806	4,274	532	12.4
Product Liability [Long-term]	1,645	1,201	444	37.0
Other Liabilities	1,021	1,087	(66)	(6.1)
Long-Term Debt	635	644	(9)	(1.4)
Total Liabilities	8,107	7,206	901	12.5
Stockholders' Equity				
Common stock	54	54	-0-	0.0
Capital in excess of par value of stock	375	397	(22)	(5.5)
Cumulative translation adjustments	(327)	(301)	(26)	(8.6)
Retained earnings	7,917	7,600	317	4.2
Less cost of treasury stock	(2,197)	(2,046)	(151)	(7.4)
Total Stockholders' Equity	5,822	5,704	118	2.1
	$13,929	$12,910	$1,019	7.9%

*Warranties, guarantees, and the like.

EXHIBIT 13-3
Comparative Balance Sheet—Horizontal Analysis

Trend percentages are computed by selecting a base year whose amounts are set equal to 100 percent. The amounts of each following year are expressed as a percentage of the base amount. To compute trend percentages, divide each item for following years by the corresponding amount during the base year:

$$\textbf{Trend \%} = \frac{\textbf{Any year \$}}{\textbf{Base year \$}}$$

Bristol-Myers Squibb Company showed sales, cost of goods sold, and gross profit for the past six years as follows:

(In millions)	1995	1994	1993	1992	1991	1990
Net Sales	$13,767	$11,984	$11,413	$11,156	$10,571	$9,741
Cost of products sold	3,637	3,122	3,029	2,857	2,717	2,665
Gross profit	10,130	8,862	8,384	8,299	7,854	7,076

We want trend percentages for a five-year period starting with 1991. We use 1990 as the base year. Trend percentages for net sales are computed by dividing each net sales amount by the 1990 amount of $9,741 million. Trend percentages for Cost of products sold are calculated by dividing each Cost of products sold amount by $2,665 (the base-year amount), and trend percentages for Gross profit are calculated by dividing each gross profit amount by $7,076 (the base-year amount). The resulting trend percentages follow (1990, the base year = 100%):

	1995	1994	1993	1992	1991	1990
Net Sales	141%	123%	117%	115%	109%	100%
Cost of products sold	136	117	114	107	102	100%
Gross profit	143	125	118	117	111	100%

Bristol-Myers Squibb's sales and cost of goods sold have trended upward. Gross profit has increased steadily, with the most dramatic growth during 1991 and 1995. This information suggests that gross profit is increasing steadily.

Vertical Analysis

Objective 2

Perform a vertical analysis of financial statements

Horizontal analysis highlights changes in an item over time. However, no single financial analysis technique provides a complete picture of a business. Another method of analyzing a company is vertical analysis.

Vertical analysis of a financial statement reveals the relationship of each statement item to a specified base, which is the 100% figure. Every other item on the financial statement is then reported as a percentage of that base. For example, when an income statement is subjected to vertical analysis, net sales is usually the base. Suppose under normal conditions a company's gross profit is 70% of net sales. A drop in gross profit to 60% of net sales may cause the company to report a net loss on the income statement. Management, investors, and creditors view a large decline in gross profit with alarm. Exhibit 13-4 shows the vertical analysis of Bristol-Myers Squibb's income statement as a percentage of net sales.

EXHIBIT 13-4
Comparative Income Statement—Vertical Analysis

BRISTOL-MYERS SQUIBB COMPANY
Statement of Earnings (Adapted)
Years Ended December 31, 1995 and 1994

	1995		1994	
(Dollar amounts in millions)	**Amount**	**Percent**	**Amount**	**Percent**
Net sales	$13,767	100.0%	$11,984	100.0%
Cost of products sold	3,637	26.4	3,122	26.1
Gross profit	10,130	73.6	8,862	73.9
Operating expenses:				
Marketing, selling, and administrative	3,670	26.7	3,166	26.4
Advertising and product promotion	1,646	12.0	1,367	11.4
Research and development	1,199	8.7	1,108	9.2
Special charge	950	6.9	750	6.3
Provision for restructuring	310	2.2	—	
Other	(47)	(0.3)	(84)	(0.7)
Earnings before income taxes	2,402	17.4	2,555	21.3
Provision for income taxes	590	4.2	713	(5.9)
Net earnings	$ 1,812	13.2%	$ 1,842	15.4%

BRISTOL-MYERS SQUIBB COMPANY
Balance Sheet
December 31, 1995 and 1994

(Dollar amounts in millions)	1995 Amount	1995 Percent	1994 Amount	1994 Percent
Assets				
Current Assets:				
Cash and cash equivalents	$ 1,645	11.8%	$ 1,642	12.7%
Time deposits and marketable securities	533	3.8	781	6.0
Receivables, net of allowances	2,356	16.9	2,043	15.8
Inventories	1,451	10.4	1,397	10.8
Prepaid expenses	1,033	7.4	847	6.7
Total Current Assets	7,018	50.3	6,710	52.0
Property, Plant, and Equipment—net	3,760	27.0	3,666	28.4
Insurance Recoverable	959	6.9	968	7.5
Other Assets	973	7.0	627	4.8
Excess of cost over net tangible assets received in business acquisitions [Goodwill]	1,219	8.8	939	7.3
	$13,929	100.0%	$12,910	100.0%
Liabilities				
Current Liabilities:				
Short-term borrowings	$ 575	4.1%	$ 725	5.6%
Accounts payable	848	6.1	693	5.4
Accrued expenses [payable]	1,939	13.9	1,481	11.5
U.S. and foreign income taxes payable	744	5.4	740	5.7
Product liability	700	5.0	635	4.9
Total Current Liabilities	4,806	34.5	4,274	33.1
Product Liability [Long-term]	1,645	11.8	1,201	9.3
Other Liabilities	1,021	7.3	1,087	8.4
Long-Term Debt	635	4.6	644	5.0
Total Liabilities	8,107	58.2	7,206	55.8
Stockholders' Equity				
Common stock	54	0.4	54	0.4
Capital in excess of par value of stock	375	2.7	397	3.1
Cumulative translation adjustments	(327)	(2.3)	(301)	(2.3)
Retained earnings	7,917	56.8	7,600	58.9
Less cost of treasury stock	(2,197)	(15.8)	(2,046)	(15.9)
Total Stockholders' Equity	5,822	41.8	5,704	44.2
	$13,929	100.0%	$12,910	100.0%

EXHIBIT 13-5
Comparative Balance Sheet—Vertical Analysis

In this case,

$$\textbf{Vertical analysis \%} = \frac{\textbf{Each income statement item}}{\textbf{Net sales}}$$

So, for example, the vertical analysis percentage for Cost of products sold for 1995 equals 26.4% ($3,637/$13,767 = 0.264). Exhibit 13-5 shows the vertical analysis of the balance sheet amounts as a percentage of total assets.

The vertical analysis of Bristol-Myers Squibb's income statement (Exhibit 13-4) shows no unusual relationships. The gross profit percentage declined a bit in 1995, as did net income's percentage of sales. However, there is no cause for alarm.

The vertical analysis of Bristol-Myers Squibb's balance sheet (Exhibit 13-5) also yields few surprises. Current assets' percentage of total assets declined in 1995, while current liabilities' percentage rose a little. The worst news on the balance sheet is the increase in product liability. The MD&A explained that the company's product liability resulted from claims against the company for its former breast-implant products. Bristol-Myers Squibb disposed of the subsidiary that manufactured the breast-implant products.

Recall from Chapter 3 (page 143) that the current ratio = total current assets divided by total current liabilities.

Despite the ongoing litigation, the company's financial position remains strong. For example, the current ratio is 1.46 ($7,018 million/$4,806 million). The company has very little long-term debt, and retained earnings (profit from operations) is the largest single source of financing.

STOP & THINK During 1995, Bristol-Myers Squibb's ratio of current assets to total assets decreased from 52.0% to 50.3 percent. The current liability percentage increased from 33.1% to 34.5 percent. Use these figures to predict whether Bristol-Myers Squibb's *current ratio* increased or decreased during 1995. Did the company's *debt ratio* increase or decrease during 1995? How can you tell?

Answer

The current ratio decreased during 1995, as follows:

	1995	1994
Current assets' percentage / Current liabilities' percentage	50.3% / 34.5% = 1.46	52.0% / 33.1% = 1.57
Total current assets (millions) / Total current liabilities (millions)	$7,018 / $4,806 = 1.46	$6,710 / $4,274 = 1.57

The debt ratio (total liabilities divided by total assets) increased from 55.8% in 1994 to 58.2% in 1995. The percentage of total liabilities reveals these percentages for the debt ratio. (Do the math yourself to double-check this.)

Common-Size Statements

Objective 3

Prepare common-size financial statements for benchmarking against the industry average and key competitors

The percentages in Exhibits 13-4 and 13-5 can be presented as a separate statement that reports only percentages (no dollar amounts). Such a statement is called a **common-size statement.**

On a common-size income statement, each item is expressed as a percentage of the net sales amount. Net sales is the *common size* to which we relate the statement's other amounts. In the balance sheet, the common size is the total on each side of the accounting equation (total assets *or* the sum of total liabilities and stockholders' equity). A common-size statement eases the comparison of different companies because their amounts are stated in percentages.

Common-size statements may identify the need for corrective action. Exhibit 13-6 is the common-size analysis of current assets taken from Exhibit 13-5. Exhibit 13-6 shows cash as a relatively high percentage of total assets at the end of each year. Receivables are a growing percentage of total assets. What could have caused the increase in receivables? Bristol-Myers Squibb may have been lax in collecting accounts receivable, a policy that may lead to a cash shortage. The company may need to pursue collection more vigorously. Or, the company may have sold to less-creditworthy customers. In any event, the company should monitor its cash position and collection of receivables to avoid a cash shortage. Common-size statements provide information useful for this purpose.

STOP & THINK Calculate the common-size percentages for the following income statement:

Net sales	$150,000
Cost of goods sold	60,000
Gross margin	90,000
Operating expense	40,000
Operating income	50,000
Income tax expense	15,000
Net income	$ 35,000

EXHIBIT 13-6
Common-Size Analysis of Current Assets

BRISTOL-MYERS SQUIBB COMPANY
Analysis of Current Assets
December 31, 1995 and 1994

	Percent of Total Assets	
	1995	1994
Current Assets:		
Cash and cash equivalents	11.8%	12.7%
Time deposits and marketable securities	3.8	6.0
Receivables, net of allowances	16.9	15.8
Inventories	10.4	10.8
Prepaid expenses	7.4	6.7
Total Current Assets	50.3	52.0
Long-Term Assets	49.7	48.0
Total Assets	100.0%	100.0%

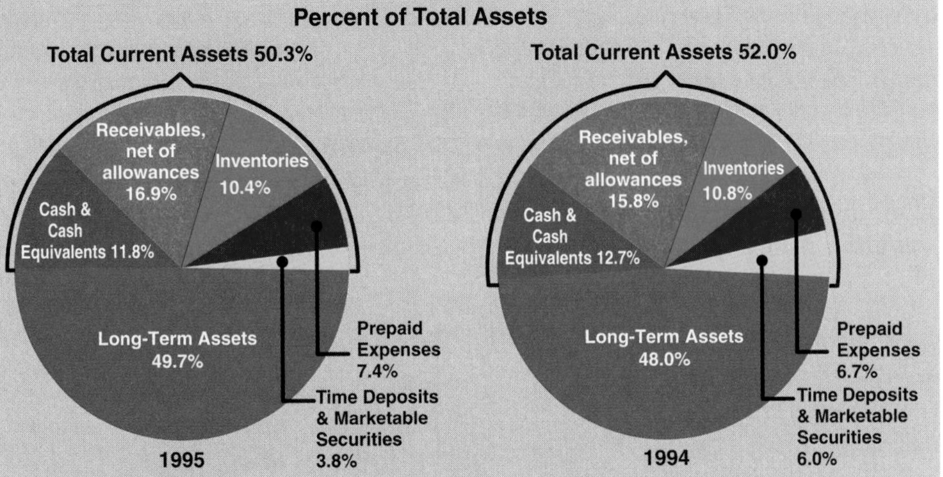

Percent of Total Assets

Answer

Net sales	100%	(= $150,000 ÷ $150,000)
Cost of goods sold	40	(= $ 60,000 ÷ $150,000)
Gross margin	60	(= $ 90,000 ÷ $150,000)
Operating expense	27	(= $ 40,000 ÷ $150,000)
Operating income	33	(= $ 50,000 ÷ $150,000)
Income tax expense	10	(= $ 15,000 ÷ $150,000)
Net income	23%	(= $ 35,000 ÷ $150,000)

Benchmarking

Benchmarking is the practice of comparing a company to a standard set by other companies, with a view toward improvement.

Benchmarking Against the Industry Average

We study a company's records to help us understand past results and predict future performance. Still, the knowledge that we can develop from a company's records is limited to that one company. We may learn that gross profit has decreased and that net income has increased steadily for the last ten years. This information is helpful, but it does not consider how businesses in the same industry have fared over the same time period. Have other companies in the same line of business increased their sales? Is there an industrywide decline in gross profit? Has cost of goods sold risen steeply for other businesses that sell the same products? Managers, investors, creditors, and other interested parties need to know how one company compares with other companies in the same line of business. For example, **Apple Computer's** gross margin has steadily declined in relation to its competitors'.

Exhibit 13-7 gives the common-size income statement of Bristol-Myers Squibb Company compared with the average for the pharmaceuticals (health-care) industry. This analysis compares Bristol-Myers Squibb with all other companies in its line of business. The industry averages were adapted from Robert Morris Associates' *Annual Statement Studies*. Analysts at **Merrill Lynch** and other companies specialize in a particular industry and make such comparisons in deciding which companies' stocks to buy or sell. For example, financial-service companies such as Merrill Lynch have health-care industry specialists, airline-industry specialists, and so on. Boards of directors evaluate top managers on the basis of how well the company compares with other companies in the industry. Exhibit 13-7 shows that Bristol-Myers Squibb compares favorably with competing companies in its industry. Its gross profit percentage is much higher than the industry average. The company does a good job of controlling total expenses, and as a result, its percentage of income from continuing operations and net income percentage are significantly higher than the industry average.

Benchmarking Against a Key Competitor

Common-size statements are also used to compare the company to another specific company. Suppose you are a member of Angela Lane's team at Baer & Foster. You are considering an investment in the stock of a manufacturer of health-care

EXHIBIT 13-7
Common-Size Income Statement Compared with the Industry Average

BRISTOL-MYERS SQUIBB COMPANY
Common-Size Income Statement for Comparison with Industry Average
Year Ended December 31, 1995

	Bristol-Myers Squibb	Industry Average
Net sales	100.0%	100.0%
Cost of products sold	26.4	55.3
Gross profit	73.6	44.7
Operating expenses	56.2	37.7
Earnings from continuing operations before income tax	17.4	7.0
Income tax expense	4.2	1.7
Earnings from continuing operations	13.2	5.3
Special items (discontinued operations, extraordinary gains and losses, and effects of accounting changes)	—	1.1
Net earnings	13.2%	4.2%

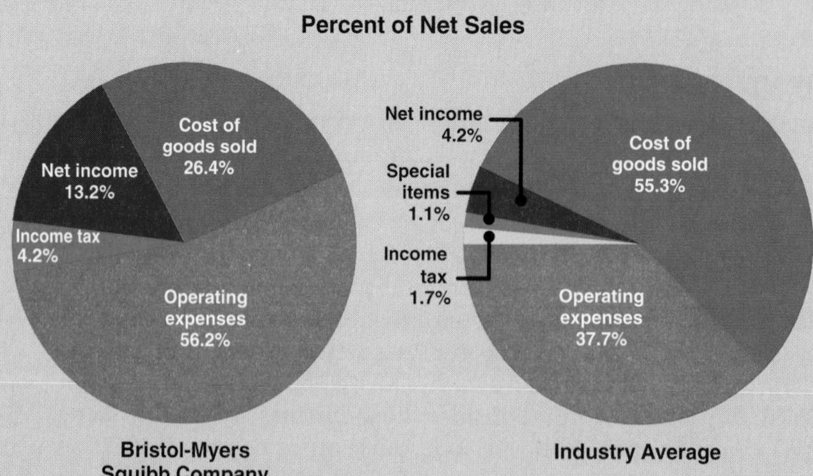

BRISTOL-MYERS SQUIBB COMPANY
Common-Size Income Statement for Comparison with Key Competitor
Year Ended December 31, 1995

	Bristol-Myers Squibb	Procter & Gamble
Net sales	100.0%	100.0%
Cost of products sold	26.4	58.4
Gross profit	73.6	41.6
Operating expenses	56.2	29.6
Earnings from continuing operations, before income tax	17.4	12.0
Income tax expense	4.2	4.0
Earnings from continuing operations	13.2	8.0
Special items (discontinued operations, extraordinary gains and losses, and effects of accounting changes)	—	—
Net earnings	13.2%	8.0%

Percent of Net Sales

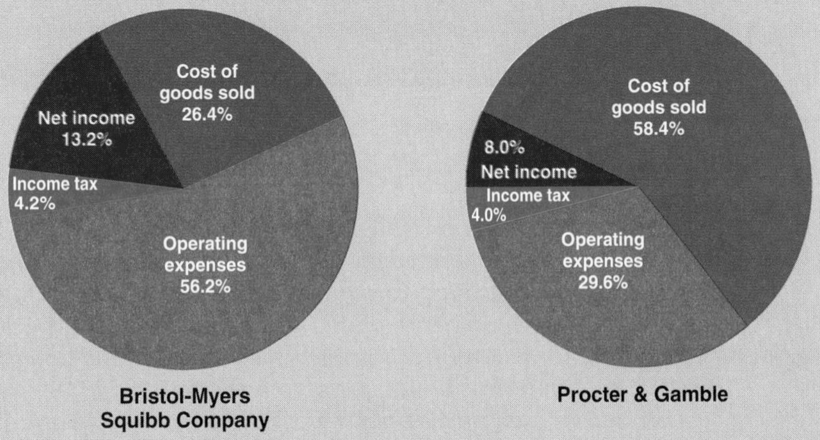

EXHIBIT 13-8
Common-Size Income Statement Compared with a Key Competitor

and other consumer products, and you are choosing between Bristol-Myers Squibb and Procter & Gamble. A direct comparison of their financial statements in dollar amounts is not meaningful because the amounts are so different (see the income statements on page 644). However, you can convert the two companies' income statements to common size and compare the percentages.

Exhibit 13-8 presents the common-size income statements of Bristol-Myers Squibb and Procter & Gamble. Procter & Gamble serves as an excellent benchmark because most of its products are market leaders. In this comparison, Bristol-Myers Squibb has higher percentages of gross profit, earnings from continuing operations, and net earnings.

Using the Statement of Cash Flows in Decision Making

Objective 4

Use the statement of cash flows in decision making

In the chapter thus far we have focused on the income statement and balance sheet. We may also perform horizontal and vertical analysis on the statement of cash flows. In Chapter 12, we discussed how to prepare the statement. To continue our discussion of its role in decision making, let's use Exhibit 13-9 on page 656.

Some analysts use cash-flow analysis to identify danger signals about a company's financial situation. For example, the statement in Exhibit 13-9 reveals what may be a weakness in DeMaris Corporation.

EXHIBIT 13-9
Statement of Cash Flows

DEMARIS CORPORATION
Statement of Cash Flows
Year Ended December 31, 19X5

Operating activities:		
Income from operations		$ 35,000
Add (subtract) noncash items:		
Depreciation	$ 14,000	
Net increase in current assets other than cash	(5,000)	
Net increase in current liabilities	8,000	17,000
Net cash inflow from operating activities		52,000
Investing activities:		
Sale of property, plant, and equipment	$ 91,000	
Net cash inflow from investing activities		91,000
Financing activities:		
Issuance of bonds payable	$ 72,000	
Payment of long-term debt	(170,000)	
Purchase of treasury stock	(9,000)	
Payment of dividends	(33,000)	
Net cash outflow from financing activities		(140,000)
Increase in cash		$ 3,000

First, operations provided a net cash inflow of $52,000, which is much less than the $91,000 generated by the sale of fixed assets. An important question arises: Can the company remain in business by generating the majority of its cash by selling its property, plant, and equipment? No, because these assets are needed to manufacture the company's products in the future. Note also that borrowing by issuance of bonds payable brought in $72,000. No company can long survive by living on borrowed funds. DeMaris must eventually pay off the bonds. Indeed, the company paid $170,000 on older debt. Successful companies such as **General Mills, DuPont,** and **Colgate-Palmolive** generate the greatest percentage of their cash from operations, not from selling their fixed assets or from borrowing money. These conditions may be only temporary for DeMaris Corporation, but they are worth investigating.

Successful companies such as General Mills, DuPont, and Colgate-Palmolive generate the greatest percentage of their cash from operations, not from selling their fixed assets or from borrowing money.

The most important information that the statement of cash flows provides is a summary of the company's sources and uses of cash. How a company spends its cash today determines its sources of cash in the future. The company may wisely use its cash to purchase assets that will generate income in the years ahead. If a company invests unwisely, however, cash will eventually run short.

DeMaris' statement of cash flows reveals problems. Exhibit 13-9 indicates that DeMaris invested in no fixed assets to replace those that it sold. The company may in fact be going out of business. Also, DeMaris paid dividends of $33,000, an amount very close to its net income. Is the company retaining enough cash to finance future operations—especially in light of the large amount of long-term debt that DeMaris paid off? Analysts seek answers to questions such as this. They analyze the information from the statement of cash flows along with the information from the balance sheet and the income statement to form a well-rounded picture of the business.

Mid-Chapter

SUMMARY PROBLEM FOR YOUR REVIEW

Perform a horizontal analysis and a vertical analysis of the comparative income statement of TRE Corporation, which makes metal detectors. State whether 19X3 was a good year or a bad year, and give your reasons.

TRE CORPORATION
Comparative Income Statement
Months Ended December 31, 19X3 and 19X2

	19X3	19X2
Total revenues	$275,000	$225,000
Expenses:		
Cost of products sold	$194,000	$165,000
Engineering, selling, and administrative expenses	54,000	48,000
Interest expense	5,000	5,000
Income tax expense	9,000	3,000
Other expense (income)	1,000	(1,000)
Total expenses	263,000	220,000
Net earnings	$ 12,000	$ 5,000

ANSWER

TRE CORPORATION
Horizontal Analysis of Comparative Income Statement
Months Ended December 31, 19X3 and 19X2

			Increase (Decrease)	
	19X3	19X2	Amount	Percent
Total revenues	$275,000	$225,000	$50,000	22.2%
Expenses:				
Cost of products sold	$194,000	$165,000	$29,000	17.6
Engineering, selling, and administrative expenses	54,000	48,000	6,000	12.5
Interest expense	5,000	5,000	—	—
Income tax expense	9,000	3,000	6,000	200.0
Other expense (income)	1,000	(1,000)	2,000	—*
Total expenses	263,000	220,000	43,000	19.5
Net earnings	$ 12,000	$ 5,000	$ 7,000	140.0%

*Percentage changes are typically not computed for shifts from a negative amount to a positive amount, and vice versa.

TRE CORPORATION
Vertical Analysis of Comparative Income Statement
Months Ended December 31, 19X3 and 19X2

	19X3		19X2	
	Amount	Percent	Amount	Percent
Total revenues	$275,000	100.0%	$225,000	100.0%
Expenses:				
Cost of products sold	$194,000	70.5	$165,000	73.3
Engineering, selling, and administrative expenses	54,000	19.6	48,000	21.3
Interest expense	5,000	1.8	5,000	2.2
Income tax expense	9,000	3.3	3,000	1.4*
Other expense (income)	1,000	0.4	(1,000)	(0.4)
Total expenses	263,000	95.6	220,000	97.8
Net earnings	$ 12,000	4.4%	$ 5,000	2.2%

*Number rounded up.

The horizontal analysis shows that total revenues increased 22.2 percent. This percentage increase was greater than the 19.5% increase in total expenses, resulting in a 140% increase in net earnings.

The vertical analysis shows decreases in the percentages of net sales consumed by the cost of products sold (from 73.3% to 70.5%) and by the engineering, selling, and administrative expenses (from 21.3% to 19.6%). These two items are TRE's largest dollar expenses, so their percentage decreases are quite important. The relative reduction in expenses raised December 19X3 net earnings to 4.4% of sales, compared with 2.2% the preceding December. The overall analysis indicates that December 19X3 was significantly better than December 19X2.

Using Ratios to Make Business Decisions

Objective 5

Compute the standard financial ratios used for decision making

An important part of financial analysis is the calculation and interpretation of ratios. A ratio expresses the relationship of one number to another number. For example, if the balance sheet shows current assets of $100,000 and current liabilities of $25,000, the ratio of current assets to current liabilities is $100,000 to $25,000. We simplify this numerical expression to the ratio of 4 to 1, which may also be written 4:1 and 4/1. Other acceptable ways of expressing this ratio include (1) "current assets are 400% of current liabilities," (2) "the business has four dollars in current assets for every one dollar in current liabilities," or simply, (3) "the current ratio is 4.0."

We often reduce the ratio fraction by writing the ratio as one figure over the other—for example, 4/1—and then dividing the numerator by the denominator. In this way, the ratio 4/1 may be expressed simply as 4. The 1 that represents the denominator of the fraction is understood, not written. Consider the ratio $175,000:$165,000. After dividing the first figure by the second, we come to 1.06:1, which we state as 1.06. The second part of the ratio, the 1, again is understood. Ratios provide a convenient and useful way of expressing a relationship between numbers. For example, the ratio of current assets to current liabilities—the current ratio—gives information about a company's ability to pay its current debts with existing current assets.

A manager, lender, or financial analyst may use any ratio that is relevant to a particular decision. Many companies include ratios in a special section of their annual financial reports. **Rubbermaid Incorporated**—the well-known manufacturer of plastic products for the home and garden, office, and industry—displays ratio data in the consolidated financial summary section of its annual report. Exhibit 13-10 shows an excerpt from that summary section. Investment services—**Moody's, Standard & Poor's, Robert Morris Associates,** and others—report these ratios for companies and industries.

Rubbermaid Incorporated—the well-known manufacturer of plastic products for the home and garden, office, and industry—displays ratio data in the consolidated financial summary section of its annual report.

The *Decision Guidelines* feature on pages 660–661 summarizes the widely used ratios that we will discuss in this chapter. The ratios may be classified as follows:

1. Ratios that measure the company's ability to pay current liabilities
2. Ratios that measure the company's ability to sell inventory and collect receivables
3. Ratios that measure the company's ability to pay long-term debt
4. Ratios that measure the company's profitability
5. Ratios used to analyze the company's stock as an investment

How much can a computer help in analyzing financial statements for investment purposes? Time yourself as you perform one of the financial-ratio problems in this chapter. Multiply your efforts by, say, 100 companies that you are comparing by means of this ratio. Now consider ranking these 100 companies on the basis of four or five additional ratios.

Online financial databases, such as **Lexis/Nexis** and the **Dow Jones News Retrieval Service,** offer quarterly financial figures for thousands of public corporations going back as far as ten years. Assume that you want to compare companies' recent earnings histories. You might have the computer compare hundreds of companies on the basis of price/earnings ratio and rates of return on stockholders' equity and total assets. The computer could then give you the names of the 20 (or however many) companies that appear most favorable in terms of these ratios. Alternatively, you could have the computer download financial statement data to your spreadsheet and compute the ratios yourself.

Accountants use computerized financial analysis a great deal. CPAs focus on the individual client. They want to know how the client is doing compared to the previous year and compared to other firms in the industry. Auditors want to detect any emerging trends in the company's ratios and compare the results of actual operations with expected results. To do so, they can download monthly financial statistics on a spreadsheet and compute the financial ratios to gain insight into the client's situation.

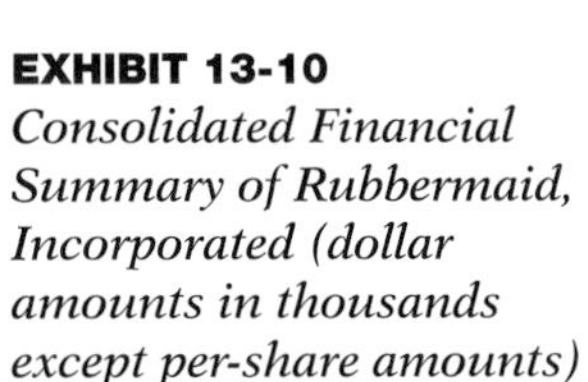

EXHIBIT 13-10
Consolidated Financial Summary of Rubbermaid, Incorporated (dollar amounts in thousands except per-share amounts)

Years Ended December 31,	19X3	19X2	19X1	19X0
Operating Results				
Net earnings	$211,413	$164,095	$162,650	$143,520
Per common share	$1.32	$1.02	$1.02	$0.90
Percent of sales	10.8%	9.1%	9.8%	9.4%
Return on average shareholders' equity	20.0%	17.5%	19.7%	20.2%
Financial Position				
Current assets	$829,744	$699,650	$663,999	$602,697
Current liabilities	$259,314	$223,246	$245,500	$235,300
Working capital	$570,430	$476,404	$418,499	$367,397
Current ratio	3.20	3.13	2.70	2.56

Decision Guidelines

Using Ratios in Financial Statement Analysis

Ratio	Computation	Information Provided
Measuring the company's ability to pay current liabilities:		
1. Current ratio	$\dfrac{\text{Current assets}}{\text{Current liabilities}}$	Measures ability to pay current liabilities with current assets.
2. Acid-test (quick) ratio	$\dfrac{\text{Cash} + \text{Short-term investments} + \text{Net current receivables}}{\text{Current liabilities}}$	Shows ability to pay all current liabilities if they come due immediately.
Measuring the company's ability to sell inventory and collect receivables:		
3. Inventory turnover	$\dfrac{\text{Cost of goods sold}}{\text{Average inventory}}$	Indicates saleability of inventory—the number of times a company sells its average inventory level during a year.
4. Accounts receivable turnover	$\dfrac{\text{Net credit sales}}{\text{Average net accounts receivable}}$	Measures ability to collect cash from credit customers.
5. Days' sales in receivables	$\dfrac{\text{Average net accounts receivable}}{\text{One day's sales}}$	Shows how many days' sales remain in Accounts Receivable—how many days it takes to collect the average level of receivables.
Measuring the company's ability to pay long-term debt:		
6. Debt ratio	$\dfrac{\text{Total liabilities}}{\text{Total assets}}$	Indicates percentage of assets financed with debt.
7. Times-interest-earned ratio	$\dfrac{\text{Income from operations}}{\text{Interest expense}}$	Measures the number of times operating income can cover interest expense.

LEARNING TIP Take some time here and make sure you really understand the relationships among the numbers on a financial statement. Horizontal and vertical analyses are one way to study such relationships. Ratios are another, even more helpful way. We compare financial statement amounts to other items to assess what the ratio indicates about the company. How do we assess a ratio? We must consider prior years, industry averages, budgeted ratios, and so on. These comparisons give a ratio added meaning.

Measuring a Company's Ability to Pay Current Liabilities

Working capital is defined as follows:

Working capital = Current assets − Current Liabilities

Working capital is widely used to measure a business's ability to meet its short-term obligations with its current assets. In general, the larger the working capital, the better able is the business to pay its debt. Recall that capital, or owners' equity, is total assets minus total liabilities. Working capital is like a "current"

Ratio	Computation	Information Provided
Measuring the company's profitability:		
8. Rate of return on net sales	$\frac{\text{Net income}}{\text{Net sales}}$	Shows the percentage of each sales dollar earned as net income.
9. Rate of return on total assets	$\frac{\text{Net income} + \text{Interest expense}}{\text{Average total assets}}$	Measures how profitably a company uses its assets.
10. Rate of return on common stockholders' equity	$\frac{\text{Net income} - \text{Preferred dividends}}{\text{Average common stockholders' equity}}$	Gauges how much income is earned with the money invested by common shareholders.
11. Earnings per share of common stock	$\frac{\text{Net income} - \text{Preferred dividends}}{\text{Number of shares of common stock outstanding}}$	Gives the amount of net income per one share of the company's common stock.
Analyzing the company's stock as an investment:		
12. Price/earnings ratio	$\frac{\text{Market price per share of common stock}}{\text{Earnings per share}}$	Indicates the market price of $1 of earnings.
13. Dividend yield	$\frac{\text{Dividend per share of common (or preferred) stock}}{\text{Market price per share of common (or preferred) stock}}$	Shows the precentage of a stock's market value returned as dividends to stockholders each period.
14. Book value per share of common stock	$\frac{\text{Total stockholders' equity} - \text{Preferred equity}}{\text{Number of shares of common stock outstanding}}$	Indicates the recorded accounting amount for each share of common stock outstanding.

version of total capital. The working capital amount considered alone does not give a complete picture of the entity's working capital position, however. Consider two companies with equal working capital:

	Company A	Company B
Current assets	$100,000	$200,000
Current liabilities	50,000	150,000
Working capital	$ 50,000	$ 50,000

Both companies have working capital of $50,000, but Company A's working capital is as large as its current liabilities. Company B's working capital is only one-third as large as its current liabilities. Which business has a better working capital position? Company A, because its working capital is a higher percentage of current assets and current liabilities. To use working-capital data in decision making, it is helpful to develop ratios. Two decision-making tools based on working capital data are the *current ratio* and the *acid-test ratio*.

CURRENT RATIO The most common ratio using current-asset and current-liability data is the **current ratio,** which is current assets divided by current lia-

We introduced the current ratio in Chapter 3 (page 143.)

bilities. Recall the makeup of current assets and current liabilities. Inventory is converted to receivables through sales, the receivables are collected in cash, and the cash is used to buy inventory and pay current liabilities. A company's current assets and current liabilities represent the core of its day-to-day operations. The current ratio measures the company's ability to pay current liabilities with current assets.

Exhibit 13-11 gives the comparative income statement and balance sheet of Palisades Furniture, Inc. The current ratios of Palisades Furniture, Inc., at December 31, 19X7 and 19X6, follow, along with the average for the retail furniture industry:

Formula	Palisades' Current Ratio 19X7	Palisades' Current Ratio 19X6	Industry Average
$\text{Current ratio} = \dfrac{\text{Current assets}}{\text{Current liabilities}}$	$\dfrac{\$262{,}000}{\$142{,}000} = 1.85$	$\dfrac{\$236{,}000}{\$126{,}000} = 1.87$	1.80

The current ratio decreased slightly during 19X7. Lenders, stockholders, and managers closely monitor changes in a company's current ratio. In general, a higher current ratio indicates a stronger financial position. A higher current ratio suggests that the business has sufficient liquid assets to maintain normal business operations. Compare Palisades Furniture's current ratio of 1.85 with the industry average of 1.80 and with the current ratios of some well-known companies:

Company	Current Ratio
Chesebrough-Pond's, Inc.	2.50
Wal-Mart Stores, Inc.	1.51
The Superior Oil Company	1.46
General Mills, Inc.	1.05

What is an acceptable current ratio? The answer depends on the nature of the industry. The norm for companies in most industries is between 1.60 and 1.90, as reported by Robert Morris Associates. Palisades Furniture's current ratio of 1.85 is within the range of those values. In most industries, a current ratio of 2.0 is considered good.

EXHIBIT 13-11
Comparative Financial Statements

PALISADES FURNITURE, INC.
Comparative Income Statement
Years Ended December 31, 19X7 and 19X6

	19X7	19X6
Net sales	$858,000	$803,000
Cost of goods sold	513,000	509,000
Gross profit	345,000	294,000
Operating expenses:		
Selling expenses	126,000	114,000
General expenses	118,000	123,000
Total operating expenses	244,000	237,000
Income from operations	101,000	57,000
Interest revenue	4,000	—
Interest expense	(24,000)	(14,000)
Income before income taxes	81,000	43,000
Income tax expense	33,000	17,000
Net income	$ 48,000	$ 26,000

ACID-TEST RATIO The **acid-test** (or **quick**) **ratio** tells us whether the entity could pay all its current liabilities if they came due immediately. That is, could the company pass this *acid test?* To do so, the company would have to convert its most liquid assets to cash.

We saw in Chapter 5 (pages 241–242) that the higher the acid-test ratio, the better able is the business to pay its current liabilities.

To compute the acid-test ratio, we add cash, short-term investments, and net current receivables (accounts and notes receivable, net of allowances) and divide by current liabilities. Inventory and prepaid expenses are the two current assets *not* included in the acid-test computations because they are the least liquid of the current assets. A business may not be able to convert them to cash immediately to pay current liabilities. The acid-test ratio uses a narrower asset base to measure liquidity than the current ratio does.

Palisades Furniture's acid-test ratios for 19X7 and 19X6 follow:

Formula		Palisades' Acid-Test Ratio 19X7	Palisades' Acid-Test Ratio 19X6	Industry Average
Acid-test ratio	= (Cash + short-term investments + net current receivables) / Current liabilities	($29,000 + $0 + $114,000) / $142,000 = 1.01	($32,000 + $0 + $85,000) / $126,000 = 0.93	0.60

The company's acid-test ratio improved considerably during 19X7 and is significantly better than the industry average. Compare Palisades' 1.01 acid-test ratio with the acid-test values of some well-known companies (shown on page 664):

EXHIBIT 13-11
Comparative Financial Statements (Continued)

PALISADES FURNITURE, INC.
Comparative Balance Sheet
December 31, 19X7 and 19X6

	19X7	19X6
Assets		
Current assets:		
Cash	$ 29,000	$ 32,000
Accounts receivable, net	114,000	85,000
Inventories	113,000	111,000
Prepaid expenses	6,000	8,000
Total current assets	262,000	236,000
Long-term investments	18,000	9,000
Property, plant, and equipment, net	507,000	399,000
Total assets	$787,000	$644,000
Liabilities		
Current liabilities:		
Notes payable	$ 42,000	$ 27,000
Accounts payable	73,000	68,000
Accrued liabilities	27,000	31,000
Total current liabilities	142,000	126,000
Long-term debt	289,000	198,000
Total liabilities	431,000	324,000
Stockholders' Equity		
Common stock, no par	186,000	186,000
Retained earnings	170,000	134,000
Total stockholders' equity	356,000	320,000
Total liabilities and stockholders' equity	$787,000	$644,000

Company	Acid-Test Ratio
Chesebrough-Pond's, Inc.	1.25
Whirlpool Corporation	0.92
General Motors, Inc.	0.91
Wal-Mart Stores, Inc.	0.08

How can a leading company such as Wal-Mart function with so low an acid-test ratio? Wal-Mart has almost no receivables. Its inventory is priced low to turn over very quickly. The norm ranges from 0.20 for shoe retailers to 1.00 for manufacturers of paperboard containers and certain other equipment, as reported by Robert Morris Associates. An acid-test ratio of 0.90 to 1.00 is acceptable in most industries.

STOP & THINK Palisades Furniture's current ratio is 1.85, which looks strong, while the company's acid-test ratio is 1.01, also strong. Suppose Palisades' acid-test ratio were dangerously low, say 0.48. What would be the most likely reason for the discrepancy between a high current ratio and a weak acid-test ratio?

Answer: It would appear that the company is having difficulty selling its inventory. The level of inventory must be relatively high, and the inventory is propping up the current ratio. The rate of inventory turnover may be low. This leads us into the next topic.

Measuring a Company's Ability to Sell Inventory and Collect Receivables

The ability to sell inventory and collect receivables is fundamental to business success. Recall the operating cycle of a merchandiser: cash to inventory to receivables and back to cash. In this section we discuss three ratios that measure the company's ability to sell inventory and collect receivables.

If you need to, refer to the discussion of the operating cycle in Chapter 3, page 137.

INVENTORY TURNOVER Companies generally seek to achieve the quickest possible return on their investments, including their investments in inventory. The faster inventory sells, the sooner the business creates accounts receivable, and the sooner it collects cash.

Inventory turnover is a measure of the number of times a company sells its average level of inventory during a year. A high rate of turnover indicates relative ease in selling inventory; a low turnover indicates difficulty in selling. In general, companies prefer a high inventory turnover. A value of 6 means that the company's average level of inventory has been sold six times during the year. This is generally better than a turnover of 3 or 4. However, a high value can mean that the business is not keeping enough inventory on hand, and inadequate inventory can result in lost sales if the company cannot fill a customer's order. Therefore, a business strives for the *most profitable* rate of inventory turnover, not necessarily the *highest* rate.

We introduced inventory turnover in Chapter 6, pages 285–286. Average inventory is computed as follows: (Beginning inventory + Ending inventory)/2.

To compute the inventory turnover ratio, we divide cost of goods sold by the average inventory for the period. We use the cost of goods sold—not sales—in the computation because both cost of goods sold and inventory are stated *at cost*. Sales is stated at the sales value of inventory and therefore is not comparable with inventory cost.

Palisades Furniture's inventory turnover for 19X7 is

Formula	Palisades' Inventory Turnover	Industry Average
$\text{Inventory turnover} = \dfrac{\text{Cost of goods sold}}{\text{Average inventory}}$	$\dfrac{\$513{,}000}{\$112{,}000} = 4.58$	2.70

Cost of goods sold appears in the income statement (Exhibit 13-11). Average inventory is figured by averaging the beginning inventory ($111,000) and ending inventory ($113,000). (See the balance sheet, Exhibit 13-11.) If inventory levels vary greatly from month to month, compute the average by adding the 12 monthly balances and dividing the sum by 12.

Inventory turnover varies widely with the nature of the business. For example, most manufacturers of farm machinery have an inventory turnover close to three times a year. In contrast, companies that remove natural gas from the ground hold their inventory for a very short period of time and have an average turnover of 30. Palisades Furniture's turnover of 4.58 times a year is high for its industry, which has an average turnover of 2.70. Palisades' high inventory turnover results from its policy of keeping little inventory on hand. The company takes customer orders and has its suppliers ship directly to some customers.

Inventory turnover rates can vary greatly within a company. At **Toys "Я" Us,** diapers and formula turn over more than 12 times a year, while seasonal toys turn over less than 3 times a year. The entire Toys "Я" Us inventory turns over an average of 3 times a year. The company's inventory is at its lowest point on January 31 and at its highest point around October 31.

To evaluate fully a company's inventory turnover, we must compare the ratio over time. A sudden sharp decline or a steady decline over a long period suggests the need for corrective action.

ACCOUNTS RECEIVABLE TURNOVER **Accounts receivable turnover** measures a company's ability to collect cash from credit customers. In general, the higher the ratio, the more successfully the business collects cash, and the better off its operations are. However, a receivable turnover that is too high may indicate that credit is too tight, causing the loss of sales to good customers. To compute the accounts receivable turnover, we divide net credit sales by average net accounts receivable. The resulting ratio indicates how many times during the year the average level of receivables was turned into cash.

Palisades Furniture's accounts receivable turnover ratio for 19X7 is computed as follows:

Formula	Palisades' Accounts Receivable Turnover	Industry Average
$\text{Accounts receivable turnover} = \dfrac{\text{Net credit sales}}{\text{Average net accounts receivable}}$	$\dfrac{\$858{,}000}{\$99{,}500} = 8.62$	22.2

The net credit sales figure comes from the income statement. Palisades Furniture makes all sales on credit. If the company makes both cash and credit sales, this ratio is best computed by using only net credit sales. Average net accounts receivable is figured by adding the beginning accounts receivable balance ($85,000) and the ending balance ($114,000), then dividing by 2. If the accounts receivable balances exhibit a seasonal pattern, compute the average by using the 12 monthly balances.

Palisades' receivable turnover of 8.62 is much lower than the industry average. The explanation is simple: The company is a home-town store that sells to local people who tend to pay their bills over a period of time. Many larger furniture stores sell their receivables to other companies called *factors,* a practice that keeps receivables low and receivable turnover high. But companies that factor (sell) their receivables receive less than face value of the receivables. Palisades Furniture follows a different strategy.

We examined the factoring of accounts receivable in Chapter 5, page 240.

STOP & THINK The sales of Comptronix, a manufacturer of computerized metering equipment, grew far faster than its receivables. Would this situation create an unusually high or an unusually low accounts receivable turnover?

Answer: Receivable turnover would be unusually high. This high ratio would look strange in relation to the company's past measures of receivable turnover.

DAYS' SALES IN RECEIVABLES Businesses must convert accounts receivable to cash. All else equal, the lower the Accounts Receivable balance, the more successful the business has been in converting receivables into cash, and the better off the business is.

The **days'-sales-in-receivables** ratio tells us how many days' sales remain in Accounts Receivable. To compute the ratio, we follow a two-step process. First, divide net sales by 365 days to figure the average sales amount for one day. Second, divide this average day's sales amount into the average net accounts receivable.

Recall from Chapter 5 (page 242) that days' sales in receivables indicates how many days it takes to collect the average level of receivables.

The data to compute this ratio for Palisades Furniture, Inc., for 19X7 are taken from the income statement and the balance sheet (Exhibit 13-11):

Formula	Palisades' Days' Sales in Accounts Receivables	Industry Average
Days' Sales in AVERAGE Accounts Receivable:		
1. One day's sales = $\frac{\text{Net sales}}{\text{365 days}}$	$\frac{\$858{,}000}{\text{365 days}} = \$2{,}351$	
2. $\text{Days' sales in average accounts receivable} = \frac{\text{Average net accounts receivable}}{\text{One day's sales}}$	$\frac{\$99{,}500}{\$2{,}351} = 42 \text{ days}$	16 days

Days' sales in average receivables can also be computed in a single step: $99,500/($858,000/365 days) = 42 days.

Palisades' ratio tells us that 42 average days' sales remain in accounts receivable and need to be collected. The company will increase its cash inflow if it can decrease this ratio. To detect any changes over time in the firm's ability to collect its receivables, let's compute the days'-sales-in-receivables ratio at the beginning and the end of 19X7:

Days' Sales in ENDING 19X6 Accounts Receivable:

$$\textbf{One day's sales} = \frac{\$803{,}000}{\text{365 days}} = \$2{,}200 \qquad \textbf{Days' sales in ENDING 19X6 accounts receivable} = \frac{\$85{,}000}{\$2{,}200} = \textbf{39 days at beginning of 19X7}$$

Days' Sales in ENDING 19X7 Accounts Receivable:

$$\textbf{One day's sales} = \frac{\$858{,}000}{\text{365 days}} = \$2{,}351 \qquad \textbf{Days' sales in ENDING 19X7 accounts receivable} = \frac{\$114{,}000}{\$2{,}351} = \textbf{48 days at end of 19X7}$$

This analysis shows a drop in Palisades Furniture's collection of receivables; days' sales in accounts receivable has increased from 39 at the beginning of the year to 48 at year end. The credit and collection department should strengthen its collection efforts. Otherwise, the company may experience a cash shortage in 19X8 and beyond.

The days' sales in receivables for Palisades is higher (worse) than the industry average because the company collects its own receivables. Many other furniture stores sell their receivables and carry fewer days' sales in receivables. Palisades Furniture remains competitive because of its personal relationship with its customers. Without their good paying habits, the company's cash flow would suffer.

Measuring a Company's Ability to Pay Long-Term Debt

The ratios discussed so far give us insight into current assets and current liabilities. They help us measure a business's ability to sell inventory, to collect receivables, and to pay current liabilities. Most businesses also have long-term debts. Bondholders and banks that loan money on long-term notes payable and bonds payable take special interest in the ability of a business to meet its long-term obligations. Two key indicators of a business's ability to pay long-term liabilities are the *debt ratio* and the *times-interest-earned ratio.*

DEBT RATIO Suppose you are a loan officer at a bank and you are evaluating loan applications from two companies with equal sales revenue and total assets. Sales and total assets are the two most common measures of firm size. Both companies have asked to borrow $500,000 and have agreed to repay the loan over a ten-year period. The first firm already owes $600,000 to another bank. The second owes only $250,000. Other things equal, to which company are you more likely to lend money at a lower interest rate? Company 2, because the bank faces less risk by loaning to Company 2. That company owes less to creditors than Company 1 owes.

This relationship between total liabilities and total assets—called the **debt ratio**—tells us the proportion of the company's assets that it has financed with debt. If the debt ratio is 1, then debt has been used to finance all the assets. A debt ratio of 0.50 means that the company has used debt to finance half its assets and that the owners of the business have financed the other half. The higher the debt ratio, the higher the strain of paying interest each year and the principal amount at maturity. The lower the ratio, the lower the business's future obligations. Creditors view a high debt ratio with caution. If a business seeking financing already has large liabilities, then additional debt payments may be too much for the business to handle. To help protect themselves, creditors generally charge higher interest rates on new borrowing to companies with an already-high debt ratio.

We introduced the debt ratio in Chapter 3, page 143.

Calculation of the debt ratios for Palisades Furniture at the end of 19X7 and 19X6 is as follows:

Formula	Palisades' Debt Ratio 19X7	Palisades' Debt Ratio 19X6	Industry Average
Debt ratio = $\frac{\text{Total liabilities}}{\text{Total assets}}$	$\frac{\$431{,}000}{\$787{,}000} = 0.55$	$\frac{\$324{,}000}{\$644{,}000} = 0.50$	0.61

Palisades Furniture expanded operations by financing the purchase of property, plant, and equipment through borrowing, which is common. This expansion explains the firm's increased debt ratio. Even after the increase in 19X7, the company's debt is not very high. Robert Morris Associates reports that the average debt ratio for most companies ranges around 0.57–0.67, with relatively little variation from company to company. Palisades' 0.55 debt ratio indicates a fairly low-risk debt position compared to the retail furniture industry average of 0.61.

TIMES-INTEREST-EARNED RATIO The debt ratio measures the effect of debt on the company's *financial position* (balance sheet) but says nothing about its ability to pay interest expense. Analysts use a second ratio—the **times-interest-earned ratio**—to relate income to interest expense. To compute this ratio, we divide income from operations by interest expense. This ratio measures the number of times that operating income can *cover* interest expense. For this reason, the ratio is also called the *interest-coverage ratio.* A high times-interest-earned ratio indicates ease in paying interest expense; a low value suggests difficulty.

Calculation of Palisades' times-interest-earned ratios is as follows:

Formula	Palisades' Times-Interest-Earned Ratio 19X7	Palisades' Times-Interest-Earned Ratio 19X6	Industry Average
$\text{Times-interest-earned ratio} = \frac{\text{Income from operations}}{\text{Interest expense}}$	$\frac{\$101{,}000}{\$24{,}000} = 4.21$	$\frac{\$57{,}000}{\$14{,}000} = 4.07$	2.00

The company's times-interest-earned ratio increased in 19X7. This is a favorable sign, especially since the company's short-term notes payable and long-term debt rose substantially during the year. Palisades Furniture's new plant assets, we conclude, have earned more in operating income than they have cost the business in interest expense. The company's times-interest-earned ratio of around 4.00 is significantly better than the 2.00 average for furniture retailers. The norm for U.S. business, as reported by Robert Morris Associates, falls in the range of 2.0 to 3.0 for most companies.

On the basis of its debt ratio and its times-interest-earned ratio, Palisades Furniture appears to have little difficulty *servicing its debt*—that is, paying its liabilities.

Measuring a Company's Profitability

The fundamental goal of business is to earn a profit. Ratios that measure profitability play a large role in decision making. These ratios are reported in the business press, by investment services, and in companies' annual financial reports.

Suppose you are a personal financial planner who helps clients select stock investments. One client has $100,000 to invest in a chemical company. Over the next few years, you expect **Dow Chemical** to earn higher rates of return on its investments than analysts are forecasting for the chemical manufacturer **Monsanto.** Which company's stock will you recommend? Probably Dow's—for reasons you will better understand after studying four rate-of-return measurements.

RATE OF RETURN ON NET SALES In business, the term *return* is used broadly and loosely as an evaluation of profitability. Consider a ratio called the **rate of return on net sales,** or simply *return on sales.* (The word *net* is usually omitted for convenience, even though the net sales figure is used to compute the ratio.) This ratio shows the percentage of each sales dollar earned as net income. The rate-of-return-on-sales ratios for Palisades Furniture are calculated as follows:

Formula	Palisades' Rate of Return on Sales 19X7	Palisades' Rate of Return on Sales 19X6	Industry Average
$\text{Rate of return on sales} = \frac{\text{Net income}}{\text{Net sales}}$	$\frac{\$48{,}000}{\$858{,}000} = 0.056$	$\frac{\$26{,}000}{\$803{,}000} = 0.032$	0.008

Companies strive for a high rate of return. The higher the rate of return, the more net sales dollars are providing income to the business and the fewer net sales dollars are absorbed by expenses. The increase in Palisades Furniture's return on sales is significant and identifies the company as more successful than the average furniture store. Compare Palisades' rate of return on sales to the rates of some other companies:

Company	Rate of Return on Sales
Chesebrough-Pond's, Inc.	0.076
General Motors	0.054
Kraft, Inc.	0.047
Wal-Mart Stores, Inc.	0.036

As these numbers indicate, the rate of return on sales varies widely from industry to industry.

One strategy for increasing the rate of return on sales is to develop a product that commands a premium price, such as **Häagen-Dazs** ice cream, **Sony** products, and **Maytag** appliances. Another strategy is to control costs. If successful, either strategy converts a higher proportion of sales into net income and increases the rate of return on net sales.

A return measure can be computed on any revenue and sales amount. Return on net sales, as we have seen, is net income divided by net sales. *Return on total revenues* is net income divided by total revenues. A company can compute a return on other specific portions of revenue as its information needs dictate.

RATE OF RETURN ON TOTAL ASSETS The **rate of return on total assets,** or simply *return on assets,* measures a company's success in using its assets to earn a profit. Creditors have loaned money to the company, and the interest they receive is the return on their investment. Shareholders have invested in the company's stock, and net income is their return. The sum of interest expense and net income is thus the return to the two groups that have financed the company's operations, and this amount is the numerator of the return-on-assets ratio. Average total assets is the denominator. Computation of the return-on-assets ratio for Palisades Furniture is as follows:

We first discussed the rate of return on total assets in Chapter 9, page 447.

Formula	Palisades' 19X7 Rate of Return on Total Assets	Industry Average
$\text{Rate of return on assets} = \dfrac{\text{Net income} + \text{Interest expense}}{\text{Average total assets}}$	$\dfrac{\$48{,}000 + \$24{,}000}{\$715{,}500} = 0.101$	0.049

Net income and interest expense are taken from the income statement (Exhibit 13-11). To compute average total assets, we take the average of beginning and ending total assets from the comparative balance sheet. Compare Palisades Furniture's rate of return on assets to the rates of some other companies:

Company	Rate of Return on Assets
The Gap, Inc.	0.170
Wal-Mart Stores, Inc.	0.129
General Mills, Inc.	0.124
The Superior Oil Company	0.080

As you can see, the rate of return on assets varies widely from industry to industry.

RATE OF RETURN ON COMMON STOCKHOLDERS' EQUITY A popular measure of profitability is **rate of return on common stockholders' equity,** which is often shortened to **return on stockholders' equity,** or simply *return on equity.* This ratio shows the relationship between net income and common stockholders' investment in the company—how much income is earned for every $1 invested by the common shareholders. To compute this ratio, we first subtract preferred dividends from net income. This calculation provides net income available to the common stockholders, which we need to compute the ratio. We then divide net income available to common stockholders by the average stockholders' equity during the year. Common stockholders' equity is total stockholders' equity minus preferred equity. The 19X7 rate of return on common stockholders' equity for Palisades Furniture is calculated as follows:

We examined this ratio in detail in Chapter 9. For a review, see page 448.

Formula		Palisades' 19X7 Rate of Return on Common Stockholders' Equity	Industry Average
Rate of return on common stockholders' equity	= $\frac{\text{Net income} - \text{Preferred dividends}}{\text{Average common stockholders' equity}}$	$\frac{\$48{,}000 - \$0}{\$338{,}000} = 0.142$	0.093

We compute average equity by using the beginning and ending balances [($356,000 + $320,000)/2 = $338,000]. Common stockholders' equity is total equity minus preferred equity.

Observe that Palisades' return on equity (0.142) is higher than its return on assets (0.101). This difference results from borrowing at one rate—say, 0.08, or 8%—and investing the funds to earn a higher rate, such as the firm's 0.142, or 14.2%, return on stockholders' equity. This practice is called **trading on the equity,** or using **leverage.** It is directly related to the debt ratio. The higher the debt ratio, the higher the leverage. Companies that finance operations with debt are said to *leverage* their positions. Leverage increases the risk to common stockholders.

For a review of these terms, see Chapter 8, page 394.

For Palisades Furniture and for many other companies, leverage increases profitability. This is not always the case, however. Leverage can have a negative impact on profitability. If revenues drop, debt and interest expense still must be paid. Therefore, leverage is a double-edged sword, increasing profits during good times but compounding losses during bad times.

Compare Palisades Furniture's rate of return on common stockholders' equity with the rates of some leading companies:

Company	Rate of Return on Common Equity
Wal-Mart Stores, Inc.	0.25
Chesebrough-Pond's, Inc.	0.20
General Motors	0.20

Palisades Furniture is not as profitable as these leading companies—perhaps because they must satisfy millions of stockholders worldwide. Palisades Furniture, on the other hand, is a much smaller company with stockholders who do not demand so high a return on their equity.

Earnings per Share of Common Stock *Earnings per share of common stock,* or simply **earnings per share (EPS),** is perhaps the most widely quoted of all financial statistics. EPS is the only ratio that must appear on the face of the income statement. EPS is the amount of net income per share of the company's outstanding *common* stock. Earnings per share is computed by dividing net income available to common stockholders by the number of common shares outstanding during the year. Preferred dividends are subtracted from net income because the preferred stockholders have a prior claim to their dividends. Palisades Furniture, Inc., has no preferred stock outstanding and thus has no preferred dividends. Computation of the firm's EPS for 19X7 and 19X6 follows (the company had 10,000 shares of common stock outstanding throughout 19X6 and 19X7):

Recall from Chapter 11, page 524, that GAAP requires corporations to disclose EPS figures on the income statement.

Formula		Palisades' Earnings per Share 19X7	19X6
Earnings per share of common stock	= $\frac{\text{Net income} - \text{Preferred dividends}}{\text{Number of shares of common stock outstanding}}$	$\frac{\$48{,}000 - \$0}{10{,}000} = \$4.80$	$\frac{\$26{,}000 - \$0}{10{,}000} = \$2.60$

Palisades Furniture's EPS increased 85 percent. Its stockholders should not expect such a significant boost in EPS every year. Most companies strive to increase EPS by 10–15% annually, and the more successful companies do so. But even the most dramatic upward trends include an occasional bad year.

Analyzing a Company's Stock as an Investment

Investors purchase stock to earn a return on their investment. This return consists of two parts: (1) gains (or losses) from selling the stock at a price that differs from the investors' purchase price, and (2) dividends, the periodic distributions to stockholders. The ratios we examine in this section help analysts evaluate stock in terms of market price or dividend payments.

PRICE/EARNINGS RATIO The **price/earnings ratio** is the ratio of the market price of a share of common stock to the company's earnings per share. This ratio, abbreviated P/E, appears in the *Wall Street Journal* stock listings. P/E ratios play an important part in decisions to buy, hold, and sell stocks. They indicate the market price of $1 of earnings.

Calculations for the P/E ratios of Palisades Furniture, Inc., follow. The market price of its common stock was $50 at the end of 19X7 and $35 at the end of 19X6. These prices can be obtained from a financial publication, a stockbroker, or some other source outside the accounting records.

Formula	Palisades' Price/Earnings Ratio 19X7	19X6
P/E ratio = $\frac{\text{Market price per share of common stock}}{\text{Earnings per share}}$	$\frac{\$50.00}{\$4.80} = 10.4$	$\frac{\$35.00}{\$2.60} = 13.5$

Given Palisades Furniture's 19X7 P/E ratio of 10.4, we would say that the company's stock is selling at 10.4 times earnings. The decline from the 19X6 P/E ratio of 13.5 is not a cause for alarm because the market price of the stock is not under Palisades Furniture's control. Net income is more controllable, and it increased during 19X7. Like most other ratios, P/E ratios vary from industry to industry. P/E ratios range from 8 to 10 for electric utilities (**Pennsylvania Power and Light,** for example) to 40 or more for "glamor stocks" such as **Auto Zone,** an auto parts chain, and **Oracle Systems,** which develops computer software.

The higher a stock's P/E ratio the higher its *downside risk*—the risk that the stock's market price will fall. Many investors interpret a sharp increase in a stock's P/E ratio as a signal to sell the stock.

DIVIDEND YIELD **Dividend yield** is the ratio of dividends per share of stock to the stock's market price per share. This ratio measures the percentage of a stock's market value that is returned annually as dividends, an important concern of stockholders. *Preferred* stockholders, who invest primarily to receive dividends, pay special attention to this ratio.

Palisades Furniture paid annual cash dividends of $1.20 per share of common stock in 19X7 and $1.00 in 19X6, and market prices of the company's common stock were $50 in 19X7 and $35 in 19X6. Calculation of the firm's dividend yields on common stock is as follows:

Formula	Dividend Yield on Palisades' Common Stock 19X7	19X6
Dividend yield on common stock[1] = $\frac{\text{Dividend per share of common stock}}{\text{Market price per share of common stock}}$	$\frac{\$1.20}{\$50.00} = 0.024$	$\frac{\$1.00}{\$35.00} = \$0.029$

[1]Dividend yields may also be calculated for preferred stock.

An investor who buys Palisades Furniture common stock for $50 can expect to receive almost 2½% of the investment annually in the form of cash dividends. Dividend yields vary widely, from 5% to 8% for older, established firms (such as **Procter & Gamble** and **General Motors**) down to the range of 0–3% for young, growth-oriented companies. Palisades Furniture's dividend yield places the company in the second group.

BOOK VALUE PER SHARE OF COMMON STOCK **Book value per share of common stock** is simply common stockholders' equity divided by the number of shares of common stock outstanding. Common shareholders' equity equals total stockholders' equity less preferred equity. Palisades Furniture has no preferred stock outstanding. Calculations of its book-value-per-share-of-common-stock ratios follows. Recall that 10,000 shares of common stock were outstanding at the end of years 19X7 and 19X6.

		Book Value per Share of Palisades' Common Stock	
Formula		19X7	19X6
Book value per share of common stock	$= \frac{\text{Total stockholders' equity} - \text{Preferred equity}}{\text{Number of shares of common stock outstanding}}$	$\frac{\$356{,}000 - \$0}{10{,}000} = \$35.60$	$\frac{\$320{,}000 - \$0}{10{,}000} = \$32.00$

Recall from Chapter 9, pages 444–447, that book value depends on historical costs, while market value depends on investors' outlook for dividends and an increase in the stock's value.

Book value indicates the recorded accounting amount for each share of common stock outstanding. Many experts argue that book value is not useful for investment analysis. It bears no relationship to market value and provides little information beyond stockholders' equity reported on the balance sheet. But some investors base their investment decisions on book value. For example, some investors rank stocks on the basis of the ratio of market price to book value. To these investors, the lower the ratio, the more attractive the stock. These investors are called "value" investors, as contrasted with "growth" investors, who focus more on trends in a company's net income.

Limitations of Financial Analysis: The Complexity of Business Decisions

Objective 6

Use ratios in decision making

Business decisions are made in a world of uncertainty. As useful as ratios are, they have limitations. We may liken their use in decision making to a physician's use of a thermometer. A reading of 101.6° Fahrenheit indicates that something is wrong with the patient, but the temperature alone does not indicate what the problem is or how to cure it.

In financial analysis, a sudden drop in a company's current ratio signals that *something* is wrong, but this change does not identify the problem or show how to correct it. The business manager must analyze the figures that go into the ratio to determine whether current assets have decreased, current liabilities have increased, or both. If current assets have dropped, is the problem a cash shortage? Are accounts receivable down? Are inventories too low? Only by analyzing the individual items that make up the ratio can the manager determine how to solve the problem. The manager must evaluate data on all ratios in the light of other information about the company and about its particular line of business, such as increased competition or a slowdown in the economy.

Legislation, international affairs, competition, scandals, and many other factors can turn profits into losses, and vice versa. To be most useful, ratios should be analyzed over a period of years to take into account a representative group of these factors. Any one year, or even any two years, may not be representative of the company's performance over the long term.

Economic Value Added—A New Measure of Performance

The top managers of **Coca-Cola, Quaker Oats, AT&T,** and other leading companies use **economic value added (EVA)** to evaluate a company's operating performance. EVA combines the concepts of accounting income and corporate finance to measure whether the company's operations have increased stockholder wealth. EVA can be computed as follows:

Objective 7

Measure economic value added by a company's operations

$$\textbf{EVA} = \textbf{Net income} + \textbf{Interest expense} - \textbf{Capital charge}$$

where

$$\textbf{Capital charge} = \left(\begin{array}{c}\textbf{Notes}\\\textbf{payable}\end{array} + \begin{array}{c}\textbf{Loans}\\\textbf{payable}\end{array} + \begin{array}{c}\textbf{Long-term}\\\textbf{debt}\end{array} + \begin{array}{c}\textbf{Stockholders'}\\\textbf{equity}\end{array}\right) \times \begin{array}{c}\textbf{Cost of}\\\textbf{capital}\end{array}$$

All amounts for the EVA computation, except the cost of capital, are taken from the financial statements. The **cost of capital** is a weighted average of the returns demanded by the company's stockholders and lenders. The cost of capital varies with the company's level of risk. For example, stockholders would demand a higher return from a start-up computer software company than from AT&T because the new company is untested and therefore more risky. Lenders would also charge the new company a higher interest rate because of this greater risk. Thus, the new company has a higher cost of capital than AT&T. The cost of capital is a major topic in finance classes. In the following discussions we merely assume a value for the cost of capital (such as 10%, 12%, or 15%) to illustrate the computation of EVA and its use in decision making.

The idea behind EVA is that the returns to the company's stockholders (net income) and to its creditors (interest expense) should exceed the company's capital charge. The **capital charge** is the amount that stockholders and lenders *charge* a company for the use of their money. A positive EVA amount indicates an increase in stockholder wealth, and the company's stock should remain attractive to investors. If the EVA measure is negative, the stockholders will probably be unhappy with the company's progress and sell its stock, resulting in a decrease in the stock's price. Different companies tailor the EVA computation to meet their own needs.

The Coca-Cola Company is a leading user of EVA. Coca-Cola's EVA for 1995 can be computed as follows, assuming a 12% cost of capital for the company (dollar amounts in millions):

$$\begin{aligned}\textbf{Coca-Cola's EVA} &= \begin{array}{c}\textbf{Net}\\\textbf{income}\end{array} + \begin{array}{c}\textbf{Interest}\\\textbf{expense}\end{array} - \left[\left(\begin{array}{c}\textbf{Loans and}\\\textbf{notes payable}\end{array} + \begin{array}{c}\textbf{Long-term}\\\textbf{debt}\end{array} + \begin{array}{c}\textbf{Stockholders'}\\\textbf{equity}\end{array}\right) \times \begin{array}{c}\textbf{Cost of}\\\textbf{capital}\end{array}\right]\\ &= \$2{,}986 + \$272 - [(\$2{,}371 + \$1{,}141 + \$5{,}392) \times 0.12]\\ &= \$3{,}258 - \$8{,}904 \times 0.12\\ &= \$3{,}258 - \$1{,}068\\ &= \$2{,}190\end{aligned}$$

By this measure, Coca-Cola's operations during 1995 added $2.19 billion ($2,190 million) of value to its stockholders' wealth after meeting the company's capital charge. This performance is outstanding. Coca-Cola's positive EVA measures explain why the company's stock price increased an average of 29% per year over the ten-year period from 1985 to 1995. A $100 investment in Coca-Cola stock in 1985 had grown to a value of $1,287 in 1995.

Efficient Markets, Management Action, and Investor Decisions

An **efficient capital market** is one in which market prices fully reflect all information available to the public. Stocks are priced in full recognition of all publicly accessible data, so it can be argued that the stock market is efficient. Market efficiency has implications for management action and for investor decisions. It means that managers cannot fool the market with accounting gimmicks. If the information is available, the market as a whole can translate accounting data into a "fair" price for the company's stock.

Suppose you are the president of Anacomp Company. Reported earnings per share are $4, and the stock price is $40—so the P/E ratio is 10. You believe the corporation's stock is underpriced in comparison with other companies in the same industry. To correct this situation, you are considering changing your depreciation method from accelerated to straight-line. The accounting change will increase earnings per share to $5. Will the stock price then rise to $50? Probably not. The company's stock price will probably remain at $40 because the market can understand the accounting change. After all, the company merely changed its method of computing depreciation. There is no effect on the company's cash flows, and its economic position is unchanged.

In an efficient market, the search for "underpriced" stock is fruitless unless the investor has relevant private information. Moreover, it is unlawful to invest on the basis of *inside* information. For outside investors, an appropriate strategy seeks to manage risk, diversify, and minimize transaction costs. The role of financial statement analysis consists mainly of identifying the risks of various stocks to manage the risk of the overall investment portfolio.

SUMMARY PROBLEM FOR YOUR REVIEW

The following financial data are adapted from the annual report of The Gap, Inc., which operates The Gap, Banana Republic, and Old Navy clothing stores.

THE GAP, INC.
Five-Year Selected Financial Data

Operating Results*	19X5	19X4	19X3	19X2	19X1
Net sales	$2,960	$2,519	$1,934	$1,587	$1,252
Cost of goods sold and occupancy expenses, excluding depreciation and amortization	1,856	1,496	1,188	1,007	814
Interest expense (net)	4	4	1	3	3
Income from operations	340	371	237	163	126
Income taxes	129	141	92	65	52
Net earnings	211	230	145	98	74
Cash dividends	44	41	30	23	18
Financial Position					
Merchandise inventory	366	314	247	243	193
Total assets	1,379	1,147	777	579	481
Working capital	355	236	579	129	434
Current ratio	2.06:1	1.71:1	1.39:1	1.69:1	1.70:1
Stockholders' equity	888	678	466	338	276
Average number of shares of common stock outstanding (in thousands)	144	142	142	141	145

*(Dollar amounts in thousands)

Required

Compute the following ratios for 19X5 through 19X2, and evaluate The Gap's operating results. Are operating results strong or weak? Did they improve or deteriorate during the four-year period?

1. Gross profit percentage
2. Net income as a percentage of sales
3. Earnings per share
4. Inventory turnover
5. Times-interest-earned ratio
6. Rate of return on stockholders' equity

ANSWERS

Requirement	19X5	19X4	19X3	19X2
1. Gross profit percentage	$\frac{\$2,960 - \$1,856}{\$2,960}$ = 37.3%	$\frac{\$2,519 - \$1,496}{\$2,519}$ = 40.6%	$\frac{\$1,934 - \$1,188}{\$1,934}$ = 38.6%	$\frac{\$1,587 - \$1,007}{\$1,587}$ = 36.5%
2. Net income as a percentage of sales	$\frac{\$211}{\$2,960} = 7.1\%$	$\frac{\$230}{\$2,519} = 9.1\%$	$\frac{\$145}{\$1,934} = 7.5\%$	$\frac{\$98}{\$1,587} = 6.2\%$
3. Earnings per share	$\frac{\$211}{144} = \$1.47$	$\frac{\$230}{142} = \$1.62$	$\frac{\$145}{142} = \$1.02$	$\frac{\$98}{141} = \$0.70$
4. Inventory turnover	$\frac{\$1,856}{(\$366 + \$314)/2}$ = 5.5 times	$\frac{\$1,496}{(\$314 + \$247)/2}$ = 5.3 times	$\frac{\$1,188}{(\$247 + \$243)/2}$ = 4.8 times	$\frac{\$1,007}{(\$243 + \$193)/2}$ = 4.6 times
5. Times-interest-earned ratio	$\frac{\$340}{\$4}$ = 85 times	$\frac{\$371}{\$4}$ = 93 times	$\frac{\$237}{\$1}$ = 237 times	$\frac{\$163}{\$3}$ = 54 times
6. Rate of return on stockholders' equity	$\frac{\$211}{(\$888 + \$678)/2}$ = 26.9%	$\frac{\$230}{(\$678 + \$466)/2}$ = 40.2%	$\frac{\$145}{(\$466 + \$338)/2}$ = 36.1%	$\frac{\$98}{(\$338 + \$276)/2}$ = 31.9%

Evaluation: During this four-year period, The Gap's operating results were outstanding. Operating results improved, with all ratio values but return on stockholders' equity higher in 19X5 than in 19X2. Moreover, all the performance measures indicate high levels of income and return to investors.

SUMMARY OF LEARNING OBJECTIVES

1. *Perform a horizontal analysis of comparative financial statements.* Banks loan money, investors buy stocks, and managers make decisions on the basis of accounting information. *Horizontal analysis* is the study of percentage changes in financial statement items from one period to the next. To compute these percentage changes, (1) calculate the dollar amount of the change from the base (earlier) period to the later period, and (2) divide the dollar amount of change by the base-period amount. *Trend percentages* are a form of horizontal analysis.

2. *Perform a vertical analysis of financial statements.* *Vertical analysis* of a financial statement reveals the relationship of each statement item to a specified base, which is the 100% figure. In an income statement, net sales is usually the base. On a balance sheet, total assets is usually the base.

3. *Prepare common-size financial statements for benchmarking against the industry average and key competitors.* A form of vertical analysis, *common-size statements* report only percentages, no dollar amounts. Common-size statements ease the comparison of different companies and may signal the need for corrective action. *Benchmarking* is the practice of comparing a company to a standard set by other companies, with a view toward improvement.

4. *Use the statement of cash flows in decision making.* The statement of cash flows can be very useful in decision making. Analysts use cash-flow analysis to identify danger signals about a company's financial situation. The most important information provided by the cash-flow statement is a summary of the company's sources and uses of cash.

5. *Compute the standard financial ratios used for decision making.* An important part of financial analysis is the calculation and interpretation of financial ratios. A ratio expresses the relationship of one item to another. The most important financial ratios measure a company's ability to pay current liabilities (current ratio, acid-test ratio); its ability to sell inventory and collect receivables (inventory turnover, accounts receivable turnover, days' sales in receivables); its ability to pay long-term debt (debt ratio, times-interest-earned ratio); its profitability (rate of return on net sales, rate of return on total assets, rate of return on common stockholders' equity, earnings per share of common stock); and its value as an investment (price/earnings ratio, dividend yield, book value per share of common stock).

6. *Use ratios in decision making.* Analysis of financial ratios over time is an important way to track a company's progress. A change in one of the ratios over time may signal the existence of a problem. It is up to the company's managers to find the source of this problem and take actions to correct it.

7. *Measure economic value added by a company's operations.* *Economic value added (EVA)* measures whether a company's operations have increased its stockholders' wealth. EVA can be defined as the excess of net income and interest expense over the company's capital charge, which is the amount that the company's stockholders and lenders charge for the use of their money. A positive amount of EVA indicates an increase in stockholder wealth; a negative amount indicates a decrease.

ACCOUNTING VOCABULARY

accounts receivable turnover *(p. 665).*
acid-test ratio *(p. 663).*
benchmarking *(p. 653).*
book value per share of common stock *(p. 672).*
capital charge *(p. 673).*
common-size statement *(p. 652).*
cost of capital *(p. 673).*
current ratio *(p. 661).*
days' sales in receivables *(p. 666).*
debt ratio *(p. 667).*
dividend yield *(p. 671).*
earnings per share (EPS) *(p. 670).*
economic value added (EVA) *(p. 673).*
efficient capital market *(p. 674).*
horizontal analysis *(p. 647).*
inventory turnover *(p. 664).*
leverage *(p. 670).*
long-term solvency *(p. 647).*
price/earnings ratio *(p. 671).*
quick ratio *(p. 663).*
rate of return on common stockholders' equity *(p. 669).*
rate of return on net sales *(p. 668).*
rate of return on total assets *(p. 669).*
return on stockholders' equity *(p. 669).*
short-term liquidity *(p. 647).*
times-interest-earned ratio *(p. 667).*
trading on the equity *(p. 670).*
vertical analysis *(p. 650).*
working capital *(p. 660).*

QUESTIONS

1. Identify two groups of users of accounting information and the decisions they base on accounting data.
2. Name the three broad categories of analytical tools that are based on accounting information.
3. Briefly describe horizontal analysis. How do decision makers use this analytical tool?
4. What is vertical analysis, and what is its purpose?
5. What is the purpose of common-size statements?
6. State how an investor might analyze the statement of cash flows. How might the investor analyze investing-activities data?
7. Why are ratios an important tool of financial analysis? Give an example of an important financial ratio.
8. Identify two ratios used to measure a company's ability to pay current liabilities. Show how they are computed.
9. Why is the acid-test ratio given that name?
10. What does the inventory turnover ratio measure?
11. Suppose the days'-sales-in-receivables ratio of Gomez, Inc., increased from 36 at January 1 to 43 at December 31. Is this a good sign or a bad sign? What might Gomez management do in response to this change?
12. Company A's debt ratio has increased from 0.50 to 0.70. Identify a decision maker to whom this increase is important, and state how the increase affects this party's decisions about the company.
13. Which ratio measures the *effect of debt* on (a) financial position (the balance sheet) and (b) the company's ability to pay interest expense (the income statement)?
14. Company A is a chain of grocery stores, and Company B is a computer manufacturer. Which company is likely to have the higher (a) current ratio, (b) inventory turnover, and (c) rate of return on sales? Give your reasons.
15. Identify four ratios used to measure a company's profitability. Show how to compute these ratios and state what information each ratio provides.
16. The price/earnings ratio of General Motors was 6, and the price/earnings ratio of American Express was 45. Which company did the stock market favor? Explain.
17. McDonald's Corporation paid cash dividends of $0.78⅔ (78 and ⅔ cents) per share when the market price of the company's stock was $58. What was the dividend yield on McDonald's stock? What does dividend yield measure?

18. Hold all other factors constant and indicate whether each of the following situations generally signals good or bad news about a company:
    a. Increase in current ratio
    b. Decrease in inventory turnover
    c. Increase in debt ratio
    d. Decrease in interest-coverage ratio
    e. Increase in return on sales
    f. Decrease in earnings per share
    g. Increase in price/earnings ratio
    h. Increase in book value per share
19. Explain how an investor might use book value per share of stock in making an investment decision.
20. Describe how decision makers use ratio data. What are the limitations of ratios?
21. What is EVA, and how is it used in financial analysis?

EXERCISES

Computing year-to-year changes in working capital **(*Obj. 1*)**

E13-1 What were the amount of change and the percentage change in Western Bell Corporation's working capital during 19X6 and 19X7? Is this trend favorable or unfavorable?

	19X7	19X6	19X5
Total current assets	$312,000	$290,000	$280,000
Total current liabilities	150,000	117,000	140,000

Horizontal analysis of an income statement **(*Obj. 1*)**

E13-2 Prepare a horizontal analysis of the following comparative income statement of Syntex Incorporated. Round percentage changes to the nearest one-tenth percent (three decimal places):

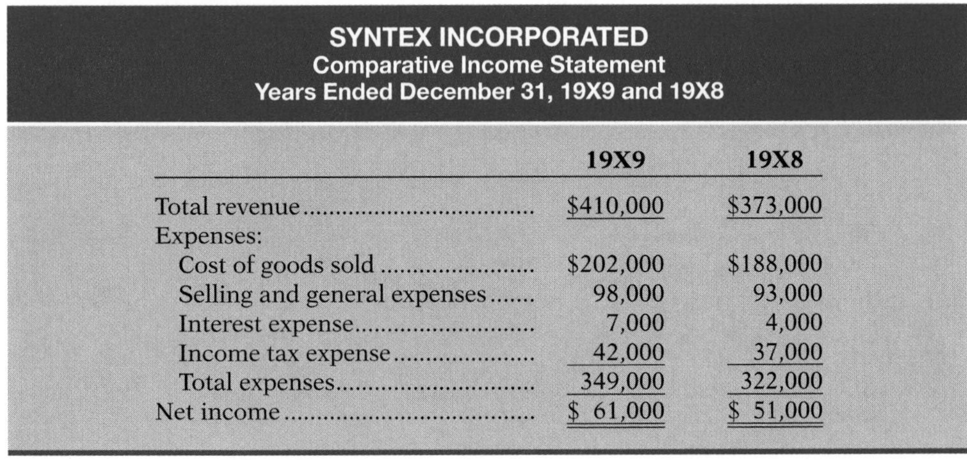

SYNTEX INCORPORATED
Comparative Income Statement
Years Ended December 31, 19X9 and 19X8

	19X9	19X8
Total revenue.....................................	$410,000	$373,000
Expenses:		
Cost of goods sold	$202,000	$188,000
Selling and general expenses	98,000	93,000
Interest expense............................	7,000	4,000
Income tax expense......................	42,000	37,000
Total expenses..............................	349,000	322,000
Net income	$ 61,000	$ 51,000

Why did net income increase by a higher percentage than total revenues during 19X9?

Computing trend percentages **(*Obj. 1*)**

E13-3 Compute trend percentages for Maxim Corporation's net sales and net income for the following five-year period, using year 1 as the base year. Round to the nearest full percent.

(In thousands)	Year 5	Year 4	Year 3	Year 2	Year 1
Net sales	$1,410	$1,187	$1,106	$1,009	$1,043
Net income	117	114	83	71	85

Which grew faster during the period, net sales or net income?

Vertical analysis of a balance sheet **(*Obj. 2*)**

E13-4 Copy World, Inc., has requested that you perform a vertical analysis of its balance sheet to determine the component percentages of its assets, liabilities, and stockholders' equity.

COPY WORLD, INC. Balance Sheet December 31, 19X3	
Assets	
Total current assets	$ 72,000
Long-term investments	35,000
Property, plant, and equipment, net	217,000
Total assets	$324,000
Liabilities	
Total current liabilities	$ 58,000
Long-term debt	118,000
Total liabilities	176,000
Stockholders' Equity	
Total stockholders' equity	148,000
Total liabilities and stockholders' equity	$324,000

Preparing a common-size income statement
(Obj. 3)

E13-5 Prepare a comparative common-size income statement for Syntex Incorporated, using the 19X9 and 19X8 data of Exercise 13-2 and rounding percentages to one-tenth percent (three decimal places).

Analyzing the statement of cash flows
(Obj. 4)

E13-6 Identify any weaknesses in the company revealed by the statement of cash flows of Nemmer Electric, Inc.

NEMMER ELECTRIC, INC. Statement of Cash Flows For the Current Year		
Operating activities:		
Income from operations		$ 52,000
Add (subtract) noncash items:		
Depreciation	$ 23,000	
Net increase in current assets other than cash	(15,000)	
Net increase in current liabilities exclusive of short-term debt	11,000	19,000
Net cash inflow from operating activities		71,000
Investing activities:		
Sale of property, plant, and equipment		101,000
Financing activities:		
Issuance of bonds payable	$ 114,000	
Payment of short-term debt	(171,000)	
Payment of long-term debt	(79,000)	
Payment of dividends	(42,000)	
Net cash outflow from financing activities		(178,000)
Decrease in cash		$ (6,000)

Computing five ratios
(Obj. 5)

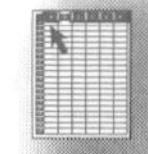

E13-7 The financial statements of Alamo Iron Works include the following items:

	Current Year	Preceding Year
Balance sheet:		
Cash	$ 17,000	$ 22,000
Short-term investments	11,000	26,000
Net receivables	64,000	73,000
Inventory	87,000	71,000
Prepaid expenses	6,000	8,000
Total current assets	185,000	200,000
Total current liabilities	121,000	91,000
Income statement:		
Net credit sales	$454,000	
Cost of goods sold	257,000	

Required

Compute the following ratios for the current year: (a) current ratio, (b) acid-test ratio, (c) inventory turnover, (d) accounts receivable turnover, and (e) days' sales in average receivables.

Analyzing the ability to pay current liabilities ***(Obj. 5, 6)***

E13-8 Academy Control Systems has asked you to determine whether the company's ability to pay its current liabilities and long-term debts has improved or deteriorated during 19X2. To answer this question, compute the following ratios for 19X2 and 19X1: (a) current ratio, (b) acid-test ratio, (c) debt ratio, and (d) times-interest-earned ratio. Summarize the results of your analysis in a written report.

	19X2	19X1
Cash	$ 21,000	$ 47,000
Short-term investments	28,000	—
Net receivables	102,000	116,000
Inventory	226,000	263,000
Prepaid expenses	11,000	9,000
Total assets	503,000	489,000
Total current liabilities	205,000	241,000
Total liabilities	261,000	273,000
Income from operations	165,000	158,000
Interest expense	36,000	39,000

Analyzing profitability ***(Obj. 5, 6)***

E13-9 Compute four ratios that measure ability to earn profits for New York Packaging, Inc., whose comparative income statement follows:

NEW YORK PACKAGING, INC.
Comparative Income Statement
Years Ended December 31, 19X6 and 19X5

	19X6	19X5
Net sales	$174,000	$158,000
Cost of goods sold	93,000	86,000
Gross profit	81,000	72,000
Selling and general expenses	48,000	41,000
Income from operations	33,000	31,000
Interest expense	21,000	10,000
Income before income tax	12,000	21,000
Income tax expense	4,000	8,000
Net income	$ 8,000	$ 13,000

Additional data:

	19X6	19X5
Average total assets	$204,000	$191,000
Average common stockholders' equity	$ 96,000	$ 89,000
Preferred dividends	$ 3,000	$ 3,000
Shares of common stock outstanding	20,000	20,000

Did the company's operating performance improve or deteriorate during 19X6?

Evaluating a stock as an investment ***(Obj. 5, 6)***

E13-10 Evaluate the common stock of Stroud Security Systems as an investment. Specifically, use the three stock ratios to determine whether the stock has increased or decreased in attractiveness during the past year.

	19X8	19X7
Net income	$ 58,000	$ 55,000
Dividends (half on preferred stock)	28,000	28,000
Common stockholders' equity at year end (80,000 shares)	530,000	500,000
Preferred stockholders' equity at year end	200,000	200,000
Market price per share of common stock at year end	$10.12	$7.75

Using economic value added to measure corporate performance
(Obj. 7)

E13-11 Two companies with very different economic-value-added (EVA) profiles are **IHOP**, the restaurant chain, and **Texaco**, the giant oil company. Adapted versions of the two companies' 1995 financial statements are presented here (in millions):

	IHOP	Texaco
Balance sheet data:		
Total assets	$252	$24,937
Interest-bearing debt	$ 35	$ 4,240
All other liabilities	109	11,178
Stockholders' equity	108	9,519
Total liabilities and equity	$252	$24,937
Income statement data:		
Total revenue	$164	$36,787
Interest expense	9	483
All other expenses	139	35,697
Net income	$ 16	$ 607

Required

1. Before performing any calculations, which company do you think would represent the better investment? Give your reason.
2. Compute the EVA for each company, and then decide which company's stock you would rather hold as an investment. Assume each company's cost of capital is 12 percent.

CHALLENGE EXERCISES

Using ratio data to reconstruct a company's income statement
(Obj. 2, 3, 5)

E13-12 The following data (dollar amounts in millions) are from the financial statements of **McDonald's Corporation**, which operates more than 13,000 restaurants in 65 countries.

Average stockholders' equity	$3,605
Interest expense	$ 413
Preferred stock	-0-
Operating income as a percent of sales	24.04%
Rate of return on sales	11.13%
Rate of return on stockholders' equity	20.50%
Income tax rate	37.53%

Required

Complete the following condensed income statement. Report amounts to the nearest million dollars.

Sales	$?
Operating expense	?
Operating income	?
Interest expense	?
Pretax income	?
Income tax expense	?
Net income	$?

Using ratio data to reconstruct a company's balance sheet
(Obj. 2, 3, 5)

E13-13 The following data (dollar amounts in millions) are from the financial statements of **Wal-Mart Stores, Inc.**, the largest retailer in the world:

Total liabilities	$11,806
Preferred stock	$ -0-
Total current assets	$10,196
Accumulated depreciation	$ 448
Debt ratio	57.408%
Current ratio	1.51

Required

Complete the following condensed balance sheet. Report amounts to the nearest million dollars.

Current assets		$?
Property, plant, and equipment	$?	
Less Accumulated depreciation	?	?
Total assets		$?
Current liabilities		$?
Long-term liabilities		?
Stockholders' equity		?
Total liabilities and stockholders' equity		$?

PROBLEMS

(GROUP A)

Trend percentages, return on sales, and comparison with the industry ***(Obj. 1, 5, 6)***

P13-1A Net sales, net income, and total assets for Monica Hearn, Inc., for a six-year period follow:

(In thousands)	19X6	19X5	19X4	19X3	19X2	19X1
Net sales	$347	$313	$266	$281	$245	$241
Net income	27	21	11	18	14	13
Total assets	296	254	209	197	181	166

Required

1. Compute trend percentages for each item for 19X2 through 19X6. Use 19X1 as the base year. Round to the nearest percent.
2. Compute the rate of return on net sales for 19X2 through 19X6, rounding to three decimal places. In this industry, rates above 5% are considered good, and rates above 7% are outstanding.
3. How does Hearn's return on net sales compare with that of the industry?

Common-size statements, analysis of profitability, and comparison with the industry ***(Obj. 2, 3, 5, 6)***

P13-2A Top managers of Bull's Eye Archery Company have asked your help in comparing the company's profit performance and financial position with the average for the sporting goods industry. The accountant has given you the company's income statement and balance sheet and also the following data for the sporting goods industry.

BULL'S EYE ARCHERY
Income Statement
Compared with Industry Average
Year Ended December 31, 19X3

	Bull's Eye	Industry Average
Net sales	$957,000	100.0%
Cost of goods sold	653,000	65.9
Gross profit	304,000	34.1
Operating expenses	257,000	28.1
Operating income	47,000	6.0
Other expenses	2,000	0.4
Net income	$ 45,000	5.6%

BULL'S EYE ARCHERY
Balance Sheet
Compared with Industry Average
December 31, 19X3

	Bull's Eye	Industry Average
Current assets	$448,000	74.4%
Fixed assets, net	127,000	20.0
Intangible assets, net	42,000	0.6
Other assets	13,000	5.0
Total	$630,000	100.0%
Current liabilities	$246,000	35.6%
Long-term liabilities	144,000	19.0
Stockholders' equity	240,000	45.4
Total	$630,000	100.0%

Required

1. Prepare a two-column common-size income statement and balance sheet for Bull's Eye. The first column of each statement should present Bull's Eyes common-size statement, and the second column should show the industry averages.
2. For the profitability analysis, compute Bull's Eye's (a) ratio of gross profit to net sales, (b) ratio of operating income (loss) to net sales, and (c) ratio of net income (loss) to net sales. Compare these figures with the industry averages. Is Bull's Eye's profit performance better or worse than the average for the industry?

Using the statement of cash flows for decision making ***(Obj. 4)***

3. For the analysis of financial position, compute Bull's Eye's (a) ratio of current assets to total assets and (b) ratio of stockholders' equity to total assets. Compare these ratios with the industry averages. Is Bull's Eye's financial position better or worse than average for the industry?

P13-3A You are evaluating two companies as possible investments. The two companies, similar in size, are in the commuter airline business. They fly passengers from Minneapolis and Milwaukee to smaller cities in their area. Assume that all other available information has been analyzed and that the decision regarding which company's stock to purchase depends on the information given in their statements of cash flows, which appear below.

NORWEGIAN EXPRESS
Statement of Cash Flows
For the Years Ended November 30, 19X9 and 19X8

	19X9		19X8	
Operating activities:				
Income from operations		$184,000		$131,000
Add (subtract) noncash items:				
Total		64,000		62,000
Net cash inflow from operating activities		248,000		193,000
Investing activities:				
Purchase of property, plant, and equipment	$(303,000)		$(453,000)	
Sale of property, plant, and equipment	46,000		39,000	
Sale of long-term investments	—		33,000	
Net cash outflow from investing activities		(257,000)		(381,000)
Financing activities:				
Issuance of long-term notes payable	$ 131,000		$ 83,000	
Issuance of short-term notes payable	43,000		35,000	
Payment of short-term notes payable	(66,000)		(18,000)	
Net cash inflow from financing activities		108,000		100,000
Increase (decrease) in cash		$ 99,000		$ (88,000)
Cash summary from balance sheet:				
Cash balance at beginning of year		$116,000		$204,000
Increase (decrease) in cash during the year		99,000		(88,000)
Cash balance at end of year		$215,000		$116,000

WISCONSIN AIRWAYS, INC.
Statement of Cash Flows
For the Years Ended November 30, 19X9 and 19X8

	19X9		19X8	
Operating activities:				
Income (loss) from operations		$ (67,000)		$154,000
Add (subtract) noncash items:				
Total		84,000		(23,000)
Net cash inflow from operating activities		17,000		131,000
Investing activities:				
Purchase of property, plant, and equipment	$ (120,000)		$ (91,000)	
Sale of property, plant, and equipment	118,000		39,000	
Sale of long-term investments	52,000		4,000	
Net cash inflow (outflow) from investing activities		50,000		(48,000)
Financing activities:				
Issuance of short-term notes payable	$ 122,000		$ 143,000	
Payment of short-term notes payable	(179,000)		(134,000)	
Payment of cash dividends	(45,000)		(64,000)	
Net cash outflow from financing activities		(102,000)		(55,000)
Increase (decrease) in cash		$ (35,000)		$ 28,000
Cash summary from balance sheet:				
Cash balance at beginning of year		$131,000		$103,000
Increase (decrease) in cash during the year		(35,000)		28,000
Cash balance at end of year		$ 96,000		$131,000

Required

Discuss the relative strengths and weaknesses of Norwegian and Wisconsin. Conclude your discussion by recommending one of the company's stocks as an investment.

Effects of business transactions on selected ratios ***(Obj. 5, 6)***

P13-4A Financial statement data on TriState Optical Company include the following items:

Cash	$ 47,000	Accounts payable	$ 96,000
Short-term investments	21,000	Accrued liabilities	50,000
Accounts receivable, net	102,000	Long-term notes payable	146,000
Inventories	274,000	Other long-term liabilities	78,000
Prepaid expenses	15,000	Net income	119,000
Total assets	933,000	Number of common shares outstanding	22,000
Short-term notes payable	72,000		

Required

1. Compute TriState's current ratio, debt ratio, and earnings per share.
2. Compute each of the three ratios after evaluating the effect of each transaction that follows. Consider each transaction *separately*.
   - **a.** Borrowed $76,000 on a long-term note payable.
   - **b.** Sold short-term investments for $44,000 (cost, $66,000); assume no tax effect of the loss.
   - **c.** Issued 14,000 shares of common stock, receiving cash of $168,000.
   - **d.** Received cash on account, $6,000.
   - **e.** Paid short-term notes payable, $51,000.
   - **f.** Purchased merchandise of $48,000 on account, debiting Inventory.
   - **g.** Paid off long-term liabilities, $78,000.
   - **h.** Declared, but did not pay, a $51,000 cash dividend on the common stock.

Use the following format for your answer:

Requirement 1		**Current Ratio**	**Debt Ratio**	**Earnings per Share**
Requirement 2	**Transaction (letter)**	**Current Ratio**	**Debt Ratio**	**Earnings per Share**

Using ratios to evaluate a stock investment ***(Obj. 5, 6)***

P13-5A Comparative financial statement data of Dunn's Brass Foundry follow.

DUNN'S BRASS FOUNDRY
Comparative Income Statement
Years Ended December 31, 19X6 and 19X5

	19X6	19X5
Net sales	$667,000	$599,000
Cost of goods sold	378,000	283,000
Gross profit	289,000	316,000
Operating expenses	129,000	147,000
Income from operations	160,000	169,000
Interest expense	57,000	41,000
Income before income tax	103,000	128,000
Income tax expense	34,000	53,000
Net income	$ 69,000	$ 75,000

DUNN'S BRASS FOUNDRY
Comparative Balance Sheet
December 31, 19X6 and 19X5
(Selected 19X4 amounts given for computations of ratios)

	19X6	19X5	19X4
Current assets:			
Cash	$ 37,000	$ 40,000	
Current receivables, net	208,000	151,000	$138,000
Inventories	352,000	286,000	184,000
Prepaid expenses	5,000	20,000	
Total current assets	602,000	497,000	
Property, plant, and equipment, net	287,000	276,000	
Total assets	$889,000	$773,000	707,000

(Continued)

(Continued)

	19X6	19X5	19X4
Total current liabilities	$286,000	$267,000	
Long-term liabilities	245,000	235,000	
Total liabilities	531,000	502,000	
Preferred stockholders' equity, 4%, $20 par	50,000	50,000	
Common stockholders' equity, no par	308,000	221,000	148,000
Total liabilities and stockholders' equity	$889,000	$773,000	

Other information:

1. Market price of Dunn's common stock: $30.75 at December 31, 19X6, and $40.25 at December 31, 19X5.
2. Common shares outstanding: 15,000 during 19X6 and 14,000 during 19X5.
3. All sales on credit.

Required

1. Compute the following ratios for 19X6 and 19X5:
   - **a.** Current ratio
   - **b.** Inventory turnover
   - **c.** Accounts receivable turnover
   - **d.** Times-interest-earned ratio
   - **e.** Return on assets
   - **f.** Return on common stockholders' equity
   - **g.** Earnings per share of common stock
   - **h.** Price/earnings ratio
   - **i.** Book value per share of common stock
2. Decide whether (a) Dunn's financial position improved or deteriorated during 19X6 and (b) the investment attractiveness of its common stock appears to have increased or decreased.
3. How will what you learned in this problem help you evaluate an investment?

Using ratios to decide between two stock investments; measuring economic value added ***(Obj. 5, 6, 7)***

P13-6A Assume that you are considering purchasing stock in a company in the hospital supply industry. You have narrowed the choice to Scott & White and Pediatric Supply and have assembled the following data:

Selected income statement data for current year:

	Scott & White	Pediatric Supply
Net sales (all on credit)	$519,000	$603,000
Cost of goods sold	387,000	454,000
Income from operations	72,000	93,000
Interest expense	8,000	—
Net income	38,000	56,000

Selected balance sheet and market price data at end of current year:

	Scott & White	Pediatric Supply
Current assets:		
Cash	$ 39,000	$ 25,000
Short-term investments	13,000	6,000
Current receivables, net	164,000	189,000
Inventories	183,000	211,000
Prepaid expenses	15,000	19,000
Total current assets	414,000	450,000
Total assets	938,000	974,000
Total current liabilities	338,000	366,000
Total liabilities	691,000*	667,000*
Preferred stock, 4%, $100 par	25,000	
Common stock, $1 par (150,000 shares)		150,000
$5 par (20,000 shares)	100,000	
Total stockholders' equity	247,000	307,000
Market price per share of common stock	$47.50	$9

*Notes and bonds payable: Scott & White, $303,000
Pediatric Supply, $4,000

Selected balance sheet data at beginning of current year:

	Scott & White	Pediatric Supply
Current receivables, net	$193,000	$142,000
Inventories	197,000	209,000
Total assets	909,000	842,000
Preferred stock, 4%, $100 par	25,000	
Common stock, $1 par (150,000 shares)		150,000
$5 par (20,000 shares)	100,000	
Total stockholders' equity	215,000	263,000

Your investment strategy is to purchase the stocks of companies that have low price/earnings ratios but appear to be in good shape financially. Assume that you have analyzed all other factors, and your decision depends on the results of the ratio analysis to be performed.

Required

1. Compute the following ratios for both companies for the current year and decide which company's stock better fits your investment strategy.
   1. Current ratio
   2. Acid-test ratio
   3. Inventory turnover
   4. Days' sales in average receivables
   5. Debt ratio
   6. Times-interest-earned ratio
   7. Return on net sales
   8. Return on total assets
   9. Return on common stockholders' equity
   10. Earnings per share of common stock
   11. Book value per share of common stock
   12. Price/earnings ratio
2. Compute each company's economic-value-added (EVA) measure, and determine whether their EVAs confirm or alter your investment decision. Each company's cost of capital is 10 percent. Round all amounts to the nearest $1,000.

(GROUP B)

Trend percentages, return on common equity, and comparison with the industry ***(Obj. 1, 5, 6)***

P13-1B Net sales, net income, and common stockholders' equity for Bear Utilities, Inc., for a six-year period follow.

(In thousands)	19X7	19X6	19X5	19X4	19X3	19X2
Net sales	$761	$714	$641	$662	$642	$634
Net income	61	45	32	48	41	40
Ending common stockholders' equity	386	354	330	296	272	252

Required

1. Compute trend percentages for each item for 19X3 through 19X7. Use 19X2 as the base year. Round to the nearest percent.
2. Compute the rate of return on average common stockholders' equity for 19X3 through 19X7, rounding to three decimal places. In this industry, rates of 13% are average, rates above 16% are good, and rates above 20% are outstanding.
3. How does Bear's return on common stockholders' equity compare with the industry?

Common-size statements, analysis of profitability, and comparison with the industry ***(Obj. 2, 3, 5, 6)***

P13-2B Alto Auto Glass has asked your help in comparing the company's profit performance and financial position with the average for the auto parts retail industry. The proprietor has given you the company's income statement and balance sheet and also the industry average data for retailers of auto parts.

ALTO AUTO GLASS
Income Statement
Compared with Industry Average
Year Ended December 31, 19X6

	Alto	Industry Average
Net sales	$781,000	100.0%
Cost of goods sold	497,000	65.8
Gross profit	284,000	34.2
Operating expenses	163,000	19.7
Operating income	121,000	14.5
Other expenses	5,000	0.4
Net income	$116,000	14.1%

ALTO AUTO GLASS
Balance Sheet
Compared with Industry Average
December 31, 19X6

	Alto	Industry Average
Current assets	$350,000	70.9%
Fixed assets, net	74,000	23.6
Intangible assets, net	4,000	0.8
Other assets	22,000	4.7
Total	$450,000	100.0%
Current liabilities	$207,000	48.1%
Long-term liabilities	62,000	16.6
Stockholders' equity	181,000	35.3
Total	$450,000	100.0%

Required

1. Prepare a two-column common-size income statement and balance sheet for Alto. The first column of each statement should present Alto's common-size statement, and the second column should show the industry averages.
2. For the profitability analysis, compute Alto's (a) ratio of gross profit to net sales, (b) ratio of operating income to net sales, and (c) ratio of net income to net sales. Compare these figures with the industry averages. Is Alto's profit performance better or worse than the industry average?
3. For the analysis of financial position, compute Alto's (a) ratio of current assets to total assets, and (b) ratio of stockholders' equity to total assets. Compare these ratios with the industry averages. Is Alto's financial position better or worse than the industry averages?

Using the statement of cash flows for decision making ***(Obj. 4)***

P13-3B You have been asked to evaluate two companies as possible investments. The two companies, Allied Assets for Lease, Inc., and Northern Leasing Corporation, are similar in size. They buy computers, airplanes, and other high-cost assets to lease to other businesses. Assume that all other available information has been analyzed, and the decision regarding which company's stock to purchase depends on the data in their statements of cash flows (below and page 687).

Required

Discuss the relative strengths and weaknesses of each company. Conclude your discussion by recommending one company's stock as an investment.

ALLIED ASSETS FOR LEASE, INC.
Statement of Cash Flows
For the Years Ended September 30, 19X5 and 19X4

	19X5		19X4	
Operating activities:				
Income from operations		$ 37,000		$ 74,000
Add (subtract) noncash items:				
Total		14,000		(4,000)
Net cash inflow from operating activities		51,000		70,000
Investing activities:				
Purchase of property, plant, and equipment	$ (13,000)		$ (3,000)	
Sale of property, plant, and equipment	86,000		79,000	
Sale of long-term investments	13,000		—	
Net cash inflow from investing activities		86,000		76,000
Financing activities:				
Issuance of short-term notes payable	$ 73,000		$ 19,000	
Issuance of long-term notes payable	31,000		42,000	
Payment of short-term notes payable	(181,000)		(148,000)	
Payment of long-term notes payable	(55,000)		(32,000)	
Net cash outflow from financing activities		(132,000)		(119,000)
Increase in cash		$ 5,000		$ 27,000
Cash summary from balance sheet:				
Cash balance at beginning of year		$ 31,000		$ 4,000
Increase in cash during the year		5,000		27,000
Cash balance at end of year		$ 36,000		$ 31,000

NORTHERN LEASING CORPORATION Statement of Cash Flows For the Years Ended September 30, 19X5 and 19X4				
	19X5		19X4	
Operating activities:				
Income from operations		$ 79,000		$71,000
Add (subtract) noncash items:				
Total		19,000		—
Net cash inflow from operating activities		98,000		71,000
Investing activities:				
Purchase of property, plant, and equipment	$(121,000)		$(91,000)	
Sale of long-term investments	13,000		18,000	
Net cash outflow from investing activities		(108,000)		(73,000)
Financing activities:				
Issuance of long-term notes payable	$ 46,000		$ 43,000	
Payment of short-term notes payable	(15,000)		(40,000)	
Payment of cash dividends	(12,000)		(9,000)	
Net cash inflow (outflow) from financing activities		19,000		(6,000)
Increase (decrease) in cash		$ 9,000		$ (8,000)
Cash summary from balance sheet:				
Cash balance at beginning of year		$ 72,000		$80,000
Increase (decrease) in cash during the year		9,000		(8,000)
Cash balance at end of year		$ 81,000		$72,000

Effects of business transactions on selected ratios
(Obj. 5, 6)

P13-4B Financial statement data of Mennonite Industries, Inc., include the following items:

Cash	$ 22,000
Short-term investments	19,000
Accounts receivable, net	83,000
Inventories	141,000
Prepaid expenses	8,000
Total assets	657,000
Short-term notes payable	49,000
Accounts payable	103,000
Accrued liabilities	38,000
Long-term notes payable	160,000
Other long-term liabilities	31,000
Net income	71,000
Number of common shares outstanding	40,000

Required

1. Compute Mennonite's current ratio, debt ratio, and earnings per share.
2. Compute each of the three ratios after evaluating the effect of each transaction that follows. Consider each transaction *separately*.
   a. Purchased merchandise of $26,000 on account, debiting Inventory.
   b. Paid off long-term liabilities, $31,000.
   c. Declared, but did not pay, a $22,000 cash dividend on common stock.
   d. Borrowed $85,000 on a long-term note payable.
   e. Sold short-term investments for $18,000 (cost, $11,000); assume no income tax on the gain.
   f. Issued 5,000 shares of common stock, receiving cash of $120,000.
   g. Received cash on account, $19,000.
   h. Paid short-term notes payable, $32,000.

Use the following format for your answer:

Requirement 1		**Current Ratio**	**Debt Ratio**	**Earnings per Share**
Requirement 2	**Transaction (letter)**	**Current Ratio**	**Debt Ratio**	**Earnings per Share**

Using ratios to evaluate a stock investment
(Obj. 5, 6)

P13-5B Comparative financial statement data of Wahl Furniture Co. follow.

WAHL FURNITURE CO.
Comparative Income Statement
Years Ended December 31, 19X4 and 19X3

	19X4	19X3
Net sales	$462,000	$427,000
Cost of goods sold	229,000	218,000
Gross profit	233,000	209,000
Operating expenses	136,000	134,000
Income from operations	97,000	75,000
Interest expense	11,000	12,000
Income before income tax	86,000	63,000
Income tax expense	30,000	27,000
Net income	$ 56,000	$ 36,000

WAHL FURNITURE CO.
Comparative Balance Sheet
December 31, 19X4 and 19X3
(selected 19X2 amounts given for computation of ratios)

	19X4	19X3	19X2
Current assets:			
Cash	$ 96,000	$ 97,000	
Current receivables, net	112,000	116,000	$103,000
Inventories	172,000	162,000	207,000
Prepaid expenses	16,000	7,000	
Total current assets	396,000	382,000	
Property, plant, and equipment, net	189,000	178,000	
Total assets	$585,000	$560,000	598,000
Total current liabilities	$206,000	$223,000	
Long-term liabilities	119,000	117,000	
Total liabilities	325,000	340,000	
Preferred stockholders' equity, 6%, $100 par	100,000	100,000	
Common stockholders' equity, no par	160,000	120,000	90,000
Total liabilities and stockholders' equity	$585,000	$560,000	

Other information:

1. Market price of Wahl common stock: $49 at December 31, 19X4, and $32.50 at December 31, 19X3
2. Common shares outstanding: 10,000 during 19X4 and 9,000 during 19X3.
3. All sales on credit.

Required

1. Compute the following ratios for 19X4 and 19X3:
   a. Current ratio
   b. Inventory turnover
   c. Accounts receivable turnover
   d. Times-interest-earned ratio
   e. Return on assets
   f. Return on common stockholders' equity
   g. Earnings per share of common stock
   h. Price/earnings ratio
   i. Book value per share of common stock
2. Decide (a) whether Wahl's financial position improved or deteriorated during 19X4 and (b) whether the investment attractiveness of its common stock appears to have increased or decreased.
3. How will what you learned in this problem help you evaluate an investment?

P13-6B Assume that you are purchasing an investment and have decided to invest in a company in the air-conditioning and heating business. You have narrowed the choice to Smajstrla, Inc., and DuBois Corp. and have assembled the following data:

Using ratios to decide between two stock investments; measuring economic value added ***(Obj. 5, 6, 7)***

Selected income statement data for current year:

	Smajstrla, Inc.	DuBois Corp.
Net sales (all on credit)	$497,000	$371,000
Cost of goods sold	258,000	209,000
Income from operations	138,000	79,000
Interest expense	19,000	—
Net income	72,000	48,000

Selected balance sheet and market price data at end of current year:

	Smajstrla, Inc.	DuBois Corp.
Current assets:		
Cash	$ 19,000	$ 22,000
Short-term investments	18,000	20,000
Current receivables, net	46,000	42,000
Inventories	100,000	87,000
Prepaid expenses	3,000	2,000
Total current assets	186,000	173,000
Total assets	328,000	265,000
Total current liabilities	98,000	108,000
Total liabilities	131,000*	108,000*
Preferred stock: 5%, $100-par	20,000	
Common stock, $1-par (10,000 shares)		10,000
$2.50-par (5,000 shares)	12,500	
Total stockholders' equity	197,000	157,000
Market price per share of common stock	$112	$51

*Notes payable: Smajstrla, $86,000
Dubois, $ 1,000

Selected balance sheet data at beginning of current year:

	Smajstrla, Inc.	DuBois Corp.
Current receivables, net	$ 48,000	$ 40,000
Inventories	88,000	93,000
Total assets	270,000	259,000
Preferred stock, 5%, $100-par	20,000	—
Common stock, $1-par (10,000 shares)		10,000
$2.50-par (5,000 shares)	12,500	
Total stockholders' equity	126,000	118,000

Your investment strategy is to purchase the stocks of companies that have low price/earnings ratios but appear to be in good shape financially. Assume that you have analyzed all other factors and your decision depends on the results of the ratio analysis to be performed.

Required

1. Compute the following ratios for both companies for the current year, and decide which company's stock better fits your investment strategy.
   1. Current ratio
   2. Acid-test ratio
   3. Inventory turnover
   4. Days' sales in average receivables
   5. Debt ratio
   6. Times-interest-earned ratio
   7. Return on net sales
   8. Return on total assets
   9. Return on common stockholders' equity
   10. Earnings per share of common stock
   11. Book value per share of common stock
   12. Price/earnings ratio

2. Compute each company's economic-value-added (EVA) measure, and determine whether their EVAs confirm or alter your investment decision. Each company's cost of capital is 12 percent. Round all amounts to the nearest $1,000.

EXTENDING YOUR KNOWLEDGE

DECISION CASES

Identifying action to cut losses and establish profitability ***(Obj. 2, 5, 6)***

Case 1. Suppose you manage Wheel Sports, Inc., a sporting goods and bicycle shop, which lost money during the past year. Before you can set the business on a successful course, you must analyze the company and industry data for the current year to learn what is wrong. The company's data follow.

Wheel Sports Balance Sheet Data

	Wheel Sports	Industry Average
Cash and short-term investments	3.0%	6.8%
Trade receivables, net	15.2	11.0
Inventory	64.2	60.5
Prepaid expenses	1.0	0.0
Total current assets	83.4	78.3
Fixed assets, net	12.6	15.2
Other assets	4.0	6.5
Total assets	100.0%	100.0%
Notes payable, short-term, 12%	17.1%	14.0%
Accounts payable	21.1	25.1
Accrued liabilities	7.8	7.9
Total current liabilities	46.0	47.0
Long-term debt, 11%	19.7	16.4
Total liabilities	65.7	63.4
Common stockholders' equity	34.3	36.6
Total liabilities and stockholders' equity	100.0%	100.0%

Wheel Sports Income Statement Data

	Wheel Sports	Industry Average
Net sales	100.0%	100.0%
Cost of sales	(68.2)	(64.8)
Gross profit	31.8	35.2
Operating expense	(37.1)	(32.3)
Operating income (loss)	(5.3)	2.9
Interest expense	(5.8)	(1.3)
Other revenue	1.1	0.3
Income (loss) before income tax	(10.0)	1.9
Income tax (expense) saving	4.4	(0.8)
Net income (loss)	(5.6)%	1.1%

Required

On the basis of your analysis of these figures, suggest four courses of action Wheel Sports might take to reduce its losses and establish profitable operations. Give your reasons for each suggestion.

Understanding the components of accounting ratios ***(Obj. 5, 6)***

Case 2. Consider the following business situations.

a. Krista Chen has asked you about the stock of a particular company. She finds it attractive because it has a high dividend yield relative to another stock she is also considering. Explain to her the meaning of the ratio and the danger of making a decision based on it alone.

b. Rocketdyne's owners are concerned because the number of days' sales in receivables has increased over the previous two years. Explain why the ratio might have increased.

c. Mark Lott is the controller of Hunan Industries, Inc., whose year end is December 31. Lott prepares checks for suppliers in December and posts them to the appropriate accounts in that month. However, he holds on to the checks and mails them to the suppliers in January. What financial ratio(s) are most affected by the action? What is Lott's purpose in undertaking this activity?

ETHICAL ISSUE

River Front Restaurant Company's long-term debt agreements make certain demands on the business. River Front may not purchase treasury stock in excess of the balance of Retained Earnings. Also, Long-Term Debt may not exceed Stockholders' Equity, and the current ratio may not fall below 1.50. If River Front fails to meet these requirements, the company's lenders have the authority to take over management of the corporation.

Changes in consumer demand have made it hard for River Front to attract customers. Current liabilities have mounted faster than current assets, causing the current ratio to fall to 1.47. Before releasing financial statements, River Front management is scrambling to improve the current ratio. The controller points out that an investment can be classified as either long-term or short-term, depending on management's intention. By deciding to convert an investment to cash within one year, River Front can classify the investment as short-term—a current asset. On the controller's recommendation, River Front's board of directors votes to reclassify long-term investments as short-term.

Required

1. What effect will reclassifying the investments have on the current ratio? Is River Front's financial position stronger as a result of reclassifying the investments?
2. Shortly after the financial statements are released, sales improve and so, then, does the current ratio. As a result, River Front management decides not to sell the investments it had reclassified as short-term. Accordingly, the company reclassifies the investments as long-term. Has management behaved unethically? Give your reason.

FINANCIAL STATEMENT CASES

Measuring profitability and analyzing stock as an investment ***(Obj. 5, 6)***

Case 1. Use the financial statements and the data labeled Eleven-Year Consolidated Financial Summary that appear at the end of the Lands' End, Inc., financial statements (Appendix A at the end of the book) to answer the following questions.

Required

1. From the Eleven-Year Consolidated Financial Summary, chart these ratios over the three most recent fiscal years, 1996, 1995, and 1994:
   a. Percent of pretax income to net sales (similar to rate of return on sales)
   b. Net income per share
   c. Rate of return on common stockholders' equity
   d. Rate of return on total assets
2. Compute these ratios at the end of each of the three most recent fiscal years:
   a. Current ratio
   b. Debt ratio
3. Compute inventory turnover for each of the three most recent fiscal years. You will have to reconstruct ending inventory at January 31, 1994, and January 31, 1993, from the changes in the Inventory account given on the statement of cash flows.
4. Evaluate the company's progress (or lack of progress) in profitability and its ability to turn over inventory and to pay current and long-term liabilities during this three-year period.

Measuring profitability and analyzing stock as an investment ***(Obj. 5, 6)***

Case 2. Obtain the annual report of a company of your choosing.

Required

1. Use the financial statements and the multiyear summary data to chart the company's progress during the three most recent years, including the current year. Compute the following ratios that measure profitability and are used to analyze stock as an investment:

   Profitability Measures

   a. Rate of return on net sales
   b. Rate of return on common stockholders' equity
   c. Rate of return on total assets

   Stock Investment Measure

   d. Price/earnings ratio (If given, use the average of the "high" and "low" stock prices for each year)
2. Is the trend in the profitability measures consistent with the trend in the stock analysis measure? Evaluate the company's overall outlook for the future.

GROUP PROJECTS

Project 1. Select an industry in which you are interested, and use the leading company in that industry as the benchmark. Then select two other companies in the same industry. For each category of ratios in the *Decision Guidelines* feature on pages 660–661, compute at least two ratios for all three companies. Write a two-page report that compares the two companies with the benchmark company.

Project 2. Select a company and obtain its financial statements. Convert the income statement and the balance sheet to common size, and compare the company you selected to the industry average. Robert Morris Associates' *Annual Statement Studies,* Dun & Bradstreet's *Industry Norms & Key Business Ratios,* and Prentice Hall's *Almanac of Business and Industrial Financial Ratios,* by Leo Troy, publish common-size statements for most industries.

INTERNET EXERCISE

BRISTOL-MYERS SQUIBB

Financial statement analysis is as much art as it is science. There is no single "correct" way to analyze a firm; rather, the company's circumstances guide the analyst in determining which of the many analytical tools to employ and emphasize. Remember: The objective of financial statement analysis is to better understand the company by evaluating its current position, where it is headed, and how it is going to get there.

Bristol-Myers Squibb recently replaced its chief executive officer (CEO). The new CEO established some tough financial goals for Bristol-Myers Squibb to achieve by the turn of the century. An analysis of Bristol-Myers Squibb's financial statements will indicate whether the firm is on its way to meeting those goals.

Required

1. Go to **http://www.bms.com/,** the home page of Bristol-Myers Squibb. This site provides information regarding the company's history, mission, and businesses. It is also the home of its headache center and links to a women's cyberclub.
2. Find the company's latest annual report by clicking on **For Our Investors.**
3. Click on the most recent **Annual Report** and answer the following questions.
   a. In the **Letter to Stockholders,** what does the CEO identify as the financial goals of Bristol-Myers Squibb? Which financial ratios would most likely reflect the results of these goals?
   b. Compute the ratios from your answer in (a) above for the past two years. Does it appear that Bristol-Myers Squibb is achieving its goals?
   c. Bristol-Myers Squibb is a conglomerate of numerous companies competing in various lines of business. What are Bristol-Myers Squibb's lines of business?
   d. Do Bristol-Myers Squibb's various business lines have similar levels of profitability, capital intensity, size, and international markets? How does the answer to this question affect your financial analysis of the firm as a whole?

APPENDIX A

The Annual Report of Lands' End, Inc.

1996 Annual Report

LANDS' END®
DIRECT MERCHANTS

Lands' End *is a leading direct merchant of traditionally styled, casual clothing for men, women, and children, accessories, domestics, shoes, and soft luggage. The company's products are offered through regular mailings of its monthly primary catalog and its specialty catalogs. Lands' End is known for providing products of exceptional quality at prices representing honest value, enhanced by a commitment to excellence in customer service. Our reputation, our franchise, our pledge–these are built on this simple but strong foundation...*

Quality...

Quality is all-important at Lands' End. It is our first principle of doing business: We do everything we can do to make our products better. In August, we completed the first of our core product improvements and introduced our new mesh knit shirt, shown on the cover of this report. It features new fabric, a set-on placket, and jersey taping at the neck and shoulder seams. In September, we followed with a new line of fabrics for all our women's knit garments. We've gone back to the drawing board on our denim jeans and will introduce a better-fitting jean later this year. We also plan improvements in other core products, such as our Super-T shirt, our Squall jackets, our seamless neck turtlenecks, and our cotton Drifter sweaters.

We believe that upgrading fabrics, adding features and raising the quality standard of our products will result in continued customer confidence and will differentiate us from our competition.

Honest value...

As direct merchants, we travel all over the world to find what we believe are the best fabrics and quality construction available in the market. We do not buy branded merchandise–instead we deal directly with the mills and manufacturers who make our products according to our specifications. They have proved that they are extremely competent, cost-conscious and committed to the same level of quality as we are. Working with them as partners allows us to eliminate unnecessary markups required by dealing with middlemen.

We are able to offer honest value to our customers because we operate efficiently. We feel that our people are the greatest group of intelligent, hard-working and dedicated employees that can be found anywhere. While their contribution may not be measurable in dollars and cents, we are certain it has a significant impact on our financial success.

And always, always...customer service.

We believe that if we take care of each customer, one at a time, the business will take care of itself. Our customers trust us to provide fast shipment and no-hassle returns. We expand on that trust by offering monogramming, free hemming, specialty shoppers–services you would get from a friend. Our friendly telephone operators are happy to send out fabric samples or our Book of Caring telling how to keep clothes looking their best. Our specialty shoppers will help match colors or select gifts for friends or family. And as we expand into international markets, our customer service philosophy remains all important.

Our customers trust us, and we will not let them down. By continuing to focus on their expectations for quality, value and service, and by exceeding those expectations in every way possible, we will continue to earn their trust.

Financial Highlights

683 734 870 992 1,032

92 93 94 95 96

fiscal year

Net sales Dollars in millions

Net sales rose to $1.032 billion in fiscal 1996, an increase of 4 percent. Over the last five years, net sales increased at an average compound annual growth rate of 11.4 percent.

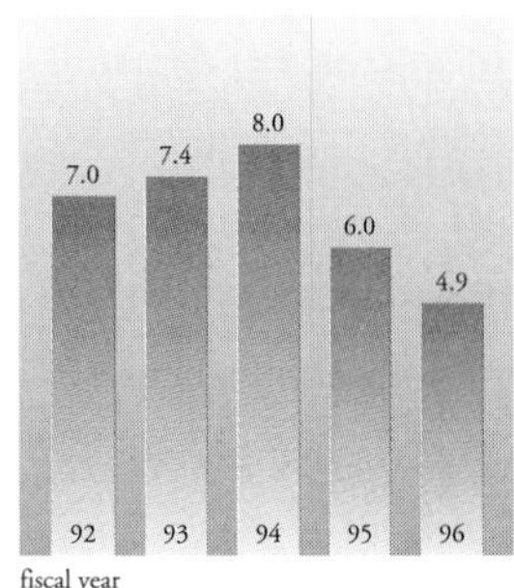

Pretax return on sales Percent

Pretax return on sales declined to 4.9 percent in the year just ended.

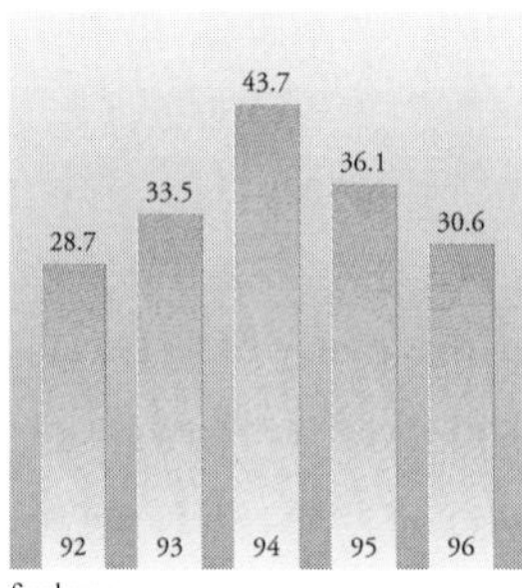

Net income Dollars in millions

Net income was $30.6 million in fiscal 1996, compared with $36.1 million a year ago. Fiscal 1996 includes a charge of $1.1 million; fiscal 1995 includes a charge of $2.1 million.

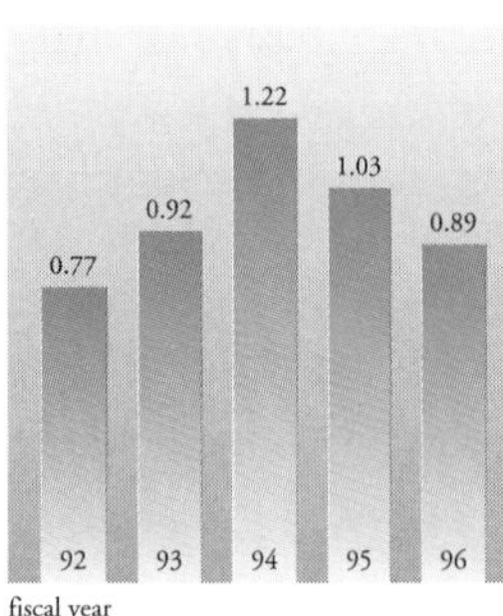

Net income per share Dollars

Net income per common share was $0.89, down 14 percent from fiscal 1995. Without the effect of the factors noted in net income, EPS was $0.92 this year versus $1.09 in fiscal 1995.

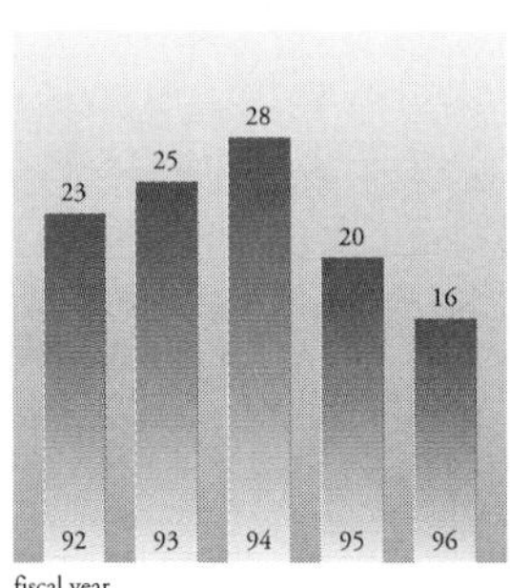

Return on average shareholders' investment Percent

Return on average shareholders' investment was 16 percent in fiscal 1996, down from 20 percent last year, and averaged about 22 percent over the last five years.

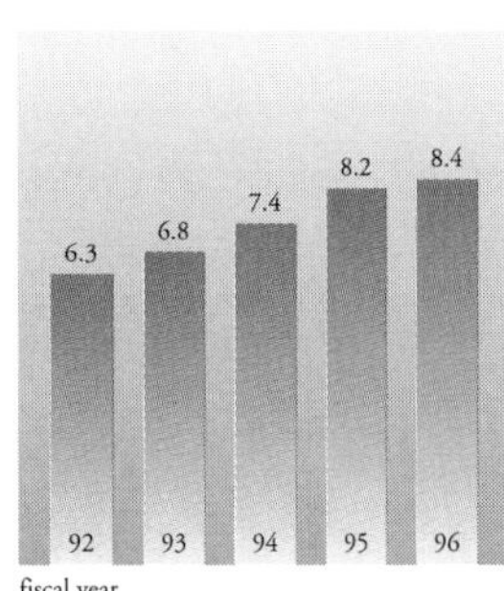

36-month buyers Millions

We have 8.4 million customers who have made at least one purchase during the past 36 months, and our complete mailing list contains more than 22 million names.

Inside this report

Dear Shareholder,

Fiscal 1996 was a difficult year for Lands' End. Our sales advanced 4 percent to $1.032 billion, and our earnings fell 15 percent to $30.6 million. Catalog retailers faced the tough combination of significantly increased postage and paper prices, in conjunction with soft apparel demand.

Through the first three quarters of the year, our profits declined by over 50 percent. Cost increases were particularly troublesome, with paper and postage increases alone adding about $20 million in expenses. We responded by cutting pages and circulation and by focusing on improving the productivity of the catalogs. The combination of these efforts contributed to a slight fourth quarter year-on-year improvement in profits.

There were other areas of focus in addition to short-term profitability – areas of even more importance and with longer range implications. We believe that to compete effectively in today's crowded marketplace, we must develop a special relationship with our customer. We do this by religiously following some very simple principles relating to product quality, customer service and employee relationships. This year, we've made progress in each of these key areas.

My major concern throughout the year was for our reputation for quality. Product quality is one of the key foundations on which we've built our business, and we believe that we have set the standard for quality in many of the areas in which we compete.

Maintaining such levels of quality takes company-wide focus and commitment. I became convinced that we were at risk of losing our edge and needed to refocus our efforts on quality. In some of our flagship products, competition had caught up. We needed to quickly regain our leadership positions in these key areas. Our profits could be restored, but our reputation, if lost, could never quite be replaced.

So we stepped up all of our quality-improvement programs. Everyone involved with product rolled up their sleeves and set about creating new standards. Our product experts, some of the best in the business, challenged every assumption and every step in the process to produce some of the finest products we've seen in recent history.

Michael J. Smith

We started with our core products, some of which already have appeared in our catalog – our mesh knit polo, our Interlochen polo, our Super-T t-shirt. The question asked of each product manager was "How can we make this product better?" We were concerned not so much with short-term costs as with our long-term standing with our customers.

I believe that long term, our future success as a company depends on our ability to deliver high-quality product at a value not seen elsewhere, with warm, friendly customer service. We've been encouraged so far by the response to our product quality and customer service initiatives. Returns declined this past year, especially in the second half of the year. And customer letters that we receive have turned increasingly positive with respect to both quality and service.

We improved our initial customer fulfillment, the percent of items in stock when a customer orders. Out-of-stocks are always a source of irritation for the customer, as well as very costly for the company. We ended the year near our goal of 90 percent initial fulfillment and established a five-year high. This not only saves on shipping costs of backorders, but more important, it provides us with a clear competitive service advantage. In addition, this fulfillment level was achieved while keeping inventory levels in line.

Internally, we focused on improving the systems for managing the business in such areas as planning, tracking, product development, and analysis. The increasing complexity of our business had constantly challenged our ability to effectively manage it. We've made significant progress in this area during the past year, and I see us completing most of our current projects by the end of this year.

Looking towards the future, product quality, customer service and the cultivation of an idea-driven, entrepreneurial environment are the pillars that will support both our short-term and long-term strategies.

Within this context, in addition to the foundation pieces referred to above, there are some areas that will receive particular attention this coming year. First, we will continue to improve product quality and the processes that affect quality. We are especially focusing on improving consistency of the fit of our products.

Second, we need to improve profitability. Since much of the paper price increases came in the second half of last year, we need to implement productivity improvements of several million dollars simply to cover those expenses that will be anniversaried this year. Productivity improvements will come from stronger, more compelling product, more effective selling presentations and improved marketing efforts.

Third, we need to improve our flexibility and responsiveness. We need to implement new ideas and make changes to our business faster than we can today. Our size should be an advantage and not an impediment to competitiveness.

Fourth, we need to focus on customer acquisition to rebuild some of the momentum lost during last year's sluggish period.

And finally, we need to build on our recruitment, training and development programs to ensure that we will have sufficient management depth. We have a unique culture and way of doing business that takes time to learn. We need to develop a topnotch pool of managers who are bright, creative leaders and who embrace the Lands' End way of doing business.

These areas are all important to improving our competitiveness in today's difficult environment, and we are working hard on each one of them. In doing so, we are committed to maintaining our customer focus. Our customers are our lifeblood and the key to any future success.

We have a special relationship with our customer that requires a certain way of doing business. When we do something they like, they let us know. When we mess up, they take us to task. And when they have ideas about our business, they write to tell us about them. We do not take this relationship lightly.

We have some very simple guidelines to follow that our founder Gary Comer expressed years ago. We refer to them often. These can best be summed up from a memo sent to all employees and reprinted in a catalog years ago. Gary wrote, "Don't worry about what is best for the company – worry about what is best for the customer."

While quite a simple statement, it carries with it an importance and meaning far beyond mere words. It implies an outlook, a way of thinking – an attitude about coming to work. This attitude comes naturally to our people. They make decisions every day as to how to best serve the customer. They do it without lengthy rules and regulations and without a cumbersome approval process. They do it on their own. We could not have made the progress we did this year without such an outstanding group of people.

We believe this focus on quality, on our customer and on our people is the best path to success. It keeps customers happy and coming back. It keeps employees motivated and excited. And it creates a unique and well-defined position that differentiates us from others.

This is all very simple in concept. But it is the execution that makes the difference – execution with passion, creativity and commitment. These qualities bring the company to life for our customers and make Lands' End more than just a place to buy clothes.

Thank you for your time and support.

Michael J. Smith
President and Chief Executive Officer

Our catalog businesses

Core Business In the past year, our core domestic business, represented by our primary and prospecting catalogs, has been the focus of our attention. These catalogs offer our full line of traditionally styled, classic casual apparel for men and women, as well as accessories and soft luggage. With the increases in paper prices and postage rates and the increasingly competitive retail market, we must make each page more productive to reach a higher level of profitability. By concentrating on a strong line merchandising position and making each and every presentation more compelling to the buyer, we believe we can reverse the decline experienced in fiscal 1996 in this major segment of our business that accounted for roughly two-thirds of our total sales this year. While it is more difficult to grow a large business than a smaller one, we believe there are opportunities to expand our sales through new products and through line extensions, such as big and tall sizes for men, and to add new buyers to our customer base. We are continuing our investments in information systems to help us in our ongoing challenge to utilize the information in our database to mail catalogs more efficiently and profitably.

Specialty Businesses The Lands' End Kids collection of comfortable, casual clothing for children and infants is the largest of our specialty businesses. Lands' End has a large list of upscale mail-order-responsive parents, and we mailed our Kids catalog to this group six times in fiscal 1996.

Coming Home, our specialty catalog for bed and bath, has become known for its innovative products, such as the "Sheet That Fits" and 100 percent Supima® cotton towels that are five inches longer than the market standard. We mailed Coming Home nine times in fiscal 1996. This year we are expanding our line of custom window treatments, utilizing our exceptional customer service standards to provide a competitive edge.

Our Beyond Buttondowns catalog, mailed four times in fiscal 1996, offers a broad assortment of classic tailored clothing for men. The exceptional fabrics and fine tailoring of our suiting separates, dress shirts, ties, handcrafted shoes, and accessories make Beyond Buttondowns a one-stop shopping experience for men's tailored dressing.

Our Textures catalog features a selection of finely tailored clothing for the workplace and was mailed twice in fiscal 1996. We continue to test separate mailings and bound-in pages within the primary catalog to determine the shopping method our customers prefer.

International Businesses We launched operations in Japan in the fall of 1994, and in fiscal 1996 we mailed six issues of our Japanese-language, yen-denominated catalog with great success. The Japanese market has responded to our catalogs even more strongly than we anticipated. We have focused on laying the infrastructure in the areas of inventory control and systems to support this strong response, and we are pleased with the progress we've made in our customer service levels. This year we will move our leased distribution center to a larger facility to allow us to manage additional growth.

Sales in the United Kingdom continue to grow. We recently opened a small outlet store near our leased headquarters in Oakham, England, to manage inventory overstocks and have purchased a site to allow us flexibility for future development. We have started hiring staff and selecting a site in Germany to establish telephone operations for a launch there within the next 12 months.

While sales from our foreign-based operations have not yet reached 10 percent of total consolidated sales, they have made an improvement in profit contribution. We are optimistic about our long-term future in these exciting, growing markets.

Through our Pan International business, we send regular mailings of our primary and prospecting catalogs to our friends in Canada and to customers in more than 175 countries throughout the world, and these export sales turned in a strong sales performance for our core business in fiscal 1996. We will be discontinuing our licensing agreement with Myer Direct in Australia and plan to develop this counter-seasonal business through our Dodgeville operations instead. The growth we have seen in this section of our business reinforces the belief that our exceptional quality products, our honest value position and our customer service stance have appeal elsewhere in the world.

New Businesses Corporate Sales continues to bring the high-quality merchandise for which Lands' End is known to the business-to-business market, utilizing our embroidery capabilities to design and monogram unique emblems and logos for corporations, clubs, teams, and other groups. Offering the best in customer service, the Corporate Sales motto is "Just Ask."

The Territory Ahead, based in California, offers upscale casual clothing with a strong design and fashion flair. In fiscal 1996, The Territory Ahead expanded its focus on women's product, which was enthusiastically received by customers.

In October 1995, we launched the Willis & Geiger catalog, a respected brand since the early 1900s. Willis & Geiger's rich history as the adventure outfitter for Teddy Roosevelt, Charles Lindbergh and Admiral Byrd is brought into the present through its outstanding collection of clothing and accessories for today's outdoor adventurer.

Did you know?

On our busiest day–
we had almost 115,000 phone calls;
we packed and shipped about
140,000 orders.

In our busiest month–
we hemmed more than 350,000 pants;
we wrapped approximately 100,000 gifts.

There are 69 steps involved in making our Pinpoint Oxford men's dress shirt.

Our distribution center in Dodgeville is as large as 16 football fields.

During the year more than 3,000 people stopped by to visit headquarters while visiting in Wisconsin.

Our contributions committee sent more than 1,000 teddy bears to sick children and their families.

Handling the challenges–and the opportunities

As always, there are many challenges ahead. The apparel retailing environment is competitive, crowded, and highly promotional. We believe we have the best group of employees any company could have. They are naturally friendly, talented and efficient, and they always take care of our customer. Their charge is to make sure that we do all we can to offer products that are more compelling, to deliver our message more effectively and to develop mailing strategies that are more efficient.

Product Focus The Lands' End brand is one of the largest, most respected names in apparel retailing in the United States. Classically inspired, traditionally styled clothing of the highest quality is our heritage and our future. Whether we are developing new lines of tailored clothing for men and women or improving lines of casualwear for our more informal workplaces and weekends, we will always do our best to incorporate innovations in fabric, construction and detail that add value and excitement and differentiate Lands' End from the competition.

We have a strong merchandising, design and quality staff focused on product development. Our people travel all over the U.S. and the world to find the best fabrics – from Arizona's long-staple cotton for our men's dress shirts to Peruvian cotton for our Interlochen shirts; from Massachusetts for exceptional Polartec® fleece used in our sportswear and outerwear to England for authentic Harris tweed jackets. We take great care in selecting our manufacturers and form strong partnerships with them. Our quality assurance staff is constantly on the go, visiting the mills and factories to make sure that everything is going right, right from the start – a lot easier than trying to make it right later.

There are areas where we can be even stronger. We are focusing on our core products to capitalize on them and plan to offer a wider assortment of "cut-above" and specialty products. To add interest and excitement to the catalog, we are also featuring additional appearances of our Find of the Month, one-time-only offerings of remarkable value. We believe these and other approaches will be welcomed by our current customers and will help us bring new customers into the fold.

"Find of the Month"

What's a "Find"? It's a remarkable value that appears in only one issue of our catalog! Something we track down in an out-of-the-way place, buy at opportunistic savings, then offer to you on a "one-time-only" basis.

Creative Presentations On the creative side, we are making our presentations stronger by focusing on the strengths of line merchandising and doing a better job in explaining the benefits of each of our products and how they differ from what is found in the marketplace. We also plan to add more editorial and feature articles – another way to make our catalogs interesting and different from others our customers find in their mailboxes and another way to be welcome in our customers' homes.

Mailing Strategies Increases in paper prices and postage have driven up our cost of catalogs dramatically. The added catalog costs have made it necessary to reduce the number of pages we mail, to use catalog space even more judiciously and to make each page as productive as possible. We reduced our prospect mailings in fiscal 1996 because it was simply too expensive to bring in new customers through additional mailings. Combined with weaker customer reaction to our offerings, this resulted in adding fewer new customers to our housefile. We have allocated resources to develop new, creative and innovative ways to reach new customers through our prospector catalog and to develop programs that will help retain and reactivate those who have purchased in the past.

We have established our new corporate database, and this is one of our biggest challenges and opportunities. We are trying to develop better methods of accessing our database to discover the best mailing strategy for our customers – the best combination of monthly and specialty catalogs to mail to obtain optimum sales and optimum profitability. We have tests in progress, and we'll continue to try new and different approaches. We're working hard to determine the best ways to mail to our huge list of customers. We'll continue to invest resources in our information systems to make progress in this most important area.

New Channels of Distribution We also continue to explore new channels of distribution. In July 1995, we established a Lands' End home page on the Internet's World Wide Web and offer more than 100 core products that can be purchased on-line. While this method of shopping is still in its infancy, we have seen a lot of interest from those who like to spend time surfing the Net, and nobody knows how it will develop. We continue to explore the development of CD-ROMs and other methods of interactive shopping – all in order to be wherever our customers want us to be and to learn the best ways to bring our products to them.

The U.S. apparel market totals about $135 billion, and mail-order apparel sales account for about $10 billion of that total. The appeal of catalog shopping continues to be strong. Customers are seeking the best possible quality, the best possible value, and the best possible service, and they will continue to do so. We offer all three. We always have. We always will. That is our challenge and our opportunity.

Results of operations for fiscal 1996, compared with fiscal 1995

Consolidated statements of operations presented as a percentage of net sales:

For the period ended	**February 2, 1996**	January 27, 1995	January 28, 1994
Net sales	**100.0%**	100.0%	100.0%
Cost of sales	**57.0**	57.6	59.1
Gross profit	**43.0**	42.4	40.9
Selling, general and administrative expenses	**38.0**	36.0	32.8
Charges from sale of subsidiary	**0.2**	0.4	–
Income from operations	**4.8**	6.0	8.1
Interest expense, net	**(0.3)**	(0.2)	–
Other	**0.4**	0.2	(0.1)
Income before income taxes and cumulative effect of change in accounting	**4.9**	6.0	8.0
Income tax provision	**1.9**	2.4	3.1
Net income before cumulative effect of change in accounting	**3.0**	3.6	4.9
Cumulative effect of change in accounting for income taxes	**–**	–	0.1
Net income	**3.0%**	3.6%	5.0%

Net sales for the 53-week year just ended totaled $1.032 billion, compared with $0.992 billion in the prior 52-week year, an increase of 4 percent. Net sales for the first 52 weeks of fiscal 1996 rose 3 percent, compared to fiscal 1995. Sales in the United States from the company's core monthly and prospecting catalogs, which accounted for about two-thirds of total net sales, were lower than the prior year. Sales from the company's international and new businesses accounted for more than the entire rise in sales for the year. During the year, worldwide, catalog mailings were higher than in the prior year, while overall pages mailed were slightly lower. The number of full-price catalogs mailed increased 5 percent to 200 million in fiscal 1996 from 191 million in fiscal 1995.

The company ended the year with inventory of $165 million, down 2 percent from fiscal 1995 ending inventory of $169 million. For the year, the company was able to ship about 90 percent of items ordered by customers at the time the order was placed, compared with 88 percent for fiscal 1995.

Gross profit increased

Gross profit increased 5 percent to $444 million in fiscal 1996, compared with $421 million in fiscal 1995. As a percentage of net sales, gross profit rose to 43.0 percent in fiscal 1996, compared with 42.4 percent in fiscal 1995. The increase in gross profit margin was mainly due to lower merchandise costs, primarily from improvements in sourcing, as well as from a greater proportion of sales from higher margin businesses. Liquidation of out-of-season and overstocked merchandise was about 11 percent of net sales in fiscal 1996, compared to 10 percent in the prior year.

Costs of inventory purchases increased approximately 1.8 percent in fiscal 1996, compared to 0.1 percent in fiscal 1995.

Selling, general and administrative expenses

Selling, general and administrative (SG&A) expenses rose 10 percent in fiscal 1996 to $392 million, from $358 million in fiscal 1995. As a percentage of sales, SG&A increased to 38.0 percent in fiscal 1996 from 36.0 percent in fiscal 1995. The rise in the SG&A ratio was primarily due to higher paper prices and postal rates and lower sales per catalog mailed in the United States. Those expenses increased about $20 million. The costs of producing and mailing catalogs represented about 43 percent of total SG&A in fiscal 1996 and 41 percent in fiscal 1995. Other operating expenses as a percentage of sales were about the same as last year. While payroll costs were relatively higher, this was mostly offset by lower bonuses and consulting fees.

Depreciation and amortization expense was up 21 percent from the prior year, to $12.5 million, mainly for computer software and equipment. Rental expense was up 34 percent to total $11.6 million, primarily due to increased computer-related rentals and building rentals.

Utilization of credit lines remained stable

Borrowing under our short-term lines of credit was consistent with last year due to stabilized inventory levels. These funds were mainly used to meet peak inventory requirements. In addition, the company purchased approximately $20 million in treasury stock and spent $15 million in capital expenditures. The company's lines of credit peaked at $104 million in October 1995, compared with a peak of $106 million in the prior year. At February 2, 1996, the company had only short-term debt outstanding for a foreign subsidiary of $9.3 million and no long-term debt outstanding.

Net income decreased

Net income was $30.6 million, down 15 percent from the $36.1 million the company earned in fiscal 1995. Earnings per common share for the year just ended were $0.89, compared with $1.03 per share in the prior year. Net income for the year includes $2.4 million in foreign currency exchange gains, recorded as other income.

As previously reported, during the fourth quarter of fiscal 1996, the company took an after-tax charge to earnings of $1.1 million, or a reduction of $0.03 per share, in connection with the sale of its wholly owned subsidiary, MontBell America, Inc. This is in addition to the after-tax charge of $2.1 million, or a reduction of $0.06 per share, taken as a reserve in the fourth quarter of fiscal 1995 in anticipation of the sale of the subsidiary. Without the effect of these after-tax charges, net income for fiscal 1996 was $31.7 million, or $0.92 per share, compared with $38.2 million, or $1.09 per share, in fiscal 1995.

Results of operations for fiscal 1995, compared with fiscal 1994

Net sales increased 14 percent to $992 million in fiscal 1995, compared with $870 million in fiscal 1994. The increase was primarily due to improved customer reaction to the catalogs and a 23 percent increase in the number of regular and specialty catalogs mailed from 155 million to 191 million in fiscal 1995. About half of the increase in net sales in fiscal 1995 came from the company's regular monthly catalogs, prospector catalogs, and specialty catalogs in the United States. Specialty catalogs include the Kids catalog, featuring children's clothing; Coming Home, a catalog focusing on products for bed and bath; Beyond Buttondowns, a men's tailored clothing and accessories catalog; and the Textures catalog, featuring tailored clothing for women. In addition, over 30 percent of the sales increase was attributed to the strong sales growth from the company's international businesses as well as from two new businesses, The Territory Ahead and Corporate Sales.

The company ended fiscal year 1995 with inventory of $169 million, up 13 percent from fiscal 1994 ending inventory of $150 million. Higher inventory levels throughout the year resulted in higher interest expense, but enabled the company to ship nearly 88 percent of items ordered by customers at the time the order was placed, compared with 85 percent for fiscal 1994.

Gross profit increased

Gross profit increased 18 percent to $421 million in fiscal 1995, compared with $356 million in fiscal 1994, primarily due to the 14 percent increase in consolidated net sales, as well as to the increase in gross profit margin. As a percentage of net sales, gross profit rose to 42.4 percent in fiscal 1995, compared with 40.9 percent in fiscal 1994. The increase in gross profit margin was mainly due to lower merchandise costs from improvements in domestic and offshore sourcing, partially offset by steeper markdowns of liquidated merchandise. Liquidation of out-of-season and overstocked merchandise was about 10 percent of net sales in each of the last two years.

Costs of inventory purchases increased approximately 0.1 percent in fiscal 1995, compared with 0.8 percent in fiscal 1994. The impact of inflation continued to be low for the merchandise purchased by the company.

Selling, general and administrative expenses
Selling, general and administrative (SG&A) expenses rose 25 percent in fiscal 1995 to $358 million, from $286 million in fiscal 1994, principally due to the 14 percent increase in net sales. Associated with higher sales were advertising expenses (attributed to customer prospecting and increased catalog mailings), fixed expenses (due to investment spending in international and new businesses), and increased variable expenses (primarily due to higher payroll and shipping and handling costs). The costs of producing and mailing catalogs represented about 41 percent of total SG&A in fiscal 1995 and in fiscal 1994.

As a percentage of sales, SG&A increased to 36.0 percent in fiscal 1995 from 32.8 percent in fiscal 1994. The rise in the SG&A ratio was primarily due to the company's investment spending to develop international and new businesses, to expand customer acquisition programs in anticipation of the 1995 postal rate and paper price increases, to enhance its customer service by offering two-day UPS delivery service, and to upgrade its information systems.

Depreciation and amortization expense was up 24 percent from the prior year, to $10.3 million. Rental expense was up 19 percent to total $8.6 million, primarily due to increased computer hardware and building rentals.

Increased utilization of credit lines
Higher inventory levels for the majority of the year resulted in more borrowing and higher interest expense throughout the year. In addition, the company purchased approximately $28 million in treasury stock and spent $27 million in capital expenditures. The company's lines of credit peaked at $106 million in October 1994, compared with a peak of $54 million in the prior year. At January 27, 1995, the company had short-term debt outstanding for a subsidiary of $7.5 million and no long-term debt outstanding.

Net income decreased
Net income was $36.1 million, down 17 percent from the $43.7 million the company earned in fiscal 1994. Earnings per common share for the year just ended were $1.03, compared with $1.22 per share in the prior year.

During the fourth quarter of fiscal 1995, the company set up a reserve for the anticipated sale of its subsidiary, MontBell America, Inc., that reduced net income by $2.1 million, or $0.06 per share. During the first quarter of fiscal 1994, the company adopted Statement of Financial Accounting Standards No. 109, "Accounting for Income Taxes," which added $1.3 million of net income, or $0.04 per share, to the results in fiscal 1994. Without the effect of these two factors, net income for fiscal 1995 was $38.2 million, or $1.09 per share, compared with $42.4 million, or $1.18 per share, in fiscal 1994.

The Christmas season is our busiest

The company's business is highly seasonal. The fall/winter season, which the company regards as a five-month period ending in December, includes the peak selling season during the Thanksgiving and Christmas holidays in the company's fourth quarter. In the longer spring/summer season, orders are fewer and the merchandise offered generally has lower unit selling prices than products offered in the fall/winter season. As a result, net sales are usually substantially greater in the fall/winter season, and SG&A as a percentage of net sales is usually higher in the spring/summer season. In addition, as the company continues to refine its marketing efforts by experimenting with the timing of its catalog mailings, quarterly results may fluctuate.

Nearly 40 percent of the company's annual sales came in the final three months (November, December, and January) of fiscal years 1996 and 1995. About 85 percent and 65 percent of before-tax profit was realized in the same three months of fiscal 1996 and 1995, respectively.

Liquidity and capital resources

To date, the bulk of the company's working capital needs have been met through funds generated from operations and from short-term bank loans. The company's principal need for working capital has been to meet peak inventory requirements associated with its seasonal sales pattern. In addition, the company's resources have been used to purchase treasury stock and make asset additions.

During fiscal 1995, the board of directors evaluated its dividend practice whereby it had paid annual dividends. Given the company's intent to buy back additional shares, the board determined that the current dividend practice was no longer desirable, and payment of a cash dividend is not planned for the foreseeable future.

The company continues to explore investment opportunities arising from the expansion of its international businesses and the development of new businesses. While this investment spending has had some negative impact on earnings, it is not expected to have a material effect on liquidity.

At February 2, 1996, the company had unsecured domestic credit facilities totaling $110 million, all of which was unused. The company also maintains foreign credit lines for use in foreign operations totaling the equivalent of approximately $19 million, of which $9.3 million was used at February 2, 1996. The company has a separate $20 million bank facility available to fund treasury stock purchases and capital expenditures. This facility runs through December 31, 1996.

Since June 1989, the company's board of directors has authorized the company from time to time to purchase a total of 8.2 million shares of treasury stock, of which 1.3 million, 1.4 million, and 0.1 million shares have been purchased in the fiscal years ended February 2, 1996, January 27, 1995, and January 28, 1994, respectively. The total cost of the purchases was $20.0 million, $28.0 million and $2.9 million for fiscal 1996, 1995 and 1994, respectively. There is a balance of 0.7 million shares available to the company to purchase as of February 2, 1996.

Capital investment

Capital investment was about $15 million in fiscal 1996. Major projects included new computer hardware and software, leasehold improvements for new retail stores and material handling equipment.

In the coming year, the company plans to invest about $16 million in capital improvements. Major projects will include new computer hardware and software, material handling equipment and leasehold improvements for new retail stores. The company believes that its cash flow from operations and borrowings under its current credit facilities will provide adequate resources to meet its capital requirements and operational needs for the foreseeable future.

Possible future changes

A 1992 Supreme Court decision confirmed that the Commerce Clause of the United States Constitution prevents a state from requiring the collection of its use tax by a mail order company unless the company has a physical presence in the state. However, there continues to be uncertainty due to inconsistent application of the Supreme Court decision by state and federal courts. The company attempts to conduct its operations in compliance with its interpretation of the applicable legal standard, but there can be no assurance that such compliance will not be challenged.

In recent challenges, various states have sought to require companies to begin collection of use taxes and/or pay taxes from previous sales. The company has not received assessments from any state.

The Supreme Court decision also established that Congress has the power to enact legislation that would permit states to require collection of use taxes by mail order companies. Congress has from time to time considered proposals for such legislation. The company anticipates that any legislative change, if adopted, would be applied only on a prospective basis.

The possible future changes discussed above are forward looking, subject to numerous uncertainties and accordingly, not necessarily indicative of actual future results.

Consolidated Statements of Operations

(In thousands, except per share data)	For the period ended February 2, 1996	January 27, 1995	January 28, 1994
Net sales	**$1,031,548**	$992,106	$869,975
Cost of sales	**588,017**	571,265	514,052
Gross profit	**443,531**	420,841	355,923
Selling, general and administrative expenses	**392,484**	357,516	285,513
Charges from sale of subsidiary	**1,882**	3,500	–
Income from operations	**49,165**	59,825	70,410
Other income (expense):			
Interest expense	**(2,771)**	(1,769)	(359)
Interest income	**253**	307	346
Other	**4,278**	1,300	(527)
Total other income (expense), net	**1,760**	(162)	(540)
Income before income taxes and cumulative effect of change in accounting	**50,925**	59,663	69,870
Income tax provision	**20,370**	23,567	27,441
Net income before cumulative effect of change in accounting	**30,555**	36,096	42,429
Cumulative effect of change in accounting for income taxes	**–**	–	1,300
Net income	**$ 30,555**	$ 36,096	$ 43,729
Net income per share before cumulative effect of change in accounting	**$ 0.89**	$ 1.03	$ 1.18
Cumulative per share effect of change in accounting	**–**	–	0.04
Net income per share	**$ 0.89**	$ 1.03	$ 1.22

The accompanying notes to consolidated financial statements are an integral part of these consolidated statements.

Consolidated Balance Sheets

(In thousands)	**February 2, 1996**	January 27, 1995
Assets		
Current assets:		
Cash and cash equivalents	**$ 17,176**	$ 5,426
Receivables	**8,064**	4,459
Inventory	**164,816**	168,652
Prepaid advertising	**15,824**	7,506
Other prepaid expenses	**5,295**	3,713
Deferred income tax benefits	**10,914**	8,412
Total current assets	**222,089**	198,168
Property, plant and equipment, at cost:		
Land and buildings	**72,248**	69,798
Fixtures and equipment	**83,880**	74,745
Leasehold improvements	**2,912**	1,862
Total property, plant and equipment	**159,040**	146,405
Less – accumulated depreciation and amortization	**60,055**	49,414
Property, plant and equipment, net	**98,985**	96,991
Intangibles, net	**2,423**	2,453
Total assets	**$323,497**	$297,612
Liabilities and shareholders' investment		
Current liabilities:		
Lines of credit	**$ 9,319**	$ 7,539
Accounts payable	**62,380**	52,762
Reserve for returns	**4,555**	5,011
Accrued liabilities	**23,751**	25,959
Accrued profit sharing	**1,483**	1,679
Income taxes payable	**13,256**	9,727
Current maturities of long-term debt	**–**	40
Total current liabilities	**114,744**	102,717
Deferred income taxes	**7,212**	5,379
Long-term liabilities	**349**	388
Shareholders' investment:		
Common stock, 40,221 shares issued	**402**	402
Donated capital	**8,400**	8,400
Additional paid-in capital	**26,165**	25,817
Deferred compensation	**(1,193)**	(1,421)
Currency translation adjustments	**360**	284
Retained earnings	**260,109**	229,554
Treasury stock, 6,561 and 5,395 shares at cost, respectively	**(93,051)**	(73,908)
Total shareholders' investment	**201,192**	189,128
Total liabilities and shareholders' investment	**$323,497**	$297,612

The accompanying notes to consolidated financial statements are an integral part of these consolidated balance sheets.

Consolidated Statements of Shareholders' Investment

(In thousands)	For the period ended February 2, 1996	January 27, 1995	January 28, 1994
Common Stock			
Beginning balance	**$ 402**	$ 201	$ 201
Two-for-one stock split	**–**	201	–
Ending balance	**$ 402**	$ 402	$ 201
Donated Capital Balance	**$ 8,400**	$ 8,400	$ 8,400
Additional Paid-in Capital			
Beginning balance	**$ 25,817**	$ 24,888	$ 24,857
Tax benefit of stock options exercised	**348**	1,130	31
Two-for-one stock split	**–**	(201)	–
Ending balance	**$ 26,165**	$ 25,817	$ 24,888
Deferred Compensation			
Beginning balance	**$ (1,421)**	$ (2,001)	$ (1,680)
Issuance of treasury stock	**–**	–	(564)
Amortization of deferred compensation	**228**	580	243
Ending balance	**$ (1,193)**	$ (1,421)	$ (2,001)
Foreign Currency Translation			
Beginning balance	**$ 284**	$ 246	$ –
Adjustment for the year	**76**	38	246
Ending balance	**$ 360**	$ 284	$ 246
Retained Earnings			
Beginning balance	**$229,554**	$193,460	$153,324
Net income	**30,555**	36,096	43,729
Cash dividends paid	**–**	–	(3,592)
Issuance of treasury stock	**–**	(2)	(1)
Ending balance	**$260,109**	$229,554	$193,460
Treasury Stock			
Beginning balance	**$ (73,908)**	$ (47,909)	$ (45,714)
Purchase of treasury stock	**(20,001)**	(27,979)	(2,861)
Issuance of treasury stock	**858**	1,980	666
Ending balance	**$ (93,051)**	$ (73,908)	$ (47,909)
Total Shareholders' Investment	**$201,192**	$189,128	$177,285

The accompanying notes to consolidated financial statements are an integral part of these consolidated statements.

Consolidated Statements of Cash Flows

(In thousands)	For the period ended February 2, 1996	January 27, 1995	January 28, 1994
Cash flows from operating activities:			
Net income before cumulative effect of change in accounting	**$ 30,555**	$ 36,096	$ 42,429
Adjustments to reconcile net income to net cash flows from operating activities –			
Depreciation and amortization	**12,456**	10,311	8,286
Deferred compensation expense	**228**	580	243
Deferred income taxes	**(669)**	(2,645)	(1,684)
Loss on disposal of fixed assets	**1,544**	901	684
Changes in assets and liabilities excluding the effects of acquisitions and divestitures:			
Receivables	**(4,888)**	(264)	(3,179)
Inventory	**1,423**	(16,544)	(41,769)
Prepaid advertising	**(8,318)**	(580)	(2,504)
Other prepaid expenses	**(1,611)**	1,177	(3,211)
Accounts payable	**9,618**	(2,093)	16,765
Reserve for returns	**(456)**	1,104	(98)
Accrued liabilities	**(2,208)**	8,509	3,701
Accrued profit sharing	**(196)**	(597)	642
Income taxes payable	**3,877**	(1,671)	1,601
Other	**37**	177	502
Net cash flows from operating activities	**41,392**	34,461	22,408
Cash flows from investing activities:			
Cash paid for capital additions and businesses acquired	**(13,904)**	(32,102)	(17,321)
Proceeds from divestiture	**1,665**	–	–
Net cash flows used for investing activities	**(12,239)**	(32,102)	(17,321)
Cash flows from financing activities:			
Proceeds from short-term and long-term debt	**1,780**	7,539	80
Payment of long-term debt	**(40)**	(40)	–
Purchases of treasury stock	**(20,001)**	(27,979)	(2,861)
Issuance of treasury stock	**858**	1,978	101
Cash dividends paid	**–**	–	(3,592)
Net cash flows used for financing activities	**(17,403)**	(18,502)	(6,272)
Net increase (decrease) in cash and cash equivalents	**11,750**	(16,143)	(1,185)
Beginning cash and cash equivalents	**5,426**	21,569	22,754
Ending cash and cash equivalents	**$ 17,176**	$ 5,426	$ 21,569
Supplemental cash flow disclosures:			
Interest paid	**$ 2,833**	$ 2,828	$ 364
Income taxes paid	**16,896**	27,595	27,475

The accompanying notes to consolidated financial statements are an integral part of these consolidated statements.

Notes to Consolidated Financial Statements

Note 1. Summary of significant accounting policies

Nature of business
Lands' End, Inc., (the company) is a direct marketer of traditionally styled apparel, domestics (primarily bedding and bath items), soft luggage, and other products. The company's primary market is the United States, and other markets include the Pacific Basin area, Europe and Canada.

Use of estimates
The preparation of financial statements in conformity with generally accepted accounting principles requires management to make estimates and assumptions that affect the reported amounts of assets and liabilities and disclosure of contingent assets and liabilities at the date of the financial statements and the reported amounts of revenues and expenses during the reporting periods. Actual results could differ from those estimates.

Principles of consolidation
The consolidated financial statements include the accounts of the company and its subsidiaries after elimination of intercompany accounts and transactions.

Year-end
The company's fiscal year is comprised of 52-53 weeks ending on the Friday closest to January 31. Fiscal 1996 was a 53-week year that ended on February 2, 1996. The additional week was added in the fourth quarter of fiscal 1996. Fiscal 1995 ended on January 27, 1995, and fiscal 1994 ended on January 28, 1994.

Fair values of financial instruments
The fair value of financial instruments does not materially differ from their carrying values.

Inventory
Inventory, primarily merchandise held for sale, is stated at last-in, first-out (LIFO) cost, which is lower than market. If the first-in, first-out (FIFO) method of accounting for inventory had been used, inventory would have been approximately $22.4 million and $18.9 million higher than reported at February 2, 1996, and January 27, 1995, respectively.

Advertising
The company expenses the costs of advertising for magazines, television, radio, and other media the first time the advertising takes place, except for direct-response advertising, which is capitalized and amortized over its expected period of future benefits.

Direct-response advertising consists primarily of catalog production and mailing costs that have not yet been fully amortized over the expected revenue stream, which is within three months from the date catalogs are mailed.

Advertising costs reported as prepaid assets were $15.8 million and $7.5 million as of February 2, 1996, and January 27, 1995, respectively. Advertising expense was $188.3 million, $162.0 million and $131.5 million reported for fiscal years ended February 2, 1996, January 27, 1995, and January 28, 1994, respectively.

Depreciation
Depreciation expense is calculated using the straight-line method over the estimated useful lives of the assets, which are 20 to 30 years for buildings and land improvements and five to 10 years for leasehold improvements and furniture, fixtures, equipment, and software. The company provides one-half year of depreciation in the year of addition and retirement.

Intangibles
Intangible assets consist primarily of goodwill which is being amortized over 40 years on a straight-line basis. Other intangibles are amortized up to a period of five years. Total accumulated amortization of these intangibles was $0.4 million and $0.3 million at February 2, 1996, and January 27, 1995, respectively.

Net income per share
Net income per share is computed by dividing net income by the weighted average number of common shares outstanding during each period. The weighted average common shares outstanding were 34.2 million, 35.2 million and 35.9 million for fiscal years 1996, 1995 and 1994, respectively. Common stock equivalents include awards, grants and stock options which have been issued by the company. The common stock equivalents do not significantly dilute basic earnings per share.

Reserve for losses on customer returns
At the time of sale, the company provides a reserve equal to the gross profit on projected merchandise returns, based on its prior returns experience.

Financial instruments with off-balance-sheet risk
The company is party to financial instruments with off-balance-sheet risk in the normal course of business to reduce its exposure to fluctuations in foreign currency exchange rates and to meet financing needs.

The company enters into forward exchange contracts to hedge anticipated foreign currency transactions during the upcoming seasons. The purpose of the company's foreign currency hedging activities is to protect the company from the risk that the eventual dollar cash flows resulting from these transactions will be adversely affected by changes in exchange rates. At February 2, 1996, the company had forward exchange contracts, maturing through January 1997, to sell approximately 1.8 billion Japanese yen and 3.0 million British pounds and to purchase approximately 2.2 million Canadian dollars. The gains and losses on the outstanding forward exchange contracts are reflected in the financial statements in the period in which the currency fluctuation occurs.

The company also uses import letters of credit to purchase foreign-sourced merchandise. The letters of credit are primarily U.S. dollar-denominated and are issued through third-party financial institutions to guarantee payment for such merchandise within agreed-upon time periods. At February 2, 1996, the company had outstanding letters of credit of approximately $20.0 million, all of which had expiration dates of less than one year.

The counterparties to the financial instruments discussed above are primarily two large financial institutions; management believes the risk of counterparty nonperformance on these financial instruments is not significant.

Foreign currency transactions
Financial statements of the foreign subsidiaries are translated into U.S. dollars in accordance with the provisions of Statement of Financial Accounting Standards (SFAS) No. 52. Translation adjustments are accumulated in a separate component of stockholders' equity. Foreign currency transaction gains reflected on the Consolidated Statements of Operations were $4.1 million and $0.8 million in fiscal 1996 and 1995, respectively. Foreign currency gains and losses for fiscal 1994 were not material.

Postretirement benefits
The company does not currently provide any postretirement benefits for employees other than profit sharing and a 401(k) plan (see Note 7).

Reclassifications
Certain financial statement amounts have been reclassified to be consistent with the fiscal 1996 presentation.

Accounting Standards
In 1995, Statement of Financial Accounting Standards (SFAS) No. 121, "Accounting for the Impairment of Long-Lived Assets and for Long-Lived Assets to Be Disposed Of," was issued. The company will adopt SFAS No. 121 during the first quarter of fiscal 1997. The company does not anticipate that adoption of this standard will have a material impact on the consolidated financial statements.

Note 2. Shareholders' investment

Two-for-one stock split
In May 1994, the company declared a two-for-one split (effected as a stock dividend) in the company's common stock. The stock split resulted in an increase in the stated capital of the company from $201,103 to $402,206 with a corresponding reduction in paid-in capital. All share data reflects the May 1994 two-for-one stock split.

Capital stock
The company currently has 160 million shares of $0.01 par value common stock. The company is authorized to issue 5 million shares of preferred stock, $0.01 par value. The company's board of directors has the authority to issue shares and to fix dividend, voting and conversion rights, redemption provisions, liquidation preferences, and other rights and restrictions of the preferred stock.

Treasury stock
The company's board of directors has authorized the purchase of a total of 8.2 million shares of the company's common stock. A total of 7.5 million, 6.2 million and 4.8 million shares had been purchased as of February 2, 1996, January 27, 1995, and January 28, 1994, respectively.

Treasury stock summary:

For the period ended	**February 2, 1996**	January 27, 1995	January 28, 1994
Beginning balance	**5,394,972**	2,154,235	2,082,035
Two-for-one stock split	–	2,154,235	–
Purchase of stock	**1,282,326**	1,380,502	89,800
Issuance of stock	**(116,000)**	(294,000)	(17,600)
Ending balance	**6,561,298**	5,394,972	2,154,235

Stock awards and grants
The company has a restricted stock award plan. Under the provisions of the plan, a committee of the company's board of directors may award shares of the company's common stock to its officers and key employees. Such shares vest over a 10-year period on a straight-line basis from the date of the award.

In addition, the company granted shares of its common stock to individuals as an inducement to enter the employ of the company.

The following table reflects the activity under the stock award and stock grant plans:

	Awards	Grants
Balance at January 29, 1993	141,320	12,000
Granted	27,200	–
Forfeited	(3,600)	–
Vested	(15,760)	(2,000)
Balance at January 28, 1994	149,160	10,000
Granted	–	–
Forfeited	(15,940)	(10,000)
Vested	(17,860)	–
Balance at January 27, 1995	115,360	–
Granted	–	–
Forfeited	**(2,700)**	–
Vested	**(15,980)**	–
Balance at February 2, 1996	**96,680**	**0**

The granting of these awards and grants has been recorded as deferred compensation based on the fair market value of the shares at the date of grant. Compensation expense under these plans is recorded as shares vest.

Stock options

The company has 2.5 million shares of common stock, either authorized and unissued shares or treasury shares, that may be issued pursuant to the exercise of options granted under the company's stock option plan. Options are granted at the discretion of a committee of the company's board of directors to officers and key employees of the company. No option may have an exercise price less than the fair market value per share of the common stock at the date of grant.

Activity under the stock option plan is as follows:

	Options	Average Exercise Price	Exercisable Options
Balance at January 29, 1993	1,060,000	$ 9.81	216,000
Granted	637,200	$19.12	
Exercised	(8,000)	$12.69	
Balance at January 28, 1994	1,689,200	$13.31	340,000
Granted	–	–	
Exercised	(294,000)	$ 6.72	
Forfeited	(928,800)	$15.27	
Balance at January 27, 1995	466,400	$13.56	195,480
Granted	**342,100**	**$16.50**	
Exercised	**(116,000)**	**$ 7.40**	
Forfeited	**(70,800)**	**$17.55**	
Balance at February 2, 1996	**621,700**	**$15.87**	**150,240**

The above options vest over a five-year period from the date of grant. The outstanding options expire as follows:

2001	72,000
2002	40,000
2003	181,600
2005	328,100
	621,700

In 1995, the Financial Standards Board issued SFAS No. 123, "Accounting for Stock-Based Compensation," which establishes financial accounting and reporting standards for stock-based employee compensation. The company plans to adopt the disclosure requirements of this statement, and to continue to apply the accounting provisions of Accounting Principles Board Opinion No. 25 to stock-based employee compensation arrangements, as is allowed by the statement. The disclosure will be adopted effective with the fiscal 1997 financial statements.

Note 3. Income taxes

Effective January 30, 1993, the company adopted SFAS No. 109, "Accounting for Income Taxes." The cumulative effect of adopting the standard was recorded as a change in accounting principle in the first quarter of fiscal 1994 with an increase to net income of $1.3 million or $0.04 per common share.

The components of the provision for income taxes for each of the periods presented are as follows (in thousands):

Period ended	**February 2, 1996**	January 27, 1995	January 28, 1994
Current:			
Federal	**$17,996**	$22,154	$24,607
State	**3,043**	4,058	4,518
Deferred	**(669)**	(2,645)	(1,684)
	$20,370	$23,567	$27,441

The difference between income taxes at the statutory federal income tax rate of 35 percent and income tax reported in the statements of operations is as follows (in thousands):

Period ended	**February 2, 1996**	January 27, 1995	January 28, 1994
Tax at statutory federal tax rate	**$17,825**	$20,882	$24,421
State income taxes, net of federal benefit	**2,018**	2,156	2,818
Other	**527**	529	202
	$20,370	$23,567	$27,441

Temporary differences which give rise to deferred tax assets and liabilities as of February 2, 1996, and January 27, 1995, are as follows (in thousands):

	February 2, 1996	January 27, 1995
Deferred tax assets:		
Catalog advertising	**$(1,415)**	$(1,539)
Inventory	**8,602**	7,052
Employee benefits	**1,918**	1,243
Reserve for returns	**1,822**	1,406
Other	**(13)**	250
Total	**$10,914**	$ 8,412
Deferred tax liabilities:		
Depreciation	**7,980**	5,379
Foreign operating loss carryforwards	**(527)**	(807)
Valuation allowance	**527**	807
Other	**(768)**	–
Total	**$ 7,212**	$ 5,379

The valuation allowance required under SFAS No. 109 has been established for the deferred income tax benefits related to certain subsidiary loss carryforwards, which management currently estimates may not be realized. These carryforwards do not expire.

Note 4. Lines of credit

The company has unsecured domestic lines of credit with various U.S. banks totaling $110 million. There were no amounts outstanding at February 2, 1996, and January 27, 1995.

In addition, the company has unsecured lines of credit with foreign banks totaling the equivalent of $19 million for a wholly owned foreign subsidiary. There was $9.3 million outstanding at February 2, 1996, at interest rates averaging 1.6 percent.

Note 5. Long-term debt

There was no long-term debt as of February 2, 1996, and January 27, 1995.

The company has an agreement which expires December 31, 1996, with a bank for a $20 million credit facility available to fund treasury stock purchases and capital expenditures. As of February 2, 1996, the company was in compliance with lending conditions and covenants related to this debt facility.

Note 6. Leases

The company leases store and office space and equipment under various leasing arrangements. The leases are accounted for as operating leases. Total rental expense under these leases was $11.6 million, $8.6 million and $7.3 million for the years ended February 2, 1996, January 27, 1995, and January 28, 1994, respectively.

Total future fiscal year commitments under these leases as of February 2, 1996, are as follows (in thousands):

1997	$10,322
1998	7,905
1999	5,368
2000	3,940
2001	2,393
After 2001	5,136
	$35,064

Note 7. Retirement plan

The company has a retirement plan which covers most regular employees and provides for annual contributions at the discretion of the board of directors. Also included in the plan is a 401(k) feature that allows employees to make contributions, and the company matches a portion of those contributions. Total expense provided under this plan was $3.2 million, $3.5 million and $3.7 million for the years ended February 2, 1996, January 27, 1995, and January 28, 1994, respectively.

As of October 1, 1995, the "Lands' End, Inc. Retirement Plan" was amended to allow certain participants to invest their elective contributions, employer matching contributions and profit sharing contributions in a "Lands' End, Inc. Stock Fund" established primarily for investing in common stock of the company at the fair market value.

Note 8. Acquisitions and divestiture

In July 1994, the company formed a wholly owned subsidiary that acquired the marketing rights and assets of MontBell America, Inc., which designs, develops and distributes premier technical outdoor clothing and equipment through the wholesale channel to outdoor specialty stores, primarily in the United States.

During the fourth quarter of fiscal 1996, the company sold the marketing rights and assets of MontBell America, Inc., to a wholly owned subsidiary of Outdoor Industry Group, Inc., of San Francisco. In connection with this sale, the company has taken an after-tax charge to earnings of $1.1 million in fiscal year 1996. This is in addition to the after-tax charge of $2.1 million taken as a reserve in January of fiscal 1995 in anticipation of the sale.

In March 1993, the company purchased a majority interest in The Territory Ahead, a catalog company that offers private label sportswear, accessories and luggage. Beginning in 2003, the minority shareholders have the option to require the company to purchase their shares, and the company will have the option to require the minority shareholders to sell their shares in The Territory Ahead. The price per share would be based on the fair market value of The Territory Ahead.

Results of operations of MontBell America, Inc., and The Territory Ahead were not material to the company, and as a result, no pro forma data is presented. The transactions were accounted for using the purchase method. The excess of the purchase price over the fair value of net assets was recorded as goodwill. The operating results of MontBell America, Inc., and The Territory Ahead are included in the consolidated financial statements of the company from their respective dates of acquisition.

Note 9. Sales and use tax

A 1992 Supreme Court decision confirmed that the Commerce Clause of the United States Constitution prevents a state from requiring the collection of its use tax by a mail order company unless the company has a physical presence in the state. However, there continues to be uncertainty due to inconsistent application of the Supreme Court decision by state and federal courts. The company attempts to conduct its operations in compliance with its interpretation of the applicable legal standard, but there can be no assurance that such compliance will not be challenged.

In recent challenges various states have sought to require companies to begin collection of use taxes and/or pay taxes from previous sales. The company has not received assessments from any state. The amount of potential assessments, if any, cannot be reasonably estimated.

The Supreme Court decision also established that Congress has the power to enact legislation which would permit states to require collection of use taxes by mail order companies. Congress has from time to time considered proposals for such legislation. The company anticipates that any legislative change, if adopted, would be applied only on a prospective basis.

Note 10. Consolidated Quarterly Analysis (unaudited)

(In thousands, except per share data)	Fiscal 1996				Fiscal 1995			
	1st Qtr.	**2nd Qtr.**	**3rd Qtr.**	**4th Qtr.**	1st Qtr.	2nd Qtr.	3rd Qtr.	4th Qtr.
Net sales	**$207,122**	**$189,064**	**$235,887**	**$399,475**	$187,012	$179,833	$246,209	$379,052
Gross profit	**90,677**	**82,069**	**98,991**	**171,794**	79,230	76,731	99,512	165,368
Pretax income	**2,192**	**2,813**	**2,941**	**42,979**	8,058	5,651	6,331	39,623
Net income	**$ 1,307**	**$ 1,695**	**$ 1,766**	**$ 25,787**	$ 4,878	$ 3,413	$ 3,833	$ 23,972
Net income per share	**$ 0.04**	**$ 0.05**	**$ 0.05**	**$ 0.77**	$ 0.14	$ 0.10	$ 0.11	$ 0.69
Common shares outstanding	**34,686**	**34,536**	**33,784**	**33,659**	35,791	34,893	34,879	34,875
Market price of shares outstanding:								
Market high	**19½**	**17**	**17¾**	**15½**	27¾	24 1/16	20½	19
Market low	**15**	**14⅝**	**14⅜**	**12⅞**	22⅝	17⅜	16⅞	13

Responsibility for Consolidated Financial Statements

The management of Lands' End, Inc. and its subsidiaries has the responsibility for preparing the accompanying financial statements and for their integrity and objectivity. The statements were prepared in accordance with generally accepted accounting principles applied on a consistent basis. The consolidated financial statements include amounts that are based on management's best estimates and judgments. Management also prepared the other information in the annual report and is responsible for its accuracy and consistency with the consolidated financial statements.

The company's consolidated financial statements have been audited by Arthur Andersen LLP, independent certified public accountants. Management has made available to Arthur Andersen LLP all the company's financial records and related data, as well as the minutes of shareholders' and directors' meetings. Furthermore, management believes that all representations made to Arthur Andersen LLP during its audit were valid and appropriate.

Management of the company has established and maintains a system of internal control that provides for appropriate division of responsibility, reasonable assurance as to the integrity and reliability of the consolidated financial statements, the protection of assets from unauthorized use or disposition, and the prevention and detection of fraudulent financial reporting, and the maintenance of an active program of internal audits. Management believes that, as of February 2, 1996, the company's system of internal control is adequate to accomplish the objectives discussed herein.

Two directors of the company, not members of management, serve as the audit committee of the board of directors and are the principal means through which the board supervises the performance of the financial reporting duties of management. The audit committee meets with management, the internal audit staff and the company's independent auditors to review the results of the audits of the company and to discuss plans for future audits. At these meetings, the audit committee also meets privately with the internal audit staff and the independent auditors to assure its free access to them.

Michael J. Smith
Chief Executive Officer

Stephen A. Orum
Chief Financial Officer

Report of Independent Public Accountants

To the Board of Directors and Shareholders of Lands' End, Inc.:

We have audited the accompanying consolidated balance sheets of Lands' End, Inc. (a Delaware corporation) and its subsidiaries as of February 2, 1996, and January 27, 1995, and the related consolidated statements of operations, shareholders' investment and cash flows for each of the three years in the period ended February 2, 1996. These financial statements are the responsibility of the company's management. Our responsibility is to express an opinion on these financial statements based on our audits.

We conducted our audits in accordance with generally accepted auditing standards. Those standards require that we plan and perform the audit to obtain reasonable assurance about whether the financial statements are free of material misstatement. An audit includes examining, on a test basis, evidence supporting the amounts and disclosures in the financial statements. An audit also includes assessing the accounting principles used and significant estimates made by management, as well as evaluating the overall financial statement presentation. We believe that our audits provide a reasonable basis for our opinion.

In our opinion, the financial statements referred to above present fairly, in all material respects, the financial position of Lands' End, Inc. and subsidiaries as of February 2, 1996, and January 27, 1995, and the results of their operations and their cash flows for each of the three years in the period ended February 2, 1996, in conformity with generally accepted accounting principles.

As explained in Note 3 to the consolidated financial statements, effective January 30, 1993, the company changed its method of accounting for income taxes.

Arthur Andersen LLP

Arthur Andersen LLP
Milwaukee, Wisconsin
March 8, 1996

The following selected financial data have been derived from the company's consolidated financial statements, which, except pro forma amounts, have been audited by Arthur Andersen LLP, independent public accountants. The information set forth below should be read in conjunction with "Management's Discussion and Analysis" and the consolidated financial statements and notes thereto included elsewhere herein.

(In thousands, except per share data)	**1996**	1995	1994[2]
Income statement data:			
Net sales	**$1,031,548**	$992,106	$869,975
Pretax income	**50,925**	59,663	69,870
Percent to net sales	**4.9%**	6.0%	8.0%
Net income before cumulative effect of change in accounting	**30,555**	36,096	42,429
Cumulative effect of accounting change	**–**	–	1,300
Net income	**30,555**	36,096	43,729
Net income (pro forma for 1986 and 1987)	**30,555**	36,096	43,729
Per share of common stock:[1]			
Net income per share before cumulative effect of change in accounting	**$ 0.89**	$ 1.03	$ 1.18
Cumulative effect of change in accounting	**–**	–	0.04
Net income per share	**$ 0.89**	$ 1.03	$ 1.22
Cash dividends per share	**–**	–	$ 0.10
Common shares outstanding	**33,659**	34,826	35,912
Balance sheet data:			
Current assets	**$ 222,089**	$198,168	$192,276
Current liabilities	**114,744**	102,717	91,049
Property, plant, equipment and intangibles, net	**101,408**	99,444	81,554
Total assets	**323,497**	297,612	273,830
Noncurrent liabilities	**7,561**	5,767	5,496
Shareholders' investment	**201,192**	189,128	177,285
Other data:			
Net working capital	**$ 107,345**	$ 95,451	$101,227
Capital expenditures	**14,780**	27,005	16,958
Depreciation and amortization expense	**12,456**	10,311	8,286
Return on average shareholders' investment	**16%**	20%	28%
Return on average assets	**10%**	13%	18%
Debt/equity ratio	**–**	–	–

(1) Net income per share (pro forma for 1986 and 1987) was computed after giving retroactive effect to the 108-for-one stock split in August 1986, the two-for-one stock split in August 1987, the two-for-one stock split in May 1994, and assuming the shares sold in the October 1986 initial public offering were issued at the beginning of fiscal 1986.

(2) Effective January 30, 1993, the company adopted Statement of Financial Accounting Standards (SFAS) No. 109, "Accounting for Income Taxes," which was recorded as a change in accounting principle at the beginning of fiscal 1994 with an increase to net income of $1.3 million or $0.04 per share.

Fiscal year							
1993	1992	1991	1990	1989	1988[3]	1987[4]	1986
$733,623	$683,427	$601,991	$544,850	$454,644	$335,740	$264,896	$226,575
54,033	47,492	29,943	47,270	52,142	38,328	28,486	21,584
7.4%	7.0%	4.1%	8.7%	11.4%	11.4%	10.7%	9.5%
33,500	28,732	14,743	29,071	32,282	22,120	18,650	21,584
–	–	–	–	–	685	–	–
33,500	28,732	14,743	29,071	32,282	22,805	18,650	21,584
33,500	28,732	14,743	29,071	32,282	22,805	14,605	11,270
$ 0.92	$ 0.77	$ 0.38	$ 0.73	$ 0.81	$ 0.56	$ 0.37	$ 0.28
–	–	–	–	–	0.01	–	–
$ 0.92	$ 0.77	$ 0.38	$ 0.73	$ 0.81	$ 0.57	$ 0.37	$ 0.28
$ 0.10	$ 0.10	$ 0.10	$ 0.10	$ 0.10	$ 0.10	–	–
36,056	36,944	38,436	39,762	40,080	40,080	40,080	39,920
$137,531	$131,273	$107,824	$ 99,714	$103,681	$ 78,256	$ 57,660	$ 35,687
67,315	74,548	60,774	43,915	51,530	38,860	32,920	18,002
74,272	74,527	77,576	67,218	47,471	28,723	26,822	19,841
211,803	205,800	185,400	166,932	151,152	106,979	84,482	55,528
5,100	4,620	7,800	8,413	7,674	11,445	13,685	10,321
139,388	126,632	116,826	114,604	91,948	56,674	37,877	27,205
$ 70,216	$ 56,725	$ 47,050	$ 55,799	$ 52,151	$ 39,396	$ 24,740	$ 17,685
9,965	5,347	17,682	25,160	15,872	5,862	9,603	6,843
7,900	7,428	7,041	5,251	3,916	3,185	2,576	1,867
25%	23%	13%	28%	43%	48%	45%	48%
16%	15%	8%	18%	25%	24%	21%	22%
–	1%	3%	4%	7%	15%	28%	38%

(3) In the fourth quarter of fiscal 1988, the company elected early adoption of the provisions of SFAS No. 96, "Accounting for Income Taxes," as recommended by the Financial Accounting Standards Board. The effect of the change for the year was to increase net income $715,000 including the cumulative effect of $685,000 or $0.01 per common share which was reflected in the first quarter.

(4) The company has been subject to corporate income taxes since October 6, 1986. For earlier periods shown, the company elected to be treated as an S Corporation and accordingly was not subject to corporate income taxes. The net income and net income per share for such periods reflect a pro forma tax provision as if the company had been subject to corporate income taxes.

Directors

Richard C. Anderson
Vice Chairman
Lands' End, Inc.
Director since 1979

Gary C. Comer
Founder and Chairman
Lands' End, Inc.
Director since 1963

David B. Heller
President
Advisory Research, Inc.
An investment advisory firm
Director since 1986

Howard G. Krane
Partner
Kirkland & Ellis
A law firm
Director since 1986

John N. Latter
Financial consultant
Director since 1978

Michael J. Smith
President and
Chief Executive Officer
Lands' End, Inc.
Director since 1994

Committees of the Board

Audit

John N. Latter, Chairman
David B. Heller

Compensation

Howard G. Krane, Chairman
Gary C. Comer
David B. Heller
John N. Latter

Performance Compensation

David B. Heller, Chairman
John N. Latter

Officers

Gary C. Comer
Chairman
Founder

Richard C. Anderson
Vice Chairman
12 years service

***Michael J. Smith**
President and
Chief Executive Officer
13 years service

***Stephen A. (Chip) Orum**
Executive Vice President,
Chief Operating Officer and
Chief Financial Officer
5 years service

***Francis P. Schaecher**
Senior Vice President
Operations
14 years service

Michael P. Atkin
Vice President
Marketing
8 years service

Joan T. Brown
Vice President
Quality Assurance
9 years service

Frank A. Buettner
Vice President
International
16 years service

Ronald T. Campo
Vice President
Specialty Businesses
3 years service

John F. Keenan
Vice President
Employee Relations
14 years service

Jane M. McAndrew
Vice President
International Merchandising
9 years service

Stephen V. McCardell
Vice President
Inventory
10 years service

Mary C. Nordloh
Vice President and
Creative Director
12 years service

Cory R. Owens
Vice President
Production
14 years service

Suresh C. Patel
Vice President
Global Planning and Logistics
8 years service

Kelly A. Ritchie
Vice President
Human Resources
12 years service

Daniel J. Rourke
Vice President
Information Services
4 years service

Joe F. Sirianni, Jr.
Vice President
Merchandising
11 years service

David T. Zentmyer,
Vice President
Corporate Sales
14 years service

Pamela M. Patzke
General Counsel
3 years service

Michael L. Krentz
Treasurer and
Assistant Secretary
13 years service

*Executive Committee Member

Annual Meeting
The 1996 annual meeting of shareholders will be held on Wednesday, May 22, at Lands' End headquarters in Dodgeville, Wisconsin, beginning at 10:00 a.m.

Form 10-K Report
A copy of the company's annual report on Form 10-K, filed with the Securities and Exchange Commission, is available without charge upon request to your investor relations contact in Dodgeville.

Interim Reports
The company does not send quarterly reports to shareholders. Instead, the quarterly earnings release distributed to the financial community and business media is mailed to all shareholders. This will allow shareholders to receive interim information in a more timely manner and at a lower cost to the company. If you do not receive the quarterly earnings releases, please get in touch with your investor contact.

Securities Information
The Firstar Trust Company, Milwaukee, Wisconsin 53202, is the transfer agent, registrar and dividend dispersing agent for Lands' End stock. Phone 414-287-3920. Lands' End stock is listed on the New York Stock Exchange. The stock tables in most daily newspapers list the company as "LandsE." Ticker symbol: LE.

Headquarters
Lands' End, Inc.
Lands' End Lane
Dodgeville, Wisconsin 53595
608-935-9341

Subsidiaries
Lands' End Japan, K.K.
Shinyokohama Tobu AK Building 5F
3-23-3 Shinyokohama
Kohoku-ku, Yokohama
222 Japan
Gary R. Steuck, President
011-81-45-476-0830

Lands' End Direct Merchants UK Limited
Pillings Road
Oakham, Rutland LE15 6NY
Henry Heavisides, Managing Director
011-44-1572-722553

The Territory Ahead
27 East Mason Street
Santa Barbara, California 93101
Bruce Willard, President
805-962-5558

Corporate Secretary
Robert S. Osborne
Kirkland & Ellis
Chicago, Illinois 60601

Investor Contact
Charlotte LaComb
Lands' End, Inc.
Dodgeville, Wisconsin 53595
608-935-4835

Customer Information
Brian Finnegan
Lands' End, Inc.
Dodgeville, Wisconsin 53595
800-356-4444

Internet
Visit our Web site at:
http://www.landsend.com
or e-mail us at:
mailbox@landsend.com
(Please include your phone number.)

Catalog
If you know someone you'd like to introduce to our quality products, call us toll-free at 800-356-4444. Our operators will gladly add a friend's name to our mailing list for a free trial subscription to our catalog.

Design: Boller Coates & Neu
Color separations: NCL Graphics
Printing: Bruce Offset Company

Printed on recycled paper 

Trademarks
Lands' End,® Sheet That Fits,® Super-T™ shirts, Squall™ jackets, and Drifter™ sweaters, as used in this report, are trademarks of Lands' End, Inc.

APPENDIX B

Time Value of Money: Future Value and Present Value

The following discussion of future value lays the foundation for our explanation of present value in Chapter 8 but is not essential. For the valuation of long-term liabilities, some instructors may wish to begin on page 723.

The term *time value of money* refers to the fact that money earns interest over time. *Interest* is the cost of using money. To borrowers, interest is the expense of renting money. To lenders, interest is the revenue earned from lending. We must always recognize the interest we receive or pay. Otherwise, we overlook an important part of the transaction. Suppose you invest $4,545 in corporate bonds that pay 10% interest each year. After one year, the value of your investment has grown to $5,000. The difference between your original investment ($4,545) and the future value of the investment ($5,000) is the amount of interest revenue you will earn during the year ($455). If you ignored the interest, you would fail to account for the interest revenue you have earned. Interest becomes more important as the time period lengthens because the amount of interest depends on the span of time the money is invested.

Let's consider a second example, this time from the borrower's perspective. Suppose you purchase a machine for your business. The cash price of the machine is $8,000, but you cannot pay cash now. To finance the purchase, you sign an $8,000 note payable. The note requires you to pay the $8,000 plus 10% interest one year from the date of purchase. Is your cost of the machine $8,000, or is it $8,800 [$8,000 plus interest of $800 ($8,000 × 0.10)]? The cost is $8,000. The additional $800 is interest expense and not part of the cost of the machine. (Recall from Chapter 7, pages 323–325, that interest expense is *not* ordinarily included in the cost of a machine.) If you ignored the interest, you would understate the amount of interest expense.

Future Value

The main application of future value is the accumulated balance of an investment at a future date. In our first example above, the investment earned 10% per year. After one year, $4,545 grew to $5,000, as shown in Exhibit B-1. If the money were invested for five years, you would have to perform five such calculations. You would also have to consider the compound interest that your investment is earning. *Compound interest* is not only the interest you earn on your principal

EXHIBIT B-1
Future Value: An Example

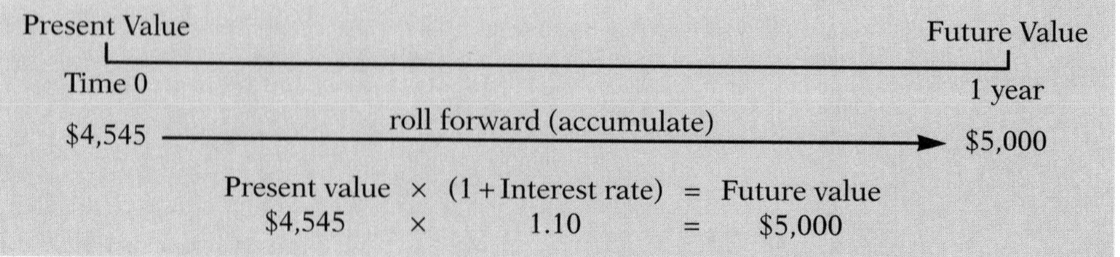

amount, but also the interest you receive on the interest you have already earned. Most business applications include compound interest. The following table shows the interest revenue earned on the original $4,545 investment each year for five years at 10 percent:

End of Year	Interest	Future Value
0	—	$4,545
1	$4,545 × 0.10 = $455	5,000
2	5,000 × 0.10 = 500	5,500
3	5,500 × 0.10 = 550	6,050
4	6,050 × 0.10 = 605	6,655
5	6,655 × 0.10 = 666	7,321

Earning 10%, a $4,545 investment grows to $5,000 at the end of one year, to $5,500 at the end of two years, and $7,321 at the end of five years. Throughout this appendix we round off to the nearest dollar.

Future-Value Tables

The process of computing a future value is called *accumulating* because the future value is *more* than the present value. Mathematical tables ease the computational burden. Exhibit B-2, Future Value of $1, gives the future value for a single sum (a present value), $1, invested to earn a particular interest rate for a specific number of periods. Future value depends on three factors: (1) the amount of the investment, (2) the length of time between investment and future accumulation, and (3) the interest rate. Future-value and present-value tables are based on $1 because unity (the value 1) is so easy to work with.

In business applications, interest rates are always stated for the annual period of one year unless specified otherwise. In fact, an interest rate can be stated for any period, such as 3% per quarter or 5% for a six-month period. The length of the period is arbitrary. For example, an investment may promise a return (income) of 3% per quarter for six months (two quarters). In that case, you would be working with 3% interest for two periods. It would be incorrect to use 6% for one period because the interest is 3% compounded quarterly, and that

EXHIBIT B-2
Future Value of $1

Future Value of $1

Periods	4%	5%	6%	7%	8%	9%	10%	12%	14%	16%
1	1.040	1.050	1.060	1.070	1.080	1.090	1.100	1.120	1.140	1.160
2	1.082	1.103	1.124	1.145	1.166	1.188	1.210	1.254	1.300	1.346
3	1.125	1.158	1.191	1.225	1.260	1.295	1.331	1.405	1.482	1.561
4	1.170	1.216	1.262	1.311	1.360	1.412	1.464	1.574	1.689	1.811
5	1.217	1.276	1.338	1.403	1.469	1.539	1.611	1.762	1.925	2.100
6	1.265	1.340	1.419	1.501	1.587	1.677	1.772	1.974	2.195	2.436
7	1.316	1.407	1.504	1.606	1.714	1.828	1.949	2.211	2.502	2.826
8	1.369	1.477	1.594	1.718	1.851	1.993	2.144	2.476	2.853	3.278
9	1.423	1.551	1.689	1.838	1.999	2.172	2.358	2.773	3.252	3.803
10	1.480	1.629	1.791	1.967	2.159	2.367	2.594	3.106	3.707	4.411
11	1.539	1.710	1.898	2.105	2.332	2.580	2.853	3.479	4.226	5.117
12	1.601	1.796	2.012	2.252	2.518	2.813	3.138	3.896	4.818	5.936
13	1.665	1.886	2.133	2.410	2.720	3.066	3.452	4.363	5.492	6.886
14	1.732	1.980	2.261	2.579	2.937	3.342	3.798	4.887	6.261	7.988
15	1.801	2.079	2.397	2.759	3.172	3.642	4.177	5.474	7.138	9.266
16	1.873	2.183	2.540	2.952	3.426	3.970	4.595	6.130	8.137	10.748
17	1.948	2.292	2.693	3.159	3.700	4.328	5.054	6.866	9.276	12.468
18	2.026	2.407	2.854	3.380	3.996	4.717	5.560	7.690	10.575	14.463
19	2.107	2.527	3.026	3.617	4.316	5.142	6.116	8.613	12.056	16.777
20	2.191	2.653	3.207	3.870	4.661	5.604	6.728	9.646	13.743	19.461

amount differs from 6% compounded semiannually. *Take care in studying future-value and present-value problems to align the interest rate with the appropriate number of periods.*

Let's see how a future-value table like the one in Exhibit B-2 is used. The future value of $1.00 invested at 8% for one year is $1.08 ($1.00 × 1.080, which appears at the junction of the 8% column and row 1 in the Periods column). The figure 1.080 includes both the principal (1.000) and the compound interest for one period (0.080).

Suppose you deposit $5,000 in a savings account that pays annual interest of 8 percent. The account balance at the end of one year will be $5,400. To compute the future value of $5,000 at 8% for one year, multiply $5,000 by 1.080 to get $5,400. Now suppose you invest in a 10-year, 8% certificate of deposit (CD). What will be the future value of the CD at maturity? To compute the future value of $5,000 at 8% for 10 periods, multiply $5,000 by 2.159 (from Exhibit B-2) to get $10,795. This future value of $10,795 indicates that $5,000, earning 8% interest compounded annually, grows to $10,795 at the end of 10 years. Using Exhibit B-2, you can find any present amount's future value at a particular future date. Future value is especially helpful for computing the amount of cash you will have on hand for some purpose in the future.

Future Value of an Annuity

In the preceding example, we made an investment of a single amount. Other investments, called *annuities,* include multiple investments of an equal periodic amount at fixed intervals over the duration of the investment. Consider a family investing for a child's education. The Dietrichs can invest $4,000 annually to accumulate a college fund for 15-year-old Helen. The investment can earn 7% annually until Helen turns 18—a three-year investment. How much will be available for Helen on the date of the last investment? Exhibit B-3 shows the accumulation—a total future value of $12,860.

EXHIBIT B-3
Future Value of an Annuity

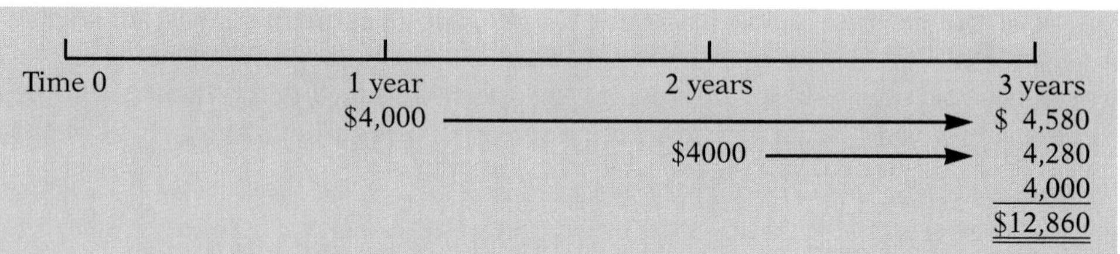

The first $4,000 invested by the Dietrichs grows to $4,580 over the investment period. The second amount grows to $4,280, and the third amount stays at $4,000 because it has no time to earn interest. The sum of the three future values ($4,580 + $4,280 + $4,000) is the future value of the annuity ($12,860), which can also be computed as follows:

End of Year	Annual Investment		Interest		Increase for the Year	Future Value of Annuity
0	—		—		—	0
1	$4,000		—		$4,000	$ 4,000
2	4,000	+	($4,000 × 0.07 = $280)	=	4,280	8,280
3	4,000	+	($8,280 × 0.07 = $580)	=	4,580	12,860

These computations are laborious. As with the Future Value of $1 (a lump sum), mathematical tables ease the strain of calculating annuities. Exhibit B-4, Future Value of Annuity of $1, gives the future value of a series of investments, each of equal amount, at regular intervals.

What is the future value of an annuity of three investments of $1 each that earn 7 percent? The answer, 3.215, can be found at the junction of the 7% col-

Future Value of Annuity of $1										
Periods	**4%**	**5%**	**6%**	**7%**	**8%**	**9%**	**10%**	**12%**	**14%**	**16%**
1	1.000	1.000	1.000	1.000	1.000	1.000	1.000	1.000	1.000	1.000
2	2.040	2.050	2.060	2.070	2.080	2.090	2.100	2.120	2.140	2.160
3	3.122	3.153	3.184	3.215	3.246	3.278	3.310	3.374	3.440	3.506
4	4.246	4.310	4.375	4.440	4.506	4.573	4.641	4.779	4.921	5.066
5	5.416	5.526	5.637	5.751	5.867	5.985	6.105	6.353	6.610	6.877
6	6.633	6.802	6.975	7.153	7.336	7.523	7.716	8.115	8.536	8.977
7	7.898	8.142	8.394	8.654	8.923	9.200	9.487	10.089	10.730	11.414
8	9.214	9.549	9.897	10.260	10.637	11.028	11.436	12.300	13.233	14.240
9	10.583	11.027	11.491	11.978	12.488	13.021	13.579	14.776	16.085	17.519
10	12.006	12.578	13.181	13.816	14.487	15.193	15.937	17.549	19.337	21.321
11	13.486	14.207	14.972	15.784	16.645	17.560	18.531	20.655	23.045	25.733
12	15.026	15.917	16.870	17.888	18.977	20.141	21.384	24.133	27.271	30.850
13	16.627	17.713	18.882	20.141	21.495	22.953	24.523	28.029	32.089	36.786
14	18.292	19.599	21.015	22.550	24.215	26.019	27.975	32.393	37.581	43.672
15	20.024	21.579	23.276	25.129	27.152	29.361	31.772	37.280	43.842	51.660
16	21.825	23.657	25.673	27.888	30.324	33.003	35.950	42.753	50.980	60.925
17	23.698	25.840	28.213	30.840	33.750	36.974	40.545	48.884	59.118	71.673
18	25.645	28.132	30.906	33.999	37.450	41.301	45.599	55.750	68.394	84.141
19	27.671	30.539	33.760	37.379	41.446	46.018	51.159	63.440	78.969	98.603
20	29.778	33.066	36.786	40.995	45.762	51.160	57.275	72.052	91.025	115.380

EXHIBIT B-4
Future Value of Annuity of $1

umn and row 3 in Exhibit B-4. This amount can be used to compute the future value of the investment for Helen's education, as follows:

Amount of each periodic investment	×	**Future value of annuity of $1 (Exhibit B-4)**	=	**Future value of investment**
$4,000	×	**3.215**	=	**$12,860**

This one-step calculation is much easier than computing the future value of each annual investment and then summing the individual future values. In this way, you can compute the future value of any investment consisting of equal periodic amounts at regular intervals. Businesses make periodic investments to accumulate funds for equipment replacement and other uses—an application of the future value of an annuity.

Present Value

Often a person knows a future amount and needs to know the related present value. Recall Exhibit B-1, in which present value and future value are on opposite ends of the same time line. Suppose an investment promises to pay you $5,000 at the *end* of one year. How much would you pay *now* to acquire this investment? You would be willing to pay the present value of the $5,000 future amount.

Like future value, present value depends on three factors: (1) the *amount of payment (or receipt)*, (2) the length of *time* between investment and future receipt (or payment), and (3) the *interest rate*. The process of computing a present value is called *discounting* because the present value is *less* than the future value.

In our investment example, the future receipt is $5,000. The investment period is one year. Assume that you demand an annual interest rate of 10% on your investment. With all three factors specified, you can compute the present value of $5,000 at 10% for one year:

$$\textbf{Present value} = \frac{\textbf{Future value}}{\textbf{1 + Interest rate}} = \frac{\$5{,}000}{1.10} = \$4{,}545$$

By turning the data around into a future-value problem, we can verify the present-value computation:

Amount invested (present value)	$4,545
Expected earnings ($4,545 × 0.10)	455
Amount to be received one year from now (future value)	$5,000

This example illustrates that present value and future value are based on the same equation:

$$\textbf{Future value} = \textbf{Present value} \times (1 + \textbf{Interest rate})$$

$$\textbf{Present value} = \frac{\textbf{Future value}}{1 + \textbf{Interest rate}}$$

If the $5,000 is to be received two years from now, you will pay only $4,132 for the investment, as shown in Exhibit B-5. By turning the data around, we ver-
* ify that $4,132 accumulates to $5,000 at 10% for two years:

Amount invested (present value)	$4,132
Expected earnings for first year ($4,132 × 0.10)	413
Value of investment after one year	4,545
Expected earnings for second year ($4,545 × 0.10)	455
Amount to be received two years from now (future value)	$5,000

You would pay $4,132—the present value of $5,000—to receive the $5,000 future amount at the end of two years at 10% per year. The $868 difference between the amount invested ($4,132) and the amount to be received ($5,000) is the return on the investment, the sum of the two interest receipts: $413 + $455 = $868.

Present-Value Tables

We have shown the simple formula for computing present value. However, figuring present value "by hand" for investments spanning many years is time-consuming and presents too many opportunities for arithmetic errors. Present-value tables ease our work. Let's reexamine our examples of present value by using Exhibit B-6: Present Value of $1.

For the 10% investment for one year, we find the junction of the 10% column and row 1 in Exhibit B-6. The figure 0.909 is computed as follows: $1/1.10 = 0.909$. This work has been done for us, and only the present values are given in the table. To figure the present value for $5,000, we multiply 0.909 by $5,000. The result is $4,545, which matches the result we obtained by hand.

For the two-year investment, we read down the 10% column and across row 2. We multiply 0.826 (computed as $0.909/1.10 = 0.826$) by $5,000 and get $4,130, which confirms our earlier computation of $4,132 (the difference is due to rounding in the present-value table). Using the table, we can compute the present value of any single future amount.

Present Value of an Annuity

Return to the investment example beginning at the asterisk above. That investment provided the investor with only a single future receipt ($5,000 at the end of two years). *Annuity investments* provide multiple receipts of an equal amount at fixed intervals over the investment's duration.

EXHIBIT B-5
Present Value: An Example

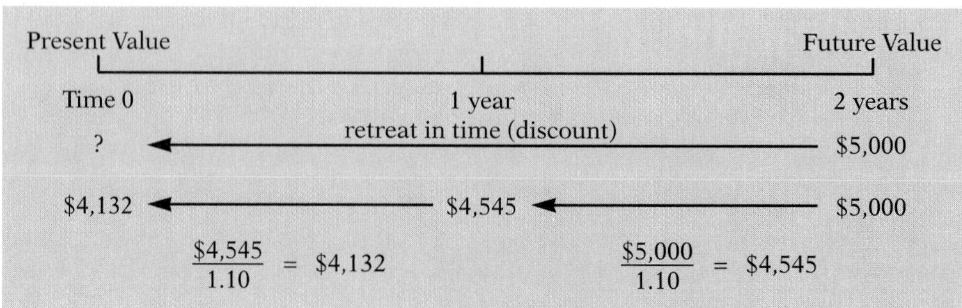

Present Value of $1									
Periods	**4%**	**5%**	**6%**	**7%**	**8%**	**10%**	**12%**	**14%**	**16%**
1	0.962	0.952	0.943	0.935	0.926	0.909	0.893	0.877	0.862
2	0.925	0.907	0.890	0.873	0.857	0.826	0.797	0.769	0.743
3	0.889	0.864	0.840	0.816	0.794	0.751	0.712	0.675	0.641
4	0.855	0.823	0.792	0.763	0.735	0.683	0.636	0.592	0.552
5	0.822	0.784	0.747	0.713	0.681	0.621	0.567	0.519	0.476
6	0.790	0.746	0.705	0.666	0.630	0.564	0.507	0.456	0.410
7	0.760	0.711	0.665	0.623	0.583	0.513	0.452	0.400	0.354
8	0.731	0.677	0.627	0.582	0.540	0.467	0.404	0.351	0.305
9	0.703	0.645	0.592	0.544	0.500	0.424	0.361	0.308	0.263
10	0.676	0.614	0.558	0.508	0.463	0.386	0.322	0.270	0.227
11	0.650	0.585	0.527	0.475	0.429	0.350	0.287	0.237	0.195
12	0.625	0.557	0.497	0.444	0.397	0.319	0.257	0.208	0.168
13	0.601	0.530	0.469	0.415	0.368	0.290	0.229	0.182	0.145
14	0.577	0.505	0.442	0.388	0.340	0.263	0.205	0.160	0.125
15	0.555	0.481	0.417	0.362	0.315	0.239	0.183	0.140	0.108
16	0.534	0.458	0.394	0.339	0.292	0.218	0.163	0.123	0.093
17	0.513	0.436	0.371	0.317	0.270	0.198	0.146	0.108	0.080
18	0.494	0.416	0.350	0.296	0.250	0.180	0.130	0.095	0.069
19	0.475	0.396	0.331	0.277	0.232	0.164	0.116	0.083	0.060
20	0.456	0.377	0.312	0.258	0.215	0.149	0.104	0.073	0.051

EXHIBIT B-6
Present Value of $1

Consider an investment that promises *annual* cash receipts of $10,000 to be received at the end of each of three years. Assume that you demand a 12% return on your investment. What is the investment's present value? That is, what would you pay today to acquire the investment? The investment spans three periods, and you would pay the sum of three present values. The computation is as follows:

Year	Annual Cash Receipt	Present Value of $1 at 12% (Exhibit B-6)	Present Value of Annual Cash Receipt
1	$10,000	0.893	$ 8,930
2	10,000	0.797	7,970
3	10,000	0.712	7,120
Total present value of investment			$24,020

The present value of this annuity is $24,020. By paying this amount today, you will receive $10,000 at the end of each of the three years while earning 12% on your investment.

This example illustrates repetitive computations of the three future amounts, a time-consuming process. One way to ease the computational burden is to add the three present values of $1 (0.893 + 0.797 + 0.712) and multiply their sum (2.402) by the annual cash receipt ($10,000) to obtain the present value of the annuity ($10,000 × 2.402 = $24,020).

An easier approach is to use a present value of an annuity table. Exhibit B-7 on page 726 shows the present value of $1 to be received periodically for a given number of periods. The present value of a three-period annuity at 12% is 2.402 (the junction of row 3 and the 12% column). Thus, $10,000 received annually at the end of each of three years, discounted at 12%, is $24,020 ($10,000 × 2.402), which is the present value.

Present Value of Bonds Payable

The present value of a bond—its market price—is the present value of the future principal amount at maturity plus the present value of the future contract interest payments. The principal is a *single amount* to be paid at maturity. The interest is an *annuity* because it occurs periodically.

Periods	4%	5%	6%	7%	8%	10%	12%	14%	16%
				Present Value of Annuity of $1					
1	0.962	0.952	0.943	0.935	0.926	0.909	0.893	0.877	0.862
2	1.886	1.859	1.833	1.808	1.783	1.736	1.690	1.647	1.605
3	2.775	2.723	2.673	2.624	2.577	2.487	2.402	2.322	2.246
4	3.630	3.546	3.465	3.387	3.312	3.170	3.037	2.914	2.798
5	4.452	4.329	4.212	4.100	3.993	3.791	3.605	3.433	3.274
6	5.242	5.076	4.917	4.767	4.623	4.355	4.111	3.889	3.685
7	6.002	5.786	5.582	5.389	5.206	4.868	4.564	4.288	4.039
8	6.733	6.463	6.210	5.971	5.747	5.335	4.968	4.639	4.344
9	7.435	7.108	6.802	6.515	6.247	5.759	5.328	4.946	4.607
10	8.111	7.722	7.360	7.024	6.710	6.145	5.650	5.216	4.833
11	8.760	8.306	7.887	7.499	7.139	6.495	5.938	5.453	5.029
12	9.385	8.863	8.384	7.943	7.536	6.814	6.194	5.660	5.197
13	9.986	9.394	8.853	8.358	7.904	7.103	6.424	5.842	5.342
14	10.563	9.899	9.295	8.745	8.244	7.367	6.628	6.002	5.468
15	11.118	10.380	9.712	9.108	8.559	7.606	6.811	6.142	5.575
16	11.652	10.838	10.106	9.447	8.851	7.824	6.974	6.265	5.669
17	12.166	11.274	10.477	9.763	9.122	8.022	7.120	6.373	5.749
18	12.659	11.690	10.828	10.059	9.372	8.201	7.250	6.467	5.818
19	13.134	12.085	11.158	10.336	9.604	8.365	7.366	6.550	5.877
20	13.590	12.462	11.470	10.594	9.818	8.514	7.469	6.623	5.929

EXHIBIT B-7
Present Value of Annuity of $1

Let's compute the present value of the 9% five-year bonds of Chrysler Corporation (discussed on page 384). The face value of the bonds is $100,000, and they pay 4½% contract (cash) interest semiannually (that is, twice a year).[1] At issuance, the market interest rate is expressed as 10% annually, but it is computed at 5% semiannually. Therefore, the effective interest rate for each of the 10 semiannual periods is 5 percent. We thus use 5% in computing the present value (PV) of the maturity and of the interest. The market price of these bonds is $96,149, as follows:

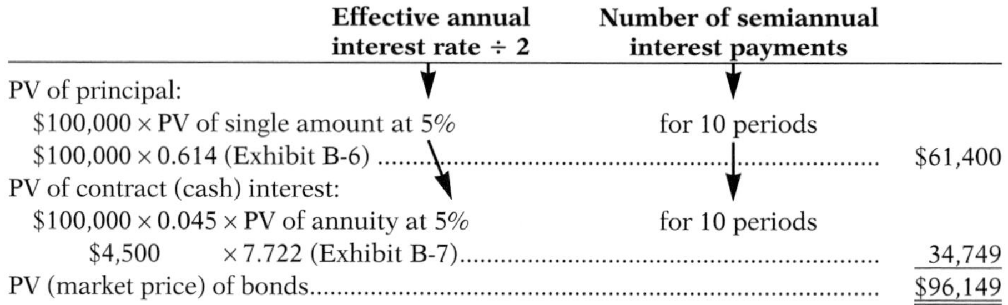

	Effective annual interest rate ÷ 2	Number of semiannual interest payments	
PV of principal:			
$100,000 × PV of single amount at 5%		for 10 periods	
$100,000 × 0.614 (Exhibit B-6)			$61,400
PV of contract (cash) interest:			
$100,000 × 0.045 × PV of annuity at 5%		for 10 periods	
$4,500 × 7.722 (Exhibit B-7)			34,749
PV (market price) of bonds			$96,149

The market price of the Chrysler bonds shows a discount because the contract interest rate on the bonds (9%) is less than the market interest rate (10%). We discuss these bonds in more detail on pages 385–388.

Let's consider a premium price for the 9% Chrysler bonds. Assume that the market interest rate is 8% (rather than 10%) at issuance. The effective interest rate is thus 4% for each of the 10 semiannual periods:

	Effective annual interest rate ÷ 2	Number of semiannual interest payments	
PV of principal:			
$100,000 × PV of single amount at 4%		for 10 periods	
$100,000 × 0.676 (Exhibit B-6)			$ 67,600
PV of contract (cash) interest:			
$100,000 × 0.045 × PV of annuity at 4%		for 10 periods	
$4,500 × 8.111 (Exhibit B-7)			36,500
PV (market price) of bonds			$104,100

[1]For a definition of contract interest rate, see page 382.

We discuss accounting for these bonds on pages 388–390. It may be helpful for you to reread this section ("Present Value of Bonds Payable") after you've studied those pages.

Capital Leases

How does a lessee compute the cost of an asset acquired through a capital lease? (See page 395 for a definition of capital leases.) Consider that the lessee gets the use of the asset but does *not* pay for the leased asset in full at the beginning of the lease. A capital lease is therefore similar to an installment purchase of the leased asset. The lessee must record the leased asset at the present value of the lease liability. The time value of money must be weighed.

The cost of the asset to the lessee is the sum of any payment made at the beginning of the lease period plus the present value of the future lease payments. The lease payments are equal amounts occurring at regular intervals—that is, they are annuity payments.

Consider the 20-year building lease of Walgreen Co. that we discuss on pages 396 and 397. The lease requires 20 annual payments of $10,000 each, with the first payment due immediately. The interest rate in the lease is 10%, and the present value of the 19 future payments is $83,650 ($10,000 × PV of annuity at 10% for 19 periods, or 8.365 from Exhibit B-7). Walgreen's cost of the building is $93,650 (the sum of the initial payment, $10,000, plus the present value of the future payments, $83,650). The entries for a capital lease are illustrated on pages 396–397.

APPENDIX PROBLEMS

PB-1 For each situation, compute the required amount.

a. Langefeld Enterprises is budgeting for the acquisition of land over the next several years. Langefeld can invest $300,000 today at 9 percent. How much cash will Langefeld have for land acquisitions at the end of five years? At the end of six years?

b. Mercer Associates is planning to invest $10,000 each year for five years. The company's investment adviser believes that Mercer can earn 6% interest without taking on too much risk. What will be the value of Mercer's investment on the date of the last deposit if Mercer can earn 6 percent? If Mercer can earn 8 percent?

PB-2 For each situation, compute the required amount.

a. Eastman Kodak's operations are generating excess cash that will be invested in a special fund. During 19X2, Kodak invests $11,287,000 in the fund for a planned advertising campaign for a new product to be released six years later, in 19X8. If Kodak's investments can earn 10% each year, how much cash will the company have for the advertising campaign in 19X8?

b. Eastman Kodak Company will need $20 million to advertise a new type of photo film in 19X8. How much must Kodak invest in 19X2 to have the cash available for the advertising campaign? Kodak's investments can earn 10% annually.

c. Explain the relationship between your answers to *a* and *b*.

PB-3 Determine the present value of the following notes and bonds:

1. A $40,000, five-year note payable with contract interest rate of 9%, paid annually. The market interest rate at issuance is 10%.

2. Ten-year bonds payable with maturity value of $100,000 and contract interest rate of 12%, paid semiannually. The market rate of interest is 10% at issuance.

3. Same bonds payable as in number 2, but the market interest rate is 8 percent.

4. Same bonds payable as in number 2, but the market interest rate is 12 percent.

PB-4 On December 31, 19X1, when the market interest rate is 8%, Interstate Express Co. issues $300,000 of 10-year, 7.25% bonds payable. The bonds pay interest semiannually.

Required

1. Determine the present value of the bonds at issuance.
2. Assume that the bonds are issued at the price computed in Requirement 1. Prepare an effective-interest-method amortization table for the first two semiannual interest periods.
3. Using the amortization table prepared in Requirement 2, journalize issuance of the bonds and the first two interest payments and amortization of any premium or discount.

PB-5 Yokohama Children's Home needs a fleet of vans to transport the children to singing engagements throughout Japan. Nissan offers the vehicles for a single payment of 6,300,000 yen due at the end of four years. Toyota prices a similar fleet of vans for four annual payments of 1,500,000 yen at the end of each year. The children's home could borrow the funds at 6%, so this is the appropriate interest rate. Which company should get the business, Nissan or Toyota? Base your decision on present value, and give your reason.

PB-6 Goldblatt Institute acquired equipment under a capital lease that requires six annual lease payments of $10,000. The first payment is due when the lease begins, on January 1, 19X6. Future payments are due on January 1 of each year of the lease term. The interest rate in the lease is 16 percent.

Required

1. Compute Goldblatt's cost of the equipment.
2. Journalize the (a) acquisition of the equipment, (b) depreciation for 19X6 (use the straight-line method), (c) accrued interest at December 31, 19X6, and (d) second lease payment on January 1, 19X7.

APPENDIX C

Summary of Generally Accepted Accounting Principles (GAAP)

Every technical area has professional associations and regulatory bodies that govern the practice of the profession. Accounting is no exception. In the United States, generally accepted accounting principles (GAAP) are influenced most by the Financial Accounting Standards Board (FASB). The FASB has seven full-time members and a large staff. Its financial support comes from professional associations such as the American Institute of Certified Public Accountants (AICPA).

The FASB is an independent organization with no government or professional affiliation. The FASB's pronouncements, called *Statements of Financial Accounting Standards,* specify how to account for certain business transactions. Each new *Standard* becomes part of GAAP, the "accounting law of the land." In the same way that our laws draw authority from their acceptance by the people, GAAP depends on general acceptance by the business community. Throughout this book, we refer to GAAP as the proper way to do financial accounting.

The U.S. Congress has given the Securities and Exchange Commission (SEC), a government organization that regulates the trading of investments, ultimate responsibility for establishing accounting rules for companies that are owned by the general investing public. However, the SEC has delegated much of its rule-making power to the FASB. Exhibit C-1 outlines the flow of authority for developing GAAP.

The Objective of Financial Reporting

The basic objective of financial reporting is to provide information that is useful in making investment and lending decisions. The FASB believes that accounting information can be useful in decision making only if it is *relevant, reliable, comparable,* and *consistent.*

Relevant information is useful in making predictions and for evaluating past performance—that is, the information has feedback value. For example, PepsiCo's disclosure of the profitability of each of its lines of business is relevant for investor evaluations of the company. To be relevant, information must be timely. *Reliable* information is free from significant error—that is, it has validity. Also, it is free from the bias of a particular viewpoint—that is, it is verifiable and

EXHIBIT C-1
Flow of Authority for Developing GAAP

Concepts, Principles, and Financial Statements	Quick Summary	Text Reference
Concepts		
Entity concept	Accounting draws a boundary around each organization to be accounted for.	Chapter 1, page 11
Going-concern concept	Accountants assume the business will continue operating for the foreseeable future.	Chapter 1, page 12
Stable-monetary-unit concept	Accounting information is expressed primarily in monetary terms.	Chapter 1, page 12
Time-period concept	Ensures that accounting information is reported at regular intervals.	Chapter 3, page 109
Conservatism concept	Accountants report items in the financial statements in a way that avoids overstating assets, owners' equity, and revenues and avoids understating liabilities and expenses.	Chapter 6, page 280
Materiality concept	Accountants perform strictly proper accounting only for items that are significant to the company's financial statements.	Chapter 6, page 280
Principles		
Reliability (objectivity) principle	Accounting records and statements are based on the most reliable data available.	Chapter 1, page 11
Cost principle	Assets and services, revenues and expenses are recorded at their actual historical cost.	Chapter 1, page 12
Revenue principle	Tells accountants when to record revenue (only after it has been earned) and the amount of revenue to record (the cash value of what has been received).	Chapter 3, page 110
Matching principle	Directs accountants to (1) identify all expenses incurred during the period, (2) measure the expenses, and (3) match the expenses against the revenues earned during the period. The goal is to measure net income.	Chapter 3, page 111
Consistency principle	Businesses should use the same accounting methods from period to period.	Chapter 6, page 279
Disclosure principle	A company's financial statements should report enough information for outsiders to make informed decisions about the company.	Chapter 6, page 279
Financial Statements and Notes		
Balance sheet	Assets = Liabilities + Owners' Equity at a point in time.	Chapters 1 and 11
Income statement	Revenues and gains – Expenses and losses = Net income or net loss for the period.	Chapters 1 and 11
Statement of cash flows	Cash receipts – Cash disbursements = Increase or decrease in cash during the period, grouped under operating, investing, and financing activities.	Chapters 1 and 12
Statement of retained earnings	Beginning retained earnings + Net income (or – Net loss) – Dividends = Ending retained earnings.	Chapter 1
Statement of stockholders' equity	Shows the reason for the change in each stockholders' equity account, including retained earnings.	Chapter 11
Financial statement notes	Provide information that cannot be reported conveniently on the face of the financial statements. The notes are an integral part of the statements.	Chapter 11

EXHIBIT C-2
Summary of Important Accounting Concepts, Principles, and Financial Statements

neutral. *Comparable* and *consistent* information can be compared from period to period to help investors and creditors track the entity's progress through time. These characteristics combine to shape the concepts and principles that make up GAAP. Exhibit C-2 summarizes the concepts and principles that accounting has developed to provide useful information for decision making.

APPENDIX D

Accounting for Partnerships

A **partnership** is an association of two or more persons who co-own a business for profit. This definition stems from the Uniform Partnership Act, which nearly every state in the United States has adopted to regulate partnership practice.

Forming a partnership is easy. It requires no permission from government authorities and involves no legal procedures. When two persons decide to go into business together, a partnership is automatically formed.

Different Types of Partnerships

Partnerships come in all sizes. Many partnerships have fewer than 10 partners. Some medical and law firms have 20 or more partners. The largest CPA firms are international organizations with almost 2,000 partners.

General Partnerships

A **general partnership** is the basic form of partnership organization. Each partner is an owner of the business with all the privileges and risks of ownership. The general partners share the profits, losses, and the risks of the business. The partnership *reports* its income to the governmental tax authorities (the Internal Revenue Service in the United States), but the partnership itself pays *no* income tax. The profits and losses of the partnership pass through the business to the partners, who then pay personal income tax on their income.

Limited Partnerships

A **limited partnership** has at least two classes of partners. There must be at least one *general partner,* who takes primary responsibility for the management of the business. The general partner also takes the bulk of the risk of failure in the event the partnership goes bankrupt (liabilities exceed assets). In real estate limited partnerships, the general partner often invests little cash in the business. Instead, the general partner's contribution is his or her skill in managing the organization. Usually, the general partner is the last owner to receive a share of partnership profits and losses. But the general partner may earn all excess profits after satisfying the limited partners' demands for income.

The *limited partners* are so named because their personal obligation for the partnership's liabilities is limited to the amount they have invested in the business. Usually, the limited partners have invested the bulk of the partnership's assets and capital. They therefore usually have first claim to partnership profits and losses, but only up to a specified limit. In exchange for their limited liability, their potential for profits usually has an upper limit as well.

Most of the large accounting firms are organized as **limited liability partnerships,** or **LLPs,** which means that each partner's personal liability for the business's debts is limited to a certain amount. The LLP must carry a large insurance policy to protect the public in case the partnership is found guilty of malpractice. Medical, legal, and other firms of professionals can also be organized as LLPs.

Characteristics of a Partnership

Starting a partnership is voluntary. A person cannot be forced to join a partnership, and partners cannot be forced to accept another person as a partner. Although the partnership agreement may be oral, a written agreement between the partners reduces the chance of a misunderstanding. The following characteristics distinguish partnerships from sole proprietorships and corporations.

For a review of the definitions of a *proprietorship* and a *corporation,* see Chapter 1, pages 8 and 9.

THE WRITTEN PARTNERSHIP AGREEMENT A business partnership is like a marriage. To be successful, the partners must cooperate. But business partners do not vow to remain together for life. Business partnerships come and go. To make certain that each partner fully understands how a particular partnership operates and to lower the chances that any partner might misunderstand how the business is run, partners may draw up a **partnership agreement,** also called the **articles of partnership.** This agreement is a contract between the partners, so transactions involving the agreement are governed by contract law. The articles of partnership should make the following points clear:

1. Name, location, and nature of the business
2. Name, capital investment, and duties of each partner
3. Method of sharing profits and losses by the partners
4. Withdrawals of assets allowed to the partners
5. Procedures for settling disputes between the partners
6. Procedures for admitting new partners
7. Procedures for settling up with a partner who withdraws from the business
8. Procedures for liquidating the partnership—selling the assets, paying the liabilities, and disbursing any remaining cash to the partners

LIMITED LIFE A partnership has a life limited by the length of time that all partners continue to own the business. If Marva Turner, a partner of the business Turner & Lail, withdraws from the business, the partnership of Turner & Lail will cease to exist. A new partnership may emerge to continue the same business, but the old partnership will have been *dissolved.* **Dissolution** is the ending of a partnership. The addition of a new partner dissolves the old partnership and creates a new partnership.

MUTUAL AGENCY **Mutual agency** in a partnership means that every partner can bind the business to a contract within the scope of the partnership's regular business operations. If Brad Lail enters into a contract with a business to provide accounting service, then the firm of Turner & Lail—not only Lail—is bound to provide that service. If Lail signs a contract to purchase lawn services for his home, however, the partnership will not be bound to pay. Contracting for personal services is not a regular business operation of the partnership.

UNLIMITED LIABILITY Each partner has an **unlimited personal liability** for the debts of the partnership. When a partnership cannot pay its debts with business assets, the partners must use their personal assets to meet the debt.

Suppose the Turner & Lail firm has had an unsuccessful year and the partnership's liabilities exceed its assets by $20,000. Turner and Lail must pay this amount with their personal assets. Because each partner has *unlimited* liability, if a partner is unable to pay his or her part of the debt, the other partner (or partners) must make payment. If Lail can pay only $5,000 of the liability, Turner must pay $15,000.

Unlimited liability and mutual agency are closely related. A dishonest partner or a partner with poor judgment may commit the partnership to a contract under which the business loses money. In turn, creditors may force *all* the partners to pay the debt from personal assets. Hence, a business partner should be chosen with care. Partners can avoid unlimited personal liability for partnership obligations by forming a limited partnership.

Co-Ownership of Property Any asset—cash, inventory, machinery, and so on—that a partner invests in the partnership becomes the joint property of all the partners. Also, each partner has a claim to his or her share of the business's profits.

No Partnership Income Taxes A partnership pays no income tax on its business income. Instead, the partnership's net income is divided and becomes the taxable income of the partners. Suppose Turner & Lail, Certified Public Accountants, earned net income of $180,000, shared equally by the two partners. The firm would pay no income tax *as a business entity.* Turner and Lail, however, would pay income tax as individuals on their $90,000 shares of partnership income.

Partners' Owner's Equity Accounts Accounting for a partnership is much like accounting for a proprietorship. We record buying and selling, collecting, and paying for a partnership just as we do for a business with only one owner. But because a partnership has more than one owner, the partnership must have more than one owner's equity account. Every partner in the business—whether the firm has two or 2,000 partners—has an individual owner's equity account. Often, these accounts carry the name of the particular partner and the word *capital.* For example, the owner's equity account for Brad Lail would read "Lail, Capital." Similarly, each partner has a withdrawal account. If the number of partners is large, the general ledger may contain the single account Partners' Capital, or Owners' Equity. A subsidiary ledger can be used for individual partner accounts.

For more on subsidiary ledgers, see Chapter 5, page 229, and Appendix F, page 755.

S Corporations An **S Corporation** is a corporation that is taxed in the same way that a partnership is taxed. Therefore, S corporations are often discussed in conjunction with partnerships. This form of business organization derives its name from Subchapter S of the United States Internal Revenue Code.

An ordinary (Subchapter C) corporation is subject to double taxation. First, the corporation pays corporate income tax on its income. Then, when the corporation pays dividends to the stockholders, they pay personal income tax on their dividend income. An S corporation pays no corporate income tax. Instead, the corporation's income flows through directly to the stockholders, who pay personal income tax on their share of the S corporation's income. The one-time taxation of an S corporation's income is an important advantage over an ordinary corporation. Thus, from a tax standpoint, an S corporation operates like a partnership.

To qualify as an S corporation, the company can have no more than 75 stockholders, all of whom must be citizens or residents of the United States. Accounting for an S corporation resembles that of accounting for a partnership because the allocation of corporate income follows the same procedure used by partnerships.

Initial Investments by Partners

Let's see how to account for a partnership's multiple owner's equity accounts—and learn how they appear on the balance sheet—by looking at how to account for the starting up of a partnership.

Partners in a new partnership may invest assets and liabilities in the business. These contributions are entered in the books in the same way that a proprietor's assets and liabilities would be recorded. Subtraction of each person's liabilities from his or her assets yields the amount to be credited to that person's capital account. Often the partners hire an independent firm to appraise their assets and liabilities at current market value at the time a partnership is formed. This outside evaluation assures an objective accounting for what each partner brings into the business.

Assume that Dave Benz and Joan Hanna form a partnership to manufacture and sell computer software. The partners agree on the following values based on an independent appraisal.

Benz's contributions:

- Cash, $10,000; inventory, $70,000; and accounts payable, $85,000 (the appraiser believes that the current market values for these items equal Benz's values)
- Accounts receivable, $30,000, less allowance for doubtful accounts of $5,000
- Computer equipment: cost, $600,000; market value, $450,000

Hanna's contributions:

- Cash, $5,000
- Computer software: cost, $18,000; market value, $100,000

The partners record their initial investment at the current market values.

Benz's investment:

June 1	Cash	10,000	
	Accounts Receivable	30,000	
	Inventory	70,000	
	Computer Equipment	450,000	
	Allowance for Doubtful Accounts		5,000
	Accounts Payable		85,000
	Benz, Capital		470,000
	To record Benz's investment in the partnership.		

Hanna's investment:

June 1	Cash	5,000	
	Computer Software	100,000	
	Hanna, Capital		105,000
	To record Hanna's investment in the partnership.		

The initial partnership balance sheet reports the amounts as shown in Exhibit D-1.

EXHIBIT D-1
Partnership Balance Sheet

BENZ AND HANNA
Balance Sheet
June 1, 19X5

Assets			**Liabilities**	
Cash		$ 15,000	Accounts payable	$ 85,000
Accounts receivable	$30,000			
Less Allowance for doubtful accounts	5,000	25,000	**Capital**	
Inventory		70,000	Benz, capital	470,000
Computer equipment		450,000	Hanna, capital	105,000
Computer software		100,000	Total liabilities	
Total assets		$660,000	and capital	$660,000

Sharing Partnership Profits and Losses

How to allocate profits and losses among partners is one of the most challenging aspects of managing a partnership. If the partners have not drawn up an agreement or if the agreement does not state how the partners will divide profits and losses, then by law the partners must share profits and losses equally. If the agreement specifies a method for sharing profits but not losses, then losses are shared in the same proportion as profits. For example, a partner who was allocated 75% of the profits would likewise absorb 75% of any losses.

In some cases, an equal division is not fair. One partner may perform more work for the business than the other partner, or one partner may make a larger capital contribution. In our example, Joan Hanna might agree to work longer hours for the partnership than Dave Benz to earn a greater share of the profits. Benz could argue that he should share in more of the profits because he contributed more net assets ($470,000) than Hanna did ($105,000). Hanna might contend that her computer software program is the partnership's most important asset and that her share of the profits should be greater than Benz's share. Agreeing on a fair sharing of profits and losses in a partnership may be difficult. We now discuss options available in determining partners' shares.

Sharing Based on a Stated Fraction

Partners may agree to any profit-and-loss-sharing method they desire. For example, they may state a particular fraction of the total profits and losses that each individual partner will share. Suppose the partnership agreement of Ian Cagle and Justin Dean allocates two-thirds of the business profits and losses to Cagle and one-third to Dean. If net income for the year is $90,000 and all revenue and expense accounts have been closed, the Income Summary account has a credit balance of $90,000:

We discussed Income Summary in Chapter 3, p. 133.

Income Summary	
	Bal. 90,000

The entry to close this account and allocate the profit to the partners' capital accounts is

Dec. 31	Income Summary	90,000	
	Cagle, Capital ($90,000 × ⅔)		60,000
	Dean, Capital ($90,000 × ⅓)		30,000
	To allocate net income to partners.		

Consider the effect of this entry. Does Cagle get cash of $60,000 and Dean cash of $30,000? No. The increase in the partners' capital accounts cannot be linked to any particular asset, including cash. Instead, the entry indicates that Cagle's ownership in *all* the assets of the business increased by $60,000 and Dean's by $30,000.

If the year's operations resulted in a net loss of $66,000, the Income Summary account would have a debit balance of $66,000. In that case, the closing entry to allocate the loss to the partners' capital accounts would be

Dec. 31	Cagle, Capital ($66,000 × ⅔)	44,000	
	Dean, Capital ($66,000 × ⅓)	22,000	
	Income Summary		66,000
	To allocate net loss to partners.		

Sharing Based on Capital Contributions

Profits and losses are often allocated in proportion to the partners' capital contributions in the business. Suppose that Jim Antoine, Erika Barber, and Rico Cabañas are partners in ABC Company. Their capital accounts have the following balances at the end of the year, before the closing entries:

Antoine, Capital	$ 40,000
Barber, Capital	60,000
Cabañas, Capital	50,000
Total capital balances	$150,000

Assume that the partnership earned a profit of $120,000 for the year. To allocate this amount on the basis of capital contributions, compute each partner's percentage share of the partnership's total capital balance. Simply divide each partner's contribution by the total capital amount. These figures, multiplied by the $120,000 profit amount, yield each partner's share of the year's profits:

$$\textbf{Antoine: } \left(\frac{\$40{,}000}{\$150{,}000}\right) \times \$120{,}000 = \$\ 32{,}000$$

$$\textbf{Barber: } \left(\frac{\$60{,}000}{\$150{,}000}\right) \times \$120{,}000 = 48{,}000$$

$$\textbf{Cabañas: } \left(\frac{\$50{,}000}{\$150{,}000}\right) \times \$120{,}000 = 40{,}000$$

$$\textbf{Net income allocated to partners} = \$120{,}000$$

The closing entry to allocate the profit to the partners' capital accounts is

Dec. 31	Income Summary	120,000	
	Antoine, Capital		32,000
	Barber, Capital		48,000
	Cabañas, Capital		40,000
	To allocate net income to partners.		

After this closing entry, the partners' capital balances are

Antoine, Capital ($40,000 + $32,000)	$ 72,000
Barber, Capital ($60,000 + $48,000)	108,000
Cabañas, Capital ($50,000 + $40,000)	90,000
Total capital balances after allocation of net income	$270,000

Partner Drawings

Like anyone else, partners need cash for personal living expenses. Partnership agreements usually allow partners to withdraw cash or other assets from the business. Drawings from a partnership are recorded exactly as for a proprietorship. Assume that both Randy Lewis and Gerald Clark are allowed a monthly withdrawal of $3,500. The partnership records the March withdrawals with this entry:

Mar. 31	Lewis, Drawing	3,500	
	Clark, Drawing	3,500	
	Cash		7,000
	Monthly partner withdrawals.		

During the year, each partner's drawing account accumulates 12 such amounts, a total of $42,000 ($3,500 × 12). At the end of the period, the general ledger shows the following accounts balances immediately after net income has been closed to the partners' capital accounts. Assume the following beginning balances for Lewis ($80,000) and Clark ($100,000) at the start of the year and the following allocation of $82,000 ($44,200 + $37,800) profit:

Lewis, Capital

	Jan. 1 Bal.	80,000
	Dec. 31 Net. inc.	44,200

Clark, Capital

	Jan. 1 Bal.	100,000
	Dec. 31 Net inc.	37,800

Lewis, Drawing	
Dec. 31 Bal. 42,000	

Clark, Drawing	
Dec. 31 Bal. 42,000	

The withdrawal accounts must be closed at the end of the period. The closing entry credits each partner's drawing account and debits each capital account. Proprietorships follow the same process.

Admission of a Partner

A partnership lasts only as long as its partners remain in the business. The addition of a new member or the withdrawal of an existing member dissolves the partnership. We turn now to a discussion of how partnerships dissolve—and how new partnerships arise.

Often a new partnership is formed to carry on the former partnership's business. In fact, the new partnership may retain the dissolved partnership's name. Price Waterhouse, for example, is an accounting firm that retires and hires partners during the year. Thus, the former partnership dissolves and a new partnership begins many times. But the business retains the name and continues operations. Other partnerships may dissolve and then re-form under a new name. Let's look now at the ways that a new member may gain admission into an existing partnership.

Admission by Purchasing a Partner's Interest

A person may become a member of a partnership by gaining the approval of the other partner (or partners) for entrance into the firm *and* by purchasing a present partner's interest in the business. Let's assume that Beverly Fisher and Renata Garcia have a partnership that carries these figures:

Cash	\$ 40,000	Total liabilities	\$120,000
Other assets	360,000	Fisher, capital	110,000
		Garcia, capital	170,000
Total assets	\$400,000	Total liabilities and capital	\$400,000

Business is going so well that Fisher receives an offer from Barry Dynak, an outside party, to buy her \$110,000 interest in the business for \$150,000. Fisher agrees to sell out to Dynak, and Garcia approves Dynak as a new partner. The firm records the transfer of capital interest in the business with this entry:

Apr. 16	Fisher, Capital	110,000	
	Dynak, Capital		110,000
	To transfer Fisher's equity in the business to Dynak.		

The debit side of the entry closes Fisher's capital account because she is no longer a partner. The credit side opens Dynak's capital account because Fisher's equity has been transferred to Dynak. The entry amount is Fisher's capital balance (\$110,000) and not the \$150,000 price that Dynak paid Fisher to buy into the business. The full \$150,000 goes to Fisher, including the \$40,000 difference between her capital balance and the price received from Dynak. In this example, the partnership receives no cash because the transaction was between Dynak and Fisher, not between Dynak and the partnership. Suppose Dynak pays Fisher less than Fisher's capital balance. The entry on the partnership books is not affected. Fisher's equity is still transferred to Dynak at book value (\$110,000).

The old partnership has dissolved. Garcia and Dynak draw up a new partnership agreement with a new profit-and-loss-sharing ratio and continue business operations. If Garcia does not accept Dynak as a partner, Dynak does not become a partner and thus gets no voice in management of the firm. However, under the Uniform Partnership Act, the purchaser shares in the profits and losses of the firm and in its assets at liquidation.

Admission by Investing in the Partnership

A person may be admitted as a partner by investing directly in the partnership rather than by purchasing an existing partner's interest. The new partner contributes assets—for example, cash, inventory, or equipment—to the business. Assume that the partnership of Robin Ingel and Michael Jay has the following assets, liabilities, and capital:

Cash	$ 20,000	Total liabilities	$ 60,000
Other assets	200,000	Ingel, capital	70,000
		Jay, capital	90,000
Total assets	$220,000	Total liabilities and capital	$220,000

Laureen Kahn offers to invest equipment and land (Other Assets) with a market value of $80,000 to persuade the existing partners to take her into the business. Ingel and Jay agree to dissolve the existing partnership and to start up a new business, giving Kahn one-third interest—$80,000/($70,000 + $90,000 + $80,000) = ⅓—in exchange for the contributed assets. The entry to record Kahn's investment is

July 18	Other Assets	80,000	
	Kahn, Capital		80,000
	To admit L. Kahn as a partner with a one-third interest in the business.		

After this entry, the partnership books show the following:

Cash	$ 20,000	Total liabilities	$ 60,000
Other assets ($200,000 + $80,000)	280,000	Ingel, capital	70,000
		Jay, capital	90,000
		Kahn, capital	80,000
Total assets	$300,000	Total liabilities and capital	$300,000

Kahn's one-third interest in the partnership does not necessarily entitle her to one-third of the profits. The sharing of profits and losses is a separate element in the partnership agreement.

ADMISSION BY INVESTING IN THE PARTNERSHIP—BONUS TO THE OLD PARTNERS The more successful a partnership, the higher the payment the partners may demand from a person entering the business. Partners in a business that is doing quite well might require an incoming person to pay them a bonus. The bonus increases the current partners' capital accounts.

Suppose that Hiro Nagasawa and Ralph Osburn's partnership has earned above-average profits for 10 years. The two partners share profits and losses equally. The partnership balance sheet carries these figures:

Cash	$ 40,000	Total liabilities	$100,000
Other assets	210,000	Nagasawa, capital	70,000
		Osburn, capital	80,000
Total assets	$250,000	Total liabilities and capital	$250,000

The partners agree to admit Glen Parker to a one-fourth interest with his cash investment of $90,000. Parker's capital balance on the partnership books is $60,000, computed as follows:

Partnership capital before Parker is admitted ($70,000 + $80,000)	$150,000
Parker's investment in the partnership	90,000
Partnership capital after Parker is admitted	$240,000
Parker's capital in the partnership ($240,000 × ¼)	$ 60,000

The entry on the partnership books to record Parker's investment is

Mar. 1	Cash	90,000	
	Parker, Capital		60,000
	Nagasawa, Capital ($30,000 × ½)		15,000
	Osburn, Capital ($30,000 × ½)		15,000
	To admit G. Parker as a partner with a one-fourth interest in the business.		

Parker's capital account is credited for his one-fourth interest in the partnership. The other partners share the $30,000 difference between Parker's investment ($90,000) and his equity in the business ($60,000). This difference is called a *bonus*. It is accounted for as income to the old partners and is therefore allocated to them on the basis of their profit-and-loss ratio.

The new partnership's balance sheet reports these amounts:

Cash ($40,000 + $90,000)	$130,000	Total liabilities	$100,000
Other assets	210,000	Nagasawa, capital	
		($70,000 + $15,000)	85,000
		Osburn, capital	
		($80,000 + $15,000)	95,000
		Parker, capital	60,000
Total assets	$340,000	Total liabilities and capital	$340,000

Withdrawal of a Partner

A partner may withdraw from the business for many reasons, including retirement or a dispute with the other partners. The withdrawal of a partner dissolves the old partnership. The partnership agreement should contain a provision to govern how to settle with a withdrawing partner. In the simplest case, a partner may withdraw and sell his or her interest to another partner in a personal transaction. The only entry needed to record this transfer of equity debits the withdrawing partner's capital account and credits the purchaser's capital account. The dollar amount of the entry is the withdrawing partner's capital balance, regardless of the price paid by the purchaser. The accounting when one current partner buys a second partner's interest is the same as when an outside party buys a current partner's interest.

If the partner withdraws in the middle of an accounting period, the partnership books should be updated to determine the withdrawing partner's capital balance. The business must measure net income or net loss for the fraction of the year up to the withdrawal date and allocate profit or loss according to the agreed-upon ratio. After the books have been closed, the business then accounts for the change in partnership capital.

The withdrawing partner may receive his or her share of the business in partnership assets other than cash. The question arises regarding what value to assign to the partnership assets: book value or current market value. The settlement procedure may specify an independent appraisal of assets to determine their current market value. If market values have changed, the appraisal will result in revaluing the partnership assets. The partners then share in any market-value changes that their efforts caused.

Suppose that Keith Isaac is retiring in midyear from the partnership of Green, Henry, and Isaac. After the books have been adjusted for partial-period income but before the asset appraisal, revaluation, and closing entries, the balance sheet reports the following:

Cash		$ 39,000	Total liabilities	$ 80,000
Inventory		44,000	Green, capital	54,000
Land		55,000	Henry, capital	43,000
Building	$95,000		Isaac, capital	21,000
Less accum. depr.	35,000	60,000	Total liabilities and	
Total assets		$198,000	capital	$198,000

An independent appraiser revalues the inventory at $38,000 (down from $44,000) and the land at $101,000 (up from $55,000). The partners share the differences between the market values of these assets and their prior book values on the basis of their profit-and-loss ratio. The partnership agreement has allocated one-fourth of the profits to Susan Green, one-half to Charles Henry, and one-fourth to Isaac. (This ratio may be written 1:2:1 for one part to Green, two parts to Henry, and one part to Isaac.) For each share that Green or Isaac has, Henry has two. The entries to record the revaluation of the inventory and land are

July 31	Green, Capital ($6,000 × ¼)	1,500	
	Henry, Capital ($6,000 × ½)	3,000	
	Isaac, Capital ($6,000 × ¼)	1,500	
	Inventory ($44,000 – $38,000)		6,000
	To revalue the inventory and allocate the loss in value to the partners.		
31	Land ($101,000 – $55,000)	46,000	
	Green, Capital ($46,000 × ¼)		11,500
	Henry, Capital ($46,000 × ½)		23,000
	Isaac, Capital ($46,000 × ¼)		11,500
	To revalue the land and allocate the gain in value to the partners.		

After the revaluations, the partnership balance sheet reports the following:

Cash		$ 39,000	Total liabilities	$ 80,000
Inventory		38,000	Green, capital	
Land		101,000	($54,000 – $1,500 + $11,500)	64,000
Building	$95,000		Henry, capital	
Less accum. depr.	35,000	60,000	($43,000 – $3,000 + $23,000)	63,000
			Isaac, capital	
			($21,000 – $1,500 + $11,500)	31,000
Total assets		$238,000	Total liabilities and capital	$238,000

The books now carry the assets at current market value, which becomes the new book value, and the capital accounts have been adjusted accordingly. Isaac has a claim to $31,000 in partnership assets. How is his withdrawal from the business accounted for?

Withdrawal at Book Value

If Keith Isaac withdraws by receiving cash equal to the book value of his owner's equity, the entry will be

July 31	Isaac, Capital	31,000	
	Cash		31,000
	To record withdrawal of K. Isaac from the partnership.		

This entry records the payment of partnership cash to Isaac and the closing of his capital account upon his withdrawal from the business.

Withdrawal at Less Than Book Value

The withdrawing partner may be so eager to leave the business that he or she is willing to take less than his or her equity. This situation has occurred in real estate and oil-drilling partnerships. Assume that Keith Isaac withdraws from the business and agrees to receive partnership cash of $10,000 and the new partnership's note for $15,000. This $25,000 settlement is $6,000 less than Isaac's $31,000 equity in the business. The remaining partners share this $6,000 difference—which is a bonus to them—according to their profit-and-loss ratio. However, because Isaac has withdrawn from the partnership, a new agreement—and a new profit-and-loss ratio—must be drawn up. In forming a new partnership, Henry and Green may decide on any ratio that they see fit. Let's assume they agree that Henry will earn two-thirds of partnership profits and losses and Green one-third. The entry to record Isaac's withdrawal at less than book value is

July 31	Isaac, Capital	31,000	
	Cash		10,000
	Note Payable to K. Isaac		15,000
	Green, Capital ($6,000 × ⅓)		2,000
	Henry, Capital ($6,000 × ⅔)		4,000
	To record withdrawal of K. Isaac from the partnership.		

Isaac's account is closed, and Henry and Green may or may not continue the business.

Withdrawal at More Than Book Value

The settlement with a withdrawing partner may allow him or her to take assets of greater value than the book value of that partner's capital. Also, the remaining partners may be so eager for the withdrawing partner to leave the firm that they pay him or her a bonus to withdraw. In either case, the partner's withdrawal causes a decrease in the remaining partners' book equity. This decrease is allocated to the remaining partners on the basis of their profit-and-loss ratio.

The accounting for this situation follows the pattern illustrated for withdrawal at less than book value—with one exception. The remaining partners' capital accounts are debited because the withdrawing partner receives more than his or her book equity.

Death of a Partner

Like any other form of partnership withdrawal, the death of a partner dissolves a partnership. The partnership accounts are adjusted to measure net income or loss for the fraction of the year up to the date of death, then closed to determine the partners' capital balances on that date. Settlement with the deceased partner's estate is based on the partnership agreement. The estate commonly receives partnership assets equal to the partner's capital balance. The partnership closes the deceased partner's capital account with a debit. This entry credits a payable to the estate.

Alternatively, a remaining partner may purchase the deceased partner's equity. The deceased partner's equity is debited, and the purchaser's equity is credited. The amount of this entry is the ending credit balance in the deceased partner's capital account.

Liquidation of a Partnership

Admission of a new partner or withdrawal or death of an existing partner dissolves the partnership. However, the business may continue operating with no perceived change to outsiders such as customers and creditors. Business **liquidation,** however, is the process of going out of business by selling the entity's assets and paying its liabilities. The final step in liquidation of a business is the *distribution of the remaining cash to the owners.* Before the business is liquidated, its books should be adjusted and closed. After closing, only asset, liability, and partners' capital accounts remain open.

Liquidation of a partnership includes three basic steps:

1. Sell the assets. Allocate the gain or loss to the partners' capital accounts on the basis of the profit-and-loss ratio.
2. Pay the partnership liabilities.
3. Disburse the remaining cash to the partners on the basis of their capital balances.

In practice, the liquidation of a business can stretch over weeks or months. Selling every asset and paying every liability of the entity takes time. After the 80 partners of **Shea & Gould,** one of New York's best-known law firms, voted to dissolve their partnership in January 1994, the firm remained open for an extra year to collect bills and pay off liabilities.

To avoid excessive detail in our illustrations, we include only two asset categories—Cash and Noncash Assets—and a single liability category—Liabilities.

Our examples assume that the business sells the noncash assets in a single transaction and pays the liabilities in a single transaction.

Assume that Jane Aviron, Elaine Bloch, and Mark Crane have shared profits and losses in the ratio of 3:1:1. (This is equal to a 3/5, 1/5, 1/5 ratio, or a 60%, 20%, 20% sharing ratio.) They decide to liquidate their partnership. After the books are adjusted and closed, the ledger contains the following balances:

Cash	$ 10,000	Liabilities	$ 30,000
Noncash assets	90,000	Aviron, capital	40,000
		Bloch, capital	20,000
		Crane, capital	10,000
Total assets	$100,000	Total liabilities and capital	$100,000

Sale of Noncash Assets at a Gain

Assume that the Aviron, Bloch, and Crane partnership sells its noncash assets (shown on the balance sheet at $90,000) for cash of $150,000. The partnership realizes a gain of $60,000, which is allocated to the partners on the basis of their profit-and-loss-sharing ratio. The entry to record this sale and allocation of the gain is

Oct. 31	Cash	150,000	
	Noncash Assets		90,000
	Aviron, Capital ($60,000 × 0.60)		36,000
	Bloch, Capital ($60,000 × 0.20)		12,000
	Crane, Capital ($60,000 × 0.20)		12,000
	To sell noncash assets in liquidation and allocate gain to partners.		

The partnership must next pay off its liabilities:

Oct. 31	Liabilities	30,000	
	Cash		30,000
	To pay liabilities in liquidation.		

In the final liquidation transaction, the remaining cash is disbursed to the partners. *The partners share in the cash according to their capital balances.* (In contrast, *gains and losses* on the sale of assets are shared by the partners on the basis of their profit-and-loss-sharing ratio.) The amount of cash left in the partnership is $130,000—the $10,000 beginning balance plus the $150,000 cash sale of assets minus the $30,000 cash payment of liabilities. The partners divide the remaining cash according to their capital balances:

Oct. 31	Aviron, Capital ($40,000 + $36,000)	76,000	
	Bloch, Capital ($20,000 + $12,000)	32,000	
	Crane, Capital ($10,000 + $12,000)	22,000	
	Cash		130,000
	To disburse cash to partners in liquidation.		

A convenient way to summarize the transactions in a partnership liquidation is given in Exhibit D-2.

After the disbursement of cash to the partners, the business has no assets, liabilities, or owners' equity. All the balances are zero. By the accounting equation, partnership assets *must* equal partnership liabilities plus partnership capital.

STOP & THINK The liquidation of the Dirk & Cross partnership included the sale of assets at a $150,000 loss. Lorraine Dirk's Capital balance of $45,000 was less than her $60,000 share of the loss. Allocation of losses to the partners created a $15,000 deficit (debit balance) in Dirk's Capital account. Identify two ways that the partnership could deal with the negative balance (a capital deficiency) in Dirk's Capital account.

	Cash	+	Noncash Assets	=	Liabilities	+	Capital: Aviron (60%)	+	Capital: Bloch (20%)	+	Capital: Crane (20%)
Balance before sale of assets	$ 10,000		$90,000		$30,000		$40,000		$20,000		$10,000
Sale of assets and sharing of gain	150,000		(90,000)				36,000		12,000		12,000
Balances	160,000		-0-		30,000		76,000		32,000		22,000
Payment of liabilities	(30,000)				(30,000)						
Balances	130,000		-0-		-0-		76,000		32,000		22,000
Disbursement of cash to partners	(130,000)						(76,000)		(32,000)		(22,000)
Balances	$ -0-		$ -0-		$ -0-		$ -0-		$ -0-		$ -0-

EXHIBIT D-2
Partnership Liquidation—Sale of Assets at a Gain

Answer: Two possibilities are

1. Dirk could contribute assets to the partnership in an amount equal to her capital deficiency.
2. Joseph Cross, Lorraine Dirk's partner, could absorb Dirk's capital deficiency by decreasing his own capital balance.

Partnership Financial Statements

Partnership financial statements are much like those of a proprietorship. However, a partnership income statement includes a section showing the division of net income to the partners. For example, the partnership of Leslie Gray and DeWayne Hayward might report its statements for the year ended December 31, 19X6, as shown in Panel A of Exhibit D-3. A proprietorship's statements are presented in Panel B for comparison.

EXHIBIT D-3
Financial Statements of a Partnership and a Proprietorship

PANEL A—Partnership

GRAY AND HAYWARD CONSULTING
Income Statement
For the Year Ended December 31, 19X6

Revenues		$ 460
Expenses		(270)
Net income		$ 190
Allocation of net income:		
To Gray	$114	
To Hayward	76	$ 190

GRAY AND HAYWARD CONSULTING
Statement of Owners' Equity
For the Year Ended December 31, 19X6

	Gray	Hayward
Capital, December 31, 19X5	$ 50	$ 40
Additional investments	10	—
Net income	114	76
Subtotal	174	116
Drawings	(72)	(48)
Capital, December 31, 19X6	$102	$ 68

PANEL B—Proprietorship

GRAY CONSULTING
Income Statement
For the Year Ended December 31, 19X6

Revenues	$ 460
Expenses	(270)
Net income	$ 190

GRAY CONSULTING
Statement of Owner's Equity
For the Year Ended December 31, 19X6

Capital, December 31, 19X5	$ 90
Additional investment	10
Net income	190
Subtotal	290
Drawings	(120)
Capital, December 31, 19X6	$170

(Continued)

(Continued)

GRAY AND HAYWARD CONSULTING Balance Sheet December 31, 19X6	
Assets	
Cash and other assets	$170
Owners' Equity	
Gray, capital	$102
Hayward, capital	68
Total capital	$170

GRAY CONSULTING Balance Sheet December 31, 19X6	
Assets	
Cash and other assets	$170
Owner's Equity	
Gray, capital	$170

Large partnerships may not find it feasible to report the net income of every partner. Instead, the firm may report the allocation of net income to active and retired partners and average earnings per partner. For example, Exhibit D-4 shows how the CPA firm Main Price & Anders reported its earnings.

EXHIBIT D-4
Reporting Net Income for a Large Partnership

MAIN PRICE & ANDERS Combined Statement of Earnings For the Year Ended August 31, 19X7	**(In thousands)**
Fees for professional services	$914,492
Earnings for the year	$297,880
Allocation of earnings:	
To partners active during the year—	
Resigned, retired, and deceased partners	$ 19,901
Partners active at year end	253,270
To retired and deceased partners—retirement and death benefits	8,310
Not allocated to partners—retained for specific partnership purposes	16,399
Earnings for the year	$297,880
Average earnings per partner active at year end (1,336 partners)	$ 223

ACCOUNTING VOCABULARY

articles of partnership *(p. 732).*
dissolution *(p. 732).*
general partnership *(p. 731).*
limited liability partnership (LLP) *(p. 731).*
limited partnership *(p. 731).*
liquidation *(p. 741).*
mutual agency *(p. 731).*
partnership *(p. 731).*
partnership agreement *(p. 732).*
S corporation *(p. 733).*
unlimited personal liability *(p. 732).*

EXERCISES

Recording a partner's investment

ED-1 Rebecca Stepanik has operated an apartment-location service as a proprietorship. She and Kristen Clem have decided to reorganize the business as a partnership. Stepanik's investment in the partnership consists of cash, $2,100; accounts receivable, $10,600, less allowance for uncollectibles, $800; office furniture, $2,700, less accumulated depreciation, $1,100; a small building, $55,000, less accumulated depreciation, $27,500; accounts payable, $3,300; and a note payable to the bank, $10,000.

To determine Stepanik's equity in the partnership, she and Clem hire an independent appraiser. This outside party provides the following market values of the assets and liabilities that Stepanik is contributing to the business: cash, accounts receivable, office furniture, accounts payable, and note payable (the same as Stepanik's book value); allowance for uncollectible accounts, $2,900; building, $71,000; and accrued expenses payable (including interest on the note payable), $1,200.

Required

Make the entry on the partnership books to record Stepanik's investment.

ED-2 Matt Looney and Dave Briseño form a partnership, investing $40,000 and $70,000, respectively. Determine their shares of net income or net loss for each of the following situations:

Computing partners' shares of net income and net loss

a. Net loss is $44,000, and the partners have no written partnership agreement.

b. Net income is $66,000, and the partnership agreement states that the partners share profits and losses on the basis of their capital contributions.

c. Net loss is $77,000, and the partnership agreement states that the partners share profits on the basis of their capital contributions.

ED-3 Clay Brown is admitted to a partnership. Prior to his admission, the partnership books show Bob Reitmeier's capital balance at $100,000 and Lisa Jayne's capital balance at $50,000. Compute each partner's equity on the books of the new partnership under the following plans:

Admitting a new partner

a. Brown pays $60,000 for Jayne's equity. Brown's payment is not an investment in the partnership but instead goes directly to Jayne.

b. Brown invests $50,000 to acquire a one-fourth interest in the partnership.

c. Brown invests $70,000 to acquire a one-fourth interest in the partnership.

ED-4 Make the partnership journal entry to record the admission of Brown under plans *a*, *b*, and *c* in Exercise D-3. Explanations are not required.

Recording the admission of a new partner

ED-5 After the books are closed, Allen & Bowden's partnership balance sheet reports capital of $60,000 for Allen and $70,000 for Bowden. Allen is withdrawing from the firm. The partners agree to write down (decrease) partnership assets by $40,000. They have shared profits and losses in the ratio of one-third to Allen and two-thirds to Bowden. If the partnership agreement states that a withdrawing partner will receive assets equal to the book value of his owner's equity, how much will Allen receive? Bowden will continue to operate the business as a proprietorship. What is Bowden's beginning capital on the proprietorship books?

Withdrawal of a partner

ED-6 The partnership of Lee, Molnari, and Nix is dissolving. Business assets, liabilities, and partners' capital balances prior to dissolution follow. The partners share profits and losses as follows: Kim Lee, 25%; Sandra Molnari, 55%; and Ray Nix, 20%.

Liquidation of a partnership

Required

1. Create a spreadsheet or solve manually—as directed by your instructor—to show the ending balances in all accounts after the noncash assets are sold for $145,000 and for $95,000. Determine the unknown amounts (noted by "?"):

	A	B	C	D	E	F
1			LEE, MOLNARI, AND NIX			
2			Sale of Noncash Assets			
3			(For $145,000)			
4						
5		Noncash		Lee	Molnari	Nix
6	Cash	Assets	Liabilities	Capital	Capital	Capital
7						
8	$ 6,000	$126,000	$77,000	$12,000	$37,000	$6,000
9	145,000	(126,000)		? †	?	?
10						
11	$151,000	$ -0-	$77,000	$?	$?	$?
12						
13						($A9–$B8) * .25
14			(For $95,000)			
15						
16						
17		Noncash		Lee	Molnari	Nix
18	Cash	Assets	Liabilities	Capital	Capital	Capital
19						
20	$ 6,000	$126,000	$77,000	$12,000	$37,000	$6,000
21	95,000	(126,000)		? ††	?	?
22						
23	$101,000	$ -0-	$77,000	$?	$?	$?
24						
						($A21–$B20) * .25

2. Identify two ways the partners can deal with the negative ending balance in Nix's capital account.

PROBLEMS

Writing a partnership agreement

PD-1 Dolores Sanchez and Leticia Gaitan are discussing the formation of a partnership to import dresses from Guatemala. Sanchez is especially artistic, so she will travel to Central America to buy merchandise. Gaitan is a super salesperson and has already lined up several large stores to which she can sell the dresses.

Required

Write a partnership agreement to cover all elements essential for the business to operate smoothly. Make up names, amounts, profit-and-loss-sharing percentages, and so on as needed.

Investments by partners

PD-2 Jo Ringle and Mel LeBlanc formed a partnership on March 15. The partners agreed to invest equal amounts of capital. LeBlanc invested his proprietorship's assets and liabilities (credit balances in parentheses):

	LeBlanc's Book Value	Current Market Value
Accounts receivable	$ 12,000	$12,000
Allowance for doubtful accounts	(740)	(1,360)
Inventory	43,850	31,220
Prepaid expenses	2,400	2,400
Store equipment	36,700	26,600
Accumulated depreciation	(9,200)	(-0-)
Accounts payable	(22,300)	(22,300)

On March 15, Ringle invested cash in an amount equal to the current market value of LeBlanc's partnership capital. The partners decided that LeBlanc would earn 70% of partnership profits because he would manage the business. Ringle agreed to accept 30% of profits. During the period ended December 31, the partnership earned $80,000. Ringle's drawings were $32,000, and LeBlanc's drawings were $36,000.

Required

1. Journalize the partners' initial investments.
2. Prepare the partnership balance sheet immediately after its formation on March 15.

Computing partners' shares of net income and net loss

PD-3 Robin Dewey, Kami Karlin, and Dean DeCastro have formed a partnership. Dewey invested $20,000; Karlin, $40,000; and DeCastro, $60,000. Dewey will manage the store, Karlin will work in the store three-quarters of the time, and DeCastro will not work in the business.

Required

1. Compute the partners' shares of profits and losses under each of the following plans.
   a. Net income is $87,000, and the articles of partnership do not specify how profits and losses are shared.
   b. Net loss is $47,000, and the partnership agreement allocates 45% of profits to Dewey, 35% to Karlin, and 20% to DeCastro. The agreement does not discuss the sharing of losses.
2. Revenues for the year ended September 30, 19X4, were $572,000, and expenses were $485,000. Under plan *a*, prepare the partnership income statement for the year.
3. How will what you learned in this problem help you manage a partnership?

Recording changes in partnership capital

PD-4 Airborne Systems is a partnership owned by three individuals. The partners share profits and losses in the ratio of 30% to Eve Koehn, 40% to Earl Neiman, and 30% to Ivana Marcus. At December 31, 19X6, the firm has the following balance sheet:

Cash		$ 25,000	Total liabilities	$103,000
Accounts receivable	$ 16,000			
Less allowance for uncollectibles	1,000	15,000		
Inventory		92,000	Koehn, capital	38,000
Equipment	130,000		Nieman, capital	49,000
Less accumulated depreciation	30,000	100,000	Marcus, capital	42,000
Total assets		$232,000	Total liabilities and capital	$232,000

Koehn withdraws from the partnership on this date.

Required

Record Koehn's withdrawal from the partnership under the following plans:

1. Koehn gives her interest in the business to Lynn Albelli, her cousin.
2. In personal transactions, Koehn sells her equity in the partnership to Matt Bullock and Shelley Jones, who each pay Koehn $15,000 for half her interest. Neiman and Marcus agree to accept Bullock and Jones as partners.
3. The partnership pays Koehn cash of $5,000 and gives her a note payable for the remainder of her book equity in settlement of her partnership interest.
4. Koehn receives cash of $20,000 and a note payable for $20,000 from the partnership.
5. The partners agree that the equipment is worth $150,000 and that accumulated depreciation should remain at $30,000. After the revaluation, the partnership settles with Koehn by giving her cash of $10,000 and inventory for the remainder of her book equity.

Liquidation of a partnership

PD-5 The partnership of Whitney, Kosse, & Itasca has experienced operating losses for three consecutive years. The partners, who have shared profits and losses in the ratio of Fran Whitney, 15%; Walt Kosse, 60%; and Emil Itasca, 25%, are considering the liquidation of the business. They ask you to analyze the effects of liquidation under various possibilities regarding the sale of the noncash assets. They present the following condensed partnership balance sheet at December 31, end of the current year:

Cash	$ 7,000	Liabilities	$ 63,000
Noncash assets	163,000	Whitney, capital	24,000
		Kosse, capital	66,000
		Itasca, capital	17,000
Total assets	$170,000	Total liabilities and capital	$170,000

Required

The noncash assets are sold for $175,000. Prepare a summary of liquidation transactions (as illustrated in Exhibit D-2).

APPENDIX E

Modern Accounting Information Systems: A Comparison of Computerized and Manual Accounting Systems

Computerized accounting systems have replaced manual systems in many organizations. As you read this appendix, observe the differences between a computerized system and a manual system.

Inputs into an accounting system are data from source documents, such as sales receipts, bank deposit slips, and fax orders. Inputs are usually grouped by type. For example, a firm would enter cash sale transactions separately from credit sales and purchase transactions.

Computerized accounting systems require that data inputs be arranged in specific formats. The system will not accept transactions that are missing dates, account numbers, or other critical information. Transactions for which debits do not equal credits are also rejected.

In a manual system, *processing* includes journalizing transactions, posting to the accounts, and preparing the financial statements. A computerized system also processes data but without the intermediate steps (journal, ledger, and trial balance).

See Chapters 2 and 3 for a review of these terms.

The *outputs* of an accounting system are the reports used for decision making, including the financial statements (income statement, balance sheet, statement of cash flows, and so on). Businesses make better decisions because of the reports their accounting systems produce. From the computer's point of view, a trial balance is also a report. But a manual system would treat the trial balance as a processing step leading to the statements. Exhibit E-1 diagrams the relationships among the components of a computerized accounting system.

EXHIBIT E-1
Overview of a Computerized Accounting System

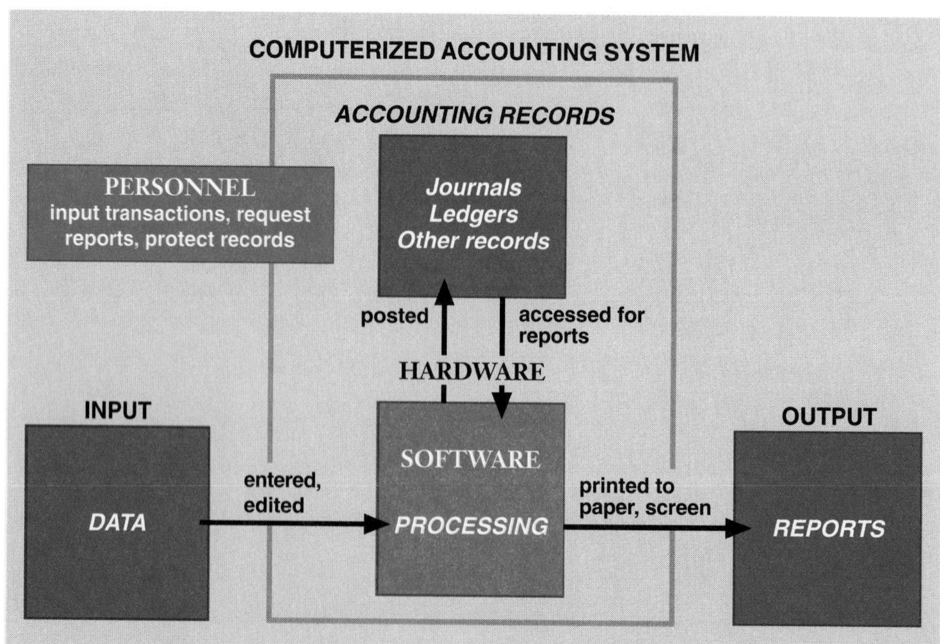

In a computerized accounting system, the software controls how the hardware operates. Input enters the system, subject to editing for the balancing of debits and credits, numerical limits, and so on. The computer then accesses the accounting records, or files, and updates (posts) to them. Reports are displayed on the screen and printed in response to operator command. All steps are under the control of the software and the operator (accountant).

Accounting Systems Design: The Chart of Accounts

Design of the accounting system begins with the chart of accounts. It is efficient to represent a complex account title, such as Accumulated Depreciation—Photographic Equipment, with a concise account number (for example, 16570).

We saw the chart of accounts in Chapter 2, page 77.

Recall that asset accounts generally begin with the digit 1, liabilities with the digit 2, owner equity accounts with the digit 3, revenues with 4, and expenses with 5. Exhibit E-2 diagrams one structure for computerized accounts. Assets are divided into current assets, fixed assets (property, plant, and equipment), and other assets. Among the current assets, we illustrate only three general ledger accounts: Cash in Bank (Account No. 111), Accounts Receivable (No. 112), and Prepaid Insurance (No. 115). Accounts Receivable holds the *total* dollar amount receivable from all customers. To ensure collection and follow-up, companies also keep records of the amount receivable from each customer. (We discuss the individual customer records in Appendix F.)

The account numbers in Exhibit E-2 get more detailed as we move from top to bottom. For example, Customer A's account number is 1120001, in which 112 represents Accounts Receivable and 0001 refers to Customer A.

The choice of number groups for account categories is not as critical in a manual system as it is in a computerized system, except for the ease of looking up accounts in the accounting records. But computerized accounting systems rely on *number ranges* to translate accounts and their balances into properly organized financial statements and other reports. For example, the accounts numbered 101–399 (assets, liabilities, and owner equity) are sorted to the balance sheet; the accounts numbered 401–599 (revenues and expenses) go to the income statement.

Classifying Transactions

Recording transactions in an accounting system requires an additional step that we have skipped thus far. A business of any size must *classify* transactions by type for efficient handling. In a manual system, credit sales, purchases on account, cash receipts, and cash payments are treated as four separate categories,

EXHIBIT E-2
Structure for Computerized Accounts

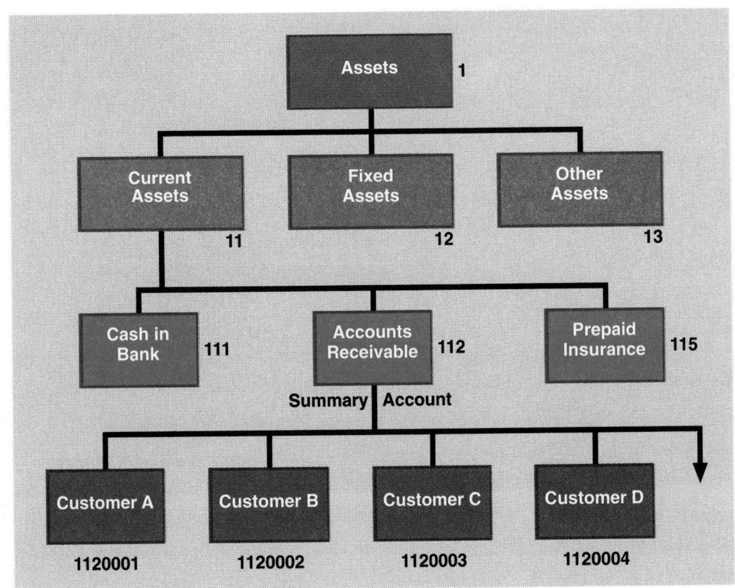

with each type entered into its own special journal. For example, credit sales are recorded in a special journal called a *sales journal.* Cash receipts are entered into a *cash receipts journal,* and so on. Transactions that do not fit any of the special journals, such as the adjusting entries at the end of the period, are recorded in the general journal, which serves as the "journal of last resort." (For more details on special journals, see Appendix F.)

Computerized systems require a company to preclassify transactions. Suppose you are accruing salary expense (debit Salary Expense; credit Salary Payable). In a manual system, you record the data in the general journal and post to the general ledger. But there is no "set of books" in a computerized system. To record this entry, you choose the appropriate processing environment from a menu within the system software. A *menu* is a list of options for choosing computer functions.

Menu-Driven Accounting Systems

Computerized systems are organized by function, or task. Access to functions is arranged in terms of menus. In such a *menu-driven* system, you first access the most general group of functions, called the *main menu.* You then choose from one or more submenus until you finally reach the function you want. Most computerized systems have similar functions, but their menu structures differ.

Exhibit E-3 illustrates one type of menu structure. The top row of the exhibit shows the main menu. The computer operator (or accountant) has chosen the General option (short for General Ledger), as shown by the highlighting. This action opened a submenu of four items—Transactions, Posting, Account Maintenance, and Closing. The Transactions option was then chosen (highlighted).

Posting in a computerized system can be performed continuously as transactions are being recorded (**on-line processing**) or later for a group of similar transactions (**batch processing**). In either case, posting is automatic. Batch processing of accounting data allows accountants to check the entries for accuracy before posting them. In effect, the transaction data are "parked" in the computer to await posting, which simply updates the account balances.

Accounting Reports

Outputs—accounting reports—are the final stage of data processing. In a computerized system, the financial statements can be printed automatically. For example, the Reports option in the main menu gives the operator various report

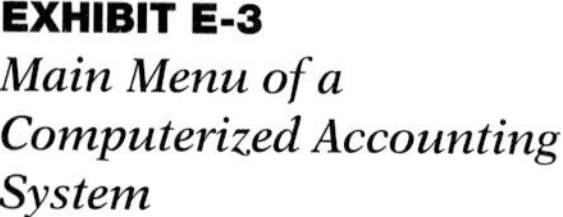

EXHIBIT E-3
Main Menu of a Computerized Accounting System

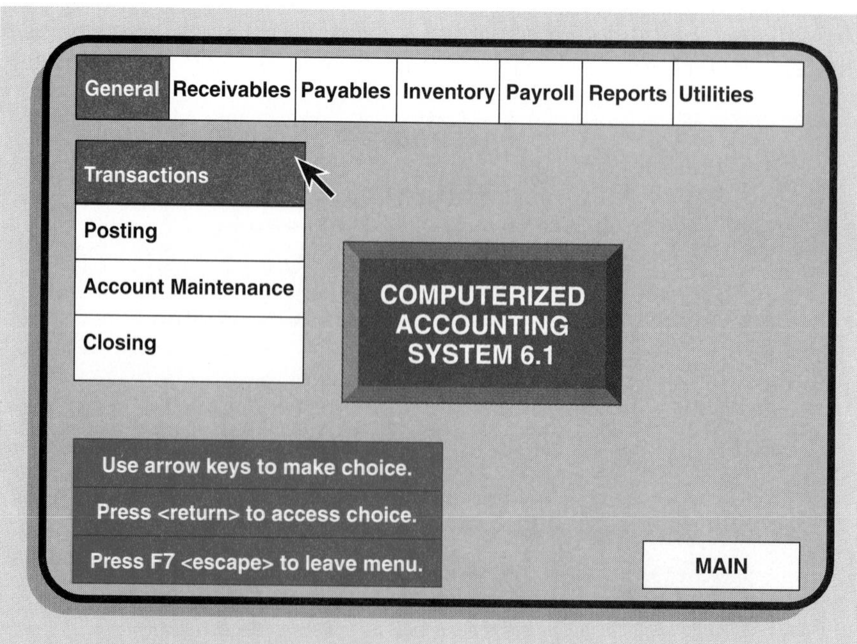

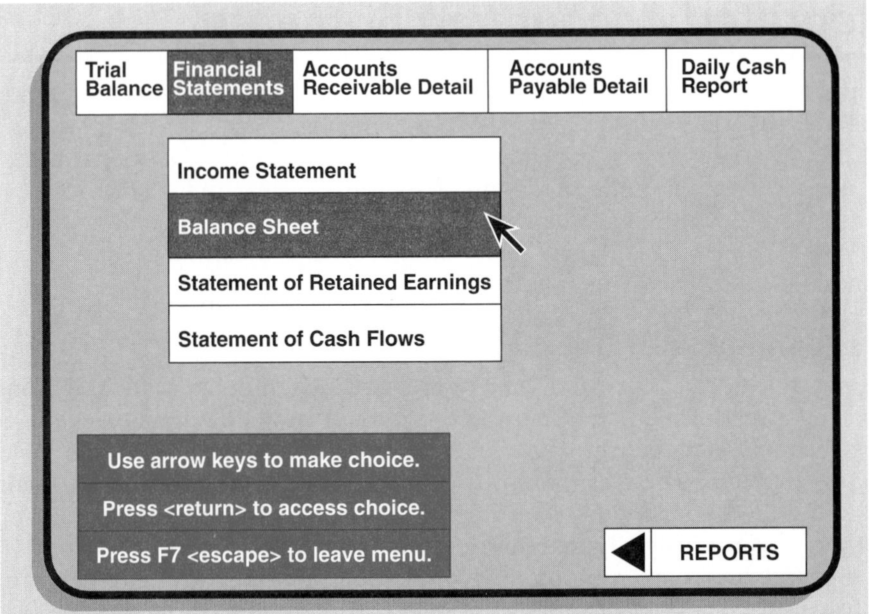

EXHIBIT E-4
Reports Submenu of a Computerized Accounting System

choices, which are expanded in the Reports submenu of Exhibit E-4. In the exhibit the operator is working with the financial statements, specifically the balance sheet, as shown by the highlighting.

STOP & THINK Why does every business need an accounting information system? Give several reasons.

Answer: Managers and owners of businesses must make decisions, and they need information to run the organization. The business's accounting system provides much of this information. Likewise, lenders and outside investors use accounting information in their lending and investment decisions. And most businesses are subject to some form of taxation. An accounting system provides tax information as well.

Summary of the Accounting Cycle: Computerized and Manual

Exhibit E-5 summarizes the accounting cycle in a computerized system and in a manual system. As you study the exhibit, compare and contrast the two types of systems.

EXHIBIT E-5
Comparison of the Accounting Cycle in a Computerized and a Manual System

Computerized System	Manual System
1. Start with the account balances in the ledger at the beginning of the period.	1. Same.
2. Analyze and classify business transactions by type. Access appropriate menus for data entry.	2. Analyze and journalize transactions as they occur.
3. Computer automatically posts transactions as a batch or when entered online.	3. Post journal entries to the ledger accounts.
4. The unadjusted balances are available immediately after each posting.	4. Compute the unadjusted balance in each account at the end of the period.
5. If needed, the trial balance can be accessed as a report.	5. Enter the trial balance on the work sheet, and complete the work sheet.
6. Enter and post adjusting entries. Print the financial statements. Run automatic closing procedure after backing up the period's accounting records.	6. Prepare the financial statements. Journalize and post the adjusting entries. Journalize and post the closing entries.
7. The next period's opening balances are created automatically as a result of closing.	7. Prepare the postclosing trial balance. This trial balance becomes step 1 for the next period.

Integrated Accounting Software

Computerized accounting packages are organized by **modules,** separate but integrated units—compatible units that function together. Changes affecting one module will affect others. For example, entry and posting of a sales transaction will update two modules: Accounts Receivable/Sales and Inventory/Cost of Goods Sold. Accounting packages, such as Business Works, Peachtree, DacEasy, One-Write Plus, and RealWorld Accounting, come as a complete set of accounting modules to form an integrated system.

Spreadsheets and Database Programs

You may have been preparing your homework assignments manually. Imagine preparing a work sheet for General Motors. Each adjustment changes the company's financial statement totals. Consider computing General Motors' revenue amounts by hand. The task would be overwhelming. For even a small business with only a few departments, the computations are tedious and time-consuming, and therefore expensive. Furthermore, errors are likely.

Spreadsheets are computer programs that link data by means of formulas and functions. These electronic work sheets were invented to automate budget updates. Spreadsheets are organized as a rectangular grid composed of hundreds or thousands of grid points called *cells,* each defined by a row number and a column number. A cell can contain words (called labels), numbers, or formulas (relationships among cells). The *cursor,* or electronic highlighter, indicates which cell is active. When the cursor is placed over any cell, information can be entered there for processing.

Exhibit E-6 shows a simple income statement on a spreadsheet screen. The words were entered in cells A1 through A4. The dollar amount of revenues was entered in cell B2 and expenses in cell B3. A formula was placed in cell B4 as follows: +B2–B3. This formula subtracts expenses from revenues to compute net income in cell B4. If revenues in cell B2 increase to $105,000, net income in B4 automatically increases to $45,000. No other cells will change.

EXHIBIT E-6
A Spreadsheet Screen

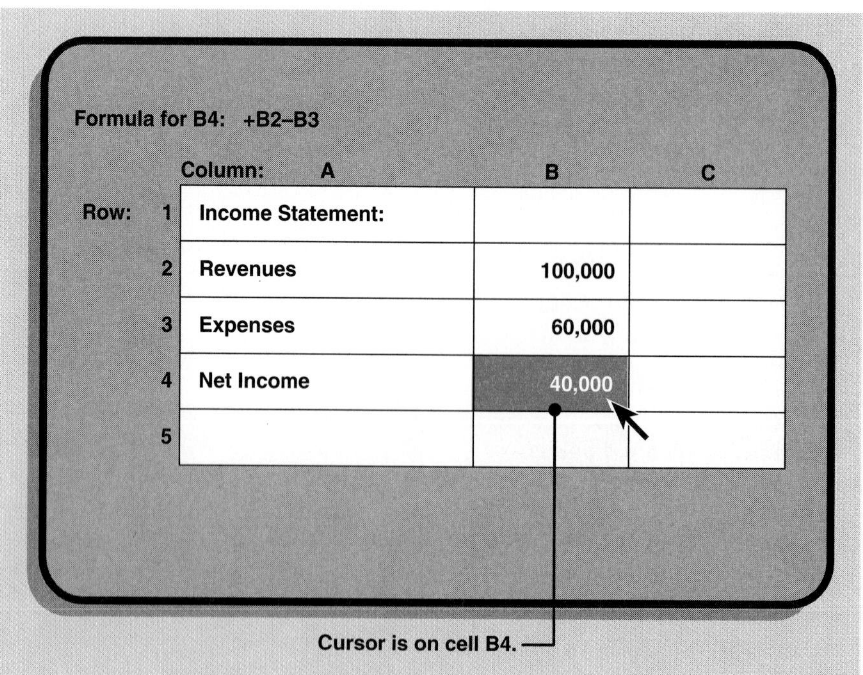

EXHIBIT E-7
Basic Arithmetic Operations in Spreadsheets

Operation	Symbol
Addition	+
Subtraction	–
Multiplication	*
Division	/
Addition of a range of cells	@SUM(beginning cell..ending cell) or =SUM(beginning cell:ending cell)
Examples:	
Add the contents of cells A2 through A9	@SUM(A2..A9)
Divide the contents of cell C2 by the contents of cell D1	+C2/D1

Spreadsheets are ideally suited to preparing a budget. Consider Procter & Gamble, whose Health-Care Sector has an annual advertising budget of $300–400 million. If Procter & Gamble adds $40–50 million for the development of its new Crest Complete toothbrush and $2 million for a new stand-up tube of Crest, its advertising expenses will increase. The company will also forecast an increase in sales revenue, cost of goods sold, and other expenses. A spreadsheet computes all these changes automatically in response to the increase in advertising. The spreadsheet lets Procter & Gamble's managers track the relative profitability of each product. Their budget can stay abreast of the latest developments. Armed with current data, the managers can make informed decisions.

We can add or delete whole rows and columns of data and move blocks of numbers and words on a spreadsheet. The power and versatility of spreadsheets are apparent when enormous amounts of data are entered on the spreadsheet with formula relationships. Change only one number, and save hours of manual recalculation. Exhibit E-7 shows the basic arithmetic operations in some popular spreadsheet programs such as Lotus 1–2–3.

Computerized accounting packages often come with the ability to export data to spreadsheets. For example, the western branch office of the B.F. Goodrich Company in Los Angeles may export a list of accounts receivable (thousands of customers and their balances) as a spreadsheet to the home office in Akron, Ohio. The spreadsheet can sort the B.F. Goodrich customers by name, size of balance, sales to the customer during the last quarter, and so on. Other software called **database programs** organize information so that it can be summarized in a variety of report formats. A database program can merge information from various sources to generate even more complex reports than spreadsheets can handle. Some of the common database programs are dBase, Access, and Paradox.

Overview of an Accounting Information System

The purpose of an accounting system is to provide information for decision making. The financial statements and other reports are used by managers, creditors, and others who evaluate the businesses. Each entity designs its accounting system to meet its own needs for information while keeping the cost of the system within its budget. Exhibit E-8 on page 754 diagrams a typical accounting system for a merchandising business.

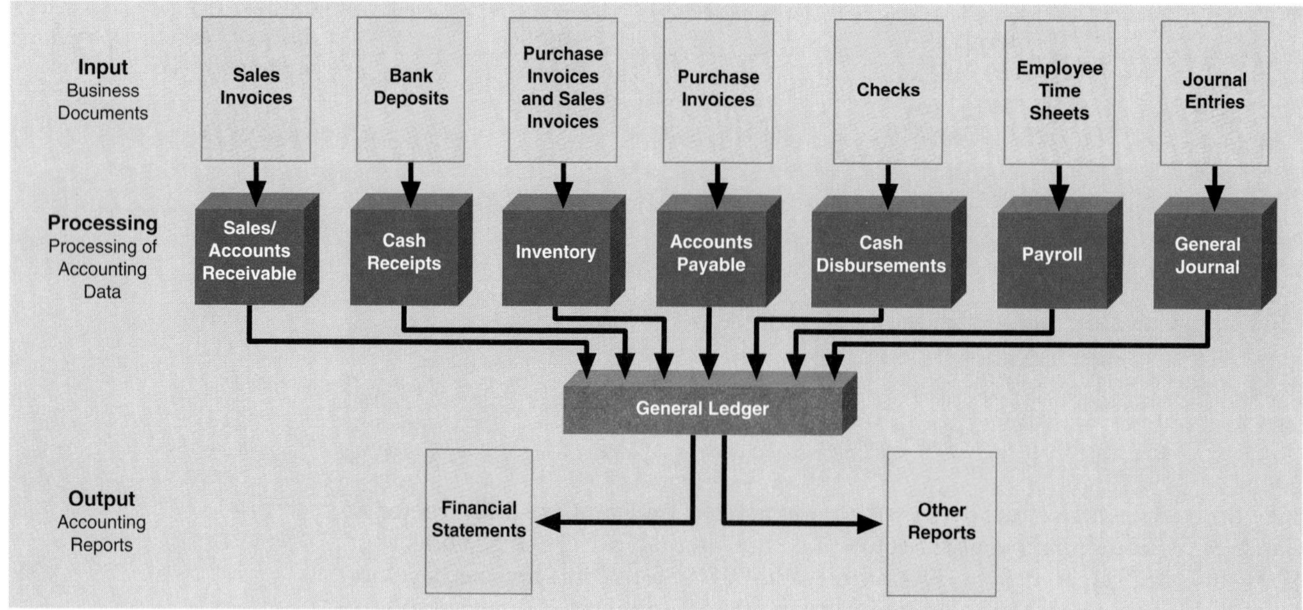

EXHIBIT E-8
Overview of an Accounting System

ACCOUNTING VOCABULARY

batch processing *(p. 750).*
database program *(p. 753).*
module *(p. 752).*
on-line processing *(p. 750).*
spreadsheet *(p. 752).*

APPENDIX F

Special Accounting Journals

The journal entries illustrated in this book have all been made in the general journal. The **general journal,** which we usually simply call "the journal," is used to record all transactions that do not fit one of the special journals. A **special journal** is an accounting journal designed to record one specific type of transaction, such as credit sales. Credit sales can be recorded in the special journal called the sales journal. In practice, it is inefficient to record all transactions in the general journal, so we use special journals.

For a review of journals, ledgers, and posting, see Chapter 2, pages 66–74.

Both manual systems and computerized systems must organize transaction entries by type. Special journals and accounting modules accomplish that task. In a computerized system, accountants do not enter transaction data directly into these journals. Instead, they input data through various modules, such as the Accounts Receivable module for credit sales. But the underlying accounting principles are the same in manual and computerized systems.

In all likelihood, you will be working with a computerized system. We would rather you *not* view the process as a black box. Thus, to help you understand the basic accounting, this appendix takes you through the steps in a manual system.

Most of a business's transactions fall into one of four categories. The four categories of transactions, the related special journal, and the posting abbreviations are as follows:

Transaction	Special Journal	Posting Abbreviation
1. Sale on account	Sales journal	S
2. Cash receipt	Cash receipts journal	C R
3. Purchase on account	Purchases journal	P
4. Cash disbursement	Cash disbursements journal	C D

Adjusting and closing entries are entered in the general journal. Its posting abbreviation is J.

Sales Journal

Most merchandisers sell at least some of their inventory on account. These *credit sales* are entered in the **sales journal.** Credit sales of assets other than inventory—for example, buildings—occur infrequently and are recorded in the general journal.

Exhibit F-1 on page 756 illustrates a sales journal (Panel A) and the related posting to the ledgers (Panel B) of Austin Sound Stereo Center. Each entry in the Accounts Receivable/Sales Revenue column of the sales journal in Exhibit F-1 is a debit (Dr.) to Accounts Receivable and a credit (Cr.) to Sales Revenue, as the heading above this column indicates. For each transaction, the accountant enters the date, invoice number, and customer account along with the transaction amount. This streamlined way of recording sales on account saves a vast amount of time that, in a manual system, would be spent entering account titles and dollar amounts in the general journal.

In recording credit sales in the text, we did not keep a record of the names of credit-sale customers. In practice, the business must know the amount receivable from each customer. How else can the company keep track of who owes it money, when payment is due—and how much?

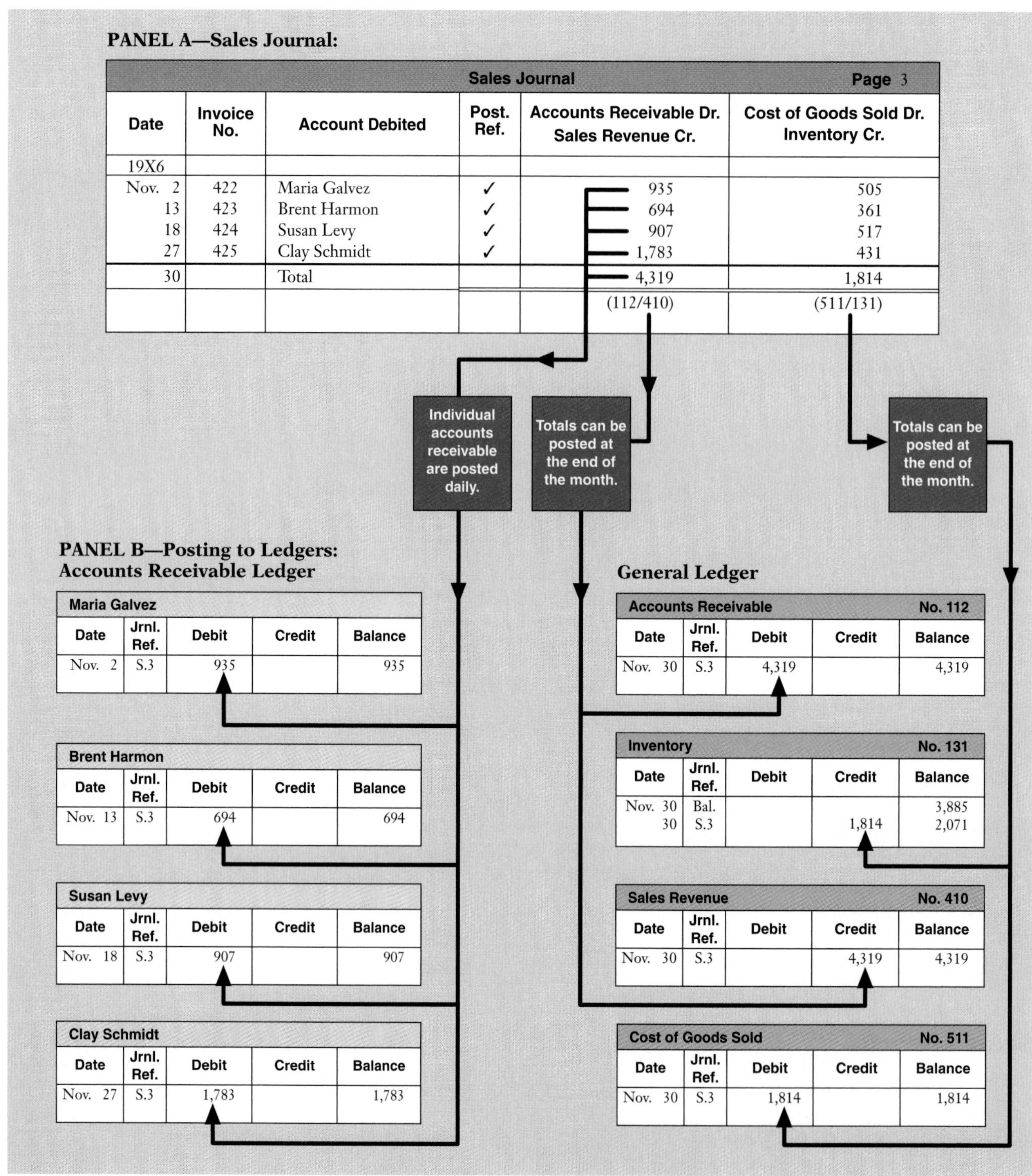

PANEL A—Sales Journal:

Sales Journal					Page 3
Date	Invoice No.	Account Debited	Post. Ref.	Accounts Receivable Dr. Sales Revenue Cr.	Cost of Goods Sold Dr. Inventory Cr.
19X6					
Nov. 2	422	Maria Galvez	✓	935	505
13	423	Brent Harmon	✓	694	361
18	424	Susan Levy	✓	907	517
27	425	Clay Schmidt	✓	1,783	431
30		Total		4,319	1,814
				(112/410)	(511/131)

PANEL B—Posting to Ledgers:
Accounts Receivable Ledger

Maria Galvez				
Date	Jrnl. Ref.	Debit	Credit	Balance
Nov. 2	S.3	935		935

Brent Harmon				
Date	Jrnl. Ref.	Debit	Credit	Balance
Nov. 13	S.3	694		694

Susan Levy				
Date	Jrnl. Ref.	Debit	Credit	Balance
Nov. 18	S.3	907		907

Clay Schmidt				
Date	Jrnl. Ref.	Debit	Credit	Balance
Nov. 27	S.3	1,783		1,783

General Ledger

Accounts Receivable				No. 112
Date	Jrnl. Ref.	Debit	Credit	Balance
Nov. 30	S.3	4,319		4,319

Inventory				No. 131
Date	Jrnl. Ref.	Debit	Credit	Balance
Nov. 30	Bal.			3,885
30	S.3		1,814	2,071

Sales Revenue				No. 410
Date	Jrnl. Ref.	Debit	Credit	Balance
Nov. 30	S.3		4,319	4,319

Cost of Goods Sold				No. 511
Date	Jrnl. Ref.	Debit	Credit	Balance
Nov. 30	S.3	1,814		1,814

EXHIBIT F-1
Sales Journal and Posting to Ledgers for Austin Sound

Consider the first transaction in Panel A. On November 2, Austin Sound sold stereo equipment on account to Maria Galvez for $935. The invoice number is 422. All this information appears on a single line in the sales journal. No explanation is necessary. The transaction's presence in the sales journal means that it is a credit sale (debited to Accounts Receivable, Maria Galvez) and credited to Sales Revenue. To gain additional information about the transaction, we would look up the actual invoice.

In a computerized system, accountants do not enter credit sales in a sales journal. The transaction data may be input through point-of-sales terminals, as in a **Sears** or **JC Penney** store. When managers wish to review credit sales, they can print a report that resembles the sales journal. The report may show the date and amount of each transaction, the invoice number, and the customer name. The other special journals discussed in this appendix are similar to the reports generated by a computerized system.

Austin Sound uses a *perpetual* inventory system. At the time of recording the sale, Austin Sound also records the cost of the goods sold and the decrease in inventory. Many computerized accounting systems are programmed to read both the sales amount (from the bar code on the package of the item sold) and the cost of goods sold. A separate column of the sales journal holds the cost of goods sold and inventory amount—$505 for the sale to Maria Galvez. If Austin Sound used a *periodic* inventory system, it would not record cost of goods sold and the decrease in inventory at the time of sale. The sales journal would need only one column to debit Accounts Receivable and to credit Sales Revenue for the amount of the sale.

POSTING TO THE GENERAL LEDGER The ledger we have used so far is the **general ledger,** which holds the accounts reported in the financial statements. We will soon introduce other ledgers.

Posting from the sales journal to the general ledger can be done *monthly.* In Exhibit F-1 (Panel A), the total credit sales for November are $4,319. This column has two headings, Accounts Receivable and Sales Revenue. When the $4,319 is posted to these accounts in the general ledger, their account numbers are written beneath the total in the sales journal. In Panel B of Exhibit F-1, the account number for Accounts Receivable is 112, and the account number for Sales Revenue is 410. These account numbers are entered beneath the credit sales total in the sales journal to signify that the $4,319 has been posted to the two accounts.

The debit to Cost of Goods Sold and the credit to Inventory for the monthly total of $1,814 can also be posted at the end of the month. After posting, these accounts' numbers are entered beneath the total to show that Cost of Goods Sold and Inventory have been updated.

POSTING TO THE SUBSIDIARY LEDGER The $4,319 sum of the November debits to Accounts Receivable does not identify the amount receivable from any specific customer. Most businesses would find it unmanageable to keep a separate Accounts Receivable account in the general ledger for each customer. A business may have thousands of customers. Consider the **Consumers Digest Company,** a Chicago-based firm that publishes the bimonthly magazine *Consumers Digest.* The Consumers Digest Company has a customer account for each subscriber.

To streamline operations, businesses place the accounts of their individual credit customers in a subsidiary ledger, called the Accounts Receivable ledger. A **subsidiary ledger** is a book of accounts that provides supporting details on individual balances, the total of which appears in a general ledger account. The customer accounts are arranged in alphabetical order.

We saw subsidiary ledgers in Chapter 5, page 229.

Amounts in the sales journal are posted to the subsidiary ledger *daily* to keep a current record of the amount receivable from each customer. The amounts are debits. Daily posting allows the business to answer customer inquiries promptly. Suppose Maria Galvez telephones Austin Sound on November 11 to ask how much money she owes. The subsidiary ledger readily provides that information.

When each transaction amount is posted to the subsidiary ledger, a check mark or some other notation is entered in the posting reference column of the sales journal.

JOURNAL REFERENCES IN THE LEDGERS When amounts are posted to the ledgers, the journal page number is printed in the account to identify the source of the data. All transaction data in Exhibit F-1 originated on page 3 of the sales journal, so all journal references in the ledger accounts are S.3. The "S." indicates sales journal.

Trace all the postings in Exhibit F-1. The most effective way to learn about accounting systems and special journals is to study the flow of data. The arrows indicate the direction of the information. The arrows also show the links between the individual customer accounts in the subsidiary ledger and the Accounts Receivable account. These links are summarized as follows:

Accounts Receivable debit balance	$4,319
Customer Accounts Receivable	
Customer	**Balance**
Maria Galvez	$ 935
Brent Harmon	694
Susan Levy	907
Clay Schmidt	1,783
Total accounts receivable	$4,319

Accounts Receivable in the general ledger is a **control account,** an account whose balance equals the sum of the balances of a group of related accounts in a subsidiary ledger. The individual customer accounts are subsidiary accounts. They are "controlled" by the Accounts Receivable account in the general ledger.

STOP & THINK Suppose Austin Sound had 400 credit sales for the month. How many postings to the general ledger would be made from the sales journal? (Ignore Cost of Goods Sold and Inventory.) How many would there be if all sales transactions were routed through the general journal?

Answer: There are only two postings from the sales journal to the general ledger: one to Accounts Receivable and one to Sales Revenue. There would be 800 postings from the general journal: 400 to Accounts Receivable and 400 to Sales Revenue. This difference clearly shows the benefit of using a sales journal.

Additional data can be recorded in the sales journal. For example, a company may add a column to record sales terms, such as 2/10 n/30. The design of the journal depends on managers' needs for information.

For a review of sales discounts, see Chapter 4, page 189, and Chapter 6, page 315.

Cash Receipts Journal

Cash transactions are common in most businesses because cash receipts from customers are the lifeblood of business. To record cash receipt transactions, accountants use the **cash receipts journal.**

Exhibit F-2, Panel A, illustrates the cash receipts journal. The related posting to the general and subsidiary ledgers is shown in Panel B. The exhibit illustrates November transactions for Austin Sound Stereo Center.

Every transaction recorded in this journal is a cash receipt, so the first column is for debits to the Cash account. The next column is for debits to Sales Discounts on collections from customers. In a typical merchandising business, the main sources of cash are collections on account and cash sales. Thus, the cash receipts journal has credit columns for Accounts Receivable and Sales Revenue. The journal also has a credit column for Other Accounts, which lists sources of cash other than cash sales and collections on account. This Other Accounts column is also used to record the names of customers from whom cash is received on account.

In Exhibit F-2, cash sales occurred on November 6, 19, and 28. Observe the debits to Cash and the credits to Sales Revenue ($517, $853, and $1,802). Each sale entry is accompanied by an entry that debits Cost of Goods Sold and credits Inventory for the cost of the merchandise sold. The column for this entry is at the far right side of the cash receipts journal. Some companies may record this entry separately.

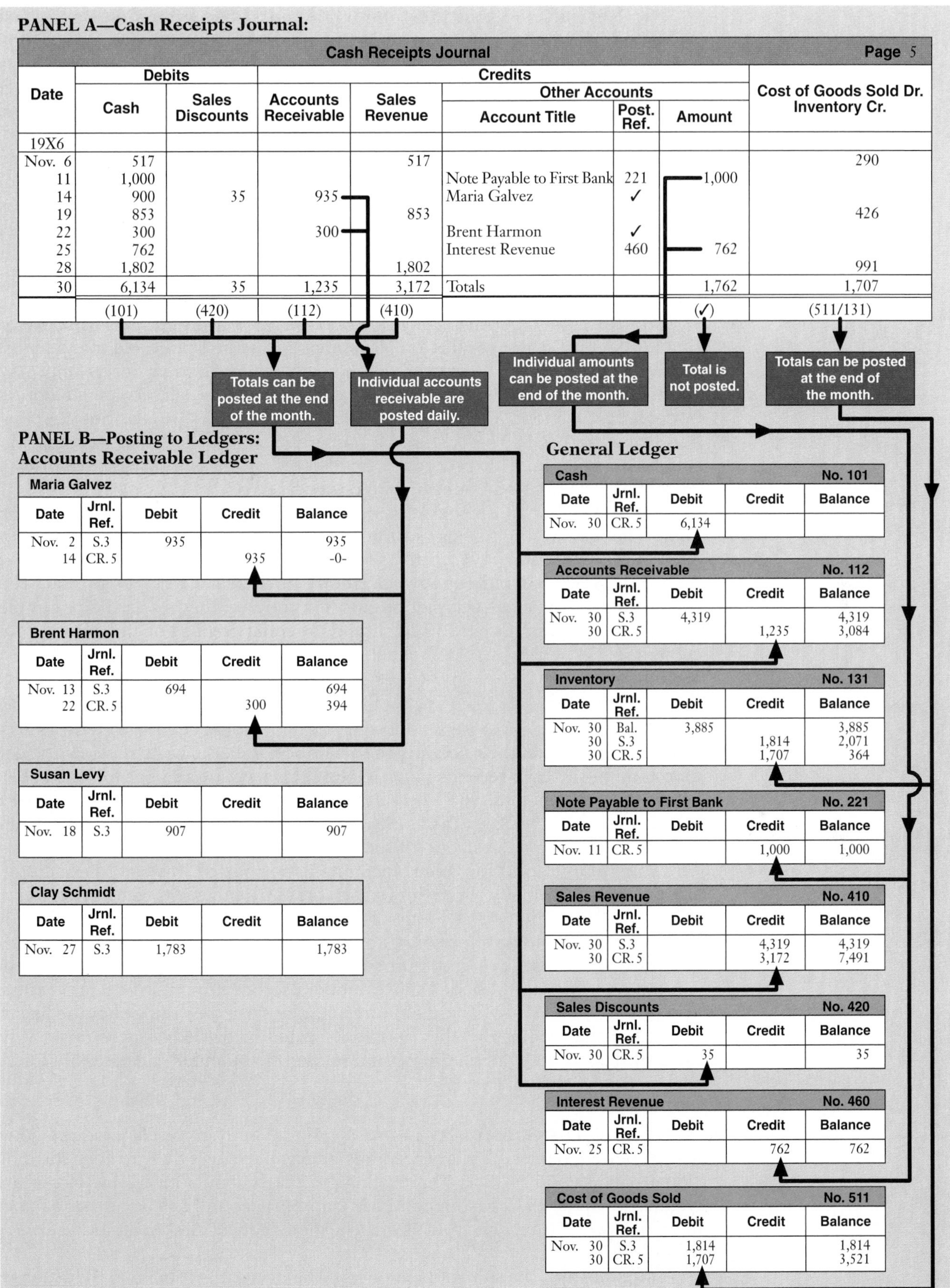

PANEL A—Cash Receipts Journal:

Cash Receipts Journal								Page 5
	Debits		Credits					
					Other Accounts			
Date	Cash	Sales Discounts	Accounts Receivable	Sales Revenue	Account Title	Post. Ref.	Amount	Cost of Goods Sold Dr. Inventory Cr.
19X6								
Nov. 6	517			517				290
11	1,000				Note Payable to First Bank	221	1,000	
14	900	35	935		Maria Galvez	✓		
19	853			853				426
22	300		300		Brent Harmon	✓		
25	762				Interest Revenue	460	762	
28	1,802			1,802				991
30	6,134	35	1,235	3,172	Totals		1,762	1,707
	(101)	(420)	(112)	(410)			(✓)	(511/131)

PANEL B—Posting to Ledgers:
Accounts Receivable Ledger

Maria Galvez				
Date	Jrnl. Ref.	Debit	Credit	Balance
Nov. 2	S.3	935		935
14	CR. 5		935	-0-

Brent Harmon				
Date	Jrnl. Ref.	Debit	Credit	Balance
Nov. 13	S.3	694		694
22	CR. 5		300	394

Susan Levy				
Date	Jrnl. Ref.	Debit	Credit	Balance
Nov. 18	S.3	907		907

Clay Schmidt				
Date	Jrnl. Ref.	Debit	Credit	Balance
Nov. 27	S.3	1,783		1,783

General Ledger

Cash				No. 101
Date	Jrnl. Ref.	Debit	Credit	Balance
Nov. 30	CR. 5	6,134		

Accounts Receivable				No. 112
Date	Jrnl. Ref.	Debit	Credit	Balance
Nov. 30	S.3	4,319		4,319
30	CR. 5		1,235	3,084

Inventory				No. 131
Date	Jrnl. Ref.	Debit	Credit	Balance
Nov. 30	Bal.	3,885		3,885
30	S.3		1,814	2,071
30	CR. 5		1,707	364

Note Payable to First Bank				No. 221
Date	Jrnl. Ref.	Debit	Credit	Balance
Nov. 11	CR. 5		1,000	1,000

Sales Revenue				No. 410
Date	Jrnl. Ref.	Debit	Credit	Balance
Nov. 30	S.3		4,319	4,319
30	CR. 5		3,172	7,491

Sales Discounts				No. 420
Date	Jrnl. Ref.	Debit	Credit	Balance
Nov. 30	CR. 5	35		35

Interest Revenue				No. 460
Date	Jrnl. Ref.	Debit	Credit	Balance
Nov. 25	CR. 5		762	762

Cost of Goods Sold				No. 511
Date	Jrnl. Ref.	Debit	Credit	Balance
Nov. 30	S.3	1,814		1,814
30	CR. 5	1,707		3,521

EXHIBIT F-2
Cash Receipts Journal and Posting to Ledgers for Austin Sound

On November 11, Austin Sound borrowed $1,000 from First Bank. Cash is debited, and Note Payable to First Bank is credited in the Other Accounts column because no specific credit column is set up to account for borrowings. For this transaction, it is necessary to print the account title, Note Payable to First Bank, in the Other Accounts/Account Title column to record the source of cash.

On November 25, Austin Sound collected $762 of interest revenue. The account credited, Interest Revenue, would be printed in the Other Accounts column. The November 11 and 25 transactions illustrate a key fact about business. Different entities have different types of transactions; they design their special journals to meet their particular needs for information. In this case, the Other Accounts credit column is the catchall used to record all nonroutine cash receipt transactions.

On November 14, Austin Sound collected $900 from Maria Galvez. Referring to Exhibit F-1, we see that on November 2, Austin Sound sold merchandise for $935 to Galvez. The terms of sale allowed a $35 discount for prompt payment, and she paid within the discount period. Austin's cash receipt is recorded by debiting Cash for $900 and Sales Discounts for $35 and by crediting Accounts Receivable for $935. The customer's name appears in the Other Accounts/Account Title column. This procedure enables the business to keep track of each customer's account in the subsidiary ledger.

On November 22, the business collected $300 on account from Brent Harmon, who was paying for part of the November 13 purchase. No discount applied to this collection.

Total debits should equal total credits in the cash receipts journal. This equality holds for each transaction and for the monthly totals. For example, the first transaction has a $517 debit and an equal credit. For the month, total debits ($6,134 + $35 = $6,169) equal total credits ($1,235 + $3,172 + $1,762 = $6,169).

Posting to the General Ledger The column totals can be posted monthly. To indicate their posting, the account number is written below the column total in the cash receipts journal. Note the account number for Cash (101) below the column total $6,134, and trace the posting to Cash in the general ledger. Likewise, the Sales Discounts, Accounts Receivable, and Sales Revenue column totals are also posted to the general ledger.

The column total for Other Accounts is not posted. Instead, these credits are posted individually. In Exhibit F-2, the November 11 transaction reads "Note Payable to First Bank." This account's number (221) in the Post. Ref. column indicates that the transaction amount was posted individually. The checkmark instead of an account number below the column indicates that the column total was not posted. The November 25 collection of interest revenue is also posted individually. These amounts can be posted to the general ledger at the end of the month. But they should be dated in the ledger accounts on the basis of their actual date in the journal so that the amounts can be easily traced back to the journal.

Posting to the Subsidiary Ledger Amounts from the cash receipts journal are posted to the subsidiary accounts receivable ledger daily to keep the individual balances up to date. The postings to the accounts receivable ledger are credits. Trace the $935 posting to Maria Galvez's account. It reduces her balance to zero. The $300 receipt from Brent Harmon reduces his accounts receivable balance to $394.

After posting, the sum of the individual balances that remain in the accounts receivable subsidiary ledger equals the general ledger balance in Accounts Receivable ($3,084). Austin Sound may prepare a November 30 list of account balances from the subsidiary ledger to follow up on slow-paying customers:

Customer Accounts Receivable	
Customer	Balance
Brent Harmon	$ 394
Susan Levy	907
Clay Schmidt	1,783
Total accounts receivable	$3,084

Good accounts receivable records help a business manage its cash.

Purchases Journal

A merchandising business purchases inventory and supplies frequently. Such purchases are usually made on account. The **purchases journal** is designed to account for all purchases of inventory, supplies, and other assets *on account.* It can also be used to record expenses incurred on account. Cash purchases are recorded in the cash disbursements journal.

Exhibit F-3 on page 762 illustrates Austin Sound's purchases journal (Panel A) and posting to the general and subsidiary ledgers (Panel B). This purchases journal has columns for credits to Accounts Payable and debits to Inventory, Supplies, and Other Accounts.[1] A periodic inventory system would replace the Inventory column with a column titled "Purchases." The Other Accounts columns accommodate purchases of items other than inventory and supplies. Each business designs its journals to meet its own needs for information and efficiency. Accounts Payable is credited for all transactions recorded in the purchases journal.

On November 2, Austin Sound purchased from JVC Corporation stereo inventory costing $700. The creditor's name (JVC Corporation) is entered in the Account Credited column. The purchase terms of 3/15 n/30 are also printed to help identify the due date and the discount available. Accounts Payable is credited and Inventory is debited for the transaction amount. On November 19, a credit purchase of supplies is entered as a debit to Supplies and a credit to Accounts Payable.

Note the November 9 purchase of fixtures from City Office Supply. The purchases journal contains no column for fixtures, so the Other Accounts debit column is used. Because this was a credit purchase, the accountant enters the creditor name (City Office Supply) in the Account Credited column and Fixtures in the Other Accounts/Account Title column.

The total credits in the purchases journal ($2,876) equal the total debits ($1,706 + $103 + $1,067 = $2,876). This equality proves the accuracy of the entries in the purchases journal.

To pay debts efficiently, a company must know how much it owes particular creditors. The Accounts Payable account in the general ledger shows only a single total, however, and therefore does not indicate the amount owed to each creditor. Companies keep an accounts payable subsidiary ledger. The accounts payable subsidiary ledger lists the creditors in alphabetical order, along with the amounts owed to them. Exhibit F-3, Panel B, shows Austin Sound's accounts payable subsidiary ledger, which includes accounts for Audio Electronics, City Office Supply, and others. After posting, the total of the individual balances in the subsidiary ledger equals the balance in the Accounts Payable control account in the general ledger.

POSTING FROM THE PURCHASES JOURNAL Posting from the purchases journal is similar to posting from the sales journal and the cash receipts journal. Exhibit F-3, Panel B, illustrates the posting process.

[1]This is the only special journal that we illustrate with the credit column placed to the left and the debit columns to the right. This arrangement of columns focuses on Accounts Payable, which is credited for each entry to this journal, and on the individual supplier to be paid.

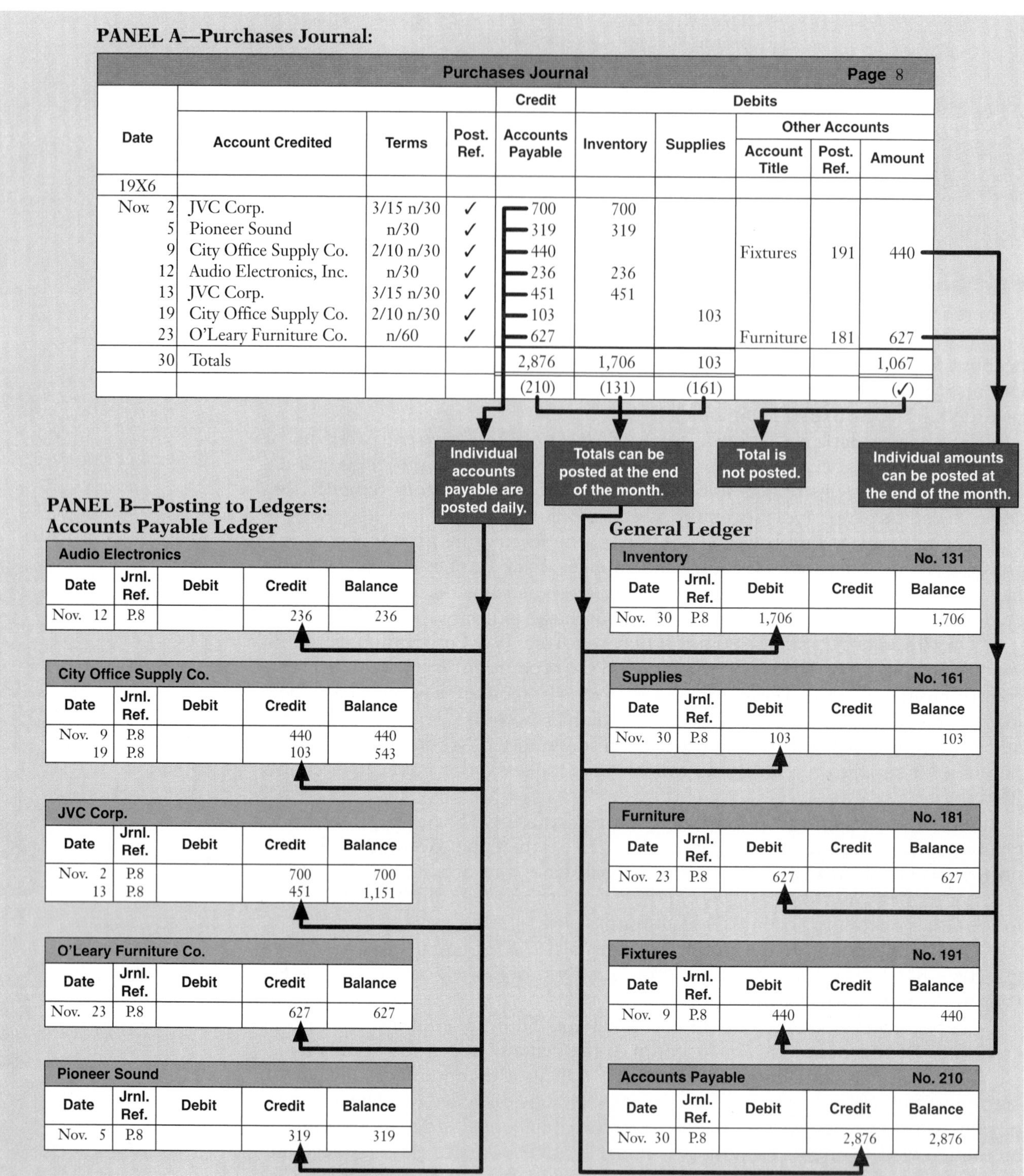

PANEL A—Purchases Journal:

				Credit	Debits				
Purchases Journal									**Page** 8
							Other Accounts		
Date	Account Credited	Terms	Post. Ref.	Accounts Payable	Inventory	Supplies	Account Title	Post. Ref.	Amount
19X6									
Nov. 2	JVC Corp.	3/15 n/30	✓	700	700				
5	Pioneer Sound	n/30	✓	319	319				
9	City Office Supply Co.	2/10 n/30	✓	440			Fixtures	191	440
12	Audio Electronics, Inc.	n/30	✓	236	236				
13	JVC Corp.	3/15 n/30	✓	451	451				
19	City Office Supply Co.	2/10 n/30	✓	103		103			
23	O'Leary Furniture Co.	n/60	✓	627			Furniture	181	627
30	Totals			2,876	1,706	103			1,067
				(210)	(131)	(161)			(✓)

PANEL B—Posting to Ledgers:
Accounts Payable Ledger

Audio Electronics

Date	Jrnl. Ref.	Debit	Credit	Balance
Nov. 12	P.8		236	236

City Office Supply Co.

Date	Jrnl. Ref.	Debit	Credit	Balance
Nov. 9	P.8		440	440
19	P.8		103	543

JVC Corp.

Date	Jrnl. Ref.	Debit	Credit	Balance
Nov. 2	P.8		700	700
13	P.8		451	1,151

O'Leary Furniture Co.

Date	Jrnl. Ref.	Debit	Credit	Balance
Nov. 23	P.8		627	627

Pioneer Sound

Date	Jrnl. Ref.	Debit	Credit	Balance
Nov. 5	P.8		319	319

General Ledger

Inventory — No. 131

Date	Jrnl. Ref.	Debit	Credit	Balance
Nov. 30	P.8	1,706		1,706

Supplies — No. 161

Date	Jrnl. Ref.	Debit	Credit	Balance
Nov. 30	P.8	103		103

Furniture — No. 181

Date	Jrnl. Ref.	Debit	Credit	Balance
Nov. 23	P.8	627		627

Fixtures — No. 191

Date	Jrnl. Ref.	Debit	Credit	Balance
Nov. 9	P.8	440		440

Accounts Payable — No. 210

Date	Jrnl. Ref.	Debit	Credit	Balance
Nov. 30	P.8		2,876	2,876

EXHIBIT F-3
Purchases Journal and Posting to Ledgers for Austin Sound

Individual accounts payable from the purchases journal are posted daily to the *accounts payable subsidiary ledger*. Column totals and Other Accounts from the purchases journal can be posted to the *general ledger* at the end of the month. In the ledger accounts, P.8 indicates the source of the posted amounts—that is, page 8 of the purchases journal.

STOP & THINK Contrast the number of general ledger postings from the purchases journal in Exhibit F-3 with the number that would be required if the general journal were used to record the same seven transactions.

Answer: Use of the purchases journal requires only five general ledger postings—$2,876 to Accounts Payable, $1,706 to Inventory, $103 to Supplies, $440 to Fixtures, and $627 to Furniture. Without the purchases journal, there would have been 14 postings, two for each of the seven transactions.

Cash Disbursements Journal

Businesses make most cash disbursements by check. All payments by check are recorded in the **cash disbursements journal.** Other titles of this special journal are the *check register* and the *cash payments journal.* Like the other special journals, it has multiple columns for recording cash payments that occur frequently.

Exhibit F-4, Panel A, illustrates the cash disbursements journal, and Panel B shows the postings to the general and subsidiary ledgers of Austin Sound. This cash disbursements journal has two debit columns—for Accounts Payable and

EXHIBIT F-4
Cash Disbursements Journal and Posting to Ledgers for Austin Sound

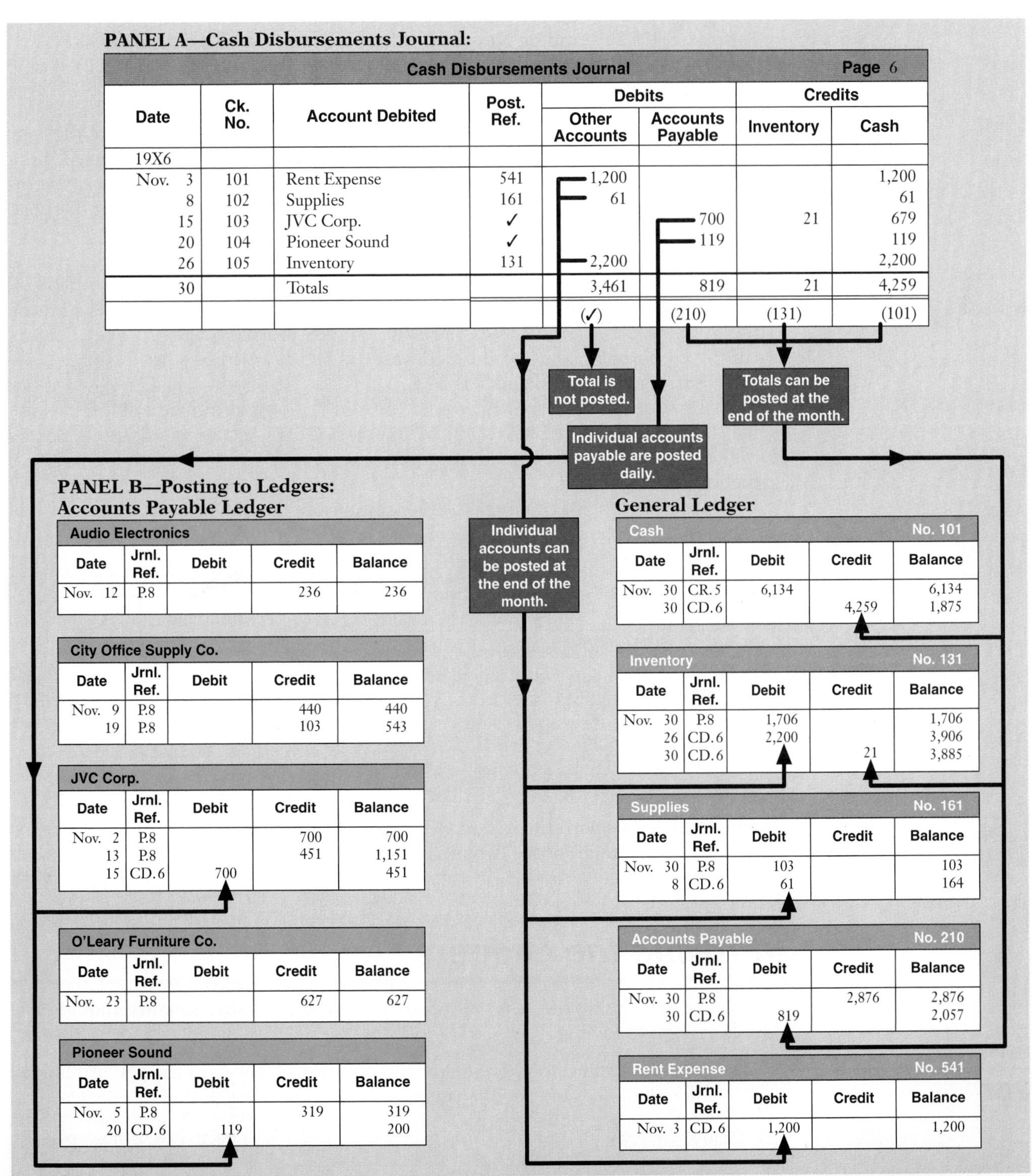

PANEL A—Cash Disbursements Journal:

Cash Disbursements Journal — Page 6

Date	Ck. No.	Account Debited	Post. Ref.	Debits: Other Accounts	Debits: Accounts Payable	Credits: Inventory	Credits: Cash
19X6							
Nov. 3	101	Rent Expense	541	1,200			1,200
8	102	Supplies	161	61			61
15	103	JVC Corp.	✓		700	21	679
20	104	Pioneer Sound	✓		119		119
26	105	Inventory	131	2,200			2,200
30		Totals		3,461	819	21	4,259
				(✓)	(210)	(131)	(101)

PANEL B—Posting to Ledgers:

Accounts Payable Ledger

Audio Electronics

Date	Jrnl. Ref.	Debit	Credit	Balance
Nov. 12	P.8		236	236

City Office Supply Co.

Date	Jrnl. Ref.	Debit	Credit	Balance
Nov. 9	P.8		440	440
19	P.8		103	543

JVC Corp.

Date	Jrnl. Ref.	Debit	Credit	Balance
Nov. 2	P.8		700	700
13	P.8		451	1,151
15	CD.6	700		451

O'Leary Furniture Co.

Date	Jrnl. Ref.	Debit	Credit	Balance
Nov. 23	P.8		627	627

Pioneer Sound

Date	Jrnl. Ref.	Debit	Credit	Balance
Nov. 5	P.8		319	319
20	CD.6	119		200

General Ledger

Cash — No. 101

Date	Jrnl. Ref.	Debit	Credit	Balance
Nov. 30	CR.5	6,134		6,134
30	CD.6		4,259	1,875

Inventory — No. 131

Date	Jrnl. Ref.	Debit	Credit	Balance
Nov. 30	P.8	1,706		1,706
26	CD.6	2,200		3,906
30	CD.6		21	3,885

Supplies — No. 161

Date	Jrnl. Ref.	Debit	Credit	Balance
Nov. 30	P.8	103		103
8	CD.6	61		164

Accounts Payable — No. 210

Date	Jrnl. Ref.	Debit	Credit	Balance
Nov. 30	P.8		2,876	2,876
30	CD.6	819		2,057

Rent Expense — No. 541

Date	Jrnl. Ref.	Debit	Credit	Balance
Nov. 3	CD.6	1,200		1,200

Other Accounts—and two credit columns—for Cash and purchase discounts, which are credited to the Inventory account in a perpetual inventory system. This special journal also has columns for the date and for the check number of each cash payment.

Suppose a business makes numerous cash purchases of inventory. What additional column would its cash disbursements journal need to be most useful? A column for Inventory, which would appear under the Debits heading, would streamline the information in the journal.

All entries in the cash disbursements journal include a credit to Cash. Payments on account are debits to Accounts Payable. On November 15, Austin Sound paid JVC on account, with credit terms of 3/15 n/30 (for details, see the first transaction in Exhibit F-3). Therefore, Austin took the 3% discount and paid $679 ($700 less the $21 discount). The discount is credited to the Inventory account.

The Other Accounts column is used to record debits to accounts for which no special column exists. For example, on November 3, Austin Sound paid rent expense of $1,200, and on November 8, the business purchased supplies for $61.

As with all other journals, the total debits ($3,461 + $819 = $4,280) should equal the total credits ($21 + $4,259 = $4,280).

POSTING FROM THE CASH DISBURSEMENTS JOURNAL Posting from the cash disbursements journal is similar to posting from the cash receipts journal. Individual creditor amounts are posted daily, and column totals and Other Accounts can be posted at the end of the month. Exhibit F-4, Panel B, illustrates the posting process.

Observe the effect of posting to the Accounts Payable account in the general ledger. The first posted amount in the Accounts Payable account (credit $2,876) originated in the purchases journal, page 8 (P.8). The second posted amount (debit $819) came from the cash disbursements journal, page 6 (CD.6). The resulting credit balance in Accounts Payable is $2,057. Also, see the Cash account. After posting, its debit balance is $1,875.

Amounts in the Other Accounts column are posted individually (for example, Rent Expense—debit $1,200). When each Other Accounts amount is posted to the general ledger, the account number is entered in the Post. Ref. column of the journal.

To review their accounts payable, companies list the individual creditor balances in the accounts payable subsidiary ledger:

Creditor Accounts Payable

Creditor	Balance
Audio Electronics	$ 236
City Office Supply	543
JVC Corp.	451
O'Leary Furniture	627
Pioneer Sound	200
Total accounts payable	$2,057

This total agrees with the Accounts Payable balance in the general ledger in Exhibit F-4. Agreement of the two amounts indicates that the resulting account balances are correct.

Proving the Ledgers

At the end of the period, after all postings have been made, equality should exist between the following:

1. Total debits and total credits of the account balances in the general ledger. These balances are used to prepare the trial balance.

2. The balance of the Accounts Receivable control account in the general ledger and the sum of individual customer accounts in the accounts receivable subsidiary ledger.
3. The balance of the Accounts Payable control account in the general ledger and the sum of the individual creditor accounts in the accounts payable subsidiary ledger.

The process of checking for these equalities is called *balancing the ledgers,* or *proving the ledgers*. It is an important control procedure because it helps ensure the accuracy of the accounting records.

Documents as Journals in a Manual Accounting System

Many small businesses streamline their accounting systems to save money by using their business documents as the journals. For example, Austin Sound could let its sales invoices serve as its sales journal and keep all invoices for credit sales in a loose-leaf binder. At the end of the period, the accountant simply totals the sales on account and posts that amount to Accounts Receivable and Sales Revenue. Also, the accountant can post directly from invoices to customer accounts in the accounts receivable subsidiary ledger. This "journal-less" system reduces accounting costs because the accountant does not have to write in journals the information already in the source documents.

Computers and Special Journals

Computerizing special journals to create accounting modules requires no drastic change in the accounting system's design. Systems designers create a special screen for each accounting application (module)—credit sales, cash receipts, credit purchases, and cash payments. ⇐ The special screen for credit sales would ask the computer operator to enter the following information: date, customer number, customer name, invoice number, and dollar amount of the sale. These data can generate debits to the subsidiary accounts receivable and files from which are generated monthly customer statements that show account activity and ending balance. For purchases on account, additional computer files keep the subsidiary ledger information on individual vendors.

⇐⇐⇐ For a discussion of accounting modules, see Appendix E, page 752.

ACCOUNTING VOCABULARY

cash disbursements journal *(p. 763).*
cash receipts journal *(p. 758).*
control account *(p. 758).*
(general) journal *(p. 755).*
general ledger *(p. 757).*
purchases journal *(p. 761).*
sales journal *(p. 755).*
special journal *(p. 755).*
subsidiary ledger *(p. 757).*

PROBLEMS

PF-1 The general ledger of Roberson, Inc., includes the following accounts, among others:

Using the sales, cash receipts, and general journals

	Account Number
Cash	11
Accounts Receivable	12
Inventory	13
Notes Receivable	15
Supplies	16
Land	18
Sales Revenue	41
Sales Discounts	42
Sales Returns and Allowances	43
Interest Revenue	47
Cost of Goods Sold	51

All credit sales are on the company's standard terms of 2/10 n/30. Transactions in May that affected sales and cash receipts were as follows:

May 2 Sold inventory on credit to Wadkins Co., $1,700. Roberson's cost of these goods was $1,200.
4 As an accommodation to a competitor, sold supplies at cost, $85, receiving cash.
7 Cash sales for the week totaled $1,890 (cost, $1,640).
9 Sold merchandise on account to A. L. Prince, $7,320 (cost, $5,110).
10 Sold land that cost $10,000 for cash of $10,000.
11 Sold goods on account to Sloan Electric, $5,104 (cost, $3,520).
12 Received cash from Wadkins Co. in full settlement of its account receivable from May 2.
14 Cash sales for the week were $2,106 (cost, $1,530).
15 Sold inventory on credit to the partnership of Wilkie & Blinn, $3,650 (cost, $2,260).
18 Received inventory sold on May 9 to A. L. Prince for $600. The goods shipped were unsatisfactory. These goods cost Roberson $440.
20 Sold merchandise on account to Sloan Electric, $629 (cost, $450).
21 Cash sales for the week were $990 (cost, $690).
22 Received $4,000 cash from A. L. Prince in partial settlement of his account receivable.
25 Received cash from Wilkie & Blinn for its account receivable from May 15.
25 Sold goods on account to Olsen Co., $1,520 (cost, $1,050).
27 Collected $5,125 on a note receivable, of which $125 was interest.
28 Cash sales for the week totaled $3,774 (cost, $2,460).
29 Sold inventory on account to R. O. Bankston, $242 (cost, $170).
30 Received goods sold on May 25 to Olsen Co. for $40. The inventory was damaged in shipment. The salvage value of these goods was $10.
31 Received $2,720 cash on account from A. L. Prince.

Required

1. Roberson records sales returns and allowances in the general journal. Use the appropriate journal to record the above transactions in a sales journal (omit the Invoice No. column), a cash receipts journal, and a general journal.
2. Total each column of the cash receipts journal. Show that the total debits equal the total credits.
3. Show how postings would be made from the journals by writing the account numbers and checkmarks in the appropriate places in the journals.

Using the purchases, cash disbursements, and general journals

PF-2 The general ledger of Gibbs, Inc., includes the following accounts:

Cash	111
Inventory	131
Prepaid Insurance	161
Supplies	171
Furniture	187
Accounts Payable	211
Rent Expense	564
Utilities Expense	583

Transactions in August that affected purchases and cash disbursements were as follows:

Aug. 1 Purchased inventory on credit from Cowtown Co., $3,900. Terms were 2/10 n/30.
1 Paid monthly rent, debiting Rent Expense for $2,000.
5 Purchased supplies on credit terms of 2/10 n/30 from Ross Supply, $450.
8 Paid electricity bill, $588.
9 Purchased furniture on account from A-1 Office Supply, $4,100. Payment terms were net 30.
10 Returned the furniture to A-1 Office Supply. It was the wrong color.
11 Paid Cowtown Co. the amount owed on the purchase of August 1.
12 Purchased inventory on account from Wynne, Inc., $4,400. Terms were 3/10 n/30.
13 Purchased inventory for cash, $655.
14 Paid a semiannual insurance premium, debiting Prepaid Insurance, $1,200.
15 Paid our account payable to Ross Supply, from August 5.
18 Paid gas and water bills, $196.
21 Purchased inventory on credit terms of 1/10 n/45 from Software, Inc., $5,200.

Aug. 21 Paid account payable to Wynne, Inc., from August 12.
22 Purchased supplies on account from Office Sales, Inc., $274. Terms were net 30.
25 Returned to Software, Inc., $1,200 of the inventory purchased on August 21.
31 Paid Software, Inc., the net amount owed from August 21, less the return, on August 25.

Required

1. Gibbs, Inc., records purchase returns in the general journal. Use the appropriate journal to record the preceding transactions in a purchases journal, a cash disbursements journal (omit the Check No. column), and a general journal.
2. Total each column of the special journals. Show that the total debits equal the total credits in each special journal.
3. Show how postings would be made from the journals by writing the account numbers and checkmarks in the appropriate places in the journals.

Check Figures—Chapter 1

E1-1 No check figure
E1-2 No check figure
E1-3 No check figure
E1-4 A. $166,200
B. $51,900
C. $31,900
E1-5 4. $6,856 million
E1-6 1. Net income $15,000
2. Net income $53,000
3. Net loss $10,000
E1-7 1. $7.1 billion
2. $2.34 billion
E1-8 No check figure
E1-9 Total assets $18,750
Retained earnings $4,000
E1-10 1. Net income $86,200
2. Dividends $69,100
E1-11 Ending cash $124.2 million
E1-12 Net income $1,400
Retained earnings 7/31/X1 $200
E1-13 Total assets $35,450
E1-14 Net cash flow from operating activities $1,450
E1-15 No check figure
E1-16 No check figure
P1-1A No check figure
P1-2A 1. Net income $3.7 billion
P1-3A Alpha expenses $195,000
Beta ending assets $180,000
Omega investments $10,000
P1-4A Total assets $108,000
P1-5A Total assets $104,000
Retained earnings $5,000
P1-6A Net income $69,000
Total assets $92,000
P1-7A 1. d. $3,043 m. $598
j. $86 s. $12,216
P1-1B No check figure
P1-2B 1. Net income $4.2 billion
P1-3B Red expenses $155,000
White ending assets $160,000
Blue investments $20,000
P1-4B Total assets $70,000
P1-5B Total assets $160,000
Retained earnings $49,000
P1-6B Net income $128,000
Total assets $313,000
P1-7B 1. d. $12,213 m. $2,740
j. $45 s. $37,541
Decision Case 1 No check figure
Decision Case 2 No check figure
Financial Statement Case 1 No check figure
Financial Statement Case 2 No check figure

Check Figures—Chapter 2

E2-1 No check figure
E2-2 No check figure
E2-3 No check figure
E2-4 Total assets $35,800
E2-5 No check figure
E2-6 Net income $2,000
E2-7 Ending cash $21,600
E2-8 Trial balance $63,300
E2-9 No check figure
E2-10 Trial balance $140,100
Net income $12,650
E2-11 Trial balance $61,100
E2-12 Cash balance $500
E2-13 Trial balance $13,700
Net loss $1,600
E2-14 Trial balance $18,400
E2-15 No check figure
E2-16 a. Net income $5,100
c. Collections $63,100
E2-17 No check figure
P2-1A No check figure
P2-2A Net income $1,900
Total assets $28,850
P2-3A Cash balance $12,600
P2-4A Total assets $54,500
P2-5A 2. Cash $17,000
Total owed $35,200
P2-6A Trial balance $33,500
P2-7A Trial balance $63,300
P2-8A Accounts receivable $2,540
Trial balance $62,500
P2-9A Trial balance $98,200
P2-1B No check figure
P2-2B Net income $4,240
Total assets $38,920
P2-3B Cash balance $7,690
P2-4B Total assets $145,100
P2-5B 2. Cash $195,400
Total owed $210,900
P2-6B Trial balance $24,100
P2-7B Trial balance $47,900
P2-8B Accounts receivable $10,270
Trial balance $57,600
P2-9B Trial balance $97,300
Decision Case 1 Trial balance $16,200
Net income $4,650
Decision Case 2 No check figure
Decision Case 3 No check figure
Financial Statement Case 1 No check figure
Financial Statement Case 2 No check figure

Check Figures—Chapter 3

E3-1 No check figure
E3-2 No check figure
E3-3 No check figure
E3-4 Overall-net income overstated by $7,700
E3-5 1. Insurance Expense $1,200
E3-6 No check figure
E3-7 Service Revenue balance $5,300
E3-8 Net income $11,550
Total assets $35,080
E3-9 Supplies expense $8,500
E3-10 Net income $34,900
E3-11 Net income $9,800
E3-12 Total assets $35,600
Current ratio 1.33
E3-13 No check figure
E3-14 Net income $1,690
Total assets $16,790
E3-15 a. Service revenue $4,200
b. Cash collected $7,600
E3-16 Net income $49,000
Total assets $111,200
P3-1A Cash loss before tax $5,300
Accrual income before tax $1,000
P3-2A No check figure
P3-3A No check figure
P3-4A No check figure
P3-5A Net income $49,030
Total assets $42,810
P3-6A Net income $3,255
Total assets $49,075
P3-7A Total assets $78,200
Current ratio 1.19
P3-8A d. Overall: net income overstated by $6,240
f. Net income $42,660
P3-9A 3. Current ratio 2.04
Debt ratio 0.67
P3-1B Cash loss before tax $500
Accrual income before tax $1,600
P3-2B No check figure
P3-3B No check figure
P3-4B No check figure
P3-5B Net income $54,470
Total assets $105,030
P3-6B Net income $4,300
Total assets $46,100
P3-7B Total assets $108,800
Current ratio 1.37
P3-8B d. Overall: net income overstated by $1,640
f. Net income $14,230
P3-9B Current ratio 2.76
Debt ratio 0.81
Decision Case 1 Stockholders' equity $135,400
Decision Case 2 Stockholders' equity $30,120
Financial Statement Case 1 1996: Current ratio 1.94
Debt ratio 0.38
Financial Statement Case 2 No check figure
Group Project Net income $2,450
Total assets $2,590

Check Figures—Chapter 4

E4-1 No check figure
E4-2 No check figure
E4-3 No check figure
E4-4 No check figure
E4-5 No check figure
E4-6 Adjusted balance $1,941
E4-7 Adjusted balance $5,161
E4-8 No check figure
E4-9 No check figure
E4-10 No check figure
E4-11 No check figure
E4-12 New financing needed $15.8 million
E4-13 No check figure
E4-14 No check figure
E4-15 New financing needed $503 million
P4-1A No check figure
P4-2A No check figure
P4-3A Adjusted balance $8,657
P4-4A Adjusted balance $4,003.33
P4-5A No check figure
P4-6A Cash available for investments $78.4 million
P4-7A No check figure
P4-1B No check figure
P4-2B No check figure
P4-3B Adjusted balance $13,670
P4-4B Adjusted balance $19,368.77
P4-5B No check figure
P4-6B New financing needed $63.6 million
P4-7B No check figure
Decision Case 1 No check figure
Decision Case 2 Adjusted bank balance $19,258
Adjusted book balance $19,858
Financial Statement Case 1 No check figure
Financial Statement Case 2 No check figure

Check Figures—Chapter 5

E5-1 No check figure
E5-2 No check figure
E5-3 No check figure
E5-4 No check figure
E5-5 No check figure
E5-6 2. Net receivable $23,600
E5-7 2. Net receivable $25,930
E5-8 2. Net receivable $256,103
E5-9 a. Net receivable $132,400
b. Net receivable $133,100
E5-10 Dec. 31 Interest Revenue $795
E5-11 Apr. 1 Interest Revenue $200

E5-12 No check figure

E5-13 19X6 acid-test ratio 0.88; days' sales in receivables 37 days

E5-14 Collection period 3 days

E5-15 No check figure

E5-16 Net income without credit cards $75,000; with credit cards $93,150

P5-1A Short-term investments $325,400

P5-2A Interest revenue $23,000 Purchase of short-term investments $804,000

P5-3A No check figure

P5-4A 4. Net receivable: direct write-off method $268,700; allowance method $262,000

P5-5A 3. Net receivable 19X4 $125,591; 19X3 $115,300

P5-6A Dec. 31 Interest Revenue $128

P5-7A 19X9 Current ratio 1.83; Days' sales in receivables 18 days

P5-1B Short-term investments $419,000

P5-2B Interest revenue $6,000 Purchase of short-term investments $955,000

P5-3B No check figure

P5-4B Net receivable: direct write-off method $84,900; allowance method $80,300

P5-5B 3. Net receivable 19X9 $286,937; 19X8 $263,160

P5-6B Dec. 31 Interest Revenue $500

P5-7B 19X8 Current ratio 1.67 Days' sales in receivables 20 days

Decision Case 1 Net income 19X8 $57,000; 19X7 $45,750

Decision Case 2 No check figure

Financial Statement Case 1 a. Collections $1,027,943,000

Financial Statement Case 2 No check figure

Check Figures—Chapter 6

E6-1 Gross margin $1,573,798,000

E6-2 Budgeted purchases $7,230 million

E6-3 COGS: Wtd.-avg $3,174; FIFO $3,120; LIFO $3,230

E6-4 COGS $3,230 both methods

E6-5 LIFO advantage $33

E6-6 (b) $145,300; (d) $27,100

E6-7 COGS $735; End. invy. $760

E6-8 Net income FIFO $28,000; LIFO $23,100; FIFO $11,900; LIFO $7,000

E6-9 No check figure

E6-10 No check figure

E6-11 Gross margin $113,651

E6-12 Gross margin $39,900

E6-13 Net income 19X8 $28,800; 19X9 $39,600

E6-14 Est. cost of inventory destroyed $43,600

E6-15 Company A Gross margin % 39.9%; Invy. turnover 3.5 times

E6-16 No check figure

E6-17 3. Net earnings without liquidation $162 million

E6-18 19X2 Invy. turnover 7.67 times

E6-19 FIFO Net income $75,090

P6-1A 3. Net income $402,000

P6-2A 1. Budgeted purchases $731,000

P6-3A Gross margin $3,050

P6-4A COGS: Wtd.-avg. $12,473; FIFO $12,199; LIFO $12,790

P6-5A Gross margin: Wtd.-avg. $62,461; FIFO $62,970; LIFO $62,030

P6-6A No check figure

P6-7A Net income: 19X4 $18,000; 19X5 $56,000; 19X6 $63,000

P6-8A Gross margin $2,562,000

P6-9A Wal-Mart Gross margin % 20.4%; Invy. turnover 5.0 times

P6-10A FIFO Gross margin $2,766 million

P6-1B 3. Net income $474,000

P6-2B 1. Budgeted purchases $766,000

P6-3B Gross margin $1,394

P6-4B COGS: Wtd.-avg. $56,609; FIFO $55,720; LIFO $57,374

P6-5B Gross margin: Wtd.-avg. $2,435; FIFO $2,587; LIFO $2,289

P6-6B No check figure

P6-7B Net income: 19X1 $23,000; 19X2 $13,000; 19X3 $13,000

P6-8B Gross margin $2,160,000

P6-9B General Motors Gross margin % 11.9%; Invy. turnover 11.7 times

P6-10B FIFO Gross margin $5,445 million

Decision Case 1 Net income without purchase: FIFO $249,000; LIFO $213,000; with purchase: FIFO $249,000; LIFO $189,750

Decision Case 2 No check figure

Financial Statement Case 1 FIFO COGS $584,517,000

Financial Statement Case 2 No check figure

Check Figures—Chapter 7

E7-1 Land $219,900

E7-2 Interest capitalized $70,400

E7-3 Machine 1 $11,680

E7-4 No check figure

E7-5 SL $2,500/yr; UOP $0.10/mile; DDB $6,500 19X1

E7-6 Extra cash to invest $32,571

E7-7 Year 15 $20,000; Year 16 $26,667

E7-8 Gain on sale $1,296

E7-9 Cost of new truck $276,000

E7-10 Depletion $63,000

E7-11 Amortization: Part 1 $190,000; Part 2 $380,000

E7-12 Payment for other assets $81 million

E7-13 Amortization $900,000

E7-14 No check figure

E7-15 No check figure

E7-16 2. Equipment: Year 1 F 2.4 million under; Year 2 F1.8 million under

E7-17 3. Acquisitions $2,504.8 million

P7-1A 1. Land $277,100; Land improvements $66,500; Sales building $986,150

P7-2A Dec. 31 depr. exp.—old building $80,000

P7-3A No check figure

P7-4A 1. SL $44,000/yr.; UOP $1.10/unit; DDB 19X2 $57,600

P7-5A 3. Cost of plant assets sold $5,583 million

P7-6A Part 1. 2. Net income $16,650
Part 2. 2. Goodwill $1,800,000

P7-7A 3. Gain or loss $0

P7-1B 1. Land $568,250; Land improvements $106,400; District office building $1,646,100

P7-2B Dec. 31, depr. exp.—old building $1,920,000

P7-3B No check figure

P7-4B 1. SL $9,000/yr.; UOP $0.54/mile; DDB 19X2 $15,556

P7-5B 3. Cost of plant assets sold $11,922,000

P7-6B Part 1. 2. Net income $83,340
Part 2. 2. Goodwill $1,135,000

P7-7B 3. Gain or loss $0

Decision Case 1 Net income: Waldorf $89,400; Seattle $66,600

Decision Case 2 No check figure

Financial Statement Case 1 2. Depreciation $12,426,000

Financial Statement Case 2 No check figure

Check Figures—Chapter 8

E8-1 2. Est. Warranty Pay. bal. $8,940

E8-2 Dec. 31 Interest Payable $1,120

E8-3 1. Total liabilities $11,720

E8-4 Income Tax Payable $120 million

E8-5 Debt ratio 0.53

E8-6 No check figure

E8-7 Pay current liabilities of $20,000

E8-8 Total current liabilities $131,900

E8-9 1. c. Dec. 31 Interest Expense $33,750

E8-10 1. Dec. 31, 19X4 Interest Expense $14,943

E8-11 1. Sep. 30,1999 Interest Expense $11,602

E8-12 12-31-X2 Interest Expense $54,945

E8-13 3. Paid-in Cap. in Excess of Par $116,200

E8-14 2. Paid-in Cap. in Excess of Par $33,500

E8-15 EPS: Plan A $7.98; Plan B $4.26

E8-16 1. Dec. 31 Interest Expense $5,183

E8-17 b. $70,000

E8-18 4. $27,050,000 5. Year 1 Interest expense $26,895,000

E8-19 1. Increase in debt $555 million
2. Excess of new debt over payments of old debt $542 million
3. Loss on Retirement of Debt $13 million

P8-1A No check figure

P8-2A Dec. 31 Interest Expense $6,054

P8-3A No check figure

P8-4A 19X5 Interest Expense $87,500

P8-5A 3. c. Interest Expense $14,417
4. Bonds' carrying amount $485,625

P8-6A 3. Bonds' carrying amount $174,768,000

P8-7A 3. Bonds' carrying amount $94,984

P8-8A Dec. 31, 1998 Carrying amount:
Bonds payable $973,000
Lease liability $54,421

P8-9A No check figure

P8-10A 1. Total current liabilities $118,000; Total long-term liabilities $493,000

P8-1B No check figure

P8-2B Dec. 31 Interest Expense $15,094

P8-3B No check figure

P8-4B 19X7 Interest Expense $93,333

P8-5B 3. b. Interest Expense $11,325
4. Notes' carrying amount $305,500

P8-6B 3. Bonds' carrying amount $124,423,000

P8-7B 3. Bonds' carrying amount $157,344

P8-8B Dec. 31, 1998 Carrying amount:
Bonds payable $473,000
Lease liability $68,040

P8-9B No check figure

P8-10B 1. Total current liabilities $26,200; Total long-term liabilities $367,000

Decision Case 1 EPS: Plan A $6.66; Plan B $6.27; Plan C $6.53

Decision Case 2 No check figure

Financial Statement Case 1 No check figure

Financial Statement Case 2 No check figure

Check Figures—Chapter 9

E9-1 No check figure

E9-2 Total paid-in capital $116,500

E9-3 Capital in excess of par-common $71,926

E9-4 Total stockholders' equity $305,500

E9-5 Total paid-in capital $1,145,000

E9-6 Total stockholders' equity $542,000

E9-7 Dec. transactions increased stockholders' equity by $4,500

E9-8 4. $48.85 per share 5. $751 million

E9-9 Series A Pfd. $23,200
Common $99,200

E9-10 Total stockholders' equity $327,500

E9-11 Total stockholders' equity $890,000

E9-12 No check figure

E9-13 Total stockholders' equity $490,000

E9-14 1. BV per share: Preferred $63.62; Common $19.36

E9-15 Return on assets .094
Return on common .138

E9-16 No check figure

E9-17 Check figures are the Jan. 31, 19X2, balances

E9-18 Cap. in excess of par $14,279,000

P9-1A No check figure

P9-2A Total stockholders' equity $410,300

P9-3A Total stockholders' equity $430,000

P9-4A No check figure

P9-5A Total stockholders' equity $5,216,000

P9-6A 5. Common dividend $25,840

P9-7A No check figure

P9-8A Total assets $456,000
Retained earnings $58,000

P9-9A No check figure
P9-1B No check figure
P9-2B Total stockholders' equity $314,900
P9-3B Total stockholders' equity $648,000
P9-4B No check figure
P9-5B Total stockholders' equity $8,750,000
P9-6B 5. Common dividend $15,000,000
P9-7B No check figure
P9-8B Total assets $732,000
Retained earnings $201,000
P9-9B No check figure
Decision Case 1 Total stockholders' equity:
Plan 1 $415,900; Plan 2 $400,900
Decision Case 2 No check figure
Financial Statement Case 1 No check figure
Financial Statement Case 2 No check figure

Check Figures—Chapter 10

E10-1 c. Unrealized Gain $400
E10-2 2. Unrealized Loss $8,750
E10-3 No check figure
E10-4 Gain on sale of investments $345,000
E10-5 2. Long-term investments $187,200
E10-6 Consol. total assets $734,000
E10-7 3. Investment carrying amount $18,708
E10-8 No check figure
E10-9 Translation adjustment $(2,000)
E10-10 Net cash used in investing activities $(759) million
E10-11 No check figure
E10-12 3. Loss on sale $7,313,000
E10-13 Dividends received $9 million
E10-14 No check figure
P10-1A 2. Long-term investments, at equity $1,168,300
P10-2A 2. Long-Term Investments in Affiliates $909,000
P10-3A 3. Consol. debt ratio 0.899
P10-4A 1. Consol. total assets $933,000
P10-5A 1. Consol. total assets $1,024,000
P10-6A 2. Long-term investments in bonds $615,857
P10-7A Cost of bond investment $486,123
P10-8A 1. Foreign-currency transaction loss, net $1,500
P10-9A 1. Translation adjustment $138,000
P10-10A No check figure
P10-1B 2. Long-term investments, at equity $920,935
P10-2B 2. Long-Term Investments in Affiliates $1,195,000
P10-3B 3. Consol. debt ratio 0.893
P10-4B 1. Consol. total assets $746,000
P10-5B 1. Consol. total assets $969,000
P10-6B 2. Long-term investments in bonds $464,314
P10-7B Cost of bond investment $387,578
P10-8B 1. Foreign-currency transaction gain, net $900
P10-9B 1. Translation adjustment $(37,000)
P10-10B No check figure
Decision Case 1 No check figure
Decision Case 2 No check figure
Financial Statement Case 1 No check figure
Financial Statement Case 2 No check figure

Check Figures—Chapter 11

E11-1 Net income $658 million
E11-2 Net income $15,200
E11-3 No check figure
E11-4 No check figure
E11-5 EPS = $1.11
E11-6 EPS = $1.02
E11-7 Deferred income tax balance: 19X6 $14,000 cr.; 19X7 $0
E11-8 No check figure
E11-9 Retained earnings Dec. 31, 19X9 $443.8 million
E11-10 Total stockholders' equity $1,090,000
E11-11 Retained earnings Dec. 31, 19X7 $820.9 million
E11-12 Total stockholders' equity Dec. 31, 19X6 $5,532,000
E11-13 No check figure
E11-14 2. Affiliates' net losses $616 million
E11-15 No check figure
E11-16 4. Inventory turnover 30 times
E11-17 1. Total debt $148,624 million
3. Fair value of debt $152,890 million
E11-18 No check figure
E11-19 Case B Deferred income tax credit balance: 19X1 $2,400; 19X2 $4,000
E11-20 2. U.S. automotive sales 44.5%
U.S. financial services 41.5%
P11-1A Net income $68,800; total stockholders' equity $547,800
P11-2A Est. value of stock $960,000
P11-3A 1. EPS = $3.87
P11-4A Comprehensive income $97,800
P11-5A Taxable income: 19X3 $200,000; 19X4 $230,000;
Net income: 19X3 $136,500; 19X4 $143,000
P11-6A 1. $800 million 5. 10%
P11-7A No check figure
P11-1B Net income $44,000; total stockholders' equity $557,000
P11-2B Est. value of stock $871,429
P11-3B EPS = $0.57
P11-4B Comprehensive income $58,200
P11-5B Taxable income: 19X7 $215,000; 19X8 $265,000;
Net income: 19X7 $149,500; 19X8 $162,500
P11-6B 1. $560,000 million 5. 5%
P11-7B No check figure
Decision Case No check figure
Financial Statement Case 1 Est. value of a share of stock $14.19

Check Figures—Chapter 12

E12-1 No check figure
E12-2 4 oper. activities; 3 invest. activities; 6 finan. activities

E12-3 4 oper. activities; 3 invest. activities; 4 finan. activities

E12-4 Net cash outflow from oper. $2,000

E12-5 No check figure

E12-6 Net cash inflow from oper. $82,000

E12-7 Payments for inventory $81,000

E12-8 Cash proceeds of sale $8,000

E12-9 Net cash outflow from oper. $2,000

E12-10 No check figure

E12-11 Net cash inflow from oper. $82,000

E12-12 $26,000

E12-13 No check figure

E12-14 No check figure

P12-1A No check figure

P12-2A Net cash inflow from oper. $129,700

P12-3A Net cash inflow from oper. $69,600

P12-4A Net cash inflow from oper. $69,600

P12-5A Net cash inflow from oper. $80,200

P12-6A Net cash inflow from oper. $90,600

P12-7A Net cash inflow from oper. $72,800

P12-8A Net cash inflow from oper. $61,100

P12-1B No check figure

P12-2B Net cash outflow from oper. $(38,000)

P12-3B Net cash inflow from oper. $75,600

P12-4B Net cash inflow from oper. $75,600

P12-5B Net cash inflow from oper. $84,000

P12-6B Net cash inflow from oper. $50,500

P12-7B Net cash inflow from oper. $67,200

P12-8B Net cash inflow from oper. $67,400

Decision Case 1 Net cash inflow from oper. $140,000

Decision Case 2 No check figure

Financial Statement Case 1 2a. $1,027,943,000
2c. $574,563,000

Financial Statement Case 2 No check figure

P12A-1 Panel A—Transaction analysis totals $1,510,200

P12A-2 Panel A—Transaction analysis totals $93,200

P12A-3 Panel A—Transaction analysis totals $234,300

P12A-4 Panel A—Transaction analysis totals $1,356,800

Check Figures—Chapter 13

E13-1 19X6: Increase of $33,000 and 23.6%

E13-2 Revenue increased 9.9%
Total expenses increased 8.4%

E13-3 Year 5: Net sales 135%; Net income 138%

E13-4 Total stockholders' equity 45.7%

E13-5 19X8: Net income 13.7%

E13-6 No check figure

E13-7 (a) 1.53 (b) 0.76 (e) 55 days

E13-8 19X1: (a) 1.80 (b) 0.68 (c) 0.56 (d) 4.05

E13-9 19X5: (a) 0.082 (b) 0.12 (c) 0.112 (d) $0.50

E13-10 19X7: (a) 15.1 (b) 0.023 (c) $6.25

E13-11 2. EVA IHOP $8 million

E13-12 Sales $6,639 million

E13-13 Stockholders' equity $8,759 million

P13-1A 19X6: 1. Net sales 144%
2. 0.078

P13-2A Net income 4.7%
Stockholders' equity 38.1%

P13-3A No check figure

P13-4A 2b. Current ratio 2.00; Debt ratio 0.49; EPS $4.41

P13-5A 19X5: (b) 1.20 (e) 0.157 (h) 7.7

P13-6A Scott & White: (3) 2.04 (4) 126 days (9) 0.180 (12) 25.7

P13-1B 19X7: 1. Net sales 120%
2. 0.165

P13-2B Net income 14.9%
Stockholders' equity 40.2%

P13-3B No check figure

P13-4B 2e. Current ratio 1.47; Debt ratio 0.57; EPS $1.95

P13-5B 19X3: (b) 1.18 (e) 0.083 (h) 9.8

P13-6B Smajstrla: (3) 2.74; (4) 35 days (9) 0.502 (12) 7.9

Decision Case 1 No check figure

Decision Case 2 No check figure

Financial Statement Case 1 1994: 1c. 28% 2b. 0.35
3. 3.92

Financial Statement Case 2 No check figure

Check Figures—Appendixes B, D, and F

Appendix B

PB-1 a. 5 years $461,700

PB-2 a. $20,000,564

PB-3 1. $38,488

PB-4 Bond carrying amount 12-31-X2 $285,629

PB-5 Present value: Toyota 5,197,500 ¥

PB-6 2. b. Deprec. exp. $7,123
2. c. Interest exp. $5,238

Appendix D

ED-1 Stepanik, Capital $67,900

ED-2 c. Looney net loss $28,000

ED-3 c. Reitmeier capital $107,500

ED-4 Credit Jayne, Capital for $7,500

ED-5 Allen receives $46,667

ED-6 Molnari, Capital $47,450 and $19,950

PD-1 No check figure

PD-2 LeBlanc, Capital $48,560; Ringle, Capital $48,560

PD-3 a. Net income: Dewey $29,000; Karlin $29,000, DeCastro $29,000

PD-4 4. Debit: Koehn, Capital $38,000;
Neiman, Capital $1,143; Marcus, Capital $857

PD-5 Cash to: Whitney $25,800; Kosse $73,200; Itasca $20,000

Appendix F

PF-1 Debit cash for $35,933

PF-2 Credit Accounts Payable for $18,324

Glossary

Accelerated depreciation method. A depreciation method that writes off a relatively larger amount of the asset's cost nearer the start of its useful life than the straight-line method does *(p. 330).*

Account. The detailed record of the changes that have occurred in a particular asset, liability, or stockholders' equity during a period. The basic summary device of accounting *(p. 52).*

Account format. A balance-sheet format that lists assets on the left and liabilities and stockholders' equity on the right *(p. 141).*

Account payable. A liability backed by the general reputation and credit standing of the debtor *(p. 13).*

Account receivable. An asset, a promise to receive cash from customers to whom the business has sold goods or for whom the business has performed services *(p. 13).*

Accounting. The information system that measures business activities, processes that information into reports and financial statements, and communicates the results to decision makers *(p. 5).*

Accounting cycle. The process by which accountants produce an entity's financial statements for a specific period *(p. 108).*

Accounting equation. The most basic tool of accounting: Assets = Liabilities + Owners' Equity *(p. 13).*

Accounts receivable turnover. Ratio of net credit sales to average net accounts receivable. Measures ability to collect cash from credit customers *(p. 665).*

Accrual-basis accounting. Accounting that recognizes (records) the impact of a business event as it occurs, regardless of whether the transaction affected cash *(p. 108).*

Accrued expense. An expense incurred but not yet paid in cash *(pp. 119, 373).*

Accrued liability. A liability incurred but not yet paid by the company. Another name for *accrued expense (p. 373).*

Accrued revenue. A revenue that has been earned but not yet received in cash *(p. 120).*

Accumulated Depreciation. The cumulative sum of all depreciation expense from the date of acquiring a plant asset *(p. 117).*

Acid-test ratio. Ratio (of the sum of cash plus short-term investments plus net current receivables) to (total current liabilities). Tells whether the entity can pay all its current liabilities if they come due immediately. Also called the *quick ratio (pp. 241, 663).*

Adjusted trial balance. A list of all the ledger accounts with their adjusted balances *(p. 125).*

Adjusting entry. Entry made at the end of the period to assign revenues to the period in which they are earned and expenses to the period in which they are incurred. Adjusting entries help measure the period's income and bring the related asset and liability accounts to correct balances for the financial statements *(p. 113).*

Adverse. An audit opinion stating that the financial statements are unreliable *(p. 546).*

Aging of accounts receivable. A way to estimate bad debts by analyzing individual accounts receivable according to the length of time they have been receivable from the customer *(p. 233).*

Allowance for Doubtful Accounts. Also called *Allowance for Uncollectible Accounts (p. 232).*

Allowance for Uncollectible Accounts. A contra account, related to accounts receivable, that holds the estimated amount of collection losses. Another name for *Allowance for Doubtful Accounts (p. 232).*

Allowance method. A method of recording collection losses based on estimates of how much money the business will not collect from its customers *(p. 232).*

Amortization. The systematic reduction of a lump-sum amount. Expense that applies to intangible assets in the same way depreciation applies to plant assets and depletion applies to natural resources *(p. 343).*

Articles of partnership. The contract between partners specifying such items as the name, location, and nature of the business; the name, capital investment, and duties of each partner; and the method of sharing profits and losses by the partners. Also called the *partnership agreement (p. 732).*

Asset. An economic resource that is expected to be of benefit in the future *(p. 13).*

Audit. A periodic examination of a company's financial statements and the accounting systems, controls, and records that produce them *(p. 175).*

Authorization of stock. Provision in a corporate charter that gives the state's permission for the corporation to issue—that is, to sell—a certain number of shares of stock *(p. 425).*

Available-for-sale securities. All investments not classified as held-to-maturity or trading securities *(pp. 227, 472).*

Bad-debt expense. Another name for *uncollectible-account expense (p. 231).*

Balance sheet. List of an entity's assets, liabilities, and owners' equity as of a specific date. Also called the *statement of financial position (p. 18).*

Bank collection. Collection of money by the bank on behalf of a depositor *(p. 180).*

Bank reconciliation. A document explaining the reasons for the difference between a depositor's records and the bank's records about the depositor's bank account *(p. 180).*

Bank statement. Document showing the beginning and ending balances of a particular bank account listing the month's transactions that affected the account *(p. 178).*

Batch processing. Computerized accounting for similar transactions in a group or batch *(p. 750).*

Benchmarking. The practice of comparing a company to a standard set by other companies, with a view toward improvement *(p. 653).*

Board of directors. Group elected by the stockholders to set policy for a corporation and to appoint its officers *(pp. 10, 421).*

Bonds payable. Groups of notes payable (bonds) issued to multiple lenders called *bondholders (p. 379).*

Book value (of a plant asset). The asset's cost minus accumulated depreciation *(p. 117).*

Book value (of a stock). Amount of owners' equity on the company's books for each share of its stock *(p. 446).*

Book value per share of common stock. Common stockholders' equity divided by the number of shares of common stock outstanding. The recorded amount for each share of common stock outstanding *(p. 672).*

Brand name. See *trademark, trade name (p. 344).*

Budget. A quantitative expression of a plan that helps managers coordinate the entity's activities *(p. 195).*

Bylaws. Constitution for governing a corporation *(p. 421).*

Callable bonds. Bonds that the issuer may call (pay off) at a specified price whenever the issuer wants *(p. 391).*

Capital. Another name for the *owners' equity* of a business *(p. 13).*

Capital charge. The amount that stockholders and lenders charge a company for the use of their money. Calculated as (notes payable + loans payable + long-term debt + stockholders' equity) times the cost of capital *(p. 673).*

Capital expenditure. Expenditure that increases an asset's capacity or efficiency or extends its useful life. Capital expenditures are debited to an asset account *(p. 346).*

Capital lease. Lease agreement that meets any one of four criteria: (1) The lease transfers title of the leased asset to the lessee. (2) The lease contains a bargain purchase option. (3) The lease term is 75% or more of the estimated useful life of the leased asset. (4) The present value of the lease payments is 90% or more of the market value of the leased asset *(p. 395).*

Capitalize. To include a related cost as part of an asset's cost *(p. 324).*

Cash-basis accounting. Accounting that records only transactions in which cash is received or paid *(p. 108).*

Cash disbursements journal. Special journal used to record cash payments by check *(p. 763).*

Cash equivalents. Highly liquid short-term investments that can be converted into cash with little delay *(p. 585).*

Cash flows. Cash receipts and cash payments (disbursements) *(p. 584).*

Cash receipts journal. Special journal used to record cash receipts *(p. 758).*

Chairperson. Elected by a corporation's board of directors, usually the most powerful person in the corporation *(p. 422).*

Chart of accounts. List of all a company's accounts and their account numbers *(p. 77).*

Charter. Document that gives a business the state's permission to form a corporation *(p. 420).*

Check. Document instructing a bank to pay the designated person or business the specified amount of money *(p. 178).*

Classified balance sheet. A balance sheet that shows current assets separate from long-term assets, and current liabilities separate from long-term liabilities *(p. 138).*

Clean. See *unqualified (p. 546).*

Closing entries. Entries that transfer the revenue, expense, and Dividends balances from these respective accounts to the Retained Earnings account *(p. 133).*

Closing the accounts. The process of preparing the accounts to begin recording the next period's transactions. Closing the accounts consists of journalizing and posting the closing entries to set the balances of the revenue, expense, and dividends accounts to zero *(p. 132).*

Common-size statement. A financial statement that reports only percentages (no dollar amounts); *(p. 652).*

Common stock. The most basic form of capital stock. Common stockholders own a corporation *(pp. 14, 424).*

Comprehensive income. A company's change in total stockholders' equity from all sources other than from the owners of the business *(p.526).*

Conservatism. The accounting concept by which the least favorable figures are presented in the financial statements *(p. 280).*

Consignment. Transfer of goods by the owner (consignor) to another business (consignee) that, for a fee, sells the inventory on the owner's behalf. The consignee does not take title to the consigned goods *(p. 271).*

Consistency principle. A business must use the same accounting methods and procedures from period to period *(p. 279).*

Consolidated statements. Financial statements of the parent company plus those of majority-owned subsidiaries as if the combination were a single legal entity *(p. 478).*

Contingent liability. A potential liability that will become an actual liability only if a potential event does occur *(p. 241).*

Contra account. An account that always has a companion account and whose normal balance is opposite that of the companion account *(p. 117).*

Contract interest rate. Interest rate that determines the amount of cash interest the borrower pays and the investor receives each year. Also called *stated interest rate (p. 382).*

Contributed capital. See *paid-in capital (pp. 14, 423).*

Control account. An account whose balance equals the sum of the balances of a group of related accounts in a subsidiary ledger *(p. 758).*

Controller. The chief accounting officer of a business *(p. 173).*

Controlling (majority) interest. Ownership of more than 50% of an investee company's voting stock *(p. 477).*

Convertible bonds (or notes). Bonds (or notes) that may be converted into the issuing company's common stock at the investor's option *(p. 392).*

Convertible preferred stock. Preferred stock that may be exchanged for another class of stock *(p. 430).*

Copyright. Exclusive right to reproduce and sell a book, musical composition, film, other work of art, or computer program. Issued by the federal government, copyrights extend 50 years beyond the author's life *(p. 344).*

Corporation. A business owned by stockholders. A corporation is a legal entity, an "artificial person" in the eyes of the law *(p. 9).*

Cost of capital. A weighted average of the returns demanded by the company's stockholders and lenders *(p. 673).*

Cost of goods sold. The cost of the inventory that the business has sold to customers. Also called *cost of sales (p. 263).*

Cost of sales. Another name for *cost of goods sold (p. 263).*

Credit. The right side of an account *(p. 64).*

Creditor. The party to whom money is owed *(pp. 222, 237).*

Cumulative preferred stock. Preferred stock whose owners must receive all dividends in arrears before the corporation can pay dividends to the common stockholders *(p. 439).*

Current asset. An asset that is expected to be converted to cash, sold, or consumed during the next 12 months, or within the business' normal operating cycle if longer than a year *(pp. 18, 137).*

Current liability. A debt due to be paid within one year or within the entity's operating cycle if the cycle is longer than a year *(pp. 20, 138).*

Current portion of long-term debt. Amount of the principal on a loan that is payable within one year *(p. 372).*

Current ratio. Current assets divided by current liabilities. Measures a company's ability to pay current liabilities with current assets *(pp. 143, 661)*.

Database program. Computer program that organizes information so that it can be systematically accessed in a variety of report formats *(p. 753)*.

Days' sales in receivables. Ratio of average net accounts receivable to one day's sale. Indicates how many days' sales remain in Accounts Receivable awaiting collection. Also called the *collection period (pp. 242, 666)*.

Debentures. Unsecured bonds—bonds backed only by the good faith of the borrower *(p. 380)*.

Debit. The left side of an account *(p. 64)*.

Debt instrument. A payable, usually some form of note or bond payable *(p. 222)*.

Debt ratio. Ratio of total liabilities to total assets. States the proportion of a company's assets that is financed with debt *(pp. 143, 667)*.

Debtor. The party who has a debt *(pp. 222, 237)*.

Default on a note. See dishonor of a note.

Deferral. See *prepaid expense (p. 113)*.

Deficit. Debit balance in the Retained Earnings account *(p. 437)*.

Depletion expense. That portion of a natural resource's cost that is used up in a particular period. Depletion expense is computed in the same way as units-of-production depreciation *(p. 342)*.

Deposit in transit. A deposit recorded by the company but not yet by its bank *(p. 180)*.

Depreciable cost. The cost of a plant asset minus its estimated residual value *(p. 328)*.

Depreciation. Expense associated with spreading (allocating) the cost of a plant asset over its useful life *(p. 116)*.

Direct method. Format of the operating activities section of the statement of cash flows; lists the major categories of operating cash receipts (collections from customers and receipts of interest and dividends) and cash disbursements (payments to suppliers, to employees, for interest and income taxes) *(p. 588)*.

Direct write-off method. A method of accounting for bad debts in which the company waits until the credit department decides that a customer's account receivable is uncollectible and then debits Uncollectible-Account Expense and credits the customer's Account Receivable *(p. 236)*.

Disclaimer. An audit opinion stating that the auditor was unable to reach a professional opinion regarding the quality of the financial statements *(p. 546)*.

Disclosure principle. A business's financial statements must report enough information for outsiders to make knowledgeable decisions about the business. The company should report relevant, reliable, and comparable information about its economic affairs *(p. 279)*.

Discount (on a bond). Excess of a bond's maturity (par value) over its issue price *(p. 381)*.

Discounting a note payable. A borrowing arrangement in which the bank subtracts the interest amount from the note's face value. The borrower receives the net amount *(p. 369)*.

Dissolution. Ending of a partnership *(p. 732)*.

Dividend yield. Ratio of dividends per share of stock to the stock's market price per share. Tells the percentage of a stock's market value that the company returns to stockholders as dividends *(p. 671)*.

Dividends. Distributions (usually cash) by a corporation to its stockholders *(p. 424)*.

Double-declining-balance (DDB) depreciation. An accelerated depreciation method that computes annual depreciation by multiplying the asset's decreasing book value by a constant percentage, which is 2 times the straight-line rate *(p. 331)*.

Double-entry system. An accounting system that uses debits and credits to record the dual effects of each business transaction *(p. 63)*.

Double taxation. Corporations pay income taxes on corporate income. Then, the stockholders pay personal income tax on the cash dividends that they receive from corporations *(p. 421)*.

Doubtful-account expense. Another name for *uncollectible-account expense (p. 231)*.

Due date. See *maturity date.*

Earnings per share (EPS). Amount of a company's net income per share of its outstanding common stock *(pp. 393, 524, 670)*.

Economic value added (EVA). Used to evaluate a company's operating performance. EVA combines the concepts of accounting income and corporate finance to measure whether the company's operations have increased stockholder wealth. EVA = net income + interest expense − capital charge *(p. 673)*.

Effective interest rate. Another name for *market interest rate (p. 382)*.

Efficient capital market. A capital market in which market prices fully reflect all information available to the public *(p. 674)*.

Electronic funds transfer (EFT). System that transfers cash by electronic communication rather than by paper documents *(p. 178)*.

Entity. An organization or a section of an organization that, for accounting purposes, stands apart from other organizations and individuals as a separate economic unit *(p. 11)*.

Equity method for investments. The method used to account for investments in which the investor has 20–50% of the investee's voting stock and can significantly influence the decisions of the investee *(p. 475)*.

Equity securities. Stock certificates that represent the investor's ownership of shares of stock in a corporation *(p. 222)*.

Estimated residual value. Expected cash value of an asset at the end of its useful life. Also called *residual value, scrap value,* or *salvage value (p. 328)*.

Estimated useful life. Length of a service that a business expects to get from an asset. May be expressed in years, units of output, miles, or other measures *(p. 328)*.

Expense. Decrease in retained earnings that results from operations; the cost of doing business; opposite of revenues *(p. 14)*.

Extraordinary gain or loss. Also called *extraordinary items,* these gains and losses are both unusual for the company and infrequent *(p. 523)*.

Extraordinary item. A gain or loss that is both unusual for the company and infrequent *(p. 523)*.

Extraordinary repair. Repair work that generates a capital expenditure *(p. 346)*.

Financial accounting. The branch of accounting that provides information to people outside the firm *(p. 7)*.

Financial statements. Business documents that report financial information about a business entity to decision makers *(p. 6)*.

Financing activities. Activities that obtain from investors and creditors the cash needed to launch and sustain the business; a section of the statement of cash flows *(pp. 4, 587)*.

First-in, first-out (FIFO) method. Inventory costing method by which the first costs into inventory are the first costs out to cost of goods sold. Ending inventory is based on the costs of the most recent purchases *(p. 273)*.

Foreign-currency exchange rate. The measure of one country's currency against another country's currency *(p. 488)*.

Foreign-currency translation adjustment. The balancing figure that brings the dollar amount of the total liabilities and stockholders' equity of the foreign subsidiary into agreement with the dollar amount of its total assets *(p. 492)*.

Franchises and licenses. Privileges granted by a private business or a government to sell product or service in accordance with specified conditions *(p. 344)*.

Free cash flow. The amount of cash available from operations after paying for planned investments in plant, equipment, and other long-term assets *(p. 612)*.

General journal. Journal used to record all transactions that do not fit one of the special journals *(p. 755)*.

General ledger. Ledger of accounts that are reported in the financial statements *(p. 757)*.

General partnership. A form of partnership in which each partner is an owner of the business, with all the privileges and risks of ownership *(p. 731)*.

Generally accepted accounting principles (GAAP). Accounting guidelines, formulated by the Financial Accounting Standards Board, that govern how accountants measure, process, and communicate financial information *(p. 10)*.

Goodwill. Excess of the cost of an acquired company over the sum of the market values of its net assets (assets minus liabilities) *(p. 345)*.

Gross margin. Sales revenue minus cost of goods sold. Also called *gross profit (p. 264)*.

Gross margin method. A way to estimate inventory based on a rearrangement of the cost-of-goods-sold model: Beginning inventory + net purchases = Cost of goods available for sale. Cost of goods sold = Ending inventory. Also called *gross profit method (p. 284)*.

Gross margin percentage. Gross margin divided by net sales revenue. Also called the *gross profit percentage (p. 285)*.

Gross profit. Another name for *gross margin (p. 264)*.

Gross profit method. See gross margin method.

Gross profit percentage. See *gross margin percentage*.

Hedging. To protect oneself from losing money in one transaction by engaging in a counterbalancing transaction *(p. 491)*.

Held-to-maturity investments. Bonds and notes that an investor intends to hold until maturity *(p. 483)*.

Held-to-maturity securities. Debt instruments that pay interest. The investor plans to hold those securities until they mature *(p. 223)*.

Horizontal analysis. Study of percentage changes in comparative financial statements *(p. 647)*.

Imprest system. A way to account for petty cash by maintaining a constant balance in the petty cash account, supported by the fund (cash plus disbursement tickets) totaling the same amount *(p. 194)*.

Income statement. A financial statement listing an entity's revenues, expenses, and net income or net loss for a specific period. Also called the *statement of operations (p. 16)*.

Income summary. A temporary "holding tank" account into which revenues and expenses are transferred prior to their final transfer to the Retained Earnings account *(p. 133)*.

Incorporators. Persons who organize a corporation *(p. 421)*.

Indirect method. Format of the operating activities section of the statement of cash flows; starts with net income and reconciles to cash flows from operating activities. Also called the *reconciliation method (p. 588)*.

Intangible asset. An asset with no physical form, a special right to current and expected future benefits *(p. 322)*.

Interest. The borrower's cost of renting money from a lender. Interest is revenue for the lender, expense for the borrower *(p. 237)*.

Interest-coverage ratio. See *times-interest-earned ratio.*

Interim reporting. Financial reporting for a period of less than one year *(p. 542)*.

Internal control. Organizational plan and all the related measures adopted by an entity to safeguard assets, encourage adherence to company policies, promote operational efficiency, and ensure accurate and reliable accounting records *(p. 172)*.

Inventory profit. Difference between gross margin figured on the FIFO basis and gross margin figured on the LIFO basis *(p. 274)*.

Inventory turnover. Ratio of cost of goods sold to average inventory. Indicates how rapidly inventory is sold *(p. 285)*.

Investing activities. Activities that increase or decrease the long-term assets available to the business; a section of the statement of cash flows *(pp. 4, 587)*.

Investment capitalization rate. An earnings rate used to estimate the value of an investment in the capital stock of another company *(p. 520)*.

Investor's total return on an investment. Made up of the change in the stock price (increase or decrease), plus the dividends received divided by beginning stock price *(p. 541)*.

Journal. The chronological accounting record of an entity's transactions *(p. 66)*.

Last-in, first-out (LIFO) method. Inventory costing method by which the last costs into inventory are the first costs out to cost of goods sold. This method leaves the oldest costs—those of beginning inventory and the earliest purchases of the period—in ending inventory *(p. 273)*.

Lease. Rental agreement in which the tenant (lessee) agrees to make rent payments to the property owner (lessor) in exchange for the use of the asset *(p. 394)*.

Leasehold. Prepayment of rent that a lessee (renter) makes to secure the use of an asset from a lessor (landlord) *(p. 344)*.

Ledger. The book of a company's accounts and their balances *(p. 69)*.

Legal capital. Minimum amount of stockholders' equity that a corporation must maintain for the protection of creditors. For corporation's with par-value stock, legal capital is the par value of the stock issued *(p. 425)*.

Lessee. Tenant in a lease agreement *(p. 394)*.

Lessor. Property owner in a lease agreement *(p. 394)*.

Leverage. Another name for *trading on equity (p. 670)*.

Liability. An economic obligation (a debt) payable to an individual or an organization outside the business *(p. 13).*

LIFO reserve. The difference between the LIFO cost of an inventory and what it would be under FIFO *(p. 316).*

Limited liability. No personal obligation of a stockholder for corporation debts. A stockholder can lose no more on an investment in a corporation's stock than the cost of the investment *(p. 420).*

Limited liability partnership (LLP). A form of partnership in which each partner's personal liability for the business' debts is limited to a certain amount *(p. 731).*

Limited partnership. Has at least two classes of partners—one general partner, who takes primary responsibility for the management of the business and the limited partners, whose personal obligation for the partnership's liabilities is limited to the amount they have invested in the business *(p. 731).*

Liquidation. The process of going out of business by selling the entity's assets and paying its liabilities. The final step in liquidation of a business is the distribution of any remaining cash to the owners *(p. 741).*

Liquidity. Measure of how quickly an item can be converted to cash *(p. 137).*

Long-term asset. An asset that is not a current asset *(p. 138).*

Long-term investment. Any investment that does not meet the criteria of a short-term investment; any investment that the investor expects to hold longer than a year or that is not readily marketable *(p. 471).*

Long-term liability. A liability that is not a current liability *(p. 138).*

Long-term solvency. An organization's ability to generate enough cash to pay long-term debts as they mature *(p. 647).*

Lower-of-cost-or-market (LCM) rule. Requires that an asset be reported in the financial statements at whichever is lower—its historical cost or its market value (current replacement cost for inventory) *(p. 280).*

Majority interest. See *controlling interest (p. 477).*

Management accounting. The branch of accounting that generates information for the internal decision makers of a business, such as top executives *(p. 8).*

Market interest rate. Interest rate that investors demand for loaning their money. Also called *effective interest rate (p. 382).*

Market value (of a stock). Price for which a person could buy or sell a share of stock *(p. 445).*

Market value method of accounting (for investments). Used to account for all available-for-sale securities. These investments are reported at their current market value *(p. 472).*

Marketable security. Another name for *short-term investment (pp. 222, 471).*

Matching principle. The basis for recording expenses. Directs accountants to identify all expenses incurred during the period, to measure the expenses, and to match them against the revenues earned during that same period *(p. 111).*

Materiality concept. A company must perform strictly proper accounting only for items and transactions that are significant to the business's financial statements *(p. 280).*

Maturity. The date on which a debt instrument matures—that is, becomes payable *(p. 222).*

Merchandising company. A company that earns most of its revenue by selling products *(p. 263).*

Minority interest. A subsidiary company's equity that is held by stockholders other than the parent company *(p. 481).*

Module. Separate compatible units of a computerized accounting package that are integrated to function together *(p. 752).*

Multi-step income statement. An income statement that contains subtotals to highlight important relationships between revenues and expenses *(p. 142).*

Mutual agency. Every partner can bind the business to a contract within the scope of the partnership's regular business operations *(p. 732).*

Net earnings. Another name for *net income* or *net profit (p. 14).*

Net income. Excess of total revenues over total expenses. Also called *net earnings* or *net profit (p. 14).*

Net loss. Excess of total expenses over total revenues *(p. 14).*

Net profit. Another name for *net income* or *net earnings (p. 14).*

Nominal account. Another name for a *temporary account (p. 133).*

Nonsufficient funds (NSF) check. A "hot" check, one for which the payer's bank account has insufficient money to pay the check. NSF checks are cash receipts that turn out to be worthless. *(p. 180).*

Note payable. A liability evidenced by a written promise to make a future payment *(p. 13).*

Note receivable. An asset evidenced by another party's written promise that entitles the note's holder to receive cash in the future *(p. 13).*

Objectivity principle. See *reliability principle.*

Off-balance-sheet financing. Acquisition of assets or services with debt that is not reported on the balance sheet *(p. 397).*

On-line processing. Computerized processing of related functions, such as the recording and posting of transactions, on a continuous basis as these transactions occur *(p. 750).*

Operating activities. Activity that creates revenue or expense in the entity's major line of business; a section of the statement of cash flows. Operating activities affect the income statement *(pp. 3, 586).*

Operating cycle. Time span during which cash is paid for goods and services that are sold to customers who pay the business in cash *(p. 137).*

Operating lease. Usually a short-term or cancelable rental agreement *(p. 394).*

Ordinary repair. Repair work that creates a revenue expenditure, which is debited to an expense account *(p. 347).*

Outstanding check. A check issued by the company and recorded on its books but not yet paid by its bank *(p. 180).*

Outstanding stock. Stock in the hands of stockholders *(p. 423).*

Owners' equity. The claim of the owners of a business to the assets of the business. Also called *capital* for proprietorships and partnerships and *stockholders' equity* for corporations. Sometimes called net assets *(p. 13).*

Paid-in capital. The amount of stockholders' equity that stockholders have contributed to the corporation. Also called *contributed capital (pp. 14, 423).*

Par value. Arbitrary amount assigned by a company to a share of its stock *(p. 425).*

Parent company. An investor company that owns more than 50% of the voting stock of a subsidiary company *(p. 477).*

Partnership. An association of two or more persons who co-own a business for profit *(pp. 9, 731).*

Partnership agreement. Another name for the *articles of partnership (p. 732).*

Patent. A federal government grant giving the holder the exclusive right for 20 years to produce and sell an invention *(p. 343).*

Payroll. Employee compensation, a major expense of many businesses *(p. 373).*

Pension. Employee compensation that will be received during retirement *(p. 398).*

Percentage of sales approach. A method of estimating uncollectible receivables as a percentage of net credit sales (or net sales) *(p. 232).*

Periodic inventory system. An inventory system in which the business does not keep a continuous record of the inventory on hand. Instead, at the end of the period, the business makes a physical count of the inventory on hand and applies the appropriate unit costs to determine the cost of the ending inventory *(p. 264).*

Permanent account. Asset, liability, and stockholders' equity that are *not* closed at the end of the period *(p. 133).*

Perpetual inventory system. An inventory system in which the business keeps a continuous record for each inventory item to show the inventory on hand at all times *(p. 265).*

Petty cash. Fund containing a small amount of cash that is used to pay minor expenditures *(p. 194).*

Plant asset. Long-lived assets, such as land, buildings, and equipment, used in the operation of the business. Also called *fixed assets (pp. 116, 322).*

Postclosing trial balance. List of the company's accounts and their balances at the end of the period after the journalizing and posting of the closing entries. The postclosing trial balance ensures that the ledger is in balance for the start of the next accounting period. *(p. 136).*

Posting. Copying amounts from the journal to the ledger *(p. 69).*

Preferred stock. Stock that gives its owners certain advantages, such as the priority to receive dividends before the common stockholders and the priority to receive assets before the common stockholders if the corporation liquidates *(p. 424).*

Premium (on a bond). Excess of a bond's issue price over its maturity (par) value *(p. 381).*

Prepaid expense. A category of miscellaneous assets that typically expire or get used up in the near future. Examples include prepaid rent, prepaid insurance, and supplies. Also called a *deferral (p. 113).*

Present value. Amount a person would invest now to receive a greater amount at a future date *(p. 381).*

President. Chief operating officer in charge of managing the day-to-day operations of a corporation *(p. 422).*

Pretax accounting income. Income before tax on the income statement *(p. 527).*

Price/earnings ratio. Ratio of the market price of a share of common stock to the company's earnings per share. Measures the value that the stock market places on $1 of a company's earnings *(p. 671).*

Principal. The amount borrowed by a debtor and lent by a creditor *(p. 237).*

Prior-period adjustment. A correction to beginning balance of retained earnings for an error of an earlier period *(p. 529).*

Proprietorship. A business with a single owner *(p. 8).*

Purchase allowance. A decrease in the cost of purchases because the seller has granted the buyer a subtraction (an allowance) from the amount owed *(p. 266).*

Purchase return. A decrease in the cost of purchases because the buyer returned the goods to the seller *(p. 266).*

Purchases journal. Special journal used to record all purchases of inventory, supplies, and other assets on account *(p. 761).*

Quick ratio. Another name for the *acid-test ratio (pp. 241, 663).*

Rate of return on common stockholders' equity. Net income minus preferred dividends, divided by average common stockholders' equity. A measure of profitability. Also called *return on equity (pp. 448, 669).*

Rate of return on net sales. Ratio of net income to net sales. A measure of profitability. Also called *return on sales (p. 668).*

Rate of return on total assets. Net income plus interest expense, divided by average total assets. This ratio measures a company's success in using its assets to earn income for the persons who finance the business. Also called *return on assets (pp. 447, 669).*

Real account. Another name for a *permanent account (p. 133).*

Receivable. A monetary claim against a business or an individual, acquired mainly by selling goods and services and by lending money *(p. 228).*

Reconciliation method. Another name for the *indirect method* of determining cash flows from operating activities *(p. 605).*

Reliability principle. Requires that accounting information be dependable (free from error and bias). Also called the objectivity principle *(p. 11).*

Report format. A balance-sheet format that lists assets at the top, followed by liabilities and stockholders' equity below *(p. 142).*

Retained earnings. The amount of stockholders' equity that the corporation has earned through profitable operation of the business and has not given back to stockholders *(pp. 14, 423).*

Return on assets. Another name for *rate of return on total assets (p. 447).*

Return on equity. Another name for *rate of return on common stockholders' equity (p. 448).*

Return on stockholders' equity. Another name for *rate of return on common stockholders' equity (p. 669).*

Revenue. Increase in retained earnings from delivering goods or services to customers or clients *(p. 14).*

Revenue expenditure. Expenditure that merely maintains an asset in its existing condition or restores the asset to good working order. Revenue expenditures are expensed (matched against revenue) *(p. 346).*

Revenue principle. The basis for recording revenues; tells accountants when to record revenue and the amount of revenue to record *(p. 110).*

S Corporation. A corporation taxed in the same way as a partnership *(p. 733).*

Sales. Another name for *sales revenue.*

Sales journal. Special journal used to record credit sales *(p. 755).*

Securities. Note receivable or stock certificates that entitle the owner to the benefits of an investment *(p. 222).*

Segment of a business. One of various separate divisions of a company *(p. 522)*.

Serial bonds. Bonds that mature in installments over a period of time *(p. 380)*.

Shareholder. Another name for *stockholder (pp. 9, 420)*.

Short presentation. A way to report contingent liabilities in the body of the balance sheet, after total liabilities but with no amount given. The contingent liabilities are explained in a note to the balance sheet *(p. 377)*.

Short-term investment. Investment that a company plans to hold for one year or less. Also called *marketable securities (pp. 222, 471)*.

Short-term liquidity. An organization's ability to meet current payments as they come due *(p. 647)*.

Short-term note payable. Note payable due within one year *(p. 368)*.

Single-step income statement. An income statement that lists all the revenues together under a heading such as Revenues or Revenues and Gains, Expenses appear in a separate category titled Expenses, Costs and Expenses, or perhaps Expenses and Losses *(p. 142)*.

Special journal. An accounting journal designed to record one specific type of transaction *(p. 755)*.

Specific-unit-cost method. Inventory cost method based on the specific cost of particular units of inventory *(p. 271)*.

Spreadsheet. A computer program that links data by means of cells, formulas, and functions; an electronic worksheet *(p. 752)*.

Stated interest rate. Another name for the *contract interest rate (p. 382)*.

Stated value. An arbitrary amount assigned to no-par stock; similar to par value *(p. 425)*.

Statement of cash flows. Reports cash receipts and cash disbursements classified according to the entity's major activities: operating, investing, and financing *(pp. 21, 584)*.

Statement of financial position. Another name for balance sheet *(p. 18)*.

Statement of operations. Another name for *income statement (p. 16)*.

Statement of retained earnings. Summary of the changes in the retained earnings of a corporation during a specific period *(p. 18)*.

Statement of stockholders' equity. Reports the changes in all categories of stockholders' equity during the period *(p. 533)*.

Stock. Shares into which the owners' equity of a corporation is divided *(pp. 9, 420)*.

Stock dividend. A proportional distribution by a corporation of its own stock to its stockholders *(p. 440)*.

Stock split. An increase in the number of authorized, issued, and outstanding shares of stock coupled with a proportionate reduction in the stock's par value *(p. 443)*.

Stockholder. A person who owns stock in a corporation. Also called a *shareholder (pp. 9, 420)*.

Stockholders' equity. The stockholders' ownership interest in the assets of a corporation *(pp. 14, 422)*.

Straight-line (SL) method. Depreciation method in which an equal amount of depreciation expense is assigned to each year (or period) of asset use *(p. 329)*.

Strong currency. A currency whose exchange rate is rising relative to other nations' currencies *(p. 489)*.

Subsidiary company. An investee company in which a parent company owns more than 50% of the voting stock *(p. 477)*.

Subsidiary ledger. Book of accounts that provides supporting details on individual balances, the total of which appears in a general ledger account *(p. 757)*.

Taxable income. The basis for computing the amount of tax to pay the government *(p. 527)*.

Temporary account. Another name for a *nominal account*. The revenue and expense accounts that relate to a particular accounting period and are closed at the end of the period are temporary accounts. For a corporation, the Dividends account is also temporary *(p. 133)*.

Term. The length of time until a debt instrument matures *(p. 222)*.

Term bonds. Bonds that all mature at the same time for a particular issue *(p. 380)*.

Time-period concept. Ensures that accounting information is reported at regular intervals *(p. 110)*.

Times-interest-earned ratio. Ratio of income from operations to interest expense. Measures the number of times that operating income can cover interest expense. Also called the *interest-coverage ratio (p. 667)*.

Trademark, trade name. A distinctive identification of a product or service. Also called a *brand name (p. 344)*.

Trading on the equity. Earning more income on borrowed money than the related interest expense, thereby increasing the earnings for the owners of the business. Also called *leverage (pp. 394, 670)*.

Trading securities. Stock investments that are to be sold in the near future with the intent of generating profits on the sale *(pp. 224, 472)*.

Transaction. An event that both affects the financial position of a business entity and can be reliably recorded *(p. 54)*.

Treasury stock. A corporation's own stock that it has issued and later reacquired *(p. 433)*.

Trial balance. A list of all the ledger accounts with their balances *(p. 74)*.

Uncollectible-account expense. Cost to the seller of extending credit. Arises from the failure to collect from credit customers. Also called *doubtful-account expense* or *bad-debt expense (p. 231)*.

Underwriter. Organization that purchases the bonds from an issuing company and resells them to its clients or sells the bonds for a commission, agreeing to buy all unsold bonds *(p. 380)*.

Unearned revenue. A liability created when a business collects cash from customers in advance of doing work for the customer. The obligation is to provide a product or a service in the future *(p. 121)*.

Units-of-production (UOP) method. Depreciation method by which a fixed amount of depreciation is assigned to each unit of output produced by the plant asset *(p. 330)*.

Unlimited personal liability. When a partnership (or proprietorship) cannot pay its debts with business assets, the partners (or the proprietor) must use personal assets to meet the debt. If a partner cannot pay this debt, then the other partner(s) must make the payment. Does not apply in limited liability partnerships *(p. 732)*.

Unqualified (clean). An audit opinion stating that the financial statements are reliable *(p. 546)*.

Vertical analysis. Analysis of a financial statement that reveals the relationship of each statement item to a specified base, which is the 100% figure *(p. 650)*.

Weak currency. A currency whose exchange rate is falling relative to that of other nations *(p. 489)*.

Weighted-average cost method. Inventory costing method based on the weighted-average cost of inventory during the period. Weighted-average cost is determined by dividing the cost of goods available for sale by the number of units available. Also called the *average-cost method (p. 272)*.

Working capital. Current assets minus current liabilities; measures a business's ability to meet its short-term obligations with its current assets *(p. 660)*.

Company Index

Real companies are in bold type.

Subject Index

A

B

C

D

E

F

G

H

I

J

K

L

M

N

O

P

Q

R

S

T

U

V

W

Y